PENGUIN REFERENCE

The Penguin Concise Guide to Opera

Amanda Holden studied music at Oxford and at the Guildhall School in London, where she subsequently taught for several years. In 1987 she began work on the first edition of this book and wrote her first opera translation, of Verdi's *Falstaff*. Since then she has completed about fifty more translations and texts for the opera stage, theatre and concert hall. Her librettos include *The Silver Tassie* for which, with the composer Mark-Anthony Turnage, she received the Olivier award for Outstanding Achievements in Opera in 2001.

The Penguin Concise

GUIDE TO OPERA

Edited by Amanda Holden

PENGUIN BOOKS

PENGUIN BOOKS

Published by the Penguin Group
Penguin Books Ltd, 80 Strand, London WC2R 0RL, England
Penguin Group (USA) Inc., 375 Hudson Street, New York, New York 10014, USA
Penguin Group (Canada), 10 Alcorn Avenue, Toronto, Ontario, Canada M4V 3B2
(a division of Pearson Penguin Canada Inc.)
Penguin Ireland, 25 St Stephen's Green, Dublin 2, Ireland
(a division of Penguin Books Ltd)
Penguin Group (Australia), 250 Camberwell Road,
Camberwell, Victoria 3124, Australia (a division of Pearson Australia Group Pty Ltd)
Penguin Books India Pvt Ltd, 11 Community Centre,
Panchsheel Park, New Delhi – 110 017, India
Penguin Group (NZ), cnr Airborne and Rosedale Roads, Albany,
Auckland 1310, New Zealand (a division of Pearson New Zealand Ltd)
Penguin Books (South Africa) (Pty) Ltd, 24 Sturdee Avenue,
Rosebank 2196, South Africa

Penguin Books Ltd, Registered Offices: 80 Strand, London WC2R 0RL, England

www.penguin.com

First published by Viking as *The Viking Opera Guide* 1993
Abridged edition with revisions first published by Viking as
The Penguin Opera Guide 1995
Published in Penguin Books 1997
The New Penguin Opera Guide published 2001
The Penguin Concise Guide to Opera published 2005
1

Designed by Andrew Barker
Set in 7.5/9 pt PostScript ITC Stone
Typeset by Rowland Phototypesetting Ltd, Bury St Edmunds, Suffolk
Printed in England by Clays Ltd, St Ives plc

Contents

Preface

The Penguin Concise Guide to Opera provides an introduction to the standard opera canon as well as to the other works you are most likely to encounter in opera houses around the world. So this book will take you from Monteverdi's *Orfeo* – the earliest acclaimed opera, first performed in 1607 – to Thomas Adès's *The Tempest* – premiered at Covent Garden in 2004 – via all the works that hold a place in the repertoire: it could be subtitled *Your 250 Best Operas*.

It is now 20 years since I wondered whether I could interest a publisher in my idea for a comprehensive opera guide containing all the best operas ever written. This book is the fourth edition of that book (the first was *The Viking Opera Guide*, 1993) and the second concise version. It is mainly derived from *The New Penguin Opera Guide* (2001) and anyone whose appetite is whetted can proceed to the larger volume and discover the works of 750 more opera composers!

This selection aims to be an easy way into opera for any remotely curious beginner as well as the ideal guide for anyone who has heard a few operas and seeks to know more about them. Though some assume it is an acquired taste, opera need not be intimidating – listen to operas rather than to anyone who might try to put you off them. I was recently in the balcony of the Albert Hall in London for a performance of Puccini's *Madam Butterfly*. By the end, the couple beside me, who had never seen an opera before, were in floods of tears. Music is uniquely able to plumb the depths and heights of human emotions that are impossible to express in words, while opera, which couples music with words and adds all the panoply of the stage, can achieve an alchemy that both mirrors and transcends all human experience.

In the 17th and 18th centuries the majority of operas were contemporary works, written for special occasions or patrons, and most of them disappeared after their premieres. Accordingly, very few Mozart operas were performed immediately after his death, the operas of Handel and Rameau sank without trace after their heydays in England and France, and Monteverdi's even earlier operas were consigned to oblivion. In the 19th century a few opera composers – Rossini, Donizetti, Tchaikovsky, Verdi and Wagner – became superstars, with an eager public for every new work. Due to the huge popularity of a few works, a repertoire began to emerge. Then, as the 20th century began, there was a huge explosion of activity. New operas by Puccini, Richard Strauss, Janáček, Berg, Weill and Britten, to name but the most prominent, displayed a more visceral approach to the drama. Furthermore, in the second half of the century, a vast number of neglected operas began to dominate the scene alongside an even greater diversity of work by contemporary composers totally freed from the confines of tradition. I was surprised and excited after choosing these 250 works to discover that well over 100 of them were premiered in the 20th century. Despite the conservative cries of doom and gloom, opera is alive and healthy.

The old opera guides on my shelves encompass the great favourites as well as a motley crew of composers who are now totally forgotten. This book contains works by eighteen living composers whose works have been premiered by major houses. Only time will decide which of these become classics and which others end up in the charity shop of music history.

Meanwhile, the start of the 21st century is a wonderful vantage point from which to survey the richest and most multi-faceted of musical genres. Opera houses now stage a vast variety of works each year, and all but the most recent operas in this book are currently available on CD. Life has never been more luxurious for the opera fan.

I would like to give thanks for *Opera*, the redoubtable monthly magazine that has chronicled opera the world over since 1950, and to Rodney Milnes, a former editor of *Opera* and my generous mentor, for all his excellent advice. I am grateful to Andrew Clements and George Hall who have also advised me and written all the new material that brings this volume right up to date, and to my editor Nigel Wilcockson and his team at Penguin, who are exemplary in their zeal, support and non-interference.

Amanda Holden
Highbury, London

About This Book

The Penguin Concise Guide to Opera contains 102 composer articles, each including separate entries examining their most frequently performed works. The (alphabetically listed) articles encompass all the best-known opera composers – Mozart, Puccini, Verdi and Wagner – other mainstream composers not mainly known for their operas, such as Beethoven and Debussy, as well as operetta composers and contemporary successes. Each opera entry is complemented with recommended recordings.

A biographical introduction begins each article, explaining the composer's relevance to opera. Their most popular works are examined in separate entries in chronological order of composition. Operas without entries are listed at the end of the article with year of premiere (dates in brackets record completion of composition, if that is significantly earlier than the premiere date).

The length of each opera entry has been graded according to merit. Each one includes TITLE (in original language and English translation), GENRE, NUMBER OF ACTS and DURATION (to the nearest 15 minutes), LIBRETTIST and SOURCE OF LIBRETTO and WORLD PREMIERE dates and venues, followed by UK and US premieres. The paragraphs that follow contain background to the work, SYNOPSIS and musical commentary. There is also RECORDING information: when several recordings exist a selection represents the best old and new recordings (record labels are the most recent, including reissues; dates give year of recording). Major operas receive a full CAST list; these are abbreviated for operas on the edge of the repertoire; less important works are examined in less detail.

To look up an opera, turn to the Index of Opera Titles at the back of the book. Titles are listed here in their original form and in English translation.

ABBREVIATIONS are at the front of the book; a list of CONTRIBUTORS (credited in their articles by initial) with their biographical information is at the back.

Russian dates are New Style; transliteration follows modern usage, except where familiarity seems more apposite – for example, this book uses Prokofiev not Prokofyev and Tchaikovsky not Chaikovsky. Titles in languages other than French, German, Italian or Spanish are first given in English translation.

A.H.

Abbreviations

a	alto
arr.	arranged
b	bass
b	born
bar	baritone
b-bar	bass-baritone
BBC	British Broadcasting Corporation
boy s	boy soprano/treble
BPO	Berlin Philharmonic Orchestra
c	contralto
C	Chamber
CBSO	City of Birmingham Symphony Orchestra
CCh	Chamber Choir
Ch	Chorus, Choir, Choeur, etc
CO	Chamber Orchestra
COE	Chamber Orchestra of Europe
coll.	collaborator, collaboration
Cons	Conservatoire
ct	counter-tenor
d	died
DG	Deutsche Grammophon
EBS	English Baroque Soloists
ECO	English Chamber Orchestra
ed.	editor
edn	edition
Eng	English
ENO	English National Opera
Ens	Ensemble
f.s.	full score
h	hour, hours
inc.	incomplete
IRCAM	Institut de recherche et de coordination acoustique/musique
ISCAM	International Society for Contemporary Music
jr	junior
LPO	London Philharmonic Orchestra
LSCh	London Symphony Chorus
LSO	London Symphony Orchestra
m	minutes
mc	mezzo contralto
ms	mezzo soprano
Nat	National
n.d.	no date
no.	number
NPO	New Philharmonia Orchestra
nr	near
NT	National Theatre
O	Orchestra, Orchestre, Orchester, etc.
OAE	Orchestra of the Age of Enlightenment
Op	Opera, Opéra, etc.
orch.	orchestrated by, orchestrator
orig.	original
ORTF	Orchestre de la Radio et Télévision Française
PCh	Philharmonic Choir
pf	pianoforte
PO	Philharmonic Orchestra
R	radio
RAI	Radio Audizioni Italiane
RCh	radio choir/chorus
RCM	Royal College of Music
rev.	revised
RO	radio orchestra
RPO	Royal Philharmonic Orchestra
RSO	Radio Symphony Orchestra
s	soprano
satb	soprano, alto, tenor, bass
SCh	Symphony Chorus

SO	Symphony Orchestra
Soc	Society
t	tenor
Th	Theatre, Theater, etc.
trans.	translated by, translator
VPO	Vienna Philharmonic Orchestra
WDR	Westdeutsche Rundfunk (West German Radio)
WNO	Welsh National Opera

Mark Adamo

b 1 August 1962, Philadelphia, US

Adamo started writing stories at the age of seven and at high school taught himself the piano. He later studied at New York University, where his gifts as a playwright won him the Paulette Goddard Remarque Scholarship. He then took a degree course in composition at the Catholic University of America in Washington DC, where he received the Theodore Presser Award. He has maintained an interest in writing, but the instant success of his first opera, written to his own libretto, established him as one of the most prominent American composers of his generation. *Little Women* transferred from the Studio division of Houston Grand Opera to the main company itself and has been repeated in a clutch of productions throughout the United States and in Mexico. Houston's administrator, David Gockley, quickly commissioned two more works from Adamo, of which the first, *Lysistrata*, was premiered in March 2005.

Little Women

Opera in two acts (2h)
Libretto by the composer after the novel by Louisa May Alcott (1869)
Composed 1995–7
PREMIERE 13 March 1998, Opera Studio, Houston

In the Prologue Jo, aged 21, looks back on her happy teenage years in her family home and her close relationships with her sisters, Meg, Amy and the ailing Beth. Laurie touches a tender spot as Jo's own former admirer who then married her sister, Amy. Time slips back and we see Laurie and the girls conversing and playing games. To Jo's disapproval, Laurie reveals the growing attention Meg is receiving from his tutor, Mr Brooke. Mr Brooke proposes to Meg and, despite Jo's and Aunt Cecilia's determined opposition, she marries him. At the ceremony, Laurie proposes to Jo and she turns him down. As her close family ties start to dissolve, Jo moves to New York to embark on a literary career and there meets Friedrich Bhaer, whose foreign sophistication arouses her interest. She returns to Concord to be with her sister Beth as she dies. The final scene returns us to the attic of the Prologue, where Jo and Laurie reprise their earlier conversation and reconcile. After Jo again revisits the lost past, Bhaer arrives and she takes his hand.

Little Women is an ensemble piece with strongly individualized roles for all the characters. An orchestra only slightly larger than that used by Britten in his chamber operas points up one element in Adamo's heritage; another is the musical theatre of Stephen Sondheim. The result is a well-crafted score that, if rarely striking in itself, matches effectively with its subject.

RECORDING Lloyd, Tappan, Novacek, DiDonato, Jones, Shelton, Belcher,

Houston Grand Op O, P. Summers, Ondine, 2000 (live)

G.H.

John Adams

John Coolidge Adams; *b* 15 February 1947, Worcester, Massachusetts, US

Adams is among the leading opera composers to emerge in the late 20th century and, it has been claimed, the most frequently performed living American composer of our time. Often described as a minimalist, he has moved even further away than have Reich, his ertswhile mentor, and Glass, the other major figure in so-called minimalist opera, from the pared-down rigour characteristic of this approach in the 1960s and 1970s. Indeed, Adams's success as an opera composer lies precisely in the extent to which he has incorporated narrative, characterization and other aspects commonly thought essential to opera, but antithetical to minimalism, to forge an operatic style on minimalist foundations.

While only ten years younger than Glass, Adams could be said to have become the foremost figure in a second generation of composers inspired by the early explorations of sustained sounds and repetition undertaken by La Monte Young and Terry Riley in the late 1950s and early 1960s. They built their experimental work on a solid conventional training in Western classical music, and Adams has allied himself more consistently with this heritage, though he has more recently become interested in the wide range of other musics – non-Western, jazz, rock – from which the minimalist approach in part derived. Following Adams's move from the East Coast to the West in 1972, his music first became more experimental – notably during the earlier part of his period as a teacher at the San Francisco Conservatory (1972–82) – and then increasingly related to the styles and techniques of a range of 19th- and early 20th-century Romantic composers. His invention in the mid-1980s of an operatic style owing at least as much to earlier operatic and even oratorio traditions as to avant-garde genres of music theatre and performance art thus appears quite natural. And it is by bringing a new vigour and purpose to composing music for drama that does not avoid a clear narrative basis that Adams has found his full maturity.

Adams's style from as far back as the late 1970s is, in fact, characterized by its individual development of a repetitive idiom in which direct emotional expression is, unusually, not avoided, and in which allusions to – or even direct quotations from – other musics have played an increasingly significant part; *Shaker Loops* for string septet (1978) represents the emergence of this style. An avoidance of extensive reliance on tuned percussion or keyboard instruments (mainstays of at least the earlier Reich and Glass) is significant. Even more important is an increasing concern with melody, harmonic motion and regular metre (which Adams shares with these composers but takes even further).

The development of this approach has taken him naturally to opera. Here he was at first aided by the American poet Alice Goodman, who provided him with texts closely reflecting the composer's own musical approach in their deployment of everyday language; in their second collaboration, *The Death of Klinghoffer*, this is integrated with references to great literature of the past. But Adams has been most strongly influenced and assisted by the American director Peter Sellars, who has had a considerable impact on both the initial inspiration and the first productions of all four of Adams's stage works so far. The later two of these – the 'Songplay' *I was Looking at the Ceiling and Then I Saw the Sky*, and the Nativity Oratorio *El Niño* – move away from the 'grand opera' of *Nixon* and *Klinghoffer* to explore other ways of combining music and theatre.

Adams's forthcoming full-length opera, *Doctor Atomic*, commissioned by San Francisco Opera and to be premiered there on 1 October 2005, is based on the career of J. Robert Oppenheimer, the leader of the Manhattan Project, which developed the first atomic bomb.

Nixon in China

Opera in three acts (2h 30m)
Libretto by Alice Goodman
Composed 1985–7
PREMIERES 22 October 1987, Brown Theater, Wortham Center, Houston; UK: 1 September 1988, Playhouse Theatre, Edinburgh
CAST Chou En-lai *b*, Richard Nixon *b*, Henry Kissinger (also Lao Szu) *b*, Nancy T'sang (First Secretary to Mao) *ms*, Second Secretary to Mao *ms*, Third Secretary to Mao *ms*, Mao Tse-tung *t*, Pat Nixon *s*, Chiang Ch'ing (Madame Mao Tse-tung) *s*, Wu Ching-hua *dancer*, Hung Chang-ching (Party Representative) *silent*; *satb* chorus of Chinese militia, guests at banquet, citizens of Peking, trio of citizens (also singing the roles of participants in *The Red Detachment of Women* and the voice of Ching-hua); dancers in *The Red Detachment of Women*

Peter Sellars's idea of basing an opera on the visit of American President Richard Nixon to the Chinese Chairman Mao Tse-tung in February 1972 resulted in a close collaboration with the librettist Alice Goodman and the choreographer Mark Morris as well as with Adams himself. The original Houston production toured extensively and was televised.

SYNOPSIS
Act I: Nixon – with an entourage that includes his wife Pat and Dr Henry Kissinger – arrives at Peking airport for his historic visit to China in February 1972. His first audience with Chairman Mao finds the Chinese leader philosophical and inscrutable, but a banquet the same evening brings the two sides together more successfully.

Act II: Pat Nixon goes sightseeing and the Nixons watch a performance of the ballet *The Red Detachment of Women*, presided over by Madame Mao, in the course of which fact and fiction become hopelessly confused; the singer playing Kissinger is required to take a leading role in the ballet's action.

Act III consists of one long scene in which the six main protagonists, on the Americans' last night in Peking, ruminate on the events that have taken place and on their significance for themselves as individuals more than as political figures.

Nixon in China demonstrates, in a more extended form than ever before in Adams's music, the move from stylistic allusion – to Romantic music in particular – to actual quotation. Also notable is the integration of musical and dramatic incident and the related use of music for characterization. As the action develops following the performance of *The Red Detachment* ballet in Act II, for instance, an arpeggio figure is quickly speeded up and soon develops into the perfect complement to the onset of a tropical storm.

The increasing emphasis on the protagonists as real people, in an opera that could easily have developed purely as a political pageant in poster colours, is most clearly demonstrated in the final act. And it is here that another expansion of Adams's style is to be found: the virtual abandonment of minimalist repetition and its replacement by a new, highly lyrical manner, predominantly slow but very sensitive to the ebb and flow of action and, especially, text. Emphasis is placed firmly on a natural and free-flowing setting of Goodman's libretto, underpinned by a harmonic language of great variety and subtlety.

RECORDING Page, Sylvan, Hammons, Maddalena, Ch & O of St Luke's, de Waart, Nonesuch, 1988

The Death of Klinghoffer

Opera in a prologue and two acts
(2h 15m)
Libretto by Alice Goodman
Composed 1989–91

PREMIERES 19 March 1991, Théâtre de la Monnaie, Brussels; US: 5 September 1991, Brooklyn Academy of Music, New York; UK: 18 January 2002, Barbican Hall, London (concert)

CAST Alma Rumor *ms*, Jonathan Rumor *t*, Harry Rumor *b*, Captain *b*, Swiss Grandmother *s*, First Officer *b*, Molqi *t*, Mamoud *b*, Austrian Woman *s*, Leon Klinghoffer *b*, 'Rambo' *b*, British Dancing Girl *s*, Omar *ms*, Marilyn Klinghoffer *c*; dancers (both ensemble and solo, including the doubling of some of the solo singing roles); *satb* chorus

As with the same team's previous opera, *The Death of Klinghoffer* is based on a recent world event: in this case the hijacking, in 1985, of the cruise liner *Achille Lauro* by Palestinian terrorists and their eventual murder of a paralysed American Jewish tourist. Goodman drew for her libretto on the Bible and the Koran, as well as on her own personal transmutations of everyday language. The original production by Sellars was shared between six European and American opera houses but was not performed, as intended, at Glyndebourne. In the USA, much more than at its European premiere, *Klinghoffer*'s political ramifications stirred up strong feelings, especially in the immediate aftermath of the 1991 Gulf War.

SYNOPSIS

A lengthy prologue portrays a wealthy American family relaxing at home and talking about travel abroad; this is preceded by a Chorus of Exiled Palestinians and followed by a Chorus of Exiled Jews.

Act I: The cruise liner *Achille Lauro* has been hijacked just a few hours out of Alexandria. The purpose of the hijackers is at first unclear. The hostages are rounded up; the ship's Captain is guarded by Mamoud, and both soon start to reflect on their situation.

Act II: The liner awaits permission to enter the Syrian port of Tartus. The passengers have now been moved on deck, but the wheelchair-bound Leon Klinghoffer is forced to remain apart. The Palestinians begin to quarrel. Klinghoffer is shot. The Captain and the hijackers come to an arrangement that will allow the ship to return to Alexandria, where the Palestinians will be able to disembark. Klinghoffer's body is thrown overboard. After their arrival in port, the Captain tells Mrs Klinghoffer of her husband's death.

As in the final act of *Nixon in China*, *Klinghoffer* takes as its main subject matter the private thoughts and emotions of its characters. The two main acts allow the action to unfold via a libretto consisting mainly of individual statements and meditations. The opera thus falls into a sequence of arias and choruses inspired, according to Sellars, by Bach's Passions. The arias offer reflections of the individual protagonists in the *Achille Lauro* drama, with the Captain of the ship emerging as the character with whom one might most readily sympathize. In this opera, however, unlike *Nixon*, Sellars and his associates deliberately eschew attempts at characterization in order to focus more strongly on the issues and make the audience question their own preconceptions.

Musically, the opera continues for the most part the approach first observed in the final act of *Nixon*. Occasional use is made of what the composer himself calls his 'trickster' style – the other aspect of Adams's recent development in his non-operatic works – as in the aria for a British Dancing Girl in Act II, which draws on popular styles in a more overtly minimalist way. But, for the most part, the music is more reflective, more melodic, contrapuntal and sometimes more dissonant, marking something of a watershed in Adams's style and responding acutely to the nuances of Goodman's text. Still present, though, is a virtuosic approach to orchestration, aided in the premiere production by a specially devised sound-distribution system. The use of video to provide close-up views added a further dimension. Even more than *Nixon, The Death of Klinghoffer* distances Adams's mature style from its minimalist roots.

RECORDING Friedman, Sylvan, Maddalena, Felty, Hammons, Young, Perry, Nadler, Eng Op Ch, Op Nat de Lyon O, Nagano, Nonesuch, 1991
OTHER OPERATIC WORKS *I Was Looking at the Ceiling and Then I Saw the Sky*, 1995; *El Niño*, 2000; *Doctor Atomic*, 2005

K.P.

Thomas Adès

Thomas Joseph Edmund Adès;
b 1 March 1971, London

Adès emerged in the 1990s as one of the most promising British composers of his generation. He studied at the Guildhall School in London before reading music at Cambridge University, where his composition teachers included Goehr and Holloway; he confirmed his individuality with a *Chamber Symphony* (1990), composed while he was an undergraduate. The series of vividly imagined works that followed boosted his reputation still further; they included *Living Toys* for ensemble (1994) and the string quartet *Arcadiana* (1994) as well as his first opera, *Powder Her Face*, though at the time of its premiere the sensationalism and sexual explicitness of the subject matter overshadowed the craft and imaginative power of the score. Adès's development as a composer has progressed in parallel with the increasing success of his career as a pianist and conductor; in 1999 he became artistic director of the Aldeburgh Festival. His orchestral work *Asyla* won the Grawemeyer Prize for Composition in 1999, and the song-cycle *America* was a millennium commission from the New York Philharmonic Orchestra. In 2000 he was awarded the Siemens Prize for Music, and in 2004 the Royal Opera, Covent Garden, presented the premiere of Adès's second stage work, *The Tempest*.

Powder Her Face

Opera in two acts (2h)
Libretto by Philip Hensher
Composed 1994–5
PREMIERES 1 July 1995, Everyman Theatre, Cheltenham; US: 25 April 1997, Zellerbach Auditorium, Berkeley, California (concert); 25 July 1997, Wheeler Opera House, Aspen, Colorado (stage)
CAST Duchess *s*, Maid/Confidante/Waitress / Mistress / Journalist / Rubbernecker/Society Journalist *s*, Electrician/Lounge Lizard/Waiter/Rubbernecker/Delivery Boy *t*, Hotel Manager/Duke/Laundryman/Guest/Judge *bar*

The colourful life of Margaret Sweeny, later Duchess of Argyll, whose divorce from the Duke, eventually settled in 1963, scandalized Britain, is the framework for a sometimes surreal series of episodes, viewed in flashback from the end of the Duchess's life.

SYNOPSIS
Act I: Mocked by an Electrician and a Maid in a hotel bedroom in 1990, the Duchess takes refuge in memories of her glamorous past. A male figure is seen in the doorway as the action switches back to 1934. The Duchess has divorced her first husband and is about to marry the Duke; the Lounge Lizard sings her favourite song as the Duke himself enters. A Waitress describes the marriage of the Duke and Duchess in 1936, as the rest of the cast enact a series of tableaux depicting the ceremony and its aftermath. In a London hotel room in 1953

the Duchess fellates a room-service Waiter; a flashbulb goes off as he climaxes. The Duke's mistress persuades him to ruin his wife, and they find the incriminating photographs.

Act II: Rubberneckers eagerly discuss the divorce proceedings in 1955; the Judge delivers his verdict, branding the Duchess as having the 'morals of a bed post' and praising the Duke's tolerance. The Duchess is interviewed by a journalist in the hotel room that by 1977 has become her home; as delivery men come and go, she laments the loss of elegance and style in the modern world. Returning to 1990, the Hotel Manager presents the destitute Duchess with a notice to quit within the hour. She recalls her past happiness but is terrified of the future; a final attempt to seduce the Manager fails. As she leaves, the Electrician and the Chambermaid emerge from beneath the bed and trash the room.

The libretto's pitiless portrayal of the Duchess has a whiff of misogyny about it; even her pathetic state in the final scene fails to turn the portrait into a sympathetic one. But Adès's virtuosic score, with a tendency to use instruments at the extremes of their ranges, captures its heartless brittleness exactly. The music, alternating set pieces with instrumental interludes, contains pastiches of 1930s dance tunes but also shows its debts to Britten and Weill, Richard Strauss, Ligeti and Kurtág; Stravinsky's *The Rake's Progress* is quoted directly. The sharply characterized vocal writing includes coloratura for the Maid and lines of greater suavity and breadth for the Duchess; the Judge's summing-up is presented as a Bergian passacaglia that reaches a climax of expressionist frenzy.

RECORDING Gomez, Anderson, Morris, Bryson, Almeida Ens, Adès, EMI, 1996

The Tempest

Opera in three acts (2h 15m)
Libretto by Meredith Oakes after the play by William Shakespeare (1611)
Composed 2002–4
PREMIERE 10 February 2004, Covent Garden, London
CAST Prospero *high bar*, Ariel *high s*, Caliban *t*, Miranda *ms*, Ferdinand *t*, King *t*, Antonio *t*, Stefano *b-bar*, Trinculo *ct*, Sebastian *bar*, Gonzalo *b-bar*; *satb chorus* Court

In both its musical and dramatic structure and its approach to linear narrative, Adès's second opera, commisssioned by the Royal Opera, Covent Garden, is much more conventional than *Powder Her Face*. Oakes's libretto preserves every aspect of the original play, but offers a demotic paraphrase in rhyming couplets of Shakespeare's high-flown verse.

SYNOPSIS

Act I: Prospero, deposed as Duke of Milan by his brother Antonio and exiled to an island that he has transformed into a magical kingdom, conjures up a storm to sink a passing ship carrying the King of Naples and his court, including Antonio. His spirit Ariel reports on the survivors and leads them to Prospero's kingdom. Caliban states his claim to the island, but is banished to his cave by Prospero. Ariel lures Ferdinand, the king's son, away from the other survivors; Miranda, daughter of Prospero, encounters Ferdinand and, to her father's fury, is enchanted by the sight of another human being. Prospero imprisons Ferdinand.

Act II: The survivors of the shipwreck come ashore and are taunted by Ariel. The King laments the loss of his son, but Gonzalo's and Antonio's efforts to comfort him are confused by Ariel. Though Caliban is ridiculed by the courtiers, he calms their fear of the island's sounds and voices but is silenced by Prospero's magic when asked who his master is. Caliban pleads for the help of Stefano and Trinculo in regaining his island. Ferdinand is liberated by Miranda, and Prospero realizes that he cannot prevent their love.

Act III: Ariel has led the King and his court across the island, still teased and denounced by Ariel. Prospero realizes the horror his magical powers have unleashed but summons Ariel to bless the union of Miranda and Ferdinand. Caliban's attempted rebellion is easily quashed, and when Ariel describes how Antonio and the King are suffering, Prospero promises to show mercy. Prospero appears to the Court, the King begs his forgiveness, and Ferdinand and Miranda are revealed. A union between Milan and Naples is announced; Prospero offers forgiveness to Antonio but is rebuffed, and breaks his staff so relinquishing his magic powers. Ariel is released and, despite Prospero's pleas, flies off to freedom. Caliban is alone on the island again.

Apart from some vague allusions to renaissance dance music in Act III, Adès's score, transparent and full of glinting instrumental colours, contains no parody or pastiche. Each of the three acts is anchored by a substantial set-piece aria, for Ariel, Caliban and Gonzalo in turn, which provide oases of limpid tonality in a musical world that otherwise shifts and changes very rapidly. The principals are crisply characterized vocally: stratospheric and increasingly wordless coloratura writing for Ariel, lyrical tenor lines for Caliban, smoothly contoured phrases for Miranda and Ferdinand. Only the largely declamatory writing for Prospero lacks real vividness; he has no large-scale vocal number to himself. The resolution of the final act is achieved against the background of a huge, slowly moving chaconne in the orchestra, which comes as the culmination of a series of harmonic sleights of hand underpinning the entire drama.

A.C.

Franco Alfano

b 8 March 1875, Posillipo, Naples;
d 27 October 1954, San Remo

Although best known outside Italy as the man who completed Puccini's *Turandot*, Alfano won considerable success south of the Alps with his own works, which were not by any means all operas. Like most leading Italian composers of his generation, he sought a more equal balance between operatic and non-operatic composition, after the long period when opera had dominated his country's musical life. He was also active as a pianist and teacher.

Nevertheless, after studies in Naples and Leipzig, plus short periods of residence in Berlin and Paris, he won his biggest popular success with the relatively traditional opera *Risurrezione*, which had reached its 1000th Italian performance by 1951. Though less favoured by the public, his best subsequent operas – especially *La leggenda di Sakùntala*, commonly regarded as his masterpiece – show greater musical individuality and enterprise: by the time *Sakùntala* was written, Alfano had absorbed important lessons from Richard Strauss, the Russian nationalists, Ravel and (especially) Debussy. None of his later operas won the popularity of *Risurrezione* or the critical acclaim of *Sakùntala*, though the uneven *Cyrano de Bergerac* has shown renewed life of late, thanks to the influence of star tenors who sense its theatrical possibilities.

Alfano's completion of *Turandot*, based (not altogether satisfactorily) on Puccini's sketches, gives little idea of the quality and character of his own best work. Nevertheless, the discovery that the usually performed version contains drastic cuts led critics (notably Mosco Carner) to make forceful pleas for restoring the original, which was first performed at the Barbican Hall, London, on 3 November 1982.

Cyrano de Bergerac
Cyrano of Bergerac

Comédie héroïque in four acts (2h)
Libretto by Henri Cain after the play by Edmond Rostand (1897)
Composed 1933–5
PREMIERES 22 January 1936, Teatro Reale, Rome (in Italian); 29 May 1936, Opéra Comique, Paris (in the orig. French); US: 13 May 2005, Metropolitan, New York

Paris, 1640. The proud Cyrano is ever at the service of his friends, but his repulsive nose precludes him from declaring his love for his cousin Roxane. She loves Christian, a cadet in the same Gascon regiment as Cyrano, whom he generously takes under his wing. Cyrano offers to woo Roxane on his behalf, and she is entranced by her lover's new eloquence. At the siege of Arras Roxane tells Christian (now her husband) that it is his eloquence that she loves not his looks. Before he dies in battle, Christian admits to Cyrano that it is he whom his wife truly loves. Fifteen years later, Cyrano, mortally wounded by an assassin, visits Roxane in the convent where she has retired. He reads Christian's final letter to her, and, finally realizing the truth, she declares her love for him as he dies.

Alfano's eclectic score draws upon French as well as Italian influences and uses some neo-Baroque elements. Its highly theatrical alternation of swashbuckling and melancholy outweighs the unevenness of its invention.

RECORDING Uhl, Sadnik, McNamara, Newerla, Pauly, Kiel Op Ch & PO, Frank, CPO, 2002 (live)
OTHER OPERAS *Miranda*, (1896); *La fonte di Enschir*, 1898; *Risurrezione*, 1903; *Il principe Zilah*, 1909; *L'ombra di Don Giovanni*, 1914, rev. as *Don Juan de Manara*, 1941; *La leggenda di Sakùntala* 1921; *Madonna Imperia*, 1927; *L'ultimo lord*, 1930; *Il dottor Antonio*, 1949

J.C.G.W./G.H.

Dominick Argento

b 27 October 1927, York, Pennsylvania, US

Initially self-taught as a composer, Argento commenced serious studies after leaving the army in 1947. From the Peabody Institute in Baltimore (where he worked with Nicolas Nabokov), he progressed to lessons with Hugo Weisgall, the locally based, Bohemian-born composer, whose compositional sophistication became a feature of his own works. Further periods of study with Dallapiccola in Florence and with Henry Cowell (again at Peabody) were later followed by a spell at the Eastman School, where his teachers included Alan Hovhaness and Howard Hanson. A Ph.D. marked the end of a long apprenticeship that prepared him to be one of the most technically well equipped American composers of his generation.

Meanwhile, his first opera, *Sicilian Limes*, had been performed and withdrawn, and a second, *The Boor*, more successfully received. Settling in Minneapolis, Argento commenced a teaching career at the University of Minnesota that continued in step with his increasing success as a composer, especially of operas. In 1965 he and his librettist John Olon-Scrymgeour founded the Center Opera Company (subsequently the Minnesota Opera), which staged the premieres of three of his works. The steadily rising interest aroused by them, however, eventually brought forth commissions from other companies in the United States as well as follow-up stagings overseas.

Argento's development has been marked by a constant ability to extend his range in terms of subject-matter and style. His careful craftsmanship never gets in the way of his fluency, nor has a discrete use of serial techniques (in *The Voyage of Edgar Allan Poe* and *The Aspern Papers*) ever hampered his lyricism. One of the most admired as well as most successful of American opera composers, he has shown a consistent understanding of what is effective in music written for the theatre.

Postcard from Morocco

Opera in one act (1h 30m)
Libretto by John Donahue
Composed 1971
PREMIERES 14 October 1971, Cedar Village Theater, Minneapolis; UK: 28 July 1976, King's College, London

Written for seven singers, a group of mimes and an orchestra of eight players, the opera sets a semi-surreal libretto in which only one character is named while almost all the others double parts designated by the possessions they carry with them – A Lady with a Hand Mirror, A Man with a Cornet Case and so forth. The period implied is 1914 (giving occasion to parodies of popular song, Viennese operetta and a café orchestra playing Wagner). The location is less clearly defined, though the librettist suggests a scene 'like an old postcard from a foreign land showing the railway station of Morocco'. In this true ensemble piece Argento has considerable fun with a range of styles and textures that mirror the swiftly changing moods of the absurdist plot.

RECORDING Brandt, Roche, Hardy, Marshall, Sutton, Busse, Foreman, Center Op of Minnesota Ens, Brunelle, CRI, 1971
OTHER OPERATIC WORKS *Sicilian Limes*, 1954 (withdrawn); *The Boor*, 1957; *Colonel Jonathan the Saint*, (1960), 1971; *Christopher Sly*, 1963; *The Masque of Angels*, 1964; *The Shoemaker's Holiday*, 1967; *The Voyage of Edgar Allan Poe*, 1976; *A Water Bird Talk*, 1977; *Miss Havisham's Fire*, 1979, rev. 2001; *Miss Havisham's Wedding Night*, 1981; *Casanova's Homecoming*, 1985; *The Aspern Papers*, 1988; *The Dream of Valentino*, 1994

G.H.

B

Samuel Barber

b 9 March 1910, West Chester, Pennsylvania, US; *d* 23 January 1981, New York

Barber was one of the most successful American composers of the mid-20th century. Confidently conservative in style, his romantic music has stood its ground through changes of fashion and seems as enduring as that of Aaron Copland or Gershwin, although it is less distinctively American in style.

Barber's family background was conducive to his musical development. His mother was a good pianist, and his aunt, the opera singer Louise Homer, was married to a composer. Barber began composing when he was seven and his first attempts at an opera date from three years later. In 1924 Barber became a student of singing, piano and conducting as well as composition at the newly founded Curtis Institute in Philadelphia. There he met Menotti, who became an essential colleague, librettist and near-lifelong companion. After graduating Barber went to study singing in Vienna, gave recitals and radio broadcasts and recorded his own song, *Dover Beach* (composed 1931), for voice and string quartet.

At Curtis, Barber received a thorough traditional grounding in composition from Rosario Scalero. His student works were polished and well received, enabling him to gain awards for European travel. He soon attracted the attention of major conductors such as Rodzinski and Toscanini. The latter conducted the first performance of the famous *Adagio* for strings (arranged from the String Quartet, 1936), which has become a classic.

All this augured well for Barber's progression to opera, as did his early orchestral pieces related to dramatic subjects, such as the *School for Scandal* overture and the *Music for a Scene from Shelley*, as well as his ballets, *Medea* (1946) and *Souvenirs* (1952). Barber was concerned to communicate directly. In a late interview he said, 'There's no reason music should be difficult for an audience to understand, is there?'

Vanessa

Opera in four acts, Op. 32 (2h)
Libretto by Gian Carlo Menotti, based on a story in *Seven Gothic Tales* by Isak Dinesen (1934)
Composed 1956–7, rev. 1964
PREMIERES 15 January 1958, Metropolitan, New York; rev. version: 3 March 1964, Metropolitan, New York; UK: 8 July 1999, Bloomsbury Theatre, London
CAST Vanessa *s*, Erika *ms*, The Old Baroness *c*, Anatol *t*, The Old Doctor *bar*, Nicholas *b*, Footman *b*; *satb* chorus of servants, guests, peasants, children, musicians

Menotti, as a seasoned man of the theatre, contributed significantly as both librettist and director of *Vanessa*. Elegant sets and costumes were designed by Cecil Beaton and the casting – as can readily be confirmed in the original recording –

was superb. Barber had written *Knoxville: Summer of 1915* (1948) for Eleanor Steber, and she was chosen for the title role (Callas had refused it on the grounds that the work had no melody and she could not be expected to fall in love with a man who had slept with the mezzo-soprano). Menotti's plot has overtones of Ibsen, which suited Barber's nostalgic tendencies and inspired arias, dances and dramatic moments in his strongest vein.

Remarkably for a first opera, *Vanessa* was a resounding success. Winthrop Sargeant considered it a 'near masterpiece in the genre', and Paul Henry Lang predicted that its impeccable vocal writing and sumptuous orchestration would be an 'eye-opener for Europeans'. Although there were reservations about its derivative nature when it was performed at the Salzburg Festival later in 1958, *Vanessa* seems likely to survive.

SYNOPSIS

The action takes place at Vanessa's country house in an unspecified northern country, *c.*1905.

Act I: Vanessa, her mother the Baroness and her niece Erika are waiting for the return of Vanessa's lover, Anatol, who left 20 years ago. When he arrives he turns out to be the son of her lover and also called Anatol; his father is dead.

Act II: Anatol and Vanessa are becoming increasingly attached, although Anatol had seduced Erika on the night of his arrival. Erika decides to give him up.

Act III: At a splendid ball Anatol and Vanessa pledge their love in public: Erika collapses.

Act IV: Erika, pregnant by Anatol, is recovering after attempting suicide. Vanessa and Anatol, married, prepare to leave for Paris. Erika settles down to wait for Anatol indefinitely, as had Vanessa at the start of the opera.

Although Barber sticks to the traditional forms of opera (arias, duets, ensembles, etc.), his musical language is far-ranging, encompassing folklike and parodistic elements within the predominantly lyrical whole. Barber and Menotti revised the opera to a three-act version in 1964, but the original version is more commonly performed.

RECORDING Brewer, Graham, Burden, BBC Singers & SO, Slatkin, Chandos, 2003
OTHER OPERAS *A Hand of Bridge*, 1959; *Antony and Cleopatra*, 1966, rev. 1975

P.D.

Béla Bartók

Béla Viktor János Bartók; *b* 25 March 1881, Nagyszentmiklós, Hungary (now Sînnicolau Mare, Romania); *d* 26 September 1945, New York

Bartók wrote only one opera, but it is the major work of his early maturity. *Duke Bluebeard's Castle* would doubtless have had successors but for the obstacles it encountered; these not only deterred him from writing for the stage but for a time blocked his creative faculty altogether. In 1911, at the time of its composition, Bartók was becoming established as a leading figure in Hungarian music, albeit through performance of early works that were no longer representative of his current style. In 1910 the first performance of his String Quartet No. 1, together with the experimental Bagatelles and the First Romanian Dance for piano, had been greeted with incomprehension verging on hostility, and when he entered his new opera for a competition sponsored by the Budapest Lipótvarós Club, it was rejected as unperformable and denied a prize.

The opera is nevertheless the most integrated of all Bartók's works written before the First World War and the first to show a completely personal synthesis of the various strains in his music up to that time. Seven years earlier he had been writing chamber works in a post-

Brahmsian manner. Then, in about 1905, he made his first contact with the ancient peasant music of Hungary, a music remote from the Hungarian style copied by Brahms, Liszt and others; and a year or two later he came across the latest piano music of Debussy (the *Estampes* and *Images*). The Bagatelles of 1908 show in rather anecdotal form some of the effects of these encounters. Folk-tunes with drumming accompaniments alternate with pieces using streams of common chords or series of irregular scale patterns that seem to mimic the modal scales of peasant music. In the first Bagatelle the left and right hands play in different keys, a semitone apart. But the String Quartet No. 1, written at about the same time, sticks to a lyrical manner not wholly remote from the Expressionism of contemporary Viennese music, though with folksong ingredients too. In the opera, which was Bartók's first work for voices, these apparently incompatible elements fused to create a unique masterpiece of Hungarian Symbolism.

Duke Bluebeard's Castle

A kékszakállú herceg vára

Opera in one act (1h)
Libretto by Béla Balázs, after the story by Charles Perrault (1697)
Composed March–September 1911; ending rev. 1912, 1918, 1921
PREMIERES 24 May 1918, Budapest Opera; US: 8 January 1946, Dallas (concert); 2 October 1952, State Theater, New York (stage); UK: 16 January 1957, Sadler's Wells, London
CAST Prologue (The Bard) *speaker*, Judith *s*, Duke Bluebeard *bar*, Bluebeard's 3 former wives *silent*

Balázs's play owes a good deal to Maeterlinck's *Ariane et Barbe-bleue*, set by Paul Dukas in 1907, and was apparently written in the same spirit as that play – that is, without commission but in the conscious hope that it would be set as an opera: 'I wrote [it] for Béla Bartók and Zoltán Kodály because I wanted to give them an opportunity to write works for the stage.' It treats the well-known legend of Bluebeard in Symbolistic fashion as an allegory of the incommunicable privacy of our inmost selves, and hence as a tragedy of Expressionism well adapted to the dying years of Romanticism. It must have had special resonance for Bartók, an intensely withdrawn but passionate man who had, moreover, recently married (the opera is dedicated to his wife, Márta Ziegler).

Duke Bluebeard's Castle had to wait until after the success of Bartók's ballet *The Wooden Prince* (1917) for its first production, and after 1918 there were no further Hungarian productions for nearly 20 years because the reactionary regime of Admiral Horthy would not allow the socialist Balázs's name to be credited, and Bartók would not allow performances if it were not. Recent revivals have shown, however, that the work's supposed untheatricality is a myth; static it may be, but the strong visual imagery more than compensates.

SYNOPSIS

The short spoken Prologue (often omitted in performance) hints that the well-known tale is to be retold as a parable of the inner self; the curtain then rises on a 'vast, circular Gothic hall' with seven large doors. When Bluebeard and Judith enter through another door at the top of the stairs, the 'dazzling white opening' is the only light in the darkened hall.

A short orchestral introduction sets the gloomy scene. Judith, who is still in her wedding dress, has married Bluebeard against her family's wishes. She finds his castle cold and dark and the walls ooze moisture. Bluebeard reminds her that she could have married into a 'brighter castle, girt with roses', but she insists that she will bring brightness to his castle. An orchestral transition clearly supports Bluebeard's denial of this possibility.

Judith now notices the seven doors

and demands that they be unlocked. She hammers on the first door, and as she does so a deep sigh is heard from behind it 'like the wind in a long, low corridor'. As the door swings open to reveal Bluebeard's torture chamber a blood-red light glares on to the stage. Undeterred, Judith insists on opening the second door. This time Bluebeard's armoury is revealed in 'a lurid reddish-yellow light'. Once again the 'blood' motif intrudes, as Judith sees blood on the weapons. But as she presses Bluebeard for the remaining keys, he senses the joy of release from oppressive secrets. He allows her three more keys. The doors open to display first his treasury and then his garden, bathed in a blue-green light. Yet again, the image of blood returns as Judith sees spots of red on the flowers. Finally the fifth door opens on to Bluebeard's vast and beautiful domains, portrayed in the grandest and loudest music in the whole work.

This is the architectural centre of the opera, and its visual climax in terms of light. The mood now returns gradually to the gloom and darkness of the start. Bluebeard tries to distract Judith from the remaining two doors, but she persists. She sees blood even on the lands that for him are radiant with light. Reluctantly he yields the sixth key, and as she turns it in the lock another deep sigh warns of sinister revelations, and a shadow passes over the hall. The door conceals a silent lake of tears. Judith now exerts her feminine guile to coax the final key out of Bluebeard. She questions him about his past lovers and suddenly guesses that the blood on his possessions signifies that he has murdered them all. Bluebeard gives her the key. The seventh door opens (at this point doors five and six should swing shut), and his three former wives, richly adorned, process slowly out. The first, he says, he met in the morning, the second at midday, the third in the evening. 'You', he tells Judith as the three women vanish back through the door, 'I met at night.' He dresses her in the crown, mantle and jewels she herself brought from the treasury (the third door closes as he does so), and she slowly follows the other wives through the seventh door, which closes behind her. 'The darkness of night creeps back across the stage, and engulfs Bluebeard.'

In musical style, *Duke Bluebeard's Castle* is still an early work which shows Bartók's debt to German and Austrian late-Romanticism. But it also reveals influences that were to help turn him into an abrasive modernist. Debussy is an obvious model for passages such as the massive parallel chords at the opening of the fifth door (cf. *La cathédrale engloutie* in the first book of *Préludes*, published in 1909), while echoes of Strauss's *Ein Heldenleben*, a work Bartók had once transcribed for piano, are unmistakable in the biting semitone clashes of the 'blood' motif. Yet *Bluebeard* is hardly a derivative score. It has an individuality that comes partly, perhaps, from Bartók's study of Hungarian folk music, with its strange modal scales, which seem to rub off on the opera's harmony as well as on its melody. The sharpened fourth note, which produces the interval C–F♯, is a common feature of the folksongs Bartók was collecting at this time, as is the descending perfect fourth, and both leave their mark on the very opening of the opera. Also typical of Hungarian peasant music are rhythmic details such as the decorated first beat, which produces the characteristic 'snap' or 'turn', and the so-called parlando rubato style of word-setting, which ensures that the incessant Hungarian accent on the first syllable rarely becomes monotonous, though it makes translation hard. Balázs himself modelled his regular octosyllabic lines on peasant verse.

Balázs's imagery, on the other hand, aligns him with modern Expressionism, with its strong colour symbolism; and with the German art nouveau, or Jugendstil, of which images of blood, flowers, castles and crowns were the stock in trade. Bartók adapts the gentle colourings of Debussian Impressionism to provide vivid but not-so-gentle musical equivalents of this imagery. In this respect *Bluebeard* is a kind of stage tone poem. It also has a strong built-in symbolism of its own, based on the opposition of keys and tonal centres. The score follows the arch form of the libretto. The darkness–light–darkness cycle is exactly matched by the tonal scheme, F♯–C–F♯, with its centre at the opening of the fifth door and its ending in the 'darkness' music of the start. Bartók's later instrumental music offers many more instances of this type of plan: the first movement of the *Music for Strings, Percussion and Celesta* (A–E♭–A), its third movement, and the larger arch structures of the Third and Fourth String Quartets. The actual key symbolism of *Bluebeard*, however, is unique in Bartók. F♯ stands for Bluebeard's world, while the outside world represented by Judith inhabits the region of F and C. But the symbolism is made ambiguous. For example, the C major of the fifth door is Bluebeard's pretence at normality, while Judith sees the shadow of blood on it (F♯). Bluebeard's first note is F♯; Judith's is F, but the wives are in C minor, though now belonging exclusively to his world. Bluebeard's last two notes are F♯ and C, and the last orchestral note C♯. The same ambiguity is constantly present in the harmony, which achieves psychological depth by mixing elements rather than segregating them.

RECORDINGS 1. Ludwig, Berry, LSO, Kertész, Decca, 1965; 2. Troyanos, Nimsgern, BBC SO, Boulez, CBS, 1976; 3. Varady, Fischer-Dieskau, Bavarian State O, Sawallisch, DG, 1979

S.W.

Ludwig van Beethoven

b 16 December 1770, Bonn; *d* 26 March 1827, Vienna

Amid the abundance and supreme self-confidence of Beethoven's oeuvre, his solitary opera cuts a strangely isolated and equivocal figure. In large-scale instrumental forms, Beethoven wrote prolifically and with a mastery surpassed by none. Yet he achieved only one opera – and this not from any lack of interest in writing for the theatre. (Music for the stage forms a surprisingly large part of his output – *Egmont* and the *Prometheus* ballet music are only the most obvious examples – and at intervals throughout his career we find him searching for a congenial opera libretto.) Moreover, this one opera took more than ten years to reach its final shape and went through three separate versions and no fewer than four overtures. Compared with the speed and assurance with which he wrote the Eroica Symphony, the Violin Concerto, the Razumovsky quartets, this degree of uncertainty suggests a clear distinction between a composer in his element in the symphonic medium and out of it in the operatic form.

So the argument frequently goes. *Fidelio* has regularly fallen foul of academic commentators. It is as if the work's detractors needed to free themselves of the burden of Beethoven's greatness by finding some field of composition in which he was not a master but could, on the contrary, be criticized and even patronized with impunity. Yet looked at without prejudice (including the prejudice against opera with spoken dialogue), *Fidelio* in its final form is as characteristic and as powerfully wrought as anything Beethoven wrote. It took him longer to perfect, not only because to begin with he lacked experience of the operatic medium but also because the subject – the unjustly imprisoned man, the fearless, dedicated woman –

moved him too much and struck such resounding chords in the depth of his being. But he got it right in the end.

Fidelio, oder Die eheliche Liebe

Fidelio, or Married Love

Opera in two acts (19 scenes) (2h 15m)
Libretto by Joseph Sonnleithner and Georg Friedrich Treitschke, after the libretto by Jean-Nicolas Bouilly for *Léonore ou L'amour conjugal* by Pierre Gaveaux (1789)
Composed 1804–5, rev. 1806 and 1814
PREMIERES original three-act version: 20 November 1805, Theater an der Wien, Vienna; first rev. version, in two acts: 29 March 1806, Theater an der Wien; second rev. version: 23 May 1814, Kärntnertortheater, Vienna; UK: 18 May 1832, King's Theatre, Haymarket, London; US: 9 September 1839, Park Theater, New York
CAST Leonore (Fidelio) *s*, Florestan *t*, Rocco *b*, Marzelline *s*, Jaquino *t*, Don Pizarro *bar*, Don Fernando *b-bar*, first prisoner *t*, second prisoner *bar*; *satb* chorus of officers, soldiers, state prisoners, people

Vienna first heard the rescue operas of the French Revolution school in the spring of 1802. These opéras comiques – operas with spoken dialogue, of which Cherubini's *Lodoïska* and *Les deux journées* were the prime examples – startled the Viennese with their dramatic force, realism and topicality and, for the next few years, dominated the Viennese stage. They made a profound impression on Beethoven, whose orchestral style, not only in *Fidelio* but generally, shows clear signs of the influence of Cherubini's massive, driving tuttis, insistent rhythms, incisive accents and cross-accents, and strong dynamic contrasts. By early 1803 he had signed a contract with the Theater an der Wien.

For some reason it was for a work not after the current French model but on an ancient Roman subject, entitled *Vestas Feuer*, the libretto by Emanuel Schikaneder (perhaps Beethoven accepted it because of his admiration for *The Magic Flute*). He composed a couple of scenes – musical material from one of them was later used for the *Fidelio* duet 'O namenlose Freude!' – but by the end of 1803 he had abandoned it and turned to a French libretto by J. N. Bouilly (librettist of Luigi Cherubini's *Les deux journées*), which had been set a few years earlier by the French composer Pierre Gaveaux (and which both Paer and Mayr set at about the same time as Beethoven).

The plot was based on an actual event that had happened not long before in France during the Terror: a woman disguises herself as a man in order to free her husband from a gaol where he is being held as a political prisoner. The poet Joseph Sonnleithner wrote a German version, and Beethoven worked on it during 1804 and the first half of 1805. Composition coincided with his abortive love affair with Josephine von Brunswick, and there is little doubt that his longing for a woman who would commit herself unreservedly to him gave added intensity to his portrait of Leonore, just as his self-identification with the lonely, persecuted Florestan – immured in the darkness of his cell, as Beethoven felt himself imprisoned in his growing deafness – contributed to the extraordinary force and vividness of the dungeon scene.

Despite its many beauties the first version of *Fidelio* (usually known as *Leonore*, the title Beethoven wanted to give the work) was not a success when it was performed in November 1805. Vienna was occupied by Napoleon's army. Most of Beethoven's supporters were absent, having fled the city, and by the time they came back the opera had been taken off. But it was also felt that the work had failed because it was too long, in particular because the early scenes dragged. For the revival in March–April 1806 Beethoven was persuaded, by Stephan von Breuning and others, to make cuts, some of them quite drastic. In this form (in two acts instead of three) it was more successful, but Beethoven, in dispute with the management, withdrew his score after only two performances.

It was not heard again for eight years. (A Prague production planned for 1807 came to nothing. It was probably for this production that Beethoven wrote the overture known as *Leonore No. 1*.) In 1814 when his fame (thanks to the enormously popular orchestral extravaganza *Wellington's Victory*) was at its height in Vienna, the Kärntnertortheater asked permission to revive *Fidelio*. He agreed, but insisted on a thorough revision. This time the opera was a triumphant success. The remodelling of the libretto was carried out by G. F. Treitschke, the theatre's stage manager and resident poet, in close collaboration with the composer. Treitschke removed several numbers from Act I and provided texts for a new final scene for the act, a new recitative ('Abscheulicher!') before the great aria 'Komm, Hoffnung' in which Leonore reasserts her faith in her heroic mission, a new final section for Florestan's scena, and a rewritten opening to the final scene of the opera (which was moved from the dungeon to the castle parade ground). It is to this revision that we owe two of the most exalted passages in the work: the farewell to the light of day sung by the prisoners as they return to their cells at the end of Act I (replacing the energetic but conventional original number) and Florestan's radiant vision of his wife.

In addition, the whole score was subjected to minute overhaul. *Fidelio* is a shorter opera than *Leonore*, not only because there are fewer numbers but because of a general tightening up. The excessive repetitions that marred the original score, especially in the domestic scenes of Act I, were stripped away. (Its prolixity is one reason why *Leonore*, though sometimes revived, cannot seriously be regarded as a valid alternative to *Fidelio*.) But the changes go deeper than simple abbreviation. Again and again Beethoven altered the declamation or the rhythmic emphasis, so that the voice part made its point more tellingly and the rhythms became more varied and vital. To take only the most striking example, the dungeon quartet was transformed; though most alterations may be small, the cumulative effect is crucial. Already a very powerful piece of dramatic music in 1805, it becomes overwhelming in its final form.

A few changes made in 1806 were retained; but some of the most extreme were rejected. In particular, both the dungeon trio and the great F major ensemble in the final scene were reshaped, becoming the same length as in the hurriedly cut version of 1806 but now perfectly formed, no longer mutilated.

The work's key structure was also changed. In *Leonore* C major, the key of freedom and salvation, was established at the outset as the home key; in *Fidelio* it emerges gradually. The new overture (*Fidelio*) is in E (the key of Leonore's aria). During the first act B♭, the prison key, becomes increasingly prominent, and the second act begins in its dominant minor, F. C is touched on from time to time, but as a foreign key, though often at moments of transcendent meaning (the sacrament of bread in the dungeon trio, Leonore's holy resolve to save the prisoner even if he is not her husband). It is only in the final scene that its triumph is achieved. This new evolutionary treatment of tonality is an aspect of the more flexible and dramatic conception of opera that Beethoven had acquired by the time he revised his score.

Even more important, he reduced the weight of the orchestration. The original version is much more thickly scored, less epic in sound, more lyrical, more Romantic. For example, in *Leonore* the introduction to the dungeon scene creates an almost Wagnerian effect. Beethoven's revision of it, which also shortened it by nine bars, altered its character profoundly. The texture was thinned out: string tremolos were confined to four bars, the trombones were removed altogether. So were the trumpets; they were now kept back until the quartet, to blaze forth the more brilliantly at the moment when the prisoner defies his assassin. Horns and timpani were left on their own to evoke a far more awesome sense of cold, vaulted darkness; in this austerer texture, too, the melodic cries in octave doublings on the woodwind which sound from the surrounding gloom stand out more sharply. This leaner, starker but also more glowing sonority is characteristic of the final version as a whole; it is true to the original idea behind the opera whereas the luxuriance of 1805 was not. The grief and passion and heroism of the drama, the sense of feelings stretched almost to breaking point, the central concept of human suffering in the context of divine providence, achieved their destined sound in 1814.

SYNOPSIS

Florestan, who disappeared two years ago and is believed dead, has been incarcerated secretly by his political enemy Don Pizarro. Florestan's wife, Leonore, in search of him, disguises herself as a young man and, under the name Fidelio, enters the service of the prison where Pizarro is governor.

Act I: The prison courtyard on a fine spring morning. Marzelline, the gaoler's daughter, is ironing. Jaquino, the turnkey, in the intervals of dealing with packages arriving at the postern gate, tries to get her to name a day for their wedding, but she rebuffs him ('Jetzt, Schätzchen, jetzt sind wir allein'). She used to like Jaquino, but everything has changed; now her dream is of married bliss with Fidelio ('O wär ich schon mit dir vereint'). Rocco, the gaoler, enters, followed by Fidelio (Leonore) who is carrying heavy chains from the blacksmith. Rocco praises Fidelio's zeal and hints broadly that he understands the reason for it. They all reflect on what this new turn of events means for them ('Mir ist so wunderbar'). Rocco offers Fidelio his daughter's hand but points out that a sound marriage depends as much on money as on love ('Hat man nicht auch Gold beineben'). Leonore begs Rocco, as a mark of trust, to let her help him in the cells. Rocco agrees to ask the governor, though there is one cell, occupied by a prisoner on starvation rations, where he will never be allowed to take Fidelio. Pizarro arrives with an armed escort. One of the letters he is given warns him that the Minister, Don Fernando, has heard rumours of injustice and is coming to inspect the gaol. Pizarro decides to kill Florestan ('Ha! welch' ein Augenblick!'). He posts a trumpeter on the tower overlooking the road from Seville and orders Rocco to prepare the unnamed prisoner's grave. Leonore overhears their conversation. Appalled by Pizarro's inhuman cruelty, she reaffirms her faith in the power of love ('Abscheulicher! . . . Komm, Hoffnung'). Leonore persuades Rocco to let the prisoners out into the garden. With Jaquino she unlocks the cell doors, and the prisoners emerge wonderingly into the light of day ('O welche Lust!'). Rocco returns with the news that Fidelio is to be allowed to help dig the grave of the mysterious prisoner. Leonore weeps at the thought that it may be her husband's but convinces Rocco that it is her duty to go with him. Pizarro, discovering that the prisoners have been let out, angrily orders them back, and they return to their cells ('Leb' wohl, du warmes Sonnenlicht').

Act II: A deep dungeon. Florestan sits in darkness lit by a small lamp; he is chained to a stone, but his spirit is unbroken. Half delirious with hunger, he has a vision of an angel in the likeness of Leonore, surrounded by bright light and leading him to freedom ('Gott! welch' Dunkel hier! . . . In des Lebens Frühlingstagen'). He rises to follow her but the chain drags him back and he collapses unconscious. Rocco and Leonore enter the dungeon and, while the prisoner sleeps (his face invisible), clear the opening of a disused cistern. Leonore resolves to save the man whoever he is. When Florestan wakes, she recognizes him. Rocco gives him a little wine and is persuaded by Leonore to overlook orders and let her give him some bread ('Euch werde Lohn'). At a signal from Rocco, Pizarro appears. He is about to stab Florestan when Leonore springs forward and shields him, crying 'First kill his wife!' ('Töt' erst sein Weib!'). She draws a pistol. At that moment, far above, a trumpet sounds. It sounds a second time, louder, as the door leading to the cell opens. Jaquino calls out from the top of the steps that the Minister has arrived. Alone, Leonore and Florestan, reunited, thank God for their deliverance ('O namenlose Freude!'). The parade ground of the fortress. The Minister addresses the people: he has come to free them from tyranny. Pizarro is taken away by guards. Leonore unlocks Florestan's chains and all give thanks to God who did not forsake them ('O Gott! welch' ein Augenblick!'). Led by Florestan, the released prisoners and the people join in a hymn of praise to the noble woman who saved her husband's life ('Wer ein holdes Weib errungen').

The mixture of domestic comedy and heroic melodrama, which Beethoven took from Cherubini and which remains central to the work even in the shortened final version, has worried commentators. But it is fundamental to the whole conception, which is that love, devotion, courage, faith are not exclusively 'operatic' qualities, to be presented only in lofty romantic settings, but human attributes that may flower in the most humdrum surroundings. It is right that *Fidelio* should begin with Marzelline ironing, that Leonore's first words – spoken, not sung – should concern the cost of repairs carried out by the blacksmith, and that we learn of her perilous quest only by degrees. The process by which the singspiel atmosphere of the early scenes is gradually left behind and the musical language deepens and intensifies in preparation for the great dungeon scene – a process that culminates in the mysterious final bars of Act I – is the work of a master of music drama, however heterodox.

For the same reasons the two huge *Leonore* overtures of 1805 (*No. 2*) and 1806 (*No. 3*), virtual symphonic poems that anticipate the heroic issues of the opera, make way for a much shorter piece, a true prelude to the action – to quote Tovey, 'dramatic, brilliant, terse, and with an indication of some formidable force in the background'. The practice of playing the *Leonore No. 3* overture between the dungeon scene and the finale – a practice, still not uncommon, that goes back at least to the middle of the 19th century and therefore antedates Mahler, who is often said to have originated it – is wrong on at least two counts. It imposes an alien sound on *Fidelio* – the heavier 1805–6 orchestration that Beethoven deliberately changed in 1814 – and it destroys the effect that is created by going straight from the sublimities of the Leonore–Florestan duet to the festive, breezy march that begins the finale.

To bring us back to earth again in the final scene of the opera, after the torrential force of the dungeon quartet and the incandescence of the ensuing duet, is a stroke of the highest realism. But realism cannot have the last word. The opera ends in a mighty hymn to liberty and the noble, all-enduring woman, sung by the whole company, soloists and chorus, in a blazing C major that dissolves the personal drama into a vision of universal love; a conclusion that has been criticized as being more cantata than opera. But *Fidelio* could not end in any other way. This has been at the heart of the work from the moment that Leonore's aria was followed immediately by the prisoners' chorus; and the final progression from the particular to the universal is the natural and logical conclusion. It brings to flower the seed of selfless love planted in the darkness of the dungeon (and in the key of C major) at the most apparently hopeless point of Leonore's quest, as she digs the grave of the man who may be her husband and realizes that ultimately it does not matter who he is: even if he is not Florestan and her journey has been in vain, 'I will loose your chains whoever you are, unhappy man, by God I will save you and set you free.'

RECORDINGS *Leonore* (1805) Martinpelto, Oelze, Begley, Schade, M. Best, Hawlata, Miles, Monteverdi Ch, O Revolutionnaire et Romantique, Gardiner, Archiv, 1996 (inc. nos from later versions); *Fidelio* 1. Rysanek, Seefried, Haefliger, Fischer-Dieskau, Frick, Bavarian State Op Ch & O, Fricsay, DG, 1957; 2. Ludwig, Hallstein, Vickers, Berry, Frick, Philharmonia Ch & O, Klemperer, EMI, 1962; 3. Margiano, Bonney, Seiffert, Polgár, Leiferkus, COE, Harnoncourt, Teldec, 1994

D.C.

Vincenzo Bellini

Vincenzo Salvatore Carmelo Francesco Bellini; *b* 3 November 1801, Catania, Sicily; *d* 23 September 1835, Puteaux, Paris

Together with Rossini, Donizetti and Verdi, Bellini is one of the four great figures of Italian Romantic opera whose work remains fundamental to the repertoire of all Italian and most international opera houses. Less prolific and less versatile than the other three, he nevertheless produced in the late 1820s a group of operas that were seminal in establishing in Italy a distinctively Romantic musical language; and in the masterpieces of the early 1830s – *La sonnambula* (1831), *Norma* (1831) and *I puritani* (1835) – he brought the art of bel canto opera to its apogee.

Bellini's early musical education was at the hands of his father Rosario and his grandfather Vincenzo Tobia, both professional musicians in Catania. In 1819 he was enrolled as a pupil at the Conservatorio di San Sebastiano in Naples, where, from 1822, the teaching of Nicola Zingarelli, the director, exerted a lasting influence. Zingarelli introduced Bellini to the best of the Neapolitan masters of the past and to the instrumental music of Haydn and Mozart, but his shrewdest pedagogical stroke was to invite him to put away his contrapuntal studies and concentrate on refining his skills as a melodist, listening to the dictates of his heart and striving to express them in pure and simple song. Zingarelli apparently felt it necessary to 'protect' his students from Rossini, whose music dominated the repertoire in the public theatres of the city, and it was only as a final-year student, in 1824, that Bellini first heard a Rossini opera (*Semiramide*). Nevertheless, relations between Bellini and Zingarelli remained exceptionally affectionate: the old maestro followed his young protégé's career with pride, and in due course was thanked in princely fashion with the dedication of *Norma*.

It was customary each year to give one of the outstanding students the experience of composing a short opera and staging it in the conservatory theatre. Bellini's début, *Adelson e Salvini*, came early in 1825 and was so successful that he was commissioned to compose a full-length opera (*Bianca e Gernando*) for the Teatro San Carlo the following year. The impresario there, Domenico Barbaja, was also involved in the running of La Scala in Milan. Inevitably therefore, Bellini's success in Naples led to his being invited to go north and compose his third opera, *Il pirata* (1827), for La Scala, to a libretto by Felice Romani, the most admired theatre poet of the age. The two men got along famously, and their partnership was to prove one of the most remarkable in operatic history: all seven of the remaining operas Bellini composed in Italy had Romani libretti, and all but *Zaira* (1829) and *Beatrice di Tenda* (1833) triumphed gloriously. Their first works together, *Il pirata* and *La straniera* (1829), bizarre and violent in plot and set to music of matching emotional abandon, marked the beginning of full-blooded Romanticism in Italian opera. But tragedy in the most elevated Classical style also came within their range (*Norma*); and so did sentimental tenderness (*La sonnambula*).

Until the early months of 1833, Bellini

had enjoyed a prodigiously successful Italian career, and by now his fame had spread throughout Europe and reached America. From an early date he could and did demand high fees for his operas, not simply out of greed, but because he was, for Italy, a new kind of composer, one who felt a need for a greater measure of independence than did most of his predecessors; he liked to work slowly and was disinclined to assume the kind of official teaching or administrative posts they had virtually always filled. The fiasco of *Beatrice di Tenda* in March 1833 and the attendant breakdown of his partnership with Romani was a severe blow. At the same time his personal life was in a state of upheaval; a long-standing love affair with Giuditta Turina, having been discovered by her husband, had become a source of embarrassment and inconvenience. An invitation to visit London to help produce three of his operas was probably doubly welcome therefore. After a successful trip, he made no hasty return to Italy, but lingered in Paris, traditionally a Mecca for Italian composers.

Bellini's last opera, *I puritani*, was composed for the Théâtre-Italien. Like so many Italians before him, he found it enormously stimulating to compose for Paris: the scope of his work seemed to expand, its manner to become more urbane and cosmopolitan. During the composition he was often with Rossini, who, though he no longer held an official position at the Théâtre-Italien, remained the presiding genius of operatic life in Paris. A relationship that began, as far as Bellini was concerned, out of calculated self-interest developed into one of genuine mutual respect, and Bellini benefited much from the older composer's advice. But working on the opera showed him more clearly than ever how badly he needed a librettist of Romani's calibre, and in the last year of his life he made energetic attempts to re-establish a working relationship with his old comrade-in-arms. The success of *I puritani* gave Bellini a position in Parisian musical life 'second only to Rossini' (letter to Francesco Florimo, 21 September 1834); but there is no reason to doubt that, but for an untimely and wretched death from acute gastro-enteritis, complicated by an abscess of the liver, he would soon have returned to Italy.

I Capuleti e i Montecchi

The Capulets and the Montagues

Tragedia lirica in two acts (four parts) (2h 15m)
Libretto by Felice Romani (a reworking of his libretto, *Giulietta e Romeo*, written for Nicola Vaccai in 1825), after the 16th-century novella *Giulietta e Romeo* by Matteo Bandello and a play of the same name by Luigi Sceola (1818)
Composed January–March 1830
PREMIERES 11 March 1830, La Fenice, Venice; UK: 20 July 1833, King's Theatre, Haymarket, London; US: 4 April 1837, St Charles Theater, New Orleans
CAST Capellio *b*, Giulietta *s*, Romeo *ms*, Tebaldo *t*, Lorenzo *bar* or *b*; *satb* chorus of Capulets, Montagues, maidens, soldiers, squires

At the end of 1829, while Bellini was in Venice to supervise a revival of *Il pirata*, Giovanni Pacini withdrew from a contract to write an opera for the same 1829–30 Carnival season. The impresario Lanari persuaded Bellini to come to his rescue by composing a new opera in considerable haste – something he was normally most reluctant to do. The task proved possible partly because Romani was able quickly to rework to Bellini's satisfaction a libretto originally set by Nicola Vaccai four years earlier and partly because, having written off *Zaira*, Bellini had a store of good music waiting to find a more congenial dramatic home. Eight movements are based on material from the ill-fated Parma opera, and a further one is a revision of 'Dopo l'oscuro nembo' from *Adelson e Salvini*. The opera was ecstatically received: in Bellini's own words, '*Zaira* was revenged in *I Capuleti e i Montecchi*'. At a revival in

Paris in 1832 Maria Malibran, apparently at Rossini's suggestion, replaced the final scene of the opera with the corresponding scene from Vaccai's setting, a piece of high-handedness that was long imitated. Despite its theme, Bellini's opera is only tenuously linked to Shakespeare: Romani made some use of Jean-François Ducis's then fashionable French adaptation of Shakespeare, but his primary sources were Bandello's novella and Sceola's play.

SYNOPSIS
Act I: Thirteenth-century Verona. As warfare threatens again between Guelphs and Ghibellines, Capellio, chief of the Capulets, scorns the offer of a pact, to be sealed by the marriage of his daughter Giulietta with Romeo, and agrees that her wedding with Tebaldo should take place without delay. Having failed to persuade Giulietta to elope with him, Romeo and his supporters enter the city in disguise and interrupt the festivities. Romeo reveals himself as Tebaldo's rival.

Act II: Giulietta is persuaded by the family doctor Lorenzo that her only chance of escaping marriage with Tebaldo is to take a sleeping draught so powerful that she will be taken for dead; when she revives in the family burial vault, he and Romeo will be waiting for her. But Lorenzo's plan goes wrong: he himself is arrested, and Romeo, believing Giulietta to be really dead, comes to her tomb and takes poison. She awakes as he is dying, and when Capellio and Lorenzo rush in in a desperate bid to avert catastrophe they find her, broken-hearted and lifeless, lying on Romeo's body.

Though so much of *I Capuleti e i Montecchi* consists of 'parody' (the reworking of pre-existent music to fit a new text and a new dramatic context) – and parody was doubtless a labour-saving device – Bellini took infinite trouble over the procedure, scrupulously reassessing every detail of the original in the light of its new purpose. After the 'philosophical' austerity of his previous two operas, *Il pirata* and *La straniera*, Bellini's lyricism begins to relax and smile a little once more: the swaying 9/8 and 12/8 rhythms, the charming ornamental flourishes at cadences, the many dulcet passages where voices and instruments move in parallel thirds, are all characteristic of his full maturity. The orchestration was much admired by contemporary critics: a striking feature is the several instrumental preludes built around a 'song-without-words' type of instrumental solo. The *stretto* of the Act I finale ('Se ogni speme è a noi rapita'), where the lovers sing a long ecstatic cantabile melody in unison, is one of the earliest and most eloquent examples of what was soon to become a hackneyed device; when Berlioz heard a performance of the opera in Florence in 1831 he was, despite his impatience with what he mistakenly took to be a travesty of his beloved Shakespeare, bowled over by the 'wonderful *élan* and intensity' of this passage. Wagner, for whom the performance of Wilhelmine Schröder-Devrient as Romeo had been one of the great artistic experiences of his youth, acknowledged the influence of Bellini's opera on the second act of *Tristan und Isolde*.

RECORDINGS 1. Gruberova, Baltsa, Raffanti, Howell, Tomlinson, Covent Garden Ch & O, Muti, EMI, 1984; 2. Mei, Kasarova, Vargas, Chiummo, Alberghini, Munich RCh & O, R. Abbado, RCA, 1997 (adds alternative ending written by Vaccai for Malibran); 3. Hong, Larmore, Groves, Lloyd, Scottish CCh & CO, Runnicles, Teldec, 1998

La sonnambula

The Sleepwalker

Melodramma in two acts (3h)
Libretto by Felice Romani, after the scenario by Eugène Scribe for Jean-Pierre Aumer's ballet *La somnambule, ou L'arrivée d'un nouveau seigneur* (1827) (music by Ferdinand Hérold)
Composed January–March 1831
PREMIERES 6 March 1831, Teatro

Carcano, Milan; UK: 28 July 1831, King's Theatre, Haymarket, London; US: 13 November 1835, Park Theater, New York
CAST Count Rodolfo *b*, Teresa *ms*, Amina *s*, Elvino *t*, Lisa *s*, Alessio *b*, Notary *t*; *satb* chorus of peasants

At the end of February 1830, while Bellini was preparing the Venetian premiere of *I Capuleti e i Montecchi*, Victor Hugo's *Hernani* had been performed amid clamorous controversy at the Comédie-Française in Paris. Echoes of *Hernani*'s triumph, which signalled the taking over of the French theatre by the representatives of Romanticism and Liberalism, were heard all over Europe, and in the late summer and autumn Bellini and Romani worked on an operatic adaptation. But in the wake of the series of political insurrections that had occurred during the year, Italian theatre censorship was tightened up, *Ernani* was abandoned, and the two colleagues turned from a revolutionary subject to what was ostensibly the most socially reactionary of all their operas. *La sonnambula* is an Arcadian idyll in which a group of simple Swiss villagers are saved from the consequences of their folly by the benign protection of Count Rodolfo, the 'signor del villaggio'. With its pastoral setting, its Utopian vision of a harmoniously ordered society and a happy ending reached by way of situations of great poignancy, rather than by the intrigues of comedy, *La sonnambula* is close in spirit to the first classic of the semiseria genre, Giovanni Paisiello's *Nina* of 1789.

The principal role in *La sonnambula* was composed for Giuditta Pasta, one of the very greatest of the many remarkable sopranos of that era, a consummate artist with whom Bellini established a working relationship as fruitful as that he enjoyed with Rubini (who took the role of Elvino). He once paid tribute to her 'encyclopedic' artistry, and proved the point by composing for her not only the gracefully tender Amina, but the more austere and powerfully dramatic roles of Norma and Beatrice di Tenda. Thanks to the combination of the exquisite lyricism of Bellini's full maturity and the incomparable vocal arts of Pasta and Rubini the early performances of *La sonnambula* provided some of the most blissful evenings in the annals of Italian opera. The Russian composer Glinka, who witnessed them, left in his *Memoirs* a vivid account of the scenes in the theatre and of the 'tears of emotion and ecstasy' that were continually shed.

SYNOPSIS

Act I: The scene is set in a Swiss village. Scene 1: Outside Teresa's mill the village is celebrating the approaching marriage of the orphan Amina to the wealthy farmer Elvino; only the jealous Lisa, hostess of the local inn, finds it difficult to join in ('Tutto è gioia, tutto è festa'). Amina thanks her friends, especially Teresa, who has loved her like a mother ('Come per me sereno . . . Sovra il sen la man mi posa'). Elvino, who has been praying at his mother's tomb, arrives a little late. But now the civil wedding can proceed ('Prendi: l'anel ti dono'); tomorrow it will be solemnized in church. A stranger enters; though the villagers do not know him, he is in fact Rodolfo, their feudal lord, who, on the death of his father, is returning home after a long absence during which he was himself mourned for dead. Learning that the castle is far off, he decides to stay overnight in Lisa's inn. The village scene brings youthful memories flooding back ('Vi ravviso, o luoghi ameni'), and the sight of the young bride reminds him of his own lost love ('Tu non sai con quei begli occhi'). Evening falls; before making their way home, the villagers tell the sceptical Rodolfo of a ghost that has been haunting the vicinity. Elvino is jealous at the attention Rodolfo was paying his bride, but left alone with Amina he is soon reassured ('Son geloso del zefiro errante'). Scene 2: In a room in the inn, Rodolfo is enjoying his homecoming, and when Lisa comes to inquire after his comfort, he flirts with her. They are interrupted when the window opens and Amina enters. Lisa hides, dropping a handkerchief; then, believing that Amina has come for an assignation with the Count, she hurries out to alert Elvino. Meanwhile, Rodolfo realizes that Amina is sleepwalking; tempted as he is to take advantage of her, he is touched by the words she utters in her dream and goes out, leaving her asleep on the sofa. Villagers come to pay homage to the noble guest and are perplexed to find no one but a sleeping woman. When Lisa returns with Elvino, the sleeper is revealed as Amina; she awakes, to find herself denounced for her shamelessness. Though she protests her innocence ('D'un pensiero a d'un accento'), Elvino declares that there can now be no wedding; only Teresa is moved by Amina's plight.

Act II, Scene 1: A wood. The villagers' affection for Amina has revived, and they set out to the castle to ask Rodolfo to clear up the mystery. Amina and Teresa are also going there, but as they pass Elvino's farm Amina's strength fails her. They meet Elvino, who repulses her again and takes back his ring; even the joyful return of the villagers and their assurances of Amina's innocence cannot soften his bitterness ('Tutto è sciolto' – 'Ah! perchè non posso odiarti?'). Scene 2: The village. The unhappy Alessio, a peasant who loves Lisa, learns that Elvino has decided to marry her instead of Amina; Lisa exults in her good fortune ('De' lieti auguri a voi son grata'). Rodolfo explains to Elvino the phenomenon of somnambulism; but neither he nor the villagers credit such unlikely tales. When Teresa produces the handkerchief Lisa dropped in Rodolfo's room, Elvino is ready to despair of womankind; but now they are all astonished to see Amina indeed sleepwalking across the roof of the mill. When she reaches the ground she can be heard praying for Elvino and lamenting the loss of his love ('Ah! non credea mirarti'). Rodolfo prompts Elvino to replace the ring he took from Amina's finger. When she wakes, she finds Elvino kneeling at her feet and her friends rejoicing. The lovers are escorted away to church for the wedding ('Ah! non giunge uman pensiero').

La sonnambula is Bellini's first mature masterpiece: the little world of Amina and Elvino is embodied in music of a rare unity of spirit, yet within that unity the melodic invention is of a prodigal richness. Nothing is lost of the expressive directness his music had gained during his 'philosophical' years; but it is now combined with a new elegance and sensibility, heard at its most beguiling in the duet 'Son geloso del zefiro errante'. Aria forms have become more varied, with less dependence on the tight, symmetrical A–A'–B–A' design of the previous years. Bellini's determination to make even the most conventional and formal parts of the opera dramatically meaningful is vividly shown in the introduction to Elvino's 'Tutto è sciolto', where a recitative sung by Amina – a commentary on Elvino's emotional state – is superimposed on the orchestral melody, a device used again with powerful effect in *Norma*. The sense that the leading characters are part of a close-knit community is conveyed musically by the continual interaction of soloists and chorus: in the majority of the arias and ensembles the solo voices are at some stage or other set in high relief against a background in which colour and harmony are due as much to the chorus as to the orchestra. In writing for Pasta, Bellini was stimulated to extend the expressive range of his lyricism. The magnificent amplitude of Amina's opening cavatina – which embraces ecstatic introspection, tender recitative-like musings and exuberant virtuosity – is new in his work; and in the closing scene her heart-broken 'Ah! non credea mirarti' has good claims to be regarded as the supreme example of those 'long, long, long melodies' that Verdi so much admired.

RECORDINGS 1. Callas, Valletti, Modesti, La Scala Ch & O, Bernstein,

Cetra, 1955 (live); 2. Sutherland, Pavarotti, Ghiaurov, London Op Ch, Nat PO, Bonynge, Decca, 1980; 3. Orgonášová, Giménez, Ellero D'Artegna, Netherlands RCh & CO, Zedda, Naxos, 1992 (live)

Norma

Tragedia lirica in two acts (3h)
Libretto by Felice Romani, after the tragedy *Norma* by Alexandre Soumet (1831) and drawing on *Les martyrs* by Chateaubriand (1809)
Composed September–December 1831
PREMIERES 26 December 1831, La Scala, Milan; UK: 20 June 1833, King's Theatre, Haymarket, London; US: 1 April 1836, St Charles Theater, New Orleans
CAST Pollione *t*, Oroveso *b*, Norma *s*, Adalgisa *s*, Clotilde *ms*, Flavio *t*, 2 children (sons of Norma and Pollione) *silent*; *satb* chorus of druids, bards, eubages, priestesses, virgins, warriors, soldiers

Of all Bellini's operas *Norma* is the one whose reputation has been least affected by changes in fashion. For his librettist, Felice Romani, it was 'the most beautiful rose in the garland'; and this view was shared by Richard Wagner, who, in his Riga years (1837–9), wrote an eloquent essay on what he called 'indisputably Bellini's most successful composition' (as well as an insert aria for Oroveso, 'Norma il predisse'). He went on to praise Romani's libretto, 'which soars to the tragic heights of the ancient Greeks . . . all the passions, so characteristically ennobled by Bellini's melodies, are thereby given a majestic foundation and support, [and] form themselves into grandiose and distinct pictures, that remind us involuntarily of the creations of Gluck and Spontini'. The mastery of Romani's text was not lightly achieved. Bellini, now at the height of his powers and self-confidence, was exacting in his demands, and many sections of the libretto were written over and over again before they satisfied him.

The role of Norma was designed for Giuditta Pasta. It would be ideal, Bellini told her, for a singer with her 'encyclopedic' range of expression; and he encouraged her, once she had read Romani's text, to let him know if she had any thoughts on the part which he ought to bear in mind when he was composing. A well-authenticated anecdote reports that she at first disliked 'Casta Diva', finding it ill-suited to her voice; that Bellini promised he would rewrite it, if she practised it faithfully every day for a week and still felt the same; that Pasta agreed, was slowly won over by the splendour of the music and, having sent Bellini a charming gift as an expression of contrition, went on to make her performance of it one of the highlights of the score.

Norma enjoyed a less instantaneous success than most of Bellini's operas; the composer blamed hostile factions in the audience for what he felt had been 'a solemn fiasco'. But it rapidly overcame that initial coolness, enjoying 34 performances before the end of the season and conquering the whole of Europe in the space of a few years. In view of the reputation the opera now enjoys as one of the most demanding in the repertoire, it is astonishing to see the central position it held in popular music-making in the mid-19th century. When Glinka was in Murcia, southern Spain, in 1845, he witnessed a performance given by a local children's theatre; at much the same time Charles Dickens visited Carrara, where he heard an act of the opera performed in the local theatre with a chorus provided by labourers from the marble quarries. On several occasions during the Risorgimento we hear of music from *Norma* serving as the focus for patriotic demonstrations. In 1848, for example, at a service in the cathedral at Palermo to celebrate the liberation of Sicily from the Bourbons, the blessing of the tricolour was accompanied by a performance of 'Guerra, guerra!', the 'war hymn' from Act II of the opera.

SYNOPSIS

Act I: Gaul during the Roman Occupation, *c.*50 BC. Scene 1: The sacred forest of the druids; night. Gaulish warriors and druids, led by the chief druid, Oroveso, process to the oak of Irminsul; at moonrise they expect the druidess Norma, Oroveso's daughter, to signal a revolt against the Romans ('Ite sul colle'). Pollione, the Roman pro-consul, and Flavio enter. Pollione's love for Norma has been quenched by a new passion for Adalgisa, an acolyte in the temple of Irminsul; and, despite an ominous dream, he is determined to take her to Rome and marry her ('Meco all'altar di Venere'). Summoned by a gong, the Gauls reassemble. Norma is angered by their impatience, for all will be lost if they strike too soon; then, while priestesses gather the sacred mistletoe, she invokes the moon ('Casta Diva, che inargenti'). But in reality she still longs to win back Pollione's love ('Ah! bello a me ritorna'). Left alone, Adalgisa prays for relief from the emotions that torment her; but when Pollione appears, urging her to abandon the cruel gods of the North, she agrees to elope the following night ('Va crudele ... Vieni in Roma'). Scene 2: Norma's dwelling. Pollione has been recalled to Rome, and Norma is troubled by the sight of the children she has secretly borne him. Adalgisa comes to confess her love and seek Norma's guidance; Norma, oblivious of the object of Adalgisa's passion and touched by the story, readily releases her from her vows ('Sola, furtiva, al tempio ... Ah sì! fa core, abbracciami'). But when Pollione arrives, the truth is clear. Adalgisa is appalled to learn that he is Norma's seducer and swears she would rather die than let him abandon Norma. As they argue the temple gong sounds; Pollione is warned that for him it signifies death ('Oh! di qual sei tu vittima ... Vanne, sì, mi lascia, indegno').

Act II, Scene 1: The same. Norma watches over her sleeping children, dagger in hand; would it not be better to kill them than to have them carried off to Rome as slaves ('Dormono entrambi')? Since she must die to atone for her guilt, she solemnly entrusts the children to Adalgisa. But in a long, emotional dialogue she is persuaded that all may yet be well: Adalgisa vows to love Pollione no more, but to bring him back to Norma ('Deh! con te, con te li prendi ... Mira, o Norma ... Sì, fino all'ore estreme'). Scene 2: A desolate spot close to the druids' forest. The Gauls eagerly await Pollione's departure, but are dismayed to hear from Oroveso that an even harsher pro-consul has been appointed to succeed him; they must be patient a little longer ('Ah! del Tebro al giogo indegno'). Scene 3: The temple of Irminsul. Learning that Adalgisa's mission to Pollione failed, Norma strikes the sacred shield to summon the Gauls. The hour has come for the Romans to be destroyed ('Guerra, guerra!'); all that is wanting is a victim to sacrifice to the god. Pollione is reported captured while sacrilegiously breaking into the virgins' temple enclosure. Norma insists that she be left alone to question him: unafraid of death, he refuses to renounce Adalgisa ('In mia man alfin tu sei'). Norma calls back the Gauls, orders a pyre to be prepared, and reveals that she is herself the sacrificial victim. Her nobility revives Pollione's love; but Oroveso is deeply ashamed, and only Norma's most eloquent prayers can persuade him to accept guardianship of her children. She is stripped of her sacred insignia, veiled in black, anathematized and led off with Pollione to the flames ('Qual cor tradisti ... Deh! non volerli vittime').

The greatest opera by Bellini is not necessarily the most sophisticated. The noblest pages of *Norma* tend to be sustained by a harmonic vocabulary of no more than three or four basic chords; and it is the dissonant tensions set up between this 'primitive', impassive harmony and the singing voices that soar above that give the music its weight of expressiveness (the arioso 'Teneri figli' encapsulates the style in a few bars). Similarly, Bellini makes no attempt with his orchestra to emulate the verve and wit of Rossini, let alone to explore the new worlds of sound opened up by his French and German contemporaries. There are some beautifully apt orchestral colours in the score – the cool, sacral flute in 'Casta Diva', for example, or the combination of pure string tone and ominously rumbling timpani in 'Qual cor tradisti' – but Bellini's most astonishing achievement in Norma is, amid all the more obvious excitements of musical Romanticism, to have asserted his belief that the true magic of opera depended on a kind of incantation in which dramatic poetry and song are perfectly fused.

'In mia man' – a duet without ensemble singing, in which the melody passes dialogue-like from voice to voice – is an ideal place to observe Bellini's art of conjuring poetry, character and drama into song. For 26 bars, as Norma and Pollione are stalemated in a conflict of wills, the music remains virtually motionless, using a vocabulary of three chords and giving not the slightest hint of a modulation; a glimpse of possible freedom has the music opening up to the relative C major; and when Pollione declines the proffered bargain, it returns inexorably to the home key; the music turns to the minor, and the delivery of the text accelerates nervously as Norma begins to realize that she has no chance of conquering Pollione's will. And all the time, the melody is exquisitely sculpted around the words, highlighting crucial phrases by tessitura, rhetorical word-repetition or 'madrigalisms'. Such perfect fusion of music with dramatic meaning is to be found everywhere in Bellini's mature works.

Norma follows *I Capuleti e i Montecchi* in discarding the popular convention of an aria finale, complete with cabaletta, for the prima donna. In fashioning the closing scene to match the dramatic catastrophe, Bellini apparently had to overcome the resistance of a nervous impresario. But, in his own words, 'these last two pieces ('Qual cor tradisti' and 'Deh! non volerli vittime') are of so original a type and so effective, that they have silenced any enemies I might have had . . . I think they are the best pieces I have composed so far.'

RECORDINGS 1. Callas, Ludwig, Corelli, Zaccaria, La Scala Ch & O, Serafin, EMI, 1954; 2. Sutherland, Horne, Alexander, Cross, LSCh & LSO, Bonynge, Decca, 1964

I puritani

The Puritans

Opera seria (melodramma serio) in three parts (2h 45m)
Libretto by Count Carlo Pepoli, after the historical drama *Têtes rondes et cavaliers* (1833) by Jacques-Arsène Polycarpe François Ancelot and Joseph-Xavier Boniface ('Xavier Saintine'), in turn derived from the novel *Old Mortality* by Sir Walter Scott (1816)
Composed April 1834–January 1835; rev. December 1834–January 1835
PREMIERES 25 January 1835, Théâtre-Italien, Paris; UK: 21 May 1835, King's Theatre, London; US: 22 July 1843, Chestnut St Theater, Philadelphia; rev. version: 14 December 1985, Barbican Centre, London (concert); 1 April 1986, Teatro Petruzzelli, Bari
CAST Lord Gualtiero Valton *b*, Sir Giorgio *b*, Lord Arturo Talbo *t*, Sir Riccardo Forth *bar*, Sir Bruno Robertson *t*, Enrichetta di Francia *s*, Elvira *s*; *satb* chorus of soldiers of Cromwell, heralds and armigers of Lords Talbo and Valton, Puritans, lords and ladies, ladies-in-waiting, pages, servants

When Bellini settled in Paris in August 1833, he was besieged by inquiries about possible new operas; the only project that came to fruition, however, was a commission from the Théâtre-Italien. Bellini began work on *I puritani* in April 1834, 'after a year of real solid rest'; and he composed it at a more leisurely pace than any of his earlier operas, 'orchestrating it with such indescribable care that I feel very great satisfaction on looking at every piece I complete'. During the composition he consulted Rossini continually; one of Rossini's several services was to persuade the Théâtre-Italien to install an organ for the quartet in Part I.

Bellini met Count Carlo Pepoli at the Paris salon of Princess Belgioioso. A political exile from Italy, he was a fluent versifier who had written poems for Rossini's *Soirées musicales*. But Bellini soon found he was no Romani; his exasperation with Pepoli was to lead to a memorable outburst in which he explained his philosophy in drastic terms: 'Carve in your head in letters of adamant: the music drama must draw tears, inspire terror, make people die, through singing.' Even after the unqualified triumph of the opera he continued to deplore the way in which the strong theatrical situations were undermined by the poor dialogue, the 'repetitive, commonplace and sometimes stupid turns of phrase'.

The four principal singers – Giulia Grisi (Elvira), Giovanni Battista Rubini (Arturo), Antonio Tamburini (Riccardo) and Luigi Lablache (Giorgio) – formed as fine an ensemble as has ever been assembled in an opera house; they are remembered to this day as the '*Puritani* Quartet' because none of the other operas they sang together was so beautifully tailored to match their peculiar gifts or occasioned so delirious a triumph. Such was the enthusiasm at the premiere and so insistent the demand for encores, especially of the duet 'Suoni la tromba', that immediately afterwards Bellini had to make a number of substantial cuts to prevent the opera overrunning. Already at rehearsals the effect of the duet 'Suoni la tromba' had been so great that it was decided to turn it into a finale: the original second act was subdivided into two, and Elvira's 'mad scene' – the *scena ed aria* 'O rendetemi la speme' – which had followed the duet, was moved to its present position lest it fell flat after the frenzy that 'Suoni la tromba' seemed bound to provoke.

While in Paris, Bellini was asked by the San Carlo in Naples for a new opera for Maria Malibran, who had just enjoyed a spectacular triumph there in *Norma*. Short of time, Bellini agreed to make an alternative version of *I puritani*, in which Elvira became a mezzo-soprano and Riccardo a tenor. He worked on this in December and January of 1834–5; but the revised score arrived in Naples too late to be fitted into the season and was not performed anywhere until 1985. It includes music cut from the Paris version after the encore-protracted premiere, but not 'Suoni la tromba', on which Bellini was still working in January 1835.

SYNOPSIS

Part I: A fortress near Plymouth. Scene 1: A spacious glacis outside the fortress. Day breaks, reveille sounds, the guard is changed and the soldiers look forward to victory over the Stuarts ('Quando la tromba squilla'); a morning hymn is heard from the fortress, and all rejoice at the thought of the forthcoming marriage of Elvira, daughter of the Puritan governor-general Sir Gualtiero Valton. Riccardo, a colonel in the Puritan army, confides his sorrows to Bruno, a fellow officer: Elvira had been promised to him; but returning to Plymouth after years of soldiering, he finds that she loves Lord Arturo Talbo, a Cavalier, and that her father is unwilling to force his own wishes on her ('Ah! per sempre io ti perdei ... Bel sogno beato'). Scene 2: Elvira's apartment. Giorgio, Elvira's uncle, turns her melancholy into joy by telling how he has persuaded her father to allow her to marry Arturo ('Sorgea la notte folta'). Cries from the courtyard announce Arturo's arrival. Scene 3: The armoury. The chorus acclaims the bridal pair; Arturo compares his present happiness with the time he had to woo Elvira secretly ('A te, o cara, amor talora'). Valton has been commanded to escort a lady – a suspected Stuart spy – to appear before Parliament. Arturo speaks with her. She proves to be Enrichetta, the widowed queen, and Arturo vows to save her. Elvira now reappears, in part adorned for the wedding, but carrying her veil. Singing of her happiness, she playfully drapes the veil round Enrichetta ('Son vergin vezzosa'). This gives Arturo an idea of how the queen might be rescued, and as soon as Elvira and her companions have left, he veils her and hurries her away. When they are challenged by the jealous Riccardo, Enrichetta, fearing bloodshed, reveals herself; Riccardo allows them to make their escape. The wedding party reappears, and Valton sounds the alarm and organizes the pursuit. Shock and grief strike Elvira senseless, and in a dreamlike delirium she imagines herself being married to Arturo ('Oh, vieni al tempio, fedele Arturo').

Part II: The fortress. A room with an outlook over the English camp. As Giorgio is describing Elvira's ravings ('Cinta di fiori') Riccardo brings news that Parliament has condemned Arturo to the scaffold. The mad Elvira enters, dreaming still of her lost love ('Qui la voce sua soave . . . Vien, diletto, è in ciel la luna'). Giorgio urges Riccardo to save Arturo; otherwise he will have Elvira's death on his conscience ('Il rival salvar tu dei'). Finally Riccardo agrees; but if Arturo is in the Royalist ranks fighting against them on the morrow, he must die ('Suoni la tromba').

Part III: Countryside close to the fortress. A loggia in a garden shrubbery; nightfall. Three months have elapsed. While a storm rages and sounds of distant gunfire are heard, Arturo enters and hears Elvira singing. Despite the danger from passing groups of soldiers, he takes up the song ('A una fonte afflitto e solo'). When she appears he falls at her feet, begging forgiveness, and explaining what has happened. The lovers embrace ecstatically ('Vieni fra le mie braccie'). But Elvira's mind darkens once more: she imagines that Arturo is again leaving her, and her screams bring Riccardo, Giorgio and the rest hurrying in. Riccardo announces the sentence passed on Arturo, the word 'death' so shocking Elvira that she recovers her senses. In the face of death the lovers stand united, and even Riccardo is moved to compassion ('Credeasi, misera'). The Puritan soldiery are demanding summary execution when a messenger arrives: the Civil War is over, the Stuarts have been defeated, and a general pardon is issued.

Giulia Grisi was a superb singer, but she lacked the 'encyclopedic' talents of Pasta, and Bellini had no thought of composing for her a tragedy in the grand manner of *Norma*. In *I puritani* all his old sweetness and pathos return; he himself described the opera as 'fundamentally in the style of *La sonnambula* or Paisiello's *Nina*, with a dash of military robustness, and something of Puritan severity'. It derives the robust and severe qualities from the pervasive march rhythm and from the ever-present sound of brass and drums.

The music that Bellini heard in Paris convinced him that, though the French were almost as skilful as the Germans in their use of the orchestra, they had 'little understanding of what real song was'. Certainly a more sumptuous feast of song than *I puritani* can hardly be imagined. It ranges in style from the sparkling coloratura of 'Son vergin vezzosa' (which may well have been inspired more by the idea of Malibran's voice than of Grisi's) to such ecstatically long-drawn cantabiles as 'A te, o cara'; from the plangent nostalgia of 'Ah! per sempre' to the blood-stirring fervour of 'Suoni la tromba'. Rubini's part in particular is one of the truly fabulous tenor roles, demanding a high C♯ at his first appearance on stage, and moving into the vocal stratosphere in the final scene, with a D in his duet with Elvira, and an F in the last finale.

But Bellini also relished showing the Parisians that he too was capable of orchestral and harmonic finesse. French taste encouraged him to go further than before in breaking down the frontiers between lyrical numbers and recitatives and between solos and ensembles. In the

Introduzione he seems to attempt to match French rhythmic sophistication: there are as many changes of metre in this single piece as in whole acts of some Bellini operas. All these elements contribute to make *I puritani* the most sophisticated and brilliant of Bellini's operas. No wonder Rossini, who had once found *Il pirata* 'a little bit lacking in brilliance', was impressed, and regarded this last opera as being, along with *Norma*, the most unmistakable proof of Bellini's greatness.

The *Largo maestoso* from the Part III finale ('Credeasi, misera'), adapted by August-Mathieu Panseron to the text of the Lachrymosa, was sung at Bellini's funeral in Les Invalides on 2 October 1835.

RECORDINGS 1. Callas, di Stefano, Panerai, Rossi-Lemeni, La Scala Ch & O, Serafin, EMI, 1953; 2. Sutherland, Pavarotti, Capuccilli, Ghiaurov, Covent Garden Ch, LSO, Bonynge, Decca, 1973; 3. Gruberova, Lavender, Ellero d'Artegna, Kim, Bavarian RCh, Munich RO, Luisi, Nightingale Classics, 1993 (live)
OTHER OPERAS *Adelson e Salvini*, 1825; *Bianca e Fernando*, 1826; *Il pirata*, 1827; *La straniera*, 1829; *Zaira*, 1829; *Beatrice di Tenda*, 1833

D.K.

Alban Berg

Alban Maria Johannes Berg;
b 9 February 1885, Vienna;
d 24 December 1935, Vienna

Although Schoenberg also wrote operas, Berg is the only member of the so-called Second Viennese School whose music can regularly be heard in the opera house. True, his personality was warmer and more outgoing and his style more naturally lyrical than Schoenberg's or Webern's. But one might just as well say that he was simply more interested in the theatre and the voice. From the start, he wrote songs: some 50 survive from before his 20th birthday, and he wrote another 40-odd during and just after his years of study with Schoenberg. Song-writing was displaced by the long-drawn-out composition of his first opera, *Wozzeck* (1914–22); and *Lulu* occupied him from 1928 until his death in 1935, with interruptions for the cantata *Der Wein* (1929) and the Violin Concerto (1935).

Berg came from a cultivated, well-to-do bourgeois Viennese family where reading and plays were part of everyday life. He read widely, knew the best writing of his day, and kept up with the theatre. Both his libretti are direct adaptations of successful stage plays: Büchner's *Woyzeck*, whose Viennese premiere Berg attended in May 1914; and Wedekind's 'Lulu' plays, the first of which Berg had read in 1904, while he saw the second performed the following May. This is in marked contrast with Schoenberg, whose stage works are mostly musical enactments of psychological states or abstract concepts. Yet Berg was strongly under Schoenberg's influence from their first meeting in 1905 until his death 30 years later. Schoenberg claimed it was through his teaching that Berg learned how to write extended instrumental movements, and it was certainly under his tutelage that Berg composed his Piano Sonata, Op. 1, and the String Quartet, Op. 3. Schoenberg seems to have opposed *Wozzeck* as an operatic subject, and in general the relationship between master and pupil preserved hidden tensions, apparent in Berg's letters, which, while sycophantic, still give little ground on creative matters.

Musically Berg was certainly indebted to Schoenberg's classically based teaching, with its insistence on good formal models and coherent musical argument. But his style owes more to the pluralism of Mahler, with its rich strata of association, than to the tortured intellectualism of Schoenberg. Later, in adopting Schoenberg's serial method (*Lyric Suite*, 1926), he adapted it to the point where it loses its strict cohesive function, evident in Schoenberg's music of the time, and takes on a quasi-secret quality that links it with the hidden ciphers in the music of Schumann as well as with other features of Berg's own music, such as the large-scale palindromes and symmetries in the *Chamber Concerto*, *Lyric Suite* and *Lulu*, the secret setting of Baudelaire's *De profundis clamavi* in the finale of the *Lyric Suite*, and the cryptic numbers (10 and 23), which play a part in this latter work. Of course, Berg's serialism has a cohesive function too. But it is typical of him that, in the *Lyric Suite* and *Lulu*, he derives a succession of note rows from the original one, whereas Schoenberg, no less typically, always confined himself to a single row in any one work. These derivatives often have a strong tonal feeling, as indeed do the original rows; Berg never shared the view that a tonal focus was something to avoid in truly progressive music (whether serial or not).

For all the free-sounding Romanticism and natural sweep of his best music, Berg composed slowly and with great effort. Work on *Wozzeck* was constantly interrupted, first by the First World War, in which he served as an officer cadet and later as an official in the War Ministry, and then by the heavy demands of Schoenberg's Society for Private Musical Performance (1918–21) as well as administrative duties in connection with the Berg family estate. Later, while at work on *Lulu*, he suffered poor health (he was a severe asthmatic), and like most Viennese had to endure a drastic decline in his living standards as a result of the hyperinflation of the mid-1920s. Finally, after the accession of the Nazis to power in January 1933, his music was branded decadent and excluded from performance in Germany, as well as, increasingly, in Austria, which deprived him of any strong practical incentive to finish *Lulu*. The opera was nevertheless virtually complete when, on Christmas Eve 1935, he died of blood poisoning after a short illness resulting from an abscess on his back. It seems certain that, if penicillin had been available (it came into use in 1941), Berg's life could have been saved.

Wozzeck

Opera in three acts (15 scenes) (1h 30m)
Libretto by the composer from the play *Woyzeck* by Georg Büchner (1837)
Composed 1914–22
PREMIERES 14 December 1925, Staatsoper, Berlin; US: 19 March 1931, Academy of Music, Philadelphia; UK: 14 March 1934, Queen's Hall, London (concert); 22 January 1952, Covent Garden, London (stage)
CAST Wozzeck *bar*, Drum-Major *heroic t*, Andres *lyric t*, Captain *buffo t*, Doctor *buffo b*, 2 Apprentices *deep b*, *high bar*, Idiot *high t*, Marie *s*, Margret *c*, Marie's son *treble*, Soldier *t*; *satb* chorus of girls, wenches, youths and soldiers and children

The composition of *Wozzeck* took almost eight years, but Berg worked on it for only a fraction of that time. After seeing the play in 1914, he made some musical sketches and set about adapting Büchner's text, but was then interrupted by the war and returned to the opera only during 1917 and 1918. Act I was finished by summer 1919, Act II in August 1921, and the final act during the following two months (the orchestration took a further six). During this whole period Berg wrote nothing else, except to complete the *Three Orchestral Pieces* (1913–15), with whose final movement (*Marsch*) the opera shares its style and even some material. The first performance was conducted by Erich Kleiber, who programmed it on his own initiative, with no fewer than 34 orchestral and 14 full rehearsals. It was a *succès de scandale*, with disturbances during the performance and a mixed press afterwards, but it led to a stream of productions in Germany and Austria, before the Nazis consigned it to the dustbin of 'decadent art' after 1933.

For its time, *Wozzeck* now seems a

highly modern and topical subject. But the play was in fact some 77 years old when Berg saw it in Vienna (its world premiere was in Munich the previous year). Its author, Georg Büchner, had died of typhus in 1837 at the age of 23, leaving *Woyzeck* unfinished and in an unclear and disorganized state. It was first edited into a coherent text by Karl Emil Franzos in 1879, and this edition was further reorganized by Paul Landau for a 1909 publication which formed the basis of the stage premieres and of Berg's libretto. In adapting this text, Berg cut out a few scenes and conflated two or three others, but he retained the essential character of the play, with its many short scenes, its abrupt and sometimes brutal language, and its stark, if haunted, realism – so unusual for its day, but reflecting the fact that Büchner's source was an actual incident (of 1824) in which an ex-soldier had been executed for the murder of his unfaithful mistress.

Büchner, a post-1830 revolutionary thinker, made his Woyzeck a representative of the downtrodden proletariat; a soldier, because soldiers have always been slaves to a cruel and mindless system, but also the helpless victim of modern social experimentation, which is more general and insidious in its effects. It is this aspect of the character that Berg portrays most movingly. Wozzeck's fumbling attempts to articulate his thoughts, and to comprehend and control his passions, reverberate in the music, while the social 'machine', with its fads and statistics masking an essential unconcern for the individual, rolls on in the fugues, rhythmic mechanisms and ostinato effects that Berg also loved.

SYNOPSIS

The square-bracketed designations are from a chart drawn up by Berg's pupil Fritz Mahler; they are not included in the score.

Act I [Five Character Pieces], Scene 1 [Suite]: The Captain's room: Wozzeck is shaving him. The Captain, a high, yapping, grotesque tenor, philosophizes about eternity. Wozzeck acquiesces to everything in a flat monotone, but when the Captain impugns his morality, Wozzeck quotes the Bible and adds: 'We poor folk . . . I could be virtuous if I were a gentleman with a hat and a watch and an eye-glass and could talk posh.' Scene 2 [Rhapsody]: An open field outside the town. Wozzeck and Andres, another soldier, are cutting sticks. Wozzeck senses mysterious forces around them and sees in the sunset 'a fire rising from earth to heaven, and an uproar descending like the last trump'. Andres pooh-poohs him and sings a hunting song. Scene 3 [Military March and Lullaby]: Marie's room. In the street Margret comments on Marie's candid admiration for the Drum-Major. Marie turns angrily back into the house and sings her child a bitter lullaby. Wozzeck looks in through the window and tries to describe his experience in the field, but will not look at his child, and hurries off to barracks. Scene 4 [Passacaglia]: The Doctor's study. The Doctor, a caricature of scientific positivism, uses Wozzeck as guinea pig for dietary experiments. When Wozzeck tries to explain his visions, the Doctor is delighted with his 'aberratio mentalis partialis, second species' and gives him a rise of one groschen. Scene 5 [Rondo]: The street outside Marie's door. Marie is again admiring the Drum-Major. After token resistance, she takes him into her house.

Act II [Symphony in Five Movements], Scene 1 [Sonata Movement]: Marie's room. She is admiring a pair of ear-rings given her by the Drum-Major. When the child wakes up, she sings him a song about a gypsy. Wozzeck comes in and is at once suspicious of the ear-rings, but gives Marie his pay, leaving her guilt-stricken. Scene 2 [Fantasia and Fugue]: A street in the town. The Captain and Doctor meet and talk, the Doctor pretending to see in the Captain's florid complexion and bloated physique signs of fatal illness. Wozzeck arrives and they torment him by hinting at Marie's infidelity. Scene 3 [Largo]: The street outside

Marie's door. Wozzeck confronts her, obliquely and apocalyptically, with her infidelity. As obliquely, she denies it, defying him to hit her: 'Rather a knife in my body than a hand on me.' Scene 4 [Scherzo]: The garden of an inn. A band plays a ländler to which the customers dance, and two apprentices sing drunkenly. Marie dances with the Drum-Major, watched jealously by Wozzeck. There is a hunting chorus and a song for Andres with guitar. Finally an idiot, reading the future, smells blood on Wozzeck. Scene 5 [Rondo con introduzione]: Guardroom in the barracks. Wozzeck, unable to sleep, complains to Andres of inner voices and a vision of a flashing knife blade. The Drum-Major arrives drunk and boasts of his success with Marie. The two men fight, and Wozzeck is knocked down.

Act III [Six Inventions], Scene 1 [Invention on a Theme]: Marie's room. Marie reads from the Bible about the woman taken in adultery and Mary Magdalene. In between, the child presses against her, and she tells him a story about a hungry orphan. Scene 2 [Invention on a Note]: A woodland path by a pond. Marie and Wozzeck walk past. Wozzeck kisses her menacingly, then as the moon rises he stabs her in the throat. Scene 3 [Invention on a Rhythm]: A tavern. A frenzied polka on an out-of-tune piano. Wozzeck is drowning his guilt and sings a folksong. Margret draws attention to the blood on his hand, and he rushes out in a panic. Scene 4 [Invention on a Six-note Chord]: Woodland path by the pond. Wozzeck returns for the knife, which he throws into the pond. Then, frightened by the moon, he decides to throw the knife in farther, wades in and drowns. The Captain and Doctor pass, comment on the eerie scene and hurry away. [Orchestral Interlude: Invention on a Key.] Scene 5 [Invention on a Regular Quaver Motion]: The street outside Marie's door. Her child is playing with other children. A child announces that Marie's body has been found, and they all run off, followed by Marie's child.

Though technically 'atonal' (no key signatures and few definite key centres), *Wozzeck* is really ambivalent in this respect. Its musical world is Viennese Expressionism, with its violently dissonant gestures, dense textures and steep dynamic gradients. Schoenberg's sprechgesang technique figures prominently. But the music also hints at a simpler, more homely tonal language, which stands for normal life, or elusive happiness, or other concepts opposed to the excess, misery and inhumanity we witness on the stage. Marie's lullaby, Andres's hunting song and, above all, the great D minor interlude in Act III have this quality. Berg also uses conventional music – ländler, march, out-of-tune polka – ironically, in Mahler fashion (the inn scene in Act II is perhaps the most Mahlerian music Berg ever wrote). In the same way he uses background forms for both structure and irony. It is an open question whether the sonata form of Act II, Scene 1 or the rondo of Act II, Scene 5 could ever be heard as such, but there is no mistaking the sarcasm of the fugue in Act II, Scene 2 or the obsessiveness of the passacaglia in Act I, Scene 4, with its 21 variations on a ground (a patent influence on Britten's *Peter Grimes*). Meanwhile, the demoniac repeated Bs in the murder scene and the wild ostinato rhythms in the tavern scene that follows are obviously straight dramatic devices dignified by formal tags.

A unique feature is the cinematic time flow. Not only do the short scenes intercut like a film montage, but this even leads in Act III to an experimental handling of actual clock time. By cutting from the murder to the tavern (where Wozzeck is already drinking) back to the murder scene (where he is just arriving to look for the knife), Berg both speeds up the action and seems to override the physical limitations of the medium (how can Wozzeck already be in the tavern?). This device is in fact an adaptation of a real ambiguity of sequence in the play (which admittedly Büchner might have rectified in due course), and it influenced later operas like Zimmermann's *Die Soldaten*, where cinematic devices are used to suggest multiple layers of action.

In other ways *Wozzeck* is an authentic renewal of the German tradition of symphonic drama. The five scenes in each act play continuously, linked by interludes, and organized by leitmotifs and recurrent harmonies. And while Berg perfected the hypermodern idea of symbolic characterization ('Captain', 'Doctor', 'Drum-Major', etc.), his musical portraiture is as fine and precise as anything in German opera since Mozart. The humanizing of the potentially subhuman Wozzeck and Marie through the music they sing is one of the great miracles of 20th-century theatre.

RECORDINGS 1. Behrens, Zednik, Grundheber, Haugland, Vienna State Op Ch, VPO, Abbado, DG, 1987 (live); 2. Silja, Zednik, Waechter, Malta, Vienna State Op Ch, VPO, Dohnányi, Decca, 1981; 3. Denoke, Skovhus, Hamburg State Op Ch & Hamburg State PO, Metzmacher, EMI, 1998 (live)

Lulu

Opera in three acts (2h 45m)
Libretto by the composer from two plays, *Erdgeist* (1895) and *Die Buchse der Pandora* (1903; first performed 1918) by Frank Wedekind
Composed 1928–35; Act III ed. and orch. by Friedrich Cerha, 1974
PREMIERES Acts I and II, plus fragments of Act III: 2 June 1937, Zurich; UK: 1 October 1962, Sadler's Wells, London; US: 7 August 1963, Santa Fe; complete version: 24 February 1979, Opéra, Paris; UK: 16 February 1981, Covent Garden, London; US: 28 July 1979, Opera Theater, Santa Fe
CAST [Perle, 1985] Lulu *high s*, Countess Geschwitz *dramatic ms*, Wardrobe Mistress/Schoolboy/Groom *c*, Medical Specialist/Banker/Professor *high b*, Painter/Negro *lyric t*, Dr Schön/ Jack the Ripper *heroic bar*, Alwa *youthful heroic t*, Schigolch *high character b*, Animal Tamer/Acrobat *heroic b with buffo flavour*, Prince/Manservant/ Marquis *buffo t*, Stage Manager *low buffo b*, Clown *silent*, Stagehand *silent*, Police Commissioner *spoken role*, 15-year-old Girl *opera soubrette*, Her Mother *c*, Designer *ms*, Journalist *high bar*, Servant *deep bar*; pianist, attendants to the Prince, policemen, nurses, wardresses, dancers, party guests, servants, workers *silent*

After the premiere of *Wozzeck* Berg was soon on the look-out for another libretto. He made abortive sketches for an opera called *Und Pippa tanzt* (1928, based on a play by Gerhart Hauptmann) but then decided on an adaptation of Wedekind's 'Lulu' plays. As before, he himself carried out the textual surgery, which had to be much more extensive than with Büchner; and this time he adapted as he composed. The opera was complete in short score by April 1934, apart from a few passages in Act II (87 bars in all) where accompanying detail was implicit rather than explicit. He then started work on the full score, beginning with what was to be the symphonic suite – the only music from *Lulu* he ever heard performed (11 December 1935; Kleiber had previously conducted it in Berlin, 30 November 1934), and which included the *Variations* and *Adagio* from Act III. Finally he scored the opera from the start, and had reached bar 268 of Act III (out of 1,326) at the time of his final illness.

To complete *Lulu* therefore involved mainly orchestration, plus a small amount of added harmony and counterpoint, much of it facilitated by the large amount of musical recapitulation involved. A vocal score of Act III (by Erwin Stein) was actually ready for press in 1936, by which time the composer's widow, Helene, had asked Schoenberg and Webern (in vain) to finish and edit the full score. Only later did she adopt the obstructive attitude that kept the material of Act III virtually unavailable until after her death in August 1976. Meanwhile *Lulu* was performed as a torso, normally with only the end of Act III, mimed to the music of the *Adagio* from the suite (the procedure adopted in Zurich in 1937). Cerha's completion was ready by 1974, but not heard until 1979 in Paris (conducted by Pierre Boulez), since when the full version has been widely produced.

SYNOPSIS

Prologue The Animal Tamer introduces the beasts in his menagerie (identified by the music as characters in the opera). Lulu, the snake, 'created to make trouble', is carried on and presented in person.

Act I, Scene 1: The Painter's studio. Lulu is having her portrait painted, watched by Dr Schön (an 'editor-in-chief') and his son Alwa, a composer. The dialogue makes clear the men's interest in Lulu, or hers in them. She offers sarcastic respects to Schön's fiancée. When he and Alwa leave, the Painter makes a heavy pass at Lulu, chasing her round the studio. There is a bang on the door, which collapses to admit her husband, the Medical Specialist. Seeing the two together, he has a stroke and dies. Lulu, seemingly detached from events, allows herself to be taken over by the Painter. Scene 2: A very elegant drawing room. The Painter, now married to Lulu, is rich from the sale of pictures (fixed, it transpires, by Schön). News of Schön's engagement arrives in the post. The doorbell rings, and the asthmatic old tramp Schigolch comes in as the Painter retires to his studio. Lulu's father figure, Schigolch, is delighted to see her living in luxury. He soon leaves, as Schön arrives. Schön wants to end their affair and live respectably with his wife-to-be. They are interrupted by the Painter, to whom, as Lulu exits, Schön obliquely explains the true situation. Shocked, the Painter goes out, ostensibly to confront Lulu, in reality to cut his own throat. Alwa arrives and they break down the door to reach the body. Seeing his own engagement 'bleeding to death', Schön calls the police, as Lulu insists, 'You'll marry me all the same.' Scene 3: A theatre dressing room. Lulu is dancing in Alwa's latest work. They drink champagne and discuss Schön, their own first meeting, and the Prince who wants to marry Lulu and take her to Africa. As she returns to the stage, Alwa ponders writing an opera about her. Cheering is heard from the auditorium as the Prince enters, soon followed by Lulu, who has seen Schön in the audience with his fiancée and has shammed a fainting fit. Left alone with Schön, she threatens to go to Africa with the Prince, and taunts Schön over his engagement. At last Schön realizes he cannot leave her. She forces him to write a letter to his fiancée breaking off their engagement.

Act II, Scene 1: A magnificent room (in Schön's house). Lulu and Schön are now married. The lesbian Countess Geschwitz has come to invite Lulu to the lady artists' ball, but quickly leaves in the face of Schön's disapproval. Schön and Lulu go out together. The Countess returns and hides. Schigolch and two other admirers, the Acrobat and the Schoolboy, come in from the balcony; Lulu also comes back in, and they talk. Next Alwa is announced and the admirers hide, as Alwa declares his love for her. Schön overhears and also notices the Acrobat, at whom he points a revolver; he then takes Alwa out, while the Acrobat finds a new hiding-place. Schön returns and gives Lulu the gun to shoot herself as the Acrobat makes his escape. Schön now discovers the Countess and locks her in the next room. Continuing his argument with Lulu he again tries to force her to shoot herself, but as the Schoolboy intervenes she shoots Schön instead. As Lulu implores Alwa to save her, the police arrive. Interlude: A silent film depicts Lulu's arrest, trial and imprisonment, her deliberate infection with cholera and her escape from the isolation hospital disguised as the Countess. Scene 2: The same room, shuttered and dusty. Alwa, the Countess and the

Acrobat await Schigolch, who is to take the Countess to the hospital to change places with Lulu. The Acrobat is to marry Lulu and take her to Paris as his performing partner. Alwa offers the Countess money, Schigolch arrives and leaves with the Countess, after which the Acrobat himself demands money from Alwa. Next the Schoolboy arrives, but is sent packing in the belief that Lulu is dead. Schigolch then returns with Lulu, who is so physically spoilt by illness that the Acrobat abandons the plan and goes off to the police. Schigolch departs to collect train tickets. Left alone, Alwa and Lulu declare their love.

Act III, Scene 1: A spacious salon (in a Paris casino). A gambling party is in progress. As the company exit to the gaming room, talk is mainly of their booming Jungfrau shares. The Marquis threatens to expose Lulu unless she agrees to be sold to a Cairo brothel. The company returns from the gaming room, all having won. The Acrobat also tries to blackmail Lulu, who meanwhile abuses the Countess Geschwitz as a pervert. A telegram informs the Banker of the collapse of the Jungfrau shares. Schigolch now arrives, also asking for money; but he agrees to lure the Acrobat to his hotel and murder him. After a brief exchange with the Acrobat, the Marquis goes for the police. Lulu contrives that the Acrobat and the Countess go off together to Schigolch's hotel. As the company learns of the share collapse, Lulu changes clothes with the Groom and leaves with Alwa just before the police arrive. Scene 2: An attic room (in London). Alwa and Schigolch await the return of Lulu, now a prostitute, with a client. They hide as she comes in with a Professor, and while they are in her room Schigolch goes through his pockets. When the Professor has gone, Countess Geschwitz arrives with the portrait of Lulu (which has featured in every scene). Alwa nails it up, and Lulu goes back out, followed by the Countess. Alwa tells Schigolch that Lulu has infected him with a disease to which she herself is immune. She returns with a second client, a Negro. There is an altercation about payment, and the Negro kills Alwa. Schigolch goes off to the pub, the Countess returns, contemplating suicide. Lulu comes in with her third client, Jack the Ripper. They go into her room, where he murders her. On the way out he stabs the Countess, who dies as the curtain falls.

Wedekind's ramshackle and contrived narrative was a challenge to Berg that he was partly, but not wholly, successful in meeting. Too many characters have to be accommodated, and at times (Act II, Scene 1; Act III, Scene 1) they get in each other's way. There are too many stock dramatic devices – the doorbell, the telegram, the exchange of garments – not all strictly germane – the Jungfrau shares. And Berg's use of hidden structural process is incredibly elaborate: a treasure trove for analysts but of mixed significance in the theatre. Unlike the abstract forms in *Wozzeck*, those in *Lulu* are deployed sectionally over large spans of music, intercutting with other processes: for instance, Lulu's conversations with Schön about his engagement (Act I, Scenes 2 and 3) form a large sonata movement whose exposition and development are separated by well over 500 bars of music; similarly Alwa's declarations of love in Act II, Scenes 1 and 2 comprise a rondo, and there are two large sets of variations in Act III. In between come shorter, self-contained units with such titles as 'Chorale', 'English Waltz', 'Cavatina', or vague generic names like 'Chamber Music I', 'Ensemble I'. Some of them employ strict technical devices, such as canon, or isorhythm ('Monoritmica', like the 'Invention on a Rhythm' in *Wozzeck*). The somewhat modish film sequence in Act II is a musical palindrome, marking the high point from which Lulu begins her descent to degradation. Embracing everything is a complex scheme of 'leading sections', in which recapitulation serves to remind us of previous incidents, while at the same time giving structure. This comes to a head in the final scene, which is substantially built on such reminiscence, reflecting Berg's idea that Lulu's clients should be the avenging spirits of her former husbands.

Berg's serial technique is another aspect of this plurality of formal procedures. Unlike Schoenberg in *Moses und Aron* (1930–32), he uses several 12-note rows, as well as smaller unordered sets, derived from each other by a variety of more or less convoluted operations. They not only bind the music harmonically and thematically, but also act as leitmotifs: each character has his or her own set or series. But the serial treatment itself is extremely free (as in *Der Wein* and the Violin Concerto); and there is a strong tonal emphasis built into the basic ('Lulu') series, brought out in the derivatives, and dwelt on by the music's harmony and texture.

Whatever the importance of this apparatus, *Lulu* works in the end because of its direct musical beauty and richness of portraiture. As a universal morality about the power of sensual experience, it depends on a broad range of characterization: Lulu has to conquer all sorts and conditions of men. And for this Berg, with his emotional breadth and intellectual focus, was brilliantly equipped. As with the best operas of Strauss, there is a cornucopian feeling about the work as a whole, and an endless fascination in its detail (not least orchestral: the *Lulu* sound is unique). Whether Berg would have significantly tightened or revised the score remains an open question. It would surely have remained an essentially diverse experience, with all the virtues and defects of its genre.

RECORDINGS 1. Lear, Johnson, Grobe, Fischer-Dieskau, Deutsche Op O, Berlin, Böhm, DG, 1968 (live): Acts I and II only (plus the *Variations* and *Adagio*); 2. Stratas, Minton, Riegel, Mazura, Blankenheim, Paris Op O, Boulez, DG, 1979

S.W.

Luciano Berio

b 24 October 1925, Oneglia, Italy;
d 27 May 2003, Rome

Born into a family of professional musicians, Berio was trained from an early age by both grandfather and father and entered the Milan Conservatory in 1945. His strong sense of the potential of the human voice, first instilled in childhood as he listened to his father giving singing lessons, was fortified during his six years of study at the conservatory by work as an accompanist and as a conductor in provincial opera houses, and above all by his marriage, in 1950, to the singer Cathy Berberian, who was to become so notable an interpreter of his works.

Berio began work for Italian Radio and Television (RAI) in 1952, and there developed an electronic studio. The experience, first encountered at this time, of counterpointing dense layers of sound was to have far-reaching consequences in all aspects of his work. He left RAI in 1961 to take up a series of teaching appointments, first on the West then the East Coast of the United States. A decade later he returned to Italy, but from 1974 to 1980 established a second base in Paris, where he directed the electro-acoustic section of IRCAM. In 1987 he founded the research institute, Tempo Reale, in Florence.

It is a reflection of the vivid, gestural nature of Berio's music in the 1950s that his first work for the stage was for mimes. In 1952–3 he had written two pieces, one orchestral, the other electronic, both entitled *Mimusique*. Having received a commission from the 1955 Teatro delle Novità festival in Bergamo he asked Roberto Leydi to devise a scenario around the orchestral *Mimusique*, adding further music where appropriate. The result, *Tre modi per sopportare la vita*, was a rather wooden Brechtian parable. When the 1959 Venice Biennale requested a mime piece, Berio dusted off his composite score and requested a new scenario from Italo Calvino. This, the final version, was entitled *Allez Hop* – the cry of a travelling showman, one of whose performing fleas escapes and provokes instructive mayhem.

This first series of ventures established a way of working that was to be repeated in most of Berio's future work in the theatre: only once he had established a general musico-dramatic conception – and indeed often composed a good deal of the music for it – would he turn to a collaborator to find specific images that would give it theatrical focus. Although both of the mime pieces mentioned above told stories, they were the last of Berio's theatrical works to do so. Thereafter, a more complex, 'musical' proliferation of visual and verbal materials that found their theoretical counterpart in Umberto Eco's discussions of the 'open work' became the hallmark of his theatre.

The gradual unfolding of Cathy Berberian's extraordinary gifts as a performer had a profound impact on the development of Berio's sense of theatre. The electronic works that he produced with her – *Thema* (*Omaggio a Joyce*) in 1958 and, above all, *Visage* in 1960–61 – revealed a complex theatre of the voice that was independent of narrative and, in the case of *Visage*, of words. Furthermore the theatricalization of the concert hall in *Circles*, where circular processes proliferate not just within the music, but also visually, on stage, pointed directly onwards to his first piece of vocal theatre, *Passaggio*.

Indeed, many of Berio's works of the mid-1960s underline the theatrical aspect of concert-hall performance: notably *Sequenza III* for voice, and *Sequenza V* for trombone. More significant in developing a 'theatre of the mind' was *Laborintus II* (1965). This multi-layered homage to Dante, in which Berio and Sanguineti were able to experiment richly with the fragmentation and counterpointing of texts, was in principle 'open' to theatrical realization, but in the main has proved more effective in the concert hall.

Laborintus II and *Sinfonia* (for 8 solo voices and orchestra, 1968–9) were the essential stepping-stones from *Passaggio* to Berio's next theatrical work, *Opera* (1969–70). Precisely because of its rich, multi-layered nature, *Opera* has also proved a challenge to effective theatrical realization – yet the difficulties that Berio encountered with it enabled him to see his way towards a form of large-scale theatre in which skeletal narrative structures and proliferating imagery are held in fruitful tension. In consequence, between 1977 and 1984 he was able to produce two full-scale operatic works, *La vera storia* and *Un re in ascolto*, which have held the stage with conviction. The 'Musical Actions' *Outis* and *Cronaca del luogo*, both exploring beyond conventional narrative frames, set the seal upon this innovative trajectory. In 2000 Berio paid homage to the composer whose music, broadcast on wartime radio, had framed his childhood. Using the original sketches, he made a new conclusion to Puccini's incomplete opera *Turandot*. Its stage premiere took place on 25 May 2002 at the Dorothy Chandler Pavilion in Los Angeles.

La vera storia

The True Story

Opera in two parts ('a full evening')
Libretto by Italo Calvino
Composed 1977–81
PREMIERES 9 March 1982, La Scala, Milan; UK: 14 May 1994, Royal Festival Hall, London (semi-staged)
CAST Leonora *s*, Luca *t*, Ada *ms*, Ivo/Commandant *bar*, The Condemned Man *b*, Ugo/Priest *t*, at least 2 street-singers, passers-by I, II and IV, passer-by III *s*, 3 voices in the street; *satb* chorus of at least 60 voices; speakers, mimes, dancers, acrobats

Berio started with his own musico-dramatic conception, and indeed had already begun work on the music before he invited Calvino to fine down the project into a concrete libretto. Part I is built from three interacting, but now closely related levels. The first of these concerns the popular feast, or *festa*, embodied in four large choral sections that show collective life in all its ambivalence: anarchic ebullience, sadism in the face of a public execution, rebellion against an oppressive regime and, when that rebellion is crushed by the authorities, stoic resignation.

Within this framework, Berio and Calvino use individual protagonists to operate what is in effect a structural analysis of the conventions of 19th-century opera. Individual protagonists have names, but little more. They act out a series of stock situations whose emotional urgency is taken entirely seriously, but unembellished by narrative detail. Clearly *Il trovatore* lies in the background: a baby is stolen in an act of revenge, two brothers – one powerful, one not – fight for the love of a passive heroine. The music abets the analytical process: characters wedded to action sing clean, urgent lines, while those to whom circumstance denies the chance of action proliferate into melismatic settings of richly poetic texts. A third level of commentary, some of it decidedly ironic, is provided by a series of six popular ballads, of which the last two, both reflecting Berio's studies of folk music, acquire remarkable intensity.

Part II synthesizes the disjunct verbal and musical material of Part I into a powerful and continuous flow. It reinterprets the framework of Part I in grimly contemporary terms. But in the urban police state of Part II the power of the authorities is omnipresent: the popular solidarity of the Part I *festa* has been silenced; the chorus on stage is almost mute (their powers of articulation being transferred to disembodied voices in the orchestra, and where individuals dare to raise their voice, they are no longer 'characters from an opera' but nameless 'passers-by'. The same story of police brutality and revenge, of revolt and suppression is enacted, but now under circumstances where, if the voice of stoic resignation that ended Part I is to be heard at all, it behoves the creatures of operatic fiction from Part I to re-enter at the end of Part II and sing on behalf of a silent and utterly crushed chorus. It is one of Berio's bleakest and most powerful conceptions.

Un re in ascolto

A King Listens

Musical action in two parts (1h 30m)
Libretto by the composer, after Italo Calvino, W. H. Auden and Friedrich Gotter
Composed 1979–84
PREMIERES 7 August 1984, Kleines Festspielhaus, Salzburg; UK: 9 February 1989, Covent Garden, London
CAST Prospero *bar*, Producer *t*, Friday *actor*, Female Protagonist *s*, Soprano I (with her Pianist), Soprano II, Mezzo-Soprano, 3 singers *t*, *bar*, *b*, Nurse *s*, Wife *ms*, Doctor *t*, Lawyer *b*, Singing Pianist; *satb* chorus; Mime (Ariel), Messenger, Stage Designer and Assistants, Seamstress, A Lady to Saw in Half, Acrobats, Clown, 3 Dancers and others, *silent*; Accordion-player

Un re in ascolto started life as a parable, proposed by Calvino, about a king who deciphers the collapse of his kingdom and the infidelity of his queen from what he hears listening in his palace. Berio transmuted this figure into an elderly theatrical impresario, so closely at one with his latest project – a search for 'another theatre' for which *The Tempest* is to serve as a vehicle – that he himself is called Prospero, and his theatre becomes his island. Prospero listens because he is auditioning a series of three singers in the hope of finding the ideal female protagonist for his production. But his hopes of finding his fantasies made flesh are confounded – indeed, each woman addresses to him the same disturbingly personal message. He can never hope to capture the essential 'otherness' of a desired woman within his own world.

Meanwhile, his new project is slipping from his control. An ambitious producer is turning it into an extravaganza quite alien to his own aspirations. In desperate revolt he finally starts to tear down some of the producer's scenery, but collapses.

At the start of Part II he is found where he fell (Berio originally intended the whole musical action to be continuous). Realizing that he is dying, those nearest to him react with predictable self-interest, but his players initiate a ragged ceremony of watching with the dying man. Prospero, by now wholly absorbed in his own dreams, takes on the role of the 'listening king' from which Berio and Calvino started – but does so recognizing that his kingdom is not essentially that of lights and scenery but rather that of 'the sea of music'. Thus fortified, he can now confront one final apparition. The female Protagonist for whom he was searching enters to confront him with a summation of all that he has heard during the three auditions: the distance between them is immutable. His players bid him farewell, and, left alone on the island of his theatre, Prospero dies.

Recurrent musical threads run through *Un re in ascolto*. The female Protagonist's aria sums up the musical as well as the verbal materials of *Auditions I* and *II*. Three of the four *Concertati* for Prospero's players share common materials. Above all, Prospero's five arias on listening (settings of monologues by Calvino that survived from the original project) all use the same restricted pitch field, and in consequence abound in similar melodic gestures. But it is above all the subtlety of Berio's mature harmonic language, accommodating as it does many echoes from previous generations, that gives *Un re in ascolto* its singular expressive power.

RECORDING Wise, Sima, Zednik, Adam, VPO, Maazel, Col Legno, 1984
OTHER OPERATIC WORKS *Passaggio*, 1963; *Opera*, 1970; *Outis*, 1996; *Cronaca del luogo*, 1999

D.O.-S.

Hector Berlioz

Louis Hector Berlioz; *b* 11 December 1803, La Côte St André, Isère, France; *d* 8 March 1869, Paris

Opera should have been at the centre of Berlioz's composing career, as it was of his life. The musical culture in which he grew to maturity was dominated by it. Once he had decided to be a composer (against the will of his doctor father, who wanted him to take up medicine), opera became his goal. Everything conspired to make him see music – requiem mass, secular cantata, above all opera – as a dramatic, expressive art: his own instincts; the precepts of his teacher Jean-François Le Sueur; the example of Gluck and Spontini and also of Salieri, Sacchini, Méhul and Cherubini (whose works he immersed himself in from his first arrival in Paris in 1821 and whose cause he defended against the, to him, frivolous, undramatic values of Rossini); and, in the mid-1820s, the discovery of Weber through the performances of *Der Freischütz* at the Odéon. A large part of Berlioz's apprenticeship was practically lived in the opera house (and in the library, where he pored over and analysed the scores he had heard). Even the revelation of Beethoven at the Conservatoire Concerts from 1828 onwards – the crucial event in the evolution of his musical personality and the catalyst that precipitated the *Symphonie fantastique* – did not alter the fundamentally dramatic bias of his outlook. Symphony became a branch of dramatic music, to be developed in the direction opened up by Beethoven's Fifth, Sixth and Ninth. But opera remained a major preoccupation.

Yet it was symphonic and choral, non-operatic music that, in the event, absorbed the greater part of his compositional energies. Though the *Symphonie fantastique* and its successors, *Harold en Italie*, *Roméo et Juliette* and the *Symphonie funèbre et triomphale*, may contain quasi-theatrical elements, as do – even more so – the 'dramatic legend'

La damnation de Faust and the oratorio *L'enfance du Christ*, they were all conceived as concert works. In a career of 40 years Berlioz completed only four operas (five, if we count the lost ballad opera *Estelle et Némorin* of 1823): the first version of *Les francs-juges* (a medieval drama of tyranny and intrigue composed in 1824–6 and musically influenced by Méhul), *Benvenuto Cellini*, *Les Troyens* and *Béatrice et Bénédict*.

It was certainly not for want of trying that he did not write more. Throughout his career there was usually some operatic project or other under consideration. Subjects he actively contemplated included *Antony and Cleopatra*, *Romeo and Juliet* (many years after the composition of his symphony on the play) and Scott's *The Talisman*. Undoubtedly Berlioz was more choosy than most of his contemporaries (in the end he became, like Wagner, his own librettist), and also more idealistic and demanding in his attitude to performance. The low standards with which his work as music critic brought him into contact daily may at times have discouraged him from writing operas. But the chief reason was simply the hostility and scepticism of the Paris operatic establishment. In the age of Auber, Meyerbeer and Halévy, Berlioz was not regarded as a good commercial investment: he was an eccentric, and besides – in the pigeonholing way of musical opinion in Paris – he was a 'symphonist' and therefore unfitted for writing opera.

The failure of *Benvenuto Cellini*, which was due to a combination of factors, among them the extreme technical difficulty of the score and the unfashionably colloquial style of the libretto, effectively ended Berlioz's hopes of establishing himself as an opera composer in Paris. He never had another commission there. As a brilliant and widely read critic and as a protégé of the influential daily newspaper the *Journal des débats*, he could not be entirely ignored; and for a few years, during the 1840s, he was in negotiation with the Opéra to set a Scribe libretto, *La nonne sanglante* ('The Bleeding Nun') based on M. G. Lewis's Gothic novel *The Monk*. The surviving numbers show him making some effort to accommodate his style to the tastes of the Opéra. But neither party had much belief in the collaboration; the project languished, and the libretto was eventually set by Gounod.

In the last 25 years of his career Berlioz's only direct involvement with the Paris Opéra was as musical consultant to productions of operas by Weber and Gluck. In 1841 he composed recitatives for *Der Freischütz* (spoken dialogue being forbidden at the Opéra) and orchestrated Weber's piano rondo *Invitation to the Dance* for the obligatory ballet; and in 1861 he supervised a revival of *Alceste* (repeated in 1866). This followed the Théâtre-Lyrique's immensely successful revival, in 1859, of *Orphée*, with Pauline Viardot, in an edition by Berlioz that adapted Gluck's Paris revision of the score to the title role's original alto pitch. It is in this edition that the opera is still usually given.

Berlioz's most regular operatic activity consisted in reviewing the endless succession of mostly ephemeral works that came and went on the Paris stage. The theatrical adaptation of *La damnation de Faust*, which he planned to give (under the title *Méphistophélès*) in London in the late 1840s, during his period as musical director of Adolphe Jullien's English Grand Opera at Drury Lane, remained only an idea: Jullien went bankrupt before work could begin on it or on another unspecified opera intended for Jullien. Of Berlioz's last two operas, *Béatrice et Bénédict* was commissioned by a foreign theatre. *Les Troyens* he wrote, in the first place, for himself. Then, having completed libretto and score in two years, he spent five years trying to get it staged, and in the end had to settle for performances of Acts III to V only, themselves in truncated form, by an opera house whose resources were inadequate.

Berliozian opera does not lend itself to generalization. In his output as a whole each major work inhabits its own poetic world, with an atmosphere and a style unique to it. The three completed operas of his maturity are quite unlike each other. *Béatrice et Bénédict*, outwardly, is a conventional opéra comique, breaking no new ground. *Benvenuto Cellini* is a most unconventional combination of comedy and grand opera and musically a work of great originality – in terms of rhythm especially, years ahead of its time. *Les Troyens* harks back to classical tragédie lyrique and its successor, Spontinian grand opera, but it fuses them with the expressive language of Berliozian musical Romanticism at its most fully developed and highly charged. It has taken the musical world a good hundred years to realize that the work that resulted from this idiosyncratic mixture is among the supreme achievements of the 19th century – in Tovey's words, 'one of the most gigantic and convincing masterpieces of music-drama'.

Benvenuto Cellini

Opera semiseria in two acts (2h 45m)
Libretto by Léon de Wailly and Auguste Barbier, after Cellini's *Memoirs* (1558–66; published 1728)
Composed 1836–8, rev. 1851–3
PREMIERES 10 September 1838, Académie Royale de Musique (Opéra), Paris; rev. version: 20 March 1852, Hoftheater, Weimar; UK: 25 June 1853, Covent Garden, London; US: 3 May 1975, Boston
CAST Benvenuto Cellini *t*, Giacomo Balducci *b*, Teresa *s*, Ascanio *ms*, Fieramosca *bar*, Pope Clement VII *b*, Francesco *t*, Bernardino *bar*, Pompeo *bar*, innkeeper *t*; *satb* chorus of metalworkers, foundrymen, maskers, guards, monks, the Pope's retinue, Balducci's female servants and neighbours, people of Rome; dancers

Berlioz apparently did not read the *Memoirs* of Benvenuto Cellini ('that bandit of genius,' as he called him) until after his return from Italy in 1832. Yet in an important sense the opera springs from the 15 months he spent there as winner of the Prix de Rome. It celebrates Italy – not the Italy he experienced during his time in Rome (like Mendelssohn, who was there at the same time, he found contemporary Italian culture depressingly decadent and lethargic) but its Renaissance counterpart, an ideal Italy where art is proud and vital and held in high public esteem. The Renaissance artist-hero was a cult among the Romantics (cf. Delacroix's *Michelangelo in his Studio*). The libretto freely adapted by Barbier and Wailly from Cellini's *Memoirs* (with commedia dell'arte additions), showed the triumph of the unorthodox, embattled artist over obstructive officialdom and conventional, academic art – a subject with which Berlioz could identify strongly – in a setting that evoked the colour and energy of 16th-century Rome.

In its original opéra comique form, with spoken dialogue, the libretto was turned down by the director of the Opéra-Comique in 1834. The following year a revised version, in which Alfred de Vigny had a hand, was accepted by the Opéra, and the work was given there three years later (with Pope Clement VII replaced, at the insistence of the censor, by a cardinal). It had a stormy reception and ran for only four performances (followed by three of Act I only plus a ballet). The opera remained unperformed for 13 years, and in 1844 Berlioz used material from it for his concert overture *Le carnaval romain*. On becoming kapellmeister at Weimar, Liszt, a great admirer of the work, chose it as his second major production (the first was Wagner's *Lohengrin*). For the first Weimar performances, in March 1852, Berlioz revised the score, shortening it slightly, simplifying some of its technical difficulties and, with German taste in mind, removing or toning down its more burlesque elements. Before it was given again, in November 1852, Liszt suggested more drastic surgery in the form of a large cut in the final act, removing many scenes so as to achieve a much swifter denouement. Berlioz concurred; but in order to save a few of the numbers involved he placed them earlier in the action.

This shorter, three-act 'Weimar version' was the one in which the work was generally known and performed for the next hundred years. Recently, however, there has been a return to the fuller two-act form and more logical scene order of the Paris *Cellini* of 1838 (as well as to the inclusion of the Pope) and even, beyond that, to spoken dialogue, as in the original opéra-comique conception. (On this point it is significant that for a production proposed by the Théâtre-Lyrique in 1856, the opera was to have been given with spoken dialogue instead of recitatives.) The Paris version including spoken dialogue and the Pope was the form in which Covent Garden presented the opera in 1966; and most subsequent performances, as well as the complete recording based on Covent Garden material, have done the same. So does the following synopsis.

SYNOPSIS

Act I, Tableau 1: Shrove Monday, Rome; Balducci's house, evening. Balducci, the Papal Treasurer, is unhappy because the Pope has commissioned the Florentine metalworker Cellini, instead of the official papal sculptor, Balducci's prospective son-in-law Fieramosca, to make a statue of Perseus. Maskers, Cellini among them, annoy Balducci by singing a Carnival song under his window. He goes off angrily. Cellini and Teresa, Balducci's daughter, decide to elope the following night. Fieramosca overhears their plan ('Demain soir, mardi gras'). When Balducci returns, Cellini gets away, but Fieramosca is given a drubbing. Tableau 2: Shrove Tuesday evening; Piazza Colonna, with tavern courtyard and, opposite, Cassandro's open-air theatre. Cellini and his metalworkers sing to the glory of their art ('Honneur aux maîtres ciseleurs'). They plot public revenge on the Papal Treasurer for the meagre advance payment for Perseus: one of Cassandro's actors will impersonate him in the satirical pantomime about to be performed. Fieramosca and his friend Pompeo plan to foil the abduction of Teresa. Fieramosca brags of his fencing skill ('Ah! qui pourrait me résister'). The revellers gather for Cassandro's show, *King Midas with the Ass's Ears*. Among them are Balducci, Teresa, Cellini, Ascanio (Cellini's apprentice), Fieramosca and Pompeo – the last four dressed as monks. Balducci is furious and a fight breaks out between the 'monks'. Cellini kills Pompeo. He is seized and about to be taken away when the Sant' Angelo cannon proclaims the end of Carnival. All lights are extinguished and in the confusion Cellini escapes.

Act II, Tableau 3: Ash Wednesday; Cellini's studio, dawn. As a religious procession passes, Teresa and Ascanio pray for Cellini's safety ('Sainte Vierge Marie'). A moment later he appears: they must get away to Florence immediately. Before they can leave, Balducci enters with Fieramosca and denounces Cellini ('Ah! je te trouve enfin'). Their quarrel is interrupted by the arrival of the Pope, impatient to see if his Perseus is finished. He grants general absolution ('A tous péchés pleine indulgence') but gives Cellini an ultimatum: pardon and Teresa if the statue is cast that day. If not, he will hang. Tableau 4: That evening, in Cellini's foundry in the Colosseum, Ascanio looks forward to their 'bronze offspring's baptism of fire' ('Tra la la, mais qu'ai-je donc?'). Cellini gives way to weariness and longs for the simple life ('Seul pour lutter . . . Sur les monts'). Fresh setbacks now threaten him. Fieramosca insists on their fighting a duel. In Cellini's absence the men down tools. But their mood changes when Fieramosca reappears and tries to bribe them to leave Cellini's service; Fieramosca is forced to help in the foundry. The Pope arrives and commands the casting to begin. Suddenly Fieramosca announces that they are running out of metal. But Cellini orders his men to throw all his finished works of art into the crucible. The metal fills the waiting mould and the statue is cast. The Pope acknowledges divine sanction for Cellini's labours, and all praise the art of the master metalworkers.

Berlioz's own verdict on *Benvenuto Cellini* – 'a variety of ideas, a vitality and zest and a brilliance of musical colour such as I shall perhaps never find again' – hardly seems excessive when the work is performed well. These qualities were, of course, its undoing. The music's rhythmic complexity, its constantly changing pulse and syncopation of orchestral colour, and the sheer pace at which things happen – the means by which the composer evokes the agitated, exuberant life and times of his hero – made it exceptionally difficult to perform. The final section of Fieramosca's fencing aria, to take one example, is metred successively in 7, 6 and 5 – this long before conductors were taught to deal with such irregularities.

Even now it is a virtuoso score, for chorus (male chorus especially) as well as orchestra. The best numbers are also among the most demanding: notably the huge, and hugely vivacious, tumultuous Carnival scene (in which, as Liszt said 'for the first time in opera the crowd speaks with its great roaring voice') and the swift-moving yet lyrically expansive Act I trio 'Demain soir, mardi gras', music as scintillating as anything by Berlioz. Other striking numbers or passages include the E major prayer sung by Teresa and Ascanio against a background of liturgical chanting, with its softly glowing woodwind scoring; the firecracker finale of the sextet (the whole ensemble shows Berlioz's gift for comic music); the pungent Musorgsky-like recital of the innkeeper's bill for wine; the graphically evocative rhythms and colours of the forging scene; Harlequin's beautiful love song (cor anglais, harp, cello, with comments from the crowd) contrasted with Pasquarello's parody cavatina on ophicleide (tuba) and thumping bass drum, complete with ludicrously prolonged final cadence. The opera's characteristic blend of grandeur and levity is epitomized in the dramatic and musical treatment of the Pope – a personage at once awesome and profoundly cynical, who, however, places supreme value on art.

RECORDING Eda-Pierre, Berbié, Gedda, Massard, Bastin, Soyer, Covent Garden Ch, BBC SO, C. Davis, Philips, 1973

Les Troyens
The Trojans

Grand opera in five acts (3h 45m)
Libretto by the composer, based on Books 1, 2 and 4 of the *Aeneid* by Virgil (*c*.19 BC)
Composed 1856–8, rev. 1859–60
PREMIERES Acts III–V, *Les Troyens à Carthage*: 4 November 1863, Théâtre-Lyrique, Paris; Acts I–II, *La prise de Troie*: 6 December 1890, Grossherzogliches Hoftheater, Karlsruhe; Acts I–V, condensed: 18 May 1913, Königliches Hoftheater, Stuttgart; US: Acts I–V, condensed: 27 March 1955, New England Opera Theater, Boston; UK: Acts I–II, *La prise de Troie*: 18 March 1935, Acts III–V, *Les Troyens à Carthage*: 19 March 1935, Theatre Royal, Glasgow; Acts I–V, with a few cuts: 6 June 1957, Covent Garden, London; complete: 3 May 1969, King's Theatre, Glasgow; US: complete: 26 September 1983, Metropolitan, New York
CAST Cassandre *ms*, Chorèbe *bar*, Enée *t*, Ascagne *s*, Panthée *b*, Priam *b*, Ghost of Hector *b*, Hécube *s*, Hélénus *t*, Polyxène *s*, Andromache *silent*, Astyanax *silent*, Greek captain *b*, Didon *ms*, Anna *c*, Iopas *t*, Narbal *b*, Hylas *t*, Mercure *bar* or *b*, 2 Trojan soldiers 2 *b*, priest of Pluto *b*; *satb* chorus of Trojans, Greeks, Tyrians, Carthaginians, nymphs, satyrs, fauns, sylvans, invisible spirits

The roots of Berlioz's culminating masterpiece lie far back in his boyhood, in the passion for Virgil's *Aeneid* that he conceived while studying Latin under his father's tuition. The characters of the

Aeneid became familiar inhabitants of his inner world; they were so real to him, he later wrote, that 'I imagine they knew me, so well do I know them'. Though the idea of basing an opera on the fall of Troy and the founding of Rome must have often been in his mind in the intervening years, it was not until the early 1850s that he began to think really seriously of doing so. At first he resisted it, knowing that in the climate of the time the likelihood of the Paris Opéra accepting such a work, by a composer of his dubious reputation, let alone performing it adequately, was practically nil. But in 1856, prompted by the recent unexpected success of his oratorio *L'enfance du Christ* and by the urgings of Princess Carolyne Sayn-Wittgenstein, Liszt's mistress, with whom he had discussed the project on his visits to Weimar (and who made it her mission to get the work written), he changed his mind. Beginning in May 1856, he wrote *Les Troyens*, poem and score, in less than two years.

In structure and language the libretto is influenced by the example of Berlioz's beloved Gluck. At the same time it borrows important features (though not its ancient-world subject) from Parisian grand opera: among them the five-act form, the central role of the chorus, the spectacular crowd scenes and the large forces, including stage bands. A further influence is Shakespeare, not only in the Act IV love duet, whose text is inspired by Lorenzo's and Jessica's 'In such a night' in *The Merchant of Venice*, but, generally, in the mixture of genres and juxtaposition of sharply contrasted scenes and in the wide geographical scope of the action. Berlioz described the work as 'Virgil Shakespeareanized'. Reshaped with great skill, the *Aeneid* – chiefly Books 1, 2 and 4, but other parts of the epic as well – provides the material for most of the text, part of which is a direct translation from the Latin.

If the libretto of *Les Troyens* contains elements that were old-fashioned by the standards of the day, the music is Berlioz at his most audacious and richly expressive; it is both a summing up – a merging of the two main streams of his compositional life, the operatic and the dramatic-symphonic – and a reaching out into new territory.

Despite its grand scale *Les Troyens* is not an exceptionally long opera. But before a note had been heard it had acquired the reputation of being so; and that reputation seemed confirmed when Berlioz subsequently made two operas of it, *La prise de Troie* and *Les Troyens à Carthage*. The Théâtre-Lyrique, whose offer he had accepted when the Opéra continued to make no serious move to put on *Les Troyens*, decided that the work's demands were too great for its resources and insisted on his dividing it in two; and, so that he could hear it before he died, he reluctantly agreed. In the event only *Les Troyens à Carthage* was given and, even then, extensive cuts were made during the run of 21 performances. For nearly a century *Les Troyens*, when it was played in the theatre, was given mostly as a two-part work on successive evenings, or if on one evening, in drastically shortened form. It was not until the near-complete *Troyens* at Covent Garden in 1957 that Berlioz's original conception was vindicated: that of a single epic of the destiny of a people and its tragic consequences in the lives of individual human beings.

SYNOPSIS

Act I, Troy: The abandoned Greek camp outside the walls. The Trojans celebrate their deliverance from ten years of siege. They hurry off to look at the huge wooden horse left by the Greeks, many believe, as an offering to Pallas Athene. Cassandra, the Trojan prophetess and daughter of King Priam, foresees the fate of Troy – the people, led by the king, going blindly to their doom, and with them her betrothed, the young Asian prince Corebus, whom she will not live to marry ('Malheureux roi'). When Corebus appears she rejects his soothing words and, as her vision takes shape, prophesies the destruction of Troy. She urges Corebus to save his life by leaving at once. He dismisses her terrors ('Quittenous dès ce soir'). Trojan leaders lay offerings of thanks at a field altar but their rejoicing breaks off at the arrival of Andromache, widow of Hector, the Trojan hero and son of Priam. Aeneas rushes in and describes the appalling death of the priest Laocoon, devoured by sea serpents as he was inciting the people to burn the wooden horse. The whole assembly is struck with horror ('Châtiment effroyable'). Aeneas interprets the portent as Athene's anger at the sacrilege. Priam orders the horse to be placed beside the temple of the goddess. Cassandra's warning cries are ignored. The torchlit procession draws near, chanting the sacred hymn of Troy ('Du roi des dieux, ô fille aimée'). Suddenly it halts: from within the horse has come a sound like the clash of arms. But the people, possessed, take it as a happy omen. Cassandra hears the procession pass into the city.

Act II, Tableau 1: A room in Aeneas' palace. The ghost of Hector appears to Aeneas and tells him that he must escape and found a new Troy in Italy ('Ah! fuis, fils de Vénus'). Corebus enters at the head of a band of armed men. He reports that the citadel is holding out. They resolve to defend it to the death. Tableau 2: A hall in Priam's palace; at the back a high colonnade. Women pray before an altar to Vesta ('Ha! puissante Cybèle'). Cassandra prophesies that Aeneas will found a new Troy in Italy. But Corebus is dead, and she would rather take her own life than fall into the hands of the Greeks. Those women too frightened to face death are driven out. The rest, in growing exaltation, vow to die with Cassandra ('Complices de sa gloire'). Cassandra stabs herself. Greek soldiers announce that Aeneas has escaped with the treasure of Troy. With a last cry of 'Italie!', some of the women throw themselves from the colonnade, others stab or strangle themselves. Fire engulfs the palace.

Act III: Carthage (the city founded by Dido after she fled from Tyre and her brother Pygmalion, murderer of her husband Sychaeus); a hall in Dido's palace, decorated for a festival, on a brilliant day after storms. The people celebrate their city and their queen ('Gloire à Didon') and promise to defend her against the Numidian king, Iarbas. Builders, sailors and farmworkers are presented with symbolic gifts. Alone with her sister Anna, Dido confesses to a mysterious sadness. She denies she is pining for love, and resists her sister's argument that she should marry again. But to herself she admits the appeal of Anna's words ('Sa voix fait naître dans mon sein'). Iopas, the court poet, announces the arrival of an unknown fleet, driven ashore by the storm. Dido, recalling her own wanderings ('Errante sur les mers'), gives the strangers audience. Trojan chiefs enter, and Ascanius, Aeneas' son, presents trophies from Troy. Panthus explains Aeneas' mission: to found a new Troy in Italy. Narbal rushes in with the news that Iarbas and his hordes have attacked. Aeneas, till now disguised, offers the dazzled queen an alliance and, after entrusting Ascanius to her care, leads Trojans and Carthaginians to battle.

Act IV, Tableau 1 (*Royal Hunt and Storm*): A forest near Carthage. Naiads bathing in a stream take fright at the sound of hunting horns and vanish as huntsmen enter the clearing. A storm breaks. Dido and Aeneas, separated from the rest, take refuge in a cave and there acknowledge and consummate their love, while satyrs and wood nymphs utter cries of 'Italie!'. The storm passes. Tableau 2: Dido's garden by the sea; night. Narbal and Anna discuss the situation, he full of foreboding, she optimistic: 'Fate calls Aeneas to Italy' – 'Love is the greatest of the gods'. Dido, Aeneas and the court watch dances performed to celebrate victory over the Numidians. Iopas, to soothe the queen's restless mood, sings of the fruits of the earth ('O blonde Cérès'). Dido learns from Aeneas that Andromache has married Pyrrhus, son of Achilles the slayer of her husband Hector. She feels absolved ('Tout conspire a vaincre mes remords'). All contemplate the beauty of the night ('Tout n'est que paix et charme'). Alone, Dido and Aeneas pour out their love ('Nuit d'ivresse et d'extase infinie'). As they leave, Mercury appears by a column on which Aeneas' arms are hung and, striking the shield, calls three times 'Italie!'.

Act V, Tableau 1: The harbour of Carthage; night. Hylas, a young Phrygian sailor, sings of his longing for the forests of Mount Ida ('Vallon sonore'). Panthus and the Trojan chiefs agree they must delay their departure for Italy no longer. Two Trojan sentries fail to see why they should go. Aeneas enters, determined to leave but torn by love and remorse ('Inutiles regrets'). The ghosts of dead Trojan heroes appear and urge him to be gone. He rouses the sleeping army. Dido, distraught, confronts him. But her entreaties and her curses are equally vain. Tableau 2: A room in the royal palace. The Trojan fleet is seen setting sail. Dido orders a pyre, on which she will burn all memorials of Aeneas. Alone, she resolves on her death and takes farewell of life, friends and city ('Je vais mourir – Adieu, fière cité'). Tableau 3: A terrace overlooking the sea. Narbal and Anna pronounce a ritual curse on Aeneas. Dido ascends the pyre. To the horror of all she stabs herself with Aeneas' sword. Before doing so, she has prophesied the coming of a great conqueror – Hannibal – who will avenge her wrongs. But her final vision is of Eternal Rome.

As a musical epic and a dramatization of Virgil, *Les Troyens* necessarily encompasses a wide variety of scenes and atmospheres. It is Berlioz's richest, most eventful score, embracing at one extreme the panoply of the *Royal Hunt and Storm* and the procession of the wooden horse and at the other the chamber-music intimacy of Dido's 'Adieu, fière cité'. But the composer is at great pains to unify its wealth of incident, not only by large-scale tonal design but also by means of innumerable recurring motifs, melodic, harmonic and rhythmic, of which the *Trojan March*, the fateful hymn heard in Acts I, III and V, is only the most obvious. Musically as well as verbally, the central idea of Roman destiny is a constant presence.

At the same time, contrast is a fundamental principle governing the musico-dramatic structure of the work. There is, first and most striking, the contrast between the musical idioms of Acts I and II (Troy) and III and IV (Carthage) – the one harsh, jagged, possessed, rhythmically on a knife edge; the other warm, expansive, sensuous. Then there is the contrast between one act and the next: Act I spacious and, for much of its course, static, followed by the violent, highly compressed Act II – Troy on its final fatal night – itself giving way to the Arcadian picture of peaceful Carthage in Act III, which, however, like Act I ends with a fast-moving, highly dramatic and martial finale. Act IV is a sustained lyrical interlude, a time out of war, but ending with a grim reminder of the great questions of fate and war which will come to a head in Act V, the act that draws together and completes the preceding four.

There are also continual smaller scale contrasts of musical character and dramatic perspective: the Trojans' rejoicing interrupted by the mime scene for the grieving Andromache, with its long clarinet melody, classical as a Grecian frieze, itself followed abruptly by Aeneas' brief, hectic narration of the death of Laocoon and the horror-struck ensemble it provokes; the sudden shift of focus from high romance and affairs of state to the feelings of ordinary people caught up in the tides of history, as Hylas the young sailor sings of his longing for his lost homeland; the Trojan chiefs' earnest discussion of policy giving way to the low-life grumbling of two sentries, for whom 'Italy' means nothing more significant than danger and discomfort, and whose homely dialogue in turn yields to the anguished, exalted mood of Aeneas' monologue, with its extended melodic lines, panting rhythms and heroic orchestration.

The central theme of the work is embodied in music of truly heroic temper. Yet Berlioz has no illusions about great 'causes' and what they can do to the lives of individuals. The juggernaut of Roman destiny marches across the personal fates of two contrasted but complementary tragic heroines, Cassandra and Dido. Cassandra is virtually Berlioz's own creation, developed from a few glimpses in the Aeneid into the fiery protagonist of the opera's first two acts; she is the personification of Troy's doom, which she foresees but is powerless to prevent. The role of Dido is the composer's tribute – a tribute of extraordinary radiance, tenderness and expressive intensity – to the mythical but to him totally real person who had first possessed his imagination 40 years before.

RECORDINGS 1. Lindholm, Veasey, Vickers, Glossop, Wandsworth School Boys' Ch, Covent Garden Ch & O, C. Davis, Philips, 1969; 2. De Young, Lang, Heppner, Mattei, LSCh & O, C. Davis, LSO Classics, 2000

Béatrice et Bénédict

Opéra comique in two acts (1h 30m)
Libretto by the composer, after the play *Much Ado About Nothing* by William Shakespeare (1599)
Composed 1860–62, rev. 1863
PREMIERES 9 August 1862, Neues Theater, Baden-Baden; 4 June 1890, Opéra-Comique, Paris; UK: 24 March 1936, Glasgow; US: 21 March 1960, Carnegie Hall, New York (concert); 3 June 1964, Cramton Auditorium, Howard University, Washington DC (stage)
CAST Béatrice *s*, Bénédict *t*, Héro *s*, Claudio *bar*, Don Pedro *b*, Léonato *spoken role*, Ursule *ms*, Somarone *b*; *satb* chorus of people of Sicily, musicians, choristers, lords and ladies at the governor's court; dancers

As early as 1833 Berlioz had contemplated composing an opera on *Much Ado About Nothing*. In the event it was to be his last major work, written nearly 30 years later to inaugurate the new opera house at the fashionable spa town of Baden-Baden in Germany. Since the mid-1850s the manager of the casino, Edouard Bénazet, had engaged Berlioz to give an annual gala concert at the height of the season, with an élite orchestra assembled for the occasion and rehearsed for as long as was necessary. In 1858 Bénazet commissioned an opera from him. The libretto, by Edouard Plouvier, concerned an episode from the Thirty Years War. Berlioz, however, felt little enthusiasm for it, and persuaded Bénazet to release him from his contract (Plouvier's libretto was set by Henry Litolff) and to agree instead to an opera, with spoken dialogue, on *Much Ado*.

Béatrice et Bénédict ('Bénédict' was the standard French form of Shakespeare's 'Benedick') was composed to a text by Berlioz himself, closely based, for the most part, on the play. The Baden-Baden performances of August 1862 were followed by a production, in German, at Weimar in the spring of 1863, with two numbers added to the second act (the women's trio and the distant chorus). In this form the opera was revived at Baden-Baden the following August.

Berlioz had first thought in terms of a one-act opera. Even at its full length *Béatrice* contains only 15 numbers, separated by mostly very short dialogue scenes. The work is a divertissement on one aspect of the play. Composing it, he said, was 'a relaxation after *Les Troyens*' – 'I have taken as my text part of Shakespeare's tragi-comedy.' There is no Don John, no sinister sub-plot, no Dogberry and the watch; and Claudio remains a shadowy figure. The drama consists in 'persuading Beatrice and Benedick that they love each other', and in contrasting with their complex but ultimately more rewarding relationship the conventionally starry-eyed romance of the 'sentimental couple', Hero and Claudio. Somarone, the portrait of a pedantic, fussily conscientious court musician of the old school, is Berlioz's invention, derived from Shakespeare's Balthasar, whose song 'Sigh no more, ladies' comes at the same point in the action as Somarone's *Epithalame grotesque*, and prompts the same comment from Benedick: 'An he had been a dog that should have howled thus, they would have hanged him.'

SYNOPSIS

Act I: In the park of the governor, Leonato, the inhabitants of Messina joyfully await the return of the victorious army from the Moorish wars. Hero, Leonato's daughter, learns that Claudio has come back loaded with honours. Beatrice inquires about 'Signor Mountanto' – that is, Benedick, between whom and Beatrice (Leonato explains) 'there is a kind of merry war – they never meet but there's a skirmish of wits'. After a *sicilienne*, the people disperse. Hero reflects on the happiness of being reunited with Claudio ('Je vais le voir'). Beatrice and Benedick mock each other in a duet whose teasing manner does not conceal an exasperated mutual interest ('Comment le dédain'). Don Pedro congratulates Claudio. Does the example not tempt Benedick? But Benedick is impervious to their jests; he will die a bachelor ('Me marier'). Don Pedro and Claudio decide to find a way of tricking Beatrice and Benedick into loving one another. Court musicians rehearse the epithalamium that the choirmaster Somarone has written for the bridal couple. Benedick overhears an apparently serious discussion between Don Pedro, Leonato and Claudio about the wonderful behaviour of Beatrice, who has actually fallen in love with him. Benedick, astonished but impressed, resolves to requite her ('Ah! je vais l'aimer'). Hero and Ursula, too, laugh about the deception practised on Beatrice, who has been made to overhear that Benedick has fallen hopelessly in love with her. The two girls sink into a sweetly melancholy reverie on the beauty of the night and the impending wedding ('Nuit paisible et sereine').

Entr'acte reprise of the *sicilienne*.

Act II: A room in the governor's palace. From near by come the shouts of soldiers calling for drink, and Somarone's voice improvising a song in honour of Sicilian wines ('Le vin de Syracuse'). Beatrice enters, in great agitation. She recalls her unexpected sadness when Benedick left for the wars, and her dreams of him during his absence ('Il m'en souvient'). Then, with sudden decision, she faces her feelings: 'Contempt, farewell and maiden pride, adieu: Benedick, love on – I will requite you.' Hero and Ursula affect astonishment to see Beatrice at once agitated and strangely softened. With her they sing of the happiness of a bride about to marry the man she loves ('Je vais d'un coeur aimant'). Alone, Beatrice listens to a distant chorus summoning the bride. Benedick enters, and the two skirmish in a new key. Their embarrassed exchange is cut short by the wedding march. Claudio and Hero sign the contract. The scrivener produces a second one. 'Who else is marrying?' asks Don Pedro. Beatrice and Benedick confront each other. Each denies loving the other 'more than reason'. Avowals of love in their own hands are produced to confound them. A sign is brought in with the words, 'Here you may see Benedick the married man', which all sing to the music to which Benedick (trio, Act I) swore he'd never marry. Unabashed, Benedick ripostes by acknowledging the power of love and the giddiness of mankind ('L'amour est un flambeau').

Berlioz described *Béatrice et Bénédict* as 'a caprice written with the point of a needle'. It is his most light-fingered score, echoing in a gentler vein the rhythmic high spirits and wit of *Benvenuto Cellini*, and bathed in a kind of late-afternoon glow. The woodwind-writing is piquant and luminous. Prominent also are pizzicato strings and finely shaped violin lines of the utmost delicacy. Trombones play only in the latter part of the overture, the middle section of Beatrice's aria, the 13-bar *enseigne* (No. 14) and the final tutti. Tambourines and guitar add a touch of exotic colour. The exuberant overture alludes to half-a-dozen different numbers. Its angular, lilting theme in triplets, full of cross-rhythms, reappears in the final number, in which Benedick and Beatrice, declaring a temporary truce, sing of love as a 'will o' the wisp', a brief but enchanting gleam that 'comes from nowhere and then vanishes, to the distraction of our souls'. The other best numbers include the men's trio 'Me marier', with its nimble musical repartee; the charming women's trio 'Je vais d'un coeur aimant' in Berlioz's favourite slow 6/8 time; also in 6/8, the nocturne sung by Hero and Ursula, music of great economy used to evoke a mood of deep enchantment; and the noble, long-breathed andante (interrupted by martial sounds reminiscent of *Les Troyens*) in which Beatrice recalls her sadness when Benedick left for the wars.

RECORDINGS 1. Baker, Eda-Pierre, Watts, Tear, John Alldis Ch, LSO, C. Davis, Philips, 1977; 2. Graham, McNair, Robbin, Viala, Op Nat de Lyon Ch & O, Nelson, Erato, 1991 (includes dialogue)
OTHER OPERATIC WORK *La Damnation de Faust*, 1846

D.C.

Leonard Bernstein

b 25 August 1918, Lawrence, Massachusetts, US; *d* 14 October 1990, New York

Bernstein worked with huge success in the fields of both classical music and the Broadway musical theatre. He wrote ballets, musicals and later in life returned to opera. Some of his works, such as *Candide*, have been performed both in theatres and in opera houses. One of his most distinctive contributions was the development of a new direction for popular music theatre in *West Side Story*.

He first achieved fame as a conductor (studying with Reiner and serving as assistant to Koussevitzky and Rodzinski). A last-minute substitution for Bruno Walter with the New York Philharmonic in November 1943 led to a huge demand for Bernstein as both conductor and composer. Within months, he had composed the highly successful one-act ballet *Fancy Free*, and he followed it with an impressive series of concert pieces over the following years. His position as principal conductor of the New York Philharmonic from 1956 to 1966 (the first American-born conductor to hold that post) and his television appearances as a commentator on music made him one of the most familiar faces in American music. In the years following his departure from the Philharmonic, he became one of the most prominent international conductors of his time.

At the same time, Bernstein involved himself with musical theatre on an ever-increasing level of musical complexity and sophistication. He achieved success in many genres, and all but one of his stage works (an unsuccessful collaboration with Alan Jay Lerner) have retained an active stage life. He several times expressed the belief that a living American operatic form could evolve only from its popular musical theatre, and his own efforts contributed to that development. He ranks among the handful of popular composers who had the ability to orchestrate their own musicals (though he in fact delegated part, sometimes all, of this work to others). His first efforts for the Broadway stage aspired to be little more than well-crafted entertainments, but beginning with *Candide* he took pains to unify his theatre scores motivically and to find opportunities for extended musical development. The essay 'Why Don't You Run Upstairs and Write a Nice Gershwin Tune?' from his book *The Joy of Music* reveals his disappointment that after two musicals he had not produced a truly popular song, but *West Side Story* (in particular, its film version) changed that. Unfortunately, thereafter he composed only sporadically for the musical stage.

Candide

Comic operetta in two acts (2h 30m: 1988 version)
Revised version in one act
Libretto by Lillian Hellman (rev. versions, by Hugh Wheeler), based on the novel by François Voltaire (1756); lyrics by Richard Wilbur; additional lyrics by John Latouche, Dorothy Parker, Hellman, Bernstein and (in rev. versions) Stephen Sondheim
Composed 1954–6, rev. 1973, 1988–9
PREMIERES 1 December 1956, Martin Beck Theater, New York; UK: 30 April 1959, Saville Theatre, London; US: published rev. version: 18 December 1973, Chelsea Theater Center, Brooklyn, New York

The journey of Voltaire's eponymous hero from naïve optimism to disillusioned knowledge of the world's evil is told in a mock-operetta style. Its music covers a wide range, from allusions to various popular styles (tango, *schottische*, waltz) through mock operetta, to some passages of fully operatic weight. Its most familiar portions are the pseudo-Rossinian overture (probably Bernstein's most performed concert piece) and the coloratura soprano aria, both sincere and parodistic, 'Glitter and be Gay'.

Far more popular in revival (sometimes by opera companies) than during its brief Broadway run in 1956, *Candide* has undergone sweeping revisions since its troubled conception. The music used in the Broadway premiere (pre-production manuscripts included many songs and lyrics not used in that production) corresponds to that in the published vocal score and, with some sections omitted, to the original-cast recording. For the first London production, Bernstein supplied a new song ('We are Women'). Then, in a series of US West Coast productions, the libretto was revised and different music used, culminating in a full-scale revival which began in San Francisco and ended in Washington DC, closing before its intended Broadway opening.

The 1973 revision, conceived and directed by Harold Prince, moved to Broadway in 1974 and had a successful run there. It became the usual performing version thereafter. Hugh Wheeler supplied a new libretto to replace Hellman's, in one act and with a quite different sequence of events (more faithful to Voltaire in some respects), often more farcical in tone, and with Pangloss and the Governor combined into a single role to be played by Voltaire as narrator. Five numbers were omitted and Stephen Sondheim supplied minor lyric revisions as well as words for three new songs.

John Mauceri, who had assembled the music for the 1973 production, performed the same service for New York City Opera when it added *Candide* to its repertoire. This was closely based on the 1973 version (Prince was still directing), but in two acts and with the five missing songs restored, mostly in new contexts (sometimes with new lyrics, by Wilbur).

A 1988 Scottish Opera production, with yet another reconsidered libretto (still credited to Hugh Wheeler) and additional restorations, established another new text. This adaptation by John Wells and Mauceri aimed to include as much of Bernstein's music as possible and was able for the first time since 1971 to use the locations, if not the words, of Hellman's libretto. A 1989 concert and a recording by the composer in London used primarily the Scottish Opera version but introduced revisions and restorations of its own.

RECORDING Anderson, Hadley, Gedda, Ludwig, Green, London

Symphony Ch & O, Bernstein, DG, 1989 (contains the most music of any *Candide* recording, and the composer's final thoughts on it)

OTHER OPERATIC WORKS *On the Town*, 1944; *Trouble in Tahiti*, 1952; *Wonderful Town*, 1953; *West Side Story*, 1957; *Mass*, 1971; *1600 Pennsylvania Avenue*, 1976; *A Quiet Place*, 1983, rev. 1984

J.A.C.

Harrison Birtwistle

(Sir) Harrison Birtwistle; *b* 15 July 1934, Accrington, Lancashire, England

Birtwistle has made a more significant contribution to opera than any other British musician of his generation. He studied at the Royal Northern College of Music (1952–5) and was a member of the New Music Manchester Group along with Alexander Goehr, Peter Maxwell Davies, John Ogdon and Elgar Howarth. The Group performed new music, in line with the preoccupation with Webern characteristic of young Continental composers of the time; medieval techniques of composition also formed a strong area of interest. However, the earliest works Birtwistle himself acknowledges date only from 1957, and his first operatic work, *Punch and Judy*, was not written until 1967.

Birtwistle worked as a school teacher until a Harkness Fellowship in 1965 enabled him to take up musical studies in America and devote himself to composition. *Punch and Judy* was followed by *Down by the Greenwood Side* in 1969, and in 1973 he embarked on *The Mask of Orpheus*, a project that would not be completed for another ten years. All these works exhibit the interests in mythic narration (whether from Classical or English sources), ritualistic patterning and different ways of organizing time that are essential features of Birtwistle's musical thinking. While the subject matter of all these pieces includes murder, the violence is tempered by a melody-based style and by dramatic resolutions incorporating the idea of regenerative life force.

From 1975 to 1983 Birtwistle was the first Musical Director of the National Theatre, and then continued in the advisory post of Associate Director, Music, for a further five years. *Bow Down* (1977), which sits midway between theatre and opera, was the result of a collaboration between the company's actors and musicians, while among the incidental music he composed there, the score for Peter Hall's celebrated production of *The Oresteia* (1981) was the most significant, and also left its mark on the way in which he conceived the staging of *The Mask of Orpheus*, which was completed in 1984. In that year *Yan Tan Tethera*, originally commissioned for television, was also composed. It was followed by the large-scale orchestral work *Earth Dances* (1986), the more rhetorical world of which prepared the way for the gestural vocabulary that characterizes *Gawain*, yet another of Birtwistle's explorations of myth and narrative. In *The Second Mrs Kong*, however, the myth is an invented one, and it is the collision of two worlds, one fictional, the other historically rooted, that generates what is arguably the most direct and emotionally searching of all his operas. Birtwistle explored other aspects of myth and myth-making in his 'dramatic tableaux' *The Last Supper* (2000), while an obliquely operatic return to the world of classical mythology, *The Io Passion*, received its premiere at the Aldeburgh Festival in June 2004.

If Stravinsky and Messiaen are two composers for whom Birtwistle acknowledges great respect, they also suggest themselves as the nearest comparisons in this century for a composer who has created a distinctive voice in working and reworking musical concepts with clarity and vision as well as extremism.

Punch and Judy

Comical tragedy or tragical comedy in one act (1h 45m)
Scenario and libretto by Stephen Pruslin
Composed 1966–7
PREMIERES 8 June 1968, Jubilee Hall, Aldeburgh; US: 12 February 1970, Minnesota Opera, Minneapolis
CAST Punch *high bar*, Judy/Fortune-Teller *ms*, Pretty Polly/Witch *high s*, Choregos/Jack Ketch *low bar*, Doctor *basso profundo*, Lawyer *high t*, 5 mime dancers

Birtwistle's first operatic work became something of a *cause célèbre* when Benjamin Britten and Peter Pears vacated their box some time before the end of the premiere. One reviewer remembered the performance as seeming 'almost gratuitously offensive'; another described it as 'the baby's tantrum beneath our civilized sociability'. Birtwistle himself has referred to it as a central work in his output, acting as a source for other pieces. The music has the Expressionistic energy of other music-theatre pieces from the 1960s (such as Maxwell Davies's *Eight Songs for a Mad King*), harnessed to a stylized plot that focuses on elemental and violent urges. Punch's desire to destroy leads to four murders (Melodramas), and is linked to the desire to possess by the three Quests for Pretty Polly. These Quests are unsuccessful, and only by escaping from the rules of his own games does Punch eventually win his love.

The work divides into nine sections, plus a prologue and an epilogue. Four sections are Melodramas, and three are Quests. The action opens with Choregos, the Punch-and-Judy man, opening his booth. Melodrama I begins as Punch enters, carrying the baby. He sings a lullaby and then throws the baby into the fire, with the war cry that precedes each of his murders. Judy enters, finds the baby dead, and confronts Punch in a word game. Punch then murders Judy. Punch embarks on his first Quest for Pretty Polly. He journeys east, and serenades her with a gavotte. She rejects his offered sunflower, however, with the words, 'The flaw in this flower is a flicker of flame'.

Melodrama II follows, in which Punch confronts the Lawyer and Doctor in three riddle games. After this legal and medical disputation, Punch murders the Doctor with a hypodermic syringe and the Lawyer with a quill pen. He then sets off again on the second Quest for Pretty Polly, travelling west on a hobby-horse. Pretty Polly dances to his allemande. This time she rejects his offer of a gem.

For the third Melodrama, Punch takes on Choregos himself, 'crowning' him by breaking a trumpet, cymbal and drum over his head. He then locks him in his bass-viol case. This time, though, the war cry falters as Punch's creator falls out of the case dead. At this point a Nightmare begins. Punch travels north, where his victims turn on him to exact revenge, Judy appearing as a Fortune-Teller and Pretty Polly as a Witch. He manages to escape from the Nightmare on the hobby-horse; but on the third Quest for Pretty Polly, journeying south, his pavan fails even to make her appear.

In the final Melodrama, Punch again confronts Choregos, who returns in the guise of Jack Ketch, the legendary hangman. After an interview game, Punch is condemned to death; at the last moment, however, he tricks Jack Ketch into trying the noose on himself; as the hangman is hanged, Pretty Polly appears; the final section, 'Punch Triumphans', sees Punch finally united with his love in a maypole dance.

Despite the violence of both subject matter and musical gesture, there are moments of great lyricism and humour in the work. The repeated prayer, 'Let the winds be gentle, let the seas be calm', and the paradox that precedes each death, 'The sweetness of this moment is unendurably bitter', are examples of 'musical signposts' for the audience, along with the use of sequences of colours, dance forms, games and so forth through the different sections. The incessant verbal playing ('Witness, avenging gods, my Choregos in stringent suffering strung on a violent viol vile,' sings Judy) sometimes suffers in the musical turbulence; but by and large, this first theatre piece shows a musical inventiveness that creates great contrasts within a consistent language.

RECORDING Bryn-Julson, De Gaetani, Langridge, Roberts, Wilson-Johnson, Tomlinson, London Sinfonietta, Atherton, Decca, 1980

Gawain

Opera in two acts (3h)
Libretto by David Harsent, after the anonymous 14th-century poem *Sir Gawain and the Green Knight*
Composed 1989–91
PREMIERE 30 May 1991, Covent Garden, London
CAST Gawain *bar*, The Green Knight/Sir Bertilak de Hautdesert *b*, Morgan le Fay *s*, Lady de Hautdesert *ms*, Arthur *t*, Guinevere *s*, A Fool *bar*, Agravain *b-bar*, Ywain *t*, Bishop Baldwin *ct*, Bedevere *actor*; *satb* chorus of clerics; offstage: *satb* chorus

The first work by Birtwistle to bear the title 'opera' is a massive work that represents the culmination of his interest in the folklore of the Green Man. The first of his works to be produced at Covent Garden, its premiere was broadcast by radio and recorded for television.

Harsent's libretto is strikingly faithful to the medievalism of the original poem, though it presents the whole action as controlled by Morgan le Fay, who is on stage but invisible to the other characters for almost the whole opera.

SYNOPSIS
Act I: Arthur's court is celebrating New Year when the Green Knight enters. He issues a challenge for someone to strike a blow at his neck with his axe and to receive a return blow a year later. Eventually Gawain accepts, and strikes the Knight's head from his body. The Knight himself picks up the head, tells Gawain to meet him at the Green Chapel, and leaves. During a long representation of the changing seasons, Gawain is prepared for his quest.

Act II: Gawain's journey. He eventually reaches the castle of Sir Bertilak and Lady de Hautdesert, who tell him that the Green Chapel is near by. For three days he is entertained: Bertilak hunts all day while his wife attempts, unsuccessfully, to seduce Gawain. Each evening, fulfilling a pact between them, the two men exchange the day's winnings: a stag, a boar and a fox, for one, two and then three kisses. However, on the third day Gawain also secretly accepts a protective girdle from Lady de Hautdesert. Gawain then goes to the Green Chapel. The Green Knight feigns two blows, and cuts Gawain only slightly with the third. The Knight is then revealed to be Bertilak, and the cut is retribution for keeping the girdle. Gawain returns to Arthur's court, convinced of his cowardice and refusing to be seen as 'that hero' who was sent out.

There are points of contact between the medieval and contemporary verse. The alliteration of the original is occasionally echoed, as in Gawain's words to the Green Knight, 'My life is light – easier to lift than the axe', and the overall effect of the libretto derives from the features of the original that must have drawn Birtwistle to it: the mixture of mythic figures (the Green Man; the 'magic site' of the Chapel, a barrow; the Christian symbolism and the repetitions and parallelisms of the text) and the equivocal denouement, which is preserved without any attempt at more modern didactic point-making.

The half-hour masque that concludes Act I aroused much comment at the premiere, and some found it tedious. Emblematic figures, including Father Time and nature spirits, process carrying symbols of seasonal growth, harvest and death, while the Fool and the knights strip, wash and arm Gawain for his journey. Although Birtwistle later revised this section, the difficulties it originally gave critics seemed to stem from its deliberate adoption of ritually repeated blocks of time in the context of an otherwise straightforward narrative, rather than a misjudgement of its length.

The opera is at first sight much more conservative in form than earlier Birtwistle works. There are none of the alternative narratives of *The Mask of Orpheus*, and no repetition of blocks of action, except for the masque of the seasons and the beheading itself, where the Green Knight enters for a second time to expedite the special effect. The music accompanies the action in a fairly direct manner, with the moments of violence or tenderness set alongside onomatopoeia (the Green Knight's horse's clip-clopping shoes, or, in the hunting scenes, abundant horn calls; these last are used leitmotivically elsewhere – for instance, slowed down in the texture of the overture). But if the opera lacks the experimental form of *The Mask of Orpheus*, it should not be assumed that this is a retrograde stylistic step. Birtwistle's gritty and consistent harmonic language owes much to the techniques of *Earth Dances* (1986), frequently proliferating melodic lines stratified into separate layers of orchestral texture; this consistency allows great diversity of rhythm and sonority without falling into the bathos that any treatment of myth and metaphor courts. There are moments of parody (Gawain's first kiss is accompanied by a sugary cello phrase), stylistic reference (notably to Stravinsky's *The Rite of Spring*) and occasional rhythmic relaxation (for instance in Morgan le Fay's and Lady de Hautdesert's dance). The typical Birtwistle interest in altered repetitions of material follows the parallelisms of the text itself, and melodic repetition is skilfully deployed, for instance for Morgan le Fay's recurring lines, 'This is the hour of legacy or loss./ This is the hour of vanity or choice.'

RECORDING Angel, Howells, le Roux, Tomlinson, Covent Garden Ch & O, Howarth, Collins, 1994 (live)

The Second Mrs Kong

Opera in two acts (nine scenes)
(2h 15m)
Libretto by Russell Hoban
PREMIERE 24 October 1994, Glyndebourne, Sussex
CAST Kong *t*, Pearl *s*, Anubis/Death of Kong *b-bar*, Vermeer *bar*, Mirror/Mirror Echo *lyric s*, Inanna (Mrs Dollarama) *ms*, Mr Dollarama *bar*, Swami Zumzum *light t*, Orpheus *ct*, the Sphinx *c*, Four Models/Four Temptations 2 *s*, 2 *ms*, Euridice *lyric s*, Monstrous Messenger/ Joe Shady *b*; *satb* chorus of The Dead

Reading the works of Russell Hoban, Birtwistle was attracted by their brevity and structure, and their up-to-date way of dealing with myth – a recurring characteristic of much of the composer's work – led him to approach Hoban for a libretto. They began with the idea of the King Kong of the 1933 film, a subject that intrigued them both, and what emerged after many drafts is a concise, wittily allusive (and elusive) libretto about the impossibility of love, peopled by a weird assortment of characters – familiar, surreal and mythological.

SYNOPSIS
Act I: Anubis, the jackal-headed boatman, brings the souls of the dead to the world of shadows. Some of them (the Dollaramas and Zumzum) relive their more bizarre memories; Vermeer recalls his meeting with the woman in his picture, *The Girl with the Pearl Earring*. The film of *King Kong* arrives, but Kong himself knows he doesn't belong here as he is merely an idea. Vermeer paints Pearl. A mirror promises to take her into the future; she hears Kong calling out. In the 20th century, Vermeer's picture becomes a popular icon, and Pearl, now part of a stockbroker's furniture, searches for Kong with the help of a computer. They

fall in love. Kong escapes the world of shadows and sets off, with Orpheus as his pilot, to find Pearl among the living.

Act II: Kong and Orpheus are attacked by four temptations (Doubt/Fear/Despair/Terror). Orpheus loses his head but Kong rescues it. They avoid the pursuing dead and also the Sphinx. Orpheus's singing charms a telephone on which Kong speaks to Pearl. Kong fights off the threatening figure of the Death of Kong and realizes that, being an idea, he cannot die. Pearl and Kong meet but find they cannot reach one another. They recall falling in love.

The Second Mrs Kong is less complex and both more lyrical and immediately accessible than its two operatic predecessors, but its subject matter and sense of humour never obscure the seriousness and compassion behind its quirkily imaginative ideas. The vocal lines are easy on the ear; the ingenious orchestration, omitting trombones, includes an accordion, a cimbalom and two saxophones. According to the composer, the opera 'sits' on the thick texture of the score, which is constructed upon two whole-tone scales. The opera's director/designer Tom Cairns played a vital part in the gestation of the work and the successful premiere of this masterpiece of the 1990s.

OTHER OPERATIC WORKS *Down by the Greenwood Side*, 1969; *Bow Down*, 1977; *The Mask of Orpheus*, 1986; *Yan Tan Tethera*, 1986; *The Last Supper*, 2000; *The Io Passion*, 2004

R.S./A.H./A.C.

Georges Bizet

Alexandre-César-Léopold [Georges] Bizet; *b* 25 October 1838, Paris; *d* 3 June 1875, Le Bougival, nr Paris

Bizet began and ended his career before the public with operas, though he also wrote orchestral music, piano pieces, songs, and choral and incidental music. None of his operas was immediately successful in Paris, but from the start his work was original enough to be taken seriously. The faith placed in Bizet by a few well-placed contemporaries has been amply justified by the brilliant posthumous triumph of his operatic masterpiece, *Carmen*, an enduring place in the repertoire for *Les pêcheurs de perles*, and a growing appreciation for several of his other operas.

Bizet achieved a vibrant and original amalgam of memorable melody, piquant harmony, vivid orchestration and, on occasion, a realistic, dramatic power that has rarely been equalled in opera. Though contemporary critics frequently applied the label 'Wagnerian' to Bizet's operas, the composer kept his distance from Wagner's theories and chose to work within the number- and scene-opera tradition; however, his orchestra plays a more active role in presenting melody and countermelody than that of earlier French composers, and its tone colours are essential to the varying of motifs for dramatic ends.

Like most French composers, Bizet formed his skills largely at the Conservatoire (1847–57), where he studied composition with Fromental Halévy; Gounod, perhaps the most potent single influence on his development, came to know Bizet outside that institution. The connection involved not only some composition lessons, but also arrangements of Gounod's works. Bizet's delightful Symphony in C, composed at this time (1855), is clearly modelled on Gounod's Symphony in D.

Bizet's early operas are charming, comic works, where the models of Rossini and Donizetti show through clearly. As he expanded his range in the 1860s to more dramatic and serious topics, his scores show the influence of others, notably Gounod, Félicien David, Meyerbeer, Halévy, Verdi and Weber. Although they are generally more uneven, these scores teem with ideas. Abandoned or lost projects from the period 1868–71 obscure the route by which Bizet achieved true artistic maturity. From the 1870s there are just two mature opéras comiques (*Djamileh* and *Carmen*) and an abandoned grand opera *Don Rodrigue*, which remains largely unscored; since rehearsal revisions were normally an essential stage in Bizet's creative process, it is difficult to speculate on the final form this torso might have taken.

Bizet's first two completed operas were written while he was still a student at the Conservatoire. *La maison du docteur* (*c.*1855) was probably composed for private performance with his fellow students, but *Le Docteur Miracle* (1856) was given at the Bouffes-Parisiens theatre as one of the prizewinners in a competition conducted by Offenbach to promote comic opera. A few months later Bizet capped a brilliant student career by winning the Prix de Rome with his cantata *Clovis et Clotilde* (1857). This enabled him to spend nearly three years in Rome, from January 1858 to July 1860. During this time he worked on *Don Procopio*, which he submitted as his first *envoi* as a Prix de Rome winner (officially this should have been a sacred work). He considered further operatic projects and began some, but completed none until the one-act opéra comique *La guzla de l'émir* (1862, now lost), which, as a Prix de Rome *envoi* (his last), was due to be performed at the Opéra-Comique, though it was never produced. Instead Bizet turned his attention to *Les pêcheurs de perles*, which in late March or early April 1863 was commissioned by Léon Carvalho, the influential director of the Théâtre-Lyrique.

Bizet wrote most of the three-act score in only four to five months, presumably incorporating large parts of *La guzla de l'émir*. Treated severely by the critics, *Les pêcheurs de perles* enjoyed little public support. It did not hold the stage for long, and was virtually forgotten until the 1880s; however, Carvalho immediately encouraged Bizet to complete *Ivan IV*. At the outset this grand opera, modelled largely on Meyerbeer, was apparently intended for Baden-Baden (as was, perhaps, the mysterious fragment, *La prêtresse* (*c.*?1860), whose florid vocal lines are akin to Leïla's in *Les pêcheurs de perles*). To Bizet's great disappointment and eventual bitterness, *Ivan* was never staged owing both to Carvalho's budget problems and to the Opéra's unwillingness to open its doors to a beginner. Carvalho's substitute project, *La jolie fille de Perth* (1866–7), took shape while Bizet was crushed by hackwork for publishers. Critics reacted more favourably to it than to *Les pêcheurs de perles*, for here Bizet turned to a style more natural to him and aimed for charm rather than power.

In 1868 Bizet wrote to a friend that an extraordinary artistic change was taking place in him, but unfortunately no complete original opera score survives from the period 1868–71. The Franco-Prussian War disrupted all artistic activities, but with his marriage to Halévy's daughter Geneviève in June 1869, Bizet had new responsibilities that took time and emotional energy away from composition. The responsibility of his beautiful but neurotic wife, and a mother-in-law who suffered at times from attacks of insanity, though it matured and deepened him, was hardly an ideal situation. Furthermore, the considerable financial advantages he anticipated from a generous marriage contract did not materialize. To show loyalty to his former teacher, therefore, Bizet completed and orchestrated Halévy's opera *Noé* (1868–9). During this period Bizet also looked at or began work on a half-dozen libretti, but he completed only *La coupe du roi de Thulé* for a competition at the Opéra; there were rumours of corruption as the jury passed over scores by Bizet, Guiraud, Massenet and others for the effort of an amateur. Bizet soon reused some of the best ideas from his score, much as he had earlier begun to recycle material from *Ivan IV*. In 1870–71 he sketched two opéras comiques, *Grisélidis* and *Clarisse Harlowe*, but abandoned both when the Opéra-Comique and its new co-director,

Camille Du Locle, withdrew from an earlier commitment to produce a new full-length work.

Bizet's operatic ventures in the 1870s were tied largely to Du Locle and the Opéra-Comique. He was delighted at the prospect of changing a genre he regarded as old-fashioned and insipid. His one-act opéra comique *Djamileh* (1871–2) is rich in beautiful scoring and dramatic subtlety but was attacked by Parisian critics as 'Wagnerian' and had little success. Du Locle immediately asked Bizet, none the less, to collaborate with the experienced team of Henri Meilhac and Ludovic Halévy on a full-length work; Bizet soon proposed Prosper Mérimée's novella *Carmen*. That summer, however, Bizet turned his attention to providing incidental music and mélodrames for Daudet's Provençal tragedy, *L'arlésienne* (1872) at Carvalho's new theatre, the Vaudeville. Though the play failed, Bizet's exquisite suite soon became popular with Parisian concert audiences.

A grand opera, *Don Rodrigue* (1873, based on the Cid legend) was abandoned prior to orchestration, partly because the Opéra was destroyed by a fire (October) and partly because the Opéra administration chose to mount Membrée's *L'esclave* instead. Bizet had continued to work on *Carmen* and orchestrated it quickly in the summer of 1874. He knew certain critics were prejudiced against him but had thought this score would finally convert them: 'They make out that I am obscure, complicated, tedious, more fettered by technical skill than lit by inspiration. Well, this time I have written a work that is all clarity and vivacity, full of colour and melody.' After the premiere in March 1875 the more even-handed critics praised individual pieces, but even they often predicted that the work would not attract the public. Bizet fell ill with an attack of quinsy shortly afterwards and never completely regained his health; obsessed by thoughts of death, suffering from rheumatism and an ear infection, he none the less continued planning an oratorio, *Geneviève de Paris*. Three months later, after two heart attacks, he died aged 36, just before *Carmen* began to conquer the entire operatic world. Its enormous popularity encouraged revivals of other Bizet operas in the 1880s and 1890s. *Carmen* remains one of the greatest operas ever written; in an era dominated by Verdi and Wagner, Bizet achieved, within the traditional frame of the number opera, an original and vital solution to the balance of music and drama.

Les pêcheurs de perles

The Pearlfishers

Opera in three acts (four tableaux) (1h 45m)
Libretto by Eugène Cormon and Michel Carré
Composed and rev. April–September 1863
PREMIERES 30 September 1863, Théâtre-Lyrique, Paris; UK: 22 April 1887, Covent Garden, London (as *Léïla*); US: 25 August 1893, Academy of Music, Philadelphia
CAST Zurga *bar*, Nadir *t*, Léïla *s*, Nourabad *b*; *satb* chorus of pearlfishers, Indians and Brahmins

Bizet signed a contract with Carvalho in late March or early April 1863 to complete a three-act opera that would go into rehearsal in August, with an anticipated premiere in mid-September. He responded imaginatively to the setting (originally Mexico, but changed to Ceylon [Sri Lanka]), but to meet the tight schedule had to borrow from several earlier works (including *Ivan IV*) and probably cannibalized most of his last *envoi de Rome*, the one-act opéra comique, *La guzla de l'émir*. Until the rehearsals were under way the opera apparently contained spoken dialogue for several scenes in the first two acts. Other rehearsal revisions centred on the Act II love duet and, in particular, the problematic final scene.

The critical reception of the premiere

was largely negative, but Berlioz, writing his last review for the *Journal des débats*, found 'a considerable number of beautiful, expressive pieces filled with fire and rich colouring'. *Les pêcheurs de perles* had 18 performances (respectable for a début work) but was not revived until 1886. At about that time the publisher Choudens began tampering with the score. The wonderful Act I tenor–baritone duet lost its triple-metre closing allegro for a dramatically nonsensical return to the more attractive opening andante (audiences are still loath to give up this posthumous version). To compensate for various cuts Godard wrote a new, but extremely weak, Act III trio, 'O lumière sainte'. Editors also altered both stage action and music in the final scene: first they had Zurga being burned at the stake; later he was stabbed in the back by an Indian. The 1975 edition returns largely to the 1863 vocal score, with orchestration by Arthur Hammond for restored portions (since the autograph manuscript has been missing since the 1890s); however, the discovery of an 1863 short score has made approximate reconstruction of Bizet's orchestration possible.

SYNOPSIS

Act I: On a wild beach in Ceylon the pearlfishers are preparing for the fishing season. Zurga reminds them that it is time to elect a chief. They unanimously choose him and swear absolute obedience. His old friend Nadir the hunter suddenly appears, and Zurga invites him to stay. They recall their last trip, where at the temple in Kandi both had seen and fallen in love with a beautiful young woman leading a religious ceremony ('Au fond du temple saint'); both had sworn never to approach her so that nothing would trouble their friendship ('Amitié sainte'). A canoe arrives bringing that year's unknown, veiled, virgin priestess (Léïla), who will sing and pray for the safety of the pearlfishers during this season. They all welcome her and attend the initiation ritual where Léïla swears to give up friend, husband and lover, even though at the last minute she has recognized Nadir. Nourabad, the high priest, conducts Léïla to the temple as the sun is setting. Left alone, Nadir admits that despite his oath he had returned to hear Léïla's songs; he remembers the magic of the experience ('Je crois entendre encore') and falls asleep. Léïla now appears on the crag that looks out to sea and begins her prayers ('O Dieu Brahma, O maître souverain'), but her thoughts turn to Nadir, who wakes, comes closer, and recognizes his beloved.

Act II: Léïla's forbidden ruined temple. Léïla tells Nourabad how, still a child, she had risked her life to protect a fugitive; this man had given her a necklace as a memento. Left alone, Léïla rejoices that Nadir is again watching over her ('Comme autrefois, dans la nuit sombre'). Nadir arrives and in their happiness the couple forget the danger they risk ('Ton coeur n'a pas compris le mien'). As a storm rumbles in the distance, Nourabad and the guards discover the lovers and catch Nadir as he attempts to flee. Zurga plans to allow the guilty couple to leave – until he recognizes Léïla. Blind with jealousy, he too cries for vengeance. All pray to Brahma, and Nadir and Léïla are led away.

Act III, Scene 1: Zurga, alone in his tent, regrets his rage against his old friend ('O Nadir, tendre ami de mon jeune âge') and recalls Léïla's radiant beauty. She comes to beg for mercy for Nadir ('Je frémis, je chancelle, de son âme cruelle'), but succeeds only in reigniting Zurga's jealous anger when she reveals her love for Nadir. As Léïla is led away she asks a young pearlfisher to give her necklace to her mother; Zurga then recognizes this as the gift he had presented to the brave young girl who saved his life many years earlier. Scene 2: Nadir watches as the pearlfishers dance, anticipating the execution ('Dès que le soleil'). Léïla and Nadir prepare to face death in each other's arms. Suddenly Zurga enters, hatchet in hand, and announces a fire in the camp. After the Indians have left, he releases Nadir and Léïla and reveals that he started the fire to aid their escape and repay his debt to Léïla. The lovers flee, and Zurga leans against an idol of Brahma while frightened Indians escape through the forest, their children in their arms.

In early 1867 Bizet modestly referred to his début work as 'an opera much discussed, attacked, defended . . . in all, an honourable, brilliant failure . . .'. He correctly assessed his first two acts as stronger than the third and his lyric passages and exotic numbers (usually quite imaginatively scored) as more successful than the uneven dramatic portions.

Each of the major soloists has at least one strong solo number, usually indebted to Gounod in style. Among them, Nadir's Act I romance is perhaps the loveliest, not only for its melody but also for its poetic orchestration (cor anglais, muted violins and two solo cellos). The depth of Nadir's obsession is brought out by understatement – high Bs taken pianissimo for his 'mad rapture' much as a high pianissimo B♭ later illustrated Don José's obsession with Carmen.

That Bizet had already developed a fine sense of the grand moment is demonstrated by his preparation for the famous tenor–baritone melody in Act I. He moves from Nadir's eloquent recitative evoking their experience in Kandi to a chromatic descent as Zurga describes that evening, through shimmering muted strings and murmured vocal lines to the tune itself, in flute and harp on the long-delayed tonic. Most wonderfully, however, a rising chromatic section with Zurga's shorter phrases maintains tension until the men finally present the marvellous, Gounod-indebted melody, gloriously harmonized. The 'goddess' motif, though rather long for its purpose, recurs frequently, rescored and often doubled in speed, whenever the two men's friendship is influenced by Léïla.

Portions of the work are indebted to other composers; critics in 1863 cited Gounod, David, Halévy and Verdi, among others. But despite the score's unevenness, its lyric beauty and unforgettable moments have won *Les pêcheurs de perles* a place in the standard repertoire.

RECORDINGS 1. 1893 version: Alarie, Simoneau, Bianco, Ch Elisabeth Brasseur, Lamoureux O, Fournet, Philips, 1953; 2. Cotrubas, Vanzo, Sarabia, Soyer, Paris Op Ch & O, Prêtre, EMI, 1977; 3. 1863 version: Hendricks, Aler, G. Quilico, Courtis, Capitole Toulouse Ch & O, Plasson, EMI, 1989 (complete)

Carmen

Opéra comique in four acts (2h 45m)
Libretto by Henri Meilhac and Ludovic Halévy, after the novella by Prosper Mérimée (1845, rev. 1846)
Composed 1873–5; recitatives by Ernest Guiraud, 1875; ballets from *L'arlésienne* (farandole and chorus) and *La jolie fille de Perth* (*Danse bohémienne*) inserted by Guiraud
PREMIERES 3 March 1875, Opéra-Comique, Paris; UK: 22 June 1878, Her Majesty's Theatre, London; US: 23 October 1878, Mapleson Academy of Music, New York
CAST Moralès *bar*, Micaëla *s*, Don José *t*, Zuniga *b*, Carmen *ms*, Frasquita *s* (or *ms*), Mercédès *s* (or *ms*), Lillas Pastia *spoken role*, Escamillo *bar*, Le Remendado *t*, Le Dancaïre *t* (or *bar*), guide *spoken role*, soldier *spoken role*; *satb* chorus of soldiers, men and women of Seville, cigarette-factory girls, gypsies, street vendors; street urchins *trebles*

Bizet himself seems to have proposed Mérimée's *Carmen* as the source for his librettists. The experienced team, Meilhac and L. Halévy, made numerous astute changes to the narrative and provided the necessary opportunities for a variety of musical numbers. They invented the episodic, messenger role of

Micaëla (the pure, bourgeois opéra-comique heroine) to serve as a foil to Carmen, the gypsy, an unrepentant sinner who prizes the freedom to control her own life over all else. Escamillo's role was greatly expanded, and Don José, after his gradual descent from dutiful corporal/son to deserter/smuggler, commits only one murder, the final crime of jealous rage (in Mérimée's novella he commits at least three). The extent of Bizet's involvement in shaping the libretto is unknown (though he certainly contributed much of the *habanera* text and Carmen's death song in the Card Trio). The novella itself was widely admired, but placing such a subject on the Opéra-Comique stage was a bold step in a theatre that depended on a bourgeois clientele. Furthermore, in his quest to renovate the genre, Bizet wrote a score rich in ensembles and choruses, more demanding and complex than his performers and audience were used to. Not surprisingly, the chorus (asked to smoke, quarrel, or enter by twos and threes instead of marching in *en masse* to sing simple tunes) threatened to strike after two months of rehearsal; even the orchestra claimed certain passages were unplayable. Some revisions during rehearsals accommodated the performers' limitations; but most of them also refined and sharpened the dramatic impact of each scene. The soloists came to believe strongly in the work, particularly Galli-Marié (Carmen) and Lhérie (Don José), and with Bizet they resisted the director's and librettists' attempts to tone down their performance.

At the premiere audience response cooled as drama and music moved further away from the traditional opéra comique. Most of the press condemned the plot as too immoral to be staged and, though they praised certain pieces (like the Act II entr'acte and Micaëla's air), they found Bizet's score both overlong and 'scientific'. *Carmen* was not the great success Bizet had hoped for, but there were 35 performances that spring and 13 more the next season, many more than any of his other operas. *Carmen* had succeeded in 18 other countries before the Opéra-Comique revived the work in 1883; yet by the end of 1904 there had been 1000 performances in that house alone. In most other theatres, *Carmen* was performed with competent recitatives by Bizet's good friend Ernest Guiraud to texts supplied by Halévy; Bizet himself apparently intended to write such recitatives to make the work more widely performable. Ever since the publication of a flawed critical edition in 1964, however, which included some twenty passages that Bizet changed or removed during rehearsals and which reinstated Moralès's couplets and the Act III duel duet (cuts that seem to date back to 1875), most music directors have opted for a performing version which includes some of the rejected passages alongside the text Bizet published in the same month as *Carmen*'s premiere.

SYNOPSIS

Act I: Outside the tobacco factory in Seville soldiers amuse themselves by watching the passers-by ('Sur la place chacun passe'). Micaëla approaches looking for Don José; when she is told he will arrive with the changing of the guard, she flees their assiduous gallantry. The soldiers then return to their initial pastime. Their sergeant Moralès notices a young bourgeois wife accepting a billet doux behind her elderly husband's back ('Attention! Chut!'). Children imitate the guard as they enter ('Avec la garde montante'); this group includes Don José and his new superior officer Zuniga. The bell sounds and the women factory-workers come outside to take their break, smoking cigarettes ('La cloche a sonné; nous, des ouvrières'); their arrival delights the men who apparently wait for them each day. When the gypsy Carmen finally makes her grand entrance, she describes the fickle nature of her love to her many admirers (*habanera*: 'L'amour est un oiseau rebelle'). She speaks provocatively to Don José, and throws a flower at him before she and the others are summoned inside by the factory bell. José is disturbed by her effrontery, but picks up the flower. Micaëla returns to bring a kiss from José's mother ('Parle-moi de ma mère'), as well as a letter which suggests Micaëla as a suitable wife. José is about to throw away Carmen's flower, but the women suddenly rush out of the factory arguing ('Au secours! n'entendez-vous pas'); Carmen has cut another worker's face. When she refuses to answer Zuniga ('Coupe-moi, brûle-moi, je ne te dirai rien'), he orders José to take her to prison. Left alone with José, she uses all her practised wiles on him. He can no longer resist when she tempts him with the prospect of becoming her next lover (*seguidilla*: 'Près des remparts de Séville'), and helps her to escape.

Act II: Carmen and her gypsy friends, Frasquita and Mercédès, entertain officers in Lillas Pastia's tavern ('Les tringles des sistres tintaient'). Zuniga tells Carmen that José has been released after a month in prison; she is delighted. The toreador Escamillo enters with his entourage and drinks with the patrons ('Votre toast . . . je peux vous le rendre'). Though Carmen does not encourage Escamillo's attentions, she tells him that it is always pleasant to hope. When all but the three gypsy women and Pastia have left, Le Remendado and Le Dancaïre enter and describe their plan for that night ('Nous avons en tête une affaire'). They are all astonished when Carmen refuses to participate because she is 'in love'. They urge her to recruit her new lover and leave as they hear José approaching ('Halte-là!'). To celebrate his release Carmen orders a feast and then dances for José ('Je vais danser en votre honneur'), but her joy quickly turns to fury when José announces he must leave because the call to barracks is sounding; she is unmoved when he shows her the flower he has saved ('La fleur que tu m'avais jetée') and claims that if he loved her he would follow her to the mountains ('Là-bas, là-bas dans la montagne'). José is about to leave when Zuniga returns, hoping to find Carmen alone. When ordered to get out, José, blind with jealousy, attacks his superior officer. He now has no choice but to leave the army and reluctantly throws in his lot with the gypsies.

Act III: The smugglers gather in the mountains ('Ecoute, écoute, compagnon, écoute'). Carmen and José argue again. Mercédès and Frasquita pass the time by telling their fortunes with cards ('Mêlons! Coupons!'); when Carmen joins in, she reads death again and again, first for herself, then for José. The smugglers depart to set about their task while the women distract the customs officials ('Quant au douanier, c'est notre affaire'). José stays behind on guard. A guide brings in a frightened but determined Micaëla ('Je dis que rien ne m'épouvante'); she hides when José fires a shot, and Escamillo enters, calmly examining the bullet hole in his hat. He has heard that Carmen has tired of her latest lover and has come to seek her out ('Je suis Escamillo, toréro de Grenade'). Drawing his knife, the furious José challenges the toreador. Escamillo spares him, but falls in the second round. José is ready to kill him, but Carmen arrives with Le Dancaïre and stops the fight. Escamillo invites her to his next bullfight in Seville and leaves. Micaëla is discovered and tells José that his mother is dying. He leaves with her after threatening Carmen.

Act IV: Outside the bullring in Seville merchants hock their wares ('A deux cuartos'). The participants in the bullfight march past ('Les voici! Voici la quadrille!'), and Escamillo arrives with a radiantly happy and beautifully dressed Carmen. Frasquita and Mercédès warn her that José is hiding in the crowd, but Carmen is determined to face him. The crowd follows the procession into the bullring leaving Carmen alone. José confronts Carmen and implores her to leave with him, but she says she no longer loves him; she would rather die than give up her freedom. She is eager to witness Escamillo's triumph, but José blocks her path. When she furiously throws away his ring, José draws his knife and stabs her while Escamillo is fêted in the bullring. As everyone comes out José, confessing his crime, throws himself on the body of his beloved Carmen.

Bizet's ability to create effective local colour is vividly represented in this score. The accelerating gypsy dance that opens Act II is an orchestral tour de force in which dissonance and sliding harmonies paint the scene of Lillas Pastia's underworld tavern as surely as any set design. Carmen's mesmerizing entrance piece, the *habanera*, winds sensually and chromatically above a pedal that provides tonal stability and symbolizes her irresistible sexuality. The *seguidilla* was Bizet's own invention, but its combination of guitar-like accompaniment, dance rhythm and remarkably ambiguous tonality seem just as 'Spanish' as the borrowed tunes. For Escamillo's entrance aria, Bizet adopted a deliberately popular manner as overstated as the toreador himself. In contrast, the susceptible Don José sings very little in Act I; his first solo is the simple, unaccompanied soldier's march in Act II, sung backstage.

Bizet's orchestration had become quite distinctive in his earlier works, but Richard Strauss regarded *Carmen* as sheer perfection: 'If you want to learn how to orchestrate, don't study Wagner's scores, study the score of *Carmen* . . . What wonderful economy, and how every note and every rest is in its proper place.' Woodwind instruments receive particular attention: the flute is associated with Carmen in the *seguidilla* and elsewhere and has the famous solo in the lovely entr'acte preceding Act III. The cor anglais makes a rare appearance as José shows Carmen the flower he has kept with him through his month in prison, and flutes and bassoons play a delicate counterpoint to Mercédès's and Frasquita's warning to Carmen just before the final tragedy.

As in earlier operas Bizet imaginatively rescores his motifs for dramatic effect. The flickering 'Carmen' motif (with an augmented second) and its alternate form, the 'fate' motif (with a slower tempo) are used economically. (The 'fate' motif itself appears only at the end of the prelude and in one number of each act.) Unexpected harmonies and modulations advance the drama in virtually every number. The featherlight Act II quintet moves effortlessly from a distant G major back to the tonic refrain in D♭ major. Bizet's contemporaries were shocked by the cadential harmonies of the Flower Song, which are unrelated to the key that surrounds them; after the seamless beauty of the melody itself and Don José's *pianissimo* high B♭, this harmonic gesture (to the words 'je t'aime') underlines how utterly José is bewitched by Carmen.

Though Bizet's final scenes had often previously fallen short, those in *Carmen* contain his most dramatic and original inspiration (he revised three of the four repeatedly during rehearsals). Certainly the idea for offstage trumpets (duty) playing in counterpoint to Carmen's sensual dance (love) in Act II is a brilliant stroke, but even more powerful is the combination of different styles and recurring motifs in the finale of Act III. Escamillo's suavely popular refrain, Micaëla's Gounod-like message from José's mother, Don José's impassioned threats and the 'fate' motif build to a climax of great intensity. In the Act IV duet Bizet achieved a dramatic potency that has rarely been equalled in any opera, and in the final section the regular phrasing and diatonic harmonies of the joyful, backstage choruses contrast starkly with the rapid interchange of the protagonists. The bright F♯ major of the 'Toreador' refrain, celebrating the death of the bull, forms a supremely ironic commentary on the murder outside the bullring. The realism and tragic power that so shocked Bizet's Parisian contemporaries had a profound influence on the verismo composers just a few years later, and has moved countless others ever since. 'I do not know any other instance where tragic humour, which constitutes the essence of love, is expressed . . . in a more shattering phrase than in Don José's last words . . .' (Nietzsche, *Randglossen zu Carmen*, pub. posth. 1912).

RECORDINGS 1. Michel, Angelici, Jobin, Dens, Op Comique Ch & O, Cluytens, EMI, 1950 (Choudens edn; with dialogue); 2. Guiot, Callas, Gedda, Massard, René Duclos Ch, Paris Op O, Prêtre, EMI, 1964 (Choudens edn); 3. Te Kanawa, Troyanos, Domingo, Van Dam, John Alldis Ch, LPO, Solti, Decca, 1975 (Dean–Solti edn; with dialogue)
OTHER OPERATIC WORKS *La maison du docteur*, (*c*.1855), 1989; *Le Docteur Miracle*, 1857; *Don Procopio*, (1859), 1906; *L'amour peintre* (inc.; lost), (1860); *La prêtresse* (inc.), (?1860); *La guzla de l'émir* (lost), (1862); *Ivan IV*, (1865), 1951; *La jolie fille de Perth*, 1867; *Malbrough s'en va-t-en guerre* (operetta, Act I by Bizet, coll. with Legouix, Jonas, Delibes; lost), 1867; *La coupe du roi de Thulé* (manuscript largely missing), (1869), 1955 (BBC broadcast of fragments); *Noé* (completion of F. Halévy's opera), (1868–9) 1885; *Clarisse Harlowe*, (sketches, 1871); *Grisélidis*, (sketches, 1870–71); *Sol-si-re-pif-pan* (operetta; lost), 1872; *Djamileh*, 1872; *Don Rodrigue* (inc.), (1873)

L.A.W.

Arrigo Boito

Enrico Arrigo Boito; *b* 24 February 1842, Padua; *d* 10 June 1918, Milan

Boito's reputation rests on three distinct achievements: first, his contribution as Verdi's librettist for *Otello* and *Falstaff*, as well as for the revised *Simon Boccanegra*; second, his own two operas (*Mefistofele* and *Nerone*); and third, to a lesser extent, his books of poems, *Libro dei versi* and *Re Orso*. Educated at the Milan Conservatory, where he studied composition with Alberto Mazzucato, he and his lifelong friend Franco Faccio, the composer–conductor, won scholarships for study abroad. In Paris, Boito met both Rossini and Verdi, and for the latter he supplied the text for the cantata *Inno delle nazioni*. Returning to Milan, he wrote musical journalism and continued work on his *Faust* opera, a project he had begun as a student in Milan.

It was at a dinner following the premiere of Faccio's first opera, *I profughi fiamminghi* (1863), that the idealistic young Boito made the notorious comment comparing the defiled altars of Italian opera to the splattered walls of a brothel. Verdi assumed Boito included him among the defilers (in fact he was just being over-enthusiastic about Faccio's opera) and took umbrage. (That Verdi was deeply offended is proved by his allusions to this sentiment, never getting the words quite right, in a number of his letters over the succeeding years.) Boito's faith in his friend's skill continued, and in 1865 he wrote his first opera libretto, significantly on a Shakespearean subject, *Hamlet*, for Faccio.

Three years later the opportunity arose for Boito himself to demonstrate his hopes for the future of Italian music drama with his *Mefistofele*. The work precipitated a historic fiasco at La Scala and was withdrawn after two rowdy performances. Proudly hiding his humiliation, Boito spent the next years writing libretti for others (including, as 'Tobia Gorrio', *La Gioconda* for Ponchielli) and supplying a number of translations of songs and operas, including Wagner's *Rienzi* and *Tristan*. At Bologna in 1875 the drastically revised *Mefistofele* proved successful.

Through Faccio and the music publisher Giulio Ricordi, a rapprochement was arranged with Verdi in 1879, with the agreement that Boito would provide a text for *Otello* without any firm commitment on the part of the composer. As a test, Boito was invited to prepare a revision of Piave's text for *Simon Boccanegra*. That task successfully accomplished, work progressed on *Otello*, but not without some crises. However, by the time *Otello* had its triumphant premiere at La Scala in 1887, Boito had forged a firm friendship with Verdi and their collaboration on *Falstaff* (1893) went much more smoothly. Boito proposed *King Lear* as their next project and began a libretto, but, though he had planned for decades to write an opera on the play (he got as far as sketching a complete scenario in 1850), Verdi finally realized that, at past 80, such an undertaking was beyond him. Boito's relationship with Verdi remained close, and he was present when Verdi died.

As early as 1862, Boito had sketched plans for an opera on the subject of Nero, but other commissions had always prevented his working on it consistently. Shortly after Verdi's death, he published his five-act libretto for *Nerone*, which was hailed as a major literary achievement. With the passage of time, Boito suffered from increasing difficulty in concentration, and diminished confidence in his ability to compose this work. When he died, *Nerone* was still incomplete, 56 years after its conception. Although much of the score existed, including sketches for the discarded fifth act, the work required considerable preparation. This was supervised by Toscanini, who conducted the posthumous premiere at La Scala in 1924.

Mefistofele

Mephistopheles

Opera in a prologue, four acts and an epilogue (originally a prologue and five acts) (2h 15m)
Libretto by the composer, after *Faust* by Johann von Goethe (1808, 1832)
Composed 1860–67, rev. 1871, 1875, 1881
PREMIERES 5 March 1868, La Scala, Milan; rev. version: 4 October 1875, Teatro Comunale, Bologna; second rev. version: 13 May 1876, Teatro Rossini, Venice; UK: 6 July 1880, Her Majesty's Theatre, London; US: 16 November 1880, Boston; definitive version: 25 May 1881, La Scala, Milan
CAST Mefistofele *b*, Faust *t*, Margherita *s*, Elena *s*, Marta *c*, Pantalis *c*, Wagner *t*, Nereo *t*; *satb* chorus of heavenly host, burghers, witches, sirens; ballet

Boito's revisions, after the failure of the 1868 version of *Mefistofele* (which he conducted himself), included omitting a scene at the emperor's court and an intermezzo sinfonico. Although most of the changes were made for an 1875 production at Bologna, the score did not emerge in its final form until 1881. The opera includes the prologue in heaven and the Helen of Troy scene from the second part of Goethe's *Faust* (both ignored by Gounod in his *Faust*, 1859).

SYNOPSIS

Prologue: The devil, Mefistofele, wagers with God that he can win the soul of Faust, while the chorus praises the Lord.

Act I: In Kermesse, the aged scholar Faust and his disciple Wagner first see Mefistofele, disguised as a grey friar. Later, in his study, Faust contemplates nature, but Mefistofele appears, introduces himself as the spirit of negation, rejuvenates Faust, and persuades him to sign the fatal pact.

Act II: While Mefistofele flirts with Marta, Faust woos her friend Margherita and wins the promise of a later assignation. He gives her a narcotic for her mother so that they won't be disturbed. Mefistofele brings Faust to the Brocken mountains to witness the orgiastic Walpurgis Night.

Act III: Margherita languishes in prison, condemned for the death of her mother, who was poisoned by Faust's sleeping draught, and for drowning the child she bore Faust. Faust comes to her cell, hoping to save her, but the appearance of Mefistofele fills her with dread. Dying, she remains constant in her Christian faith.

Act IV: In Classical Greece, whither Mefistofele has transported Faust, Elena (Helen of Troy) has a vision of the destruction of Troy. Faust woos her, anticipating a fusion of the Classic and Romantic spirits.

The epilogue shows the aged Faust longing for death. Despite Mefistofele's warnings, he invokes divine forgiveness and dies redeemed.

The projected plan for the work was without equal in Italian opera in the latter half of the 19th century, but, unfortunately, Boito's incapacity as a composer (his frequent inability to develop musical ideas) prevented him from realizing his ambition fully. Boito's revisions, gigantic in scope, brought *Mefistofele* far closer to the conventional operatic forms of the time, emphasizing the romance of Faust and Margherita and the conflict of good and evil. The success the opera enjoyed in its less overtly 'futuristic' version reassured Boito after its initial failure. The music, although at times inspired, on the whole lacks spontaneity – particularly the rhythm. *Mefistofele* survives today, principally in Italy and the United States, as a vehicle for star basses.

RECORDINGS 1881 version 1. Tebaldi, Cavalli, Del Monaco, Siepi, Accademia di Santa Cecilia Ch & O, Serafin, Decca, 1958; 2. Freni, Caballé, Pavarotti, Ghiaurov, London Op Ch, Nat PO, De Fabritiis, Decca, 1983
OTHER OPERA *Nerone*, (1918), 1924

W.A.

William Bolcom

William Elden Bolcom; *b* 26 May 1938, Seattle

Bolcom is one of America's most versatile composers, writing songs, operas and instrumental works over more than 40 years. He studied at Stanford University with Milhaud in 1958 and later with Messiaen in Paris, before settling in New York, where he was prominent in the 1970s ragtime revival. Major works include an oratorio *Songs of Innocence and Experience* (1984), based on William Blake, and the operas *Dynamite Tonite* (1963) and *McTeague* (Chicago, 1992). Since 1973, Bolcom has taught at the University of Michigan, Ann Arbor.

A View from the Bridge was the second opera to be commissioned from Bolcom by the Chicago Lyric Opera, following *McTeague*, the company's first commission for a new work from an American composer. A third commission by Chicago, *A Wedding*, based on the film by Robert Altman, was premiered in December 2004.

A View from the Bridge

Opera in two acts (2h 45m)
Libretto by Arnold Weinstein and Arthur Miller, based on the play by Miller (1955, rev. 1957)
Composed 1997–8
PREMIERE 9 October 1999, Civic Opera House, Chicago

Bolcom's successful opera is closely based on Miller's play, set in 1950s New York among Italian working-class immigrants. A local lawyer, Alfieri, tells the story of two illegal immigrants, Marco and Rodolpho, who arrive in Brooklyn where they are housed by fellow Italians Eddie Carbone and his wife Beatrice. The ambitious Rodolpho falls in love with the Carbones' daughter Catherine, to the consternation of Eddie, who becomes increasingly desperate to stop the affair. After a drunken evening, Eddie betrays Marco and Rodolpho to the authorities and becomes a pariah in his community and within his own family. Marco and Eddie fight and Eddie is stabbed to death.

Bolcom's eclecticism is evident throughout, with spare and violent atonality eliding into 1950s pop music and back again. Nothing in the angular chords that open the opera suggest that this is in fact a stage work with big tunes, notably Rodolpho's tender aria of immigrant aspiration 'The New York Lights' in Act I, and a doo-wop quartet of hard-drinking dockers in Act II.

RECORDING Rambaldi, Malfitano, Turay, Josephson, Nolen, McCrory, Lyric Op of Chicago Ch & O, Russell Davies, New World, 2000
OTHER OPERATIC WORKS *Dynamite Tonite*, 1963; *Greatshot*, 1969; *The Beggar's Opera* (J. Gay), 1979 (completion of adaptation begun by Milhaud, 1937); *Casino Paradise*, 1990; *McTeague*, 1992; *A Wedding*, 2004

M.J.K.

Aleksandr Borodin

Aleksandr Porfiryevich Borodin; *b* 12 November 1833, St Petersburg, Russia; *d* 27 February 1887, St Petersburg

Borodin, whose mere handful of mainly instrumental compositions are regularly performed in the concert hall and whose only opera, *Prince Igor*, is a household name, was an untrained spare-time composer and proud of the fact. Despite the repeated reproaches of his musical friends for not devoting more time to fulfilling his outstanding musical gifts, he resolutely maintained that he was essentially a 'Sunday composer' and that his professional work obliged him to consider composition simply as a relaxation and indulgence.

Borodin trained as a chemist and at the age of 31 became Professor of Organic Chemistry at the Medico-Surgical Academy in St Petersburg. An exceptionally genial and attractive man, he took his professional duties very seriously and spent most of his time in research, teaching, committee work and looking after the well-being of his students. These biographical details are particularly relevant to *Prince Igor* for they largely explain the otherwise incomprehensible fact that he failed to complete the opera after 17 years of sporadic work on it. At his sudden death aged 53, the overture had been improvised but not written down, some of the numbers were in a very sketchy form, quite a lot remained unorchestrated and, worst of all, the third act had large chunks missing, including the libretto itself. For this reason *Igor* will always be a problem opera; its extended, diffuse dramatic shape is far from satisfactory and the libretto sometimes lapses into banality. Nevertheless it is packed with magnificent music, wonderful opportunities for solo and choral singing, and the *Polovtsian Dances* that conclude Act II undoubtedly constitute one of the most overwhelming scenes in all opera.

Prince Igor

Knyaz' Igor'

Opera in four acts with a prologue (3h 30m)
Libretto by the composer, based on a scenario by V. V. Stassov
Composed 1869–70, 1874–87
PREMIERES 4 November 1890, Mariinsky Theatre, St Petersburg; UK: 8 June 1914, Drury Lane, London; US: 30 December 1915, Metropolitan, New York
CAST Prince Igor *bar*, Yaroslavna *s*, Vladimir *t*, Prince Vladimir Galitsky *high b*, Khan Konchak *b*, Khan Gzak *silent*, Konchakovna *c*, Ovlur *t*, Skula *b*, Eroshka *t*, Nurse *s*, Polovtsian Girl *s*; *satb* chorus of Russian princes and princesses, boyars and their wives, elders, Russian warriors, attendant girls, the people, Polovtsian Khans, Konchakovna's friends, Konchak's slaves, Russian prisoners-of-war, Polovtsian guards

In 1869 Borodin asked Vladimir Stassov, art historian and literary mentor to the 'Mighty Handful' composers, to suggest a suitable subject for an opera. Stassov recognized Borodin's qualities as an essentially lyrical composer who had inherited Glinka's sympathy with Russia's epic past and astutely prepared a detailed scenario based on the 12th-century national epic *The Lay of Igor's Army*. In this Prince Igor of Seversk (now in the

Ukraine) decides to make a show of strength by leading his army against the Polovtsi, a nomadic tribe of Turkish origin which habitually ravaged southern Russia. A battle takes place in which the army is all but annihilated and Igor and his son captured. Eventually he escapes and is reunited with his wife Yaroslavna. The original purpose of the epic was to use the campaign to underline the political and spiritual disunity of the separate principalities of Kiev and to show the need for a united Russia. Borodin was delighted with the idea, but unfortunately decided to write the libretto himself and instead of finalizing the text before beginning composition, wrote it piecemeal as he went along. In the process, the original intention of the epic was watered down and Igor himself, because of his courageous, impulsive but essentially weak character, becomes almost an anti-hero.

SYNOPSIS

Prologue: The town square in Putivl, 1185. Igor, with his son Vladimir, prepares to set out with his army, despite the entreaties of his wife Yaroslavna and an ill-omened eclipse of the sun.

Act I, Scene 1: Skula and Eroshka, deserters from Igor's army, ingratiate themselves with Yaroslavna's dissolute brother, Prince Galitsky, who boasts of his hedonistic life, 'Greshno taits ya skuki nye lyublyu' ('I hate a dreary life'). Scene 2: In a touchingly expressive arioso, Yaroslavna describes her loneliness, fear of civil strife and troubled dreams. Boyars enter and solemnly inform her of Igor's defeat and captivity; at the same time the Polovtsi begin to attack Putivl.

Act II: Khan Konchak's camp in the eastern steppe. Vladimir has already fallen in love with Konchak's daughter, Konchakovna, and apostrophizes her in a beautifully lyrical aria, 'Medlenno dyen ugasal' ('Slowly the daylight faded'). Igor's thoughts are filled with remorse and longing for Yaroslavna, 'Ni sna, ni otdykha' ('No rest, no sleep'). The barbaric but magnanimous Khan Konchak cannot understand his captive's depression, 'Zdorov li, knyaz?' ('Unhappy, Prince?'), and, in order to entertain him, arranges for his slaves to dance and sing for him (Polovtsian Dances).

Act III: After hearing of the attack on Putivl, Igor decides to escape, although Vladimir is reluctant to leave Konchakovna and is captured. Konchak admires Igor for his audacity and unites the two lovers.

Act IV: Yaroslavna laments Igor's captivity and the devastation of Putivl (vividly described in a hauntingly elegiac unaccompanied chorus), but is overjoyed when he arrives back safely to general rejoicing.

The great strength of *Prince Igor* lies in the distinguished and noble quality of its music rather than its emotional force or sense of dramatic involvement. Act II in particular consists of one outstanding number after another (the arias of Konchakovna, Vladimir, Igor, Konchak), culminating in the barbaric splendour of the Polovtsian Dances. The music has a richly lyrical quality that never becomes cloying, and the writing for solo voices, chorus and orchestra is always freshly minted. Although constructed very much as a series of set tableaux, the opera is generally successful in putting over the big-boned, epic quality of the story, and the characters of Yaroslavna and Konchak in particular are finely delineated in their text and music.

After Borodin's death his self-appointed musical executors, Rimsky-Korsakov and Glazunov, were faced with the task of putting the noble torso of *Igor* into performable shape. With Glazunov filling in most of the empty gaps (including writing out the overture from memory), while Rimsky undertook the equally onerous task of editing and orchestrating the rest, they soon produced the only edition of the opera that has ever been published. Although it includes Borodin's Polovtsian March and Trio (featuring the second subject of the overture), Glazunov's bravely attempted reconstruction of Act III is frequently cut in performance, resulting in the omission of the all-important dramatic episode of Igor's escape.

RECORDINGS 1. Evstatieva, Milcheva, Kaludov, Martinovich, Ghiaurov, Ghiuselev, Sofia Nat Op Ch & Festival O, Tchakarov, Sony, 1990; 2. Gorchakova, Borodina, Grigorian, Kit, Minzhilkiev, Ognovenko, Kirov Op Ch & O, Gergiev, Philips, 1993 (complete)
OTHER OPERATIC WORKS *The Valiant Knights* (*Bogatyry*) (pastiche opera-farce), 1867; *Mlada* (sketches for Act IV of composite opera-ballet, 1872).
D.L.-J.

Benjamin Britten

Edward Benjamin, Lord Britten of Aldeburgh; *b* 22 November 1913, Lowestoft, Suffolk; *d* 4 December 1976, Aldeburgh, Suffolk

Britten was the first major composer to be born in England for 300 years who was first and foremost an opera composer. The premiere of *Peter Grimes* at Sadler's Wells Theatre on 7 June 1945 is generally accounted a watershed in the history of British music. Although there had been hostility to its production among members of the company, the opera's impact on the public and on most of the critics was likened to a fresh, invigorating storm and it was immediately recognized as the start of a new dawn for British opera as well as of a brilliant dramatic career for its composer. Within three years it had been produced in the major opera houses of Europe, including Milan, where Tullio Serafin conducted it, and in the United States, where its first conductor was Leonard Bernstein.

There was general astonishment in 1945 that Britten's first opera should be so stageworthy and show such theatrical and dramatic flair. It was then not widely known that during his sojourn in North America from 1939 to 1942 he had composed what he called an 'operetta', *Paul Bunyan*, to a libretto by his friend W. H. Auden. This was performed by university students and was remarkable for its assimilation of the American idiom, so that it had both the zip and immediate melodic appeal of a Broadway musical and also absorbed other elements from spirituals, folk ballads and choral music. *Paul Bunyan* marked out its creator as a 'natural' for stage subjects. With hindsight it can be seen that there was a nascent opera composer in some of the concert works by which his name first became known to British audiences before the Second World War; for example, the symphonic cycle *Our Hunting Fathers* (1936), for voice and orchestra, also to a text compiled and partly written by Auden, is intensely dramatic.

Although *Peter Grimes* was staged at the Royal Opera House, Covent Garden in 1947, Britten's immediate operatic future was not to be in large opera houses. He was first associated with Glyndebourne, Sussex, where *The Rape of Lucretia* was first performed in July 1946. A second chamber opera, *Albert Herring*, followed a year later, but by then a provincial tour of *The Rape of Lucretia* had been a financial disaster, and although John Christie, the owner of Glyndebourne, stood the loss, he stated that this was as far as he would go. Early in 1947 the English Opera Group, with Britten, Eric Crozier and the artist John Piper as artistic directors, was launched as a non-profit-making company.

Touring again proved costly, and in 1948 Britten, Peter Pears and Crozier founded a festival at Aldeburgh, Suffolk, where they lived. Thereafter many of Britten's works were written specifically for this festival, held in June each year. But as it happened, Britten's next three major operas were not composed for

Aldeburgh. For the 1951 Festival of Britain he wrote *Billy Budd* for Covent Garden, a return to the large orchestra and chorus of *Peter Grimes*. With its all-male cast and grim story, it was not at first a popular success, but revivals in the 1970s and 1980s established it, in the opinion of many, as Britten's greatest opera. It was followed by *Gloriana*, commissioned by Covent Garden for the Coronation of Elizabeth II in 1953. This, too, was a relative failure, the first-night audience being offended by the supposed *lèse-majesté* of the treatment of Queen Elizabeth I and her relationship with the Earl of Essex. Wounded, Britten returned to chamber opera, and composed *The Turn of the Screw*, based on Henry James's ghost story, for the Venice Biennale in 1954.

In 1956 Britten visited Bali, where he was profoundly impressed by the sounds of the gamelan. These were not entirely strange to him, since he had been introduced to them in 1939 by Colin McPhee. Henceforward, however, exotic Eastern sounds became a feature of his orchestration, giving rise even to such a homely invention as the 'slung mugs' representing rain in *Noye's Fludde* (1957). Memories of the gamelan lend a supernatural glitter to the score of *A Midsummer Night's Dream* (1960), but find full expression in the three church parables, *Curlew River*, *The Burning Fiery Furnace* and *The Prodigal Son*, composed between 1964 and 1968. Another major influence here was Britten's first encounter with the art of the Noh play in Japan in 1956. In these three works, highly sophisticated as they are musically, Britten achieved his ideal of providing operas that could be performed almost by improvisation in the surroundings of a village church or hall.

Britten's deep pacifist convictions, fuelled by the Vietnam War, led him to select an antimilitaristic short story by Henry James – *Owen Wingrave* – for his next opera, written for television but soon transferred to Covent Garden. His last opera – composed in a grim race against time when his doctors diagnosed a serious heart condition for which surgery was essential – was based on Thomas Mann's *Death in Venice*. This was produced at Snape Maltings, the Aldeburgh Festival's concert hall and opera house, although the composer was too ill to attend the rehearsals and first performance.

Peter Grimes

Opera in a prologue and three acts (2h 15m)
Libretto by Montagu Slater, after the poem *The Borough* by George Crabbe (1810)
Composed January 1944–10 February 1945
PREMIERES 7 June 1945, Sadler's Wells, London; US: 6 August 1946, Berkshire Music Center, Lenox, Massachusetts (Tanglewood)
CAST Peter Grimes *t*, Boy (John) *silent*, Ellen Orford *s*, Captain Balstrode *bar*, Auntie *c*, Niece 1 *s*, Niece 2 *s*, Bob Boles *t*, Swallow *b*, Mrs Sedley *ms*, Revd Horace Adams *t*, Ned Keene *bar*, Hobson *b*, Dr Crabbe *silent*; *satb* chorus of townspeople and fisherfolk

The plan for an opera on the subject of Peter Grimes originated when Britten and Pears, staying on the West Coast of America, read an article by E. M. Forster about George Crabbe in the *Listener* (29 May 1941). It made them homesick for Aldeburgh, the subject of Crabbe's poem *The Borough*, and anxious to read his poetry. Pears found an edition in San Diego and Britten at once saw the operatic possibilities of the section dealing with the sadistic fisherman Peter Grimes, accused of ill-treating and murdering his apprentices. Grimes appealed to Britten as an outsider in society, the first of several of his operatic heroes (or anti-heroes) who embody this experience: a reflection of Britten's own position as a homosexual and conscientious objector.

When Britten was offered a commission of $1000 from the Koussevitzky

Music Foundation for a full-length opera, he and Pears began to sketch a scenario before they sailed back to Britain in March 1942. There he approached the playwright Montagu Slater, with whom he had worked on left-wing plays in the 1930s. This was a prickly collaboration, since Slater worked slowly and did not always meet Britten's wishes. Some of the libretto was rewritten during rehearsals by Eric Crozier (who produced the first performance), Britten and Pears.

In 1944 Britten played parts of the opera to the soprano Joan Cross, who was managing the Sadler's Wells opera company during its arduous wartime tours. She became 'possessive' (her own word) about the work and decided it was the ideal opera to reopen Sadler's Wells Theatre in London when the war ended. But she encountered fierce hostility from within the company. Tired and bored by four years of provincial touring of a limited repertoire, they found this modern score unattractive and, some of them claimed, unsingable and unplayable. Nevertheless, Cross had her way. Pears sang the title role, Cross sang Ellen Orford, the designs were by Kenneth Green, and Reginald Goodall conducted. Tension backstage on the first night was high. However, most of the reviews were ecstatic, like the public's response, and *Peter Grimes* was launched on its international career. Pears's Grimes was one of his strongest characterizations, never losing sight of Britten's interpretation of the character as a romantic figure. Another major assumption of the role, rougher and harsher, was that of the Canadian tenor Jon Vickers. Tyrone Guthrie's Covent Garden production in 1947 was outstanding for its handling of the crowd scenes and powerful creation of the atmosphere of a witch hunt. *Peter Grimes* has remained the most popular of Britten's operas.

SYNOPSIS

Prologue: An inquest is held in the Moot Hall of the Borough into the death of the young apprentice of the fisherman Peter Grimes, who explains that on the way to London to sell a huge catch they were blown off course and ran out of drinking water. After three days the boy died. The coroner, Mr Swallow, returns a verdict of accidental death but advises Grimes not to get another apprentice. After the court has been cleared, Ellen Orford, who has befriended Grimes, pleads with him, in vain, to leave the Borough with her.

Act I

Interlude I [Dawn]

Scene 1: Morning by the sea, in a street outside the Moot Hall and the Boar public house. Women are mending the nets ('Oh, hang at open doors the nets'). Borough personalities arrive: the Methodist fisherman Bob Boles, the Boar's landlady Auntie and her two 'nieces' (as they are euphemistically called), Mrs Sedley, widow of an East India Company employee, the Rector, and Balstrode, a retired merchant sea captain. When Grimes calls for help to haul up a boat, only Balstrode and Ned Keene, the apothecary, go to his aid. Keene tells Grimes he has found another apprentice at the workhouse. Hobson the carrier will fetch him. Ellen agrees to accompany Hobson to look after the boy. She rebukes those who criticize her ('Let her among you without fault cast the first stone'). The entire cast sings together of the approaching storm which 'will eat the land'. Balstrode advises Grimes to join the merchant fleet, but Grimes says he is rooted in the Borough. He describes the boy's death ('Picture what the day was like') and says his ambition is to make enough money from fishing to buy a shop and marry Ellen ('They listen to money'). Grimes sings of Ellen ('What harbour shelters peace?').

Interlude II [Storm]

Scene 2: Inside the Boar, Mrs Sedley awaits Hobson's return with her consignment of laudanum. Each new arrival tells of storm damage along the coast. Quarrels break out, quietened by Balstrode ('We live and let live, and look, we keep our hands to ourselves'). Grimes enters, wet and dishevelled, and begins a soliloquy ('Now the Great Bear and Pleiades'). Boles, drunk, tries to attack him, but Balstrode intervenes and Keene starts up a catch ('Old Joe has gone fishing'). Hobson, Ellen and the boy (John) arrive and Grimes immediately takes the boy to his hut on the cliff.

Act II

Interlude III [Sunday Morning]

Scene 1: In the street again, on a Sunday morning some weeks later, Ellen and the boy sit watching the churchgoers and listening to the hymns ('Glitter of waves'). Ellen notices a tear in the boy's coat and a bruise on his neck. Grimes comes to collect the boy – he has seen a shoal. Ellen pleads for the boy to have a day's rest and tells Grimes the Borough's gossips will never be silenced – their own dreams were a mistake. In anguish, he strikes her and runs after the boy. This scene has been observed by Keene, Boles and others, who stir up anger against Grimes ('Grimes is at his exercise'). Ellen explains her compassion but is shouted down. The Rector proposes a visit to Grimes's hut by the men alone, but the crowd follows ('Now is gossip put on trial'). Only Auntie, the nieces and Ellen remain ('From the gutter, why should we trouble at their ribaldries?').

Interlude IV [Passacaglia]

Scene 2: In his hut, Grimes dresses the boy to go to sea. He thinks of the life he had planned with Ellen ('In dreams I've built myself some kindlier home'). But he also imagines he can see his dead former apprentice staring at him. He sees the Rector's procession coming up the hill and blames the boy and Ellen for gossiping. He opens the cliff door and the boy scrambles out and falls. Grimes goes after him. The Rector and his companions find an empty tidy hut. Looking out of the open door they comment on the landslide. They leave, saying they have misjudged Grimes.

Act III

Interlude V [Moonlight]

Scene 1: A few days later, on a summer evening in the village street, sounds of a dance are heard. The nieces run from the hall, followed by Swallow ('Assign your prettiness to me'). Mrs Sedley tackles Keene about the missing Grimes and his apprentice ('Murder most foul it is'). He dismisses her but she hides and hears Balstrode tell Ellen that Grimes's boat has returned, although there is no sign of him or the boy. Ellen has found the boy's jersey, on which she had embroidered an anchor ('Embroidery in childhood'). They vow to help Grimes. Mrs Sedley has overheard this conversation and summons Swallow to tell him Grimes's boat is back. Shouting 'Peter Grimes!' the crowd sets off on a manhunt.

Interlude VI [Fog]

Scene 2: To the distant sounds of a foghorn and the voices of the mob, Grimes enters, weary and demented. Ellen and Balstrode approach him. Balstrode tells him to take his boat out of sight of shore and sink it. Next morning the Borough resumes normal life. Swallow says the coastguard has reported a boat sinking. 'One of these rumours,' Auntie says.

The principal character in *Peter Grimes* is the Borough. Although the opera has a major central figure in Grimes, it repeats the pattern of *Paul Bunyan* in having a number of smaller, vividly drawn parts. Grimes is probably the least well drawn, for while he is given magnificent music, the romanticizing of Crabbe's brutal fisherman into a misjudged victim of society is at odds with the plot. But such is the power and conviction of Britten's score that this in no way lessens the opera's impact.

In many respects, *Grimes* is less 'original' than *Paul Bunyan*. It is a brilliant synthesis – as is *Bunyan* – of the influences that made Britten the composer he was. It sounds fresh and 'different', but on closer acquaintance one realizes that the novelty is really Britten's ability, also displayed in works such as *Les illuminations* (1939) and the *Serenade* (1943), to present old forms and musical devices as if they were new. *Peter Grimes* is an opera in the great tradition – with a storm and a mad scene – but it owes something also to Berg's *Wozzeck*.

Britten unified the opera symphonically through six extended orchestral interludes. The pre-act interludes are atmospheric pieces, describing the scene and mood to follow, while those between the scenes are psychological commentaries on the plot and in particular on Grimes himself. The storm (Interlude II), for instance, is not only a wonderful depiction of an east-coast gale, but a penetrating analysis of the conflicts in Grimes's mind as he moves towards madness. The finest interlude is the Passacaglia, a favourite form of Britten's. His word-setting is one of the opera's great features – the Prologue, for example, with its naturalistic recitative contrasted with Grimes's arioso.

RECORDINGS 1. C. Watson, J. Watson, Elms, Pears, Pease, Evans, Covent Garden Ch & O, Britten, Decca, 1958; 2. Harper, Bainbridge, Payne, Vickers, Summers, Allen, Covent Garden Ch & O, C. Davis, Philips, 1978; 3. J. Watson, Gunson, Collins, Langridge, Opie, R. Williams, LSCh, City of London Sinfonia, Hickox, Chandos, 1995

The Rape of Lucretia

Opera in two acts (1h 45m)
Libretto by Ronald Duncan, based on the play *Le viol de Lucrèce* by André Obey (1931)
Composed 1945–6; rev. 1947
PREMIERES 12 July 1946, Glyndebourne, Sussex; US: 1 June 1947, Shubert Theater of Chicago Opera, Chicago
CAST Male Chorus *t*, Female Chorus *s*, Collatinus *b*, Junius *bar*, Tarquinius *bar*, Lucretia *c*, Bianca *ms*, Lucia *s*

In March 1946, when the team that had championed *Peter Grimes* in 1945 resigned from Sadler's Wells – among them the soprano Joan Cross, the producer Eric Crozier and Britten's lifelong friend and interpreter Peter Pears – Britten joined them in forming a new company to perform new works at the least possible expense, implying chamber operas. At first the company was called the Glyndebourne English Opera Company and *The Rape of Lucretia* was premiered at Glyndebourne, which itself had been closed during the war. Its general manager, Rudolf Bing, persuaded its owner, John Christie, that an association with Britten and his colleagues would be worthwhile. Britten agreed to compose an opera for eight singers and twelve musicians for a limited Glyndebourne season in the summer of 1946. Crozier suggested the subject of the rape of Lucretia, and Britten chose as his librettist his friend Ronald Duncan, for whose verse play *This Way to the Tomb* he had composed incidental music in 1945. For the first performances at Glyndebourne, the opera was produced by Crozier and the designer was John Piper, who was later to design several other Britten operas. Two casts were assembled, with Kathleen Ferrier and Nancy Evans alternating as Lucretia, and Ernest Ansermet and Reginald Goodall as conductors. The company then took the opera on tour in the provinces and to Holland. For the 1947 Glyndebourne performances of *The Rape of Lucretia*, the libretto was revised and a substitute aria was composed for Collatinus in Act I. After Ferrier's death in 1953, the outstanding Lucretia was Janet Baker, who sang the role on stage and recorded it in 1970. Like *Peter Grimes*, *The Rape of Lucretia* was performed widely in Europe and North America.

SYNOPSIS
Act I, Scene 1: The Male and Female Choruses recount how 'the Etruscan upstart' Tarquinius Superbus seized power in Rome and how his son Tarquinius Sextus has become a warrior leader and 'treats the proud city as if it were his

whore'. Their perspective on the action of the opera is in relation to an event still 500 years in the future – Christ's birth and death. The curtain rises to show an army camp outside Rome. In the generals' tent, Collatinus, Junius and Tarquinius are drinking and talking about women. On the previous night, six generals had ridden back to Rome to check on their wives' fidelity. The only wife found virtuously at home was Collatinus' wife, Lucretia. Junius, whose wife was found with a negro, quarrels violently with the unmarried Tarquinius. Collatinus parts them and proposes a toast to Lucretia. Junius rushes from the tent. He is sick of hearing Lucretia's name because Collatinus will win over political supporters from him on the strength of her chastity. Collatinus joins Junius and rebukes him for his attitude to Lucretia. They shake hands, at which point a drunken Tarquinius leaves the tent and mocks Junius as a cuckold. Collatinus brings them together, leaving the two generals to discuss women and power. Women are whores by nature, Junius says. Not Lucretia, Tarquinius retorts, adding 'I'll prove her chaste' and calling for his horse. In an interlude, the Male Chorus describes Tarquinius' ride to Rome ('Tarquinius does not wait'). Scene 2: In Lucretia's house in Rome that evening she is sewing while her servants Bianca and Lucia are spinning. She thinks she hears a knock at the gate, but Lucia finds no one there. Before folding the linen, Lucretia sings, 'How cruel men are to teach us love!' The three women prepare to go to bed while the Male and Female Choruses describe Tarquinius' arrival in Rome and his violent knock on Lucretia's door. He asks Lucretia for wine and says his horse is lame. She shows him to a room for the night.

Act II, Scene 1: A short introduction by the Choruses and offstage voices describes the Etruscan domination of Rome. Then Lucretia is seen asleep in her bedroom with Tarquinius approaching the bed (Male Chorus: 'When Tarquin desires, then Tarquin will dare'). Tarquinius kisses her and she, dreaming of her husband, draws him to her. She wakes and repulses him ('How could I give, Tarquinius, since I have given to Collatinus?'). They struggle until he draws his sword and rapes her. The Choruses, in an interlude, invoke Christ's compassion. Scene 2: In the hall of Lucretia's home, Lucia and Bianca extol the beauty of the morning and arrange flowers ('Oh, Lucia, please help me fill my vase with laughing daffodils'). Bianca has heard Tarquinius gallop away before dawn. Lucretia enters in a trancelike state. She says she hates the flowers and gives an orchid to Lucia for a messenger to take to Collatinus with a message that a Roman harlot has sent it. She makes a wreath from the remaining orchids ('Flowers bring to every year the same perfection'). Bianca tries to stop the messenger, but Collatinus has already arrived with Junius, who alerted him after seeing Tarquinius leave the camp and return at dawn. Lucretia enters in purple mourning ('Now there is no sea deep enough to drown my shame'). She tells Collatinus what has happened. He forgives her, but she stabs herself to death. In an epilogue the Choruses ask, 'Is it all?' and conclude that Jesus Christ is all.

Britten unifies the score by two motifs, one for Tarquinius, the other for Lucretia, constructed from a diminished fourth. These dominate the work in various subtle guises. The Male and Female Choruses have a chorale-like motif, which establishes their credentials as Christian commentators. The scoring for the small orchestra is a masterpiece of colour and imaginative sonority, with the harp's contribution a major feature. Like several Britten scores, *The Rape of Lucretia* is full of nocturnal imagery and onomatopoeic sounds – the chirp of crickets, the croaking of bullfrogs. When the Female Chorus describes the sleeping Lucretia, the evocative instrumentation is alto flute, bass clarinet and muted horn.

The full sound of the chamber orchestra is deployed to brilliant effect in the accompaniment to the Male Chorus's description of Tarquinius' Ride, a remarkable piece of graphic scoring. Lyrical passages abound in the opera: the sensuous trio for the women as they fold the linen and the music, full of summer morning heat, of 'O what a lovely day' at the start of the tragic final scene. Here Britten again employs one of his favourite devices, the passacaglia.

RECORDINGS 1. Baker, Harper, Pears, Luxon, Shirley-Quirk, ECO, Britten, Decca, 1970; 2. Rigby, Pierard, N. Robson, Maxwell, Miles, City of London Sinfonia, Hickox, Chandos, 1993

Albert Herring

Comic opera in three acts (2h 15m)
Libretto by Eric Crozier, after the short story *Le rosier de Madame Husson* by Guy de Maupassant (1888)
Composed 1946–7
PREMIERES 20 June 1947, Glyndebourne, Sussex; US: 8 August 1949, Berkshire Music Center, Lenox, Massachusetts (Tanglewood)
CAST Albert *t*, Lady Billows *s*, Mrs Herring *ms*, Florence Pike *c*, Vicar (Mr Gedge) *bar*, The Mayor (Mr Upfold) *t*, Miss Wordsworth *s*, Superintendent Budd *b*, Sid *bar*, Nancy *ms*, Emmie *s*, Cis *s*, Harry *treble*

Albert Herring was written as a companion piece to *The Rape of Lucretia* for performance by the same vocal and instrumental forces of the English Opera Group. It was first performed at Glyndebourne, whose owner John Christie disliked it intensely and is said to have greeted members of the first-night audience with the words: 'This isn't our kind of thing, you know.' Nevertheless, nearly 40 years later, in 1985, the Glyndebourne production by Peter Hall was one of the most successful the opera has had. Having shown the tragic aspects of Aldeburgh life in the early years of the 19th century in *Peter Grimes*, Britten now showed its comic side, taking the opportunity to poke fun at a lady bountiful, moral hypocrisy, village fêtes, mayors, vicars, schoolmarms and policemen. The gift for parody, which he had exhibited in *Paul Bunyan* and in several of his instrumental compositions, was again to the fore in *Albert Herring* and ranged from the Sullivanesque to self-quotation. In spite of criticism in Britten's own country that the opera was 'cosily provincial' in its treatment of stock characters, *Albert Herring* has proved popular in translation in several European countries. Like the best comedies, it has a dark side.

SYNOPSIS
Act I, Scene 1: The Mayor and Vicar of Loxford, the schoolmistress Miss Wordsworth and Police Superintendent Budd are meeting Lady Billows in her breakfast room on 10 April 1900 to select a May Queen. Lady Billows announces that she is putting up a prize of 25 sovereigns. Each member of the committee puts forward a candidate, but each name is torpedoed by Florence Pike, Lady Billows's housekeeper, who knows something disreputable about them all. Budd suggests a King of the May and nominates Albert Herring, who works for his mother in her greengrocery. Encouraged by the vicar and by a general chorus of 'Albert is virtuous', Lady Billows agrees. Scene 2: Mrs Herring's shop. Sid the butcher's assistant taunts Albert for being under his mother's thumb and tells him of delights in store if he breaks the apron strings – 'Courting a girl is the king of all sports'. Nancy from the bakery joins them and Sid makes an assignation with her for that night ('Meet me at quarter past eight'). Left alone, Albert muses that Sid might be right that he misses all the fun. Lady Billows, with the rest of the committee, arrives ('We bring great news to you upon this happy day!'). Albert regards his election as May King as 'daft' and tells his mother he will

refuse. But Mrs Herring has heard about the 25-sovereign prize.

Act II, Scene 1: Inside the marquee near the vicarage. A trestle table has been set for eleven places. Sid tells Nancy that he plans to put a generous tot of rum into Albert's lemonade ('Just loosen him up and make him feel bright'). The bigwigs now arrive with Albert, who is wearing a straw hat crowned with a wreath of orange blossom. The children sing their welcome to him and present flowers to Lady Billows, Albert and Mrs Herring. Lady Billows orates about the evils of carnal indulgence, gambling and the havoc wrought by gin. After receiving various prizes, Albert calls for three cheers for Lady Billows, drains his glass and promptly has hiccups. Scene 2: The shop. Albert, tipsy rather than drunk, recalls the feast he has just eaten – 'but oh! the taste of that lemonade'. He has been disturbed by Nancy – 'why did she stare each time I looked towards her?' He then hears Sid whistle in the street outside. Nancy joins Sid and Albert overhears them discussing him, saying he'll be all right once he's sown a few wild oats. They kiss and go off to the common. Albert tosses a coin and decides to leave. His mother returns, calls him and gets no reply. 'Fast asleep, poor kid. Worn out by all this fuss.'

Act III: The shop, the following afternoon. Albert is missing and the whole town is searching for him. Nancy, who has a guilty conscience, quarrels with Sid, who doesn't think Albert is dead. Superintendent Budd asks Mrs Herring for a photograph of Albert to send round the police stations. She gives him one in a frame ('It was took on the pier at Felixstowe'). Lady Billows demands that Scotland Yard and Conan Doyle should be called in. The Mayor solemnly carries in a tray. Underneath a cloth cover is Albert's orange-blossom wreath, found on a road crushed by a cart. All now assume Albert is dead and sing a threnody 'In the midst of life is death'. As it ends a dishevelled and mud-stained Albert returns. They turn on him and cross-examine him. He has spent three of his 25 pounds and has been with girls; he got drunk in one pub, until he was ejected, and started a fight in another. He turns on his mother – 'you squashed me down and reined me in'. Lady Billows prophesies he will pay for his sins of the flesh. Albert is left with Sid and Nancy and the village children, who now see him in a new light.

Albert Herring is a brilliantly successful comic opera, almost Rossinian in the speed and dexterity of Britten's treatment of recitatives. Contrapuntal treatment of certain episodes – fugal and canonic – is also extremely adept. The orchestral interludes are as racy, witty and illustrative as anything Britten wrote, and his use of parody and quotation is inspired. The children's street-game song, the hymnlike 'Albert the Good' and the zany patriotism of Lady Billows's speech in the marquee are superb examples of Britten's fertile melodic invention. The committee meeting in Act I is a notable example of Britten's gift for characterization. Each character is given an apposite aria, from the Vicar's quasi-ecclesiastical vocalizing to Miss Wordsworth's ballad-like twitterings. When Albert's lemonade is laced with rum and when he drinks it, the love-potion motif from Wagner's *Tristan* coils upwards and when Budd the policeman confides to Sid that he'd find 'a criminal case of rape' preferable to a manhunt, the orchestra quotes Lucretia's motif.

The musical climax is the nine-part threnody in Act III. This begins as a parody of a chant, but it quickly becomes a deeply felt lament, with each of the characters making an individual contribution and, towards the end, joining together in an elaborate piece of polyphonic writing over a pedal B♭. It is at this moment, when the opera turns serious, that one experiences it most strongly as a nostalgic recreation of a vanished England.

RECORDING Fisher, Wilson, Cantelo,

Rex, Pears, Brannigan, Ward, ECO, Britten, Decca, 1964

Billy Budd

Opera in four acts; rev. as two acts, 1960 (2h 45m)
Libretto by E. M. Forster and Eric Crozier, adapted from the story *Billy Budd, Foretopman* by Herman Melville (1891)
Composed 1950–51, rev. 1960
PREMIERES four-act version: 1 December 1951, Covent Garden, London; US: 19 October 1952, NBC Television Opera Workshop, New York (excerpts); 7 December 1952, Indiana University Opera Theater, Bloomington, Indiana; two-act version: 13 November 1960 (BBC broadcast); 9 January 1964, Covent Garden; US: 4 January 1966, Carnegie Hall, New York (concert); 6 November 1970, Civic Opera House, Chicago (stage)
CAST Captain Vere *t*, Billy Budd *bar*, Claggart *b*, Mr Redburn *bar*, Mr Flint *b-bar*, Lieutenant Ratcliffe *b*, Red Whiskers *t*, Dansker *b*, Donald *bar*, Novice *t*, Squeak *t*, Novice's friend *bar*, Captain's cabin boy *spoken role*, Bosun *bar*, 1st mate *bar*, 2nd mate *bar*, Maintop *t*, Arthur Jones *bar*, 4 midshipmen *boys' voices*; *tb* chorus of officers, sailors, powder monkeys, drummers, marines

Britten himself suggested the subject of *Billy Budd* to Crozier and Forster, who began work on the text in 1949; Crozier was responsible for the technical scenes and the dialogue, Forster for the 'big slabs of narrative'. The libretto is almost wholly in prose, since Forster could not write poetry, though some verses from Melville were interpolated, such as the ballad 'Billy in the Darbies', which is appended to the original story. Melville's first draft (1888) was a short story, *Baby Budd, Sailor*. This was expanded to a novella, *Billy Budd, Foretopman*, and completed in April 1891, a few months before the author's death. Melville was moved to write the story by events in 1842 aboard the United States brig-of-war *Somers* (and known as the Mackenzie Case), but he transferred the action to the Royal Navy just after the mutinies at Spithead and The Nore in 1797. Britten was attracted by this tale of innocence destroyed, of good crushed by evil and of an 'outsider' against society.

Britten's relationship with both librettists underwent crises during the composition of the opera, which is certainly a masterpiece born of creative tensions. The fourth draft was finished at the end of 1949. Britten began to compose the music in earnest six months later. The first performance at Covent Garden was to have been conducted by Josef Krips, but he withdrew at a late stage and Britten himself took over. Although the opera was fully appreciated by a handful of critics, it was generally received with a cold respect, and it was not until nearly 20 years later that it became a real success with the public.

Billy Budd had been planned in two acts, but for reasons Britten himself could not remember, it was made into four. Three interruptions of the action for intervals weakened the dramatic flow, and in 1960 Britten reverted to the two-act format. In doing so, he deleted a scene at the end of Act I, when Captain Vere addresses his crew with a rousing death-or-glory speech. In the revised version, the crew discuss Vere – 'he cares for us, he wishes us well' – and Billy sings, 'Star of the morning . . . I'd die to save you.'

SYNOPSIS

Act I: The action takes place on board the *Indomitable*, a seventy-four, during the French wars of 1797. Prologue: Captain Vere, as an old man, looks back over his life. He has found 'always some flaw' in the good that has come his way, 'some stammer in the divine speech'. Scene 1: The main deck and quarter-deck. A cutter returns to the ship with three press-ganged recruits. One is Billy Budd, a foundling and an able seaman, whose answers reveal that he stammers. But Claggart, the master-at-arms, calls him 'the jewel of great price'. He is placed in the foretop and is exultant ('Billy Budd, king of the birds!'). During this aria he sings farewell to the merchantman, 'Farewell, old *Rights o' Man*'. This disturbs the officers, who associate the phrase 'Rights of Man' with Thomas Paine's seditious book, a sensitive issue after the mutinies. Claggart calls Squeak, the ship's corporal, and orders him to keep an eye on Billy and to 'tangle up his hammock, mess his kit, spill his grog'. Dansker, an old seaman, warns Billy to beware of Claggart, known as Jemmy Legs. Scene 2: Captain Vere's cabin, a week later. Vere sends for the officers Redburn and Flint to take wine with him. They look forward to being in action ('Don't like the French') and mention Billy's shout of 'Rights o' Man'. Vere dismisses their fears: 'No danger there.' Scene 3: The berth deck. The seamen are singing ('Blow her away'). Billy and Red Whiskers try to persuade Dansker to join in, but he says he's too old. All he misses is tobacco. Billy offers to lend him some and goes to his kitbag. He begins to stammer as he finds Squeak there. Squeak draws a knife. Billy knocks him down just as Claggart appears. Dansker tells him what happened, and Claggart has no option but to have Squeak put in irons. Left alone, Claggart sings his evil Credo about Billy: 'Would that I never encountered you . . . I have you in my power and I will destroy you.' The Novice joins him and, after some hesitation, agrees to tempt Billy with money to lead a mutiny. Furious, Billy strikes out. The scene has been witnessed by Dansker, who tells him, 'Jemmy Legs is down on you.'

Act II, Scene 1: The main deck and quarter-deck some days later. Claggart asks to see Vere, who is visibly irritated by his sycophantic and long-winded manner of presenting his complaint. He still has not reached the point when they are interrupted by a shout of 'Enemy sail on starboard bow'. The crew goes to action stations ('This is the moment'), but the French ship escapes in a mist. Claggart returns to his charge and tells how the Novice was offered gold by Billy to join a mutiny. Vere ridicules him, but agrees to see Billy. Scene 2: Vere's cabin. Vere calls in Claggart, who formally accuses Billy of mutiny. Billy is aghast, stammers and shoots out his right fist, which strikes Claggart's forehead. Claggart falls dead. Vere calls in the three officers to hold a drumhead court martial. Billy pleads with Vere to save him, but Vere stays silent. Scene 3: A bay of the gun deck, shortly before dawn. Billy, in irons, sings his ballad, 'Look! Through the port comes the moonshine astray!' Dansker brings him food. The whole ship is seething, he says, and some of the crew plan to rescue Billy. Billy says they must not or they will hang too. Alone, he sings, 'I've sighted a sail in the storm, the far-shining sail.' Scene 4: The main deck and quarter-deck at 4 a.m. The crew assembles in silence. Billy cries, 'Starry Vere, God bless you!' As he is hanged, an ugly muttering from the crew grows louder. The officers order, 'Down all hands.' Epilogue: Vere as an old man describes the trial of Billy and laments, 'I could have saved him. He knew it. But he has saved me. I was lost in the infinite sea, but I've sighted a sail in the storm, the far-shining sail . . .'

Billy Budd is among Britten's greatest achievements (some are tempted to rank it the greatest). The struggle between good and evil, Billy and Claggart, is symbolized by the opposition of the chords of B♭ major and B minor, which is heard in the strings that accompany Vere's musings at the start of the opera. This opposition permeates the whole score. The tonal ambiguity stands, too, for the moral uncertainty that is a feature of the opera, particularly affecting the character of Vere. Yet the music is firmly tonal, with certain keys acting almost as leitmotifs for the characters concerned. Claggart's key is F minor, for example.

The opera's harmonic range is extraordinarily wide and its structure is taut and tense, the themes often similar in melodic outline as if to stress the obsessive nature of the piece.

The atmosphere is claustrophobic, but there is no sense of monotony because of the richness and variety of the orchestral score. *Billy Budd* has the largest orchestra of any of Britten's operas; it requires, for example, six percussionists. Claggart's evil is represented by the darker, lower sonorities – trombones, tuba, double bassoon. Billy's stammer is brilliantly depicted by a trill on a muted trumpet and a roll on the block. Potent use is made of the saxophone, while the large wind band is associated with the sea itself and with the harsh life aboard a man-of-war. For deeper human qualities, the strings are used with poignant effect, and Britten's writing for the chorus in the shanties is powerfully moving. Not the least skilful feature of the score is the most obvious – that it is for male voices only, without any sense of limitation or monotony.

The opera is Verdian in its juxtaposition of the public and the private – the external life of the ship and the personal dramas of Vere, Billy and Claggart. Each is given a solo aria of outstanding beauty and memorability. Yet perhaps the most compelling episode in the score is the celebrated passage when Vere tells Billy of his sentence: the stage is empty and the orchestra plays 34 slow chords, each varying in colour and dynamics and eventually reaching an F major that seems to wipe away Claggart's vile influence.

RECORDINGS 1. Pears, Glossop, Langdon, Brannigan, Ambrosian Op Ch, LSO, Britten, Decca, 1967 (two-act version); 2. Rolfe Johnson, Hampson, Halfvarsen, Van Allan, Hallé Ch & O, Nagano, Erato, 1997 (four-act version); 3. Langridge, Keenlyside, Tomlinson, Bayley, LSCh & O, Hickox, Chandos, 1999 (two-act version)

Gloriana

Opera in three acts (2h 30m)
Libretto by William Plomer, based on *Elizabeth and Essex* by Lytton Strachey (1928)
Composed 1952–3
PREMIERES 8 June 1953, Covent Garden, London; US: 8 May 1955, Music Hall, Cincinnati, Ohio (concert); 6 June 1984, Lila Cockrell Theater, San Antonio, Texas (stage)
CAST Queen Elizabeth I *s*, Earl of Essex *t*, Countess of Essex *ms*, Lord Mountjoy *bar*, Penelope, Lady Rich *s*, Sir Robert Cecil *bar*, Sir Walter Raleigh *b*, Henry Cuffe *bar*, Lady-in-Waiting *s*, Blind ballad singer *b*, Recorder of Norwich *b*, Housewife *ms*, Spirit of the Masque *t*, Master of Ceremonies *t*, City Crier *bar*; *satb* chorus of citizens, maids of honour, ladies and gentlemen of the household, courtiers, masquers, old men, men and boys of Essex's following, councillors; Time *male dancer*, Concord *female dancer*; country girls, rustics, fishermen, morris dancer, dancers; pages, ballad singer's runner, Sir John Harington, French ambassador, Archbishop of Canterbury, phantom kings and queens, actors

When Princess Elizabeth became Queen in February 1952 her cousin the Earl of Harewood, founder editor of *Opera* magazine (and later director of the Edinburgh Festival and managing director of ENO), suggested to Britten that he should compose an opera on the subject of Queen Elizabeth I and the Earl of Essex to mark the Coronation the following year. Royal permission was obtained, and Britten laid aside all other creative work in order to complete the opera in time for the premiere on 8 June 1953 when Joan Cross sang the role of Elizabeth I and Peter Pears that of Essex.

Gloriana came at an unfortunate moment in Britten's career. Because of his success and his acceptance by a wide public, there was intense jealousy of him in musical circles (heightened by his appointment as a Companion of Honour at the age of 39) and enmity because of his homosexuality, which was then still a criminal offence. These were undoubtedly factors in the cool reception of *Gloriana*, but the gala audience comprised mainly diplomats and civil servants for many of whom any opera, let alone one by a 20th-century composer, would have been an alien and tedious experience. Because the character of Elizabeth I was not sycophantically treated in the opera, it was said that *Gloriana* was a tasteless choice for the occasion. Later performances were warmly received, but the work had been given a bad name and was soon dropped from the Covent Garden repertoire. When it was revived, in a slightly revised version, by the Sadler's Wells company in 1966 (with Sylvia Fisher in the title role) it enjoyed a popular success. But for many years after its first performance, *Gloriana* remained the only Britten opera not to have been recorded in full.

SYNOPSIS

Act I, Scene 1: The Earl of Essex and Lord Mountjoy, rivals for the Queen's favour, quarrel at a tournament. The Queen rebukes them and they are uneasily reconciled. Scene 2: Sir Robert Cecil warns the Queen against Essex's lack of restraint. Essex sings two lute songs to the Queen and urges his claim to be made Viceroy of Ireland.

Act II, Scene 1: Essex, Mountjoy, Cecil and others attend the Queen, who is in Norwich on a royal progress. They watch a rustic masque. Scene 2: At Essex House in the Strand, Mountjoy awaits his lover, Essex's sister Lady Rich. They are joined by Essex and his wife. Essex complains of delay over the Ireland decision and all four agree that when the Queen dies they will decide her successor. Scene 3: At a dance in the Palace of Whitehall the Queen humiliates the gorgeously gowned Lady Essex by ordering the ladies to change their linen and herself returning in Lady Essex's dress, which does not fit her. But a moment later she appoints Essex Lord Deputy of Ireland.

Act III, Scene 1: Essex's Irish campaign has failed. He bursts in on the Queen while she is dressing and is without her wig. She orders him to be kept under guard. Scene 2: Essex is proclaimed a traitor after trying to persuade the citizens of London to rebel. Scene 3: Essex has been condemned to death, but the Queen does not sign the warrant for his execution until she is angered by Lady Rich's haughty demeanour. The opera ends with the Queen speaking, not singing, while six brief episodes of her life pass before her.

Gloriana is a succession of tableaux and brilliantly succeeds in giving a dignified and touching portrait of the Queen both as a public and a private individual. All the other characters are subsidiary, even Essex himself. The music is often subtle, as when the first lute song, 'Quick music is best', is undermined in the bass by the motif that stands for the Queen's cares of state. The sedition scene (Act II, Scene 2) is Verdian in its dramatic effectiveness, and there is no denying the impact of the Queen's spoken epilogue, unorthodox as it may be. In the ceremonial music – the Norwich masque and at the Palace ball – Britten evokes the Tudor age without a trace of pastiche.

RECORDING Barstow, Kenny, Jones, Langridge, Opie, J. Summers, WNO Ch & O, Mackerras, Argo, 1992

The Turn of the Screw

Opera in a prologue and two acts (1h 45m)
Libretto by Myfanwy Piper, after the story by Henry James (1898)
Composed 1954
PREMIERES 14 September 1954, La Fenice, Venice; UK: 6 October 1954, Sadler's Wells, London; US: 19 March 1958, New York College of Music, New York

CAST Prologue *t*, Governess *s*, Flora *s*, Mrs Grose *s*, Quint *t*, Miss Jessel *s*, Miles *treble*

The idea for an opera based on Henry James's ghost story was given to Britten by Myfanwy Piper, wife of the artist John Piper, who had been a friend of Britten since 1935 and had provided designs for several of the operas. The theme of *The Turn of the Screw* appealed particularly to Britten – corruption and innocence. It tells of two orphaned Victorian children, brother and sister, living in an Essex country house, who come under the evil influence of the ghosts of their guardian's former valet and the governess he seduced. A new governess discovers what is happening and tries to counteract it, with disastrous consequences. James never states what happens between haunters and haunted, but the story and the opera imply some sexual or erotic relationship, and the impression of evil is all the greater for remaining unspecified. In James the ghosts never speak; Mrs Piper's outstandingly skilful libretto provides words for them to sing and Britten directed that the audience should see them. The reader of the story is left to decide whether the ghosts exist or are figments of the repressed imagination of the distraught Governess (Britten's finest soprano role). James himself said he did not know. The dialogue between the ghosts at the beginning of Act II is an invention of Mrs Piper. She quotes a line from W. B. Yeats, 'The ceremony of innocence is drowned'. For Britten this was the heart of the matter.

The opera was written to a commission from the 1954 Venice Biennale. Beginning to write the music in February 1954, Britten had composed the first three scenes when he decided there should be a prologue. Another late insertion was the letter scene, one of the finest in the work. Britten worked on the opera very fast: Imogen Holst, who copied the vocal score several pages at a time and posted them to the publisher, was amazed by Britten's confidence in parting with the start of a scene before he had composed the end of it. He conducted the English Opera Group in the first performance in Venice with a fine cast fortunately preserved in a recording.

SYNOPSIS

Prologue (to be played in front of a drop curtain) A male narrator relates 'a curious story' written 'long ago' by a woman: it tells how she agreed to become governess to two orphaned children in the country on condition that she would never write to their handsome young guardian because he was so busy.

Act I

Theme

Scene 1: The Journey. The Governess is in a coach travelling to Bly ('Nearly there. Very soon I shall know'). How will the old housekeeper welcome her?

Variation I

Scene 2: The Welcome. On the porch at Bly Mrs Grose, the housekeeper, and the excited children, Flora and Miles, await the Governess ('Mrs Grose! Mrs Grose! Will she be nice?'). They practise curtseying and bowing. The Governess finds them charming and beautiful.

Variation II

Scene 3: The Letter. News comes that Miles has been expelled from school. Mrs Grose tells the Governess that she has known him to be wild, but not bad. They watch the children innocently singing 'Lavender's blue' and decide the school has erred. The Governess says she will not tell the guardian.

Variation III

Scene 4: The Tower, 'evening, sweet summer'. The Governess is strolling in the grounds of Bly ('How beautiful it is'). She is enchanted more each day by her 'darling children'. Yet she has heard a cry in the night and a footstep outside her door. Suddenly she sees a man on the tower ('Who is it, who?').

Variation IV

Scene 5: The Window. In the hall Flora and Miles are riding a hobby-horse ('Tom, Tom, the piper's son'). The

Governess again sees the man in the window. She describes the apparition to Mrs Grose, whose reaction is 'Quint! Peter Quint! Is there no end to his dreadful ways?' She explains that Quint was the master's former valet. He was 'free with everyone', spent hours with Miles, and 'had his will' with the lovely Miss Jessel, the children's previous governess, who left when pregnant and died. Quint also died when he fell on an icy road. The Governess, horrified, vows to protect the children.

Variation V

Scene 6: The Lesson. The Governess is giving Miles a Latin lesson in the schoolroom. He sings her a plaintive rhyme ('Malo I would rather be. Malo in an apple tree').

Variation VI

Scene 7: The Lake. On a sunny morning the Governess, with a book, and Flora, with a doll, sit by the lake in the park. Flora names the seas she knows, ending with the Dead Sea. She sings to her doll ('Go to sleep, my dolly dear') while the Governess reads. The Governess sees the ghost of Miss Jessel on the other side of the lake and realizes Flora has seen her too ('They are lost! Lost!').

Variation VII

Scene 8: At Night. Miles, in his nightgown, is in the garden near the tower. Quint's voice calls to him ('I'm all things strange and bold'). Later Miss Jessel, by the lake, calls to Flora. The colloquy between the ghosts and children is interrupted by the Governess and Mrs Grose. Miles tells the Governess, 'You see, I am bad.'

Act II

Variation VIII

Scene 1: Colloquy and Soliloquy (The setting is 'nowhere'). Quint and Miss Jessel reproach each other and sing that 'The ceremony of innocence is drowned.' They disappear, and the Governess sings ('Lost in my labyrinth') of the evil she fears.

Variation IX

Scene 2: The Bells. In the churchyard, Flora and Miles sing a mock-Benedicite. Mrs Grose is reassured by 'how sweet they are together', but the Governess tells her 'they are not playing, they are talking horrors' and are 'with the others'. Mrs Grose urges her to write to their guardian, but she refuses. As Flora goes into the church, Miles hangs back ('Do you like the bells? I do!'). He asks the Governess when he is returning to school. He mentions 'the others' to her. She knows she has been challenged and decides to leave Bly.

Variation X

Scene 3: Miss Jessel. The Governess enters the schoolroom to find Miss Jessel sitting at the desk and bemoaning her suffering ('Here my tragedy began'). The Governess defies her and she vanishes. The Governess decides to stay, but writes to the guardian ('Sir – dear Sir – my dear Sir').

Variation XI

Scene 4: The Bedroom. Miles is singing 'Malo'. The Governess tells him she has written to his guardian. Quint's voice calls to the boy, who shrieks and the candle goes out. ''Twas I who blew it,' Miles tells the alarmed Governess.

Variation XII, in which Quint is seen hovering ('So! She has written . . . It is there on the desk . . . Easy to take.').

Scene 5: Quint. Quint tempts Miles to steal the letter. Miles creeps into the schoolroom and takes the letter back to his bedroom.

Variation XIII

Scene 6: The Piano. In the schoolroom the Governess and Mrs Grose listen admiringly to Miles playing the piano ('O what a clever boy') while Flora makes a cat's cradle. Flora slips away and the two women set off to find her while Miles, his ruse successful, plays triumphantly.

Variation XIV

Scene 7: Flora. Flora is found by the lake. Miss Jessel appears ('Flora! Do not fail me!') and is seen by the Governess but not by Mrs Grose and Flora, or so they say ('I can't see anybody'). Flora, shouting abuse at the Governess, is led away by Mrs Grose. The Governess bewails Mrs Grose's desertion.

Variation XV

Scene 8: Miles. Mrs Grose is taking Flora away from Bly after a night listening to her outpourings of 'things I never knew or hope to know'. She reveals that Miles took the Governess's letter. The Governess is left behind ('O Miles – I cannot bear to lose you!'). The boy saunters in ('So, my dear, we are alone'). 'I stay as your friend,' she tells him. But he is listening for Quint. As the Governess questions Miles, Quint tells him not to betray their secrets. The boy becomes hysterical and admits he took the letter. 'Say the name of him who made you take it,' she says, 'and he will go for ever.' Miles screams, 'Peter Quint, you devil!' Quint disappears. The Governess realizes Miles is dead in her arms. She lays him on the ground and sings his 'Malo' tune as a requiem.

The title of James's story gave Britten the clue for the musical plan of the opera. The tension is maintained and heightened by turns of the musical screw – that is, by the use of variation form. The prologue and 15 scenes are linked by 16 orchestral interludes – the theme and 15 variations – which are as vocal as any words in creating atmosphere. The theme (the 'screw') is 12-note, but it is not a Schoenbergian note row and is not treated as such. The opera's tonal conflict 'turns' between A minor and A♭ major – a conflict similar to that in *Billy Budd*. The first seven scenes are in the white-note keys of the octave. Only in the last scene of Act I, when the two ghosts are heard for the first time, does the first black-note key appear.

Britten's scoring for chamber orchestra in this opera is as beautiful and imaginative as he ever achieved. The use of harp and low woodwind is especially striking, while his obsession with bells contributes powerfully to the opera's potent spell. Britten's employment of children's nursery rhymes, the lyrical writing of the letter by the Governess, her ecstatic aria as she strolls through the grounds of Bly, the mock-Benedicite, the brilliant pastiche Mozart that Miles (originally performed by David Hemmings, later a film actor) plays at the piano and his poignant 'Malo' song are among the highlights.

RECORDINGS 1. Vyvyan, Cross, Mandikian, Dyer, Pears, Hemmings, Eng Op Group, Britten, Decca, 1955; 2. Donath, June, Harper, Watson, Ginn, Langridge, Tear, Covent Garden O, C. Davis, Philips, 1981

A Midsummer Night's Dream

Opera in three acts (2h 30m)
Libretto by Benjamin Britten and Peter Pears, adapted from the play by William Shakespeare (*c*.1593–4)
Composed October 1959–April 1960
PREMIERES 11 June 1960, Jubilee Hall, Aldeburgh; US: 10 October 1961, War Memorial Opera House, San Francisco
CAST Oberon *ct* or *c*, Tytania *coloratura s*, Puck *boy acrobat, spoken role*, Theseus *b*, Hippolyta *c*, Lysander *t*, Demetrius *bar*, Hermia *ms*, Helena *s*, Bottom *b-bar*, Quince *b*, Flute *t*, Snug *b*, Snout *t*, Starveling *bar*, Cobweb *treble*, Peaseblossom *treble*, Mustardseed *treble*, Moth *treble*; *treble* or *s* chorus of fairies

For the 1960 Aldeburgh Festival, the stage and pit of the Jubilee Hall were enlarged and other improvements were made. Britten wanted to compose a new opera as a celebration, but in the time left it was impossible to commission a libretto. So he and Pears adapted Shakespeare's *A Midsummer Night's Dream*, cutting the play by about half and simplifying the action. Some of Puck's lines are given to the chorus of fairies and other lines are reallocated among the singers. Britten said he did not feel in the least guilty about the cuts: 'The original Shakespeare will survive.' The whole project was completed in seven months, during part of which Britten was ill, though he conducted the first performance.

SYNOPSIS

Act I: The wood, deepening twilight. Oberon, King of the Fairies, has quarrelled with his Queen, Tytania, because she has 'a lovely boy' as attendant, stolen from an Indian king, and Oberon wants him. Tytania defies him and Oberon plans his revenge, ordering Puck to fetch him a herb of which the juice, sprinkled on a sleeping human's eyelids, will make the sleeper 'madly dote upon the next live creature that it sees'. Hermia, in love with Lysander, has been ordered by her father to marry Demetrius, who loves her. She and Lysander plan to flee outside Athens where the ruling will not apply. As they leave, Demetrius and Helena enter. Demetrius tells Helena he does not love her; he is looking for Lysander and Hermia – 'The one I'll slay, the other slayeth me.' Puck returns with the herb. Oberon, who has been eavesdropping, tells of his plan for Tytania ('I know a bank where the wild thyme blows') and orders Puck to find Demetrius – 'Thou shalt know the man by the Athenian garments he hath on' – and to anoint his eyes when he can ensure that 'the next thing he espies' will be Helena. The rustics arrive to rehearse a play, *Pyramus and Thisbe*, to be performed before Duke Theseus of Athens on the occasion of his marriage to Hippolyta. Parts are allotted – Bottom the weaver is to be Pyramus – and they agree to rehearse later. Lysander and Hermia are lost and settle to sleep. Puck sprinkles Lysander's eyelids with juice. When Demetrius and Helena arrive, Helena awakens Lysander who declares his love for her and follows her. Hermia finds herself alone and goes in search of Lysander. Tytania and her retinue arrive. When she is asleep, Oberon squeezes the juice on her eyes.

Act II: The wood, dark night. The rustics arrive for their rehearsal. Bottom leaves the clearing (followed by Puck) and returns wearing the head of an ass. Tytania awakes and falls in love with him. When Hermia and Demetrius return, it is obvious that Puck has bewitched the wrong man. Oberon orders him to search for Helena. As Demetrius lies down to sleep, Oberon squeezes juice on his eyes. Lysander is still protesting his sincerity to Helena when Demetrius awakes, declaring passion for Helena, who thinks everyone is playing a joke on her. Hermia returns and the women, formerly close friends, mock and insult each other. Oberon orders Puck to lead the four astray in the wood and to put the juice on Lysander's eyes to restore the status quo.

Act III, Scene 1: The wood, early next morning. Oberon, now that he has acquired Tytania's boy attendant, frees her and Bottom from the spell. Bottom rejoins his companions. The four lovers awaken and are reconciled, Lysander with Hermia and Demetrius with Helena. Scene 2: Theseus' palace. The Duke tells Hermia he will overrule her father and allow her to marry Lysander. The rustics' play is enacted, after which the couples retire. The fairies and Puck occupy the room ('Now the hungry lion roars'). Oberon and Tytania enter and, with the fairies, sing, 'Now until the break of day, through this house each fairy stray'. They leave the stage to Puck, who addresses the audience: 'Give me your hands, if we be friends, and Robin shall restore amends.'

In *A Midsummer Night's Dream*, Britten found themes congenial to him: night and sleep, the juxtaposition of the natural and the supernatural, marvellous lyric poetry, and the opportunity for a rich display of musical parody. He responded with some of his most inventive, enchanting and evocative music. Each of the three strata of beings in the opera – fairies, lovers and rustics – has its own sound-world, each with distinctive instrumental timbres – harps, celesta, harpsichord and percussion for the fairies, strings and woodwind for the lovers, bassoon and deep brass for the rustics. Two other inspirations contribute to the opera's success: Puck is a spoken role, accompanied by trumpet cadenzas and drums, and Oberon is assigned to a counter-tenor, an otherworldly sound that is both sinister and beguiling. The fairies' music has an acerbic quality. Britten said he had 'always been struck by a kind of sharpness in Shakespeare's fairies'. *A Midsummer Night's Dream* is as melodious a score as he ever wrote. His setting of 'I know a bank' is exquisite, as is the love music for Tytania and Bottom. The rustics' play is a closely organized opera buffa, notable for its witty parodies of Italian opera. And over the whole score lies the magic of the wood, brought before our eyes in the opera's first bars, with its slow portamento sighs depicting the rustling leaves and creaking branches. Although Britten never used serial method as such, the series of major triads, connected by glissandi on the strings, which so vividly depict the wood, covers all 12 notes of the chromatic scale. As they are in false relation to one another, Britten again (as in *Billy Budd*) creates a tonal ambiguity which is continued in the music given to the fairies on their first appearance, Lydian G major spiced with D major and F♯ major. At the end of the opera, in the haunting 'Now until the break of day', a radiant Mahlerian F♯ major is achieved. On the journey to that magical moment, Britten creates a Shakespearean opera to rank with Verdi's masterpieces.

RECORDINGS 1. Harwood, Harper, Veasey, Watts, Deller, Pears, Brannigan, Downside & Emanuel School Boys' Chs, LSO, Britten, Decca, 1966; 2. McNair, J. Watson, Philogene, H. Summers, Asawa, Ainsley, Lloyd, New London Children's Ch, LSO, C. Davis, Philips, 1995

Death in Venice

Opera in two acts (2h 30m)
Libretto by Myfanwy Piper, based on the novella *Der Tod in Venedig* by Thomas Mann (1912)
Composed spring 1971–March 1973; rev. 27 August 1973 and early 1974

PREMIERES 16 June 1973, The Maltings, Snape; US: 18 October 1974, Metropolitan, New York
CAST Gustav von Aschenbach *t*, Traveller/Elderly Fop/Old Gondolier/Hotel Manager/Hotel Barber/Leader of the Players/Voice of Dionysus *b-bar*, Voice of Apollo *ct*; *satb* chorus of youths and girls, hotel guests and waiters, gondoliers and boatmen, street vendors, touts and beggars, citizens of Venice, choir in St Mark's, tourists, followers of Dionysus; chorus includes (*s*) Danish lady, Russian mother, English lady, French girl, strawberry-seller, lace-seller, newspaper-seller, strolling player; (*c*) French mother, German mother, Russian nanny, beggar woman; (*t*) hotel porter, 2 Americans, 2 gondoliers, glass-maker, strolling player; (*bar and b*) ship's steward, lido boatman, Polish father, German father, Russian father, hotel waiter, guide in Venice, restaurant waiter, gondolier, priest in St Mark's, English clerk in the travel bureau; dancers: Polish mother, Tadzio, 2 daughters, governess, Jaschiu, boys and girls, strolling players, beach attendants

The idea of an opera based on Mann's *Death in Venice* had been in Britten's mind for some years. In November 1970 he approached Myfanwy Piper for a libretto and began work on the music in the spring of 1971. He completed the short score just before Christmas 1972. For most of the time he was ill, and in the autumn of 1972 his doctors decreed that he needed an operation to replace a deficient heart valve. He made a bargain with them – he would have the operation provided they allowed him to finish *Death in Venice* first. The full score was completed in March 1973. The opera had become an obsession. Not only was it a subject with which he was passionately involved, but he wanted to complete it as a tribute to Peter Pears.

During the operation (in May 1973), Britten had a slight stroke which permanently affected his right hand. He was not well enough to supervise rehearsals of the opera, conducted by Steuart Bedford, nor to attend the first performance at the Maltings. He first saw it at a special, semi-private performance on 12 September and later attended the first London performance at Covent Garden on 18 October. He attended the recording sessions in spring 1974 although very ill, and saw the opera again at the 1975 Aldeburgh Festival and at Covent Garden on 7 July 1975. Thus he heard Pears give the performance of his life in the long, taxing and testing role of Aschenbach and John Shirley-Quirk, equally impressive, in the seven baritone roles.

SYNOPSIS

Act I, Scene 1: Munich. Aschenbach, a famous novelist and now a widower, is walking in a Munich suburb and musing on the apparent drying up of his creativity ('My mind beats on and no words come'). He enters a cemetery and reads the texts on the façade of the chapel. He becomes aware of a Traveller, who sings of exotic sights in far-off lands ('Marvels unfold! . . . Go, travel to the South'). Aschenbach decides to have a holiday in the sun. Scene 2: On the boat to Venice. Youths are leaning over the rail shouting to their girls on shore. An Elderly Fop joins the youths as they sing of 'Serenissima' and starts a popular song, 'We'll meet in the Piazza'. Aschenbach comes on to the deck and is disgusted by the rouged 'young–old horror'. Arrival in Venice is described in an overture based on the Serenissima theme. Scene 3: The journey to the Lido. Aschenbach is in a gondola and sings his own praise of Serenissima. The Old Gondolier is not rowing him the way he wants to go. They pass a boatload of boys and girls singing 'Serenissima . . . Bride of the sea'. On arrival at the quayside, Aschenbach is met by a Boatman and the Hotel Porter. The Old Gondolier has disappeared, without payment. Aschenbach soliloquizes ('Mysterious gondola . . . black, coffin black, a vision of death itself'). Scene 4: The first evening at the hotel. The Manager shows Aschenbach his room with its superb view of the lagoon. He watches the other guests assemble for dinner – French, American, German, Polish, Danish, English and Russian. The Polish family enters, with the boy Tadzio, whose beauty is immediately noticed by Aschenbach ('Surely the soul of Greece lies in that bright perfection'). Scene 5: On the beach. Aschenbach watches children playing games and buys some strawberries. Tadzio arrives and joins the games. Scene 6: The foiled departure. Aschenbach crosses to Venice from the Lido. The city is hot and crowded and the sirocco is blowing. Back at the hotel, he decides to leave. Just before he goes, Tadzio walks through the hall. Aschenbach learns that his luggage has been sent on to the wrong destination, so he returns to the hotel. The Manager has kept his room and reminds him that the wind is now blowing from a healthier quarter. Through the window Aschenbach sees Tadzio playing on the beach ('That's what made it hard to leave. So be it'). Scene 7: The Games of Apollo. On the Lido beach, Aschenbach watches the boys' beach games as if they were in an Olympian world. The Voice of Apollo is heard ('He who loves beauty worships me'). Competing in a variety of games, Tadzio wins each time. Aschenbach, excited, wants but fails to speak to the boy, who passes him and smiles ('Ah, don't smile like that! No one should be smiled at like that'). On an empty stage, Aschenbach exclaims 'I love you'.

Act II: Aschenbach analyses his outburst. Scene 8: The Hotel Barber's shop. While trimming Aschenbach's hair, the garrulous barber mentions 'the sickness'. Scene 9: The pursuit. Aschenbach crosses to Venice where people are reading notices advising precautions against infection. In a newspaper he reads denials of rumours of cholera in Venice. He follows the Polish family into St Mark's and later in a gondola ('They must not leave . . .'). He is in thrall to

Tadzio. Scene 10: The Strolling Players. At the hotel, Aschenbach attends an entertainment by strolling players. He taxes their leader about the plague, but is rebuffed. Scene 11: The Travel Bureau. An English clerk is frank with Aschenbach: there is cholera and he should leave. Scene 12: The Lady of the Pearls. Aschenbach decides to warn Tadzio's mother, but he cannot bring himself to speak. Scene 13: The dream. In his sleep he hears the voices of Apollo and Dionysus, who depict the struggle in his mind. Scene 14: The empty beach. Aschenbach watches Tadzio and his friends as they play games desultorily. Scene 15: The Hotel Barber's shop. Aschenbach has his hair dyed and his face made up. Scene 16: The last visit to Venice. Rejuvenated, Aschenbach takes a gondola to Venice, jauntily singing the youths' song from Scene 2. He again trails the Polish family but loses them. Buying strawberries, he finds them musty. In a soliloquy he recalls Socrates ('Does beauty lead to wisdom, Phaedrus?'). Scene 17: The departure. The guests are leaving the hotel. Aschenbach goes to the deserted beach where Tadzio loses a fight with one of his friends. Aschenbach calls out and Tadzio beckons him, but the writer slumps dead in his chair.

Death in Venice is a tour de force of Britten's compositional skill. The long role of Aschenbach combines a Monteverdi-like recitative with Schoenbergian Sprechstimme and Mahlerian melody. The atmosphere of decay and decadence is as uncannily evoked as are the sounds of Venice itself. Britten again employs three strata of sound: piano accompaniment for the recitatives, a gamelan percussion for Tadzio and his friends, and the full orchestra for Venice and for the other characters. The silent Polish family are dancers. For the Voice of Apollo a counter-tenor is used. Thus the fantasy of *A Midsummer Night's Dream* and the austerity of the parables are tributaries flowing into this rich and compelling elegy.

RECORDINGS 1. Bowman, Pears, Shirley-Quirk, Eng Op Group, ECO, Bedford, Decca, 1974 2. Chance, Langridge, Opie, BBC Singers, City of London, Sinfonia, Hickox, Chandos, 2004

OTHER OPERATIC WORKS *Paul Bunyan*, 1941; *The Little Sweep*, 1949; *Noye's Fludde*, 1958; *Curlew River*, 1964; *The Burning Fiery Furnace*, 1966; *The Prodigal Son*, 1968; *Owen Wingrave*, 1971

M.K.

Ferruccio Busoni

Ferruccio Dante Michelangelo Benvenuto Busoni; *b* 1 April 1866, Empoli, Italy; *d* 27 July 1924, Berlin

Busoni enjoyed no regular schooling and matured young. Although born in Italy, he grew up in a central European cultural environment and spent most of his adult life in German-speaking countries. He acquired a specialist's knowledge of Bach and Liszt, adored Mozart and felt a growing antipathy towards Wagner. Schoenberg and many other contemporary composers interested him intensely, yet he remained independent of all schools and 'isms', hence acquiring a reputation for aloofness. During his lifetime his worldwide reputation as a virtuoso pianist completely eclipsed his activities as a composer. In recent years a growing familiarity with his works has helped penetrate the barrier of his alleged intellectualism and established him as an important figure in 20th-century music.

His first operatic project, based on Hertz's *King René's Daughter*, dates from 1883; it came to nothing. In 1884 Busoni negotiated unsuccessfully for a stage adaptation of Gottfried Keller's *A Village Romeo and Juliet* (later set by Delius). During a period of study at Leipzig, he began to compose his first opera, *Sigune, oder Das stille Dorf*. He completed the short score but orchestrated only the prelude before abandoning the work in about 1892. Some of the music was salvaged in the *Konzertstück*, for piano and orchestra, while an important motif, connected with the building of a cathedral, appears in the *Pezzo serioso* of the monumental Piano Concerto (1904). The Piano Concerto closes with a chorus of offstage male voices to a text from Oehlenschläger's play *Aladdin*. This too is the remains of a theatrical plan, a setting of *Aladdin*, 'not as an opera but as a Gesamtkunstwerk with drama, music, dance [and] magic'.

During the 1890s Busoni composed relatively little, expending much energy on perfecting his piano technique and widening his repertoire. The world premiere of Verdi's *Falstaff* in 1893 revived his belief in the future of Italian music and influenced his developing style. During this period he worked on the libretto for an opera about the Wandering Jew, *Ahasver*. Although he later abandoned the plan, he was to vary the central theme – the profoundly gifted outsider who strives for immortality – in several subsequent operatic projects, arriving at a definitive version in *Doktor Faust*. Variants of the same idea are to be found in *Der mächtige Zauberer*, *Leonardo da Vinci* and *Dante*. Libretti or sketches for these have survived; several further ideas for opera subjects are mentioned in Busoni's copious correspondence. Although Busoni made sporadic approaches to writers such as G. B. Shaw, D'Annunzio and Hofmannsthal, he actually wrote all his opera texts himself, in German.

In 1907 Busoni published his controversial *Outline of a New Aesthetic of Music* together with the libretto of *Die Brautwahl*. Although *Die Brautwahl* ultimately failed, Busoni was convinced that opera was the 'universal domain' of contemporary music and that his own musical language was intrinsically theatrical. In the revised edition of the *New Aesthetic* (1916) he elaborates on his idea of opera as a multimedia spectacle, which should 'rely on the incredible, untrue or unlikely'. The opera of the future, he writes, should use music only where it is indispensable, particularly for the portrayal of the supernatural or the unnatural, hence as a magic mirror (opera seria) or a distorting mirror (opera buffa). These theories, coupled with his earliest memories of Italian puppet theatre, form the foundation of his three remaining operas, *Arlecchino*, a one-act 'musical caprice', its companion piece, *Turandot*, and *Doktor Faust*. *Turandot* and *Arlecchino* are grouped together as *la nuova commedia dell'arte*, while *Doktor Faust* is based largely on the early German puppet play of *Faust*.

During the years immediately preceding the First World War Busoni came into contact with progressive artists in various fields – the Viennese Secessionists, the Italian Futurists, D'Annunzio, Rilke, Schoenberg and Varèse, to name but a few – and he entered on a period of experiment. The earliest studies for *Doktor Faust*, the *Sonatina seconda* for piano and *Nocturne symphonique*, Op. 43, for orchestra, date from this time. Apart from their dense, brooding textures, these works are notable for a new harmonic and rhythmic boldness and a distinctive instrumental chiaroscuro. The war effected a gradual change of direction, which finally led Busoni in 1918 to proclaim *Junge Klassizität* ('Young Classicality') as his artistic aim. 'Many experiments have been made in this young century,' he wrote. 'Now . . . it is time to form something durable again.' *Arlecchino* was his first brilliant essay in the new style.

Junge Klassizität is a concept that embraces many possibilities, for Busoni believed that the achievements of past generations could be combined with all new developments and that a full flowering of Western music would hence lie in the distant future. The libretto of *Doktor Faust* expresses this belief in allegorical form and can be interpreted as the composer's definitive artistic and philosophical statement.

Doktor Faust

Opera in two preludes, two intermezzi and three scenes (3h)
Libretto by the composer
Composed 1916–24 (inc.); completed by Philipp Jarnach (1925) and Antony Beaumont (1984)
PREMIERES Jarnach version: 21 May 1925, Dresden, Sächsisches Staatstheater; UK: 17 March 1937, Queen's Hall, London (concert); US: 1974, Pioneer Center for the Performing Arts, Reno, Nevada; Beaumont version: 2 April 1985, Teatro Comunale, Bologna; UK: 25 April 1986, Coliseum, London
CAST Faust *bar*, Mephistopheles *t*, Wagner *b*, Duke of Parma *t*, Duchess of Parma *s*, Master of Ceremonies *b*, Gretchen's Brother *bar*, Lieutenant *t*, 3 Students from Cracow *t*, 2 *bar*, Theology Student *bar*, Law Student *b*, Student of Natural Philosophy *bar*, Beelzebub *t*, Megaeros *t*, Gravis *b*, Levis *bar*, Asmodus *bar*, Student *t*, Poet *spoken role*, Helen of Troy *silent*, Boy *silent*; offstage: 3 *s*; *satb* chorus of churchgoers, soldiers, courtiers, huntsmen, Catholic and Lutheran students, countryfolk; dancers

Busoni consciously conceived *Doktor Faust* as his most significant work and his life's crowning achievement. Before finally deciding on *Faust* he had actively considered several alternatives, including the Wandering Jew, Leonardo da Vinci and Don Juan. He wrote the libretto between 1910 and 1915, the major portion coming to him impulsively during Christmas of 1914. Work on the score was begun in 1916, although the first musical studies for the opera date from 1912. Ill health began to impede Busoni's progress from 1921 onwards, and when he died in 1924 two substantial passages were still incomplete, the apparition of Helen of Troy to Faust in Scene 2 and the closing monologue of the final scene. In 1974 hitherto unknown sketches for these missing sections were bequeathed to the Prussian State Library in Berlin by Philipp Jarnach. Antony Beaumont's completion, based on this material, comes closer to Busoni's own concept than Jarnach's hastily written interpretation.

SYNOPSIS

The opera opens with an orchestral introduction (*Symphonia*), in which invisible voices chime out the word 'Pax' like bells, and a spoken prologue in which the poet outlines the genesis of the libretto and stresses its puppet origins. The opening scenes take place in Faust's study at Wittenberg. Wagner, his factotum, admits three students from Cracow, who bring a magic book, *Clavis Astartis Magica*. Following the instructions of the book, Faust summons the servants of Lucifer; they appear to him as six tongues of fire. Mephistopheles, the highest of them, claims to be 'swifter than the thoughts of man'. He draws up a pact, which Faust signs with his own blood, against an offstage chorus of Eastertide churchgoers. Faust collapses. The scene changes to a Romanesque chapel (scenic intermezzo), where Gretchen's brother vows to revenge himself on Faust. Mephistopheles engineers his brutal murder.

For the main body of the work the scene changes to the ducal park in Parma. As the climax to the duke's wedding celebrations, Faust is presented as a celebrity and astonishes the guests with magic tricks. He conjures up three visions from antiquity (Samson and Delilah, Solomon and the Queen of Sheba, Salome and John the Baptist) which express his love for the duchess. With the aid of Mephistopheles he soon succeeds in winning her. The duchess sings of her infatuation for Faust and flees with him. Disguised as court chaplain, Mephistopheles advises the duke to remarry, raising his clawed hand in ghastly benediction. A sombre orchestral sarabande marks the turning-point in the drama (symphonic intermezzo). In a tavern in Wittenberg, Faust mediates in an argument between Catholic and Protestant students, but his words lead only to uproar and dissent. Mephistopheles, disguised as a courier, brings the dead body of the duchess's child. He sets it alight and out of the flames emerges Helen of Troy. Faust tries in vain to grasp the visionary figure. Again he is confronted by the students from Cracow, who tell him that he is to die at midnight. The scene changes to Wittenberg town square, snow is falling. Mephistopheles, as night-watchman, calls the hour: it is ten o'clock. Students skittishly serenade Wagner, who has succeeded Faust as rector of the university. Faust gives alms to a beggarwoman, but she is revealed as the ghost of the duchess, who urges him to 'finish the work before midnight'. Faust transfers his soul to the dead child, dying as midnight strikes. The child arises in his place and strides out into the night. Mephistopheles is defeated.

The score is assembled from numerous musical studies, ranging from unfinished fragments (lieder, piano pieces, etc.) to substantial published works. Diverse as the sources are, they are unified by a 'Faustian' musical vocabulary: tonal music of extreme harmonic subtlety, with predominantly polyphonic textures and clear, sophisticated orchestral sonorities.

Busoni distinguished between Wagnerian music drama and his own (epic) theatre, in which words and music are intended to fulfil their own, separate functions. In 1922 he published his essay 'Outline of a Preface to the Score of *Doktor Faust*', in which he stressed that each section of his score is shaped into an organic, if unorthodox symphonic form: the festivities at Parma are formed into a dance suite, the tavern scene features a scherzo, chorale and fugue. The introspective, Faustian element is countered in each main scene by lighter, extrovert episodes; hence the work can be understood as a mystery play, part folk festival, part Passion. Among those rarefied stage works concerned with artistic creativity and higher philosophical questions (such as Wagner's *Die Meistersinger*, Schoenberg's *Moses und Aron*, Pfitzner's *Palestrina*) *Doktor Faust* occupies a prominent place.

RECORDING Jenis, Begley, Kerl, Hanschel, Hollop, Fischer-Dieskau, Op Nat de Lyon Ch & O, Nagano, Erato, 1997/8 (incl. both Jarnach & Beaumont endings)
OTHER OPERATIC WORKS *Sigune, oder Das stille Dorf* (not orch.), (1892); *Die Brautwahl*, 1912; *Arlecchino, oder Die Fenster*, 1917; *Turandot*, 1917

A.B.

C

Alfredo Catalani

b 19 June 1854, Lucca, Italy; *d* 7 August 1893, Milan

Catalani is an isolated figure in late 19th-century Italian opera. Eschewing both the Verdian vein of French-influenced international opera and the melodramatic excesses of the emerging verismo school, he pursued a brand of Germanic Romanticism, yet endowed it with an authentic Italian flavour. He was just coming into his own when he died of tuberculosis at 39.

His first musical studies, in Lucca with Puccini's uncle, Fortunato Magi, were followed by further lessons in Paris under Bazin. Later, he settled in Milan, where he continued his studies in composition at the conservatory with Antonio Bazzini. In 1875 he wrote an eclogue (in effect a one-act opera), *La falce* (to a text by Boito), as his graduation exercise, which won him the support of the publisher Giovannina Lucca, who then underwrote his career for several years.

Encouraged by a modest monthly stipend from Lucca, he embarked on an opera, *Elda*, finishing the first version in 1876, but continuing to revise it until it was premiered in Turin in 1880. Next came *Dejanice* (1883) and *Edmea* (1886); the latter won him favourable critical attention, despite one of Ghislanzoni's more implausible libretti. *Edmea* is the first of Catalani's scores to hint at his natural inclination towards idiosyncratic Romanticism. The same year he was appointed professor of composition at the Milan Conservatory on the death of Ponchielli, but because of his ill health he was granted the post only on a year's probation.

When Lucca's publishing house was merged with that of Ricordi in 1888, Catalani failed to find favour with the new regime, and his final works were brought to fruition largely through his own efforts. He embarked on a full-scale revision of *Elda*. Retitled *Loreley*, it was introduced at the Teatro Regio, Turin, early in 1890. It subsequently became the first of Catalani's works to be widely performed outside Italy. His last opera, *La Wally* (1892), to a text by Illica (commissioned and paid for by Catalani himself), was even more successful. With *La Wally*, he finally earned the good will of Giulio Ricordi, but by then it was too late.

Catalani struggled to find himself at a time when Italian stages were dominated by the final works of Verdi and by the emergence of the *veristi*. He laboured by trial and error to achieve what came more easily to other opera composers with a stronger instinct for the stage. His ability to create poetically atmospheric orchestral music, as in the 'Dance of the Ondine' in Act III of *Loreley* and the prelude to Act III of *La Wally*, compensates to some extent for his difficulty in projecting clearly individualized personalities for his characters.

La Wally

Dramma musicale in four acts (2h)
Libretto by Luigi Illica, after the novel *Die Geyer-Wally* by Wilhelmine von Hillern (1875)
Composed 1890–91
PREMIERES 20 January 1892, La Scala, Milan; US: 6 January 1909, Metropolitan, New York; UK: 27 March 1919, Manchester
CAST Wally *s*, Stromminger *b*, Afra *ms*, Walter *s*, Giuseppe Hagenbach *t*, Vincenzo Gellner *bar*, messenger *t* or *b*; *satb* chorus of Tyroleans, shepherds, peasants, hunters, old women, village children

Premiered within months of Verdi's *Falstaff* and Puccini's *Manon Lescaut, La Wally* is the clearest example of the 'alternative' direction Italian opera might have taken had not Catalani's death intervened. It is the composer's most successful opera and – initially thanks to the championing of Toscanini, who conducted its premiere (and named his daughter Wally) – has become an established, if infrequently performed, part of the repertoire.

SYNOPSIS
Act I: The setting is the Tyrolean Alps, and the plot turns on the triangle of the independent but vulnerable Wally, Gellner, whom her father, Stromminger, wants her to marry, and Hagenbach, whom she loves. At Stromminger's 70th birthday party, Wally rejects Gellner and her father turns her out.

Act II: After her father's death, Wally, now wealthy, comes to a festival at Sölden. There, Gellner urges her to accept him, but Wally is still fascinated by Hagenbach, with whom she dances a *valzer del bacio*. Wally confesses she loves him, but Hagenbach's kiss is derisive, whereupon she orders Gellner to kill him.

Act III: That night Wally wishes she could take back her words. Hagenbach comes to ask pardon, but Gellner intercepts him, and hurls him down a ravine. Wally clambers down and saves Hagenbach. Once more she retreats to the heights, leaving her possessions to the woman she believes Hagenbach loves.

Act IV: High in the Alps, Hagenbach comes to Wally and, their mutual misunderstanding resolved, they rejoice in their love. An ominous storm has gathered and they both perish in an avalanche.

Catalani took advantage of the setting to introduce some local colour into his music, for example, the 'Edelweiss' song sung by Walter, a village boy, in Act I, and the Tyrolean dances in Act II; Wally's 'Ebben? Ne andro lontan', the best known of all Catalani's arias, is an adaptation of the melody of Catalani's *Chanson groënlandaise*, but its Nordic character is not so pronounced as to make it seem out of place here. While these individual set numbers may be singled out, one of the most significant features of the score is its continuity. Catalani abandoned the number-opera structure of his earlier operas and, no doubt influenced by Wagner and perhaps by Verdi's *Otello*, created instead an opera where the music flows seamlessly, incorporating and then developing motifs of dramatic significance.

RECORDING Tebaldi, Del Monaco, Cappuccilli, Diaz, Monte Carlo Op Ch & O, Cleva, Decca, 1968
OTHER OPERAS *La falce*, 1875; *Elda*, 1880; *Dejanice* 1883; *Edmea*, 1886; *Loreley*, 1890

W.A.

Francesco Cavalli

Pietro [Pier] Francesco Caletti [Caletto, Caletti-Bruni, Caletti di Bruno] detto il Cavalli; *b* 14 February 1602, Crema; *d* 14 January 1676, Venice

One of the major composers of the 17th century, Cavalli played a crucial role in establishing opera as a genre. Although opera had been 'invented' in the 1590s, performances had largely been isolated events mounted for special court occasions. In 1637, however, the concept of public opera, with regular seasons financed by ticket sales, emerged in Venice. This idea stimulated a wave of creativity that quickly won opera a permanent place in the musical world, with Venice as its centre. After the death of Monteverdi (1643), Cavalli became the leading opera composer in Venice; he wrote 32 between 1639 and 1673. Unlike those of his contemporaries, most of his works survive: the Biblioteca Marciana, Venice, preserves 28 manuscript scores from Cavalli's own collection, some autograph, and many bearing his corrections. Moreover, as opera spread throughout Italy in the 1640s and 1650s, Cavalli's works played a vital part in initiating the tradition of opera performance in numerous cities (including Naples). His fame reached beyond Italy to England, Austria and, particularly, France, and in 1660 he was commissioned to write an opera, *Ercole amante*, for the wedding of Louis XIV. In an era that constantly demanded new operas, Cavalli's were unusual for their sustained popularity; today many have been revived with considerable success.

Cavalli received his first musical training from his father, G. B. Caletti, maestro di cappella of the Crema Cathedral. In 1616 the boy was brought to Venice by Federico Cavalli, governor of Crema; Francesco later adopted his patron's name. Shortly after his arrival in Venice, Francesco joined the choir at St Mark's, where Monteverdi was the new maestro di cappella. This was the beginning of a lifelong association with St Mark's in which Cavalli rose from soprano to tenor to second organist (1639) to first organist (*c*.1645), and finally maestro di cappella (1668).

Cavalli's opera career began in 1639, when he signed a contract with Venice's first opera theatre, S. Cassiano; besides composing, he initially helped finance and manage the company. In 1641 Cavalli teamed up with Giovanni Faustini, librettist and later impresario, with whom he collaborated (on ten operas) until the latter's death in 1651; he subsequently worked for Faustini's brother Marco, who took over as impresario. He composed seven operas to libretti by Nicolò Minato, and three to works by G. F. Busenello, author of *L'incoronazione di Poppea*. Cavalli apparently helped revise Monteverdi's music to *Poppea*: the Marciana collection includes a score with his annotations.

In 1660 Cavalli accepted Mazarin's invitation to Paris. This journey was ill-fated from the start: preparations for the celebration were over budget and behind schedule, and Mazarin died before they were completed. *Ercole amante*'s premiere was delayed until 1662; in the meantime, a revival of *Xerse* was staged. Both were adapted to French taste by Lully, who added long ballet entrées. Cavalli's music received little comment, and he departed vowing never to write another opera. He did ultimately finish six more, but two of the last three fell victim to the fickle tastes of the Venetian public. Even so, as maestro of St Mark's, he died in 1676 the most respected musician in Venice. The expressive quality of his music and his gift for dramatic portrayal mark him as a worthy successor to Monteverdi.

La Calisto

Callisto

Dramma per musica in a prologue and three acts (2h 30m)

Libretto by Giovanni Faustini
PREMIERES 28 November 1651, Teatro S. Apollinare, Venice; UK: 25 May 1970, Glyndebourne, Sussex (rev. Raymond Leppard); US: 12 April 1972, Cincinnati University
CAST Callisto *s*, Jove *bar*, Diana *s*, Endymion *a*, Mercury *t*, 7 *s*, 2 *a*, *bar*; *satb* chorus of celestial spirits

Calisto is probably Cavalli's best-loved opera today, thanks to Leppard's 1970 revival. In its day, however, it was one of Cavalli's least successful works: attendance at the premiere was meagre, and the opera was shelved after 11 performances. Moreover, Faustini – who was serving as both librettist and impresario – died suddenly in the middle of the run. Whatever the reasons for the opera's initial failure, however, the overall quality of the work is extremely high: as Cavalli's fifteenth opera and his ninth collaboration with Faustini, *Calisto* reveals both men working at the peak of their creative powers.

The libretto fuses together the myth of Jove's seduction of Callisto with that of Diana's affair with Endymion. Although mythological plots were out of fashion at the time, these two stories are laden with potential for love intrigue in the contemporary style: Faustini portrays the gods and goddesses as more or less real humans, with plenty of human flaws.

SYNOPSIS

Act I: As a follower of the virgin goddess Diana, the nymph Callisto is sworn to chastity. To win her, Jove cleverly turns himself into Diana (a deceit devised by Mercury); the naïve Callisto is then obedient to his every command, and overwhelmed by the delight of their encounter. Diana, meanwhile, has fallen in love with the shepherd Endymion, despite her own vows of chastity.

Act II: Juno, suspecting her errant husband is up to his usual tricks, quickly discovers the truth. Diana's secret affair is discovered by Pan, who had long adored her. Pan and his band of satyrs torment Endymion.

Act III: Juno, in revenge, turns Callisto into a bear. In the end, Endymion is rescued by his beloved goddess, and Jove reveals his true identity to Callisto. Although he cannot undo Juno's spell, he elevates Callisto to the stars as the constellation Ursa Major.

Cavalli clearly designed Endymion to be the star of this show: he is awarded some of the most beautiful and substantial numbers (including three out of four accompanied arias) as well as the most moving recitative. Particularly fine is 'Lucidissima face', his salute to the moon goddess Diana. Callisto is another character given to lyricism: as she moves between prim defiance, exultation, despair, confusion, and humble adoration of her great lover, Cavalli captures each moment with a beautifully wrought aria. The final *Poppea*-like duet between Jove and Callisto is one of many delightful ensembles in this work.

The wood deities, Pan, Sylvan, and the Young Satyr, provide *Calisto* with an unusual flavour. These are wild, passionate creatures, yet the Satyr is comic as well. Following a tradition for rustic poetry, Faustini concluded each line with a dactyl. Cavalli followed this rhythm, and intensified the strangeness of these 'half-beasts' by eschewing recitative, writing entirely in melodious arioso style.

RECORDINGS 1. Cotrubas, Kubiak, Baker, Bowman, Cuenod, Gottlieb, Davià, Trama, Glyndebourne Festival Ch, LPO, Leppard, Argo, 1971; 2. Bayo, Pushee, Visse, Keenlyside, Lippi, Concerto Vocale, Jacobs, Harmonia Mundi, 1994
OTHER OPERATIC WORKS *Le nozze di Teti e di Peleo*, 1639; *Gli amori d'Apollo e di Dafne*, 1640; *Didone*, 1641; *La virtù de'strali d'Amore*, 1642; *L'Egisto*, 1643; *L'Ormindo*, 1644; *Doriclea*, 1645; *Giasone*, 1649; *Orimonte*, 1650; *L'Oristeo*, 1651; *Rosinda*, 1651; *Eritrea*, 1652; *Veremonda*

l'amazzone di Aragona, 1652/3; *Orione*, 1653; *Ciro*, 1654 (rev. by Cavalli and Aureli of work by F. Provenzale and G. C. Sorrentino); *Xerse*, [1654/5]; *Statira principessa di Persia*, 1655/?6; *L'Erismena*, 1656; *Artemesia*, 1656/?7; *Hipermestra*, (1654), 1658; *Elena*, 1659/60; *L'Ercole amante*, 1662; *Scipione Affricano*, 1664; *Mutio Scevola*, 1665; *Pompeo magno*, 1666; *Eliogabalo*, (1667/8); 6 other operas, music lost

J.W.B.

Emmanuel Chabrier

Alexis-Emmanuel Chabrier; *b* 18 January 1841, Ambert, Puy-de-Dôme, France; *d* 13 September 1894, Paris

Despite early evidence of his musicality, Chabrier's family insisted on a legal training for him. After graduation he took a civil service post in Paris but continued to compose. Cultivated and gregarious, his circle was more Bohemian than bureaucratic. As well as musicians, he enjoyed the friendship of painters, including Manet (Chabrier was the first owner of his painting *The Bar aux Folies-Bergères*), and poets, including Verlaine with whom he collaborated in the early 1860s on two uncompleted operettas: *Fisch-Ton-Kan* and *Vaucochard et fils 1er*. A grand opera, *Jean Hunyade*, followed in 1867 and was also left unfinished.

His particular musical character began to focus in the late 1870s with a pair of further comic pieces – *L'étoile* (1877) and *Une éducation manquée* (1879). Their apparent frivolity was compatible with a passion for Wagner: indeed the experience of hearing *Tristan* in Munich (1879) precipitated (as well as the wicked set of piano-duet quadrilles on its principal motifs) the decision to resign his civil service post and devote himself entirely to composition. A trip to Spain in 1882 seems almost purposely to have realized Nietzsche's call to purge Bayreuth with the Mediterranean. Its most famous result came the following year with the orchestral rhapsody, *España*.

Other highlights from his brief maturity include the *Dix pièces pittoresques* (1881) for solo piano and the *Trois valses romantiques* for two pianos (1883); the orchestral *Joyeuse marche* (1888); two ravishing works for women's voices and orchestra, *La Sulamite* (1884) (seminal to Debussy's *Damoiselle élue*) and the *Ode à la musique* (1890), as well as a handful of songs to which Ravel and Poulenc were the appreciative heirs. His later operatic ventures, serious as well as comic, run alongside this small but choice output – *Gwendoline, Le roi malgré lui* and the unfinished *Briséïs*. He undoubtedly pinned his most ardent hopes on them and gave them his all – his love was unreciprocated. From the early 1890s his health deteriorated rapidly, and he died aged 53 of general paralysis of the insane.

Chabrier's operatic career shows that, though the comic muse came to him with greater naturalness, there is real substance in his musical make-up to justify his ambition in tackling exalted subjects. And though only *L'étoile* can be called even marginally a repertoire piece, all five add, in different ways, to the range and stature of this complex and greatly underestimated composer.

L'étoile

The Star

Opéra bouffe in three acts (1h 30m)
Libretto by Eugène Leterrier and Albert Vanloo
Composed 1877
PREMIERES 28 November 1877, Théâtre des Bouffes-Parisiens, Paris; US: 18 August 1890, Broadway Theater, New York (arr. Sousa); UK: 7 January 1899, Savoy Theatre, London (arr. Sousa as *The Merry Monarch*); 14 April 1970, John Lewis Theatre, London (as *The Lucky Star*)
CAST Ouf *t*, Siroco *b*, Hérisson de Porc-Epic *bar*, Aloès *ms*, Tapioca *t*,

Lazuli *s* (*travesti* role), Princess Laoula *s*, maids of honour (Oasis, Asphodèle, Youca, Adza, Zinnia, Koukouli) 6 *s*, Mayor and Chief of Police *spoken roles*; *satb* chorus of people, watchmen, courtiers

For all the (to us) charm of Chabrier's first completed opera, it was at first regarded as excessively complicated for an opéra bouffe. It was accused of Wagnerian orchestration (Henri Duparc, who admired it, later called it 'a French *Meistersinger*'), and both the orchestra and the chorus had difficulty preparing their music. Its original run of 40 performances at the Bouffes-Parisiens was regarded as disappointing, and it was not seen again in Paris until 1941.

SYNOPSIS

Act I: Ouf the First roams his city in disguise to find a suitable subject to execute as a 39th birthday treat. Enter, also disguised, Hérisson, his wife Aloès, secretary Tapioca and Laoula, daughter of the neighbouring monarch. Their mission, of which she is unaware, is to marry Laoula to Ouf. The pedlar Lazuli has already fallen for her. Scolded for flirting with the two ladies (who are disguised as each other) he insults Ouf, who thus finds the desired candidate for death by impalement. Just in time Siroco, the king's astrologer, reveals that Ouf's fate and Lazuli's are inextricably linked. Lazuli is escorted with honour into the palace.

Act II: Lazuli longs to escape and join Laoula. Ouf, still unaware of the two women's exchange, furthers the lovers' marriage by having the superfluous husband, Hérisson, imprisoned. Lazuli and Laoula depart happily together, leaving Aloès and Ouf in friendly contact, to the discomposure of Hérisson who has now escaped. This confusion is resolved, and Hérisson orders the pedlar to be shot. Gunfire is heard from the lake. Laoula is brought in, but no Lazuli, so Ouf and Siroco accept that this day will be their last.

Act III: Lazuli, who has swum to safety, returns to overhear Ouf and his astrologer drowning their sorrows in green chartreuse and then, when Hérisson enters, an explanation. The men leave; the girls return. Their sadness is dispelled when Lazuli reveals himself, suffering only from a sneeze. A second elopement is planned. But Ouf returns, anxious to implant an heir without delay (an earlier prediction said he would lose his throne if his successor was not sired before he turned 40). Functionaries arrive to perform the marriage. Then when Siroco's latest erratic stargazing tells Ouf that his death is imminent, he releases Laoula and declares the pedlar his heir. His disappointment is lost in the general rejoicing.

The attractions of this charming piece include the tender *Romance de l'étoile* where Lazuli first declares his love (its words possibly by Verlaine) and the delicious Tickling trio which follows. The words for the gruesome punishment which gives the otherwise kindly king such pleasure can surely be attributed in all their salacious innuendo to Verlaine: 'Le Pal / Est de tous les supplices / Le principal / Et le plus fécond en délices.' (The official librettists changed the last line to 'le moins rempli de délices'.) The note of tenderness is struck again in Act III with Laoula's *Couplets de la rose* (at the moment when all hope of Lazuli has abandoned her for the second time). Parody of Donizetti/Bellini, lurking everywhere, surfaces in the Green Chartreuse duet a little earlier. But the music's main language is French, the accent unmistakably Chabrier's.

RECORDING Alliot-Lugaz, Raphanel, Damonte, Gautier, Le Roux, Bacquier, David, Op Nat de Lyon Ch & O, Gardiner, HMV, 1984

OTHER OPERAS *Fisch-Ton-Kan* (inc.), (1864), 1941; *Vaucochard et fils 1er* (inc.), (1864), 1941; *Jean Hunyade* (inc.), (1867); *Le sabbat* (inc.), (1877); *Une education manqué*, 1879; *Les muscadins* (inc.), (1880); *Gwendoline*, 1886; *Le roi malgré lui*, 1887; *Briséïs*, 1897

R.G.H.

Gustave Charpentier

b 25 June 1860, Dieuze, Meurthe, France; *d* 18 February 1956, Paris

The son of a baker who had moved with his family from his native Lorraine to Tourcoing at the time of the Franco-Prussian War, Charpentier entered the Lille Conservatoire at the age of 15. Success there led to a municipal scholarship to the Paris Conservatoire in 1881. He studied composition with Massenet, and in 1887 won the prestigious Prix de Rome. During his three-year stay in Rome he produced a colourful orchestral suite, *Impressions d'Italie*, which won widespread notice, and a symphonie-drame in four movements, *La vie du poète*, for solo voices, chorus and orchestra, set to his own text. He also began work on the libretto and score for an opera set in working-class Paris and in the village of Montmartre, where he had lived as a student.

After his return to Paris Charpentier's affinities with the poets gave birth to four Baudelaire settings for voice and piano, and three songs for voice and orchestra on texts by Verlaine. Fashionable interest in the 18th century found expression in a *Sérénade à Watteau*, for solo voices, chorus and orchestra. The manuscript score of a second orchestral suite was accidentally destroyed and the work was lost. His *Fête du couronnement de la Muse*, intended for an open-air ceremony in Montmartre organized by the composer himself, was performed in Lille and Paris in 1898. In the meantime Charpentier continued work on his opera, in collaboration with some literary friends, including the writer Saint Pol-Roux. He incorporated the music of the *Fête du couronnement* as the central scene of the third act. After some delay attributable to its unusual nature, the completed work, now named *Louise*, was accepted by the Opéra-Comique, and at its premiere in February 1900 was an immediate success, attracting enthusiastic audiences from all social classes. It made its way round the opera houses of the world, and was conducted by Mahler in both Vienna and New York. It also launched the career of the young Scottish singer Mary Garden, who stepped into the leading role in the course of the eighth performance.

In 1902, in accordance with his philosophy and interests, Charpentier founded the Conservatoire Populaire Mimi Pinson, designed to provide a free education in the arts for the working girls of Paris. Thereafter the cultivation of his image as an artist became a substitute for creative production: the only other work of significance that he wrote was *Julien*, a poème lyrique in four acts and a prologue, again to his own libretto. *Julien*, conceived as a sequel to *Louise*, was performed at the Opéra-Comique in June 1913. The score was largely a reworking of the earlier *Vie du poète*, with additional material borrowed from *Louise*. The later work, which substituted fantasy for realism, shared the limitations but lacked the strengths of its predecessor. In 1913 it was already a relic of a bygone age, and it did not survive its initial productions in Paris, Prague and New York. It may have been some consolation for the composer that in the previous year he was elected to succeed his friend and teacher Massenet as a member of the Académie des Beaux Arts. Other stage projects came to nothing, and the rest of his life was uneventful.

Louise

Roman musical in four acts (five tableaux) (2h 15m)
Libretto by the composer
Composed *c.*1889–96
PREMIERES 2 February 1900, Opéra-Comique, Paris; UK: 18 June 1909, Covent Garden, London; US: 3 January 1908, Manhattan Opera, New York
CAST Louise *s*, Her Mother *ms*, Julien

t, Louise's Father *bar*, 19 female soloists, 20 male soloists; *satb* chorus of Paris citizens, street sellers, workmen, dressmakers, beggars, street urchins, people of Montmartre, Bohemians, etc.

SYNOPSIS

Act I: The action is set in Paris in 1900. Louise, a young dressmaker, is torn between her love for the poet Julien and her attraction to his Bohemian way of life, and her loyalty to her devoted but narrow-minded working-class parents.

Act II: At first Julien fails to persuade Louise to abandon her family for freedom and happiness, but she eventually runs away with him.

Act III: In a carnival atmosphere Louise is crowned Queen of Bohemia and Muse of Montmartre. But her mother interrupts the celebrations and persuades her to return to see her father, who is dangerously ill.

Act IV: Although her father recovers, he is broken by disappointment and bitterness, and her parents use all means to prevent Louise from leaving. But the freedom and pleasures of the life she has tasted are too compelling. After a violent dispute her father orders her from the home. She flees to her lover and his world, and her despairing parent curses the city that has taken her from him.

The attraction of *Louise* lies in its unique amalgam of disparate elements and influences. It owes something to the late 19th-century French school of social realism, as exemplified in the novels of Zola: the portrayal of the bleak existence of the poor and deprived is unadorned. At the same time the pill is sweetened by the romantic portrayal of the Bohemian life of Montmartre, and by the heroine's proclaimed desire, daring in its day, for sensual pleasure. The musical style too is eclectic, with influences ranging from Berlioz and Wagner to Gounod and Massenet, and incorporating a naturalistic treatment of Paris street cries. Some aspects of the work, in particular the Symbolist elements, are undoubtedly dated. But at his best, as in the well-known air 'Depuis le jour' and in the crowd scenes, Charpentier displays a genuine melodic gift and a lively theatrical sense, which have ensured for *Louise* a distinctive place in the repertoire of French opera.

RECORDINGS 1. Monmart, Laroze, Michel, Musy, Paris Op Comique Ch & O, Fournet, Philips, 1956; 2. Cotrubas, Berbié, Domingo, Bacquier, Ambrosian Op Ch, NPO, Prêtre, Sony, 1975; 3. Lott, Pruett, Gorr, Blanc, Op Nat de Belgique Ch & O, Cambreling, Erato, 1982

OTHER OPERATIC WORKS *L'amour au faubourg*, (*c*.1913); *Orphée* (inc.), (1913); *Julien*, 1913

B.D.

Luigi Cherubini

Maria Luigi Carlo Zenobi Salvatore Cherubini; *b* 14 September 1760, Florence; *d* 15 March 1842, Paris

Cherubini's background was typical of that of a talented young Italian musician of his time. The son of a harpsichordist at the Teatro della Pergola in Florence, he showed precocious talent. His intermezzo *Il giuocatore* (1775) demonstrates a thorough mastery of the idiom made popular by Pergolesi's *La serva padrona*. Cherubini came to the attention of the Grand Duke of Tuscany who, in 1778, sent him to study with Giuseppe Sarti, one of the leading composers of the day. In 1780 Cherubini received a commission for a full-length opera seria, *Il Quinto Fabio*, and other operas followed. His early works, generally, show a competence without any particular originality or promise of greater things to come. Like many of his contemporaries he sought fortune abroad and in 1784 accepted an invitation to London where an opera buffa, *La finta principessa* (1785), and an opera seria, *Il Giulio Sabino* (1786), were presented at the King's Theatre in the Haymarket. Neither was successful, due, at least in part, to inadequate performances. So in 1787 Cherubini, encouraged by his compatriot, the violinist and composer Viotti, a leading figure on the French musical scene, took up residence in Paris, which was to become his permanent home.

When Cherubini arrived in the French capital the battle for supremacy at the Opéra between the supporters of Piccinni and Gluck, representing traditional and reform opera respectively, was still raging. Cherubini was engaged by Marmontel, a leading traditionalist, to set his libretto on the theme of Demophoon, a typically classic theme of love, conflict, sacrifice and rescue already familiar in a version by Metastasio. Cherubini's work was weighed against a rival treatment of the same plot by Vogel, a dedicated follower of Gluck, and was found wanting. Not for the last time Cherubini was saddled with an incompetent libretto, and his imperfect understanding of the French language attracted critical condemnation. But despite its uncertainties *Démophoön* foreshadows Cherubini's mature style in its richly orchestrated accompaniments, its effective choral writing, and the sustained power of the dramatic conclusion.

Cherubini's association with Viotti and the queen's perfumer, Léonard, in forming a new opera company at the Théâtre de Monsieur, intended principally for the promotion of imported Italian opera buffa, established his position as an important influence in the musical life of Paris. The new theatre opened to acclaim in January 1789. With the advent of the Revolution the directors of the company realized that a change of name and of artistic policy was desirable. They commissioned a new building in the rue Feydeau, and the Théâtre Feydeau, as it came to be known, played a prominent role in the theatrical life of Paris throughout the turbulent final decade of the century. The new politically minded audiences rejected traditional opera on Classical themes (unless the themes were consonant with the principles of Republicanism), looking instead for subjects of contemporary relevance, with heroic deeds, highly charged action, exotic settings and cataclysmic climaxes. A vehicle for the new style was to hand in opéra comique, a medium combining music with spoken dialogue, whose flexible possibilities had already been explored by Grétry and his contemporaries in the preceding decades. Cherubini adapted his style at once to this genre. His solidly grounded musical training (not always matched by that of his French contemporaries), a symphonic mode of thinking, and an imaginative command of orchestral colour and texture served him well. His first attempt, *Lodoïska*, a rescue opera set in Poland, won instant acclaim. First performed in 1791, it remained the longest-running opera of the decade. Its successor, *Eliza*, written at the height of the Terror in 1794, is a romantic story set in the Swiss Alps. Cherubini's next work, *Médée*, of 1797, took up in the more liberal post-revolutionary period a central Classical legend, in a score of almost unparalleled intensity. In *Les deux journées*, which opened the new century in January 1800, the composer adopted a simpler idiom to proclaim a message of social and political reconciliation.

This opera, though not his last, marked the apogee of Cherubini's theatrical career. In 1803 his opéra-ballet *Anacréon* was staged at the Opéra. Its failure was attributed by the composer to a cabal; but it suffers from an inane plot, which was not rescued by some excellent dance music, a dramatic storm and a sparkling overture much admired by Weber. However, an extended season of his earlier works performed in Vienna the previous year had won him the admiration and applause of the Viennese public, not least among them Beethoven, and Cherubini wrote his next opera, *Faniska* (1806), to a commission for Vienna. This was a rescue opera in the tradition of *Lodoïska* on a text by Beethoven's librettist Sonnleithner. It was initially well received by all, including the aged Haydn, who warmly embraced the composer at the premiere; but the opera did not establish itself. Nor did his next full-length opera, *Les abencérages* (1813), based on a medieval Spanish theme, despite the colour and opulence of the score.

The anachronistic *Ali-Baba*, performed 20 years later, was a reworking of much earlier material. It was a total failure, exciting the gleeful derision of Berlioz. Meanwhile the disillusioned Cherubini had turned to church music; the two settings of the Requiem Mass are among his best works. He had been associated with the National Conservatoire since its creation in 1795, and in 1822 was appointed director. Thereafter administrative and public duties limited his musical output. By the time of his death in 1842 his operas had long since disappeared from the French stage, as the young Wagner, writing from Paris in the previous year, remarked with caustic disapproval.

Cherubini's influence on the course of opera in his adopted country after 1800 was slight. But in the German-speaking countries it was more important. *Lodoïska* and *Les deux journées* were widely performed in Europe in the early years of the new century. A season of the four principal operas staged in Vienna in 1802 had a profound effect on Beethoven, who regarded Cherubini as his greatest contemporary – one not confined to his obvious indebtedness to Cherubini in *Fidelio*. Weber, another great admirer, also drew inspiration from him, notably in *Der Freischütz*. It is difficult, however, to arrive at an overall assessment of Cherubini's operatic achievement because of the comparative neglect from which his work has suffered.

Médée

Medea

Opera in three acts (2h 15m)
Libretto by François-Benoît Hoffman, after the tragedy by Pierre Corneille (1635)
PREMIERES 13 March 1797, Théâtre Feydeau, Paris; UK: 6 June 1865, Her Majesty's Theatre, London (in Italian, with recitatives by Luigi Arditi); US: 8 November 1955, New York (concert); 7 July 1973, State Theater, New York (stage); UK: original version: 28 July 1984, Opera House, Buxton
CAST Médée *s*, Dircé *s*, Néris *ms*, Jason *t*, Créon *b*, Captain of the Guard *bar*, 2 servants *s*, *ms*; 2 children *silent*; *satb* chorus of servants of Dircé, Argonauts, priests, warriors, people of Corinth

Médée, by virtue of its dramatic and musical range and intensity, is Cherubini's masterpiece. It is also the only work out of the two thousand or so theatrical productions during the revolutionary decade in France to maintain a place in the repertoire, albeit until recently in a bowdlerized version. It has links with the pre-revolutionary classical opera of Gluck and his contemporaries and immediate successors. But in other respects it anticipates the 19th-century conception of tragic opera. The libretto focuses throughout on the personality and situation of the tormented sorceress, torn between her hatred of Jason, who has deserted and betrayed her, and her love for her children, who have been taken from her. The symphonic treatment of the accompaniment heightens the emotional tension, as do the enormous demands on the technique and stamina of the leading role. The obligatory final catastrophe, the immolation of the children and the destruction of the temple, remains unsurpassed in its dramatic and psychological power. Although coolly received at its premiere, *Médée* later won the admiration of Beethoven, Weber, Schumann, Wagner and Brahms.

SYNOPSIS

Act I: The action takes place at Corinth. Outside the palace of King Créon, preparations are in train for the wedding of the king's daughter Dircé to Jason, who stole the Golden Fleece from Colchis, with the aid of the sorceress Médée. Médée betrayed her family and people to help him, and subsequently bore him two children, before he abandoned her. Dircé is fearful of Médée's wrath. Médée appears, demands that Jason return to her and is rebuffed. She curses Jason and swears a terrible vengeance.

Act II: Inside the palace Médée is in despair. Her servant Néris urges her to leave. Créon appears and banishes her from the city. Médée, whose schemes of vengeance are taking shape, begs to be allowed to spend a last day with her children. Créon grants her request. Apparently more calm, she asks Néris to take to Dircé two wedding gifts, a cloak and a diadem given to her by Apollo.

Act III: Between the palace and a temple. Néris brings the children out of the palace to Médée, who embraces them. Sounds of lamentation come from the palace. The bride is dead, poisoned by Médée's gifts. The enraged populace storms out, seeking revenge. Médée, Néris and the children take refuge in the temple. Soon a horrified Néris re-emerges, followed by Médée, brandishing the bloodstained knife with which she has slain her sons, and attended by Furies. Jason dies, to her imprecations. The temple is consumed by fire, and Médée and her Furies disappear in the flames.

The role of Médée was written for a singer of quite exceptional gifts, Mme Scio, principal soprano at the Théâtre Feydeau. The range and sustained power necessary to fulfil the requirements of the part ensure that the singer increasingly dominates the action, from her anticipated first appearance in the middle of Act I, to her virtually continuous presence in the final act, in which the interruption of spoken dialogue is reduced to a minimum. The other principals are perceived in relation to the sorceress and have limited scope; they are none the less clearly delineated in musical terms. The marches in the first two acts are fine examples of their type. The mood of each act is established by the preceding orchestral music. The turbulent one-section overture, in F minor, bears some striking resemblances to the later *Egmont* overture of Beethoven (1810).

RECORDINGS 1. Callas, Scotto, Pirazzini, Picchi, Modesti, La Scala Ch & O, Serafin, EMI, 1957 (in Italian); 2. Tamar, Ciofi, Damonte, Lombardo, Courtis, Sluk CCh of Bratislava, International O of Italian Op, Fournillier, Nuova Era, 1995

OTHER OPERATIC WORKS *Il giuocatore* (intermezzo, 1775); untitled intermezzo, 1778; *Il Quinto Fabio* (orig. lost), 1779, rev. 1783; *Armida abbandonata*, 1782; *Mesenzio re d'Etruria*, 1782; *Lo sposo di tre e marito di nessuna*, 1783; *Olimpiade*, (c.1783); *L'Alessandro nell'Indie*, 1784; *L'Idalide*, 1784; *Demetrio*, 1785; *Il Giulio Sabino*, 1786; *Ifigenia in Aulide*, 1788; *Démophoön*, 1788; *La Molinarella*, 1789; *Lodoïska*, 1791; *Eliza, ou le voyage aux glaciers de Mont St Bernard*, 1794; *L'hôtellerie portugaise*, 1798; *La punition*, 1799; *La prisonnière*, 1799; *Les deux journées, ou Le porteur d'eau*, 1800; *Epicure*, 1800 (coll. with Méhul); *Anacréon, ou L'amour fugitif*, 1803; *Achille à Scyros*, 1804; *Faniska*, 1806; *Pigmalione*, 1809; *Il crescendo*, 1810; *Les abencérages, ou L'étendard de Grenade*, 1813; *Ali-Baba, ou Les quarante voleurs*, 1833; 6 others lost

B.D.

Francesco Cilea

b 23 July 1866, Palmi, Italy;
d 20 November 1950, Varazze, Italy

Cilea is remembered principally for his opera *Adriana Lecouvreur* and certain arias from *L'arlesiana*. Continued success in the opera house eluded him, and he devoted much of his time to teaching, finally becoming the director of the Naples Conservatory, where he had been a student (1881–9). His first opera, *Gina*, was premiered when he was still enrolled there and received enough attention to win him a contract with the publishing house of Sonzogno. His second, *La Tilda* (1892), an overwrought work seeking to capitalize on the vogue for verismo subjects, was a setback.

Better fortune attended *L'arlesiana* (1897), where Caruso's success with Federico's 'Lament' helped establish Cilea as a relatively prominent member of his generation of Italian composers. Yet when this opera failed to maintain its initial success, Cilea began to rework it and over the next 40 years he made a number of modifications.

Cilea reached the high point of his career with *Adriana Lecouvreur* (1902), but failed to repeat its success with his remaining operas. Of these, *Gloria* was premiered at La Scala under Toscanini (1907) but survived for only two performances. In 1932 Cilea revised it for Naples, but without happier results. His last opera, *Il matrimonio selvaggio*, was not performed.

Cilea possessed an undeniable melodic gift, as 'Io sono l'umile ancella' from *Adriana Lecouvreur* shows, but his powers of invention were limited. Brief motivic ideas recur but are rarely developed into a cohesive musical fabric. His operas give the overall impression that the musical materials have been stretched perilously thin.

Adriana Lecouvreur

Opera in four acts (2h 15m)
Libretto by Arturo Colautti, after the play *Adrienne Lecouvreur* by Eugène Scribe and Ernest Legouvé (1849)
Composed 1901–2
PREMIERES 6 November 1902, Teatro Lirico, Milan; UK: 8 November 1904, Covent Garden, London; US: 5 January 1907, French Opera House, New Orleans
CAST Adriana Lecouvreur *s*, Maurizio *t*, Prince de Bouillon *b*, L'abate di Chazeuil *bar*, Quinault *b*, Poisson *t*, Princess de Bouillon *ms*, Mlla Jouvenot *s*, Mlla Dangeville *ms*, Michonnet *bar*, Major Domo *t*; 4 acted roles; *satb* chorus of ladies, gentlemen, stagehands, servants; ballet

The plot is melodramatic fiction, but the title character (and some of the others) were real people: Adrienne Lecouvreur (1692–1730) was a star actress at the Comédie Française in Paris. The libretto is quite condensed and rife with unexplained allusions. During the rehearsal period, Cilea had tightened up the score, omitting some episodes that would have rendered the complex plot easier to follow.

SYNOPSIS

Act I: In the green room of the Comédie, Adriana tells the stage manager Michonnet, who loves her faithfully, that she is enamoured of Maurizio (who is, unknown to her, Comte de Saxe and pretender to the throne of Poland). Adriana and Maurizio meet briefly and, before she leaves to perform onstage, she gives him a bouquet of violets as a memento. Later, the Prince de Bouillon intercepts a note asking Maurizio for a meeting; he assumes the note is from Maurizio's mistress, the actress Duclos, but it is in fact written by his own wife. The Prince invites the whole company to his house for a post-theatre party.

Act II: In a fever of jealous anticipation the princess awaits her rendezvous with Maurizio. When he arrives, she is obsessed with the idea that he loves another woman; to placate her Maurizio gives her the violets. When the guests are heard arriving, the princess hides in an inner room. Later, Adriana, at Maurizio's request, helps her to leave under cover of darkness, but, while neither is aware of the other's identity, each suspects the other of being her rival.

Act III: At a sumptuous party given by the princess, she identifies Adriana's voice as that of her suspected rival and shows her the fading bouquet. In retaliation, the actress recites a scene from Racine's *Phèdre*, thereby making pointed allusions to the princess's promiscuity, an insult the princess vows to avenge.

Act IV: It is Adriana's name-day, and among the presents she receives is a mysterious box containing violets, which she mistakenly assumes is a token of farewell from Maurizio. He arrives, delighted to see her, but she is dying, killed by the violets that the princess has soaked in poison.

Though not consistently strong musically, *Adriana* continues to maintain itself on the fringes of the repertoire principally because it contains a challenging dramatic soprano role that is not particularly taxing on the upper register.

RECORDINGS 1. Scotto, Obraztsova, Domingo, Milnes, Ambrosian Op Ch, Philharmonia O, Levine, CBS, 1977; 2. Sutherland, Ciurca, Bergonzi, Nucci, WNO Ch & O, Bonynge, Decca, 1988
OTHER OPERAS *Gina*, 1889; *La Tilda*, 1892; *L'arlesiana*, 1897; *Gloria*, 1907; *Il matrimonio selvaggio*, (1909)

W.A.

Domenico Cimarosa

Domenico Nicola Cimarosa [Cimmarosa]; *b* 17 December 1749, Aversa, Italy; *d* 11 January 1801, Venice

Together with Paisiello, Cimarosa was the most popular opera composer in the late 18th century. He produced some 60 opere buffe and 20 opere serie, many of which quickly entered the repertoire of opera houses throughout Europe.

Cimarosa studied with Pietro Antonio Gallo in Naples at the Conservatorio di S. Maria di Loreto, and later with the leading opera composer Niccolò Piccinni. His first opera, *Le stravaganze del conte*, was premiered in Naples in Carnival 1772. He produced a number of comic operas for the Teatro dei Fiorentini, Naples, and (from 1778) for Rome; his first major triumph was *L'italiana in Londra* (1778). He was appointed supernumerary organist of the Neapolitan royal chamber in November 1779, and by the early 1780s he was also a visiting maestro at the Ospedaletto di SS. Giovanni e Paolo, Venice. In 1787 Cimarosa moved to St Petersburg to replace Giuseppe Sarti as maestro di cappella to Empress Catherine II (a post held earlier by Paisiello). His period in Russia was an unhappy one – the court theatre was under severe financial difficulties and Catherine seems to have disliked Cimarosa's music – and when his contract expired in 1791 he moved to Vienna. Emperor Leopold II (whom Cimarosa had known as Grand Duke Leopold of Tuscany) appointed him kapellmeister in place of Antonio Salieri, and Cimarosa's most successful opera, *Il matrimonio segreto*, was staged at the court theatre on 7 February 1792.

The death of Leopold II some three weeks later left Cimarosa unemployed, and he returned to Italy in 1793. In 1796, he was appointed first organist to Ferdinand IV, King of Naples, and he continued to write operas for Naples, Rome and Venice. In 1799 the composer came under a political cloud for espousing the libertarian cause of the short-lived 'Parthenopean Republic'. He was arrested and threatened with execution, although after four months in prison the sentence was commuted to exile. Cimarosa moved to Venice, where he died of stomach cancer perhaps contracted during his imprisonment (although some suspected poison). His last opera, *Artemisia*, was left incomplete on his death.

Cimarosa's output includes instrumental works, sacred music, oratorios and cantatas, but operas predominate. His facility as a composer was legendary, but doubtless he also made extensive reuse of material (which has not yet been fully studied) and relied on assistants (for example, to compose recitatives). His first Neapolitan period focused on opera buffa – Cimarosa's first opera seria, *Cajo Mario*, dates from 1780 – and, with some notable exceptions (including *Gli Orazi ed i Curiazi*, 1796), he remained most sympathetic to the comic style. His opere buffe (encompassing intermezzi, farse, commedie per musica and dramme giocose) gradually adopted a standard two-act format, balancing tuneful arias with action ensembles. Their popularity is documented by the large number of performances and adaptations: the resulting spread of manuscript and printed sources remains a scholarly minefield. Cimarosa's style was much admired by Goethe, Stendhal (who noted his 'glittering array of comic verve, of passion, strength and gaiety'), and Hanslick; many compared him (often favourably) with Mozart. But the two composers came from very different operatic traditions, and Cimarosa's significance lies in his development of a Neapolitan tradition following on from Piccinni that eventually led, through Paisiello, to Rossini.

Il matrimonio segreto

The Secret Marriage

Dramma giocoso in two acts (3h)
Libretto by Giovanni Bertati, after *The Clandestine Marriage* by George Colman and David Garrick (1766)
PREMIERES 7 February 1792, Burgtheater, Vienna; UK: 11 January 1794, King's Theatre, Haymarket, London (libretto rev. Lorenzo da Ponte); US: 4 January 1834, Italian Opera House, New York; UK: 17 March 1959, St Pancras Town Hall, London
CAST Geronimo *b*, Elisetta *ms*, Carolina *s*, Fidalma *c*, Count Robinson *b*, Paolino *t*

Cimarosa's best-known opera, so popular that, at its premiere, Emperor Leopold II reputedly ordered that a second performance take place after dinner – the longest encore in operatic history. In the two years after its premiere, the opera was widely performed in Europe and translated into several languages. Cimarosa later claimed that it was not his best work: he preferred *Artemisia regina di Caria*. But Verdi called it a 'true musical comedy, which has everything an opera buffa should', and Hanslick proclaimed it 'full of sunshine'.

SYNOPSIS

Act I: Geronimo, a wealthy, albeit deaf, Bolognese merchant, has two daughters, Elisetta and Carolina: their household is run by his sister, Fidalma. Carolina is secretly married to Paolino, who is loved by Fidalma. Count Robinson arrives to wed Elisetta but falls for Carolina, who fails to convince him of her many faults. Geronimo, delighted at the count's supposed interest in Elisetta, organizes a banquet in his honour, but remains confused by the shenanigans.

Act II: Geronimo and the count agree a marriage with Carolina; Paolino goes to Fidalma for help, but she misinterprets his words as a proposal of marriage, and he faints into her arms. Carolina enters inopportunely and takes some convincing of Paolino's love for her. The count seeks to estrange Elisetta by painting himself as an ogre; she and Fidalma respond by trying to send Carolina to a convent. Paolino and Carolina decide to run away but are caught by Elisetta, who summons the household. The assumption is that the man with Carolina is the count, but he makes a surprise entrance from another room (shades here of the Countess in Act IV of *Le nozze di Figaro*), and Paolino and Carolina eventually confess. The count agrees to marry Elisetta, and all ends happily.

While some elements of the opera's music are Mozartian, others anticipate the works of Rossini – for instance, the patter of fast words sung on a repeated note, comic nonsense sounds ('ba ba ba') and the overall structure of the work, which, in keeping with the latest developments in Italian opera, contains an extended finale and numerous ensembles. The first performance included Mozart's 'Al desio di chi t'adora' (K. 577; written for the 1789 revival of *Figaro*) and a 'Scena Livornese', alluding to Cimarosa's meeting with Leopold II as Grand Duke of Tuscany when the composer was en route to St Petersburg. Both are now omitted.

RECORDINGS 1. Sciutti, Ratti, Stignani, Alva, Badioli, Calabrese, La Piccola Scala O, Sanzogno, Columbia, 1955; 2. Patterson, J. Williams, Banditelli, Matteuzzi, Eastern Netherlands O, Bellini, Arts, 1991

OTHER OPERAS *Le stravaganze del conte*, 1772 (Act III also given separately as *Le magie di Merlina e Zoroastro*); *La finta parigina*, 1773; *I sdegni per amore*, 1776; *I matrimoni in ballo*, 1776, (rev. as Act III of *Il credulo*, 1786); *La frascatana nobile* (*La finta frascatana*), 1776; *I tre amanti*, 1777, (rev. as *Le gare degl'amanti*, 1783); *Il fanatico per gli antichi romani*, 1777; *L'Armida immaginaria*, 1777; *Gli amanti comici, o sia La famiglia in scompiglio*, ?1778, (rev. 1796; as *Il matrimonio in commedia*, 1797; as *La famiglia stravagante, ovvero Gli amanti comici*, 1798); *Il ritorno di Don Calandrino*, 1778, (rev. as *Armidoro e Laurina*, 1783); *Le stravaganze d'amore*, 1778; *L'italiana in Londra*, 1778; *Il matrimonio per raggiro* (*La donna bizzarra*), ?1779, (rev. 1802), related to *L'apprensivo raggirato*, 1798; *L'infedeltà fedele*, 1779; *Le donne rivali*, 1780, (rev. as *Le due rivali*, 1791); *Caio Mario*, 1780; *I finti nobili*, 1780; *Il falegname*, 1780, (rev. as *L'artista*, 1789); *Il capriccio drammatico*, ?1781, related to *L'impresario in angustie*, 1786, (rev. da Ponte, 1794); *Il pittor parigino*, 1781, (rev. as *Il barone burlato*, 1784; as *Le brame deluse*, 1787; as *Der Onkel aus Amsterdam*, 1796); *Alessandro nell'Indie*, 1781; *L'amante combattuto dalle donne di punto*, 1781, (rev. as *La biondolina*, 1781; as *La giardiniera fortunata*, 1805); *Giunio Bruto*, 1781; *Giannina e Bernadone*, 1781; *Il convito*, 1782, (rev. as *Der Schmaus*, 1784); *L'amor costante*, 1782, (rev. as *Giulietta ed Armidoro*, 1790); *L'eroe cinese*, 1782; *La ballerina amante*, 1782, (rev. as *L'amante ridicolo*, 1789); *La Circe*, 1783; *I due baroni di Rocca Azzurra*, 1783; *La villana riconosciuta*, 1783, (rev. as *La villanella rapita*, 1793); *Oreste*, 1783; *Chi dell'altrui si veste presto si spoglia*, 1783, (rev. as *Nina e Martuffo*, 1825); *I matrimoni impensati* (*La bella greca*), 1784; *L'apparenza inganna, o sia La villeggiatura*, 1784; *La vanità delusa* (*Il mercato di Malmantile*), 1784; *L'Olimpiade*, 1784; *I due supposti conti, ossia Lo sposo senza moglie*, 1784, (rev. as *Lo sposo ridicolo*, 1786); *Artaserse*, 1784; *Il marito disperato* (*Il marito geloso*), 1785, (rev. as *Die bestrafte Eifersucht*, 1794; as *L'amante disperato*, 1795); *La donna sempre al suo peggior s'appiglia*, 1785; *Il credulo*, 1786, (see *I matrimoni in ballo*, 1776; rev. as *Il credulo deluso*, 1791); *Le trame deluse*, 1786, (rev. as *L'amor contrastato*, 1788; as *Li raggiri scoperti*, 1799); *L'impresario in angustie*, 1786; *Volodimiro*, 1787; *Il fanatico burlato*, 1787, (rev. as *Der adelsüchtige Bürger*, 1791); *La felicità inaspettata*, 1788; *La vergine del sole*, ?1788; *La Cleopatra*, 1789; *Amor rende sagace*, 1793, related to *Le astuzie femminili*, 1794; *I traci amanti*, 1793, (rev. as *Il padre alla moda, ossia Lo sbarco di Mustanzir Bassà*, 1795; as *Gli turchi amanti*, 1796); *Le astuzie femminili*, 1794; *Penelope*, 1795; *Le nozze in garbuglio*, 1795; *L'impegno superato*, 1795; *La finta ammalata*, 1796; *I nemici generosi*, 1796, (rev. as *Il duello per complimento*, 1797); *Gli Orazi ed I Curiazi*, 1796; *Achille all'assedio di Troia*, 1797, related to *Gli Orazi ed i Curiazi*, 1797; *L'imprudente fortunato*, 1797; *Artemisia regina di Caria*, 1797; *L'apprensivo raggirato*, 1798; *Il secreto*, 1798; *L'intrigo della lettera*, 1798; *Artemisia* (inc.), 1801; 26 other undated or doubtful operas

T.C.

Luigi Dallapiccola

b 3 February 1904, Pisino d'Istria, Slovenija; *d* 19 February 1975, Florence, Italy

Dallapiccola was the son of an Istrian schoolmaster, and his teenage education was disrupted when his father's school was closed by the Austrian authorities and the family was interned at Graz. Only at the close of the First World War, when Istria was ceded to Italy, was the family able to return to Pisino. In 1922 Dallapiccola moved to Florence, which was to be his home for the rest of his life. He studied at the conservatory there, where in 1934 he became professor of piano as a second study – a post that he held until his retirement. His compositions of the late 1930s and 1940s showed first a tentative, and then an increasingly convinced use of serial techniques, and after the Second World War Dallapiccola emerged as the most authoritative advocate of that tradition in Italy.

In his theatrical work, Dallapiccola was heir to a theatre of philosophical challenge perhaps most strikingly exemplified in Busoni's *Doktor Faust*. He sought to infuse the Italian lyric tradition with a distinctive complexity of musical and dramatic thought and, in so doing, markedly influenced a younger generation of post-war composers, particularly with *Il prigioniero*, whose first performances in 1949 and 1950 were an important index of reviving cultural fortunes in Italy.

Il prigioniero

The Prisoner

[Opera in] a prologue and one act (55m)
Libretto by the composer, after the story *La torture par l'espérance* from *Nouveaux contes cruels* by Count Philippe-Auguste Villiers de l'Isle-Adam (1888), with additions after the novel *La légende d'Ulenspiegel* by Charles de Coster (1868) and other sources
Composed 1944–8
PREMIERES 1 December 1949, RAI broadcast; 20 May 1950, Teatro Comunale, Florence; US: 15 March 1951, Juilliard School of Music, New York; UK: 27 July 1959, Sadler's Wells, London

Dallapiccola first considered the theatrical potential of Villiers de l'Isle-Adam's story in 1939, at the instigation of his Jewish wife, Laura. That story is a more specific study of anti-Semitic persecution than is the libretto that Dallapiccola derived from it, for it centres on a rabbi tortured by the Inquisition in Saragossa. Drawing his imagery from de Coster's extraordinary epic of Flemish defiance to Spanish rule, *La légende d'Ulenspiegel*, Dallapiccola substituted for the rabbi an imprisoned Flemish freedom fighter, simply designated the Prisoner. Introducing two new figures, the Mother and the Gaoler, he fleshed out the spare simplicity of Villiers de l'Isle-Adam's narration so as to emphasize the theme of resistance to tyranny (embodied in the opera in the brooding but unseen presence of Philip II).

Dallapiccola's ground plan is symmetrical. The Prisoner's Mother enters before the curtain to sing a prologue, recounting her nightly dream of Philip II. She is engulfed by the first choral intermezzo, symbolizing the power of the Inquisition. The three main scenes follow: the Mother visits the Prisoner – as she rightly guesses – for the last time. Next comes the central scene of the Prisoner's temptation by the 'Gaoler' (Dallapiccola's point of departure when setting to work on the music). The Gaoler addresses him as *fratello* ('brother'), urges him to hope, and tells of a Flemish uprising. He departs, leaving the Prisoner's door unlocked. The third scene charts his fearful progress as, taking advantage of this opportunity, he makes his way along seemingly endless subterranean corridors: miraculously, two passing monks fail to notice him. A second choral intermezzo reasserts the presence of the Inquisition with thunderous force. Finally, in a scene that balances the first of the opera, the Prisoner emerges into a nocturnal garden. Ecstatic beneath the night sky, the Prisoner advances to embrace a great cedar tree. Arms shoot out from the tree, and a familiar voice intones 'fratello': it is the Grand Inquisitor who, posing as a gaoler, has put the Prisoner to the ultimate torture: that of hope. As a fire begins to flicker in the background, he leads him towards it.

The work is knit together by three different note rows, each used thematically, and by short motifs in part derived from them. The first is associated with the Prisoner's prayer, 'Signore, aiutarmi a camminare' ('Lord, help me to walk'), the second with hope, and thus with the 'fratello' motif that announces the insidious presence of the 'Gaoler'. The third row, rich in tonal associations, is that of freedom on which the Gaoler's 'aria in three strophes' depicting the revolt in Flanders is based. A further motif depicts Roelandt, the great bell of Ghent (destroyed by Philip II's father, Charles V), which the Prisoner is induced to believe may yet ring again. As he makes his way down the corridor, Dallapiccola summarizes his mental state by three ricercars: one on the prayer note row, one on the 'fratello' motif and one on the 'Roelandt' motif. Such associations and interactions are typical of the opera: in consequence, the score repays repeated listening.

RECORDING Bryn-Julson, Haskin, Hynninen, Swedish RCh & SO, Salonen, Sony, 1995
OTHER OPERATIC WORKS *Volo di notte*, 1940; *Job*, 1950; *Ulisse*, 1968

D.O.-S.

Peter Maxwell Davies

(Sir) Peter Maxwell Davies;
b 8 September 1934, Manchester, England

Davies has said that he was set on the path to becoming a composer when, at the age of four, he was taken to a Gilbert and Sullivan operetta, and he has written more for the theatre than any other leading composer of his generation: operas, ballets, school operas, and small-scale works of 'music theatre', a genre he helped establish in the late 1960s. Perhaps the importance to him of the stage springs out of his concern with hypocrisy and betrayal, both intellectual and moral: each of his major dramatic works is concerned with an individual's search for personal authenticity in a mirror world of truth and falsehood, and the theatre – where real people assume roles, where musical thought can be traduced by stage action and vice versa – provides the ideal location for his questioning, ironical imagination.

The musical roots of that imagination

lie in the great Austro-German tradition, which Davies absorbed as a boy, and in the alternatives of medieval, Indian and modern music, which he encountered as a student in Manchester, where he was part of an extraordinary group of young musicians who interested themselves in the latest music of Boulez, Stockhausen and Nono (other members of the group included Birtwistle and Goehr). In essence his musical world was established by the mid-1950s. It depended on an equivalence between medieval and serial techniques, on a Schoenbergian reverence for developing form and on a keenness to upset convention by means of complex rhythms, wild sonorities and harmonic double-thought. The idea for the opera *Taverner* came while he was still a student, though he did not begin the score until 1962, meanwhile concerning himself mostly with instrumental pieces and with school music (associated with his time as music master at Cirencester Grammar School, 1959–62).

While working on *Taverner* he found his music becoming more and more extravagant, its ironies exploding into manifest parody: plainsong themes could be converted into Victorian hymns or foxtrots; any and every musical intention could be mocked and guyed. It was out of this deeply unsettled and unsettling time that offshoots from the opera began to appear as pieces of music theatre, extending the debate about how a man can separate himself (or how a musical idea can separate itself) from masquerades, imitations, forced roles and madness. In order to put on their music-theatre pieces, Davies and Birtwistle founded the Pierrot Players in 1967 (the group continued, after Birtwistle's departure, as The Fires of London, 1970–87), and for that ensemble – consisting of the forces of Schoenberg's *Pierrot lunaire* together with a percussionist – Davies produced a host of dramatic works, chamber pieces and arrangements (or in some cases travesties).

In the early 1970s Davies settled in an isolated croft on the Orkney island of Hoy, and the fierce seascapes and stark landscapes of the islands effected an immediate change in his musical language. Expressionist extremes were abandoned and the transformational processes were further refined, making consistent use of 'magic squares'. He founded the St Magnus Festival in 1977, and much of his work in that decade, including the chamber operas *The Martyrdom of St Magnus* and *The Lighthouse* (which has become one of the most frequently performed of all late-20th-century operas), was informed by Orcadian history and literature, especially the works of George Mackay Brown. The composition of his First Symphony (1976) signalled another change of emphasis in Davies's output. For the next two decades his output was increasingly dominated by orchestral works, including eight symphonies (the last of them, *Antarctic Symphony*, was premiered in 2001) and the series of ten *Strathclyde Concertos* (1986–96), composed for the principals of the Scottish Chamber Orchestra – one of the orchestras that Davies conducted regularly in the 1980s and 1990s.

Davies composed a series of educational works for the communities on Orkney – he moved to another island, Sanday, in 1999 – but other forays into music theatre became less and less frequent. Though the quasi-autobiographical *Resurrection* harked back to the world of expressionism and parody of the 1960s, the ever-increasing fluency of his language tended to lay less emphasis on dramatic potency and much more on musical process and thematic transformations. Nevertheless, *The Doctor of Myddfai*, his first full-length opera since *Taverner*, appeared in 1996 and the 'dramatic sonata' *Mr Emmet Takes a Walk* in 2000, after which Davies announced that he would write no more theatre works.

In 2004 Davies was created Master of the Queen's Music, a post he agreed to hold for a maximum of ten years.

The Lighthouse

Chamber opera in one act with prologue (1h 15m)
Libretto by the composer
Composed 1979
PREMIERES 2 September 1980, Moray House Gymnasium, Edinburgh; US: 1 November 1983, Boston Shakespeare Company, Boston
CAST Officer 1/Sandy *t*, Officer 2/Blazes *bar*, Officer 3/Arthur *b*

The work is scored for very similar forces to those used in *The Martyrdom of St Magnus*, but the pageantry of that work is replaced by atmospheric grimness, by evocations of the cold northern sea at night and by parodies that heighten the passions and nightmares of the characters.

The prologue is set at a court of inquiry into the disappearance of three lighthouse keepers from their station. Questions are posed by solo horn, which may sound from the audience, and three officers give answer. Gradually they move from straight testimony into fantastical imaginings of evil during a flashback to the lighthouse; but then we snap back to the courtroom.

In the main act the three singers become the vanished keepers. They have been together for months, long enough to know each other well and to know how to taunt each other: their relationship is highly unstable. To reduce the tension they sing songs. Blazes begins with a rough ballad of street violence, accompanied by violin and banjo; Sandy, with cello and upright piano, sings of making love; and Arthur, with brass and clarinet, belts out a hymn. But the songs serve only to resurrect in their minds ghosts from the past, and as fog descends each of them becomes convinced that he is being claimed by the Beast. They prepare to meet its dazzling eyes, which become the lights of the relief vessel, and the three men reappear as officers, finding at the lighthouse only an infestation of rats. They leave, and at the end the last hours of the three keepers begin to play over again.

RECORDING Mackie, Comboy, Keyte, BBC PO, Maxwell Davies, Collins, 1994
OTHER OPERAS *Taverner*, 1972; *The Martyrdom of St Magnus*, 1977; *Resurrection*, 1988; *The Doctor of Myddfai*, 1996; **OTHER MUSIC-THEATRE WORKS** *Notre Dame des Fleurs* (mini-opera), (1966) 1973; *Eight Songs for a Mad King*, 1969; *Blind Man's Buff*, 1972; *Miss Donnithorne's Maggot*, 1974; *Le jongleur de Notre Dame*, 1978; *The No. 11 Bus*, 1984; *Mr Emmet Takes a Walk*, 2000; **CHILDREN'S OPERAS** *The Two Fiddlers*, 1978; *Cinderella*, 1980; **CHILDREN'S MUSIC-THEATRE WORKS** *The Rainbow*, 1981; *Jupiter Landing*, 1989; *The Great Bank Robbery*, 1989; *Dinosaur at Large*, 1989; *Dangerous Errand*, 1990; *The Spiders' Revenge*, 1991; *A Selkie Tale*, 1992

P.A.G.

Claude Debussy

Achille-Claude Debussy; *b* 22 August 1862, St Germain-en-Laye, nr Paris; *d* 25 March 1918, Paris

The son of a suburban Parisian shopkeeper who was imprisoned for his part in the Commune of 1871, Debussy studied piano (with Verlaine's mother-in-law, Mme Mauté, and later at the Conservatoire) and turned seriously to composition only when hopes of a virtuoso career receded in the late 1870s. Though to this day best known for his piano and orchestral music, and even though he completed only one opera, he was almost continuously preoccupied with music for the theatre in some form from the early 1880s until shortly before he died. Very few of these projects came to fruition, but they show that Debussy was fascinated by musical theatre and, under favourable conditions, a brilliant exponent of it. His single opera and the one purpose-made ballet of which he composed and orchestrated every note, *Jeux* (1912–13), are both masterpieces. Many other projects, on the other hand, were never even sketched, partly because he perhaps had no real intention of composing them, partly because of his intense self-criticism and partly because other work intervened or circumstances changed. For French composers, the theatre has always been a much stronger presence than for their German or British colleagues, and to some extent Debussy's involvement was an automatic reaction to context. But it was also a genuine creative preoccupation, connected with an early enthusiasm for Wagner, and then with his interest in Symbolist literature and his friendship with some of its best-known exponents (including Mallarmé). It was this literary connection which gave rise to the two abortive Edgar Allan Poe projects of the years following *Pelléas et Mélisande*.

Debussy's earliest proper theatre score is *Rodrigue et Chimène*, which was substantially composed in short score between 1888 and 1892, when it gave way to the first version of the orchestral *Nocturnes*, the *Prélude à l'après-midi d'un faune*, and soon *Pelléas et Mélisande*. Before this, Debussy's most successful works had been songs, including the compact and atmospheric Verlaine settings of the *Ariettes oubliées* (1885–8), and the more elaborate *Cinq poèmes de Baudelaire* (1887–9), with their Wagnerian turn of phrase. *Rodrigue et Chimène* is the sort of first opera one might expect of the composer of the Baudelaire songs. Its conventionally heroic subject suggests many other post-Wagner French operas, and while its harmonic language is that of mature early Debussy, its gesture often lacks the finesse and restraint of the composer at his subtlest. It was in about 1890 that Debussy described to his former composition teacher Ernest Guiraud the sort of operatic text he would like to set: 'The ideal would be two associated dreams. No place, no time. No big scene. No compulsion on the musician, who must complete and give body to the work of the poet. Music in opera is far too predominant. Too much singing and the musical settings are too cumbersome. The blossoming of the voice into true singing should occur only when required . . . My idea is of a short libretto with mobile scenes. No discussion or arguments between the characters whom I see at the mercy of life or destiny.' This is remarkably prescient of Maeterlinck's *Pelléas* (as yet neither published nor performed), and a direct rebuttal of the *Rodrigue* kind of opera.

The composition, revision and orchestration of *Pelléas* preoccupied Debussy from 1893 until its first performance in April 1902, and during this period he started no other significant new works except the *Chansons de Bilitis* (1897–8) and *Pour le piano* (1894–1901). But once *Pelléas* reached the stage, he entered a completely new phase of mainly instrumental composition, in which he explored the formal and imaginative possibilities of innovations that had first been prompted, in song or opera, by words. This is the time of the great piano collections, the *Estampes* (1903), *Images* (1905, 1907) and *Préludes* (1910, 1912–13), *L'isle joyeuse* (1904), and the orchestral masterpieces *La mer* (1903–5) and *Images* (1905–12). Yet for much of the same period, Debussy tinkered with a one-act opera on Poe's *The Devil in the Belfry*, somewhat later turning to *The Fall of the House of Usher*, sketches for which occupied him, on and off, for the last decade of his life. It is hard to imagine what Debussy could have made of Poe's absurd tale about the devil who makes the midday chimes strike thirteen and thereby brings chaos to the well-ordered life of the Dutch village of Vondervotteimittis. But *Usher*, as a subject, is a direct descendant of Debussy's early Symbolist obsessions. (Poe was a hero of the French Symbolist movement, and was translated by Baudelaire.) It might have made a superbly mysterious successor to *Pelléas*, if Debussy had solved its problems before the rectal cancer that tormented him from 1909 onwards finally made sustained creative concentration impossible.

Pelléas et Mélisande

Drame lyrique in five acts (12 tableaux) (3h 15m)
Libretto by the composer; abridgement of the play by Maurice Maeterlinck (1892)
Composed ?September 1893–17 August 1895; rev. January 1900 (or earlier)–1902 (orch. ?November 1901–January 1902; interludes composed March–April 1902)
PREMIERES 30 April 1902, Opéra-Comique, Paris; US: 19 February 1908, Manhattan Opera Company, New York; UK: 21 May 1909, Covent Garden, London
CAST Mélisande *s*, Pelléas *t*, Golaud *bar*, Arkel *b*, Geneviève *ms*, Yniold *s*, Doctor *b*, Shepherd *bar*, 3 poor men *silent*, servants *silent*; offstage: *atb* chorus of sailors

Debussy attended the first performance of Maeterlinck's play at the Théâtre des Bouffes-Parisiens on 17 May 1893. But he had probably already read it and considered setting it to music, having even before that (1891) applied unsuccessfully to Maeterlinck for permission to set his earlier play *La Princesse Maleine*. Over *Pelléas*, the playwright was more accommodating. Debussy set to work initially on the big final scene of Act IV, setting the text as it stood, without cuts. Then, finding his music too Wagnerian, he at once revised the scene, before returning to the start of the drama and composing it through roughly in sequence, omitting four of Maeterlinck's scenes and making extensive cuts to the remainder. At this stage he was seeking a new way of rendering into music Maeterlinck's curious mixture of high-sounding realism and interior symbolism, and finally came up, as he wrote to Ernest Chausson on 2 October 1893, 'with a technique which seems to me quite extraordinary, that is to say, Silence (don't laugh!) as a means of expression!'

Early proposals for performance came to nothing, and even though the new director of the Opéra-Comique, Albert Carré, accepted the work in principle in the spring of 1898, it was another three years before it was firmly scheduled for production. During this time Debussy made substantial revisions, especially to Act IV, and after the work's acceptance he again revised that act, as well as at last carrying out the orchestration. Also, during the rehearsal period, he composed the somewhat Wagnerian orchestral interludes to cover the numerous scene changes (performance is still possible, though unusual, without them). At this stage a row blew up with Maeterlinck over the casting of Mélisande, for whom the Scottish soprano Mary Garden was announced in December 1901. Maeterlinck's determination that his mistress Georgette Leblanc should have the part drove him to the extremes of a formal complaint to the Société des Auteurs, an open letter to *Le Figaro* expressing the hope that the opera would fail, and the printing of a satirical 'synopsis', which was distributed to the audience at the public dress rehearsal on 28 April 1902, which may well have fuelled the near riot at that performance.

Despite these troubles and the work's unusual character, the official premiere passed off well, and *Pelléas* quickly entered the repertoire of the Opéra-Comique. Debussy himself supervised the rehearsals, and even had a hand in the beautiful pre-Raphaelite designs of Lucien Jusseaume and Eugène Ronsin. The first cast was generally strong, and the music sympathetically conducted by André Messager. But casting nevertheless has remained problematic; Pelléas has been sung variously by tenors and baritones (the first Pelléas, Jean Périer, was a 'baryton Martin', a voice like Debussy's own in which the lighter head tone is prominent). But later there was even talk of playing Pelléas as a *travesti* role for soprano. The original Yniold was a boy treble named Blondin, but his performance prompted such hilarity at the public dress rehearsal that a number of cuts were made in his part for the official premiere. (His scene with the sheep in Act IV, however, had probably already been omitted, and was first performed in public only in autumn 1902, when the part was sung by a woman, Suzanne Dumesnil.)

SYNOPSIS

Arkel is King of Allemonde, Geneviève his daughter, and Golaud and Pelléas her sons by different marriages. Yniold is Golaud's son by his first wife, who is now dead.

Act I, Scene 1: Golaud, lost in the forest while out hunting, comes upon the frail Mélisande, who is lost too and crying. She recoils from him, evades his questions, and refuses to let him retrieve her crown, which he sees glistening in the pool. Eventually she tells him her name, and he persuades her to go with him. Scene 2: Golaud has written to Pelléas about Mélisande, whom he married six months ago. Golaud fears Arkel (who wished a political remarriage for him). But Arkel, when Geneviève reads him the letter, accepts the will of fate. Pelléas asks to visit a dying friend, but Arkel insists he await Golaud's return. Scene 3: Mélisande is walking in the grounds with Geneviève. They remark on the darkness of the surrounding forests. Pelléas joins them, and they turn their attention to the sea (where the ship that brought Mélisande can be seen and heard departing). Pelléas announces that he is going away the next day.

Act II, Scene 1: Pelléas and Mélisande are by a fountain in the park. Mélisande leans over and tries to touch the water, but only her long hair can reach it. Playing with the ring Golaud gave her, she drops it into the water as a harp softly sounds the distant chime of noon. Scene 2: Golaud has been thrown by his horse on the stroke of noon. Nursing him that night, Mélisande complains of being unhappy in the castle, and Golaud tries to find out why. He notices that her ring is missing, and furiously orders her to find it, taking Pelléas with her. Scene 3: Pelléas and Mélisande pretend to look for the ring in a sea cave, but they are scared when they find three starving beggars asleep on the ground.

Act III, Scene 1: Mélisande is combing her hair at a tower window. Pelléas appears and persuades her to lean out so far that her hair tumbles down the wall. He makes passionate simulated love to it, winding her hair round himself and then tying it to the branches of a willow. As he does so Mélisande's white doves fly out of the tower. Golaud appears and chides them for their 'childishness'. Scene 2: Golaud takes Pelléas into the vaults. But the air is stifling, and they climb back out – Scene 3 – emerging into the fresh midday air. Golaud lectures Pelléas about his behaviour with Mélisande, who is pregnant. Scene 4: Below Mélisande's window Golaud questions Yniold roughly about her and Pelléas. To each question Yniold replies with a child's elusiveness. A lamp is lit in Mélisande's room and Golaud lifts Yniold to spy on her. Pelléas is with her, but they are merely gazing silently at the lamp.

Act IV, Scene 1: Pelléas and Mélisande agree to meet by the fountain. He is going away. His father (who never appears in the opera) has been ill but is now recovering and has ordered him to travel. Scene 2: Arkel expects the recovery of Pelléas's father to revitalize the castle, he tells Mélisande. But Golaud appears and picks a quarrel with her, accusing her of deception. He takes her by the hair and drags her from side to side, despite Arkel's protests. Scene 3: At the fountain, Yniold is looking for his ball. A shepherd passes with his flock, Yniold asks him why the sheep have stopped bleating. 'Because this isn't the way to the stable.' Scene 4: Pelléas and Mélisande meet for the last time. Passionately they declare their love. But in the distance the castle gates clang shut, and Mélisande realizes that Golaud has followed her in the darkness and is watching them from behind a tree. As they kiss with utter abandon, Golaud runs out and kills Pelléas with his sword.

Act V: Mélisande, having given birth to a daughter, lies dying, attended by the doctor and Arkel. Golaud is stricken with remorse, but asks her in desperation if her and Pelléas's love was guilty. It was not, she says; but Golaud accuses her of lying and remains uncertain to the end. The serving women file silently in and, at the moment of Mélisande's death, fall to their knees.

The most celebrated feature of *Pelléas* is its unique vocal declamation, which carries the text on a continuous, fluid cantilena, somewhere between chant and recitative, a note to a syllable. There are no arias or set pieces. Debussy consciously avoided both the broad formal and gestural clichés of French and Italian Romantic opera, and the heavy arioso style of Wagner, though he was certainly influenced by the 'endless melody' of *Tristan*. The refinement and subtlety of the word-setting come partly from the French language, with its discreet and flexible accentuation, and are a natural extension of Debussy's Verlaine and Baudelaire songs. But they are also a response to the dreamlike world of Maeterlinck's play, a world of doomed children at the mercy of passions they only dimly apprehend. The play's 'tableau' design, so different from the purposeful symphonic structures of Wagner, must also have appealed to Debussy. His own style was moving towards a kind of suspended-animation harmony in which gentle discords are relished for their sensual beauty rather than their grammar (just as in Proust individual words and phrases take on an almost magical significance while the sentence structure fades into the background). The fact that many of Debussy's favourite chords are Wagnerian in type merely emphasizes the restraint with which he uses them.

In fact *Pelléas* deploys an incredibly small number of harmonic and melodic ideas for such a long work. Leitmotifs are used sparingly. There are motifs for the main characters (some of them distinctly Wagnerian in cut) and for aspects of the drama, like the spirit of remote antiquity conveyed by the solemn modal chords of the prelude; and there are one-off musical ideas for Maeterlinck's symbols, like the crown in Act I or the white doves in Act III. Harmony is used to fix or intensify atmosphere, almost like a kind of musical scenery or lighting. So the menacing scene in the vaults is entirely in whole tones, while the sparkling sunlight and water of the next scene are conveyed throughout in pentatonic harmony which looks forward to piano pieces like *Reflets dans l'eau* or *Cloches à travers les feuilles*. The 'static' character of this kind of writing is tempered by some of the most exquisitely varied orchestration in any opera. The sound is soft and restrained, but the texture is mobile and vividly graphic, and the music rises to dramatic climaxes that are all the more effective for their rarity.

Pelléas is a key work for the 20th century. Musically, it established an approach to form, harmony and texture which profoundly influenced composers as various as Stravinsky, Messiaen (who was given the score at the age of nine) and Puccini, who was fascinated by its 'extraordinary harmonic qualities and . . . transparent instrumental texture'. Operatically, it was a shot across the bows of stage realism, as represented by works such as Gustave Charpentier's *Louise* or Massenet's *Werther*. The play's strangeness, admittedly, is a matter more of style than of content, and hidden meanings are less important than the evasive treatment of the commonplace: it is really a bourgeois tragedy slowed down, with a few poetic non sequiturs and a strong atmosphere. But these are qualities that lend themselves to musical treatment. It is significant that Maeterlinck's play also attracted avant-garde composers outside France and Belgium: Schoenberg's tone poem was written in 1902–3, and the link with Expressionism comes out in his *Erwar-*

tung (1909). But where Maeterlinck's play has dated, the music it inspired has not, which is only fitting, as Symbolism in France began as an imitation of music, and specifically that of Wagner.

RECORDINGS 1. Joachim, Jansen, Etcheverry, Cabanel, Paris Conservatoire O, Désormière, Pathé-Marconi, 1941; 2. Söderström, Shirley, McIntyre, Ward, Covent Garden O, Boulez, CBS, 1969/70
OTHER OPERATIC WORKS *Rodrigue et Chimène*, (1893, inc.); *La chute de la Maison Usher*, (1917, inc.)

S.W.

Léo Delibes

Clément Philibert Léo Delibes;
b 21 February 1836, St Germain du Val, France; *d* 16 January 1891, Paris

Delibes came to Paris from the provinces at the age of 12 after the death of his father. Musical on his mother's side, he studied at the Conservatoire, though his evident melodic gift gained him no outstanding distinctions there. His teachers included the organist–composer Benoist and the stage composer Adam. His own career was divided between church, as chorister and organist, and stage, as ballet and opera composer. Among about 30 stage works his four most important scores are *Le roi l'a dit*, *Lakmé* and the ballets *Coppélia* (1870) and *Sylvia* (1876).

If these four works endure, the remainder testifies more to his industry than to his genius as a composer. Adam's interest in his pupil, a boy chorister at La Madeleine and at the Opéra (he sang in the cathedral scene at the premiere of Meyerbeer's *Le prophète* in 1849), saw Delibes, at the age of 17, appointed organist at Saint-Pierre de Chaillot and accompanist at the Théâtre-Lyrique, a modest establishment directed by Hervé, who supplied all its music. These posts brought Delibes into contact with some of the popular composers of the day, notably Victor Massé, who, late with his work on *La Reine Topaze*, employed the youth as copyist. With the amused blessing of Adam, Delibes also took over from Hervé the setting of *Deux sous de charbon*, completing it within a few days. Delibes was 19 when this first work was given at the Folies-Nouvelles in 1856. Fourteen others followed in as many years.

However, between *Le roi l'a dit* (1873) and *Sylvia* (1876), the only notable composition was the song 'Les filles de Cadix'. His music for the theatre was engendered by the need to earn a living and support his widowed mother. His musical ambitions were restricted by these considerations, for after a good start his academic career at the Conservatoire had been disappointing. It seems that he never even thought of competing for the Prix de Rome. Yet the initial success of *Le roi l'a dit* spread his fame abroad and official honours came his way. Finally, in 1881, he succeeded Reber as a professor at the Conservatoire at the insistence of the director, Ambroise Thomas, to whom Delibes disclaimed any knowledge of fugue and counterpoint. Urged to practise those skills, he did, and became an unusually conscientious and dedicated teacher. Essentially ebullient yet shy and unsure, Delibes had a need to be loved that was gratified. The successes of *Jean de Nivelle* (1880) and *Lakmé* (1883) were conclusive; the posthumous performance (1893) of *Kassya* (completed by Massenet) proved an anti-climax.

Lakmé

Opera in three acts (2h 15m)
Libretto by Edmond Gondinet and Philippe Gille, after the novel *Le mariage de Loti* by Pierre Loti (1882)
Composed 1883
PREMIERES 14 April 1883, Opéra-Comique, Paris; US: 4 October 1883, Grand Opera House, Chicago; UK: 6 June 1885, Gaiety Theatre, London

CAST Lakmé *s*, Mallika *ms* or *c*, Mistress Bentson *ms*, Ellen *s*, Rose *ms*, Gerald *t*, Nilakantha *b*, Frederic *bar*, Hadji *t*, Gypsy *t*, Chinese merchant *t*, Pickpocket *bar*; *satb* chorus of Indians, Brahmins, Chinese merchants; ballet

In *Lakmé* Delibes, already successful as a composer of memorably tuneful ballets, fulfilled his ambition to produce a successful serious opera. Its title role attracted the finest sopranos of the time, such as Patti and Tetrazzini, and its survival is due largely to the vehicle it provides for the coloratura soprano voice.

SYNOPSIS

The plot centres around the fanatical hatred of the Brahmin priests in 19th-century India for the English invaders, who forbid them to practise their religion.

Act I: Gerald and Frederic, two English officers, find themselves in a sacred grove. Catching sight of Lakmé, daughter of the Brahmin priest Nilakantha, Gerald falls in love with her. He is seen by Nilakantha, who swears vengeance on the intruder who has desecrated holy ground.

Act II: Gerald and Frederic meet in a crowded marketplace, whence Gerald has been shadowed by Nilakantha. He commands Lakmé to sing an old Brahmin song ('The Bell Song') so that the intruder will again be drawn to her and Nilakantha will be able to identify him. At the sight of Gerald, Lakmé faints, but she later manages to warn him of her father's plans for vengeance. Nevertheless, during a procession, Gerald is stabbed and slightly injured.

Act III: Lakmé is nursing Gerald in a forest hut, where Frederic finds him and calls him back to duty. Lakmé, realizing that she will lose Gerald, takes poison, and dies just as her father rushes in to find her.

Delibes's desire to please caused him to conform without question to procedures already well worn in the field of opéra comique. *Lakmé* is composed of separate numbers, devoid of musical links between them, with a contrived symmetry of form in each and a subordinate, purely accompanimental role for the orchestra throughout. It has, on the other hand, a melodic fluency that has proved irresistible to singers and listeners alike, a transparency of texture and a French elegance that places it poles apart from the Wagnerian influences of the time to which Delibes's more forward-looking compatriots were prone.

RECORDINGS 1. Sutherland, Berbié, Vanzo, Bacquier, Monte Carlo Op Ch & O, Bonynge, Decca, 1967; 2. Dessay, Haidan, Kunde, Van Dam, Toulouse Capitole Ch & O, Plasson, EMI, 1997

OTHER OPERATIC WORKS *Deux sous de charbon, ou Le suicide de Bigorneau*, 1856; *Deux vieilles gardes, ou Double garde, ou Un malade qui se porte bien*, 1856; *Six demoiselles à marier*, 1856; *Maître Griffard, ou Les deux procureurs*, 1857; *La fille du golfe*, (1859); *L'omelette à la Follembuche*, 1859; *Monsieur de Bonne-Etoile*, 1860; *Les musiciens de l'orchestre* (coll. with Offenbach, Erlanger, Hignard), 1861; *Les eaux d'Ems*, 1861; *Mon ami Pierrot, ou L'enfance de Pierrot*, 1862; *Le jardinier et son seigneur* (*Le lièvre*), 1863; *La tradition*, 1864; *Grande nouvelle*, 1864; *Le serpent à plumes*, 1864; *Le boeuf Apis*, 1865; *Malbrough s'en va-t-en guerre* (Act IV of coll.), 1868; *L'écossais de Chatou, ou Montagnards écossais*, 1869; *La cour du roi Pétaud*, 1869; *Le roi l'a dit*, 1873; *Jean de Nivelle*, 1880; *Kassya* (inc.; orch. by Massenet), 1893; 2 lost opéras bouffes

F.A.

Gaetano Donizetti

Gaetano Domenico Maria Donizetti; *b* 29 November 1797, Bergamo; *d* 8 April 1848, Bergamo

Although a handful of Donizetti's 65 operas have always maintained a place in the international repertoire, his reputation has undergone some profound changes. From a position of dominance at the time of his death, when one in every four Italian operas performed in Italy was one of his, his standing declined seriously in the last decades of the 19th century, when his music was often dismissed as facile and imitative. Since the Second World War, however, an extraordinarily widespread re-examination of most of his output has established his importance as a vital link in the development of Italian opera.

To see Donizetti at his true value, it is essential to understand him in terms of his period. Coming from poor parents, he was fortunate to have his talent recognized early, and to acquire as good a musical training (at the hands of Simon Mayr and Padre Mattei) as was then available in Italy. To support himself he had to accept every possible commission offered him. Writing sometimes as many as four operas a year and confronted with the exigencies of an audience that insisted on freshness without eccentricity, he deliberately set out to attain a mastery over the range of operatic types and genres then current in Italy. Not least of Donizetti's attributes as an opera composer was the effectiveness of his writing for every range of voice.

Donizetti first established himself as a potential talent with *Zoraide di Grenata* (Rome, 1822), which was successful enough to win him a contract with the impresario Barbaja, who brought him to Naples. The next eight years have been described as his 'apprenticeship', a period of experimentation and unflagging productivity. The turning point of his career was the great success of *Anna Bolena* (Milan, 1830), which won him commissions from all the leading Italian opera houses. Although he never totally renounced comedy (two of his greatest opere buffe, *L'elisir d'amore* (1832) and *Don Pasquale* (1843) were written after *Anna Bolena*), he now chiefly confined himself to tragedy. Some of these works, among them *Lucrezia Borgia* and *Lucia di Lammermoor*, soon made him a household name.

In 1838 Donizetti left Naples for Paris, drawn there not only by the possibility of prestige and larger fees, but also by the greater freedom of subject matter permitted there. In 1842 he was named hofkapellmeister to the Habsburg court in Vienna and for the next three years divided his time between the French and Austrian capitals, with occasional trips to Italy. In 1846 signs of mental deterioration forced his confinement to a sanatorium at Ivry, but later, paralysed and almost totally bereft of speech, he was brought home to Bergamo, where he was nursed by friends until his death.

As a man, Donizetti was gregarious, good-humoured and well disposed toward his fellow composers, whom he recognized as working against the obstacles of the censors and the court-controlled theatres. His letters are filled with his spontaneous reactions to his increasingly tragic life. None of his three children lived more than a few days, and his beloved wife Virginia died at the age of 29 in 1837 in the midst of a horrifying outbreak of cholera; he never remarried. Thereafter, a morbid streak in his character became more pronounced. His death was ultimately caused by a long-standing syphilitic infection.

It was Donizetti more than anyone else who raised the temperature of drama in Italian opera. Throughout his career, but particularly after 1830, he engaged in as near open warfare with the censors as he dared without losing his livelihood as an opera composer. He protested against the niggling restrictions that long forbade religious topics on the stage. He wanted to show rulers as human beings with human failings and not as mere benign figureheads. His many operas on English subjects, particularly those dealing with the Tudors, were able to pass muster with the Italian censors because they dealt with Protestant, rather than Catholic, kings and queens. *La favorite*, with its scenes of convent life and the delivery of a papal bull, was first given in Italy in mutilated form, as was *Dom Sébastien*, which included a funeral procession with a great catafalque on stage. Parisian authorities were more tolerant; for instance, *Poliuto*, banned in Naples for showing the martyrdom of a Christian saint, was given at the Opéra as *Les martyrs*.

Working within the conventions of his day, Donizetti found a variety of ways to adapt them to his manifold dramatic purposes: as in his fondness for elegiac cabalettas, sometimes slower in tempo than the arias they follow, or in his knack of creating ambiguity between the major and minor modes, and in his way of heightening an emotion by smoothly modulating into an unexpected key (as in Lucia's 'Spargi d'amaro pianto' or Norina's 'E' duretta la lezione' in Act III of *Don Pasquale*). In his late works Donizetti felt freer to foreshorten or even dismember the conventional structures; for instance, in these works he often abandoned the tradition of the aria-finale.

It is difficult to conceive of the phenomenon of Verdi without the foundation stone of Donizetti's works. Verdi's exploitation of the possibilities of the baritone persona finds its antecedents in such powerful roles as Cardenio in *Il furioso*, and in the title roles of *Tasso* and *Belisario*. In such scores as *Lucia*, *La favorite* and *Maria di Rohan* one discovers foreshadowing of the concept of *tinta* that Verdi came to insist on. While not suggesting that there is any conscious imitation, one can scarcely exaggerate the centrality of Donizetti to the tradition of Italian melodramma from which Verdi sprang and which he carried to loftier heights.

Anna Bolena

Anne Boleyn

Tragedia lirica in two acts (3h 15m)
Libretto by Felice Romani, after Ippolito Pindemonte's translation (1816) of the play *Henri VIII* by Marie-Joseph de Chenier (1791) and the play *Anna Bolena* by Alessandro Pepoli (1788)
Composed 1830

PREMIERES 26 December 1830, Teatro Carcano, Milan; UK: 8 July 1831, King's Theatre, Haymarket, London; US: 12 November 1839, Théâtre d'Orléans, New Orleans

CAST Anna Bolena *s*, Giovanna Seymour *ms*, Smeton *ms*, Percy *t*, Enrico VIII *b*, Rochefort *b*, Hervey *t*; *satb* chorus of courtiers

Anna Bolena established Donizetti among the leading composers of his day and introduced him to the audiences of Paris and London. It used to be a critical commonplace that this work marked a watershed in Donizetti's oeuvre and that here, in his thirtieth opera, he found at long last his personal style. Today, however, as more and more of his earlier works have been revived, *Anna Bolena* appears, rather, to be the logical culmination of tendencies implicit in his development. The critical factor seems to have been that Donizetti had at his disposal a superior libretto, one that moved him deeply. He also had the incentive of striving to win over the Milanese, till then unimpressed by successes won elsewhere. The element of consistency in Donizetti's development can be demonstrated by his having adapted an aria from his first opera, *Enrico di Borgogna*, as the basis of Anna's famous larghetto in the Tower scene ('Al dolce guidami'). The work retained its currency for nearly 50 years and then lapsed into oblivion, until its successful revival at La Scala with Maria Callas provided the incentive for performances elsewhere.

SYNOPSIS

Act I, Scene 1: The courtiers suspect that the king's fickleness bodes ill for Anna, an impression strengthened by the conscience-stricken Giovanna Seymour. Anna enters and bids her musician Smeton sing, but he, infatuated with Anna, offers an amorous ditty, reminding her of Percy, her first love ('Come innocente, giovane'). Anna retires, leaving Seymour alone; soon she is joined by the king. She wants this to be their last meeting, declaring that honour forbids the continuation of their relationship. Accused of being more in love with the throne than with him, Seymour begs the king to free her conscience ('Ah! qual sia cercar non oso'). Scene 2: Unknown to Anna, the king has laid her a trap, by arranging a hunting party at which she will unexpectedly encounter Percy, returned from exile. Percy questions Anna's brother, Lord Rochefort, about the rumours of Anna's unhappiness ('Da quel diche, lei perduta'). When the hunt appears, Percy approaches to thank the king, but he withdraws his hand; when Percy kisses Anna's hand, she feels his tears of gratitude on it ('Io sentii sulla mia mano'). As the hunt moves on, all hail this auspicious day. Enrico is happy too; but he has been hunting a different prey. Scene 3: Smeton surreptitiously enters the queen's apartment, carrying her miniature in a locket. Hearing someone approach, Smeton hides. Rochefort asks Anna to grant Percy a brief interview. When Percy appears, Anna's admission that the king now hates her prompts him to declare his love ('S'ei t'abborre, io t'amo ancora'). Frightened, Anna firmly refuses his request to see her again. Percy draws his sword, and Smeton, misinterpreting Percy's intentions, rushes out, drawing his. Anna faints. The king arrives, enraged, and summons guards. Smeton offers to die as proof of the compromised queen's innocence, and when he tears open his jacket, Anna's miniature falls out at the king's feet. Anna begins an eloquent sextet ('In quegli sguardi impresso'); she wants to explain, but the king declares she must defend herself in court. Anna is shocked ('Anna! ai giudici!') and realizes that her fate is already sealed.

Act II, Scene 1: In Anna's apartment in the Tower, her ladies comment on Anna's plight ('Oh! dove mai ne andarono'). Anna appears and prays for consolation. Seymour enters to inform her that the king has promised to spare her life if she will acknowledge her guilt. Anna's astonishment turns to fury when she hears Seymour beg it not only in the king's name but in that of the woman who will succeed her on the throne. Anna calls on heaven to punish her rival. When Seymour tearfully prostrates herself, Anna realizes the identity of her rival and orders her to leave, but Seymour cannot contain her remorse ('Dal mio cor punita io sono'). Scene 2: Hervey announces that Smeton has confessed to adultery with Anna, having been told that such a declaration would spare her life. Anna and Percy are led in. When Enrico tells her of Smeton's confession, Anna turns the charge of adultery back on him. Percy is willing to die to spare her life, reminding her that she was once married to him. They are led off, leaving Enrico furious. Seymour comes to beg him to forget her and be merciful. Scene 3: In the Tower, Percy tells Rochefort that he should live to defend Anna's memory ('Vivi tu'). Anna longs for her childhood home and first love ('Al dolce guidami'). Summoned to the scaffold, Anna sings a prayer ('Cielo, a' miei lunghi spasimi'). Cannons announce the king's marriage to Seymour, and Anna calls for heaven's mercy on the guilty couple ('Coppia iniqua!').

Romani clearly outlined the conflicts between the characters, giving Donizetti many opportunities for psychologically apposite expressiveness. This is particularly true in the great duet for Seymour and Enrico in Act I and in that for Anna and Seymour in the opening scene of Act II. The contrast between the devious menace of Enrico and the straightforward remorse of Seymour is reinforced by the unusual device of having Seymour repeat one of her melodies from the larghetto section in the cabaletta, a convincing expression of her failure to be convinced by Enrico's arguments. In the scene between the women, the emotional range is even greater, each shift of feeling being persuasively characterized as this pair, who have every reason to distrust each other, come to a rapprochement.

From the start of his career, Donizetti had demonstrated a considerable flair for writing ensembles, more persuasive in the slow movements than in the rapid pendants, where he was as yet restricted by the conventional *settinari* (seven-syllable verses). Especially effective is the canonic quintet, 'Io sentii sulla mia mano' (adapted from the score of *Otto mesi in due ore*, 1827) near the close of Act I, Scene 2. Even more so is the sextet 'In quegli sguardi impresso' in the next scene on Anna's regaining consciousness, where the interweaving of the parts creates a mood of welling intensity. On almost as high a level is the trio for Anna, Percy and Enrico in Act II Scene 2, 'Fin dall'età più tenera', where the indignation of Anna, the nostalgia of Percy, and the fury of the king are neatly contrasted.

The musical climax of the work comes in the Tower scene, which consists primarily of two full-scale arie-finali. Percy's 'Vivi tu' is full of pathos, but that mood is given even deeper expression in Anna's 'Al dolce guidami', with its purling cor anglais obbligato and yearning figurations. The *tempo di mezzo* of her scena flowers into a lyrical outpouring at 'Cielo, a' miei lunghi spasimi' (a variant of the melody of 'Home, Sweet Home'), with the solo voice supported by three other voices and a chamber-size accompaniment. The cabaletta, 'Coppia iniqua!', conveys with its driving rhythms and succession of trills the emotional delirium that brings Anna to the point of death.

RECORDINGS 1. Callas, Simionato, G. Raimondi, Rossi-Lemeni, La Scala Ch & O, Gavazzeni, EMI, 1957 (live, cut); 2. Sutherland, Mentzer, Hadley, Ramey, WNO Ch & O, Bonynge, Decca, 1987; 3. Gruberova, Ziegler, Bros, Palatchi, Hungarian R & TV Ch & O, Boncompagni, Nightingale, 1994

L'elisir d'amore

The Love Potion

Opera comica in two acts (2h)
Libretto by Felice Romani, after the text for Auber's *Le philtre* by Eugène Scribe (1831), in turn after *Il filtro* by Silvio Malaperta
Composed 1832
PREMIERES 12 May 1832, Teatro Canobbiana, Milan; UK: 10 December 1836, Lyceum, London; US: 18 June 1838, Park Theater, New York
CAST Adina *s*, Nemorino *t*, Sergeant Belcore *bar*, Dr Dulcamara *buffo*, Giannetta *s*; *satb* chorus of peasants and soldiers

L'elisir d'amore is the earliest of Donizetti's operas never to have left the standard repertoire, and during his lifetime it was the most frequently performed of his works. Although Romani's libretto is at times a literal translation of Scribe's text for Auber's *Le philtre*, it contains a number of significant passages that have no counterpart in the French libretto: the Adina–Nemorino duet, 'Chiedi all'aura', the tenor's 'Adina, credimi', and his famous 'Una furtiva lagrima'. All of these additions contribute an element of pathos that Donizetti believed to be a necessary constituent of truly satisfying comedy. Another modification was moving the setting of Scribe's plot from the Basque countryside to rural northern Italy, Donizetti's native soil.

SYNOPSIS

Act I: The gentle Nemorino is hopelessly in love with Adina, who amuses the harvesters by reading to them the story of Queen Iseult and the love potion ('Della crudele Isotta'). Sergeant Belcore and his platoon enter, and he gallantly presents Adina with a nosegay ('Come Paride vezzoso'). Nemorino is upset by Adina's apparent susceptibility to Belcore. She tells a disconsolate Nemorino that she will never love him ('Chiedi all'aura'); he protests that he would die for her. The quack Dr Dulcamara arrives to peddle his nostrums ('Udite, udite, o rustici!'). Nemorino, remembering the story of Iseult, buys a bottle of love potion, which he is assured will work in 24 hours ('Obbligato, ah! si obbligato'). Tipsy from the elixir, which in reality is Bordeaux, Nemorino gains in confidence ('Esulti pur la barbara'), but his spirits are crushed when he hears Adina agree to marry Belcore that very evening ('Adina, credimi').

Act II: The wedding feast is under way, and Dulcamara sings a mock barcarolle with the bride-to-be ('Io son ricco, tu sei bella'). Adina forestalls the notary, however, since Nemorino is not present to witness the ceremony. Penniless, Nemorino is desperate to buy more elixir, and on impulse he allows Belcore to enlist him into the army, because an enrollee receives a bounty ('Venti scudi'). Giannetta and the village girls have heard that Nemorino's rich uncle has died, leaving him his heir, and they fawn over him, a response that Nemorino attributes to the elixir. The sight of these attentions astonishes Adina. From Dulcamara she learns the story of Nemorino and the potion, but she assures him her own charms are a more potent weapon in winning a man ('Quanto amore'). Nemorino has observed that Adina has been affected by seeing him with the girls, but he would rather die than live without her ('Una furtiva lagrima'). Adina tells him that she has bought back his enlistment ('Prendi: per me sei libero') and at last confesses that she loves him. The village turns out to celebrate their betrothal, while Dulcamara takes his leave, firmly convinced that his potion has unexpected powers.

Donizetti's score alternates sparkling tunes with emotional melodies. There is not a weak number in the whole opera. The patter song for Dulcamara has an orotund garrulity about it that is irresistible. The scene between Nemorino and the village girls can seem a comic anticipation of that between Parsifal and the Flower Maidens. Donizetti's gift for pungent characterization animates the duet between the smarmy Dulcamara and Adina, confident of her own female wiles. The tenderness of the first Adina–Nemorino duet and their successive arias in Act II, particularly Nemorino's 'Una furtiva lagrima', with its haunting bassoon obbligato and climactic shifts from minor to major mode, are the jewels of this delightful score. Unlike most opere buffe, *L'elisir* presents us with two characters that develop before our eyes. Nemorino learns to assert himself, and Adina comes to see that a constant heart is preferable to the fickle one of a practised womanizer in uniform.

RECORDINGS 1. Carteri, Alva, Panerai, Taddei, Vercelli, La Scala Ch & O, Serafin, EMI, 1958;
2. Sutherland, Pavarotti, Cossa, Malas, Ambrosian Singers, ECO, Bonynge, Decca, 1970: includes a cabaletta, 'Nel dolce incanto', written for Malibran;
3. Gheorghiu, Alagna, Scaltriti, Alaimo, Op Nat de Lyon Ch & O, Pidò, Decca, 1996

Maria Stuarda
Mary Stuart

Opera seria in two acts (2h 30m)
Libretto by Giuseppe Badari, after the translation by Andrea Maffei of the tragedy by Friedrich von Schiller (1800)
Composed 1834
PREMIERES 18 October 1834, Teatro San Carlo, Naples (as *Buondelmonte*; libretto adapted by the composer and Pietro Salatino); original version: 30 December 1835, La Scala, Milan; 15 October 1958, Bergamo; UK: 1 March 1966, St Pancras Town Hall, London; US: 16 November 1964, Carnegie Hall, New York (concert); 7 March 1972, State Theater, New York (stage)
CAST Maria *s*, Elisabetta *s*, Leicester *t*, Talbot *bar*, Anna *ms*, Lord Cecil *bar*; *satb* chorus of courtiers, huntsmen, soldiers, servants

After *Maria Stuarda* was banned in Naples by the king while in rehearsal in

1834, Donizetti used most of the score as *Buondelmonte*, but this version has never been revived. Malibran sang the premiere of the original version at La Scala but, as she did not follow the censor's changes, the opera was soon prohibited. In 1865, after Donizetti's death, it was performed in Naples with two substitute numbers taken from Donizetti's lesser works. In contrast to its limited performance history in the 19th century, *Maria Stuarda* has entered the repertoire since its revival at Bergamo in 1958. The discovery of the autograph in a Swedish collection in 1987 has made possible the preparation of an authentic edition.

SYNOPSIS
Act I, Scene 1: At Westminster, Elisabetta suspects Leicester's affections are elsewhere engaged. Talbot shows Leicester a portrait and letter from Maria, who is imprisoned at Fotheringay, begging for an interview with the queen. When Leicester asks Elisabetta to grant Maria's request, her jealousy cannot be disguised, but she does not refuse. Scene 2: At Fotheringay, Maria envies the clouds their freedom to sail towards France. Leicester comes to prepare her for the queen's visit. Elisabetta enters and regards her young rival with ill-concealed hostility. When Elisabetta insults Maria, she is stung in turn, declaring that Elisabetta is a 'vile bastard' whose 'foot sullies the English throne'. Furious, Elisabetta orders Maria seized.

Act II: Elisabetta debates whether to sign Maria's death warrant, urged on to it by Cecil. When Leicester comes to beg clemency, he is told that he is to witness Maria's execution. Scene 2: At Fotheringay, Maria does not flinch when Cecil delivers the fatal warrant. She turns to Talbot, who wears a cassock beneath his cloak, and confesses her sins. Maria asks her friends to join her in a prayer for all those who have wronged her. Leicester watches helplessly while Maria is led to the block.

Maria Stuarda, which used to have a reputation as an opera that even Malibran could not save, has proved a grateful vehicle for a number of recent singers. Today, it stands as a clear example of Donizetti's eagerness, in the face of the increasingly repressive censors of the 1830s, to expand the range of powerful subject matter for the opera stage. The explosive scene between the two queens, which has no basis in history, is unparalleled in operas of the period for its dramatic immediacy. The hushed, elegiac aria of Maria to the clouds, 'Oh! nube che lieve', is both a masterly piece of tone-painting and a shrewdly low-key anticipation of the fireworks that follow. Donizetti's skill at combining features of the solo aria with a duet, keeping within the conventions but using them in unpredictable ways, is shown in Leicester's aria in the opening scene and in Maria's 'Lascio contento al carcere' as she confesses herself to Talbot. The prayer for Maria with chorus, a magnificent reworking of a musical idea from the early *Il paria*, builds to a fine climax. The whole final scene, including Maria's aria-finale with its unexpected modulations, is one of the composer's major achievements.

RECORDINGS 1. Sutherland, Tourangeau, Pavarotti, Soyer, Morris, Teatro Comunale Bologna Ch & O, Bonynge, Decca, 1974/5; 2. Baker, Plowright, Rendall, Tomlinson, Opie, ENO Ch & O, Mackerras, Chandos, 1982 (in English); 3. Gruberova, Baltsa, Araiza, Ellero D'Artegna, Alaimo, Bavarian RCh, Munich PO, G. Patané, Philips, 1989

Lucia di Lammermoor

Dramma tragico in three acts (2h 30m)
Libretto by Salvatore Cammarano, after the novel *The Bride of Lammermoor* by Sir Walter Scott (1819); French version by Alphonse Royer and 'Gustave Vaez' (Jean-Nicolas Gustave van Nieuvenhuysen)
Composed 1835; rev. (in French) 1839
PREMIERES 26 September 1835, Teatro

San Carlo, Naples; UK: 5 April 1838, Her Majesty's Theatre, Haymarket, London; 1839 version: 6 August 1839, Théâtre de la Renaissance, Paris; US: 28 December 1841, Théâtre d'Orléans, New Orleans
CAST Lucia *s*, Edgardo *t*, Enrico *bar*, Raimondo Bide-the-Bent *b*, Arturo *t*, Alisa *ms*, Normanno *t*; *satb* chorus of huntsmen and wedding guests

Lucia has never lost its place in the popular affection, although there has been a change from the days when it was regarded primarily as a vehicle for a coloratura soprano until, in the wake of the impact of Callas, it has come to be appreciated as a compelling Romantic melodrama. Far from being a conventional score, it is filled with original touches. The prevailing orchestral colour, dominated by horns, and the subtle repetition of brief motivic ideas lend the score its distinctive *tinta*. The psychological and dramatic appositeness of its striking contrasts in situation and melody, now idyllic, now propulsively energetic, add to its richness. Clearly, *Lucia* is one of the scores that Verdi knew during his formative years.

When it was new, *Lucia* was regarded as the last word in Romantic sensibility. And as such it was used by Flaubert in the famous episode when Emma Bovary meets Léon again at the theatre in Rouen; he even wove phrases from the French libretto into the narrative.

SYNOPSIS
Act I, Scene 1: Enrico Ashton learns from his huntsmen that his sister Lucia has been meeting his hated rival Edgardo Ravenswood and has fallen in love with him. This disclosure sends Enrico into a murderous rage ('Cruda, funesta smania'). Scene 2: Lucia and her old nurse Alisa are waiting by a fountain, where she has a secret rendezvous with Edgardo. Lucia tells Alisa that she has seen the ghost of her ancestress who was murdered by a Ravenswood ('Regnava nel silenzio'). When her lover arrives, she sends Alisa off to keep watch. Edgardo wants to ask Enrico to forget their family feud, but Lucia is terrified of her brother's temper. When Edgardo tells her he must go to France (to aid the Stuart cause), she is desolate, but they exchange rings ('Verranno a te sull' aure').

Act II, Scene 1: Enrico and his friend Normanno have forged a letter to convince Lucia of Edgardo's infidelity. When Lucia enters, Enrico tells her of his desperate political position and that only her marrying Arturo can save him ('Il pallor funesto'). Weeping, Lucia protests, but she is badly shaken when Edgardo shows her the forged letter. The chaplain Raimondo further weakens Lucia's resolution by reminding her of her obligations to her family. Scene 2: The guests greet Arturo on his arrival for the wedding ('Per te l'immenso giubilo'). Half-fainting, Lucia has just signed the wedding contract when Edgardo unexpectedly returns to claim her ('Chi mi frena in tal momento'). When Enrico shows him the signed contract, Edgardo curses Lucia, whereupon Enrico demands vengeance.

Act III, Scene 1: During a storm, Enrico comes to Edgardo's ruined hall to challenge him to a duel. Scene 2: The wedding festivities are interrupted by Raimondo's disclosure that Lucia has murdered Arturo. Crazed, she appears, bloodstained dagger in hand, believing that she is about to marry Edgardo ('Alfin son tua'), and collapses. Scene 3: Edgardo comes to his family tombs to meet Enrico. Waiting, he thinks he no longer wants to live since Lucia has proved faithless ('Fra poco a me ricovero'). Learning of her death, he looks forward to their reunion in heaven ('Tu che a Dio spiegasti l'ali') and stabs himself.

Lucia is filled with memorable melodies, but it is easy to overlook their dramatic appositeness and psychological depth. For instance, during the accompanied recitative preceding the famous mad scene, Lucia's mental confusion is underscored by the recurrence of earlier themes in altered form; the one tune she manages to keep straight is that of her Act I duet with Edgardo: 'Verranno a te'. A striking contrast is afforded by the merry chorus at the beginning of Act III Scene 2, followed by Raimondo's grim narrative, 'Dalle stanze ove Lucia', with its uneasy modulations. It is followed by the elegiac chorus in E major, 'Oh, qual funesto avvenimento', which, like Edgardo's final aria, testifies to Donizetti's unusual skill in expressing grief in the major mode. Although much of the score of *Lucia* uses conventional compound structures, the dramatic propulsiveness of the plot, combined with Donizetti's melodic inventiveness, endows the work with surprising strength.

RECORDINGS 1. Sutherland, Pavarotti, Milnes, Covent Garden Ch & O, Bonynge, Decca, 1971: complete; 2. Caballé, Carreras, Sardinero, Ambrosian Op Ch, NPO, Lopez-Cobos, Philips, *c.*1976: follows the autograph scrupulously, without added embellishments and restores the original higher keys to Lucia's Act I arias, her duet with Enrico, and the mad scene; 3. Gruberova, Kraus, Bruson, Lloyd, Ambrosian Op Ch, RPO, Rescigno, EMI, 1983

Roberto Devereux

Opera seria in three acts (2h)
Libretto by Salvatore Cammarano, after the play *Elisabeth d'Angleterre* by François Ancelot (1832) and with some indebtedness to the text by Felice Romani for *Il conte d'Essex* by Mercadante (1833), also derived from Ancelot's play
Composed 1837, rev. 1838
PREMIERES 29 October 1837, Teatro San Carlo, Naples; rev. version: 27 December 1838, Théâtre-Italien, Paris; UK: 24 June 1841, London; US: 15 January 1849, Astor Place Opera House, New York
CAST Elisabetta *s*, Sara, Duchess of Nottingham *ms*, Roberto Devereux (Essex) *t*, Nottingham *bar*, Cecil *t*, Gualtiero (Walter Raleigh) *b*, Page *b*, Nottingham's confidant *b*; *satb* chorus of courtiers

Composed at the time of his wife's death, *Roberto Devereux* reflects Donizetti's effort to assuage his grief by losing himself in a work of great power. Twentieth-century revivals of this opera have proved that its dramatic intensity can still grip audiences. For its demands on a potent singing actress, the role of Elisabetta is worthy of mention alongside Bellini's Norma. The score also shows Donizetti's growing avoidance of lengthy sections of chordally accompanied recitative.

SYNOPSIS
Act I: At Westminster, Roberto is threatened with arrest for treason for his recent debacle in Ireland, but Elisabetta loves him and is determined to save him, giving him a ring that will guarantee his freedom. Unknown to the queen, however, Roberto is deeply in love with Sara, who during his absence has been forced into a loveless union with his friend Nottingham. Later, Roberto visits Sara to say farewell, and he entrusts her with Elisabetta's ring, while she gives him a scarf in return.

Act II: The ministers of the queen are meeting to decide Roberto's fate. They have searched his apartments and bring the queen the scarf. When Nottingham sees it, remembering that he has observed his wife working on it, he bursts into a jealous rage. Deeply offended herself at this apparent evidence of Roberto's infidelity, the queen is furious. Roberto is sent to the Tower.

Act III: Nottingham confronts his wife, ordering her seclusion at home, thereby making it impossible for her to send the ring to Elisabetta. In the Tower, Roberto hopes he can restore Sara's reputation before he is executed. At Westminster, Elisabetta is miserable, wondering why she has not received the ring, wanting Roberto to be spared. As a cannon shot announces Roberto's execution, Sara rushes in with the ring, followed by Nottingham, who declares he detained Sara so that he might have his revenge. The queen orders their arrest and then, haunted by visions of Roberto's ghost and her own demise, announces her abdication.

Although the plot plays fast and loose with history, the opera carries its own brand of dramatic conviction. The overture, added for Paris, capitalizes on the tune of 'God Save the Queen'. The terse second act develops considerable tension, exploding at the end into an impulsive trio-finale. Act III opens with a powerful asymmetrical duet for Sara and Nottingham. Roberto's fine aria in the Tower scene, preceded by an almost Beethovenesque prelude, exemplifies Donizetti's canny writing for the tenor voice. Even more wonderful is Elisabetta's aria-finale, 'Vivi, ingrato', which expands in a long arc of restrained emotion, capped by a propulsive cabaletta.

RECORDING Gruberova, Ziegler, Bernardini, Kim, Rhine Op Ch, Strasbourg PO, Haider, Nightingale, 1994

La fille du régiment

The Daughter of the Regiment

Opéra comique (with spoken dialogue) in two acts (1h 30m)
Libretto by J. F. A. Bayard and Jules-Henri Vernoy de Saint-Georges
Composed 1839; Italian opera buffa version (with recitatives) 1840
PREMIERES 11 February 1840, Opéra-Comique, Paris; as an opera buffa: 3 October 1840, La Scala, Milan; US: 2 March 1843, Théâtre d'Orléans, New Orleans; UK: 27 May 1847, Her Majesty's Theatre, Haymarket, London
CAST Marie *s*, Marquise *ms*, Tonio *t*, Sergeant Sulpice *b*, Hortensius *b*, Corporal *b*, Farmer *t*; *spoken roles*: Duchesse de Crakentorp, Notary; *satb* chorus of soldiers, peasants, guests of the Marquise

One of the most popular of Donizetti's comedies, *La fille* shows no signs of weakening its hold on the public's affections. It is a tribute to the composer's grasp of the Gallic spirit that this opera became a staple of the French repertoire and that Marie's cabaletta in Act II, 'Salut à la France!', attained the status of a patriotic song. Although in the summer of 1840 Donizetti adapted the work as an Italian opera buffa with sung recitatives, dropping the typically French couplets and inserting some other material, including an aria from *Gianni di Calais* (1828), this variant has never seriously challenged the appeal of the original opéra-comique version, in which the work is almost always performed today.

SYNOPSIS

Act I: Brought up by the soldiers of the 21st Regiment of the French Army and adopted by them as their 'daughter', the *vivandière* Marie confesses to gruff old Sulpice that she is much taken with a strapping Tyrolean, Tonio, who saved her life when she nearly fell off a precipice. The attraction is mutual, for Tonio has been lurking around the encampment hoping to talk to Marie. Seized as a spy, the young fellow is claimed by Marie as her personal prisoner, and in their ensuing duet ('De cet aveu si tendre') their true feelings for one another emerge. Hoping to marry Marie, Tonio is surprised to learn that her husband must be a member of the regiment, tidings that cause him promptly to enlist. The regiment celebrates his decision, calling on Marie to sing the regimental song ('Chacun le sait, chacun le dit'). The aged Marquise de Birkenfeld, strangely discomfited by the presence of the campaigning so near her château, learns from Sulpice that a certain Captain Robert had been a member of this very regiment. On the strength of this information, she claims to be Marie's aunt and insists on removing the girl from what in her eyes is a very unsuitable environment. Now in uniform, Tonio has come to claim his bride, but

Marie is forced to leave by the marquise's intervention ('Il faut partir, mes bons compagnons d'armes').

Act II: At the château, Marie is bored by lessons in dancing and in singing vapid romances, her reluctance strengthened by the presence of Sulpice, whom the marquise has taken in to recover from a wound. Longing for her old freedom and harassed by her aunt's insistence on respectability and that she marry a silly young duke, Marie is overjoyed when the 21st Regiment arrives at the château. Tonio, who has been promoted on the battlefield, pleads with the marquise for Marie's hand. He has been investigating her true parentage and now demands an explanation. During the reception to announce Marie's engagement to the duke, the marquise suffers a change of heart and confesses to the startled company that Marie is in fact her own daughter and consents to her marriage to Tonio. Amid general rejoicing, the opera ends with a patriotic chorus, 'Salut à la France'.

The score is filled with effective numbers. Particularly noteworthy are Marie's regimental song, 'Chacun le sait' (surprisingly adapted from an ensemble in *Il diluvio universale*, 1830), and her farewell to Tonio, 'Il faut partir', a finely crafted melody with a cor anglais obbligato that serves as the opening movement of the mid-point finale. A prime moment of comedy is provided by her lesson scene, in which the marquise tries to teach her an old tune by Garat, while Sulpice cannot resist teasing her into a reprise of 'Chacun le sait'. Tonio has both 'Pour mon âme' in Act I, with its redoubtable series of high Cs, and his tender plea to the marquise in Act II, 'Pour me rapprocher de Marie'. The character of the intrepid Marie stands squarely behind Verdi's portrait of another *vivandière*, Preziosilla in *La forza del destino*. Far from the least attractive aspect of *La fille du régiment* is Donizetti's skill and economy in contrasting military atmosphere with the tone of polite society, established at once by the charming *tyrolienne* that serves as a prelude to Act II.

RECORDINGS 1. Sutherland, Sinclair, Pavarotti, Malas, Covent Garden Ch & O, Bonynge, Decca, 1968; 2. Anderson, T'Hézan, Kraus, Trempont, Paris Op Ch & O, Campanella, EMI, 1986

La favorite

The Favourite

Grand opera in four acts (2h 30m, excluding the ballet)
Libretto by Alphonse Royer, Gustave Vaëz and Eugène Scribe after the play *Le Comte de Comminge* by Baculard d'Arnaud (1764) among other sources, on to which Scribe grafted the story of Leonora de Guzman
Composed 1840
PREMIERES 2 December 1840, Opéra, Paris; US: 9 February 1843, Théâtre d'Orléans, New Orleans; UK: 18 October 1843, Drury Lane, London
CAST Léonor *ms*, Inès *s*, Fernand *t*, Alphonse *bar*, Balthazar *b*, Don Gaspard *t*; *satb* chorus of monks and courtiers; ballet

In December 1839 Donizetti had completed a four-act semiseria entitled *L'ange de Nisida* for the Théâtre de la Renaissance, but the management declared bankruptcy before that work could be produced, leaving Donizetti with an unperformed score that, because of the nature of its plot (dealing with a royal mistress of the Bourbons), would offend the Italian censors. In the summer of 1840 when he was in Milan concocting the Italian adaptation of *La fille du régiment*, he was summoned back to Paris to produce a full-length work for the Opéra. Only the existence of *L'ange* and some other unperformed works allowed the resourceful Donizetti to complete *La favorite* and meet his deadline. Most of the major arias were newly composed, being tailored to the vocal characteristics of the cast.

SYNOPSIS

Act I: Castile, 1340. Fernand informs Balthazar, his father and the superior of a monastic order, that he must renounce his novitiate because he has fallen in love with a beautiful woman without being aware of her identity ('Une ange, une femme inconnue'). Balthazar's austere admonitions serve only to strengthen the young man's resolve. Blindfolded, Fernand is taken to the island of Léon, where he is greeted by Inès and other ladies. Léonor appears and tells Fernand that she appreciates his feelings, but she refuses to tell him who she is and asks him to forget her. As a farewell present she hands him a royal commission and leaves. Alone, Fernand determines to win military glory so that he can ask for her hand.

Act II: Alphonse, king of Castile, thinks longingly of Léonor as he walks through the gardens of Alcazar ('Léonor, viens!'). He intends to divorce his wife and make his mistress his queen. Léonor comes to him and sadly begs him to release her from what is an intolerably humiliating position. Alphonse attempts to cheer her up with some dancing (ballet). Balthazar, who is father to the queen as well as to Fernand, arrives at court with a papal bull of excommunication, which will take effect if the king pursues his intention of putting his consort aside. When Alphonse proudly refuses to heed this injunction, Balthazar pronounces an anathema before the horrified courtiers.

Act III: Covered with honour for having defeated the Moors, Fernand comes to make obeisance to the king. Complacently, the king offers to grant any favour that Fernand might request. When the young man asks for Léonor's hand, Alphonse, who cannot believe that Fernand is ignorant of the lady's compromised position, ironically accedes to this happy solution of his dilemma and commands the ceremony be performed at once ('Pour tant d'amour'). Léonor loves the young man's sincerity, but she feels unworthy of him ('O, mon Fernand'). She asks Inès to deliver a note revealing her true position, but one of the courtiers, Don Gaspard, detains Inès so that Fernand goes into the adjacent chapel uninformed. While the ceremony is taking place, the courtiers comment on the dishonourable affair. When Fernand emerges from the chapel, Alphonse confers noble titles on him. The courtiers, however, refuse to acknowledge him as their equal. Balthazar arrives and from him Fernand learns the truth. Fernand confronts the king; refusing the titles given him, and breaking his sword and casting it at the royal feet, he leaves to resume the cloistered life.

Act IV: Monks dig the grave of the queen, who has just died. Fernand is still haunted by the memory of Léonor ('Ange si pur'). After he leaves to be received into full membership of the order, Léonor, disguised as a novice, appears, ill and conscience-stricken, hoping for a last glimpse of Fernand. When he returns, he starts to order her away, but then, seeing the genuineness of her contrition, he can think only of being with her. For a time, she shares his vain illusion, but her strength fails her and she dies at his feet.

In spite of its diverse sources, the score of *La favorite* is remarkably cohesive. Unlike most grand operas of its period, it has an almost austere and solemn colour, yet it contains much smouldering feeling, particularly in the final act, much admired by Toscanini. The sensuous, aristocratic nature of Alphonse is admirably depicted. Once one accepts the odd premiss that Fernand, as the queen's brother, should be ignorant of the identity of his brother-in-law's mistress, the plot is convincing. Although this opera has usually been performed in a not very exact Italian translation and in a version inauthentic in a number of details, the publication of the facsimile edition raises hopes that *La favorite* will regain its former pride of place.

RECORDINGS 1. Lapeyrette,

R. Lassalle, Albers, anon. Ch & O, Ruhlmann, Marston, 1912: in French; 2. Furmansky, Kasarova, Vargas, Michaels-Moore, Colombara, Piccoli, Bavarian RCh, Munich RO, Viotti, RCA, 1999: in French; 3. Cossotto, Pavarotti, Bacquier, Ghiaurov, Teatro Comunale Bologna Ch & O, Bonynge, Decca, 1974: in Italian

Don Pasquale

Opera buffa in three acts (2h)
Libretto by Giovanni Ruffini and the composer, after the libretto by Angelo Anelli for *Ser Marc'Antonio* by Pavesi (1810)
Composed 1842
PREMIERES 3 January 1843, Théâtre-Italien, Paris; UK: 29 June 1843, Her Majesty's Theatre, Haymarket, London; US: 7 January 1845, Théâtre d'Orléans, New Orleans
CAST Norina *s*, Ernesto *t*, Dr Malatesta *bar*, Don Pasquale *b*, Notary *b*; *satb* chorus of servants

Donizetti's comic masterpiece is the last of the golden tradition of opera buffa of the first half of the 19th century to remain in the international repertoire. Designed for the principal quartet of the Théâtre-Italien, *Don Pasquale* has a concentration and comic sweep, humanized by touches of Donizettian pathos, that sets it in a class by itself. At this point in his busy, occasionally frantic, career Donizetti had accumulated a background of practical theatrical experience unmatched by that of any of his rivals, and this experience in combination with his musical talent produced a work whose freshness has never faltered. In the light of this achievement, it is difficult to realize that before the year was out the illness that would dim his mental capacities would manifest itself.

SYNOPSIS
Act I, Scene 1: Don Pasquale impatiently awaits his friend and doctor, determined to disinherit his nephew Ernesto, who to his uncle's displeasure has fallen in love with the widow Norina. Pasquale wishes to consult Dr Malatesta about undertaking a marriage himself and siring some more direct heirs. When Malatesta appears, he informs Pasquale that he knows of the perfect bride for him ('Bella siccome un angelo'), whom he claims to be none other than his own sister, though he intends to employ his cousin Norina as the supposed bride. Pasquale confronts his nephew about his refusal to marry the woman his uncle approves of, ordering his nephew out of the house and announcing his own impending marriage ('Prender moglie!'). Realizing that his own hopes of marrying Norina are ruined ('Sogno soave e casto'), Ernesto suggests that his uncle should consult Dr Malatesta about this implausible prospect; he is astounded when he learns that the doctor has already given his whole-hearted approval. Scene 2: Norina reads a tale of chivalric love, laughing over its absurdity, and expressing her conviction that real femininity is far more persuasive ('So anch'io la virtù magica'). Dr Malatesta comes to see Norina to enlist her assistance in his plan to bring Pasquale to his senses. She is to pretend to be his sister 'Sofronia', fresh from a convent, and they agree on the details of the impersonation ('Pronta io son').

Act II: The disillusioned Ernesto has made his preparations to depart ('Cercherò lontana terra'). In a fever of impatience, Pasquale awaits the bride. The doctor leads in a demure young lady wearing a veil, a spectacle that titillates the susceptible Pasquale ('Sta a vedere'). 'Sofronia' is upset to find herself in a room with a strange man, and, on being questioned, she admits to sewing as her only pastime. Malatesta produces a notary (in reality his nephew Carlino) and a wedding contract is drawn up by which Pasquale endows his bride with half his worldly goods. This arrangement is barely concluded when Ernesto appears to bid his uncle farewell; he is dismayed by Norina's apparent infidelity. No sooner is the contract signed than 'Sofronia' changes character completely, appointing Ernesto her *cavaliere servante*. When Pasquale objects, she insists on having her way. The old man is stunned by this turn of events ('E' rimasto là impietrato'). She demands more servants, carriages and other extravagances, leaving Pasquale close to apoplexy.

Act III, Scene 1: Don Pasquale is dismayed at the accumulation of bills run up by his bride. She appears in evening dress, announcing she is going to the theatre. When he objects, she advises him to go to bed. At the height of the altercation, she slaps his face. Now thoroughly disillusioned, Pasquale contemplates the results of his impulsiveness ('E' finita, Don Pasquale'). Seeing his discomfiture, Norina feels sorry for him and advises him to get a good night's sleep ('Via, caro sposino'). As she leaves, she drops a note, which Pasquale picks up and reads. Horrified to learn that an assignation in the garden is planned for that very evening, Pasquale summons Malatesta. The servants comment on the turmoil of the household ('Che interminabile andirivieni!'). When Malatesta appears, he and the doctor plot how they will catch Norina and unmask her infidelity ('Cheti, cheti, immantinente'). Scene 2: Ernesto serenades his beloved ('Com'è gentil'). Norina steals in, and they sing a tender duet ('Tornami a dir che m'ami'). Pasquale surprises them, but Malatesta resolves the imbroglio by persuading his friend to agree to annul his own marriage and allow Ernesto to marry Norina. Although he feels he has been made a fool of, Pasquale is so relieved to be free of 'Sofronia' that he blesses the young lovers.

Although *Don Pasquale* makes some use of music that had already been used in other contexts, the score seems perfectly homogenous. Written in a relatively short time, the music was carefully worked out, as the compositional sketches testify. The overture sparkles and quotes several themes that appear later in the opera: notably Ernesto's Act III serenade and Norina's self-analysing aria from Act I. Malatesta's aria in the opening scene, 'Bella siccome un angelo', in which he describes the charms of his mythical sister, is a fine example of bel canto irony. The high spirits of the work are neatly epitomized in the duet for Norina and Malatesta that closes Act I, wherein he coaches her in the part she must play to bamboozle Pasquale. Act II, with its unflagging build-up to an hilarious climax, is for many the summit of Donizetti's achievement. Act III contains its own share of riches in three irresistible duets and an apt finale to point the moral of the piece: that December should not tempt fate with May. Instead of the traditional secco recitative, the connective passages are string-accompanied. The mid-point finale is a solo quartet without choral reinforcement; indeed, the chorus appears only in the two scenes of Act III.

RECORDINGS 1. Saraceni, Schipa, Poli, Badini, La Scala Ch & O, Sabanjo, Music Memoria, 1932; 2. Mei, Lopardo, Aleen, Bruson, Bavarian RCh, Munich RO, R. Abbado, RCA, 1993

OTHER OPERAS *Il Pigmalione*, (1816) 1960; *L'ira d'Achille*, (1817); *Enrico di Borgogna*, 1818; *Una follia*, 1818; *Il falegname di Livonia, o Pietro il grande, czar delle Russie*, 1819; *Le nozze in villa*, 1820/21; *Zoraida di Granata*, 1822; *La zingara*, 1822; *La lettera anonima*, 1822; *Chiara e Serafina*, 1822; *Alfredo il grande*, 1823; *Il fortunato inganno*, 1823; *L'ajo nell'imbarazzo, o Don Gregorio*, 1824; *Emilia di Liverpool*, 1824; *Alahor in Granata*, 1826; *Elvida*, 1826; *Gabriella di Vergy*, (1826) 1869; *Olivo e Pasquale*, 1827; *Otto mesi in due ore*, 1827; *Il borgomastro di Saardam*, 1827; *Le convenienze ed inconvenienze teatrali*, 1827; *L'esule di Roma, ossia Il proscritto*, 1828; *Alina, regina di Golconda*, 1828; *Gianni di Calais*, 1828; *Il paria*, 1829; *Il giovedì grasso*, 1829; *Elisabetta al castello di Kenilworth*, 1829; *I pazzi per progetto*, 1830; *Il diluvio* *universale*, 1830; *Imelda de' Lambertazzi*, 1830; *La romanzesca e l'uomo nero*, 1831; *Gianni di Parigi*, (1831), 1839; *Francesca di Foix*, 1831; *Fausta*, 1832; *Ugo, Conte di Parigi*, 1832; *Sancia di Castiglia*, 1832; *Il furioso all'isola di San Domingo*, 1833; *Parisina*, 1833; *Torquato Tasso*, 1833; *Lucrezia Borgia*, 1833; *Rosmonda d'Inghilterra*, 1834; *Gemma di Vergy*, 1834; *Marino Faliero*, 1835; *Belisario*, 1836; *Il campanello di notte*, 1836; *Betly, ossia La campanna svizzera*, 1836; *L'assedio di Calais*, 1836; *Pia de' Tolomei*, 1837; *Maria de Rudenz*, 1838; *Poliuto*, (1838), 1848 (as *Les Martyrs*, 1840); *Il duca d'Alba*, (1839 inc.) completed Matteo Salvi, 1882; *Elisabetta*, (mid-1840s), 1997 (concert); *L'ange de Nisida*, (1839); *Adelia*, 1841; *Rita, ou Le mari battu*, (1841), 1860; *Maria Padilla*, 1841; *Linda di Chamounix*, 1842; *Caterina Conaro*, 1844; *Maria di Rohan*, 1843; *Dom Sébastien*, 1843

W.A.

Antonín Dvořák

Antonín Leopold Dvořák;
b 8 September 1841, Nelahozeves, nr Kralupy; *d* 1 May 1904, Prague

Dvořák's operatic education came largely from playing the viola in the orchestra of the Prague Provisional Theatre from its opening in 1862 until 1871, by which time he had written his first opera, *Alfred*. To say that his operatic career spanned most of his life as a composer is accurate but misleading. *Alfred* was written within five years of his first substantial surviving compositions such as the first two symphonies and the song-cycle *Cypresses* (*Cypřiše*); *Armida* was his last completed composition, premiered only a few weeks before his death. However, the pattern of work that spans these two operas is irregular: between 1882, when he completed *Dimitrij*, and 1897, when he wrote *The Devil and Kate*, Dvořák composed only one new opera. During this 15-year period he was at the height of his powers, writing his three last symphonies, the Cello Concerto, the late chamber music and most of his choral music. His turning away from opera was partly a sign of his frustration with the medium and his lack of success in making any mark abroad with it, and perhaps a recognition that his natural talents lay elsewhere. There were also the practical circumstances that some of this time was spent outside Bohemia – his numerous trips to England (where large-scale choral works were preferred to operas), his three-year stint in America (where he went to the opera only twice and even wrote to a friend that he regretted all the time he had spent writing operas). Nor was there much demand for operas from Prague, which preferred to fill its brand new National Theatre, at least in the opening decade, with lavishly produced foreign novelties and ballets rather than native operas.

Therefore Dvořák's opera-writing falls into two distinct halves: at the beginning of his life and at the end, bridged by *The Jacobin* in the middle. Dvořák's earlier operatic period epitomizes many of the trends in contemporary Czech opera. His first opera, *Alfred* (1870), was in German, looking back to earlier German-orientated Prague composers. Its subject matter, like that of *Vanda* (1875), was concerned with national conflicts: English against Danes in *Alfred*; Poles against Germans in *Vanda*. This series of large-scale serious operas reaches a climax with *Dimitrij* (1881–2). *Vanda* was written originally in five acts; *Dimitrij* was planned in five acts, though later reduced to four. This, together with their 'political' subject matter, suggests a debt to French grand opera, a model evident in many other aspects of composition, such as the deployment of double choruses and large-scale concerted finales.

Dvořák's three other operas of the 1870s, *King and Charcoal Burner*, *The Stubborn Lovers* and *The Cunning Peasant*, are all instead of the 'village comedy' type of Czech operas of the period. They are all on a smaller scale, the second and third in one and two acts respectively. The musical idiom is lighter and owes more to Lortzing and Nicolai than to Meyerbeer. Uniting both lines of development is an emphasis on instrumental music. All the operas have overtures; most have instrumental dances and recurring motifs to provide unity. It is remarkable that the libretti of these six operas were all by different librettists, in some cases writers completely unknown to Dvořák.

In *Dimitrij* Dvořák had worked closely with the librettist, Marie Červinková-Riegrová, and she provided him with the libretto for his next opera, *The Jacobin* (1887–8). Though Dvořák was not to write another new opera until 1897, the years after *Dimitrij* saw revision of three operas, among them a final version of *King and Charcoal Burner*, and some additions to *The Jacobin*. But the most radical revision was that of *Dimitrij*, rewritten in a sternly 'declamatory' version that jettisoned many of the ensembles. The inspiration behind this was Dvořák's later recognition of Wagnerian music drama: if there are Wagnerian traits in the earlier operas they are a good generation behind the time, the Wagner of *Tannhäuser* and *Lohengrin*.

With this radically changed aesthetic Dvořák approached the three operas written in his final period, which together with a series of tone poems formed the entire output of his final eight years. *The Devil and Kate* avoids duets, though the role of the chorus is undiminished and the piece is studded with recognizable set numbers. Orchestrally there is a great expansion – perhaps too great to accommodate the slender folktale on which it is based. In Dvořák's next opera, *Rusalka*, without doubt his masterpiece, the chorus has less work, but there are a number of real duets, while by the final opera, *Armida*, he had slipped back into an aesthetic not noticeably different from that of his first opera over 30 years earlier.

This is symptomatic of the problems with Dvořák's operas. He inherited a conception of opera that was, by current European standards, out of date, and, despite a flirtation with Wagnerian music drama in the 1890s, it did not really change or develop. Though he used recurring themes, they are those of a symphonist attempting to unify a long complex work rather than those of a musical dramatist using leitmotifs to supply extra-musical information. Dvořák's early operas tend to be hit or miss affairs, over-dependent on the strength of their libretti. His own compositional personality was not sufficiently developed to override this in the way that it does in later works. With the exception of the flagging *Armida*, his operas from *Dimitrij* onwards all have distinct and forceful musical personalities, which have spoken directly to the Czech public, over the heads of the strongly anti-Dvořák lobby that, in the early years of the century, was keen to promote almost any composer other than Dvořák as 'Smetana's successor'. Some of the results of this official disdain are still evident in the niggardly provision of scores and recordings of the earlier works.

Rusalka

Lyric fairy tale in three acts (3h)
Libretto by Jaroslav Kvapil, after the tale *Undine* by Friedrich Heinrich Carl de la Motte Fouqué (1811)
Composed 1900
PREMIERES 31 March 1901, National Theatre, Prague; US: 10 November 1935, Sokol Slav Hall, Chicago; UK: 9 May 1950, Peter Jones Theatre, London
CAST Prince *t*, Foreign Princess *s*, Rusalka *s*, Water Goblin *b*, Ježibaba *ms*, 3 *s*, *c*, 2 *t*; *satb* chorus of wood sprites, the Prince's entourage, guests at the castle

SYNOPSIS
Act I: Rusalka (a water nymph) wishes to become human to gain the love of the Prince. Ježibaba the witch makes two

conditions for her magic: that Rusalka be dumb and that her lover be true – otherwise both will be damned. Despite the warnings of the anxious Water Goblin, Rusalka proceeds on this hazardous path; her Prince is captivated by her appearance, and takes her off with him.

Act II: At court the dumb Rusalka is no match for the brilliant and evil Foreign Princess. Rumours circulate about Rusalka's supernatural origins, and the Prince rejects her.

Act III: Rusalka, a pale shadow of her former self, mourns her state. Her Prince, now repentant, returns. She is able to speak to him and explain that he will die if she kisses him. He begs her to do so. At her kiss, he perishes, and Rusalka, released from the curse, disappears into the lake.

Rusalka stands out clearly above all of Dvořák's operas as his most successful and most popular. Unlike the rather thin tale on which *The Devil and Kate* is based, the Undine legend that lies behind *Rusalka* has a haunting resonance which is magically matched by Dvořák's music. The composer found a vein of melodic poignancy that memorably sets off his heroine: for many years Rusalka's 'Hymn to the moon' was all that was known abroad of Dvořák's vast operatic output. The libretto itself cleverly grafted on to its sources (which include Andersen's *Little Mermaid*) a folk periphery that identifies the work as distinctively Czech. Characters such as the doleful Water Goblin and the malicious witch were by then well known from Erben's ballads and had recently formed the basis of two of Dvořák's tone poems. Kvapil changed the chief characters too, notably Rusalka herself, who is here essentially a suffering Slavonic heroine (rather like Dargomyzhsky's Rusalka), rather than the skittish Undine in Lortzing's opera. Dvořák responded well to all aspects of the libretto with the result that the work has an impressive range of characterization, from its poignant heroine and evocative nature scenes to the brilliant court scenes in Act II, and some surprisingly effective comic relief with the mock-serious witch, a kitchen boy and a gamekeeper. For all the Wagnerian ripeness of the harmony and orchestration, Dvořák discarded some of the Wagnerian aesthetic that lay behind *The Devil and Kate* and his revision of *Dimitrij*. The duets he now included were some of his most committed and passionate.

RECORDINGS 1. Beňačková, Drobková, Soukupová, Ochman, Novák, Prague Philharmonic Ch, Czech PO, Neumann, Supraphon, 1982/3; 2. Fleming, Urbanová, Zajick, Heppner, Hawlata, Kühn Mixed Ch, Czech PO, Mackerras, Decca, 1998

OTHER OPERAS *Alfred*, (1870) 1938; *King and Charcoal Burner* (*Kráhl a uhlíř*), 1874; *The Stubborn Lovers* (*Tvrdé palice*), 1874; *Vanda*, 1876; *The Cunning Peasant* (*Šelma sedlák*), 1878; *Dimitri* (*Dmtrij*), 1882; *The Jacobin* (*Jakobin*), 1889; *The Devil and Kate* (*Čert a Káča*), 1899; *Armida*, 1904

J.T.

Manuel de Falla

Manuel María de los Dolores de Falla y Matheu; *b* 23 November 1876, Cadiz, Spain; *d* 14 November 1946, Alta Gracia de Córdoba, Argentina

Falla was the outstanding Spanish composer of the 20th century. His music evolved from the easy outpourings of *La vida breve* to the burning economy of the Harpsichord Concerto (1926) and the pungent austerity of *Atlántida*. Meanwhile regionalism made way for a wider view, still intensely Spanish but of supranational relevance. Falla was born and educated in Cadiz, where, apart from the vital background of Andalusian folksong, there was little but salon music and decent amateur endeavour. When his family moved in 1896 to Madrid, Falla entered the conservatory, completing the seven-year course in two years. The only outlet for an ambitious young composer was the theatre, where light opera in the form of zarzuelas held sway. Unwillingly Falla conformed, writing six zarzuelas, three of them in collaboration with Amadeo Vives. Only *Los amores de la Inés* was performed (1902). Of greater importance was the revelation of the music of Felipe Pedrell (1841–1922), persuaded by Falla to take him as a pupil. In 1904 Falla entered and won two competitions, one a piano contest, the other for one-act operas for which he submitted *La vida breve*. The authorities' failure to implement the promised Madrid production of the winning piece caused Falla much frustration. His dream of going to Paris was not realized until 1907. Once there he met Dukas, Debussy, Ravel and other French musicians as well as his compatriot Albéniz. After a long wait *La vida breve* was performed in Nice, Paris and finally, after Falla had returned there in 1914 at the outbreak of war, in Madrid. He completed *Nights in the Gardens of Spain* for piano and orchestra and wrote the two ballets, *El amor brujo* and *The Three-Cornered Hat*.

After his parents' deaths in 1919 Falla moved to Granada, paradoxically ceasing to write overtly Andalusian music. His strange character intensified: he was a devout Catholic, superstitious, a conservative who abhorred violence and militarism. Since he had many friends of liberal tendencies, during the Civil War he suffered mental agony. His health deteriorated. When he left Spain for Argentina in 1939, *Atlántida*, a score that had already occupied him for more than a decade, was unfinished, and remained incomplete at his death. In Granada Falla wrote some incidental music for two autos sacramentales, Calderón's *El gran teatro del mundo* and Lope de Vega's *La vuelta de Egipto*. Many operatic collaborations with friends, including the poet Lorca and the painter Zuloaga, were discussed but not started. A curious project towards the end of his second Madrid period was a three-act comic opera *Fuego fatuo* (Will-o'-the-wisp) with a libretto by María Martinez Sierra and music adapted from Chopin's piano works by Falla. Only the outer acts of the three were finished before the scheme was abandoned. In 1976 Antoni Ros Marbá made an orchestral suite out of the completed acts.

La vida breve

Life is Brief

Lyric drama in two acts (four tableaux) (1h 15m)
Libretto by Carlos Fernández Shaw
Composed 1904
PREMIERES 1 April 1913, Casino Municipal, Nice (in French); US: 6 March 1926, Metropolitan, New York; UK: 9 September 1958, King's Theatre, Edinburgh
CAST Salud *s*, La abuela (grandmother) *ms* or *c*, Paco *t*, Uncle Sarvaor *bar* or *b*, Manuel *bar*, Carmela *ms*, singer *bar*, 3 street-sellers 2 *s*, *ms*, 2 offstage voices 2 *t*; *satb* chorus of townsfolk (wedding guests)

Falla and the zarzuela writer Fernández Shaw had agreed to collaborate and had started work on their project when the one-act opera competition was announced by the Royal Academy of San Fernando in 1904. Even so, *La vida breve* had to be written quickly. The opera won the prize, but the Madrid production held out as an inducement did not materialize. When Falla showed the score to musicians in Paris they (Dukas especially) were favourably impressed, but not until 1913 was the opera accepted. By then Falla had for practical reasons divided the opera into two acts, touched up the orchestration, expanded the second scene and the second dance and, on the advice of Debussy, shortened the ending. The success of the Nice premiere induced the Opéra-Comique to change its mind; the further acclaim in Paris caused Madrid to open its doors at last. The success of the first performance in Spanish, on 14 November 1914 in Madrid, was triumphant.

SYNOPSIS

Act I: Granada, at the turn of the century. Salud lives with her grandmother in the gypsy quarter above the town. She is anxiously awaiting Paco, a local playboy who has seduced her and promised marriage. The grandmother is reassuring but warns Salud against loving too much. Voices of workmen in a nearby forge are heard, lamenting the miserable poor, born to be anvils, not hammers. Salud enlarges on their words in an aria. Paco arrives, protesting love. Unnoticed by the couple, Sarvaor steals in and confirms to the grandmother the truth of a rumour about Paco's impending marriage to a well-off girl in the town. Paco and Salud arrange to meet next day. The following scene takes place in mime as night falls over Granada. Paco takes leave of Salud. The grandmother restrains Sarvaor from following him.

Act II, Scene 1: The front of a house in the town. Night. Through the windows the patio can be seen, illuminated for the wedding of Paco to Carmela. A *cantaor* sings in their honour. During the following dance (familiar in transcriptions as Spanish Dance No. 1) Salud appears. She sings of her grief at Paco's betrayal and of her wish to die. Her grandmother and Sarvaor join her. Salud repeats the workmen's hammer-and-anvil comparison. Scene 2: Inside the patio Paco, Carmela and her brother Manuel (the host) are the centre of a throng of wedding guests. There is a second dance, with wordless chorus. Sarvaor appears leading Salud; she holds back, then suddenly denounces Paco. As she advances towards him she falls dead at his feet.

The libretto veers between passionate feelings violently expressed and another form of verismo – a detailed depiction of the sights and sounds of Granada, a remarkable case of empathy (reminiscent of Gustave Charpentier's depiction of Paris in *Louise*) since Falla had not visited the town when he wrote the opera. The music, written in haste when Falla was bursting with invention, is irresistible in spite of stylistic inconsistency. The depiction of Salud, the only character drawn in the round, is highly individual. There is a quality of youthful exuberance in the opera which Falla neither achieved nor sought again.

RECORDINGS 1. de los Angeles, Cossutta, Orfeón Donostiarra Ch, Nat O of Spain, Frühbeck de Burgos, EMI, 1966; 2. Berganza, Carreras, Ambrosian Op Ch, LSO, Navarra, DG, 1978

El retablo de Maese Pedro

Master Peter's Puppet Show

Musical and scenic version of an episode from *El Ingenioso Cavallero Don Quixote de la Mancha* in one act (30m)
Libretto by the composer after *Don Quixote* by Miguel de Cervantes (1605 and 1615)
Composed 1919–22
PREMIERES 23 March 1923, Teatro San Fernando, Seville (concert); 25 June 1923, Princesse Edmond de Polignac's house, Paris (private); UK: 13 October 1924, Victoria Rooms, Clifton, Bristol; US: 29 December 1925, New York
CAST Don Quixote *bar* or *b*, Maese Pedro *t*, El trujaman (the boy) boy *s*, 5 mime roles, several puppets

In 1919 Princesse Edmond de Polignac asked Falla to write a chamber opera for performance in her house in Paris. Falla, who had arranged the music for some private puppet shows in Granada devised by Lorca, suggested a puppet opera based on an episode in *Don Quixote*. The princess gave permission for a concert performance in Seville (conducted by Falla) a few months before the private Paris premiere. On the latter occasion Hector Dufranne sang Don Quixote, the conductor was Wladimir Golschmann, and Wanda Landowska played the harpsichord.

SYNOPSIS

On a trestle table in the yard of a Spanish inn the travelling showman Master Peter presents a puppet play. The boy, interrupted from time to time by pedantic objections from Don Quixote in the audience, intones the narration. The play is set in the time of Charlemagne. The emperor's daughter Melisendra is a captive of the Moors at Saragossa in Spain. The emperor rebukes her husband, Don Gayferos, for not going to her rescue. From her prison in a tower Melisendra scans the horizon. A Moor steals a kiss and is sentenced by the king, Marsilius, to punishment, which is duly effected. Gayferos sets out on horseback for Spain. The hills resound with horn- and trumpet-calls. Gayferos reaches Saragossa and reveals himself. Melisendra leaps from her tower into his arms. They ride off towards France. When Quixote sees Moors in pursuit of the Christian couple, he rises in fury. Believing the spectacle to be real, he wrecks the puppets with his sword before declaring himself 'knight errant and captive of the most fair Dulcinea' to whom he sings a prayer. Finally he addresses the public on the virtues of knight-errantry.

The opera can be performed by two sets of puppets (large ones for Quixote, Master Peter, his boy and the onlookers, small ones for the players) with the three singers in the orchestra, or by the singers and mimes for the 'real' characters and small puppets for the players. Another possibility is to use singers and mimes with children in the place of puppets – all masked.

El retablo, in every way a more sophisticated work than *La vida breve*, ranks with Stravinsky's *L'histoire du soldat* as a seminal piece of music theatre. The spontaneity and wide range of expression conceal a carefully prepared synthesis of national, historical and popular elements. Typical are the writing for the boy, whose narrations, delivered in shrill monotone, were based on plainsong and street cries, and the way in which Falla lifts the final scene for Quixote on to a different plane. The scoring, for example in Gayferos's ride through the Pyrenees, shows Falla at his most masterly. So finely calculated are the proportions that the opera feels longer and bigger than it really is.

RECORDING Smith, Oliver, Knapp, London Sinfonietta, Rattle, Decca, 1980
OTHER OPERATIC WORKS Operas: *El conde de Villamediana* (lost, 1887); *Fuego fatuo* (Acts I and III; Act II, inc. 1919); *Atlántida*, (inc. 1946), 1961; Zarzuelas: *Los amores de la Inés*, 1902; *Prisionero de guerra* (coll. with Vives; inc.), (1904); lost zarzuelas: *La Juana y la Petra, or La casa de Tócame Roque* (1902); *Limosna de amor* (?1903); *El cornetín de órdenes* (with Vives), (1903); *La Cruz de Malta* (with Vives), (?1903)

R.H.C.

Carlisle Floyd

Carlisle Sessions Floyd Jr; *b* 11 June 1926, Latta, South Carolina, US

Born into the family of a Methodist minister, Floyd grew up amongst the type of community that would later form the background to more than one of his operas. A serious piano student, he followed his teacher Ernst Bacon (himself a composer interested in American subjects and folk music) to Syracuse, New York, in 1945; he also had lessons with Rudolf Firkusny. Floyd became head of the piano faculty at Florida State University in 1947, remaining there until 1976 when he moved to Houston as Professor of Composition (he had also taught composition latterly at Florida) and to assume the co-directorship of the Houston Opera Studio.

Floyd began to compose operas to his own texts in 1949: the first, *Slow Dusk*, was derived from one of his own short stories and premiered at Syracuse University. The success of *Susannah* in 1955 at Florida University was repeated the following year at the New York City Opera, and established at a stroke Floyd's position as a leading American opera composer. It remains a favourite with both professional companies and student bodies. In March 1999 it was granted the honour of a staging at the New York Metropolitan.

Floyd continued to produce operas, almost all of them based on local subjects, up to the beginning of the 1980s, then switched to other (mainly vocal) media, returning to the genre after a gap of nearly two decades. His works have enjoyed mixed success, but a number of them have been repeatedly revived within the US. While only *Susannah* and *Of Mice and Men* have had much of a career overseas, the number of their European admirers seems to be on the increase. Very much on the conservative wing of American music, Floyd can nevertheless be seen as a careful craftsman with a natural and formidable instinct for what works on stage.

Susannah

Musical drama in two acts (1h 30m)
Libretto by the composer, after the Apocrypha
Composed 1953–4
PREMIERES 24 February 1955, Florida State University, Tallahassee; UK: 27 July 1961, Civic Hall, Orpington

Floyd has recently admitted that although he knew the outlines of the story, he had not actually read the biblical account of Susanna when he wrote his opera. The simple tale shows an innocent young woman persecuted by the members of the Evangelical sect in her small-town community when discovered bathing naked by the Elders of the church. The fierce visiting preacher, Rev. Olin Blitch, becomes her chief persecutor and then seducer, falling victim to her brother's bullet after Susannah has told him what has occurred. The directness and sincerity of Floyd's style suit his subject well, even though the quality of his material is uneven. At its best, however, he as librettist provides himself as composer with strong situations and responds with apt and effective musical atmosphere and characterizations. Opportunities present themselves for revival hymn-singing, folk-songs and dances: all are seized upon and managed with skill in purely musical terms and the instant memorability of several numbers has clearly aided the score's popularity. The two major roles – those of Susannah and Blitch – also offer marvellous opportunities for talented singing-actors.

RECORDING Studer, Hadley, Chester, Ramey, Op Nat de Lyon Ch & O, Nagano, Virgin, 1993/4

OTHER OPERAS *Slow Dusk*, 1949; *The Fugitives* (withdrawn), 1951; *Wuthering Heights*, 1958; *The Passion of Jonathan Wade*, 1962, rev. 1991; *The Sojourner and Mollie Sinclair*, 1963; *Markheim*, 1966; *Of Mice and Men*, 1970; *Bilby's Doll*, 1976; *Willie Stark*, 1981; *Cold Sassy Tree*, 2000

G.H.

G

John Gay

b September 1685, Barnstaple, Devon, England; *d* 4 December 1732, London

John Gay is unique among the figures treated in this book in that he is not known to have composed a bar of music in his life; but he invented opera's most significant mutant form. Ballad opera, of which Gay's *The Beggar's Opera* is the first and the best, led to German singspiel, French opéra bouffon and the Anglo-American musical. His musical attainments did not extend beyond recorder-playing, but this gave him access to the innumerable songbooks of the day, which provided transpositions of the tunes within the compass of that instrument. He went to London as apprentice to a silk mercer; a small legacy enabled him to break the indenture and, in 1708, to embark on a literary career. He became a lifelong friend of Alexander Pope.

From the start Gay's work exploited a deliberate incongruity of form and content; a mordant sense of social reality was given point by being expressed in an effortlessly decorous literary attire. He wrote the libretto for Handel's *Acis and Galatea* (1718), which is notable for its firm and economical construction and for the reanimation of stock material by dint of drastic pruning. At about this time Gay started to explore the possibilities of the broadside ballad: 'Sweet William's Farewell to Black-ey'd Susan' (1720) rapidly acquired tunes by four rival composers. The idea of a 'Newgate Pastoral' had been mooted by Dean Swift, in a letter to Pope, as early as 1715. In 1724 Newgate became especially topical: the highwayman Jack Sheppard was finally captured and hanged, and the informer and receiver Jonathan Wild was knifed in court by one of his victims. Gay celebrated this in 'Newgate's Garland', a ballad to be sung to the tune of 'Packington's Pound', which prefigures the method, setting and substance of *The Beggar's Opera*. But whereas 'Newgate's Garland' is a single song, *The Beggar's Opera* is a three-act drama with spoken dialogue and 69 airs all to existing tunes: English, Irish and Scots traditional melodies, and popular songs by recent composers, including Purcell, Handel, Henry Carey and Bononcini.

In a sequel, *Polly*, Macheath is transported to the West Indies, marries Jenny Diver, and, disguised as a black man, turns pirate. He has been followed to the Caribbean by Polly who, disguised as a man, becomes an honorary member of an Indian tribe, which captures him. It is amusing but bland, and Gay seems to have used up his stock of catchy and pointed tunes. It was banned by the Lord Chamberlain and sold well in consequence; when it was eventually produced it flopped, as did a posthumous ballad opera on a classical theme, *Achilles*.

The Beggar's Opera

Ballad opera in three acts (orig. version: 3h)
Libretto by John Gay

PREMIERES 29 January 1728, Lincoln's Inn Fields Theatre, London; US: 3 December 1750, Nassau Street Theater, New York; UK: Austin arrangement: 5 June 1920, Lyric Theatre, Hammersmith, London; Britten arrangement: 24 May 1948, Arts Theatre, Cambridge
CAST Peachum *b*, Lockit *b*, Macheath *t*, Filch *t*, Mrs Peachum *ms*, Polly Peachum *s*, Lucy Lockit *s*; *sa* chorus of women of the town; *tb* chorus of Macheath's gang

There was nothing new about plays with an extensive musical component nor in writing fresh words to existing tunes; Gay's originality lay in seeing how the principle could be extended, making song the predominant element, advancing the action rather than serving merely as its reflection. *The Beggar's Opera* was an immediate success, running for 32 nights consecutively, and 62 in the season altogether. Though there are some contemporary allusions (Lockit as Walpole, the prime minister; Polly and Lucy as Faustina and Cuzzoni, the rival prima donnas from the Italian Opera), Gay did not attempt to make them run consistently through the piece. The satire is general: what distinguishes a military hero from a highwayman in uniform, a woman who marries for money from a prostitute, a politician from a venal gaoler, an operatic aria from a good vernacular song? Many of the original words to the tunes would have been familiar to the audience, and the subversion of the sentiments these express is also part of Gay's design.

It has been claimed, improbably, that Gay originally intended the airs to be unaccompanied. In the event Dr Pepusch, harpsichordist at Lincoln's Inn Fields, provided basses for the songs and a lively overture, which has for its allegro an anticipation of Lucy's 'I'm like a ship on the ocean tossed'. The songs would probably have been introduced by the orchestra and doubled as appropriate. Dr Burney, no great admirer of Pepusch, thought his basses 'so excellent that no sound contrapuntist will ever attempt to alter them'. Nevertheless, in almost every subsquent generation some such effort has been made. Notable 20th-century versions were those of Frederick Austin (with text edited by Arnold Bennett) and Benjamin Britten. The work also inspired the completely rewritten Brecht–Weill collaboration, *Die Dreigroschenoper*. Both Weill and Britten radically miscomprehended Gay's intentions by giving acerbic accompaniments to pretty tunes, thus upsetting the whole ironic balance of words and music in the original, but Austin did not make this mistake. Jeremy Barlow was the first to attempt a scholarly historical reconstruction.

SYNOPSIS

In a spoken introduction the Beggar apologizes for failing to make his opera 'throughout, unnatural, like those in vogue; for I have no Recitative'; otherwise it 'must be allowed an Opera in all its Forms'.

Act I takes place in the house of Peachum, an informer and receiver of stolen goods. He is anxious to arrange 'a decent Execution against next sessions' and has his eye on Robin of Bagshot, who proves to be a favourite of his wife's. Mrs Peachum voices her suspicion that their daughter, Polly, is involved with the handsome, free-handed highwayman, Captain Macheath. Taxed with this Polly confesses her love and her desire to preserve her honour: 'Virgins are like the fair Flower in its Lustre'. Meanwhile Mrs Peachum has discovered the awful truth: Polly has actually married Macheath and, worse, still loves him. Her parents attempt to make Polly see sense, impeach Macheath and have him hanged. She demurs: 'For on the Rope that hangs my Dear/ Depends poor Polly's life'. Macheath opportunely calls, and Polly persuades him he must flee.

Act II commences in a tavern near Newgate. Macheath's gang lay their plans and set out singing 'Let us take the Road' to the march from Handel's

Rinaldo. Macheath, insatiate for women, summons the ladies of the town. Two favourites, while fondling him, take his pistols and signal for Peachum and the constables to enter and seize him. Macheath is removed to Newgate and the custody of Mr Lockit. He is then confronted by Lucy, Lockit's daughter, whom he has seduced and abandoned. Trapped, he agrees to marry her and they go in search of the chaplain. Peachum and Lockit come to blows over the division of the reward for Macheath's capture, but eventually compose their differences, recognizing their 'Mutual Interest'. Lucy and Macheath return, only to encounter a distracted Polly, resolved to stay with her husband 'till Death'. The quarrel between the girls reaches its climax in 'Why how now, Madam Flirt'; finally Peachum has to tear his daughter away, which gives Macheath the chance to persuade Lucy to help him escape.

Act III begins in Newgate. Lockit berates Lucy for her folly and goes to find Peachum. Macheath meets his gang in a gaming house and is recognized by Diana Trapes, who informs Peachum. In Newgate Lucy, torn by 'Jealousy, Rage, Love and Fear', tries to poison Polly, but when Macheath is brought in, recaptured, Polly drops the laced cordial. Lockit and Peachum hurry him to the Old Bailey. The final scene takes place in the condemned cell where Macheath laments his fate ('O cruel, cruel, cruel Case/Must I suffer this disgrace?'). Other wives arrive: 'Four Women more, Captain, with a Child apiece'. 'This is too much,' says Macheath, and the Player agrees, imploring the Beggar to make the piece end as an opera should, happily. The Beggar agrees, a reprieve is granted, and Macheath and Polly lead off the concluding chorus and dance.

RECORDINGS 1. Prietto, Lipton, Noble, Argo C Ens, R. Austin, Argo, 1955; 2. Mills, Dawson, Walker, Honeyman, Thompson, Broadside Band, Barlow, Hyperion, 1991

OTHER OPERATIC WORKS *Polly* (1728), 1779; *Achilles*, 1733

R.L.

George Gershwin

Jacob Gershvin; *b* 26 September 1898, Brooklyn, New York; *d* 11 July 1937, Hollywood, California

Piano and theory studies at an early age led George Gershwin to work as a pianist when he was 15. His compositional studies remained haphazard and short-lived throughout his life (his longest period of study with a single teacher was his work with Joseph Schillinger from 1932 to 1936). From working as a song-plugger for a publishing house, he quickly moved to composing songs of his own and getting them interpolated into musicals written by others. He soon had the opportunity to supply whole scores for revues, and for George White's *Scandals* of 1922 he provided a 20-minute 'jazz opera', *Blue Monday*.

Gershwin continued to challenge himself by writing instrumental music, and established himself as a leading composer of musicals for the most popular performers of his day; from 1924 onwards he almost always wrote to lyrics by his older brother Ira. His writing for Gertrude Lawrence and the Astaires conformed to the standard structure of musicals of the period, rarely going beyond the 32-bar form. Noteworthy, however, are his harmonic deftness (often evident at the return to the original theme) and the exceptional care he devoted to verses.

His first venture beyond Broadway conventions, *Strike Up the Band* (1927), was initially a failure, but it was successfully revived three years later, and was followed by two other ventures in similar vein (*Of Thee I Sing* and *Let 'Em Eat Cake*). The libretti satirize (in a broadly entertaining way) certain aspects of American life; Gershwin made the most of this by creating scores with links to the quick-witted style of operetta created by Gilbert and Sullivan, as opposed to the more sentimental Viennese-derived strain that had flourished on Broadway. These operettas, though intended for show, rather than operatic, voices, indulged in such luxuries as passages of recitative and ensemble finales that did not reprise the songs (Leonard Bernstein, in *The Joy of Music*, pointed out the parallels between the Act I finales of *The Mikado* and *Of Thee I Sing*), and a greater variety of musical idioms. The use of marches, waltzes, patter and other styles meant that these musicals contained fewer hits than Gershwin's more conventional efforts. But they constituted more satisfying overall entities, extending to greater care in the construction of overtures.

Other commercial Broadway enterprises were not totally abandoned during this period: *Girl Crazy* launched an extraordinary number of hit songs. But the real culmination of Gershwin's work for the musical stage was his opera *Porgy and Bess*. In some technical respects it reveals (as had his concert and stage work since 1932) the skills he had learned from Schillinger in terms of handling thematic development, transition and transformation in an efficient way. From another vantage point it reveals Gershwin reconciling his more ambitious theatrical forms with the abundance of memorable melodies that had characterized his earlier shows; few operas or musicals contain as many famous and unforgettable excerpts as *Porgy*. As he had also achieved success in the film musical during the 1930s, future possibilities seemed limitless for Gershwin, but his life ended tragically early when he died of a brain tumour in 1937.

Gershwin's music retains an indelible place in modern culture. He created songs unsurpassed in the fertility of their melodic invention, the variety of their structures, and the perfection of their craftsmanship. Most of his stage musicals, observing the stage conventions of their time and devised in part as vehicles for distinctive performers, have not borne revival in recent times without extensive alteration – despite the enormous appeal of their music. Perhaps the recent increase in historical performance styles may lead to a revival of Gershwin's musicals on their own terms. Purely on musical grounds, there should always be occasional attempts to bring his earlier shows back to the stage; *Strike Up the Band*, with its merry treatment of an anti-war theme, might well merit first attention. Whether such revivals happen or not, *Porgy and Bess* has secured Gershwin his place as a stage composer of consequence.

Porgy and Bess

Opera in three acts (3h)
Libretto by DuBose Heyward, based on the play *Porgy* by Dorothy and DuBose Heyward; lyrics by DuBose Heyward and Ira Gershwin
Composed 1934–5
PREMIERES 10 October 1935, Alvin Theater, New York; UK: 9 October 1952, Stoll Theatre, London
CAST Porgy *b-bar*, Bess *s*, Crown *bar*, Serena *s*, Clara *s*, Maria *c*, Jake *bar*, Sporting Life *t*, Mingo *t*, Robbins *t*, Peter *t*, Frazier *bar*, Annie *ms*, Lily *ms*, Strawberry woman *ms*, Jim *bar*, Undertaker *bar*, Nelson *t*, Crab man *t*; *spoken roles*: Mr Archdale, Detective, Policeman, Coroner, Scipio (boy); Jasbo Brown *pianist*; *satb* chorus of residents of Catfish Row (including divisi and soli)

Having wanted to base an opera on DuBose Heyward's novel *Porgy* since reading it in 1926, Gershwin had to wait while it enjoyed success as a play. In 1933 a contract was signed, and the two men began their collaboration, mostly by correspondence, with Ira brought in later to help with some individual lyrics. During the composition of the score, Gershwin travelled to South Carolina to absorb the milieu at first hand; once back in New York, he tried out passages of the score with cast members as he selected them. The title roles were created by Todd Duncan, a baritone not previously associated with the popular idiom, and Anne Brown, a young Juilliard student; John W. Bubbles, a vaudeville star, played Sporting Life. A private concert performance in Carnegie Hall was followed by a try-out run in Boston during which cuts and alterations were made. The New York production's run was 124 performances – short by Broadway standards, but quite extraordinary for an opera, old or new. Reviews from both music and drama critics expressed mostly condescension, and the general perception was that *Porgy* failed as opera, however appealing its popular excerpts.

As the score had been printed before Gershwin's rehearsals began, it contains music that he cut before the New York opening, but *Porgy*'s operatic identity remained unmistakable. Revivals after Gershwin's death established *Porgy* as a success – and also inaugurated a history of textual meddling. A 1941 production went far beyond any of the composer's cuts, reducing the cast and chorus, providing a new orchestration for a smaller orchestra, and replacing most of the connecting orchestral passages with spoken dialogue. A highly successful revival in the 1950s, which toured the world and included among its principals Leontyne Price and William Warfield (it was still touring in the 1960s), restored more music (often as underscoring) but still reshaped *Porgy* as a two-act operetta. Two recordings made in 1976, both complete according to the published score, marked an important new step, drawing attention again to the work's operatic stature and establishing the merit of many of the passages that had seldom been heard. Productions at the Metropolitan, New York, and at Glyndebourne have espoused equally complete texts. Perhaps, now that these and similar presentations have proven the stature and quality of *Porgy and Bess*, it may become possible to consider whether some of Gershwin's own cuts might not be considered improvements after all.

SYNOPSIS

The action takes place in the early 20th century, in Charleston, South Carolina. The principal location is the waterfront courtyard called Catfish Row, formerly an elegant mansion, now a Negro tenement.

Act I, Scene 1: The sounds of a honky-tonk piano ('Jasbo Brown Blues'), the young mother Clara's lullaby ('Summertime') and a crap game permeate Saturday night in Catfish Row. Clara's husband Jake, a fisherman, jokingly quiets their baby ('A Woman is a Sometime Thing'), and all greet the crippled beggar Porgy as he arrives in his goat-cart. The mean-tempered stevedore Crown arrives with his woman Bess, and joins the game. It develops into a fight in which Crown kills Robbins and flees, leaving Bess to fend for herself. Porgy takes her in. Scene 2: All the Catfish Row residents (now including a subdued Bess) come to Robbins's room to mourn with his widow Serena ('Gone, gone, gone') and contribute money for the burial ('Overflow'). A policeman investigating Robbins's death takes Peter, a honey salesman, into custody for questioning. Serena mourns her loss ('My Man's Gone Now'), and Bess leads the group in a triumphant spiritual ('Leavin' for the Promised Land').

Act II, Scene 1: Several weeks later, Jake and the other fishermen work on their nets ('It Take a Long Pull To Get There'). Bess's love has brought happiness to Porgy's life for the first time ('I Got Plenty o' Nuttin"). Events of the morning include Sporting Life's attempts to peddle 'happy dust' (frustrated by the shopkeeper Maria), the fraudulent lawyer Frazier's offer to divorce Bess from Crown ('Woman to Lady'), and the visit of a sympathetic white man, Mr Archdale, who promises to get Peter out of gaol ('Buzzard Song'). All are preparing for the church picnic, but Bess is content to stay behind with Porgy ('Bess, You Is My Woman'). As the picnic parade forms ('Oh, I Can't Sit Down'), Porgy and Maria persuade her to go and enjoy herself. Scene 2: At the picnic on Kittiwah Island ('I Ain't Got No Shame'), Sporting Life presents his cynical philosophy ('It Ain't Necessarily So'). Bess misses the boat back, detained by Crown. He has been hiding on the island and tries to persuade Bess to come back to him. She refuses ('What You Want wid Bess?'), but ultimately is helpless against his insistence. Scene 3: Jake and his men leave for an extended fishing trip. Bess is heard calling out in the delirium in which she has remained for the week since she was found on the island. Peter returns from gaol, and he, Serena, Lily (Peter's wife), and Porgy pray for Bess's recovery ('Oh, Doctor Jesus'). Time passes as the cries of strawberry-, honey- and crab-sellers are heard, and Bess awakes, restored to health. She tells Porgy she wants to stay with him, not Crown, and he assures her that she need fear Crown no longer ('I Loves You, Porgy'). A terrible storm rises. Scene 4: In Clara's room all are gathered to pray for safety from the hurricane ('Oh, de Lawd Shake de Heavens'). Even Crown shows up, shocking everyone with his irreverence ('A Red-Headed Woman'). When Jake's empty boat is seen outside and Clara runs out to find him, Crown is the only one who will go after her. The others resume their prayers.

Act III, Scene 1: Back in the courtyard, the prayers of everyone for Clara, Jake and Crown are heard as night falls ('Clara, Clara'). Bess is now caring for Clara's baby. Crown crawls back to claim Bess, but in the ensuing fight Porgy manages to kill him. Scene 2: Policemen investigating Crown's death get no help from anyone and finally take Porgy with them to identify the body. Sporting Life plays on Bess's fear that she is left alone, offering to take her with him to a new life up north ('There's a Boat Dat's Leavin' Soon for New York'). She resists, but finally takes the dope he offers and gives in. Scene 3: Porgy returns, triumphant after his release from gaol. When Bess fails to appear, he becomes desperate ('Oh Bess, Oh Where's My Bess'). The others finally tell him that she has gone to New York with Sporting Life; he resolves to follow her there and get her back. As the curtain falls, he starts on his journey ('Oh, Lawd, I'm on My Way').

With this score, Gershwin proved that the gifts he possessed – a gift for capturing emotion musically, theatrical flair, and the ability to accommodate and accentuate the skills of his chosen performers (in his first try at writing for classically trained voices, he succeeded masterfully) – count for far more in operatic composition than some of the academic techniques he lacked. His songwriting genius had not deserted him, of course; *Porgy* contains one hit after another. But each is precisely suited to its place in the drama, and hardly any observe the standard 32-bar form. If some of the connecting material sounds more dutiful than inspired, much of it fulfils its purpose effectively; different textures and rhythms are tellingly contrasted, and a few significant motifs recur potently at key points (Porgy, Crown, Sporting Life, and the 'happy dust' are among the motivically defined elements). Larger musical recurrences play a role too: Porgy's solos in the first scene contain seeds of music to come in Act II (harmony for 'I Got Plenty o' Nuttin'', a melody for 'Bess, You Is My Woman'), and a jazzy strain associated with Catfish Row's social life is turned into a gentle barcarolle for the fishermen's fateful departure. As representative examples of resourcefulness in making the most of the libretto's potential, one might mention the powerful succession of recitative, arioso and duet that comprises the scene between Bess and Crown (written by Heyward as a simple prose dialogue), the six simultaneous unmeasured prayers of the hurricane scene and the rhythmic and vocal contrasts that shape 'My Man's Gone Now'. Indeed, the entire scene containing this impassioned solo shows Gershwin's genius at achieving overall unity through variety: linked choral passages, expressive recitative, one section of spoken dialogue, and two arias (with chorus) combine to create a uniquely varied picture of grief. Even with its minor imperfections and infelicities acknowledged, *Porgy* stands as the most vital and completely successful of American operas. One of the great might-have-beens of 20th-century music is the thought of the scores Gershwin could have gone on to write if he had lived beyond the age of 38.

RECORDING Dale, Lane, Shakesnider, Marshall, Smith, Albert, Houston Grand Op Ch & O, DeMain, RCA, 1976
MUSICALS *La-La-Lucille!*, 1919; *A Dangerous Maid*, 1921; *Blue Monday*, 1922; *Our Nell* (coll. with William Daly), 1922; *Sweet Little Devil*, 1924; *Primrose*, 1924; *Lady, Be Good!*, 1924; *Tell Me More*, 1925; *Tip-Toes*, 1925; *Song of the Flame* (coll. with Herbert Stothart), 1925; *Oh, Kay!*, 1926; *Strike Up the Band*, 1927; *Funny Face*, 1927; *Rosalie* (coll. with Sigmund Romberg), 1928; *Treasure Girl*, 1928; *Show Girl*, 1929; *Girl Crazy*, 1930; *Of Thee I Sing*, 1931; *Pardon My English*, 1933; *Let 'Em Eat Cake*, 1933

J.A.C.

Umberto Giordano

b 28 August 1867, Fóggia, Italy;
d 12 November 1948, Milan

Giordano studied at the Naples Conservatory and became caught up in the verismo movement after the sensational success of Mascagni's *Cavalleria rusticana* (1890). His first opera in this vein, *Mala vita* (1892), which tells of a labourer who vows to reform a prostitute if the Virgin will heal his tuberculosis, created a scandal for its sordidness. It was revised and performed five years later, retitled *Il voto*, but failed to improve Giordano's standing. In the meantime Giordano's next opera, *Regina Diaz* (1894), saw the composer retreat from verismo into the outworn world of romantic melodrama. However, this fared no better than *Mala vita* and it survived for only two performances. The same year Giordano left Naples for Milan with hopes of better fortune.

Success came at last with *Andrea Chénier* (1896). The French Revolutionary subject and Illica's literate libretto moved Giordano to write music of passionate conviction. It was followed by *Fedora* (1902), based on a play by Sardou; its ingenious and powerful second act has helped maintain the work on Italian stages. These works represent a plateau of accomplishment that Giordano never attained again. A few of Giordano's later operas have survived on gramophone records or in occasional revivals. *Marcella* is remembered for one aria, 'O santa liberta!', for which Italian tenors have a weakness.

Giordano was not without talent, but he lacked the essential resourcefulness and inventiveness to develop beyond his own limitations. He had two veins: one, an emphatic, occasionally strident, emotionalism: and the other, a graceful and predictable nattering that rarely rises above the level of salon music. The shifting of gears between these is all too often crude.

Andrea Chénier

Dramma di ambiente storico in four acts (2h 15m)
Libretto by Luigi Illica
Composed 1894–6
PREMIERES 28 March 1896, La Scala, Milan; US: 13 November 1896, Academy of Music, New York; UK: 16 April 1903, Camden Town Hall, London
CAST Andrea Chénier *t*, Carlo Gérard *bar*, Maddalena di Coigny *s*, Contessa

di Coigny *ms*, Bersi *ms*, Madelon *ms*, Roucher *b*, Pietro Fléville *bar*, Fouquier-Tinville *bar*, Mathieu *bar*, the Abbé *t*, an 'Incroyable' *t*, Majordomo *b*, Schmidt *b*; *satb* chorus of courtiers, ladies, soldiers, servants, peasants, prisoners, merchants, etc.

A successful combination of naturalism and historical drama, *Andrea Chénier* has remained a popular repertoire piece since its premiere. Illica's libretto – which, he claimed in a note in the vocal score, did not draw on historical fact but was based on ideas suggested by the editors of the real-life Chénier's poetic works – had originally been written for Alberto Franchetti. Franchetti ceded it to Giordano, who made use of the French Revolutionary background, spicing the opera with quotations of period tunes. The characters are scarcely developed, but the opera is kept alive with effective solos for the three principals and a surging final duet.

SYNOPSIS

Act I: The Contessa de Coigny is giving a soirée, at which her daughter Maddalena is struck by the ardent libertarianism of the poet Chénier, but the fête is interrupted by peasants in revolt, led by a servant, Gérard, who tears off his livery. The intruders are sent away, and the Countess's guests resume their gavotte.

Act II: Five years later, Chénier is disillusioned by the excesses of the Terror, and his friend Roucher, who has procured him a passport, urges him to go abroad. He hesitates because an unknown woman has written to him, asking for an appointment that very evening. It is Maddalena who seeks out Chénier's protection. Gérard, now Robespierre's agent, appears and tries to abduct Maddalena, but Chénier wounds him, while Roucher spirits the girl away. When Gérard is asked to identify his assailant, he generously says he cannot.

Act III: Chénier has been arrested, and Gérard denounces him as a counter-revolutionary. Maddalena comes to Gérard and begs him to save Chénier, even at the cost of giving herself to him. At his trial, in spite of Chénier's stirring self-defence, Gérard is unable to prevent the sentence of death.

Act IV: Chénier awaits execution at the prison of St Lazare. With Gérard's help Maddalena comes, substituting herself for another prisoner, to die with Andrea.

Giordano's quest for veristic naturalism led to the inclusion of the Revolutionary songs 'Ça ira', the 'Carmagnole' and 'La Marseillaise' and contrasting (but historically equally accurate) 18th-century dances and pastoral music. Set against these are the beautiful lyrical melodies for which the opera is famous: Chénier's 'Improvviso', Gérard's 'Nemico della patria', Maddalena's 'La mamma morta' and the final duet, 'Vicino a te'. The chorus, representing the 'people' in their many guises, plays a larger than usual part, the violence of some of their music – their part is marked *urlando* (yelling) at one point – making a significant contribution to the verismo nature of the work.

RECORDINGS 1. Scotto, Domingo, Milnes, John Alldis Ch, Nat PO, Levine, RCA, 1976; 2. Caballé, Pavarotti, Nucci, WNO Ch, Nat PO, Chailly, Decca, 1982–4

OTHER OPERAS *Marina*, (*c*.1889); *Mala vita*, 1892; *Regina Diaz*, 1894; *Il voto* (rev. of *Mala vita*), 1897; *Fedora*, 1898; *Giove a Pompeii* (coll. with Franchetti), (*c*.1901), 1921; *Siberia*, 1903; *Marcella*, 1907; *Mese mariano*, 1910; *Madame Sans-Gêne*, 1915; *La cena delle beffe*, 1924; *Il re*, 1929; *La festa del Nilo* (inc.), (n.d.)

W.A.

Philip Glass

b 31 January 1937, Baltimore, Maryland

Glass is the leading composer of so-called minimalist opera to emerge in the late 20th century. Since the 1980s he has also been one of the most widely performed composers in the world. During 1988, for instance, no fewer than eight of his full-length stage works with more or less continuous music (the simplest way of defining the 'operatic' in an output by then as varied as it was already alarmingly extensive) were performed. Several works have had more than one production, unusual these days for any living composer. Glass's operas are indisputably successful, though their merits are hotly disputed.

Glass's compositions – like those of his fellow Americans La Monte Young, Terry Riley and Steve Reich, who were exploring repetition and often clearly audible structural processes even earlier than he was – have become known as 'minimalist'. Certain similarities to the art of such figures as the sculptor Richard Serra (for whom Glass once acted as an assistant) provide justification for the label, though ironically the term 'minimalism' was not regularly applied to such music until the early 1970s, by which time Glass and others had begun to move away from their early repetitive rigour.

In 1967 Glass returned to the US from lengthy trips to Europe, where he had studied with Nadia Boulanger, and India. Between then and 1978 he wrote most of his compositions for the small amplified ensemble of flutes, saxophones and electric keyboards that still plays his music today, even though much of his energy since has been devoted to writing for the conventional opera house. While the earlier works' high energy level and sheer volume derived in part from rock music, their driving force technically was a rhythmic notion of additive process that came from classical North Indian music.

Glass's reputation was achieved primarily through his contribution to the New York 'downtown' scene, which flourished in the 1960s and 1970s, with its crossing of the boundaries between artforms – music, theatre, film, performance art and even the 'fine' arts of painting and sculpture – and its disregard for the usual division between the 'cultivated' and 'vernacular' traditions. Much of Glass's early music was written to accompany stage performances, partly due to the close involvement of his first wife, JoAnne Akalaitis, and their work with the experimental theatre group Mabou Mines, who were active first in Paris (the couple's base in the mid-1960s) and later in New York, where the group's early association with Samuel Beckett continued. The influence of non-Western theatrical traditions, including those of Indian Khatikali, gave rise to an increasingly close collaboration between the writers, designers, directors, actors and musicians in the creation of the group's productions.

The culmination of this activity came with *Einstein on the Beach*, the brainchild of the American Robert Wilson. Though sometimes described as an opera, *Einstein* is perhaps more logically regarded as a manifestation of what Wilson himself referred to as the 'theatre of images'. After *Einstein*, Glass's best-known stage works moved closer to conventional notions of opera, substituting aspects more familiar from 18th- and 19th-century operatic practice. This category includes all the works described below.

The 'theatre of images', however, continues to play a key role in Glass's post-*Einstein* music-theatre works. All these avoid the forces normally found in the opera house; some were written for the composer's own ensemble. Perhaps more significantly, the handling of both dramatic and musical continuity aligns them more closely with the world of *Einstein* than with a conventional definition of opera. The extent to which they remain disputed territory (even in the composer's own mind) is itself, however, an important dimension of their vitality. Glass also continues to be particularly active as a composer of 'incidental' music for films and television, as well as works for the concert hall.

Einstein on the Beach

Opera in four acts [and five 'kneeplays'] (4h 30m)
Spoken texts by Christopher Knowles, Samuel M. Johnson and Lucinda Childs
Composed 1974–5
PREMIERES 25 July 1976, Théâtre Municipal, Avignon; US: 21 November 1976, Metropolitan, New York
CAST *s*, *t*, Einstein *violinist*, actors, dancers; *satb* chorus (16 voices including second solo *s* and *t*) sometimes in the pit, sometimes part of the action

Behind the conception and realization of *Einstein on the Beach* lay Robert Wilson's approach to performance art. Wilson's starting points are usually visual rather than textual: here a set of drawings to which Glass would respond by writing music, which in turn influenced a reworking of the drawings, which inspired further music and so on. The common description of Wilson as 'director-designer' scarcely does justice to his actual role.

Einstein, according to its creators, concerns not only the German physicist Albert Einstein but also 'science, technology and ecology'. It eventually became the first part in a trilogy of operas by Glass, each taking a major historical figure and a major human issue for its theme. Since narrative and characterization in the usual sense are absent, it is impossible to give a conventional synopsis. Choreographed movement of various kinds, by no means confined to 'dance', is more important than the text. In addition, the close relationship between dramatic structure and *mise-en-scène* inherent in Wilson's approach presents any other director with unusual problems.

The work is 'about' Einstein, the discoverer of relativity, whose activity as a keen amateur violinist leads to his portrayal not as a singer but (in Wilson's original production at least) as an elderly man who punctuates the action with extended violin solos. A train, which forms the first of three recurring images – the others are a courtroom and a spaceship – also suggests that Einstein's theory of relativity is, however obliquely, being practised on the audience; so also do such things as the slow eclipse of a handless clock by a large black disc in the first trial scene. Yet at the time of its composition, Glass said that he and Wilson merely 'tried to find out where Einstein was in the piece'. Act I offers the train and a trial scene; Act II the spaceship, hovering above a field of dancers, and then the train again, this time at night. In Act III the courtroom also resembles a prison, and the spaceship moves closer to the dancers. In Act IV all three images are developed more drastically: the train, for example, turning into a building.

While all this can be taken as the main action, the five 'kneeplays', which form the prologue, interludes and epilogue to the four acts, seem of equal significance, even though the first kneeplay is already in progress as the audience enters the auditorium. Their subject matter is, however, related only tenuously to that of the main acts. In the original production, two women sat at tables downstage right; in the fourth kneeplay they lay on glass tables, and for the fifth they became two lovers sitting on a park bench. Other images counterpointed their action (or inaction); all somehow related to experiments in relativity or more directly to Einstein himself.

The recitation of numbers and *solfège* syllables accounts for a significant part of the 'text'. In Wilson's production, eleven other texts were included, the majority provided by Christopher Knowles, an autistic boy whom Wilson had encountered while working with handicapped children. None of their imagery relates in any obvious way to the stage picture; their respect for grammar is somewhat intermittent. The only text – the single one written by Lucinda Childs – even to mention either Einstein or the beach (only the latter, in fact) confines mention of the subject to avoiding the beach. Yet narrative, as well as grammatical, sense is by no means entirely forsaken in these texts, which are all spoken, never sung.

Musically, *Einstein* is crucially 'on the edge'. It retains not only a high degree of repetition but much of the non-developmental, 'non-narrative' approach of true minimalism. But while additive and cyclic rhythmic processes remain its driving forces, the more harmonically and melodically directed approach of Glass's later operas also begins to emerge. The impression that the grammar of a more familiar tonality is under reinvestigation is reinforced, in particular, by the use of chord sequences with clearly defined movement in the bass line.

RECORDINGS 1. LaBarbara, Zukovsky, Childs, Sutton, Johnson, Mann, Philip Glass Ens, Riesman, CBS, 1979;
2. Beckenstein, Geissinger, Childs, Sutton, Johnson, Grib, Philip Glass Ens, Riesman, Nonesuch, 1993

Satyagraha: M. K. Gandhi in South Africa

Opera in three acts (2h 15m)
Libretto (in Sanskrit) by Constance DeJong and the composer, adapted by DeJong from the *Bhagavad-Gîtâ*
PREMIERES 5 September 1980, Stadsschouwburg, Rotterdam; US: 29 July 1981, Artpark, Lewiston, New York State; UK: 19 February 1996, Bath Spa University, Bath
CAST Miss Schlesen *s*, Mrs Naidoo *s*, Kasturbai *ms*, M. K. Gandhi *t*, Mr Kallenbach *bar*, Parsi Rustomji *b*, Mrs Alexander *c*, Arjuna *t*, Krishna *b*; *silent*: Count Leo Tolstoy, Rabindranath Tagore, Martin Luther King; *satb* chorus of two hostile armies (Indians and Europeans), an Indian crowd, 8 European men; *silent*: 6 Indian workers, 6 Indian residents, 2 contemporary policemen

Satyagraha became the second opera in Glass's trilogy. Based on Mahatma Gandhi's early years in South Africa, according to the composer it deals with 'politics: violence and non-violence'. 'Satyagraha' literally means 'truth-force' but has come to stand for the concept of 'passive resistance'. The *Bhagavad-Gîtâ*, source of the libretto, is the Sanskrit religious text that was Gandhi's 'dictionary of daily reference'.

SYNOPSIS
Satyagraha covers the period from Gandhi's arrival in South Africa in 1893 to the New Castle March of 1913 (the event that brought the 'Satyagraha' movement to an end in that country) as though it were a single day.

Act I introduces turn-of-the-century South Africa via a somewhat ambiguous invocation of the *Bhagavad-Gîtâ*; Gandhi's workers build Tolstoy Farm and demonstrate against the imposition of identification cards.

Act II: White resistance to Gandhi's arrival in Durban is thwarted by the wife of the superintendent of police; the newspaper *Indian Opinion* is set up and distributed; and identification cards are ceremonially burned in retaliation against the government's retraction of its promise to repeal the Black Act.

Act III: The striking miners of New Castle and their families march with the 'Satyagraha' army in peaceful protest against racial discrimination.

Satyagraha establishes the crucial differences between Glass's early, minimalist music and his later, post-minimalist output. The opera is specifically concerned with the life of Gandhi who, while hardly subjected to conventional dramatic development, becomes a clearly delineated focus of attention. The structure of the opera is much more conventional than that of *Einstein*, with scenes and acts forming a sequence of tableaux. The use of Sanskrit encourages reflection on the moral lessons of each scene rather than engagement in the dynamic of narrative; the scenes of Gandhi's early life portrayed here do not, in any case, appear chronologically. In addition, the 'figurative counterpart' placed above the action of each of the opera's three acts – Count Leo Tolstoy, Rabindranath Tagore and Martin Luther King – suggests the historical continuity of the broad philosophy for which Gandhi's movement stood.

Taken as a whole, however, the opera charts a readily comprehensible, conventionally motivated plot. Movement on stage plays a significant role, but the main thrust is conveyed through the conventions of solo aria, duets, trios, etc. and choral singing, in ways closely resembling those adopted by the traditional lyric stage. The more harmonically and melodically directed approach already noted in *Einstein* is here clarified by chaconne-like structures underpinning an often continuous flow of vocal melody.

RECORDING Cummings, Woods, Liss, Perry, Macfarland, Reeve, New York City Op Ch & O, Keene, Sony, 1985

Akhnaten

Opera in [a prologue,] three acts [and an epilogue] (2h 15m)
Libretto by the composer in association with Shalom Goldman, Robert Israel and Richard Riddell; drawn from Egyptian and Akkadian sources (some in English translation), Psalm 104 (in Hebrew) and sentences from Fodor's and Frommer's guides to Egypt
Composed 1980–83
PREMIERES 24 March 1984, Kleines Haus, Württembergischer Staatstheater, Stuttgart; US: 12 October 1984, Wortham Theater Center, Houston; UK: 17 June 1985, Coliseum, London
CAST Akhnaten *ct*, Nefertiti *c*, Queen Tye *s*, Horemzhab *bar*, Aye *b*, High Priest of Amon *t*, Amenhotep *spoken role*, 6 daughters of Akhnaten and Nefertiti, 3 *s*, 3 *a*, funeral party, 4 *t*, 4 *b*; offstage: tourist guide (voice-over); *tb* chorus of mourners, priests of Amon, priests of Aten, soldiers etc.; *satb* chorus of people of Thebes, Akhnaten's entourage; offstage chorus: people of Egypt, soldiers, outlawed priest of Amon; *silent*: funeral cortège, tourists; dancers; onstage musicians

Akhnaten, the final panel in the trilogy of operas beginning with *Einstein on the Beach*, has as its subject the Egyptian pharoah of the 14th century BC and, more widely, 'religion: orthodoxy and reaction'. Sigmund Freud's *Moses and Monotheism* (1939) and Immanuel Velikovsky's *Oedipus and Akhnaton* (1960) were both crucial influences on the composer and his team of assistant librettists. Shalom Goldman compiled the text from original sources, and the opera is sung in ancient languages – Egyptian, Akkadian and Hebrew – as well as 'the language of the audience', which also serves for narration.

SYNOPSIS

The opera shows the rise and fall of Akhnaten in a series of tableaux. During an orchestral prelude, the narrator reads from ancient Pyramid Texts to set the scene.

Act I: The funeral of Amenhotep III, Akhnaten's father. Akhnaten's coronation is followed by a hymn announcing the revolution to come.

Act II: Akhnaten launches an attack on the Amon temple, sings a love duet with his queen Nefertiti, participates in a dance to mark the inauguration of the city of Akhetaten and sings his own 'Hymn to the Sun'.

Act III: The progressive withdrawal of Akhnaten and his family from the world and the pharaoh's downfall are represented; the final scene moves to the present, as tourists visit what little remains of Akhnaten's former city.

The epilogue depicts the ghosts of Akhnaten and his entourage amid the ruins.

Akhnaten continues in the tradition of post-minimalist opera established by *Satyagraha*. Dramatically, it is concerned with a central character who – though somewhat distanced by voice-type (David Freeman's Houston–London production also drew attention to Akhnaten's reputedly hermaphrodite aspect) – is sympathetically drawn and develops as a real human being. His pivotal 'Hymn to the Sun' in Act II is sung in 'the language of the audience', thus encouraging even greater identification. The sequence of scenes – here chronological, unlike in *Satyagraha* – may still be treated ritualistically (as in Achim Freyer's original production); Freeman, however, attempted to demonstrate its propensity for dramatic development in tandem with the evolution of character.

Akhnaten has a wider musical range than its predecessor. The approach to harmony is often much darker and more chromatic. Careful consideration of overall key-structure and the use of leitmotifs join the basic techniques already established in *Satyagraha*. Orchestration, too, is more subtle; the lack of violins provoked some original responses to the inevitably darker colouring, as well as an appropriate emphasis at times on somewhat militaristic wind and percussion; Akhnaten himself is frequently accompanied by a solo trumpet. The love duet for Akhnaten and his queen Nefertiti and Akhnaten's 'Hymn to the Sun' are powerfully lyrical utterances.

RECORDING Esswood, Vargas, Liebermann, Hannula, Hauptmann, Holzapfel, Warrilow, Stuttgart State Op Ch & O, Russell Davies, Sony, 1987

The Fall of the House of Usher

Chamber opera in a prologue and two acts (1h 30m)
Libretto by Arthur Yorinks, based on the short story by Edgar Allan Poe (1839)
Composed 1987
PREMIERES 18 May 1988, American Repertory Theater, Cambridge, Massachusetts; UK: 9 August 1989, St Donat's Castle, Llantwit Major, Wales

Poe's story of demented lust in a crumbling castle is well known; its air of Gothic horror and what Debussy (who never finished his *Usher* opera) called its 'sombre melancholy' are ideally suited to the more chromatic and doom-laden style Glass first developed in *Akhnaten*. The highly charged emotional content and structural compression of Poe's tale seem particularly well suited to the ambiguous ways in which Glass's exploration of familiar-sounding harmonic devices deals with tonal progression. Famously trounced by nearly all British critics, such an idiom perhaps works best when illustrating single emotional and dramatic states, as here.

Sunk in the weird introspection of Poe's text, which Glass sets with considerable rhythmic subtlety, *Usher* to some extent reclaims the more ambiguous territory between conventional opera and openly modernist notions of music theatre, while doing full justice to a narrative of cumulative power and terrifying denouement. As a result, it is one of Glass's best works since *Einstein*.

OTHER OPERATIC WORKS *Attacca – A Madrigal Opera*, 1980, as *The Panther* (music theatre), 1982; *the CIVIL warS: a tree is best measured when down*, 1984; *The Photographer* (music theatre), 1982; *The Juniper Tree* (coll. with Robert Moran), 1985; *A Descent into the Maelstrom*, 1986; *The Making of the Representative for Planet 8*, 1988; *1,000 Airplanes on the Roof* (music theatre), 1988; *Hydrogen Jukebox* (music theatre), 1990; *White Raven*, (1991), 1998; *The Voyage*, 1992; *Orphée*, 1993; *La Belle et la Bête*, 1994; *Les enfants terribles* (music theatre), 1996; *The Marriages between Zones Three, Four, and Five*, 1997; *Monsters of* Grace, 1998; *In the Penal Colony*, 2000; *Galileo Galilei*, 2002

K.P.

Mikhail Glinka

Mikhail Ivanovich Glinka; *b* 1 June 1804, Novospasskoye, Russia; *d* 15 February 1857, Berlin

Glinka was by no means the first Russian to compose opera, yet he was indisputably the founder of the Russian operatic tradition. Born into a minor landowning family, he was educated in St Petersburg, then settled into the role of a dilettante in the city's salons. Though he had had no proper musical education, he composed a good many undemanding songs and piano pieces, and shared in the current Russian taste for French opera, as well as for Rossini. But by the end of the 1820s Italian opera in general was becoming his central interest, and in 1830 he left for a three-year residence in Italy. He met Bellini, soaked himself in the Italian tradition, but by the end of his stay was turning against it; as he himself put it: 'I could not sincerely be Italian. A longing for my own country led me gradually to the idea of writing in a Russian manner.' On his return journey he delayed five months in Berlin for the only formal composition study of his whole life. The following year he began his first opera, *Ivan Susanin* (better known as *A Life for the Tsar*), and it was a sensation at its first performance in 1836.

Glinka promptly chose Pushkin's *Ruslan and Lyudmila* as the subject of his next opera, but the poet's death in a duel thwarted Glinka's hope that Pushkin himself would be the librettist. As it was, the totally unsystematic, even incompetent way in which the libretto was compiled, coupled with Glinka's equally unsystematic compositional process, could only result in a work hopelessly flawed, and it was a relative failure at its premiere in 1842.

Glinka's two operas are very different pieces. *A Life for the Tsar*, with its grand choruses and formal ballet, depended heavily on the French operatic tradition; but it treated a subject that was thoroughly Russian, and besides achieving an often remarkable synthesis of Italian and Russian melodic characteristics, Glinka devised a novel arioso-cum-recitative idiom for narrative and dialogue that was to become a fundamental element in many later Russian operas (*A Life for the Tsar* is the first Russian opera not to use spoken dialogue). The opera is very effective on the stage. By contrast, *Ruslan and Lyudmila* is dramatically a disaster. Nevertheless it represents a very remarkable achievement. Uneven the music may be, but there was abundant stimulus to the imagination in this fantastic tale of the supernatural set in a heroic past, and Glinka's music, at its imaginative best, was not only strikingly original and sometimes very beautiful, but also so new in a specially Russian way that later Russian composers could find in it a richness of stimuli and suggestion for their own creative ventures. *Ruslan and Lyudmila* could indeed claim to be the most seminal work in Russian music.

Ruslan and Lyudmila

Ruslan i Lyudmila

Opera in five acts (3h 15m)
Libretto by Konstantin Bakhturin (scenario); mostly Valerian Shirkov, but also Nestor Kukolnik, Nikolay Markevich, Mikhail Gedeonov; after the poem by Aleksandr Pushkin (1820)
Composed 1837–42
PREMIERES 9 December 1842, St Petersburg; UK: 4 June 1931, Lyceum, London; US: 26 December 1942, Town Hall, New York (concert); 5 March 1977, Boston (stage)
CAST Svetozar *b*, Lyudmila *s*, Ruslan *bar*, Ratmir *c*, Farlaf *b*, Gorislava *s*, Finn *t*, Naina *ms*, Bayan *t*, Chernomor *silent*; *satb* chorus of courtiers, the Gigantic Head, Naina's maidens, and Chernomor's followers

Glinka began work on *Ruslan and Lyudmila* in 1837, and had completed several numbers before ever a scenario had been devised. His disorganized lifestyle ensured that the compositional process was even more disorderly and spasmodic than that of *A Life for the Tsar*, with the libretto provided by a succession of amateur writers (though incorporating some lines of Pushkin), and composition spread over five years. Interest in the work was fanned by public performances of separate numbers and Liszt was highly approving when Glinka showed him some of the score early in 1842. But despite radical changes during production, it was tepidly received. Appreciation of the opera seems, however, to have increased fairly steadily. Connoisseurs apparently appreciated its unusual qualities, and it retained an intermittent place in the repertoire. By 1893 it had been performed 300 times in St Petersburg, but there have been few productions outside Russia.

SYNOPSIS

Act I: At the court of Svetozar, Prince of Kiev, celebrations are in progress before the marriage of his daughter, Lyudmila, to Ruslan, a warrior. The Bayan (a minstrel) sings of the trials in store for Ruslan, though he predicts the victory of true love. Nostalgically, Lyudmila bids farewell to her parents' home, and consoles her unsuccessful suitors, the eastern prince Ratmir and the Varangian warrior Farlaf. Suddenly all darkens; when light is restored, Lyudmila has vanished. Svetozar promises her hand and half his kingdom to the one who rescues her.

Act II: In his cave Finn, a good magician, reveals to Ruslan that Lyudmila's abductor is the dwarf Chernomor (whose strength lies in his enormously long beard) and warns Ruslan against the evil enchantress Naina. The scene changes to a deserted place where Naina instructs a very frightened Farlaf to wait at home; she will help him defeat Ruslan and gain Lyudmila. Finally, on a deserted battlefield Ruslan reaffirms his resolve, then defeats a gigantic head and draws from beneath it a sword; the head explains he is Chernomor's brother and one of his victims, and that the sword's magic can defeat the dwarf.

Act III: In Naina's enchanted palace her maidens are directing their allure at a travel-weary Ratmir, to the distress of his slave, Gorislava, who loves him. Ruslan appears and is smitten with Gorislava, but Finn intervenes, breaks the seductive spell, unites Ratmir and Gorislava, and all set out to rescue Lyudmila.

Act IV: Confined in Chernomor's enchanted garden, Lyudmila voices her despair and defiance, rejecting her captor's blandishments. On Ruslan's approach Chernomor casts a spell over her and goes out to fight with Ruslan. Chernomor's followers observe the offstage encounter, in which Ruslan catches hold of Chernomor's beard, then cuts it off. Triumphantly he returns onstage with it, but is in despair when he finds Lyudmila in an enchanted sleep. He decides to take her back to Kiev.

Act V: Ratmir sings of his love for Gorislava. Farlaf steals Lyudmila and speeds to Kiev. Meanwhile Finn gives Ratmir the magic ring that will waken Lyudmila. In Kiev Farlaf cannot rouse her, but when Ruslan arrives with Ratmir he breaks the spell with the aid of the ring. General rejoicing.

The fantasy and romance of Pushkin's *Ruslan and Lyudmila* had a natural appeal to Glinka; the problem was that the subject was totally unsuited to operatic treatment, and the work's fate was sealed when a friend, Konstantin Bakhturin, devised its scenario 'in a quarter of an hour while drunk'. For some four years Glinka worked intermittently on such individual incidents as caught his fancy; by the time he came to knit these together, far too much music of the wrong kind had been composed, and for all the drastic surgery during rehearsals, nothing could hide the unevenness or remedy the often misshapen structure. Dramatically, *Ruslan and Lyudmila* is an irreparable disaster, and some of the characterization is weak; Farlaf in particular is little more than a conventional opera-buffa figure.

Yet, at its musical best, *Ruslan and Lyudmila* contains some of the most strikingly original invention of 19th-century opera, some separate incidents are brilliantly treated, and some characters transcend the ludicrous situations in which they find themselves. The opera's Russianness is far deeper than that of *A Life for the Tsar*, springing not from the absorption of folk and chant idioms into what was still basically a Western idiom, but from the sometimes novel materials and free structures that Glinka's vivid and totally Russian imagination created. Hence the prodigious seminal importance of the opera. In addition, the clear and bright scoring, which contributes so much colour to the whole opera, established the fundamental style of Russian orchestration.

Though *Ruslan and Lyudmila* is mostly an opera of brilliant moments, Act I does have real consistency, establishing for Russian music its special heroic idiom, which is extended further in Ruslan's great Act II aria. (Act I also contains the famous passage where, to depict the disorientation caused by Chernomor's magic as he abducts Lyudmila, Glinka disrupts the music's tonal course with a descending whole-tone scale.) Earlier in Act II Naina's music introduces something of the special Russian 'magic' idiom, while the oriental idiom appears for the first time in Act III, notably in the voluptuous Persian chorus and the first part of Ratmir's aria. Between these is Gorislava's plangent cavatina, but there is a greater concentration of excellent music in Act IV: in Lyudmila's spirited scena and aria, for instance, and in the languorous delicacy of the choruses for Chernomor's houris – though most immediately arresting, perhaps, are Chernomor's splendidly grotesque march and the fierce oriental *lezhginka*. The most memorable movement in Act V is Ratmir's sultry romance.

RECORDING Netrebko, Gorchakova, Diadkova, Ognovienko, Bezzubenkov, Kirov Ch & O, Gergiev, Philips, 1995 (live)

OTHER OPERA *A Life for the Tsar* (*Zhizn za tsarya*), 1836

D.B.

Christoph Willibald Gluck

Christoph Willibald Ritter von Gluck; *b* 2 July 1714, Erasbach, nr Berching; *d* 15 November 1787, Vienna

Gluck came from a family of foresters who worked for the minor nobility. His precocious musical talent led to studies in music (and law) in Prague, probably sponsored by Prince Lobkowitz (father of Beethoven's patron), and travel to Italy where he studied with G. B. Sammartini. His first operas were written for Milan and Venice; he then tried his luck in London, producing two operas in 1746. Years later he told Burney how he admired Handel and English musical taste (this may have been flattery as Gluck was to say much the same in France about Lully). His search for a permanent position took him to Saxony and Denmark. Recurring visits to Vienna, his wife's home, enabled him to ingratiate himself with the imperial family, some of whom became his pupils. The first of many operas commissioned by the Vienna court was *La Semiramide riconosciuta* (1748); Gluck settled there by about 1750.

His earliest output consisted of conventional opere serie, mainly to libretti by Metastasio. He wrote no opera buffa. Among his earliest surviving music are solidly composed da capo arias, not without anticipations of his later style; some pieces reappear in his greatest works. Recycling material was common enough at the time not to excite remark, and Gluck, never as fluent as his Italian contemporaries, was certainly justified in searching for better dramatic contexts for his most original conceptions. Some passages display a rugged boldness, as well as a grand melodic span, which were to continue to influence musicians as late as Berlioz.

From Vienna, Gluck made occasional journeys to fulfil commissions in Italy and at last, most significantly, in Paris. His Viennese work quickly took him away from opera seria, although he continued to produce courtly entertainments. He owed the variety of his experience during the 1750s to the favour of the imperial theatre administrator, Count Durazzo, whose *L'innocenza giustificata* he set (1755), a gesture directed against the Caesarean poet, Metastasio. Durazzo fell in with the fashion for French culture, and gave Gluck the job of adapting and later composing a series of opéras comiques for the court theatre.

Such diverse experiences stood the composer in good stead in the 1760s when he was drawn towards reform movements in dramatic music. His first significant collaboration was in the ballet *Don Juan* by Angiolini (1761), after which came three operas to libretti by Calzabigi: *Orfeo ed Euridice*, *Alceste* and *Paride ed Elena*. Besides his masterpiece of opéra comique, *Le rencontre imprévue* (1764), Gluck wrote other occasional works in the 1760s. He has sometimes been accused of backsliding from the radical position adopted in *Orfeo* and *Alceste*. There is, however, no reason to perceive *Orfeo*, an occasional work related to the courtly genres, as an irreversible step. Gluck composed no full-scale opera seria after 1756 (*Antigono*, which won him the papal knighthood of the Golden Spur); even *Telemaco* (1765) can be associated with the spirit of reform.

With the publication of *Alceste*, however, Calzabigi penned a dedicatory preface, which Gluck signed and which is their manifesto of reform. The ideas they had assimilated from French opera and the Parmesan and Viennese reform operas of Traetta are justified as a return to the natural and poetic origins of opera, at the expense of mere musicianship and especially of the virtuoso singer: 'I sought to restrict music to its true purpose of expressing the poetry and reinforcing the dramatic situation, without interrupting the action or hampering it with superfluous embellishments.' Later, in an open letter to the French press, Gluck said that in *Armide* he had striven to be 'more painter and poet than musician'. Consequences of the reform were the greater attention paid to orchestra, chorus and dance; this, however, corresponded with French tragédie lyrique. In *Orfeo* and *Paride*, but not *Alceste* and *Telemaco*, Gluck orchestrated all the recitatives; and in *Alceste* he managed without a castrato. *Alceste* was followed by *Paride ed Elena*, which Gluck must have valued less, since he did not adapt it for Paris; instead he used parts of it (and *Telemaco*) in new operas.

If the architect of reform was Calzabigi, Gluck supported him wholeheartedly. In Paris he took control of his less experienced librettists; yet even when, like Mozart and Verdi, he demanded verses for music already composed, he kept in mind the needs of the drama rather than merely the music. Largely through the influence of his pupil Marie Antoinette (then Dauphine, later in 1774 Queen of France), he was contracted to present six French operas, including thorough recompositions of *Orfeo* and *Alceste* (he also adapted two opéras comiques). *Armide* completed his rapprochement with French tradition by using an old libretto. The threat from the partisans of Italian music, who brought Piccinni to Paris, was met by wholesale plunder of Gluck's own Italian music in his last and perhaps greatest masterpiece, *Iphigénie en Tauride*. He had not permanently affected the taste of Vienna, and Italy remained largely indifferent to his reforms. But, as Lully's partisans had feared, he killed off the old French opera; and he withstood the pressure of the Italians who displaced native talents at the Opéra. The failure of *Echo et Narcisse* (1779) sent him home in disgust, but his works continued to dominate the repertoire into the next century.

Gluck's last operatic undertaking was his only one in German, a version of *Iphigénie en Tauride*. He handed *Les Danaïdes* to his protégé Salieri, and abandoned a setting of Klopstock's *Hermannschlacht*, but he wrote some songs and a *De profundis* before his death in 1787. He remained a talisman of dramatic art for several generations. Cherubini, Spontini, Weber and others paid him tribute; Berlioz (his most eloquent partisan), Wagner and Strauss supervised performances. A scholarly edition of his French operas was undertaken by musicians close to Berlioz. Major critical and historical studies have been undertaken this century, and a complete edition of his works is well advanced.

Orfeo ed Euridice / Orphée

Orpheus and Eurydice/Orpheus

First version
Azione teatrale per musica in three acts (1h 45m)
Libretto by Raniero da Calzabigi
Composed 1762
PREMIERES 5 October 1762, Burgtheater, Vienna; UK: 7 April 1770, King's Theatre, Haymarket, London
CAST Orpheus *a* (*castrato*), Euridice *s*, God of Love (Amore) *s*; *satb* chorus of shepherds and nymphs, furies and infernal spirits, heroes and heroines from Elysium, followers of Orfeo; ballet of furies and blessed spirits

Second version
Tragédie opéra (drame héroïque) in three acts (2h)
Libretto by Pierre Louis Moline, after Raniero da Calzabigi
Composed 1774
PREMIERES 2 August 1774, Opéra (Académie Royale de Musique), Salle des Tuileries, Paris; US: 24 June 1794, Charleston
CAST Orpheus *high t* (*haute-contre*), Euridice *s*, God of Love (Amore) *s*; *satb* chorus of shepherds and shepherdesses, nymphs, demons and furies, blessed spirits, heroes and heroines; ballet of furies and blessed spirits

The performance of *Orfeo* on the Emperor Franz's name-day in 1762 involved a rare galaxy of talent and must be accounted one of the major events in 18th-century musical theatre. Calzabigi, with full support from the administrator Durazzo, was the guiding spirit (as Gluck admitted); he manipulated a familiar subject and genre with the intention of restoring naturalness and simplicity to dramatic music. Thus *Orfeo* in no sense proposes the reform of Metastasian opera seria. The choreographer Angiolini, for whom Gluck had composed a revolutionary action ballet (*Don Juan*) the year before, was also an innovator in his field; the sets were by the ubiquitous Quaglio brothers, and the title role was sung by Gaetano Guadagni, who ten years before had worked with Handel in London and studied acting with Garrick.

The festa or azione teatrale, like the serenata, an Italian opera on a mythological subject with chorus and dancing, was a feature of courtly celebrations (Gluck had written several already and was to write more). But its musical style was similar to opera seria, particularly in the virtuoso writing for voices. Calzabigi probably designed *Orfeo* to capitalize on Gluck's particular musical strengths and on his recent dramatic experience. It was preceded by Durazzo's reform gesture (*L'innocenza giustificata*) and by Gluck's French comedies, which trained the composer in directness of utterance. *Don Juan* permitted Gluck to explore extremes of expression, particularly in the final scenes. Calzabigi had been inspired by traditional French opera, notably Rameau; Gluck knew the reform operas of Traetta, whose *Armida*, based on the French libretto Gluck later used in Paris, was given in Vienna in 1761. From this source came the richly developed tableaux in which chorus, solo singing and dance are alternated and combined. The subject had been used, symbolically, at a critically early stage in the development of opera, and Gluck, unknowingly, revived something of the spirit of those early 17th-century operas by Peri, Caccini and Monteverdi, particularly in the first two acts, by restoring to recitative its original function as the most expressive and articulate part of the protagonist's role. Yet *Orfeo* feels like a new start rather than the climax of a remarkable tradition. To posterity it has remained, perhaps to an unfair degree, Gluck's masterpiece.

After performances in Italy and England, much abused by additional music, a second authentic version (*Orphée*, 1774) clinched Gluck's reputation in Paris after the disputed success of *Iphigénie en Aulide*. Gluck enlarged his work to occupy a whole evening; he compromised the spirit of the original by adding a bravura air for Orpheus to end the first act and introducing new ballets, most notably the long *Dance of Furies* taken from *Don Juan* and the famous *Dance of the Blessed Spirits* for flute and strings, perhaps his most eloquent instrumental solo.

SYNOPSIS (1762 VERSION)

Act I, Scene 1: Orpheus and the traditional pastoral chorus of nymphs and shepherds are grouped round Eurydice's tomb. The mournful C minor chorus, 'Ah, se intorno a quest'urna funesta', is punctuated by Orpheus' cries: he can only utter Eurydice's name. In a grouping of movements characteristic of reform works, the chorus is used to frame a recitative for Orpheus and a dance-pantomime, during which the tomb is strewn with flowers. Orpheus, alone, sings of his grief, 'Chiamo il mio ben così'. The three verses alternate with powerfully expressive recitatives. He complains that only Echo hears him; her wordless replies are confided to an echo orchestra with chalumeaux. Orpheus shakes off his despair and resolves to recover Eurydice from the dead. Scene 2: Love appears to encourage him, for his music can overcome any obstacle. After a short aria Love disappears, and Orpheus, in recitative, determines to carry the adventure through. (In the 1774 version Love has two songs; and Orpheus ends with the aria 'L'espoir renaît dans mon âme', a piece that aroused controversy; its Italian style led to the accusation that Gluck had stolen it from Bertoni. It actually comes from *Il Parnaso confuso* and *Le feste d'Apollo*.)

Act II, Scene 1: A hideous landscape near the banks of the river Cocytus. After a fierce sinfonia, Orpheus' lyre (represented by the harp) is heard approaching. It arouses the Furies' wrath; they dance frenziedly and sing of the hellish watchdog Cerberus (whose barking is represented by orchestral glissandi). When Orpheus explains his mission they interrupt with cries of 'No!', but as his singing grows in eloquence they display signs of compassion and finally allow him passage. (The 1774 version at this point somewhat incongruously inserts the magnificent *Dance of Furies* which originally ended the ballet *Don Juan*.) Scene 2: A delectable landscape in Elysium. Ballo. (This was expanded in the 1774 version to became the *Dance of the Blessed Spirits*.) The chorus and a soloist, sometimes taken to be Eurydice, sing of their bliss in such a place ('Cet asile aimable'). Orpheus, alone, sings of the beauty around him and its emptiness for him, because he cannot find Eurydice ('Che puro ciel'). Eurydice is brought to him, blindfold; the chorus ('Vieni a regni del riposo' repeated as 'Torna, o bella, al tuo consorte') exhorts her to return to Orpheus.

Act III, Scene 1: A dark, twisted path in a repellent landscape, leading away from Hades. Eurydice is overjoyed at her release, but Orpheus, in fulfilment of conditions imposed by Love (in Act I, Scene 2), has to let go of her hand and must not look at her. She reproaches him for his apparent coldness, and he suffers her unjust suspicions (the first long recitative dialogue of the opera is followed by the duet 'Vieni, appaga il tuo consorte'). Eventually she feels that death was preferable ('Che fiero momento'). Orpheus can bear it no longer; he turns to look at her, and she dies. His grief is embodied in the aria 'Che farò senza Euridice?' Scene 2: Love reappears in time to prevent his suicide; Eurydice is revived and the couple are united on earth to the happiness of their friends. Scene 3: All join in praise of Love. (In the 1774 version Orpheus joins in the central part of Eurydice's arias and a trio is added from *Paride ed Elena*; many changes were made in the dances, and the work is considerably longer as a result.)

For all the importance of Calzabigi in directing Gluck towards a new type of opera, *Orfeo* owes its perennial freshness to Gluck's musical imagination. When Bertoni set the text, very beautifully but in a conventional idiom (Venice, 1776), the loss of Gluckian directness led to loss of magic and dramatic insight. The aim is truth to nature, in the 18th-century sense of 'imitation' – not only of natural phenomena but of human passions. The new directness of expression appears in the absence of da capo forms. Instead, Orpheus sings songs, strophic ('Chiamo il mio ben così') or rondo ('Che farò senza Euridice?') in form. 'Che puro ciel', potentially an aria text, is an obbligato recitative; and Orpheus overcomes the Furies by short, even fragmentary outpourings of lyrical intensity. These forms may derive from Renaissance or baroque traditions, particularly 18th-century French ones, but the directness is also from opéra comique, and the gestural exactness of the musical language, not only in the dances, derives from Angiolini's ballet d'action.

The experiment of building scenes out of blocks of interlocked ideas is taken further in *Alceste*, but is never more eloquent than in the dying away of the Furies' music. Gluck's other innovations include the abolition of simple recitative (the orchestra plays throughout), an experiment not resumed until *Paride*, and a richness of orchestral colouring unprecedented in his work and very unusual anywhere before the 1770s. Cornetti and chalumeaux, in their brief appearances, provide a haunting, antique colour; in 'Che puro ciel' a complex layered sonority includes solo flute, oboe, bassoon, horn and cello over a triplet continuum. The choral sonorities are remarkable, and the dances, in their appositeness to each scene, reveal an exceptional choreographic imagination.

Most prophetic, perhaps, is the continuity. Cadences are only occasionally omitted or elided, but many numbers are too short to be self-contained, and in a good performance they flow into each other, forming single, extended complexes. But in addition to painting unforgettably Eurydice's tomb, Hades and Elysium, Gluck discovered accents of grief, resignation, pleading, hope and despair that make his conception of the mythological singer the equal of Monteverdi's and raised the possibilities of the musical language of his generation to a level otherwise attained only by his exact contemporary C. P. E. Bach (who wrote no operas).

Orpheus was produced in most European centres but the original version fell from favour. Berlioz, in 1859, restored the 1762 tessitura to the title role by assigning it to a woman, Pauline Viardot-García. Tenors still take the role occasionally, in the 1774 keys, but the majority of performances adopt Berlioz's sensible, albeit inauthentic, compromise solution, which involves restoring the 1762 key scheme, while retaining music added in 1774, transposed where necessary. The role has been taken by, among others, Kathleen Ferrier and Janet Baker; it is now increasingly sung and recorded by male falsettists/counter-tenors.

RECORDINGS 1. McNair, Sieden, Ragin, Monteverdi Ch, EBS, Gardiner, Philips, 1991: 1762 version, in Italian; 2. Delunsch, Harousseau, Croft, Les

Musiciens du Louvre Ch & O, Minkowski, Archiv, 2002 (live): 1774 version, in French; 3. von Otter, Hendricks, Fournier, Monteverdi Ch, Op Nat de Lyon O, Gardiner, EMI, 1989: 1859 (Berlioz) version, in French; 4. Larmore, Upshaw, Hagley, San Francisco Op Ch & O, Runnicles, Teldec, 1995: 1859 (Berlioz) version, in French

Alceste

First version
Tragedia per musica in three acts (2h 15m)
Libretto by Raniero da Calzabigi, after Euripides
Composed 1766–7
PREMIERE 26 December 1767, Burgtheater, Vienna
CAST Admeto *t*, Alceste *s*, Eumelo and Aspasia (children of Admeto and Alceste) 2 *s*, Evandro *t*, Ismene *s*, herald *b*, High Priest of Apollo *bar*, oracle *b*, infernal god *b*; *satb* chorus of courtiers and citizens, female attendants on Alceste, priests of Apollo, infernal deities

Second version
Tragédie lyrique in three acts (2h 45m)
Libretto by Marie-François-Louis Gand Leblanc du Roullet, after Raniero da Calzabigi
Composed 1775
PREMIERES 23 April 1776, Opéra, Paris; UK: 30 April 1795, London; US: 11 March 1938, Wellesley College, Massachusetts
CAST Admète *t*, Alceste *s*, High Priest of Apollo *b*, Evandre *t* (*haute-contre*), herald at arms *b*, Hercule *b*, 4 Coryphées *satb*, Apollon *bar*, Oracle *b*, infernal god *b*, 2 children of Admète and Alceste 2 *silent*; *satb* chorus of officers of the palace, female attendants on Alceste, Thessalians, infernal deities, priests and priestesses in the temple of Apollo

Euripides' *Alkestis* is a tragi-comedy; but unlike Quinault and Lully, Calzabigi omitted the humour and concentrated on the loftiest sentiments whose unrelenting expression make the original (1767) version both the most radical reforming gesture of Gluck's career and the most persistently mournful opera ever written. Possibly the subject was intended to convey sympathy to the Empress Maria Theresa, widowed in 1765; the libretto is dedicated to her.

Alceste was performed by an opera-buffa troupe rather than singers used to the musical finery of opera seria; for the first time in a full-scale Italian opera, Gluck dispensed with a castrato. A buffo troupe would also be more amenable to being expected to act. Thus Sonnenfels said of Bernasconi, who sang Alceste, that 'her gestures followed only the movements of the heart'. The ballets were by Noverre, who sympathized less with Gluck and Calzabigi than had Angiolini; he presented a final 'grotesque ballet', which some, at least, enjoyed more than the opera. Nevertheless, *Alceste* made a profound impression on the public, which included the 11-year-old Mozart and his father. It is the most challenging gesture of the Viennese reformers, but its severity is such that Gluck should not have been surprised, as he complained in the dedicatory preface to *Paride ed Elena*, that it had found no imitators. As an attempted reform of Italian opera seria, it must be accounted a failure; but in its French form, although preceded by *Iphigénie en Aulide*, it exerted considerable influence.

Alceste was the second Gluck opera revived with Pauline Viardot-García in the title role (Paris, 1861). Subsequent revivals have likewise usually used the French version, even if translated back into Italian: with Cigna under Gui (Florence, 1935) and Callas under Giulini (Milan, 1954). An exception was Flagstad's performance of the Italian original. *Alceste* in the French version was the last new opera role undertaken by Janet Baker (Covent Garden, under Mackerras, 1981).

SYNOPSIS

Act I begins with the proclamation that

Admetus, the young king of Thebes, is dying; his wife Alceste is drawn into scenes of communal mourning (1767: 'Io non chiedo, eterni dei'; 1776: 'Grands Dieux! Du destin qui m'accable'). After an imposing religious ceremony, Apollo's oracle pronounces: Admetus can live if someone dies in his place. The people flee (1767: 'Che annunzio funesto/Fuggiamo'; 1776: 'Quel oracle funestre/Fuyons'). Only his wife Alceste has the courage to take this step. In the 1776 version her immense recitative is replaced by an incisive recitative and the new aria, which provides a resolution of her dilemma: to die for Admetus is not a sacrifice ('Non, ce n'est point un sacrifice'). She offers herself to the underworld gods ('Ombre, larve, compagne di morte'). The 1767 version concludes Act I with a short scene for Evander and the chorus, whereas the aria 'Divinités du Styx' provides a more fitting ending to the act in the 1776 version.

Act II (1767 version): Alceste, dismissing Ismene, approaches the gods to beg respite so that she can see Admetus again (this scene is omitted in the French version, much of its music passing to Act III). In both versions, choral singing and dancing celebrate the recovery of Admetus, but nobody knows its price. When Alceste arrives her tears seem incomprehensible; in the French version she appears in the midst of the ballet, making explicit the irony behind this rejoicing, which Rousseau found so incongruous. Gradually the truth is revealed. In a magnificent tableau she bids farewell to life; the act ends with the aria 'Ah per questo' ('Ah, malgré moi'), embedded in a splendid choral refrain in F minor ('O come rapida').

Act III (1767 version): Admetus tries in vain to force Alceste to renounce her sacrifice and let him die ('Misero! E che farò!'). Alceste bids farewell and dies ('Piangi o Patria', a choral tableau of mourning with solos, reminiscent of Act III of Lully's *Alceste*). But Apollo comes to revoke his dreadful oracle: Alceste, as well as Admetus, can live after all. The revised version initially mounted in Paris in 1776 was threatened with failure, so further revisions were undertaken, and the final French version reverts more nearly to Euripides by bringing in Hercules, who owes Admetus a debt of hospitality. The act begins with the mourning tableau ('Pleure, o patrie') abbreviated. Hercules arrives and learns the truth; he determines to rescue Alceste (Gluck refurbished an aria from *Ezio*). The scene changes to the underworld. Alceste, in music from the 1767 Act II, meets the infernal deities; Admetus appears to offer his own life ('Alceste, au nom des dieux'). The infernal deities call on Alceste; Hercules overpowers them and Alceste is returned to life with the blessing of Apollo.

Perhaps because *Orfeo* is concerned with a superhuman being, but *Alceste* with human society, the latter did more to set the pattern for tragic opera in years to come. Its elevated tone is reflected in Italian and French tragedies, notably Mozart's *Idomeneo* and Cherubini's *Médée*. The D minor overture and its link with Act I anticipate both *Idomeneo* and *Don Giovanni*. It has been argued that the arpeggio motif that begins the *Alceste* overture is a sort of leitmotif, anticipating the crucial preparation for the speech of the oracle. The thematic connection with the opera is less explicit than in some of Mozart's operas, or in *Iphigénie en Aulide*, but the oracle scene was certainly Mozart's model for the sacrifice scene in *Idomeneo*. One might go further and suggest that the presentation of the nobly suffering heroine is suggestive of the redeeming women of Romanticism, although the music and forms are neoclassical.

Gluck himself was the most constructive critic of the Italian version. Magnificent as it is, its high-flown sentiments and huge static tableaux of repeated choruses surrounding recitative, arias and dance, demand absolute submission: if the tension is lost for a moment, it is bound to appear tedious. Tovey observed that Gluck had got rid of the abuses of opera seria by simplifying the drama almost out of existence. Rousseau made an extensive critique of the Italian score: much as he admired it, he deplored the multi-movement arias (which were to arouse opposition from the Piccinnists), and he criticized the cheerful divertissement which greets the king's recovery. For Paris, Gluck kept his style of aria, although he eliminated arias for minor characters and the touching intrusion of the children into one of Alceste's arias. But as well as introducing new dances (some taken from works written in the meantime, *Le feste d'Apollo* and *Paride ed Elena*) he changed the divertissement along lines suggested by Rousseau, omitted much repetition and added new material, including a superb aria for Alceste in Act I. Like that of *Iphigénie en Aulide*, which intervened between the two versions, the design is fluid; grandeur is lost but theatricality enhanced.

The Italian version follows *Telemaco* rather than *Orfeo* by returning to simple recitative. In proportion to the orchestral (obbligato) recitative it is, however, much reduced from the opera seria norm. In the French version the recitatives are orchestrated throughout. Gluck's orchestration attains a new depth and richness in the tutti, particularly in the infernal scenes, which are totally different from those in *Orfeo*. The Romantic orchestra, or at least its treatment of the darker colours, finds its origin here, with Gluck's sonorous scoring for full woodwind and trombones, soon taken up in French opera by Piccinni. The orchestra, particularly in 'Ombre, larve, compagne di morte', is made to stand for the voices of the infernal deities, another foretaste of Romantic practice. Yet the orchestration continues the functional, symbolic use of instrumental timbre applied in *Orfeo*. The trombones are used to colour mourning and underworld scenes, while the cors anglais characterize only the former, and chalumeaux the latter. Low flutes colour the ritual march in Act I (which Mozart remembered in *Die Zauberflöte*). Standard orchestration, flutes, oboes, horns, bassoon and strings, with occasional trumpets and timpani, represents normality.

RECORDINGS 1. 1767 version: Ringholz, Lavender, Degerfeld, Drottningholm Court Th Ch & O, Östman, Naxos, 1998; 2. 1776 version: Norman, Gedda, Gambill, Nimsberg, Bavarian RCh & SO, Baudo, Orfeo, 1982

Iphigénie en Aulide

Iphigenia in Aulis

Tragédie-opéra in three acts (2h 30m)
Libretto by Marie-François-Louis Gand Leblanc du Roullet after the tragedy *Iphigénie* by Jean-Baptiste Racine (1674)
Composed *c.*1771–3
PREMIERES 19 April 1774, Opéra, Paris; UK: 24 November 1933, Playhouse Oxford; US: 22 February 1935, Philadelphia
CAST Agamemnon *bar*, Clitemnestre *s*, Iphigénie *s*, Achille *t*, Patrocle *b*, Calchas *b*, Arcas *b*, Diane *s*, 3 Greek women 3 *s*, a slave from Lesbos *s*; *satb* chorus of Greek soldiers and people, Thessalian soldiers, guards, attendants on the princess, women from Aulis, slaves from Lesbos, priestesses of Diana; dancers

Gluck's first French opera was written speculatively, in the hope of arousing interest in Paris. His campaign bore fruit only four years after the first performance of *Paride ed Elena* in 1770. His objective was to found a new school in the cultural capital of Europe, in the interests of wider diffusion of his reform of serious opera. In so far as the old French operas rapidly dropped out of the repertoire after 1774, and his new works were widely performed in the original language or in translation, he succeeded. Gluck also created a revolution at the Paris Opéra by insisting that the principals (who included Sophie Arnould in the title role and the most distinguished French tenor and baritone of the time, Legros and Larrivée), and even the chorus, should act; according to contemporary reports, he had to behave like a sergeant-major to achieve this. He retained elements of French operatic tradition that had been taken over into the Calzabigian reform, notably the integration of choral and dance music, short and freely structured solo vocal numbers, and the serious use of orchestra, and could thus readily adapt *Orpheus* and *Alceste* for Paris; but in the *Iphigénies* and *Armide* he eschewed the monumentality of the latter and the slowness of action in all three Calzabigi operas.

The subject of the sacrifice of Iphigenia had been treated in several Italian operas and by Algarotti in his *Saggio sopra l'opera in musica* (1755). In essence, the story was intended to justify the murder of Agamemnon by his wife Clytemnestra on his return from Troy: Euripides invented the substitution of an animal for the human sacrifice by the offended goddess Artemis (Diana), and the translation of Iphigenia to Tauris. Du Roullet's libretto is adapted from Racine's *Iphigénie*, in which Iphigenia is married to Achilles; Eriphile, whose real name is also Iphigenia, turns out to be the intended sacrifice. Du Roullet's plot is less contrived, although the ending does not prepare for the Tauris drama.

Du Roullet's procedure became standard for the adaptation of neoclassical tragedy into opera. The plot is simplified (two major characters, Eriphile and Ulysses, are omitted); events only described in the play (notably the denouement) are enacted to satisfy the requirement for choral involvement; danced divertissements are introduced. Other operas that treat plays in this manner included Grétry's *Andromaque* (1780), Salieri's *Les Horaces* (1786), Lemoyne's *Phèdre* (1786), and Gluck's (1779) and Piccinni's (1781) *Iphigénie en Tauride*.

Iphigénie en Aulide was never as successful as *Tauride*, but it retained a hold on the repertoire into the 19th century. Its most remarkable revival was organized by Wagner in Dresden (1847); in places this amounted to a recomposition in line with his own development (Mahler revived it in Vienna in 1904). Perhaps the most significant post-war revival was staged in 1965 using 18th-century sets discovered in the theatre at Drottningholm.

SYNOPSIS

Act I: The Greeks are held up in Aulis by unfavourable winds on their way to attack Troy; a sacrifice is needed to propitiate Artemis. Agamemnon agonizes over his dilemma ('Diane impitoyable'); Iphigenia is sent for on the pretext of marrying her to Achilles, but in reality as the sacrifice. Calchas urges Agamemnon to do his duty; the Greek soldiers are heard fiercely demanding the sacrifice, but he is defiant ('Peuvent-ils ordonner'). Agamemnon believes Arcas has forestalled his daughter's coming, but the chorus is heard greeting her and her mother. His next ruse is to tell Clytemnestra that Achilles has changed his mind. Iphigenia is devastated at the news, and greets her lover coldly; but his ardour overcomes her resistance.

Act II: Preparations are made for the wedding, but Arcas reveals the truth; Achilles promises to defend Iphigenia, but she is submissive. Achilles confronts Agamemnon (duet, 'De votre audace téméraire'). The infuriated king orders the sacrifice, but repents ('O toi, l'objet le plus aimable').

Act III: The first part of the act is punctuated by the angry chorus of Greeks demanding blood. Iphigenia intends to submit to fate, despite Achilles' intention to fight and Clytemnestra's anguish. At the altar, after a solemn hymn, the sacrifice is prepared, but Achilles bursts in with his troops, threatening Calchas' life. The miraculous ignition of the pyre and a change of wind permits a happy ending.

For the Paris revival of 1775 minor changes were made in Act II, and at the end Artemis herself appears to bring about the happy ending and urge the Greeks on to the destruction of Troy (this was the version performed at the Paris Opéra into the 19th century, but not published until 1873). The ending, like that of *Tauride*, anticipates the 1790s vogue for operas ending in a rescue.

As the inception of the Gluckist era in France, *Iphigénie en Aulide* has a special place in operatic history. It is also, however, a logical development of his Viennese reform operas; in particular the overture is his finest, its contrasting thematic ideas, arranged in a free form, apparently representing the conflicting demands of authority and human affection that motivate the characters of the opera. In place of the sheer beauty of *Orfeo* and the grandeur of *Alceste*, Gluck concentrates on the variety and development of characterization, particularly of the title role and Agamemnon. To the almost saintly Iphigenia, who, however, is admirably severe when she believes herself jilted in Act I, and the noble yet devious king are added a one-dimensional but vivid Achilles and a Clytemnestra whose anguish and fury in her arias (Act II, 'Par un père cruel'; Act III, 'Jupiter, lance la foudre') is worthy of the artistic, as well as actual, mother of Electra in Mozart's *Idomeneo*.

Gluck was criticized for surrendering beauty (particularly in the ballets, which are inferior to those in *Orphée*) to the portrayal of strong feeling; it was argued that opera is an art of illusion, and tragedy belonged in the spoken theatre. These qualities, which made *Iphigénie* only a qualified triumph, are precisely those that we value today. Both the orchestration and the recitative (albeit orchestrated throughout) are simpler than in the Calzabigi operas, perhaps because Gluck trusted the Paris orchestra less, and perhaps because he saw no place for trombones in an opera that in its original form had no true *merveilleux*. The forms are remarkably fluid, a personal adoption of a French model, which was to influence the later revision of *Alceste*. In addition to arias, none long, some very short, there are fine ensembles and complex scenes built out of arioso and recitative (especially those involving Agamemnon).

RECORDING Dawson, von Otter, Aler, Van Dam, Monteverdi Ch, Op Nat de Lyons O, Gardiner, Erato, 1990

Iphigénie en Tauride

Iphigenia in Tauris

First version
Tragédie lyrique in four acts (2h)
Libretto by Nicolas-François Guillard, after Euripides and the tragedy by Claude Guimond de la Touche (1757)
Composed 1778
PREMIERES 18 May 1779, Opéra, Paris; UK: 7 April 1796, King's Theatre, Haymarket, London; US: 25 November 1916, Metropolitan, New York

Second version
Tragisches singspiel in four acts (2h)
Libretto by Johann Baptist von Alxinger, after Nicolas-François Guillard
PREMIERE 23 October 1781, Burgtheater, Vienna
CAST Iphigenie *s*, Thoas *b*, Oreste *bar* (1781: *t*), Pylade *t* (*haute-contre*), 2 priestesses *s*, Diana *s*, a Scythian *b* (1781: *t*), a temple servant *b* (1781: *le ministre b*), 1779 only: a Greek woman *s*; *satb* chorus of priestesses, Scythians, Eumenides, Greeks, Thoas' guards

Gluck's last triumph at the Paris Opéra returns to Trojan War material. That Artemis (Diana) should save Iphigenia from sacrifice in Aulis and take her to Scythia (Crimea) as a priestess seems to negate the ending of the earlier opera; but the two themes were separately and incompatibly treated by Euripides, whose light-toned drama lies behind the more serious operas on the subject. The French pair (Piccinni's followed in 1781) were directly derived from Guimond de la Touche's play of 1757, still in repertoire at the Comédie Française in the 1770s. By coincidence, Goethe's poetic drama on the subject was written at the same time as Gluck's opera. The second version, in German, is only a little altered. Its designation 'tragisches singspiel' uses the latter word in its original sense, implying simply 'opera'; there is no spoken dialogue.

Iphigénie en Tauride continues to be one of the most often revived of Gluck's operas. In the early 19th century the role was taken by Mme Branchu. The opera was a particular favourite of Berlioz; he wrote enthusiastically to Hallé (who gave a performance in Manchester in 1860) about 'O malheureuse Iphigénie'; this aria was also singled out for praise by Tovey. Richard Strauss rearranged the operas, with additional orchestration and some musical 'modernization', in 1900 (repeated New York, 1916); but his version was considerably less radical than Wagner's of *Aulide*. Most of the major opera companies have put on the work since the Second World War. Callas took the title role under Giulini (Milan, 1957) and Gorr under Solti at the Edinburgh Festival in 1961, subsequently transferring to Covent Garden. The Paris Opéra revived it in 1965 with Régine Crespin.

SYNOPSIS

Act I: Gluck prophetically began this opera without an overture. Instead the orchestra depicts calm at dawn, followed by the storm that (we learn later) brings Orestes to Tauris. Through this the voices of Iphigenia and her priestesses are heard imploring the gods' protection. The storm dies away; but Iphigenia declares that it is still raging in her heart. She has dreamed of the death of her father and mother, and then that she herself will raise the sacrificial knife to kill her brother. She turns to Artemis, who has brought her to Tauris, in prayer ('O toi, qui prolongeas mes jours'). The savage Thoas is afflicted by foreboding ('De noirs pressentiments'); when two strangers appear, driven inland by the storm, he demands their immediate sacrifice in accordance with local custom.

Act II (Guillard originally wrote a five-act drama; on Gluck's insistence two acts were conflated into Act II): Orestes has been driven by the avenging Furies to seek absolution for killing his mother by recovering the statue of Artemis, profaned by human sacrifice in Tauris. The other captive is his close friend Pylades. They are separated by guards, and Orestes, after a delusory moment of peace ('Le calme rentre dans mon coeur'), falls into a fit in which the Furies accuse him. At its climax his mother Clytemnestra's ghost appears and seems to merge into the real Iphigenia who comes to question him. Although unaware of Orestes' identity, Iphigenia feels drawn to him; she persuades him to tell her the history of her family, which he ends by announcing his own death. Lamenting his end ('O malheureuse Iphigénie'), she turns for solace to ritual ('Contemplez ces tristes apprêts').

Act III: Iphigenia resolves to free one captive, to take a message to her sister Electra. She hopes Orestes will be saved, but after a magnanimous dispute, in which Orestes cites his own madness as a reason for dying, Pylades agrees to go; he may find help and attempt a rescue ('Divinité des grandes âmes').

Act IV: Iphigenia prays for release from her hated duty ('Je t'implore et je tremble'). At the sacrificial altar Iphigenia and Orestes recognize each other; Thoas enters in a rage, singing an air of invective, which Gluck required his librettist to supply, and is about to slaughter the victim and priestess together when Pylades appears with the crew of the Greek ship, kills Thoas and overcomes the superstitious barbarian guards. Artemis descends to confirm that her statue must no longer be profaned by human blood. (A ballet, *Les scythes enchaînés*, was added by Gossec, Gluck by this date (1779) apparently regarding such things as *hors d'oeuvre*.)

One remarkable aspect of this opera is the absence of sexual love. Gluck concentrates on his heroine, magnificently drawn in four contrasted arias, and on Orestes, whose frenzies, the result of the remorseless grip on his conscience of matricide (symbolized by the Furies) bring the trombones into play. The reminder, by the throbbing violas, that his peace ('Le calme rentre dans mon coeur') is illusory, is Gluck's most famous (though by no means unique) piece of psychological instrumentation. When it was criticized for the calm with which Orestes was speaking, Gluck replied: 'He is lying: he killed his mother.'

Iphigénie en Tauride may well be considered the most perfect of Gluck's serious operas. Yet he made even more use than usual of material salvaged from earlier works. The 1765 ballet *Semiramis* formed the basis for the Furies' music; Iphigenia's longer arias are from *La clemenza di Tito* and *Antigono* via *Telemaco*, which also supplied Orestes' Act II aria 'Dieux! qui me poursuivez' via *Le feste d'Apollo*; and the opening is derived from *L'île de Merlin*. The incorporation of Italian arias gives an expansiveness to the characterization which is markedly different from *Aulide* or *Armide*, though not unlike *Alceste*. None of these arias, however, retains its full da capo form, and they are balanced by shorter pieces. Iphigenia has an aria in each act; those in the first and third are considerably shorter, as are the arias for Thoas and Pylades. The small chorus of priestesses is handled with unprecedented freedom, intervening for single words as well as short choruses, and providing an additional dynamic and emotional resource at the climax of 'O malheureuse Iphigénie'.

The divertissement is confined to the first act, a short abrasive set of choral and dance movements using 'Turkish' percussion instruments, following up the demonstration of national characteristic in *Paride*. Gluck continued to work in massive tableaux, notably in Act II; first Orestes' scene with the Furies, then Iphigenia's mourning, the central part of the original aria being converted into the chorus 'Contemplez ces tristes apprêts' (in the German version this is omitted, being replaced to considerably less effect by a sinfonia). The work also possesses a symphonic dimension unusual in Gluck, which, however, functions like a ritornello, connecting the opening storm music with the denouement (the intervention of Thoas to the arrival of Artemis), also in D major: the continuity of the music here exceeds even that of the climax of *Aulide*.

Gluck continued to cultivate flexibility of form, especially in recitatives, where the use of string texture, while prohibiting fast delivery, enabled him to exert an iron control over the tension even in the longest speeches. He makes more use than ever of sustained chordal accompaniment, which permits an immediate response from the orchestra to a crucial word or gesture. The principal formal achievement of this opera is the integration of arias derived from Italian works into a framework that seems entirely French. The revived *Alceste*, and earlier still Philidor in *Ernelinde*, provided precedents, but Gluck shortened his arias while retaining their expansiveness of gesture. This enabled him to move flexibly between recitative, aria and chorus.

RECORDINGS 1. Montague, Aler, Allen, Monteverdi Ch, Op Nat de Lyon O, Gardiner, Philips, 1985; 2. Goerke, Cole, Gilfry, Boston Baroque, Pearlman, Telarc, 1999

OTHER OPERAS *Artaserse*, 1741 (2 arias survive); *Demetrio*, 1742 (8 arias survive); *Demofoonte*, 1743; *Il Tigrane*, 1743 (11 arias and 1 duet survive); *La Sofonisba*, 1744 (11 arias and 1 duet survive); *Ipermestra*, 1744; *Poro*, 1744 (overture, 4 arias and 1 duet survive); *Ippolito*, 1745 (11 arias and 1 duet survive); *La caduta de'giganti*, 1746; *Artamene*, 1746 (6 arias survive); *Le nozze d'Ercole e d'Ebe*, 1747; *La Semiramide riconosciuta*, 1748; *La contesa de'numi*, 1749; *Ezio*, 1750; *Issipile*, 1752 (4 arias survive); *La clemenza di Tito*, 1752; *Le Cinesi*, 1754; *La danza*, 1755;

L'innocenza giustificata, 1755; *Antigono*, 1756; *Il re pastore*, 1756; *La fausse esclave*, 1758; *L'ile de Merlin, ou Le monde renversé*, 1758; *La Cythère assiégée*, 1759; *Le diable à quatre, ou La double métamorphose*, 1759; *L'arbre enchanté, ou Le tuteur dupé*, 1759, rev. 1775; *L'ivrogne corrigé*, 1760; *Tetide*, 1760; *Le cadi dupé*, 1761; *Il trionfo di Clelia*, 1763; *La rencontre imprévue*, 1764; *Il Parnaso confuso*, 1765; *Telemaco, o sia l'isola di Circe*, 1765; *La corona*, (1765); *Il prologo*, 1767 (overture and 3 numbers to precede Traetta's *Ifigenia in Aulide*); *Le feste d'Apollo*, 1769; *Paride ed Elena*, 1770; *Armide*, 1777; *Echo et Narcisse*, 1779

J.R.

Charles Gounod

Charles François Gounod; *b* 17 June 1818, Paris; *d* 18 October 1893, St-Cloud, nr Paris

Gounod, widely celebrated for a few years at the height of his career as France's leading composer, could count among his teachers two grand old men of French musical pedagogy in the 1830s, Antonin Reicha and Jean-François Lesueur. Thorough academic training fertilized his prodigious musical facility and led to the Prix de Rome at the early age of 20. Exposure to Italian cultural treasures on the prizewinner's trip left an indelible mark on Gounod, who was also a gifted painter. Unlike many of his contemporaries, he looked to Classical culture in a general way as a model of balance and control for his own work. And impregnated with Classical ideals about the higher role of art in society, he expressed alarm in letters home about the despoliation of music through commercialism. Not surprisingly, Gounod never became comfortable in business matters. His career was also unusual in that, on his return to Paris, he did not seek to achieve success in the world of opera, preferring to devote himself to sacred music and even seriously contemplating the priesthood.

It was entirely characteristic that Gounod was drawn to a Classical subject, the death of the poet Sappho, for his first opera. *Sapho* was composed for the great mezzo Pauline Viardot, who championed the composer after he turned away from the seminary in 1848. Though it was a box-office failure during its first run at the Opéra in 1851, *Sapho* was enough of a *succès d'estime* to lead to another commission at the same house, *La nonne sanglante* (1854) to a libretto by Eugène Scribe. That work was no more enduring, mainly because of a poorly wrought libretto, but Gounod's continuing prominence was assured not only by favourable critical response to his music but also by his appointment in 1852 as director of an important choral society, the Orphéon de la Ville de Paris. He began a number of operatic projects following the demise of *La nonne*, including an *Ivan le terrible* which he never completed; that libretto eventually passed into the hands of his young friend Bizet. The planning of *Faust* (1859), Gounod's first collaboration with Jules Barbier and Michel Carré, began in 1856 with encouragement from the newly appointed director of the Théâtre-Lyrique, Léon Carvalho. Before that work was staged, however, Gounod completed a very fine operatic adaptation of Molière's *Le médecin malgré lui* (1858). *Faust* itself was well received during its first run, though publishers were slow to take interest. A few weeks after the premiere, Gounod and his librettists struck an agreement with the Choudens firm. By arranging performances in other cities, that publisher set about effectively marketing *Faust*. Stagings at French provincial theatres were followed by productions in Germany, many of them under the title of *Margarete* to distance the work from Goethe and to reflect more accurately its substance.

Carvalho, eager to follow on the success of *Faust* with a new work by Gounod, persuaded him to reroute *Philémon et Baucis* (1860) from its intended destination, the summer theatre at Baden-Baden, to the Théâtre-Lyrique. Gounod rather artificially enlarged the scope of *Philémon* for the Parisian stage, and it did not fare well until it was reduced to its original proportions many years later at the Opéra-Comique. In place of *Philémon et Baucis*, he supplied the Baden stage with *La Colombe* (1860). Demonstrating remarkable productivity for a composer of his generation, Gounod soon completed the five-act *La Reine de Saba* (1862) after a story by Nerval, for the Opéra. For the first time in his career (and possibly that of any French composer) several reviewers described the music as *wagnérien*, a term that would be used with similar lack of discrimination in France until the end of the century. In part because of expectations roused by the success of *Faust*, the opera was Gounod's most resounding failure to date. His subsequent stage work, *Mireille* (1864), did little better at first; nevertheless, on revival and after extensive modifications it eventually did entrench itself in French houses.

Another failure would almost certainly have led precipitously to the end of Gounod's operatic career. In *Roméo et Juliette* he scored a much-needed critical triumph that was vigorously sustained at the Théâtre-Lyrique box office by an initial run during the Paris World Exhibition of 1867, when the city was well populated by tourists. Personal turmoil brought about by a move to England after the war of 1870 and by a temporary estrangement from his wife produced a lengthy hiatus before his next operatic premiere. Because of a long-distance dispute with the management of the Opéra-Comique Gounod never completed the setting that he began of Molière's *Georges Dandin*, a most interesting project since he used Molière's prose text throughout instead of a more conventional verse reworking. Another project during these years was an adaptation of *Polyeucte*, Corneille's play about Christian martyrdom in Rome. A messy dispute over ownership of the complete autograph full score with Georgina Weldon, a singer of modest accomplishments with whom Gounod had become personally entangled while in England, caused a delay in a staging of that work.

After Gounod's return to France, Léon Carvalho, now hoping to replicate earlier Théâtre-Lyrique successes as director of the Opéra-Comique, commissioned *Cinq-Mars* (1877) from him. It disappointed, as did *Polyeucte* when it was finally unveiled on the stage of the Opéra in 1878. The latter failure was a bitter pill since Gounod himself valued the work highly, no doubt largely because of its fusion of Classical setting with Christian theme and the difficult personal circumstances surrounding its genesis. With scarcely better luck, he attempted radically different subject matter in his subsequent opera, *Le tribut de Zamora* (1881), a story set in Spain that prominently featured a madwoman's recovery of reason. By this time it was clear that Gounod's operatic career would not be resuscitated; he had not renewed himself musically and was left behind by younger composers such as Massenet. A major overhaul of *Sapho* in 1884, with the addition of much new music, was Gounod's final operatic endeavour. That he could even undertake a recasting of his first opera late in his career is testimony to the short stylistic distance between his first opera and last.

Faust

Opéra in five acts (3h 30m)
Libretto by Jules Barbier and Michel Carré, after the play *Faust et Marguerite* by Michel Carré (1850) and the play *Faust*, Part I, by Johann von Goethe, in the French translation by Gérard de Nerval (1828)
Composed 1856–9; ballet 1868–9
PREMIERES 19 March 1859,

Théâtre-Lyrique, Paris; UK: 11 June 1863, Her Majesty's Theatre, Haymarket, London; US: 18 November 1863, Academy of Music, Philadelphia
CAST Faust *t*, Méphistophélès *b*, Wagner *bar*, Valentin *bar*, Siébel *s*, Marguerite *s*, Marthe *ms*; *satb* chorus of young girls, labourers, students, burghers, matrons, invisible demons, church choir, witches, queens and courtesans of antiquity, celestial voices

Gounod's enthusiasm for Goethe's *Faust* was of long standing by the time he set about planning his opera with Barbier and Carré in 1856; he had even composed a setting of the church scene in the late 1840s (the present location of that autograph is unknown). Since Goethe's play offered little character interaction beyond the three principals (Faust, Gretchen and Mephistopheles), Michel Carré allowed his own earlier adaptation of Goethe's *Faust* for the Théâtre du Gymnase-Dramatique, with its significantly expanded roles for Valentin and Siébel, to serve as the proximate source for the project. Gounod's opera follows Carré's light boulevard play quite closely, but reintroduces weightier elements from Goethe, such as Valentin's death, the *Walpurgisnacht* and Marguerite's imprisonment. The return to Goethean elements missing from Carré's play, however, seems to have been motivated in many instances as much, if not more, by purely musical and operatic considerations as by the principle of fidelity to the German playwright. Direct comparison of Gounod's opera with the Goethe play risks obscuring the opera's many qualities.

The work that Gounod originally composed was much longer than the one performed on the opening night. Many numbers, including an Act II duet for Valentin and Marguerite, a more extended *Nuit de Walpurgis* episode, and a mad scene for Marguerite alone in the last act – doubtless not well suited to the voice of Marie Miolan-Carvalho, creator of the role – were cut in the first rehearsal. At a late rehearsal stage, the 'Soldiers' Chorus' was lifted from Gounod's aborted *Ivan le terrible* to replace a set of couplets composed for Valentin in Act IV. Upheavals to *Faust* continued as its popularity spread. The original spoken dialogue between set pieces was soon replaced on most stages by recitatives supplied by the composer. In some productions the church scene appeared near the beginning of Act IV instead of in its original position after Valentin's death. For the second set of performances at Her Majesty's Theatre in 1864, the English baritone Charles Santley requested an arrangement of a melody from the orchestral prelude that became 'Avant de quitter ces lieux'; that piece has remained part of the work ever since, despite Gounod's reservations about it. Finally, Gounod composed the well-known ballet music when the work travelled from the Théâtre-Lyrique to the Opéra in 1869.

SYNOPSIS

Act I: Faust, despondent and alone in his study, resolves to take poison but hesitates when he hears a pastoral chorus. An invocation to Satan conjures up a rather dapper buffo Méphistophélès. Faust yearns above all for sensual gratification, and Méphistophélès readily promises to fulfil the philosopher's desires in return for service in the nether world. When Faust hesitates, Méphistophélès conjures up a vision of Marguerite at her spinning wheel. Faust signs the document and is transformed into a young nobleman, singing of the pleasures that await him ('A moi les plaisirs').

Act II: At the fair townspeople sing a virtuoso chorus ('Vin ou bière'). Valentin appears, clutching a medallion given him by his sister Marguerite; he is about to leave for battle and instructs his friends, including Wagner and Siébel, to look after her. Méphistophélès joins the group and provides blasphemous entertainment with a song about the golden calf ('Le veau d'or'). Valentin is incited to anger when Méphistophélès makes light of his sister, but his sword breaks in mid-air. Alarmed, the men brandish the crossed pommels of their weapons before him in a gesture of Christian exorcism. Temporarily emasculated, Méphistophélès is left alone on stage, but is soon joined by Faust and a group of waltzing villagers ('Ainsi que la brise légère'). When Marguerite appears among them, Faust offers her his arm; she modestly rejects his advance.

Act III: Siébel leaves a bouquet for Marguerite in her garden. Faust, playing well the role of romantic idealist, apostrophizes her home and the protective embrace of nature ('Salut! demeure chaste et pure'). More worldly wise, Méphistophélès positions a jewel box near Siébel's flowers. Marguerite enters and sings a ballad tinged with modal inflexions about the King of Thule. She then discovers both the bouquet and jewel box and erupts in a buoyant cabaletta (the 'Jewel Song' – 'Je ris de me voir') as she tries on earrings and a necklace. Her guardian Marthe is not immune to male attentions either and when Faust and Méphistophélès join the pair, she is attracted to the devil. Marguerite allows herself to be embraced by Faust in a duet ('Laisse-moi, laisse-moi contempler ton visage') but is suddenly overcome with shame. Encouraged by Méphistophélès, Faust completes the seduction.

Act IV: Marguerite has given birth to Faust's child and is ostracized by girls in the street below. She sits down to spin ('Il ne revient pas') and Siébel, ever faithful, attempts to encourage her. The scene shifts to a public square for the return of Valentin, bombastic and self-assured ('Soldiers' Chorus'). While Valentin is inside the house, Méphistophélès trenchantly plays a lover delivering a serenade beneath Marguerite's window. Faust declares his responsibility for Marguerite's fall and successfully engages Valentin in a duel. As he dies, Valentin blames Marguerite and damns her for eternity. The next scene shows Marguerite attempting to pray in a church. She eventually succeeds, despite the musical efforts of a chorus of demons, but faints when Méphistophélès unleashes a final imprecation.

Act V: It is the *Nuit de Walpurgis* in the Harz mountains, and Faust is first mesmerized by will-o'-the-wisps and witches and then titillated by legendary courtesans of antiquity. A vision of Marguerite redirects his thoughts to her. She has been imprisoned for infanticide. Through Méphistophélès, Faust obtains the keys to her cell. They sing a love duet about past bliss, and he begs her to flee ('Oui c'est toi je t'aime'). With Méphistophélès impatiently goading the two to follow him, Marguerite resists and calls for divine protection ('Anges purs! anges radieux'). Faust looks on with despair and falls to his knees in prayer as her soul rises to heaven.

Faust was considered a difficult work by many during its first run of performances. In part this was due to a full flowering of Gounod's mature melodic style, one that eschewed mechanistic spinning out of rhythmic motifs and an abundance of coloratura in favour of a tapering of relatively simple surface rhythms around the expressive nuances of the text. Gounod also avoided certain conventions – for example, the introductory chorus and concertato-type finale. It is easy to forget just how unusual the opening scene was in its day, with its long passages of arioso singing by Faust punctuated by offstage music. Marguerite's appearance late in Act II is a refreshingly understated first entry for the prima donna. The magnificent orchestral peroration at the curtain of Act III, a grand statement of a tune previously heard only at softer dynamic levels and fragmented, is another impressive moment, one that proved highly influential on later composers. To conclude with the threefold tonal rise on 'Anges purs! anges radieux!' was an electrifying, and unprecedented, inspiration.

Marguerite is the most fully developed

musical character in *Faust*. Her awakened sensuality is hinted at through recitative interruptions in 'The Ballade of the King of Thule' and later more fully exposed as she leans out of her window wishing for Faust's return. Her role displays a naturalism uncommon on the French stage at the time, as in her account of her sister's death in the Act III quartet where, with a brief turn to recitative in the prevailing arioso, she spontaneously recalls rushing to the side of the crib. Her spinning song compares favourably with other settings of this text, and she achieves truly heroic musical stature in both the church scene and final trio. Méphistophélès is something of a demonic Leporello, light-hearted but dangerously cynical, a characteristic given effective musical form (particularly through orchestration) in the Act IV serenade.

RECORDINGS 1. Boué, Noré, Bourdin, Rico, RPO & Ch, Beecham, Preiser, 1947/8; 2. Studer, Leech, Hampson, Van Dam, French Army Ch, Toulouse Capitole Ch & O, Plasson, EMI, 1991

Roméo et Juliette

Romeo and Juliet

Opera in a prologue and five acts (3h 15m)
Libretto by Jules Barbier and Michel Carré, after the play by William Shakespeare (1596)
Composed 1865–7
PREMIERES 27 April 1867, Théâtre-Lyrique, Paris; UK: 11 July 1867, Covent Garden, London (in Italian); US: 15 November 1867, New York
CAST Paris *bar*, Tybalt *t*, Capulet *b*, Juliette *s*, Roméo *t*, Mercutio *bar*, Benvolio *t*, Gertrude *ms*, Frère Laurent *b*, Stéphano *s*, The Duke *b*, Frère Jean *b*; *satb* chorus of servants, retainers and kinsfolk to the Capulet and Montaigu households; masquers

In view of the widely recognized success of the love music in *Faust*, a setting of Shakespeare's *Romeo and Juliet* was a natural project for Gounod. Many episodes that do not centre directly on the relationship of the two protagonists in the play were cut by Gounod and his librettists, with the result that the encounters between the two main characters consume a far greater proportion of the opera than of the play. There is also a glaring discrepancy in the tomb scene: where in Shakespeare Juliet stirs only after Romeo has died, in Gounod (as well as other 19th-century versions, including Berlioz's dramatic symphony) she awakens in time to sing a final duet with him. In other respects Barbier and Carré followed Shakespeare closely, borrowing directly from existing French translations.

Like so many of Gounod's operas, *Roméo et Juliette* underwent much revision. The celebrated *valse-ariette*, 'Je veux vivre', was written at the request of Marie Miolan-Carvalho late in the rehearsal period. Because of her relatively light voice, the dramatic aria originally intended as the centrepiece for the role, 'Amour ranime mon courage' in Act IV, though printed in the first edition, was not performed at the first run and is still rarely given today. The great confrontation between the Capulets and Montaigus at the end of Act III was repeatedly revised: in the first edition, for example, the entry and departure of the duke were accompanied by a pompous stage band that was soon cut. For the revival at the Opéra in 1888 Gounod composed a new musical phrase for Romeo and the chorus to bring down the curtain at the end of that episode, the imposing 'O jour de deuil', and also supplied a ballet for the next act.

SYNOPSIS (FOLLOWING THE FIRST EDITION)

The curtain opens to a declaimed choral prologue summarizing the tragedy about to be enacted.

Act I: The assembled guests at a masked ball in the Capulet residence admire the beauty of Juliet when she is escorted into the hall by her father.

Romeo Montaigu and his friends, Mercutio and Benvolio, emerge from hiding. Mercutio makes light of Romeo's dark premonitions with an account of the fantastic realm of the fairy queen Mab ('Mab, la reine des mensonges'). Juliet reappears accompanied by her nurse Gertrude and maintains that she is uninterested in marriage ('Je veux vivre'), but after exchanging a few words with Romeo, she realizes that their destinies are intertwined. The guests return, and Capulet restrains Tybalt from venting his anger at the trespassing Montaigus.

Act II: Romeo has stealthily made his way into the Capulet garden and apostrophizes Juliet as the morning sun ('Ah! lève-toi soleil'). Shortly after she appears, he reveals his presence. Their tender words are interrupted by Capulet servants who run through the garden in search of the Montaigu page Stéphano, a comic foil to the elegiac tone of the act. The lovers agree to marry and reluctantly separate when Juliet is called in by Gertrude.

Act III: Frère Laurent sings of nature's wonders and is soon joined by Romeo and Juliet. As the two kneel, he administers the sacrament of marriage. The scene changes to a street in front of the Capulet house where Stéphano is seen taunting the rival family ('Que fais-tu, blanche tourterelle'). The page's horseplay gives rise to serious consequences: Capulets come out; Montaigus appear and a succession of duels follows, during which Romeo mortally wounds Tybalt. Romeo is exiled from Verona by the duke.

Act IV: After spending the night with Juliet, Romeo suddenly breaks from her embrace on hearing the morning lark, and Juliet sadly admits that they must separate again. Capulet gives his daughter the news that she is to marry Paris. Frère Laurent explains how she might escape with Romeo by means of a ruse enacted through a potion that will make her appear dead. She summons her courage before drinking the liquid ('Amour ranime mon courage', a dramatic air often omitted). In the next scene Juliet is led into the family ballroom to the strains of a wedding march. She suddenly collapses.

Act V: In the underground crypt of the Capulets, Frère Laurent learns from Frère Jean that Romeo has not received his letter explaining the ruse. After an instrumental interlude, Romeo appears. Believing Juliet to be dead he takes poison. At that moment, she awakens and the two sing of their love, largely through reminiscences of previous music, since a past is all that they now have. As he weakens, Juliet uncovers a sword hidden in her clothes and stabs herself.

The highlights of the score are the four duets for the two protagonists, certainly an unusual (and possibly unprecedented) number of tenor–soprano duets in a single opera: Massenet would follow suit in *Manon* and *Werther*. The passage for *divisi* cellos at the outset of the Act IV duet (surely a model for Verdi in the Act I duet of *Otello*) is a small tone poem about the wedding night; that entire duet exudes an air of sensuousness that was quite new to the French stage in its day. The concluding duet is one of Gounod's least conventional operatic numbers, at least in form: despite its length, it has few passages of ensemble singing or even of voice-dominated music constructed of phrases with regular lengths.

The opera also contains many other fine musical numbers. Romeo's ternary *cavatine* 'Ah! lève-toi, soleil' is justly renowned; its outer sections feature prominently a chromatic descent against a bass pedal note that illustrates the fading-star metaphor of the text without sacrificing lyric intensity. Mercutio's Queen Mab *ballade* is brilliantly orchestrated, and in the Act III confrontation between the Montaigus and Capulets Gounod achieves a kind of momentum and excitement that is sometimes missing from his work.

RECORDINGS I. Malfitano, Kraus, G.

Quilico, Bacquier, Van Dam, Toulouse Capitole Ch & O, Plasson, EMI, 1983; 2. Gheorghiu, Alagna, Keenlyside, Fondary, Van Dam, Toulouse Capitole Ch & O, Plasson, EMI, 1995
OTHER OPERAS *Sapho*, 1851; *La nonne sanglante*, 1854; *Ivan le terrible* (inc.), (1858); *Le médecin malgré lui*, 1858; *Philémon et Baucis*, 1860; *La Colombe*, 1860; *La reine de Saba*, 1862; *Mireille*, 1864; *George Dandin* (inc.), (1874); *Cinq-Mars*, 1877; *Polyeucte*, 1878; *Maître Pierre* (inc.), (1878); *Le tribut de Zamora*, 1881.

S.H.

H

George Frideric Handel

Georg Friedrich Händel; *b* 23 February 1685, Halle an der Saale; *d* 14 April 1759, London

Although Handel is best known in the English-speaking world for his oratorios and orchestral works, he was primarily an opera composer. Until he was in his mid-fifties, his career centred on the opera house: he took a leading role in the musical management of London's repertoire opera companies, and between 1710 and 1740 he composed new operas at a rate averaging more than one major work per year. Working within the musical conventions of Italian opera seria, Handel mainly set libretti that had already been used by other composers in Italy, though he adapted them to the needs of his own performers and, to some extent, to the tastes of his audiences. The well-developed and mature genre of opera seria to which Handel attached himself in his early twenties was already being enriched by elements from French opera (Handel's operas normally begin with a 'French' *ouverture*) and influences from French drama. To this form Handel brought formidable composition skills, particularly in the control and extension of melody and harmony, that took the baroque operatic aria to a peak of its development: and, since opera seria relied on the exposition of character and of emotional states through arias, in both of which Handel was supremely skilled, his operas mark the highest point in the genre itself.

In the town of his birth Handel received a firm technical education in music at the hands of Friedrich Wilhelm Zachow, the organist of the Market Church. Just before his 17th birthday he registered as a student at Halle University, and soon after received his first musical appointment as organist of the Calvinist Domkirche. However, he apparently nursed musical ambitions that could not be fulfilled in Halle, and two years later left to join the opera house in Hamburg, initially as a violinist. He had already met one of the opera house's leading young musicians, Johann Mattheson, during a visit to Hamburg and Lübeck in 1703, and may have made preliminary contact with its leading composer, Keiser, through his family connections in the area near Halle.

At Hamburg Handel advanced quickly from second violinist to keyboard accompanist. Early in 1704 he was involved in a duel with Mattheson over the occupancy of the harpsichord at the end of Mattheson's *Cleopatra*. The next year saw the production of Handel's own first operas, *Almira* and *Nero*: the first was a success, but the second ran for only three performances. After this, Handel seems to have withdrawn somewhat from the opera company, though he composed one further opera, apparently so extensive that it was divided over two nights when it was first performed in 1708 (*Florindo* and *Dafne*) – but by then

Handel had left Hamburg for Italy. Handel's Hamburg operas have not survived intact: *Almira* is the only one for which a sufficiently complete score survives for modern performance.

Handel's Italian visit lasted from the autumn of 1706 to the early months of 1710. Since he wanted to meet as many contemporary Italian musicians as possible, and to hear their music, he spent periods in a number of different centres. Considerable time was spent in Rome, where Handel enjoyed enlightened patronage and composed many chamber cantatas, developing in them the operatic forms of recitative and aria. But opera itself was absent from Rome owing to papal opposition. At Florence, on the other hand, opera flourished under the patronage of Ferdinando de' Medici. Handel probably heard works by Alessandro Scarlatti, Perti and Orlandini there, and became acquainted with the libretti of Antonio Salvi, a physician to the Florentine court. It was for Florence that he composed his first all-Italian opera, *Rodrigo*. Venice gave him the opportunity to hear operas by Gasparini, Lotti, Albinoni, Caldara and Alessandro Scarlatti, and to produce his own *Agrippina*.

During the Carnival season Venice was a resort for foreign diplomats as well as musicians. There Handel may have made contacts that brought him successively to Hanover and London, among them Agostino Steffani, who had directed the court opera in Hanover during its heyday in the 1690s. When Handel accepted a post at Hanover in June 1710 he must have recognized that the court opera was in abeyance for the foreseeable future, and it was apparently agreed that he would enjoy generous leave of absence to pursue his operatic ambitions elsewhere. Before the year was out, Handel was in London, and early the next year *Rinaldo* was produced at the Queen's Theatre, Haymarket. After a single dutiful return to Hanover, he settled permanently in London in 1712.

Handel's long operatic career in London falls into a number of phases. Although an overall musical continuity is apparent in the type of music presented, the administrations of successive opera companies lurched from one artistic or financial crisis to another. The decade preceding Handel's arrival had seen almost continuous chaos in the management of the London patent theatres: only recently had the idea of all-sung Italian opera become a reality, and the Haymarket Theatre its regular venue. Musical quality, some novel stage effects and the presence of the leading castrato Nicolini brought success to Handel's first London opera, *Rinaldo*, and contributed to the permanent establishment of Italian opera in London. But managements came and went: sometimes, like Owen Swiney in 1713, they took the money with them. John Jacob Heidegger as manager brought some stability to the situation, but his efforts were temporarily beaten by a political division among the patrons in 1717, which came at the end of a period of gradual financial attrition.

The reunification of the sources of patronage, symbolized by the reconciliation between George I and the Prince of Wales in March 1720, coincided with the most determined attempt to establish Italian opera in London on a permanent footing. The Royal Academy of Music, established by Charter in 1719, named Handel as 'Master of the Orchestra', and he was given instructions to undertake a European tour to engage singers, including the castrato Senesino. The Academy presented repertoire seasons, whose programmes included operas by several composers and pasticcios assembled from other works. In the first years of the Academy Handel had to share musical authority with other composers, most importantly Giovanni Bononcini, but gradually responsibility devolved to Handel alone. Unfortunately, the Academy was eventually overcome by problems of artistic and financial management. By 1728 the commitment of its original patrons had probably run its course, and could not be revived even by the unedifying rivalry between the supporters of the opera company's two leading ladies, Francesca Cuzzoni and Faustina Bordoni. After a break during 1728–9, Handel and Heidegger resumed opera seasons under their own management, taking over the Academy's scenery and costume stock. Handel once again visited the Continent to collect singers, including the soprano Strada and the castrato Bernacchi; but within the year the latter had been replaced by the return of Senesino.

However, when a rival opera company, The Opera of the Nobility, was established in 1733 Senesino joined the opposition, taking most of the rest of the cast with him. After one season of rivalry, Handel had to cede the premier Haymarket opera house (known as the King's Theatre since the accession of George I in 1714) to the Nobility Opera, taking his own opera company to Covent Garden. The period of the two opera companies, which lasted until 1737, was an uncomfortable one for Handel, but it brought forth some fine operas. In Carestini and Conti he found technically accomplished successors to Senesino, and his programmes were more diverse than those of the Nobility Opera. From 1732 onwards he mixed English oratorios, odes and serenatas with his Italian operas and in 1734–5 his operas were considerably enhanced by Madame Sallé's dance company.

On the collapse of the Nobility Opera, Handel reoccupied the King's Theatre for two seasons in 1738–9: the emphasis was on opera in the first season and oratorio in the second. Then Handel moved his performances to a less central venue, the theatre in Lincoln's Inn Fields, for two seasons: English works were given in the first season, but the second included new Italian operas, *Imeneo* and *Deidamia*. There Handel gave his last London opera performance in February 1741: the next year *Imeneo* saw a final revival at his hands as part of his concert season in Dublin. When Handel returned to London, his theatre career centred around English works. He looked back only once, when he inserted five of his Italian opera arias into a revival of *Semele* in December 1744, probably to accommodate Italian singers. It may be significant that this occurred in the one English work that, although performed 'after the manner of an oratorio', was composed to a libretto originally written *c.*1706 for an English opera and intended for one of London's major theatres.

None of Handel's English works was given a staged performance in the theatre under the composer: *Acis and Galatea* and *Esther* were probably acted in their earlier versions, at private performances, but when they came to the public theatre Handel presented them as a serenata and an oratorio respectively, without stage action. The genre of theatre oratorio that Handel developed in his later years was differently paced, and differently constructed, from his operas: opinions are divided as to whether staged performances are successful.

Handel revived several of his operas, with consequent changes of cast and musical contents. The versions and voice types listed are those of the first performances; major changes on subsequent revivals are noted in the descriptions. Voices are described according to the clefs used by Handel for the original singer (soprano, alto, tenor, bass), and roles originally composed for castrati are noted as such. The operas generally end with a *coro* sung by all the soloists. The presence of other chorus movements (generally sung by the soloists alone until Handel's operas of the mid-1730s) is noted for the relevant operas. Handel composed his operas to a normal time-span of about three hours' music: the performances must have lasted about four hours with the intervals.

Agrippina

Drama per musica in three acts (3h)
Libretto by Vincenzo Grimani, based on events *c.*AD 40–50 as related by Tacitus and Suetonius
Composed 1709
PREMIERES ?January 1710, Teatro Grimani di San Giovanni Crisostomo (now Teatro Malibran), Venice; UK: 27 June 1963, Unicorn Theatre, Abingdon; US: 16 February 1972, Philadelphia (concert); 14 March 1985, Fort Worth (stage)
CAST Agrippina *s*, Poppea *s*, Nerone *s* (*castrato*), Ottone *a*, Claudio *b*, Narciso *a* (*castrato*), Pallante *b*, Lesbo *b*, Giunone *c*

Agrippina is arguably Handel's first operatic masterpiece. The plot is an anti-heroic satirical comedy. The characters (and their follies) are vividly portrayed with a light touch; yet the seriousness of the motivations and issues that produce the dramatic tensions are never undercut. The libretto is one of the best that Handel ever set and, unusually, was written specially for him. Handel probably composed the score in Venice late in 1709: the Carnival season began on 26 December, and *Agrippina* was apparently the second opera of the season.

SYNOPSIS

Act I: Agrippina, wife of the Roman emperor Claudio, schemes that Nerone, her son by a previous marriage, should succeed to the throne. Hearing that Claudio has been drowned, she arranges to have Nerone proclaimed, but the ceremony is interrupted by news of the arrival of Claudio, who has been rescued by his lieutenant Ottone: in return Claudio has named Ottone as his successor. Ottone declares his love for Poppea. Agrippina, knowing that Claudio is also attracted to Poppea, suggests to Poppea that Ottone has agreed to yield her to Claudio in return for the succession.

Act II: Poppea sets Claudio against Ottone, but subsequently discovers that she has been deceived by Agrippina. Meanwhile, Agrippina plays on Claudio's belief in Ottone's treachery and persuades him that he should name Nerone as his successor.

Act III: Poppea receives three admirers, successively hiding Ottone and Nerone behind curtained doorways, and awaiting Claudio. To him she says that she was mistaken in her previous identification and that his traitorous rival is Nerone, not Ottone: to prove this, she reveals Nerone's presence in the room, and Claudio dismisses him in a fury. Agrippina realizes that Poppea has denounced Nerone, and that her own schemes are in danger of exposure. She responds to Claudio's accusations by saying that she acted for the safety of the city and the throne, and taxes him with being improperly influenced by Poppea. When she claims that Ottone loves Poppea, Claudio lays the blame for his actions on Nerone, and summons all three. He accuses Nerone of hiding in Poppea's room, and orders them to marry, meanwhile naming Ottone to the succession. Ottone renounces the throne in order to reclaim Poppea: Claudio approves the exchange of Ottone's and Nerone's ambitions, and invokes Juno to bless the marriage of Ottone and Poppea. (Giunone is not listed in the original printed libretto: the final scene, in which she appears, may have been cut before the first performance.)

Agrippina was a success: according to John Mainwaring, Handel's first biographer, 'The theatre, at almost every pause, resounded with shouts of *Viva il caro Sassone*. They were thunderstruck with the grandeur and sublimity of his style: for never had they known till then all the powers of harmony and modulation so closely arrayed, and forcibly combined.' The arias in *Agrippina* are shorter and more numerous than in Handel's later operas, but this is appropriate to the nature of the story, and the opera marks a great advance on *Rodrigo* in the balance and pacing of the scenes. The portrayal of Agrippina herself is particularly well managed in the second half of Act II, and Handel's music keeps pace with the succession of comic denouements in Act III.

RECORDINGS 1. Bradshaw, Saffer, Minter, Hill, Isherwood, Capella Savaria, McGegan, Harmonia Mundi, 1991; 2. Jones, Brown, Miles, EBS, Gardiner, Philips, 1991/2

Rinaldo

Opera in three acts (3h)
Libretto by Giacomo Rossi, to a scenario by Aaron Hill, after *Gerusalemme liberata* by Torquato Tasso (1575)
Composed December 1710–January 1711; rev. 1731
PREMIERES 24 February 1711, Queen's Theatre, Haymarket, London; US: 16 October 1975, Jones Hall, Houston
CAST Rinaldo *a* (*castrato*), Goffredo *a*, Eustazio *a* (*castrato*), Almirena *s*, Armida *s*, Argante *b*, Magician *a* (*castrato*), Herald *t*, Woman *s*, Mermaids *s*

Handel first arrived in London towards the end of 1710. His music had preceded him: movements from the *Rodrigo* overture had provided incidental music to *The Alchemist* (by Ben Jonson) earlier that year, and an aria from *Agrippina* was introduced into a performance of Alessandro Scarlatti's *Pirro e Demetrio* in December, probably with Handel's co-operation. It can safely be presumed that Handel had received a firm invitation to compose for the Haymarket company before he set out for London. The composer obviously wished to make his mark on London; the opera management for its part welcomed the opportunity for an original work in their programme, which had hitherto been founded on second-hand Italian scores.

In the preface to the printed libretto of *Rinaldo*, Rossi claimed that Handel had composed the opera in a fortnight, and this is possible since he reworked many of his previous Italian arias into the score. No doubt it had been prudent for Handel to leave the composition until he arrived in London and could see him cast in action. The preface by Aaron Hill (manager of the Queen's Theatre) to the libretto indicated his attempt to remedy what he regarded as the defects in the Italian operas hitherto seen in London: 'First, That they had been compos'd for Tastes and Voices, different from those who were to sing and hear them on the English Stage; And Secondly, That wanting the Machines and Decorations, which bestow so great a Beauty on their Appearance, they have been heard and seen to very considerable Disadvantage.'

As the *Spectator* commented, with only slight exaggeration, on 6 March 1711: 'The opera of *Rinaldo* is filled with Thunder and Lightning, Illuminations, and Fireworks.' Hill exploited the full resources of the stage machinery at the Haymarket. His intention seems to have been to match the virtuosity of the Italian singers with extravagant scenic effects derived from the English masque tradition. In addition to the singers, *Rinaldo* required a full complement of spirits, fairies and armies.

SYNOPSIS
Act I: The Christian camp outside the gates of Jerusalem. Rinaldo reminds Goffredo, the Captain General of the Crusade force, that he has been promised the hand of Almirena, Goffredo's daughter, if the city is conquered. Argante's mistress Armida (an 'Amazonian' enchantress, and Queen of Damascus) arrives from the air in a fiery chariot and tells him that success depends on detaching Rinaldo from the Christian army. In a delightful grove with singing birds, Almirena and Rinaldo affirm their love. Armida enters and leads Almirena away. When Rinaldo offers resistance, the two ladies are carried away in a black cloud, and Rinaldo is left disconsolate ('Cara sposa, amanta cara'). Goffredo and his brother Eustazio enter; Eustazio advises that they consult a hermit in order to de-

feat Armida. Rinaldo calls on winds and tempests to assist him ('Venti, turbini').

Act II: On the seashore Goffredo and Rinaldo complain about the distance they must travel to find the hermit, but Eustazio assures them that they are close to their destination. A spirit in the shape of a lovely woman lures Rinaldo into a boat, telling him that she has been sent by Almirena. Rinaldo's companions try to prevent him from entering the boat, but he breaks free of them. The boat immediately sails away. In the garden in the enchanted palace of Armida, Almirena complains of her abduction. Argante makes advances, saying that he can prove his affection by breaking Armida's spell, even though this will provoke the enchantress's wrath, but Almirena pleads to be left alone ('Lascia ch'io pianga'). Armida rejoices at Rinaldo's capture, but when he is led in, in defiant mood, Armida annoys him further by offering her own love. When this is refused, Armida changes her appearance to that of Almirena: Rinaldo is at first taken in, but when the deception is revealed Rinaldo leaves angrily. Armida is torn between her passion for Rinaldo and her anger that he will not respond to her ('Ah, crudel'). On Argante's arrival, she changes her appearance to that of Almirena again in order to disguise her own distress, only to expose Argante's designs on Almirena. Resuming her own appearance she upbraids Argante: the alliance between them is at an end and it is now Armida's turn to call for revenge ('Vò far guerra').

Act III: A mountain prospect with the hermit's cave at the bottom and an enchanted palace at the top. The Magician–Hermit tells Goffredo and Eustazio that Rinaldo and Almirena are prisoners in the palace, but enormous force will be necessary to release them. The Christians' first attempt is repelled by 'ugly spirits', but they escape back to the cave, and the Magician gives them 'fatal Wands' that can conquer witchcraft. They climb the mountain and strike the gates of the palace, whereupon the palace, spirits and mountain vanish, and Goffredo and Eustazio are found hanging on to the sides of a vast rock in the middle of the sea. Armida, in her garden, makes to stab Almirena with a dagger; Rinaldo draws his sword to attack Armida, but is restrained by two spirits. Goffredo and Eustazio arrive and Armida invokes the furies, but with help of the Christians' wands the garden vanishes, transformed into the area near the city gate at Jerusalem. Rinaldo is united with his companions and, when Armida again attempts to stab Almirena, he attacks her again: Armida vanishes. Argante and Armida are reconciled. Eustazio announces the approach of the pagan army, and the Christian army gathers (Rinaldo: 'Or la tromba'). In the battle, Rinaldo swings the balance in favour of the Christians. Argante and Armida are captured, Rinaldo and Almirena are united. Armida, deciding that heaven may not intend her destruction, breaks her magic wand: she and Argante profess the Christian faith and are released by Goffredo.

With such an episodic scenario, the strength of *Rinaldo* lies in the power of individual events, their variety and contrast, rather than in dramatic continuity. Although his musical style had advanced enormously during the preceding six years, Handel was almost thrown back into the operatic world of *Almira*. He may have missed a few dramatic tricks, but he matched visual spectacle with its musical equivalent: tuneful hit numbers such as 'Lascia ch'io pianga', the song for the mermaids and the now famous march for the Christian army in Act III. It mattered not that the tunes were second-hand, for the audience had not heard Handel's previous works. Presumably the libretto was adapted, even in places distorted, to accommodate the texts for some of these arias, though from the musical point of view the old tunes were considerably improved. And, where the plot allowed, dramatic characterization was strong:

one of the high points is Armida's scene near the end of Act II, beginning with the forceful accompanied recitative 'Dunque i lacci d'un volto' and ending in 'Vò far guerra', which was a showpiece for Handel too, at the harpsichord in the orchestra pit.

Rinaldo maintained its popularity through several seasons following 1711. Inevitably there were some changes to the score as casts varied: the part of Goffredo was taken over by successive sopranos and that of Argante by an alto castrato, and new arias were added. One of the factors contributing to the initial success of the opera had been the presence of the castrato Nicolini in the title role. When Handel revived *Rinaldo* in April 1731 this part fell to the equally famous Senesino and the rest of the cast was also differently balanced (Goffredo as a tenor, Armida a contralto and the Magician a bass); Handel rewrote virtually the whole score.

RECORDING Bartoli, Orgonasova, Fink, Daniels, Taylor, Finley, Academy of Ancient Music, Hogwood, Decca, 1999

Giulio Cesare

Julius Caesar

Opera in three acts (3h 15m)
Libretto by Nicola Francesco Haym, after *Giulio Cesare in Egitto* by Giacomo Francesco Bussani set by Sartorio (1676) and a 1685 version of the same libretto
Composed 1723–4
PREMIERES 20 February 1724, King's Theatre, Haymarket, London; US: 14 May 1927, Smith College, Northampton, Massachusetts
CAST Giulio Cesare *a* (*castrato*), Cleopatra *s*, Cornelia *c*, Sesto Pompeo *s*, Tolomeo *a* (*castrato*), Achilla *b*, Nireno *a* (*castrato*), Curio *b*; *satb* chorus of Egyptians, conspirators

Handel probably began the composition of *Giulio Cesare* in the summer of 1723, soon after the last performance of *Flavio* on 15 June. Compared to the compactness of *Flavio*, *Giulio Cesare* is on an enormous scale: it is one of the longest and most elaborate of Handel's operas. In *Flavio* Senesino received four arias: as *Giulio Cesare* he had eight, as did Cuzzoni playing Cleopatra. During composition Handel subjected the music of Act I to a series of massive revisions, partly to accommodate cast changes but also apparently as a result of alterations to the libretto. Circumstantial evidence suggests that Haym, probably in collaboration with Handel, evolved and revised the libretto with careful thought, drawing ideas from more than one literary source and paying careful attention to dramatic coherence and characterization. The intricate plot and careful organization of the finished libretto make for an elaborate and delicately balanced opera: performances of a shortened version can be a rather bewildering experience.

Giulio Cesare and *Tamerlano* together form the climax of Handel's operas from the Royal Academy period, and indeed are among the greatest opera-seria creations by any composer, applying the formal conventions of the genre to superb and sustained dramatic effect. *Giulio Cesare* is also the Handel opera that has seen most modern revivals, perhaps because its title gives promise of recognizable historical subject matter.

SYNOPSIS
Cesare has defeated Pompeo at Pharsalia in Greece, and pursued him to Egypt: the events forming the historical basis for the action took place 18–17 BC.

Act I: Cesare is welcomed by the Egyptians. He has agreed to an appeal by Pompeo's wife and son (Cornelia and Sesto) for a peaceful settlement. When gifts arrive, brought by Achilla on behalf of Tolomeo (who is joint ruler of Egypt with his sister Cleopatra), among them is the severed head of Pompeo. Cesare sends Achilla back with a message of contempt and disgust. Cornelia tries to kill herself, then faces an unwelcome proposal of marriage from Curio, the Roman tribune. Sesto swears to avenge his father's murder. Meanwhile Cleopatra, horrified to hear of Pompeo's murder, decides to seek an alliance with Cesare against her brother. On Tolomeo's arrival Achilla reports Cesare's reaction to the gifts and promises to kill Cesare, provided he can claim Cornelia as his reward. Cesare reflects on the transitoriness of human greatness. Cleopatra, in the guise of 'Lidia', a noble Egyptian maiden whose fortune has been stolen by Tolomeo, enters and appeals to Cesare for justice. He promises redress, captivated by her beauty. Cornelia pays her last respects to her husband's ashes and snatches his sword from the trophies, crying vengeance on Tolomeo; but Sesto seizes the sword and determines to take the task on himself. Tolomeo invites Cesare to occupy the royal apartments that have been prepared for him; Cesare recognizes that he must be cautious ('Va tacito e nascosto'). Sesto challenges Tolomeo to a duel: Tolomeo orders Sesto's arrest and consigns Cornelia to work in the garden of the seraglio. Achilla offers to secure the release of Cornelia and her son if she will consent to marry him, but she rejects the idea with contempt.

Act II: Cleopatra has arranged an elaborate set piece for the seduction of Cesare ('V'adoro pupille'). It works as planned, and Cesare is promised an assignation with 'Lidia', who will introduce him to Cleopatra. Cornelia, in the seraglio garden, repels advances from Achilla and Tolomeo; she threatens suicide but is restrained by Sesto. Cleopatra's eunuch Nireno brings Tolomeo's order that Cornelia be taken to the harem. Cleopatra waits for Cesare in another garden. After some flirtation, the pair are interrupted by Curio, who tells Cesare that he is betrayed and people are calling for his murder. Cleopatra reveals her true identity and says that her royal presence will quell the tumult: but she fails, and urges Cesare to leave. He refuses and goes to face his assailants. Cleopatra asks the gods to preserve him and to have pity on her ('Se pietà di me non senti'). In the seraglio Tolomeo indicates that Cornelia is his choice. Sesto enters and snatches Tolomeo's sword from the table, but Achilla appears and takes it from him. Achilla tells Tolomeo to prepare for war: Cesare is believed drowned, and Cleopatra has fled to the Romans, who are mustering against Tolomeo. Tolomeo dismisses Achilla as a traitor when the latter reminds him that Cornelia had been promised as his reward for killing Cesare, and then departs expecting a quick victory over the Romans. Sesto attempts to stab himself, but is restrained by his mother: he renews his vengeance against Tolomeo.

Act III: Achilla, exasperated by Tolomeo's broken promise, leads his soldiers to join Cleopatra. In the ensuing battle Tolomeo's forces are victorious and Cleopatra is taken prisoner. Alone, and mourning for Cesare, she bewails her fate ('Piangerò la sorte mia'): she is led away. But Cesare is not dead: he appears, having escaped drowning by swimming from the harbour. He has lost contact with his troops and prays for help ('Aure, deh, per pietà'). Achilla, mortally wounded, gives Sesto a seal that will guarantee the loyalty of his troops and tells him of a secret passageway to Tolomeo's palace. Cesare witnesses the scene, takes the seal from Sesto, and hurries off to assemble his forces. As Cleopatra bids her friends farewell Cesare appears with his soldiers to rescue her. Cesare and Cleopatra are reunited. In the 'Royal Hall', Cornelia once again has to repel Tolomeo's attentions: she draws a dagger and is about to attack him when Sesto enters with drawn sword and claims the right of revenge. In the ensuing duel, Tolomeo is killed. At the port of Alexandria Cesare and Cleopatra welcome Cornelia and Sesto as friends and proclaim their own undying love: everyone celebrates the return of peace.

In addition to a succession of fine arias, the score contains a remarkable novelty in the set-piece scene at the beginning of Act II. The nine Muses are represented on Mount Parnassus, and Handel provided an onstage band, which may have had nine players to consort with Cleopatra/Lidia/Virtue. Another unusual feature was the use of four horns in the opening and closing scenes of the opera. The original (1724) run of *Giulio Cesare* had 13 performances, and it achieved double figures again in Handel's revivals of 1725 and 1730. For the revivals Handel subjected his score to the usual alterations necessitated by changing casts; but mostly these alterations weakened the original conception.

RECORDINGS 1. Schlick, Larmore, Rørholm, Ragin, Fink, Zanasi, Concerto Köln, Jacobs, Harmonia Mundi, 1991; 2. Dawson, Laurens, James, Bowman, Vissem, La Grande Écurie et la Chambre du Roy, Malgoire, Auvidis, 1995

Tamerlano

Tamburlaine

Opera in three acts (3h)
Libretto by Nicola Francesco Haym, after *Il Tamerlano* (1711) and *Il Bajazet* (1719) both by Agostino Piovene, both set by Gasparini; based on the play *Tamerlan, ou La mort de Bajazet* by Jacques Pradon (1675)
Draft composition score dated 3–23 July 1724
PREMIERES 31 October 1724, King's Theatre, Haymarket, London; US: 26 January 1985, Indiana University Opera Theater, Bloomington
CAST Tamerlano *a* (*castrato*), Andronico *a* (*castrato*), Bajazet *t*, Leone *b*, Asteria *s*, Irene *c*

Tamerlano is significant not only as one of Handel's finest Academy operas, but also as one of the few opere serie with a leading role for the tenor voice. Opposite Senesino playing the part of Tamerlano, the self-made ruler of the Tartar empire, Handel cast the tenor Francesco Borosini as Bajazet, the Turkish sultan defeated by Tamburlaine in 1402 who subsequently died while still in captivity to the Tartar. Borosini's contribution to the opera extended beyond that of a soloist. When Handel completed his draft composition score at the end of July 1724, he had been composing to a libretto adapted from Piovene's 1711 libretto for a Venice production with music by Gasparini. In 1719 a much revised version of Gasparini's opera was performed in Reggio, with a significantly changed title: *Il Tamerlano* became *Il Bajazet*, and the strengthened role of Bajazet was played by Borosini. When Borosini arrived in London in September 1724 to take up his place in the opera company, he provided Handel and Haym with the libretto and score of the 1719 version. Stimulated by this, Handel revised his own score, in particular incorporating new scenes at the beginning and end of the opera based on the 1719 libretto.

Plays on the subject of Tamburlaine already had a niche on the 18th-century London stage: the theatres regularly performed one (most often Nicholas Rowe's) around the beginning of November, to coincide with the triple anniversaries of the foiling of the Gunpowder Plot, the birthday of King William III and his landing in Torbay in 1688. No doubt a political allegory was intended or imposed in these plays, but Handel's opera seems innocent of any such interpretation: nevertheless, the treatment of a familiar subject was no doubt intended as good box office.

SYNOPSIS

Bajazet has been defeated and captured by Tamerlano, who is betrothed to Irene, Princess of Trebizond. Tamerlano and Andronico (a Greek prince in alliance with Tamerlano) have both, unknown to each other, fallen in love with Asteria, Bajazet's daughter. The action takes place in Prusa, the first city that Tamerlano occupied after defeating the Turks.

Act I: Bajazet despises his conqueror and attempts suicide, but desists when Andronico reminds him that this would leave Asteria an orphan ('Forte e lieto'). Rather than return to the throne of Byzantium, Andronico opts to remain with Tamerlano to learn more about warfare. Tamerlano hopes to use Andronico to break down Bajazet's resistance to his suit, in return for which Andronico will receive the hand of Irene. Andronico is appalled that his action in bringing Asteria to plead for her father's life should have this consequence. Tamerlano agrees to release Bajazet, on condition that he can marry Asteria. Bajazet rejects this proposal, and Asteria accuses Andronico (who has spoken for Tamerlano) of taking Tamerlano's part in order to gain Irene and a kingdom for himself. She tells Andronico that she no longer loves him. Irene, arriving at the palace, is surprised when Tamerlano does not come to greet his bride-to-be: she is yet more surprised to learn that Andronico is to be her husband instead. Alone, Andronico reflects that he can save Bajazet's life only by concealing his love for Asteria and bearing her anger ('Benchè mi sprezzi').

Act II: Tamerlano claims that he now has Asteria's heart: he tells Andronico to look forward to the double wedding. Andronico and Asteria each accuse the other of sacrificing their love for a throne. Irene, disguised as a messenger at the suggestion of Andronico, reproaches Tamerlano for his betrayal, and refuses his offer of the alternative suit. Tamerlano responds that if Asteria does not prove a satisfactory consort, then he will embrace Irene. Andronico vows to kill both Tamerlano and himself if Asteria marries Tamerlano. Asteria herself approaches Tamerlano's throne, with murder in her heart. Bajazet enters to prevent the marriage of his daughter: Tamerlano orders Bajazet to prostrate himself – Asteria can mount the throne over his body. Asteria refuses to do so, nor will Bajazet rise when Tamerlano orders him to. Asteria asks her father's forgiveness, but he refuses and turns his back on the throne as she advances to it. Irene enters, still disguised, and says that Irene will not appear until she has a share in Tamerlano's throne: Tamerlano replies that she will have to force Asteria to leave the throne. Bajazet orders his daughter to descend, or he will renounce her and end his own life, but Asteria at first makes no move. She has to decide between marriage to Tamerlano and renewed imprisonment: she chooses the latter. Tamerlano orders the execution of both father and daughter.

Act III: Tamerlano says that he still loves Asteria, and orders Andronico to tell her that her place at the throne is still vacant. Andronico reveals his own love for Asteria, which she reciprocates ('Vivo in te'). When Tamerlano orders Bajazet's execution, Asteria pleads for her father's life. Father and daughter are sentenced to the indignity of being dragged forcibly to Tamerlano's table, where Tamerlano orders Asteria to kneel as a slave with his drinking cup. Asteria poisons the cup and offers it to Tamerlano, but Irene, who has seen her place the poison, restrains him from drinking and reveals both Asteria's plan and her own identity. Tamerlano tells Asteria that he will drink if Andronico and Bajazet will do so first: she decides instead to take the poison herself, but Andronico dashes the cup from her hands. Tamerlano orders her to be sent to the slaves' seraglio and now promises to marry Irene, who accepts him. Bajazet takes poison; he says farewell to Asteria, and dies breathing fury against Tamerlano. Andronico offers to kill himself, but Tamerlano restrains him: Bajazet's death has been sufficient bloodshed. He yields Asteria to Andronico, and will marry Irene himself.

The quality of Handel's music is no less high than in *Giulio Cesare*, but *Tamerlano* has not gained popularity on the strength of individual arias, though Andronico's 'Bella Asteria' had some circulation in the 18th century. This is perhaps rather surprising, since 'Se non mi vuol amar' (Asteria), 'Par che mi nasca' (Irene), 'A suoi piedi' (Bajazet) and 'Cor di padre' (Asteria) are among Handel's finest arias. The final scenes of Acts II and III are powerful musico-dramatic sequences. At the end of Act II, when Asteria appeals to Bajazet, Andronico and Irene in turn, they reply in short but pointed exit arias. The end of Act III is dominated by Bajazet's last scene: before the opera's first performance Handel cut out a substantial amount of music (including a fine aria, 'Padre amato', for Asteria) so that no concerted numbers remained between Bajazet's death scene and the final minor-key *coro* (sung by the soloists). The scoring of *Tamerlano* is fairly restrained, but there are some novelties. Recorders and flutes double in the duet 'Vivo in te'; the obbligato part in Irene's Act II aria 'Par che mi nasca in seno' was composed for clarinets, misnamed 'cornetti' in Handel's autograph. The unusual prominence of the tenor role limited the opera's appearance in Handel's opera repertoire: he revived *Tamerlano* only once, in 1731.

RECORDING Argenta, Findlay, Ragin, Chance, N. Robson, Schirrer, EBS, Gardiner, Erato, 1985 (live)

Rodelinda

Opera in three acts (3h 15m)
Libretto by Nicola Francesco Haym, adapted from *Rodelinda* by Antonio Salvi set by Perti (1710) after *Pertharite* by Pierre Corneille (1652)
Draft composition score completed 20 January 1725
PREMIERES 13 February 1725, King's Theatre, Haymarket, London; US: 9 May 1931, Smith College, Northampton, Massachusetts
CAST Rodelinda *s*, Bertarido *a* (*castrato*), Grimoaldo *t*, Garibaldo *b*, Eduige *a*, Unolfo *a* (*castrato*)

Rodelinda was cast for the same singers as *Tamerlano*, with a major part for the tenor Borosini as well as leading roles for Senesino and Cuzzoni. For the subject, Haym returned to another libretto dealing with Lombard history: the infant Flavio appears here (as a non-singing role) in company with his mother Rodelinda. The action of the opera relies on a complex dynastic background. On the death of Ariberto of Lombardy (AD 681) his kingdom was divided between his sons Bertarido and Gundeberto. A war developed between the brothers; Gundeberto was mortally wounded, and called on the assistance of Grimoaldo, Duke of Benevento, promising him the hand of his sister Eduige. Faced with an attack from Grimoaldo, Bertarido fled to Hungary, leaving his family behind: he put out reports of his own death, planning to return disguised in order to rescue his wife, Rodelinda, and son. Grimoaldo is supported by Garibaldo, Duke of Turin, who had rebelled against Bertarido.

SYNOPSIS
Act I: Rodelinda mourns her supposedly dead husband. Grimoaldo proposes to Rodelinda that he will restore her to her husband's inheritance if she will marry him, but she rejects him. Garibaldo professes his love for Eduige, who has been rejected by Grimoaldo, but his real ambitions are set on her inheritance. Bertarido, in disguise, returns and sees Rodelinda receive a further proposal of marriage from Grimoaldo, accompanied by a threat that her non-compliance would lead to the young Flavio's death. Rodelinda agrees to Grimoaldo's terms, intending to ask for the traitor Garibaldo's death once she is in a position of influence. Bertarido is horrified by Rodelinda's acceptance of Grimoaldo.

Act II: Eduige is embittered by Grimoaldo's rejection. Rodelinda, saying that she cannot be mother of the lawful king and wife of a tyrant at the same time, tells Grimoaldo to murder Flavio before her eyes. In spite of encouragement from Garibaldo, Grimoaldo recoils from this. Eduige recognizes Bertarido and learns that his prime purpose is to regain his family, not his throne: after

Bertarido's death, Eduige had a claim to Bertarido's kingdom. Unolfo tells his friend Bertarido that Rodelinda is faithful to him: the reunion between husband and wife ('Io t'abbraccio') is interrupted by the arrival of Grimoaldo, who puts Bertarido under arrest and sentences him to death.

Act III: Eduige and Unolfo plan Bertarido's escape. Grimoaldo is encouraged by Garibaldo to have Bertarido executed, but hesitates because this would alienate Rodelinda. Bertarido laments his fate ('Chi di voi'). Eduige throws a sword into the dungeon. Unolfo goes to release Bertarido, but in the darkness Bertarido wounds him, mistaking him for a potential executioner. Unolfo leads Bertarido to freedom by a secret passage. Rodelinda and Flavio, arriving at the dungeon, find blood (Unolfo's) and Bertarido's cloak: Rodelinda laments her husband's apparent fate ('Se'l mio duol'). Having bandaged Unolfo's wound, Bertarido then sets off to find Rodelinda. Grimoaldo approaches, tormented by jealousy, anger and love: eventually he falls asleep in the garden. Garibaldo takes the sleeping Grimoaldo's sword and goes to kill him, but Bertarido, who has been watching unobserved, intervenes and kills Garibaldo. On his return, Bertarido throws his sword at Grimoaldo's feet. Rodelinda, entering, is amazed to find her husband alive. Explanations ensue. Grimoaldo renounces his claim to Bertarido's inheritance and takes up Gundeberto's former kingdom, with Eduige as his queen.

Rodelinda, though less hot-headed as a heroine than Asteria in *Tamerlano*, is a strong and faithful wife. Borosini played Grimoaldo, a tyrant with a softer side that recoils from murdering the young Flavio: as in *Tamerlano*, he received a powerful 'distraction' scene in Act III. Senesino, as Bertarido, had a no less remarkable prison scene. Bertarido's aria, 'Dove sei', familiar as a concert aria to the sentimental text 'Art thou troubled?', remains as an example of the 'capital and pleasing airs' that Burney recognized as one of the strengths of the score. After the initial season, Handel revived *Rodelinda* twice, in 1725 and in 1731; as with *Tamerlano*, opportunities for revival may have been limited by the necessity for a good tenor.

RECORDINGS 1. Schlick, Schubert, Cordier, Wessel, Prégardien, Schwarz, La Stagione Frankfurt, Schneider, Deutsche Harmonia Mundi, 1990 (live); 2. Daneman, Robbin, Taylor, Blaze, Thompson, Purves, Raglan Baroque Players, Kraemer, Virgin Veritas, 1996

Orlando

Opera in three acts (3h)
Libretto after *L'Orlando, overo La gelosia pazzia* by Carlo Sigismondo Capeci set by Domenico Scarlatti (1711) based on the epic poem *Orlando furioso* by Lodovico Ariosto (1516)
Draft composition score completed 20 November 1732
PREMIERES 27 January 1733, King's Theatre, Haymarket, London; US: 18 January 1971, Carnegie Hall, New York (concert); 16 December 1981, Cambridge, Massachusetts (stage)
CAST Orlando *a* (*castrato*), Angelica *s*, Medoro *a*, Dorinda *s*, Zoroastro *b*

Orlando returns to the sort of drama that Handel had developed 20 years before, involving a supernatural dimension and transformation scenes: this contrasts with the operas that had been his concern since the start of the Academy in which the characters, however much fired by jealousy or passion, generally behave rationally. A spectacular element had been creeping back into Handel's opera productions since *Alessandro* (1726): for example, the opera house must have invested in a collapsible city wall, which featured in siege scenes in several operas. At all periods the London opera companies probably employed a fair number of non-singing 'supers', who represented servants or armies as required, and once (in *Admeto*) furies. In *Orlando* they made the significant transition to genii in the service of the magician Zoroastro, a substantial role written for the bass Montagnana, whose part was enhanced by a contrast in vocal ranges: his was the only low voice.

Unlike *Tolomeo*, *Orlando* had a libretto that had been developed considerably from Capeci's original: the identity of the adapter is not known (this is generally the case with Handel's new libretti after 1729), though it has been suggested that Handel worked from a version that Haym may have prepared before his death in 1729 or even that Handel himself had a hand in the adaptation. One factor in the shaping of the opera may have been the revival, if only temporarily, of English opera by a company in a theatre near to the opera house: perhaps opera was not, for the moment, such a 'foreign' medium. In December 1732 Aaron Hill, the artistic impresario who had promoted *Rinaldo*, wrote a letter to Handel encouraging him to take up opera in English. By then the score of *Orlando* had already been written and, like *Rinaldo*, it embodied spectacular scenes of the type that had been developed by the English masque.

SYNOPSIS

Act I: The magician Zoroastro surveys the stars at night and predicts from them that the knight errant Orlando will not always be a 'Foe to Glory'. Orlando, entering, promises that he will follow Glory rather than Love, but after the magician has gone he recants and dedicates himself to the service of Love. In a wood the lovers Angelica, queen of Catai, and Medoro, an African prince, are seen together; Angelica tells Medoro that he shall share her empire as well as her heart: Medoro has supplanted her former attachment to Orlando. After Angelica has gone, Medoro is detained by the shepherdess Dorinda, to whom he had previously paid court: Dorinda still loves him, but finds his reaction evasive. Zoroastro warns Angelica of Orlando's jealousy. Seeing Medoro approaching, she appeals for help. Zoroastro conjures up a fountain to conceal Medoro, and the scene is transformed, leaving Orlando alone in a garden ('Fammi combattere'). Angelica and Medoro embrace, and are seen by Dorinda: Angelica presents her with a jewel, which Dorinda thinks a poor substitute for Medoro himself.

Act II: In a wood, Dorinda laments her situation. Orlando accuses her of linking his name with Isabella, a princess he rescued, but Dorinda says that she believed him attached to Angelica, who is now betrothed to another man. Orlando is horrified by the last piece of news and falls victim to anger and jealousy ('Cielo! se tu il consenti'). Zoroastro urges Angelica and Medoro to escape ('Tra caligni profonde'). As Medoro leaves, he carves their names on a tree. Orlando sees these names and follows in hot pursuit. He finds Angelica in the wood and tries to catch her, but a large cloud descends and bears her away. Orlando now crosses the bounds of reason: he imagines himself following the lovers to the underworld, finding Medoro in the arms of Proserpina, who weeps for him. Zoroastro appears in his chariot, scoops up Orlando and rides off into the air.

Act III: Medoro takes refuge in Dorinda's cottage and rather shamefacedly confesses to her that he loves Angelica. Orlando meets Dorinda, but has clearly taken leave of his senses, entering into an imaginary battle with the murderer of Angelica's brother. Dorinda tells Angelica of Orlando's pitiful condition and reflects on the pains brought about by love ('Amor è qual vento'). Zoroastro changes the scene to a 'horrid Cavern' ('Sorge infausta'). Dorinda, weeping, tells Angelica that Orlando has demolished her cottage, leaving Medoro in the wreckage. Orlando thirsts for revenge. He throws Angelica into the cave, which is transformed into the Temple of Mars, then sinks exhausted to sleep. Zoroastro announces that the time has arrived for

Orlando to be released from the power of love. He waves his wand, and four genii descend with an eagle carrying a golden vessel in its beak. Zoroastro takes the vessel and sprinkles liquor from it over Orlando's face. Orlando revives, restored to his senses, and is told by Dorinda that he has murdered Angelica and Medoro. Filled with remorse, Orlando determines to kill himself; but the lovers appear, having been saved by Zoroastro. Orlando announces that he has triumphed over 'himself and Love', and presents Angelica to Medoro. Dorinda, reconciled to her own situation, invites everyone to her cottage to celebrate the 'Festival of Love'.

The high point of *Orlando* is the mad scene at the end of Act II, an extended scena in a recognized theatrical tradition, but which may also be related to English musical progenitors such as Purcell's 'Mad Bess' ('From Silent Shades'). The 5/8 passage as Orlando imagines himself reaching Pluto's throne is a novelty, but more telling overall are the obsessive recurrences of a simple gavotte melody ('Vaghe pupille') as Orlando fights for coherence. The opening scenes for Zoroastro and Orlando are hardly less remarkable: in them recitatives and set numbers flow naturally into each other. Although there are some conventional (though dramatically strong) set-piece da capo arias, the action often breaks anticipated moulds, and there are some particularly effective duets. Act I ends with a remarkable 'romantic triangle' trio ('Consolati, o bella') of great subtlety. All five soloists have strong roles, though Medoro receives fewer musical opportunities than the others. In *Orlando* Handel applied the fast-moving dramatic skills of *Partenope* and *Sosarme* to a richly symbolic libretto, which showed off the powers of Senesino (Medoro), Strada (Angelica) and Montagnana (Zoroastro) to best advantage. It ran for 10 performances in 1733. That Handel never revived it is attributable to the confusion that overcame his opera company at the end of the season, when he lost Senesino and Montagnana to a rival operation.

RECORDING Joshua, Mannion, Summers, Bardon van der Kamp, Les Arts Florissants, Christie, Erato, 1996

Ariodante

Opera in three acts (3h)
Libretto after *Ginevra, principessa di Scozia* by Antonio Salvi set by Perti (1708), itself after cantos IV–VI of the epic poem *Orlando furioso* by Lodovico Ariosto (1516)
Draft composition score completed 24 October 1734
PREMIERES 8 January 1735, Covent Garden, London; US: 29 March 1971, Carnegie Hall, New York (concert); 14 September 1971, Washington (stage)
CAST Ariodante *s* (*castrato*), Ginevra *s*, Polinesso *a*, Lurcanio *t*, Dalinda *s*, Il re *b*, Odoardo *t*; *satb* chorus of shepherds and shepherdesses; dancers

For his 1734–5 season Handel was driven from the Haymarket Theatre by the Opera of the Nobility and set up his company at John Rich's new theatre in Covent Garden, which had opened in December 1732. No doubt Handel had some misgivings about leaving London's premier opera house, which had been his musical home for a quarter of a century. But he took with him an excellent cast, including Carestini and Strada, and the first season was enlivened by the participation of a group of French dancers under the direction of Madame Sallé. Handel made good use of the dancers: ballets were written into Handel's new operas *Ariodante* and *Alcina*, and *Il pastor fido* was revived with a prologue (*Terpsicore*), in which dancing played the major part. At Covent Garden also Handel seems to have regularly employed an independent chorus, which gave a new sound to *coro* movements: these had formerly been rendered by the soloists alone.

Ariodante is set in Edinburgh, with the king of Scotland and Guinevere (Ginevra), his daughter, among the persons represented; but the basis of Salvi's story was from Ariosto's *Orlando furioso*. Handel may have seen Perti's opera on Salvi's libretto in Florence in 1708. The outlines of Ariosto's tale provided popular subject matter for dramatists, including Shakespeare in *Much Ado About Nothing*.

SYNOPSIS

Act I: In the royal palace Ginevra prepares to meet Ariodante, a vassal prince with whom she is in love. Polinesso, Duke of Albany, declares his love for Ginevra. She rejects him, but her lady-in-waiting Dalinda hints he would find a better response from her. Polinesso wonders whether he can use Dalinda's infatuation to take revenge on Ginevra. In the palace garden Ginevra and Ariodante pledge their love. The king interrupts them and, approving of Ariodante, tells Ginevra to prepare for her wedding the next day. Polinesso persuades Dalinda to dress as Ginevra that night and to admit him to the princess's apartments. Dalinda rebuffs Ariodante's brother Lurcanio, who is in love with her. Ariodante and Ginevra share their joy with shepherds and shepherdesses.

Act II: At night, Ariodante encounters Polinesso, who suggests that Ginevra is unfaithful to him, and offers to prove it. Ariodante vows to kill himself if the accusation proves true – if false, he will kill Polinesso. Polinesso tells Ariodante to hide and watch. Unknown to them both, Lurcanio is also concealed in the garden. Dalinda, dressed as Ginevra, is seen to admit Polinesso to Ginevra's apartments. Ariodante resolves to end his own life, but Lurcanio urges him to avenge his betrayal. In the palace the king is declaring Ariodante his heir when the courtier Odoardo brings the news that Ariodante has thrown himself into the sea and is dead. On hearing the news Ginevra faints. Lurcanio produces to the king a sworn statement of what he saw that night and accuses Ginevra of unfaithfulness: he offers a challenge to anyone prepared to defend Ginevra. Ginevra herself cannot understand why she is harshly disowned by the king. Furies torment her dreams.

Act III: Ariodante, wandering alone, hears cries for help and finds Dalinda, pursued by assassins sent by Polinesso. He drives them off and learns from her the story of Polinesso's deceit. Dalinda herself turns against Polinesso. At the palace, Polinesso offers himself as Ginevra's champion: the king accepts him despite Ginevra's fierce opposition. In the combat Lurcanio mortally wounds Polinesso – it looks as if the heavens are signalling Ginevra's guilt. A stranger in a helmet with lowered visor comes to her defence. It is Ariodante, who says that he has knowledge of Ginevra's innocence, which he will reveal if the king will pardon Dalinda in advance. Odoardo reports that the dying Polinesso confessed his crime. Dalinda agrees to accept Lurcanio as her lover. The king brings Ariodante to Ginevra, releases her from her confinement, and celebrations begin for the two pairs of lovers, with dances for the 'Knights and Ladies'.

In *Ariodante* Handel managed to combine an intimate atmosphere, in which the cross-currents of personal attractions and conflicts flow strongly, with a platform for Carestini's skill, which reached its apogee in his arias 'Con l'ali di costanza', 'Scherza infida' (at the climax of one of Handel's most powerful scenes, in the garden at the beginning of Act II), 'Cieca notte' and 'Dopo notte'. The recitatives are short and the arias extended, reflecting exactly the balance between the simple actions and the great effects they have on the participants. At the other extremity of scale, there are few more effective scene-setting introductions in opera than the 'moonrise' sinfonia at the beginning of Act II – a mere ten bars. With ravishing arias, some splendid duets (including one in Act I, 'Prendi, prendi', in which the king interrupts Ariodante and Ginevra as they are about to embark on their da capo), spectacular dancing integrated with the plot (particularly at the end of Act II) and, incidentally, a good libretto, *Ariodante* is one of the most rewarding of Handel's operas. But it relied to some extent on the individual skills of Carestini. Handel revived the opera only once, in 1736, in a revised form to accommodate another castrato, Conti.

RECORDINGS 1. Mathis, Burrowes, Baker, Bowman, Ramey, London Voices, ECO, Leppard, Philips, 1978; 2. Gondek, Saffer, Hunt, Lane, Cavallier, Wilhelmshaven Vocal Ens, Freiburg Baroque O, McGegan, Harmonia Mundi, 1995; 3. Dawson, Cangemi, von Otter, Podles, Sedov, Musiciens du Louvre, Minkowski, Archiv, 1997

Alcina

Opera in three acts (3h 30m)
Libretto based on *L'isola d'Alcina* by ?Antonio Fanzaglia set by Broschi (1728) after cantos VI–VII of the epic poem *Orlando furioso* by Lodovico Ariosto (1516)
Draft composition score completed 8 April 1735
PREMIERES 16 April 1735, Covent Garden, London; US: 16 November 1960, Dallas Civic Opera, Dallas
CAST Alcina *s*, Ruggiero *s* (*castrato*), Morgana *s*, Bradamante *a*, Oronte *t*, Melisso *b*, Oberto *s* (*boy treble*); *satb* chorus

Alcina was the last of Handel's operas to be derived from Ariosto's *Orlando furioso*. Handel probably collected the libretto during his visit to the Continent in 1729; as usual, it was considerably rearranged to suit London conditions (recitatives were abbreviated and arias were tailored to the singers' abilities). Of the four Handel operas on libretti derived from Ariosto's epic poem, three (*Rinaldo*, *Orlando* and *Alcina*) include an enchantress and/or enchanter among the leading characters. The nature of the story, set here on Alcina's enchanted island, gave plenty of opportunities for spectacle and scene transformation. As in *Ariodante*, Marie Sallé's ballet troupe was integrated effectively into the opera. Names added by Handel to one of the *coro* movements show that the main cast singers were supplemented by at least one more soprano, an alto (or two), three tenors and two basses in the chorus movements.

Alcina seems to have done well for Handel in the period of rivalry between his company and the Opera of the Nobility; in the original run it had 18 performances. As Burney commented later, *Alcina* was 'an opera with which Handel seems to have vanquished his opponents, and to have kept the field near a month longer than his rival Porpora was able to make head against him'. Burney's further comments are also interesting: 'Upon the whole, if any one of Handel's dramatic works should be brought on the stage, entire, without a change or mixture of airs from his other operas, it seems as if this would well sustain such a revival.' *Alcina* was indeed one of the first operas to re-enter the repertoire and to sustain some place in modern productions of Handel's operas, though it is rarely revived 'entire'.

SYNOPSIS

Alcina has fallen in love with the knight Ruggiero and has detained him on her enchanted island.

Act I: Bradamante, Ruggiero's betrothed, arrives at the island in an attempt to rescue him, accompanied by her guardian Melisso; she is disguised as her brother Ricciardo. Bradamante and Melisso are discovered by Morgana, Alcina's sister, who is attracted to 'Ricciardo'. The original scene (a mountain) breaks open to reveal Alcina adorning herself while Ruggiero holds her mirror. The new arrivals introduce themselves and are welcomed by Alcina. 'Ricciardo' asks Ruggiero if he remembers him, the brother of his betrothed, but, under

Alcina's spell, Ruggiero has no recollection of any lover but Alcina ('Di te mi rido'). Oronte, Alcina's general, tells Ruggiero that, with the arrival of 'Ricciardo', he may suffer the same fate as the thousands of Alcina's previous lovers who have been turned into streams, beasts, trees and rocks. When challenged, Alcina tells Ruggiero that he still pleases her, for the moment. Ruggiero tries to encourage 'Ricciardo' to return home. Bradamante reveals her true identity, but Ruggiero thinks that this is just one of Alcina's tricks.

Act II: In a hall of the palace Melisso, disguised as Ruggiero's tutor Atlante, gives Ruggiero a magic ring which returns him to his senses. He renews his devotion to Bradamante, but decides to conceal this from Alcina. Before the statue of Circe, Alcina is about to change 'Ricciardo' into a beast, when Morgana, who believes 'Ricciardo' is in love with her, and Ruggiero together persuade her to desist. Oberto, Bradamante's nephew, who has come to the island in search of his lost father, Astolfo, asks Alcina for help, and is told that he shall see Astolfo soon. Bradamante tells Oberto that his father has been changed into a lion. Oronte tells Alcina that he is preparing to leave with the new guests; he taunts Morgana with the faithlessness of her new lover. At first inclined to disbelieve him, Morgana then finds Bradamante and Ruggiero together ('Verdi prati'). In a 'Subterraneous Appartment', Alcina tries to use her powers to detain Ruggiero, but to no avail – he is protected by the ring ('Ombre pallide').

Act III: In a courtyard of the palace, Oronte and Morgana, previously lovers, are reconciled. Alcina tries unsuccessfully to dissuade Ruggiero from leaving ('Ma quando tornerai'). A ship awaits Ruggiero and Bradamante, but Bradamante declares that she will not leave until Alcina's enchantments are broken ('Mi restano le lagrime') and life has been restored to her victims. Outside Alcina's palace are the dens of the wild beasts and the urn that contains the 'whole power of the Inchantment'. Ruggiero goes to break the urn with his ring. Alcina and Morgana try to restrain him, but he throws the urn down, whereupon 'the Scene wholly disappears, changing to the Sea, which is seen thro' a vast subterraneous Cavaern where many Stones are chang'd into Men; among them is Astolfo, who embraces Oberto: They form the Chorus and the Dance'.

'Verdi prati' in Act II, which expresses perfectly Ruggiero's regret that the beautiful landscape of the island is about to decay, caught the public's imagination at an early stage: with its sarabande-like rhythm and measured phrases it is reminiscent of Handel's first 'hit' in London, 'Lascia ch'io pianga' from *Rinaldo*. Reputedly, Carestini dismissed the aria when it was first presented to him as being insufficiently brilliant. In the opera its effect is heightened because it is followed immediately by Alcina's attempt to hold Ruggiero by enchantment. Throughout the opera Handel's command of contrast and pacing is masterly, making the most of the interplay between rational and irrational elements in the plot. Remarkably, he makes no attempt to cover a potential weakness in the plot – the fact that Alcina is effectively beaten by the end of Act II – by hurrying over the denouement. Her developing character, through to her final aria ('Mi restano le lagrime'), is among Handel's most subtly drawn creations. Act III begins with a chain of magnificent and luxuriant da capo arias, which serve to emphasize the change of pace in the final scenes, when a trio, recitatives, choruses and dances follow in quick succession to complete Alcina's downfall. Although Carestini (Ruggiero) and Strada (Alcina) naturally dominated the score and the stage, the other roles are also quite substantial – even the 15-year-old treble 'Young Mr Savage' as Oberto had a man-size part to sing. Handel revived *Alcina* at the beginning and end of his 1736–7 season, though without the dances at the later perfomances since the arrangement with Madame Sallé's troupe had ended. It may be that the scenic effects of *Alcina* were particularly geared to the facilities of the Covent Garden Theatre. Handel never revived the opera after he returned to the King's Theatre in 1738.

RECORDINGS 1. Sutherland, Sciutti, Berganza, Sinclair, Alva, LSO, Bonynge, Decca, 1962; 2. Auger, Harrhy, Jones, Kuhlmann, Davies, City of London Baroque Sinfonia, Hickox, EMI, 1985; 3. Fleming, Dessay, Graham, Kuhlmann, Robinson, Les Arts Florissants, Christie, Erato, 1999 (live)

Serse

Xerxes

Opera in three acts (3h)
Libretto after *Xerse* by Silvio Stampiglia set by Giovanni Bononcini (1694), itself based on *Serse* by Nicolò Minato set by Cavalli (1654)
Draft composition score completed 14 February 1738
PREMIERES 15 April 1738, King's Theatre, Haymarket, London; US: 12 May 1928, Northampton, Massachusetts
CAST Serse *s* (*castrato*), Arsamene *s*, Amastre *c*, Ariodate *b*, Romilda *s*, Atalanta *s*, Elviro *b*; *satb* chorus of soldiers, sailors, politicians, priests

To the 1737–8 opera season at the Haymarket Theatre Handel contributed two new operas, *Faramondo* and *Serse*, and a third work, *Alessandro Severo*, which was musically a 'self-pasticcio' using arias from Handel's previous operas. Otherwise, the programme consisted of revivals of operas by other composers, apparently to the taste of the former Nobility Opera patrons. The fact that Handel did not revive any of his own operas probably indicates that he was not in artistic control of the season as a whole. With *Serse* Handel returned to the librettist who had provided *Partenope*, with results in a similar spirit. If the tone of *Faramondo* is ambiguous, as the hero seems too innocently virtuous to be taken entirely seriously, there is no doubt about the ironic slant of *Serse*. The dialogue is quite light in tone; there are no great causes or heroics. In addition to dealing in comic situations, the opera includes one unambiguously comic character, the servant Elviro, 'a facetious Fellow'. Even the paragraph 'To the Reader' that takes the place of the conventional 'Argument' in the printed word-book seems to be a parody of the normal historical and literary justification: 'The contexture of this Drama is so very easy, that it wou'd be troubling the reader to give him a long argument to explain it. Some imbecilities, and the temerity of Xerxes (such as his being deeply enamour'd with a plane tree, and the building a bridge over the Hellespont to unite Asia to Europe) are the basis of the story, the rest is fiction.'

SYNOPSIS
Act I: Serse, king of Persia, enjoys the shade provided by the plane tree in a garden ('Ombra mai fu'). His brother Arsamene enters looking for Romilda, with whom he is in love, whose singing is heard coming from elsewhere in the garden: the sound impels Serse to love. Arsamene tries to deter his brother by saying that her social station (she is the daughter of a vassal, Ariodate) makes her unworthy of the king's attentions. Undeterred, Serse instructs his brother to convey his affectionate intentions to Romilda, much to Arsamene's consternation. Romilda's sister Atalanta, who has her own designs on Arsamene, is present when Arsamene carries out his duty. When Arsamene later interrupts Serse's attempt to command Romilda into matrimony, Serse banishes him from the court. Romilda rejects Serse's love. Amastre, Serse's betrothed, arrives disguised as a man and overhears Serse reflecting that his plans for a liaison with Romilda will entail deserting Amastre. Arsamene sends his servant Elviro with a love letter to Romilda, asking for a meeting. Atalanta tries to make Romilda

doubt Arsamene's constancy. Romilda declares that she will not love Arsamene if he proves unfaithful ('Se l'idol mio'), but warns Atalanta against trying to steal Arsamene from her.

Act II: In the city square Elviro, who is masquerading as a flower-seller ('Ah! chi voler fiora'), tells Amastre of the situation between Serse, Arsamene and Romilda. Atalanta intercepts Arsamene's letter to Romilda, and then persuades Serse that the letter was written to herself. Serse determines to force Arsamene to marry Atalanta, and shows the letter to Romilda as proof of Arsamene's infidelity. Romilda is overcome with jealousy, but will still not accept Serse as a husband. Serse seems convinced that Arsamene loves Atalanta, conveniently leaving Romilda available for himself, but Arsamene protests his continuing devotion to Romilda. Outside the town Serse meets Amastre, still dressed as a man. He tries to enlist her into his military service, but the conversation is interrupted by the arrival of Romilda. When Serse tries to force his claim on Romilda, Amastre intervenes and says that she will champion Romilda against Serse's pressure.

Act III: Romilda taxes Arsamene with writing to Atalanta: the deception is revealed. Atalanta claims that Serse arrived so suddenly that she had to pretend to be the recipient in order to screen Romilda. Serse again makes an approach to Romilda, which she counters by saying that her father's permission is needed. Serse tells Ariodate that Romilda is to be given a 'consort of our royal blood'. Ariodate gives his consent and agrees to receive the suitor in his apartment soon, assuming that Serse had been referring to Arsamene. Romilda claims that she is already committed to Arsamene. Serse is not sure whether to believe her, but orders Arsamene's arrest. Arsamene goes to the temple, where he meets Ariodate who, believing that he is following Serse's command, marries Arsamene to Romilda. When Ariodate goes to Serse, to thank him for the honour done to his family, Serse discovers what has taken place. As he accuses Ariodate of treachery, a page brings Serse a letter purporting to come from Romilda: it is from Amastre, who threatens suicide on account of Serse's infidelity. Serse commands Arsamene to kill his new wife, giving him a sword for the purpose. Amastre takes the sword and turns it on Serse himself, at the same time revealing her true identity. Serse is reconciled to her and, repenting the violence of his rage, approves the union of Arsamene and Romilda.

Like *Berenice*, the title of *Serse* has remained in public consciousness through one melody – Serse's first arietta, 'Ombra mai fu': few of those who recognize 'Handel's *Largo*' (though designated larghetto by the composer) are aware of its origin in Serse's paean to a plane tree. The score of *Serse* is indebted in some details to Giovanni Bononcini's setting of the same text, though considerably transformed by Handel. As a whole, *Serse* exhibits more variety in its arias than any other Handel opera: in complete contrast to 'Ombra mai fu' there are some full bravura da capo arias (such as Serse's 'Più che penso', 'Se bramate d'amar' and 'Crude furie'). But da capo arias account for only about half of the score: many arias are through-composed (e.g. Amastre's 'Anima infida' and Atalanta's 'Voi mi dite') and several are curtailed or modified in form by dramatic exigencies (such as Romilda's 'O voi che penate!'). Even the duets deviate from the conventional 'lovers' reunion' type: in 'Troppo oltraggi la mia fede' (Act III) Romilda and Arsamene are actually separating emotionally, while in 'Gran pena è gelosia' (Act II) Serse and Amastre sing their own separate (but related) thoughts, unaware that the other person is present. Elviro's first scene in Act II is amusingly punctuated by snatches of song as he interrupts his conversations with flower-seller's cries in local dialect.

Perhaps because the plot lacks substantial political overtones, the characters are clearly delineated both individually and in their relationships. The central characters are seriously motivated by love, though Serse's behaviour has a touch of exaggeration, which makes it impossible to take him entirely seriously. A lighter touch is provided not only by Elviro but also by Atalanta (who is clearly capricious and likely to get up to fraudulent tricks) and Ariodate. As in *Partenope*, Handel achieved exactly the appropriate musical means to express both the characterization and the plot. That Handel never revived the opera is easily explained: he never again had seven evenly matched soloists for an opera season.

RECORDINGS 1. Hendricks, Rodde, Watkinson, Wenkel, Esswood, La Grand Écurie et la Chambre du Roy, Malgoire, Sony, 1979; 2. Smith, Milne, Malafronte, Bickley, Asawa, Hanover Band, McGegan, Conifer, 1997

Semele

Dramatic entertainment in three acts (3h)
Libretto after that by William Congreve (*c.*1705–6) for John Eccles (unperformed; published 1710)
Draft composition score completed 4 July 1743
PREMIERES 10 February 1744, Covent Garden, London; US: January 1959, NW University, Evanston, Illinois
CAST Jupiter *t*, Cadmus *b*, Athamas *a*, Somnus *b*, Apollo *t*, Juno *c*, Iris *s*, Semele *s*, Ino *c*; *satb* chorus of priests and augurs, lovers and zephyrs, nymphs and swains; (the score also includes one aria for Cupid *s*, probably cut before the first performance)

Two secular-subject works that Handel performed 'after the manner of an Oratorio' have some claim to attention as near-operas – *Semele* and *Hercules* – and of the two *Semele* has more relevance here because its source libretto was actually written for an opera. (That for *Hercules* was written for a play.) The original text was published in 1710, as 'Semele, an Opera', in a sumptuous edition of Congreve's works. Handel's adapter followed most of Congreve's text fairly faithfully, but cut and adapted sections and added some new material (partly drawn from other works by Pope and Congreve himself), including a new scene at the end of Act II. Although Handel performed the work in 'oratorio' style, it is perhaps significant that he ended his first draft of the end of Act II with 'Fine dell' Atto 2do', but a second draft with 'Fine della parte 2da': the uncertainty between 'parts' and 'acts' seems to reveal an equivocation in Handel's view of the work.

SYNOPSIS
Act I: The action begins in Boeotia, at the Temple of Juno, where the marriage of Semele, daughter of Cadmus, king of Thebes, and Athamas, a prince of Boeotia, is about to be solemnized. Semele seems reluctant: she does not want to forgo her present liaison with Jupiter. Suddenly thunder is heard (a sign of Jupiter's activity), and the fire on the altar is extinguished: eventually the altar sinks from sight, and the wedding is abandoned in face of these omens. Ino, Semele's sister, reveals her love for Athamas, and Cadmus reports that, as his party was leaving Juno's temple, an eagle swooped down and carried Semele away; Jupiter now enjoys Semele's favours 'above' ('Endless pleasure, endless Love').

Act II: Juno is incensed by Jupiter's affair with Semele, and she determines to destroy the woman who has displaced her. She decides that she will need help from Somnus, the god of sleep. In her palace Semele awakes ('O Sleep, why dost thou leave me?'); Jupiter enters and the two renew their affection. But Semele is not entirely happy: she is only a mortal, and feels frightened when Jupiter leaves her. In order to distract Semele from wishing for immortality, Jupiter brings Ino to Semele for company: he transforms the scene to Arcadia ('Where'er you walk') and leaves the sisters together to enjoy the harmony of the spheres.

Act III: Juno and her attendant messenger Iris visit Somnus' cave and (with some difficulty) awaken him. Among Juno's requests to Somnus is one that Ino should be immobilized by sleep so that Juno can impersonate her when she visits Semele: in return Juno guarantees to Somnus the lady that he desires, Pasithea. Juno, disguised as Ino, goes to Semele; she asks whether Jupiter has consented to Semele's request to join the immortals. Semele replies that she is still mortal, and Juno gives her a mirror in order to admire her own features. Semele gains confidence from what she sees in the mirror and Juno suggests that Semele should use her attractions to make Jupiter approach her bed 'Not . . . In Likeness of a Mortal, but like himself, the mighty Thunderer': by that means, Juno says, Semele will 'partake of immortality' and be called from the mortal state. Juno leaves as she hears Jupiter approach. Jupiter allows himself to be lured into promising to grant whatever Semele requests. When Semele asks him to appear 'like Jove', Jupiter tries to dissuade her, but to no avail. Jupiter knows that if he appears as he really is, Semele will be consumed by his fire. And thus it turns out: Semele sees Jupiter afar in his true form, and dies. The chorus reflects on ambition that overreaches itself. Ino, returned to the world of mortals, relates that in a dream Hermes told her that it was Jove's wish that she should now marry Athamas. Athamas enters willingly into the union. A cloud descends on Mount Citheron, in which Apollo is discovered. He predicts that better times lie ahead, and specifically refers to the creation of Bacchus – 'From Semele's ashes a Phoenix shall rise'.

In terms of the dramatic and musical expectations familiar from Handel's operas, the libretto of *Semele* is entirely coherent. However, allowance must be made for the features that are more effective in unstaged performances and which inevitably affect the dramatic pacing. Semele's aria 'The morning lark', for example, is really a concert-room piece; here Handel effectively invites us to forget the onward pressure of the plot and just listen to the music. Similarly, although the choruses are so arranged that they are sung by participants in the drama (priests, zephyrs and so on), the chorus movements inevitably delay the action, but no musician would want to be deprived of 'Nature to each allots his proper sphere' in any performance of *Semele*. Perhaps because *Semele* sat uneasily with the general tone of Handel's developing oratorio seasons, the composer revived it only briefly in December 1744 after its original run of four performances earlier that year. Modern circumstances provide more flexibility than Handel himself had for choice between staged or unstaged treatments.

RECORDINGS 1. Burrowes, Kwella, Denley, Penrose, Jones, Rolfe Johnson, Davies, Thomas, Lloyd, Monteverdi Ch, EBS, Gardiner, Erato, 1981; 2. Battle, McNair, Horne, Chance, Aler, Ramey, Ambrosian Op Ch, ECO, Nelson, DG, 1990: the first complete recording
OTHER OPERATIC WORKS *Almira*, 1705; *Rodrigo*, 1707; *Il pastor fido*, 1712; *Teseo*, 1713; *Silla*, 1713; *Amadigi*, 1715; *Radamisto*, 1720; *Muzio Scevola*, 1721; *Floridante*, 1721; *Ottone*, 1723; *Flavio*, 1723; *Scipione*, 1726; *Alessandro*, 1726; *Admeto*, 1727; *Riccardo Primo*, 1727; *Siroe*, 1728; *Tolomeo*, 1728; *Lotario*, 1729; *Partenope*, 1730; *Poro*, 1731; *Ezio*, 1732; *Sosarme*, 1732; *Arianna*, 1734; *Parnasso in Festa*, 1734; *Atalanta*, 1736; *Arminio*, 1737; *Giustino*, 1737; *Berenice*, 1737; *Faramondo*, 1738; *Imeneo*, 1740; *Deidamia*, 1741; operas lost or surviving only in fragments: *Nero* (*Die durch Blut und Mord erlangte Liebe*) (music lost), 1705; *Florindo* (*Der beglückte Florindo*), and *Daphne* (*Der verwandelte Dephne*), (1706), music partially lost, performed as two operas, 1708;

Genserico (*Olibrio*) (inc.), (1728); *Titus l'Empereur* (inc.), (1731); London pasticcio operas constructed by Handel from his own music: *Oreste*, 1734; *Alessandro Severo*, 1738; *Jupiter in Argos* (*Giove in Argo*), 1739; London pasticcio operas with music by other composers, arr. (with some new composition of recitatives, etc.) Handel: *Elpidia*, 1725; *Ormisda*, 1730; *Venceslao*, 1731; *Lucio Papirio*, 1732; *Catone*, 1732; *Semiramide riconosciuta*, 1733; *Cajo Fabricio*, 1733; *Arbace*, 1734; *Didone abbandonata*, 1737

D.J.B.

Karl Amadeus Hartmann

b 2 August, 1905, Munich, Germany;
d 5 December 1963, Munich

Hartmann was primarily a symphonist whose musical roots are to be found in Bruckner and Mahler. He belonged to no school and founded none, developing a unique, neoclassically orientated style. It is significant that the strongest influence on him was exerted by a conductor, Hermann Scherchen, and although he studied privately with Webern, 1941–2, there is little detectable influence of the Second Viennese School. His musical language is founded on a strong sense of form and powerfully expressive gesture.

Simplicius Simplicissimus

Des Simplicius Simplicissimus Jugend
The Simplest Simpleton

Chamber opera in three scenes (1h 15m)
Libretto by Hermann Scherchen, Wolfgang Petzet and the composer, after the romance by Hans Jacob Christoffel von Grimmelshausen (1668)
Composed 1934–5, rev. 1955
PREMIERES 2 April 1948, Munich (concert); 20 October 1949, Stadttheater, Cologne (stage); rev. version: 9 July 1957, Nationaltheater, Mannheim

Grimmelshausen's romance narrates the adventures of Simplicius ('the simpleton') during the Thirty Years War. Hartmann found in this work an ideal vehicle to express his rejection of Nazi dogma and to justify the ten years of 'inner emigration' – a process of silent resistance and withdrawal – to which he subjected himself at a time when serious modern music was effectively outlawed in Germany. 'Our times are so confused, nobody can say whether he will survive them without losing his life,' says Simplicius. Hartmann wrote of his score: 'The music ranges from street ballad to chorale, interpolates songlike structures into a psalmodized recitative and frequently waxes to symphonic dimensions.' The score calls for a medium-sized orchestra with a large percussion section.

The first performance, scheduled for Brussels in 1935, had to be postponed until after the war. A striking piece of epic theatre, the work deserves to be performed more frequently.

RECORDING Donath, Büchner, König, Brinkmann, Munich Concert Ch, Bavarian RSO, Fricke, Wergo, 1985
OTHER OPERATIC WORK
Wachsfigurenkabinett (five little operas; partly orch. by Bialas, Henze and Hiller), (1930), 1988

A.B.

Jake Heggie

b 31 March 1961, West Palm Beach, Florida, US

Heggie studied composition with Ernst Bacon, then piano at the Paris Conservatoire and at the University of California. He composed for voice and piano from his teens and, until he suffered a hand injury in 1989, performed professionally. He worked at San Francisco Opera from 1993 and became composer in residence in 1998. In 1995 Heggie won the Schirmer Art Song Competition with a group of three American folksongs written for Frederica von Stade and since then has written more than 130 songs as well as solo instrumental, chamber, choral and orchestral works. Heggie's second opera, based on Graham Greene's novel *The End of the Affair* (1951), was premiered by Houston Grand Opera on 4 March 2004.

Dead Man Walking

Opera in two acts (2h 30m)
Libretto by Terrence McNally based on the book *Dead Man Walking: An Eyewitness Account of the Death Penalty in the US* by Sister Helen Prejean CSJ (1993)
Composed 1998–9
PREMIERE 7 October 2000, War Memorial Opera House, San Francisco

Heggie's first opera deals with the controversial issue of the death penalty in modern America and follows the book and the Oscar-winning movie (1995) of the same name. Its premiere attracted unusual US and worldwide attention, partly because of its topical subject.

Joe de Rocher, a convicted Louisiana murderer, is visited on Death Row and befriended by a Catholic nun, Sister Helen. The families of de Rocher's victims denounce Sister Helen for her involvement, while the prison governor and chaplain also express their doubts. De Rocher's mother fails to obtain a pardon for her son, and preparations are made for the execution, which is carried out.

Dead Man Walking is a tonal, musically conservative work which owes much to the traditions of American music theatre. The work is dominated by the role of Sister Helen, sung at the premiere by Susan Graham, and scored for a traditional symphony orchestra, including harp, piano and extensive percussion. There are also numerous sound effects, including two radio pop songs, a gospel chorus, and prolonged sounds made by the execution apparatus.

RECORDING Graham, Packard, original cast, San Francisco Op Ch & O, P. Summers, Erato, 2000

M.J.K.

Hans Werner Henze

b 1 July 1926, Gütersloh, Westphalia, Germany

Henze has said of himself that all his music starts out from and returns to the theatre. Among his earliest musical memories was of listening enthralled to a performance on record of the overture to Mozart's *Le nozze di Figaro*, and though it would be an exaggeration to assert that it was this childhood experience that established the pattern of his creative life, he has been at pains to point out on more than one occasion that the theatre is his natural domain. Even in his most seemingly abstract works the instruments often behave in an entirely theatrical way, like personages in a drama.

After a period of military service, during which for a short time he was a British prisoner-of-war, Henze continued his studies with the composer Wolfgang Fortner and the leading Schoenbergian theorist Rene Leibowitz, while consolidating his more practical commitment to the theatre working for various provincial opera companies in the West. Since then a substantial sequence of operas and music-theatre works, beginning with a couple of radio operas, before his first significant success with *Boulevard Solitude* (1951), has punctuated his prolific output like peaks in a mountain range, each with its own closely related series of orchestral, chamber and other vocal pieces.

In 1953 Henze made a sudden, and wholly characteristic decision to break with his German roots and to settle permanently in Italy, first in the Bay of Naples and then in the countryside near Rome. As a composer who has always been responsive to the distinctive qualities of landscape and accent, the impact of his Mediterranean experience was first celebrated operatically in the huge, sprawling fantasy of *König Hirsch* (first given in 1956 in a severely shortened version; Henze prepared his own abridgement in 1963, as *Il re cervo*). The next four operas each represented a different approach to the problems of inventing and sustaining an operatic form. In *Der Prinz von Homburg* (1960), the model was explicitly that of 19th-century Italian opera. In *Elegy for Young Lovers* (1961) he specified to his librettists that the scenario should include the opportunity for 'tender, beautiful noises', while *Der junge Lord* (1965) was an attempt to write an opera buffa, and in *The Bassarids* (1966) the problems of symphonic drama were confronted head on.

After the composition of *The Bassarids*, Henze's sympathy with the aims of revolutionary socialism produced another radical change of direction, abandoning the passive attitude to contemporary reality in favour of a more active and astringently defined participation in its brutal struggles; those ideas were expressed dramatically in a series of music-theatre pieces and finally in the opera for Covent Garden, *We Come to the River* (1976). Though elements of political didacticism survived into *The English Cat* (1983), by the time of *Das verratene Meer* (1990) Henze's musical and political reorientation was complete and conveyed in a musical language owing much to Berg. Both of Henze's subsequent operas are scored for an equally large orchestra, but their effect in performance is much more intimate: *Venus and Adonis* (1997) is derived from Shakespeare, while Henze produced his own libretto for *L'Upupa und der Triumph der Sohnesliebe* (2003), based on a legend from the Arabic.

Boulevard Solitude

Lyric drama in seven tableaux (1h 15m)
Libretto by Grete Weil, after a play by Walter Jockisch based on the novel *Manon Lescaut* by the Abbé Prevost (1731)
Composed 1951
PREMIERES 17 February 1952, Landestheater, Hanover; UK: 25 June 1962, Sadler's Wells, London; US: 2 August 1967, Opera Theater, Santa Fe

In the 25-year-old Henze's first full-length opera, the Abbé Prevost's famous 18th-century story of the doomed love of the passionate but weak-willed des Grieux for the morally unscrupulous Manon is updated to Paris just after the Second World War. At their first meeting in the opening scene, set in the main railway station of some large French town and introduced and accompanied by an array of evocative percussion, the cigarette-smoking Manon is on her way to a finishing school in Lausanne, and des Grieux to continue his lonely student life in Paris. Their burgeoning love in a Parisian attic is soon shattered, however, when the self-seeking Manon is forced by her rapacious brother Lescaut into a sexual liaison with a grotesque but rich old admirer, Lilaque, and then with Lilaque's young son. Des Grieux seeks oblivion in drugs, and when the elder Lilaque discovers the theft of a valuable modern painting from his son's apartment he is shot dead by Lescaut, who cunningly transfers the gun to his unsuspecting sister's hand. She is arrested and imprisoned before the opera comes full circle with a final symbolic pantomime involving many of the incidental characters first encountered in the opening scene.

Drawing on influences as heterogeneous as Cocteau, the big-band jazz of Stan Kenton, Parisian music-hall and modern opera from Weill and Milhaud to Alban Berg, the score of *Boulevard Solitude* provides a striking early example of Henze's assimilative virtuosity. With its seven short scenes linked by orchestral intermezzi, and combining 19th-century operatic conventions with modern cinematic techniques, its music combines the tonal and atonal, jazz and a blues based on a chord progression borrowed from Puccini's *La bohème*, the atonal identified with the pains of love, the tonal with the bourgeois capitalist world.

RECORDING Vassilieva, Pruett, Falkman, Brewer, Ottevaere, O des Rencontres Musicales, Anghelov, Cascavelle, 1990

Elegy for Young Lovers

Opera in three acts (2h 30m)
Libretto by W. H. Auden and Chester Kallman
Composed 1959–61
PREMIERES 20 May 1961, Schlosstheater, Schwetzingen (in German); UK: 13 July 1961, Glyndebourne; US: 29 April 1965, Juilliard School, New York
CAST Mittenhofer *bar*, Reischmann *b*, Toni *t*, Elisabeth *s*, Carolina *c*, Hilda *s*, Mauer *spoken role*

An inscription on the title page reads: 'To the memory of Hugo von Hofmannsthal, Austrian, European and Master Librettist, this work is gratefully dedicated by its three makers.' When Henze made his first tentative proposal to Auden and Kallman that they should write an English libretto for him, what he had in mind was a chamber opera with a small, subtle orchestra and dominated by tender, beautiful noises. Set in an Alpine chalet in the year 1910, requiring a cast of just six solo voices and with its three acts made up of 34 short scenes each with its own individual title, the opera's true subject matter is the creation of a poem. At its centre is the poet Gregor Mittenhofer who ruthlessly exploits the personal obsessions of everyone around him to feed his monstrous creative appetites. Every year he returns to his Alpine retreat to write his spring poem, and to renew contact with the coloratura visions of the demented widow Hilda Mack, who, still dressed in the style of the 1870s, has waited in lonely isolation at the inn for the return of her husband who disappeared on the mountain 40 years before.

SYNOPSIS
Act I: This year Mittenhofer has brought with him his wealthy patroness and unpaid secretary Carolina, his personal physician Dr Reischmann, and young companion Elisabeth, who are soon joined by Reischmann's son Toni. Morning life goes on with its everyday bustle as Mittenhofer calls impatiently for his breakfast egg and his daily injection, wheedles money out of Carolina, scolds her for her typing errors and makes notes of Hilda's hallucinatory visions. But the morning routine is suddenly interrupted when the guide Josef Mauer rushes in to tell them that a body has been found in the ice on the Hammerhorn and that it must be Frau Mack's husband. Elisabeth gently consoles the bewildered Hilda, and the act ends with her ecstatic realization that her imprisoning crystal has at last been broken and with Toni's ardent recognition of his love for Elisabeth.

Act II: Made aware by Carolina of the young couple's clearly expressed love for each other, Mittenhofer first plays on Elisabeth's feelings of guilt but then, in a change of tack, asks Reischmann to bless them and the lovers to bring him from the mountain a sprig of edelweiss that he needs to complete his poem. However, once they have departed his mood veers abruptly from apparent acceptance to furious rage.

Act III: The now completely cured Hilda says her farewells, and Elisabeth and Toni leave for the mountain slope. But though a fine, warm day has been forecast a fierce snowstorm suddenly blows up and, in a switch of scene, the young couple are seen on the Hammerhorn, resigned to a loving death in one another's arms. Finally, the scene shifts to an auditorium in Vienna where, after acknowledging the applause of his admirers, Mittenhofer silently mouths his newly finished poem, 'Elegy for Young Lovers', against the background of the offstage voices of Elisabeth, Toni, Hilda, Carolina and the doctor.

With its predominance of silvery sounds and high-tuned percussion the instrumental writing breathes an air of sharp, crystalline purity, depicting the sparkling atmosphere and the chill of the Alpine landscape in flashing, translucent colours. Each character is associated with a particular instrument or group of instruments; Mittenhofer, for instance, with horn, trumpet and trombone; Carolina with the plangent, submissive tone of a cor anglais, and Hilda with the flute, whose agile tracery, as it shadows the widely leaping intervals and brilliantly decorative figurations of her hallucinatory coloratura, is directly based on the mad scene from Donizetti's *Lucia di Lammermoor*.

In 1989 Henze made a revision of the score; some vocal lines were modified, and made less angular, but the main changes were to the scoring, with the percussion writing in particular thinned and refined, so that the soundworld is less dominated by chiming bells and other metallic sounds than it was before.

RECORDING excerpts: Gayer, Dubin, Mödl, Driscoll, Fischer-Dieskau, Hemsley, Berlin RSO & Op O, Henze, DG, 1964

The Bassarids

Opera seria with intermezzo in one act (2h 30m)
Libretto by W. H. Auden and Chester Kallman, after the play *The Bacchae* by Euripides (407 BC)
Composed 1965
PREMIERES 6 August 1966, Grosses Festspielhaus, Salzburg (in German); UK: 22 September 1968, BBC Radio 3; 10 October 1974, Coliseum, London (stage); US: 7 August 1968, Opera Theater, Santa Fe
CAST Pentheus *bar*, Dionysus *t*, Cadmus *b*, Tiresias *t*, Captain *bar*, Agave *ms*, Autonoe *s*, Beroe *ms*, 2 *silent*; intermezzo: Venus *ms*, Proserpina *s*, Kalliope *t*, Adonis *bar*; *satb* chorus of Bacchantes, Theban citizens, guards, servants

Before Henze started work on *The Bassarids*, his librettists demanded as a condition of their cooperation that he should go to a performance of *Götterdämmerung* and make his peace with Wagner. Already simmering in his imagination were ideas for a work that would no longer be influenced by the closed, Italianate forms that had mostly dominated his earlier operas, but which would instead be through-composed in a single, broadly designed span. From the great masterpiece of Euripides' old age, Auden and Kallman forged a scenario that falls naturally into four symphonic movements and whose language, Henze has written, is so richly expressive that it immediately suggested musical themes and textures.

SYNOPSIS
After the chorus has described the abdication of Cadmus as king of Thebes in favour of his grandson Pentheus a distant voice announces the arrival of Dionysus in Boeotia. Ignoring Pentheus' angry denunciation of the dangerous stranger, not only the Theban people, but also the blind seer Tiresias, Pentheus' widowed mother Agave and her sister Autonoe are all gradually seduced into the service of the new, erotic god and the religion he embodies.

In the second movement the rash, severely rationalistic Pentheus orders the captain of the guard to round up Dionysus and his disciples. But his questioning of the prisoners produces no satisfactory answers.

Playing on the king's youthful voyeurism, Dionysus, in the pivotal third movement, reveals to Pentheus by means of a lascivious charade based on the Judgment of Calliope, and seen through a magic mirror, the true nature of his repressed sexual fantasies and desires. Pentheus is persuaded to dress in women's clothes and to go to Mount Cytheron to observe for himself the Dionysian mysteries. The hunter thus becomes the hunted, and his dying screams can be heard in the darkness as the maenads, led by his own mother, tear him limb from limb. Slowly Agave is brought back to her senses, and as Henze's Dionysiac passion play reaches its tragic resolution Cadmus and his family are banished by the triumphant god from Thebes and their palace ordered to be burned to the ground.

The first section is a kind of large-scale sonata movement based on the interaction between the more harshly accented music associated with the rigid King Pentheus and the seductively sensuous music identified with the god Dionysus. The second is a scherzo made up of a suite of Bacchic dances, the third an extended adagio in two parts (which were originally separated by a lighter intermezzo, removed by the composer in 1991), the last a vast passacaglia. And woven into the musical texture at crucial moments are reminiscences of composers from Bach and Rameau to Mahler.

RECORDING Lindsley, Armstrong, Wenkel, Riegel, Tear, Schmidt, Murray, Burt, South German RCh & RIAS CCh, Berlin RSO, Albrecht, Schwann, 1991: recorded, presumably with the composer's agreement, without the third-movement intermezzo

The English Cat

A story for singers and instruments in two acts (2h 45m)
Libretto by Edward Bond, after the tale *Peines de coeur d'une chatte anglaise* by Honoré de Balzac (1840)
Composed 1980–83, rev. 1990
PREMIERES 2 June 1983, Schlosstheater, Schwetzingen; US: 13 July 1985, Opera Theater, Santa Fe; UK: 19 August 1987, Leith Theatre, Edinburgh

Henze's second operatic collaboration with playwright Edward Bond (the first being *We Come to the River*) is also his fourth opera written to an original English text. The basic idea came initially from Henze himself after he had seen a dramatization in Paris of Balzac's feline parable. The cats in Balzac's brief satirical tales encompass all the familiar human types, from the amorous Tom, the demure, empty-headed Minette and her humble, but very pretty, sister Babette, to the aristocratic Lord Puff, his spendthrift nephew Arnold and money-lender Mr Jones. Bond's version updates the setting from the Directoire to London in the Edwardian period, and he provides a didactic framework for the interwoven stories of marriage and divorce, love and infidelity, vanity, deceit, loyalty and violent death, with the invention of the Royal Society for the Protection of Rats, whose members treat their fellow cats with an adamant, cruelly self-seeking conformity when it suits their own hypocritical ends, but who refrain from eating rats and are kindly to mice in a rather superior way.

In keeping with his aristocratic position, the RSPR's president elect, Lord Puff, is expected to breed and has chosen as his bride the simple country cat Minette. Determined to preserve his inheritance, Puff's insolvent nephew Arnold tries every trick in the book to prevent their marriage, but fails. The wedding goes ahead, but Minette cannot forget the seductive attractions of the basically decent but feckless Tom. When Puff and the entire RSPR burst in to find Tom at Minette's feet, divorce proceedings are instigated. Meanwhile, Tom has been discovered to be the long-lost son and heir of the rich Lord Fairport, and when he learns that Puff's owner, Mrs Halifax, has arranged for the pathetic Minette to be drowned he quickly turns his attention to her pretty sister Babette. But just when he is about to claim his inheritance, which he has refused to hand over to the RSPR, Tom is himself murdered. The RSPR gets its money and the mouse Louise is left bemoaning its treachery.

The libretto is designed in the form of a ballad opera on the pattern established by Gay's *The Beggar's Opera*, by Brecht and by Auden in Stravinsky's *The Rake's Progress*. What Henze has called his 'sinister, oblique' music also pays its respects to Stravinsky while fleshing out the situations and characters by means of a continuously evolving variation technique modelled on the formal outlines of Beethoven's *Diabelli Variations*. The scoring is for large chamber orchestra with a lavish percussion section, in which various unusual instruments are subtly employed to underpin the distinctive traits of particular characters: Minette by a zither, Lord Puff by chamber organ and Arnold by a heckelphone or bass oboe.

RECORDING Berkeley-Steele, Coles, Watt, Platt, Pike, Parnassus Ens, Stenz, Wergo, 1991
OTHER OPERATIC WORKS *Das Wundertheater*, 1949; *Ein Landarzt*, 1951; *Das Ende einer Welt*, 1953; *König Hirsch*, 1956; *Der Prinz von Homburg*, 1960; *Der junge Lord*, 1965; *Moralities*, 1968 (three scenic cantatas); *El Cimarrón*, 1970; *Der langwierige Weg in die Wohnung der Natascha Ungeheuer* (*A Show for 17*), 1971; *La Cubana*, 1974 (vaudeville); *We Come to the River*, 1976; *Don Chisciotte della Mancia*, 1976; *Pollicino*, 1980 (children's opera); *Il ritorno d'Ulisse in patria*, 1981 (free realization of Monteverdi's opera); *Das verratene Meer*, 1990; *Venus und Adonis*, 1997; *L'Upupa und der Triumph der Sohnesliebe*, 2003

R.L.H./A.C.

Paul Hindemith

b 16 November 1895, Hanau, nr Frankfurt; *d* 28 December 1963, Frankfurt

Hindemith came to prominence in the rebuilding of German musical life after the First World War, by which time he had begun composing and was already working as a professional violinist, violist, clarinettist and pianist. As a violinist in the Frankfurt Opera orchestra he attracted the attention of the conductor Fritz Busch, who was on the look-out for new operas by young composers. In 1921 Busch conducted the Stuttgart premieres of Hindemith's one-act works, *Mörder, Hoffnung der Frauen* and *Das Nusch-Nuschi*, as a double-bill. Their provocative attitude to sexual matters in a continuing style of German Expressionism attracted public and critical attention. The next year they were supplemented by another one-act opera of a comparable nature, *Sancta Susanna*, first performed at Frankfurt in a triple-bill with the others. Taken in succession they reflect a progress in musical idiom from eclectic late Romanticism to a more disciplined control of structure and expressive character.

During the 1920s, while pursuing an active performing career, Hindemith embraced a style of severe contrapuntal neoclassicism in his music. His first three-act opera, *Cardillac*, premiered in 1926, is the major large-scale example of this (most of the others are chamber works). The following year Hindemith was appointed professor of composition at the Berlin Hochschule für Musik, where the practical application of his teaching was realized in what he termed *Gebrauchsmusik*: useful music for amateurs as well as professionals.

At this time he also took an interest in popular music as exemplified in night-club jazz and the Berlin satirical cabarets, which led to the brief *Hin und zürück* (1927) followed by the three-act *Neues vom Tage* (1929), both with a libretto by

Marcellus Schiffer, a leading cabaret writer/artist in Berlin. A concern with the position of the artist in society, partly suggested in *Cardillac* and renewed at a time when the darkening political scene in Germany brought the advent of the Nazi government, led to *Mathis der Maler* as a partly autobiographical allegory, for which he wrote his own libretto and adopted a more expressive musical style.

An outstandingly successful performance of the *Mathis der Maler Symphony*, extracted from the opera in advance of its production and conducted by Furtwängler, brought Hindemith into conflict with the Nazi authorities (Hitler having been offended by a bath scene in *Neues vom Tage*), and his Jewish connections led to a partial boycott of his music from 1934 and a full proscription in 1937. Hindemith left Germany for Switzerland, where *Mathis der Maler* was first staged in 1938, and in 1940 he went to the US, becoming a much-admired professor at Yale University and taking US citizenship in 1946.

Mathis der Maler remained unperformed on the German stage until that year. After major revisions to *Cardillac* and *Neues vom Tage* in the early 1950s (published as separate editions), Hindemith turned to another historical subject for *Die Harmonie der Welt* – a commission for the 1957 Munich Opera Festival. By this time he had moved back to Europe and was living at Blonay, by Lake Lucerne. He gave up further teaching at Zurich University to concentrate on composition and conducting and, two years before he died, wrote his remaining opera on Thornton Wilder's *The Long Christmas Dinner*, his only setting of a libretto in English.

Mathis der Maler

Mathis the Painter

Opera in seven scenes (3h 15m)
Libretto by the composer
Composed 1934–5
PREMIERES 28 May 1938, Stadttheater, Zurich; UK: 15 March 1939, Queen's Hall, London (concert); 29 August 1952, King's Theatre, Edinburgh (stage); US: 17 February 1956, Boston University, Boston
CAST Cardinal-Archbishop of Mainz *t*, Mathis *bar*, Lorenz von Pommersfelden *b*, Wolfgang Capito *t*, Riedinger *b*, Hans Schwalb *t*, Truchsess von Waldburg *b*, Sylvester von Schaumberg *t*, Graf von Helfenstein *silent*, Helfenstein's piper *t*, Ursula *s*, Regina *s*, Gräfin Helfenstein *c*; *satb* chorus of monks, Catholics, Lutherans, women, students, citizens, peasants, farm workers, demons

At a time when the Nazi regime in Germany was beginning to tighten its grip, Hindemith based his second treatment of the creative artist's position in relation to social and political issues on Mathias Grünewald (or Niethart), court painter in the early 16th century at Mainz, near where Hindemith was born. Grünewald is remembered for the large linked panels of the Isenheim altarpiece (now in the Unterlinden Museum in Colmar), scenes from which are regarded as a metaphor for the peasants' feelings towards their overlords. They prompted ideas for music and a libretto placing the artist at a crucial point in the Peasants' Revolt of 1524.

SYNOPSIS

Prelude: *Engelkonzert*

Scene 1: In the courtyard of St Anthony's monastery at Mainz, Mathis is painting a fresco; he gives his horse to Schwalb, the peasant leader, to help him and his daughter Regina to escape pursuing troops, and promises his support.

Scene 2: Mathis pleads the peasants' cause to the Cardinal-Archbishop, his patron, and is obliged to leave his service.

Scene 3: Amid preparations for the burning of Lutheran books, Mathis and Ursula pledge their love, though Riedinger, her father, plans she should marry the Cardinal.

Scene 4: Mathis protests against the

peasants' brutality; Schwalb is killed and Mathis protects Regina.

Scene 5: The Lutheran Ursula is introduced to the Cardinal as a prospective bride to help solve his financial problems; her faith wills her to submit to marriage for the sake of her cause, and the Cardinal, impressed, chooses to remain celibate while giving permission for Lutherans to declare themselves openly.

Scene 6: Mathis and Regina, in flight, rest in the Odenwald; Regina sleeps while Mathis endures visionary temptations as if he were St Anthony, finally redeemed by the Cardinal in the guise of St Paul (a subject of the altarpiece).

Scene 7: In Mathis's studio, Regina is dying, tended by Ursula. The Cardinal takes a last leave of Mathis, who puts away the tools of his art in humble acceptance of his own impending death.

Into a musical style still predominantly contrapuntal, Hindemith incorporates folksongs, such as the medieval 'Es sungen drei Engel', in the Prelude, subtitled *Concert of Angels* (another altarpiece subject), which also became the opening movement of the three-movement symphony drawn from the opera in 1934. Use is made of Gregorian chant and of pentatonic melodies modelled on it, while the tonal structure of the opera moves chromatically from C♯ in Scene 1 to E in the central scene, then reverses the process. The opera is long when given uncut and slow-moving. If the more active scenes lack theatrically effective climaxes, the more reflective passages of exaltation and despair, and the final resignation to the will of God, remain both a metaphor for the circumstances of the composer's experience and a moving expression of artistic principles.

RECORDINGS 1. Koszut, Wagemann, King, Fischer-Dieskau, Meven, Feldhoff, Bavarian RCh & O, Kubelik, HMV, 1977; 2. Rossmanith, Hass, Protschka, Hermann, Stamm, von Halem, Cologne RCh & SO, Albrecht, Wergo, 1990

OTHER OPERATIC WORKS *Mörder, Hoffnung der Frauen*, 1921; *Das Nusch-Nuschi*, 1921; *Tuttifäntchen*, 1922 (Christmas Fairytale); *Sancta Susanna*, 1922; *Cardillac*, 1926; *Hin und zurück*, 1927; *Neues vom Tage*, 1929; *Die Harmonie der Welt*, 1957; *The Long Christmas Dinner*, 1961

N.G.

Gustav Holst

Gustavus Theodore von Holst;
b 21 September 1874, Cheltenham, England; *d* 25 May 1934, London

Holst's great-grandfather was a Swede who emigrated from Riga to London with his Russian wife in the early 1800s. But Holst himself seems to have been purely English in his preoccupations and intellectual tendencies. He went to Cheltenham Grammar School, then studied with Stanford at the Royal College of Music from 1893. Much of his working life was spent school-teaching (notably at St Paul's Girls' School, where he became Director of Music in 1905), or running evening classes (at Morley College from 1907); but he was also deeply involved with amateur music-making, to which he brought a quasi-political conviction of the worth of the common man. All this practical work restricted his time for composition and eventually undermined his health, but it had a significant effect on his own music, which is notably free of the conventional academic influences of the day. Like his friend Vaughan Williams, Holst was interested in folk music, as well as in Indian culture (though not specifically Indian music); he taught himself Sanskrit, set a number of Hindu texts in his own translations, and based two operas on Hindu subjects. He was also quick to pick up the sounds of the new Continental music of the years before the First World War. His most famous work, *The Planets* (1914–16), is full of echoes of Debussy, Stravinsky, Skryabin, even Mahler and Schoenberg, worked into a characteristic fusion that is completely radical and individual in its effect.

Despite the pressure on his time, Holst produced a large, if uneven, body of work, dominated by choral and other types of music that reflect his practical bent and his work with amateurs. But he also wrote about a dozen operas, at a time when British opera hardly existed as a serious commodity at all. Not surprisingly, they are a mixed bag, and several of them remain unperformed.

Savitri

Chamber opera in one act (30m)
Libretto by the composer, after an episode from the *Mahabharata* (before AD 300)
Composed 1908–9
PREMIERES 5 December 1916, Wellington Hall, London (amateur); 23 June 1921, Lyric Theatre, Hammersmith, London; US: 23 January 1934, Palmer House, Chicago
CAST Savitri *s*, Satyavan *t*, Death *b*; offstage *sa* chorus

Holst's interest in Hindu literature seems to have begun while he was on tour with the Carl Rosa Opera Company in Scarborough in 1898, when a friend lent him a book on the subject. Back in London, he learned to decipher the Sanskrit and began to make his own translations with the help of published cribs. On this basis he wrote the libretti of both *Sita* and *Savitri*, as well as the texts for the *Vedic Hymns* (1907–8) and the *Choral Hymns from the Rig Veda* (1903–12).

SYNOPSIS
A wood at evening. In a long unaccompanied opening (there is no overture), Death announces to Savitri that he has come for her husband, the woodsman Satyavan. When Satyavan comes home from his day's work, he sings about the unreality (*Maya*, 'illusion') of the natural world. But Savitri tells him she now sees beyond *Maya* to 'the heart of every tree'. As Death approaches, Satyavan sinks to the ground lifeless. At first Savitri tries to protect her husband. But she then welcomes Death and invites him to stay. He offers her a wish for herself, and she asks for Life. When Death willingly grants her that which she has already, she points out that for her 'the life of woman, of wife, of mother' implies life for Satyavan too. Defeated, Death leaves at once, and Satyavan revives. As husband and wife go off, Death is heard singing of Savitri's freedom from illusion, 'for even Death is *Maya*'. At the very end Savitri's voice is heard singing alone.

The score has few exotic elements, and certainly none that are remotely Indian. Its modal character is partly English (from folksong), partly French, with a certain whole-tone colouring as in the recent piano works of Debussy. The music's main individuality lies in its spare but extremely delicate texture, its flexible metre, combining recitative with Holst's favourite seven-beat bars, and its use of a wordless female choir (originally a mixed choir, but changed at the suggestion of Herman Grunebaum, the work's first conductor), a device that obviously anticipates *The Planets*.

RECORDINGS 1. Baker, Tear, Hemsley, Purcell Singers, ECO, I. Holst, Decca, 1965; 2. Palmer, Langridge, Varcoe, Hickox Singers, City of London Sinfonia, Hickox, Hyperion, 1983
OTHER OPERATIC WORKS *Lansdown Castle, or The Sorcerer of Tewkesbury*, 1893; *Ianthe*, (*c*.1894); *The Revoke*, (1895); *The Magic Mirror* (inc.), (1896); *The Idea*, (*c*.1896); *The Youth's Choice*, (1902); *Sita*, (1906); *Cinderella* (1902) (lost); *Opera as She is Wrote* (fragments only), (1918); *The Perfect Fool*, 1923; *At the Boar's Head*, 1925; *The Wandering Scholar*, 1934

S.W.

Engelbert Humperdinck

b 1 September 1854, Siegburg, Germany; *d* 27 September 1921, Neustrelitz

Humperdinck's fame rests on his opera *Hänsel und Gretel*, the success of which has been constant and extraordinary since its first performance. Of his six other operatic works only *Königskinder* is of similar scale and quality, and this enjoyed success in its early years.

Humperdinck studied architecture at the University of Cologne where he became friendly with the composer Ferdinand Hiller, who recognized his musical talent and persuaded him to become a student of composition, piano and cello. Considered brilliant by his professors, he won the Mozart Scholarship in 1876; which financed further study in Munich with Franz Lachner and Joseph Rheinberger. His first works were published at this time: the *Humoreske* for orchestra (1879) and choral ballade, *Die Wallfahrt nach Kevlaar* (1879). The latter won the Mendelssohn Prize. (Humperdinck was an inveterate prizewinner and in 1881 he also won the Meyerbeer Prize of 7,600 marks – a huge sum at the time.) This enabled him to visit France and Italy where, in Naples in 1880, he met Richard Wagner. Wagner invited him to Bayreuth as his assistant and during 1881–2 he helped prepare the score of *Parsifal* for its premiere and publication. It is likely that he also composed a small fill-in passage, later discarded, for the Act III transition.

After Bayreuth and short spells in Barcelona and Cologne, he joined the music publishers Schott in Mainz (1888) for whom in 1889 he published an arrangement of Auber's opera *Le cheval de bronze*. He later took three posts in Frankfurt: professor at Hoch's conservatory, teacher of repertoire at Stockhausen's music school and critic on the *Frankfurter Allgemeine Zeitung*.

In 1896 Emperor William II bestowed on him the title of professor and, no doubt with massive royalties from *Hänsel und Gretel*, premiered with overwhelming success three years earlier, Humperdinck retired to Boppard on the Rhine in 1897 and devoted himself entirely to composition. He wrote spectacles, incidental music as well as orchestral works, songs, a string quartet and operas. In 1900 he was appointed (with only nominal duties) director of the Akademische Meisterschule in Berlin and a fellow of the Royal Academy of Arts there. With the premiere of the final operatic version of *Königskinder* at the Metropolitan in New York in 1910 his success grew abroad, but at the same time he became somewhat pigeonholed at home. His last work to create any significant public impression was his spectacle, *The Miracle*, with a scenario by Max Reinhardt, premiered at Olympia in London on 23 December 1911. However, the large London crowds flocking to it appeared to have been drawn solely by the spectacular nature of the production and the work attracted little attention from musicians.

Hänsel und Gretel

Hansel and Gretel

Märchenoper in three acts (2h)
Libretto by Adelheid Wette, after the tale by the Brothers (Wilhelm and Jacob) Grimm (1812)
Composed 1890–93
PREMIERES 23 December 1893, Court Theatre, Weimar; UK: 26 December 1894, Daly's Theatre, London; US: 8 October 1895, Metropolitan, New York
CAST Hänsel *ms*, Gretel *s*, Gertrud *ms*, Peter *bar*, Sandman *s*, Dew Fairy *s*, Witch *ms* (sometimes *t*), 6 echoes 4 *s* 2 *c*; children's chorus: 14 angels *silent*

The early 1890s saw Germany reacting to the bombast of the lesser imitators of Wagner by developing a craze for Italian verismo. But German artists soon grew restive against the lurid plots and the brashness of composers such as

Mascagni, and German audiences yearned for a work that was truly German in origin as well as popular. Humperdinck's success with *Hänsel und Gretel* may have been the result of his avoidance of the mainstream German works of Weber, Marschner and Lortzing; his opera inhabits a very different world.

In 1890 Humperdinck's sister, Adelheid Wette, devised a dramatized version of the Grimm story of *Hänsel und Gretel* for her children to perform. In her version the parents are a much less alarming pair than they are in the fairy tale, where the mother (stepmother in the first version) is actually determined to leave the children out to die in the wood. Wette softened this, perhaps because she knew that her brother's music would supply some of the fear and drama. She also introduced the characters of the Father, the Sandman and the Dew Fairy, as well as the chorus of echoes and the angels, which provided Humperdinck with scope for a ballet.

At first Wette asked her brother to compose four songs for a dramatized family play (1890). Subsequently they decided to make it a full-scale opera. The premiere, conducted by Richard Strauss, was an instant success, and within a year *Hänsel und Gretel* had been produced in over 50 theatres in Germany. It soon joined the repertoire of every lyric theatre in the German-speaking world and within 20 years had been translated into about 20 languages. Richard Strauss, a constant supporter of Humperdinck (he also conducted the premiere of Humperdinck's *Die Heirat wider Willen* in 1905), described the work as 'a masterpiece of the highest quality . . . all of it original, new and so authentically German', despite his reservation that 'the orchestration is always a little thick'.

Hänsel und Gretel was the first complete opera to be broadcast on radio (from Covent Garden, London, 6 January 1923) and the first to be transmitted live from the Metropolitan, New York (25 December 1931).

SYNOPSIS

The self-contained overture is often performed as a concert piece.

Act I: Hänsel and Gretel are at home waiting for their mother, Gertrud, to return. The interior displays the poverty of the family: Hänsel makes brooms for his broom-maker father, Peter, while Gretel knits. Both are bored, restless and hungry. To distract her brother, Gretel shows him a dance game ('Brüderchen, komm tanz' mit mir'), but their playing is harshly interrupted by the arrival of their mother. She is cross at how little work the children have completed, and in her anger she knocks over a jug of milk. She bursts into tears at losing the only food in the house, and sends the children out to pick strawberries in the nearby Ilsenstein forest. Depressed, she falls asleep but is wakened by the father singing on his way home. She is furious that he is obviously tipsy, but her mood changes at the sight of the food he has bought as the result of a successful day selling brooms. After celebrating with his wife, he suddenly becomes aware that the children are not there, and their mother admits that they have gone to the Ilsenstein for strawberries. Their father is appalled; he knows this is the home of the Witch who entices children into her cottage and then turns them into gingerbread by baking them alive in her oven ('Eine Hex', steinalt'). Both parents rush out of the house to find their children. Entr'acte: *Hexenritt* ('Witch's Ride').

Act II: Hänsel and Gretel are in the wood filling their baskets with strawberries ('Ein Männlein steht im Walde ganz still und stumm'). They eat them all, however, and soon Hänsel realizes that they are lost. They become frightened. A mist rises, and a little Sandman appears and throws sand in the children's eyes ('Der kleine Sandmann bin ich'). They kneel down to say their evening prayers ('Abends will ich schlafen gehn'). Lying on a bank beneath the trees they fall asleep in each other's arms. The mist surrounds them and becomes a staircase of clouds as 14 angels come down from heaven to guard the children through the night. This is accompanied by an extended orchestral postlude ('pantomime').

Act III opens with another orchestral prelude as dawn breaks and the Dew Fairy comes to shake dew drops over the children ('Der kleine Taumann heiss ich'). They cheerfully start to play. The mist clears to reveal a gingerbread cottage with a fence of gingerbread men ('O Himmel, welch Wunder ist hier geschehn'). Intrigued, the children eat little bits of the house, but the Witch appears and throws a rope around Hänsel's neck. Hänsel tries to free himself, but the Witch immobilizes both children with a spell ('Knusper, knusper Knäuschen'). She puts Hänsel into a cage, intending to fatten him up. She frees Gretel with another spell and makes her help light the oven. Gretel uses the Witch's spell to free Hänsel from the cage. The Witch, unaware of this, tries to make Gretel look into the oven, but Gretel pretends not to understand. When the Witch shows her what to do, the children push her into the oven and slam the door ('Juchhei! Nun ist die Hexe tot'). The oven explodes and the fence of gingerbread men becomes a row of children; other children who have been baked in the oven rise up from the earth. As they thank Hänsel and Gretel for their deliverance Gertrud and Peter appear. The Witch has been turned into gingerbread and everybody celebrates her downfall.

The influence of Wagner is evident in the use of leitmotifs (though Humperdinck uses them less strictly than Wagner), as well as in the orchestral and harmonic texture and in the symphonic character of the preludes and interludes. This does not, however, disguise the reliance on the style of traditional German children's songs, and two ('Ein Männlein steht im Walde' and 'Suse, liebe Suse') are taken from the well-known *Knaben Wunderhorn* collection. The work's originality derives from the synthesis of four opposite pairs of concepts: childhood/adulthood, fairy tale/reality, diatonic/chromatic and through-composition/episodic form. The subtle flexibility with which Humperdinck combined his resources gives the work its unique charm. As an heir to the Wagnerian tradition combined with folksong and realism – a strong influence on the composers of the time – *Hänsel und Gretel* occupies a startingly individual place in musical history.

An arrangement of *Hänsel und Gretel* by Ludwig Andersen (1927) uses spoken dialogue and a much reduced orchestra. This less vocally demanding version is often used by schools and amateur groups.

RECORDINGS 1. Schwarzkopf, Grümmer, Felbermayer, von Ilosvay, Schürhoff, Metternich, Philharmonia O, Karajan, EMI, 1952; 2. Popp, Fassbaender, Gruberova, Burrowes, Hamari, Schlemm, Berry, VPO, Solti, Decca, 1978; 3. Ziesak, Larmore, Schafer, Behrens, Schwarz, Weikl, Bavarian RSO, Runnicles, Teldec, 1994

OTHER OPERAS *Die sieben Geislein*, 1895; *Königskinder*, 1897 (melodrama); *Dornröschen*, 1902; *Die Heirat wider Willen*, 1905; *Königskinder*, 1910 (opera); *Die Marketenderin*, 1914; *Gaudeamus*, 1919

P.J.

J

Leoš Janáček

Leoš (Leo Eugen) Janáček; *b* 3 July 1854, Hukvaldy; *d* 12 August 1928, Moravská Ostrava (now Ostrava, Slovakia)

Janáček was almost 62 when his opera *Jenůfa* was finally produced in Prague, bringing him unexpected fame. By then he had written five operas, only two of which had been previously produced (in his adopted town of Brno) and the last had been abandoned in sheer despair that it would ever be performed. The success of *Jenůfa* in Prague in 1916, and its espousal by the Viennese publishers, Universal Edition, changed all this. He quickly completed his fifth opera and in 1919, at the age of 65, embarked on an astonishingly fertile last decade, which saw the composition of four major operas and a number of substantial works in other genres, such as the *Sinfonietta*, the *Glagolitic Mass* and the two string quartets. *Jenůfa* soon established his reputation in Czechoslovakia and the German-speaking world, but his later operas made less headway before the Second World War. None of his operas was produced in Britain, and the sole production in the US (*Jenůfa*, in New York, 1924) was not a success. Since the war, and especially from the 1960s and 1970s, Janáček has come to take his place as the best-known Czech operatic composer and one of the handful of the most important opera composers of the 20th century.

Janáček was trained, like his father and grandfather before him, as a schoolteacher, leaving his native Hukvaldy in northern Moravia in 1865 to attend the Augustinian monastery school in Brno, and thereafter a teacher-training course. The musical content in his schooling was substantial and was supplemented by later training at the Prague Organ School (1874–5), the Leipzig and Vienna conservatories (1879–80), and above all by Janáček's own particularly hard and systematic work. He read widely in literature and philosophy. Other formative influences were a fervent national pride that led to his changing his name 'Leo' to the Czech 'Leoš', and a fascination with the greater Slavonic world. He made a crucial trip to Russia in 1896 and founded a Russian Club in Brno which flourished up to the First World War; two of his completed operas, *Káťa Kabanová* and *From the House of the Dead* were based on works by Russian authors, Ostrovsky and Dostoevsky respectively, but he also considered settings of Tolstoy's *Anna Karenina* and his play *The Living Corpse*. In 1880, his formal education complete, Janáček returned to Brno, where he married the young Zdenka Schulzová, and taught at the Teacher Training College and elsewhere, notably at the institution he founded, the Brno Organ School. Apart from the Organ School, where he continued to teach until 1919, he retired from all his teaching posts by 1904 in order to devote himself to composition.

Until quite late in life Janáček's contact with opera was minimal. As a young boy he had sung in a performance of Meyerbeer's *Le prophète*. There was no

Czech opera in Brno at the time and no evidence he attended (or could have afforded to attend) opera in Prague during his year there as a student. So it is likely that the first operas he saw were in Leipzig in 1880: Weber's *Der Freischütz* and, seven weeks later, Cherubini's *Les deux journées*. 'I wasn't taken by it at all, except for one single place,' he commented on the latter to his future wife. His orientation towards opera came only when, in his thirties, the tiny Brno Provisional Theatre was opened (1884), the first permanent institution in Brno to stage plays and operas in Czech. Janáček's response was characteristically positive. He founded a new musical periodical, *Hudební listy*, one of whose functions was to report on the activities of the Brno theatre. Janáček was the chief music critic, and his knowledge and opinions of the somewhat restricted repertory (no Wagner, little Mozart, and much Smetana), can be charted in his reviews over the four years that the journal ran (1884–8). In the early 1900s, once he had retired from his schoolteaching, he had more time to travel to Prague and pick up the novelties there. He was particularly enthusiastic about works such as Puccini's *Madama Butterfly* and Charpentier's *Louise*, and their influence can be detected respectively in his own operas *Fate* and *Kát'a Kabanová*. At a much later date he championed Berg's *Wozzeck* at its controversial Prague premiere.

Although his last operas were written in the 1920s, Janáček was born in the middle of the 19th century and all he wrote was conditioned by a 19th-century training and attitude towards harmony and tonality. If his first opera, *Šárka*, had been a success at the time that he wrote it, Janáček might have been encouraged to remain with its musical idiom – essentially German-centred, though modified by the Czech romanticism of Dvořák and Smetana. But *Šárka* was not performed at the time and Janáček turned to other things. His preoccupation from the late 1880s with Moravian folk music, a particularly rich and distinctive resource in terms of mode and rhythm, had the long-term effect of enriching and fertilizing his musical language, though never obliterating its tonal roots. The result was a highly characteristic musical language, fresh and appealing, and one that a wide spectrum of audiences have found accessible.

A second factor in Janáček's success arises from his gifts as a musical dramatist. While his mature operas have some of the oddest subject matter of any group of operas, all of them work, in their various ways, as effective stage pieces. They are astonishingly different from one another, inhabiting many distinctive worlds and atmospheres. These range from 19th-century Russian provincial life to Moravian peasant verismo and sophisticated Prague of the 1920s; from the life of animals in the Moravian woods to a Siberian prison camp. What binds them together is their succinctness, Janáček's uncanny ability to suggest and change mood with just a few notes, his terse but passionate lyricism, a compassionate humanity, and an emotional charge as powerful as any in the 20th century.

Jenůfa

(Her Stepdaughter)
Jenůfa (Její pastorkyňa)

Opera in three acts (2h)
Libretto by the composer after the play by Gabriela Preissová (1890)
Composed 1894–1903, rev. 1907–8 (rev. and reorch. 1916 by Karel Kovařovic)
PREMIERES 21 January 1904, National Theatre, Brno; Kovařovic version: 26 May 1916, National Theatre, Prague; US: 6 December 1924, Metropolitan, New York; UK: 10 December 1956, Covent Garden, London
CAST Grandmother Buryjovka *c*, Laca Klemeň *t*, Števa Buryja *t*, Kostelnička Buryjovka *s*, Jenůfa *s*, Mill Foreman *bar*, Mayor *b*, Mayor's Wife *ms*, Karolka *ms*, Maid *ms*, Barena *s*, Jano *s*, Aunt *c*; chorus of villagers and labourers *satb*, recruits *tb*, girls *sa*

Janáček adapted his own libretto from Gabriela Preissová's controversial play, first produced in Prague 1890. The genesis of Janáček's opera is hard to document in view of his destruction of sketches and even his autograph score, but in 1894 he began work on the libretto and composed the prelude *Žárlivost* ('Jealousy'), originally planned as the work's overture though never performed as such during Janáček's lifetime. He probably completed Act I in about 1897 and then he seems to have let the project drop for a few years. He took it up again in 1901, and wrote the last two acts quite quickly.

The work was given in Brno, with some success (perhaps out of local patriotism) and was performed there and on local tours about 20 times up to 1913. Partly on the advice of the conductor of the premiere, Janáček's pupil Cyril Metoděj Hrazdira, Janáček revised the work and made several cuts, particularly in ensembles and other set numbers. The vocal score published by a local artistic society in 1908 incorporates these revisions and represents Janáček's definitive version of the piece.

Even before *Jenůfa* was accepted in Brno, Janáček had submitted the opera to the National Theatre in Prague, but the antagonism of its music director, Karel Kovařovic (allegedly hurt by Janáček's dismissive reviews of his opera *The Bridegrooms*), prevented its performance there until 1916. The Prague production under Kovařovic, however, proved a huge success. Two years later *Jenůfa* was given in Vienna in a German version by Max Brod, who subsequently translated most of Janáček's later opera texts. In the decade up to Janáček's death in 1928 *Jenůfa* became a repertoire piece in Czechoslovakia and in German-speaking countries.

The version heard in Prague in 1916 was one that had been revised, and in particular reorchestrated, by Kovařovic (a condition of its acceptance). It was subsequently published by Universal Edition in this form and until the 1980s this was the only version that could be heard. In 1982 Mackerras recorded a version based on Janácek's original score. This led to the publication in 1996 by Mackerras and Tyrrell of the 'Brno 1908' version of the score (with Kovařovic's accretions removed), in which form the work is increasingly played today.

SYNOPSIS

Act I: The Buryja mill in a remote village in Moravia. The mill-owner Števa Burjya and his older half-brother Laca are both in love with their cousin Jenůfa. But Jenůfa loves Števa, by whom she is pregnant. She anxiously awaits his return: if he is drafted into the army she will not be able to marry him and her pregnancy will be discovered. Laca watches her jealously and learns from the mill foreman that Števa has not been conscripted.

The recruits can be heard approaching, singing a conscription song ('Všeci sa ženija') and accompanied by a small village band. At their head is Števa, who demands another song ('Daleko, široko') and then leads the reluctant Jenůfa in a wild dance. At the climax, a stern figure approaches and silences the company. This is Jenůfa's stepmother, known as the 'Kostelnička' (female sacristan). She forbids any marriage between Jenůfa and Števa for a year, during which time Števa must stop his drinking.

Grandmother Buryjovka dismisses the musicians and attempts to comfort Jenůfa, a cue for a slow ensemble ('Každý párek'). The company disperses, leaving a desperate Jenůfa confronting an unrepentant Števa. Laca, who has observed this scene, believes that Števa loves Jenůfa only for her beauty and, after her proud dismissal of him, Laca slashes her cheek in a fit of desperation. He is immediately remorseful, and in a short ensemble he pours out his anguish.

Act II: The Kostelnička's cottage, five months later, winter. Jenůfa, kept in hiding by the Kostelnička, has given birth to a son. The Kostelnička sends her to bed with a sleeping draught. Having summoned Števa to the cottage, she shows him the baby and begs him to marry Jenůfa. But he offers money, not marriage, and hurries out. The next visitor is Laca. He is still anxious to marry Jenůfa, whom he believes, as does the rest of the village, to be in Vienna. The Kostelnička now tells him the truth. He is so dismayed to hear about the baby that the Kostelnička declares that the child died. She sends him away on an errand and, after a dramatic monologue in which she wrestles with her conscience ('Co chvíla'), runs from the cottage taking with her Jenůfa's baby, to drown it in the icy mill-stream.

Almost immediately, Jenůfa wakes up from her drugged sleep and discovers the baby is missing. Believing that the Kostelnička has taken it to show to the people at the mill, she offers up a prayer to the Virgin ('Zdrávas královno'). The Kostelnička returns frozen from her expedition, and tells Jenůfa that the child died while she was in a fever. Jenůfa accepts the news with tender resignation, and when Laca returns soon after, she offers no resistance to his earnest proposal of marriage. As the Kostelnička blesses the union and then curses Števa, the window of the cottage blows open and the Kostelnička, filled with foreboding, cries out in terror.

Act III: The Kostelnička's cottage, two months later. Preparations for Jenůfa's wedding to Laca are in progress, though the Kostelnička, broken by her deed, is a shadow of her former self. Guests arrive: the mayor and his wife, Števa and his betrothed (the mayor's daughter, Karolka). Jenůfa adroitly manages a reconciliation between the two half-brothers. Finally girls from the village come to sing a wedding song for Jenůfa ('Ej mamko, mamko'). Grandmother Buryja gives her blessing to the pair and just as the Kostelnička is about to add hers, a tumult is heard outside. Jano the herdboy runs on with the news that the frozen corpse of a little child has been found in the mill-stream. Jenůfa thinks it is her child, and the gathering crowd accuses her of murder. Laca holds off the mob, but it is the Kostelnička who silences the people with her own confession of guilt. At first appalled, Jenůfa begins to undertand the motives that lie behind the Kostelnička's terrible action. She forgives her stepmother, who is then led off to stand trial. Alone with Laca, Jenůfa thinks that he can no longer want her in these circumstances, but movingly, he pleads for and gains her love.

Superficially, there is much to link Janáček's second opera, *The Beginning of a Romance* (1894), and *Jenůfa*. Both were based on writings by Gabriela Preissová, both were set in the folklore-rich area of Slovakian Moravia. But whereas *The Beginning of a Romance* was tossed off in a few months, Janáček took almost a decade over his third opera, during which time he changed his whole attitude to the genre. The long pause before beginning Act II seems to have been particularly significant. Even in its final revision, the first act of *Jenůfa* shows traces of something like a number-opera. It opens with what amounts to arias for Jenůfa and then Laca; towards the end there is a substantial concertato ensemble and a trio; and the chorus plays a large and fairly conventional part, especially in the folk scenes of Act I.

But even here Janáček had discarded his naïvely propagandist view of Moravian folksong. While *The Beginning of a Romance* consists mostly of folksongs, *Jenůfa* has a number of folksong texts in appropriate places (the recruits scene of Act I; the bridal chorus in Act III), but the tunes are by Janáček (who declared that the opera had not a single folksong in it). A further factor was Janáček's developing preoccupation with 'speech-melody' – his notations of fragments of everyday speech, often documented with details of their emotional context. Speech-melodies were not used to generate melodic material for his operas, but instead helped sharpen Janáček's awareness of the contours of natural speech. This led to a new style of writing whereby musical continuity was concentrated in the still regularly structured orchestra part, with the voice reciting increasingly freely over it. It was inevitable with such an approach that Janáček would set *Jenůfa* as a prose libretto, the first such in Czech opera.

RECORDINGS 1. Jelínková, Krásová, Blachut, Žídek, Prague Nat Th O, Vogel, Supraphon, 1953; 2. Beňačková, Kniplová, Přibyl, Krejčík, Brno Janáček Op O, Jílek, Supraphon, 1977/8; 3. Söderström, Randová, Dvorský, Ochman, VPO, Mackerras, Decca, 1982

Katya Kabanova

Kát'a Kabanová

Opera in three acts (1h 45m)
Libretto by the composer, after the play *Groza* (*The Thunderstorm*) by Ostrovsky (1859), trans. Vincenc Červinka (1918)
Composed 1919–21, interludes added 1927

PREMIERES 23 November 1921, National Theatre, Brno; UK: 28 December 1948, BBC radio; 10 April 1951, Sadler's Wells, London (stage); US: 26 November 1957, Karamu House, Cleveland, Ohio (concert); 2 August 1980, Empire State Music Festival, Bear Mountain (stage)

CAST Savël Prokofjevič Dikoj *b*, Boris Grigorjevič *t*, Marfa Ignatěvna Kabanová (Kabanicha) *c*, Tichon Ivanyč Kabanov *t*, Katěrina (Kát'a) *s*, Váňa Kudrjáš *t*, Varvara *ms*, Kuligin *bar*, Glaša *ms*, Fekluša *ms*, Late-night passer-by *silent*, Woman from crowd *c*, Passer-by *t*; *tb* chorus of townspeople, *satb* offstage chorus

With *Kát'a Kabanová* Janáček entered his mature operatic period. His first five operas represent a painfully long operatic apprenticeship with only one clear-cut success (*Jenůfa*), for whose recognition he had to wait until he was almost 62. But what followed is without parallel. Janáček's amazing Indian summer – the last decade of his life – saw the composition of four major operas, on which, together with *Jenůfa*, his reputation rests today.

Kát'a Kabanová is Janáček's own adaptation of Ostrovsky's play *The Thunderstorm*, which he began considering late in 1919. The Russian material was congenial to him, but another strand in its inspiration was his identification of the principal character with a favourite operatic heroine of his, Madama Butterfly, and also with Kamila Stösslová. Janáček had met Mrs Stösslová on holiday in the Moravian spa town of Luhačovice in 1917. This marked the beginning of a passionate, though largely one-sided relationship which lasted until the end of Janáček's life, documented by the collection of over 700 letters which have only recently been published in full. According to these letters, Kamila Stösslová provided the inspiration for characters in all of Janáček's last four operas and for the gypsy girl in *The Diary of One who Disappeared*. *Kát'a Kabanová* was dedicated to her.

Composition began early in 1920 and proceeded rapidly and unproblematically until the spring of 1921, though Janáček continued to tinker with the score up to its premiere. This took place in Brno in November 1921 under much grander circumstances than that of the Brno premiere of *Jenůfa*. Following the independence of Czechoslovakia the Czechs now had control of the excellent German opera house; *Kát'a Kabanová* was conducted by František Neumann, the new head of opera, who was to preside over all of Janáček's later premieres except *From the House of the Dead*. *Kát'a Kabanová* also set a pattern for the later operas: all were given first in Brno, then in Prague, and published with Max Brod's German translation by Universal Edition. Despite the distinguished conductor of the first German production (Klemperer in Cologne, 1922), and a fine production in Berlin (1926), for which Janáček received the compliments of Schoenberg and Zemlinsky, the work made headway outside Czechoslovakia only after the Second World War. It was Janáček's first opera to be performed in the UK, and has been more frequently produced there than any other of his operas.

After difficulties in early productions with scene changes, Janáček wrote new interludes for Acts I and II, which were first given in the Prague German Theatre production in 1928. Its conductor, Hans Wilhelm Steinberg, played the first two acts through without a break, a procedure Janáček enthusiastically endorsed.

SYNOPSIS

Act I, Scene 1: Kalinovo, Russia in the 1860s. In a public park on the bank of the Volga, Kudrjáš learns from Boris, his employer Dikoj's nephew, about his passion for a married woman, Kát'a Kabanová, and they watch the Kabanov family come back from church. The family is at loggerheads. Kát'a, a woman of great sweetness of nature, is married to the weak Tichon, a merchant under the thumb of his domineering mother, known as Kabanicha. He is unable to prevent Kabanicha from tyrannizing his wife, and he meekly complies when she orders him off on a business trip.

Scene 2: In a room in the Kabanov household, Kát'a tells Varvara, a foundling girl in the household, about herself. Her narration, at first joyful as she remembers her life at home and her churchgoing, clouds over as she tells Varvara of the dreams that trouble her and of her guilty love for Boris. Tichon comes in, ready for his departure. Kát'a is anxious because of the temptations that might arise during his absence and begs him not to go or to take her with him. But he is helpless against his mother, who furthermore orders him to extract humiliating promises of good behaviour from Kát'a during his absence. Tichon departs.

Act II, Scene 1: Towards evening on the same day, in another room in the Kabanov household, Kabanicha reprimands Kát'a for not showing more grief at Tichon's departure. Varvara has already made plans for an assignation between Kát'a and Boris and gives her the key to the garden gate, which she has stolen from Kabanicha. Kabanicha is visited by Dikoj, Boris's unpleasant uncle, who derives pleasure from confessing his weaknesses to Kabanicha and receiving her scolding.

Scene 2: A hollow overlooked by the Kabanov garden, a summer evening. Kudrjáš sings a song as he waits for Varvara ('Po zahrádce děvucha'), and is surprised by the appearance of Boris, who tells him of the assignation arranged for him. Varvara joins them ('Za vodou za vodičkou') and runs off with Kudrjáš. Boris is soon joined by Kát'a, terrified by the 'sin' she is committing. Their courtship is interrupted by the other couple, whose more light-hearted relationship takes centre stage, with fragments from Boris and Kát'a's passionate love duet wafting in from offstage. Then it is time for the lovers to part and Kudrjáš calls Boris and Kát'a. The scene ends with another 'folksong' for Kudrjáš and Varvara ('Chod' si dívka do času').

Act III, Scene 1: Two weeks later. People are taking refuge from the afternoon storm in the ruins of an abandoned building overlooking the Volga. Kudrjáš exchanges insults with his employer, Dikoj. The scientifically minded Kudrjáš advises the installation of lightning conductors; Dikoj pooh-poohs this since, as he asserts, storms are a punishment sent by God. Kudrjáš is sought out by Varvara, worried about Kát'a's distraught state at the imminent return of her husband. Kát'a runs on dishevelled and will not be calmed or comforted. Tichon and Kabanicha now enter, and Kát'a, overwrought by the thunderstorm which she sees as a punishment from God, confesses her adultery with Boris to the assembled company and rushes out into the storm.

Scene 2: At twilight Tichon and a servant look in vain for Kát'a in a deserted place on the bank of the Volga. Kudrjáš and Varvara decide to leave for Moscow. Kát'a wanders on in a daze, wanting to see Boris once again and then die. Strange voices call her, but death does not come yet. Eventually Boris joins her. After a brief farewell he leaves (he is being sent off to Siberia by Dikoj), and Kát'a, now at peace with herself, finds death in the Volga. Her body is hauled out and presented to Kabanicha, who thanks the 'good people' for their kindness.

Kát'a Kabanová is Janáček's most lyrical opera. Central to the work is Janáček's conception of the heroine 'of such a soft nature that . . . if the sun shone fully on her she would melt'. Her first vocal utterance is gentle and regular, in sharp contrast to Kabanicha's noisy tirade. Similar 'Kát'a' music reappears in most scenes. Sometimes her music is confined to the orchestra, for instance her radiant appearance in Act I (modelled on the first appearance of Madama Butterfly) or the poignant music for the lovers' silent embrace in the final scene.

While Kát'a's presence is signalled by a type of music, two reminiscence themes are also important. Varvara's 'Za vodou' tune is heard in the opera even before it is given words in Act II, Scene 2. The eight strokes of the timpani represent a fate theme which is heard softly in the opening bars of the overture, and *fortissimo* at the end. Speeded up and heard on the oboe against a sleigh-bell accompaniment, it provides the music (first heard in the overture) for Tichon's departure, the event that precipitates the crisis.

Kát'a's gentle nature is contrasted not merely to the despotism of Kabanicha (Janáček's most evil female portrait), but to the light-hearted world of Varvara and Kudrjáš, characterized by their folksongs. The double love scene of Act II, Scene 2, with Kát'a's and Boris's love music heard in the distance against the more practical chatter of Varvara and Kudrjáš onstage, is one of the glories of the score. Equally fine are Kát'a's two monologues: the first (Act I, Scene 2), in which she travels imperceptibly from religious to sexual ecstasy in her vivid account of her inner life; the second (Act III, Scene 2) where her inner voices are made audible in an offstage chorus.

RECORDINGS 1. Tikalová, Blachut, Prague Nat Th O, Krombholc, Supraphon, 1959: Talich's reorchestration; 2. Söderström, Dvorský, VPO, Mackerras, Decca, 1976: includes Janáček's additional interlude music

The Cunning Little Vixen

Příhody Lišky Bystroušky
(The Adventures of the Vixen Bystrouška)

Opera in three acts (1h 30m)
Libretto by the composer, after the novel *Liška Bystrouška* by Rudolf Těsnohlídek (1920)
Composed 1922–3, additions 1924
PREMIERES 6 November 1924, National Theatre, Brno; UK: 22 March 1961, Sadler's Wells, London; US: 7 May 1964, Mannes College of Music, New York
CAST Gamekeeper *bar*, Gamekeeper's Wife/Owl *c*, Schoolmaster/Mosquito *t*, Priest/Badger *b*, Harašta *b*, Pásek *t*, Mrs Pásková *s*, Bystrouška (lit. Sharp-ears) the Vixen *s*, Zlatohřbítek (lit. Goldmane) the Fox *s*, Young Bystrouška *child s*, Frantík *s*, Pepík *s*, Lapák the Dog *ms*, Cock/Jay *s*, Chocholka the Hen *s*, Cricket *child s*, Grasshopper *child s*, Frog *child s*, Woodpecker *c*; choruses: *sa* hens (children), *sa* forest creatures, *sa* fox cubs (children); offstage *satb* chorus Voice of the forest, ballet (blue dragonfly, Vixen as a girl, midges, forest creatures, vixen cubs, hedgehog, squirrels)

During the spring of 1920 the Brno newspaper *Lidové noviny* published in daily instalments a tale about a vixen who is captured by a gamekeeper and then escapes back to the woods to find a mate for herself and raise a litter. A particular feature of the serialization was the inclusion of a large number of illustrations. These had in fact come first. *Lidové noviny* acquired Stanislav Lolek's 200 line drawings (which, in cartoon fashion, told their own story) and then instructed one of their reporters, Rudolf Těsnohlídek, to produce a text. The resulting 'novel', celebrating country life in the forests near Brno, was published in book form in 1921 and has remained popular to this day.

According to Janáček's housekeeper, Marie Stejskalová, it was she who drew the work to Janáček's attention as a possible opera text. But this could have come about through other means. Janáček took the paper and as a regular contributor himself had close contacts with its editors. In June 1921 he began dropping hints that *Liška Bystrouška* might be his next opera, but only the next year, with the premiere of *Kát'a Kabanová* out of the way, did he get down seriously to planning the libretto. He began the music in autumn 1922, and was essentially finished within a year, with the final act copied up by January 1924. The Brno premiere followed in November, a few months after Janáček's 70th birthday. The piece's foreign success dates from the celebrated Felsenstein production at the Komische Oper, Berlin in 1956.

Janáček wrote his own libretto. Invited to contribute, Těsnohlídek produced only the Gamekeeper's song in Act II – other songs came from folk texts. The first two acts, with many omissions, follow Těsnohlídek closely. But since the Vixen's wedding at the end of Act II of the opera closes the novel, the structure of Act III is Janáček's invention, though drawing on various scenes and incidents earlier in the book. The Vixen's death, within a context of the cyclical renewal of life, is Janáček's own distinctive contribution.

SYNOPSIS

Act I: The forest; summer, a sunny afternoon. The Gamekeeper, interrupting the animal life of the forest, lies down and takes a nap. While he sleeps, a young Frog tries to catch the Mosquito, but lands instead on the Gamekeeper's nose and wakes him up. The Frog has attracted the attention of Bystrouška ('Sharp-ears'), the vixen cub. The Gamekeeper catches her and takes her home.

The farmyard: autumn, late afternoon sun. Installed at the Gamekeeper's, Bystrouška exchanges stories with the Dog and defends herself both against his sexual advances, and against the baiting by the two boys, Frantík and Pepík, for which she is tied up. When night falls she appears in her dreams as a young girl.

Bystrouška's plan to entice the hens within her range begins with a harangue about their subservience to the Cock; when this fails she threatens to bury herself alive in disgust at their conservatism. The Cock is sent to investigate and is soon killed, as are all the hens in turn. Fearing retribution at the hands of the Gamekeeper and his wife, Bystrouška bites through her leash and escapes into the forest.

Act II: The forest; late afternoon. Now at large in the forest, Bystrouška ruthlessly evicts the Badger and takes over his comfortable home.

The inn. The Gamekeeper, the Schoolmaster and the Priest drink and play cards. The Gamekeeper sings a song about the passing of time ('Bývalo, bývalo') and taunts the Schoolmaster about his inactivity as a lover; in return, the Schoolmaster baits him about the escape of the Vixen.

The forest; moonlight. The Schoolmaster, tipsy, has trouble finding his way home, and mistakes the Vixen, hiding behind a sunflower, for his distant beloved, Terynka. The Priest, separately wending his way home, lets his thoughts wander back to an incident in his youth when he was wrongly accused of seducing a girl. Both men are startled by the Gamekeeper, who fires – in vain – at the Vixen.

The forest; summer, a moonlit night. The Vixen meets a handsome Fox; she tells him of how she was brought up by the Gamekeeper and of her subsequent escapades. They fall in love, observed by gossiping birds, and she is soon obliged to marry. The animals of the forest join in the general merrymaking.

Act III The forest; autumn, midday. Harašta, a poultry dealer, is heard approaching ('Déž sem vandroval'); he is accosted by the Gamekeeper, who thinks he has been poaching. Harašta tells him he is about to marry Terynka. The gamekeeper leaves a trap for the Vixen, but Bystrouška, her mate and litter make fun of the trap ('Beží liška k Táboru'). Bystrouška and her Fox contemplate their growing family and possible additions. Harašta returns. Bystrouška, pretending to be lame, lures him into the forest, where he trips over. While he is nursing his injuries, Bystrouška and her family demolish the chickens. In his anger Harašta shoots and kills the Vixen.

The inn. The Schoolmaster is tearful at the news of Terynka's marriage, and both he and the Gamekeeper regret the absence of the Priest. The Gamekeeper, feeling his age, sets off home.

The forest; as at the beginning. The Gamekeeper contemplates the beauty of the scene around him, and remembers the day of his wedding. At peace with nature and with himself, he falls asleep. In his dream, the creatures seen at the opening reappear, including a little Vixen, but when the Gamekeeper tries to catch her he succeeds only in catching a frog – the 'grandson' of the one in the first scene. His gun falls to the ground.

As always, Janáček was an economical librettist. Where direct or indirect speech was available in the novel he used it, and where there was none, he simply wrote music. Thus, in comparison with his previous opera, *Kát'a Kabanová*, based on a play, there is a far greater proportion of purely instrumental music – essential for the short interludes between the many scenes. The music contains some of Janáček's most enchanting orchestral inspirations – for instance, the dream sequence of the young Vixen in Act I or at the opening the evocation of the forest with its abundance of life. Janáček's score is articulated in half-act units held together by the recurrence of themes – such as the offstage chorus at the beginning of the second half of Act II transformed into the exuberant wedding chorus at the end – or by sets of variations.

Janáček had no inhibitions about the singing of animals. Size is more or less equated with pitch – ranging from the bass Badger to the female voice hens and forest birds and the inspired use of children's voices for the insects. Children's voices are also used delightfully for the Vixen's cubs. Dance is another important element of the score in the evocation of animal life. Apart from the Vixen herself, and memorably the little Frog at the end of the opera, interactions between the human and animal worlds are sparing, though Janáček reduced his cast slightly by indicating suggestive doublings (e.g., Priest/Badger, Schoolmaster/Mosquito).

For such a curious libretto, the work has a surprisingly large emotional range, from the comic episodes with the hens in Act I, to the erotic courtship music in Act II, and the painfully nostalgic inn scene in Act III. Most memorable of all, however, is the Gamekeeper's monologue, which dominates the end of the opera and lifts the original text to an altogether different plane.

RECORDINGS 1. Böhmová, Domanínská, Asmus, Prague Nat Th Ch & O, Neumann, Supraphon, 1957; 2. Popp, Randová, Jedlička, VPO, Mackerras, Decca, 1981

The Makropulos Affair

(The Makropulos Case)
Věc Makropulos

Opera in three acts (1h 30m)
Libretto by the composer, after the comedy by Karel Čapek (1922)
Composed 1923–5
PREMIERES 18 December 1926,

National Theatre, Brno; UK: 12 February 1964, Sadler's Wells, London; US: 19 November 1966, War Memorial Theater, San Francisco
CAST Emilia Marty (Elina Makropulos) *dramatic s*, Albert Gregor *t*, Vítek *t*, Kristina *s*, Jaroslav Prus *bar*, Janek *t*, Dr Kolenatý *b-bar*, Stage Technician *b*, Cleaning Woman *c*, Hauk-Šendorf *operetta t*, Chamber Maid *c*; offstage: male chorus

Janáček saw Karel Čapek's play *The Makropulos Affair* in Prague on 10 December 1922, three weeks after it opened, and was immediately attracted to it as a possible opera text, although he had only just started the composition of *The Cunning Little Vixen*. By February 1923 he was in correspondence with Čapek about it. Čapek himself was accommodating but there were legal problems to be overcome in securing the rights. On 10 September 1923 the composer heard from Čapek that these had been resolved and two months later set to work, even before the score of *The Cunning Little Vixen* was finalized. He worked quickly, with Act I drafted by February 1924 and the whole opera by February 1925, though, as was his usual practice, he needed two more drafts before he was satisfied with his work, which he completed almost a year later on 3 December 1925. The Brno premiere followed under Neumann in December 1926, and the Prague premiere under Ostrčil in March 1928 – the last premiere Janáček attended. Though a German production followed under Josef Krips in Frankfurt in 1929, the work took time to establish itself internationally. However, outstanding productions by Sadler's Wells (1964) and Welsh National Opera (1978), both of which were later taken into the English National Opera repertoire, have ensured a regular following in the UK.

Janáček's libretto is a skilful compression keeping the original three-act framework of Čapek's play intact (though not the division of the final act into two scenes). But whereas Čapek wrote his play as a philosophical comedy, which dispassionately explored the merits and drawbacks of a life prolonged to over 300 years, Janáček impatiently cut out much of the speculative banter, and instead concentrated on the emotional state of the extraordinary central character, the 337-year-old Elina Makropulos.

SYNOPSIS

A young Cretan girl, Elina Makropulos, is given an elixir of life devised by her father, physician to Emperor Rudolf II at his court in Prague. She flees with the formula, 'Věc Makropulos' (the Makropulos thing, document), trains as a singer and with literally centuries to perfect her technique has become one of the greatest singers of all time. Moving from country to country to avert suspicion, she has undergone frequent changes of name, though always retaining the same initials. For the past few years (the date is 1922 – she is now 337), she has been known as Emilia Marty and returns to Prague where her extraordinary lease of life began. As it happens, a celebrated lawsuit, Gregor versus Prus, is reaching the end of its 100-year life. The present claimant, Albert Gregor, maintains that his ancestor Ferdinand Gregor should have inherited a large estate on the death in 1827 of its owner, Baron Josef Ferdinand Prus. The Prus family, however, have successfully contested the claim.

Act I: Dr Kolenatý's chambers. Albert Gregor interrupts the historical ruminations of Kolenatý's clerk Vítek to find out the latest news of his case. Kristina, Vítek's daughter, returns from rehearsals at the theatre where Emilia Marty is currently appearing, infatuated by her artistry and beauty. She and Vítek leave just as Marty herself enters the office, accompanied by Dr Kolenatý. Marty wants to know about the Gregor–Prus case; her sharp questions and comments indicate an intimate knowledge of the people involved. She reveals that Ferdinand Gregor was Baron Josef Prus's illegitimate son and that a will in his favour exists somewhere in the house of the present Baron Jaroslav Prus. Gregor makes the disbelieving Dr Kolenatý go and find it. Left alone with the mysterious Marty, Gregor hears more about Ferdinand Gregor's mother, the singer Ellian MacGregor. By then he is completely captivated. She repels his amorous advances and is distraught when he confesses ignorance of the 'Greek papers' she claims he must have. Kolenatý returns with Prus – and with a will. Prus, however, insists that some evidence is still missing. To Kolenatý's amazement, Marty undertakes to provide it.

Act II: The empty stage of a large theatre. A cleaning woman and a stage hand discuss Marty's performance the night before. Prus comes to wait for Marty and, unobserved, witnesses the little scene between Kristina and her boyfriend, his son Janek – to the latter's embarrassment. Marty now appears, upsetting everyone who tries to congratulate her: the tongue-tied Janek, Gregor and Vítek, who to her great annoyance compares her to a famous past singer. But she is strangely compassionate to her final visitor, the aged and demented Hauk-Šendorf, who sees in her a likeness of his 'gypsy girl', Eugenia Montez, long since dead. After giving Kristina her autograph, she dismisses everyone except Prus. Prus excites her interest by mentioning that together with the will there were letters and 'something else' in a sealed envelope. He adds that his investigations reveal that Ferdinand Gregor's mother is given on the birth register as Elina Makropulos, not Ellian MacGregor, as stated by the document Marty has provided. Consequently no MacGregor (or Gregor) can claim the Prus estates. Marty, however, is more interested in the sealed envelope and offers to buy it. Prus angrily stalks off. Gregor now finds her. She asks him to retrieve the document that she gave to Kolenatý – it needs another name. When he continues his advances to her, she brutally repulses him and then falls asleep. He tiptoes away, and Marty wakes up to find Janek with her. She urges him to steal the sealed envelope from his father. This scene, however, has been overheard, once again, by Prus who dismisses his son and who finally agrees to give Marty the envelope in exchange for an assignation that night.

Act III: A hotel room. Prus and Marty have spent the night together. She gets her envelope, but Prus feels cheated and is broken by the news that Janek has committed suicide. Prus leaves, meeting Hauk on the way. Hauk proposes to Marty that they elope but they are forestalled by the arrival of Kolenatý and his party, who accuse her of forgery: the signature on the document she supplied has been written with modern ink. She goes to change while the others rifle her trunk, discovering a variety of historical documents relating to Ellian MacGregor, Eugenia Montez, Elina Makropulos and others. She returns, dressed and a little tipsy. When cross-examined, she insists that her name is Elina Makropulos and she is 337 years old. She tells them about her father and the elixir of life he devised and tried out on her. She had passed this on to the only man she loved, Josef Prus, but with the end of her life approaching she wished to get back the formula. Eventually the company believes her. She collapses and is taken to the bedroom, attended by a doctor. She returns 'as a shadow', at last understanding that death will be a welcome relief – life has become quite meaningless for her. She offers the Makropulos formula to Kristina who, however, sets fire to it, as Elina Makropulos dies.

Like the Vixen's, Elina's death at the end of the opera was Janáček's addition. This magnificent scene is the best illustration of how completely Janáček transformed Čapek's conversational comedy into a drama conceived on the grandest emotional scale. Here Janáček wrote one of his slow-waltz finales, a haunting, rocking tune played in the extremes of the orchestra with, in the middle, Elina's moving account of how meaningless life has become for her. Its otherworldliness is underlined by the slow pace and by the mysterious offstage male-voice choir repeating her words. This is the only substantial monologue in an opera that otherwise is characterized by its many memorable dialogues. Most striking of these is the verbal duel between Marty and Prus in Act II, complemented by their chilling, almost wordless encounter that brings down the curtain.

The success of the dialogues is due partly to the different atmospheres that Janáček creates in each of them, and partly to his virtuosity in handling the voice parts. Compared with those of *The Vixen*, or *From the House of the Dead* this is a wordy libretto, an aspect that has often been criticized. And yet Čapek's elegant prose seems to have offered Janáček a wealth of phrases, whose memorable settings realized perhaps more than in any other work Janáček's speech-melody ideal of revealing a character's inner life. This is one reason why all the minor characters come alive in this more than in any other Janáček opera. The vocal writing is accompanied by some of Janáček's most sophisticated and imaginative orchestral developments which, for instance, help to bind the huge span of the long Marty–Gregor dialogue in Act I.

RECORDINGS 1. Prylová, Žídek, Kočí, Berman, Prague Nat Th O, Gregor, Supraphon, 1965/6; 2. Söderström, Dvorský, Zítek, Švehla, VPO, Mackerras, Decca, 1978

From the House of the Dead

Z mrtvého domu

Opera in three acts (1h 30m)
Libretto by the composer, after the novel *Memoirs from the House of the Dead* by Fyodor Dostoevsky (1862)
Composed 1927–8
PREMIERES 12 April 1930, National Theatre, Brno (Chlubna and Bakala arr.); UK: 1 May 1960, BBC radio; 28 August 1964, King's Theatre, Edinburgh (stage); 28 October 1965, Sadler's Wells, London (Janáček's original version); US: 3 December 1969 (NET TV); 24 March 1983, New York Philharmonic (concert); 28 August 1990, State Theater, New York (stage)
CAST Alexandr Petrovič Gorjančikov *bar*, Aljeja *ms*, Luka Kuzmič (alias of Filka Morozov) *t*, Tall Prisoner *t*, Short Fat Prisoner *bar*, Prison Governor *b*, Elderly Prisoner *t*, Prisoner with eagle *t*, Skuratov *t*, Čekunov *b*, Drunk Prisoner *t*, Prisoner-cook *b*, Prisoner-blacksmith *b*, Priest *b*, Young Prisoner *t*, Wench-tramp *c*, Prisoner playing Don Juan and the Brahmin *b*, Kedril *t*, Šapkin *t*, Šiškov *bar*, Čerevin *t*, Guard *t*, Second Guard *b*, Voice offstage *t*; Elvira, Cobbler's Wife, Priest's Wife, Miller, Miller's Wife, Clerk, Devil *silent*; *tb* chorus of prisoners; guests and sentries *silent*

After completing *The Makropulos Affair* in 1925, Janáček appeared to have no more operatic plans. The next year, 1926, he wrote the *Sinfonietta*, the piano *Capriccio* and the *Glagolitic Mass*, and made a brief visit to England. During this trip he mentioned to Mrs Rosa Newmarch his idea for a violin concerto called 'The Pilgrimage of a Soul'. He made sketches, possibly in late 1926, and in 1927 these were revised to form the overture to his final opera, *From the House of the Dead*. Why he chose to set Dostoevsky's novel is not known apart from his general sympathy towards Russian literature, but his total absorption with the appalling world depicted in the novel and his feeling of urgency to set it are vividly documented in his letters to Kamila Stösslová. By May 1928 the full score of his opera had been copied out, though he continued to revise the fair copy. Acts I and II of this copy contain many additions and corrections by Janáček; Act III was on his desk when he died in August 1928. If he had followed the pattern of previous works, Janáček would have submitted the score to the

Brno Theatre that autumn for performance in 1929. In the event of his death, the premiere was delayed until 1930 and was complicated by the assumption that the work was incomplete, chiefly bcause of the sparsity of the verbal text and the thinness of the musical texture. Accordingly, the first producer, Ota Zítek, filled out the words and stage directions, and Janáček's pupils Osvald Chlubna and Břetislav Bakala reorchestrated the work, throwing in for good measure an apotheosis-like 'optimistic' finale.

In this version the work was published and performed. In 1964 Universal Edition reissued the score with Janáček's original grim ending (the Prisoners returning to their toils) added as an appendix, and thereafter productions began to respect this ending. Janáček's original orchestration has taken longer to establish itself despite the efforts of Rafael Kubelik (who revised the score on the basis of Janáček's autograph), Charles Mackerras and (in Brno) Václav Nosek. The final state of Janáček's opera was not, however, the autograph score, but the copyists' score that Janáček supervised and to which he made many additions himself. This score provided the basis for Mackerras's Decca recording of 1980.

SYNOPSIS

Act I: The yard in a Siberian prison camp; winter, early morning. Prisoners come in from the barracks, wash and eat. An argument breaks out between two of them. Alexandr Petrovič, a new prisoner and a 'gentleman', arrives and is interrogated by the prison Governor, who orders him to be flogged. The prisoners tease an eagle with a broken wing, but admire its defiance in captivity. The Governor's sudden return puts an end to this; he orders them off to work. Half the prisoners go off to outdoor work, singing as they go ('Neuvidí oko již těch krajů'). Others remain, including Skuratov. His singing annoys Luka, who picks a quarrel with him. Skuratov recalls his life in Moscow, and his previous trade as a cobbler. He breaks into a wild dance, then collapses. As he sews, Luka recalls his previous imprisonment, for vagrancy. He tells how he incited the other prisoners to rebellion and how he killed the officer who came to quell the disturbance. He also describes how he was flogged for this. Petrovič, who has meanwhile been similarly punished, is brought back by the guards, half dead.

Act II: The bank of the river Irtysh. Summer, a year later. Prisoners do outdoor work. Petrovič asks the Tartar boy Aljeja about his family and offers to teach him to read and write. With the day's work over, guests appear, a priest gives his blessing on this feast day, and the prisoners sit down to eat. Skuratov tells his story – how he murdered the man that his sweetheart Lujza was forced to marry. The prisoners improvise a stage on which they perform two plays: 'Kedril and Don Juan' and 'The Miller's Beautiful Wife'. Darkness falls after the plays. The Young Prisoner goes off with a prostitute. Against a nostalgic background of offstage folksongs, Petrovič and Aljeja drink tea. The Short Fat Prisoner, resenting this, picks a quarrel and attacks and wounds Aljeja. Guards rush on to restore order.

Act III, Scene 1: It is towards evening and Aljeja, who is recovering in the prison hospital, cries out in delirious fever. Čekunov waits on him and Petrovič, to the anger of the dying Luka. Šapkin describes how the police superintendant interrogated him and almost pulled his ears off. Night falls (short orchestral interlude). The silence is broken by the sighs of the Elderly Prisoner. Šiškov, encouraged by Čerevín, tells his story. He was made to marry Akulka (Akulina), a girl allegedly dishonoured by Filka Morozov, though in fact still a virgin. When Šiškov found out that she still loved Filka he killed her. Luka dies as the story ends; Šiškov recognizes him as Filka. His body is taken away by the guards. Petrovič is called for.

Scene 2: The Governor, drunk, apologizes to Petrovič before the other prisoners and tells him that he is to be released. Aljeja comes in from the hospital to say farewell. As Petrovič leaves, the prisoners release the eagle and celebrate its freedom as it flies away. The guards order them off to work.

This is Janáček's most extraordinary opera. The increasingly extreme musical style of Janáček's last years is here complemented by a dramaturgy in opera that was decades ahead of its time. Janáček's sound-vision of the work is perhaps best characterized by the initial sketches, which are often conceived in terms of voice parts, trombones and piccolos, and not very much else. For the first time he adopted his practice, used in other genres, of ruling his own stave lines, and thereby encouraging great economy of texture. The harmonic style is similarly stark. As the curtain opens a motif is heard: a short rocking theme in which each chord is enriched with a dissonant semitone. This motif haunts and characterizes the entire first act (in a more purposeful way than in any other Janáček opera); its most searing version is as a ritornello between the lines of the prisoners going off to work, singing of their exile.

From the House of the Dead has almost no story and, except for one tiny part, its cast is exclusively male and made up of a collective, rather than of interacting soloists – a chorus opera from which individual speakers step out to tell their tales and then merge in with the others again. Janáček's libretto here is more his own work than in any other opera except *Fate* (1905). He composed straight from the original Russian, translating as he went along, and made his own choice and ordering of events. While Dostoevsky's autobiographical account of his time in a Siberian prison is arranged chiefly by topic, Janáček, in order to give some idea of time passing, distributed some of the incidents (such as the account of the eagle or Petrovič's dealings with Aljeja) over the whole opera. He was particularly successful in producing emotional climaxes for the ends of the acts – for instance, his juxtaposition of Petrovič's return from his flogging to end Act I just after Luka had described a similar event in horrifying detail, or the release and celebration of the eagle's freedom paired off with the release of Petrovič (whose arrival and departure provide the slender narrative frame of the piece). An important element in each act are the monologues in which a prisoner describes his crime (Luka in Act I; Skuratov in Act II; Šiškov in Act III) – all miniature dramas with the virtuosic depiction of a cast of characters, and all strongly contrasting in tone and content with one another. Skuratov's lyrical account of his love for a German washerwoman is appropriately placed in the comparatively relaxed Act II, followed by the rough-and-tumble comedy of the two plays, given mostly in mime. The longest monologue of all, Šiškov's, told in the quietness of the prison hospital at night, is emblematic of the whole work: a harrowing tale held together by the recurrence of a transcendentally gentle theme in the same way that Janáček's warm compassion threads through and transforms his grimmest and yet most uplifting opera.

RECORDING Zahradníček, Žídek, Zítek, Jedlička, Švorc, Janská, VPO, Mackerras, Decca, 1980
OTHER OPERAS *Šárka*, (1888) 1925; *The Beginning of a Romance* (*Počátek románu*), 1894; *Fate* (*Osud*), (1905), 1934; *The Excursions of Mr Brouček* (*Výlety páně Broučkovy*), (1917) 1920

J.T.

K

Oliver Knussen

Stuart Oliver Knussen; *b* 12 June 1952, Glasgow, Scotland

The precocious son of a leading double-bass player, Knussen burst into prominence when at the age of 15 he conducted a performance of his First Symphony by the London Symphony Orchestra. He took some time to recover from this experience, yet his adult music has fulfilled a lot, if not all, of that early promise. Two further symphonies, a horn concerto and a number of shorter chamber-orchestral works (including some with soprano solo) testify to a brilliant feel for movement and sonority, and a bold sense of the voice as a dramatic instrument, all of which is borne out, within their self-imposed limitations, by his two short operas. A pupil of John Lambert and the American composer-conductor Gunther Schuller, Knussen is a perfectionist who takes a long time to finish a piece. Since the 1980s he has been increasingly successful as a conductor, and became musical director of the London Sinfonietta in 1999, championing a wide range of contemporary music.

Where the Wild Things Are

Fantasy opera in one act, (40m)
Libretto by Maurice Sendak and the composer, after the children's book by Sendak (1963)
Composed 1979–83

PREMIERES 28 November 1980, Théâtre de la Monnaie, Brussels (inc.); UK: 22 March 1982, Queen Elizabeth Hall, London (inc.; concert); 9 January 1984, Lyttelton Theatre, London (stage); US: 7 June 1984, Avery Fisher Hall, New York (concert); 27 September 1985, St Paul, Minnesota (stage)

Knussen describes the work as 'an attempt to revive and develop the fantasy opera', and he acknowledges the influence of Ravel's *L'enfant et les sortilèges*, Musorgsky's *Nursery* (and *Boris*), and Debussy's *La boîte à joujoux* (they are quoted). Sendak's picture book supplied both an intense, child's-nightmare atmosphere, and strong scenic ideas, and for the Glyndebourne production Sendak himself made designs based on his original drawings.

Max, a naughty little boy in a white wolf suit, is sent to bed by his mother without any supper. He dreams of revenge. His room turns into a forest, and a boat appears, in which he sails away to an island inhabited by Wild Things (dream monsters of a rather sinister amiability). He quells them with a look. They perform a frenzied, galumphing dance (the 'Wild Rumpus'), after which Max sends the Wild Things to bed without any supper. But he is homesick and hungry, and decides to sail home. The monsters wake up and chase him, but he sets sail safely, the sea and forest dissolve, and he is back in his bedroom. A supper tray is waiting for him, still hot.

With only one main character (Max, a high soprano), assorted monsters (with amplification) and a large mixed chamber orchestra, the stage is set for aural fantasy rather than music drama. Knussen not only quotes his favourite children's composers, but also satirizes the funny-noise school of modern music. But his score is typically discriminating and brilliantly composed, if sometimes too loud for the clear audibility of words.

RECORDING Saffer, King, Gillett, Hayes, Wilson-Johnson, S. Richardson, London Sinfonietta, Knussen, DG, 1999

Higglety Pigglety Pop!

(There must be more to life)

Second fantasy opera in one act
Libretto by Maurice Sendak and the composer, after the children's book by Sendak (1967)
Composed 1983–5, rev. 1990
PREMIERES 13 October 1984, Glyndebourne, Sussex (inc.); 5 August 1985, Glyndebourne; US: rev. version, 5 June 1990, Music Center, Los Angeles

The original story for this companion piece to *Where the Wild Things Are* is both more wordy and more sophisticated. Jennie, a discontented Sealyham dog, decides to leave home and seek her fortune, first devouring a potted plant that tries to dissuade her. She meets a Pig in sandwich-boards advertising for a leading lady for the World Mother Goose (i.e. 'nursery rhyme') Theatre. But the successful candidate must have 'experience'. She sets out to acquire it. A Cat Milkman mistakes her for Baby's new nurse, explaining that Baby's previous nurses have all been fed to the Downstairs Lion for failing to get Baby to eat. Jennie, too, fails but resolves to save the situation by taking Baby to its parents at Castle Yonder. On the way she meets the Lion, who is about to eat Baby when Jennie saves it by accidentally saying its name (a spoof reference to Puccini's *Turandot*). The Lion goes off with Baby, and Jennie sadly goes to sleep under an ash tree. But it turns out that she has now acquired the experience she needed, and she joins the World Mother Goose Theatre (the Pig, the Cat, the Lion and the maid Rhoda) in enacting the nursery rhyme that gives the opera both its title and its dramatis personae.

Less sharp in narrative than its predecessor, the work is not without a certain wan sentimentality offset by Knussen's penetrating ear for kindly musical satire. The influence of American neo-tonalists such as David del Tredici is palpable. As with the 'Wild Things', Sendak based his designs for the Glyndebourne production on the illustrations in his book.

RECORDING Buchan, Saffer, Hardy, Gillett, Wilson-Johnson, S. Richardson, London Sinfonietta, Knussen, DG, 1999

S.W.

Erich Wolfgang Korngold

b 29 May 1897, Brno, Moravia;
d 29 November 1957, Hollywood, California, US

One of the last great Romantic composers, Korngold is today remembered principally for his opera *Die tote Stadt* and for his numerous Hollywood film scores.

At the age of ten (through the influence of his father Julius Korngold, Vienna's foremost music critic) Korngold was introduced to Mahler who, declaring the boy a genius, sent him to Zemlinsky for composition lessons. When the 13-year-old Korngold's ballet *Der Schneemann* (orchestrated by Zemlinsky) was given a successful premiere at the Hofoper in 1910, the young composer was hailed as a *Wunderkind*. And by the time his first two operas, *Der Ring des Polykrates* and *Violanta*, were premiered – as a double-bill – in 1916, he had amassed a distinguished band of supporters, among them Richard Strauss,

Arthur Nikisch, Carl Flesch and Artur Schnabel, all of whom championed the young composer's works.

Appointed musical director of his regiment, Korngold was able to keep composing throughout the First World War, producing much-acclaimed incidental music to Shakespeare's *Much Ado About Nothing* (1919) and working on what was to be his most successful opera, *Die tote Stadt*. In the 1920s, much to his own enjoyment but to his father's disapproval, Korngold undertook the arrangement of several operetta scores; these included Johann Strauss II's *Eine Nacht in Venedig*, which consequently became one of the composer's most popular works. In the same year (1923) he began work on *Das Wunder der Heliane*. Korngold always considered the opera his masterpiece, but the combination of hostility between Julius Korngold and supporters of Krenek's opera *Jonny spielt auf* and the disappointment of a public who expected a repeat of *Die tote Stadt*, resulted in a less than enthusiastic response to the work.

Korngold was warned by his publisher in 1932 that the increase of anti-Semitism would make future productions of his operas inconceivable. He went to Hollywood in 1934 and the following year eagerly accepted an invitation from Warner Brothers to write an original score for the film *Captain Blood*, starring Errol Flynn. Over the next 12 years Korngold wrote 18 full-length film scores, which he referred to as 'opera without singing', winning Oscars for *Robin Hood* and *Anthony Adverse*.

Korngold returned to Vienna in 1949 but found that critical opinion no longer applauded his essentially lyrical, neo-Romantic style, favouring instead the austere atonal idiom of Schoenberg and his followers. When his fifth opera *Die Kathrin* received its Viennese premiere in 1950 (its world premiere had taken place in Stockholm in 1939), the critics condemned it as old-fashioned, although it enjoyed considerable success with the public. During his last decade Korngold returned to concert music, making certain moves in the direction of a modern style, notably in his Symphony in F♯ (1949–50). Although he had plans for a sixth opera, based on a story by Grillparzer, he completed only one more stage work, a musical comedy, *Silent Serenade* (1946). His last works included the arrangement, in 1954, of music by Wagner for *Magic Fire*, a film biography of the composer.

Die tote Stadt

The Dead City

Opera in three scenes ('Bilder') (2h)
Libretto by Paul Schott (pseudonym for Julius and Erich Korngold), after the novel *Bruges-la-Morte* by Georges Rodenbach (1892)
Composed 1917–19
PREMIERES 4 December 1920, Stadttheater, Hamburg and Opernhaus, Cologne; US: 19 November 1921, Metropolitan, New York; UK: 14 January 1996, Queen Elizabeth Hall, London (concert)
CAST Paul *t*, Marie/Mariette *s*, Frank *bar*, Brigitta *c*, Juliette *s*, Lucienne *ms*, Victorin *t*, Count Albert *t*, Fritz (a pierrot) *bar*; Gaston *mime*; *satb* chorus of spirits

With this work Korngold reached his operatic zenith. Its portrayal of the psychological damage of excessive mourning struck a chord in the aftermath of the First World War. At the same time its novel structure – much of it is a dream sequence – and memorable music heightened its impact. Korngold played a piano reduction of the score to Puccini, on a visit to Vienna in 1920, and he considered the work 'the strongest hope of new German music'. Productions were rapidly mounted throughout Europe and it was the first German opera to be performed at the Metropolitan after the war.

SYNOPSIS

Act I: Although Paul is gloomily obsessed with the memory of his dead wife

Marie (he preserves a room full of her memorabilia) he has met the vivacious Mariette and impetuously asks her to visit him. But Mariette leaves when she sees a portrait of Marie and realizes how much she resembles her. Paul is torn by his devotion to Marie and his feelings for Mariette. In a vision Marie bids him 'see and understand'.

Act II takes place in Paul's imagination: a fantastic sequence of scenes portraying the loss of his friends, Mariette being serenaded, rising from a coffin, arguing with Paul, realizing her rival is a dead woman and deciding to exorcize her predecessor's ghost.

Act III: The dream continues, with Mariette eventually desecrating Marie's possessions. Goaded beyond endurance Paul strangles her with a plait of Marie's hair. When he wakes the plait is intact and, though the memory remains, the mourning is over.

Korngold's Expressionistic opera, with its hallucinatory passages, was adventurous but proved to be a great success; it has remained his most popular opera. As with *Violanta*, the music throughout is intense, with Korngold making full use of the vast forces he had scored for. Rather than relying on full-blown melodies to propel the action, Korngold organizes his music around a number of short motifs representing various people, places or other aspects of the story. Many of these motifs include the interval of a perfect fourth (or its inversion, the perfect fifth), which consequently takes on a pivotal role in the musical structure of the entire opera. There are, nevertheless, identifiable arias – notably 'Gluck, das mir verblieb', sung first by the vision of Marie and later repeated by Paul, and the 'Pierrotlied', which is a serenade to Mariette performed by one of her admirers. Both numbers have enjoyed widespread performance independent of the opera.

RECORDING Neblett, Kollo, Prey, Luxon, Bavarian RCh, Munich RO, Leinsdorf, RCA, 1975

OTHER OPERAS *Der Ring des Polykrates*, 1916; *Violanta*, 1916; *Das Wunder der Heliane*, 1927; *Die Kathrin*, 1939

MUSICAL COMEDY *Silent Serenade* (1946); arrangements of works by Johann Strauss, Offenbach, Fall and Rossini

C.B.

Ernst Krenek

b 23 August 1900, Vienna;
d 23 December 1991, Palm Springs, California, US

Krenek was one of the most prolific creative artists of the 20th century. He responded tirelessly to its major cultural transformations and succeeded in staying in tune with most of its significant musical developments. Fascinated by the potential of the genre through most of his long working life, Krenek completed 21 operas – 11 in Europe before the outbreak of the Second World War, and 10 later in America, his new homeland – as well as other music for the stage.

Krenek's compositional output is remarkable for its stylistic range. The operas make a unique use of that colourful harmonic and textural palette established by 20th-century modernism – tonality, atonality, dodecaphony and serialism, jazz, dance music and electronic sounds. They also embody his changing attitudes to music itself: the aim of opera – its aesthetic function, role in society, the relationship of its music to extra-musical ideas – became a dominant concern in the critical and musicological work that Krenek pursued alongside composition.

Brought up by music-loving bourgeois parents in the vicinity of the Viennese Volksoper, Krenek was one of the youngest and most famous of the Imperial Academy composition class tutored by Schreker. Following his teacher to Berlin in 1920, he concentrated initially on instrumental works, rapidly developing an abstract and atonal style seemingly at odds with his training, but in line with the latest avant-garde tendencies influenced by Mahler, Bartók and Schoenberg. His interest in the written word, experience as Paul Bekker's assistant at the opera in Kassel and Wiesbaden (1925–7) and contact with recent artistic developments in Paris (which he visited in 1926) prompted him to write dramatic music relevant to contemporary taste. The tendencies of his first three stage works, in which he explored tragedy and comedy in avant-garde and populist styles, came to fruition spectacularly in his fourth, the neoclassical jazz opera *Jonny spielt auf* (1926). No other work by Krenek made such an impact on the public, and his instant fame brought sufficient financial security to enable him to compose full time.

A trio of appealing one-act works in burlesque operetta and fairy-tale mode followed in the afterglow of *Jonny*, and a comic work written in the spirit of Karl Kraus about contemporary Vienna, *Kehraus um St Stephan* (1930), were deemed too satirical to be performed. But Krenek had already moved on to more serious subjects and the world of grand opera with *Leben des Orest* (1929), which reflected his childhood affection for the classics, as had his earlier setting of Kokoschka's Expressionist retelling of the myth *Orpheus und Eurydike* (1923). For Krenek himself the most important work of his European years, if not his entire career, was *Karl V* (1933), a philosophically complex and musically innovative work – the first full-length, 12-note opera – which offended the Nazi authorities. Its premiere at the Vienna State Opera was cancelled, and the composer went into enforced exile.

In America, after an initial period of obscurity, Krenek became increasingly sought after as a university teacher and wrote the chamber operas *Tarquin* (1940), *What Price Confidence?* (1945), *Dark Waters* (1950) and *The Belltower* (1956). Twenty years after *Karl V* he returned to large-scale opera. Prompted by renewed European interest in his music and the political conflicts caused by McCarthyism, Krenek revised *Karl V* and completed two new works (for performance in Germany) inspired by Classical antiquity: *Pallas Athene weint* (1955) and *Der goldene Bock* (1963), the latter for the inauguration of Hamburg's new opera house. Krenek's later operas mark a return to his inimitable comic streak and predilection for special effects: *Ausgerechnet und verspielt* (1962), about gambling with computers, which used serial techniques and was one of two operas written for television, and the satirical parody *Sardakai* (1969). Thereafter Krenek continued to be fascinated by the possibilities of staged vocal music, working on chamber concert pieces (some using electronics) rather than opera.

Krenek explored the possibilities of opera to the full, experimenting with a variety of artistic intentions and expanding its expressive means. His earliest works were candidly Zeitoper, but his subsequent stage works were also intended to have a contemporary application, even when set in the past. According to Krenek, all his operas reveal facets of his philosophical preoccupation with various conceptions of freedom. Most of his works are conspicuously absent from today's operatic repertoire.

Jonny spielt auf

Jonny Plays On

Opera in two parts (11 scenes) (2h)
Libretto by the composer
Composed 1925–6

PREMIERES 10 February 1927, Stadttheater, Leipzig; US: 19 January 1929, Metropolitan, New York; UK: 14 November 1984, Grand Theatre, Leeds

CAST Max *t*, Anita *s*, Jonny *bar*, Daniello *bar*, Yvonne *s*, 4 *t*, *bar*, *b*; *satb* chorus of hotel guests, travellers and audience

One of the greatest hits in 20th-century operatic history, this lively and thought-provoking work is a tribute to Krenek's diverse talents. Its capacity to entertain surprised both the musical establishment and the general public in Germany, where it achieved a record number of performances on more than 30 stages in its first season. Acclaimed for both its musico-dramatic dynamism and its kaleidoscopic impression of central European culture, which lent itself well to avant-garde staging, the opera also triumphed in more than 20 foreign cities over the next two years, although initially its New York and Parisian receptions were comparatively cool.

SYNOPSIS

Part I: Max, a brooding intellectual composer (possibly a self-portrait), meets Anita, a sensual prima donna, on top of a glacier. Later at her house in a central European city they begin an affair, which results in the composition of a new opera. In Paris for its performance, Anita is unfaithful to Max with Daniello, a virtuoso violinist and womanizer. Meanwhile Jonny, a saxophonist performing at the hotel, steals Daniello's valuable violin. Blamed for the theft, Yvonne, a chambermaid, is sacked and returns with Anita to Germany as her maid. Jonny follows in pursuit having concealed the violin in Anita's banjo case.

Part II: Max yearns for Anita's return, but on learning of her infidelity he seeks solace back in the Alps, where he communes with a singing glacier. The sound of a loudspeaker transmitting a radio broadcast of Anita singing his aria, however, saves him, and he decides to seek a new life with her just as Jonny's jazz band comes on the air. A police car-chase ends up in a railway station where Daniello is crushed by the locomotive arriving in the nick of time to take all the others, led by Jonny tuning up on the violin, to America.

The music is striking in its juxtaposition of the dissonant chromaticism and traditional forms of the Second Viennese School with lyrically tonal Italianate Romanticism and a Teutonic brand of jazz constructed from simple melodies, repetitive rhythms and seventh chords. The label 'jazz opera' is slightly misleading because Krenek's usage is textural rather than organic. The different styles successfully convey Krenek's idea that only an infusion of Jonny's uninhibited and 'primitive' American jazz can revitalize European music and thus its people, to whom such music appeals more than Max's.

Krenek expressed his commitment to bridging the divide between high art and popular culture in this opera's carnivalesque spirit and symbolic associations. More attention has, however, been paid to the opera's superficial aura of the exotic, and implicitly to Krenek's youthful desire for fame, than to any deeper meaning in the work. Yet Jonny's indulgence in the fashionably escapist fantasies of *Amerikanismus* is no less significant or influential than Weill's didactic brand of Zeitoper, which promoted socio-political ideas more explicitly.

RECORDINGS 1. Popp, Lear, Blankenship, Feldhoff, Stewart, Vienna Academy Ch, Vienna Volksoper O, Hollreiser, Amadeo, 1960s; 2. Marc, Kruse, St Hill, Kraus, Scholz, Leipzig Op Ch, Leipzig Gewandhaus, Zagrosek, Decca, 1991

OTHER OPERATIC WORKS *Der Sprung über den Schatten*, 1924; *Die Zwingburg*, 1924; *Bluff*, (1925); *Orpheus und Eurydike*, 1926; *Der Diktator*, 1928; *Das geheime Königreich*, 1928; *Schwergewicht, oder Die Ehre der Nation*, 1928; *Leben des Orest*, 1930; *Kehraus um St Stephan*, (1930); *Cefalo e Procri*, 1934; *Karl V*, 1938; Tarquin, (1940), 1950; *What Price Confidence?*, (1945), 1962; *Dark Waters*, 1950; *Pallas Athene weint*, 1955; *The Belltower*, 1957; *Ausgerechnet und verspielt*, 1962; *Der goldene Bock*, 1964; *Der Zauberspiegel*, 1966; *Sardakai, oder Das kommt davon*, 1970

C.I.P.

L

Franz Lehár

b 30 April 1870, Komorn; *d* 24 October 1948, Bad Ischl, Austria

Lehár, the instigator and leading composer of 20th-century Viennese operetta, was of Czech and Hungarian descent. The son of a military bandmaster, he studied at the Prague Conservatory with Foerster, and briefly with Fibich and Dvořák, excelling at the violin. He played in his father's band (alongside Leo Fall) and later led his own ensembles for infantry regiments stationed in Trieste, Budapest and finally Vienna. During this period his grand 'Russian' opera *Kukuška* (1896) was unsuccessfully produced in Leipzig.

The popularity of his waltz *Gold und Silber* (1902) persuaded Lehár to leave the world of army bands and once again to try the theatre. That same year two of his operettas were performed at Vienna's two leading operetta theatres, *Wiener Frauen* (Theater an der Wien) and *Der Rastelbinder* (Carltheater), the latter making the more lasting impression with its provincial characters and a sensual, languorous love duet in Act II. After two less successful works, Lehár hit the jackpot in 1905 with one of the most popular operettas ever written, *Die lustige Witwe*.

Several undistinguished works followed *Die lustige Witwe*, until a series of Viennese and international triumphs began with *Der Graf von Luxemburg*, another Parisian romantic frolic (1909), *Zigeunerliebe* (1910), and *Eva*, again set in Paris, but dealing with industrial relations (1911). Works written around the First World War period proved less durable as new rival composers were garnering many more performances.

In the mid-1920s Lehár's fortunes began to rise again, thanks to his association with the Austrian tenor Richard Tauber. The singer had created a sensation taking over a leading part in *Frasquita* (1922) in Vienna, and later appeared in the Berlin premiere of *Paganini* (1925), the first of five new or refashioned romantic operettas written expressly for him. The contemporary charm and cohesive elegance of *Die lustige Witwe* gave way to quasi-historical exoticism. The romantic music instantly brought Puccini to mind, while the subsidiary comic numbers were written in a more vernacular style using modern dance rhythms that nevertheless sounded distinctively Lehárian. Though Tauber looked not remotely like Paganini or Goethe (in *Friederike*, 1928), the force of his voice and persona enraptured Europe. The climax of this partnership was reached with *Das Land des Lächelns* (1929).

The final original work was in fact an operetta transmogrified into an opera, *Giuditta* (1934). During the 1930s the composer wrote several film scores. With a Jewish wife, Lehár remained in retirement in Austria after 1938. His works were still performed (the non-Aryan librettists' names were omitted from the programmes), royalties continued to pour in, and the composer was occasionally feted by the Nazis – Hitler's favourite operetta was reputedly *Die lustige Witwe*.

Die lustige Witwe
The Merry Widow

Operetta in three acts (2h 30m)
Libretto by Viktor Léon and Leo Stein, from the play *L'attaché d'ambassade* by Henri Meilhac (1861) in the German translation (*Der Gesandschafts Attaché*, 1862) by Alexander Bergen
PREMIERES 30 December 1905, Theater an der Wien, Vienna; UK: 8 June 1907, Daly's Theatre, London; US: 21 October 1907, New Amsterdam Theater, New York
CAST Baron Zeta *t*, Count Danilo Danilowitsch *t*, Camille de Rosillon *t*, Vicomte Cascada *t*, Raoul de St Brioche *t*, Bogdanowitsch *bar*, Kromow *t*, Pritschitsch *bar*, Njegus *bar*, Hanna Glawari *s*, Valencienne *soubrette*, Sylviane *s*, Olga *s*, Praskowia *ms*, 6 *s*; *satb* chorus of Parisians and Pontevedrians, grisettes, partygoers, dancers, etc.

No operetta conjures up Habsburg Vienna, turn-of-the-century Paris or the glittering Edwardian era of eternal waltzes quite like *The Merry Widow*. Lehár's rapturous score – which he was never to equal – was his ticket to immortality and enormous profits; it created an international furore the like of which had not been seen since Sullivan's *HMS Pinafore* or *The Mikado* 20 years before.

SYNOPSIS
Act I: Baron Zeta, the Pontevedrian ambassador to Paris, anxiously awaits the fabulously wealthy Hanna Glawari, who has recently been widowed. To avoid her millions leaving Pontevedro, she must be prevented from marrying a foreigner. Hanna encounters the playboy Danilo; they once had an affair, but now that she is wealthy, he treats her coolly. Baron Zeta, oblivious of his own wife Valencienne's carrying on with Camille, informs Danilo that he must marry Hanna for the sake of his country. In the ballroom Hanna elects to dance with Danilo, despite his thoroughly obnoxious behaviour.

Act II: Hanna gives a party at her home with everyone in their national costumes. She tells her guests a story about a Vilja, a maid of the woods. Danilo and the men remark on the difficulties of handling women, but Danilo is falling in love again. Camille entices Valencienne into a pavilion in the garden. Zeta, looking through the keyhole, is surprised to see not his wife, but Hanna. She has taken Valencienne's place as much to save her friend as to tease Danilo, who angrily leaves.

Act III: Hanna explains the incident in the pavilion to Danilo, and they are drawn together by a sensuous waltz. Zeta's marital problems are settled, and when Hanna announces that she will lose her money on marriage, Danilo asks for her hand. She agrees, and then explains that the millions will pass to her husband.

Possibly the most frequently performed operetta of all time, the work offers a succession of brilliant scenes and superb finales, punctuated by operetta standards such as, in Act I, the entrance songs for both Hanna ('Bitte, meine Herr'n') and Danilo ('Da geh' ich zu Maxim'), in Act II, the 'Vilja' song, and the 'Weiber' march, and in the last act the famous waltz ('Lippen schweigen'). Just as glitteringly striking and memorable are the duets for Camille and Valencienne, including his passionate pavilion invitation in Act II, Hanna's description of life 'in the Parisian style' in the Act II finale and the potent 'Ballsirenen' waltz in the Act I finale.

For the London production Lehár added two new numbers, and, later, a long, formal overture – the original short introduction is infinitely more satisfying in setting the scene. It is generally forgotten today that Lehár's score was considered quite bold and even risqué by some. The silver age of Viennese operetta is said to have begun with *Die lustige Witwe*. Love affairs could become comparatively more realistic, and the orchestra far more lush in support. Lehár had brought operetta into the 20th century.

RECORDINGS 1. Schwarzkopf, Steffek, Gedda, Waechter, Philharmonia Ch & O, Von Matačić, EMI, 1962; 2. Harwood, Stratas, Hollweg, Kollo, Ch of Deutsche Op, BPO, Karajan, DG, 1972

OTHER OPERATIC WORKS
Operettas: *Fräulein Leutnant*, 1901; *Arabella, die Kubanerin* (inc.), (1901); *Das Club-Baby* (inc.), (1901); *Wiener Frauen*, 1902; *Das Rastelbinder*, 1902; *Der Göttergatte*, 1904; *Die Juxheirat*, 1904; *Der Schlüssel zum Paradies*, 1906; *Peter und Paul reisen im Schlaraffenland*, 1906; *Mitislaw der Moderne*, 1907; *Der Mann mit den drei Frauen*, 1908; *Der Graf von Luxemburg*, 1909; *Zigeunerliebe*, 1910; *Das Fürstenkind* (1909); *Die Spieluhr*, 1911; *Eva*, 1911; *Rosenstock und Edelweiss*, 1912; *Die ideale Gattin* (rev. of *Der Göttergatte*), 1913; *Endlich allein*, 1914; *Der Sterngucker*, 1916; *A Pacsirta* (*Wo die Lerche singt*), 1918; *Die blaue Mazur*, 1920; *Die Tangokönigin* (second rev. of *Der Göttergatte*), 1921; *Frühling*, 1922; *La danza della libellule*, 1922; *Frasquita*, 1922; *Die gelbe Jacke*, 1923; *Cloclo*, 1924; *Paganini*, 1925; *Gigolette* (rev. of *Der Sterngucker* and *La danza delle libellule*), 1926: *Der Zarewitsch*, 1927; *Friederike*, 1928; *Das Land des Lächelns*, 1929; *Frühlingsmädel* (rev. of *Der Sterngucker* and *Frühling*), 1930; *Schön ist die Welt* (rev. of *Endlich allein*), 1930; *Der Fürst der Berge* (rev. of *Das Fürstenkind*), 1932; *Giuditta*, 1934; Operas: *Der Kürassier* (inc.), (1892); *Rodrigo* (inc.), (1893); *Kukuška*, 1896, rev. as *Tatjana*, 1905; *Garbonciás diák* (rev. of *Zigeunerliebe*), 1943

R.T.

Ruggero Leoncavallo

b 23 April 1857, Naples; *d* 9 August 1919, Montecatini, Italy

Leoncavallo, the Italian composer and librettist, was admitted to the Naples Conservatory in 1866, where his principal teachers were Beniamino Cesi and Lauro Rossi. Graduating ten years later, he moved to Bologna, where he was much impressed by the poet Carducci's lectures. These had a strong influence on his literary interests and prompted the completion of a libretto entitled *Chatterton*, which he had begun as a student and which he now also set to music. He also fell under the spell of Wagner and planned to write a trilogy – both text and music – on the Italian Renaissance. Unable to interest a publisher in his proposals, he embarked on a journey to Egypt (1882) and later to Paris, supporting himself as an accompanist for *café-concerts*. In the French capital in 1888 he made friends with the baritone Maurel (the original Iago in Verdi's *Otello*), who persuaded the publisher Giulio Ricordi to take on the composer.

Ricordi was more impressed with Leoncavallo's abilities as a theatre poet than with his music, taking a dim view of *I Medici*, the only part of the proposed trilogy Leoncavallo had completed. In 1889 Leoncavallo worked with Puccini on the text for *Manon Lescaut*, but the collaboration lasted only briefly owing to differences of temperament. When Ricordi definitely refused *I Medici*, Leoncavallo, desperate to establish himself, quickly composed *Pagliacci*, modelling his work on Mascagni's *Cavalleria rusticana*, and exploiting the current trend for verismo opera. The successful premiere of *Pagliacci* in 1892, with Maurel as Tonio and with Toscanini conducting, made the composer famous overnight. *Pagliacci* became the almost inseparable companion of *Cavalleria rusticana* as a double-bill after the Metropolitan Opera

House, New York, staged the combination in December 1893.

Fame, however, did not ensure a trouble-free future for the composer. Like *Pagliacci, I Medici* was taken up by Ricordi's rival publishing house, Sonzogno, who, hoping to capitalize on *Pagliacci*'s recent success, quickly arranged a performance. But the pretentious panorama of the Renaissance failed to measure up to expectations, despite the composer's unabashed promotion of it, and the opera was deemed a failure. Daunted by this setback, Leoncavallo wisely put aside the remainder of his projected *Crepusculum* trilogy (the title was a distant nod in the direction of *Götterdämmerung*). When Puccini began work on *La bohème*, Leoncavallo simultaneously embarked on the same subject, determined to better his rival with his memories of the Parisian atmosphere he had absorbed in his years of vagabondage. Leoncavallo's score, which was premiered some 15 months after Puccini's, never proved a serious threat, however, despite some beguiling local colour and vocally grateful moments.

Despite earlier failure *I Medici* was premiered in Berlin in 1894; Kaiser Wilhelm II was greatly impressed and commissioned an opera from Leoncavallo extolling the Hohenzollerns, placing the Court Opera at his disposal. Leoncavallo worked on the opera for ten years and – he wrote to Caruso – believed it to be his masterpiece. He was sadly mistaken: despite its illustrious patron *Der Roland von Berlin* (1904) utterly failed to hold its own.

In 1906 Leoncavallo toured the United States and Canada, imitating Mascagni's visit four years earlier, and here he first turned his hand to operetta, a genre that would periodically engage him for the rest of his life.

Leoncavallo's natural aptitude for lighter music, which had already been demonstrated in his song 'Mattinata' (one of the earliest compositions written for the gramophone, it was recorded by Caruso accompanied by Leoncavallo in 1904), was rather at odds with his intense desire to be taken seriously as a composer. Hoping to repeat the now-distant success of *Pagliacci*, Leoncavallo set about the composition of *Tormenta*, based on a melodramatic play by Belvederi, set in Sardinia. The interruption of the First World War led to its abandonment, and Leoncavallo completed no further operas. His final operatic project, a grand opera *Edipo re* to a libretto by Forzano, was completed by Pennacchio and premiered 17 months after Leoncavallo's death. It made only a temporary splash and that thanks to Titta Ruffo in the title role.

Pagliacci

The Clowns

Dramma in two acts and a prologue (1h 15m)
Libretto by the composer
PREMIERES 21 May 1892, Teatro Dal Verme, Milan; UK: 19 May 1893, Covent Garden, London; US: 15 June 1893, Grand Opera House, New York
CAST Canio *t*, Nedda *s*, Tonio *bar*, Silvio *bar*, Beppe *t*; *satb* chorus of villagers

The only one of Leoncavallo's 12 operas and 10 operettas to enter the permanent repertoire, *Pagliacci*, along with its almost inseparable sidekick, Mascagni's *Cavalleria rusticana*, best convey the ethos of verismo, the realistic representation of lower-class characters in the context of 'a bleeding slice of life', to quote Tonio in the prologue of *Pagliacci* – itself a manifesto of the naturalistic aesthetic. Drawing on his memories of a *crime passionel* adjudicated by his magistrate father, Leoncavallo combined the story of a jealous husband and his unfaithful wife with a performance by a commedia dell'arte troupe, attaining a climax when real-life emotion supplants the play-acting.

SYNOPSIS
Prologue: Tonio alerts the audience that they are to see a drama taken from real life.

Act I: On the feast day of the Assumption Calabrian villagers gather to greet a company of strolling players, and Canio, the troupe's leader, invites them to attend the performance. When one of the bystanders makes a teasing reference to the desirability of Nedda, Canio's wife, he brushes the taunt aside, but not without revealing his jealous nature ('Un tal gioco'). When the others go off, Nedda stays behind, half afraid that Canio is suspicious of her, but envying the birds their freedom to come and go as they please ('Stridono lassù'). The deformed Tonio, a member of the company, appears and plays clumsy court to Nedda, but she repulses him with a whip, leaving him vengeful. Her lover Silvio appears and they plan a rendezvous for later that evening ('Decidi il mio destin'). The latter part of their conversation is overheard by Tonio, who fetches Canio. Barely restrained by Beppe from assaulting his wife on the spot, Canio demands to know her lover's name, but Nedda will not tell him. Canio starts to paint his face and put on his clown's costume, although his heart is breaking ('Vesti la giubba').

Act II: After a brief prelude (originally intended as an intermezzo), the audience gathers for the performance. First Harlequin (Beppe) serenades his beloved Colombine (Nedda). Next, with heavy irony Taddeo (Tonio) declares his love for the 'pure' Colombine, but Harlequin arrives and leads him off by the ear. He returns to enjoy a festive supper with Colombine, but soon they are interrupted by Taddeo's announcement that her husband Pagliaccio (Canio) is approaching. Harlequin leaves by the window, but Pagliaccio enters in time to hear Nedda repeating the same promise of an assignation that he heard her use in Act I. With difficulty Canio tries to sustain his comic role, but when Colombine refuses to divulge her lover's name, he can no longer control himself ('No, Pagliaccio non son!'). When Nedda continues to defy him, he stabs her in reality, and with her last breath she utters Silvio's name. Silvio, who has been in the audience, rushes to the stage, but, too late to save Nedda, he becomes Canio's second victim. Hoarsely, Canio announces 'La commedia è finita!' (Originally this line was intended for Tonio, but at least since the time of De Lucia and Caruso it has usually been spoken by the tenor.)

The score contains a wide variety of music, from Tonio's melodic prologue (which is in effect the mid-section of the Act I prelude), to Nedda's languorous 'ballatella' 'Stridono lassù' (Act I) and her sensuous duet with Silvio, to Canio's two impassioned arias: 'Vesti la giubba' and 'No, Pagliaccio non son!' The dainty music of the harlequinade (the play within the play in Act II) adds a further fillip to the score, which also manifests traces of Leoncavallo's affection for Wagner in the form of a number of symbolic recurring themes. Although each act is cast as a continuous musical entity, the solos and duets usually end in full cadences, allowing for the applause that Leoncavallo knew was a vital ingredient to a success.

RECORDINGS 1. Carlyle, Bergonzi, Taddei, La Scala Ch & O, Karajan, DG, 1965; 2. Caballé, Domingo, Milnes, John Alldis Ch, LSO, Santi, RCA, 1972; 3. Frittoli, Cura, Alvarez, Keenlyside, Netherlands RCh, Concertgebouw O, Chailly, Decca, 1999

OTHER OPERATIC WORKS Operas: *Chatterton*, (1876), rev. 1896, 2nd rev. 1905; *Songe d'un nuit d'été*, 1889 (private performance); *I Medici* (inc.), (*c.*1877–92), 1893; *La bohème*, 1897; *Zazà*, 1900; *Der Roland von Berlin*, 1904; *Maia*, (1908), 1910; *Gli zingari*, 1912; *Ave Maria* (abandoned 1915); *Edipo re*, 1920; *Tormenta* (inc.); *Prometeo*, (n.d.); Operettas: *La jeunesse de Figaro*, 1906; *Malbrouck*, 1910; *La reginetta della rose*,

1912; *Are You There?*, 1913; *La candidata*, 1915; *Prestami tua moglie*, 1916; *Goffredo Mameli*, 1916; *A chi la giarrettiera?*, 1919; *Il primo bacio*, 1923; *La maschera nuda* (inc.; completed S. Allegra), 1925

W.A.

György Ligeti

György Sándor Ligeti; *b* 28 May 1923, Diciosânmartin [or Dicsöszentmárton], Transylvania (now Tirnaveni, Romania)

Ligeti came late not only to opera but also to the music he really wanted to write. He began his musical life in Hungary where the political climate did not allow experiment. In 1956 he moved to Vienna and quickly became involved with western Europe's most avant-garde circles, writing electronic music at the WDR studios in Cologne and producing in the 1960s a stream of works very different from the total serialism then in vogue. With the orchestral piece *Atmosphères* (1961) and the organ composition *Volumina* (1961–2, rev. 1966) Ligeti created huge swirling clouds of sound by writing an immensely complex web of closely packed polyphony. He went on to explore this further in his celebrated *Requiem* (1963–5, used in the soundtrack of the film *2001: A Space Odyssey*), *Lontano* (1967, for orchestra), *Melodien* (1971, for chamber orchestra) and the Concerto for flute, oboe and orchestra (1972).

His operatic music belongs to a different line of thinking, a joking, perhaps cynical view of the world that produced the *Poème symphonique* (1962) for 100 metronomes set at different tempi, which lasts as long as it takes for them all to run down, *Continuum* for harpsichord (1968), where different metres are superimposed so that the music is in a perpetual rhythmic and colouristic flux determined by pitch changes, and *Clocks and Clouds* for female chorus and orchestra (1972–3), where the sound of metronomes becomes gradually less distinct.

The two dramatic entertainments from the early 1960s, *Aventures* and *Nouvelles aventures*, are like late manifestations of Dadaism, for though the texts are meaningless phonetics, when allied to the music they make a disconcerting blend of the playful and the menacing. After their success Ligeti wanted to write a larger-scale 'imaginary opera' to a meaningless text, but neither that idea nor his next operatic project, a version of the Oedipus myth, came to anything, though they amalgamated to some extent in the opera he did eventually write, *Le grand macabre*, a surrealist opera about death, conceived as a farce.

In the five years after the completion of *Le grand macabre* Ligeti wrote virtually nothing, and the works that finally emerged after that creative silence, from the *Horn Trio* (1982) and the series of piano *Etudes* (1985 onwards), signalled a radical change of direction. Formally and stylistically the music looked backwards, though as ever with Ligeti the past has been revisited from a highly personal perspective, and incorporates elements from musics outside the Western tradition. Whether or not, though, he will ever complete a long-planned second opera, originally intended to be based upon Shakespeare's *The Tempest*, but then transformed into a 'revue or musical' based upon Lewis Carroll's Alice books, remains to be seen.

Le grand macabre

Opera in two acts (original version); opera in four scenes (revised version) (2h)
Libretto by the composer and Michael K. J. A. Meschke, freely adapted from the farce *La balade du grand macabre* by Michel de Ghelderode (1934)
Composed 1972–7, revised 1996
PREMIERES first version: 12 April 1978, Royal Opera, Stockholm; UK: 2 December 1982, Coliseum, London; revised

version: 28 July 1997, Grosses Festspielhaus, Salzburg
CAST Piet the Pot *high buffo t*, Clitoria (rev. Amanda) *s*, Spermando (rev. Amando) *ms*, Nekrotzar *bar*, Astradamors *b*, Mescalina *dramatic ms*, Venus *high s*, White Minister *spoken role* (rev. *buffo t*), Black Minister *spoken role* (rev. *buffo bar*), Prince Go-Go *ct*, Chief of the Secret Police (rev. Gepopo) *coloratura s*, Ruffiak, Schobiak and Schabernak 3 *bar*; *satb* chorus of people of Breughelland; offstage *satb* chorus of the spirits; echo of Venus *sa* chorus; boys' chorus (omitted in rev. version); extras: men of the secret police, executioners, pages and servants at the court of Prince Go-Go, Nekrotzar's infernal entourage

The opera was commissioned by the Stockholm Royal Opera in 1965 but took 13 years to be written and reach the stage. It was an immediate success and was quickly taken up by European opera houses. The plot is surreal, though its essence is that the only certainty of life is that it will end in death, and one might as well eat, drink and be merry. The setting is also surreal: a place ruled over by an obese boy prince and populated by, among others, a transvestite visionary astronomer with a sadistic and sexually enterprising wife and a chief of police who is a manic coloratura soprano. It is called Breughelland, but it could perhaps be reality.

SYNOPSIS (REV. VERSION)
Scene 1: After a palindromic prelude for car horns, one of the citizens of Breughelland, the alcoholic Piet the Pot, sings the praises of his homeland while Amanda and Amando look for somewhere to make love; a mysterious figure, Nekrotzar, the figure of death (the *grand macabre* himself), announces that the end of the world will occur at midnight. He forces Piet to help him in his task of world destruction.

Scene 2: The astronomer Astradamors has to feign death to escape his appalling wife Mescalina's voracious and painfully unorthodox sexual appetites; she revives him by dropping a spider on him. Through his telescope he sees a fast-approaching comet and other signs of Armageddon, while his wife, in a drunken stupor, implores Venus to send her a man who will satisfy her desires. Nekrotzar is the man, and while Piet and her husband look on Mescalina dies in ecstasy. A satisfied Nekrotzar takes Piet off to destroy the palace, leaving a happy Astramadors.

Scene 3: The boy prince tries to chair a meeting between his two ministers, but the absurdities of politics are beyond him so they play schoolboy games, understood by everyone, until the secret police burst in. They are all dressed as birds and their leader Gepopo is a dazzling coloratura soprano. She tells the prince that the people are in revolt and are marching on the palace. He pacifies the people but they are all thrown into a panic when Nekrotzar threatens impending doom. Though drunk, before he passes out he utters the words that will bring the world to an end.

Scene 4: No one is really sure whether the end of the world has actually happened. Nekrotzar seems to think it has not, or if it has there are too many survivors. He tries to escape but is chased by the voracious Mescalina who remembers him well. He realizes his mission is a failure and dissolves. The two lovers emerge from their love nest, oblivious of the great events that have passed. Everyone realizes the moral: if death is coming for you, you cannot escape it, so do not fear it, ignore it.

The music is more in the quick-cutting comic style of *Aventures* than the almost static cloudlike sound of works such as *Lontano*. There are many direct references to other works as well as a feeling that the frequently tongue-in-cheek characterization is rooted in the past. The music of the two lovers, Amanda and Amando, has a Monteverdian richness as entwined as their bodies and the opera ends with a baroque conceit, a grand passacaglia. Nekrotzar's entrance in Act II is preceded by the opera's most obvious quotation and transformation, the 'Prometheus' theme from the finale of Beethoven's 'Eroica' Symphony.

In 1996 Ligeti extensively revised the score. The orchestration was generally lightened, and many instrumental doublings removed, while much of the spoken dialogue in the original was cut and other passages recomposed as recitative. The division into two acts was abandoned, so that the work now plays continuously, while the proportioning of a number of sections was changed. The result, Ligeti wrote, was that 'the piece in its entirety now corresponds much more to an opera than to a singspiel'.

RECORDINGS 1. (original version) Walmsley-Clark, Fredricks, Smith, Haage, Weller, Austrian RCh & SO, Howarth, Wergo, 1987 (live); 2. (2nd version) Claycomb, Hellekant, Ragin, Clark, White, London Sinfonietta Voices, Philharmonia O, Salonen, Sony, 1998 (live)

OTHER OPERATIC WORK *Aventures/ Nouvelles aventures*, 1966

C.B.

M

Bohuslav Martinů

Bohuslav Jan Martinů; *b* 8 December 1890, Polička; *d* 28 August 1959, Liestal, Switzerland

After Janáček, Martinů is the major representative of 20th-century Czech opera. Despite maintaining strong links with his homeland, most of Martinů's creative life (1923–59) was spent away from his native Czechoslovakia. Following three desultory years (1907–10) at the Prague Conservatory, from which he was expelled, Martinů made a career as a teacher and as a violinist with the Czech Philharmonic Orchestra, graduating from sporadic appearances (from 1913) to a post as second violinist (1920–23). After a brief period of study with Josef Suk at the Prague Conservatory, Martinů was awarded a Czech government scholarship from October 1923 to study with Roussel in Paris, which he had visited on a Czech Philharmonic tour in 1919; he remained there for the next 17 years, marrying his French wife Charlotte Quennehen in 1931. In 1940, having been blacklisted by the Nazis, Martinů left Paris for the south of France and in 1941 fled with Charlotte to the United States, where he stayed, apart from long summer holidays in Europe, until 1953.

After the war Martinů planned to return to Czechoslovakia, but a serious fall in 1946 and the communist take-over in 1948 deterred him. Although the music of his last years was deeply affected by his native land, Martinů's style – characterized by springy, syncopated melodies, motor rhythms, warm, predominantly diatonic melodies often allied to clear symphonic impetus – proved both durable and distinctive. Early encounters with the music of Debussy and the English madrigal led to a fascination with French-tinted harmony and complex counterpoint. Jazz and Stravinsky were important to Martinů in the 1920s, overlaid with the influence of Bach and the baroque concerto grosso in the 1930s; although by this time his style was fully formed, he remained open to influences as varied as Notre Dame polyphony, Haydn and Monteverdi.

Music for the theatre occupied Martinů almost throughout his career, some of his earliest works being ballets. Of his 14 completed operas (*Le jour de bonté*, 1930, and *Plainte contre inconnu*, 1953, are substantial torsos), six, including his first, were full length (*The Soldier and the Dancer*, *The Three Wishes*, *The Plays of Mary*, *Julietta*, *Mirandolina* and *The Greek Passion*). Martinů set his face against Wagnerian music drama and the nationalist subject matter of his Czech predecessors, favouring variety and experiment deriving from his fascination with literature and theatre. His experimental work encompasses contemporary incident, Latin comedy and improvisation in *The Soldier and the Dancer*, jazz and surrealism in *Les larmes du couteau*, film in *The Three Wishes*, medieval mystery plays in *The Plays of Mary*, commedia dell'arte in *The Suburban Theatre* and *Mirandolina*, and neoclassicism in *Alexandre bis* and *Ariadne*. Martinů was also a pioneer of opera for radio (*The Voice of the Forest* and, his most frequently performed opera, *Comedy on a Bridge*) and television (*What Men Live By* and *The Wedding*). The more elusive background to the surreal *Julietta* and the political realism of *The Greek Passion* have not prevented these two works from becoming Martinů's most widely performed full-length operas.

Julietta: or The Book of Dreams

Julietta: Snář

Lyric opera in three acts (2h 15m)
Libretto by the composer, after the play *Juliette, ou La clé des songes* by Georges Neveux (1930)
Composed 1936–7
PREMIERES 16 March 1938, National Theatre, Prague: UK: 5 April 1978, Coliseum, London
CAST Julietta *s*, Michel *t*, Man in helmet *bar*, Man at window *b*, Old Arab *b*, 19(9) other minor roles (maximum number given first, minimum in brackets), 2(1) *s*, 5(2) *ms*, 5(2) *t*, 2(1) *bar*, 5(3) *b*; 6 townsfolk/3 gentlemen, *women's voices*

According to Miloš Šafránek, Martinů saw Neveux's surrealist play *Juliette* in 1932. Martinů wrote the libretto himself with the author's permission, deeply impressing Neveux with his understanding of the work's effect on stage. The subject was a radical departure from Martinů's previous operas and remained a favourite with the composer. In his introduction to the published vocal score Martinů said of *Julietta*: 'The libretto and play are not a philosophical dissertation, but an extraordinarily beautiful and poetic fantasy in the form of a dream.' Martinů responded well to the sharply observed wit and fantasy of his own libretto in what may be described as his operatic masterpiece. The plot, which Martinů himself found difficult to relate, is built up of many apparently disjointed episodes.

SYNOPSIS

Act I: Michel, a travelling bookseller from Paris, has returned to a small harbour town to find a girl, Julietta, whose voice has haunted his memory since a previous visit. The strange behaviour of the inhabitants of the town is explained by their lack of memory: they live in a continuous present seeking to acquire the reminiscences of others for themselves. Michel, with his memory, is understandably, if inevitably somewhat sporadically, an object of fascination. Eventually he finds Julietta. Although it is not clear that she remembers him he is greeted as a lost lover, and the act ends with her asking him to meet her in a wood.

Act II: A series of surreal incidents forms a prelude to the meeting of Julietta and Michel. Michel's memories, feeding Julietta's fantasies, form the basis of the exchange. When she eventually runs away from him he shoots at her, but it is not clear whether the shot has hit her. The act concludes when Michel, uncertain why he came to the town, is preparing to leave by boat when he hears Julietta's voice again.

Act III: In the Central Office of Dreams many come to experience dreams. Michel, wanting to return to his, hears Julietta calling. As the office closes, Michel rushes back into his dream to find himself once again in the harbour town as at the start of the opera.

Julietta is characterized by subtle orchestral colouring and an acute command of situation. In an opera where large numbers of brief stage appearances form the substance of the action, the composer provides highly effective character studies. Julietta herself, by emerging forcefully as a heroine, does not threaten the dreamlike qualities of the whole. Her exchanges with Michel in Act II are a virtuoso mixture of aspiring lyricism and ironic bathos. Throughout, Martinů preserves the fantasy atmosphere of Neveux's original although, as he was to recognize in a production at Wiesbaden in 1959, the opera maintains dramatic tension and explores disturbing psychological depths.

RECORDING Tauberová, Žídek, Otava, Kalaš, Prague NT Ch & O, Krombholc, Supraphon, 1964

The Greek Passion

Řecké pašije

Opera in four acts: first version (1h); second version (1h 45m)
Libretto by the composer after the novel *Christ Recrucified* by Nikos Kazantzakis (1948), trans. Jonathan Griffin
Composed 1954–7; second version 1957–9
PREMIERES first version: 20 July 1999, Festspielhaus, Bregenz; UK: 25 April 2000, Covent Garden, London; second version: 9 June 1961, Opernhaus, Zurich; UK: 29 April 1981, New Theatre, Cardiff
CAST (second version) Manolios *t*, Katerina *s*, Grigoris *b-bar*, Fotis *b-bar*, Kostandis *bar*, Yannakos *t*, Lenio *s*, Panait *t*, 8 minor roles (3 *s*, *c*, 2 *t*, *bar*, *b*), Ladas *spoken role*; *satb* chorus of villagers and refugees; children's chorus; original version additional cast: Captain/Aga *b*, Dimitri *bar*, Schoolmaster *t*

By 1954 Martinů was looking for a libretto with a Czech subject. He was diverted, however, by his discovery of Nikos Kazantzakis's novel, *Zorba the Greek*. *Zorba* proved impractical and Martinů began a libretto on Kazantzakis's novel, *Christ Recrucified*, retitling it *The Greek Passion*. The first version, intended for Kubelik at Covent Garden, was complete by 1957 but rejected by the Opera House authorities. A much-revised second version, intended for the Zurich Festival, was composed between 1957 and 1959. The material of the first version was dispersed and its true nature remained obscure until Aleš Březina reconstructed it for the Bregenz Festival of 1999. Despite the Greek setting, the musical language is close to the Czech cantatas of the composer's late years.

SYNOPSIS (SECOND VERSION)
Act I: A Greek village, Lykovrissi, in the early 20th century. On Easter morning the priest, Grigoris, distributes parts for next year's Passion play. Katerina, a young widow, is chosen as Mary Magdalene, Manolios, a shepherd, as Christ, and Panait, Katerina's lover, as Judas. As the characters dwell on the significance of their roles night falls and a band of refugees, driven from their homes by Turks, arrives exhausted in the village. Grigoris, suspecting conflict and impoverishment for Lykovrissi, orders them to leave. The act ends with Katerina offering help and Manolios suggesting that the refugees settle near by.

Act II: It becomes clear that Katerina is obsessed with Manolios. The miser Ladas persuades the pedlar Yannakos, who is to play the apostle Peter, to offer money for the valuables of the needy refugees. Witnessing the simple dignity and hope of the refugees, Yannokos is ashamed of his attempt to cheat them and presents them instead with Ladas's money.

Act III: Manolios's and Katerina's relationship comes to a head when he persuades her that their love can be only spiritual. She learns to accept the fulfilment of the love of Mary Magdalene for Christ. Manolios, becoming still more Christ-like, persuades the villagers to help the refugees as the village elders plot to prevent him.

Act IV: As the villagers celebrate a wedding, Grigorios excommunicates Manolios and denounces him. After explaining his actions as the substitute of Christ, Manolios is killed by Panait as the refugees approach. Both parties mourn the death of Manolios and the refugees prepare to leave the village.

Although built as a series of tableaux, the second version of *The Greek Passion* has a powerful sense of dramatic continuity. The characters grow at the same pace as the Passion tragedy, leading to a denouement of extraordinary power. Much of the force of the work in the outer acts is generated by the use of the chorus. The musical language, shaded by the use of Greek Orthodox chant and the gentle lyricism associated with Martinů's last decade, is warmly diatonic. The first version of the opera is broader in design, makes more reference to the Turkish elements in Kazantzakis's novel, and in many places is both more consciously dramatic and experimental, particularly in the use of speech, than the second version; the main difference in plot is that Act IV concludes at Christmas many months after the murder of Manolios – as the villagers celebrate the festival in comfort, the refugees go in search of a new home.

RECORDINGS first version: Stemme, Ventris, Daszak, Ruuttunen, Moscow CCh, Bregenz Children's Ch, Vienna SO, Schirmer, Koch Classics, 1999 (live); second version: Field, Mitchinson, Davies, Tomlinson, Czech PCh, Kühn Children's Ch, Brno State PO, Mackerras, Supraphon, 1981
OTHER OPERAS *The Soldier and the Dancer* (*Voják a tanečnice*), 1928; *Les larmes du couteau* (*Slzy nože*), (1928), 1969; *Trois souhaits, ou Les vicissitudes de la vie* (*Trojí přání, aneb vrtkavosti života*), (1929), 1971 (film opera); *The Plays of Mary* (*Hry o Marii*), 1935; *La jour de bonté*, 1930 (inc.); *The Voice of the Forest* (*Hlas lesa*), 1935; *The Suburban Theatre* (*Divadlo za branou*), 1936; *Comedy on a Bridge* (*Veselohra na mostě*), 1937 (radio opera); *Alexandre bis* (*Dvakrát Alexandr*), (1937), 1964; *What Men Live By* (*Čím lidé žijí*), 1953 (TV opera); *The Marriage* (*Ženitba*), 1953 (TV opera); *Plainte contre inconnu*, 1953; *Mirandolina*, (1954), 1959; *Ariadne* (*Ariane/Ariadna*), (1958), 1961

J.A.S.

Pietro Mascagni

b 7 December 1863, Livorno, Italy;
d 2 August 1945, Rome

Although younger than his contemporaries Puccini and Leoncavallo, Mascagni was the first to taste triumph, and fame came to him in an unlikely way. Against family opposition (his father wanted him to continue the family bakery business), he was determined to follow a musical career, and at the age of 19 was admitted to the Milan Conservatory to study composition, where his teachers included Ponchielli. Dismissed during his second year for his failure to complete assignments, he supported himself by playing the double-bass at the Teatro Dal Verme in Milan (where he played in the premiere of Puccini's *Le villi*) and conducting opera at Cremona. Unable to interest a publisher in his attempts at writing for the stage, he settled down in Cerignola (Puglia) to give music lessons. In 1889 he saw an advertisement for Sonzogno's second competition for one-act operas. He was fired with enthusiasm and quickly wrote *Cavalleria rusticana*. Once it was completed, however, he was besieged with doubts and had all but decided to submit Act IV of his *Guglielmo Ratcliff* instead. But unbeknown to him, his wife dispatched the score of *Cavalleria rusticana* and it was awarded the first prize.

Together with the other two winning works, *Cavalleria rusticana* was performed at the Teatro Costanzi in Rome in May 1890. Mascagni was fortunate to have in the cast two of the most popular singers in Italy: the tenor Stagno and his fiery wife Gemma Bellincioni. *Cavalleria* scored an immediate success, and amazingly soon it was heard in theatres all over the world.

Mascagni was instantly famous and was soon acknowledged the harbinger of the group that came to be known as the *veristi* or the 'Young Italian School' (among its leaders would be Leoncavallo, Puccini, Giordano and Cilea).

Predictably, anticipation was great for his next work, but instead of trying to emulate *Cavalleria*, he brought out a naïve idyll set in Alsace, *L'amico Fritz* (1891). In no way an outright failure, this work puzzled and disappointed those who expected Mascagni to exploit the vein of *Cavalleria*.

A string of operas followed over the next decade, ranging in subject from a maritime drama (*Silvano*) to the Japanese *Iris*. But a repeat of the success of *Cavalleria* eluded him, and, restlessly seeking to prove himself as something more than a one-opera composer and to avoid the generally unfavourable attitude of Italian critics, Mascagni decided to give the premieres of his next two operas outside his native country. *Amica*, to a French text by de Choudens, was premiered at Monte Carlo in 1905 but failed to sustain itself. Better fortune greeted *Isabeau* (Buenos Aires, 1911), a sensational variant of the Godiva story, although its success, too, was short-lived. With *Parisina* (1913) Mascagni attempted another premiere in Italy, but, yet again, neither this long-winded score nor that of the sentimental *Lodoletta* (1917) exerted much appeal. The closest Mascagni came to a major success in the later part of his career was *Il piccolo Marat*, based on a French Revolutionary subject, though the opera still failed to enter the repertoire.

In 1929, however, Mascagni's opportunistic nature was confirmed when he succeeded Toscanini as musical director of La Scala, as he had no scruples against beginning performances with the fascist hymn. In 1932 he reworked the score of an early cantata and brought out *Pinotta* in the unlikely precincts of the San Remo Casino. His last opera, *Nerone*, was introduced at La Scala in 1935 with much preliminary hullabaloo. After the obligatory first round of productions on Italian stages, it started to gather dust, which has scarcely been disturbed since. At Venice, Rome and Milan in 1940, on the occasion of the 50th anniversary of *Cavalleria*, Mascagni conducted his chief claim to fame, filling out the evening with excerpts from its less fortunate sisters. Mascagni did not long survive the collapse of fascism, dying in an obscure Roman hotel.

It is all too easy to dismiss Mascagni as a self-promoting opportunist and a composer of limited achievements. But there is not a score of his that is without some arresting moments, although his creative impetus was short-breathed and lacked continuity. He too readily mistook emotion for the expression of deep feeling. Yet his experiments in setting text and his choice of subjects reveal his responsiveness to the temper of his times. *Cavalleria* will remain his monument, a symbol of his accomplishment as well as his limitations.

Cavalleria rusticana

Rustic Chivalry

Melodrama in one act (1h 15m)
Libretto by Giovanni Targioni-Tozzetti and Guido Menasci, after the play by Giovanni Verga (1883)
Composed 1889
PREMIERES 17 May 1890, Teatro Costanzi, Rome; US: 9 September 1891, Academy of Music, Philadelphia; UK: 19 October 1891, Shaftesbury Theatre, London
CAST Santuzza *s* or *ms*, Lola *ms*, Mamma Lucia *c*, Turiddu *t*, Alfio *bar*; *satb* chorus of villagers

The rapidity with which *Cavalleria rusticana* spread throughout the world has been unmatched by any other opera. Within the space of little more than a year it had promulgated operatic verismo and soon spawned a host of imitations, of which only Leoncavallo's *Pagliacci* firmly established itself in the repertoire, supplying the other member of the most performed double-bill of modern times. The idea of writing an opera on Verga's dramatization of his novella was Mascagni's, and he persuaded two of his friends to provide him with the libretto. In terms of influence, the opera's chief significance lies in the fact that it presents ordinary people in credible situations and thus seems to tell a story sufficiently realistic and simple to be true to life.

SYNOPSIS

Some time before Turiddu went off to serve in the army, he had had an affair with Lola. While he was away, Lola married the carter Alfio. On his return Turiddu seduced Santuzza, who is now pregnant by him and has been excommunicated because of her condition. She loves him sincerely, but to her chagrin Lola could not endure seeing him with another and has resumed her affair with the inconstant Turiddu.

Easter morning in a village in Sicily. Before the curtain rises, Turiddu is heard singing a siciliana ('O, Lola') to his mistress (this forms the final part of the opera's prelude). The villagers comment on the season ('Gli aranci alezzano'). Alfio enters ('Il cavallo scalpita') and soon asks Turiddu's mother Lucia about her son's whereabouts. Lucia says he has gone to Francofonte to fetch some wine for the family inn. When Alfio says he has seen Turiddu near his house, Santuzza hurriedly tells Lucia to keep silent. Further conversation is halted by the Easter Hymn ('Inneggiamo il Signore; non è morto'). When all but Santuzza and Lucia have entered the church, the young woman pours out her heart to Lucia, telling her how Lola has stolen Turiddu and left her desperate. Lucia goes into the church, leaving Santuzza to wait for Turiddu. He soon appears and she implores him to come back to her, informing him that he has been seen at dawn near Lola's house ('Tu qui, Santuzza?'). Turiddu accuses her of jealousy, but then they are interrupted by Lola on her way to church ('Fior di giaggiolo'). After an exchange of barbed remarks between the women, Lola goes to attend the service. Ever more desperately, Santuzza begs him to return her love, but he rejects her forcibly, throwing her down and running into the church. Now blinded by jealous fury, she sees Alfio and pours out her story of Lola's infidelity ('Oh! Il Signor vi manda, compar Alfio'), while Alfio vows vengeance. After the intermezzo, the congregation throngs out and Turiddu urges them to have a post-ecclesiastical tipple ('Viva il vino spumeggiante'). When Alfio appears, Turiddu offers him a glass of wine, but Alfio refuses, saying it would turn to poison inside him. The villagers draw Lola away. Alfio, in the way of the traditional challenge, bites Turiddu's earlobe. Before they go off to duel behind the church, Turiddu takes leave of his mother, asking that she look out for Santuzza ('Mamma, quel vino è generoso'). The women gather in the piazza, and suddenly a female voice is heard screaming that Turiddu has been killed. Santuzza and Lucia faint.

This concise, passionate tale of Sicilian peasants, ironically occurring on Easter Sunday, elicited from Mascagni crude but effective music that seemed the inevitable mode of expression for his characters. The score, except for Turridu's serenade in the prologue, begins conventionally enough with an opening chorus and a 'characteristic' song for Alfio, soon followed by the Gounod-esque Easter Hymn. It is only with Santuzza's arioso, 'Voi lo sapete, o mamma', that the dramatic temperature begins to rise, reaching a climax with the Santuzza–Alfio duet. The tragic outcome is assured at this point, but then comes the contrast of the serene intermezzo played to an empty stage. This calm before the inevitable storm serves, oddly enough, only to increase the tension.

RECORDINGS 1. Callas, di Stefano, Panerai, La Scala Ch & O, Serafin, EMI, 1953; 2. Varady, Pavarotti, Cappuccilli, London Voices, Nat PO, Gavazzeni, Decca, 1976; 3. Scotto, Domingo, Elvira, Ambrosian Op Ch, Nat PO, Levine, RCA, 1978

OTHER OPERATIC WORKS Operas: *Pinotta* (adapted from the cantata *In* *filanda*), (*c*.1880), 1932; *I Rantzau*, 1892; *L'amico Fritz*, 1891; *Guglielmo Ratcliff*, 1895; *Silvano*, 1895; *Zanetto*, 1896; *Iris*, 1898; *Le maschere*, 1901; *Amica*, 1905; *Isabeau*, 1911; *Parisina*, 1913; *Lodoletta*, 1917; *Il piccolo Marat*, 1921; *Nerone*, 1935; Operetta: *Sì*, 1919

W.A.

Jules Massenet

Jules-Emile-Frédéric Massenet; *b* 12 May 1842, Montaud, nr St Etienne, France; *d* 13 August 1912, Paris

Massenet was one of the most successful of all French opera composers, for although his work never equalled the grandeur of Berlioz's *Les Troyens*, the genius of Bizet's *Carmen* or the profundity of Debussy's *Pelléas et Mélisande*, he provided the French operatic stage between 1867 and his death in 1912 with a series of remarkable works of great variety and invention. Two of them, *Manon* and *Werther*, are masterpieces that will always grace the repertoire, and a considerable number of others offer rewarding operatic experience in terms of vocal and orchestral technique, scenic invention, comedy, pathos, sentiment, local colour and so on. He was a thoroughly professional composer who perfected his craft at an early age and enjoyed the fruits of success. His works fell victim, for the most part, to the very different tastes of the post-1918 generation, and some have not been revived. But he embodies many enduring aspects of the *belle époque*, one of the richest eras of French cultural history.

Massenet was trained at the Paris Conservatoire, and he won the Prix de Rome in 1863. He was influenced by Meyerbeer, Berlioz, Gounod and his teacher, Thomas. He was a timpanist at the Théâtre-Lyrique for a spell, learning the craft of orchestration from the experience. His grounding in opera came less from his first two operas (both opéras comiques), *La grand' tante* (1867) and *Don César de Bazan* (1872), than from the 'sacred dramas' *Marie-Magdeleine* (1873) and *Eve* (1875), in which human passion is set against a background of religious fervour, a dramatic contrast that was to inform some of his most successful operas, notably *Hérodiade*, *Thaïs* and *Le jongleur de Notre-Dame*. In the field of grand opera with epic scenic effects and abundant local colour, he maintained a long French tradition, although none of the operas of that type (*Le roi de Lahore*, *Hérodiade*, *Le Cid*, *Le mage*, *Ariane*) was able to equal his intimate tragedies (*Manon*, *Werther*), his veristic dramas (*La navarraise*, *Thérèse*) or his comedies (*Cendrillon*, *Don Quichotte*). The variety of his work is indeed astonishing since there is no ready category for a magical opera such as *Esclarmonde*, nor for the unusual blend of sex and religion found in *Thaïs*, nor for the monastic mystery *Le jongleur de Notre-Dame*.

Massenet was strictly regular in his working habits, a characteristic of many highly productive composers, and he usually composed with great speed, keeping revision to a minimum. He would sometimes have a vocal score printed before a work went into rehearsal. Many of his full scores are annotated with great precision concerning dates and locations. He worked with a variety of librettists, although the obliging Henri Cain was a regular partner. He liked to find unusual settings for his operas, ranging from Classical mythology to the contemporary, and his fondness for the 18th century is manifest. He relished providing special music, such as ballets or set-piece songs within the drama, or 'symphonies' to suggest dramatic action. He had a rare understanding of the human voice and worked enthusiastically for certain singers, usually sopranos with whom gossip was wont to link his name. For Sybil Sanderson, for instance, he felt a particular tenderness and wrote some remarkable roles, notably Esclarmonde and Thaïs; for Georgette Wallace (whose stage name was Lucy Arbell) he similarly composed with great sympathy; her chief roles were Ariane, Thérèse and Dulcinée. He always notated vocal parts with extreme precision, a practice he may have learned from studying Verdi's scores.

His affection for his leading ladies has led many to suppose that Massenet depicted only his female characters with real understanding, but this notion is easily refuted. The role of Athanaël in *Thaïs* is hard to project convincingly, but there is no mistaking the depth of Des Grieux's agony in *Manon*, or of Werther's, or of Jean's in *Sapho*. *Le jongleur de Notre-Dame* offers a rich variety of male types, and both Don Quichotte and Sancho Panza evoke the audience's sympathy with a few deft strokes.

Massenet's fondness for religious scenes was derived not from faith but simply from an acute sense of the dramatic in religious ritual and devotions, a striking feature of Catholicism. He loved the 18th-century style, using Handelian mannerisms freely, often for minor characters of the buffo type. He could equally call on medieval pastiche when required. He liked to evoke the world of magic in the manner of Rimsky-Korsakov, or the world of children, as he does in both *Werther* and *Cendrillon*. He could slip easily from tragedy to sentiment to high comedy. His sense of theatrical timing is hard to fault, an operatic instinct he shared with Verdi and Puccini. His structural skill is best observed in the way single scenes are constructed, using tonality and motifs – both vocal and orchestral – to build movements of rounded musical shape and appropriate dramatic pace.

While he aroused the envy of other composers who lacked his success (Saint-Saëns) or his fertility (Debussy), Massenet enjoyed popular acclaim in France and abroad. As a teacher he had a considerable influence on the younger generation, especially on Alfred Bruneau, Charpentier and Florent Schmitt, all of them sharply individual in their approach to opera. His best work was written in the last two decades of the 19th century, and although some of his later operas maintained this high level, the lack of any modernity began to disappoint audiences seduced by the shock of Richard Strauss, Paul Dukas and Schmitt, or by the mysterious murmurings of Debussy. His main works survived in the repertoire, though, and will continue to do so as long as great singing and high operatic craft are held in esteem.

Manon

Opéra comique in five acts (six tableaux) (2h 30m)
Libretto by Henri Meilhac and Philippe Gille, after the novel *Manon Lescaut* by the Abbé Prévost (1731)
Composed May–October 1882, orch. March–August 1883; last scene rev., gavotte inserted in Cours-la-Reine scene, 1884; *fabliau* replaced Act III gavotte (this rev. not generally used), 1898
PREMIERES 19 January 1884, Opéra-Comique, Paris; UK: 17 January 1885, Liverpool; US: 23 December 1885, Academy of Music, New York
CAST Manon Lescaut *s*, Le Chevalier Des Grieux *t*, Lescaut *bar*, Le Comte Des Grieux *b*, Guillot de Morfontaine *t*, De Brétigny *bar*, Poussette *s*, Javotte *s*, Rosette *ms*, innkeeper *b bouffe*, two guards *t*; *spoken roles*: maid, seminary porter, sergeant, constable, gambler; *satb* chorus of elegant society, citizens of Amiens and Paris, travellers, porters, postilions, merchants, churchgoers, gamblers, cardsharpers, croupiers

Manon is Massenet's most successful opera and, with *Faust* and *Carmen*, one of the mainstays of the French repertoire to this day. The Abbé Prévost's novel had been set as an opéra comique by Auber in 1856, but this had soon faded from the repertoire. The idea for *Manon* came to Massenet in a conversation with Henri Meilhac, who had written numerous libretti for Offenbach and others in collaboration with Ludovic Halévy, but who now collaborated with Philippe Gille, a journalist and dramatist. Despite the claim of Massenet's autobiography that the opera was begun in 1881, his correspondence shows that it was not composed until after *Hérodiade* had been performed. *Manon* was conceived as a quite different opera from his two preceding grandiose works. It was to be an opéra comique with some speech over music and a more continuous and integrated structure than usual. It called for some 18th-century pastiche and a more intimate manner.

It was completed in October 1882, some of it composed in The Hague, where Massenet occupied the Abbé Prévost's own rooms, at that time a hotel. Part of the gambling scene used music originally intended for *Hérodiade*. In February 1883 a contract was signed with the publisher Hartmann, and the orchestration of the work followed. At the premiere in January 1884 Talazac was Des Grieux and Marie Heilbronn was Manon, although Massenet had hoped to engage the very young Marguerite Vaillant-Couturier for the role. The conductor was Danbé. *Manon* remained a regular item of the Opéra-Comique's repertoire almost without interruption until 1959. It quickly conquered the world's stages. Ten years later Massenet followed up the story of Manon with *Le portrait de Manon*, by which time Puccini had set his version of the novel as *Manon Lescaut* (1893).

SYNOPSIS

Act I: The courtyard of a hostelry at Amiens, *c.*1720. De Brétigny, a *fermier-général*, and Guillot de Morfontaine, a financier, are calling noisily for food and drink. They are accompanied by three young ladies of doubtful virtue, Poussette, Javotte and Rosette. A bell rings, announcing the forthcoming arrival of the stagecoach from Arras. People crowd into the courtyard to inspect the new arrivals, among them Lescaut, awaiting his young cousin Manon who is on her way to a convent. Lescaut's interest, it is clear, is in drinking and gambling. Travellers arrive in some confusion, and Manon is greeted by Lescaut. She chatters eagerly about her first experience of travel ('Je suis encor tout étourdie'), then Lescaut goes in search of her luggage. Guillot appears, catches sight of Manon and makes immediate advances. Lescaut, returning, is offended. He sends Guillot away and gives Manon, who is fascinated by the sophisticated world she sees around her, a few timely words of warning about unwelcome strangers ('Regardez-moi bien dans les yeux'). Des Grieux appears. He has missed the coach, which was to take him to his father ('J'ai manqué l'heure du départ'). Entranced by Manon, he introduces himself. She is captivated too. After only a little hesitation she agrees to leave with Des Grieux, taking the coach which Guillot had arranged to abduct her in. Both Lescaut and Guillot are furious when they learn what has happened. Everyone else is amused.

Act II: In the apartment in the rue Vivienne, Paris, where he and Manon are now living, Des Grieux is writing to his father to explain their relationship and to sing Manon's praises ('On l'appelle Manon'). After a noisy disturbance offstage Lescaut comes in with De Brétigny, disguised as a guardsman. Des Grieux calms Lescaut by assuring him that he plans to marry Manon and shows him the letter to his father. Meanwhile De Brétigny is tempting Manon to abandon Des Grieux for a life of pleasure and riches, a temptation she cannot easily resist. While Des Grieux goes out to post the letter, she sings a farewell to their humble life together ('Adieu, notre petite table'). When he returns he tells her of a daydream he had in which all is paradise, except Manon is not there with him ('En fermant les yeux'). Suddenly a knock is heard. Manon, who knows that Des Grieux is to be abducted, fails to stop him answering the door, yet she is overcome by grief as he is taken away.

Act III, Scene 1: The Cours-la-Reine by

the Seine. There is much merry-making with merchants selling their wares and a crowd enjoying a public holiday. Lescaut is spending freely. Manon is arm in arm with De Brétigny, enjoying his attention and wealth. A gavotte is danced ('Profitons bien de la jeunesse'). Des Grieux's father, the count, tells De Brétigny that his son plans to take holy orders and is to preach that evening at St-Sulpice. Manon sends De Brétigny away on an errand and then questions the count about Des Grieux's feelings. Guillot lays on a divertissement, danced by a troupe from the Opéra, but Manon's thoughts are now elsewhere. Scene 2: The seminary at St-Sulpice. The service is over at which Des Grieux was preaching. His father congratulates him ('Epouse quelque brave fille'), but he is still full of bitterness. He is determined to take his vows. After the count has left, Des Grieux confesses the image of Manon still haunts him ('Ah! fuyez, douce image'). He goes into the church. When he comes back he finds Manon waiting for him. The reunion overcomes all their doubts and they run off together again.

Act IV: An illicit gaming room in the Hôtel de Transylvanie. Lescaut, Guillot and their friends are at the tables when Manon and Des Grieux enter. With Lescaut's support Manon urges an unwilling Des Grieux to try his luck. She is again dazzled by the glitter of money and the lure of laughter. Guillot loses to Des Grieux, exchanges some sharp words and goes off to fetch the count and the police. Lescaut escapes but Guillot has his revenge: Des Grieux and Manon are arrested, accused of cheating.

Act V: The road to Le Havre. Des Grieux has been freed but Manon is to be deported as a prostitute. Lescaut's plan to rescue her has failed. When the guards appear, Lescaut bribes the sergeant to let Manon stay behind for a while, under guard. He then bribes the guard too and leads him away. Des Grieux and Manon are now alone, but she is too weak to flee. She dies in Des Grieux's arms.

Manon brought out the best of Massenet's operatic genius. The score shows his great feeling for human passion and also his incomparable skill in scenic management. The principle of dramatic contrast is abundantly used: in the depiction of Manon's character, torn between her devotion to Des Grieux and her fatal weakness for a glittering social milieu; in the contrast between adjacent scenes (the solitude of their room in the rue Vivienne followed by the bustle of the Cours-la-Reine, the devotional atmosphere of St-Sulpice followed by the gaming tables of the Hôtel de Transylvanie); and in the contrast of musical styles between the elegant 18th-century pastiche in the Cours-la-Reine scene and the sweeping romantic phrases with which real passion is expressed. The use of speech over music is purposeful (although in a New York performance Massenet allowed these passages to be sung), and the choral scenes are invariably handled with great skill. The opera contains a well-developed set of leitmotifs, two for Lescaut, and one each for De Brétigny and Guillot, for example. Manon's earlier motifs pass out of sight as she grows up with great rapidity. Massenet also uses orchestral motifs to identify a scene – for example, the gambling motif in Act IV and the soldiers' motif in Act V.

Des Grieux's complex characterization explodes the belief that Massenet could portray only female characters with true feeling, and once Manon has been lured into the social world it is difficult ever quite to believe in her attachment to him as wholly as in his for her. Yet because Manon is the only female character (apart from the puppet-like trio of Poussette, Javotte and Rosette) against five males with various claims on her, she cannot fail to hold our attention when she is on stage. Her plight is no less touching because she appears at times both fickle and shallow. Massenet's sense of her impudence and gaiety makes this image of the eternal feminine perfectly sympathetic.

RECORDINGS 1. de los Angeles, Legay, Dens, Borthayre, Paris Op Comique Ch & O, Monteux, EMI, 1955; 2. Cotrubas, Kraus, G. Quilico, Van Dam, Toulouse Capitole Ch & O, Plasson, EMI, 1982; 3. Giorghiu, Panzarella, Alagna, Ragon, Van Dam, la Monnaie Ch & O, Pappano, EMI, 1999

Werther

Drame lyrique in four acts (five tableaux) (2h)
Libretto by Edouard Blau, Paul Milliet and Georges Hartmann, after *Die Leiden des jungen Werthers* by Johann von Goethe (1774)
Composed 1885–7, orch. March–July 1887
PREMIERES 16 February 1892, Hofoper, Vienna; France: 16 January 1893, Opéra-Comique, Paris; US: 29 February 1894, Chicago; UK: 11 June 1894, Covent Garden, London
CAST Werther *t*, Albert *bar*, Le Bailli *b*, Schmidt *t*, Johann *bar*, Charlotte *ms*, Sophie *s*, Bruhlmann *t*, Katchen *s*, 6 children 6 *s*

Werther may claim to be Massenet's masterpiece and, next to *Manon*, his best-known opera. In a letter of September 1880 Massenet spoke of his intention to follow *Hérodiade*, then just completed, with *Werther*. The idea had emerged from a conversation in Milan in 1879 with Hartmann, Massenet's publisher, and Milliet, librettist of *Hérodiade*. The plan was shelved in favour of *Manon* and then *Le Cid*, and Milliet's role as librettist was taken over by Edouard Blau (one of *Le Cid*'s librettists). *Werther* was eventually started in 1885, but evidently it did not go well. Hartmann, knowing Massenet's need for appropriate stimuli, acquired an 18th-century apartment in Versailles for him to work in, and then, on a trip to Bayreuth in August 1886, suggested that they visit Wetzlar, north of Frankfurt, where Goethe had conceived his *Werther*; a similar absorption of the Abbé Prévost's rooms in The Hague had assisted the composition of *Manon* three years earlier.

This visit, though not the original inspiration for *Werther*, as Massenet's autobiography claims, provided a tremendous spur to the completion of the opera. But it was turned down by the Opéra-Comique as too depressing. After that theatre's destruction by fire, its new management preferred the more glamorous *Esclarmonde*. Thus *Werther* did not appear in Paris until 1893; its premiere took place in Vienna in February 1892, following the great success there of *Manon* two years before.

It soon conquered every stage and has been a repertoire work ever since. Great interpreters have included, in the role of Werther, van Dijck (the role's creator), Beyle, de Reszke, Thill, Schipa, Tagliavini, Gedda, Vanzo, Kraus, Carreras and Domingo, and in the role of Charlotte, Farrar, Lehmann, Lubin, Crespin and von Stade.

SYNOPSIS
The action takes place near Frankfurt.

Act I: 'The Bailli's House', July. On the terrace of his house the Bailli, a magistrate, is rehearsing his six small children in a Christmas carol. A widower, he is cared for by his elder daughters, Charlotte (20) and Sophie (15). Johann and Schmidt, two of his friends, come in and discuss a ball to be given that evening in Wetzlar, the possibility that Werther (a melancholy young man of 23) may be sent away as an ambassador, and the imminent arrival of Charlotte's fiancé, Albert. They leave, and soon Werther appears, entranced by the beauty of nature and by the children's singing within the house ('O nature, pleine de grâce'). He watches as Charlotte comes out of the house and busies herself with the children. The Bailli greets Werther and introduces Charlotte. All, including a number of other guests, go off to the ball, leaving Sophie to care for the children. Albert then arrives, anxious to have news of Charlotte ('Quelle prière de reconnaissance'), and goes into the house. As darkness falls, Charlotte and Werther return, arm in arm. Werther becomes increasingly amorous until the Bailli's voice is heard telling Charlotte that Albert is back. When she tells Werther she is to marry Albert since her mother made her promise to, Werther, in despair, tells her to fulfil her promise.

Act II: 'The Lime Trees'. September. The church square at Wetzlar. Johann and Schmidt are drinking outside a tavern. Charlotte and Albert, now married, arrive for church, blessing their happiness. Werther appears, cursing the happiness he has missed ('Un autre son époux!'). When Albert comes out of the church, he offers Werther consolation for any regrets he may feel at their marriage and suggests Sophie as an alternative bride. Left alone, Werther realizes he has to leave, and when Charlotte emerges from the church she begs him to go, conceding that they may meet again at Christmas. After she has gone Werther thinks at once of suicide ('Lorsque l'enfant revient d'un voyage') and leaves, telling Sophie that he will not be back. Charlotte, hearing this from Sophie, is so clearly distraught that Albert realizes that Werther is in love with her.

Act III: 'Charlotte and Werther'. Christmas Eve, 5 o'clock. Albert's house. Charlotte confesses that her thoughts are all with Werther and that his letters stir her deeply ('Werther . . . Werther . . .'). Sophie attempts to cheer her up. Charlotte breaks into a passionate prayer for spiritual aid ('Va, laisse couler mes larmes'), then Werther appears at the door. Before long she finds herself in his arms. Overcome with guilt and remorse, she rushes from the room. Werther leaves. Albert enters, calling for Charlotte. She appears, obviously distraught. A servant brings a message for Albert from Werther: since he is leaving for a distant country, would Albert lend him his pistols? Albert orders Charlotte to fetch the pistols. As soon as Albert has gone, she rushes out, praying that she is not too late.

Act IV: The same evening. Scene 1: 'Christmas Night', an orchestral tableau leading directly into Scene 2: 'The Death of Werther', in Werther's study. Werther lies mortally wounded, the pistols at his side. Charlotte rushes in, finds him and attempts to revive him. She confesses she loves him, and they kiss for the first time. As Werther dies, he hears the children singing 'Noël' and imagines he hears angels promising forgiveness.

Goethe's novel was based on the story of a young lawyer, Karl Wilhelm Jerusalem, who shot himself in October 1772 because of his unhappy love for the wife of a diplomat. Jerusalem had borrowed pistols from a friend of Goethe's who gave a full account of Jerusalem's death, quoting the text of the note asking for the loan of the pistols. This note was copied by Goethe in his novel and by Massenet in his opera.

The libretto is necessarily a free adaptation of the novel, which consists simply of Werther's letters. Some of Werther's complex pantheistic personality is lost, whereas Charlotte is a more immediate and real figure. Sophie's role is almost entirely the invention of the librettists, and the final act, bringing Charlotte and Werther together for a final death scene, is their creation too; in the novel Werther dies alone. In Goethe, Werther's malaise may be seen as the hopeless dissatisfaction of a searching, Romantic melancholic, whereas Massenet's Werther is more narrowly the victim of an amorous passion that cannot be satisfied.

Charlotte in the opera presents a wonderfully touching portrait of a girl gradually moved to pull against her mother's wishes and the constraints of her marriage (in Goethe, Charlotte never returns Werther's love with the same ardour). Her solo scene at the beginning of Act III represents one of the greatest moments of self-discovery and self-revelation in opera, and at the same time the reading of the letter in that scene pays tribute to Goethe's epistolary mode. By the end of the opera her diffidence is thrown aside and she can confess, too late, that she returns Werther's love.

As in *Manon*, Massenet finds the intimate style very much to his taste. There is no chorus and no large orchestral effects. He relies particularly on the cor anglais, and there is an unforgettable solo for the saxophone to accompany Charlotte's 'Les larmes qu'on ne pleure pas' in Act III. In contrast to *Manon*, he does not attempt any pastiche musical touches except in the rather exaggerated counterpoint that supports Johann and Schmidt. His melodic invention in creating striking motifs was at its peak, and although there are some deliberately facile melodies that seem too plain to convey their message, the match of feeling and melody is masterly. Albert's correct *bon ton* is perfectly conveyed, for example, by inner octaves in the texture. Most striking, too, is the wider harmonic palette Massenet draws on in this opera, perhaps a reflection of Wagner's influence (although that never extended to his dramaturgy), and we may detect some darker string textures possibly derived from *Parsifal*. The very opening of the *prélude*, with its strong melodic dissonances, captures the tone of the opera, followed by a plain diatonic melody that suggests the beauty of nature. Using the children's 'Noël' as contrast and also as ironic accompaniment to Werther's death might have risked banality, but Werther's vision of angels, the idea of rebirth at Christmas and the straightforward musical coherence of recalling the opera's beginning at its end, plus Massenet's incomparable skill in musical manipulation of such materials, all ensure a deeply tragic, satisfying close.

RECORDINGS 1. Vallin, Thill, Paris Op Comique O, Cohen, EMI, 1931; 2. Kasarova, Vargas, Berlin Boys' Ch, Berlin Deutsche SO, Jurowski, RCA, 1998; 3. Gheorghiu, Alagna, LSO, Pappano, EMI, 1997/8

Thaïs

Comédie lyrique in three acts (seven tableaux) (2h 15m)
Libretto by Louis Gallet, after the novel *Thaïs* by Anatole France (1890)
Composed 1892–3, rev. 1897
PREMIERES 16 March 1894, Opéra, Paris; rev. version: 13 April 1898, Opéra, Paris; US: 25 November 1907, Manhattan Opera Company, New York; UK: 18 July 1911, Covent Garden, London
CAST Athanaël *bar*, Nicias *t*, Palémon *b*, un serviteur *bar*, Thaïs *s*, Crobyle *s*, Myrtale *ms*, Albine *ms*, 12 Cenobites 6 *t*, 6 *b*, la Charmeuse *dancer*; *satb* chorus of actors, actresses, comedians, philosophers, Nicias' friends, people

Thaïs was written for Sybil Sanderson, Massenet's favourite soprano at that time. Anatole France's novel had caused a sensation in 1890, with its remarkable description of the Thebaid and its story of Paphnutius the desert monk (Athanaël in the opera), who converts the Egyptian harlot Thaïs to the faith but falls himself a victim to the very carnality he professes to reject. The libretto was written in prose, breaking with a long tradition in French opera; the idea may have come from Charpentier. The antique setting – Egypt in the early years of the Christian era – appealed greatly to Massenet, and the interlocking claims of religion and love were now established as his special dramatic domain.

SYNOPSIS
Act I: Athanaël returns to the Thebaid from Alexandria to report to his brother Cenobites that Thaïs, whom he once knew as a good child, is the leading courtesan in that sinful city. He goes to Alexandria to save her and contrives to meet her at the house of Nicias. Intrigued by the strange visitor, Thaïs puts on her most lascivious act. Athanaël flees in disgust.

Act II: Athanaël visits Thaïs and attempts to draw her away from the cult of Venus. Her conscience is troubled. Nicias and his friends find her modestly dressed when they expect her to be decked for more conviviality. They threaten Athanaël when they learn that she is destroying her house and her wealth at Athanaël's bidding, but Nicias holds them back.

Act III: Athanaël leads Thaïs to a desert retreat where she is to offer her repentance. But he imposes such duress on her that her strength is failing. Back in the Thebaid, Athanaël is troubled by impure thoughts and visions of Thaïs as she first appeared to him; he also hears voices that tell him she is dying. He hurries to her side, drawn by her beauty and confessing his carnal passion for her while she expires, full of dreams of divine felicity.

The wide success of *Thaïs* added to Massenet's great celebrity, and the famous 'Meditation' (between Acts II and III), symbolizing Thaïs's awakening conscience, is one of the most famous of all violin solos. Although written for the Opéra, the work lacks large-scale scenes of pageantry and crowd conflict, and concentrates more on the personal predicaments of its two central characters, as in *Werther*. But their simultaneous conversions – Athanaël from self-denial to lust and Thaïs from sin to saintliness – are inherently improbable, for all the passionate intensity of the music, which displays some of the most flexible and lyrical qualities in all Massenet's work. Thaïs's 'Miroir, dis-moi que je suis belle' has enjoyed great celebrity as an operatic extract.

RECORDINGS 1. Doria, Sénéchal, Massard, unnamed Ch & O, Etcheverry, Decca, 1962; 2. Fleming, Sabbatini, Hampson, Bordeaux Op Ch, O Nat Bordeaux Aquitaine, Ybel, Decca, 1997/8

Cendrillon

Cinderella

Conte de fées in four acts (six tableaux) (2h 15m)

Libretto by Henri Cain, after the story by Charles Perrault, in *Contes de ma mère l'oye* (1697)

Composed 1895

PREMIERES 24 May 1899, Opéra-Comique, Paris; US: 23 December 1902, French Opera House, New Orleans; UK: 24 December 1928, Little Theatre, London (by puppets); 25 February 1939, Playhouse, Swindon

CAST Cendrillon *s*, Madame de la Haltière *ms*, Le Prince Charmant *s*, La Fée *s*, Noémie *s*, Dorothée *ms*, Pandolfe *b* or *bar*, Le Doyen de la Faculté *t*, Le Surintendant des Plaisirs *bar*, Le Premier Ministre *b* or *bar*, Le Roi *bar*, 6 spirits 4 *s*, 2 *a*; *satb* chorus of spirits, servants, courtiers, doctors, ministers, lords, ladies; dancers

While composing *Cendrillon* Massenet again found inspiration by immersing himself in the appropriate surroundings, in this case a 17th-century house on the Seine in Normandy that had belonged to the celebrated Duchesse de Longueville; he even bought a large antique table on which to spread the pages of his manuscript.

SYNOPSIS

Act I: Mme de la Haltière and her two daughters are making ready for the royal ball. Her husband, Pandolfe, groaning at his unhappy lot, is sorry to be leaving his daughter Cinderella behind. Cinderella, alone, falls asleep. A fairy appears, provides her with a magnificent dress and gives her a glass slipper to make her unrecognizable. She must promise to leave the ball at midnight.

Act II: Prince Charming is inconsolable, not even touched by the ballets in his honour. When Cinderella arrives, everyone is captivated by her. She and Prince Charming fall in love. Midnight strikes.

Act III, Scene 1: In her flight Cinderella has lost her slipper. The trio of women upbraid Pandolfe for his bad behaviour at the ball and tell Cinderella that the prince took only a passing interest in the unknown stranger. Scene 2: Cinderella takes refuge in the fairy domain where the spirits conjure up a meeting with Prince Charming. They join in a fervent embrace.

Act IV: The prince is said to be searching for the owner of the mysterious slipper. Before the whole court Cinderella claims it as hers, and 'all ends happily', in Pandolfe's words.

Cendrillon is one of Massenet's most attractive operas. The characterization of Cinderella's long-suffering father and of her bossy stepmother is deft, and the composer relished the opportunity to write fairy music. There is some pseudo-baroque pastiche (including the use of a viola d'amore) and much witty music in the manner of Verdi's *Falstaff*. There seem to be parodies of Meyerbeer and Wagner's *Parsifal*, too, and occasional hints of Debussy's style. The love music is some of the finest he ever wrote. Cinderella's 'Vous êtes mon Prince Charmant' is one of the opera's best-known extracts. Considering its abundant opportunities for spectacular staging, it has been surprisingly neglected. It should truly be acknowledged as on a par with Humperdinck's *Hänsel und Gretel*. The role of Prince Charming is written for a voice designated *falcon* or *soprano de sentiment*.

RECORDING von Stade, Welting, Berbié, Gedda, Bastin, Ambrosian Op Ch, Philharmonia O, Rudel, CBS, 1979

Don Quichotte

Don Quixote

Comédie héroïque in five acts (1h 45m)
Libretto by Henri Cain, after the play *Le chevalier de la longue figure* by Jacques Le Lorrain (1906), based on *Don Quixote* by Miguel de Cervantes (1605, 1615)
Composed 1908–9
PREMIERES 19 February 1910, Salle Garnier, Monte Carlo; US: 27 January 1912, French Opera House, New Orleans; UK: 18 May 1912, London Opera House, London
CAST Dulcinée *ms*, Don Quichotte *b*, Sancho Panza *bar*, Pedro *s*, Garcias *s*, Rodriguez *t*, Juan *t*, le chef des bandits *spoken role*, 2 valets 2 *bar*, 4 bandits 2 *t*, 2 *bar*; *satb* chorus of lords, Dulcinée's friends, bandits, crowd

It was appropriate that Massenet's last operatic success should make gentle fun of an elderly man with a fondness for beautiful women. The mockery of Cervantes's masterpiece makes excellent operatic material, and it offered Massenet yet another opportunity for mingling sentiment and comedy, pastiche and contemporary styles. The title role was written for Chaliapin, the role of Dulcinée for Lucy Arbell.

SYNOPSIS

Act I: In a crowded square in full fiesta Dulcinée is courted by four suitors. When Don Quichotte and his faithful servant Sancho Panza arrive, one of the suitors, Juan, mocks Don Quichotte's eccentric ways, while another, Rodriguez, reminds us of the knight's noble ambitions. When all have departed Don Quichotte serenades Dulcinée, but the jealous Juan interrupts and a duel inevitably follows. Dulcinée intervenes, sends Juan on an errand and upbraids Quichotte for his hot blood. She asks him to retrieve a necklace stolen from her by the bandit Ténébrun. The Don instantly undertakes the heroic task.

Act II: The Don and his servant have set out in the morning mist. Sancho sings a fierce tirade against women. As the mist clears Quichotte mistakes some windmills for giants and, attacking them, is borne aloft on one of the sails.

Act III: Don Quichotte is close in pursuit of the bandits. While he takes his rest (standing up, like all good knights) he and Sancho are overpowered by the bandits, but their wicked hearts are quickly won by Quichotte's evocation of his mission as knight errant, and they hand over the stolen necklace.

Act IV: Dulcinée is singing of the caprice of love. Don Quichotte returns with the necklace to everyone's amazement, but his proposal of marriage is turned down on the grounds that since she must be generous in her love she could not bear to deceive him. The old knight is disconsolate, but Sancho protects him from the crowd's mockery.

Act V: Death is near as the Don promises Sancho an 'island of dreams'. He dies, fondly imagining that the planet in the heavens is a fleeting image of Dulcinée.

Don Quichotte is a highly crafted comedy full of affection and charm. There is some traditional Spanish colour and some folk pastiche, in this case a *romanesca antica* in Act IV. The scene of Don Quichotte's death mostly presents a quiet pastoral simplicity but with a touch of harmonic tension as he dies. The boisterous music of Act I recalls both *Cendrillon* and *Falstaff*, with mocking counterpoint for the suitors, a manner used later also for the windmills. The Don himself is characterized with much subtlety and sympathy, an achievement that reflects Massenet's enormous experience and skill. The opera enjoyed considerable popularity and has been revived several times in recent years.

RECORDINGS 1. Crespin, Bacquier, Ghiaurov, Suisse Romande Ch & O, Kord, Decca, 1978; 2. Berganza, Fondary, Van Dam, Toulouse Capitole Ch & O, Plasson, EMI, 1992

OTHER OPERATIC WORKS Operas: *Esmeralda* (lost or destroyed), (*c.*1865); *La coupe du roi de Thule*, 1866; *La grand tante*, 1867; *Manfred* (inc.), (*c.*1869); *Méduse* (inc.), (*c.*1869); *Don César de Bazan*, 1872; *L'adorable Bel'-Boul'* (destroyed), 1874; *Les templiers* (inc.; lost); *Bérangère et Anatole*, 1876; *Le roi de Lahore*, 1877; *Robert de France* (lost or destroyed), (*c.*1880); *Les Girondins* (lost or destroyed), (1881); *Hérodiade*, 1881; *L'écureuil du deshonneur* (early, lost or destroyed); *Montalte* (lost or destroyed), 1882–3; *Le Cid*, 1885; *Esclarmonde*, 1889; *Le mage*, 1891; *Le portrait de Manon*, 1894; *La navarraise*, 1894; *Grisélidis*, (1894), 1901; *Sapho*, 1897; *Le jongleur de Notre-Dame*, 1902; *Chérubin*, 1905; *Ariane*, 1906; *Thérèse*, 1907; *Bacchus*, 1909; *Roma*, 1912; *Panurge*, 1913; *Amadis*, (1911), 1922; *Cléopâtre*, 1914; Sacred and profane dramas: *Les erinnyes*, 1873, rev. 1876; *Marie-Magdelaine* (originally performed as oratorio, 1873), 1906; *Eve*, 1875; *Narcisse*, 1877; *La Vierge*, 1880; Orchestration of Delibes's last opera, *Kassya*, 1893

H.M.

Gian Carlo Menotti

b 7 July 1911, Cadegliano, Italy

For at least a generation, in the years following the Second World War, Menotti was the most acclaimed American composer of opera. He has a natural sense of theatre, which stems from his Italian background, and has always shown an intuitive grasp of character and situation.

By the time he was 11, Menotti had written his first opera, *The Death of Pierrot*, and regularly attended theatre and opera in Milan where the family lived. On Toscanini's advice he went to the Curtis Institute in Philadelphia where, in 1928, Menotti met Samuel Barber, who became his close companion: they both studied composition with Rosario Scalero, who gave a solid grounding based on Brahms rather than on opera.

Menotti and Barber travelled in Italy and Austria, and in Vienna Menotti began composing the one-act opera buffa *Amelia al ballo* (later known as *Amelia goes to the Ball*). The Curtis Institute and New York performances were so successful that the Metropolitan Opera placed it in a double-bill with Richard Strauss's *Elektra* in 1938. The *New York Times* recognized 'something that has not materialized so far from an American-born composer' and admired Menotti's tuneful flexibility and spontaneity. This success brought the composer an NBC radio commission for *The Old Maid and the Thief*, which became a favourite among students and amateurs, and a production at the Metropolitan of an opera seria, *The Island God*, which flopped.

The highly original double-bill of *The Medium* and *The Telephone*, both, as usual, to Menotti's own ingenious texts, was a huge success. These were premiered separately and then united on Broadway. When the backers were losing money Toscanini again intervened in Menotti's destiny – his three visits to the operas provided enough publicity to boost a long run.

The Consul as a gripping topical tragedy maintained Menotti's high profile as, in a completely different way, did the charm of *Amahl and the Night Visitors*, which gained special fame through being the first opera written expressly for television. After *The Saint of Bleecker Street* (1954), and in the changing climate of the 1960s, Menotti's work began to be received with less enthusiasm and often downright hostility in the press. He changed his focus slightly, writing *Labyrinth* for television; a church opera, *Martin's Lie*, and *Help, Help, the Globolinks!*, a children's opera, for Hamburg. He also wrote the libretti for two of Samuel Barber's operas. Seven more operas, three for children, were premiered during the 1970s; since then he has written four more operas, of which *The Boy Who Grew Too Fast* (1982) has been the most successful.

In 1958 Menotti inaugurated the Festival of Two Worlds at Spoleto and in 1977 expanded it to Charleston, South Carolina. He enjoyed the entrepreneurial activity involved, although some connected it with a decline in his own work. The power of his earlier operas has never been in question, but in an interview for his 60th birthday in 1971, Menotti tried to disguise his bitterness about the impact of changing fashions on his reputation. However, some of his operas seem likely to survive.

Amahl and the Night Visitors

Opera in one act (45m)
Libretto by the composer
Composed 1951

PREMIERES 24 December 1951, NBC Studios, New York (television); 21 February 1952, Bloomington University, Indiana (stage); UK: 6 December 1963, Royal College of Music, London

In this perennial Christmas favourite, Amahl, a boy cripple, sits outside his hut watching the brilliant new star. The Three Kings, looking for hospitality, arrive with presents for the Holy Child they are seeking. During the night Amahl's mother tries to steal part of the treasure and there is a struggle. Eventually Amahl offers his crutch as a gift, is miraculously healed, and joins the Kings in search of the Christ Child.

Hieronymous Bosch's painting *The Adoration of the Magi* gave Menotti the idea for this opera, which, since its television premiere, has been broadcast annually at Christmas in the US. The opera's appeal to young audiences has made it a popular choice with amateur operatic groups. Menotti composed melodious, short numbers and scored the opera for a small orchestra; he insists that the part of Amahl should always be sung by a boy and not taken by a soprano.

RECORDING Haywood, Rainbird, Dobson, Maxwell, Watson, Covent Garden Ch & O, Syrus, That's Entertainment, 1978

OTHER OPERAS *Amelia al ballo*, 1937; *The Old Maid and the Thief*, 1939; *The Island God*, 1942; *The Medium*, 1946; *The Telephone*, 1946; *The Consul*, 1950; *The Saint of Bleecker Street*, 1954; *Maria Golovin*, 1958; *Labyrinth*, 1963; *Le dernier sauvage*, 1963; *Martin's Lie*, 1964; *Help, Help, the Globolinks!*, 1968; *The Most Important Man*, 1971; *Tamu-Tamu*, 1973; *The Egg*, 1976; *The Hero*, 1976; *The Trial of the Gypsy*, 1978; *Chip and his Dog*, 1979; *La Loca*, 1979; *A Bride from Pluto*,

1982; *The Boy Who Grew Too Fast*, 1982; *Goya*, 1986; *Giorno da Nozze*, 1988; *The Singing Child*, 1993

P.D.

Claudio Monteverdi

Claudio Giovanni Antonio Monteverdi; *b* 15 May 1567, Cremona; *d* 29 November 1643, Venice

Monteverdi was undoubtedly the most significant composer of opera as it emerged in the first decade of the 17th century. He studied in Cremona with Marc'Antonio Ingegneri, choirmaster of the cathedral, whose solid teaching in the traditional polyphonic style was apparent in Monteverdi's earliest publications.

In 1590, Monteverdi moved to Mantua to join the court musicians of Duke Vincenzo Gonzaga. Although employed as a string-player, he continued to publish madrigals and must have become involved in court entertainments. Mantua, then one of the most exciting musical centres in northern Italy, was host to some of the best composers of the period, including, as head of the ducal chapel, Giaches de Wert (1535–96). Wert, perhaps the leading madrigalist of his generation, significantly influenced Monteverdi's maturing style. Moreover, the Gonzaga dukes (Vincenzo and later his two sons, Francesco and Ferdinando) were keen patrons of music as more than just an essential adjunct of court life. They provided a climate in which all the arts flourished in their city.

Monteverdi participated in the grand performance of Battista Guarini's *Il pastor fido* in Mantua in late 1598. He also accompanied Duke Vincenzo on several trips outside his kingdom, including to Hungary and Flanders, and perhaps to Florence for the wedding celebrations of Maria de' Medici and Henri IV of France in October 1600: the festivities included the first opera to survive complete, *Euridice* by Jacopo Peri. In 1601 Monteverdi finally received a long-sought-for appointment as the head of the duke's musical establishment.

Monteverdi's first opera was *Orfeo*, to a libretto by the court secretary Alessandro Striggio. Although Monteverdi built on the example of the Florentines, by his cautious approach to their revolutionary stance and his own flexibility, he removed the element of dilettante experimentation from the new genre of *dramma per musica* and established it as a more powerful force in its own right. *Orfeo* was presumably intended to emphasize Mantua's cultural rivalry with Florence. Exchanges between the two cities were hardly surprising: Duke Vincenzo's wife, Eleonora, was a Medici princess, and Prince Ferdinando spent a good deal of his early life in Florentine circles and was closely involved with musicians there, especially Marco da Gagliano. For the wedding festivities of Prince Francesco Gonzaga and Margherita of Savoy, celebrated in May–June 1608, Monteverdi contributed an opera, *Arianna*, to a libretto by Ottavio Rinuccini (who had collaborated with Peri), plus a dance-entertainment, the *Ballo delle ingrate*.

Monteverdi resented what he felt was the shabby treatment accorded him by the Mantuan court, and he disliked the unhealthy climate there. Events were further marred by personal tragedy; after the death first of his wife and then of his favourite pupil Caterina Martinelli (who was to have sung the title-role in *Arianna*), Monteverdi began to look elsewhere for work. His *Sanctissimae Virgini missa . . . ac vespere* (the *Vespers* of 1610) clearly advertises his availability, and on 19 August 1613 he was appointed director of music at the Basilica of St Mark in Venice.

Monteverdi now enjoyed the fame, responsibility and security of what was possibly the leading musical position in Italy. He was also working for a republic rather than a court. His former employers continued to press him for music for operas, ballets and tournaments, but many of these requests remained unanswered. Monteverdi blamed the pressures of time and his duties at St Mark's, but in fact he now disliked catering for court tastes, where entertainments had to be peopled with mythological, allegorical and (super)natural characters. As he wrote to Striggio in 1616 about one such entertainment, *Le nozze di Tetide*: 'I have noticed that the interlocutors are Winds, Cupids, little Zephyrs and Sirens . . . [but] how can I, by such means, move the passions? Ariadne moved us because she was a woman, and similarly Orpheus because he was a man, and not a wind.' Monteverdi did in fact provide some more entertainment music for Mantua, but in his heart he had left the court behind.

Inevitably, Monteverdi's duties in Venice led him to concentrate on church music. However, as he grew older and relied more on his assistants to provide liturgical music, his thoughts returned to the stage. In the Carnival of 1624 he presented the *Combattimento di Tancredi e Clorinda*, adapting a poet who had been one of his favourite sources for madrigal texts, Torquato Tasso. He was also involved in the entertainments for the wedding of Duke Odoardo Farnese of Parma and Margherita de' Medici, which was celebrated in Parma in 1628, with a prologue, four intermedi and a licenza for the performance of Tasso's *Aminta* as well as music for a tournament. Monteverdi also wrote music for other entertainments in Venice and also Vienna.

However, Monteverdi's most striking achievements for the stage came in the last years of his life. In 1637, the first public opera house opened at the Teatro S. Cassiano in Venice, encouraging a new type of opera catering not for a court but for a paying public instead. This led to inevitable changes both in subject matter and in musical content. Subjects, whether mythological or historical, had to be more accessible and appealing; musical resources, particularly in terms of the chorus and orchestra, had to be pared down to ensure maximum profitability; tuneful arias had to dominate over recitative; and the success or failure of an opera depended ever more on the virtuoso qualities of its lead singers. The resulting changes were striking and far-reaching.

Monteverdi first revised his *Arianna* for the Teatro S. Moisè in Carnival 1640: his choice of a work always close to his heart is significant, but *Arianna* was a court opera and cannot have been entirely appropriate for the new audience. It was far better to begin anew, as he did with *Il ritorno d'Ulisse in patria*, performed in the same season. Here Monteverdi stayed with the mythological world of the court, but now the cast are real-life characters experiencing and conveying immediate, human emotions.

For his second Venetian opera, Monteverdi turned from Homer to Virgil: his *Le nozze d'Enea in Lavinia* (now lost) was staged at the Teatro SS. Giovanni e Paolo in Carnival 1641. However, the gradual move towards more concretely historical subject matter was completed only with his last work, *L'incoronazione di Poppea*. With *Orfeo*, Monteverdi had participated in the very birth of opera, marking the genre's first maturity. With *Poppea*, he celebrated a revolution of no less significance that inaugurated a new age in operatic history.

Orfeo

Orpheus

Favola in musica in a prologue and five acts (1h 45m)
Libretto by Alessandro Striggio Jnr, after *Euridice* by Ottavio Rinuccini (1600)
PREMIERES 24 February 1607, Palazzo Ducale, Mantua; UK: 8 March 1924, Institut Français, London (concert); 7 December 1925, Playhouse, Oxford (stage); US: 14 April 1912, Metropolitan Opera, New York (concert); 11 May 1929, Smith College, Northampton, Massachusetts (stage)

CAST La Musica *s*, Orfeo *t*, Euridice *s*, Silvia *s*, Speranza (Hope) *s*, Caronte (Charon) *b*, Plutone (Pluto) *b*, Proserpina *s*, Apollo *t*; *satb* chorus of nymphs and shepherds, infernal spirits

Orfeo was first performed under the auspices of Prince Francesco Gonzaga and the Accademia degli Invaghiti. The title-role was taken by Francesco Rasi, a famous virtuoso from Arezzo who had also sung in Peri's *Euridice* (1600); the other roles (and choruses) were taken by nine singers, most of whom were employees of the Mantuan court. There was a second performance a week later and a third was planned, though this seems not to have taken place. Unlike the early Florentine operas, the work is clearly divided into acts, although these were probably played without a break. The libretto published for the first performance contains an ending different from the score and closer to the myth: after Orpheus has vowed to renounce women, a crowd of Bacchantes enter, berating him for his decision and singing in praise of Bacchus. The two endings may reflect different conditions at different performances, although it is not clear which was used when.

SYNOPSIS

Prologue: After three statements of the opening fanfare-like 'toccata' (which reappears in the 1610 *Vespers*), Music enters to a ritornello for strings. This ritornello returns at key points in the opera where music and its power come into play. The prologue consists of five short stanzas sung over the same bass-line, each separated by a shortened version of the ritornello. The theme of the opera is the power of music, which can 'soothe each troubled heart and ... inflame the coldest minds now with noble anger, now with love'.

Act I: In the fields of Thrace, Orpheus is to be married to Eurydice. He sings a hymn to his beloved ('Rosa del ciel') and nymphs and shepherds rejoice in song and dance.

Act II: Eurydice has left with her companions. Orpheus sings to the woods, which once heard his laments but now ring to his joy ('Ecco pur ch'a voi ritorno ... Vi ricordi, o boschi ombrosi'). But the mood of celebration, so carefully built up over this first part of the opera, is shattered by the sudden entrance of Sylvia, the messenger ('Ahi caso acerbo!'). Her tale slowly emerges ('In un fiorito prato'); Eurydice has died from a snake-bite. Orpheus, at first scarcely believing the shattering news, laments his bride ('Tu se' morta') and then resolves to recover her from Hades. The chorus repeats 'Ahi caso acerbo', Sylvia decides to enter solitary exile and the act ends in lamentation.

Act III: A sinfonia of sombre brass instruments marks the change of scene to the Inferno. Orpheus is led by Hope to the gates of Hades, where she must leave him ('Lasciate ogni speranza, voi ch'entrate', 'Abandon all hope, you who enter' quoting Dante). Orpheus reaches the river Styx and the boatman Charon, who, singing to the rough sound of the regal, refuses to let him pass. The shepherd summons up all his musical powers to meet his greatest task, and the ensuing aria, 'Possente spirto', is the literal centrepiece and the climax of the opera. The text is in *terza rima* stanzas (as used by Dante), and each is set as a variation over the same bass, with florid vocal ornamentation reinforcing Orpheus's magical powers. Various instruments (two violins, two cornetts, a double harp) provide ritornellos and echo-like interjections. As Charon remains unmoved, Orpheus changes tack, adopting a much simpler style accompanied by strings. Eventually, the boatman is lulled to sleep by a sinfonia for strings, and Orpheus takes the oars. The chorus comments on the power of man to triumph over all obstacles.

Act IV: Pluto, king of the underworld, and his wife Proserpine have heard Orpheus's lament. She pleads on Orpheus's behalf, and Pluto grants that Eurydice return to earth, with the condition that Orpheus leads her from the underworld without looking back. The chorus comments on the mercy to be found even in Hades. Orpheus takes up a joyful song in praise of his lyre ('Qual onor di te fia degno') over a walking bass and two-violin accompaniment. But as he moves earthwards, he has doubts; is Eurydice really behind him? He turns to look, only to see her disappearing before his eyes. Orpheus returns to earth alone, and the final chorus comments on the paradox of a man who can conquer Hades but not his own emotions.

Act V: In the fields of Thrace, Orpheus laments his second loss of Eurydice; only an echo responds, and he decides to renounce women. Suddenly the heavens open and Apollo, Orpheus's father, appears in a chariot. He consoles his son, and in a duet ('Saliam cantando al cielo') they both return to heaven, where Orpheus will see Eurydice in the stars. The chorus rejoices in Orpheus's apotheosis and dances a final moresca.

Both composer and librettist clearly knew Peri's *Euridice*. Alessandro Striggio was certainly in Florence when it was first performed, and so, probably, was Monteverdi. Striggio's libretto contains many echoes of Rinuccini in both structure and content, although significantly he avoids much of Rinuccini's self-indulgent artistry in favour of a more concise dramatic presentation as seen in their different narrations of Euridice's death. Monteverdi's recitative, too, owes much to Peri.

However, *Orfeo* also has much broader roots. There are many references to the tradition of the Florentine *intermedi*: the spectacular stage effects, the mythological subject matter, the allegorical figures, the number and scoring of the instruments and the extended choruses. The opera also harks back to classical tragedy in the five-part division, the use of a messenger and the commenting choruses at the ends of acts, and to the pastoral tragi-comedies of Tasso and Guarini. Similarly, Monteverdi's music is redolent of 16th-century techniques: the choruses are madrigalian in style, the technique of variation over a repeated bass was typical of earlier improvisatory procedures, and even in his new recitative, Monteverdi exploits expressive devices first explored in his polyphonic madrigals, including carefully crafted vocal lines, dissonances and chromaticism.

These backward-looking, Renaissance aspects of the opera are reinforced by its various humanist messages about the power of man and music. But *Orfeo* also looks forward to the Baroque. Monteverdi demonstrates his openness to the new styles developed by his Florentine contemporaries, and also to other techniques then being developed, particularly in the duple- and triple-time arias and in the duet textures for voices and/or instruments (as in Monteverdi's *Scherzi musicali* of 1607). Another novel aspect of his score is the detail with which Monteverdi notes his precise intentions in matters of instrumentation and ornamentation (e.g., the ornaments in 'Possente spirto' are written out): here he asserts his control over elements previously left to the performer. As a result, *Orfeo* contains an intriguing mixture of old and new elements. Rather than rejecting previously perfected techniques in an iconoclastic search for novelty, Monteverdi reinterprets the old in the light of the new (and vice-versa) to produce a powerful synthesis of undeniable dramatic force. Moreover, and unlike the Florentines, Monteverdi is unquestionably a masterful composer. His attention to the drama, to large-scale structure (witness his symmetrical patterning and tonal planning) and to expressive detail demonstrate his skills to the full; and they produced what is arguably the first great opera.

RECORDINGS 1. Kwella, Smith, Rogers, Bolognesi, Chiaroscuro, London Baroque, Medlam, EMI, 1983; 2. Baird, von Otter, Rolfe Johnson, Robson, Monteverdi Ch, EBS, Gardiner,

Archiv, 1987; 3. Larmore, Fink, Peeters, Scholl, Dale, Concerto Vocale, Jacobs, WDR, 1995

Il ritorno d'Ulisse in patria

The Return of Ulysses

Opera in a prologue and three acts (3h)
Libretto by Giacomo Badoaro (1602–54), after the *Odyssey* XIII–XXIII by Homer (*c.*700 BC)
PREMIERES Carnival, February 1640, Teatro S. Cassiano, Venice; UK: 16 January 1928, BBC broadcast; 16 March 1965, St Pancras Town Hall, London (stage); US: 18 January 1974, Opera House, Kennedy Center, Washington DC
CAST L'Humana fragilità (Human Frailty) *s*, Tempo (Time) *b*, Fortuna (Fortune) *s*, Amore (Cupid) *s*, Ulisse (Ulysses) *t*, Penelope *s*, Telemaco (Telemachus) *t*, Antinoo (Antinous) *b*, Pisandro (Peisander) *t*, Anfinomo (Amphinomus) *a*, Eurimaco (Eurymachus) *t*, Melanto (Melantho) *s*, Eumete (Eumaeus) *t*, Iro (Irus) *t*, Ericlea (Eurycleia) *ms*, Giove (Jupiter) *t*, Nettuno (Neptune) *b*, Minerva *s*, Giunone (Juno) *s*; *satb* chorus of Phaeacians, celestial spirits, maritime spirits

Ulisse was Monteverdi's first new opera for Venice, and it reveals him coming to terms both with the demands of the new public theatres and with the stylistic developments of his younger contemporaries. Its authenticity, once doubted, now seems clear. The score survives in manuscript in Vienna but there are significant differences between this score and the surviving manuscript copies of the libretto. The text is a straightforward adaptation of Homer, and Badoaro exploited all the devices now becoming standard in Venetian opera: the moralizing prologue, comic characters (Iro and Ericlea, Melanto and Eurimaco (cf. Damigella and Valletto in *Poppea*)) and spectacular scenic effects. However, the subject matter of the opera also has a somewhat archaic, courtly feel: notably the prominence of the gods and an almost 'super-human' hero in the manner of *Orfeo*. The opera seems to have been a success: it was also staged in Bologna in 1640 and again in Venice in 1641.

SYNOPSIS

Prologue: Human Frailty acknowledges its submission to Time, Fortune and Cupid, as the following drama will reveal.

Act I: In her palace in Ithaca, Penelope awaits the return of her husband Ulysses from the Trojan Wars. She cannot be consoled by her nurse, Eurycleia. Melantho, a maid, and Eurymachus, a shepherd, comment on the pains yet pleasures of their own love ('De' nostri amor concordi'). Neptune, supported by Jupiter, condemns the rescue of Ulysses by the Phaeacians. They have brought him back to Ithaca, leaving him sleeping on the beach. As a punishment, Neptune turns their ship into a rock. Ulysses awakes ('Dormo ancora') and believes himself to have been abandoned. Minerva enters disguised as a shepherd ('Cara e lieta gioventù') and tells Ulysses that the island is his home. She reveals herself to his amazement ('O fortunato Ulisse') and tells him to bathe in a sacred fountain (a chorus of naiads is missing in the score). Here Ulysses will change into an old man so as to enter his palace unrecognized and outwit Antinous, Peisander and Amphinomus, the suitors who have insinuated themselves into the offices of state and are seeking his wife's hand. Meanwhile, Minerva will bring back Ulysses' son Telemachus from Sparta. Ulysses again rejoices ('O fortunato Ulisse'). Melantho urges Penelope to forget Ulysses and love another ('Ama dunque'). Eumaeus, a shepherd faithful to Ulysses, tends his flocks and argues with the social parasite Irus. Ulysses, now disguised, enters and warns Eumaeus of the imminent return of his sovereign ('Ulisse, Ulisse è vivo').

Act II: Minerva brings Telemachus on her chariot. Eumaeus welcomes the prince ('O gran figlio d'Ulisse') and presents the old man, who, he says, has news of his father's return. A ray of light descends from heaven to reveal Ulysses in his true form. Father and son are joyfully reunited in a duet ('O padre sospirato/O figlio desiato'), and they plan their return to the palace. Melantho and Eurymachus discuss Penelope's continued devotion to Ulysses. The suitors enter to pursue their advances ('Ama dunque'), but Penelope staunchly resists ('Non voglio amar'). Eumaeus announces the imminent return of Telemachus and Ulysses, and the suitors are disconcerted. They plot to kill Telemachus, but the sight of Jupiter's eagle flying overhead warns them against the plan. They decide instead to redouble their wooing of Penelope ('Amor è un'armonia'). Minerva outlines to Ulysses a plan to remove the suitors, and Eumaeus recounts to Ulysses Penelope's lasting fidelity. Ulysses rejoices ('Godo anch'io'), and they plan to go to the palace. Meanwhile, Telemachus discusses his recent travels with Penelope. Antinous and Irus meet Eumaeus and Ulysses, now disguised as a beggar. Antinous treats them badly and Ulysses is provoked to fight Irus, thrashing his fat adversary. Penelope orders that the beggar be made welcome. The suitors redouble their efforts to gain her favours with rich gifts. She proclaims that she will marry whoever manages to string Ulysses' great bow. The suitors agree willingly ('Lieta, soave gloria'), but all three fail the test. The beggar asks to enter the competition, while renouncing the prize, and succeeds in stringing the bow. Invoking Minerva's protection, Ulysses looses arrows at the suitors and kills them all.

Act III: Irus grieves for his colleagues in a splendid take-off of the typical lament scene (a following scene for Mercury and the ghosts of the suitors is missing). Penelope refuses to believe Eumaeus' claim that the beggar who bent the bow was indeed Ulysses ('Ulisse, Ulisse è vivo'), and even Telemachus cannot convince her. Minerva and Juno decide to plead with Jupiter on Ulysses' behalf ('Ulisse troppo errò'). Neptune is pacified, and choruses of celestial and maritime spirits praise the new accord ('Giove amoroso'). Eurycleia ponders how best to act with Penelope, who still refuses the assurances of Eumaeus and Telemachus ('Troppo incredula'). Even when Ulysses enters in his true form she fears a trick. Eurycleia claims that it is indeed he ('È questo, è questo Ulisse'): she has seen him in his bath and recognized a scar. But Penelope is finally convinced only when Ulysses correctly describes the embroidered quilt on their nuptial bed ('Hor sì ti riconosco . . . Illustratevi, o cieli'). Husband and wife are rejoined in a blissful love duet ('Sospirato mio sole').

There are clear parallels between *Ulisse* and the styles found in Monteverdi's other later works (for example the *genere concitato* first seen extensively in the *Combattimento*). The opera also contains several echoes of *Orfeo*; the recitative laments (for example Penelope at the opening of Act I), the virtuosic ornamental writing for Minerva and Juno, the five-part sinfonias, and even the care for large-scale symmetrical structures. But whereas in *Orfeo* it was the recitative that carried the bulk of the action, with arias, duets and so on, interposed only where they could be used realistically (rather as songs in a play), now the style is one of a flexible shifting between recitative, arioso and aria. The duple- and triple-time arias, whether just short phrases or more developed structures, are points of intensification prompted by the drama, by the need to emphasize particular words and by the emotional effect. They also reflect changes in the verse structure of the text. The sensuous triple-time melodies, so much more developed than the simple hemiola patterns of *Orfeo*, are a truly modern characteristic. Indeed, at the age of 73 Monteverdi shows himself to be remarkably au fait with the most up-to-date Venetian idioms.

RECORDINGS 1. Lerer, Eliasson, Concentus Musicus Wien, Harnoncourt, Teldec, 1971; 2. Fink, Prégardien, Concerto Vocale, Jacobs, Harmonia Mundi, 1992

L'incoronazione di Poppea

The Coronation of Poppaea

Opera in a prologue and three acts (3h 30m)
Libretto by Giovanni Francesco Busenello (1598–1659), after Tacitus, Suetonius and perhaps Seneca
PREMIERES Carnival 1643, Teatro SS. Giovanni e Paolo, Venice; UK: 6 December 1927, Playhouse, Oxford; US: 27 April 1926, Smith College, Northampton, Massachusetts
CAST Fortuna (Fortune) *s*, Virtù (Virtue) *s*, Amore (Cupid) *s*, Poppea (Poppaea) *s*, Nerone (Nero) *s*, Ottavia (Octavia) *ms*, Seneca *b*, Ottone (Otho) *a*, Drusilla *s*, Arnalta *a*, Nutrice (Nurse) *a*, Lucano (Lucan) *t*, Valletto (a valet) *s*, Damigella (a maidservant) *s*, Liberto *t*, Littore (a lictor) *b*, 2 soldiers 2 *t*, Pallade (Pallas Athene) *s*, Mercurio (Mercury) *b*, Venere (Venus) *s*; *atb* chorus of consuls and tribunes, Seneca's companions, cupids

Poppea is the first known opera to adopt a factual historical subject: it is set in Rome in AD 64. The earthy, sensuous plot, tempered by Busenello's trenchant view of the world, is typical of new Venetian trends. Certainly there are no high-minded allegories here, and important precedents are established by the oft-remarked 'immorality' of the plot, by the comic interludes and by the emphasis on virtuoso singers (Ottavia was sung by the young Anna Renzi, who later had an outstanding operatic career in Venice).

The surviving sources are complex. We have a scenario associated with the first performances, some manuscript libretti of uncertain date and Busenello's edition of the libretto in his *Delle hore ociose* (Venice, 1656). The music survives in two manuscripts: one in Naples, perhaps associated with a performance by the travelling Febiarmonici in 1651 (a libretto printed for this performance also survives); the other in Venice, largely copied in the early 1650s by Francesco Cavalli's wife, with performance alterations and annotations by Cavalli himself. These various sources differ, sometimes considerably. The music was first definitely assigned to Monteverdi in 1681 (although the Venice manuscript also bears an attribution of uncertain date) and the extent of his authorship is not entirely clear. Certainly there seems little doubt that *Poppea* as it survives mixes the work of various composers. The text of the final duet between Nero and Poppaea was used in a revival of Benedetto Ferrari's *Il pastor reggio* (Bologna, 1641; now lost), and in an entertainment (1647) by Filiberto Laurenzi. There is also music almost certainly by Cavalli (the opening sinfonia is reworked from his *Doriclea* of 1645) and by Francesco Sacrati (the sinfonias in the consul scene in Act III appear in his *La finta pazza* of 1641). These and other problems pose obvious difficulties for modern productions. The leading exponent of mid-17th-century Venetian opera in the 1960s, Raymond Leppard, viewed these manuscripts as essentially skeletons that were then, and should be now, fleshed out in various ways. He added lavish string accompaniments and made extensive cuts and alterations. One can sympathize with the intent (such pragmatism was clearly characteristic of 17th-century operatic performances), but Leppard's overly romantic 'realizations' have now gone out of favour. Latterly productions have followed the surviving scores and contemporary resources more closely, with the result that the dramatic and musical effect, although considerably less opulent, is more stringent and arguably more effective.

SYNOPSIS (VENICE MANUSCRIPT)
Prologue: Fortune, Virtue and Cupid dispute their respective powers. Cupid

claims to be master of the world, as the story of Nero and Poppaea will prove.

Act I: Otho arrives at his house and sees Nero's soldiers outside, asleep. He realizes that his betrothed, Poppaea, is together with Nero and curses her faithlessness. The soldiers are aroused and complain about their job and the decline of Rome. Nero and Poppaea enter: they take a sensuous farewell as Poppaea emphasizes her love for him ('Signor, sempre mi vedi') and seeks to guarantee their marriage. She is left alone with her nurse, Arnalta, to discuss tactics and ignores Arnalta's common-sense warnings, for Cupid is on her side ('Per me guerreggia Amor e la Fortuna'). Arnalta is left to grumble at her mistress's folly ('Ben sei pazza'). In the emperor's palace Octavia, Nero's wife, acknowledges her humiliation ('Disprezzata regina'), while her nurse suggests that she should take a lover. Seneca, shown in by Octavia's valet, urges restraint and appeals to her dignity: Valletto responds by cursing Seneca's pedantry. As Seneca reflects on Octavia's power and the transitory nature of life ('Le porpore regali e le grandezze'), Pallas Athene appears to warn him of his impending death. Seneca welcomes the news. Nero debates his plans about Octavia and Poppaea with Seneca ('Son risoluto al fine'). The philosopher urges reason, but Nero is inflamed to anger. Poppaea enters to calm him down ('Come dolci signor, come soavi'), suggesting that Seneca must be killed. Otho confronts Poppaea over her infidelity, but she dismisses him ('Chi nasce sfortunato di se stesso si dolga e non d'altrui'). He tries to come to his senses ('Otton, torna in te stesso') and vows revenge. Then he turns to Drusilla, who has always loved him, and swears that he will favour her over Poppaea.

Act II: Seneca praises Stoic solitude. Mercury appears, warning him again of death, which the philosopher accepts happily ('O me felice'). Liberto, a freedman, enters with Nero's command: Seneca must die by the end of the day. He welcomes his fate, despite the urgings of his companions ('Non morir, Seneca') and they leave to prepare the bath in which he will open his veins. The tension is broken by a flirtatious scene between Valletto and Damigella. Nero and Lucan celebrate the news of Seneca's death with wine and song ('Son rubini amorosi'). Otho rededicates himself to Poppaea, whom he still loves ('Sprezzami quanto sai'), but Octavia orders him to assume female garb and kill her. He cannot refuse. Drusilla delights in her love for Otho ('Felice cor mio'), and Octavia's nurse wishes she were in her place. Otho enters and explains his plan for Poppaea: Drusilla gives him her clothes. Meanwhile Poppaea rejoices in Seneca's death ('Hor che Seneca è morto') and prays for Cupid to support her. Arnalta lulls her to sleep ('Oblivion soave') as Cupid watches overhead. Otho, dressed as Drusilla, enters and tries to kill Poppaea, but he is prevented by Cupid. She wakes and gives the alarm as Otho escapes. Cupid proclaims his success ('Ho difeso Poppea').

Act III: Drusilla joyfully anticipates Poppaea's death, but she finds herself arrested for the attempted murder (Otho was wearing her clothes), and Nero sentences her to death. Otho in turn confesses his guilt, despite Drusilla's persistent attempts to protect her beloved, and Nero banishes them. Nero and Poppaea rejoice now that the way is clear for their marriage ('Non più s'interporrà noia a dimora'). Octavia enters and, in a lament, bids a halting farewell ('Addio Roma'). Arnalta revels in the exaltation of her mistress as empress of Rome (these two scenes are reversed in some sources). Nero crowns Poppaea ('Ascendi, o mia diletta'), and the consuls and tribunes pay homage. Cupid proclaims his triumph to his approving mother, Venus ('Io mi compiaccio, o figlio') echoed by a chorus of cupids. Nero and Poppaea have a final ecstatic duet ('Pur ti miro, pur ti godo').

The uncertain status of *Poppea*, upsetting though it may be for devotees of the single-composer masterpiece, is itself revealing. First, the fact that Monteverdi can be so easily conflated with his contemporaries and successors suggests the similarity of styles exploited in Venetian opera around the middle of the 17th century. Second, it emphasizes the priorities of contemporary opera production, where the librettist and stage designer held sway over such lesser functionaries as musicians. In comparison with *Ulisse*, *Poppea* has a drastically pared-down orchestration and places much more emphasis on the tuneful melodies given to the lead singers. Again the style is one of a flexible shifting between recitative, arioso and aria, although here the arias become more extensive and structurally self-contained. To be sure, Monteverdi, if it is he, can still provide some splendid recitative, such as Octavia's great Act III lament, harking back to *Orfeo* and *Arianna*. But the splendidly lyrical arias now carry the emotional and musical weight of the drama and point the way forward to the prime concerns of later baroque opera.

RECORDINGS 1. Donath, Berberian, Söderström, Luccardi, Concentus Musicus Wien, Harnoncourt, Teldec, 1973/4; 2. Borst, Larmore, Laurens, Schopper, Concerto Vocale, Jacobs, Harmonia Mundi, 1990; 3. McNair, von Otter, Chance, Hanchard, Ellero D'Artegna, EBS, Gardiner, Archiv, 1993 (live)

OTHER STAGE WORKS SURVIVING IN WHOLE OR PART *De la bellezza le dovute lodi*, 1607; *Arianna* (one aria survives), 1608; *Ballo delle ingrate*, 1609; *Tirsi e Clori*, 1616; 'Su le penne de' venti il ciel varcando' (prologue for G. B. Andreini's *La Maddalena*), 1617; *Combattimento di Tancredi e Clorinda*, 1624; *Volgendo il ciel per l'immortal sentiero*, 1638

T.C.

Douglas S. Moore

Douglas Stuart Moore; *b* 10 August 1893, Cutchogue, New York; *d* 25 July 1969, Greenport, New York

Born into a notable New England family, Moore had a long musical training with a succession of distinguished teachers: Horatio Parker at Yale, Vincent d'Indy in Paris, Ernest Bloch in Cleveland and (apparently less profitably) Nadia Boulanger back in the French capital. From 1921 he was curator of music at the Cleveland Museum of Art, and acted at the Cleveland Playhouse. His friendship with the poet Vachel Lindsay led him to concentrate firmly on American subjects for his music, which included songs popular and serious as well as choral, orchestral and chamber works before his later focus on music for the stage.

His arrival at Columbia University in 1926 began a long association with American academic life (he retired as chairman of the music department in 1962), which he combined not only with composition but a series of appointments on various musical committees. His own stage works were diverse and practically conceived, and include pieces for children as well as the soap-opera parody *Gallantry*. Though his achievement is variable in tone and quality, his ingenuity and directness balance a lack of finesse, and *The Ballad of Baby Doe* continues to maintain a lively presence on American stages.

The Ballad of Baby Doe

Opera in two acts (2h)
Libretto by John Latouche
Composed 1954–5
PREMIERES 7 July 1956, Opera House, Central City, Colorado; UK: 11 March 1996, Bloomsbury Theatre, London

Moore first sensed the possibilities of the riches-to-rags career of Colorado's silver king Horace Tabor, his respectable first wife Augusta and his second, the warm-hearted former floozie Baby Doe, in 1935, when he read recent accounts of the latter's death at the Matchless Mine, the last remaining fragment of Tabor's once-prosperous empire. It was the Central City Opera Association that brought the subject to his attention again in 1953, commissioning the work that has proved to be his most enduring composition.

In 1880, when the story begins, self-made Tabor has already virtually bought up the town of Leadville, Colorado, and his latest purchase of the Matchless Mine somewhat compensates him for his loveless marriage to the frosty Augusta. Struck by the attractions of a newcomer to Leadville, Baby Doe, he begins a relationship with her that his wife deplores but eventually comes to terms with. He and Baby Doe nevertheless divorce their respective spouses, but their subsequent attempt to enter into a Catholic marriage causes a scandal. The removal of the US currency from the silver standard ruins Tabor, who dies after insisting that Baby hold fast to the mine no matter what. Decades later, as an old woman, she freezes to death at the derelict site.

Moore had the benefit of a straightforward and moving tale that employed elements of America's history as capably and resonantly as a film by John Ford. The work he produced is resolutely in the vein of traditional American opera, and none the worse for its occasional nods in the direction of Broadway. His genuine lyricism and dramatic acumen ensured that characters that might seem stereotypical from the text alone are fleshed out by the music. Generations of American singers have prospered in the opera; the title role was a favourite of Beverly Sills.

RECORDING Grissom, Krueger, Steele, Paris, Blaisdell, Freiman, Central City Op Ch & O, Moriarty, Newport Classic, 1996

OTHER OPERATIC WORKS *Oh, Oh, Tennessee* (1925); *Jesse James* (inc.), (1928); *White Wings*, (1935) 1949; *The Headless Horseman*, 1937; *The Devil and Daniel Webster*, 1939; *The Emperor's New Clothes*, 1949, rev. 1956; *Puss in Boots*, 1950; *Giants in the Earth*, 1951, rev. 1963; *Gallantry*, 1958; *The Wings of the Dove*, 1961; *The Greenfield Christmas Tree*, 1962; *Carry Nation*, 1966

G.H.

Wolfgang Amadeus Mozart

Joannes Chrysostomus Wolfgangus Theophilus Mozart; *b* 27 January 1756, Salzburg; *d* 5 December 1791, Vienna

Mozart is the most famous of all infant prodigies, the little boy who charmed kings and princes as his music continues to charm us today. But far more remarkable than his precocity was his development by the time he was 30 into the composer of works of the greatest beauty, depth and humanity.

After three operas composed by the time he was 12, Mozart had the extraordinary honour of being commissioned to compose the opera seria *Mitridate* for the royal ducal theatre of Milan in 1770 when he was 14, with two more operas for 1771 and 1772. His own personality gradually gained the upper hand over the Italian models he had assimiliated. The next years were frustratingly short of opera commissions. Salzburg had no regular theatre or opera, only occasional touring companies and formal gala occasions, for one of which he wrote the totally undramatic *Il re pastore*. Fortunately, the court of the Bavarian Elector in Munich gave him the chance of composing *La finta giardiniera* in 1775 and *Idomeneo* – his first truly great opera – in 1781. Soon after, he left the service of the Prince Archbishop of Salzburg in a stormy scene and settled in Vienna, where his first major task was the composition of *Die Entführung aus dem Serail* (1782), a resounding success. Yet, neither the beautiful music of this singspiel, nor the Italian operas begun but soon abandoned because of their hopeless libretti, prepare us for his next major opera, *Le nozze di Figaro* (1786). There is no accounting for perfection, but the genius of the librettist Lorenzo da Ponte (to be confirmed in the next two operas which lacked the benefit of Beaumarchais's brilliant play as a basis) played its part, along with Mozart's greater maturity, deeper experience of life and the intense application of a unique intelligence. After *Don Giovanni* (1787) and *Così fan tutte* (1790) to da Ponte's libretti, Mozart wrote two totally different operas, both produced within three months of his death in 1791. In *Die Zauberflöte* he miraculously combines a new simplicity with great seriousness and comedy; *La clemenza di Tito* is at the same time a backward glance at opera seria and a work of neoclassical nobility ushering in the new century.

The creation of *Le nozze di Figaro* coincided with two comparable achievements, the series of great piano concertos and the six quartets dedicated to Haydn, but he had a special love for opera: its influence is audible throughout his instrumental music in many a 'vocal' phrase and in the dramatic juxtapositions of mood. The influence of Mozart the instrumental composer on the operas is equally important. Whereas his highly successful contemporary, Paisiello, regarded modulation as an unsatisfactory substitute for melody, patterns of tonality form the architecture of Mozart's mature operas, both in the total plan and within the individual sections. Could Mozart expect a listener lacking absolute pitch (as most of us do) to take in his schemes of tonality, even when an 18th-century opera-goer was lucky to see a work more than once in a lifetime? The answer must be yes, perhaps subconsciously, since the whole use of sonata form is based on that assumption.

Apart from the formal consideration that operas and finales ended in the key they started with and apart from the traditional keys, C and D for martial occasions, E♭ for solemn ones and so on, Mozart had his own instinct. The most sensual key for him was A major, for most seductions were performed or attempted in it. In *Die Zauberflöte*, C minor always refers to death, while A♭, not the relative major (E♭) but its subdominant, usually brings relief, as in the opening scene. The same key relationship, a tone higher, takes on a structural role in *Don Giovanni*, where D minor, the key of the Commendatore and his vengeance opposes and finally overcomes B♭ major and D major, the Don's principal keys.

The supreme example of Mozart's architecture is perhaps the Act II finale of *Figaro*, which presents a chain of crises appearing and being resolved in turn, each depicted in a 'movement' in sonata form with its rise of tension at the modulation to the dominant and then the reconciliation of the return to the tonic key. The key relationship between the movements is also significant in this finale: from Figaro's entrance in the fourth section it moves to the subdominant every time (G–C–F–B♭–E♭) each move therefore expressing a lowering of tension, but this always proves to be momentary since a new problem soon appears.

Although Mozart rigorously adheres to the harmonic structure (of sonata, rondo or ternary form), his operas become ever freer about the recapitulation of the melodies. From the time of *Figaro*, Mozart is less liable to repeat words and music for the sake of musical form. New events and emotions arise, requiring new music. By the time of *Die Zauberflöte* the recapitulation of melodies may be vestigial, just a hint to give the listener his bearings.

Not only do keys have a special significance, but melodic phrases or intervals reappear throughout Mozart's vocal music to express similar moods: in *Die Zauberflöte* the exultant rising major sixth that opens Tamino's aria 'Dies Bildnis' is echoed by the equally rapturous 'Tamino mein' sung by Pamina in the Act II finale. These are in different keys, but there is a link of melody and key in the vengeance sworn by Donna Anna's 'Fuggi crudele' in *Don Giovanni* and the Queen of the Night's 'Der Hölle Rache' in *Die Zauberflöte*. Attempts to codify a distinct musical language as used by Mozart go too far, since his thinking was deep and instinctive, but nearly everything in his great opera scores, melody, harmony and orchestration, has a dramatic purpose as well as a purely musical one.

Mitridate, re di Ponto

Mithridates, King of Pontus

Opera seria in three acts (3h 30m)
Libretto by Vittorio Amedeo Cigna-Santi, originally set by Quirino Gasparini (1767), after the tragedy by Jean Racine (1673) trans. into Italian by Giuseppe Parini (*c.*1765)
Composed September–December 1770
PREMIERES 26 December 1770, Teatro Regio Ducal, Milan; UK: 17 March 1979, Logan Hall, London (concert); US: 15 August 1985, Avery Fisher Hall, New York (concert); Ireland: 27 October 1989, Theatre Royal, Wexford (stage); US: 30 June 1991, Loretto-Hilton Centre, St Louis (stage)
CAST Mitridate *t*, Aspasia *s*, Sifare *s*, Farnace *a*, Ismene *s*, Marzio *t*, Arbate *s*, guards and Roman soldiers *silent*

In March 1770 the 14-year-old Mozart presented three magnificent arias at a soirée of Count Firmian's in Milan. This led to his first commission, for an opera seria for one of Italy's three principal theatres. It had a powerful orchestra, including 28 violins, as opposed to the 12 he would find at the Vienna Burgtheater and the six at the premiere of *Die Zauberflöte*. Mozart duly handed in the recitatives by the end of October, but the arias had to be tailored to the singers. The primo uomo (principal castrato) in the role of Sifare did not arrive until the end of November. The tenor Guglielmo d'Ettore (Mitridate) was the most troublesome – Mozart had to rewrite his opening aria three times. The premiere, which lasted six hours (including ballets by another hand), was a great success. The opera was given 22 times and the composer was re-engaged for the following year.

Mithridates VI Eupator (132–63 BC), King of Pontus (on the Black Sea), was finally defeated by the Romans after a reign of 50 years and many conquests. Like *Figaro*, this libretto has the advantage of being based on a great play. The tension of the drama is maintained throughout in a way that was impossible for tragedies of 18th-century origin with their genteel, rather bloodless behaviour. Unusually for Racine, nobody dies except the fierce old king; it thus conforms to the Age of Enlightenment's wish for a happy ending.

SYNOPSIS

Act I: King Mitridate has left his empire in the care of his sons Sifare and Farnace while he is away at the wars. Deceived by a rumour of his father's death, Farnace declares his love to the king's betrothed, Aspasia. She seeks the protection of Sifare. Mitridate returns with Ismene as a bride for Farnace. When he hears of Farnace's guilt, he determines to kill him.

Act II: Aspasia and Sifare declare their love for each other and mourn that she must marry the king.

Act III: When Farnace's treacherous plotting with the Romans is discovered, he reveals in his despair that Sifare is his father's real rival. Mitridate traps Aspasia into confessing her love for Sifare and condemns them both to death. Ismene holds off the king's wrath for long enough to let both sons beat off the Roman attack. Mitridate, mortally wounded, rejoices at their loyalty and their coming betrothals.

An Italian composer would have avoided some of Mozart's mistakes, such as setting Aspasia's pleading in the first aria to fierce coloratura or giving the angry king staccatos in the manner of opera buffa. Gasparini's setting of the same libretto is less attractive, but his version of Mitridate's last aria, 'Vado incontro al fato', with its six top Cs, was used in place of Mozart's frankly weaker one. One can always admire Mozart's craftsmanship – for example, in Sifare's first aria, 'Soffre il mio cor', the organization of short phrases of the orchestral ritornello, some of which return at the end of the exposition while others are reserved for the end of the aria, or the coloratura subtly varied at its return. He also does his best to characterize – Mitridate's ferocity with great leaps and dynamic contrasts, the gentleness of Sifare opposed to the far more angular music of his impulsive brother. But when in doubt he turns out a well-made, all-purpose piece with a busy orchestra over a drumming bass and a good deal of coloratura, his general stand-by until after *Il re pastore* (1775).

The formal patterns of the day demanded long arias, even with the shortened da capo form. Another type, a succession of slow and fast sections, is used tellingly by Mozart when Mitridate speaks gently to Sifare, then fiercely to Aspasia in 'Tu, che fedel mi sei', but formal convention weakened the drama by demanding a complete repeat (in appropriate keys). The Italian composers generally kept their arias shorter than Mozart at this stage.

There is, however, more and more music of great beauty as the opera proceeds. There are two agitato pieces in minor keys with no contrasting section to destroy the mood and some delicious lyrical music, especially in Sifare's 'Lungi da te' with horn obbligato (inspired by contact with the orchestra, for there is an earlier version without the horn) and in the one duet, 'Se viver non degg'io', in which Aspasia and Sifare declare their doomed love. The original version, presumably rejected by the singers, is even more beautiful. The greatest piece is 'Pallid' ombre' with its accompanied recitatives, sung by Aspasia when she receives the king's poisoned cup. Her long incantation has the earnestness of Gluck's *Alceste*. When she sings at the lowest range of the voice, it is as a means of intense expression and not to show what the singer could do.

RECORDINGS 1. Auger, Gruberova, Cotrubas, Baltsa, Hollweg, Mozarteum-O, Hager, Philips, 1977; 2. Dessay, Bartoli, Asawa, Sabbatini, Les Talens Lyriques, Rousset, Decca, 1998

La finta giardiniera

The Pretend Gardener

Dramma giocoso in three acts (3h 30m)
Libretto by ?Giuseppe Petrosellini, originally for Anfossi (1774)
Composed December 1774; accompanied recitatives rev. by Mozart for German singspiel version, *Die verstellte Gärtnerin* (*Die Gärtnerin aus Liebe*), 1779–80, libretto trans. ?Johann Franz Joseph Stierle the elder
PREMIERES 13 January 1775, Salvatortheater, Munich; UK: 7 January 1930, Scala Theatre, London; US: 18 January 1927, Mayfair Theater, New York; singspiel version: ?1 May 1780, Komödienstadl, Augsburg
CAST Don Anchise (the Podestà) *t*, La Marchesa Violante/'Sandrina' *s*, Belfiore *t*, Arminda *s*, Ramiro *s* or *ms*, Serpetta *s*, Roberto/'Nardo' *b*

Commissioned for the Munich Carnival, Mozart's opera was twice postponed and then had only three performances amid problems with an ailing prima donna and a 'large but rather untidy orchestra'. It was not done again in his lifetime except in the German translation, nor could the Italian version be performed in our own day until the missing recitatives of Act I were found in a copy in Moravia in the 1970s. Piccinni's *Buona figliuola* (1760) had started the fashion for opera buffa with a sentimental story, the operatic daughter of Richardson's virtuous maltreated Pamela and, like *La finta giardiniera*, an aristocratic girl working as a gardener's assistant (they all clung to this pastoral activity rather than descend to housework). Petrosellini, the probable author, had written several libretti in this vein, including *L'incognita perseguita* and *La Metilde ritrovata*. Mad scenes were also popular: Haydn was to write them for *La vera costanza* (1778) with a similar plot and *Orlando paladino* (1782), but the afflicted persons were the tenor heroes (in the tradition of Ariosto's *Orlando furioso*) until Paisiello's *Nina, o sia La pazza per amore* (1789) changed all that. Belfiore and Sandrina proclaim their madness by believing themselves to be all sorts of mythological figures. Auden took up the same idea for the chilling Bedlam finale in Stravinsky's *The Rake's Progress* (1951).

SYNOPSIS

Act I: Don Anchise, the Podestà (mayor) of Lagonero, has fallen in love with the new gardener's assistant, Sandrina, to the annoyance of the jealous maid, Serpetta. Sandrina is really the disguised Marchesa Violante, who has fled from her violent lover, the Count Belfiore. She is accompanied by her servant Roberto under the name of Nardo. The Podestà's haughty niece, Arminda, arrives to receive her bridegroom, none other than Count Belfiore. Arminda is recognized by her moping cavalier, Ramiro. Reproaches all round.

Act II: Sandrina, meaning to test Belfiore, denies that she is Violante, but when the Podestà appears with a warrant for the arrest of Belfiore on the charge of having murdered Violante, she saves him by admitting that she is Violante. Left alone with him, she denies it again. At this point Belfiore, who has always acted a little strangely, goes completely mad. The jealous Arminda and Serpetta contrive to abandon Sandrina in a wild forest, but Nardo, who has been wooing the maid, discovers the plot and goes to the rescue, followed by the entire cast. Unfortunately, Sandrina now seems to have gone mad as well.

Act III: Sandrina and Belfiore awaken to refound sanity and love. Arminda makes do with Ramiro and Serpetta accepts Nardo. The Podestà decides to wait until another Sandrina turns up.

Serpetta and Nardo are the traditional buffo soubrette and valet; the Podestà is a buffo tenor (not bass) with the hoary old cliché of an aria imitating various musical instruments; Arminda and Ramiro are the opera seria characters; but the heroine wavers between the Marchesa Violante she is and the Sandrina she pretends to be; Belfiore is mainly cast in a buffo light, for his first entry reminds us of Ferrando and Guglielmo taking their mock tender leave in *Così fan tutte*, and the aria 'Da Scirocco a Tramontana', boasting of his good breeding, is certainly comic. Perhaps his mad scenes were meant to be comic too. The idea that the count needs a process of trial and purification to make him worthy of Violante is in the tradition of great comedies. While the librettist hops awkwardly in and out of the comic and serious implications, the score shows the beginning of Mozart's ability to combine these two aspects of life – later to become the cornerstone of his operatic masterpieces.

Musically, Mozart had taken another gigantic step in the two years since *Lucio Silla*. 'Most of the pieces show the imprint of Mozart's style so clearly,' wrote Abert, 'that it would be impossible to think of any other composer.' The arias are mostly in sonata form and mostly of suitable length; there are no da capos. Where there is a change of tempo it is for the sake of the text or to heighten the tension towards the end of an aria. Some of Serpetta's arias would not be out of place among Despina's in *Così fan tutte*. The most striking novelty is in the Act I and II finales, with their rich palette of harmony, instrumentation and rhythm, far beyond anything achieved or indeed even considered by his Italian contemporaries. For the two allegro sections in the Act I finale Mozart employs a loose rondo form, in which the characters impart their own flavour to the main tune by singing it in the minor, or by continuing it in a different way. The excitement mounts as all the voices join in. The finale to Act II, linked by orchestral sections or accompanied recitatives to the three previous arias, provides 26 minutes of continuous music, compared to the great *Figaro* Act II finale of under 20 minutes. It opens in darkness (like the Act IV finale in *Figaro*), though here with an andante sostenuto in E♭, the traditional key for an *ombra* scene, as in *Lucio Silla*. The nocturnal sounds of the forest, expressed by the orchestra, are broken by single voices here and there, until Ramiro enters followed by servants with torches. They are accompanied by a busy violin figure until the scene is lit up to the sound of flutes and horns and everybody's identity is revealed. There are so many touches of Mozart's real genius that one cannot help regretting the weaknesses of the libretto.

RECORDINGS 1. Donath, Norman, Cotrubas, Troyanos, Hollweg, Prey, NDR Ch & O, Schmidt-Isserstedt, Philips, 1972: singspiel version; 2. Conwell, Sukis, Ihloff, Fassbaender, Moser, di Cesare, McDaniel, Mozarteum-Orchester, Hager, Philips, 1980; 3. Gruberova, Margiono, Upshaw, Bacelli, Heilmann, Concentus Musicus Wien, Harnoncourt, Teldec, 1991 (cut)

Il re pastore

The Shepherd King

Serenata in two acts (2h)
Libretto by Pietro Metastasio (1751)
Composed March–April 1775
PREMIERES 23 April 1775, Archbishop's Palace, Salzburg; UK: 8 November 1954, St Pancras Town Hall, London; US: 7 July 1971, Norfolk, Virginia
CAST Alessandro *t*, Aminta *s* (*castrato*), Elisa *s*, Tamiri *s*, Agenore *t*

Two operas on libretti by Metastasio were commissioned by Archbishop Colloredo for the visit of the youngest archduke, Maximilian Franz. The text chosen by (or for) Mozart had been set a dozen times, chiefly for occasions honouring Habsburg princes. (The well-meaning bungler Alexander, as depicted here, predicts the career of the archduke's elder brother, the Emperor Joseph II.) The opera, or serenata, was virtually performed as a cantata with a minimum of scenery and movement. After this, Mozart was not to see a new opera performed for five years. He began to loathe Salzburg, where musicians were held in no regard and where there was no opera or theatre.

Metastasio cites the ancient historians Cursius and Justinian as his sources for the story that Alexander the Great placed an obscure gardener named Abdolonymus on the throne of Sidon. But this name 'made him sound like a hypochondriac with a stomach ache', so Metastasio changed him into the shepherd Aminta.

SYNOPSIS

Act I: Having freed Sidon from the usurper Strato, Alexander determines to put the rightful heir on the throne. With the help of Agenore, he discovers him in Aminta, who was unaware of his origins. Agenore recognizes his own beloved Tamiri, Strato's daughter, disguised as a shepherdess. Aminta, only concerned with his beloved Elisa, is dismayed by Alexander's news. He and Elisa reaffirm their love.

Act II: Agenore refuses to admit Elisa to the new king, but Aminta has no desire for the crown. Alexander tells the devastated Agenore that he will arrange for Aminta to marry Tamiri, thus making everybody happy. In the end Tamiri and Elisa pluck up courage to tell him that he is actually making everybody miserable. Aminta hands in his royal robes: let Tamiri reign with another, he says, for he himself prefers Elisa's love to a crown. Alexander appoints Tamiri and Agenore to rule over Sidon, promising Aminta and Elisa the next kingdom he comes upon (another unconsciously ironic reflection on the Habsburgs).

The nature of the occasion and of the libretto precluded anything dramatic in the music, but the melodies are more truly Mozartian than in his earlier opera-seria music. Since his main preoccupation at this time was with instrumental music, it is not surprising to find Mozart using instrumental form for some of the arias, sharing the theme of Aminta's first aria with the G major Violin Concerto (September 1775) and providing extremely enjoyable scoring, including the virtuoso flutes of Alexander's 'Se vincendo vi rendo felice'. The duet exactly follows the pattern of all his previous opera-seria duets, and the finale is strictly formal in its writing for the 'chorus' of soloists. The most moving music is in Aminta's protestation of love, the famous rondeaux 'L'amerò, sarò costante' with solo violin and an accompaniment of flutes, cors anglais, bassoons, horns and muted strings. Almost as touching is Tamiri's simple rondo 'Se tu di me fai dono' that follows it.

RECORDING Blasi, McNair, Vermillion, Hadley, Ahnsjö, Academy of St Martin in the Fields, Marriner, Philips, 1989

Idomeneo

Dramma per musica in three acts (3h 30m) and ballet (30m)
Libretto by Giambattista Varesco, after the libretto by Antoine Danchet for the tragédie en musique *Idomenée* by André Campra (1712), itself after the tragedy by Crébillon *père* (1705)
Composed October 1780–January 1781
PREMIERES 29 January 1781, Cuvilliés Theater, Munich; UK: 12 March 1934, Theatre Royal, Glasgow (amateur); 20 June 1951, Glyndebourne, Sussex; US: 4 August 1947, Berkshire Music Center, Lenox, Massachusetts (Tanglewood)
CAST Idomeneo *t*, Idamante *s* (or *t*), Ilia *s*, Elettra *s*, Arbace *t*, High Priest *t*, Oracle *b*; *satb* chorus of Trojan captives, Cretan sailors, Cretan people, priests; ballet

The artistic Karl Theodor had succeeded to the Bavarian Electorate in 1778 and brought his famous orchestra and opera company with him from Mannheim. Mozart's letters home from his arrival in Munich (on 8 November 1780) until his father joined him (on 25 January 1781) give a fascinating detailed account of the creation of his first operatic masterpiece. His problems with the 67-year-old tenor Raaff and the untalented 'amato castrato del Prato', his Idomeneo and Idamante ('the two worst actors any stage has ever borne'), were not without influence on the music he wrote for them. Mozart's dramatic instinct and common sense are in evidence when he remarks that 'the thunder is presumably not going to cease for Mr Raaff's aria' or 'it seems naïve to think that everybody hurries off (after the Oracle has spoken) just to leave Mme Elettra alone'. The music for the Oracle was written at least four times, for he believed that it must be short to be credible, adding that the Ghost in *Hamlet* would have benefited from greater brevity. In the interests of dramatic tightness he cut three arias from Act III at a late stage (among many smaller cuts). The opera was given only three performances, but Mozart continued to believe in it: nothing came of his hope of making a German opera of it with a bass Idomeneo in Vienna in 1781, but there was one revival by aristocratic amateurs in the Palais Auersperg, Vienna, in March 1786 (when he was completing the score of *Figaro*). For this Mozart made some important changes: Idamante was now apparently a tenor (though the music is mysteriously written in the soprano, not the tenor, clef) and has a new aria with violin obbligato ('Non temer, amato bene', K.

490). The Act III duet was almost wholly rewritten to its great advantage ('Spiegarti non poss'io', K. 489), and small adjustments were made to the trio and quartet.

Gluck's *Iphigénie en Aulide* and *Alceste* were the most famous of the sacrifice operas, but the genre continued into the 19th century. Melchior von Grimm, who had been Mozart's patron in Paris in 1778–9, remarked that sacrifice operas were 'a very interesting spectacle to behold and offered many situations at once strong and pathetic and suitable for music'. There was certainly more pathos than drama to be got out of them, for all humans can do is submit to the gods. The too pliant and generous Idamante plays the Metastasian role of dying cheerfully for a father he has only just met. Yet the story does contain, at least potentially, the perennial tragedy of the young generation condemned to death by the vows or treaties of their elders.

SYNOPSIS

Act I: The action takes place in Crete after the Trojan War. In the royal palace the captive Trojan princess Ilia laments her fate ('Padre, germani, addio!'), but the Cretan prince Idamante loves her ('Non ho colpa') and sets all the Trojan captives free to prove it. Arbace brings the news that Idomeneo has been drowned at sea. The fierce Greek princess Elettra is jealous of Ilia's power over Idamante ('Tutte nel cor vi sento'). On a storm-swept shore the pitiful cries of the sailors ('Pietà! Numi, pietà!') finally give way to the appearance of Neptune himself (in a pantomima), calming the storm in answer to Idomeneo's prayer. As the king comes ashore he is profoundly unhappy at the vow he has just taken, to sacrifice the first being he meets ('Vedrommi intorno'). His victim, the friendly young man who comes to his aid, turns out to be his son Idamante, saddened that his father seems to reject him ('Il padre adorato ritrovo'). The Cretan people celebrate Idomeneo's safe return.

Act II: In the palace alone with Arbace, Idomeneo resolves to send Idamante to safety in Argos with Elettra. Ilia involuntarily reveals her love for his son ('Se il padre perdei'), which increases his despair at the storm in his soul ('Fuor del mar'). Only Elettra rejoices at her coming departure with the prince, hurrying down to the harbour to join the chorus ('Placido è il mar') and the leave-taking of the king and his son ('Pria di partir'). But suddenly Neptune, infuriated by Idomeneo's attempts to break the vow, sends a monster in a storm ('Qual nuovo terrore!'). Idomeneo begs Neptune to punish him alone, but the tempest continues and the people flee in terror ('Corriamo, fuggiamo').

Act III: In the royal garden Ilia sings to the breeze of her love for Idamante ('Zeffiretti lusinghieri'), and when he promises to kill the monster or die in the attempt, she at last confesses her love. The momentary happiness of their duet ('S'io non moro a questi accenti') is followed by the bleak tragedy of the quartet ('Andrò ramingo e solo'), when Idomeneo once more urges his son's departure. Arbace now warns him that the people demand action and threaten revolt. Idomeneo goes to meet them in a large square before the palace. Urged by the High Priest, he at last reveals that the victim is his own son, to the sorrow of the people ('Oh voto tremendo!'). The scene of the sacrifice is the temple of Neptune near the shore. After Idomeneo's prayer ('Accogli, oh re del mar') there is a momentary ray of hope at the news that Idamante has killed the monster. But he is brought on as the willing sacrificial victim. Idomeneo's sword is already raised when Ilia rushes in to implore him to kill her, an enemy of Greece, instead. Now the nobility of Ilia and Idamante melts Neptune's anger, and the Oracle announces that they shall henceforth reign in Crete. This is followed by universal rejoicing with the notable exception of Elettra, a prey to the furies who had tormented her brother, Orestes ('D'Oreste, d'Aiace ho in seno i tormenti').

Seen as a whole, *Idomeneo* is a flawed masterpiece without the tension of a great tragedy, but Mozart's score contains some of the greatest operatic music ever written. Traditional elements of opera seria struggle with innovations based on Gluck and the tragédie lyrique, especially in the great dramatic choruses. Infinitely expressive accompanied recitatives link the arias and ensembles to form long stretches of continuous music, leaving few opportunities for the old applauded exit aria: they also bind the music by quoting themes from arias just heard or yet to come and achieve great tension by merging into rhythmic arioso at the approach of an aria or of some important revelation. Ilia has the most beautiful of the arias; her 'Se il padre perdei' early in Act II is one of Mozart's very greatest, accompanied by a concertante wind quartet, not as a virtuoso or merely colourful element but to express every hidden emotion. Mozart avoided giving del Prato coloratura or other problems and made up for this with his orchestration – for example, the string runs and chromatic wind to express Idamante's perplexity in 'Non ho colpa'. Idomeneo has the noble prayer 'Accogli, oh re del mar' with the unison chant of the priests and a unique accompaniment of pizzicato strings with a web of interlinking woodwind, but also the return to an earlier style in the coloratura of 'Fuor del mar', ineptly triumphant even if it is meant to represent the storm in his heart. The two other characters have virtually no impact on the story at all. The confidant Arbace sings two very conventional arias, which were heavily cut by Mozart and can easily be omitted. But Elettra has the most varied and difficult role in Mozart (along with the equally fierce Vitellia in *La clemenza di Tito*): she can sing of the joys of love as sweetly as any Zaide ('Idol mio', or in her solo in 'Placido è il mar'), but her first and last arias express fury beyond the limits of sanity, especially in the manic laugh that concludes the latter. No wonder conductors are reluctant to follow Mozart in cutting her 'D'Oreste' at the end of the opera. Unfortunately nobody ever takes the slightest bit of notice of Elettra, which is perhaps why she goes mad.

The Act II duet is little more than a charming pastoral piece: Mozart's 1786 version is the most pertinent criticism of it. The trio ('Pria di partir'), a beautiful piece of conflicting emotions, is, however, overshadowed by the quartet ('Andrò ramingo e solo'), one of Mozart's great tragic utterances – he himself later burst into tears while singing it with friends. The dramatic choruses at the appearance of the monster in Act II and at the revelation of Idamante's fate in Act III are of incomparable eloquence. And there is also the sheer happy lilt of the barcarolle 'Placido è il mar'.

If Mozart tailored each aria to his singer, how much more he must have fitted the score to his admired Mannheim orchestra. Mozart never created such a rich orchestral part in any other opera. His father wondered how the musicians could survive three hours of it (four hours would be closer if the ballet was performed complete): 'I know your style. Every musician needs astonishing continuous concentration.' Mozart is suddenly freed from the old conventions, the woodwind are wholly independent; he lovingly uses the clarinet for the first time in an opera, as well as the virtuoso oboe of his friend Ramm and all the power of four horns, two trumpets and timpani. One must also imagine all the effects of thunder, lightning, crowd movements, swift scene changes and a monster and a god out of the machine, as produced by the experts of the Munich theatre.

For the first time Mozart uses little phrases, not quite leitmotifs, but expressions of a particular emotion, such as the anxious trill-like trembling we hear in Elettra's first aria and in Idamante's first two arias and throughout the chorus 'Qual nuovo terror', or the falling phrase associated with Idamante's fate and first heard towards the end of the overture. Lacking Gluck's bold simplicity, Mozart hints at subtler shades of emotion with an orchestral, melodic and harmonic richness far beyond his contemporaries. The premiere took place two days after his 25th birthday.

RECORDINGS 1. Popp, Baltsa, Gruberova, Pavarotti, Vienna State Op Ch, VPO, Pritchard, Decca, 1983; 2. McNair, von Otter, Martinpelto, Rolfe Johnson, Monteverdi Ch, EBS, Gardiner, Archiv, 1990 (live)

Die Entführung aus dem Serail

The Abduction from the Harem

Singspiel in three acts (2h 15m)
Libretto by Gottlieb Stephanie the Younger, after *Bellmont und Constanze, oder Die Entführung aus dem Serail* by Christoph Friedrich Bretzner set by Johann André (1781)
Composed July 1781–May 1782
PREMIERES 16 July 1782, Burgtheater, Vienna; UK: 24 November 1827, Covent Garden, London; US: 16 February 1860, Brooklyn Athenaeum, New York
CAST Bassa Selim *spoken role*, Konstanze *s*, Blonde *s*, Belmonte *t*, Pedrillo *t*, Osmin *b*, Klaas, a sailor *spoken role*, guards *silent*; *satb* chorus of janissaries and attendants

The composition of *Die Entführung aus dem Serail*, commissioned for Joseph II's singspiel company under Stephanie's direction, took an unusually long time to complete, although Mozart composed three major numbers for it in one day. It had been intended for a visit by the Russian Grand Duke at the end of 1781, which kept being postponed. The opera was Mozart's main preoccupation between May 1781, when he broke with the Archbishop of Salzburg and settled in Vienna, and his marriage in August 1782. He wrote three long letters to his father in the autumn of 1781 that give a vivid insight into his creative thinking. He describes how he expressed the emotions, the very heartbeats of Belmonte in 'O wie ängstlich, o wie feurig' and the unbridled fury of Osmin: at the end of 'Solche hergelauf'ne Laffen' he is 'beside himself, so the music must be too, but because passion, however strong, must never be expressed to the extent of disgusting the hearer and music must remain music, I have chosen a key [for 'Erst geköpft, dann gehangen'] that is not a stranger to F [the key of the aria], but a friend, not the closest one D minor, but A minor'. The actual words of Stephanie's undistinguished text did not really worry him, for Osmin's aria 'was already walking around' in his head before he saw the libretto. He thought that a good composer who understood the stage, helped by the right poet, could steer the drama in the right direction, that words should be the obedient daughters of the music and that rhyming texts were a waste of time. But there has probably never been a really satisfactory production of *Die Entführung* and Mozart must bear the main responsibility for this. Stephanie added little to Bretzner's text. They even copied the idea of a speaking Selim: a tenor had been planned for the role, but Mozart must have turned against the thought of three tenors. This means that the only musical opposition comes from the comic Osmin. In the opera that was their model Bretzner and his composer Johann André had produced a lively ensemble for the elopement scene in Act III: Mozart began a finale for Act II presumably to contain the elopement, with an unfinished duet for Belmonte and Pedrillo ('Welch ängstliches Beben'), but eventually the elopement and recapture of the lovers was allowed to take place in silence. Thus, both the main action of the opera and its main character, Selim, in the sense that the plot hangs on his moods and their changes, remain without music. In spite of this the opera was an instant success and was played in 40 cities during Mozart's lifetime. Goethe, who had himself written libretti for singspiels, said: '*Die Entführung* knocked everything else sideways.' Weber saw that Mozart's artistic experience had reached maturity in *Die Entführung*. The Emperor apparently remarked: 'An awful lot of notes, my dear Mozart.'

SYNOPSIS

Act I: The Spanish nobleman Belmonte has arrived on the Barbary or Turkish coast to search for his betrothed Konstanze, who was captured by pirates, together with her maid Blonde and his servant Pedrillo ('Hier soll ich dich denn sehen'). With great difficulty he learns from the grumpy overseer Osmin that he is standing before the palace of Bassa Selim ('Wer ein Liebchen hat gefunden'). When Pedrillo appears, Osmin expresses his lethal loathing for him ('Solche hergelauf'ne Laffen'). When he has gone, Belmonte learns that Konstanze is alive and well: his emotion is boundless ('Konstanze! . . . O wie ängstlich'). The Bassa arrives with his retinue ('Singt dem grossen Bassa Lieder') and begins to woo Konstanze once more, but her heart belongs to another from whom she was cruelly parted ('Ach, ich liebte'). Selim gives her one more day to change her mind. She leaves, and Pedrillo introduces Belmonte to the Bassa as a talented architect. Selim takes him on, but Belmonte and Pedrillo have the greatest difficulty in getting past Osmin to enter the palace ('Marsch, marsch, marsch!')

Act II: Outside Osmin's house in the palace garden. Blonde has been assigned to Osmin but soon shows that she has the upper hand. 'I am a free-born Englishwoman,' she tells him and proceeds to tease him into submission ('Ich gehe, doch rate ich dir'). Konstanze still has nothing to say to the Bassa except to express her sorrow ('Welcher Wechsel herrscht in meiner Seele . . . Traurigkeit ward mir zum Lose'), but when he threatens her with torture, she replies defiantly ('Martern aller Arten'). Blonde is delighted to hear from Pedrillo that they are to escape that very night ('Welche Wonne, welche Lust'). Pedrillo summons up as much courage as he can ('Frisch zum Kampfe!'), then proceeds to get Osmin drunk to be out of the way ('Vivat Bacchus!'). Belmonte meets his beloved at last ('Wenn der Freude Tränen fliessen'). The women assure their lovers that they have always been faithful to them despite all the hazards of life in a harem ('Ach Belmonte, ach mein Leben!').

Act III: Outside the palace Pedrillo sings an old ballad as a signal ('Im Mohrenland gefangen war') and the two men succeed in abducting the women, but a guard discovers the ladder and they are soon brought before Osmin, who is seething with vengeful fury ('O, wie will ich triumphieren'). Condemned to die by the Bassa, Belmonte reveals that his father is Lostados, governor of Oran. 'He is my greatest enemy,' Selim answers, 'who has robbed me of my beloved, my wealth, my fatherland.' Belmonte and Konstanze await their death, each longing to die for the other ('Welch ein Geschick . . . Meinetwegen sollst du sterben'). But the Bassa has no wish to emulate the despised Lostados, so he pardons them and sends all four home. The opera ends in the gratitude and rejoicing of everybody except Osmin.

The wonderful freshness of the musical invention more than makes up for the dramatic weakness. Mozart gave the magnificent buffo bass Ludwig Fischer, in the part of Osmin, music of great brilliance and range with frequent descents to evil thoughts and bottom D. The Konstanze, Caterina Cavalieri, was famous for her coloratura and her two-octave leaps: Mozart admitted that he had to sacrifice something to her 'fluent throat' and that he had to express the mood within the limitations of an Italian bravura aria. Her second aria ('Traurigkeit') with its recitative is one of his most moving creations, but when he came to the great showpiece of the opera, 'Martern aller Arten', Mozart abandoned dramatic relevance by adding a virtuoso concertante quartet of flute, oboe, violin and cello. Belmonte opens with a lied, taken from the middle section of the overture, and then Mozart gives him 'O wie ängstlich' – 'everybody's favourite, including mine'. The famous tenor Johann Valentin Adamberger demanded four arias, so he sings one on meeting Konstanze, when a duet would have been far more appropriate, and another in Act III, which is generally omitted. The duet in Act III avoids tragic tones except in the opening recitative, for the lovers are quietly exulting in thoughts of self-sacrifice. Pedrillo's arias are both full of character: in the first a not very courageous little man is trying to wind himself up to the necessary courage for the daring rescue. The romance, sotto voce, with only pizzicato strings, is one of Mozart's strangest compositions: the first three lines pass though the keys of D, A, C, G, F♯ minor and F♯ major. The soubrette Blonde is lyrical and vixenish as the occasion demands.

The quartet, though it does not fit the customary picture of an Act II finale as a crescendo of noise and confusion, is one of Mozart's most enchanting creations. The beginning and end express generalized joy, but the middle part contains its own little drama: the two tenors ask the sopranos, not without due hesitation and embarrassment, if in spite of all the temptations and threats they have remained faithful to them. The women's reactions reassure them. This is not so much a quartet as two simultaneous duets – the two noble lovers with their legato lines, the servants in staccato phrases, the culmination being in Blonde's triplet fireworks (she is still smarting at the insult) against the blissful reconciliation of the others. At the very heart of the quartet there is a serene siciliana in A major of only 15 bars, in which Mozart celebrates the profound happiness of love. He was about to marry his Constanze despite a father rather less forgiving than the Bassa.

One should mention the vivid Turkish music, with its C major, its repeated little phrases and, of course, percussion, which fills the overture and the choruses. The characters take their leave in a charming vaudeville, a form borrowed from opéra comique.

RECORDINGS 1. Auger, Schreier, Moll, Leipzig RCh, Dresden Staatskapelle, Böhm, DG, 1974; 2. Organásová, Olsen, Hauptmann, Monteverdi Ch, EBS, Gardiner, Archiv, 1991; 3. Schäfer, Bostridge, Ewing, Les Arts Florissants, Christie, Erato, 1998

Der Schauspieldirektor

The Impresario

Comedy with music in one act (music only: 30m)
Text by Gottlieb Stephanie the Younger
Composed January–February 1786
PREMIERES 7 February 1786, Orangerie, Schloss Schonbrunn, Vienna; UK: 30 May 1857, St James's Theatre, London; US: 9 November 1870, Stadttheater, New York
CAST Buff *b*, Monsieur Vogelsang *t*, Mme Herz *s*, Mlle Silberklang *s*; *spoken roles*: Frank, Eiler, Mme Pfeil, Mme Krone, Mme Vogelsang

In the midst of one of the most astonishing creative periods of Mozart's life, which included the composition of *Figaro*, the piano concertos K. 482, K. 488 and K. 491 and a dozen other major works, came the imperial command for a few songs for a comedy to be presented at a court festivity in honour of the governor-general of the Austrian Netherlands, the Archduchess Christine and her husband. The 80 guests were given lunch in the centre of the hall, then this German comedy on a stage at one end followed by an opera buffa, *Prima la musica poi le parole* by Casti, with music by Salieri, at the other end. Mozart wrote an overture and four vocal numbers. Stephanie, director of the National Singspiel, obviously saw himself in the role of the good-natured impresario Frank (though Mozart was one of the few who spoke well of him). The two prima donnas, Caterina Cavalieri (Salieri's mistress and the first Konstanze in *Die Entführung*) as Mlle Silberklang and Aloysia Lange (née Weber, Mozart's sister-in-law and first love) as Mme Herz, must have had a sense of humour to take part in this parody on the vanity of singers.

SYNOPSIS

The impresario Frank, assisted by the buffo singer Buff, is forming a theatrical company to play in Salzburg. Two actresses perform for him and are engaged. Then Mme Herz sings a pathetic arietta ('Da schlägt die Abschiedsstunde') and Mlle Silberklang a rondo ('Bester Jüngling!') to exhibit their strongest points. Each then gives brilliant vocal backing to her claim for the higher fee, but Monsieur Vogelsang manages to effect a truce ('Ich bin die erste Sängerin'). When Frank threatens to abandon the whole plan of forming a company, all unreasonable demands are instantly withdrawn. In a vaudeville ('Jeder Künstler strebt nach Ehre') everybody, including Buff, recognizes the need for the ambition of artists, provided that it is not at the expense of their colleagues.

Mozart would have preferred to compose the opera buffa (if his work on *Figaro* had permitted it), but he made the very best of his trivial task. The overture is a brilliant, symphonic work with rich orchestration. The pathos of the first aria anticipates the parodies of *Così*: the horn imitating the tolling bell is an especially good touch. A sketch of the vocal line, of which only the first five bars remain in the final version, is a rare surviving example to show us how much Mozart sometimes departed from his initial ideas. Mlle Silberklang has a delicious wind-band accompaniment and the same coloratura figure that is the undoing of many a Donna Anna in 'Non mi dir' in *Don Giovanni*. The trio is a very funny scene in which each lady sings about the nobility of her art while trying to defeat her rival with ever higher notes. The closing song is a simple rondo in gavotte time.

RECORDING Nador, Laki, Hampson, van der Kamp, Concertgebouw O, Harnoncourt, Teldec, 1986

Le nozze di Figaro

The Marriage of Figaro

Opera buffa in four acts (3h)
Libretto by Lorenzo da Ponte, after the comedy *La folle journée, ou Le mariage de Figaro* by Pierre-Augustin Caron de Beaumarchais (1784)
Composed October 1785–April 1786
PREMIERES 1 May 1786, Burgtheater, Vienna; UK: 2 May 1812, Pantheon, London; US: 10 May 1824, Park Theater, New York
CAST Il Conte di Almaviva *bar*, La Contessa di Almaviva *s*, Susanna *s*, Figaro *b*, Cherubino *s* (or *ms*), Marcellina *s*, Bartolo *b*, Basilio *t*, Don Curzio *t*, Barbarina *s*, Antonio *b*; *satb* chorus of peasants and the Count's tenants

We know very little about the process of composition of *Figaro*, for none of Mozart's letters survives from the months that preceded the first performance on 1 May 1786. When da Ponte came to relate his tale many years later in his autobiography, he was himself the hero of the story: it was he who hurried to the emperor and persuaded him to permit the musical version of a play that had been banned as subversive and he who later foiled the typical Viennese plots. But even da Ponte admitted that the idea of setting *Figaro* came from Mozart. The play had everything to commend it, not least the thrill of having been banned. It used most of the old ingredients of comedy, but in a new way: there was a pair of lovers, but they were a valet and a lady's maid; the comic servant has become his master's successful rival; in the concluding scene of clemency, common to nearly all of Mozart's operas, it is the Count, the representative of emperor, bassa or god, who has to beg for it. We are in the new topsy-turvy world of the French Revolution. Cherubino is a new invention, 'drunk with love' (according to Kierkegaard), the first of the many *travesti* roles that succeeded the youths impersonated by castrati. Beaumarchais, who recognized the potential frisson, specified that 'he could be played only by a young and very pretty woman'. The play is brilliantly theatrical, for each act has its coup de théâtre: the discovery of the page in Act I, Susanna emerging from the closet in Act II, the revelation of Figaro's parentage in Act III and the Countess as dea ex machina in Act IV – and how quietly, almost casually, Mozart brings each one about. The actual plotting does not bear too much scrutiny. How many people in the audience realize that there are actually three mysterious pieces of paper at different points? Unlike *Così fan tutte* with its schematic plot, *Figaro* teems with plots, as life does: all the characters are involved with intrigues of their own, sometimes even against their allies, as when Susanna and Figaro set out to teach each other a lesson in Act IV. But the main plot is clear: although the Count is doing everything to cancel or postpone the wedding because of his feelings for Susanna, Figaro and Co. defeat him and bring him back to his wife.

Da Ponte apologized in his preface to the libretto for having had to reduce the number of acts, characters and bons mots in the interests of the music. He also had to omit *Figaro*'s more politically subversive remarks, though the tone of 'Se vuol ballare' is defiant enough. The essential difference between the play and the opera was perceptively described by Stendhal in his *Lettre sur Mozart* (1814): 'Mozart, with his overwhelmingly sensitive nature, has transformed into real passions the superficial inclinations which amuse the easy-going inhabitants of Aguas Frescas in Beaumarchais . . . In this sense then it might be said that Mozart could not have distorted the play more. I do not really know if music is capable of depicting French flirtation and frivolity for the course of four acts and in all the characters: I should say it was difficult, for music needs strong emotions, whether of joy or unhappiness . . . the wit remains only in the situations: all the characters have been filled with feeling and passion . . . Mozart's opera is a sublime mixture of wit and melancholy, which has no equal.'

The cast included the great actor Francesco Benucci as Figaro (later the first Vienna Leporello and the first Guglielmo), Francesco Bussani as Bartolo and Antonio (later the first Vienna Commendatore and Masetto and the first Don Alfonso), his wife, Dorotea, as Cherubino (later the first Vienna Zerlina and the first Despina), the 12-year-old Anna Gottlieb as Barbarina (later the first Pamina) as well as the English Nancy Storace as Susanna and the Irish Michael Kelly as Basilio and Don Curzio.

On 29 August 1789 began a series of performances of a revival in Vienna with a new cast for which Mozart made a number of revisions, including changes in the Count's aria and in the Countess's second aria. The new Susanna, Caterina Cavalieri, made him replace her two arias with 'Un moto di gioia' and 'Al desio'.

SYNOPSIS

Act I: A half-furnished room in Count Almaviva's Castle of Aguas Frescas near Seville. The Count's valet, Figaro, and Susanna, the Countess's maid, are preparing for their wedding ('Cinque, dieci, venti'). How convenient, thinks Figaro, for us to be between the Count and the Countess; and how convenient, Susanna adds, for the Count, who has started making advances to her – not that Figaro should doubt her for a moment ('Se a caso madama la notte ti chiama'). Left alone, Figaro is distraught but vengeful ('Se vuol ballare signor Contino'). When he has gone out, Dr Bartolo and his housekeeper, Marcellina, enter: though old enough to be his mother, she is trying to force Figaro into marriage in acquittal of a loan he cannot repay. Bartolo is eager to help her in order to avenge himself on Figaro, who had planned the abduction of his ward Rosina, now the Countess ('La vendetta'). Susanna returns and she and Marcellina soon abandon ironic politeness ('Via resti servita, madama brillante') until Marcellina storms out. Cherubino darts in. He is in love with all women ('Non so più cosa son, cosa faccio') but most of all with his godmother, the Countess. Hearing the Count approach, he hides behind the armchair. The Count at once begins to flirt with Susanna but, hearing the music master Don Basilio outside, he too hides behind the armchair – though not before Cherubino has had time to jump into the armchair and be covered up by Susanna with a dress. Basilio taunts Susanna about Cherubino's passion for the Countess. At this the Count springs up in a rage ('Cosa sento!'); Basilio enjoys the mischief and Susanna nearly swoons. The Count complacently relates how he has recently discovered Cherubino in the room of the gardener's young daughter, Barbarina, hiding under the tablecloth. Acting out the story, he lifts the dress from the armchair and is stunned to see the page again. There is to be no pardon this time and Figaro had better know about his bride's relations with the page, thunders the Count, a little uneasy that Cherubino had witnessed his scene with Susanna. Figaro leads in the peasants to praise the Count for abolishing the wicked old feudal rights over his female tenants. The Count, with great presence of mind, postpones the wedding and sends Cherubino off with a commission to his regiment. Figaro warns Cherubino in a rousing finale ('Non più andrai') that a soldier's life is very different from that of an 'amorous great butterfly'.

Act II: The grand bedroom of the Countess. She is alone, regretting the loss of her husband's love ('Porgi amor'). Figaro unfolds his plan to bring him back to fidelity: he will send the Count an anonymous letter claiming that the Countess has made a secret assignation with a lover; at the same time Susanna is to make an assignation with him, but they will send Cherubino dressed as a girl in place of her. All this will at least distract the Count from averting their marriage. When he has left, Cherubino arrives to perform his latest love song ('Voi che sapete') and to be fitted with his disguise by Susanna ('Venite . . . inginocchiatevi'). The Countess is touched to find that he has wrapped a ribbon of hers round his arm. Suddenly the Count is heard knocking on the door and demanding entry. Susanna happens to be out in the dressing room, so the Countess quickly shuts Cherubino into a closet and opens the door to the Count. She cannot allay his suspicions when a noise is heard from the closet. 'It is only Susanna,' she claims. In a trio ('Susanna, or via sortite') the Count orders Susanna to come out, the Countess is affronted by his behaviour and Susanna, who has come into the room unseen by both of them, observes the situation. As soon as the Count has gone off with the Countess to fetch a hammer to break the closet door down, Susanna releases the page. After a moment of panic ('Aprite presto aprite'), he jumps out of the window. The Count returns and the Countess confesses that he will not find Susanna in the closet but Cherubino. The finale opens with the Count ordering Cherubino out and threatening to kill him. When Susanna emerges, all innocence, the Count and Countess are equally surprised, but he asks to be forgiven for his suspicions. Figaro now arrives to remind him that it is time for the wedding ceremony. The Count confronts him with the anonymous letter, but Figaro denies any knowledge of it. A new threat appears: Antonio, the drunken gardener, complains that somebody had jumped out of the Countess's window on to his geraniums. To allay suspicion Figaro admits that it was he. 'In that case,' says Antonio, 'you will want these papers you dropped.' The Count challenges Figaro to tell him what they are. Prompted by the Countess and Susanna, Figaro gradually reveals that they are the page's commission, which needed the official seal. Just as the Count fears he has lost the campaign, Marcellina storms in with Bartolo and Basilio to urge her legal claim over Figaro. The Count declares that he will hear it at a proper trial in due course, to the noisy despair of Figaro's party.

Act III: A grand hall prepared for the wedding feast. The Count is puzzled by events but delighted with a surprisingly compliant Susanna, sent in to him by the Countess in pursuit of Figaro's plot ('Crudel! perchè finora'). Unfortunately, he overhears Susanna whisper to Figaro of her success and bursts out in jealous fury ('Hai gia vinta la causa! . . . Vedrò mentr'io sospiro'). The trial has gone against Figaro, who, confronted by all his enemies, reveals that his parents are unknown: it gradually emerges that he is the bastard son of Bartolo and Marcellina. The rejoicing over this reunion ('Riconosci in questo amplesso'), not shared by the baffled Count, is interrupted by Susanna with the money to pay off Marcellina. Seeing him in the embrace of her rival, she slaps his face, but the necessary explanations soon bring general contentment. The Countess comes in alone to sing of her hope of regaining her husband's love ('E Susanna non vien! . . . Dove sono . . .') and then to dictate to Susanna a letter of assignation to the Count ('Che soave zeffiretto'). The village girls bring her flowers. Cherubino, who has joined them in disguise, is unmasked by Antonio and the Count. Nevertheless, the wedding celebrations commence. Figaro is amused to see the Count pricking himself on a pin that had sealed a letter of assignation.

Act IV: The garden that night, with various arbours and pavilions. Barbarina is desperately looking for the pin the Count had given her to return to Susanna in acknowledgement of their rendezvous. Figaro wheedles this out of the innocent creature and gives way to his despair at being cuckolded on his wedding night. After Marcellina and Basilio each sing a superfluous aria (normally cut), Figaro has his diatribe about women ('Tutto è disposto . . . Aprite un po' quegl'occhi'), then hides to spy on Susanna. She sings of the coming joy of love ('Giunse alfin il momento . . . Deh vieni non tardar'), but poor Figaro does not realize that she is thinking of him, not of the Count. The moment of the Count's assignation is at hand: the plot has been modified in that the Countess will herself take Susanna's place, disguised as Susanna, while Susanna is disguised as her mistress. The amorous Cherubino opens the finale, pleased to find Susanna, as he thinks, in the dark: he tries to kiss her, but in the confusion it is the Count who gets the kiss and Figaro who receives the Count's answering slap. When the Count's seduction of the supposed Susanna is getting too close for comfort, Figaro chases them off. He eventually recognizes Susanna's voice beneath her disguise and the injustice of his suspicions. He teases her for a while by pretending to declare his love to the 'Countess' and receives another slap for his pains. They make peace and prepare to tease the Count, as Figaro flings himself down before Susanna to declare his love for 'Milady'. The Count calls the whole establishment to witness this outrageous betrayal by his wife and his servant. He is deaf to universal pleas for mercy, until at last the Countess appears, in her disguise as Susanna, and he realizes that it is he who must ask forgiveness. She grants it. There is serene happiness, which explodes into great rejoicing.

Though seven years older than the composer, Lorenzo da Ponte had written only three libretti compared to Mozart's 12 operas. Mozart doubtless played a leading role in their collaboration, but da Ponte was able to understand and satisfy his requirements to a very high degree. The fluidity and freedom of his metres and line lengths, which could blur the transition from recitative to aria, fitted in with Mozart's preference for arias of action rather than contemplation – Susanna's Act II aria ('Venite . . . inginocchiatevi') is sung while dressing Cherubino, her Act IV aria ('Deh vieni non tardar') is designed to tease the eavesdropping Figaro and Mozart's music follows the words and their meanings, not merely the metre of the verse.

Time and time again Mozart's music humanizes the farce of the libretto. *Figaro* stands out, even in Mozart's work, for having the greatest human warmth and the most natural characters, especially in the central figures. Instead of operatic conventions and vain repetitions we get something like a stream of consciousness. In 'Deh vieni non tardar', for example, the melody winds on rhapsodically, while just enough feeling of formal unity is given by the siciliana rhythm and the recapitulation of the woodwind phrases. Susanna's opening phrase, a sort of quote from 'Che Susanna ella stessa si fè' in the opening duet, is recapitulated, but in disguise – a third higher. When she changes from teasing the jealous, eavesdropping Figaro to real emotion, the serenade-like pizzicato of the violins changes magically to con arco sighs, the same accompanying figure Mozart used for the beginning of the *Lacrymosa* in the *Requiem* six years later, the last notes he ever wrote down. The letter duet, an exquisite piece in which the woodwind illustrate the breezes of the nocturnal tryst, treats the dictating of the letter absolutely realistically with suitable pauses for Susanna to write, then follows this with the two women reading the letter together and overlapping in their eagerness. Da Ponte once wrote that a finale should be a complete little opera in itself. The sextet in Act III, reputedly a great favourite of Mozart's, could stand alone as the epitome of Mozartean opera buffa. The action is, of course, a parody of the sentimental pieces of the time, in which long-lost parents and children discover each other (and still a subject for parody in Oscar Wilde's *The Importance of Being Earnest*). There is a long calm opening over a pedal for the quiet joy of the reunited family. Susanna arrives with the ransom money, not at all overjoyed at what she sees – the music has moved to the dominant and agitated violins accompany her. She relieves her feelings by slapping Figaro, but she and the Count, whose plans have been spoiled by the discovery, continue to sing in angry dotted rhythms against the serenity of the others. When we arrive at the recapitulation, back in F major, Marcellina has an entirely new text to explain things to Susanna and therefore new music, which Mozart elegantly combines with the original opening melody now played by the woodwind. The next section, in which the incredulous Susanna is introduced over and over again to Figaro's new parents, is the most delicious passage in all comic opera. But the miracle is still to come when the laughter dissolves in tears of happiness, as Susanna's voice lightly runs over the sotto voce accompaniment of the others (Mozart crossed out his original idea of doubling her line with flute and bassoon). In the end the Count and his henchman, Don Curzio, provide a mildly threatening movement, in case we should lapse into sheer blissful sentimentality.

These are just three examples, briefly described, but every piece in *Figaro* deserves more, from the magic of the overture (with no musical quotation from the opera, but instead an embodiment of its feeling of excitement and tenderness) to the finale of Act IV. Earlier operas had placed the denouement an extra act after the second big finale. Mozart and da Ponte accomplish everything within the great Act IV finale – the mounting excitement and gathering of all the characters as well as both reconciliations, Figaro's with Susanna in a playful tone, the Count's with the Countess in a still moment of the utmost beauty.

RECORDINGS 1. della Casa, Gueden, Danco, Poell, Siepi, Vienna State Op Ch, VPO, E. Kleiber, Decca, 1955; 2. Gens, Ciofi, Kirschlager, Keenlyside, Regazzo, Concerto Köln, Jacobs, Harmonia Mundi, 2003; 3. Vaness, Focile, Miles, Corbelli, Scottish CCh & O, Mackerras, Telarc, 1994

Don Giovanni

Dramma giocoso in two acts (2h 45m)
Libretto by Lorenzo da Ponte, after the opera *Don Giovanni Tenorio, o sia Il convitato di pietra* by Giovanni Bertati (1787)
Composed April–October 1787
PREMIERES 29 October 1787, Gräflich Nostitzsches Nationaltheater, Prague; 7 May 1788, Burgtheater, Vienna; UK: 12 April 1817, His Majesty's Theatre, Haymarket, London; US: 7 November 1817, Park Theater, New York
CAST Don Giovanni *b* or *bar*, Il Commendatore *b*, Donna Anna *s*, Don Ottavio *t*, Donna Elvira *s*, Leporello *b*, Zerlina *s*, Masetto *b*; *satb* chorus of peasants, *tb* chorus of servants; *silent*: peasants, servants, musicians and ministers of justice; offstage: *b* chorus of demons

The extraordinary quantity and variety of works about Don Juan must surely exceed the alleged number of his conquests. Faust and Don Juan were created by the Counter-Reformation as warnings against exceeding the bounds set for man – Faust in seeking metaphysical knowledge and power, Juan for living in unbounded sensuality without any spiritual belief. Both are finally overtaken by divine retribution. Juan first appears in *El burlador de Sevilla*, a play written in 1630 by a monk, Tirso de Molina. But the play is much more than a pious text. The story was rewritten many times before (and after) Mozart's opera, most notably as a play by Molière and as a ballet by Gluck. By the late 18th century it had become little more than an effective puppet show: the two elements that were common to all versions make for good entertainment – a libertine who seduces innumerable ladies and a statue that gets up and comes to dinner. There were at least two new operas on the subject in 1787 before Mozart's: one was seen in Rome by Goethe, who noticed the universal delight in the farcical representation of the story; the other, by Gazzaniga, performed in Venice in January 1787, became the direct model for da Ponte and, to some extent, for Mozart. There are some striking similarities in the text and sometimes even in the music, such as the use of 'Tafelmusik' for the supper scene.

The death of the Commendatore and his revenge are the essential parts of the opera. 'The rest is a parenthesis, the most beautiful and delightful parenthesis in the history of opera but still a parenthesis' (Luigi Dallapiccola). Gazzaniga's opera was based on these essentials but it was only in one act: da Ponte and Mozart had to fill out the time between the Commendatore's death and his reappearance in the form of the avenging statue. Apart from a call to repentance and a supernatural warning, which already occur in Tirso's play, no events have any real bearing on the denouement, since Don Juan is not defeated by any human revenge or pursuit. The rest of the opera is therefore filled with the opera-buffa game of disguises.

Da Ponte later claimed that Mozart had wanted to write a serious opera and had to be persuaded to add the comedy. Mozart probably never considered if he was writing about crime and punishment or divine vengeance. After all, most of his operas had concluded in the theatrical convention of divine or imperial clemency; this time the divine intervention was simply of the opposite sort. But he must have seen this as his first opportunity since *Idomeneo* to write serious, heroic, tragic, operatic music. Mozart is inevitably compared to Shakespeare, not least for the mingling of laughter and tears, but while Shakespeare used the powerful close juxtaposition of tragedy and comedy, he surely has no parallel to *Don Giovanni*'s last scene in which the great heroic duet with the Commendatore is not merely followed, as Duncan's murder is, but actually accompanied by the patter of the buffoon.

Mozart had enjoyed witnessing the

triumph of *Figaro* during his first visit to Prague in January 1787. Only the Bohemian audience seems to have understood what Mozart was, as we believe we do today. Bondini, the manager of the Italian company, commissioned *Don Giovanni* and may have even proposed the subject. *Don Giovanni* proved to be a triumph, and Mozart was cheered on entering and leaving the pit. Vienna saw it the following May with a number of changes demanded by the new cast. The ever-exigent Caterina Cavalieri as Elvira received an extra *scena ed aria* ('Mi tradì'); Benucci as Leporello lost his aria but gained a farcical duet with Zerlina ('Per queste tue manine'), which is now seldom performed; Ottavio had his aria changed for one with less coloratura ('Dalla sua pace'). Mozart made some other changes including cutting the Anna–Ottavio duet in the final scene, but there is no conclusive evidence that he authorized the cut of the entire final scene, which became the rule from the 1790s until the 1920s.

SYNOPSIS

Act I: A garden by night. Leporello is complaining that he has to keep watch in all weathers while his master is enjoying himself indoors ('Notte e giorno faticar'), when Don Giovanni rushes out, trying to escape and hide his face from a furious Donna Anna. Her father, the Commendatore, enters with a sword: Don Giovanni kills him in a duel and escapes with Leporello. Anna returns with her betrothed, Don Ottavio; distraught at finding her father dead, she swears vengeance ('Fuggi, crudele, fuggi!'). A street scene as dawn breaks. An unknown beauty accosted by Don Giovanni ('Ah chi mi dice mai') turns out to be Donna Elvira, whom he had cozened into a pretended marriage and abandoned. Leporello tells her of his master's 2065 conquests and of his technique ('Madamina, il catalogo è questo'). Don Giovanni spies a new prey in the peasant Zerlina, who appears with her bridegroom, Masetto. Masetto is removed by Leporello, and Don Giovanni has just persuaded Zerlina to follow him to his pavilion ('Là ci darem la mano') when Elvira returns to warn her off ('Ah fuggi il traditor'). She warns Anna and Ottavio too ('Non ti fidar, o misera'), but Giovanni brushes off her accusations as a sign of madness. As he leaves, Donna Anna recognizes Don Giovanni as her nocturnal assailant: she describes the attempted rape to the horrified Ottavio and implores him to join in her vengeance ('Or sai chi l'onore'). (Ottavio then usually sings 'Dalla sua pace', added for the Vienna revival.) Don Giovanni gives Leporello instructions about his party for the peasants ('Fin ch'han dal vino'). In a garden on Don Giovanni's estate, Zerlina, reproached for her flirtation with the noble stranger, mollifies Masetto ('Batti, batti, o bel Masetto'), but as soon as Giovanni appears, she grows weak again (finale, Act I), only being saved by Masetto's presence. Donna Anna, Donna Elvira and Don Ottavio, arriving masked to pursue their vengeance, are invited to join the ball. In Don Giovanni's brightly lit ballroom with servants and peasants, the masked strangers are welcomed and the three orchestras strike up: Anna and Ottavio dance the stately minuet, Zerlina and Giovanni the middle-class contredanse, and Leporello whisks Masetto off in a rustic German dance. All is confusion when Zerlina's scream is heard offstage. She rushes in distraught and Giovanni tries to pin the blame on Leporello. The guests now unmask to tell Don Giovanni that he has been found out and that vengeance is nigh.

Act II: A street. Leporello cannot stand his job any longer and tells his master he is leaving him ('Eh via buffone'). Giovanni persuades him with money but vehemently rejects the notion of giving up his mission to make all women happy. At the moment he is thinking of Elvira's maid, but it is Elvira herself who appears on the balcony. He plans to put on Leporello's clothes and seduce the maid, while Leporello in his master's clothes is to keep Elvira out of the way. When he speaks to Elvira of his love, she all too soon falls for his honeyed words again ('Ah taci ingiusto core'), while Leporello is half amused, half pitying. Don Giovanni's plan works, but he has hardly sung his serenade ('Deh vieni alla finestra') when Masetto enters with a band of peasants intending to kill Don Giovanni. The Don, disguised as Leporello, gives Masetto directions on how to find the evil-doer ('Metà di voi qua vadano') and then, getting him on his own, beats him up mercilessly. Zerlina finds Masetto and comforts him ('Vedrai, carino'). In a dark courtyard before Donna Anna's house, Leporello is tired of the amorous Elvira ('Sola, sola in buio loco'), but just as he tries to escape, Donna Anna and Don Ottavio enter with servants bearing torches and Zerlina and Masetto come in through another door. They think they have cornered Don Giovanni at last. Ottavio is quite ready to kill him. Elvira pleads for the life of 'her husband', but the others agree that he must die. At this point Leporello reveals himself and whines for mercy. When he escapes, Don Ottavio decides that it is time to call the police ('Il mio tesoro'). (At this point Elvira's scene and aria ('Mi tradì'), composed for the Vienna revival, is usually inserted.) Meanwhile Don Giovanni has been enjoying himself seducing Leporello's wife. When he laughingly boasts of this to Leporello, whom he meets in the cemetery, it is not only Leporello who is shocked: a mysterious voice tells him that his laughter will be silenced before morning. They find the statue of the Commendatore with the inscription that he waits to be avenged. Don Giovanni orders the terrified Leporello to invite the statue to supper ('O statua gentilissima'). Donna Anna tells Don Ottavio that she loves him but cannot think of marriage during her sorrow. The finale to Act II takes place in Don Giovanni's dining room. He is eating alone, waited on by Leporello and enjoying a wind band playing an opera pot-pourri, when Elvira bursts in to make one more attempt to reclaim him from his wicked life. He answers her scornfully; she runs out and is immediately heard sceaming frantically. Leporello goes to investigate and screams too; he returns to report breathlessly that the statue is arriving. Don Giovanni himself opens the door to his stone guest, who bids him amend his life and repent. He refuses, but in spite of Leporello's terrified entreaties, he accepts the statue's return invitation. As he takes its hand, his strength drains from him. The Commendatore leaves, but an invisible chorus of demons warns Don Giovanni of his coming perdition. With a terrible scream he is swallowed up amid flames. Leporello describes these events to the others. They resolve to get on with their own lives: Don Ottavio to woo Donna Anna once again, Elvira to enter a convent, Leporello to seek a new master, Zerlina and Masetto to have a jolly dinner. The opera ends with the moral that sinners meet with their just reward.

The opening andante of the overture is taken almost entirely from the scene in which the statue confronts Don Giovanni: thus Mozart daringly anticipates the crucial event of the opera, though without the trombones and without the chord of the diminished seventh. Mozart used more ensembles than his contemporaries: *Don Giovanni* in its original form has over 80 minutes of ensemble against less than 40 of arias, and even the arias are ensembles in that each one is sung to somebody or overheard.

Within the vast dramatic range of *Don Giovanni* Mozart still adheres to a semblance of the opera-buffa types. Leporello and the peasants are clearly in the buffa category; Donna Anna and Don Ottavio in the seria, hence her rondo 'Non mi dir' before the Act II finale, suitable to an opera-seria heroine. Donna Elvira has to be *mezzo carattere* (in between): for all her true pathos, she is always being made fun of by Giovanni or Leporello (except in the Vienna addition 'Mi tradì', preceded by the most beautiful of all Mozart's accompanied recitatives, but clearly alien to the original concept).

What of the Don himself? He is everything and nothing. He dominates every moment of the opera, even when not on stage, but he subordinates his own character to that of the others – he adopts Anna's music at their first appearance, then the Commendatore's when the challenges are exchanged, he falls into peasant 2/4 and 6/8 rhythms to seduce Zerlina and into Leporello's buffo terseness when persuading him to stay in his service. Apart from the brief 'Fin ch'han dal vino', the epitome of his energy (he only once draws breath in it), he does not have a real aria of his own. The 21-year-old Luigi Bassi, who created the role, is said to have complained about it. What a *Credo* he might have sung after Leporello's well-meant suggestion that he should 'lasciar le donne'! But why should he waste time (that could be much better spent) on revealing himself, when his servant can do it for him, as in 'Madamina'? In his last scene he turns into a hero, dramatically and musically, defying heaven and hell as no other operatic hero ever did.

RECORDINGS 1. Sutherland, Schwarzkopf, Sciutti, Alva, Waechter, Taddei, Cappuccilli, Frick, Philharmonia Ch & O, Giulini, EMI, 1959; 2. Auger, Jones, van der Meel, Hagegård, Cachemaille, Drottningholm Court Ch & O, Östman, L'Oiseau-Lyre, 1989; 3. Brewer, Lott, Focile, Hadley, Skovhus, Corbelli, Chiummo, Scottish CCh & O, Mackerras, Telarc, 1995

Così fan tutte, ossia La scuola degli amanti

Women are Like That

Dramma giocoso in two acts (3h)
Libretto by Lorenzo da Ponte
Composed September–December 1789
PREMIERES 26 January 1790, Burgtheater, Vienna; UK: 9 May 1811, His Majesty's Theatre, Haymarket, London; US: 24 March 1922, Metropolitan, New York
CAST Fiordiligi *s*, Dorabella *s* or *ms*, Ferrando *t*, Guglielmo *b*, Despina *s*, Alfonso *b*; *satb* chorus of soldiers, serenaders; *silent*: servants, musicians

Nothing is known about the creation of *Così* except that the commission is supposed to have followed the successful revival of *Figaro* in Vienna beginning on 29 August 1789. The performances of *Così* were interrupted by the death of the Emperor Joseph II on 20 February 1790, but there was a second run from June to August. Mozart entered the Guglielmo aria 'Rivolgete a lui lo sguardo', composed for Benucci, into his thematic index in advance of the rest, but then replaced it in the opera with the shorter and more apt 'Non siate ritrosi'.

Through most of the 19th century and a good part of the 20th *Così fan tutte* was regarded as being immoral and frivolous, utterly unworthy of Mozart's genius. Even George Bernard Shaw, one of the few people a hundred years ago to have admired Mozart much as we do today, wrote of its libretto: 'The despised book after all has some fun in it, though quite as good plays have often been improvised in ten minutes in a drawing room at charades or dumb crambo.' The story of a lover testing the fidelity of his wife or bride by approaching her in a disguise or magical transformation goes back through Ariosto to Ovid. In our own time it has become as popular as Mozart's other greatest operas, because we believe that the psychological truths beneath the play are revealed by Mozart's music. It just steers clear of the perturbing side of 18th-century tales of wagers such as *Les liaisons dangereuses* with its sensual cruelty, but it certainly does not leave the audience with a happy glow. One asks, will any of the four ever feel so deeply again? Mozart, who was responsible for deriving the title from the text (da Ponte referred to the opera as the 'school for lovers'), might equally well have called it *Così fan tutti*, but, though he can enter fully into female emotions, his obsessive insistence on repeating the multiplicity of women's deceptions in Guglielmo's 'Donne mie, la fate a tanti, a tanti, a tanti', etc., looks like personal participation.

SYNOPSIS

Act I: In a coffee-house two young officers are boasting about the fidelity of their betrothed. Their sceptical friend, Don Alfonso, wagers 100 zecchini that Dorabella and Fiordiligi would be no more faithful than any other woman, if put to the test. Ferrando and Guglielmo indignantly accept the bet and the condition to obey Alfonso's orders all day. In a garden by the seashore the daydreams of Dorabella and Fiordiligi ('Ah guarda, sorella') are interrupted by Alfonso's desperate report that Ferrando and Guglielmo have been ordered to depart at once to the wars. They come to take a tender leave ('Sento, oddio, che questo piede'): everybody is overcome by emotion ('Di, scrivermi ogni giorno'). The women and Alfonso wave to the departing ship ('Soave sia il vento'). A room in the house of the sisters. Dorabella's vehement sorrow ('Smanie implacabili') is brushed aside by the maid, Despina: do as soldiers do, she advises them, and find yourselves new lovers ('In uomini, in soldati'). Alfonso bribes her to help him to introduce his two Albanian friends to the sisters. Despina does not recognize them ('Alla bella Despinetta'), but they are, of course, Ferrando and Guglielmo in disguise and under oath to Alfonso to woo the sisters but with new partners – Ferrando, engaged to Dorabella, is to pursue Fiordiligi, and Guglielmo Dorabella. They are reassured by the women's indignant reaction to the strangers, especially by Fiordiligi's 'Come scoglio', but their satisfaction in these proofs of constancy is beginning to be mingled with the delights of play-acting and the chase. Ferrando, especially, is intoxicated by love ('Un'aura amorosa'). A more dangerous attack is made in the Act I finale: distraught at the coldness of the strong-hearted maidens, the Albanians gulp poison and drop lifeless at their feet. Despina begs the women to revive them with affection, and then reappears disguised as a doctor to restore the patients to life with an enormous magnet according to the latest principles of Dr Mesmer. They rise dazedly and beg for a kiss to complete the cure, but the sisters still just manage to resist.

Act II: The women hardly need Despina's encouragement ('Una donna a quindici anni') for they have already decided that there cannot be much harm in a mild flirtation ('Prenderò quel brunettino'). In the garden by the shore the Albanians woo them with a serenade ('Secondate, aurette amiche'). Now that Fiordiligi and Dorabella are at last in a romantic mood, the men are overcome by bashfulness. But Alfonso and Despina persuade the two pairs to link hands and to stroll off in different directions ('La mano a me date'). Guglielmo, outrageously overacting the part of the forlorn lover, finds Dorabella succumbing ('Il core vi dono'), and they exchange their lockets as tokens of love. Ferrando, seeing Fiordiligi's agitation, expresses hope of success in an aria ('Ah, lo veggio'), which is normally omitted. When he has left, Fiordiligi admits to herself the tremors of her heart ('Per pietà'). The men compare notes: Guglielmo confesses smugly that he has found Dorabella less pure than the driven snow and adds some cynical observations about women ('Donne mie, la fate a tanti'). Alfonso takes advantage of Ferrando's despair ('Tradito, schernito') to taunt him into making one more supreme attempt on Fiordiligi's honour. Dorabella is altogether happier now that she has given in and tries to persuade Fiordiligi to follow her example ('E amore un ladroncello'), but her sister is planning to escape temptation by seeking her Guglielmo on the battlefield disguised in one of his own uniforms.

There she will be safe in his arms. But Ferrando enters at that moment, and it is into his arms that she falls ('Fra gli amplessi'). Alfonso's bet is won: the two officers have to agree that women are all the same, but the finale is needed for the written proof. A grand room brightly lit, with dinner laid, etc. The wedding celebrations include a chorus and a toast sung in canon. The versatile Despina impersonates a notary to perform the mock marriage. The ink is not dry on the contract before the sound of a familiar military march freezes the ladies' blood. The Albanians flee in terror and soon Ferrando and Guglielmo return from what was clearly a very short war. But what is a notary doing here and whose is this contract of marriage? They rush off in pursuit of the Albanians and return to confront the terrified women in the costumes of the Albanians and with the whole truth. Guglielmo taunts Dorabella with the melody that had so idyllically united them. The officers pull Despina's ears to the trill of the magnetic doctor and pay Alfonso's wager. Fiordiligi and Dorabella beg to be forgiven and are soon reunited with their original lovers.

As so often in Mozart, the whole opera expresses a comic–serious duality. The division is not always clear, for the sheer beauty of the music hits the listener at a deeper emotional level than the libretto would warrant. The overture provides just the right introduction: after the shortest of andantes (with the five chords to which the men later sing the words 'Così fan tutte') there is a presto, entirely constructed of single-bar phrases of the type that usually links more important themes, creating a music of intrigue and laughter behind one's back with nothing lyrical or sweet about it. Da Ponte's originality was in taking the old plot of the disguised husband or lover testing the fidelity of his own wife or sweetheart and doubling it, providing, as it were, two diagonal seductions. The music of Act I underlines the farcical element of the schematic nature of the plot, for the men and the women tend to move in pairs like puppets – a reminiscence of the popular Salieri/Casti *La grottadi Trofonio* (1785). The ensemble writing postulated by the double action demanded a taut style based less on melody than on short motifs – for which the overture has prepared us. In 'Alla bella Despinetta', the first piece to bring all six characters on stage, the men and the women move in pairs (singing in thirds); Despina is generally linked to Alfonso though she sometimes supports the men's pleas. Musically, the whole piece is a pattern of short clichés. The effect is strangely electrifying and exactly what the situation calls for.

The despair of Dorabella and Fiordiligi explodes in two arias parodying opera seria. Despina predictably propounds the conventional cynicism of the soubrette, though with many a tender musical thought. Mozart cannot resist striking at us with moments of piercing beauty – in the burlesque leave-taking quintet 'Di scrivermi', accompanied by a laughing Don Alfonso, or in the trio 'Soave sia il vento', one of his irresistible E major 'nature' pieces. In the Act I finale the C minor 'death' scene of the poisoned lovers, with a comic bassoon to allay any fears, is followed, after the opera-buffa business of Despina disguised as the doctor, by a reawakening of the men that would be blissful enough to serve for Adam and Eve waking in Paradise.

The musicologist Hermann Abert for once missed the point when he regretted that Mozart had not continued in Act II with another delicious ensemble to complete both seductions instead of giving us a string of arias and duets. Mozart and da Ponte realized that the game became serious only in a one-to-one confrontation. So do Ferrando and Guglielmo when first left alone with their victims. Moreover, it is time to see each one as an individual. Guglielmo uses a Don Giovanni touch to get Dorabella at his mercy and still to have time for the aside, 'Poor old Ferrando!' In his total confusion the less cynical Ferrando first gives vent to the rather artificial rondo 'Ah lo veggio' on his hopes about Fiordiligi, then to the more heartfelt 'Tradito, schernito' on his despair about Dorabella. The deepest feelings are expessed by the (relatively) constant Fiordiligi in her rondo 'Per pietà', a wonderful piece with obbligato horns and woodwind, the most moving aria in the opera. The horn, usually the mocker of cuckolds, speaks of fidelity. The duet 'Fra gli amplessi', in which the music convinces us that Fiordiligi's sincerity wins Ferrando from his play-acting to true love, is the climax of the serious side of the opera. But there is one more astonishing moment during the wedding celebration in the Act II finale – 'E nel tuo, nel mio bicchiero', the toast to forgetfulness of the past. The melody is very similar to the moving 'Volgi a me' in which Ferrando had found his true voice in the duet just before, but now (a semitone lower) sung as a canon, the only one in Mozart's operas, to intensify the beauty. When it is Guglielmo's turn to join in he cannot hide his disgust at his recent betrayal by Fiordiligi's capitulation (nor can he manage the higher reaches of the melody), so he merely mutters that he wishes the drink was poison while Fiordiligi sings his line. An enharmonic change abruptly returns us to the world of farce with the appearance of Despina in the guise of the notary, then of the returning warriors humiliating the women and finally pardoning them. It is a shock to go back to stylized symmetry after all those deeper emotions have been invoked.

RECORDINGS 1. Schwarzkopf, Ludwig, Steffek, Kraus, Taddei, Berry, Philharmonia Ch & O, Böhm, EMI, 1962; 2. Lorengar, Berganza, Berbié, R. Davis, Krause, Bacquier, LPO, Solti, Decca, 1973/4; 3. Yakar, Nafé, Resick, Winbergh, Krause, Feller, Drottningholm Court Ch & O, Östman, L'Oiseau-Lyre, 1984

Die Zauberflöte

The Magic Flute

Eine Deutsche Oper in two acts
(2h 30m)
Libretto by Emanuel Schikaneder
Composed April–July and September 1791

PREMIERES 30 September 1791, Freihaustheater auf der Wieden, Vienna; UK: 6 June 1811, His Majesty's Theatre, Haymarket, London; US: 17 April 1833, Park Theater, New York

CAST Sarastro *b*, Tamino *t*, Speaker *b*, First Priest *b*, Second Priest *t*, Third Priest *spoken role*, Queen of the Night *s*, Pamina *s*, First Lady *s*, Second Lady *s*, Third Lady *s* or *c*, 3 Boys 3 *s*, Old Woman (Papagena) *s*, Papageno *b* or *bar*, Monostatos *t*, First Man in Armour *t*, Second Man in Armour *b*, 3 slaves *spoken roles*; *satb* chorus of priests, slaves, Sarastro's subjects

The premiere of *Die Zauberflöte*, after which Mozart had only another 10 weeks to live, was followed by the most successful run of any of his operas, 197 performances in two years. In his first opera for a popular rather than a court theatre, all the 18th-century irony about the war of the sexes was replaced by an exotic fairy tale with mystical elements, features of the new German Romanticism. The chivalric quest of the outset turns into a philosophical search for love and virtue. Considering the commonly held view that it is no more than a bungled children's story, the sources of the libretto are surprisingly wide and complex. The opening scene, with the rescue by the three ladies and the appearance of a strange semi-human being, is derived from the 12th-century *Yvain, ou Le chevalier au Lion* by Chrétien de Troyes, then recently translated into German; magic instruments had appeared in Wranitzky's singspiel *Oberon* (1789); the three boys and a model for Monostatos came into *Lulu, oder Die Zauberflöte*, one of the stories in Wieland's collection *Dschinnistan* (1786);

another singspiel *Der Fagottist, oder Die Zauberzither* (1791) by Wenzel Müller is also based on one of these stories but with comic additions; Jean Terrasson's recently translated novel *Sethos* (1731), with its ancient Egyptian setting, provided the basis for the trials; the essay on the *Mysteries of the Freemasons* (1784) by one of Austria's most eminent Masons, Ignaz von Born, suggested the words of Sarastro.

Emanuel Schikaneder, since playing Hamlet at 25, had also been singer, playwright, composer, producer and manager. He had first met Mozart in Salzburg in 1780, and they seem to have had a friendly relationship. He wrote later that he and Mozart had thought *Die Zauberflöte* through very busily together. In spite of the naïve versification and some poor jokes, the whole libretto has a natural strength in its very illogicality and a mysterious quality that was perceived by Goethe. Its great superiority over Schikaneder's other works is evidence for Mozart's contribution. Like Mozart, he had been a Freemason. In fact, Mozart continued to be one despite Joseph II's stringent restriction of the order in 1786 and seems to have had a devout belief in the principles of the order as well as obviously enjoying the possibility it offered of mixing with the aristocracy and the intelligentsia on equal terms. The opera made no secret of the fact that the Temple's brotherhood represented the Freemasons, as the libretto had a frontispiece full of Masonic symbols. This glorification of Masonry could not have won the opera any popularity, least of all in official circles. The general public enjoyed the stage tricks, the comedy and the music, but Mozart must have had a purpose in courageously bringing in Freemasonry: it was surely to defend it through allegory. The audience shares Tamino's bewilderment in finding Sarastro no ogre at all but wise and virtuous, while the Queen changes from apparently good to clearly evil. It has even been suggested that the plot must have been altered when Schikaneder and Mozart arrived at the Act I finale. The moral he intended is surely: do not believe what the detractors of the order say, for it is they that turn out to be evil when you look for yourself. Every element in the music of *Die Zauberflöte* and, indeed, in Mozart's late instrumental music, has been described in terms of Freemasonic symbolism – especially the use of three chords (a masonic number), the key of E♭ with its three flat signs, bound pairs of notes, counterpoint, clarinets and basset horns – but as all these are present in a great deal of non-Masonic music, it is impossible to assess the precise influence of Freemasonry on his compositions.

It is notable in the masculine world of the time in general and of the Freemasons in particular that Pamina increasingly takes on the central role, both in her suffering and when she leads Tamino through the fire and water. The three boys are a puzzle, since they were recommended as guides by the three ladies and then turn out to be ministers of goodness. They are not servants of the Temple, but rather forces of nature, the constellations that guide our paths, the voice of conscience that keeps us from suicide, the quiet reminder of what we really know. At the start of the finale to Act II they look forward to the end of superstition and the triumph of human wisdom.

Schikaneder gave Papageno – played by himself – the lion's share. The Tamino was another versatile man of the theatre, Benedikt Schack, a composer and a good musician, who could have played the flute on stage (if Mozart had allowed him the tiniest of breaths between singing and playing). The Queen was Mozart's sister-in-law, Josepha Hofer.

SYNOPSIS

Act I: A rocky region. Prince Tamino is fleeing a huge serpent ('Zu Hilfe! Zu Hilfe!'). As he faints in terror three ladies appear and kill it. They reluctantly leave the handsome stranger in order to bring their Queen the news. As Tamino comes to, Papageno, a birdcatcher dressed up as a bird, appears ('Der Vogelfänger bin ich ja'). He claims to have throttled the serpent himself, but soon regrets his lie when the three ladies appear and padlock his mouth as punishment. They give Tamino a portrait of the Queen's daughter, Pamina, with which he instantly falls in love ('Dies Bildnis ist bezaubernd schön'). The scene changes, for the next aria only, to reveal the Queen of the Night enthroned among transparent stars. She promises Tamino her daughter's hand if he will rescue her from the demon who has kidnapped her ('O zittre nicht, mein lieber Sohn'). The ladies free Papageno but order him to accompany the prince on his dangerous quest. Tamino is given a magic flute and Papageno a magic set of bells. Three mysterious boys are to show them the way. In a splendid Egyptian room Pamina is being bullied by the lustful Moor, Monostatos. At that moment Papageno wanders in: the feathered man and the black man put the fear of the devil into each other, but Papageno remains to tell Pamina about Tamino's mission and his love for her, whereupon she falls in love with the prince without as much as seeing his picture. She and Papageno sing about love ('Bei Männern, welche Liebe fühlen'). Meanwhile Tamino, guided by the three boys, has come to a grove with three temples (finale Act I). An old Priest emerges from the central temple of wisdom to dissipate Tamino's hatred for Sarastro, the ruler who has imprisoned Pamina. A distant chorus reveals that she is still alive. Tamino plays his magic flute and wild beasts come out to enjoy the music. Hearing Papageno's pipes, he rushes out. A moment later Pamina and Papageno run through in their attempt to escape, but Monostatos gleefully captures them. Now it is Papageno's turn to try his magic instrument: Monostatos and all the slaves are bewitched by the music and march off singing happily. Sarastro arrives in his chariot drawn by lions. Pamina confesses that she fled because of Monostatos's importunities. Sarastro, too, loves her more than he should, but he recognizes that she loves another. At that moment Monostatos drags in his latest capture and thus Tamino and Pamina ecstatically behold each other for the first time. Sarastro orders the two strangers to be led to the Temple of Examination. The chorus praises his wisdom.

Act II: A palm grove with pyramids. Sarastro and the assembled priests resolve to let Tamino undergo the trials for admission to the brotherhood. The gods have decided that Pamina is to be his wife. All join in a hymn ('O Isis und Osiris'). Amid thunder the scene changes to a temple court filled with broken pillars. Two priests lead in the candidates: Tamino, resolved to undergo all the trials, the first of which is to keep silent, and Papageno, caring only about food and drink and his hope of finding Papagena, the woman of his dreams. The three ladies try in vain to rally them back to the Queen ('Wie? Wie? Wie?'). In a garden where Pamina is asleep, the lustful Monostatos flees at the approach of the Queen, who orders her daughter to murder Sarastro ('Der Hölle Rache kocht in meinem Herzen'). Left alone in despair, Pamina is once more subjected to Monostatos's lewd propositions, but Sarastro drives him off and reassures her ('In diesen heil'gen Hallen'). In another hall Papageno breaks all the rules and chats to an old crone who tells him she is eighteen years and two minutes old and has a sweetheart named . . . Papageno. Before she can reveal her identity, she disappears at a thunderclap. The three boys remind him and Tamino to be steadfast ('Seid uns zum zweitenmal willkommen'). Pamina is heartbroken when Tamino will not speak to her ('Ach ich fühl's'). In the vault of the pyramids. After another hymn, Sarastro tells Pamina and Tamino that they must part but that they will meet again ('Soll ich dich, Teurer, nicht mehr sehn?'). A glass of wine is all that Papageno really asks of life: it instantly appears, but having drunk it, he is filled by thoughts of love ('Ein Mädchen oder Weibchen'). The old woman promptly reappears. Only after she reveals that the alternative is eternal incarceration does Papageno promise her his hand. She immediately turns into Papagena, only to be whisked away. The finale to Act II opens in a garden with the three boys who save Pamina from her attempted suicide. The final trial is set between two large mountains, one a volcano, the other with a waterfall. Two men in black armour lead Tamino in and tell him that whoever walks this difficult path will be purified by fire, water, air and earth and that if he overcomes the fear of death, he will be worthy to be consecrated to the mysteries of Isis. He agrees to undergo the tests and is reunited with Pamina, who guides him through fire and water, protected by the magic flute. They are welcomed by the chorus in a brightly lit temple. Back in the garden it is now Papageno who is suicidal for lack of his Papagena. Just in time the three boys remind him of his magic bells, which bring Papagena to him with the prospect of domestic bliss. The Queen and her ladies, abetted by Monostatos, make a secret onslaught on the temple, but they are routed by storms, thunder and lightning. The stage is transformed into a sun. Sarastro receives Tamino and Pamina. Night has been dispersed. The chorus gives praise and thanks.

The overture's only direct quote is in the three chords before the development, which in the opera precede the trials of Act II, but the entire sublime amalgamation of sonata form and fugue is a metaphor for the opera's mingling of narrative with philosophy.

There are traditional ingredients in *Die Zauberflöte* – five strophic numbers (three of them for Papageno), derived from the singspiel, and opera-seria arias for the Queen, but now Mozart completed the revolutionary process begun in *Figaro*. Away with the vain repetition of words for the sake of the music! The musical form had to fit the text. In 'Dies Bildnis' Tamino is led, through admiration of Pamina's portrait (first subject) and the awakening of love (second subject in the dominant), to the thought of finding her (development ending on a chord of the dominant seventh). The thought is almost too much for him (a whole bar's rest). What would he do then? Well (although he is back in the tonic key), certainly not go back to mere admiration of a portrait, as sonata form would demand. The violins lead him on with a tender phrase, while he expresses with gradually increasing confidence his hopes of embracing Pamina. There is only a vestigial recapitulation of five bars of melody to suggest the musical form. Apart from formal considerations, there is an emotional effect in hearing a melody for the second time, never more so than in those quintessentially Mozartean moments when a melody first heard in the major returns in the minor. In 'Ach, ich fühl's' neither words nor music are recaptitulated except Pamina's magical rising phrase 'meinem Herzen', which returns to the words 'so wird Ruhe', but now with the poignant sweetness of the B♭ major phrase turned to the heartbreaking sorrow of G minor. The orchestral coda of this aria seems to echo her cry of 'Sieh, Tamino', with the music fractured as though she was looking at him dazzled by tears. Mozart always maintains the harmonic pattern of sonata form or other forms: the Act I quintet is in rondo form harmonically, but the music is always new for the new events that occur, except for a few short returning phrases that give the hearer at least a suggestion of thematic form. This freedom, which is hinted at in *Figaro*, has now become universal.

A new freedom is apparent too in the finale to Act I. In this opera the finales are not scenes of mounting numbers of participants and excitement but a free expression of the words and the emotions hidden behind the words. Tamino's dialogue with the old priest goes freely from recitative to arioso, then to the distant chorus: in spite of the stern tone of their conversation, a gentle recurring phrase in the strings indicates that Tamino is drawn to the wisdom of the order. Later in the same finale the duet between Pamina and Sarastro offers another way in which the emotions are painted by the orchestra, which indicates heartbeats of different speed and intensity – Pamina's when she thinks of her mother, Sarastro, when he recognizes that she is not for him, as he had hoped, since she now loves another. The passage from recitative, to melody, and later in the next scene, to a chorus interjection, is performed with absolute freedom.

The finale to Act II contains the essence of the opera, four pieces so separate that they have even been performed in a different order. Between the scene in which Pamina is held back from suicide by the three boys and the one in which they perform the same service for Papageno is the heart of the opera – in which Tamino and Pamina undergo the ultimate tests. Mozart opens it with six solemn bars in C minor, then an old chorale melody sung by the two men in armour doubled by woodwind and trombones, all in octaves and accompanied by a four-part fugato on the strings, done with the mastery of Bach but with late 18th-century sensibility in the frequent appoggiaturas. It is one of the most overwhelming pieces in any opera, but there is more to come. After a delightfully perky allegretto, in which the two men in armour turn out to be good fellows after all and assure Tamino that Pamina is near and all will be well, comes the final, simple, exultant reunification – 'Tamino mine! What happiness!'/'Pamina mine! What happiness!' There is a very hesitant beginning by sustained horns and strings before the lovers speak again. This is the greatest of many moments that make *Die Zauberflöte* the most moving of all Mozart's operas.

The scoring is extremely simple, compared with the richness of *Idomeneo* or *Figaro*, but each piece has exactly the right orchestration – for example, no double-basses for the airborne three boys. There were various reasons for this simplicity, an orchestra less brilliant than that of the court theatre, the singspiel tradition and a less sophisticated audience, but it is a tendency shared with *La clemenza di Tito* and the instrumental works of 1791: the concentration on essentials. The music of *Die Zauberflöte* becomes increasingly concentrated as the opera proceeds – from being quite indulgent about the not very relevant, though absolutely delightful palaver of the three ladies at the start, Mozart allows Tamino and Pamina a final duet after the completion of the trials of only two bars.

RECORDINGS 1. Popp, Janowitz, Gedda, Berry, Frick, Philharmonia Ch & O, Klemperer, 1964: omits dialogue; 2. Ziesak, Jo, Heilman, Kraus, Moll, Vienna State Op Concert Ch, VPO, Solti, Decca, 1990: with dialogue; 3. Mannion, Dessay, Blochwitz, Scharinger, Hagen, Les Arts Florissants Ch & O, Christie, Erato, 1995

La clemenza di Tito

The Clemency of Titus

Opera seria in two acts (2h 15m)
Libretto by Caterino Tommaso Mazzolà, after Pietro Metastasio (1734)
Composed July–September 1791
PREMIERES 6 September 1791, Gräflich Nostitzsches Nationaltheater, Prague; UK: 27 March 1806, His Majesty's Theatre, Haymarket, London; US: 4 August 1952, Berkshire Music Center, Lenox, Massachusetts (Tanglewood)
CAST Tito *t*, Vitellia *s*, Servilia *s*, Sesto *s* or *ms*, Annio *s* or *ms*, Publio *b*; *satb* chorus of Roman people; guards

La clemenza di Tito was commissioned as part of the celebrations in Prague for the coronation of the new Emperor Leopold II as King of Bohemia. Though the Prague public loved Mozart, he was approached only when it became clear that the court composer, Salieri, was not available. He received the definite commission from Domenico Guardasoni, director of the Italian company, in July 1791 while he was working on *Die Zauberflöte*, but he may have written at least the allegro section of Vitellia's 'Non più di fiori' by April 1791, when it perhaps was performed by Josephine Duschek, and his sketches for a tenor Sesto must have preceded the July contract with the Bohemian Estates, which stipulated a castrato Sesto. When Mozart arrived in Prague on 28 August, together with his wife and his pupil Süssmayr, the score was nearly complete.

The Roman emperor Titus Vespasianus, famous for the noble qualities he had shown in his short reign (AD 79–81), was an ideal subject for a coronation opera: Leopold had been likened to a latterday Titus during his reign as Grand Duke of Tuscany. If Mozart went back to an opera-seria libretto to please the Italian taste of the new emperor, he had it converted into a 'true opera' (as he noted in his thematic index) to please himself. A third of Metastasio's text was cut; the rest was turned into three duets, three trios, three choruses and two finales for soloists and chorus, leaving just 11 arias. Metastasio's libretto had often been modified in the 40 settings it had inspired but never so radically as this. That may have been the cause of 'a certain prejudice at court against Mozart's opera', of which Guardasoni complained to the Estates. In spite of all the changes, the libretto for each ensemble concerned a single static situation without any real action or interaction of the characters. For example, in the beautiful trio 'Quello di Tito è il volto!', when the guilty Sesto appears before his betrayed emperor and friend, only inner feelings are expressed.

Metastasio's elegant plots and verses are on the whole more suited to the tangled love stories of his famous *L'Olimpiade* and *Demofoonte* than to political subjects. Titus is the only historical character in the drama. The ferocious Vitellia is derived from Hermione in Racine's *Andromaque*, who also sends her doting lover to kill the king who spurned her: she is therefore in marked contrast to the virtuous 18th-century Romans around her, until in her final great scena she turns her back on Racinian passion and becomes another self-sacrificing Metastasian heroine.

When the court left, the public took the opera to their hearts. Mozart was delighted to hear of the applause that every number received at the last performance on the day of the equally triumphant first performance of *Die Zauberflöte* in Vienna. For 30 years it remained among Mozart's most popular operas (it was the first to be performed in England), before going underground for the next 150.

SYNOPSIS

Act I: Vitellia's apartments. Vitellia, daughter of the deposed Emperor Vitellius, had hoped to marry the Emperor Titus, but he is paying court to the Jewish princess, Berenice. The opera opens as she persuades Sesto, who is in love with her, to join the conspiracy to assassinate Titus ('Come ti piace imponi'). In the forum Titus is praised by the crowd and organizes help for the victims of the eruption of Vesuvius. He tells Sesto that he has decided to send away the foreigner, Berenice, and marry Servilia, Sesto's sister. Sesto's friend, Annio, who is himself in love with Servilia, nobly keeps silent, but when he breaks the news to her, they declare their mutual love ('Ah perdona al primo affetto'). Servilia reveals this to Titus and he praises her candour. Vitellia, hearing that she has been passed over again, promises her hand in marriage to Sesto if he will instantly murder Titus. He departs reluctantly to murder his beloved emperor and friend ('Parto, parto'). No sooner has he left than Annio and the prefect Publio come to pay homage to her as the newly chosen empress. She hysterically tries to call Sesto back, while the others attribute her emotion to excessive joy ('Vengo . . . aspettate . . .'). Below the Capitol. Sesto is torn by conflicting emotions ('Oh Dei, che smania è questa') but, just as he resolves to save Titus from the conspiracy, he sees the flames leap up (finale Act I, 'Deh conservate, oh Dei'). The soloists run around in confusion, but Vitellia keeps her head enough to warn Sesto not to blurt out the truth. The Roman people are heard mourning Titus offstage.

Act II: In a garden on the Palatine hill. Annio tells Sesto that Titus has survived and advises him to seek his mercy. As the identity of the conspirators still seems to be unknown, Vitellia begs Sesto to flee. But Publio approaches to arrest him. Sesto takes a tender leave of her ('Se al volto mai ti senti'). In a great throne room. Thanks are given for Titus' survival ('Ah grazie si rendano'). He cannot believe that his friend is guilty but Publio warns him not to judge others by his own heart. Annio can only recommend mercy. Titus is torn by inner conflict ('Che orror! che tradimento!'): he envies the happy lot of a simple peasant. Sesto is led in but refuses to reveal Vitellia's complicity ('Quello di Tito è il volto!') and takes his leave of Titus ('Deh per questo istante solo'). Titus eventually tears up the death sentence, for he wishes to be seen by posterity as a clement ruler ('Se all'impero'). Servilia begs Vitellia, the empress elect, to save Sesto ('S'altro che lacrime'). Vitellia resolves to sacrifice her own happiness and life for the noble Sesto who had not betrayed her ('Ecco il punto, oh Vitellia . . . Non più di fiori'). A crowd has collected by the entrance to the arena, where the wild beasts await the condemned. As Titus is about to pass sentence on the conspirators, Vitellia flings herself at his feet and confesses that she is guiltier than anyone – mistaking his goodness for love, she had hated him for seeming to spurn her. Titus forgives them all. Amid their praise he resolves to devote himself only to the well-being of Rome ('Tu, è ver, m'assolvi Augusto').

Vitellia is the driving force in the opera: her role contains an amazing range of emotions, from wheedling to hectoring, from feigned love to real despair and hysterical terror, together with a no less amazing vocal range from bottom A to top D. The most famous piece in the opera is her rondo 'Non più di fiori' with basset horn obbligato. The rondo, always reserved for principal singers, had an important place in Italian opera in the 1780s, especially in the works of Cimarosa and Sarti. It was always in two parts, a slow and a faster, usually a sentimental gavotte. Apart from allowing himself some wild modulations at the start of the allegros, Mozart is true to the Italian model, both in this aria and in Sesto's 'Deh per questo istante'. But Sesto also has his coloratura aria with clarinet obbligato 'Parto, parto'. (Both obbligati were performed by Mozart's friend Anton Stadler, for whom he also composed the Concerto, the Quintet and the Kegelstatt Trio.) Titus is too predictably merciful ('What will posterity say of us?') and becomes ridiculously obliging when he contemplates marriage to three different women in the course of one day. Antonio Baglioni (also the first Don Ottavio) inspired a gentle lyrical style with long coloraturas. His set-piece aria, 'Se all'impero', might have been found in *Lucio Silla*, but the other arias are in the 1791 pattern of simplicity and brevity, the most beautiful being in the heart of the chorus 'Ah grazie si rendano'. Servilia's tiny gem of an aria and Annio's two affecting pictures of loyalty are surpassed by their delicate duet, 'Ah perdona al primo affetto', as irresistible as it is sentimental.

The opera lacks the rich scoring of the previous operas, whether in deference to Italian style or to the 1791 concentration on essentials found in *Die Zauberflöte*. The recitatives are most probably by Süssmayr; however, Mozart provided highly dramatic accompanied recitatives at all the decisive moments. The most striking piece is the finale to Act I, in which the people of Rome are heard far away lamenting the assassination of their beloved emperor, at first with exclamations on diminished seventh chords and then antiphonally with the quintet of soloists on stage, in poignant harmonies prophetic of the 19th century. This coronation opera opens with a brilliant overture, its first subject like cheering crowds and pealing bells, and closes with the emperor's almost ecstatic devotion to his people, an exuberant finale that must have inspired the end of Beethoven's *Fidelio*.

RECORDINGS 1. Baker, Minton, Popp, von Stade, Burrows, Covent Garden Ch & O, Davis, Phillips, 1976; 2. Varady, von Otter, McNair, Robbin, Monteverdi Ch, EBS, Gardiner, Archiv, 1991 (live); 3. Jones, Bartoli, Bonney, Montague, Heilman, Academy of Ancient Music, Hogwood, L'Oiseau-Lyre, 1993
OTHER OPERATIC WORKS *Apollo et Hyancinthus*, 1767; *La finta semplice*, 1769; *Bastien und Bastienne*, 1768; *Ascanio in Alba*, 1771; *Il sogno di Scipione*, 1772; *Lucio Silla*, 1772; *Thamos, König in Ägypten*, 1774; *Zaide*, (1780), 1866; *L'oca del Cairo*, (1783), 1860; *Lo sposa deluso, ossia La rivaltà di tre donne per un solo amante* (inc.), (1784), 1953

E.S.

Modest Musorgsky

Modest Petrovich Musorgsky;
b 21 March 1839, Karevo, Pskov District;
d 28 March 1881, St Petersburg

Musorgsky and Tchaikovsky (one year his junior) are universally acknowledged as the outstanding masters of 19th-century Russian music. There are, however, two notable factors that distinguish them. Tchaikovsky was the first of a new conservatory-trained generation of professional composers, whereas Musorgsky remained a largely self-taught amateur, albeit one of genius. The scope of their achievement also differs markedly. In contrast to Tchaikovsky's voluminous and masterly output in every genre, Musorgsky's reputation rests essentially on his 65 songs, *Pictures at an Exhibition* for piano (1874, later orchestrated by Ravel), the orchestral *St John's Night on Bare Mountain* (1867, reworked by Rimsky-Korsakov in 1886) and three operas, two of them still unfinished at his early death aged 42. Of these *Boris Godunov* is in the repertoire of every major opera company and revered as a music drama of astonishing theatrical power, integrity and trail-blazing originality.

Musorgsky's musical ability was first displayed in his prowess as a gifted pianist and improviser. While still an army cadet in St Petersburg he met Balakirev and from him received vital encouragement and the only form of compositional guidance he ever had. Operatic projects were among his very first attempts at composition (*Oedipus in Athens*, 1858–60; *Salammbô*, 1863–6); but it was as a song-writer – often to his own texts – that he first found his highly individual voice as a composer. For these he chose diverse subjects that were often humorous, satirical or taken from low life. With an astonishing directness of utterance he displayed an ability to sympathize with and depict in the most uncompromisingly vivid way those whom Dostoevsky classed as 'the humiliated and the injured'. Closely allied to this desire for musical realism was Musorgsky's determination to fashion a vocal line that reflected, with as little recourse as possible to conventional melody, the contours and intonations of human speech. As a result the songs, especially those written between 1864 and 1870, and the three great cycles, *The Nursery* (1870–72), *Sunless* (1874) and *The Songs and Dances of Death* (1875–7), are unique in their dramatic and realistic power of expression. It is significant that Musorgsky is possibly the only one of the world's supreme song-writers to achieve comparable success in opera.

Musorgsky's artistic credo, as displayed in his greatest songs, *Boris Godunov* and, to a lesser extent, *Khovanshchina* (for which broad canvases the songs served as preliminary sketches), resided in his belief in the intimate relationship between the inflexions of the spoken Russian language, the idea and emotion expressed by it and the intonation of voice and accompaniment with which it is communicated. This could create a new, fresh form of music that was part of everybody's experience and would serve as an unprecedentedly direct means of communication. At the same time he repudiated the cult of art for art's sake as displayed by the German school of conservatory-trained composers whose works in sonata form he castigated as 'musical mathematics'.

Having resigned his commission in the Guards to devote himself fully to music, Musorgsky found that the sharp drop in his private income caused by the emancipation of the serfs obliged him to undertake part-time work in the civil service. The great turning point of his career came in 1868 when a friend proposed Pushkin's *Boris Godunov* as a subject that was perfectly suited to his rapidly developing gifts. In order to put his ideas into practice in his first full-length opera, Musorgsky perfected a novel and idiosyncratic musical style that, thanks to his lack of formal training and contempt for conventional musical disciplines, is largely free from formative influences. The voices of Glinka, Aleksandr Serov, Franz Liszt and Berlioz – all highly individual composers in their own right – can be detected at times. For the most part, however, Musorgsky's predominantly chordal language, often presupposing a vocal line and incorporating audacious harmonic procedures, must have been discovered almost empirically at the piano.

The long-delayed production of *Boris* sadly proved to be the watershed of his short life. Though acclaimed by the public and fellow artists, it met with critical incomprehension and hostility, and this, together with the drudgery of his job and more personal, emotional problems, made Musorgsky increasingly introspective and dependent on alcohol. His St Petersburg musical friends tried to help him, but he became disillusioned and listless and failed to complete, let alone orchestrate, the even larger historical canvas of *Khovanshchina* and his comic Gogol opera *Sorochintsy Fair*, which he had unwisely undertaken at the same time. The well-intentioned but excessively distorting editorial work of his friend Rimsky-Korsakov to which most of his output, unfinished or finished, was subjected after his death is now increasingly rejected in favour of a return to the originality of his own texts whenever possible.

Boris Godunov

Opera in four acts with a prologue (3h 15m)
Libretto by the composer, based on the historical drama by Aleksandr Pushkin (1825) and *History of the Russian State* by Nikolai Karamzin (1824)
Composed 1868–9; rev. 1871–2
PREMIERES definitive version: 8 February 1874, Mariinsky Theatre, St Petersburg; UK: 30 September 1935, Sadler's Wells, London; Rimsky-Korsakov version: 10 December 1896, Great Hall, Conservatoire, St Petersburg; US: 19 March 1913, Metropolitan, New York; UK: 24 June 1913, Drury Lane, London; Shostakovich version: 4 November 1959, Leningrad
CAST Boris Godunov *b*, Ksenia *s*, Fyodor *ms*, Nurse *c*, Prince Vasily Ivanovich Shuisky *t*, Andrei Shchelkalov *bar*, Pimen *b*, Grigori (later the Pretender Dimitri) *t*, Marina Mnishek *ms*, Rangoni *bar*, Varlaam *b*, Missail *t*, Hostess of the Inn *ms*, Simpleton *t*, Nikitich *b-bar*, Mitukha *bar*, Boyar in attendance *t*, Khrushchov *silent*, Lavitzky *b-bar*, Chernikovsky *b-bar* (voice categories not designated by Musorgsky himself); *satb* chorus of boyars and their children, Streltsy (guards), soldiers, police officers, Polish

noblemen and ladies, Sandomir girls, blind mendicants, people of Moscow, urchins, vagabonds

Musorgsky broke off work on his experimental setting of Gogol's comedy *The Marriage* when he became fired by the idea of making an operatic version of Pushkin's *Boris Godunov*. Having condensed the Shakespeare-like, 25-scene drama down to a mere seven scenes, adding material and rewriting considerably in the process, he began the composition in October 1868, finished it in July 1869 and completed the orchestration in December – an astonishing achievement considering his lack of experience. When the opera in this compact seven-scene initial version was rejected for performance by the Mariinsky Theatre for a complex variety of reasons (novelty, fear of imperial and ecclesiastic censorship, lack of a leading female role, personal intrigues, etc.), Musorgsky set about revising it.

The two most notable features of this revision are the addition of an entirely new act (Act III) set in Poland, thereby providing the leading female role of Princess Marina, and the removal of the scene outside St Basil's Cathedral in order to accommodate a new scene depicting the advance of the Pretender's anti-Boris forces and the defection of the Russian people. Musorgsky boldly decided that this wonderful new choral scene should follow and not precede the highly impressive death of Boris scene, and thus end the opera with the simpleton singing his solitary lament over the fate of Russia. Act II, in which the character of Boris is most fully revealed, was also substantially revised. Here, in addition to writing new songs for the nurse and Fyodor, Musorgsky largely recast the tsar's great monologue, added a touchingly domestic scene between Boris and his son and recomposed the Boris–Shuisky confrontation and final hallucination scene, making the whole act incomparably richer in the process. He also rewrote parts of the Pimen cell scene (Act I, Scene 1) and added the hostess's song at the beginning of the following inn scene.

This 'definitive' version was eventually accepted for production largely thanks to the tenacity of the singer Julia Platonova, who demanded that the opera be staged as her benefit performance. At the highly successful premiere, with Melnikov as Boris, Platonova as Marina and Nápravník conducting, the scene in Chudov monastery (Pimen's cell) was omitted for censorship reasons; it was never staged during the composer's lifetime. It may be safely asserted that no other first opera that has subsequently been acknowledged as a masterpiece has ever been created with such meagre compositional experience and against such a negative cultural and political background.

SYNOPSIS

(The sequence of scenes in the initial version is shown in square brackets.)

Ivan the Terrible died in 1584 leaving two sons: Fyodor, who became tsar, and Dimitri, the tsarevich. Soon the boyar Boris Godunov was appointed regent to the weak-minded Fyodor. In 1591 Dimitri was found dying from a knife wound, and it was rumoured that Boris was responsible.

Prologue, Scene 1 [i]: The year 1598. Boris is in retreat in the Novodevichy monastery following the death of Tsar Fyodor. The apathetic people are exhorted to beg him to assume the throne by the police and the boyar Shchelkalov. A procession of pilgrims enters the monastery. The people comment cynically on developments. Scene 2 [ii]: A square in the Kremlin. To the famous orchestral evocation of bells, supplemented by real peals on stage, the chorus greets Boris as he emerges from his coronation. In a contemplative monologue Boris acknowledges the people's acclamation, but his soul is filled with foreboding.

Act I, Scene 1 [iii]: Six years later. In his cell the old monk Pimen is completing his chronicle of Russian history

('Yeshcho odno' – 'Still one more tale'). His novice Grigori is tormented with dreams of greatness. Pimen vividly recalls how the child Dimitri was discovered murdered. Grigori realizes that had he lived the tsarevich would have been his own age. Scene 2 [iv]: Grigori has fled from the monastery and is making for Poland to raise an army against Boris. He arrives at an inn on the Lithuanian border with two vagabond monks, Varlaam and Missail. Varlaam sings a racy ballad describing Ivan the Terrible's victory at Kazan. Police arrive with a warrant for Grigori's arrest but he manages to escape.

Act II [v]: The tsar's apartments in the Kremlin. Ksenia mourns the death of her betrothed while Fyodor and the nurse try to comfort and amuse her. Boris enters and speaks affectionately to his children. In his great monologue ('Dostig ya vysshei vlasti' – 'I stand supreme in power') he meditates on his crime and the sufferings of Russia. Prince Shuisky, a rival boyar, brings news that a pretender has appeared calling himself Dimitri, the resurrected tsarevich. Shuisky gives an unbearably graphic account of the murdered child's features and, aghast, Boris dismisses him. As a mechanical clock with figures begins to chime, the guilt-racked Boris breaks down, haunted by a vision of the murdered child.

Act III, Scene 1: A castle in Poland. Princess Marina has fallen in love with the pretender and her Jesuit confessor Rangoni commands her to ensnare him in order to convert Russia to Catholicism. Scene 2: Grigori/Dimitri awaits a rendezvous with Marina in the garden. After a courtly choral polonaise the guests return indoors and Marina taunts Dimitri over his infatuation with her. When she realizes that he is determined to seize the Russian throne she pours out her love for him in a short but richly melodic love duet that is one of the opera's few concessions to tradition.

[vi, omitted in the definitive version]: Outside St Basil's Cathedral, Moscow. The starving and disaffected people beg Boris to give them bread as he emerges from the cathedral. There is an astonishing confrontation between him and a simpleton, who publicly accuses him of murder. Left alone, the simpleton foretells Russia's troubled future. (Musorgsky himself orchestrated the St Basil scene, although Ippolitov-Ivanov reorchestrated it in 1926 so that it could be used as an additional scene to the Rimsky version if required.)

Act IV, Scene 1 [vii]: An emergency meeting of the Council of Boyars is in progress in the Kremlin. Shuisky's description of the overwrought state in which he had recently found the tsar is interrupted by the sudden arrival of the deranged Boris. Pimen enters and describes a miraculous cure performed at the tomb of the Tsarevich Dimitri. Boris collapses and then, left alone with Fyodor, begins his simple and intensely moving prayer and death scene ('Proshchai, moi syn, umirayu' – 'Farewell, my son, I am dying') in which he advises his son on the government of Russia and prays for God's protection for his children. Scene 2: In a forest near Kromy an unruly mob taunts a half-lynched boyar. After short scenes between a simpleton and some urchins (transferred from the discarded St Basil scene), Varlaam and Missail and two Jesuit monks, the crowd greets the arrival of the false Dimitri and follows him to Moscow. The simpleton is left alone singing a haunting lament foretelling the troubled times that lie in store for Russia.

The most immediately striking feature of the music of *Boris* is the simplicity and economy of means by which Musorgsky achieves the maximum dramatic and expressive effect. Just as in the first movement of Beethoven's Fifth Symphony, short phrases, harmonized either simply or with audacious originality, etch themselves indelibly on the memory and create an impression of human emotion in the raw. Counterpoint is largely absent, as are colouristic orchestral effects. Instead, attention is directed with unprecedented clarity to the vocal line, which graphically communicates the rapidly changing moods of the text. When a character pauses for thought, so, more often than not, does the orchestra; no opera contains more telling silences. In the same way the scenes are all made to fade out at the end, as if in anticipation of cinema technique. The only exception to this is the brilliant coronation scene in which Musorgsky makes impressive use of the folksong 'Slava' that Beethoven had earlier used in his second 'Razumovsky' Quartet.

Musorgsky understood the expressive possibilities of the human voice to the full. A more than capable singer and accompanist himself, he extracted the maximum from his singers, and his vocal line is provided with an unusually comprehensive and detailed set of dynamics, expression marks and verbal indications as to how the voice is to be used. Furthermore, in the still modern-sounding Act II 'hallucination' scene his frequent use of the term *glukho* – a word that implies a combination of muffled, toneless and dull – anticipates the technique that Schoenberg and his pupils were to term sprechgesang.

Perhaps Musorgsky's greatest innovation is his promotion of the chorus from its normal subordinate role to that of one of the most important characters in the drama; many would say the chief one. From the very opening pages the people are shown to have unusually life-like character, and much use is made of individual groups voicing their own thoughts. Given the opera's episodic construction, the treatment of the chorus lends cohesion to the whole more than anything else.

Mention must be made of the notorious editorial problem that besets *Boris*. Although Musorgsky completed and orchestrated two different versions, the second of which was successfully performed during his lifetime, the opera was for many years exclusively performed in the reorchestrated revision of Rimsky-Korsakov. Rimsky believed that the opera's disappearance from the repertoire after Musorgsky's death was largely due to its lacklustre orchestration and 'faulty' compositional technique. It is unfortunate that the appearance of his edition coincided with Chaliapin's magisterial assumption of the title role, for the two became synonymous and established a norm. Since 1945 the tendency to return to Musorgsky's own versions has greatly accelerated worldwide, although the Bolshoi Theatre in Moscow still clings to the more sumptuous Rimsky version. Quite frequently the two authentic versions are conflated in performance, for instance by incorporating the St Basil scene from the initial version into the text of the definitive version. Shostakovich made a reorchestration in 1940 which, unlike Rimsky's, at least remained faithful to the text of Musorgsky's vocal score.

RECORDINGS 1869 version: Lutsiuk, Pluzhnikov, Putilin, Okhotnikov, Kirov Op Ch & O, Gergiev, Philips, 1997; 1872 version: Borodina, Galusin, Pluzhnikov, Vaneyev, Okhotnikov, Kirov Op Ch & O, Gergiev, Philips, 1997; Rimsky-Korsakov version: Zareska, Bielicki, Gedda, Christoff (3 roles), Russian Ch of Paris, ORTF O, Dobroven, EMI, 1952

Khovanshchina

The Khovansky Affair

National music drama in five acts (3h)
Libretto by the composer
Composed 1872–80 (inc.)
PREMIERES Rimsky-Korsakov version: 21 February 1886, Kononov Auditorium, St Petersburg; UK: 1 July 1913, Drury Lane, London; US: 18 April 1928, Philadelphia; Shostakovich version: 25 November 1960, Kirov Theatre, Leningrad
CAST Prince Ivan Khovansky *b*, Prince Andrei Khovansky *t*, Prince Vasily Golitsyn *t*, Shaklovity *b-bar*, Dosifei *b*, Marfa *ms*, Susanna *s*, Scribe *t*, Emma *s*, Lutheran Pastor *bar*, Varsonofev *bar*,

Kuzka *t*, Streshnev *t*, 3 Streltsy 3 *b* (voice categories not designated by Musorgsky himself); *satb* chorus of Streltsy, Old Believers, serving girls and Persian slaves, Peter the Great's bodyguards, the people

Musorgsky began work on *Khovanshchina* as soon as he had finished revising *Boris*. He avidly collected a vast amount of historical and social detail about the turbulent period of change from 'old' to 'new' Russia in the years following Peter the Great's accession in 1682 until 1698, conflating a number of incidents in the interests of concision. Also involved are the religious sect known as Old Believers, who were violently opposed to the new reforms introduced into the ritual of the Orthodox Church. Instead of putting his libretto into a finished state before beginning composition, Musorgsky tried to work on text and music simultaneously and soon after began a similar process with *Sorochintsy Fair*. As a result the ends of Act II and V (final chorus) had not been composed by the time of his death; neither had he managed to subject the mass of disparate episodes that he had composed to rigorous revision. Nevertheless, *Khovanshchina*, though at times opaque and slow-moving, contains some very fine music and the roles of Marfa, Dosifei, Ivan Khovansky and Golitsyn are particularly rewarding. The haunting prelude to Act I, subtitled 'Dawn over the Moscow River', and the 'Dance of the Persian Slaves' from Act IV are regularly performed in the concert hall.

SYNOPSIS

The complex story of the opera largely concerns the interaction of the chief characters against the political and religious background at the time of the accession of the young Peter the Great. Ivan Khovansky and his son Andrei, in charge of the unruly Streltsy guards, are custodians of old, feudal Russia. Prince Golitsyn, wily lover of the Regent Sophia, is the representative of the new, Westernized ideas that are being introduced by Tsar Peter. The reactionary Old Believers are represented by the monk Dosifei and Marfa.

Act I: The boyar Shaklovity dictates a letter to a scribe warning the rulers and nobility that Prince Ivan Khovansky and his son Andrei are plotting against the state. Khovansky arrives amid general rejoicing and announces his determination to crush the enemies of the throne. Andrei pursues a young German girl, Emma, but Marfa, a former lover of Andrei, intervenes. A quarrel between father and son over Emma is interrupted by the arrival of Dosifei, who restores peace but foretells times of trouble ahead.

Act II: Prince Golitsyn reads a letter from Sophia and decides to be wary of her. In a divination scene Marfa foretells his disgrace and ruin. After he has dismissed her a meeting takes place between him, Khovansky and Dosifei. They are interrupted by Shaklovity who announces that the Khovanskys have been proclaimed traitors.

Act III: Marfa sings of her past love for Andrei. She is scolded by Susanna but comforted by Dosifei. The unruly Streltsy appear singing a drinking song and quarrelling with their wives. The scribe warns them that Tsar Peter's troops are advancing on them. Khovansky advises them to disperse quietly; Tsar Peter has clearly gathered the reins of power.

Act IV, Scene 1: Khovansky is entertained by his serving girls and Persian slaves. Shaklovity arrives, ostensibly to summon him to a council of state, but assassinates him as he prepares to leave. Scene 2: Golitsyn leaves Moscow for exile and Dosifei reflects on his fall and that of Khovansky. Andrei and Marfa have an altercation, and Marfa defies him to summon his Streltsy. They arrive, but carrying blocks for their own execution. An emissary from Tsar Peter pardons them.

Act V: The Old Believers' cause is lost and they prepare for death rather than compromise their faith and yield to the tsar's soldiers. They are joined by Dosifei, Marfa and Andrei who prepare to immolate themselves in a chapel in a forest clearing. The tsar's soldiers arrive in time to see everyone consumed in flames.

Although very much the work of Musorgsky throughout, *Khovanshchina* can, in a good performance, create an almost Wagnerian cumulative impact, which some find more satisfying than the more kaleidoscopic and tersely constructed *Boris*. However, even they would be obliged to concede that here the composer's genius declares itself more fitfully, and that the grandiose concept is handled with less imagination and originality than in *Boris*.

At his death Musorgsky had orchestrated only two short scenes (Marfa's short folklike aria at the start of Act III and the Streltsy scene in Act IV Scene 1). In order for the work to be performed, Rimsky-Korsakov undertook the heavy assignment of completing and orchestrating it. In trying to give the material a more manageable shape, he cut some 800 bars while also compressing, transposing and recomposing much else. His most substantial cuts (all restored in the Shostakovich version) can be summarized as follows: in Act I the extended scene (over 200 bars) between the people and the scribe immediately preceding Khovansky's arrival; in Act II Golitsyn's reading of his ex-lover's letter, his scene with a German pastor and nearly half of the scene between Golitsyn, Khovansky and Dosifei; in Act III Shaklovity's aria is shortened and the Strelets Kuzka's song with chorus is lost entirely. Rimsky's version held the stage until 1958 when Shostakovich made his own orchestration, faithfully keeping to Musorgsky's vocal score as reconstructed and published by P. Lamm and B. Asafyev in 1931. Diaghilev commissioned Stravinsky and Ravel to orchestrate additional material for the Paris premiere in 1913. Of this, only Stravinsky's reworking of the final chorus exists in published vocal score (1914).

RECORDINGS 1. Poschner-Klebel, Lipovšek, Atlantov, Popov, Kocherga, Haugland, Burchuladze, Vienna State Op Ch & O, Abbado, DG, 1990: Shostakovich's edition but with the two sections orchestrated by Musorgsky and Stravinsky's new ending;
2. Borodina, Galusin, Steblianko, Minzhilkiev, Okhotnikov, Kirov Op Ch & O, Gergiev, Philips, 1991: orch. Shostakovich

OTHER OPERATIC WORKS
Salammbô, (inc.) (1866), 1980; *The Marriage* (*Zhenit'ba*), (inc.) (1868), 1909; *Mlada*, (inc.) (1872); *Sorochintsky Fair* (*Sorochinskaya Yarmaka*), (inc.) (1881), 1913

D.L.-J.

N

Carl Nielsen

Carl August Nielsen; *b* 9 June 1865, Sortelung, nr Nørre Lyndelse on Funen, Denmark; *d* 3 October 1931, Copenhagen

Although Nielsen wrote two successful operas, he is today chiefly considered as a symphonist. He also wrote chamber music, including four fine string quartets, incidental music for more than a dozen plays, many songs and choral works.

Nielsen came from a poor family and was brought up in rural surroundings. Together with his father, he played the violin at local weddings, dances and other celebrations. At the age of 14 he left school and for five years was employed in a military band at Odense, playing the signal horn and trombone. For recreation he played Haydn and Mozart string quartets with his friends. Helped by money supplied by benefactors in Odense, he studied for two years at the Royal Conservatory in Copenhagen. From 1889 until 1905 he played second violin in the orchestra of the Royal Theatre, Copenhagen.

A grant from the Ancker Bequest enabled him to visit Germany in the autumn of 1890. He went to Dresden, where he heard *Der Ring des Nibelungen*, then to Berlin, where he attended a performance of *Die Meistersinger*. But though overwhelmed by the music of Wagner's operas, he did not succumb to their dramatic theory. In 1894 he went abroad again, to Germany and to Vienna, where he heard *Tristan und Isolde*. He also visited Brahms, who had a greater influence on Nielsen's own compositions than Wagner. Another influence was Johan Svendsen, whom Nielsen succeeded in 1908 as conductor of the Royal Opera, Copenhagen, a post he held until 1914.

The operas date from the period of his early maturity, when he had evolved a personal style of his own. Nielsen had strong views on the nature of opera. In the diary he kept while travelling in 1894 he wrote: 'The plot must be the pole that goes through a dramatic work; the plot is the trunk, words and sentences are fruit and leaves, but if the trunk is not strong and healthy, it is no use that the fruits look beautiful.'

For his two operas, Nielsen chose strong poles or trunks: the Books of Samuel in the Old Testament for the first, *Saul og David*, and a comedy by Ludvig Holberg, the 18th-century dramatist, for the second, *Maskarade*. Given their success and the composer's interest in the genre, the question must be asked, why did Nielsen stop writing operas at the age of 41? Vilhelm Andersen, the librettist of *Maskarade*, offered him an adaptation of another Holberg comedy, but he thought the subject too similar. Then in 1930, on the 125th aniversary of Hans Andersen's birth, he considered setting the dramatization of one of Andersen's fairy tales, but instead contributed incidental music and a few songs to a play, *Amor og Digteren* (*Cupid and the Poet*), about Andersen and his love for Jenny Lind.

Nielsen began work on his Second Symphony, 'The Four Temperaments', while still composing *Saul og David*; he began the third, *Sinfonia espansiva*, four years after finishing *Maskarade*, which is called to mind in the scherzo of the symphony. The Fourth Symphony, 'The Inextinguishable', would follow in another four years. There, perhaps, lies the answer to the question raised above: the symphonist had finally found his true *métier*, and opera, like the string quartet, was abandoned.

Masquerade

Maskarade

Opera in three acts (2h 15m)
Libretto by Vilhelm Andersen, after the play by Ludvig Holberg (1724)
Composed 1904–6
PREMIERES 11 November 1906, Royal Theatre, Copenhagen; US: 23 June 1972, St Paul, Minnesota; UK: 9 May 1986, Morley College, London
CAST Jeronimus *b*, Magdelone *ms*, Leander *t*, Henrik *b-bar*, Leonard *t-bar*, Leonora *s*, Pernille *s*, *s*, *t*, 3 *bar*, *b-bar*, *b*; *satb* chorus of masqueraders – officers, students, girls; dancers

By the time he had completed composition of two-thirds of *Maskarade*, Nielsen was free, after 16 years, from the nightly grind of playing in the Royal Theatre orchestra and had not yet taken up his post as conductor of the Royal Opera. This unaccustomed freedom is reflected in the exhilaration, high spirits and even frivolity of much of the music.

SYNOPSIS

Act I: Copenhagen, early 1723. Jeronimus has arranged a marriage between his son, Leander, and Leonora, daughter of his friend Leonard. Leander, however, has fallen in love with a girl he met the night before at a masquerade and refuses the match. According to Leonard, his daughter is also unwilling – she too has fallen in love with an unknown young man.

Act II: In the street outside, Leander and Leonora meet on their way to the masquerade and sing ecstatically of their love, still unaware of each other's identity. Their respective servants, Henrik and Pernille, are also taken with each other.

Act III: At the masquerade Magdelone (wife of Jeronimus) flirts and dances with Leonard, while the two pairs of young lovers express their feelings. At midnight, when everyone unmasks, Leander and Leonora discover that the marriage arranged for them is much to their taste.

Maskarade inevitably invites comparison with Mozart's *Le nozze di Figaro*, especially as regards the characters of Henrik and Mozart's Figaro. But the revolutionary side of Beaumarchais's valet is entirely missing from Holberg's, while the atmosphere of *Maskarade* is lighthearted. Nielsen's music, in particular the dance music of the third act, is sparkling and joyous. The passionate love duet for Leander and Leonora, parodied in the scene between Henrik and Pernille, reveals genuine feeling, while the ensemble pieces are as impressive as those in *Saul og David*. The opera has become a classic in Denmark.

RECORDING Bonde-Hansen, Resmark, Henning-Jensen, Skovhus, Haugland, Danish Nat RCh & SO, Schirmer, Decca, 1996
OTHER OPERA *Saul and David* (*Saul og David*), 1902

E.F.

O

Jacques Offenbach

Jacob Offenbach; *b* 20 June 1819, Cologne; *d* 5 October 1880, Paris

Offenbach, the creator of French operetta, was the second son of a German cantor who had replaced his original surname, Eberst, with that of Offenbach, the town outside Frankfurt where he had once lived. All the Offenbach children were musical, but Jacob was enough of a cello prodigy for his father to have him enrolled at the Paris Conservatoire in 1833. He soaked up Paris's rich musical-theatre attractions; his disposition for the Opéra-Comique and the works of Adam, Auber, Hérold and others was rewarded by a spell as a cellist in the theatre's orchestra.

His experience playing at private salons led to his first compositions, sentimental waltzes such as *Fleurs d'hiver*, or *Rebecca* (using synagogue motifs), and also to public cello recitals. His cello-playing was acclaimed, even by the young Queen Victoria. Offenbach's first stage music was for an 1839 Palais-Royal vaudeville, *Pascal et Chambord*, which was unsuccessful. During the political crisis of 1848, after composing further minor stage works, Offenbach returned to Germany. But, in 1850 he was back in Paris as chef d'orchestre at the Comédie-Française, a job that entailed conducting a great deal of incidental music and songs, much of which he composed himself. His first notable song, 'La chanson de Fortunio', with its haunting refrain, was written for Alfred de Musset's *Le chandelier*.

Dissatisfied with the Opéra-Comique's reluctance to mount truly comic operas, Offenbach set out to write his own, short operettas much in the style being popularized by Hervé – one-act buffooneries with a few songs sung by two or three characters. The licensing restrictions that deprived Offenbach and his early librettists of more than two or three characters, let alone a chorus, did not seem to dull the success of the first bill at the Bouffes-Parisiens in 1855. Here, at a tiny, rickety magic theatre off the Champs-Elysées, a four-part programme was riotously ended with *Les deux aveugles*, the raffish story of two sham blind beggars. Other one-act works followed, notably *Le violoneux*, and the theatre shifted its operations to winter quarters in the Passage Choiseul.

The permanent theatre opened merrily with a bill that included *Ba-ta-clan*, a musical chinoiserie of considerable cleverness and silliness by Offenbach and Ludovic Halévy (a civil servant and a nephew of Fromental Halévy, the composer of *La juive*). It indulged in musical satire (on Meyerbeer and grand Italian opera), put its contemporary Parisian characters in a fantastic (Chinese) setting, and had them sing and dance an entrancing waltz. Thus, the pattern for many of Offenbach's works was already set. Within a year, the Bouffes was offering not only new Offenbach works, but reprises of short comic works by Mozart and Rossini, as well as two winning operettas in a competition for new composers – one by Lecocq and the other by Bizet (both to the same libretto, *Le docteur Miracle*).

The opéras bouffes were popular not only in Paris, but on tours of the Bouffes company to the French provinces, London and Vienna. In Britain, as in Austria–Hungary, the frivolity of Offenbach's one-act operettas led to local translations and, later, frank imitations. Suppé's *Das Pensionat* (1860) and Sullivan's *Cox and Box* (1866) were both influenced by Offenbach's style and were instrumental in establishing the national operetta styles of both countries.

By 1858 several characters and a full chorus were permitted at the Bouffes, and on 21 October the first great, full-length, classical French operetta was produced: *Orphée aux enfers*. Its enormous success led to worldwide productions and the composition of the full-length *Geneviève de Brabant* (1859). Several accomplished short works followed, including *M. Choufleuri restera chez lui le . . .*, *Les bavards*, *Lieschen et Fritzchen*, as well as a ballet, *Le papillon*, and a work for the Opéra-Comique, the three-act *Barkouf*. Neither *Le pont des soupirs* (1861) nor *Les géorgiennes* (1864) was particularly memorable at the Bouffes, nor was Offenbach's romantic opera for the Court Opera in Vienna: *Die Rheinnixen* (1864), although one of its numbers was transformed much later into the barcarolle in *Les contes d'Hoffmann*. But with a new star, Hortense Schneider, a new theatre (the Variétés), and a new team of librettists, there was another triumph, *La belle Hélène*. The fortuitous partnership of librettists Henri Meilhac and Ludovic Halévy ensured almost perfect texts for the great works that followed: *Barbe-bleue*, *La vie parisienne* and *La Grande-Duchesse de Gérolstein*.

La princesse de Trébizonde (1869), although coming at the very height of Offenbach's powers, also marked the beginning of the end of the public's enchantment with the old opéra-bouffe style. It was tired of the old burlesque methods and operatic parodies, the puns, the travesty, and was beginning to seek a more romantic, heavier weight to its stories, though it did not tire of clever plots and jokes if well written. It also craved spectacle. *Les brigands* (1869) was a compromise between silliness, satire and romanticism of operas such as Auber's *Fra Diavolo*. The Franco-Prussian War brought to an end the frivolity of the Second Empire with its saucy operettas; Offenbach (still ashamed of his Germanic origins) fled France.

But Lecocq's prediction that operetta would be killed by Prussian shells was wrong; post-war Paris craved either an excess of spectacle or a surfeit of sentimentality. Offenbach, who returned to take over the management of the Théâtre de la Gaîté in 1873, failed, however, to find the perfect recipe for new works. *Le Roi Carotte*, although lavish, was too satirical; *Fantasio* was bland and *Les braconniers* was a weak rehash of *Les brigands*. (Lecocq's *La fille de Madame Angot*, an immense success in Paris in 1873, was exactly what Parisians wanted: a costume romance with reduced silliness and satire.) Offenbach could still write effective short works (*La leçon de chant*, *La permission de dix heures*) and risqué longer ones with modern settings (*La jolie parfumeuse*), but he increasingly channelled his enormous energies into massive, spectacular versions of older works, and new extravaganzas, at the Théâtre de la Gaîté, which after a profitable start he mismanaged into debt. An aggrandized *Orphée aux enfers* in 1874 was followed much less profitably by an amplified *Geneviève de Brabant*.

In an attempt to recapture his imperial crown, Offenbach worked again with Meilhac and Halévy (*La boulangère a des écus*, *La créole*) and then with Lecocq's writers Chivot and Duru on *Madame Favart*, and, most successfully, *La fille du tambour-major*, a work that harked back to Donizetti and even Méhul but that displayed Offenbach's late-period charms at their most delightful. But by the end of the 1870s the triumphs of Planquette and Audran were foremost in the minds and throats of the Paris operetta public and Offenbach's works fell out of favour. *Les contes d'Hoffmann* was unfinished at the time of the composer's death and was completed at the request of his family by Ernest Guiraud. Standing outside the operetta tradition, it has become, rather ironically, the most frequently performed of Offenbach's works.

Orphée aux enfers

Orpheus in the Underworld

Opéra-bouffon in two acts (1h 45m; rev. version: 2h 45m)
Libretto by Hector Crémieux and Ludovic Halévy
Composed 1858, rev. in four acts 1874
PREMIERES 21 October 1858, Bouffes-Parisiens, Paris; US: March 1861, Stadt Theater, New York; UK: 26 December 1865, Her Majesty's Theatre, Haymarket, London (as *Orpheus in the Haymarket*); rev. version: 7 February 1874, Théâtre de la Gaîté, Paris
CAST Aristée/Pluton *t*, Jupiter *bar*, Orphée *t*, John Styx *t*, Mercure *t*, Bacchus *silent*, Mars *b*, Eurydice *s*, Diane *s*, L'Opinion Publique *ms*, Vénus *s*, Cupidon *s*, Junon *s*, Minerve *s*, Cybèle *s*, Hebé *s*; *satb* chorus of gods, goddesses; ballet

Orphée aux envers was the first classical (in both senses of the term) full-length operetta, although it was supported by other pieces at its original presentation. What began as a burlesque sketch on the Orpheus legend became something far more substantial, its foolery striking the right, impudent note. The original targets were the posturing excesses of classical performances at the Comédie-Française, still considered sacrosanct during the Second Empire, and the attack was handled by contemporary party-goers in Gustave Doré-style togas. An orgiastic climax was reached during the Act II bacchanal, with a stately minuet of the gods holidaying in hell followed immediately by the *galop infernal* (the can-can).

SYNOPSIS
Act I: Orpheus and Eurydice are bored with each other; the wife particularly loathes her husband's dreadful violin-playing. The shepherd/beekeeper Aristaeus has attracted Eurydice's attentions – in fact, he is Pluto, disguised – and he sets a poisonous snake in the fields, which conveniently bites Eurydice. She dies euphorically and is happily transported to hell. Orpheus is delighted at the news, but Public Opinion requires him to journey to Jupiter to demand the return of his wife. On Mount Olympus, the gods are seditious, demanding more excitement and better food. To quell their revolt, Jupiter decides to allow them to accompany him down to the Underworld to investigate Orpheus' predicament.

Act II: Once there, Jupiter – disguised as a fly – falls for Eurydice himself. At a rowdy farewell party for the Olympians, Jupiter consents to let the less-than-enthusiastic Orpheus retrieve his wife, providing he does not turn around on his way out. Jupiter then throws a thunderbolt, causing Orpheus to turn. Eurydice is forced to remain down under as a bacchante, to everyone's joy save Public Opinion's.

Because of its irreverent merriment (snatches of Gluck's 'Che faro senza Euridice?' appear), its catchy score and, most of all, its can-can – Offenbach's most famous composition (often rather dubiously interpolated into many of his other works) – *Orphée* is constantly performed. Generally, the original two-act version is used, but since the EMI recording of the four-act 1874 aggrandizement, parts of that overblown score have been heard in recent revivals.

RECORDINGS 1. Mesplé, Rhodes, Sénéchal, Burles, Trempont, Capitole de Toulouse Ch & O, Plasson, EMI,

1978; 2. Dessay, Podles, Beuron, Fouchecourt, Naouri, Op Nat de Lyon Ch & O, Minkowski, EMI, 1997

La belle Hélène

Beautiful Helen

Opéra-bouffe in three acts (3h)
Libretto by Henri Meilhac and Ludovic Halévy
Composed 1864
PREMIERES 17 December 1864, Théâtre des Variétés, Paris; UK: 30 June 1866, Adelphi, London (as *Helen, or Taken from the Greek*); US: 14 September 1867, Chicago
CAST Paris *t*, Ménélaus *t*, Agamemnon *bar*, Calchas *b*, Achille *t*, Ajax I *t*, Ajax II *bar*, Hélène *s*, Oreste *s* or *t*, Leøna *s*, Parthenis *s*, Bacchis *ms*; *satb* chorus of guards, slaves, people, princes, princesses, mourners for Adonis, Helen's entourage

La belle Hélène marked a return to Classical antiquity for its creators, who aimed to repeat the triumph of *Orphée aux enfers* – and succeeded. The libretto and characters are far more developed, and its musical pattern subsequently became the basic mould for the classical three-act operetta. There was also a romantic or sentimental streak that Offenbach and his librettists, their followers and the Viennese later developed. Meilhac and Halévy turned the events of the rape of Helen of Sparta into a boulevard farce, but a musical farce, and it is the delirious activity of the chorus and principals in their various ensembles that makes *La belle Hélène* so deliciously immortal.

SYNOPSIS
Act I: Queen Helen of Sparta is troubled by her marriage to the weak King Menelaus, and feels she is being hounded by the Fates. The shady soothsayer Calchas tells her that he too has heard the rumours of a divine beauty contest involving a golden apple and a handsome shepherd. The shepherd appears and tells Calchas that Venus has promised him the heart of the most beautiful woman in the world. The shepherd wins a wordplay contest and reveals himself as Paris, Prince of Troy. Calchas makes sure that Paris and Helen will be alone by manufacturing a divine message that forces Menelaus to journey to Crete.

Act II: Paris steals into Helen's boudoir, disguised as a slave. Helen thinks she is dreaming, until Menelaus barges in, discovering the two in bed. She reproaches her husband for having returned without warning. Paris tactfully withdraws, vowing to return.

Act III: The royals have gone to the beach at Nauplia for their holidays. A priest arrives on a barge, to proclaim that Helen must now take a trip to Chytherea, to atone for the gods' displeasure. As soon as she sails away, the priest reveals himself as Paris, and the Trojan War is set in motion.

While the subject matter of *La belle Hélène* and its disrespectful treatment echoed that of *Orphée*, Offenbach adopted a different musical style, moving away from 18th-century pastiche towards a more modern idiom that involved a greater degree of chromaticism (often in the melodies, for example in Helen's 'Amours divins', where the stepwise falling motion perfectly captures her sadness and longing). There is even an oblique quip at Wagner's *Tannhäuser* during the competition scene, a raucous fanfare which Menelaus passes off as 'German music I commissioned for the ceremony'.

RECORDINGS 1. Norman, Alliot-Lugaz, Aler, Burles, Lafont, Bacquier, Capitole de Toulouse Ch & O, Plasson, EMI, 1984; 2. Lott, Beuron, Sénéchal, Musiciens du Louvre, Minkowski, EMI, 2000

La Périchole

Perichole

Opéra-bouffe in two (later three) acts (2h 30m)
Libretto by Henri Meilhac and Ludovic

Halévy, after the play *Le Carrosse du Saint-Sacrement* by Prosper Mérimée (1830)
Composed 1868, rev. 1874
PREMIERES two-act version: 6 October 1868, Théâtre des Variétés, Paris; US: 4 January 1869, Pike's Opera House, New York; UK: 27 June 1870, Princess's Theatre, London; three-act version: 25 April 1874, Théâtre des Variétés, Paris

La Périchole is set in 18th-century Peru. The usual Meilhac–Halévy silliness is all there, but there is also a more sentimental vein in the leading character, which Offenbach exploited in several numbers, most famously the Act I letter song. The heroine's romantic predicament was still considered quite risqué to British audiences in 1875, when the operetta shared the bill with the first run of Gilbert and Sullivan's *Trial by Jury*.

The street singers La Périchole and Piquillo, much in love, are too poor even for a marriage licence. The viceroy, Don Andrès, is taken by La Périchole's beauty and wants her to move in to his palace as a lady-in-waiting. To do this officially, she must be a married woman, so the viceroy arranges for the lovesick Piquillo – who has just received a despairing farewell letter from his beloved – to marry La Périchole, without knowing her identity. The two are so tipsy by the time of their wedding that they do not recognize one another. Piquillo eventually recognizes her as his wife, and as the viceroy's favourite, and publicly humiliates her. For this, the viceroy has Piquillo dragged down to the dungeon reserved for recalcitrant husbands. Eventually the viceroy pardons them.

Offenbach's score is rich in Spanish (if not Peruvian) suggestions – boleros, seguidillas and fandangos abut galops, waltzes and marches – and is one of his most magical creations; the finales in particular are superb. *La Périchole* was restaged at the Variétés in 1874, in three (rather than two) acts. Since then, the operetta has had a chequered career, but certain productions have been very successful.

RECORDINGS 1. Crespin, Vanzo, Trigeau, Friedmann, Bastin, Op du Rhin Ch, Strasbourg PO, Lombard, Erato, 1977; 2. Berganza, Carreras, Sénéchal, Trempont, Bacquier, Capitole de Toulouse Ch & O, Plasson, EMI, 1981

Les contes d'Hoffmann

The Tales of Hoffmann

Fantastic opera in five acts (4h)
Libretto by Jules Barbier, based on the play by Jules Barbier and Michel Carré (1851), in turn based on several tales by E. T. A. Hoffmann, in particular *Der Sandman* (1816), *Rat Krespel* (1818) and *Die Abendteuer der Silvester-Nacht* (1815)
Composed 1877–80
PREMIERES 10 February 1881, Opéra-Comique, Paris (orch., re-arranged and with recitatives by Guiraud); US: 16 October 1882, Fifth Avenue Theater, New York; UK: 17 April 1907, Adelphi Theatre, London
CAST Hoffmann *t*, Nicklausse *ms*, Olympia *s* (sometimes also sings Antonia *s*, Giulietta *s*, Stella *s*), Lindorf *b* (also sings Coppélius *bar*, Dr Miracle *bar*, Dappertutto *b* or *bar*), Andrès *t* (also sings Cochenille *t*, Pittichinaccio *t*, Frantz *t*), Spalanzani *t*, Nathanael *t*, Crespel *b* or *bar*, Luther *b*, Hermann *b* or *bar*, Schlemil *b* or *bar*, Wolfram *t*, Wilhelm *b*, voice of Antonia's mother *ms*; *satb* chorus of students, party-goers, Venetians, servants

One of the repertoire favourites, *Les contes d'Hoffmann* has been subjected to many well-intentioned alterations and, more recently, expansions seeking to provide either a satisfying evening at the opera or the format Offenbach perhaps would have wanted had he been alive at the premiere. The celebrated tales of fantasy by E. T. A. Hoffmann inspired many other composers for the stage, including Tchaikovsky, Adam, Audran, Hindemith and previously Offenbach himself (*Le Roi Carotte*, 1872).

The composition of *Les contes d'Hoffmann* (announced for the Gaîté-Lyrique season of 1877–8) taxed Offenbach's powers, especially as he was continually turning out operettas for other theatres to support his family. When bankruptcy hit the Gaîté-Lyrique, Offenbach continued composing. In May 1879, two years after he had begun the work, a musicale at his house featuring songs from the opera attracted the attention of Carvalho, manager of the Opéra-Comique. Many of the recitatives were replaced by spoken dialogue, traditionally used at the Opéra-Comique, and vocal assignments were altered. When he died Offenbach had not completed much of Act IV or the end of Act V, nor begun the orchestration.

Shortly after Offenbach's death, Ernest Guiraud was asked to finish the work for production in early 1881. The original Venetian act was dropped entirely, except for the barcarolle, and the role of Nicklausse was shortened because of the star's vocal shortcomings. Since it was Offenbach's habit to revise his works in the light of the public reaction to the premiere, we can never know what finished form *Les contes d'Hoffmann* might have taken. The closest we can come to the composer's original intentions is to follow the critical edition made by Fritz Oeser in 1977, which revokes alterations made in other performing versions and, drawing on original vocal parts and on sketches by Offenbach, restores missing passages and probably most nearly approaches the composer's conception.

SYNOPSIS

Act I: In a German tavern, adjoining an opera house, the Muse of the poet Hoffmann calls on spirits to separate him from his adored Stella, a diva. The Muse becomes Nicklausse, Hoffmann's friend. The councillor Lindorf, rival for Stella's affections, plots to undo Hoffmann. During the interval of *Don Giovanni*, the tavern becomes filled with students, who prevail on Hoffmann to sing them a song about the deformed dwarf Kleinzach ('Il était une fois à la cour d'Eisenbach'). In the middle of the song, Hoffmann unexpectedly starts indulging in a reverie about Stella. Brought back to his senses, Hoffmann sees Lindorf, and tells his friends that the councillor has previously thwarted his love affairs. Mellowed by punch, he begins to describe them.

Act II: Hoffmann is in love with a woman he thinks is the daughter of an inventor, Spalanzani. The inventor is afraid that Coppélius, who also specializes in gadgets – particularly eyes – will want a share of the profits from his latest invention, and offers to buy him out. The inventor introduces Olympia, the singing doll, to the public; Hoffmann sings of his love for her ('Ah, vivre deux'). While Olympia sings ('Les oiseaux dans la charmille'), Spalanzani winds her clockwork mechanism up whenever it runs down. Despite Nicklausse's warnings, Hoffmann is more and more enchanted by her, though somewhat surprised at her strange behaviour. When Coppélius returns, having been given a bad cheque, he destroys Olympia, and Hoffmann finally realizes his error, to the public's delight.

Act III: In Munich, Hoffmann has fallen in love with Antonia, seriously ill and hidden away by her father, Crespel, to prevent her from exerting herself. Although forbidden to, she sings ('Elle a fui, la tourterelle!'). Hoffmann finds her and the two declare their love ('C'est un chanson d'amour'). The evil Dr Miracle, who attended the death of Crespel's late wife, enters and proceeds to 'examine' Antonia by hypnosis, making her sing. Crespel forces Miracle out, but he returns, takes a violin and urges Antonia to sing with the voice emanating from her mother's portrait. Antonia collapses as Hoffmann re-enters; the doctor declares her dead.

Act IV: In Venice, Hoffmann listens to Nicklausse and the courtesan Giulietta sing a languorous barcarolle ('Belle nuit, o nuit d'amour'). Hoffmann has given up amorous adventures for the pleasures of wine. The shadowy Dappertutto tempts Giulietta with a diamond into obtaining Hoffmann's soul ('Scintille diamant'). Hoffmann falls in love with Giulietta ('O Dieu de quelle ivresse'), and they sing an ecstatic duet ('Si ta presence m'est ravie') during which Giulietta succeeds in obtaining the reflection of Hoffmann that Dappertutto demanded. Hoffmann is drawn into a duel with Schlemil, a rival for Giulietta's hand. Hoffmann kills Schlemil, and obtains the key with which Giulietta is locked up at night, only to see his beloved disappearing in a gondola with Pittichinaccio.

Act V: Back in the tavern, Nicklausse admits that Hoffmann's loves were different personifications of the same woman – Stella. She appears but leaves the tavern on Lindorf's arm. Nicklausse reassumes the character of the Muse and tells Hoffmann that his poetry will be enriched by his sorrow.

Although, shortly before his death, Offenbach sanctioned the replacement of his planned recitatives with spoken dialogue, *Les contes d'Hoffmann* is far removed from his much essayed operetta tradition. Serious in tone, it eschews the parodistic element of many previous works, instead following closely the combination of reality and fantasy, of the romantic and the grotesque, found in Hoffmann's writings. The removal of the need to ape Meyerbeer or Bellini, for example, allowed Offenbach the opportunity to formulate his own musical style – a style that was not, melodically or harmonically, hugely innovative, but could adapt more readily to a new type of dramatic pacing. Where simple strophic songs were previously presented in the most straightforward manner, here they are often the vehicles of some dramatic development – for example, Antonia's aria 'Elle a fui, la tourterelle' (Act III) or in Hoffmann's telling of the legend of Kleinzach (Act I). Nevertheless, when appropriate, Offenbach was happy to echo earlier stylistic mannerisms, for instance Olympia's doll song, 'Les oiseaux dans la charmille', which, with its vocal virtuosity, conjures up an effective portrait of a mechanical toy. The famous barcarolle, 'Belle nuit, o nuit d'amour', had originally been composed for *Die Rheinnixen*, Offenbach's ill-fated German Romantic opera, but transferred happily to its Venetian setting; the drinking song that follows was also from that source.

RECORDINGS 1. Doria, Boué, Bovy, Jobin, Bourdin, Paris Op Comique Ch & O, Cluytens, EMI, 1948; 2. Serra, Plowright, Norman, Shicoff, Van Dam, Brussels Nat Op Ch & O, Cambreling, EMI, 1988; 3. Dessay, Vaduva, Jo, Alagua, Van Dam, Op Nat de Lyon Ch & O, Nagano, Erato, 1995

OTHER OPERATIC WORKS *L'alcôve*, 1847; *Le trésor à Mathurin*, 1853 (rev. as *Le mariage aux lanternes*, 1857); *Pépito*, 1853; *Luc et Lucette*, 1854; *Oyayaie, ou La reine des îles*, 1855; *Entrez messieurs, mesdames*, 1855; *Les deux aveugles*, 1855; *Une nuit blanche*, 1855; *Le rêve d'une nuit d'été*, 1855; *Le violoneux*, 1855; *Madame Papillon*, 1855; *Paimpol et Périnette*, 1855; *Ba-ta-clan*, 1855; *Elodie, ou Le forfait nocturne*, 1856; *Le postillon en gage*, 1856; *Trombalcazar, ou Les criminels dramatiques*, 1856; *La rose de Saint-Flour*, 1856; *Les dragées du baptême*, 1856; *Le '66'*, 1856; *Le savetier et le financier*, 1856; *La bonne d'enfants*, 1856; *Les trois baisers du diable*, 1857; *Croquefer, ou Le dernier des paladins*, 1857; *Dragonette*, 1857; *Vent du soir, ou L'horrible festin*, 1857; *Une demoiselle en lôterie*, 1857; *Les deux pêcheurs*, 1857; *Mesdames de la Halle*, 1858; *Le chatte métamorphosée en femme*, 1858; *Un mari à la porte*, 1859; *Les vivandières de la grande armée*, 1859; *Geneviève de Brabant*, 1859, rev. 1867 and 1875; *Le carnaval des revues*, 1860; *Daphnis et Chloé*, 1860; *Barkouf*, 1860 (rev. as *Boule de neige*, 1871); *La chanson de Fortunio*, 1861; *Le Pont des Soupirs*, 1861, rev. 1868; *M. Choufleuri restera chez lui le . . .* (?coll. with Duc de Morny),

1861; *Apothicaire et perruquier*, 1861; *Le roman comique*, 1861; *Monsieur et Madame Denis*, 1862; *Le voyage de MM. Dunanan père et fils*, 1862; *Les bavards*, 1862; *Jacqueline*, 1862; *Il Signor Fagotto*, 1864; *Lieschen et Fritzchen*, 1864; *L'amour chanteur*, 1864; *Die Rheinnixen*, 1864; *Les Géorgiennes*, 1864; *Jeanne qui pleure et Jean qui rit*, 1864; *Le fifré enchanté, ou Le soldat magicien*, 1864; *Coscoletto, ou Le Lazzarone*, 1865; *Les refrains des bouffes*, 1865; *Les bergers*, 1865; *Barbe-bleue*, 1866; *La vie parisienne*, 1866; *La Grande-Duchesse de Gérolstein*, 1867; *La permission de dix heures*, 1867; *Robinson Crusoe*, 1867; *Le château à Toto*, 1868; *L'île de Tulipatan*, 1868; *Vert-vert*, 1869; *La diva*, 1869; *La Princesse de Trébizonde*, 1869; *Les brigands*, 1869; *La romance de la rose*, 1869; *Mam'zelle Moucheron*, (*c*.1870), rev. Delibes, 1881; *Le Roi Carotte*, 1872; *Fantasio*, 1872; *Fleurette, oder Naherin und Trompeter*, 1872; *Der schwarze Korsar*, 1872; *La leçon de chant*, 1873; *Les braconniers*, 1873; *Pomme d'api*, 1873; *La jolie parfumeuse*, 1873; *Bagatelle*, 1874; *Madame l'archiduc*, 1874; *Whittington*, 1874; *Les Hannetons*, 1875; *La boulangère a des écus*, 1875; *La créole*, 1875; *Le voyage dans la lune*, 1875; *Tarte à la crème*, 1875; *Pierrette et Jacquot*, 1876; *La boîte au lait*, 1876; *Le docteur Ox*, 1877; *La foire Saint-Laurent*, 1877; *Maître Péronilla*, 1878; *Madame Favart*, 1878; *La marocaine*, 1879; *La fille du tambour-major*, 1879; *Belle Lurette* (completed Delibes), 1880

R.T.

P

Giovanni Battista Pergolesi

b 4 January 1710, Jesi, nr Ancona;
d 16 March 1736, Pozzuoli, nr Naples

Pergolesi's stage works include four serious operas, two comic operas, two intermezzi, and a sacred drama. These were written during a period of less than six years in Pergolesi's short lifetime and were all first produced in Naples with the exception of his last opera seria, *L'Olimpiade*.

In any discussion of works attributed to Pergolesi, the question of authenticity is an overriding concern. This is particularly true of the many sacred works, instrumental pieces, and independent arias fraudulently inscribed with the celebrated name. This wholesale production of false Pergolesiana by unscrupulous publishers and copyists was a result of the resounding posthumous success of his intermezzo *La serva padrona* in Paris in 1752 and the ensuing battle of words – the so-called *querelle des bouffons* – between the partisans of French and Italian opera.

Nevertheless, with few exceptions, the authenticity of the Pergolesi oeuvre for the stage remains not only secure but well documented, even including a partial autograph of his last opera, *Il Flaminio*. Pergolesi also wrote an oratorio, *La morte di San Giuseppe*, a complete autograph of which has recently been authenticated. Among the relatively few Pergolesi misattributions for the stage are the intermezzo *Il maestro di musica* (a pasticcio based on Pietro Auletta's *Orazio*) and the comic opera *Il geloso schernito* (a 1746 work by the Venetian composer Pietro Chiarini, with an overture by Baldassare Galuppi).

Pergolesi was sent at an early age to study at the Conservatorio dei Poveri di Gesù Cristo in Naples. There he had the advantage of studying with such masters as Greco, Vinci and Durante. His sacred drama, *La conversione e morte di San Guglielmo*, was presented, probably as a conservatory exercise, at the monastery of Sant' Agnello in the summer of 1731. Later the same year, Pergolesi was commissioned to write his first opera seria, *La Salustia*, which was received with indifference when it was produced in January 1732. In sharp contrast, his first comic opera, *Lo frate 'nnamorato*, presented later in the same year, was an unqualified success.

Pergolesi's second opera seria, *Il prigionier superbo*, is best known as the conduit for the intermezzo placed between its acts, the immortal *La serva padrona* (1733). The following year saw another intermezzo, *Livietta e Tracollo*, sandwiched between the acts of Pergolesi's third, and perhaps most powerful, opera seria, *Adriano in Siria*. Pergolesi's two final works for the stage were produced in 1735: the opera seria *L'Olimpiade*, in Rome, and the commedia musicale *Il Flaminio*, in Naples.

The diversity of style among these works is remarkable: from the buffo scenes of *La conversione e morte di San Guglielmo* to the virtuosic and extended arias of *Adriano in Siria*; from the folklike canzonas of *Lo frate 'nnamorato* to the delicate and expressive arias of *L'Olimpiade*. They reflect in microcosm the vast stylistic range of much of Pergolesi's non-dramatic work: from the simple textures of his Violin Sonata to the multitudinous sonorities of his Mass in F; from the sensitivity of his *Stabat Mater* to the virtuosity of his Violin Concerto.

Aside from *La serva padrona* and the *Stabat Mater* – which have been performed almost continually since their creation – Pergolesi performances were uncommon until relatively recently. Sparked by a renewal of scholarly interest in the composer in the 1970s, there were revivals of *Il Flaminio* in 1983, *Adriano in Siria* and *Livietta e Tracollo* in 1986, and *Lo frate 'nnamorato* in 1989.

La serva padrona

The Maid is Mistress

Intermezzo in two parts (50m)
Libretto by Gennarantonio Federico
PREMIERES 28 August 1733, Teatro San Bartolomeo, Naples; UK: 27 March 1750, King's Theatre, Haymarket, London; US: 13 June 1790, Baltimore
CAST Uberto *b*, Serpina *s*, Vespone *silent*

La serva padrona is one of the most universally popular works in the operatic repertoire. Also one of the most influential of stage works, it served as a model for Jean-Jacques Rousseau in his polemic war and long served as a prototype of the opera-buffa style. The sparkling and witty score consists of a brief instrumental introduction and two separate parts, each of which contains both spoken and sung passages and includes an aria for each principal as well as a duet.

SYNOPSIS
Part I: Uberto, a bachelor, complains about the incompetence and wilfulness of his maidservant, Serpina, who rules the household with an iron hand and keeps him waiting for his chocolate. He instructs his servant, Vespone, to find him a wife, no matter how ugly, who will bow to his wishes. Overhearing this, Serpina asks her master to take her as his wife, but Uberto refuses.

Part II: Serpina conspires with Vespone to trick her master into marrying her. She tells Uberto that she intends to marry a certain Captain Tempest. When her master asks to meet this soldier suitor, she produces Vespone in disguise. Then she informs him that the silent captain requires a dowry or else he will insist that Uberto marry Serpina in his place. Uberto, choosing what he considers to be the lesser of two evils, agrees to marry his servant. When Vespone pulls off his false moustache and reveals his true identity, Uberto realizes that he loves Serpina. Her future as mistress of the house is secured.

Among the outstanding arias in the first part are Uberto's frivolous 'Sempre in contrasti' and Serpina's peevish 'Stizzoso, mio stizzoso'. A highlight of the second intermezzo is Serpina's reflective aria, 'A Serpina penserete', in which she at first appears to have a softer side. However, later in the same aria, her true nature is revealed. The music of Uberto's aria, 'Son imbrogliato io già', is capricious, with alternating buffo and serious elements, thus reflecting his uncertain feelings towards Serpina.

RECORDING Bicciré, di Stefano, La Petite Bande, Kuijken, Accent, 1996
OTHER OPERATIC WORKS *La conversione e morte di San Guglielmo*, 1731; *La Salustia*, 1732; *Lo frate 'nnamorato*, 1732; *Il prigionier superbo*, 1733; *Adriano in Siria*, 1734; *Livietta e Tracollo, ossia La contadina astuta*, 1734; *L'Olimpiade*, 1735; *Il Flaminio*, 1735

M.E.P.

Hans Pfitzner

Hans Erich Pfitzner; *b* 5 May 1869, Moscow; *d* 22 May 1949, Salzburg

Pfitzner was born in Moscow because his father, a Saxon choirmaster, happened to be working there as a violinist. The family soon returned to Germany. Once the young Pfitzner had completed his musical education, he became a teacher and then kapellmeister at the Theater des Westens in Berlin; later he was appointed director of the Strasbourg Conservatory and conductor of the symphony orchestra. From 1910 he was director of the opera there, joined in 1914 by Otto Klemperer as his deputy. His first two operas (exactly contemporary with Richard Strauss's *Guntram* and *Feuersnot*) had impressed Humperdinck and Mahler favourably, and for a few years they were performed on many German stages. As with all his stage works, their subjects were consciously Teutonic and Christian.

Pfitzner's interest turned to symphonic music. He had begun as a gentle post-Wagnerian modernist (with a lifelong devotion to the pessimistic philosopher Schopenhauer), but he felt growing dismay at the radicalism of Schoenberg and Busoni and published angry polemics against their malign influence. His *Palestrina* is plainly a declaration of loyalty to conservative tradition – about which his writings found nothing very articulate to say, beyond reiterating his faith in lyrical spontaneity. Two comparably ambitious imposing works followed later, the huge cantata *Von deutscher Seele* (1921) and the 'choral fantasy' *Das dunkle Reich* (1929).

Notoriously, the first of these came to be venerated within the Nazi movement – which had certainly not inspired it – but until 1936 Pfitzner's career certainly throve with the Nazis. There are conflicting accounts of what his real political sentiments were (as also of his character: sour and waspish; contrariwise, humane and witty). In any case, the end of the Second World War found him bombed out of his Munich house and soon to face a denazification court, his public credit severely devalued. His miserable last years were spent in a Munich old people's home. Shortly before he died, the Vienna Philharmonic Society found him a house in Salzburg, and his 80th birthday was decently celebrated in the Austro-German musical world.

The international musical world has been gingerly about reviving Pfitzner. Among German works from between the wars, Hindemith's are neglected and only Richard Strauss's have been steadily honoured: one effect of the radical revelations from the Schoenberg–Berg–Webern axis has been the dismissal of lesser conservative composers from hearing. Since Pfitzner counts (by stern recent standards) as unrigorous and sentimentally eclectic, he must survive – or not – by his individual lyrical stamp, and his knack for broad, intuitive construction. As the winds of fashion veer this way and that, his music will doubtless enjoy intensive short-term rediscoveries.

Palestrina

Musikalische Legende in three acts (3h 30m)
Libretto by the composer, after historical sources
Composed 1912–15
PREMIERES 12 June 1917, Prinzregententheater, Munich; UK: 10 June 1981, Collegiate Theatre, London; US: 14 May 1982, Berkeley (concert)
CAST Pope Pius IV *b*, 2 Cardinal Papal Legates: Giovanni Morone *bar*, Bernardo Novagerio *t*, Cardinal Christoph Madruscht, Prince Bishop of Trent *b*, Carlo Borromeo, Cardinal from Rome *bar*, Cardinal of Lothringen [Lorraine] *b*, Abdisu, Patriarch of Assyria *t*, Anton Brus von Muglitz, Archbishop of Prague *b*, Count Luna, Orator to the King of Spain *bar*, Bishop

of Budoja *t*, Theophilus, Bishop of Imola *t*, Avosmediano, Bishop of Cadiz *b-bar*, Giovanni Perluigi Palestrina *t*, Ighino *s*, Silla *ms*, Bishop Ercole Severolus, Master-of-Ceremonies at the Council of Trent *b-bar*, Singers of the Chapel of Santa Maria Maggiore 2 *t*, 3 *b*; 9 great dead composers 3 *t*, 3 *bar*, 3 *b*; angelic voices 3 *s*, Lucrezia's spirit *s*; *silent*: 2 Papal nuncios; Lainez and Salmeron (Jesuit generals); Massarelli, Bishop of Thelesia, Secretary of the Council; Giuseppe, Palestrina's aged servant; *satb* chorus of singers from the Papal Chapel, archbishops, bishops, abbots, heads of religious orders, envoys, ambassadors (procurators) of princes spiritual and temporal, theologians, scholars from all Christendom, servants, soldiers, crowd

Many a work has been designed as a magnum opus without attaining any such status, but in its crochety way *Palestrina* succeeds. Though it deploys awkwardly many performers for a very long time, it justifies its overweening proportions as creditably as it represents Pfitzner's best strengths. The proportions are wilfully odd, with two quite disparate 90-minute acts – visibly linked only by the figure of Cardinal Borromeo – followed by a third, which takes a mere 30 minutes. Preparing his libretto, Pfitzner had immersed himself in the history of the Council of Trent for two years. The 'historical' gist of his operatic conclusions is this: in 1563 the aged Palestrina composed his *Missa Papae Marcelli*, thereby reaffirming the eternal spirit of pure music and triumphantly persuading the Roman Church not to relinquish it. It is irrelevant that every clause of that proposition is now thought dubious (Palestrina was under 40 in 1563). There is no romantic interest, nor any real note of tragedy – only Palestrina's private despair and his wry acquiescence to fame. A seasoned opera company is presupposed: the central Council act depends on a ripe team of singing actors who know how to play to one another. The premiere was conducted by Bruno Walter.

SYNOPSIS

Act I: Rome, November 1563. Palestrina's pupil Silla has written a new song in the avant-garde Florentine style. His master's son Ighino joins him and they worry over the ageing composer's gloomy lethargy since the death of his wife Lucrezia. He enters with an old friend, Cardinal Borromeo, who warns him that the Council of Trent – nearing its conclusion after 18 years – may resolve to ban polyphonic church music in favour of plainchant, recoiling from fashionably over-ornamented, verbally opaque settings. Borromeo wants Palestrina to compose a Mass that will persuade Pius IV that polyphony can be properly devout. The weary composer declines: nothing has any meaning for him now. Borromeo departs angrily; but while Palestrina drowses, his great musical ancestors – Josquin, Isaac, et al. – appear to urge him on. Angels in glory prompt his *Missa Papae Marcelli* as he begins to write, and his wife's spirit comforts him. After dawn, the boys find him asleep before the completed Mass.

Act II: At Trent, the Council is lengthily embroiled in national and personal rivalries. Merely en passant, the topic of sacred music is raised; Borromeo reports that he has commanded a Mass from Palestrina, who after steadfastly refusing has been imprisoned. The act ends with a punitive slaughter of embattled hangers-on and rabble.

Act III: Back home two weeks later, the dazed composer learns that his secret Mass is being sung in St Peter's: to save him from punishment, his Santa Maria Maggiore choristers have handed over the parts to the authorities. The papal singers arrive, full of praise, and then the delighted Pope himself comes with Borromeo and an entourage to demand Palestrina's lifelong services. Borromeo exults (but Silla has decamped to Florence); the composer resigns himself to his destiny and begins to muse at the organ.

To the static outer acts, Pfitzner's idiosyncratic art lends subtle musical lines as well as pungent character, and Borromeo's long dramatic monologue in Act I is a tour de force. In our 'authenticity'-conscious time the grand close of Act I sounds touchingly dated, with its 'Palestrina' fragments drenched in celestial harps. But Pfitzner never lapses here into plaintive sentiment; and his sardonic sketch of committee futility in Act II is brilliantly calculated for variety and pace. (None of the debate is theological, but any performance must either be sung in the audience's language or enlist surtitles.) A vision is transmitted with considerable power, and it is not a simple one. At the end, Palestrina's tight-lipped reaction to his 'triumph' and the significant absence of young Silla – whose defection to the trendy Florentines is not rebuked – leave an astringent aftertaste. To the extent that *Palestrina* is a grandiose exercise in self-exposure, it eschews self-justification: it is sadder, wiser and more far-sighted than that. The wealth of invention in Pfitzner's score speaks for itself.

RECORDING Donath, Fassbaender, Gedda, Fischer-Dieskau, Ridderbusch, Bavarian RCh & SO, Kubelik, DG, 1973
OTHER OPERATIC WORKS *Der arme Heinrich*, 1895; *Die Rose vom Liebesgarten*, 1901; *Das Christ-Elflein*, 1906; *Das Herz*, 1931

D.M.

Tobias Picker

b 18 July 1954, Manhattan, New York

As a child Picker derived inspiration from 78rpm recordings and from his mother, the fashion designer and artist Henrette Simon. Piano studies, together with an interest in improvisation and composition, began at the age of eight. In 1972 he entered the Manhattan School of Music where he undertook composition lessons with Charles Wuorinen and orchestration with John Corigliano. In 1976 he moved to the Juilliard School to study with Elliott Carter and thereafter gained a place at Princeton for further lessons under Milton Babbitt.

During the 1980s Picker was awarded a series of fellowships and began to attract wide and regular attention as a composer. He was appointed the Houston Symphony's composer-in-residence (1985–90) and in 1987 occupied the same role at the Santa Fe Chamber Music Festival. By the 1990s he had created a substantial and admired body of works for orchestra, which included three symphonies and three piano concertos (he is also a fine pianist). His move into opera with *Emmeline* in 1996 was timely and successful: following its premiere other opera companies commissioned him for new scores. As well as *Fantastic Mr Fox* for Los Angeles, *Thérèse Raquin* (after Zola's novel) was premiered by the Dallas Opera in November 2001, while *An American Tragedy* (based on Theodore Dreiser) is scheduled for the Metropolitan, New York, in 2005–6.

Emmeline

Opera in two acts (2h)
Libretto by J. D. McClatchy, after the novel by Judith Rossner (1980)
Composed 1994–6
PREMIERE 27 July 1996, Opera Theater, Santa Fe

The opera is based on a retelling in novel form of a true story that occurred in Maine in the mid-19th century. Thirteen-year-old Emmeline Mosher, eldest daughter of a large but poor family, is sent away from home to work in a mill. She is seduced by the owner's son and falls pregnant, giving birth to a child that is instantly removed from her. Twenty years later, she becomes close to Matthew Gurney, a new young boarder at her parents' home. Despite their age difference they marry: only afterwards does her aunt learn his name and reveal that they are mother and son. Horrified, Matthew leaves Emmeline, and her family and community repudiate her.

This powerful and inexorable tale has obvious resonances of Greek tragedy. Reactions to the premiere production were extremely positive, and a second staging was speedily arranged at the New York City Opera. Picker's score is highly accessible, drawing on a range of influences – Copland, Stravinsky, Bernstein and minimalism – with which audiences have no problem. With its use of hymns and folktunes, it can be placed firmly within the local tradition of Moore and Floyd, and like the best of their works it is both theatrically effective and fluently composed.

RECORDING Bradley, Geyer, Ledbetter, Racette, Peterson, Owens, Santa Fe Op Ch & O, Manahan, Albany Records, 1998
OTHER OPERAS *Fantastic Mr Fox*, 1998; *Thérèse Raquin*, 2001

G.H.

Amilcare Ponchielli

b 31 August 1834, Paderno Fasolaro (now Paderno Ponchielli), nr Cremona;
d 17 January 1886, Milan

Ponchielli, of humble origins, received his first musical instruction at home. His talents were recognized early, however, and he was admitted to the Milan Conservatory on a scholarship at the age of nine. He remained there for 11 years (the last three studying composition with Alberto Mazzucato) and graduated in 1854.

He returned to Cremona as a church organist, and for the next 18 years from there and nearby Piacenza he attempted to establish himself as an opera composer. *I promessi sposi* (1856), to a libretto the composer himself probably hacked from Alessandro Manzoni's epic novel, had some local success but failed to interest directors of important theatres. An extensive revision of this score, to a new text by Emilio Praga, premiered in Milan at the Teatro dal Verme in 1872, would prove his means of escape from the provinces. Before that lucky event, he composed three more operas, none of which produced the desired impression. The first of them was rejected after being rehearsed in Turin, the second was a turning back to the outworn semiseria genre, and the third received only one performance.

The revised *I promessi sposi* was the pivotal event in Ponchielli's career. It brought him an invitation to compose a ballet for La Scala, *Le due gemelle* (1873), which won him a contract with the publishing house of Ricordi. The prima donna of the refashioned *I promessi sposi*, Teresina Brambilla, married Ponchielli in 1874 (and her relatives harried him for the rest of his life). His reputation, improving with his next work, *I lituani* (1874), was solidified by *La Gioconda* (1876). This work entered the international repertoire. His last two operas were respectfully received but have failed to find a place in the repertoire.

In 1880 Ponchielli became professor of composition at the Milan Conservatory, where he taught Puccini and, briefly, Mascagni. Two years later he assumed the additional duties of maestro di cappella at Santa Maria Maggiore in Bergamo. He held both these positions until his death.

As an opera composer, Ponchielli has frequently been dismissed as crude and vulgar, but such snap judgements do not really describe his capacities. Afflicted by torturing self-doubt, he frequently arrived at his ideas by a painful process of trial and error, as the compositional sketches for La Cieca's 'Voce di donna' in Act I of *La Gioconda* and the progressive transmogrifications that four of his operas underwent demonstrate. None the less, he is said to have composed

'The Dance of the Hours' (*La Gioconda*, Act III) at a single sitting. He possessed a gift both for creating atmosphere, as in the prisoner's chorus of *I lituani*, and for powerful dramatic confrontations, witness the final duet for Gioconda and Barnaba. His works show considerable skill in laying out large-scale structures coherently, and many passages are impressive for their adroit orchestration. His influence on Puccini is evident in the concertato in *Edgar* and in des Grieux's impassioned outburst in the embarkation scene of *Manon Lescaut*, which inevitably reminds one of Gioconda's 'Suicidio!' And the intermezzo from *Il figliuol prodigo* set an example that was not lost on Mascagni and the other *veristi*. As an Italian opera composer attempting to launch himself in the mid-1850s, Ponchielli, unlike Verdi, had no firm underpinning in the flourishing tradition of the 1830s, and as a result he laboured and forged a personal idiom, which would later serve Mascagni, Puccini and other members of the 'Young Italian School' as a point of departure.

La Gioconda

The Ballad Singer

Dramma lirico in four acts (2h 30m)
Libretto by 'Tobia Gorrio' (Arrigo Boito), loosely based on the play *Angelo, tyran de Padoue* by Victor Hugo (1835)
Composed 1874–5; rev. 1876, 1877, 1880
PREMIERES 8 April 1876, La Scala, Milan; first rev. version: 18 October 1876, Teatro Rossini, Venice; second rev. version: January 1877, Rome; definitive version: 12 February 1880, La Scala, Milan; UK: 31 May 1883, Covent Garden, London; US: 20 December 1883, Metropolitan, New York
CAST La Gioconda *s*, La Cieca *c*, Alvise Badoero *b*, Laura *ms*, Enzo Grimaldo *t*, Barnaba *bar*, Zuane *bar*, singer *b*, Isepo *t*, pilot *b*; *satb* chorus of monks, senators, sailors, shipwrights, ladies, gentlemen, populace, masquers, guards; ballet

Boito's libretto bears but a slight resemblance to Hugo's play. He transferred the action from Padua to Venice, as the latter afforded more opportunities for spectacle and local colour. He changed the names of the characters and reduced the role of Alvise (Hugo's Angelo) to a subordinate one. During the series of revisions, he telescoped motivation to the point of occasional obscurity, sacrificing credibility for harsh contrasts, laden with irony.

SYNOPSIS

Act I ('The Lion's Mouth'): The greedy Barnaba wants to possess the street-singer Gioconda, but she rejects him. In revenge, he stirs up the crowd to believe that her blind mother, La Cieca, is a witch. They are about to drag the pious old woman away, when Enzo, a Genoese noble in exile in Venice disguised as a fisherman, attempts to save her. Alvise and his wife, Laura, appear, and the Venetian leader quells the riot. In gratitude, La Cieca gives a rosary to Laura ('Voce di donna'). Enzo recognizes Laura, whom he had loved before her marriage, and Gioconda is filled with passionate gratitude toward Enzo. Barnaba, however, knows Enzo's true identity and offers to arrange for him a rendezvous with Laura on Enzo's brigantine ('Enzo Grimaldo, principe di Santafior'). Alone, Barnaba concocts a letter, denouncing Enzo to the Council of Ten.

Act II ('The Rosary'): Fishermen gather on the wharf, and Barnaba is on hand to watch developments ('Pescator'). Enzo comes on deck to await Laura ('Cielo e mar!'). Laura is rapturously greeted ('Deh, non turbare'), but when Enzo leaves to attend to their departure, Gioconda appears and faces her rival ('L'amo come il fulgor del creato!'). Suddenly Alvise's ship is seen approaching; Laura prays to the Virgin for help and, recognizing her rosary, Gioconda determines to rescue her mother's saviour. Enzo returns to find not Laura but Gioconda, who alerts him to his danger, whereupon Enzo sets fire to his ship and they escape.

Act III ('The House of Gold'): Alvise plans revenge on his unfaithful wife. He commands her to drink poison ('Morir! è troppo orribile!'), but Gioconda emerges from hiding and substitutes a sleeping potion for the poison. At Alvise's mansion, the Ca d'Oro, guests are entertained by 'The Dance of the Hours'. Enzo is shocked that these festivities are going on while Laura lies 'dead' in the next room and tries to stab Alvise. Alvise orders Enzo's arrest, but Gioconda tells Barnaba she will submit to him to save Enzo.

Act IV ('The Orfano Canal'): Gioconda contemplates suicide ('Suicidio!'). Enzo is furious when he learns she has brought Laura's body to her house. Soon Laura returns to consciousness, and Gioconda sends the lovers away to safety ('Quest' ultimo bacio'). Awaiting Barnaba, Gioconda tries to pray. He appears but, as he moves to embrace her, she stabs herself ('Ebbrezza! Delirio!'). Frustrated, Barnaba tells her corpse that he has thrown La Cieca into a canal.

La Gioconda can produce a powerful effect, especially when well sung, though oddly enough its best-known moment, the ballet divertissement 'The Dance of the Hours', is a non-vocal one. There are a number of unconventional arias: La Cieca's 'Voce di donna'; the spy Barnaba's soliloquy, 'O monumento' (Act I); Enzo's tenor romanza 'Cielo e mar!', and Gioconda's monologue in Act IV. There are also three dramatic duets: for the rivals, Gioconda and Laura, in Act II; Alvise and Laura in Act III; and at the end between the desperate Gioconda feigning gaiety and Barnaba as he gloats at the prospect of possessing her. The chorus is treated prominently in *La Gioconda*, and the concertato at the end of Act III develops momentum on a truly grandiose scale. A particular feature of Ponchielli's style is a fortissimo peroration of a prominent tune, as at the close of the concertato or at the end of the trio in Act IV, a practice not lost on the composers of the next generation.

La Gioconda, along with *Aida*, is representative of the absorption during the 1870s of the spectacular effects of French grand opera, including the insertion of ballet into the plot, coupled with overtly emotional Italian vocalism, to produce an amalgamated 'international' style. Apart from its occasional disjointedness, both musically and dramatically, *La Gioconda* exemplifies both the strengths and weaknesses of a particular aspect of Italian operatic history.

RECORDINGS 1. Callas, Cossotto, Ferraro, Cappuccilli, Vinco, La Scala Ch & O, Votto, EMI, 1959; 2. Caballé, Baltsa, Pavarotti, Milnes, Ghiaurov, London Op Ch, Nat PO, Bartoletti, Decca, 1984

OTHER OPERAS *I promessi sposi*, 1856, rev. 1872; *Bertrando dal Bormio*, (1858); *La savoiarda*, 1861, rev. 1870 (rev. as *Lina*, 1877); *Roderico, re dei Goti*, 1863; *Il parlatore eterno*, 1873; *I lituani*, 1874; *I mori di Valenza* (inc.), (1874; completed by Cadore, 1911), 1914; *Il figliuol prodigo*, 1880; *Marion Delorme*, 1885

W.A.

Francis Poulenc

Francis Jean Marcel Poulenc;
b 7 January 1899, Paris; *d* 30 January 1963, Paris

Poulenc came to opera comparatively late in his composing career; late, that is, for one who started so early. Various historical accidents pushed the young Poulenc into the musical vanguard. His family was rich and well connected, and he soon met all the fashionable composers and artists, who discovered that Poulenc's slender gifts – an infallible ear for melody, an ironic sense of humour – were just what was required by Jean Cocteau, Erik Satie and a whole band of anti-Establishment propagandists. Even his compositional shortcomings, a complete ignorance of structure, orchestration or musical orthography, seemed to suit the post-war fashion for naïveté and primitivism.

Fashion was Poulenc's making, and his undoing. It led him to Diaghilev and the Ballets Russes, to worldwide success for his earliest piano pieces and songs. But occasionally it led him to complicate and over-embellish his natural style, which was at its most authentic when at its simplest. By the early 1930s Poulenc the enfant terrible was beginning to look a little long in the tooth. His muse faltered and then deserted him completely. The missing ingredient – his rediscovery of his Catholic faith (1935) – unlocked his soul, his psyche and his music. He also rediscovered, via the baritone Pierre Bernac, his love of song, and via Paul Eluard – the most spiritual of the Surrealist poets – a new sensual and lyrical strain.

This can be further heard in the music of the war years. The brittle influence of Stravinsky gives way to that of Ravel and Chabrier: warmer, more French. *Les mamelles de Tirésias* (1944), for all its high jinks, is shot through with this new nostalgia. The final ingredient in the making of an opera composer is to be found in Poulenc's post-war compositions, which can best be described as an acknowledgement of human frailty in music. Poulenc suffered much from depression and hopelessly doomed love affairs (often with younger men). His last two operas, *Les dialogues des Carmélites* and *La voix humaine*, have the courage to depict the blacker moments of human life in terrifying detail. Poulenc ended his career completely out of step with fashion – shamelessly tonal, unembarrassed about emotion, pain, even sentimentality. He had come a long way from the cynical stylist of the early 1920s.

Les dialogues des Carmélites

Dialogues of the Carmelites

Opera in three acts (12 scenes) (2h 45m)
Libretto by the composer, from the drama by Georges Bernanos (1948)
Composed 1953

PREMIERES 26 January 1957, La Scala, Milan; US: 14 July 1957, San Francisco; UK: 16 January 1958, Covent Garden, London

CAST The Marquis de la Force *bar*, Blanche *lyric s*, The Chevalier de la Force *t*, Madame de Croissy *c*, Madame Lidoine *s*, Mother Marie of the Incarnation *ms*, Sister Constance *light s*, Mother Jeanne *c*, Sister Mathilde *ms*, Mother Gerald/Sister Claire/Sister Antoine and 5 others *choristers*, Father Confessor *t*, First Officer *t*, Second Officer *bar*, Gaoler *bar*, Thierry *bar*, M. Javelinot *bar*; *satb* chorus of nuns, officials of the municipality, officers, police, prisoners, guards, townspeople

Les dialogues des Carmélites has a provenance complicated even by operatic standards. The tale of the martyrdom of the sisters of Compiègne was first told by one of their number, Mother Marie, who survived the French Revolutionary Terror and published her memoirs. The subsequent canonization of the nuns inspired a young German Catholic, Gertrude von le Fort, to tell their story in a novel, *Die letzte am Schafott* (1931), which describes, with grim prescience, the fate of religion under totalitarianism. Le Fort gave life, and indeed her own name, to the heroine Blanche de la Force. There followed various attempts to turn the book into a play, then a film, to which end it arrived in the hands of Georges Bernanos, who was living, or more precisely dying, in South America. He invented further characters and added further personal details, even giving the dying Prioress his own age, 59, 'a good age to die'.

By a bizarre coincidence Poulenc's lover at the time was dying as the composer was writing the music for the same Prioress. Indeed, as Poulenc noted in a letter, he breathed his last just as the work was finished. The opera had been commissioned by Ricordi for La Scala, Milan, but the length of time between conception and birth indicates the complications – legal, financial (the rights were a nightmare as one can see on the title page of the score) and indeed emotional – that the opera brought with it. All this took its toll on Poulenc's health and happiness, both of which, as we can see and hear in the opera, were fragile at the best of times. It is an opera about terror. Personal terror played against state terror. It opens as it means to go on, in fear.

SYNOPSIS

Act I: Blanche's father and brother, the Marquis and Chevalier de la Force – French aristocrats – are fearful. Blanche, whom they know to be easily frightened, is not home yet and the streets are unsettled. She is indeed frightened when she arrives, but maintains a great, albeit spurious, calm as she announces her intention to join the Carmelite order. We then meet the ageing Prioress, who explains to Blanche that the Order can protect nobody. She is touched by Blanche's devotion, however, and gives her her blessing. Blanche joins the convent, where she meets Constance, a happy-go-lucky peasant girl who voices one of the opera's themes, that, when we die, perhaps we die in someone else's stead, perhaps we die their deaths. Certainly the Prioress is dying a death she does not deserve: slow, agonizing, undignified and depicted in unflinching detail in both music and words. Mother Marie is in attendance, loyal and solid, keen to avoid involuntary blasphemy. Blanche arrives to watch her new spiritual mother die in torment.

Act II: Blanche's solitary fears begin to be matched by real dangers from the outside world. The first scene opens with the first of the sung prayers that punctuate this act. It is a Requiem for the Prioress. Blanche, left alone with the body, panics; she is calmed by Mother Marie, ever watchful. The new Prioress arrives and preaches to the nuns. Blanche's brother is admitted and, in a scene that could almost be described as a love duet, attempts to take Blanche away to safety. The finale is of Verdian proportions. The sisters are led in prayer, then the Prioress warns them against the temptation of martyrdom. The noise of the Terror grows; officers arrive and the mob threatens to attack the convent. In the uproar Blanche drops the statue of the infant Jesus.

Act III: The convent is desecrated, the Order declared illegal. Blanche runs away to her late father's house, where she lives disguised as a servant. She hears that the Carmelites have been arrested. They have been imprisoned in the conciergerie where we see the new Prioress inspiring her sisters with strength and courage to face the ordeal ahead. This is depicted with extraordinary realism in the great final scene consisting of one long prayer, the Salve Regina, sung by the nuns as they go, one by one, to their death by guillotine. The crowd looks on amazed as Blanche steps forward, transfigured and joyful, to join her sisters in martyrdom.

'You must forgive my Carmelites,' wrote Poulenc. 'They can sing only tonal music.' And, indeed, compared to most operas written in the 1950s Poulenc's is astonishingly old-fashioned. His models, indeed the work's dedicatees, were Verdi, Monteverdi, Debussy and Musorgsky. The structure, the alternation of recitative and arioso, is Verdian; the recitative itself owes a huge amount to Monteverdi's *Poppea* and to Debussy's *Pelléas*. From Musorgsky Poulenc learned the sense of menace and nightmare that suffuses the whole work.

The tessituras are meticulously planned, and borrowed from grand opera. Poulenc's models were Verdi's Amneris (Mother Marie) and Desdemona (new Prioress), Wagner's Kundry (Prioress), Massenet's Thaïs (Blanche) and Mozart's Zerlina (Constance). Each of these characters has leitmotifs that stand not only for them but also for the emotions they embody, even in other characters. Thus Mother Marie's music (strong, in C major) indicates loyalty and steadfastness not only in Marie but also in Blanche. This is an apt device in an opera in which the sharing of suffering and the universality of grace loom so large. Underpinning everything are two sorts of music: first the prayers, the pulse and counterpoint of Renaissance religious music, which in a cloistered life is at once miraculous and mundane; then the music of fear (typified by a rising minor third which we hear throughout), which always threatens to destroy the age-old structures of the religious world. The Terror versus the Order. It is in the extraordinary final scene that the two are combined; the nuns sing over repeated minor thirds, drowning the mob, conquering fear, moving into posterity.

RECORDINGS 1. Duval, Crespin, Berton, Gorr, Scharley, Op de Paris Ch & O, Dervaux, EMI, 1958 (cut); 2. Dubosc, Yakar, Fournier, Dupuy, Van Dam, Gorr, Sénéchal, Op Nat de Lyon Ch & O, Nagano, Virgin, 1992
OTHER OPERATIC WORKS *Les mamelles de Tirésias*, 1947; *La voix humaine*, 1959

J.S.

Sergey Prokofiev

Sergey Sergeyevich Prokofiev; *b* 23 April 1891, Sontsovka, Ukraine; *d* 5 March 1953, Moscow

Prokofiev considered himself essentially a man of the theatre. Before graduating from the St Petersburg Conservatory in June 1914 he had already worked on five operas; he completed six more over the next 40 years and left three unfinished. He also wrote nine ballets, including two of this century's most successful (*Romeo and Juliet* and *Cinderella*), incidental music to several dramatic works, and the scores for seven films.

Only one of the operas – the first to be performed, *The Love for Three Oranges* – was a success in his lifetime. All the others had to wait until after his death before their worth could be realistically assessed, divorced from the political considerations that had affected Prokofiev throughout his life.

His first four operas were schoolboy efforts and have not been published or professionally performed. His first mature opera, *Maddalena* (1911), was written when he was still a student at the St Petersburg Conservatory. He orchestrated the first scene but left the other three in piano score when the institution's proposed performance was abandoned because the singers found the music too difficult. A similar fate befell his second opera, *The Gambler*, in 1917, though this time the music was fully orchestrated. The following year, feeling the current state of political turmoil in Russia offered him few opportunities, Prokofiev left for a tour of the US (he had also developed a fearsome reputation as a pianist), and after a successful concert in Chicago the opera house there commissioned an opera from him based on a Russian version of Gozzi's fiaba *The Love for Three Oranges*.

The premiere was beset by delays and, uncommissioned, Prokofiev began work on his next opera, *The Fiery Angel*. With the exception of *War and Peace*, this was to occupy him for longer than any other composition (1919–27), and although it was never staged during his lifetime, Prokofiev never abandoned his belief that it contained some of his best music.

In 1920 Prokofiev, still unwilling to return to Russia, had moved to Paris where his ballet *The Tale of the Buffoon* was well received at its premiere the following spring. Over the next few years he built up a successful career in Europe but, from the mid-1930s, commissions for compositions came increasingly from the USSR rather than from the West. Unlike Stravinsky and Rakhmaninov, Prokofiev had stayed away for practical rather than political reasons and so, with an apparent change in Russia's musical climate, he moved to Moscow in 1936.

He soon made his name with *Peter and the Wolf* and the patriotic film score *Alexander Nevsky*. The latter, written in collaboration with the celebrated film director S. M. Eisenstein, transformed Prokofiev's way of thinking about constructing a dramatic musical work: instead of writing long, musically developing scenes, he chose a format of many short scenes, cut together cinematically. With his imagination fired, he quickly found a suitable story for an opera, heroic and uplifting as the Soviet authorities required, full of incident but easy to follow. This was *Semyon Kotko*, the tale of a young soldier returning from the Great War to the newly founded Soviet Ukraine. Despite all Prokofiev's hopes and efforts the authorities condemned both its musical style and its dramatic content and the work was not a success.

For his next two operas Prokofiev returned to the individual kind of neoclassicism he had earlier demonstrated in the *Classical Symphony* (1916–17) and the film score *Lieutenant Kijé* (1933). In *Betrothal in a Monastery* (1940–44) and *War and Peace* (1941–52) the music recreates the period atmosphere through use of musical forms such as minuet and gavotte, using classical period phrasing and melodic contours familiar in Mozart and Haydn, and simple, but never simplistic harmonies. In these works Prokofiev adopted rhymed verse and musical set pieces – elements he had eschewed during his early, radical period. He emphasized the romantic elements in the stories, writing lyrical tunes which are a far cry from the brittle style of the early days.

But once again, Prokofiev was unlucky with performances. Russia's entry into the Second World War made opera production difficult; and after the war, despite numerous revisions carried out at the suggestion of the authorities, a satisfactory format was never arrived at and *War and Peace* was never staged in Prokofiev's lifetime in anything like a form that represented his original concept. Meanwhile, the notorious 1948 Moscow Congress of Composers condemned Prokofiev, along with virtually every Soviet composer of any distinction, for writing 'formalist' music (Zhdanov's catch-all opposite to socialist realism; Prokofiev himself defined formalism as 'music people don't understand at first hearing'). He sought official rehabilitation with his last opera, *The Story of a Real Man*, based on a patriotic true story of a wartime fighter pilot. The music includes folksongs from the hero's north Russian homeland linked by uncomplicated and bland arioso passages. As in *Semyon Kotko*, Prokofiev wrote almost cinematically, but added nothing of his own personality to the folksongs and the opera has little dramatic thrust. It was proscribed as 'modernistic, anti-melodic' and was denied a public performance until many years later.

After Prokofiev's death there was a relaxation of the official Russian position and only *The Fiery Angel* remained unknown to Soviet audiences. In the West there has been a different reaction: of the Soviet operas, only *War and Peace* is at all well known but the early operas are increasingly being performed.

Love for Three Oranges

Lyubov k tryom apel'sinam

Opera in a prologue and four acts
(1h 45m)
Libretto by the composer, after *Fiaba dell'amore delle tre melarance* by Carlo Gozzi (1761)
Composed 1919
PREMIERES US: 30 December 1921, Auditorium, Chicago (in French); USSR: 18 February 1926, Mariinsky Theatre, Leningrad; UK: 24 August 1962, King's Theatre, Edinburgh

CAST King of Clubs *b*, The Prince *t*, Princess Clarice *c*, Leandro *bar*, Truffaldino *t*, Pantaloon *bar*, Chelio *b*, Fata Morgana *s*, Princess Linetta *c*, Princess Nicoletta *ms*, Princess Ninetta *s*, a Gigantic Cook *b*, Farfarello *b*, Smeraldina *ms*, Master of Ceremonies *t*, Herald *b*, 10 Ridiculous People 5 *t*, 5 *b*, advocates of Tragedy *b* chorus, advocates of Comedy *t* chorus, advocates of Lyric Drama *st* chorus, advocates of Farce *ab* chorus, little devils *b* chorus; *satb* chorus of courtiers; *silent*: monsters, drunkards, gluttons, guards, servants, 4 soldiers

At the time of this opera's composition, Prokofiev's eclectic style ranged from the aggressiveness of the *Scythian Suite* (which sought to outdo Stravinsky's *The Rite of Spring* in its portrayal of primitive Russian life) to the quasi-18th-century elegance of the *Classical Symphony*. In Gozzi's story Prokofiev saw the chance to synthesize these elements, its fantasy world providing scope for glittering orchestration, brilliant effects and strongly differentiated characterization. Also, he thought his American audience would appreciate a mercurial setting of the type of brittle fairy story then in operatic vogue; Busoni (and soon Puccini) also selected a Gozzi fiaba, *Turandot*, for operatic treatment. Prokofiev wrote his own libretto, in Russian, from a translation of the play by Meyerhold, Vogak and Solovyov and created a whimsical opera buffa full of the fantastic and grotesque, the comic and the sad, set within a framework of utmost unreality and maximum theatricality.

The commission, from the Chicago Opera, was signed in January 1919 for production that autumn, but the work was not staged until 1921 when the soprano Mary Garden had become the theatre director. Since its European premiere, on 14 March 1925 in Cologne, it has been the most frequently performed of Prokofiev's operas.

SYNOPSIS

The King believes his son and heir will die unless he can be cured of his melancholia. His enemies, his niece Princess Clarice and the prime minister, Leandro, are determined to prevent a cure, for Leandro plans to marry Clarice and succeed to the throne. The King's magic protector is Chelio, his enemies' is the evil Fata Morgana. The action is played out before the Ridiculous People who, like a Greek Chorus, comment on the events. At crucial moments they intervene to ensure that Good prevails.

In an allegorical prologue champions of different kinds of theatre (Tragedy, Comedy, Lyric Drama and Farce) demand to see their favourite entertainment. The Ridiculous People chase them away and a herald proclaims the beginning.

Act I: Doctors tell the King that his son's melancholia is fatal. They say that laughter is the only cure, so the King commands lavish and comic entertainments. Leandro tries unsuccessfully to dissuade him. Chelio loses a symbolic card game to Fata Morgana; Good is endangered. Leandro tells Princess Clarice he has fed the Prince a diet of Tragic Verses to hasten his demise; she wants swifter action. Both are worried that the clown Truffaldino might make the Prince laugh. Smeraldina announces that her mistress, Fata Morgana, will be at the entertainment to stop Chelio from intervening.

Act II: The Prince, in his bedroom, does not laugh at Truffaldino's antics but vomits the Tragic Verses into a bucket. The Prince refuses to attend the King's festivities but, to the strains of the celebrated March, Truffaldino forces him out. The first two divertissements fail to amuse the Prince. But when Fata Morgana, disguised as an old woman, slips and falls, legs kicking in the air, the Prince laughs hysterically. So does everyone else except Clarice, Leandro and Fata Morgana, who pronounces a spell on the Prince: he will fall in love with three oranges and will scour the earth in search of them. It takes effect immediately and the Prince leaves on his quest, accompanied by Truffaldino, blown on their way by the mighty bellows of the devil Farfarello. The King is in despair.

Act III: In a desert Chelio persuades Farfarello to disclose the Prince's destination – the castle of Creonte, where the oranges are kept. Chelio's magical powers are too weak to break Fata Morgana's spell, but he warns the Prince and Truffaldino to open the oranges only near water and arms them with a magic ribbon, to distract Creonte's Gigantic Cook. They are blown into the courtyard and head for the kitchen. While the dreaded cook is distracted by the magic ribbon, the Prince steals the oranges and escapes back to the desert, followed by Truffaldino. The oranges have grown very large and their return is slow. The Prince falls asleep exhausted, as Truffaldino, forgetting Chelio's warning, cuts into one hoping for a drink. Out steps a beautiful princess who tells him she must have water otherwise she will die. Truffaldino thinks the second orange might contain some liquid, but when he cuts it out steps another thirsty princess. Both collapse and Truffaldino flees in panic. When the Prince awakes he is angry at Truffaldino's disappearance and puzzled by the two corpses. Realizing that his future is with the remaining orange and heedless of Chelio's warning, he splits it open and the beautiful Princess Ninetta steps out. They fall in love and the Ridiculous People intervene with a reviving bucket of water. The Prince leaves to arrange for the Princess's reception at the palace. Smeraldina appears, changes the Princess into a rat and usurps her place as the entire court arrives. Smeraldina insists that she is the one the Prince promised to marry and the King believes her. The court returns to the city.

Act IV: Fata Morgana accuses Chelio of cheating; though he lost the card game he continues to help his protégés. The Ridiculous People lock Fata Morgana up so that Chelio can return to the palace. The King, the Prince and Smeraldina arrive with the rest of the court. But the throne is occupied by a giant rat. As the soldiers begin to shoot at it, Chelio, to the Prince's joy and the King's confusion, turns it back into Princess Ninetta. The King finally realizes that Smeraldina, Leandro and Clarice are traitors and orders their excecution, but they escape along with Fata Morgana. In the shortest final chorus in all opera, the Ridiculous People drink a toast to the happy couple.

In its subject and its anti-realism *The Love for Three Oranges* is quite different from Prokofiev's previous operas. However, its musical construction bears similarities with his earlier works. As in *The Gambler*, Prokofiev works with short motifs and their repetition contributes to the ostinato sound of the score. In *The Love for Three Oranges* these function more by association with specific qualities of the commedia dell'arte-type characters than with their feelings. Those who are essentially good have music that is essentially diatonic, with smooth, undisturbed rhythms. The music for the evil characters is more chromatic and rhythmically unstable, with brittle orchestration. Prokofiev usually constructed even his symphonic works in this 'patchwork' way, but its success in *The Love for Three Oranges* is to a large extent due to the flamboyance of the motifs themselves and the exuberant manner in which Prokofiev combines them.

The opera's anti-realism was in tune with prevailing post-war artistic attitudes, but it is the strength of the invention and the skill of Prokofiev's handling of his material that have kept the opera in the repertoire. In 1919 Prokofiev composed an orchestral suite on *The Love for Three Oranges*, which enjoyed instant success; this was revised in 1924. It consists of six sections from the opera, including the famous March.

RECORDING Netrebko, Pluzhnikov, Akimov, Kit, Karasev, Kirov Ch & O, Gergiev, Philips, 1997/8

The Fiery Angel

Ognennyi Angel

Opera in five acts, Op. 37 (2h)
Libretto by the composer, after the historical novel by Valery Bryussov (1908)
Composed 1919–23, rev. 1926–7
PREMIERES 25 November 1954, Théâtre des Champs-Elysées, Paris (concert); 15 September 1955, La Fenice, Venice (stage); UK: 27 July 1965, Sadler's Wells, London; US: 22 September 1965, State Theater, New York; Russia: 28 December 1991, Mariinsky Theatre, St Petersburg
CAST Ruprecht *bar*, Renata *s*, Count Heinrich *silent*, Jacob Glock *t*, Agrippa of Nettesheim *t*, Mephistopheles *t*, Faust *b-bar*, 10 solo parts 2 *s*, 2 *ms*, *c*, *t*, 3 *bar*, *b*, 3 skeletons *s*, *t*, *b*, 3 neighbours *bar*, 2 *b*; *sa* chorus of nuns; *tb* chorus of Inquisitor's retinue; offstage: *satb* chorus

This study of neurotic female sexuality set in Reformation Germany is far removed from the pantomime world of Gozzi, and the music of *The Fiery Angel* has an Expressionist intensity quite unlike the dispassionate music Prokofiev had previously been writing. He spent some four years composing the short score, but with no performance in view he did not start orchestrating it in detail. In 1926, when Bruno Walter, head of the Berlin State Opera, accepted it for performance the following season, Prokofiev revised it, reorganizing Act II and much of Acts I, III and V and orchestrating the whole opera. The Berlin performance did not materialize, but Prokofiev transferred some of the music into his Symphony No. 3. In the early 1930s there was talk of the opera being staged by the Metropolitan Opera in New York and Prokofiev began preliminary work on another major revision. This was never finished, the American performance did not take place and the opera was not staged in Prokofiev's lifetime. Even though it has been widely praised as his strongest and most dramatically intense score, productions (which always use the version prepared for Berlin) have not been frequent.

SYNOPSIS

Act I: Since childhood Renata has been obsessed with her protective angel, Madiel, at first spiritually, then, after puberty, physically. For a year she lived with Count Heinrich, the man she imagined to be Madiel, but he left her. Since then she has been searching for him. She tells all this to Ruprecht after he has found her having hysterical visions, and although everyone else agrees that she is a witch, Ruprecht, who has fallen in love with her, agrees to help.

Act II: Renata and Ruprecht turn to magic in the quest for Heinrich, acquiring forbidden books and conjuring up dark spirits, though the leading proponent of black philosophy, Agrippa, refuses to assist them.

Act III: Renata has seen Heinrich, but he has again rejected her. She demands that Ruprecht avenge her honour. As Ruprecht challenges him to a duel, Renata, seeing Heinrich bathed in light, is again convinced that he is her Fiery Angel; she commands Ruprecht not to harm him, but when Ruprecht is badly wounded in the duel she is full of remorse. She vows to love him and nurse him back to health. Unseen voices mock her.

Act IV: Ruprecht has recovered and Renata leaves him again, determined to punish her own sinfulness by entering a convent. Ruprecht encounters Faust and Mephistopheles; Mephistopheles takes Ruprecht under his wing.

Act V: Renata has corrupted the nuns with her visions and obsessions with her Angel. The Inquisition tries to exorcize the evil to no avail. While Ruprecht looks on, with a triumphant Mephistopheles beside him, Renata is condemned to torture and death.

Prokofiev began *The Fiery Angel* at the only time in his life when religion featured in his intellectual considerations, and it is unique among his theatre works in being written with neither a commission nor a production in view. Its theme of obsession looks back to his pre-Revolution operas *The Gambler* and *Maddelena*. Its form – a set of more or less free-standing tableaux – looks back even further, to Musorgsky. But its musical and dramatic portrayal of ambiguity (the story comes from one of Russia's greatest Symbolist poets) was totally new for him.

Individuals, atmospheres and emotional responses are all given specific themes of characterization – most of them chromatic to some degree. There is only one unambiguously tonal (and therefore stable) character motif in the opera, and this is associated, quite improbably, with the forces of evil. The opera is seen largely through Renata's eyes, and consequently, although the text is ambivalent about whether her visions are hallucinatory, the music makes it apparent that for her they are real and terrifying. During the narrative of her life the orchestra abounds in motifs that return when she later experiences similar feelings. Among the most memorable of these are the soaring theme of her love for Madiel, and the theme – first heard in the orchestra during Ruprecht's attempted rape – which recurs whenever Renata's responses to physical masculinity are displayed.

RECORDING Gorchakova, Galusin, Leiferkus, Alexashkin, Kirov Op Ch & O, Gergiev, Philips, 1993 (live)

War and Peace

Voina i mir

Lyric dramatic scenes – opera in five acts (two parts) – an epigraph and 13 scenes, Op. 91 (4h)
Libretto by the composer and Mira Mendelson, after the novel by Leo Tolstoy (1863–9)
Composed 1941–3, rev. 1946–52

PREMIERES 16 October 1944, Moscow (eight scenes, concert with pf); 7 June 1945, Conservatory, Moscow (nine scenes, concert with orch.); two-evening version: 12 June 1946, Maly Theatre, Leningrad (Part I); July 1947, Maly Theatre, Leningrad (Part II, private performance); new one-evening version: 26 May 1953, Teatro Comunale, Florence; USSR: June 1953, Moscow (concert); 1 April 1955, Maly Theatre, Leningrad (stage; 11 scenes of 13); 8 November 1957, Stanislavsky Theatre, Moscow (13 scenes, with cuts); another 13-scene version (with epigraph): US: 13 January 1957, NBC TV, New York; USSR: 15 December 1959, Bolshoi Theatre, Moscow; UK: 19 April 1967, Town Hall, Leeds (concert); 11 October 1972, Coliseum, London (stage); US: 8 May 1974, Boston

CAST Principal characters: Prince Andrei Bolkonsky *bar*, Countess Natasha Rostova *s*, Sonya *ms*, Maria Dmitrievna Akhrosimova *c*, Count Ilya Rostov *b*, Count Pyotr Bezukhov (Pierre) *t*, Helene Bezukhova *ms*, Prince Anatol Kuragin *t*, Lt Fedya Dolokhov *bar*, Vasska Denisov *bar*, Field-Marshal Prince Kutuzov *b*, Napoleon Bonaparte *bar*, Platon Karataev *bar*; other characters: the host *t*, Major Domo *t*, Madame Peronskaya *s*, Countess Rostova, Natasha's mother *ms*, Tsar Alexander I *silent*, Maria Antonovna *silent*, Prince Bolkonsky's Major-Domo *b*, an old valet *bar*, a housemaid *s*, Maria Bolkonskaya *ms*, Prince Bolkonsky *b-bar*, Balaga *b*, Matriosha *ms*, Josef *silent*, Dunyasha *s*, Gavrilla *b*, Metivier *bar*, French abbé *t*, Tikhon *bar*, Fyodor *t*, 2 Prussian Generals *spoken roles*, Andrei's orderly *t*, 2 Russian Generals *t*, *bar*, Kaizarov *t*, Adjutant to General Compans *t*, Adjutant to Murat, King of Naples *treble*, Prince Berthier, Marshal of France *bar*, Marquis de Caulaincourt, French Ambassador to Russia *silent*, General Belliard *bar*, Adjutant to Prince Eugene *t*, Baron Gourgaud, aide-de-camp to Napoleon *b*, Monsieur de Bausset-Roquefort *t*,

General Count Bennigsen *b*, Prince Mikhail Barclay de Tolly *t*, General Yermolov *bar*, General Konovnitsin *t*, General Rayevsky *bar*, the Peasant's daughter *silent*, Captain Ramballe *b*, Lt Bonnet *t*, Mavra *c*, Ivanov *t*, Marshal Davout *b*, a French Officer *bar*, 3 madmen *t*, *bar*, *silent*, 2 French actresses *s*, *ms*; *satb* chorus of guests, citizens of Moscow, Russian soldiers, French people, partisans

In choosing to make an opera from selected scenes of one of Russian literature's most revered masterpieces (and also one that was hailed as a cornerstone of socialist realism) Prokofiev was laying himself open to attack. He felt he could infuse the heroic story with his own very popular and characteristic kind of neoclassicism. The work immediately ran into difficulties. In May 1942, with Russia and Germany at war, he was asked to strengthen the patriotic element of the 11-scene piano score he had submitted, so he added heroic marches, arias and choruses to the 'war' sections. This shifted the balance away from the affairs of the individuals to the affairs of the state; it monumentalized the opera's substance. For the first proposed staged performances in 1946 Prokofiev added two more scenes, the glittering ball in Part I and the epic war council at Fili (Scene 10). This 13-scene version was designed to be performed over two evenings, but in fact only the first eight scenes were heard in public. After that the political climate made further performances of any of the music impossible, and although Prokofiev continued revising the work until the end of his life, he never heard the complete opera and was never able to give his approval to a final version. The first Russian performances in the late 1950s were all cut.

SYNOPSIS

Part I: Peace. Epigraph: The Russian people affirm their invincibility and the sanctity of their country against all invaders. Scene 1: The young, recently widowed Prince Andrei loses his melancholia when he hears Natasha singing of her happiness at the coming of spring. Scene 2: New Year's Eve 1810. Natasha, at her first society ball, dances with Andrei and the two fall in love. But she has been noticed by the predatory Prince Anatol. Scene 3: February 1812. Natasha and Andrei are engaged but his father refuses to accept her and insults her. She fears that the year's absence imposed on Andrei will weaken their love. Scene 4: May 1812. At a party Natasha is swept off her feet by the charming Prince Anatol, even though she realizes that an affair will sully her love for Andrei. Scene 5: 12 June 1812. Dolokhov, Anatol's friend, tries to persuade him not to elope with Natasha; neither her fiancé nor his wife would acquiesce. Anatol is adamant, summons his troika driver and after a few more drinks leaves. Scene 6: The same night. The elopement is foiled by Natasha's hostess's servants but Anatol escapes. Her aunt rails at her and makes an old family friend, Count Pierre, tell her that Anatol is already married. Pierre also tells her that he has fallen in love with her himself, which confuses her further. Scene 7: The same night. Pierre goes home and finds his wife entertaining friends, including Anatol. He demands that Anatol give up Natasha and leave Moscow immediately. News arrives that Napoleon and his army have crossed the Russian border.

Part II: War. Scene 8: 25 August 1812, before the Battle of Borodino. The Russian volunteer army is assembling, convinced of its invincibility. Andrei joins up hoping to forget Natasha, whom he still loves, and expecting to die. He rejects Field-Marshal Kutuzov's offer of a post at a staff headquarters, and as he leaves with his men the first shots of battle are heard. Scene 9: Later that day, behind the French lines, Napoleon cannot believe the extent of the Russian resistance. He feels destiny is turning against him. When a cannonball lands at his feet he calmly pushes it away before it can explode. Scene 10: Field-Marshal Kutuzov, having lost the Battle of Borodino and retreated to Fili, holds a war council to discuss whether or not to defend the ancient and sacred city of Moscow and risk defeat or retreat further so as to regroup and fight again. Against all advice he decides to abandon Moscow. Alone, Kutuzov meditates on his momentous decision but is confident that the Muscovites will win in the end. Scene 11: French-occupied Moscow is virtually deserted; Count Pierre hears that Natasha's family has fled, taking with them some wounded soldiers, including Andrei (though Natasha has not recognized him). To Napoleon's anger the Muscovites fire their city. Scene 12: Behind the Russian lines. Andrei, wounded and delirious, recalls his love for Natasha. She begs his forgiveness; he longs to live only for her. But it is too late. He dies. Scene 13: November 1812. In the terrible Russian winter the French army, with its prisoners, is in chaotic retreat on the Smolensk road. Those prisoners who cannot keep up are shot. Partisans attack an escort party and free the Russians, among them Pierre. He learns that Andrei is dead and that Natasha is sick, but he dreams that his love for her might now flower. Field Marshal Kutuzov congratulates everyone on a great victory, the people cheer him and reassert their belief in themselves and their country.

In the form and style of *War and Peace* Prokofiev harks back to the historical-tableaux operas of 19th-century Russia, such as Musorgsky's *Boris Godunov* and *Khovanshchina*. The opera's structure is traditional with set-piece arias and Tchaikovskyan dances. Within each scene there are many short episodes involving different characters, a cinematic technique already encountered in Prokofiev's earlier Soviet operas but here developed more effectively. The composer brought the characters alive by relaxing his insistence that the music needed to reflect every inflexion of the original words. In fact some of the words were made to fit pre-existing music, for Prokofiev, ever a prolific inventor of ideas and an inveterate hoarder of those not used, pillaged sketchbooks and unperformed scores for *War and Peace*; one of the most pervasive themes, associated with the love of Andrei and Natasha first heard in Scene 1, was taken over from the incidental music of an unstaged dramatization of Pushkin's *Eugene Onegin* written in 1936, where it also portrayed innocent love destined to be thwarted.

The opera is fundamentally a lyrical work, with expansive melodies, infectious dances and stirring choruses. The good characters (Natasha, Andrei, Pierre) are provided with opulent orchestration; the bad ones (Anatol and his sister Helene, who together bring about Natasha's fall) have music that matches Tolstoy's description of them as 'false and unnatural' with a spare sound. Napoleon has no melodies, only broken phrases more or less unaccompanied, perhaps symbolizing his distance from the people over whom he rules; the Russian commander, Kutuzov, on the other hand, has finely proportioned themes, strong, slow-moving and full of gravitas. The parallels of these two characters with the contemporary leaders, Hitler (Napoleon) and Stalin (Kutuzov) was played up by Prokofiev on the advice of the authorities.

RECORDINGS 1. Prokina, Grigorian, Gerelo, Okhotnikov, Kirov Op Ch & O, Gergiev, Philips, 1991 (cut);
2. Morozova, Lavender, Balashov, Williams, Russian State Symphonic Capella, Spoleto Festival O, Hickox, Chandos, 1999 (live)

OTHER OPERAS *The Giant* (*Velikan*), 1900; *Desert Islands* (*Na pustinnikh ostrovakh*), (inc.), (1900–2); *A Feast in Time of Plague* (*Pir vo vremya chumi*), (1903; one scene rev. 1908–9); *Undina*, (1907); *Maddalena*, (1911), 1978; *The Gambler* (*Igrok*), 1929; *Semyon Kotko*, 1940; *Betrothal in a Monastery* (*The Duenna*) (*Obrucheniye v Monastire*), (1941), 1946; *The Story of a Real Man* (*Povest' o Nastoyashchem*), 1948

C.B.

Giacomo Puccini

Giacomo Antonio Domenico Michele Secondo Maria Puccini; *b* 22 December 1858, Lucca, Italy; *d* 29 November 1924, Brussels

Puccini is generally regarded as the greatest Italian composer of the post-Verdi generation. All but the first two of his operas remain a firm part of the operatic repertoire, and several are among the most popular ever written. During a period in which the Italian operatic tradition was finally coming to an end, he alone among his contemporaries managed to renew himself creatively, to fashion a convincing series of works, repeatedly forging a successful compromise between his native inheritance and the French and German influences that increasingly gained sway in his country.

Puccini was born into a family whose musical tradition extended back five generations. From an early age he received training in Lucca as a church musician, but a performance of Verdi's *Aida* in Pisa in 1876 apparently turned his thoughts to operatic music. In 1880 he went to Milan to study composition at the conservatory with Ponchielli. While still studying there, he achieved some critical acclaim for his final composition exercise, an orchestral *Capriccio sinfonico* (1883); Puccini later borrowed music from this early piece for his operas *Edgar* and *La bohème*. His first opera, the one-act *Le villi*, was written immediately after leaving the conservatory for a competition sponsored by the publishing house of Sonzogno. Puccini's submission failed to receive even an honourable mention but, undeterred by the lack of success, some influential friends arranged a performance of *Le villi* in a revised, two-act version (1884). This provided the impetus for Puccini's career, as soon afterwards the publisher Ricordi offered him a contract for a new opera. Part of his contract stipulated that the librettist of *Le villi*, Ferdinando Fontana, would write the new libretto; unfortunately, Fontana's melodramatic style was ill-suited to Puccini's expressive powers and, in spite of years of work, *Edgar* (1889) was never a success. The failure nearly cost Puccini Ricordi's support, but the young composer was given a second chance.

With his next work, *Manon Lescaut* (1893), Puccini found a personal voice, and with this and the next three operas, *La bohème* (1896), *Tosca* (1900) and *Madama Butterfly* (1904), all of them written to libretti by Luigi Illica and Giuseppe Giacosa, established himself as the leading Italian composer of his generation. His sense of dramatic pacing was acute, in particular his ability to juxtapose action sections with ones of lyrical repose; and he had a masterly control over balancing the various systems – words, music and staging – that make up an opera, only rarely allowing indulgence of one aspect over the others. On the purely musical level, he managed to assimilate into his personal style such weighty foreign influences as those of Massenet and Wagner; his treatment of recurring motifs, for example, is cavalier on the semantic level precisely because it takes into account the intense dramatic presence of his operatic language.

The relatively long gaps between operas were due to a number of factors. Puccini was eager to taste the fruits of his success, and spent much time indulging his passions for hunting and for the newly invented motorcar. On the professional level, work in progress was interrupted by the series of promotional tours that Ricordi arranged in order to launch Puccini's works on the national and international stage. Perhaps most seriously, however, each new creation underwent a tortured genesis. As if in vivid illustration of the fragmented condition of the Italian operatic tradition, the structure of each opera had to be achieved through a painful process of discovery, Puccini's obsession with details of dramatic pacing causing him frequently to change his mind in mid-composition, driving his long-suffering librettists almost to despair.

The three works that secured his international reputation all succeed in part by characterizing a particularly evocative ambience: Bohemian Paris in the 1830s; Rome in 1800, seething with revolutionary and religious tension; modern-day Japan. Indeed, one senses that the choice of dramatic setting always had a critical effect on stimulating his desire and ability to find fresh ideas. After *Madama Butterfly*, however, Puccini found it increasingly difficult to locate subjects that were both novel enough to kindle his imagination, and at the same time firmly enough structured to sustain dramatic treatment. Finally, three years after the premiere of *Butterfly*, Puccini discovered a subject set in the California gold rush of 1849. *La fanciulla del West* (1910) had the usual protracted genesis, and was further interrupted by a crisis in his – frequently stormy – relationship with his wife Elvira. There was an even longer gap before his next work, *La rondine* (1917), which started life as a Viennese operetta and remains (outside a few popular excerpts) the least well known of Puccini's mature operas.

Puccini's next project took up a different dramatic challenge. *Il trittico* (1918) is a group of three sharply contrasting one-act operas that together make up a complete evening: a sinister melodrama (*Il tabarro*); a sentimental religious tragedy, written entirely for women's voices (*Suor Angelica*); and a comic opera (*Gianni Schicchi*). It is clear from the relative speed with which *Il trittico* was produced that the reduced scope of these works allowed Puccini to experiment more freely with dramatic types, to immerse himself in a particular ambience without the necessity of developing a protracted narrative structure. For his final opera, *Turandot*, he returned to exoticism, but this time employed a bold mixture of dramatic types within one work, showing that his creative imagination and dramatic insights remained intact in spite of the increasing self-doubt and pessimism of his later years. Puccini died of throat cancer in 1924, leaving the final scene of *Turandot* unfinished. It was completed by Franco Alfano, a member of the younger Italian generation, and first performed in 1926.

Although Puccini has been cast as a conservative figure in early 20th-century music, he continued to respond to contemporary music when it suited his dramatic purpose. One can, for example, trace through his mature operas a gradual development in complexity of harmonic idiom and an increasingly sophisticated use of the orchestra. However, Puccini's central innovation lay in his continual attempts to fashion new types of musical drama, to invent for each new work a particular structure, a particular dynamic relationship between its various narrative strands. In spite of these efforts, and in spite of an unprecedented success with the public, Puccini has never been fully accepted by the critical establishment. His operas respond only faintly to the Wagner-influenced analytical and critical techniques that have been in vogue for so long, and this has encouraged some to accuse him of lacking complete artistic seriousness of purpose, of cynically manipulating an easily moved mass audience. But there are signs of a general change in critical attitude. As time passes and as we gain an increasingly broad perspective on the progress of 20th-century music, Puccini's reputation as a musical dramatist of the highest quality, and as a significant representative of his age, seems bound to grow.

Manon Lescaut

Lyric drama in four acts (2h)
Libretto by Ruggero Leoncavallo, Marco Praga, Domenico Oliva, Luigi Illica and Giuseppe Giacosa (with contributions by Giulio Ricordi and the composer),

based on the novel *L'histoire du Chevalier des Grieux et de Manon Lescaut* by the Abbé Prévost (1731)
Composed 1889–October 1892, rev. 1893, 1922
PREMIERES 1 February 1893, Teatro Regio, Turin; UK: 14 May 1894, Covent Garden, London; US: 29 August 1894, Academy of Music, Philadelphia
CAST Manon Lescaut *s*, Il Cavaliere Renato des Grieux *t*, Lescaut *bar*, Geronte di Ravoir *b*, Edmondo *t*, a musician *ms*, Dancing Master *t*, Lamplighter *t*, Landlord *b*, Sergeant of the archers *b*, Naval Captain *b*, Hairdresser *silent*; *satb* chorus of girls, townspeople, men and women, students, musicians, old men and abbés, courtesans, guards, naval officers, sailors

Puccini began searching for a new opera libretto soon after his second opera *Edgar* was first performed in 1889. Ruggero Leoncavallo – then better known as a librettist than a composer – was the first to sketch a text, but he soon dropped out of the project and was succeeded by an alarming succession of further librettists, each striving to accommodate a composer who was increasingly difficult to please in matters of dramatic structure and fine verbal detail. An added problem was the existence of Massenet's opera on the same subject: Puccini felt constrained to make his work sufficiently different from Massenet's, in order to avoid the charge of plagiarism. The text was eventually completed by Luigi Illica and Giuseppe Giacosa, who were destined to become the composer's most faithful – and long-suffering – collaborators. The opera underwent many subsequent revisions and even today several competing versions exist, of Act IV in particular (at one point Puccini cut the famous aria 'Sola, perduta, abbandonata . . .'). The composer probably never reached a 'definitive' form for this opera, his first international success.

SYNOPSIS

Act I: A square in 18th-century Amiens, outside an inn. A student, Edmondo, and his companions are interrupted by Des Grieux, who mocks love before joining the others in praise of carefree pleasure. A coach arrives, and Geronte (a rich, elderly adventurer), Lescaut and his sister Manon alight. Des Grieux is captivated by Manon and soon contrives a personal encounter in which he discovers that she must go to join a convent the following day. As Lescaut calls Manon into the inn, Des Grieux persuades her to meet him again later. Left alone, the young man muses over Manon's beauty and his awakening love for her ('Donna non vidi mai'). Geronte admits to Lescaut that he too is interested in Manon and plans to take her off to Paris – with Lescaut's blessing. Edmondo overhears the plot to abduct Manon and warns Des Grieux, who convinces Manon of his love and persuades her to run off with him to Paris, taking advantage of Geronte's waiting carriage. Geronte is furious that his plan has been foiled, but Lescaut calms him, assuring him that when Des Grieux's money runs out, Manon will again be available.

Act II: opens on to a luxurious boudoir in Geronte's Parisian house. Manon has left Des Grieux, tempted away by Geronte's money. Although she relishes her new-found wealth, she nostalgically recounts to Lescaut the simple joys of her humble life with Des Grieux ('In quelle trine morbide'). After a dancing lesson, Manon is left alone. Des Grieux appears – having at last discovered Manon's whereabouts – and angrily reproaches her for her desertion. In an extended love duet, she gradually reawakens his love for her, but they are discovered by Geronte. When Manon taunts the old man, he retires with a vague threat. Des Grieux urges her to run away with him, but she lingers reluctantly over her jewels, causing him to despair over her foolishness ('Ah Manon, mi tradisce il tuo folle pensier'). As they at last prepare to depart, Lescaut appears, warning them that Geronte has denounced Manon and the police are on their way to arrest her. Manon again delays, attempting to gather up some of her treasures, and in a hectic climax Geronte bursts in and triumphantly sends her off in the hands of the police.

Act III, which is preceded by an orchestral intermezzo, takes place at the port of Le Havre, where Manon is about to be deported. Lescaut and Des Grieux are waiting for dawn in order to attempt her rescue. Des Grieux locates the room where Manon is imprisoned, and tells her through the window of their plan. But the attempt quickly fails. The convicted women are brought out one by one and the crowd comments on each of them; Manon and Des Grieux sing a bitter farewell. At the last moment, as the women are led to the convict ship bound for North America, Des Grieux attempts a last desperate rescue, and then flings himself at the feet of the captain, pleading to be allowed to accompany his beloved ('Guardate, pazzo son'). The captain takes pity on him, lets him come aboard, and gives orders for the departure.

Act IV takes place in the Louisiana desert, as night is falling. Manon and Des Grieux are again on the run. Manon, in the last stages of exhaustion, faints, and Des Grieux tries desperately to revive her ('Manon, senti, amor mio'). He goes off in search of water, and Manon bemoans her fate ('Sola, perduta, abbandonata . . .'). Soon after Des Grieux returns empty-handed, she falls dead at his feet, singing to the end that her love will never die.

As befits a youthful work, *Manon Lescaut* still betrays the influences that formed Puccini's mature style. Passages in the Act II love duet, for example, recall Wagner's harmonic language (particularly that of *Tristan*), while the close of that act is strongly reminiscent of middle-period Verdi. On the other hand, in Des Grieux's Act III aria, 'Guardate, pazzo son', and elsewhere, Puccini showed himself adept at the more 'modern' style of Ponchielli. Whatever the influences, almost all the music bears the stamp of Puccini's emerging mature style. We can also see the composer's growing awareness of large-scale structure, of the careful shaping of individual acts. Act I skilfully alternates hectic action sequences with moments of lyrical repose (a type of rapid juxtaposition that was much used in the opening acts of subsequent operas). Act II, on the other hand, is made up of two sharply contrasting musical ambiences: first a nostalgic re-creation of 18th-century musical manners; then a sudden plunge into the torridly expressive world of Manon and her rejected lover. Act III is perhaps the most perfectly achieved large structure, the action sequences framing a magnificently controlled and highly original ensemble movement in which Manon and her fellow prisoners are paraded before the public. Act IV is something of a disappointment, its lack of outward action encouraging Puccini to attempt a 'symphonic' style that interferes with his usually impeccable sense of dramatic pacing. But this final uncertainty does little to shake a general feeling that with this opera Puccini found his authentic voice as a musical dramatist.

RECORDINGS 1. Callas, di Stefano, Fioravanti, Calabrese, La Scala Ch & O, Serafin, EMI, 1957; 2. Freni, Domingo, Bruson, Rydl, Covent Garden Ch, Philharmonia O, Sinopoli, DG, 1984; 3. Guleghina, Cura, Roni, La Scala Ch & O, Muti, DG, 1998

La bohème

Bohemian Life

Opera in four acts (1h 45m)
Libretto by Giuseppe Giacosa and Luigi Illica, based on *Scènes de la vie de bohème* by Henry Murger (1845) and the play *La vie de bohème* by Murger and Théodore Barrière (1849)
Composed 1893–5, rev. 1896
PREMIERES 1 February 1896, Teatro Regio, Turin; UK: 22 April 1897, Comedy Theatre, Manchester; US: 14 October 1897, Los Angeles Theater, Los Angeles

CAST Mimì *s*, Musetta *s*, Rodolfo *t*, Marcello *bar*, Schaunard *bar*, Colline *b*, Parpignol *t*, Benoit *b*, Alcindoro *b*;
Act II: *satb* chorus of students, working girls, bourgeois, shopkeepers, street vendors, soldiers, waiters, children;
Act III: Customs officer *b*, tavern drinkers 6 *s*, 3 *a*, scavengers 8 *b*, carters, milkmaids 6 *s*, peasant women 6 *s*

La bohème was, it seems, born in litigation: the first we hear of Puccini's interest in the subject is in March 1893, when he engaged in a public quarrel with Ruggero Leoncavallo over the rights to Murger's source. Around this time, the team of Luigi Illica and Giuseppe Giacosa (who had safely completed Puccini's previous opera, *Manon Lescaut*) were engaged, and work started in earnest. However, and in spite of the continuing 'race' with Leoncavallo (who insisted on continuing work on his own *Bohème*, which was eventually performed in 1897), the opera progressed slowly, in part because the success of *Manon Lescaut* obliged Puccini to undertake a number of extensive promotional tours. The composer overcame a characteristic loss of confidence in the subject (during which he toyed with an opera entitled *La lupa*, based on a short story by Giovanni Verga) and eventually completed the score in late 1895. As would become a regular feature of Puccinian creation, the protracted period of composition saw numerous changes of direction and modification: at one point an entire act (to take place in the courtyard outside Musetta's flat) was discarded; at another the decision was made to divide the original first act into two separate acts. The first performance, given in Turin to delay the inevitable trial by fire at La Scala, Milan, was conducted by the 29-year-old Arturo Toscanini. The Turin audience, fresh from the first Italian performances of *Götterdämmerung*, gave *Bohème* a lukewarm reception, but the opera very soon found its way on to the international circuit, and is today one of the three or four most often performed works in the repertoire. Some time soon after the first performance, Puccini made various adjustments to the score, notably adding the 'bonnet' episode in Act II.

SYNOPSIS

Act I: On Christmas Eve (1830) in Paris two Bohemian artists, Rodolfo (a poet) and Marcello (a painter), are working in their scantily furnished and unheated garret. They are joined by two friends, Colline (a philosopher) and Schaunard (a musician), and the group decides to visit the Café Momus. Benoit, their landlord, enters to ask for the rent, but they skilfully evade him. As the others leave, Rodolfo stays behind to finish an article, promising to join them soon. A young seamstress, Mimì, shyly knocks at the door to ask for a light for her candle. Rodolfo is charmed and prolongs the encounter; he tells her about himself, and shares with her his dreams of love ('Che gelida manina'). Mimì in turn introduces herself, describing her loneliness and her attic lodgings ('Mi chiamano Mimì'). The shouts of Rodolfo's friends from the courtyard below call him to the window; the moonlight, flooding the room, shines directly on Mimì's face, and Rodolfo is overcome with emotion ('O soave fanciulla'). He and Mimì declare their love, and together go off to join Rodolfo's friends at the Café Momus.

Act II begins in a bustling, brightly lit street in the Latin quarter where Rodolfo and Mimì meet the other Bohemians outside the Café Momus. The entrance of Marcello's erstwhile mistress, Musetta, causes a sensation: she is on the arm of a rich admirer, Alcindoro. She places herself at a neighbouring table and tries to attract Marcello's attention by singing of the amorous attention her looks inspire ('Quando me'n vo"). Marcello, after initial irritation, capitulates; Musetta creates a scene to get rid of Alcindoro and throws herself into her former lover's arms. But then, disaster: the bill is presented. Who can pay? As a military band approaches, the Bohemians disappear into the crowd. Alcindoro returns to find Musetta gone and collapses in amazement at the huge bill she has left on his table.

Act III opens outside a tavern on the fringes of Paris. It is a bleak and snowy dawn in February; street-sweepers and peasants pass by on their way to the city. Mimì, weak and afflicted by a terrible cough, enters looking for Marcello who, at that moment, comes out of the tavern. She pours out her troubles, telling him how Rodolfo torments her with his constant jealousy. When Rodolfo himself appears Mimì retreats in confusion, hoping to avoid a confrontation. Rodolfo tells Marcello a different tale: his jealous fits hide despair over Mimì's increasingly serious illness. Mimì's coughing and sobs reveal her presence just as Marcello, hearing Musetta's laugh, rushes back inside. Rodolfo and Mimì agree that they must part but sing poignantly of their love. Marcello and Musetta come out of the tavern, quarrelling heatedly. In the ensuing quartet, Marcello and Musetta exchange insults while Rodolfo and Mimì agree to stay together until the coming of spring.

Act IV returns us to the Bohemians' garret. Several months have passed. Rodolfo and Marcello are discussing Mimì and Musetta. They feign indifference, but reveal their true feelings in a duet ('O Mimì, tu più non torni'). Colline and Schaunard come in, and the four friends enact a series of charades culminating in a furious mock duel. Musetta's sudden appearance shatters the mood with news that Mimì is outside, very ill. Mimì is brought in and her condition spurs the Bohemians to scrape money together for a doctor. Colline decides to pawn his old coat, singing it an aria of mournful farewell ('Vecchia zimarra'). Left alone, Rodolfo and Mimì reminisce about their first meeting. The others return, and Mimì gently drifts into unconsciousness. As Rodolfo busies himself with her comfort, Schaunard discovers that her sleep will be permanent. The curtain falls to anguished cries from Rodolfo as he discovers the truth.

One of the greatest strengths of *La bohème* is the clarity of its overall structure. Although there are connecting musical links across the score (notably certain recurring themes), each of the four acts projects a characteristic musical atmosphere, and each is placed in telling contrast to its surroundings. Act I (as so often with Puccini, the longest and most musically dense) introduces the hectic energy of the Bohemians but closes with a prolonged period of stasis: the two autobiographical arias and the love duet of Rodolfo and Mimì. Acts II and III might be seen as complementary, the former showing the gaudy exterior of Parisian life, the latter its more sombre side; and each contrasts this evocation of ambience with a central lyrical moment (in Act II the ensemble 'Quando me'n vo", and in Act III the famous quartet). Act IV returns us to the mood of Act I, but in subtly changed colours: the opening scene for the Bohemians is even more hectic than in Act I, while the conclusion casts a veil of nostalgia over the lovers' first meeting. As mentioned above, certain musical connections heighten this sense of pattern and reprise. The raucous descending triads that open Act II are converted to the fragile descending fifths of Act III; the characteristic, bumpy rhythm associated throughout with the Bohemians predominates in both the opening scenes of Act I and IV, and fragments of the famous Act I arias form the basis of the close of the drama. In the eyes of many perceptive commentators, *La bohème* is the composer's most perfectly achieved score: the one in which subject matter and musical style are most suited, and in which the overall dramatic effect is most consistently controlled.

RECORDINGS 1. de los Angeles, Amara, Björling, Merrill, RCA Victor Ch & O, Beecham, EMI, 1956; 2. Tebaldi, D'Angelo, Bergonzi, Bastianini, Cesari,

Siepi, Santa Cecilia Academy Ch & O, Serafin, Decca, 1958; 3. Gheorghiu, Scano, Alagna, Keenlyside, Milan Conservatorio 'G. Verdi' Ch, La Scala Ch & O, Chailly, Decca, 1998

Tosca

Opera in three acts (2h)
Libretto by Giuseppe Giacosa and Luigi Illica, based on the play *La Tosca* by Victorien Sardou (1887)
Composed 1896–9
PREMIERES 14 January 1900, Teatro Costanzi, Rome; UK: 12 July 1900, Covent Garden, London; US: 4 February 1901, Metropolitan, New York
CAST Floria Tosca *s*, Mario Cavaradossi *t*, Baron Scarpia *bar*, Cesare Angelotti *b*, Sacristan *bar*, Spoletta *t*, Sciarrone *b*, Gaoler *b*, Shepherd Boy *treble*; *silent*: a Cardinal, a Judge, Roberti the executioner, a Scribe, an Officer, a Sergeant; *satb* chorus of priests, pupils, choir singers, soldiers, police agents, ladies, nobles, bourgeois, populace

The first reference to *Tosca* in Puccini's correspondence dates from more than ten years before its premiere. The subject had been suggested by Ferdinando Fontana (librettist of *Le villi* and *Edgar*), but the subject was given by Ricordi to the by now trusted team of Illica and (later) Giacosa. For Puccini, work on *Manon* and *La bohème* intervened, and the subject passed to another composer, Alberto Franchetti. But during 1895, with work on *Bohème* coming to a close, Puccini's interest in *Tosca* revived and, with Ricordi's help, Franchetti was persuaded to give up his interest in the opera. In spite of continuing reservations on the part of Giacosa about the subject's suitability, work on the opera progressed steadily. As with *Bohème*, the main interruptions were caused by Puccini's increasingly far-flung visits to supervise revivals of his previous successes. In the later stages of composition, the composer went to considerable trouble to establish a precise sense of local colour: he made a trip to Rome in 1897 to listen to the sound of church bells from the heights of the Castello Sant'Angelo, and he enlisted the help of a priest, Don Pietro Panichelli, to check certain religious details. As the opera neared completion, Ricordi attempted to persuade Puccini to revise part of Act III, in particular a passage in the love duet that Puccini had taken from a discarded passage in *Edgar*. But the composer managed to defend himself, and the opera moved into rehearsal with few further changes. Puccini had great faith in the premiere cast, which included Ericlea Darclée (Tosca), Emilio De Marchi (Cavaradossi) and Eugenio Giraldoni (Scarpia), but the first performance (conducted by Leopoldo Mugnone) was greeted by a mixed reception. In spite of this, the composer made few alterations to his score, and *Tosca* fairly soon established itself as a staple of the operatic repertoire.

SYNOPSIS
Act I opens in the church of Sant'Andrea della Valle, Rome, in June 1800. Angelotti, an escaped prisoner, takes refuge in a side chapel. A Sacristan enters, followed shortly afterwards by Cavaradossi, an artist working on a painting of the Madonna. As Cavaradossi prepares to start work, he muses over his painting; although this Madonna is blonde she reminds him of his dark mistress, the singer Tosca ('Recondita armonia'). The sound of the Sacristan leaving brings Angelotti from his hiding-place. Angelotti and the painter recognize each other, and Cavaradossi promises to help his friend to escape from Rome. They hear Tosca's voice outside; Angelotti hides again before she enters. The sound of conversation has aroused Tosca's jealousy, but Cavaradossi's assurances calm her, and they join in a passionate duet. When Tosca leaves, Angelotti reappears and he and Cavaradossi plan his flight, but a distant cannon warns them that the prison escape has been discovered; they exit hurriedly together. As a crowd gathers

for a celebratory *Te Deum*, Scarpia, the chief of police, enters with his henchman, Spoletta, and orders a search for the escaped prisoner. Tosca returns and Scarpia, suspicious of Cavaradossi and enamoured of Tosca, tries to trick her into revealing information by inciting her jealousy. When she leaves to seek out her lover, Scarpia has her followed, and, as the crowd intones the *Te Deum*, Scarpia vows to bring Cavaradossi to the gallows and Tosca into his arms ('Va, Tosca! Nel tuo cuor s'annida Scarpia').

Act II takes place in Scarpia's room in the Farnese Palace. Scarpia muses over his violent desire for Tosca ('Ha più forte sapore'). Spoletta enters to report that Angelotti has not been found, but that he has arrested Cavaradossi for suspicious behaviour. Cavaradossi is brought in and questioned, but he denies all knowledge of Angelotti's escape. Scarpia has sent for Tosca, and she comes in as Cavaradossi is led to the next room to be tortured. Tosca is left alone with Scarpia, and Cavaradossi's cries of pain eventually drive her to reveal Angelotti's hiding-place. Cavaradossi is dragged back onstage just as Napoleon's victory at Marengo is announced. The news elicits a stirring response from Cavaradossi, and the outraged Scarpia has him taken off to prison. Scarpia and Tosca are once again left alone, and Scarpia offers Tosca a hideous choice: she must submit to his lust or cause Cavaradossi's execution. She sings a despairing aria ('Vissi d'arte') but finally agrees to submit. Scarpia summons Spoletta and pretends to order a faked execution. As Scarpia writes a safe-conduct from Rome for her and Cavaradossi, Tosca surreptitiously takes a knife from the dinner table and, when Scarpia comes forward to claim his prize, plunges it into his chest. She taunts him in his death throes and, when he expires, takes the safe-conduct from his clenched hand and starts to leave. At the last moment she returns to place candles around Scarpia's body and a crucifix on his chest.

Act III opens a few hours later, just before dawn on a platform of the Castello Sant'Angelo. Church bells ring and a shepherd boy sings in the distance. Cavaradossi awaits his final hour, overcome by memories of Tosca and thoughts of his approaching death ('E lucevan le stelle'). Tosca appears and triumphantly displays their safe-conduct. She instructs him on his role in the mock execution and they sing of their love and hopes for the future. As four o'clock strikes, the firing squad arrives and Cavaradossi is prepared for execution. Tosca watches, hardly managing to restrain herself as the shots ring out and Cavaradossi falls. In an agony of suspense, she waits for the soldiers to depart. At last she tells Cavaradossi to rise, but he does not respond: Scarpia has betrayed her even in death and her lover lies dead before her. Soldiers rush on to arrest Tosca for Scarpia's murder but, with a final defiant gesture, she flings herself over the parapet.

The famous opening chords of *Tosca* (associated with Scarpia's evil), which recur during the first two acts of the opera, have been said to herald a new dramatic and musical potential in Puccini's work. In these chords and elsewhere the composer uses 'modernistic' harmonic devices to thrilling dramatic effect. Indeed, the opera as a whole attempts a dramatic level far more grandiose and impressive than *La bohème*, and in some senses it achieves its expanded goals. Act I in particular is a tour de force; in spite of a weight of stage action that made his librettists dubious of its operatic viability, Puccini managed to characterize musically all the essential elements of the drama, and even to allow time for the lyrical pauses so necessary to the development of his dramatic intentions. Act II, scarcely less dense in its activity, though necessarily more sparse in its musical invention, is again magnificently paced, with passages such as the final, orchestrally accompanied mime showing that Puccini was capable of finely calculated dramatic effect even without the stimulus of the voice. As his publisher and friend Giulio Ricordi so acutely observed, Act III is, in spite of many fine moments, hardly on a level with the other two, and tends to flag in its central love duet. However, taken as a whole and with the help of first-class singing actors, *Tosca* can reach an intensity of dramatic effect rarely equalled in Puccini's theatre.

RECORDINGS 1. Callas, di Stefano, Gobbi, La Scala Ch & O, De Sabata, EMI, 1953; 2. L. Price, di Stefano, Taddei, Vienna State Op Ch, VPO, Karajan, Decca, 1962; 3. Caballé, Carreras, Wixell, Covent Garden Ch & O, C. Davis, Philips, 1977

Madama Butterfly

Madam Butterfly

A Japanese tragedy in three acts (2h); second and third versions in two acts (Act II in two parts); fourth version in three acts
Libretto by Giuseppe Giacosa and Luigi Illica, based on the play *Madam Butterfly* by David Belasco, itself based on a short story by John Luther Long (1898)
Composed 1901–3 (in two acts); rev. (second version) 1904; further revs 1905; cuts, alterations for Paris, 1906
PREMIERES 17 February 1904, La Scala, Milan; second version: 28 May 1904, Teatro Grande, Brescia; third version: UK: 10 July 1905, Covent Garden, London; US: 15 October 1906, Savage Opera Company, Washington DC; definitive version (with minor exceptions): 28 December 1906, Opéra-Comique, Paris
CAST Madama Butterfly (Cio-Cio-San) *s*, Suzuki *ms*, Kate Pinkerton *ms*, B. F. Pinkerton *t*, Sharpless *bar*, Goro *t*, Prince Yamadori *t*, the Bonze *b*, Yakuside *b*, Imperial Commissioner *b*, Official Registrar *b*, Butterfly's mother *ms*, aunt *s*, cousin *s*, Sorrow *silent*; *satb* chorus of Butterfly's relatives and friends, servants

Puccini's first exposure to *Madama Butterfly* (in June 1900) was at a performance of David Belasco's play in London. It is clear that what initially caught the composer's interest – he knew little English – was a drama intimately tied to a striking new ambience (Japan); and we can guess that this immediately awakened musical possibilities. Very soon afterwards, Puccini expanded his vision. With the help of material from John Luther Long's novella (the source for Belasco's play), he planned to make a two-act opera: the first set in North America, the second in Japan, thus establishing a dramatic juxtaposition between two distinctive musical ambiences. Once the rights to *Butterfly* had been cleared, Illica set to work on a scenario and in March 1901 came up with a different plan: Act I would be a kind of prologue, depicting the meeting and marriage of Butterfly and Pinkerton in Japan. Act II was to be in three scenes, with episodes in Butterfly's house framing a scene at the American Consulate. Thus, in both parts, the contrast between 'European' and 'Oriental' values could be explored. This plan (elaborated by Illica and Giacosa) held good for over a year, but then, in November 1902, the composer insisted that the Consulate scene be discarded. This decision had considerable repercussions. Act II now concentrated single-mindedly on Butterfly: the other principal characters, Pinkerton and Sharpless, were now embarrassingly peripheral, so much so that it later became clear that Pinkerton's part would have to be 'artificially' filled out in the new Act II. The opera's premiere at La Scala, Milan, was a resounding failure, and in the coming years Puccini continued to revise the score, including taking out some of the detailed Japanese local colour in Act I, and adding new material for Pinkerton, notably his aria 'Addio fiorito asil', in Act II, Part II.

SYNOPSIS

The opera takes place near Nagasaki in the early 1900s.

Act I opens outside a little house on which Pinkerton, an American naval officer, has taken out a 999-year lease and is making the final arrangements with the Japanese marriage-broker, Goro, for a Japanese wedding. From a discussion with the American consul, Sharpless, we gather that according to Japanese law the marriage will not be binding. Pinkerton revels in his carefree attitude as a 'Yankee vagabondo' who takes his pleasure where he finds it ('Dovunque al mondo'); Sharpless tries in vain to warn him that his 15-year-old bride, Butterfly, is serious about the marriage. Butterfly enters amid a bustle of friends and relatives, singing happily of the love that awaits her. After shyly greeting Pinkerton, she shows him her few belongings – including the ceremonial dagger with which her father killed himself – and the commissioner performs the wedding ceremony. But the festivities are short-lived; her uncle (the Bonze) arrives and curses her for converting to Christianity, and her relatives and friends immediately join him in rejecting her. Butterfly is left alone with Pinkerton, who tries to comfort her. Her servant Suzuki prepares her for the wedding night, and she joins Pinkerton in the garden for an extended love duet ('Viene la sera'). He is enchanted with his plaything-wife and, while she speaks tenderly of her love, ardently claims his fluttering, captured butterfly.

Act II (Part I) is in the same house, several years later. Butterfly and Suzuki are alone. Pinkerton sailed for America three years ago, but Butterfly remains fiercely loyal and describes to Suzuki her dream of his return ('Un bel dì'). Sharpless, knowing that Pinkerton has taken an American wife and will soon be arriving in Nagasaki with her, attempts to prepare Butterfly for the shock. But Butterfly will not listen and remains stubbornly faithful; she shows Sharpless the child she has borne Pinkerton without his knowledge, convinced that this revelation will ensure her husband's return. Sharpless leaves, unable to face Butterfly with the truth. A cannon shot is heard and Butterfly and Suzuki see Pinkerton's ship coming into harbour. Butterfly jubilantly prepares for his return, filling the room with flowers and again donning her bridal costume. With preparations complete, the two women and the child sit down to wait for Pinkerton's arrival. Night falls; as Suzuki and the child sleep and Butterfly waits motionless, a humming chorus is heard in the distance.

Act II (Part II): It is dawn and Butterfly has fallen asleep at her post. Suzuki rouses her and she carries the sleeping child into the next room, singing a sad lullaby. Pinkerton and Sharpless arrive and ask Suzuki to talk to Pinkerton's new wife, Kate, who is waiting outside. Suzuki agrees, but the sight of her distress, together with memories of the past, overcome Pinkerton. He is filled with remorse ('Addio fiorito asil'), and he leaves rather than face the woman he deserted. Butterfly rushes in, searching desperately for Pinkerton, but she sees only the strange woman waiting in the garden. Suzuki and Sharpless manage to break the news that this is Pinkerton's wife and that her husband will never return to her. Butterfly seems to accept the blow, and agrees to give up her son, asking only that Pinkerton come in person to fetch him. Kate and Sharpless leave; Suzuki tries to comfort Butterfly, but she asks to be left alone. She takes her father's dagger from the wall and prepares to kill herself. Suzuki pushes the child into the room, and Butterfly drops the dagger, momentarily deterred. After an impassioned farewell ('O a me, sceso dal trono'), she blindfolds the child and, going behind a screen, stabs herself just as Pinkerton rushes in calling her name.

The play of varied 'local colours', always an important feature of Puccini's writing, takes on particular importance in Act I of *Madama Butterfly*, which was structurally conceived along lines very similar to those of *La bohème*. As in the earlier opera, though on a much larger scale, an opening section established a musical and dramatic atmosphere of hectic activity, which is then juxtaposed with a lyrical and comparatively static close. However, in *Butterfly* there is a central shift in musical ambience marked by the entrance of the heroine. The final duet in Act I breaks new musical ground and although, as Illica pointed out early on, it superficially resembles that of Rodolfo and Mimì in *La bohème*, it is actually a far more complex musical and dramatic structure. By mediating between contrasting musical ambiences and then gradually blending them, the duet ends with the lovers subsumed in a new musical medium, one that somehow arises from their two quite separately established styles. As mentioned earlier, Act II focuses on the heroine with (for Puccini) unprecedented concentration and leads inexorably to the tragic denouement. Whether the music of this final scene is capable of sustaining its weight of dramatic expectation is a matter of debate, but few will deny that *Butterfly* makes an important and brave attempt to break away from established dramatic patterns.

RECORDINGS 1. Callas, Danieli, Gedda, Borriello, La Scala Ch & O, Karajan, EMI, 1954; 2. Scotto, Di Stasio, Bergonzi, Panerai, Rome Op Ch & O, Barbirolli, EMI, 1967; 3. Freni, Ludwig, Pavarotti, Kerns, Vienna Staatsoper Ch, VPO, Karajan, Decca, 1974; 4. Spacagna, Graham, Di Rienzi, Parce, Hungarian State Op Ch & O, Rosekrans, Vox, 1995: includes 1904 version

La fanciulla del West

The Girl of the Golden West

Opera in three acts (2h)
Libretto by Guelfo Civinini and Carlo Zangarini, based on the play *The Girl of the Golden West* by David Belasco (1905)
Composed 1908–10
PREMIERES 10 December 1910, Metropolitan, New York; UK: 29 May 1911, Covent Garden, London
CAST Minnie *s*, Jack Rance *bar*, Dick Johnson (Ramerrez) *t*, Nick *t*, Ashby *b*, Sonora *b*, Trim *t*, Sid *bar*, Bello (Handsome) *bar*, Harry *t*, Joe *t*, Happy *bar*, Larkens *b*, Billy Jackrabbit *b*, Wowkle *ms*, Jake Wallace *bar*, Jose Castro *b*, postilion *t*; *tb* chorus of men of the camp

After considering a variety of subjects – including Victor Hugo's *The Hunchback of Notre-Dame* – and being constantly distracted by foreign and domestic travels, Puccini finally settled on another 'exotic' subject for his next opera. The composer saw Belasco's *The Girl of the Golden West* in New York in early 1907 (he was there to see the Metropolitan premieres of both *Manon Lescaut* and *Madama Butterfly*), and decided to set it to music after reading an Italian translation. His librettists Zangarini and Civinini were on occasion slow to produce, and a personal tragedy – in which a servant girl of Puccini's was driven to suicide by his wife's unfounded jealousy – forced him to put the work aside for some time. Appropriately enough, the opera received its first performance in America, where it was conducted by Toscanini and greeted with great enthusiasm. The star cast was headed by Emmy Destinn, Enrico Caruso and Pasquale Amato.

SYNOPSIS

At the foot of the Cloudy Mountains (Nubi) in California. A miners' camp at the time of the 1849–50 gold rush.

Act I takes place in the Polka Bar. The bandit Ramerrez is at large and a $5000 reward has been set for him. Sheriff Jack Rance declares his love for Minnie, the chaste darling of the miners ('Minnie, dalla mia casa'), but she rejects him, reminiscing about her parents' true love ('Laggiù nel Soledad'). A man announcing himself as Dick Johnson arrives. He has met Minnie before, and their friendly relationship angers Rance. All the men go out in search of Ramerrez, leaving Minnie alone with Johnson. In their ensuing conversation, Johnson becomes increasingly enamoured, and they agree to meet later in her cabin.

Act II begins one hour later in Minnie's cabin, where Minnie is excitedly preparing for her visitor. Johnson arrives, and as they have supper Minnie tells him how much she loves her life in the mountains ('Oh, se sapeste'). Completely enchanted, Johnson embraces her, and she succumbs ecstatically to her 'first kiss'. As he prepares to leave, he discovers that snow is falling heavily outside, and Minnie agrees to let him stay the night. As he goes off to bed, Rance arrives to tell Minnie that 'Johnson' is none other than the bandit Ramerrez. When Rance has left, Minnie angrily confronts Johnson, who pleads for her understanding, telling her how he was fated from birth for the bandit's life ('Una parola sola'), but she orders him to leave. As soon as he has gone, shots ring out and Johnson's body slumps against the door. Minnie drags him in and succeeds in hiding him in her loft. Rance again enters, searching for the bandit, and drops of blood falling on his hand eventually reveal Johnson. In a desperate ploy, Minnie plays Rance at poker: if she wins, Johnson will go free; if she loses, she will agree to marry Rance. She wins by cheating on the last hand, Rance leaves, and she collapses, laughing hysterically.

Act III takes place in a nearby forest. Rance and friends sit by a fire. News arrives that Johnson has been caught, and the miners prepare to string him up. Johnson is brought in and, after speaking tenderly of Minnie and begging the miners not to tell her how he died ('Ch'ella mi creda libero'), is led to the makeshift gallows. But Minnie arrives just in time and pleads with the miners to spare him. They eventually agree, unable to refuse her after all she has done for them, and Minnie and Johnson depart for a new life together.

Parts of *Fanciulla* present a musical-dramatic problem even more severe than that in Act I of *Tosca*: the sheer complexity of stage action allows very little time to 'place' events musically and crowds out the opportunity for those lyrical pauses and developments so necessary to Puccini's art. Clearly the composer willingly embraced this type of drama, but it is at least arguable that by the time of *Fanciulla* his powers of musical invention were less able to sustain such extreme concentration. Like *Tosca* – and perhaps even more so – the opera needs singing actors of the first quality in order to succeed on stage. What is undeniable is that *Fanciulla* is harmonically and orchestrally one of Puccini's most innovative scores, and in these two areas represents a high point in experimentation and musical daring. For this, and for many other reasons, it deserves a better relative placing in the Puccinian canon than it today enjoys.

RECORDINGS 1. Tebaldi, Del Monaco, MacNeil, Santa Cecilia, Academy Ch & O, Capuana, Decca, 1958;
2. Neblett, Domingo, Milnes, Covent Garden Ch & O, Mehta, DG, 1977

La rondine
The Swallow

Lyric comedy in three acts (1h 45m)
Libretto by Giuseppe Adami, based on the German libretto by Alfred Maria Willner and Heinz Reichert
Composed 1914–15; rev. 1919; further revs 1920
PREMIERES 27 March 1917, Salle Garnier, Monte Carlo; UK: 24 June 1929, 9 December 1965, Fulham Town Hall, London, (stage); US: 10 March 1928, Metropolitan, New York
CAST Magda de Civry *s*, Ruggero Lastouc *t*, Rambaldo Fernandez *bar*, Lisette *s*, Prunier *t*, 4 *s*, 2 *ms*, *t*, *bar*, 3 *b*; *satb* chorus of citizens, students, artists, dancers

After *La fanciulla del West* Puccini spent

some fruitless years searching for a suitable libretto for his next work. The plan for *La rondine* emerged from a proposal made in 1913 for Puccini to write a Viennese operetta for the Karltheater. Eventually Puccini agreed, though he insisted on writing a comic opera (with no spoken dialogue) and on setting the text in Italian. In due course a German text arrived and was translated by Giuseppe Adami. Puccini finished the score in October 1915, but the outbreak of the First World War had put the whole project in jeopardy, and it was some time before he could secure the rights to arrange a first performance and Italian publication. *La rondine* was finally premiered in 1917 in Monte Carlo.

SYNOPSIS
Paris and Nice during the Second Empire.

Act I takes place in a Parisian salon. Magda (the mistress of Rambaldo, a rich banker) and her maid, Lisette, playfully discuss the joys of love with Prunier, a poet. Ruggero, the son of one of Rambaldo's friends, joins the party and all decide that, for his first night in Paris, he should go to the popular night spot Bullier. When the guests leave, Prunier and Lisette decide to go out together. Magda, who is feeling wistful and has had adventures there in the past, dons a disguise and decides she too will go to Bullier.

Act II takes place in Bullier. Magda and Ruggero meet and dance, becoming strongly attracted to each other. Even though Rambaldo appears and confronts Magda, she will not break off, and eventually she and Ruggero admit their love and leave together.

Act III occurs some months later. Magda and Ruggero are living together blissfully in Nice. Ruggero tells Magda that he has written to his mother for consent to marry her, but Magda realizes that she will never receive his family's approval. Lisette and Prunier are together again, although Prunier's attempt to put Lisette on the stage in Nice has proved a disaster. Ruggero bursts in with his mother's letter, which blesses his marriage; but Magda tells him she can never become his wife and sadly decides that she must leave him for ever.

La rondine has always been the least performed of Puccini's mature operas, and this in spite of certain well-known extracts such as Magda's Act I aria 'Che il bel sogno' and the Act II concertato 'Bevo al tuo fresco sorriso'. Various reasons for its comparative lack of success have been suggested, among which the weaknesses of Ruggero's characterization and the shaky motivation of Magda's *Traviata*-like renunciation are clearly well founded. But perhaps the central problem is with the extensive subplot between Lisette and Prunier, which vies with the Magda–Ruggero plot in length and development, but in which Puccini found little to stimulate his lyrical fantasy. However, for those who know the opera well, *La rondine* cannot be easily dismissed; its restraint and lightness of touch suggest a surprising new range in Puccini's musical language, one that many regret he did not explore further.

RECORDING Gheorghiu, Mula-Tchako, Alagna, Mattiuzzi, Rinaldi, London Voices, LSO, Pappano, EMI, 1996

Il trittico

Triptych of one-act operas
PREMIERES 14 December 1918, Metropolitan, New York; UK: 18 June 1920, Covent Garden, London

The idea of combining a collection of one-act operas into a single evening had been on Puccini's mind through most of his career, but had consistently been opposed by his publisher, Ricordi. Puccini first saw Didier Gold's play *La houppelande* in Paris in 1912, and by 1913 he was in negotiations with Illica about the subject. Eventually, though, a libretto was fashioned by Giuseppe Adami, and work on *Il tabarro* began in October 1915, immediately after Puccini had completed *La rondine*. He finished this first panel of the 'triptych' in 1916, with no idea of what the companion pieces were going to be. After considering a host of topics, the answer eventually came from Giovacchino Forzano, who in early 1917 offered Puccini the libretto for a one-act opera set in a convent, *Suor Angelica*, and (soon afterwards) a second, comic subject entitled *Gianni Schicchi*. Puccini accepted both gladly and finished the remaining two operas by early 1918 – for him, something like record time. The Metropolitan in New York paid a considerable sum for the rights to the world premiere, which was given that same year conducted by Roberto Moranzoni. Though *Il trittico* is occasionally revived in its complete form, it is more usual to find two of the three operas performed as a double-bill.

Il tabarro

The Cloak

Opera in one act (55m)
Libretto by Giuseppe Adami, based on the play *La houppelande* by Didier Gold (1910)
Composed 1915–16
PREMIERES see *Il trittico* above
CAST Giorgetta *s*, Luigi *t*, Michele *bar*, La Frugola *ms*, Tinca *t*, Talpa *b*, a song-vendor *t*, 2 lovers *s*, *t*, an organ-grinder *silent*; *satb* chorus of stevedores and seamstresses

SYNOPSIS

The opera takes place in contemporary Paris. A barge is tied to a quay beside the Seine, and its owner, Michele, watches the sun set as the stevedores finish the day's work. Michele's wife Giorgetta goes about her chores, and as workers come and go and street musicians pass she steals a few moments with her lover Luigi, who is one of the stevedores. They are interrupted by Michele, who looks at them suspiciously but leaves them alone long enough for them to arrange a rendezvous for later that night. After Luigi has gone, Michele returns and speaks of the past, begging Giorgetta to return to their former love and happiness. But Giorgetta evades his caresses, and Michele grimly watches her go inside, convinced of her infidelity. He remains alone in the dark, tormenting himself with thoughts of her betrayal ('Nulla, silenzio'). In silence he lights his pipe, and Luigi, who mistakes the light for Giorgetta's pre-arranged signal, runs aboard the barge. Michele catches Luigi and, after forcing him to confess his love for Giorgetta, chokes him to death. When Giorgetta reappears, Michele conceals the corpse under his cloak; as she approaches, he removes the cloak and triumphantly reveals Luigi's lifeless body.

Il tabarro has many admirers, some even considering it the composer's finest work. The orchestration is highly innovative (as is demonstrated, for example, by the orchestral introduction, in which a texture of Debussy-like clarity and subtlety sets forth the governing ambience of the score); the musical characterization is surprisingly well defined considering the duration of the action, with even minor figures such as Il Tinca (a stevedore) and La Frugola (wife of another stevedore, Talpa) sharply focused. Perhaps most importantly, the timing of the musical drama is impeccable, with lyrical scenes always balancing the action sequences. Realistic touches, such as the motor horn in the opening, or the music-seller who offers his clients a snatch of *La bohème*, are subtly integrated into the generally sombre atmosphere and, as the major characters all grow out of this ambience, the effect of the drama is all the more compelling.

RECORDINGS 1. Mas, Prandelli, Gobbi, Rome Op Ch & O, Bellezza, EMI, 1955; 2. L. Price, Domingo, Milnes, John Alldis Ch, NPO, Leinsdorf, RCA, 1971; 3. Gulegina, Shicoff, C. Guelfi, London Voices, LSO, Pappano, EMI, 1997

Suor Angelica

Sister Angelica

Opera in one act (1h)
Libretto by Giovacchino Forzano
Composed 1917
PREMIERES see *Il trittico* above
CAST Suor Angelica *s*, La Zia Principessa *c*, Suor Genoveva *s*, Suor Osmina *s*, Suor Dolcina *s*, La Badessa (the Abbess) *ms*, La Suora Zelatrice (the monitor) *ms*, La Maestra delle novizie (the mistress of the novices) *ms*, La Suora Infermiera (the nursing sister) *ms*; *sa* chorus of alms-collectors, novices, lay sisters

SYNOPSIS

A convent in late 17th-century Italy. As the curtain opens, the nuns are finishing their prayers and joyfully go about their business, while Sister Angelica tries unsuccessfully to hide her unhappiness; in the seven years she has spent in the convent, she has heard no news of her family. But soon the Abbess announces that her aunt, a princess, has come to visit. When the aunt is ushered in, Angelica is checked by the coldness of her aunt's greeting. From their conversation we learn that Angelica has been put in the convent by her family as punishment for having an illegitimate child. As Angelica begs for compassion, her aunt coldly informs her that the child is now dead. The princess leaves Angelica alone to weep despairingly, desiring only to end her sorrows and join her child in heaven ('Senza Mamma'). The other nuns join her in ecstatic praise of the Holy Virgin; when she is again left alone, she drinks poison, singing a joyful farewell to life. Suddenly her calm is shattered: by killing herself she is damned to eternal separation from the child she loves. She prays desperately to the Madonna; angels' voices join in her prayer as the Madonna herself appears, bringing the child to lead his mother into heaven.

As the plot summary indicates, this is an unashamedly sentimental drama, and perhaps gains its full effect only in its original context, framed by the more vivid and immediate *Tabarro* and *Gianni Schicchi*. The religious setting allowed Puccini to indulge in some pastiche of the world of his musical ancestors, and if the resulting pseudo-ecclesiastical vein works well in the less elevated context of the opening section of the opera, it seems strained at the more demanding, miraculous close. But there are moments of considerable effect, in particular the tension-laden meeting between Sister Angelica and her glacial aunt – the latter certainly the most extraordinary of Puccini's female creations – and Angelica's 'Senza Mamma', which follows the princess's exit, remains one of Puccini's greatest soprano arias.

RECORDINGS 1. de los Angeles, Barbieri, Rome Op Ch & O, Serafin, EMI, 1957; 2. Scotto, Horne, Ambrosian Op Ch, NPO, Maazel, Sony, 1977; 3. Gallardo-Domas, Manca di Nissa, London Voices, Philharmonia O, Pappano, EMI, 1997

Gianni Schicchi

Opera in one act (55m)
Libretto by Giovacchino Forzano, based on an episode (Canto XXX, l. 32) in Dante's *Inferno* (*c.*1307–21)
Composed 1917–18
PREMIERES see *Il trittico* above
CAST Gianni Schicchi *bar*, Lauretta *s*, Rinuccio *t*, Nella *s*, La Ciesca *ms*, Zita *c*, Gheraldino *boy s*, Gheraldo *t*, Marco *bar*, Ser Amantio di Nicolao *bar*, Betto di Signa *b*, Simone *b*, Maestro Spinelloccio *b*, Pinellino *b*, Guccio *b*

SYNOPSIS

Late 13th-century Florence. The curtain opens on the bedroom of Buoso Donati, a rich old gentleman who has just died. His relatives are gathered round the deathbed, feigning grief to impress each other, until a rumour that Buoso has left all his money to a monastery sends them into a feverish search for his will. The young Rinuccio finds it first but withholds it from the others until he has extracted a promise from them: when they receive Buoso's money, he will be allowed to marry Lauretta, the daughter of Gianni Schicchi. The relatives hurriedly agree, but are sorely disappointed when they find out that all Buoso's money is indeed left to the Church. Rinuccio suggests turning the problem over to Gianni Schicchi, who is famed for his cunning ('Avete torto'), even though the relatives scoff at Schicchi's low birth. Schicchi himself arrives in answer to a secret summons from Rinuccio, bringing Lauretta with him. The relatives condescend to ask for Schicchi's help, but he refuses; finally Lauretta intercedes, begging her father to make her marriage to Rinuccio possible ('O mio babbino caro'). Schicchi comes up with a plan: they are to hide Buoso's death long enough for him, disguised as Buoso, to make a new will. Delighted, the relatives send for the notary, individually bribing Schicchi to give them the most favourable portion of the inheritance. Schicchi agrees to everything, reminding them that to reveal the trick will mean severe punishment according to Florentine law. When the notary arrives, Schicchi awards the lion's share of Buoso's property to his 'devoted friend, Gianni Schicchi' and the relatives are helpless to intervene. Once the notary has gone, Schicchi drives the relatives from his new home. Rinuccio and Lauretta remain on the terrace, singing of their love for each other. Schicchi returns and, seeing the young lovers, announces to the audience his satisfaction with the way Buoso's money has been used.

It is unfortunate that *Gianni Schicchi* was the only outright comic opera that Puccini wrote. Throughout his career he periodically toyed with comic subjects, but in the end refused to commit himself to anything that strayed so far from the paths in which he had achieved his greatest successes. Again, it is probably thanks to the one-act format, whose more discrete, short-term goals released the composer from his usual doubts, that we have this masterly vignette of medieval Florence. As with *Il tabarro*, the musical characterization is on a very high level, in particular the portraits of Gianni Schicchi and his daughter Lauretta; and the sheer musical invention of the opera, as well as many of its most characteristic idioms, places in the clearest possible context the debt Puccini owed to his great predecessor, Verdi, whose final opera, *Falstaff*, paved the way for Puccini's comic masterpiece.

RECORDINGS 1. de los Angeles, Del Monte, Gobbi, Rome Op O, Santini, EMI, 1958; 2. Gheorghiu, Alagna, Van Dam, LSO, Pappano, EMI, 1997

Turandot

Opera in three acts (1h 45m)
Libretto by Giuseppe Adami and Renato Simoni, after the play by Carlo Gozzi (1762)
Composed 1920–24; completed by Franco Alfano 1925–6
PREMIERES 25 April 1926, La Scala, Milan; US: 16 November 1926, Metropolitan, New York; UK: 7 June 1927, Covent Garden, London
CAST Princess Turandot *s*, the Unknown Prince (Calaf) *t*, Liù *s*, Timur *b*, Emperor Altoum *t*, Ping *bar*, Pang *t*, Pong *t*, a Mandarin *bar*, Prince of Persia *t*, executioner *silent*; *satb* chorus of imperial guards, the executioner's servants, children, priests, mandarins, dignitaries, the eight wise men, Turandot's handmaidens, soldiers, flag-carriers, musicians, ghosts of the dead, the crowd

The idea of setting Gozzi's *Turandot*, and thus of returning to the Far Eastern ambience of *Madama Butterfly*, was first mooted by Giuseppe Adami and Renato Simoni in March 1920, nearly three years after the premiere of Busoni's short opera on the same story. Puccini was enthusiastic, but the opera went through the kind of agonizing genesis that had become the norm in Puccinian creation. Endless prose and verse scenarios were proffered and rejected; and there was a crisis during which Puccini, having completed about half the work, became convinced that its shape should be radically altered: until a fairly late stage, Act I was planned – and, what is more important, musically sketched – to encompass a good deal more of the action than the version we know today, ending where the present Act II now ends, with Calaf's solving of the riddles. When the decision came to split this sequence in two, both halves had to be enlarged: Act I with the finale after Calaf's and Liù's arias, and the new Act II with the addition of an opening scene for Ping, Pang and Pong, and a grand aria for Turandot, 'In questa reggia'.

Everything up to the final scene was finished by the end of March 1924, but the closing duet between Calaf and Turandot was still to be written when the composer died in November. The opera was completed (in part by following sketches left by Puccini) by the young composer Alfano. The first performance (which did not include Alfano's ending) was conducted by Arturo Toscanini.

SYNOPSIS

The action takes place in ancient Peking. Princess Turandot has decreed that she will marry any prince who can solve three riddles, but that if he fails in the attempt he must die. Many have tried; all have failed.

Act I: The curtain opens on a crowded scene at sunset amid preparations for the execution of the latest contestant, the Prince of Persia. The young Prince Calaf recognizes his father, Timur, who is accompanied by Liù, a slave girl. (Timur's throne has been usurped, and he has escaped penniless from his kingdom.) The execution proceeds; Turandot appears on the palace balcony, luminous in the light of the newly risen moon, to give the signal of death. Calaf is dazzled by her beauty and, as the Prince of Persia's death cry rings out, Calaf determines to win Turandot for himself. The Emperor of China's three ministers, Ping, Pang and Pong, attempt to dissuade Calaf, and are joined in this by Timur and Liù. Calaf tries to comfort his father, asking Liù to continue to care for Timur ('Non piangere, Liù!'). But his purpose cannot be deflected and, crying out 'Turandot', he strikes three blows on a gong to signal the arrival of a new suitor.

Act II, Scene 1 opens in a pavilion of the palace as Ping, Pang and Pong review the endless cycle of executions they have witnessed since Turandot first issued her decree. They dream of a princess transformed by love and restoring peace to China, but a fanfare recalls them to the reality of another trial. Scene 2 takes place in the square of the royal palace. The Emperor Altoum, weary of the needless deaths, pleads with Calaf to give up the challenge, but Calaf insists on proceeding. Turandot places herself in front of the emperor's throne. She explains that, inspired by an ancient princess who was cruelly betrayed by a man, she has vowed to keep herself pure ('In questa reggia'). The trial begins. One by one, Turandot announces her riddles. To the crowd's gathering excitement, Calaf answers each one correctly. As he solves the third riddle, Turandot collapses in despair, begging her father to release her from her own decree. The emperor is unyielding, but Calaf offers her a chance of release. He gives her a riddle of his own: if she can discover his name by daybreak, he will pay the forfeit and die; if not, she will be his.

Act III, Scene 1: Calaf is lying on the steps of a pavilion in the palace garden that same night lyrically contemplating his coming victory over the princess ('Nessun dorma'). Ping, Pang and Pong arrive, desperate over Turandot's new decree by which all their lives are forfeit if the prince's name is not discovered by dawn. They tempt Calaf with a variety of delights. Calaf remains unmoved until the guards drag in Timur and Liù, who had been seen earlier in the company of Calaf. Turandot herself enters to question Timur, but Liù courageously steps forward, saying that she alone knows the secret of the prince's name. When the soldiers try to force the name from her, her love for Calaf gives her the strength to resist. Finally Liù turns to Turandot and, crying that through her sacrifice, Turandot will learn love ('Tu che di gel sei cinta'), she grabs a soldier's dagger and stabs herself, dying at Calaf's feet. Timur, heartbroken at her death, follows as her body is carried off in mournful procession. Calaf and Turandot are left alone. Their extended duet comes to a first climax as Calaf kisses Turandot passionately. Overcome with a mixture of passion and shame, she begs him to leave for ever, but instead he gives her the answer to his riddle, telling her his name and so placing his life in her hands. Trumpets announce the coming of dawn. Scene 2: In the palace square Turandot announces triumphantly to the emperor and the crowd that she knows the stranger's name. But then to everyone's surprise she cries out: 'His name is love!' and, to a reprise of 'Nessun dorma', all join in rejoicing.

Turandot has many of the qualities of Puccini's earlier operas – superb dramatic pacing in particular – but what distinguishes it from its predecessors, and is perhaps its most remarkable quality, is its extraordinary richness of musical invention; something all the more surprising from a composer who constantly complained that advancing age was sapping his creative powers. As in many of the best fin-de-siècle operas, there is in *Turandot* a riot of competing musical colours, each primarily associated with an element of the drama: the heroic prince, the proud princess, the pathetic slave girl, the bizarre ministers, even the hapless Persian suitor – all create their own musical atmosphere during the course of Act I and thus discretely dominate sections of the drama. These 'colours' are not restricted to individual characters: there are several distinct sides to the exotic ambience, for example, not merely a blanket characterization of all things 'Eastern'. There is also an unusually large system of recurring motifs and melodies: one thinks immediately of the motif that regularly accompanies Turandot's entrances, or the choruses that welcome the emperor. These are hardly ever used in a developmental way, and almost invariably return in exact repetition and within the same broad musical context. They thus serve to articulate the various contrasting blocks of colour rather than to create connections between them. And all this musical variety is wrapped in an orchestral texture whose richness and invention Puccini had not previously equalled.

RECORDINGS 1. Nilsson, Tebaldi, Björling, Tozzi, Rome Opera Ch & O, Leinsdorf, RCA, 1959; 2. Sutherland, Caballé, Pavarotti, Ghiaurov, John Alldis Ch, Wandsworth School Boys' Ch, LPO, Mehta, Decca, 1973
OTHER OPERATIC WORKS *Le villi*, 1884; *Edgar*, 1889

E.H./R.P.

Henry Purcell

b 1658 or 1659, London; *d* 21 November 1695, London

Purcell is generally regarded as the greatest English opera composer before the 20th century, yet he wrote only one true opera, *Dido and Aeneas*. A pupil of Matthew Locke and John Blow, he also endeavoured to emulate the new French and Italian styles, though his music remained conservative and distinctively English in its predilection for dissonant counterpoint. Purcell is particularly admired for his genius at setting the English language.

Purcell was appointed composer-in-ordinary (that is, with salary) for the King's Violins in 1677 and co-organist of the Chapel Royal in 1682, having already succeeded Blow as organist of Westminster Abbey in 1678, and his early career was naturally centred on the court. He served four monarchs – Charles II (to 1685), James II (1685–88) and William and Mary (1689–95) – during the turbulent years of the Exclusion Crisis and the Glorious Revolution. His earliest public works are anthems for the Chapel Royal and royal welcome songs. During these formative years he also composed much instrumental music, including the fantasias for viol consort – contrapuntal tours de force and the last of their kind – and trio sonatas, supposedly in imitation of the new Italian style but in reality continuing to explore the same English vein as the fantasias.

Purcell's first contribution to the professional stage was the incidental music for Nathaniel Lee's tragedy *Theodosius* of 1680. The songs and choruses are modelled on the music of his teacher Locke, who had dominated the London musical theatre until his death in 1677. The *Theodosius* pieces are rather stiff and awkward in comparison to the highly sophisticated instrumental music Purcell was composing at the same time and give little indication of his later achievement in dramatic song. The political upheavals and management crises of the London theatres during the 1680s afforded him few other opportunities to write for the stage, his output being restricted to anthems, coronation music and festive odes, most notably those associated with the recently established London St Cecilia's Day celebrations.

In the last five years of his life, Purcell's career turned decisively towards the theatre, largely in consequence of William's and Mary's drastic curtailment of the Royal Musick, which forced Purcell and many of his colleagues to seek employment outside the court. In 1690 he composed the music for *The Prophetess, or The History of Dioclesian*, adapted by the actor Thomas Betterton from a Jacobean tragi-comedy. *Dioclesian* (as it became known) is a semi-opera – that is, a play with substantial musical episodes or masques which are sung and danced by minor characters (spirits, soldiers, priests, fairies and the like); the main characters do not sing. The choice of Purcell as composer of *Dioclesian*, which proved a great financial and artistic success, was probably influenced by the amateur performance in 1689 of *Dido and Aeneas* at a girls' boarding school in Chelsea. The libretto was written by Nahum Tate, soon to become Poet Laureate, and the school was run by Josias Priest, a choreographer at the Theatre Royal; both were men of considerable influence in the London theatrical world.

Dioclesian attracted the attention of John Dryden, who offered Purcell the libretto of his semi-opera *King Arthur*, which was produced in 1691, another great success for the Theatre Royal. Because it was conceived as a semi-opera rather than being adapted from an old play, *King Arthur* is much more cohesive than *Dioclesian*, and here Purcell came close to matching the quality of *Dido*; two numbers, the so-called frost scene and the nostalgic song 'Fairest Isle', have achieved immortality.

Purcell's next semi-opera, *The Fairy Queen* of 1692, was to be the grandest and most lavish of all such works. Adapted anonymously from Shakespeare's *A Midsummer Night's Dream*, it includes Purcell's finest and most sophisticated dramatic music, all of which is collected into four self-contained masques; a fifth was added to a revival in 1693. But *The Fairy Queen*, which proved as popular as Purcell's previous works, nearly bankrupted the Theatre Royal because of the expense of the scenes, music and dances. No new semi-opera was planned for 1694, and Purcell concentrated instead on writing orchestral incidental music (collected in the posthumous *Ayres for the Theatre* of 1697) and songs for plays. In the latter genre he was eclipsed in popularity by his younger contemporary John Eccles, whose simple and highly dramatic songs were better suited to the actor-singers (such as the celebrated Anne Bracegirdle) than were Purcell's more difficult, highly decorated vocal music.

In early 1695 Purcell's theatrical career suffered another setback when Betterton was given permission to set up a rival theatre in a converted tennis court in Lincoln's Inn Fields. Not only did the old actor persuade most of his colleagues to follow him, but Eccles and virtually all of the professional stage singers also joined the renegades, leaving Purcell with a handful of young and inexperienced singers. He nevertheless composed a great deal of theatre music during the last year of his life, including masques and entertainments for *Timon of Athens*, *The Libertine*, *Bonduca*, a song or two for *The Tempest* and his last semi-opera, *The Indian Queen*. He did not live to complete this score, and his younger brother Daniel was called down from Oxford to compose the final masque.

Purcell's only opera thus came at the beginning of his brief theatre career. Because *Dido and Aeneas* is through-composed and seems to conform to the 19th-century ideal of musical tragedy, it has assumed a central position in Purcell's oeuvre. Yet there is no evidence that he was dissatisfied with semi-opera as a genre or frustrated at not having the opportunity to write another all-sung opera. One needs to understand the conventions of semi-opera to appreciate how much better a composer Purcell became after *Dido and Aeneas*.

Dido and Aeneas

Tragic opera in three acts (1h)
Libretto by Nahum Tate, after his tragedy *Brutus of Alba* (1678) and the fourth book of the *Aeneid* by Virgil (29–19 BC)
PREMIERES spring 1689, Josias Priest's boarding school for girls, Chelsea; US: 13 January 1924, Town Hall, New York, (concert); 18 February 1932, Juilliard School, New York (stage)
CAST Dido *s*, Belinda *s*, Second Woman *s*, Sorceress *ms* or *b-bar*, First Witch *s*, Second Witch *s*, Spirit *ms*, Aeneas *t*, Sailor *s*; *satb* chorus of courtiers, witches, sailors and cupids

The circumstances behind the composition and performance of *Dido and Aeneas* are unknown. According to the sole surviving copy of the libretto of the Chelsea production, the opera was performed 'by young gentlewomen', presumably the girls of Priest's boarding school. It was modelled very closely on John Blow's opera *Venus and Adonis*, which had also been performed by an all-female cast at Priest's school in April 1684. That *Dido* was also a spring production is suggested by a couplet of Thomas Durfey's spoken epilogue: 'Like nimble fawns, and birds that bless the spring/Unscarr'd by turning times we dance and sing.' The opera originally included a prologue (music lost) that alludes to William and Mary and welcomes the arrival of spring; so *Dido* may have formed part of the celebrations of their joint coronation on 11 April 1689. Like *Venus and Adonis*, *Dido* is highly unusual for baroque opera in having a tragic ending. Tate based the plot on Virgil's account of Aeneas at Carthage, the main difference being that in the opera the Trojan prince, rather than being prompted by the gods to sail on to Italy, is tricked into leaving Dido by an evil Sorceress, Tate's invention.

SYNOPSIS

Act I: After escaping from the sack of Troy, Prince Aeneas sets sail for Italy where he is destined to found Rome. Blown off course to Carthage, he is welcomed by Queen Dido who, being burdened by affairs of state and unspoken grief ('Ah! Belinda'), is reluctant to reveal a growing love for her guest. Urged on by her confidante Belinda and her attendants ('Fear no danger'), Dido tacitly succumbs to Aeneas and the court rejoices ('To the hills and the vales').

Act II, Scene 1: With the playing of a sombre prelude, the scene changes to a cave, where a Sorceress and her witches plot Queen Dido's downfall ('Wayward sisters'). Hoping to trick Aeneas into leaving Dido by reminding him of his destiny in Italy, they prepare the charm in an echo chorus ('In our deep vaulted cell'). Scene 2 is set in a grove where Dido and Aeneas, having consummated their love during the previous night, are entertained by Belinda and an attendant ('Thanks to these lonesome vales'/'Oft she visits this lone mountain'). The Sorceress (unseen) conjures up a thunderstorm, which sends the courtiers running for shelter ('Haste, haste to town'), while Aeneas lags behind to hear an elf disguised as Mercury order him to leave Carthage ('Stay, Prince'). He agonizes over his decision to comply with the command.

Act III: On the quayside Aeneas' men are preparing to weigh anchor ('Come away, fellow sailors'). The Sorceress and witches reappear to gloat over the impending tragedy ('Destruction's our delight'). The scene shifts back to court where Dido, having got wind of Aeneas' decision to leave, seeks Belinda's advice ('Your counsel all is urg'd in vain') before bitterly confronting the cowardly Aeneas, who offers to stay but then ignominiously departs. Dido realizes that she cannot live without him. Inconsolable ('Thy hand, Belinda'), she sings her great lament ('When I am laid in earth'), dies and is mourned by a chorus of cupids ('With drooping wings').

Dido is remarkable for the swift concision of action, its widely contrasting moods (including the comic relief of the sailors' scene) and a deeply tragic ending. For most of these features and a carefully controlled key scheme Purcell was indebted to Blow's *Venus and Adonis*. But *Dido* is much more structured; each scene is built up of units of recitative (or declamatory song), arioso, aria, chorus and dance. Purcell was thus following the formal model offered by Lully's tragédies en musique, but his chief innovation, inspired by contemporary Venetian opera, was to concentrate the greatest musical interest in the arias. Dido's are placed at the beginning and end of the opera and both are constructed over ostinato basses: 'Ah! Belinda!' in Act I also displays a da capo structure, while the famous lament is built over a repeated chromatically descending five-bar bass, also common in Italian opera of the time.

Purcell's recitatives, which have been called the finest in the English language, are regularly measured but with great flexibility of rhythm to reflect the slightest nuance of speech; important words are often decorated with elaborate melismas. The Sorceress's part, which Purcell may have conceived for bass-baritone rather than mezzo-soprano as usually heard today, is notable for being set almost entirely in recitative accompanied by four-part strings.

Perhaps because of the involvement of Josias Priest, a professional choreographer, dance dominates the score; key pieces are the triumphing dance (another ground) at the end of Act I, the witches' echo dance (in the style of a French furies' dance) in Act II, Scene 2, and the sailors' dance in Act III, each being radically different in character one from the other. And in its brief, sharply contrasting sections, the final witches' dance, which included Jack o' Lantern, resembles a Jacobean antimasque. The opera was even supposed to end with a cupids' dance, which has not survived.

The earliest score of *Dido and Aeneas* dates from nearly a century after the Chelsea performance and differs from Tate's original libretto in several significant ways. Besides the missing prologue mentioned above, the score lacks a dance and chorus of witches at the end of Act II. Many modern producers have therefore felt the need to add music between Aeneas' soliloquy and the beginning of Act III, perhaps the most successful being that arranged by Benjamin Britten from other Purcell works. The original music for this scene, along with the prologue and final cupids' dance, may have been cut from the first public production of *Dido* at Lincoln's Inn Fields Theatre, London, in 1700, when the opera was reordered and inserted into an adaptation of Shakespeare's *Measure for Measure*.

RECORDINGS 1. Baker, Clark, Sinclair, Herincx, St Anthony Singers, ECO, Lewis, Oiseau-Lyre, 1961; 2. Von Otter, Dawson, Rogers, Varcoe, Eng Concert Ch & O, Pinnock, Archiv, 1989; 3. Marin-Degor, Brua, Berg, Les Arts Florissants, Christie, Erato, 1994

SEMI-OPERAS *Dioclesian (The Prophetess, or The History of Dioclesian)*, 1690; *King Arthur, or The British Worthy*, 1691; *The Fairy Queen*, 1692; *The Indian Queen*, 1695

C.P.

Jean-Philippe Rameau

baptized 25 September 1683, Dijon, France; *d* 12 September 1764, Paris

With excusable exaggeration, the *Mercure de France* (1765) concluded its epitaph to Rameau with the words: 'Here lies the God of Harmony.' It was a fitting tribute to the man who, then as now, was seen not only as the outstanding European musical theorist of his era but as France's leading 18th-century composer. To many music-lovers he may nowadays be best known for his keyboard and chamber works. Yet his finest and most ambitious compositions are in the field of dramatic music and include some of the most powerful operas of the period between Monteverdi and Mozart.

Rameau came late to opera. Although his music covers the best part of six decades (1706–*c*.1763), all his dramatic works belong to the last three. As he later admitted: 'I have attended the theatre since I was 12, yet I first worked for the [Paris] Opéra only at 50, and even then I did not think myself capable.'

Much of Rameau's early life was spent in the comparative obscurity of the provinces. When he eventually settled in Paris at the age of 39, it was as a music theorist that he first came to public attention: the epoch-making *Traité de l'harmonie* appeared in 1722, and was followed by some three dozen books and pamphlets on music theory. During his first decade in the capital he published his two best-known keyboard collections, the *Pièces de clavessin* in 1724 and the *Nouvelles suites de pièces de clavecin* and a volume of cantatas in 1729 or 1730; he also tried his hand at incidental music (now lost) for some knockabout comedies at the fair theatres.

For all its undoubted imagination, skill and refinement, there was little in Rameau's previous output to prepare contemporary audiences for the power and complexity of *Hippolyte et Aricie*, his first opera. Never had the French been confronted with a musical style so intensely dramatic. There were those who immediately hailed Rameau as 'the Orpheus of our century'. Others, however, found the music over-complex, unnatural, misshapen – in a word, baroque. (*Hippolyte* has the dubious distinction of being the first musical work to which that epithet, still pejorative in those days, is known to have been applied.) At the Paris Opéra (the Académie Royale de Musique) two factions soon formed – the *Ramistes*, as his supporters became known, and the *Lullistes*, devotees of the traditional repertoire, who compared the new music unfavourably with that of their revered Lully. The dispute raged around all Rameau's operas of the 1730s; although it gradually subsided during the following decade, echoes could still be heard in the 1750s and beyond.

Increasingly, though, Rameau began to win the acclaim of the French musical public. In 1745 he was adopted as a court composer, with a royal pension and the title Compositeur de la chambre du roy. From that time too, he enjoyed the esteem of the intelligentsia, and his works were received at the Opéra and elsewhere with growing enthusiasm. Yet controversy was never far away; during the *querelle des bouffons* (1752–4) – a notorious pamphlet war between supporters of opera buffa and those of serious French opera – this former threat to the musical Establishment was himself attacked as an Establishment figure. And although he was increasingly regarded as the Grand Old Man of French music, criticism that his style seemed outmoded could more often be heard. While a number of Rameau's works remained in the Opéra's repertoire after his death, few survived the radical change in taste brought about by the arrival of Gluck's operas in the mid-1770s.

To his contemporaries, Rameau's operas at first seemed revolutionary. With hindsight, however, they appear securely rooted in French operatic tradition both in their subject matter and overall dramatic structure and in many musical details. Rameau's achievement was to rejuvenate that tradition by bringing to it an astonishingly fertile musical imagination, a harmonic idiom richer and more varied than that of any French predecessor, and a boldness of expression that can still seem almost overpowering. Throughout his operatic career Rameau remained receptive to new musical fashions; consequently the lofty and dignified idiom of his first operas became noticeably influenced during the 1740s and 1750s by the lighter German and Italian styles and softened by a proliferation of ornamental detail.

Even in his late seventies the composer's creative powers remained largely unimpaired, as the amazing quality of his last work, *Les Boréades*, demonstrates. But few would deny that, with the exception of that work and of *Platée and Pigmalion*, his most enduring operas almost all belong to the period 1733–44. It is especially sad that in his later years he found few libretti with the dramatic potential of *Hippolyte*, *Castor* or the 1744 version of *Dardanus*.

Hippolyte et Aricie

Hippolytus and Aricia

Tragédie en musique in five acts with prologue (2h 45m)
Libretto by Simon-Joseph Pellegrin
PREMIERES 1 October 1733, Opéra (Académie Royale de Musique), Paris; UK: 13 May 1965, Barber Institute, Birmingham; US: 11 April 1954, New York (concert); 4 April 1966, Boston (stage)
CAST Thesée *b*, Phèdre *ms*, Hippolyte *t* (*haute-contre*), Aricie *s*, Diane *s*, Pluton *b*, Tisiphone *t* (*taille*), 7 *s*, 4 *t* (2 *hautes-contre*; 2 *tailles*), 3 *b*; *satb* chorus of nymphs, forest-dwellers, priestesses of Diana, citizens of Troezen, gods of the underworld, sailors, hunters and huntresses, shepherds and shepherdesses; ballet: priestesses of Diana, gods of the underworld, furies, sailors and citizens of Troezen, hunters and huntresses, shepherds and shepherdesses, zephyrs, people of the forest of Aricia

In reworking the story of Phaedra's incestuous love for her stepson Hippolytus, Pellegrin borrowed elements (including a number of lines) from Racine's *Phèdre* (1677); he also returned to features of Racine's models, Euripides' *Hippolytos* and Seneca's *Phaedra*. His setting, however, alters the balance between the main characters, not so much in its treatment of the young lovers Hippolytus and Aricia as of Theseus, whose role becomes both more extensive and more powerful than that of Phaedra, his queen.

SYNOPSIS

Prologue: Diana is forced to concede that, one day a year, her normally chaste forest-dwellers should be permitted to serve Cupid. She promises to protect Hippolytus and Aricia.

Act I: As the last descendant of Theseus' enemy Pallas, Aricia is compelled to take vows of chastity in the Temple of Diana. Before the ceremony, she and Hippolytus discover their mutual love. When Phaedra arrives to ensure that Aricia 'takes the veil', she learns with rage of Diana's pledge to protect the lovers.

Act II: Theseus, who is presumed dead, has descended to Hades to rescue a comrade. Eventually realizing his mission is hopeless, he invokes the help of his father, Neptune. Before he can escape, the Fates make their all-important prediction: Theseus may be leaving Hades, but he will find hell in his own home.

Act III: Phaedra, believing herself a widow, reveals her love to Hippolytus but is rebuffed even when she offers him the crown. In despair, she tries to kill herself with the prince's sword. As Hippolytus seizes it back, Theseus appears. Recalling the Fates' prediction and misled by various insinuations (which his son is too honourable to counter), Theseus jumps to the conclusion that Hippolytus has attempted rape. Concealing his anguish from the loyal subjects who celebrate his return, he calls on Neptune to punish Hippolytus.

Act IV: Hippolytus has escaped with Aricia to Diana's grove. During celebrations in the goddess's honour, a sea monster carries him off. As the horrified onlookers react to his apparent death, Phaedra confesses her guilt.

Act V: Theseus eventually learns the truth from the dying Phaedra and is himself about to commit suicide when Neptune reveals that Hippolytus is alive. For accepting his son's guilt too readily, Theseus is condemned never to see him again. The scene shifts to the forest, where Diana causes Hippolytus to be reunited with his beloved.

Despite some obvious flaws, Pellegrin's libretto comes nearer to real tragedy than any other that Rameau set (Voltaire's still-born *Samson* excepted). It provides the composer with the outlines of two of his most monumental creations. The magnanimous but fatally gullible Theseus is given music of consistently elevated tone, its broad contours and rich harmonies conveying the king's noble and generous bearing. It reaches its high points in Theseus' two invocations to Neptune and in his final dignified acceptance of his punishment, all of which have a Bach-like harmonic intensity and (unusual for France) consistently patterned accompaniments. Phaedra, though less subtle or rounded than her Racinian counterpart, is still a powerful embodiment of passionate jealousy and remorse. Though initially an unsympathetic character, she gains our compassion in her anxious prayer to Venus and, above all, in her final confession of guilt; this last, with its involvement of the grief-stricken bystanders, is one of the most powerful moments of pure tragedy in the entire pre-Romantic operatic repertoire. By comparison, the eponymous young lovers seem pale, though they project a touching innocence.

The second *Trio des Parques* (Fates) in Act II has become justly famous for its bold use of enharmonic progressions – too bold, indeed, for contemporary performers, so that it had to be cut by about two-thirds. Scarcely less remarkable are the orchestral representation of thunder (Act I) and of the boiling sea (Act III), the latter with the orchestra of strings and bassoons divided into eight parts. Performance difficulties and criticism of the work's dramatic structure led to a series of damaging cuts, both before and during the first run and at successive revivals, so that in Rameau's day the work was seldom valued as highly as his other tragedies. It is, however, the most human of them all and the most consistently moving.

RECORDINGS 1. Fouchécourt, Gens, Fink, Smythe, Naouri, Les Musiciens du Louvre, Minkowski, Archiv, 1994;
2. Panzarella, Hunt, James, Padmore, Naouri, Les Arts Florissants, Christie, Erato, 1996

Les Indes galantes

The Amorous Indies

Opéra-ballet, with prologue and four entrées (2h 30m)
Libretto by Louis Fuzelier
PREMIERES prologue and first two entrées only: 23 August 1735, Opéra, Paris; third entrée added 28 August 1735; fourth entrée added 10 March 1736; modern revival (complete): 18 June 1952, Opéra, Paris; US: 1 March 1961, New York (concert); UK: 22 May 1974, Banqueting House, London (concert); 1977, Edinburgh (stage)
CAST prologue: Hébé *s*, L'Amour *s*, Bellone *b*; first entrée: Osman *b*, Emilie *s*, Valère *t* (*haute-contre*); second entrée: Huascar *b*, Phani *s*, Don Carlos *t* (*haute-contre*); third entrée: Tacmas *t* (*haute-contre*), Fatime *s*, Ali *b* (replaced in rev. by Roxane *s*), Zaïre *s* (replaced in rev. by Atalide *s*); fourth entrée: Damon *t* (*haute-contre*), Don Alvar *b*, Zima *s*, Adario *t* (*taille*); *satb* chorus (in prologue and all entrées) of French, Italian, Spanish and Polish allies, warriors, sailors, Provençal men and women, Incas, sacrificers, Peruvians, Persian musicians and slaves, Indian savages; ballet: French, Italian, Spanish and Polish young people, warriors, Hebe's retinue, cupids, sports and pleasures, Osman's African slaves, sailors and sailor girls, Pallas, Incas and Peruvians, Persians, Bostangis, flowers, male and female savages, French women dressed as Amazons, French and Indian soldiers, Indian women, colonial shepherds and shepherdesses

Ignoring the contemporary preference for opéra-ballets based on mythological themes, Fuzelier's libretto reverted to an older type involving believable modern characters, initiated by Campra's *L'Europe galante* (1697) and briefly in vogue during the first two decades of the 18th century. The Prologue retains its allegorical character in order to introduce the work's theme – aspects of love in far-flung lands: the young men of four allied nations (France, Spain, Italy and Poland) forsake the goddess Hebe and, despite Cupid's exhortations, are led off to war by Bellona. The cupids, realizing that Europe was forsaking them, decide to emigrate to the various 'Indies' (then a generic term for any exotic land). These colourful locations become the settings for the ensuing entrées.

The third entrée, added shortly after the premiere, was criticized for what the French regarded as the absurdity of disguising the hero as a woman. Two weeks later, its plot had been entirely changed and all but the final divertissement replaced with new music. The final entrée, added the following year, eventually became one of Rameau's best-loved works of the type.

SYNOPSIS

First entrée *Le turc généreux* (*The Generous Turk*): On a Turkish island in the Indian Ocean, Emilie, a young Provençal girl, has been captured and sold as a slave to the pasha Osman. Although the pasha has fallen in love with her, Emilie cannot forget her lover Valère, a French marine officer. During a sudden storm, Valère is shipwrecked on the island and captured. Osman recognizes him as the one who freed him from slavery. After first feigning anger at seeing the couple embracing, Osman shows his gratitude to Valère by releasing them both.

Second entrée *Les Incas du Pérou* (*The Incas of Peru*): In the Peruvian desert, the Incas prepare to celebrate the Festival of Sun in the shadows of a nearby volcano, while Don Carlos, a Spanish officer, and Phani, a young Peruvian princess, declare their love for each other. Phani spurns Huascar, the Inca in charge of the ceremonial. As the sun worship begins, Huascar artificially provokes the eruption of the volcano to convince her that the sun god disapproves of her love for an alien. But Carlos foils his attempt to abduct her, and the jealous Inca, now mad with rage, provokes a further eruption of the volcano and is crushed by molten rocks.

Third entrée *Les fleurs, fête persane* (*A Persian Flower Festival*): Original version: the young Persian prince Tacmas and his confidant, Ali, are each in love with one of the other's slaves: Tacmas loves Zaïre, spurning his own slave Fatime whom Ali loves. On the day of the flower festival, the four meet in a confusing encounter in Ali's garden, where Tacmas is disguised as a woman and Fatime as a Polish slave; but when it emerges that Zaïre and Fatime each love the other's master, the men exchange slaves and the two satisfied couples take part in the festival. Revised version: Fatime (here the sultana rather than a slave) suspects her husband Tacmas of infidelity with Atalide. Disguised as a Polish slave, she gains Atalide's confidence and thus learns, to her astonishment, of Tacmas's utter fidelity. The happy couple take part in the flower festival.

Fourth [new] entrée *Les sauvages* (*The Savages*): In a North American forest near the French and Spanish colonies, a tribe of Indian savages prepares to celebrate peace with its European vanquishers. Two officers – Don Alvar, a jealous Spaniard, and Damon, a fickle Frenchman – are rivals for the hand of Zima, the chief's daughter. But she, declaring that the Spaniard loves too much and the Frenchman too little, follows the instincts of a true child of nature and chooses the honourable Indian brave, Adario. Somewhat shamefacedly the Europeans join with the Indians in the ceremony of the Great Pipe of Peace.

With *Les Indes galantes*, the lightweight genre of opéra-ballet was raised to a new level. Fuzelier's libretto, though widely condemned in Rameau's day, can now be seen to have considerable merits. Each entrée has its own distinct character; each tiny plot holds rather more dramatic interest than is usual in works of this sort. Moreover, apart from the prologue, there are no supernatural interventions. Instead, Fuzelier generates much of the necessary visual and dramatic interest from his cleverly chosen exotic locations and the indigenous ceremonial they provide. (Some of the ethnic detail was culled from published reports of recent events or from first-hand experience.) In the process he manages to portray the interaction of and contrast between European and other cultures – not always to the former's advantage, as the final entrée with its lighthearted but moving tribute to the 'noble savage' demonstrates.

Rameau's response to this unusual material is superb, and the opera is surely among his very finest. He brings to *Les Incas* a dramatic intensity no less than that of the tragédies. The passage from the start of the earthquake to the end of the entrée is an almost unbroken sequence of some 350 bars, during which voices and orchestra interact with extraordinary vehemence. The entrée is dominated by Huascar, whose harsh and fanatical but wholly credible character is established with a sureness of touch not found outside *Hippolyte et Aricie*. In the other entrées and the prologue it is the grace and variety of the vocal airs and ballet music that impress most. Appropriately, the entrée *Les sauvages* includes a reworking of Rameau's harpsichord piece *Les sauvages*, itself inspired by the dancing of two American Indians in Paris in 1725, which had involved a peace-pipe dance. The movement, as indeed the whole entrée, was to become one of Rameau's most popular in the 18th century.

RECORDING Poulenard, McFadden, Fouchécourt, Crook, Deletré, Les Arts Florissants, Christie, Harmonia Mundi, 1991

Castor et Pollux

Castor and Pollux

Tragédie en musique in five acts with prologue (2h 45m)
Libretto by Pierre-Joseph Bernard
PREMIERES 24 October 1737, Opéra, Paris; rev. version (no prologue, new Act I and other changes): ?8/?11 June

1754, Opéra, Paris; UK: 27 April 1929, Glasgow (amateur); 1754 version: US: 6 March 1937, Vassar College, New York (concert); UK: 11 October 1981, Covent Garden, London (stage)
CAST Télaïre *s*, Phébé *s*, Castor *t* (*haute-contre*), Pollux *b*, Jupiter *b*, High Priest of Jupiter *t* (*taille*), 3 *s*, 2 *t* (*haute-contre*), 2 *b*; (additional soloists, *s*, *t* (*haute-contre*) and *b*, added in 1754); *satb* chorus of arts and pleasures, Spartans, athletes, priests, people, celestial pleasures, Hebe's retinue, demons, blessed spirits, stars; ballet: graces, arts, pleasures, cupids, athletes, warriors, Spartan women, Hebe's retinue, celestial pleasures, monsters, demons, blessed spirits, stars, planets and constellations

In its choice of subject matter – the brotherly love of the twins Castor and Pollux, the one mortal and the other immortal – this work is unusual, since contemporary French opera normally gave the central place to romantic love. After an initially cool reception, *Castor* was eventually regarded as Rameau's crowning achievement, especially after the triumphant revivals of 1754 and 1764.

SYNOPSIS

The prologue relates to the Peace of Vienna (1736), which ended the Polish War of Succession: Venus and Cupid, at Minerva's bidding, succeed in subduing Mars with the power of love.

Act I: Castor has been killed in battle. As the Spartans mourn, Pollux is persuaded by Telaira to ask his father Jupiter to restore Castor to life. Pollux agrees for love of Telaira, though he knows that she loves only Castor.

Act II: At first Jupiter tries to dissuade Pollux from his mission. He eventually consents to let Castor return from Hades, but on one condition – that Pollux gives up his immortality and take his brother's place there. Pollux selflessly agrees.

Act III: At the mouth of Hades, the spurned Phoebe tries to prevent Pollux from entering. Urged on by Telaira, and with Mercury's help, he braves the demons who bar his way and descends to the Underworld.

Act IV: In Elysium, Castor has found no happiness, for he still longs for Telaira. He is naturally overjoyed when Pollux arrives. Yet, despite the prospect of seeing Telaira again, he cannot bring himself to accept Pollux's sacrifices. He finally agrees to return to earth, but for one day only.

Act V: Reunited with Telaira, Castor holds to his promise despite her pleas and taunts. Eventually relenting, Jupiter restores Pollux to life. For their selflessness he grants both brothers immortality and a place in the firmament.

At the 1754 revival the dramatically irrelevant prologue was omitted, and a new expository first act inserted before the original Act I. To compensate for this, the original Acts III and IV were telescoped into one; at the same time, the libretto was pruned by well over a quarter, the compression achieved largely by reducing the amount of recitative. The resulting libretto, tauter and better paced, is arguably the best Rameau ever set. Apart from the loss of the prologue (some of it, in any case, incorporated into the revised Act IV divertissement), almost all the most memorable music remains – the mourning chorus 'Que tout gémisse'; Telaira's aria 'Tristes apprêts' grudgingly admired by Berlioz; Castor's ethereal but nostalgic soliloquy 'Séjour de l'éternelle paix' to name only a few. In general, too, the substituted music is scarcely inferior to the original: Pollux's monologue 'Nature, Amour' is replaced by an almost equally moving hymn to friendship, 'Présent des dieux'; moreover, we should scarcely suspect from the liveliness, grace and variety of the new *ariettes* and dance movements that their composer was by now over 70.

RECORDINGS 1. 1737 version: Gens, Mellon, Crook, Corréas, Les Arts Florissants, Christie, Harmonia Mundi, 1992; 2. 1754 version: Hall, Whicher,

Ainsworth, Hopkins, Op in Concert, Arcadia Ens, Mallon, Naxos, 2003

Dardanus

Tragédie en musique in five acts with prologue (2h 30m)
Libretto by Charles-Antoine Le Clerc de La Bruère
PREMIERES 19 November 1739, Opéra, Paris; as 'nouvelle tragédie' with three acts rewritten: 23 April 1744; with new alterations: 15 April 1760; UK: February 1973, Queen Elizabeth Hall, London (concert)
CAST Dardanus *t* (*haute-contre*), Iphise *s*, Anténor *b*, Teucer *b*, Isménor *b*, Venus *s*, L'Amour *s*, Arcas *t* (*haute-contre*) added in 1744; 3 *s*, *t* (*haute-contre*), 2 *b*; *satb* chorus of retinue of Venus and Cupid, retinue of Jealousy, warriors, people, magicians, Phrygians, dreams, cupids; ballet: pleasures, Jealousy and her retinue, troubles, suspicions, mortals, warriors, Phrygians, dreams

Despite its initial run of some 26 performances, *Dardanus* was harshly criticized for its absurd plot and abuse of the supernatural (the latter more or less admitted in the libretto). Rameau and La Bruère subsequently revised the work to the extent of giving Acts III, IV and V an entirely new plot. This version, staged in 1744, at first excited little comment; but when revived in 1760 with further, though less extensive, changes, it was rightly acclaimed as one of Rameau's finest achievements.

SYNOPSIS
In Greek legend, Jupiter's son Dardanus was founder of the royal house of Troy. He was assisted in this by the Phrygian king Teucer, whose daughter he then married. La Bruère's libretto invents a stormy prehistory to these events.

Act I: Dardanus is at war with Teucer; at the same time, he has fallen in love with Teucer's daughter Iphise and she with him, though neither knows the other's feelings. Meanwhile Teucer has promised Iphise to a neighbouring prince, Anténor, in return for a military alliance.

Act II: Dardanus obtains from the magician Isménor a magic ring that disguises him as the magician himself. Iphise comes to beg this pseudo-Isménor to exorcize her love for her father's enemy; in so doing, she unwittingly reveals to Dardanus the state of her emotions. Overjoyed at the revelation, Dardanus appears in his own form and declares his own love, to Iphise's consternation and dismay.

Act III: Up to this point the 1739 and 1744 versions have virtually identical plots. The former continues with Dardanus' capture. His enemies' celebrations, however, are interrupted by news that Neptune has sent a sea monster to avenge this imprisonment of a son of Jupiter. Anténor resolves to combat the monster.

Act IV: By now, Dardanus has escaped. In his sleep he is visited by Venus and her attendant Dreams, who exhort him to slay the monster. When he eventually does so, Dardanus rescues Anténor and takes advantage of the latter's gratitude to extract a promise that Iphise be allowed to refuse Anténor's hand.

Act V: After Teucer reveals Neptune's decree that Iphise should marry whoever vanquishes the monster, Anténor is eventually forced to concede to Dardanus. Venus descends to celebrate the marriage.

The last three acts of the 1744 and later versions involve fewer supernatural interventions.

Act III: The jealous Anténor devises a plan to murder the now-captive Dardanus without appearing to be the perpetrator.

Act IV: Isménor visits Dardanus' cell and foretells his rescue but warns that his liberator will instead become the victim. Consequently, when Iphise gives Dardanus the chance to escape, he refuses. It is Anténor, remorseful and now mortally wounded, who eventually makes possible Dardanus' escape. In the ensuing battle (represented as an entr'acte between Acts IV and V) Dardanus defeats Teucer.

Act V: The king defiantly refuses to give him Iphise's hand. It is only when the despairing hero asks to be struck down with his own sword that Teucer relents. As in the original, Venus descends to celebrate the union.

In purely musical terms, the first version of *Dardanus* is without doubt one of Rameau's most inspired creations. The two superb ceremonies in Acts I and II – the first where Teucer and Anténor pledge allegiance and prepare for battle, the second where Isménor displays his occult powers by changing day into night – contain music of astonishing power, at times almost frightening in its intensity. The dream sequence, Iphise's two tortured monologues, her consultation with the pseudo-Isménor, and the scene where Dardanus slays the monster, are all among Rameau's very best. The main problem with this version is that the momentum generated by such passages is continually sapped by the plot's ill-motivated twists and turns and by what come to seem increasingly puerile supernatural happenings.

In simplifying the plot and eliminating the supernatural excesses, La Bruère brings to the drama much greater human interest. The action now focuses far more on the conflicting emotions of the principal characters. Musically, it is true, the revision entails the removal of many beauties, among them the dream sequence, the monster scenes and Iphise's second monologue. (Her first monologue is drastically curtailed, too.) But the prologue and Acts I and II, with their two great ceremonies, remain largely intact, while the considerable quantity of new music generally maintains the high quality of the original. Especially notable is Dardanus' F minor prison monologue, with its amazingly bold bassoon obbligato, wonderfully contrasted with the luminous music for Isménor that immediately follows.

For all its dramatic superiority, the 1744 version has not been revived in modern times, largely because no modern edition exists. (Only the passages where it differs from the original appear in *Oeuvres complètes*.) Yet it is easily the equal of *Castor* and *Les Boréades* if not of *Hippolyte et Aricie*.

RECORDING Gens, Delunsch, Ainsley, Courtis, Smythe, Naouri, Musiciens du Louvre, Minkowski, Archiv, 1998: 1739 version, plus 2 arias from 1744 version

Platée

Plataea

Comédie lyrique in three acts with prologue (2h 15m)
Libretto by Adrien-Joseph Le Valois d'Orville, after the play *Platée, ou Junon jalouse* by Jacques Autreau
PREMIERES 31 March 1745, La Grande Ecurie, Versailles; with text rev. by Ballot de Sovot: 4 February 1749, Opéra, Paris; UK: 4 October 1983, Sadler's Wells, London; US: 24 May 1987, Dock Street Theater, Charleston
CAST Thespis *t* (*haute-contre*), Thalie *s*, L'Amour *s*, Platée *t* (*haute-contre*), Cithéron *b*, La Folie *s*, Momus *t* (*taille*), Clarine *s*, Jupiter *b*, Junon *s*, 3 *s*, *t* (*haute-contre*), 2 *b*; *satb* chorus of satyrs, maenads, frogs, nymphs, retinue of Momus, Mercury and Cithéron; ballet: satyrs, maenads, harvesting peasants with their wives and children, nymphs, aquilons of the North Wind, retinue of Momus, Mercury and Cithéron, Folly's retinue, dryads, graces, country-dwellers

Comedy had traditionally played little part in French opera. Lully soon eliminated comic episodes from his tragédies; from then until the appearance of the present work, only a handful of operas had comic themes. That for *Platée* is the mock marriage between the god Jupiter and an ugly marsh nymph. As such, it seems grotesquely ill-suited to the occasion for which it was commissioned – the wedding of the Dauphin and the evidently unattractive Spanish princess Maria Teresa – though it was well enough received at the time. Once transferred in modified form to the Paris Opéra in 1749, it became one of Rameau's best-loved works and was ultimately regarded by many (including D'Alembert) as his masterpiece.

In Le Valois d'Orville's libretto little more than the outline of Autreau's original play remains.

SYNOPSIS

The prologue, entirely the librettist's invention, is subtitled *La naissance de la Comédie* (*The Birth of Comedy*). Thespis, represented here – unusually – as the inventor of comedy, plans with Momus, god of ridicule, Thalie, Muse of comedy, and L'Amour to teach mortals and gods a moral lesson: they decide to re-enact the episode in which Jupiter cures his wife Juno of jealousy. The comedy itself, the story of which can be traced back to the ancient Greek writer Pausanius, is set throughout in a marsh at the foot of Mount Cithaeron. (It is thus the only multi-act work by Rameau without elaborate scene changes.) Here, with her attendant frogs and cuckoos, lives the marsh nymph Platée who, though incredibly ugly, is convinced of her own charms.

Act I: In consultation with King Cithaeron, Mercury conceives a plan to cure Juno's tiresome jealousy: Jupiter is to court the ludicrous nymph and go through with a mock marriage. Juno, when she is led to uncover the plan, will be made to look foolishly jealous as the object of her husband's 'affections' is revealed.

Act II: In courting Platée, Jupiter undergoes various metamorphoses – as a cloud, a donkey, an owl – to the nymph's consternation and delight. At last he appears in his own form amid a shower of fire. After making amorous advances, he arranges a divertissement in her honour, led by Momus and La Folie, whose followers are dressed respectively as babies and as Greek philosophers.

Act III: By now Juno has been alerted and arrives incognito at the mock wedding. Heavily disguised, Platée is led in on a chariot drawn by two frogs. After an interminable chaconne, danced in *le genre le plus noble*, Momus appears disguised as L'Amour with a ridiculously large bow and quiver. Just as Jupiter is about to pronounce his marriage vows, Juno snatches away Platée's veil . . . and starts to laugh. Mocked by the entire assembly, Platée retreats to her marsh.

Such a description may well give the impression that the humour of *Platée* is rather sick. On the stage, however, that is not how it seems. While we may laugh at Platée's plight, our sympathies are with the nymph throughout. Moreover, the cruelty of laughing at an ugly but hopelessly vain woman is kept at a distance by the role of Platée being sung by a tenor. (This *travesti* role, one of the very few in French operas of the period, was created by the famous *haute-contre* Pierre Jelyotte.) The work's humour comes not just from the extravagant situations but also from wicked parodies of the conventions of serious opera, its descents and transformations, its musical and poetic language. For example, the chaconne that precedes the impatient Platée's marriage is comic not just because of its absurd length or because it is danced in mock-serious style, but because it is misplaced: chaconnes belong at the culmination of the final divertissement. Musical parody takes many forms – exaggerated vocalises, misaccentuations, vocal acrobatics; imitations of frogs, cuckoos, frightened birds, donkey-Jupiter; elaborate pizzicati for La Folie's lyre, double-stoppings for her hurdy-gurdy; even glissandos when Momus presents Platée with L'Amour's gifts (tears, sorrow, cries, languor). The burlesque use of language is seen in Platée's frequent recourse to a frog-like 'Quoi!', her comic alliterations and her colloquial expressions, including the decidedly unoperatic expletive 'Ouffe!'

Yet there is more to *Platée* than a series

of comic effects, genuinely funny though many of them are. Whether mock serious, quirkily descriptive or uninhibitedly gay, Rameau's music is a constant delight. He seems to have relished particularly the chance for elaborate ensembles; those in the prologue and at the ends of Acts II and III have a breadth almost without parallel in his output.

RECORDING Smith, Ragon, De Mey, Le Texier, Françoise Herr Vocal Ens, Musiciens Du Louvre, Minkowski, Erato, 1988

Les Boréades

The Sons of Boreas

Tragédie en musique in five acts (2h 45m)
Libretto attributed to Louis de Cahusac
PREMIERES unperformed in Rameau's lifetime; 16 September 1964, Maison de la Radio, Paris (extracts; concert); 21 July 1982, Théâtre de l'Archevêche, Aix-en-Provence; UK: 14 April 1975, Queen Elizabeth Hall, London (concert); 21 November 1985, Royal Academy of Music, London (stage; abridged); 21 April 1993, Mayfair Suite, Bullring Shopping Centre, Birmingham (stage)
CAST Alphise *s*, Abaris *t* (*haute-contre*), Sémire *s*, Borilée *bar*, Calisis *t* (*haute-contre*), Adamas *b*, Borée *b*, 4 *s*, *b*; *satb* chorus of pleasures and graces, Alphise's retinue, Bactrian people, muses, arts, subterranean winds, Boreas' retinue; ballet: pleasures and graces, priests, Alphise's retinue, Oritheia and her companions, Boreas' disciples, Bactrian people, north winds, hours, seasons, zephyrs, talents

Until recently, *Les Boréades* was widely believed to have been in rehearsal at the Paris Opéra at the time of Rameau's death but then abandoned for reasons unknown. Archival evidence now reveals that the work was rehearsed more than a year earlier, in April 1763, and that it was probably intended for performance not at the Opéra but before the court at Choisy. Why this remarkable opera should have been put aside can only be guessed at, though it must have to do with changing musical tastes in the 1760s, with the opposition of Madame de Pompadour and others at court, with the fact that the music presents formidable problems, perhaps even with the burning down of the Açadémie Royale's theatre in the very month of the rehearsals. It has been suggested, too, that since the libretto includes elements that could be construed as Masonic (an initiatory voyage, a magic talisman and various Apollonian symbols) the opera might have been considered politically subversive.

SYNOPSIS

The action, set in the ancient kingdom of Bactria, concerns the love between the Queen Alphise and a noble foreigner, Abaris, who has been brought up by Adamas, high priest of Apollo, in ignorance of his origin. The obstacle to their love is a tradition that the queen must marry a descendant of Boreas, god of the north wind. Rather than lose Abaris by marrying one of the 'Boréades', Alphise abdicates, much to her subjects' surprise and regret and the god's displeasure. During a violent tempest, she is carried off to his domain among the subterranean winds. The efforts of Abaris to rescue her are assisted by the interventions of the muse Polyhymnia and the god Apollo; Abaris also has the magic arrow that Cupid had given to Alphise. Eventually Apollo reveals that Abaris is his child by a nymph daughter of Boreas, and may therefore marry Alphise with impunity.

While the libretto is ascribed to Cahusac by two independent 18th-century writers, there are problems in accepting the attribution unreservedly. The work takes considerable (and uncharacteristic) liberties with its Classical source material, while compared with *Zoroastre* (1749) it makes little of the Masonic elements. Moreover, the hymns and ballets figurés, which are such a feature of Cahusac's work, are each represented by a single, undeveloped example; at the same time, the presence of three simile arias and other anomalies have few parallels in his other works, though such arias may be found, for example, in Marmontel's libretti. It is, however, always possible that the text was among Cahusac's papers at the time of his death (1759) and that the perceived anomalies result from subsequent tinkerings by others.

That said, the libretto is among the more serviceable of those that Rameau set. Despite its overuse of the supernatural and reduction of hero and heroine to the status of mere agents in a battle between superior forces, it is paced in such a way that successive stages of the plot generate increasing dramatic momentum; this is especially so from the moment of the queen's unexpected abdication in Act III, through the tempest that dominates the rest of that act and most of the next, to the torture scenes in Act V. Rameau takes full advantage of this to produce a work with greater forward drive than any of his others, exemplified by the way his fearsome tempest continues straight through from the middle of Act III well into Act IV (and, less innovatory, his overture into the first scene). Among musical highlights in a particularly inventive score are the simile arias 'Un horizon serein' (Act I), Abaris' despairing monologue 'Lieux désolez' and the descent of Polyhymnia and the Muses (Act IV), this last one of the most ravishing single movements in the whole of his output.

RECORDING Smith, Rodde, Langridge, Aler, Lafont, Cachemaille, Le Roux, Monteverdi Ch, EBS, Gardiner, Erato, 1982
OTHER OPERATIC WORKS *Samson*, (1735) (lost); *Les Fêtes d'Hébé, ou Les talents lyriques*, 1739; *La princesse de Navarre*, 1745; *Les fêtes de Polymnie*, 1745; *Le temple de la Gloire*, 1745; *Les fêtes de Ramire*, 1745; *Les fêtes de l'Hymen et de l'Amour, ou Les dieux d'Egypte*, 1747; *Zaïs*, 1748; *Pigmalion*, 1748; *Les surprises de l'Amour*, 1748; *Naïs*, 1749; *Zoroastre*, 1749; *La guirlande, ou Les fleurs enchantées*, 1751; *Acante et Céphise, ou La sympathie*, 1751; *Linus*, (1752) (inc.); *Daphnis et Eglé*, 1753; *Lysis et Délie*, (1753) (lost); *Les sibarites*, 1753; *La naissance d'Osiri, ou La fête Pamilie*, 1754; *Anacréon* (i), 1754; *Anacréon* (ii), 1757; *Les Paladins*, 1760; *Io*, (n.d.) (inc.); *Zéphyre*, (n.d.) 1967; *Nélée et Myrthis*, (n.d.) 1974

G.S.

Maurice Ravel

Joseph Maurice Ravel; *b* 7 March 1875, Ciboure, France; *d* 28 December 1937, Paris

Ciboure is by the Pyrenees, and though Ravel's family moved to Paris when he was three months old he kept a lifelong affection for things Basque (and Spanish) through his mother. His father was a Swiss civil engineer. It is hard not to see familial traces in the composer's love of polished, ingenious mechanisms, and the frequent Spanish irruptions in his music. They are highly characteristic features of his scores – most obviously, of *L'heure espagnole* – and yet they are marginal. Ravel's basic musical language developed from his revered teacher Fauré, with vital influences from Chabrier, Debussy (up to *Pelléas*), early Satie and the New Russian School: Rimsky-Korsakov, Borodin, Balakirev. The oft-told story of his repeated failures to win the Prix de Rome at the Paris Conservatoire (at the fifth and last attempt, in 1905, he was rejected at the preliminary round, and a great scandal ensued) is misleading. Ravel was no revolutionary young Turk challenging the Establishment, but an inquiring, fastidiously original composer who was neither interested in the kind of academic exercise prescribed for that competition nor particularly good at it.

The piquant 'injustice' of the final rebuff lay in the fact that his *Jeux d'eau*, his String Quartet and the *Shéhérezade* songs were already widely admired; the terms of the Prix de Rome, however, excluded independent works from consideration.

That failure cannot have wounded him gravely, since his most prolific period followed at once. (Of all petits-maîtres Ravel was among the least prolific: rigorously self-critical throughout his 40-odd years of composing, he published only a few hours' worth of music.) Between 1905 and 1911 came the *Introduction and Allegro* for harp and ensemble, the *Sonatine*, *Miroirs*, *Gaspard de la nuit* and the *Valses nobles et sentimentales* for piano, the suite *Ma mère l'oye* for piano duet, the *Rapsodie espagnole*, the first sketches for *Daphnis et Chloé*, many songs, and *L'heure espagnole*. Ravel's name is not popularly associated with opera, no doubt because the two he completed are brief and therefore awkward to programme, and they afford no spectacular vocal or dramatic opportunities to their leading singers. In fact his thoughts turned early to the medium. In the late 1890s he had planned an opera on Maeterlinck's *Intérieur*, as well as a Hoffmann operetta *Olympia* (the robot doll of Offenbach's celebrated piece), and later – like several other composers of the day – a fairy opera after Hauptmann's *Die versunkene Glocke* (*La cloche engloutie* or *The Sunken Bell*). His sketches were not wasted, for it seems that Dr Coppelius' entry music from *Olympia* was recycled as the prelude to *L'heure espagnole*, and much later some musical ideas for *La cloche engloutie* were transferred to *L'enfant et les sortilèges*.

After the successful premieres of *L'heure espagnole* (though one critic did call it 'a mildly pornographic vaudeville') and *Daphnis* (with Nijinsky), Diaghilev asked Ravel to collaborate with Stravinsky in an unexpected operatic task. They were to produce a reorchestrated version of *Khovanshchina*, which Musorgsky had left unfinished and Rimsky-Korsakov had adapted according to his own lights. The new version was completed and performed by the Ballets Russes in 1913; unfortunately, the score has never been retrieved. Then came the First World War, in which Ravel did non-combatant military service. During that time the novelist Colette agreed to write a libretto for the Paris Opéra, and hit upon Ravel as a suitable composer for the divertissement she conceived. It took him some time to agree; he was profoundly depressed by the war, and by the death of his mother in 1917, and his glum response to Colette's original title, *Ballet pour ma fille*, was that he *had* no daughter. Eventually he warmed to the project, but his *Tombeau de Couperin* and *La valse* were completed long before *L'enfant et les sortilèges* was finally staged, with de Sabata conducting and Balanchine as maître de ballet.

Ravel's health was declining. After *L'enfant* he composed, slowly, the newly austere *Chansons madécasses* and his Violin Sonata, then the *Boléro* for the dancer Ida Rubinstein and the two concertos for piano. Between the premieres of the latter, he was involved in the taxi-cab accident that may have triggered his final collapse. He accepted a film commission to write three songs for Chaliapin as Don Quixote (he had actually begun contemplating an opera after Cervantes's novel), but was late in fulfilling it. Those songs were Ravel's last music; in summer 1933 his muscular coordination began to fail, and aphasia set in. He became unable to compose, and in the sad four years left to him could manage only some bare sketches for *Morgiane*, another ballet meant for Ida Rubinstein.

L'heure espagnole

Spanish Time

Comédie musicale in one act
(introduction and 21 scenes) (50m)
Libretto by Franc-Nohain
(Maurice-Etienne Legrand), after his
own comedy (1904)
Composed 1907–9

PREMIERES 19 May 1911, Opéra-Comique, Paris; UK: 24 July 1919, Covent Garden, London; US: 5 January 1920, Chicago
CAST Concepción *s*, Gonzalve *t*, Torquemada *t* (*Trial*), Ramiro *bar* (*baryton-Martin*), Don Inigo Gomez *b*

Franc-Nohain was surprised when Ravel asked permission to set his highly improper, cod-poetical vaudeville to music, and when at last Ravel came to play and sing him the result, the playwright's cautious reaction was that it went on rather long. In fact the composer set his own Spanish time with expert precision and crisp habanera rhythms; there are no longueurs, except in performances that seek to humanize the characters by letting them moon over their recitatives. Ravel's score expanded Franc-Nohain's comic analogy between wound-up automata and erotically driven people much further than the text could do alone, and yet kept the sung lines natural and colloquial enough to incur some disapproving sniffs in 1911 (as with his Jules Renard songs four years earlier, the *Histoires naturelles*). The vocal writing permits the ripe double meanings to be lucid, but they are never crudely underlined. Nor are the characters guyed: besides its poise and verve, the score often glows with the famous Ravel *tendresse*.

SYNOPSIS
Eighteenth-century Toledo. A muscular mule-driver, Ramiro, takes his broken watch to the shop of the clockmaker Torquemada. But it is Thursday, the day when Torquemada regulates all the town clocks; he must leave Ramiro to wait, and his wife Concepción to entertain him. Both are embarrassed: Ramiro because he is shy ('Les muletiers n'ont pas de conversation'), Concepción because she is expecting her poet lover imminently. Her husband has promised her either of two large grandfather clocks, and it occurs to her to beg the muleteer to carry one up to her bedroom. Delighted to have a task, he goes off with it just as Gonzalve drifts in, warbling poetically.

To Concepción's frustration, he is still warbling when Ramiro comes back. She declares a sudden preference for the other clock, and dispatches the muleteer to retrieve the first one; meanwhile she conceals her poet in the second, whereupon the stout banker Don Inigo Gomez arrives unannounced to court her. Ramiro, back again with the first clock, duly carries off the second clock with negligent ease and Concepción as anxious escort. Don Inigo, abandoned, decides that flirtatious whimsy is the card to play, and squeezes himself into the first clock – but prudently shuts the door when Ramiro returns alone, musing on the mysteriousness of woman. Suddenly Concepción reappears in a temper, demanding the instant removal of the second clock. While the muleteer obeys, Don Inigo pursues his lascivious strategy with the lady; the upshot is that Ramiro, all unawares, is soon hefting the first clock upstairs once more with Concepción on his heels.

The dismissed poet sings an effusive farewell to his clock dungeon, but hides again as Ramiro comes back, still musing romantically. Concepción descends in a fury – the first clock must go. While Ramiro fetches it, she voices her bitter disappointment ('Oh! la pitoyable aventure!'): Gonzalve would do nothing but rhapsodize, and now Don Inigo is inextricably stuck in his clock. Ramiro returns bearing that clock, ready and eager for the next job. She looks at him with new eyes, and proposes going upstairs again 'sans horloge . . .'. Torquemada comes home to find two gentlemen occupying his clocks and explaining brightly that they are interested customers. By the time his wife reappears, much happier, their reluctant purchases are settled. It takes Ramiro to heave Don Inigo out of his expensive prison, and he also promises to tell Concepción the time each morning when he comes by with his mules. In a final quintet, everybody agrees on a Boccaccian moral: through plain efficiency, the muleteer eventually gets his turn.

The glittering surface of Ravel's score, all Spanish snap with horological icing (continual chimes high and low, a mechanical cuckoo and clock, even three metronomes ticking throughout the prelude), disguises its pure musical invention. Ravel expressly intended to write something more like Italian buffo than French opérette, but what he devised was *sui generis* – an elegantly comic piece for orchestra and singers, through-composed in patterns as intricately and ingeniously connected as those of any watch. The music is aptly laden with displacement jokes: just as the rigorously ticking metronomes in the prelude are all at odds, so the brisk Hispanic dance-rhythms are prone to fractures, the 'popular' harmonies derailed by post-Fauré sophistication, Gonzalve's exquisite little effusions rudely interrupted, and an impossibly low note demanded from Don Inigo by the finale is supplied by a helpful double bassoon. Ravel's Spanishry here surely owes far less to his maternal memories than to Albéniz, whose music he adored (and who died in the year Ravel completed the opera).

Recent French operas had embraced the Wagnerian leitmotif method to a fault, and Ravel extends it here to absurdity. Don Inigo is identified by a pompous fanfare of short brays, Gonzalve purely by his constant mimicking of effete fin-de-siècle art song, Ramiro by a lusty rhythm on timpani – but in his two dreamy fantasies, he is also allotted the most richly developed music.

No tag is attached to Concepción, the only character who is both clever and sensible. The music for the gentle Torquemada, to whom perhaps the situation is perfectly clear and the outcome perfectly satisfactory, is of a piece with the tintinnabulating serenity of his shop. That, in turn, is not so very far removed from the magical garden of *L'enfant et les sortilèges*.

RECORDINGS 1. Duval, Hérent, Giraudeau, Vieuille, Clavensy, Paris Op Comique O, Cluytens, EMI, 1953; 2. E. Laurence, Sénéchal, Raffalli, G. Quilico, Loup, Nouvel O Philharmonique, Jordan, Erato, 1985

L'enfant et les sortilèges

The Child and the Sorceries

Fantaisie lyrique in two parts (45m)
Libretto by Colette (Sidonie-Gabrielle Colette)
Composed 1920–25
PREMIERES 21 March 1925, Salle Garnier, Monte Carlo; US: 19 September 1930, San Francisco; UK: 3 December 1958, Town Hall, Oxford
CAST The Child *ms*, Maman *c*, Louis XV chair *s*, Chinese Cup *mc*, Fire/Princess/Nightingale *light s*, Little Old Man (Arithmetic)/Tree Frog *t*, Cat *ms*, Dragonfly *ms*, Bat *s*, Little Owl *s*, Squirrel *ms*, Shepherdess *s*, Shepherd *c*, Armchair *b chantante*, Grandfather Clock *bar*, Teapot *t*, Tom Cat *bar*, Tree *b*; children's chorus of Settle, Sofa, Ottoman, Wicker Chair and Numbers; *satb* chorus of shepherds, frogs, animals and trees

Both Colette and Ravel were cat-lovers, and the feline duet at the centre of *L'enfant et les sortilèges* was conceived *con amore*. Ravel was undoubtedly pleased to have inanimate objects to animate, too, including a much noisier clock than the ones in *L'heure espagnole*, and he must have imagined the garden of the opera on the model of his own at his recently acquired villa, *Le Belvédère*, in Montfort L'Amaury. It was the composer who tilted Colette's divertissement towards the style of a revue, with her approval: his interest in American popular music had been growing and would surface again in the 'Blues' of the Violin Sonata and in both the piano concertos. (There is a curious likeness between the cup-and-teapot duet in *L'enfant* and Gershwin's 'Our love is here to stay'.) The challenges the opera presents to a producer's imagination are severe; whimsy would be ruinous in the garden scene, and it would be a rare mezzo-soprano indeed who could make a plausible child of 'six or seven years' as prescribed by the text. After seeing a Disney animated film, Ravel's brother exclaimed that *that* must be the way to do *L'enfant et les sortilèges*.

SYNOPSIS

A naughty child, dawdling over his homework, is reproved by his mother. Left alone, he flies into a tantrum and assaults everything in the room, including the family cat. Then, one after another, all the things he has maltreated come to plaintive life: the long-suffering furniture, the broken clock and the tea service, the offended fire in the grate, the printed shepherds from the slashed wallpaper, the princess from his torn story book. He regrets bitterly the lost ending of the tale ('Toi, le coeur de la rose'), but suddenly his neglected arithmetic pops up to challenge him with impossible exercises. By now quite unstrung, he expects even the cat to speak. Instead, it miaows a mock-Wagnerian erotic duet with its mate in the garden: meanwhile the scene revolves from indoors to outdoors.

At first the garden twitters and murmurs with innocent animal voices; but the trees break in to lament their cruel wounds from the child's pocket knife and a dragonfly cries after the mate whom he pinned dead to a wall. A bat grieves for a lost mate too and a squirrel – reliving its cruel captivity – tries to warn a dim frog of omnipresent danger. A utopian wildlife ballet ensues, but at the climax the squirrel addresses a poignant rebuke to the child: 'You caged me for the sake of my beautiful blue eyes, but did you know what they reflected? – The free sky and the wind, and my free brothers!' Chastened, the child feels himself rejected from this harmonious animal realm, and he whimpers for his Maman. At once some unforgiving trees and beasts close in upon him; in the commotion, a small squirrel who has been wounded limps towards the child, who binds the squirrel's paw with a ribbon. The other animals reflect on his instinctive kindness and decide to practise calling 'Maman!' on his behalf. Eventually they manage it in chorus, and a light goes on in the house. As Maman comes to the call, they sing, 'Il est bon, l'enfant, il est sage . . .'. The child holds out his arms to her, then the opera is suddenly over.

Ravel's score is far more intricately constructed than it pretends to be, with disguised connections between seemingly disparate numbers. There are interesting echoes, too: obviously from *Le jardin féerique* of *Ma mère l'oye* in the benedictory final chorus, more subtly from the Violin and Cello Sonata in the princess's opening monologue – and the winding oboe duet that starts the opera and returns reassuringly at the end suggests a delicate shadow of Musorgsky's 'Promenade' in his *Pictures at an Exhibition*. Maman first enters on the same sighing cadence that closes the opera. Two matching modulations, among the most poignantly beautiful in all Ravel's music, adorn the squirrel's plaint (after 'Sais-tu ce qu'ils reflétaient, mes beaux yeux?') and the climax of the farewell chorus.

There are extraordinary and bewitching sounds from the orchestra pit throughout, as well as a prominent piano, which ranges from furious arpeggios to plonking revue-style accompaniments. Ravel wanted it equipped with a *luthéal*, apparently a device for altering and distorting the timbre of the instrument in various ways (he wanted it for his gypsy rhapsody *Tzigane* as well); as far as anyone knows, it is now extinct.

RECORDINGS 1. Sautereau, Angelici, Scharley, Michel, French Nat RCh & O, Bour, Testament, 1947; 2. Alliot-Lugaz, Vidal, Sénéchal, Huttonlocher, Suisse Romande Ch & O, Jordan, Erato, 1986

D.M.

Aribert Reimann

b 4 March 1936, Berlin

Reimann's parents were musicians; his father was an organist and Bach specialist, and his mother, a concert singer and voice teacher. As a child he experienced the Second World War in Berlin at first hand; a brother was killed in a bombing raid and the family home was subsequently destroyed. In 1945 he fled with his parents before the advancing Russian troops. Later he experienced the desolation of the first post-war years, alleviated only in 1949 by a period spent in Stockholm. By the age of ten he had composed some first songs and piano pieces; after completing his schooling he studied composition with Boris Blacher and Ernst Pepping in Berlin from 1955 to 1960. There followed periods of study in Vienna and at the Villa Massimo in Rome. An extremely fine pianist, Reimann is in great demand as soloist and lieder accompanist.

A song-cycle with chorus and orchestra, *Lieder auf der Flucht*, and a piano sonata, both dating from 1957, were Reimann's first published works. An extensive list of subsequent compositions includes a cello concerto, two piano concertos, *Variations* for orchestra and a substantial string trio. However, Reimann's output is predominantly vocal and displays a catholic taste in poets (Celan, Byron, Shelley, Joyce, Rilke, Louize Labé, e. e. cummings). His choral works include a cantata, *Verrà la morte* (1966), and a *Requiem* (1982). He has also composed two ballets, *Die Vogelscheuchen* (1970, scenario by Günter Grass) for large orchestra (a revision of *Stoffreste*, 1957), and *Chacun sa chimère* for tenor and chamber orchestra (1981). In Germany he has received several major prizes, while the opera *Lear* has brought him worldwide recognition.

Having spent many hours accompanying his mother's voice lessons, Reimann acquired a unique understanding of singing technique. Like earlier opera composers, he rarely creates new roles until the premiere has been cast, tailoring his vocal writing to the specific qualities of the singers chosen. His seven operas are distinguished above all by their intense and brooding qualities, a tendency to sustained hysterical outbursts, complex textures and dark colours. Reimann's childhood experiences have influenced him in his frequent choice of pessimistic or apocalyptic texts.

Lear

Opera in two parts (2h 15m)
Libretto by Claus H. Henneberg, after the play *King Lear* by William Shakespeare (1605)
Composed 1976–8
PREMIERES 9 July 1978, Nationaltheater, Munich; US: 12 June 1981, War Memorial Opera House, San Francisco; UK: 24 January 1989, Coliseum, London
CAST King Lear *bar*, King of France *b-bar*, Duke of Albany *bar*, Duke of Cornwall *t*, Kent *t*, Gloucester *b-bar*, Edgar *ct*, Edmund *t*, Goneril *s*, Regan *s*, Cordelia *s*, Fool *spoken role*, servant *t*, knight *spoken role*; *tb* chorus of followers of Lear and Gloucester, soldiers, servants

Hearing a performance of his Celan cycle (1971) – 'the dark colour, massive brass agglomerations, concentrated areas in the lower strings' – Reimann became convinced of the possibility of a third opera. 'From then on all the pieces I wrote . . . were paths towards Lear,' he wrote. It was bold indeed to approach an operatic subject that Berlioz, Debussy and, above all, Verdi had contemplated and abandoned, yet the task was made possible by Claus Henneberg's skilful reduction of Shakespeare's drama to its textual bare bones, making full use of ensembles and scenic simultaneity. The German version, based on a translation by Eschenburg, also makes some use of the anonymous *Ballad of King Lear and His Three Daughters*, which served Shakespeare himself as source material.

SYNOPSIS

Part I: Lear abdicates the throne and divides his kingdom between his daughters, Regan and Goneril. Cordelia, who remains silent out of love for her father, is disinherited and married off to the King of France. Edgar, son of Gloucester, is banished on a false charge of plotting to kill his father. Kent attaches himself to Lear as faithful servant, but Goneril and Regan drive their father away. In a ferocious storm on the heath Lear becomes demented; Kent and the Fool bring him to a hovel where Edgar, feigning madness, has also taken refuge. Gloucester rescues the king and takes him to Dover.

Part II: Cornwall (Regan's husband) takes Gloucester captive, blinds him and is himself stabbed to death. Edgar leads Gloucester to Dover, where he is reunited with Lear. The king is led to Cordelia in the French camp; both are captured by Edmund and Cordelia is strangled. Goneril poisons Regan but, when Edmund is killed by Edgar in single combat, she commits suicide. Lamenting over the corpse of Cordelia, Lear dies of grief.

The strength of *Lear* lies primarily in Reimann's delineation of character. He exploits every musical resource of the voice but strictly avoids extraneous vocal effects, hence his roles are approachable by classically trained opera singers. In the interests of clarity, the vocal lines are set in orchestral frames (a 'window' technique derived from Mozart's operatic scoring), while the Fool, a spoken role, is accompanied by string quartet. The complex and frequently aggressive orchestral textures come close to those of Penderecki. There is, however, a considerable difference in the means employed, for in *Lear* every parameter of the sound picture is notated in minutest detail: the strings are divided into 48 separate parts, rhythmic structures are strictly specified (except, on occasion, in the voice parts), clusters are exactly notated, while quarter-tones are employed to compress the harmony still further.

Dietrich Fischer-Dieskau was the moving force behind *Lear* and the eloquent first interpreter of the title role. Since its highly successful premiere the work has been widely accepted as a masterpiece of the post-war German operatic repertoire.

RECORDING Varady, Dernesch, Lorand, Knutson, Götz, Fischer-Dieskau, Nöcker, Boysen, Bavarian State Op Ch & O, Albrecht, DG, 1978 (live)
OTHER OPERATIC WORKS *Ein Traumspiel*, 1965; *Melusine*, 1971; *Die Gespenstersonate*, 1984; *Troades*, 1986; *Das Schloss*, 1992; *Bernada Albas Haus*, 2000

A.B.

Nikolay Rimsky-Korsakov

Nikolay Andreyevich Rimsky-Korsakov; *b* 18 March 1844, Tikhvin, nr Novgorod, Russia; *d* 21 June 1908, Lyubensk, nr St Petersburg, Russia

By the time Anton Rubinstein founded the St Petersburg Conservatory in 1862, four young men had joined a circle dominated by the pianist–composer Mily Balakirev: César Cui, Musorgsky, Borodin and, the youngest of the group, Nikolay Rimsky-Korsakov. All had originally been destined for careers other than music, but were persuaded to compose by the force of their mentor's magnetic personality. Balakirev's circle was nicknamed *moguchaya kuchka* or Mighty Handful by their ardent supporter, the connoisseur and critic Vladimir Stasov.

In the early 1860s Balakirev started the 17-year-old naval cadet Rimsky on a full-scale symphony, but before it was completed the latter had to interrupt his studies, sailing on a lengthy cruise to the New World. It was not until after his return to St Petersburg in 1865 and the completion of a second symphony based on the legend of Antar, that he attempted his first opera, *The Maid of Pskov*.

After a change to a more sympathetic conservatory director, Rimsky joined the staff as a professor of practical composition and instrumentation in 1871. (He resigned his naval commission in 1873, and was instead appointed to the part-time civil post of inspector of naval bands.) He studied Tchaikovsky's harmony treatise avidly and immersed himself in academic music, writing a number of fugues and chamber works (of which Balakirev thoroughly disapproved), and getting to know pre-19th-century music. Balakirev's insistence, in 1876, that Rimsky should assist him with the preparation of Glinka's operas for publication helped turn his own thoughts back to opera, though the academic experience he had gained could not be forgotten. His own most lyrical operas, *May Night* and *The Snow Maiden*, soon followed.

After Musorgsky's death in 1881, Rimsky set about arranging and completing the unfinished music for performance and publication. By the time he wrote the three great orchestral pieces of the late 1880s (*Capriccio espagnol*, *Scheherazade* and the *Russian Easter Festival* overture), Rimsky's already assured orchestral technique was matched by his compositional virtuosity. After hearing Wagner's *Ring* in 1889 he determined to concentrate on writing opera. Relations with Balakirev (known for his intransigence) became increasingly strained, and he would have nothing to do with any of Rimsky's later operas; the two men broke off relations in the early 1890s.

Between 1889 and his death – a period of less than two decades – besides a prologue for *The Maid of Pskov*, Rimsky wrote eleven operas which are as wide-ranging as they are numerous. Many of them contain exceptionally fine music, and their neglect in the West (with the exception of *The Golden Cockerel*) is unwarranted. In his performances of some of them, Valery Gergiev and his Kirov troupe have shown just how successful they can be. Acquaintance with them would help to remove the stereotyped image of Rimsky-Korsakov that is prevalent outside Russia; it would also reveal the full extent of the indebtedness to his teacher of Rimsky's pupil Stravinsky, as exemplified in the latter's music up to *Les Noces* and beyond. Most of Rimsky's operas are based on Russian topics and contain folk material, and he found fantastic or mythological subjects congenial. But he was much more than a master artificer, for realistic and other elements are often satisfactorily dealt with too.

May Night

Maiskaya noch'

Opera in three acts (2h 15m)
Libretto by the composer, after the comic short story in the volume *Evenings on a Farm near Dikanka* by Nikolay Gogol (1831–2)
Composed 1878–9
PREMIERES 21 January 1880, Mariinsky Theatre, St Petersburg; UK: 26 June 1914, Drury Lane, London
CAST The Mayor *b*, Levko *t*, Hanna *ms*, Pannochka *s*, Mayor's sister-in-law *ms*, Kalenik *bar*, Distiller *t*, 3 water sprites 2 *s*, *ms*; *satb* chorus of villagers and water sprites

In basing his opera on Gogol's story, Rimsky abandoned the dramatic realism of his previous opera, *The Maid of Pskov*. With Balakirev, he had been editing the operas of Glinka, and the score is indebted to that composer in many ways, especially to his *Ruslan and Lyudmila*.

SYNOPSIS

Act I: The village Mayor disapproves of his son Levko's love for Hanna, since he wants her himself. Horrified to learn that his father is his rival, Levko gathers together a band of village lads who sing a mocking song outside the Mayor's house.

Act II: In the confusion that follows this performance, the Mayor's sister-in-law is captured in error and bundled into prison. She chides the Mayor, saying his philanderings are common knowledge in the village. He eventually calms her and restores order.

Act III: Levko sits on the shores of a nearby lake singing of his love for Hanna. Suddenly *rusalki* (water sprites) appear. Their leader, Pannochka, asks Levko to identify a witch from among them (this was Pannochka's cruel stepmother in a former mortal life, who drove Pannochka to drown herself). He succeeds and, in gratitude for being released from the evil spell, Pannochka gives Levko a document. The illiterate Mayor, when he sees it, believes this to be a decree from the Commissar sanctioning Levko's marriage to Hanna and reluctantly agrees to the wedding.

There are some excellent comic episodes, including the Mayor's ridiculous wooing of Hanna and, later on, his interruption of the reading of the 'Commissar's' letter and the bitchy chatter of his sister-in-law depicted by bustling semiquavers. Excellent folk choruses include the finale of Act I, in which Levko eggs on the villagers to play practical jokes on his father, to a driving orchestral accompaniment (piano and harp), which imitates his vigorous strumming on the bandora. The stylized musical patterns employed for the fantastic episodes are more highly organized than the rest of the material. The opera's head motif, which occurs in its most characteristic form at the opening of Act III, is strikingly similar to the opening of Weber's *Oberon*.

RECORDING Erastova, Borisova, Nam, Kulko, Nikolsky, Bolshoi Th Ch & O, Lazarev, Capriccio, 1994

The Snow Maiden

Snegurochka

Spring fairy tale in a prologue and four acts (3h 15m)
Libretto by the composer after the play, based on a folk tale, by Aleksandr Nikolayevich Ostrovsky (1873)
Composed 1880–81; rev. *c.*1895
PREMIERES 10 February 1882, Mariinsky Theatre, St. Petersburg; US: 5 January 1922, Seattle; UK: 12 April 1933, Sadler's Wells, London
CAST Snegurochka *s*, Lel' *ms*, Kupava *s*, Tsar Berendey *t*, Mizgir *bar*, Spring *ms*, Frost *b*, Bobyl' *t*, Bobylikha *ms*, Woodsprite *t*, Bermyata *b*, 2 Heralds *t*, *b*, Carnival dummy *b*, Page *ms*; *satb* chorus of peasants, birds, flowers, blind minstrels, boyars and their wives; dancers

When Ostrovsky's play was first produced in 1873, it boasted an extensive incidental score by Tchaikovsky, who regarded it as one of his favourite works. At that time, Rimsky was still under the influence of Dargomizhsky's ideals of realist opera but, six years later, he reread the play and in his memoirs, *My Musical Life*, wrote: 'its wonderful poetic beauty had become evident to me.' *The Snow Maiden* was sketched in a continuous burst of inspiration from 1 June to 12 August 1880.

SYNOPSIS

Prologue: Spring and Frost have a child, Snegurochka, who has a heart of ice. Frost, alarmed by her fondness for the shepherd boy, Lel', worries that she will learn to love, come under the influence of Yarilo the sun god and melt. To avoid this dreaded scenario, she is entrusted to the care of the Woodsprite and taken in by a peasant couple, Bobyl' and Bobylikha.

Act I: Snegurochka takes a platonic interest in the warm-hearted Lel', but he prefers Kupava, who is betrothed to a rich merchant, Mizgir. He in turn falls in love with Snegurochka and vows to win her.

Act II: Tsar Berendey is worried that Yarilo is offended, as the springs are getting colder. Kupava complains of Mizgir's behaviour to the tsar and his heralds summon the people. When the tsar sees Snegurochka, he promises to reward the man who can prove her capable of love.

Act III: At a festival in the forest, tumblers dance and Lel' sings. The tsar asks him to choose a girl, and he picks Kupava. Snegurochka is distraught. Mizgir tries to win her by force, but the Woodsprite lures him away into the forest. Snegurochka confronts Kupava and Lel'.

Act IV: At dawn on the first day of summer, Snegurochka summons her mother, Spring, from a lake and asks her for the secrets of love. Spring weaves a spell, but counsels her to stay out of the sun. Mizgir finds Snegurochka and they fall in love. The tsar and his people greet the rising sun, but a ray falls on Snegurochka. She melts and Mizgir throws himself into the lake. The tsar announces that Yarilo is now appeased and all sing a hymn to the sun.

The Snow Maiden was written at one of the happiest times of Rimsky's life and it contains some of his freshest, most consistent and lyrical music, particularly that for Snegurochka herself; Rimsky seems absolutely to identify with this semi-human creation, and her death scene is very moving. A few genuine folk melodies are used, but they blend with Rimsky's own invented folklore. The orchestration is transparent, with much grateful writing for instruments linked with characters: Lel' with clarinet, Snegurochka with flute, and the wise tsar with solo strings. The painting of nature is vivid, from the frost-bound prologue to Spring's chariot drawn by birds, the Woodsprite transforming the forest and the torrential thaw in Act IV – a procession that looks forward to Stravinsky's *Rite of Spring*. The final hymn to the sun, in 11/4 tempo, has an overwhelming impact. Dramatically, the opera is slow moving and perhaps overcrowded with picturesque and not always relevant incident. But in Rimsky's lifetime *The Snow Maiden* was one of his most popular operas, recognized as a masterpiece by Ostrovsky and even by Tchaikovsky, who overcame his fury at 'his' subject being stolen by another and confessed: 'I was in awe of Rimsky's total mastery.'

RECORDING Zemenkova, Evstatieva, Mineva, Milcheva, Andreyev, Videnov, Bulgarian RCh & SO, Angelov, Capriccio, 1985

Christmas Eve

Noch' pered Rozhdestvom

Opera in four acts (2h 15m)
Libretto by the composer, after the story by Nikolay Gogol (1831)
Composed 1894–5
PREMIERES 10 December 1895, Mariinsky Theatre, St Petersburg; US: 15 December 1977, Indiana University Opera Theater, Bloomington; UK: 24 December 1987, BBC Radio 3; 14 December 1988, Coliseum, London (stage)

Gogol's Ukrainian story tells of the young blacksmith Vakula, son of the witch Solokha, and his endeavours to woo the coquettish Oxana, whose father is a drunken Cossack with a roving eye. Oxana sets Vakula the seemingly impossible task of bringing her the empress's slippers (literally high-heeled leather boots) from St Petersburg. Returning home, Vakula finds four heavy sacks in the kitchen: the sociable Solokha has been receiving visitors – the devil, the mayor, the priest and Oxana's father – each of whom has hidden when the next arrived. Ignorant of their contents, Vakula drags them to the smithy where, after his departure, the villagers open three of them with great relish. The remaining sack Vakula takes with him and, once he realizes its contents, forces the devil to fly with him to St Petersburg, where he succeeds in obtaining the slippers. On his return he finds his efforts have been unnecessary – Oxana loves him anyway.

Tchaikovsky's opera *Vakula the Smith*, revised as *Cherevichki*, was based on the same story, and Rimsky's version, in spite of the effective use of Ukrainian folk intonations, is inferior in characterization and lyricism. In his autobiography Rimsky himself pointed out one of the basic weaknesses: 'In *Christmas Eve* the fantastic and mythological elements are so well developed as to seem to have been foisted upon the light humour and comedy of Gogol's subject to a much greater extent than in *May Night*.' As this implies, the fantastic episodes, which he himself has interpolated into the story, are the most successful in the opera.

RECORDING Shpiller, Kulagina, Tarkhov, Migai, Krasovsky, USSR Ch & O, Golovanov, LYS, 1948

Sadko

Opera-bylina in seven scenes (three or five acts) (3h)
Libretto by the composer and Vladimir Ivanovich Bel'sky, based on a bylina (epic poem) from the 11th-century 'Novgorod cycle'
Composed 1894–6
PREMIERES 7 January 1898, Solodovnikov Theatre, Moscow; US: 25 January 1930, Metropolitan, New York; UK: 9 June 1931, Lyceum, London
CAST Sadko *t*, Princess Volkhova *s*, Sea King *b*, Lyubava *ms*, Nezhata *c*, Sopel *t*, Duda *b*, Old Pilgrim *b*, Viking Merchant *b*, Indian Merchant *t*, Venetian Merchant *bar*, Two elders *t*, *b*; *satb* chorus of merchants, sea-maidens, clowns, people, itinerant friars, soothsayers, sailors, sea creatures; dancers

The subject of *Sadko* came to Rimsky while he was writing *Christmas Eve*, and though he sketched certain passages, he did not start the new work in earnest until *Christmas Eve* was finished. *Sadko* is much superior in inspiration. The opera was rejected at first – Rimsky was out of favour with the Imperial family and had antagonized Napravnik, the chief conductor at the Mariinsky Theatre. But it was taken up by Savva Mamontov, a self-made railway magnate, who had his own private opera company: *Sadko* was a fitting choice for him, with an entrepreneur as the lead role.

SYNOPSIS
Scene 1: Merchants of Novgorod sing of their prosperity. A visiting minstrel, Nezhata, sings of Volkh Vseslavich, a hero from Kiev. The merchants wonder who will sing their praises. Sadko, a gusli-player, arrives, but sings instead of setting sail and selling Russian wares abroad – difficult, as Novgorod has no navigable river. The merchants and clowns pour scorn on Sadko who vows in future to sing to the fishes. Scene 2: By Lake Ilmen at night Sadko sings sadly, attracting a flock of swans who turn into the sea princess Volkhova and her beautiful sisters. He sings for them. Volkhova says that fate decrees she should marry a mortal and tells Sadko to fish in the lake. The Sea King rises from the lake and sends his daughters away. Scene 3: Sadko's wife, Lyubava, who has waited up all night for him, is overjoyed at his return. But Sadko repulses her, full of the previous night's encounter. Scene 4: On the quayside by Lake Ilmen, in a bustling market, everyone laughs at Sadko, who bets his head against the combined wealth of the merchants that he will find golden fish in the lake. When the fish turn into gold bars in full view of all, Sadko is hailed as a hero. He then prepares for his sea journey, inviting three foreign merchants – a Viking, an Indian and a Venetian – to sing about their homelands. Sadko bids farewell and leaves. Scene 5: Twelve years later, Sadko's ship is becalmed. He offers gold to the Sea King, but a human sacrifice is required. Lots are drawn; Sadko loses and sinks to the bottom of the sea while

his ship sails away. Scene 6: In his palace under the ocean the Sea King, when he hears Sadko sing, offers him his daughter's hand in marriage, but the dancing to Sadko's gusli becomes so frenzied that it causes a terrible storm. The Pilgrim, ghost of an old warrior, stops the dance and removes the Sea King's power. Sadko and Volkhova rise to the surface. Scene 7: By Lake Ilmen at dawn, Volkhova sings a sad lullaby in farewell to the sleeping Sadko and turns into a river. Sadko wakes and is reunited with his wife as his ships sail up the new river. Sadko tells the people of his adventures and all sing praises to the Pilgrim, the seas and the Volkhov river.

Rimsky wrote an orchestral 'musical picture' symphonic poem on the subject of *Sadko* (1867, rev. 1869/1892) and material from it, including octatonic scales, provides the basis for the opera's sea music. Along with the intricate orchestration with divided strings, harps and wordless female choruses, this music comes close to the impressionism of Debussy and contrasts with the robust folk-inspired music of the other scenes. Sadko himself is characterized by declamatory chanting, evocative of how the traditional bylini may have sounded when sung. The market scene starts with a huge fresco-like rondo that encompasses people, minstrels, wandering beggars, clowns and soothsayers, and continues with glittering tone-painting for the fish's transformation into gold and the celebrated songs of the three merchants.The full finale of the entire opera comprising Sadko's tale, is often cut – a shame, as the three merchants (incongruously still in Novgorod after 12 years) pit all their songs together in exhilarating counterpoint. The scenes with Sadko's wife, Lyubava, a character added only after Rimsky had finished the score, are noticeably less inspired; this sketchy portrayal of a marriage sits oddly with the grandly epic conception of the rest of the work. *Sadko* has never become a repertoire piece, it is expensive to stage and has an exhausting title role that is upstaged by the Indian Merchant's song and Volkhova's lullaby. It is perhaps best regarded as a pageant, discursive and inconsequential at times, which offers a vital portrait of a mythical Russian past.

RECORDING Tsidipova, Tarasova, Galusin, Grigorian, Gergalov, Minzhilikiev, Alexashkin, Kirov Op Ch & O, Gergiev, Philips, 1993

The Legend of the Invisible City of Kitezh and the Maiden Fevroniya

Skazaniye o onevidimom grade Kitezhe i deve Fevronii

Opera in four acts (six scenes) (3h)
Libretto by Vladimir Ivanovich Bel'sky, based on a conflation of two Russian legends: *Kitezkaya Legenda* (11th century) and the *Saga of the Lady Fevroniya of Murom* from Meledin's Chronicles
Composed 1903–5
PREMIERES 20 February 1907, Mariinsky Theatre, St Petersburg; UK: 30 March 1926, Covent Garden, London (concert); US: 21 May 1932, Ann Arbor (concert); 4 February 1936, Philadelphia (stage); UK: 18 August 1995, Festival Theatre, Edinburgh (stage)
CAST Fevroniya *s*, Prince Yury *b*, Prince Vsevolod *t*, Grishka Kuterma *t*, Feodor Poyarok *bar*, Bedyay *b*, Burunday *b*, Sirin *s*, Alkonost *ms*, Page *c*, Gusli player *b*, Bear leader *t*, Beggar *bar*, 2 well-off people *t*, *b*; *satb* chorus of huntsmen, peasants, people, Tartars

Kitezh is Rimsky's most ambitious opera, though commentators have had problems with its abrupt juxtaposition of mysticism and realism. Rimsky and his librettist, Bel'sky, were in disagreement over its tone – Bel'sky wanting something more contemplative, and Rimsky more action. There are considerable dramatic problems and longueurs. However, the turbulent political and social divides in Russia at the time are mirrored in this juxtaposition of a utopia with the base world of Lesser Kitezh, tellingly personified in the characters of Fevroniya, a child of nature, and the broken alcoholic, Grishka Kuterma, a vivid character without precedent in Rimsky's oeuvre.

SYNOPSIS

Act I: The maiden Fevroniya (of the title) lives in a vast forest, surrounded by animals and birds. A wounded hunter stumbles upon her, and she tends his wounds. Impressed by her piety, he vows to return and marry her. One of his party, Fyodor Poyarok, reveals that he is Prince Vsevolod of Kitezh.

Act II: In the town of Lesser Kitezh two rich townsfolk bribe the drunken Grishka to disrupt the procession bringing Fevroniya to Greater Kitezh. Grishka insults her, but the scene is invaded by Tartars. They capture Fevroniya and force Grishka to lead them to the citadel of Great Kitezh. Fevroniya prays for Kitezh to be made invisible.

Act III, Scene 1: In Great Kitezh Poyarok, blinded by the Tartars, fears mistakenly that Fevroniya is leading the enemy to them. Prince Yury prays, and his son, Vsevolod, leads his retinue off to fight the Tartars. A golden mist descends, rendering the city invisible. Interlude: In the battle near Kerzhenets, Prince Vsevolod is slaughtered. Scene 2: Grishka has led the Tartars to the lakeshore opposite Great Kitezh, but as they cannot see the city they tie him to a tree. Two chieftains, Burunday and Bedyay, fight over Fevroniya. Burunday slays Bedyay. The Tartars fall into a drunken sleep, and Fevroniya releases Grishka, who is driven mad by hearing the bells of Kitezh in his head. He drags Fevroniya into the forest with him just as the Tartars awake and see the reflection of the invisible city of Kitezh in the lake. Terrified, they flee.

Act IV, Scene 1: Deep in the forest at night, Grishka imagines he sees the devil and rushes madly away, leaving Fevroniya alone. The forest transforms into a beautiful landscape of flowers and Alkonost, a bird of paradise, prophesies Fevroniya's death. The ghost of Prince Vsevolod appears and a second bird of paradise, Sirin, promises immortality to him and to Fevroniya. Interlude: Fevroniya and Vsevolod ascend to the invisible city. Scene 2: Great Kitezh has become a paradise inhabited by those killed by the Tartars and protected by the birds. Fevroniya's wedding procession hymn, previously interrupted (in Act II), is completed, but she cannot be truly happy until she has dictated a letter to the lost Grishka, telling him of the miracle and giving him God's blessing.

After the mediocrity of much of Rimsky's music following *Sadko* (*Tsar Saltan* and *Kaschei* excepted), *Kitezh* marks a decisive return to form. Its Christian message is couched in pantheistic terms, which always inspired this composer: Fevroniya's music invokes a real sense of the numinous. Wagnerian influence is explicit, which, with its mystical connotations, led the work to be dubbed 'The Russian *Parsifal*', though other than one cadential motif, reminiscent of the 'Dresden Amen' that Wagner exploits in *Parsifal*, the predominant musical echoes actually derive from the *Ring* – notably the 'Forest Murmurs' from *Siegfried*. Also significantly, this is the first Rimsky score that lacks divisions within the acts. Echoes of Musorgsky abound too, unsurprisingly as Rimsky was then preparing his second revision of Musorgsky's *Boris Godunov*. Rimsky strove for stridency and modernity in certain passages, notably the end of Act III, depicting the Tartars' terror, where the brass tolls like a great bell and the act fades on an unresolved tritone. The mixture of the epic and psychological was uncharted territory for Rimsky, and even though he is stretched beyond his limits at times, the work has a uniquely fascinating flavour, and may very well be his masterpiece.

RECORDING Gorchakova, Marusin, Galusin, Okhotnikov, Kirov Op Ch & O, Gergiev, Philips, 1994 (live)

The Golden Cockerel

Zolotoi petushok

Opera (dramatized fairy tale) in three acts with prologue and epilogue (2h)
Libretto by Vladimir Ivanovich Bel'sky, after the poem by Aleksandr Pushkin (1834)
Composed 1906–7
PREMIERES 7 October 1909, Solodovnikov Theatre, Moscow; UK: 15 June 1914, Drury Lane, London; US: 6 March 1918, Metropolitan, New York
CAST Tsar Dodon *b*, Prince Gvidon *t*, Prince Afron *bar*, General Polkan *b*, Amelfa *c*, Astrologer *t altino*, Queen of Shemakha *s*, Golden Cockerel *s*; *satb* chorus of people, boyars, guards, soldiers, cannoniers, female slaves

The designer of the first production of *The Golden Cockerel* was the Russian fairy-tale illustrator I. Ya. Bilibin, whose cartoon of Tsar Dodon, 'sovereign of the entire earth' contemplating the notion of annexing the moon – a skit on the tsarist expansionism – may well have given Rimsky the idea of using Pushkin's poem as the basis of an opera. Whereas *Tsar Saltan* is Pushkin's longest *skazka*, the ironic *Golden Cockerel*, written three years later, is one of his shortest. This was no disadvantage, since the composer and his librettist Bel'sky (who had also written the libretto for *Tsar Saltan*) were able to expand the original to suit their purpose, adding elements of irony and political satire; for example, the passage in which the astonished tsar asks what the word 'law' means does not occur in Pushkin; new also was the close of Act II, in which the Queen's slaves sing of Dodon, a tsar by rank and dress, but a slave in body and soul.

Russia had just lost the Russo-Japanese war, and the resultant unrest caused the temporary closure of the St Petersburg Conservatory and the suspension of Rimsky for his support of the students. As *The Golden Cockerel* is a satire on incompetence in war, it is not surprising that, after completion of the opera on 11 September 1907, there was trouble with the censor. This may have contributed to the recurrence of the composer's angina, of which he died, never having heard the entire opera (though he was present at concert performances of various short extracts). Perhaps in order to veil the more obvious examples of satire there was obfuscation of the 'meaning' of the tale, but to look for deeper symbolism would be fruitless.

Significantly, the premiere was in Moscow, away from the seat of government, and certain changes were made by the censor. Because some of the parts entail dancing as well as singing, in the Western premiere, on 25 May 1914 in Paris, and in subsequent London performances, Diaghilev's ballet dancers mimed the actions while the singers sat in the theatre boxes, a version originally devised by Fokine for St Petersburg. However, later interpreters of the roles of the Queen and Dodon have been able to cope with the stage business in Act II, and the opera's frequent modern performances are always in Rimsky's authentic version.

SYNOPSIS
Prologue: The Astrologer informs the audience that the fantastic tale it is about to witness has a moral.

Act I: The curtain rises on the palace of the aged Tsar Dodon, with a view of the town in the distance, which includes people walking about and armed guards soundly asleep. With Dodon are his two sons, Gvidon and Afron, General Polkan and assembled boyars. Dodon asks advice on how to counter threatened attack. Each prince in turn makes a futile proposal, which is greeted with rapturous approval by all but the crusty old general. Not knowing how to solve the problem, they suggest the possibility of consulting an augury, and as they quarrel the Astrologer appears. He gives Dodon a golden cockerel, which will crow to predict peace or, as an alarm, point in the direction of the enemy. The delighted Dodon promises the Astrologer he may have anything he wishes as a reward. When the Astrologer asks that Dodon should put this in writing, according to the law, the astonished Tsar exclaims, 'According to the law? What does that word mean? I have never heard of it. In all cases my caprice, my command – that is the law.' The Astrologer withdraws, and Dodon dismisses the boyars, climbs into bed, plays with a parrot and, with the cockerel proclaiming that all is safe, is sung to sleep by his housekeeper Amelfa. Dodon's dreams of a lovely maiden are twice interrupted by the cockerel crowing to raise the alarm. The first time his none too willing sons are sent off at the head of an army, but the second time he dons his rusty armour and, to the cheers of his subjects, himself sets off to war.

Act II: A narrow rocky pass on a misty night. The army has been defeated and among the bodies are those of Gvidon and Afron who have slain each other in the battle. Dodon and Polkan, with their force, lament but cannot avenge the dead, since they do not know where the enemy is. With the dawn, the mists rise to reveal a magnificent tent. Assuming it to belong to the enemy general, they bombard it with singular lack of success. A beautiful maiden emerges and sings an aria in praise of the sun. She tells Dodon that she is the Queen of Shemakha who can conquer all by her beauty. Polkan, who is getting in the way, is dismissed, and she seduces Dodon, eventually prevailing on him to sing and dance, and laughing at his grotesque endeavours. She accepts his hand in marriage and they start for home.

Act III: Back in Dodon's capital the procession enters – one of the most spectacular processional marches in the whole of Russian opera. But the rejoicing is interrupted by the appearance of the Astrologer who now claims his reward – the Queen of Shemakha herself. Dodon tries to excuse himself and offers alternatives; but the aged eunuch insists, stating that he wishes to take a wife. Dodon, enraged, strikes him fiercely with his sceptre and is disconcerted when he dies as a result, but the Queen of Shemakha laughs; when Dodon tries to embrace her she repulses him. Amid dark clouds and thunder, the cockerel suddenly gives a loud crow, flies down from its perch and pecks Dodon on the head. He falls down dead and when the clouds clear the Queen and the cockerel have vanished. The people lament, singing of the virtues of their dead tsar.

Epilogue: The Astrologer asks the audience not to be alarmed by the tragic outcome, for 'the Queen and I were the only living persons in it, the rest – a pale illusion, emptiness . . .'.

The many leitmotifs are used as vivid, descriptive recurrent patterns which are treated to various metamorphoses, resulting in an elaborate fresco of sound. Three of the four most important motifs occur in the prologue. First, that of the golden cockerel, a trumpet call initially juxtaposing the triads of D flat and E major. But this is no mere 'invitation to . . . hear what will presently be enacted' as in *Tsar Saltan*, for it is interwoven into the music in many different places; the second phrase becomes the soothing accompaniment to Dodon's slumbers in Act I and is sung by the frightened chorus after the alarm has been raised. Second, the chromatic motif of the Queen of Shemakha, redolent of the Orient and depicting her insidious beauty, which accompanies not only the Queen herself but also Dodon's dreams in Act I. More importantly, the Queen's motif occurs during the Astrologer's music in Act I, thus cleverly revealing that there is a subtle connection between him and the Queen. And third, the Astrologer's own motif of unrelated arpeggiated chords tinkled out by the glockenspiel and the harps in their highest register. Together with the very high tenor register of his voice, this depicts the brittleness of his old age. Finally, the most important of Tsar Dodon's prosaic motifs occurs at the very beginning of Act I and is adroitly incorporated, in inverted form, in the march at the end of that act. There is no important new material in Act III; Rimsky skilfully employs existing material in endless permutations.

If *Kitezh* was designed to be Rimsky's last great opera, *The Golden Cockerel* is a superb coda to his operatic output as a whole. The composer–magician has woven an intricate musical web of supreme mastery. But his mastery of this particular idiom has tended, outside Russia, to obscure Rimsky-Korsakov's many other qualities; indeed, he has a strong claim to be considered, with Tchaikovsky and Musorgsky – whose operas he was responsible for bringing to the notice of the world – as a founding father (after Glinka) of Russian opera.

RECORDING Stoyanova, Babacheva, Dyakovski, Stoilov, Sofia Nat Op Ch & O, Manolov, Capriccio, 1985
OTHER OPERAS *The Maid of Pskov (or Ivan the Terrible)* (*Pskovityanka*), 1873; *Mlada*, (coll. inc.) (1872); *Mlada*, 1892; *The Barber of Baghdad* (*Bagdadskii borodobrei*), (1895) (inc.); *Mozart and Salieri* (*Mozart i Sal'yeri*), 1898; *The Noblewoman Vera Sheloga* (*Boyarynya Vera Sheloga*), 1898; *The Tsar's Bride* (*Tsarskaya nevesta*), 1899; *The Tale of Tsar Saltan, of his Son the Famous and Mighty Hero Prince Gvidon Saltanovich and of the Beautiful Swan Princess* (*Skazka o Tsare Saltane, o syne evo slavnom i moguchem bogatyre knyaze Gvidone Saltanovich i o prekrasnoi tsarevne lebedi*), 1900; *Servilia* (*Serviliya*), 1902; *Kashchei the Immortal* (*Kaschchei bessmertnyi*), 1902; *The Commander* (*Pan Voyevoda*), 1904; *Sten'ka Razin*, (1906) (inc.); *Heaven and Earth* (*Zemlya i nebo*), (1906) (inc.)

E.G./J.G.

Gioachino Rossini

Gioachino Antonio Rossini;
b 29 February 1792, Pesaro;
d 13 November 1868, Paris

Rossini's theatrical works dominated the repertoire for three decades, from the 1810s through the 1830s. His comic operas were considered supreme examples of the buffo style that had flourished in 18th-century Italy; his Italian serious operas were models for generations of composers; his French operas were fêted and reviled by opposing camps in the contentious Parisian musical world. Although he ceased writing new operas before 1830 and although his serious operas had all but disappeared from public view well before his death in 1868, every operatic composer working in Italy or France during his lifetime had to come to grips with this legacy.

Both Rossini's parents were professional musicians (his mother a singer, his father a horn-player). Even before he entered the Bologna Conservatory in 1806, he had learned to play the piano and cello, performed as a singer, and composed chamber works, overtures, and sacred music. In Bologna he regularly served as maestro al cembalo in the theatre. Early commissions for operas came through the good offices of performers who were family friends and knew the boy's talents. By the end of his 21st year, Rossini had written ten operas for northern Italian theatres. Among them were a series of five one-act operas (called *farse*) for the Venetian Teatro San Moisè, which specialized in this genre; an important comic opera, *La pietra del paragone* (1812), for La Scala in Milan; and his first major serious opera, *Tancredi* (February 1813), for La Fenice in Venice.

Tancredi and Rossini's next opera, the madcap *L'Italiana in Algeri* (May 1813), had an explosive effect: here was a new voice characterized by energy and wit, overflowing with melodic ideas, and sensitive to the most delicate shades of orchestral colour. What is more, Rossini brought to his work a structural clarity that transformed Italian opera: his characteristic forms, which gradually evolved over a period of ten years, were later developed into a system of formal rules as basic for 19th-century Italian composers as the sonata principle was for German ones.

Over the next four years, Rossini composed operas for a wide variety of Italian theatres. During this period, he prepared his major comic and semi-serious operas: *Il Turco in Italia* (Milan, 1814), *Il barbiere di Siviglia* (Rome, 1816), *La Cenerentola* (Rome, 1817), and *La gazza ladra* (Milan, 1817), all of which were performed extensively throughout Europe. Working quickly, Rossini sometimes employed collaborators to prepare recitative or even musical numbers (arias for minor characters), but he frequently returned to these works and substituted new pieces of his own composition for those of the collaborators. He also borrowed from himself, usually turning to works unlikely to circulate further and making extensive revisions to suit the new dramatic and musical context.

Naples, where he had made his début in 1815 with *Elisabetta, regina d'Inghilterra*, was the composer's centre of activity from 1817 until 1822. Many modern critics consider Rossini's nine serious operas for Naples, together with his last opera for Italy, *Semiramide* (Venice, 1823), to be his most impressive achievement. Complex works, formally inventive, orchestrally lavish, vocally extravagant, the Neapolitan operas and *Semiramide* defy easy categorization: despite their external similarities, each has its individual character. The range of their sources (from Italian Renaissance verse epic through Shakespearean tragedy, French classical drama, and English Romantic poetry) is noteworthy. Some of these works (*Otello, La donna del lago, Semiramide*) were widely known; others, particularly the more experimental operas (*Armida, Ermione, Maometto II*), did not circulate. Their highly florid vocal style, written to measure for some of the finest singers of Rossini's day (including his future wife, the soprano Isabella Colbran), made them difficult to mount even in Rossini's time and almost impossible after the mid-19th century, when vocal techniques changed radically.

After *Semiramide*, Rossini took up residence in Paris, and became musical director of the Théâtre-Italien, where his operas were becoming the backbone of the repertoire. His reputation as the composer of the political 'Restoration' was enhanced by *Il viaggio a Reims* (1825), written for the coronation of Charles X. Between 1826 and 1829 he prepared four works for the Opéra. Two were revisions of Neapolitan operas; the third (*Le Comte Ory*, 1828) borrowed extensively from *Viaggio*. Only with *Guillaume Tell* (1829) did Rossini compose an entirely new opera in French, a work of monumental proportions, mediating between the worlds of Italian melodramma and French tragédie-lyrique. The artistic growth Rossini achieved in the period of 20 years between his earliest operas and this final masterpiece is extraordinary.

Guillaume Tell was Rossini's last opera. Many have speculated about the motive behind this retirement, but no single answer is sufficient. The factors were political (the change of government in France), emotional (the death of Rossini's mother, to whom he was deeply attached), economic (a wealthy man, he had no need to continue composing), physical and psychological (his bodily and mental health was deteriorating), and his favoured position at the Opéra was threatened after the 1830 Revolution and the 1831 premiere of Giacomo Meyerbeer's *Robert le diable*; also new styles of singing were becoming common, requiring modifications in his compositional technique.

From 1830 to 1836 the composer remained in Paris, overseeing the fortunes of the Théâtre-Italien and lending support to his younger Italian colleagues (Bellini, Donizetti and Mercadante). He then returned to Italy, where despite ill health he served a term as director of the Bologna Conservatory. Only in 1855 did he return to Paris, where he regained his health, resumed active composition (though not in the field of opera) and lived out his final years, an esteemed presence from another era. The musical soirées in Rossini's apartment at the Chaussée d'Antin were attended by *tout Paris*.

Rossini's reputation for more than a hundred years, that of a composer of comic opera, has changed considerably in the past few decades. Thanks to the efforts of the Fondazione Rossini of Pesaro, many of his operas, particularly the serious ones, have been edited anew. The Rossini Opera Festival of Pesaro has provided models for intelligent stagings of these works; singers have successfully mastered their vocal style, and major theatres around the world have incorporated the operas into their repertoires. Thus, the depth and breadth of Rossini's achievement can be experienced anew by modern audiences.

L'Italiana in Algeri

The Italian Girl in Algiers

Dramma giocoso per musica in two acts (2h 15m)
Libretto by Angelo Anelli, first set by Luigi Mosca (1808)
PREMIERES 22 May 1813, Teatro San Benedetto, Venice; UK: 26 January 1819, His Majesty's Theatre, Haymarket, London; US: 5 November 1832, New York
CAST Mustafà *b*, Elvira *s*, Zulma *ms*, Haly *b*, Lindoro *t*, Isabella *c*, Taddeo *b*; *tb* chorus of eunuchs, corsairs, slaves, Pappataci; *silent*: women, European slaves, sailors

Following *Tancredi* by only a few months, *L'Italiana in Algeri* was an equal success for the 21-year-old composer. The subject – the liberation, through a deception and an encounter with a lost lover, of a woman abducted by a tyrant – has roots in Greek and Roman theatre.

Because Rossini was called on to prepare the opera only at the last minute, after another composer failed to respect his contract, it was decided to employ an earlier libretto, by Angelo Anelli, first set by Luigi Mosca for La Scala, Milan, in 1808. The few modifications show the dramaturgical hand of Rossini: Anelli's entrance aria for Taddeo (preceding Isabella's appearance) and a duet for Isabella and Lindoro were eliminated, the latter with the effect that the two lovers, like Rosina and the Count in *Il barbiere di Siviglia*, never have an intimate scene. The Act II aria for Isabella was added, as were the zany sections of the large ensembles: 'Nella testa ho un campanello' in the first finale and 'Sento un fremito' in the quintet. Perhaps because of the pressing schedule, secco recitatives and probably two short arias (Haly's 'Le femmine d'Italia' and Lindoro's 'Oh come il cor di giubilo') were composed by a collaborator. For a Milanese revival in 1814 Rossini replaced the Lindoro piece with a new aria of his own composition, 'Concedi, amor pietoso'.

The first Isabella was Maria Marcolini, the popular alto who had participated in the premieres of three previous Rossini operas (*L'equivoco stravagante*, *Ciro in Babilonia* and *La pietra del paragone*). Mustafà was sung by Filippo Galli, perhaps the finest bass of the day, Lindoro by Serafino Gentili, and Taddeo by Paolo Rosich. Rossini participated in and composed music for three later revivals: in Vicenza during the summer of 1813; at Milan's Teatro Re in April 1814 and at the Teatro dei Fiorentini in Naples in the autumn of 1815.

SYNOPSIS

The action takes place in Algiers. The overture, while not melodically related to the opera, captures its spirit delightfully. Rossini never reused it elsewhere.

Act I: Elvira, the wife of Mustafà, the Bey, grieves that her husband no longer loves her. Her confidante, Zulma, and a chorus of eunuchs (tenors and basses) advise her to accept this common lot of women. Mustafà enters in a temper; he wants an Italian woman, and gives his captain, Haly, six days in which to produce one. In another part of the palace Lindoro, an Italian recently enslaved by Mustafà's corsairs, languishes for his distant love ('Languir per una bella'). Mustafà informs Lindoro that he must marry Elvira so that Mustafà can be rid of her; Lindoro describes the woman he wants to marry, and Mustafà assures him Elvira is perfect ('Se inclinassi a prender moglie'). Offshore a ship has been wrecked and its passengers taken prisoner. Among them Haly and his men discover an Italian woman, Isabella, and her companion and would-be suitor, Taddeo. Isabella has been seeking her lover, Lindoro, and laments her cruel destiny ('Cruda sorte!'). She determines to conquer the Algerians through womanly wiles. Isabella and Taddeo argue about their relationship ('Ai capricci della sorte'), but they agree to pose as niece and uncle. Back at the palace Mustafà offers to allow Lindoro to leave immediately for Italy if he takes Elvira along. Seeing his opportunity to escape, Lindoro accepts. Haly brings news of the Italian woman, and Mustafà orders his court to assemble. He anticipates his new pleasure ('Già d'insolito ardore'). As the first finale begins, Mustafà is hailed by the eunuchs. Isabella is brought in, and Mustafà and the chorus marvel at her beauty; she flirts with the Bey to entrap him. When Taddeo forces his way into the hall, Mustafà threatens to impale him, but then accepts Isabella's 'uncle'. Elvira, Zulma and Lindoro come to say farewell; Isabella and Lindoro recognize each other and all express stupefaction in a grand ensemble of onomatopoeic nonsense during which Isabella acquires Lindoro as her slave.

Act II: Mustafà has fallen in love with Isabella. Haly counsels Elvira to be patient while Isabella's wiles make a fool of the Bey. Isabella and Lindoro plan their escape; the latter rejoices at being reunited with Isabella ('Oh come il cor di giubilo'). In order to impress Isabella, Mustafà makes Taddeo his 'Kaimakan' and has him dressed in Turkish costume. Taddeo, not wishing to be a go-between, first declines the title ('Ho un gran peso sulla testa') but accepts with much obsequiousness on seeing Mustafà's anger. Isabella prepares to receive the Bey. She orders Lindoro to bring coffee for at least three and tells Elvira to observe from another room how to handle a man. Mustafà, Taddeo and Lindoro watch from within while Isabella, completing her dressing, invokes Venus to make her more lovely ('Per lui che adoro'). Mustafà arranges to signal by sneezing the moment that the others should leave him alone with Isabella; the subsequent quintet ('Ti presento di mia man') is punctuated by numerous 'atchoos', which are conspicuously ignored. The ensemble is complete when Isabella invites Elvira to take coffee with them, and Mustafà understands that he has been tricked. Haly declares that Italian women excel at making men love them ('Le femmine d'Italia'). Lindoro tells Mustafà that Isabella loves the Bey and wants to make him her 'Pappataci', an honourable title given to men who sleep and eat while allowing their women to do just as they please. Isabella has arranged a ceremony involving the other Italian captives and has given the eunuchs and guards much wine. She encourages the Italians with patriotic passion ('Pensa alla patria'). In the second finale the chorus of Pappataci dresses the Bey in wig and costume, and Isabella confers the oath in which he swears to be deaf and blind to all her enterprises. Mustafà eats and drinks as the Italians slip away to the waiting ship. Taddeo, realizing that Isabella loves Lindoro, tries to alert the Bey but the latter fulfils his duty as Pappataci; rather than face Mustafà's wrath, Taddeo joins the Italians. Elvira, Zulma and Haly reveal the deceit to Mustafà; he begs Elvira's forgiveness and renounces Italian women. The entire ensemble proclaims that a woman cannot be kept from having her way.

Within Rossini's bubbling score the scenes range from the sentimental and the patriotic to the farcical and the lunatic. Rossini's treatment of the two genres of opera seria and opera buffa permits considerable overlap and exchange of elements, so we find noble sentiments present within the comic framework. The formal designs seen in *Tancredi* reappear in *L'Italiana*, although with greater internal flexibility.

Rossini characterizes well each of Isabella's three lovers. Mustafà's aria 'Già d'insolito ardore' combines buffoonery, elegance and virtuosity. Lindoro is a sweet, sentimental tenor who describes his sadness in the beautiful cavatina 'Languir per una bella'. Rossini emphasizes its poignancy with solo horn. Taddeo is the stock buffo of the opera and as such can hardly hope to end up with Isabella. His character is displayed in rapid patter and exaggerated leaps, a musical language that mocks its own pretensions.

The Italian girl must assume multiple personalities to triumph over cruel fate. She expresses erotic tenderness in 'Per lui che adoro'. (In 1814 Rossini rewrote the original solo cello obbligato as a flute solo.) Isabella tricks Mustafà and Taddeo time and again, from her initial meeting with the Bey in the first finale, to the pretended tête-à-tête, which turns into a quintet, to the investiture of Mustafà as a Pappataci in the Act II finale. Yet she is also a woman of strength, who encourages her countrymen to escape with profound patriotic sentiments ('Pensa alla patria'). This rondo was considered subversive in an Italy with awakening hopes of nationhood – the words were often changed or the piece omitted. Despite the censors, Rossini made his point musically: in the chorus preceding 'Pensa alla patria' he embedded a quotation from the 'Marseillaise'.

RECORDINGS 1. Battle, Horne, Foti, Palacio, Trimarchi, Ramey, Zaccaria, Prague PCh, I Solisti Veneti, Scimone, Erato, 1980; 2. Bima, Valentini Terrani, Rizzi, Araiza, Dara, Ganzarolli, Corbelli, WDR Male Ch, Capella Coloniensis, Ferro, Sony, 1984; 3. Takova, Larmore, Polverelli, Giménez, Corbelli, del Carlo, Chausson, Geneva Grand Th Ch, Lausanne CO, López-Cobos, Teldec, 1997 (live)

Il Turco in Italia

The Turk in Italy

Dramma buffo per musica in two acts (2h 15m)
Libretto by Felice Romani, after the libretto by Caterino Mazzola, first set to music by Joseph Seydelman (1788)
PREMIERES 14 August 1814, La Scala, Milan; UK: 19 May 1821, His Majesty's Theatre, London; US: 14 March 1826, Park Theater, New York
CAST Selim *b*, Fiorilla *s*, Geronio *b*, Narciso *t*, Prosdocimo *b*, Zaida *s*, Albazar *t*; *satb* chorus of gypsies, Turks, masqueraders; *silent*: friends of Fiorilla, gypsies, Turks, masqueraders

The Milanese audience, believing *Il Turco in Italia* to be a mere inversion of *L'Italiana in Algeri*, with numerous self-borrowings, felt cheated by Rossini and did not receive the opera warmly. Except for a few short motifs, however, the work was newly composed, and it is one of Rossini's most carefully constructed comic operas. It is also his most Mozartian work and shows particularly the influence of *Così fan tutte*, which was being produced at La Scala immediately before the premiere of *Il Turco*.

Il Turco in Italia suffered much from severe alterations during its early career, such as the ravages perpetrated at the Théâtre-Italien in Paris for an 1820 revival, in which a dismembered torso of Rossini's score was refitted with numbers lifted from *La Cenerentola*, *L'Italiana in Algeri* and *Ciro in Babilonia*, as well as an aria not by Rossini. The composer shared some blame, for he apparently had prepared a one-act reduction for the Théâtre-Italien, but no trace of this version survives. The Parisian pastiche was published, thereby confusing critics for a century and a half. After the mid-19th century, *Il Turco in Italia* virtually disappeared from the repertoire, returning to the stage in a production with Maria Callas in 1950. The critical edition of the Fondazione Rossini has now made Rossini's original version available.

Several items in the original version are not by Rossini: the secco recitatives, the cavatina for Geronio ('Vado in traccia d'una zingara'), the aria for Albazar ('Ah! sarebbe troppo dolce') and the entire Act II finale. After the premiere Rossini made several changes to this version. Narciso's Act II aria, 'Tu seconda il mio disegno', was added some time during the first season. An alternative cavatina for Fiorilla, 'Presto amiche', and additional pieces for Narciso and Geronio were prepared in the autumn of 1815 for a revival at Rome, where Rossini also omitted the two arias (for Geronio and Albazar) by his original collaborator.

SYNOPSIS

Act I: In their camp on a solitary shore near Naples, gypsies sing about their happy life ('Nostra patria è il mondo intero'), while Zaida, former slave and fiancée of the Turk Selim, mourns her lost love. Prosdocimo the poet thinks gypsies would provide a fine introduction for the dramma buffo he must write. Geronio is searching for a fortune-teller to advise him how to cure his wife, Fiorilla, of her passion for men ('Vado in traccia d'una zingara'). When Zaida and the gypsy girls tell him he was born under the fatal constellation of the ram, he flees. The poet learns that Zaida's rivals for Selim deceived him into condemning her to death, but the Turk's confidant, Albazar, saved her. Coincidentally, the poet reports, a Turkish prince is about to visit Italy to observe European customs; perhaps Zaida will find a mediator in him. Fiorilla muses on the folly of loving only a single object ('Non si dà follia maggiore'). Selim's boat appears, and he disembarks, greeting the wonderful country he has so longed to see ('Bella Italia, alfin ti miro'). He is further delighted by the appearance of the Italian ladies, especially Fiorilla. Geronio reveals to the poet and to Narciso (who also loves Fiorilla) that the Turk is taking coffee with Fiorilla. Geronio and Narciso are both distressed at Fiorilla's inconstancy. The quartet 'Siete Turchi' develops with protestations of anger and love. Fiorilla wants Geronio to allow her complete freedom, but he will have neither Turkish nor Italian men in his house ('Per piacere alla signora'). She threatens to punish him for his cruelty by having a thousand lovers. Selim has prepared his ship to flee with Fiorilla; while the Turk waits on the shore by the gypsy camp, Zaida reveals herself to him and they are reconciled. Narciso enters, complaining of his unrequited love ('Perché mai se son tradito'). Fiorilla and her friends arrive, then Geronio. The interaction of all six characters ('Ah! che il cor non m'ingannava'), particularly the two rival women, concludes the act in what the poet describes as a *finalone*.

Act II: Geronio and the poet are drinking at an inn. Selim arrives, and the poet withdraws to observe. The Turk offers to buy Fiorilla from Geronio, according to Turkish custom; Geronio describes the better Italian custom of breaking the would-be buyer's nose ('D'un bell'uso di Turchia'), and the business conversation turns to threats of violence. As the men leave, Fiorilla and her friends arrive ('Non v'è piacer perfetto'). She has come at Selim's invitation and expects to triumph over Zaida, who arrives followed by Selim. The women ask him to choose between them, but he cannot decide. Zaida leaves him to Fiorilla; they muse on the fickleness of the opposite sex, then avow their mutual love ('Credete alle femmine'). The poet tells Geronio and Narciso that Selim plans to abduct Fiorilla from the masked ball that evening. To thwart him, Zaida will attend, dressed exactly as Fiorilla with Narciso disguised as Selim. At the ball the masked lovers pair off – Fiorilla with Narciso, Selim with Zaida. Geronio in confusion sees the two couples, and a comic quintet ensues in which Geronio demands his wife, whichever she may be ('Oh! guardate che accidente'). Even the chorus joins in calling Geronio crazy as the lovers leave him breathless and desperate. The poet suggests that the unhappy husband send Fiorilla away and pretend to sue for divorce. Albazar assures Geronio that Selim is departing with Zaida. Outside Geronio's house the poet relays this news to Fiorilla and gives her Geronio's letter of dismissal. Chastened, she divests herself of her finery and prepares to return to her parents' home ('Squallida veste, e bruna'). The poet advises Geronio to follow and pardon her. In the Act II finale they are reconciled ('Son la vite'). Selim and Zaida – taking leave of Italy – and Narciso receive Geronio's forgiveness, and the poet hopes his public will enjoy the happy ending.

Il Turco in Italia shows Rossini at his comic best. He responds to the buffoonery of the plot with an inspired and constantly amusing score. *Il Turco in Italia* is largely an ensemble opera; only in Fiorilla's role do solo arias play an important part. There is abundant madcap motion, but time and again the composer steps back and, whether for specifically dramatic or more purely musical reasons, creates moments of extraordinary beauty and sensitivity. The Act I finale begins with all the noisy bumptiousness one expects of a Rossini finale. The scene is in turmoil, motivated by the jealous battle of Fiorilla and Zaida, but suddenly the noise stops and the orchestra disappears. The solo voices sing a remarkable unaccompanied phrase, 'Quando sono rivali, rivali in amor'. The effect of the entire *stretta* depends on Rossini's explicit wide-ranging indications of dynamics with phrases developing in unexpected ways.

The quintet in which Geronio tries to find Fiorilla, while the four disguised lovers dance around him, is extraordinarily funny; but underneath a passage of unaccompanied singing, Geronio declaims his perplexity on a single note, emerging as a genuinely touching character. The little canonic allegro that follows, 'Questo vecchio maledetto', is Rossini's best piece in this genre. Its counterpoints are perfectly placed to set off the tune and help the modulations along.

The trio for Narciso, Geronio and the poet ('Un marito scimunito!'), in which the poet expresses his glee at the developing plot while the other two plan their own revenge on him, is most unusual in design. The ensemble is largely built around a four-bar orchestral phrase in semibreves, which appears both as a melody and as an accompanimental figure. Equally delightful is the duet for Fiorilla and Geronio ('Per piacere alla signora'). With wonderful mock realism Rossini follows husband and wife through their confrontation, showing them in scenes of anger and sentimentality.

RECORDINGS 1. Callas, Gedda, Stabile, Calabrese, Rossi-Lemeni, La Scala Ch & O, Gavazzeni, EMI, 1954 (cut); 2. Jo, Giménez, Fissore, Alaimo, Ambrosian Op Ch, Academy of St Martin in the Fields, Marriner, Philips, 1991; 3. Bartoli, Vargas, Corbelli, Pertusi, La Scala Ch & O, Chailly, Decca, 1997

Il barbiere di Siviglia

The Barber of Seville

Commedia in two acts (2h 15m)
Libretto by Cesare Sterbini, after the play by Pierre-Augustin Caron de Beaumarchais (1775) and the libretto by Giuseppe Petrosellini, set by Giovanni Paisiello (1782)
PREMIERES 20 February 1816, Teatro Argentina, Rome; UK: 10 March 1818,

King's Theatre, Haymarket, London; US: 3 May 1819, Park Theater, New York
CAST Count of Almaviva *t*, Bartolo *b*, Rosina *ms*, Figaro *bar*, Basilio *b*, Berta *s*, Fiorello *bar*, Ambrogio *b*, Official *b*, Notary *silent*; *tb* chorus of police, soldiers, musicians

During the years of his association with Naples, Rossini wrote several important operas for other Italian cities, including *Il barbiere di Siviglia*, the oldest opera by an Italian composer never to have disappeared from the repertoire and perhaps the greatest of all comic operas. Set to a beautifully constructed libretto and drawing effectively on an important literary source, Rossini's opera achieves melodic elegance, rhythmic exhilaration, superb ensemble writing, and original and delightful orchestration. In it Rossini, with cleverness and irony, adapted the formal models of his art to specific dramatic situations.

In Rome for the premiere of *Torvaldo e Dorliska* in December 1815, Rossini signed a contract with the Teatro Argentina to compose an opera for the conclusion of the imminent carnival season. After a subject offered by Jacopo Ferretti had been rejected, Cesare Sterbini, author of *Torvaldo*, was selected to prepare the text. The resulting libretto was *Almaviva, or The Useless Precaution*, a title chosen to distinguish it from Paisiello's well-known *Barber of Seville*. In no more than two weeks Rossini had prepared the score; probably from lack of time he adopted the overture of *Aureliano in Palmira*, which also had formed the basis for the overture to *Elisabetta, regina d'Inghilterra*. The opening-night audience reacted unfavourably to this new and hastily mounted *Barbiere*, but on the second night its brilliance won them over. For the Bologna revival of 1816 there was no necessity to maintain the original title; Rossini's *Barbiere di Siviglia* had come into its own.

The opera was known in corrupt versions from the end of the 19th century until the 1960s. Furthermore, its modern performance tradition stressed slapstick gags rather than elegant comedy. Performances since the 1970s, reflecting more closely Rossini's own score, have allowed the public to hear the work afresh.

SYNOPSIS

Act I: At dawn in Seville Count Almaviva serenades the beautiful Rosina ('Ecco ridente il cielo'). When Rosina fails to appear at her window, he pays off the musicians who, delighted by his generosity, make an enormous racket before departing. Figaro, the barber, approaches; he loves his profession, which opens every door in the city to him ('Largo al factotum'). He recognizes the count, but the latter wants his identity hidden, for he has secretly followed Rosina. Figaro says she is the ward of old Dr Bartolo, who wishes to marry her himself. Bartolo appears, locks Rosina in, and hurries off to organize the wedding. The count, not wanting Rosina to marry him for his title, pretends to be Lindoro, a poor student ('Se il mio nome'). As Rosina starts to respond, the shutters are firmly closed. Promised gold for his assistance, Figaro concocts a plan: the count will enter Bartolo's house disguised as a drunken soldier and claim lodgings ('All'idea di quel metallo'). Inside the house Rosina has written a letter to Lindoro ('Una voce poco fa'). Figaro appears, promptly followed by Bartolo. Don Basilio, music master and friend of Bartolo, brings word that Count Almaviva, attracted by Rosina's beauty, has arrived in Seville. He suggests they spread malicious rumours about the count ('La calunnia'). Bartolo prefers to marry that day, and they go off to draft the contract. Having overheard the conversation, Figaro warns Rosina. Assuring him she can handle the situation, Rosina inquires about the handsome youth she has just seen with Figaro. He tells her it was his impoverished cousin, madly in love with Rosina. Though feigning surprise when Figaro suggests she write to Lindoro, Rosina produces her finished letter ('Dunque io son'), and Figaro goes to deliver it. The suspicious Bartolo accuses Rosina of having written to her lover and threatens to lock her up ('A un dottor'). The disguised count arrives noisily ('Ehi, di casa'). He tells Bartolo he seeks lodging. When Rosina appears, the count manages to reveal that he is Lindoro. Bartolo produces an exemption from billeting, but the count dismisses it. In the uproar, he slips Rosina a letter, which she promptly exchanges with a laundry list as the servant Berta and Don Basilio enter. Figaro soon reappears, reporting that their noise can be heard throughout the city. Soldiers knock at the door. All the characters try to explain the situation, creating even more chaos. The officer arrests the count, who shows a document and is promptly set free. Bartolo explodes in anger and everyone expresses total confusion.

Act II: Another knock at the door announces the count, disguised as a music master, 'Don Alonso' ('Pace e gioia'). He claims to be a student of Don Basilio, sent because his master is ill. To gain Bartolo's confidence, he tells him he has stolen from Almaviva a note written by Rosina. With this evidence, he will try to convince Rosina that the count merely plays with her affections. Tricked, Bartolo goes to fetch his ward for her lesson. Rosina performs a 'Rondo' from a new opera, *The Useless Precaution*, and as Bartolo dozes, she and Lindoro express their mutual affection ('Contro un cor'). Bartolo awakens, bored by this 'contemporary music', and sings some 'music of my time' ('Quando mi sei vicina'). Figaro comes to shave Bartolo, who sends the barber to get shaving materials. Figaro grabs the opportunity to obtain the balcony key, then drops crockery, forcing Bartolo to come after him. Rosina and Lindoro again swear their love. As Figaro begins to shave Bartolo, Don Basilio arrives for Rosina's lesson. The lovers and Figaro provide Basilio with an ample purse, claim he has scarlet fever, and make him withdraw ('Don Basilio! Cosa veggo!'). Figaro continues to shave Bartolo while Lindoro plans with Rosina to elope at midnight. Bartolo overhears the count speak of his disguise and breaks into a rage. Alone, Berta, Dr Bartolo's housekeeper, comments on the foolishness of old men who would marry young women ('Il vecchiotto cerca moglie'). Basilio admits to Bartolo he does not know 'Don Alonso' – perhaps it was the count himself. Bartolo instructs Basilio to fetch the notary immediately. Producing Rosina's letter to Lindoro, Bartolo tells her he obtained it from Count Almaviva and persuades her to agree to marry him. A storm rages outside. As Figaro and the count enter through the balcony, Rosina accuses 'Lindoro' of intending to sell her to that vile Count Almaviva. The count throws himself at her feet and admits his true identity. The lovers express their joy, while Figaro urges them to escape ('Ah! qual colpo inaspettato'). By the time they are ready, their ladder has disappeared. Basilio enters with the notary. Figaro has him marry the count and Rosina. Offered the choice between a valuable ring and two bullets in the head, Basilio agrees to be a witness. Bartolo, too late, arrives with soldiers. Count Almaviva reveals his identity and announces that Rosina is his wife ('Cessa di più resistere'). With no choice remaining, Bartolo blesses the marriage. All wish the happy couple love and eternal fidelity ('Di sì felice innesto').

In *Il barbiere di Siviglia* Rossini most successfully uses his musical style to provide a metaphoric interpretation of, or an ironic commentary on, the unfolding drama. The basic techniques and forms of his musical vocabulary embody in a precise and often delightful way the dramatic situations and characters. For example, the 'Rossini crescendo' (a technique for building musical tension by repeating a short phrase with added instrumental forces, expansions of register, alterations in articulation and gradual increases in dynamics), though rarely inappropriate for its context, frequently lacks specific links to the drama. In Figaro's cavatina, as the orchestral crescendo gathers force, the barber describes how the demands of his clients become ever more insistent; his words come faster and faster until the momentum reaches its climax and he is left to sing unaccompanied: 'Figaro, Figaro, Figaro, Figaro . . .'. In Don Basilio's 'calumny' aria the crescendo becomes the central musical force of the number. As Basilio describes how the soft voice of rumour gradually spreads until it explodes like a cannon shot, the orchestral crescendo builds to the *colpo di cannone* of the bass drum.

In the trio near the end of Act II Rossini uses another standard musical technique to comment ironically on the action rather than describe the dramatic situation. While the lovers react with ecstasy to their new-found happiness, Figaro urges them to leave. It is standard for Rossini to echo a lyrical vocal melody in the orchestra, giving the singer a chance to breathe at the end of a phrase while maintaining melodic interest. In this trio the echo is both played by the first violins and sung by Figaro, who tries to shake Rosina and the count out of their happy delirium. Although he imitates their very words, the lovers simply do not hear him; it is as if Figaro served as nothing more than the traditional instrumental echo. Furthermore, when the lovers finally realize they must hurry, the three sing 'Presto andiamo via di qua'; as the characters wait for the music to work itself out with standard repeats of the cabaletta theme and cadential phrases, their ladder disappears from under them.

In one number after another, Rossini both captures the essence of the characters and comments ironically, even maliciously, on them. This is an opera that combines the elegance of its literary source with the buffoonery of the Italian commedia dell'arte tradition. Even with the recovery of so many of the composer's significant operas over the past 20 years, it remains Rossini's masterpiece.

RECORDINGS 1. de los Angeles, Alva, Bruscantini, Wallace, Cava, Glyndebourne Festival Ch, LPO, Gui, EMI, 1962; 2. Berganza, Benelli, Ausensi, Corena, Ghiaurov, Naples Rossini Ch & O, Varviso, Decca, 1964; 3. Bartoli, Matteuzzi, Nucci, Fissore, Burchuladze, Bologna Teatro Comunale Ch & O, G. Patané, Decca, 1988; 4. Ganassi, Vargas, Servile, Romero, de Grandis, Hungarian RCh, Faloni CO, Humburg, Naxos, 1992

La Cenerentola

Cinderella

Dramma giocoso in two acts (2h 30m)
Libretto by Giacomo (Jacopo) Ferretti, after the tale *Cendrillon* by Charles Perrault (1697), the libretti *Cendrillon* by Charles-Guillaume Etienne (1810) and *Agatina* by F. Fiorini, set by Stefano Pavesi (1814)
PREMIERES 25 January 1817, Teatro Valle, Rome; UK: 8 January 1820, King's Theatre, Haymarket, London; US: 27 June 1826, Park Theater, New York
CAST Don Ramiro *t*, Dandini *b*, Don Magnifico *b*, Clorinda *s*, Tisbe *ms*, Angelina (known as Cinderella) *ms*, Alidoro *b*; *tb* chorus of courtiers; ladies *silent*

Rossini was originally commissioned by the Teatro Valle to set a different libretto, based on a French comedy, but the ecclesiastical censors demanded so many changes that Rossini ultimately rejected it, requesting a new libretto from his friend Ferretti. Because of the shortness of time – Ferretti and Rossini chose the subject on 23 December 1816 – Ferretti did not write a new poem based on the fairytale but rather turned to two earlier libretti, written for Paris and Milan, respectively. Practically none of the elements familiar from Perrault's fairytale figures in Ferretti's libretto. His transformation of the glass slipper into a bracelet was probably to placate the Roman censors, who would not wish to see an unshod feminine foot on stage.

The opera was staged a month later.

Rossini borrowed the overture from *La gazzetta* (1816) and employed a Roman musician, Luca Agolini, to assist him in his preparations. Agolini composed all the secco recitative and three pieces: an aria for Alidoro ('Vasto teatro è il mondo') in Act I, a chorus ('Ah della bella incognita') to open Act II and an aria for Clorinda ('Sventurata! me credea') near the end of the opera. For a Roman revival in 1821 Rossini replaced Alidoro's aria with a new composition, 'Là del ciel nell'arcano profondo'.

The nature of the libretto makes *La Cenerentola* significantly different from Rossini's previous comic operas. Although Don Magnifico and Dandini are comic characters in the great Italian tradition, the principal characters, Cinderella herself and Ramiro, are sentimental, not comic. They are heirs of Richardson's Pamela, the virtuous servant girl loved and finally married by a noble patron. From Piccinni's setting of Goldoni's *La buona figliola* (1760) on through the century, Italian opera buffa more and more frequently had sentimental and pathetic heroines, expressing their emotions in a musically simple and popular style.

SYNOPSIS

Act I: In a hall of Don Magnifico's castle, his vain daughters Clorinda and Tisbe are primping. Their stepsister, Cinderella, consoles herself with a song about a king who chose a kind-hearted bride ('Una volta c'era un re'). A beggar (actually Prince Ramiro's tutor Alidoro) comes in; Cinderella gives him some breakfast, angering the stepsisters. The prince's knights enter, announcing the imminent arrival of the prince himself, who at a ball will choose the most beautiful woman as his wife. The ensuing excitement generates great confusion. The knights leave; so does the 'beggar', foretelling that Cinderella will be happy by the next day. Quarrelling for the privilege of telling their father the good news, Clorinda and Tisbe awaken him. Don Magnifico interprets a dream he was just having as a prediction of his fortune: the impoverished baron's vision of himself as grandfather of kings is apparently confirmed by his daughters' announcement ('Miei rampolli femminini'). Ramiro, having decided to explore the situation, has exchanged clothing with his attendant, Dandini. When the disguised prince enters the house, he and Cinderella fall in love immediately ('Un soave non so che'). Dandini arrives, awkwardly playing the prince ('Come un'ape ne' giorni d'aprile'). Clorinda and Tisbe are introduced to him. Cinderella begs her stepfather to take her to the ball ('Signor, una parola'), but Magnifico orders her to stay at home. Alidoro, with a list of the unmarried women of the region, asks Don Magnifico about a third daughter; he says she died. Everyone is confused. Later Alidoro reveals his identity to Cinderella and invites her to the ball, alluding to a change in her fortunes ('Là del ciel'). At the palace Dandini, still disguised as the prince, appoints Magnifico his wine steward; Magnifico proclaims new drinking laws. Clorinda and Tisbe scornfully mistreat Ramiro, believing him to be the squire. All are enchanted by the arrival of a mysterious lady. When she unveils herself they are struck by her uncanny resemblance to Cinderella.

Act II: The courtiers laugh at the sisters' distress. Magnifico imagines himself the prince's father-in-law, making money in exchange for his favours ('Sia qualunque delle figlie'). Ramiro overhears Cinderella refusing Dandini's attentions because she loves his 'squire'. Ramiro asks her to be his, but she gives him a bracelet, saying he will find her wearing its twin. If he still likes her, she will marry him. Ramiro reassumes his princely role and determines to look for Cinderella ('Sì, ritrovarla, io giuro'). Dandini encourages Magnifico's fantasies, then reveals his real identity ('Un segreto d'importanza'). Returning home, the sisters find Cinderella by the fire and berate her because she looks like the lady at the ball. Alidoro arranges an accident for the prince's carriage, which overturns in front of the house. Cinderella and Ramiro recognize each other ('Siete voi'), and everyone expresses amazement ('Questo è un nodo avviluppato'). Ramiro whisks Cinderella away, while Alidoro convinces the sisters to ask forgiveness so as to avoid ruin. At the wedding banquet Cinderella intercedes with the prince for Magnifico and her stepsisters. She reflects on how her fate has changed ('Nacqui all'affanno, al pianto').

La Cenerentola is far from a simple comic opera. Rossini adapts for his purposes not only the popular semiseria genre but even the exalted vocal style of opera seria. When we first meet Cinderella she is a naïve girl singing a little ditty: 'Once upon a time there was a king.' The disguised prince begins their duet ('Un soave non so che') with a simple melody that is a transformation of her tune. In the sextet Rossini gives Cinderella a coloratura style that none the less remains attached to simple melodic patterns ('Ah signor, s'è ver che in petto'). But in her first appearance at the ball ('Sprezzo quei don') and at the beginning of her rondo ('Nacqui all'affanno, al pianto') she emerges a queen, her florid flights approaching those we normally associate with Rossini's serious operas. Ramiro's Act II aria ('Sì, ritrovarla, io giuro') is a thoroughly elegant piece with spectacular vocal fireworks and a range that ascends repeatedly to exposed and sustained high Cs.

The opening comic aria for Don Magnifico is rather standard, with almost continuous comic patter. Dandini, however, is a more subtle comic character. When he first appears disguised as the prince, Rossini gives him a princely *coro e cavatina* in mock-heroic style, in which extravagant coloratura alternates with patently buffo declamation. The witty duet with Magnifico ('Un segreto d'importanza') is superbly set. Once the secret is out, the tentative opening phrase is transformed into a spirited allegro in which Dandini's buffo style emerges gloriously, with Magnifico babbling in confusion. More revelations lead to the sextet of confusion ('Questo è un nodo avviluppato'), one of the most inspired moments in all Rossini's operas. By using a remarkable palette of musical styles throughout the opera, Rossini leads us through each stage. In the end, Cinderella's transformation is brought about not by supernatural arts, but by the magic of music.

RECORDINGS 1. Berganza, Alva, Capecchi, Montarsolo, Scottish Op Ch, LSO, C. Abbado, DG, 1971; 2. Bartoli, Mateuzzi, Corbelli, Dara, Bologna Teatro Comunale Ch & O, Chailly, Decca, 1992; 3. Larmore, Giménez, G. Quilico, Corbelli, Covent Garden Ch & O, Rizzi, Teldec, 1994

La gazza ladra

The Thieving Magpie

Melodramma in two acts (3h 15m)
Libretto by Giovanni Gherardini, after the play *La pie voleuse* by J.-M.-T. d'Aubigny and L.-C. Caigniez (1815)
PREMIERES 31 May 1817, La Scala, Milan; UK: 10 March 1821, King's Theatre, Haymarket, London; US: October 1827, Philadelphia
CAST Fabrizio Vingradito *b*, Lucia *ms*, Giannetto *t*, Ninetta *s*, Fernando Villabella *b*, the Mayor *b*, Pippo *ms*, Isacco *t*, Antonio *t*, Giorgio *b*, Ernesto *b*, Magistrate *b*, Gaoler *silent*, Usher *silent*; *satb* chorus of men at arms, peasants, servants; a magpie

From the second half of 1817 until 1822, Rossini's creative activity was dominated by his artistic ties with Naples, where he concentrated his attention primarily on the production of serious operas. The winter and spring seasons of 1816–17, however, proved to be one of the composer's most intensely prolific periods. Working in a variety of theatres and across a number of genres, Rossini had already affirmed his genius in opera seria (with *Otello* for Naples, 1816) and opera buffa (with *La Cenerentola* for Rome). Now he returned to Milan, the scene of his earliest important success and a city where a large number of works by German and Austrian composers (Mozart, Joseph Weigl and Peter Winter) had been produced since his last visit. Mindful of the lack of enthusiasm generated by his two previous works for La Scala, Rossini devoted considerable attention to his new opera semiseria.

Gherardini, a leading personality in Milanese cultural life, had offered the libretto the preceding year to Paër, but it was not used. The plot is based on a true story: a French servant girl, accused of theft, was tried and executed. When her townspeople later discovered that the thief was a magpie, they instituted an annual mass in her memory, called the 'mass of the magpie'. In a letter to his mother, Rossini proclaimed 'the subject is wonderful'.

La gazza ladra belongs to the 'mixed' genre, born in the mid-18th century. During the revolutionary period, semiseria operas were frequently rescue operas (the most famous example being Beethoven's *Fidelio*). *La gazza ladra* is a classic example of opera semiseria, but its fusion of comic and dramatic elements is clearly weighted towards the latter.

The opera was an immediate and enormous success. It quickly circulated outside Italy, being heard throughout Europe in the following decade, and remained in the repertoire for over 50 years. Rossini himself directed revivals in Pesaro and Naples, writing some remarkable new arias for the character of Fernando.

SYNOPSIS

The opera begins with one of Rossini's finest overtures, whose opening snare drums and military tone infiltrate much of the drama. Many themes are derived directly from the opera and anticipate its emotional content.

Act I: Fabrizio Vingradito, a well-to-do tenant farmer, would like to see his son Giannetto, who is returning from military service, marry Ninetta, their serving girl and the daughter of an honourable soldier, Fernando Villabella: the young couple are in love ('Oh che giorno fortunato!'). Lucia, Fabrizio's wife, complains that the girl is irresponsible and has recently mislaid a silver fork. Ninetta enters ('Di piacer mi balza il cor'); Fabrizio and Lucia go to meet Giannetto. Isacco the pedlar arrives selling his wares ('Stringhe e ferri da calzette'), but is sent on his way by Pippo, a friend of Ninetta in Fabrizio's service. Everyone returns with Giannetto, who embraces Ninetta ('Vieni fra queste braccia'); Pippo sings a drinking song ('Tocchiamo, beviamo'). Alone in the household, Ninetta is joined by a ragged man: it is her father. Having been refused permission to visit his daughter, Fernando fought with his commander, was imprisoned and condemned to death, and now has escaped. He gives Ninetta a silver fork and spoon to sell so that he will have some money ('Come frenar il pianto!'). The mayor, coming to renew his unwelcome amorous overtures to Ninetta ('Il mio piano è preparato'), receives an urgent message; not having his eye-glasses, he asks Ninetta to read it aloud. It is an order to arrest her father, which she falsifies by changing the description of the fugitive ('M'affretto di mandarvi'). Fernando reproaches the mayor for his unwanted attentions to Ninetta ('Respiro. Mia cara!'). Meanwhile, the pet magpie, unobserved, steals a silver spoon. Lucia accuses Ninetta of stealing the missing silver fork and spoon. Pippo inadvertently reveals to the mayor that Ninetta has sold some trinkets to Isacco. The pedlar is summoned and a deposition is taken ('In casa di Messere'); Isacco has already resold the fork and spoon, but he testifies that they had the initials F.V. – those of both Fabrizio and Fernando. Ninetta, unwilling to betray her father, is arrested.

Act II: Ninetta, in prison, is visited in turn by Giannetto, to whom she declares her innocence but not the truth about her father ('Forse un dì conoscerete'); by the mayor, whose offer of freedom in return for his love she rejects ('Sì, per voi, pupille amate'); and by Pippo, to whom she gives the money to hide for her father ('E ben, per mia memoria'). Lucia reveals Ninetta's plight to Fernando, who determines to save her at the cost of his own life ('Accusata di furto'). At the trial Ninetta is sentenced to death; all react in pity and horror ('Tremate o popoli' 'Ahi qual colpo!'). Fernando bursts in; too late to help his daughter, he is himself arrested. Lucia repents of her accusations ('A questo seno'). While Pippo is counting his money in the village square, the magpie steals a coin. The mournful procession to the execution enters the square as the townspeople console Ninetta ('Infelice, sventurata'); it pauses in front of the church while Ninetta prays for her father ('Deh tu reggi'), then leaves the square. Pippo and Antonio climb to the magpie's nest in the belltower, where they discover the stolen fork and spoon. However, it seems to be too late; gunfire is heard in the distance. Then a joyful chorus announces it is a signal that Ninetta is safe. A royal pardon arrives for Fernando. All rejoice, except the mayor.

Despite the great wealth of beautiful music in *La gazza ladra*, a modern audience may find its semi-serious tone difficult to grasp. The music moves from a light-hearted, pastoral tone to one of deep tragedy, only to wrest itself back at the last moment. The two most ambiguous characters are Pippo and the mayor. The youthful Pippo announces the return of Giannetto, plays with the magpie, and sings a drinking song; then, in the prison scene, he and Ninetta perform a duet whose beauty and tenderness create a powerful dramatic tension. In the mayor's cavatina there are elements of opera buffa (in the orchestra, in the comic declamation), but in the following trio he is much more threatening. Showing his 'official' side during the Act I finale, he reveals his fury against Ninetta in a that leaves no doubt ab which he is capable. During charged quintet ('Tremate o pop qual colpo!'), he finally expresses morse but is unable to find a way out. In the finale, when it seems that Ninetta has been executed, it is to the mayor that Rossini gives the weightiest part, while in the face of communal joy, he feels intense shame.

The funeral march of the Act II finale is laden with such grief as to set aside the lighter elements. The procession approaches, the orchestra sotto voce; it draws nearer, adding chorus (always with the accompanying drums that opened the overture and called the court to session). The prayer, with its introduction for two bassoons and two horns leading to a simple melody, does not end the scene but leads to a reprise of the march, swelling to fortissimo, then dwindling until only bassoon, horn, trombone and drum remain, fading to nothing. And then the sudden change from clouds to sunlight: Ninetta and Fernando return in triumph, and one of the principal dramaturgical requirements of opera semiseria, a happy ending, is fulfilled, with each character (except the mayor) expressing joy.

RECORDINGS 1. Pizzo, Müller, Condò, Bottazzo, Signor, Romero, Rinaldi, Ambrosian Op Ch, RPO, Zedda, Warner Fonit Cetra, 1979; 2. Ricciarelli, Manca di Nissa, D'Intino, Matteuzzi, Coviello, Furlanetto, Ramey, Philharmonic Ch of Prague, Symphonic O of RAI (Turin), Gelmetti, Sony, 1989 (live, complete)

Semiramide

Semiramis

Melodramma tragico in two acts (2h 45m)
Libretto by Gaetano Rossi, after the play *Sémiramis* by Voltaire (1748)
PREMIERES 3 February 1823, La Fenice, Venice; UK: 15 July 1824, King's

...ew

...ssur *b*,
...ne *t*,
...*satb*

...*silent*:
...s, bards,
... ministers
of th... thians,
Egyptians, s...

After his definitive departure from Naples in 1822, Rossini composed only one more opera for Italy, *Semiramide*, which had its premiere at La Fenice in Venice almost exactly ten years after the premiere of *Tancredi* at the same theatre. Both were written to libretti by Gaetano Rossi, and both were based on dramas by Voltaire, parallels that were not accidental. After the more tormented and experimental Neapolitan works, Rossini sought to recapture a more classical spirit, one that would gain the favour of a wider public. *Semiramide* occupies a unique place in the Rossini canon: a consolidation of past triumphs and a step towards his future French operas. The work captivated the Venetian public, was performed everywhere in Europe, and remained in the repertoire throughout the 19th century.

SYNOPSIS

Act I: In the Babylonian Temple of Baal a throng waits for Queen Semiramide to name the successor to the throne of her husband, Nino, dead for 15 years. Idreno, King of Indus, pays homage ('Là dal Gange'), and Prince Assur, Semiramide's former lover and her accomplice in the murder of Nino, brings offerings ('Sì, sperate'); both aspire to the throne and to the hand of Princess Azema. Semiramide, awaiting the return of the young commander Arsace, whom she loves, reluctantly begins to name the successor; lightning, thunder and wind extinguish the sacred altar fire, frightening everyone. Arsace, summoned by Semiramide, arrives in Babylon hoping to marry Azema, who loves him ('Ah! quel giorno'). He brings to the high priest, Oroe, tokens of the dead Nino and a letter that reveals the truth about Nino's murder. Assur reminds Arsace that Azema was betrothed to the missing Prince Ninia, but Arsace's love knows no obstacle ('Bella imago degli dei'). In a separate aria, Idreno professes his love to Azema ('Ah dov'è, dov'è il cimento'). In the Hanging Gardens Semiramide anticipates Arsace's arrival ('Bel raggio lusinghier'). When Arsace enters he diffidently tries to tell of his love for Azema, but Semiramide believes he loves her ('Serbami ognor'). The queen demands of her subjects an oath of loyalty to the future king, and then names Arsace as king and consort. The ghost of Nino appears and says Arsace must avenge his death with the blood of the murderers ('Qual mesto gemito'). The crowd wonders who is the guilty one ('Ah! Sconvolto nell'ordine eterno').

Act II: Assur tries to force Semiramide to make him king; they each threaten to reveal the other's crime ('Se la vita ancor t'è cara'). Oroe reveals to Arsace that Nino was his father and that his mother, Semiramide, conspired with Assur. Arsace accepts the duty of avenging his father ('In sì barbara sciagura'). Idreno entreats Azema to accept him ('La speranza più soave'). Arsace tells Semiramide the marriage cannot take place and shows her the accusing scroll; she offers herself as the sacrificial victim. Arsace pities her, but he will follow his father's instructions and descend into his tomb ('Ebben . . . a te: ferisci'). Assur learns that Oroe has turned the people against him. Shaken by a vision of Nino, he vows to kill Arsace ('Deh . . . ti ferma'). He searches for Arsace in the tomb of Nino; Semiramide follows to protect Arsace; Oroe and the Magi are close behind. Groping in the darkness, the three principals are fearful ('L'usato ardir'). When Oroe tells Arsace to strike at Assur, Semiramide steps between them and is killed. Assur is arrested. The horrified Arsace, prevented by Oroe from killing himself, accepts the throne at the behest of the populace.

Continuing Neapolitan developments, *Semiramide* provides attractive vocal opportunities for accomplished singers, and without such singers it makes no sense to perform the work, for Rossini uses this vocalism to project the drama. *Semiramide* is the first of Rossini's non-Neapolitan operas to abandon secco recitative: indeed, the accompanied recitative of *Semiramide* is a model of passionate and expressive declamation.

Important differences from its Neapolitan predecessors are the presence of a conventionally constructed overture and a preponderance of arias and duets rather than ensembles. None the less, most of the striking dramatic events in *Semiramide* occur in the three great ensembles, each centred on a supernatural intervention: the expansive introduction, the monumental Act I finale and the Act II finale.

The arias and duets of *Semiramide* are all constructed according to standard Rossinian design, but in many cases each section is enormously expanded. In duets, the formal confrontation between characters takes place in an opening section, leading to a meditative cantabile. Some of the most stunning music in *Semiramide* is found here, including the famous 'Giorno d'orror! . . . e di contento' in the Act II duet for Semiramide and Arsace, after the queen learns he is her son. A short *tempo di mezzo* leads the characters to a new dramatic stance, expressed in the cabaletta. Rossini often wrote his most memorable melodies in these duet cabalettas: 'Va, superbo, in quella reggia' for Arsace and Assur, or 'Alle più care immagini' in Act I for Semiramide and Arsace. These pieces breathe a majesty and expansiveness that give the opera its sense of monumentality. Even within these numbers, however, there are remarkably original musical and dramatic effects. Most notable is Assur's mad scene preceding the Act II finale, where his tormented mind reels from one emotion to another. Rossini's music leads him graphically through these shifts.

The andantino of the Act I finale, in which all swear to obey Semiramide's command, is particularly beautiful: it uses the theme for four horns that Rossini also employs in the overture. But the centrepiece of the finale is the canonic ensemble in which all the characters react to the appearance of the ghost ('Qual mesto gemito'), a passage accompanied by an ostinato rhythmic figure in the orchestra. One of the musical ideas in this ensemble recurs several times during Act II, recalling the ghost of Nino. In the Act II finale the trio 'L'usato ardir' seems suspended in time.

Semiramide represents the apotheosis of musical neoclassicism in Italy. It is the opera to which the next generation of Italian composers returned almost compulsively, both to imitate and to abjure. Its forms provided models. Its sounds resonated in their hearts. But they rejected its classicism, its unabashed glorification of the power of music.

RECORDINGS 1. Sutherland, Horne, Serge, Rouleau, Ambrosian Op Ch, LSO, Bonynge, Decca, 1965/6 (cut); 2. Studer, Larmore, Lopardo, Ramey, Ambrosian Op Ch, LSO, Marin, DG, 1993

Il viaggio a Reims

The Journey to Rheims

Dramma giocoso in one act (3h)
Libretto by Luigi Balocchi, after the novel *Corinne, ou l'Italie* by Mme de Staël (1807)

PREMIERES 19 June 1825, Théâtre-Italien, Paris; US: 12 June 1986, Loretto-Hilton Center, St Louis; UK: 8 June 1987, Guildhall School of Music, London

CAST Corinna *s*, Marquise Melibea *c*, Countess of Folleville *s*, Madame Cortese *s*, Chevalier Belfiore *t*, Count Libenskof *t*, Lord Sidney *b*, Don Profondo *b*, Baron Trombonok *b*, Don Alvaro *b*, Don Prudenzio *b*, Don

Luigino *t*, Maddalena *s*, Delia *ms*, Modestina *ms*, Zefirino *t*, Antonio *b*, Gelsomino *t*; *satb* chorus of musicians, peasants, gardeners, dancers, servants, travellers

Rossini's last Italian opera and the first he wrote in France had its premiere as part of the festivities honouring the coronation of Charles X. Although an occasional piece, *Viaggio* was calculated to establish Rossini's reputation. Conceived for the greatest voices of the time, including Giuditta Pasta as Corinna, the work requires an exceptional cast: three prima donna sopranos, an alto, two tenors, and four baritones and basses have leading roles. Lavish costumes, magnificent sets, and a ballet for 40 dancers enhanced the splendour. Contemporary reviews were uniformly ecstatic, but Rossini was jealous of this opera. Aware that a work so tied to a particular historical occasion could not hope to circulate widely, he reused about half the music for *Le Comte Ory* in 1828. He was pressed to permit three further performances of *Viaggio*, the proceeds of the last going to charity.

The libretto is inextricably bound to the specific event for which it was written. Hope for a strong Europe at peace, under the leadership of monarchies newly restored after the decisive defeat of Napoleon in 1815, gives symbolic meaning to the international clientele at the inn, and each character during the finale brings his own country's music to the festivities.

The manuscript sources of *Viaggio* were presumed lost until, in the mid-1970s, part of Rossini's autograph was recovered at the Library of the Conservatory Santa Cecilia in Rome. Other sources were located in Paris and Vienna, permitting a reconstruction of the entire work. (The so-called overture to *Il viaggio a Reims*, a 20th-century invention, is derived from a ballet movement written for one of Rossini's French operas: *Viaggio* never had an overture.)

SYNOPSIS

Travellers on their way to the coronation in Rheims are staying overnight at the Inn of the Golden Lily. The innkeeper, Madame Cortese, and her staff assist them in preparing for the last leg of their journey ('Presto, presto ... su, coraggio!'). The Parisian Countess of Folleville, learning that the carriage bringing her wardrobe has overturned, laments her loss ('Partir, oh ciel! desio'). Baron Trombonok, keeper of the travellers' purse and a lover of music, is responsible for making final arrangements ('Sì, di matti una gran gabbia'). Other travellers arrive: Don Profondo, an antiquarian; the Spanish admiral Alvaro, who escorts the Marquise Melibea, a Polish widow; a jealous Russian general, Count Libenskof, in love with Melibea. When Madame Cortese enters to explain that their departure has been delayed, Alvaro and Libenskof are already about to duel. From behind the scenes, the Roman poetess Corinna improvises an ode to fraternal love ('Arpa gentil'), and momentary peace returns. Lord Sidney, an English officer in love with Corinna, places flowers at her door ('Invan strappar dal core'). The French chevalier Belfiore tries to woo Corinna, but she wants nothing to do with him ('Nel suo divin sembiante'). Don Profondo lists the possessions the travellers are bringing with them ('Medaglie incomparabili'). The baron and Zefirino inform the travellers that they cannot go to Rheims after all, because no horses remain to take them there ('Ah! A tal colpo inaspettato'). Madame Cortese suggests an alternative: her husband has written to describe the festivities being prepared for the king's return to the capital, and the travellers decide to proceed directly to Paris the next morning. In the meantime, they will give a public banquet that evening. Melibea and the count quarrel; he tries once again to win her hand ('D'alma celeste, oh Dio!'), and she finally yields. In the garden the banquet is under way. Musicians and dancers provide entertainment. The baron proposes a series of musical tributes to the royal family, with each singing in his or her own national style. Corinna offers an improvisation in honour of the new king, and the assembled guests (representing all the nations of Europe) proclaim the glory of Charles X and France.

Because the orchestra of the Théâtre-Italien was strengthened with soloists from the Opéra for the first performance of *Viaggio*, instrumental lines could be made particularly demanding (see, for example, the flute solo in the aria of Lord Sidney, 'Invan strappar dal core'). And because each of his singers was a master of Italian vocal style, Rossini could allow his vocal writing to luxuriate in their strengths. Moreover, the musical numbers of *Viaggio* perfectly realize the dramatic situations. The Countess of Folleville's aria of misery over the loss of her finery is delectable, precisely because of the contrast between the grandeur of the musical expression and the triviality of the dramatic cause. In Don Profondo's aria ('Medaglie incomparabili'), he is preparing a list of the effects of each traveller so that luggage can be prepared for the journey. He invokes each traveller and writes down what each will be bringing; each strophe characterizes a single person.

The 'Gran pezzo concertato a 14 voci' ('Ah! A tal colpo inaspettato') is one of the glories of *Viaggio*. A slow opening section of astonishment, largely unaccompanied, is motivated by the news that no horses are available. In the second, quick section, the letter from Madame Cortese's husband in Paris alters the dramatic situation. The final section is constructed as a formal cabaletta, in which the characters react to the altered circumstances. The overwhelming effect of the audacious scoring for fourteen solo voices may be seen most clearly in the Rossini crescendo that serves as the concluding section of the cabaletta theme. The first phrase is sung by two voices, the second by nine, and the third by all fourteen.

The national toasts of the finale are either taken from patriotic hymns or based on national musical styles. Among the melodies that flow past are Haydn's 'Gott erhalte Franz den Kaiser', 'God Save the King' and the French 'Charmante Gabrielle'. They are joined by a polonaise, a Russian hymn, a Spanish song and a tyrolese complete with yodels. The entire company joins in an apotheosis of Charles X to the well-known French song 'Vive Henri Quatre'.

RECORDING Gasdia, Cuberli, Ricciarelli, Valentini Terrani, E. Giménez, Ramey, Raimondi, Prague Philharmonic Ch, COE, C. Abbado, DG, 1984 (live, complete)

Le Comte Ory

Count Ory

Opéra [comique] in two acts (2h 15m)
Libretto by Eugène Scribe and Charles Gaspard Delestre-Poirson, after their own play (1816), based on a medieval ballad

PREMIERES 20 August 1828, Théâtre de l'Académie Royale de Musique, Paris; UK: 28 February 1829, King's Theatre, Haymarket, London; US: 22 August 1831, New York

CAST Count Ory *t*, the Tutor *b*, Isolier *ms*, Raimbaud *bar*, Countess of Formoutiers *s*, Ragonde *ms*, Alice *s*, two knights *t*, *bar*; *satb* chorus of Ory's men, ladies, Crusaders, peasants

About half of Rossini's music for *Il viaggio a Reims* resurfaced in *Le Comte Ory*. How should one think about an opera in which such a large proportion of the music derives, essentially without change, from a work whose substance is entirely different? How should one think about an opera in which the confusion of identity extends so far as to present a tenor disguised as a woman who thinks he is making love to a soprano, when in fact he is making love to an alto in the role of a man who takes the place of the soprano?

If gender is a problem in the libretto,

genre is problematic concerning the opera as a whole. Superficially *Le Comte Ory* might seem to be an opéra comique. That it was conceived not for the Théâtre de l'Opéra-Comique but for the Opéra, however, transforms it. Whereas a typical opéra comique consists of relatively short lyrical numbers separated by spoken dialogue, *Le Comte Ory* is made up of highly developed, even massive musical forms, linked by accompanied recitative. Whereas the orchestration of a contemporary typical opéra comique is relatively light, Rossini's forces are large. Despite the Italianate forms of many of its lyrical numbers, the use of accompanied recitative was at odds with the Italian practice of secco recitative for comic operas. Furthermore, there is no hint of buffoonish characters, no exaggeratedly rapid declamation. Instead, *Le Comte Ory* sparkles with Gallic wit, grace and charm.

In the medieval ballad Count Ory and his men lay siege to nuns in a convent; their notable success became evident nine months later. Scribe and Delestre-Poirson created a one-act vaudeville first performed in Paris in 1816, changing the nuns to ladies whose husbands are away on a crusade; the crusaders return before Count Ory and his men achieve their goal. This becomes essentially Act II of the opera. Act I presents events that are described in an air at the beginning of the vaudeville. The librettists grafted a first act to the vaudeville, arranging the action and poetry so that Rossini's music from *Il viaggio a Reims* could be reused. They were also compelled by the enormous differences between the two genres to rewrite the text of their vaudeville, accommodating another two numbers from *Il viaggio a Reims*. Little wonder they originally declined to have their names on the printed libretto! Yet despite its difficult birth, *Le Comte Ory* works splendidly.

SYNOPSIS

The opera takes place *c.*1200 in and around the castle of the counts of Formoutiers.

Act I: The men are on a crusade, and their women have taken a vow of chastity and locked themselves in the castle. In order to court the beautiful Countess Adèle, Count Ory disguises himself as a hermit said to specialize in affairs of the heart, and his friend Raimbaud stirs up interest among the local people. Ragonde, stewardess of the castle, announces that her mistress wishes to consult him ('Jouvencelles, venez vite'). The count's tutor, together with his page Isolier, arrive in search of him. Hearing about the hermit, the tutor becomes suspicious ('Veiller sans cesse'). Isolier, not recognizing his master, seeks advice from the 'hermit' about gaining Adèle's love. When he reveals his plan to penetrate the castle disguised as a female pilgrim, Ory decides to adopt the plan himself ('Une dame de haut parage'). Adèle comes to consult the hermit, who advises her to distrust the page of the notorious Count Ory (Isolier), with whom she confesses to be half in love ('En proie à la tristesse'). The tutor recognizes the count and unmasks him ('Ciel! Ô terreur, ô peine extrême'). A letter arrives announcing the successful conclusion of the crusade: Adèle's brother and the knights will be home the next day. The ladies invite Ory to celebrate with them, but he resolves to use the time remaining to devise another plan to conquer Adèle.

Act II: Within the walls of the castle, the women await their men's return, thankful at having escaped Ory's wiles ('Dans ce séjour calme et tranquille'). Outside a storm is raging and cries of distress are heard. Pilgrim women say they are being threatened by Ory. 'Soeur Colette', who turns out to be the count in disguise, thanks Adèle profusely ('Ah! quel respect, Madame'). Left alone, the 'pilgrim women' revel ('Ah! la bonne folie!'); having discovered the wine cellar, Raimbaud provides wine for all

('Dans ce lieu solitaire'), and they sing a lively drinking song ('Buvons, buvons'). Isolier arrives and reveals the hoax to Adèle. Taking advantage of the darkness of her bedroom, Adèle hides behind Isolier; 'Soeur Colette', deceived by her voice, makes advances to the page, whom he mistakes for the countess ('A la faveur de cette nuit obscure'). When trumpets announce the return of the crusaders, Count Ory and his men are forced to flee ('Ecoutez ces chants de victoire').

From *Il viaggio a Reims* Rossini salvaged numbers that could be transferred most easily to other dramatic situations. The introduction is from *Viaggio*, though the short overture is new; part of the air for the tutor is derived from Lord Sidney's aria; the countess's air from the contessa's aria; the first finale from the 'Gran pezzo concertato'; the duet between the count and the countess from that between Corinna and Belfiore; Raimbaud's air from Don Profondo's. Only a single piece in Act I of *Le Comte Ory* is entirely new: the duet for Ory and Isolier. In Act II, however, Rossini reused only two compositions from *Viaggio*.

Although the borrowed numbers are artfully adapted to their new surroundings, there are losses. The carefully wrought structure of Don Profondo's aria, where parallel strophes describe different characters, seems arbitrary as the musical setting for Raimbaud's narrative of his discovery of the castle's wine cellar. But most situations, while different in detail, are structurally and emotionally similar. When the drama or characters are markedly different, Rossini intervened: for the tutor, he altered the first section of Lord Sidney's aria, whose sentimentality was ill-suited to the new laments, and made changes in the cabaletta (adding, for example, the canonic obbligato for flute and clarinet in the repetition of the theme).

The jewels of the score are the pieces Rossini prepared directly for *Le Comte Ory*. The choral songs for the count and his followers, as pilgrims, are spirited in tone and subtle in their musical realization. The original ballad tune, heard twice before in the opera, becomes the central episode of the drinking chorus. The Act II trio is magical in the nocturnal and insinuating quality of the opening section, its delicate orchestral shading, its erotic chromaticism, the shifting pairings of the voices. Rossini has centred the drama in the sexual and musical shadows, disguises, and illusions of his score.

RECORDINGS 1. Barabas, Canne-Meier, Sinclair, Oncina, Roux, Wallace, Glyndebourne Festival Ch & O, Gui, EMI, 1956; 2. Jo, Montague, Aler, G. Quilico, Cachemaille, Op Nat de Lyon Ch & O, Gardiner, Philips, 1988

Guillaume Tell

William Tell

Opera in four acts (3h 45m)
Libretto by Etienne de Jouy and Hippolyte Louis-Florent Bis, after the play *Wilhelm Tell* by Johann Christoph Friedrich von Schiller (1804)
PREMIERES 3 August 1829, Théâtre de l'Académie Royale de Musique, Paris; UK: 1 May 1830, Drury Lane, London (as *Hofer, or The Tell of the Tyrol*); US: 19 September 1831, New York
CAST Guillaume Tell *bar*, Arnold *t*, Walter *b*, Melchthal *b*, Jemmy *s*, Gesler *b*, Rodolphe *t*, Ruodi *t*, Leuthold *b*, Mathilde *s*, Hedwige *c*, Huntsman *b*; *satb* chorus of Swiss, huntsmen, soldiers

With *Guillaume Tell* Rossini finally offered Parisian audiences an original opera in French. It was intended to initiate his true career as a French composer, after his years at the Théâtre-Italien and his earlier arrangements at the Opéra. During the months preceding the premiere he struggled to obtain two long-term commitments from the French government: a lifetime annuity and a ten-year contract.

Rossini wove into the historical panorama of *Guillaume Tell* pastoral elements, patriotic deeds (much in vogue on the eve of the revolutionary wave soon to sweep Europe) and superbly drawn characters. Yet the development of the libretto, freely derived from Schiller's play, was tormented. The original draft by Etienne de Jouy underwent considerable alteration at various hands. Finally, changes were made during the long rehearsal period and even after the premiere. Some were incorporated into printed editions of the opera (in preparation before the first performance). Others survived in manuscripts of the opera; they have been reconstructed for the critical edition.

What is most fascinating about *Guillaume Tell*, however, is the imaginative way in which its composer responded to the challenge of creating a work for the French Opéra without abandoning his Italian roots. Though certain elements are more 'Italian', others more 'French', it is the combination of these elements that is extraordinary. More than in any other work, Rossini integrates the bel canto lyricism and formal refinement of Italian opera with the declamatory immediacy and scenic splendour (the latter expressed in extensive choruses and ballet) characteristic of French opera. The grandiose structure, finally, is tied together with a system of musical motifs derived from popular Swiss melodies known as *ranz des vaches*.

SYNOPSIS

Act I: The action takes place in medieval Switzerland. The villagers at Bürglen, in the canton of Uri, anticipate a triple wedding, the culmination of their traditional festival ('Quel jour serein le ciel présage!'). A fisherman serenades his beloved, while Guillaume Tell laments the tyrannical rule of the Austrians and their governor, Gesler. Melchthal, patriarch of the village, urges his son Arnold to think of marriage, but Arnold, who serves in the Austrian garrison, loves the Habsburg princess Mathilde. Distant horns announce the governor's hunt. As Arnold seeks to rush off to join Mathilde, Tell reappears. He tries to gain Arnold's support against the increasingly oppressive Austrian rule ('Où vas-tu?'). Arnold swears to join Tell when the moment to strike arrives. Melchthal blesses the couples. The festivities proceed with songs, dances and an archery contest, which Jemmy (Tell's son) wins. His triumph is interrupted by Leuthold, an old herdsman. He has killed an Austrian soldier who was trying to rape his daughter. While Tell ferries Leuthold across the dangerous rapids, Austrian soldiers arrive ('Dieu de bonté'). The Swiss refuse to identify the ferryman; Rodolphe drags Melchthal away as a hostage and orders the soldiers to loot the village.

Act II: In the dusk, huntsmen pass ('Quelle sauvage harmonie'), while villagers return to their homes. Mathilde muses on her feelings for Arnold ('Sombre forêt'). When he approaches, they declare their love ('Oui, vous l'arrachez à mon âme'). As Tell and Walter appear, Mathilde hurries off, having agreed to meet Arnold the next day. The men reveal that Gesler has murdered Melchthal; Arnold swears to avenge his father ('Quand l'Helvétie est un champ de supplices'). Representatives of the three cantons arrive. The patriots vow to throw off the Austrian yoke and gain their liberty ('Des profondeurs du bois immense').

Act III: Meeting in a ruined chapel near Gesler's palace, Mathilde and Arnold bid each other farewell ('Pour notre amour, plus d'espérance'). In the main square at Altdorf the townspeople celebrate Gesler's power ('Gloire au pouvoir suprême'), while the soldiers force the Swiss to sing and dance (*pas de trois*, 'Toi qui l'oiseau', and *pas des soldats*) and to bow before a symbol of Gesler's authority. When Tell refuses to bow, Rodolphe recognizes him as the man who saved Leuthold ('C'est là cet archer redoutable'). Having heard of Tell's skill as an archer, Gesler announces that he can save his life only by shooting an apple from Jemmy's head: otherwise, father and son will die together. Sustained by his son's courage, Tell shoots his arrow through the apple ('Sois immobile'). In the general relief that follows, Tell drops a second arrow, held in reserve for the governor, should his first arrow have killed his son. Tell is thrown into chains, but Mathilde takes Jemmy under her own protection. When Gesler orders that Tell be transported across Lake Lucerne and thrown to the reptiles living in the waters of Küssnacht Castle, the riotous reaction of the Swiss is barely contained by the soldiers.

Act IV: Arnold visits his birthplace ('Asile héréditaire'). His companions announce that Tell is a prisoner. Arnold shows them where his father and Tell concealed arms for the day of insurrection. Hedwige is about to beg mercy from Gesler, when Mathilde arrives with Jemmy. The princess offers herself as a hostage in return for Tell. The storm breaks. Leuthold reports that Tell's captors have freed his hands, since he alone can control the boat in the storm. Jemmy gives the signal for the revolt. Tell reaches the shore and, with the bow handed to him by Jemmy, kills Gesler. Arnold and his forces capture the castle of Altdorf. As the storm subsides, the Swiss join in a prayer of thanksgiving for the liberation of their country ('Tout change et grandit en ces lieux').

Carefully written, harmonically daring, melodically purged of ornamentation, orchestrally opulent, *Guillaume Tell* represents a final purification of Rossini's style. Ensembles dominate and the interests of the drama are well served. The great overture is unabashedly programmatic, and Rossini's orchestral palette is fuller than ever before. The extensive spectacular elements, ballets and processions, which derive from French operatic tradition, are effectively integrated into the opera.

Many parts of *Guillaume Tell* adhere to Italian structures, most obviously the duet for Mathilde and Arnold in Act II, Mathilde's aria at the opening of Act III and Arnold's aria in Act IV – all three part of the dramatically ancillary subplot. Also frankly Italianate in design is the Act I finale, whose action comes into focus in two major ensemble movements. Within these structures, however, the music remains highly responsive to details of the drama.

Already during his Neapolitan years Rossini began integrating French elements into his style: concern with declamation, spectacle, chorus and dance. In *Tell* the recitative is extremely powerful, blending into passionate, yet lyrical declamation, enhanced by a consistently rich orchestral texture. This happens especially in complex scenes, such as the Act III finale (including Tell's admonishment to his son) and the concluding scene of the opera. The chorus is central both musically and dramatically, and much of the opera revolves about magnificent choral ensembles such as 'Vierge que les chrétiens adorent' in the Act I finale, or the final ensemble. Some of these choruses are part of large-scale divertissements with ballet.

Act II was particularly appreciated by Rossini's contemporaries, even by hostile critics such as Berlioz. He found 'sublime' the finale, in which the three Swiss cantons, each characterized musically, are called together to plan the revolt. The chorus is the central protagonist of *Guillaume Tell*: the fate of the Swiss people is the subject of the drama. Rossini's quotation and transformation of popular Swiss tunes throughout the melodic fabric of the entire work gives it a strong, unified colour. The whole opera is a rich tapestry of Rossini's most inspired music.

RECORDINGS 1. (in French) Caballé, Gedda, Bacquier, Hendricx, Kovats, Ambrosian Op Ch, RPO, Gardelli, EMI, 1972; 2. (in Italian) Freni, Pavarotti, Milnes, Mazzoli, Ghiaurov, Ambrosian Op Ch, Nat PO, Chailly, Decca, 1979
OTHER OPERATIC WORKS *Demetrio e Polibio*, (pre 1809), 1812; *La cambiale di matrimonio*, 1810; *L'equivoco stravagante*, 1811; *L'inganno felice*, 1812; *Ciro in*

Babilonia, ossia La caduta di Baldassare, 1812; *La scala di seta*, 1812; *La pietra del paragone*, 1812; *L'occasione fa il ladro*, 1812; *Il signor Bruschino, ossia Il figlio per azzardo*, 1813; *Tancredi*, 1813; *Auerliano in Palmira*, 1813; *Sigismondo*, 1814; *Elisabetta, regina d'Inghilterra*, 1815; *Torvaldo e Dorliska*, 1815; *La gazzetta*, 1816; *Otello, ossia Il moro di Venezia*, 1816; *Armida*, 1817; *Adelaide di Borgogna*, 1817; *Mosè in Egitto*, 1818; *Adina, o Il califfo di Bagdad*, (n.d.) 1826; *Ricciardo e Zoraide*, 1818; *Ermione*, 1819; *Eduardo e Cristina*, 1819; *La donna del lago*, 1819; *Bianca e Falliero, o sia Il consiglio dei tre*, 1819; *Maometto II*, 1820; *Matilde (di) Shabran, ossia Bellezza, e cuor di ferro*, 1821; *Zelmira*, 1822; *Le siège de Corinthe*, 1826; *Moïse et Pharaon, ou Le passage de la Mer Rouge*, 1827

P.G./P.B.B.

S

Camille Saint-Saëns

Charles Camille Saint-Saëns;
b 9 October 1835, Paris; *d* 16 December 1921, Algiers

The career of Saint-Saëns, one of the most gifted and versatile musicians of the 19th century, whose accomplishments were solid as well as brilliant, covered a momentous span of musical history. Born the year before the premiere of Meyerbeer's *Les Huguenots*, he died when Berg had nearly completed *Wozzeck* and Britten was a schoolboy. At the age of ten Saint-Saëns made his début as pianist in Paris playing concertos by Mozart and Beethoven. His last public appearance took place in Dieppe 75 years later. His first numbered symphony was written when he was 18. His last works, the three woodwind sonatas, were written in the final year of his life.

In between, Saint-Saëns was unremittingly active as composer and executant. In the latter capacity he was a much travelled concert pianist, organist (notably at the Madeleine church in Paris), author, teacher (not at the Conservatoire where he had studied but at the École Niedermeyer in Paris) and scholar, who did much to make Mozart's music known in France and was general editor of the complete edition of Rameau. As composer he produced over the years five symphonies, sacred and secular choral works, numerous concertos and concerted works, four orchestral tone poems and a quantity of chamber music and songs. To his regret his operas, with the exception of *Samson et Dalila*, failed to win the success he achieved in other, by Parisian standards less important, fields. Including his part (with Dukas) in the completion of Guiraud's unfinished *Frédégonde*, Saint-Saëns wrote 13 operas, two of them opéras comiques. There were in addition a ballet, *Javotte*, incidental music for several plays and a film score. As a widely cultivated man he understood what was wanted, yet with all his competence and experience he lacked the 'nose', the instinct of the theatre animal granted, for example, to Massenet, who in other forms of music was his inferior. His choice of libretti showed more education than flair, yet he skilfully adapted the procedures of grand opera to the needs of the period between the death of Meyerbeer and the conquest of France by Wagner. The operatic music of Saint-Saëns by and large has the same strengths and weaknesses as the rest – lucidity, Mozartian transparency, greater care for form than content. His facility, a quality misprized by those who lack it, tempted him to accept ideas good or bad, often memorable if rarely profound, as they came to him. There is a certain emotional dryness; invention is sometimes thin but the workmanship is impeccable.

Samson et Dalila

Samson and Delilah

Opera in three acts (four tableaux) (2h)
Libretto by Ferdinand Lemaire, after the Book of Judges
Composed 1868–77
PREMIERES 2 December 1877, Grand Ducal Theatre, Weimar; US: 25 March 1892, New York (concert); 4 January 1893, French Opera House, New Orleans (stage); UK: 25 September 1893, Covent Garden, London (concert); 26 April 1909, Covent Garden (stage)
CAST Dalila *ms*, Samson *t*, High Priest of Dagon *bar*, Abimélech *b*, an Old Hebrew *b*, a Philistine Messenger *t*, First Philistine *t*, Second Philistine *b*; *satb* chorus of Hebrews and Philistines

Saint-Saëns, who had experience of the English oratorio tradition and shared the national admiration for Mendelssohn's *Elijah*, intended to use the biblical story of Samson's betrayal and death for an oratorio. His librettist, Ferdinand Lemaire, sensing theatrical possibilities, suggested an opera. Musical friends showed little enthusiasm for the first passages the composer tried out on them. On a visit early in 1870 to Liszt in Weimar, Saint-Saëns spoke of his discouragement. Liszt, the champion of the new and unfamiliar, offered, if Saint-Saëns finished *Samson*, to produce it in Weimar. Owing to the outbreak of the Franco-Prussian War and local difficulties, Liszt could not keep that promise until 1877. Meanwhile, there had been no takers in France. The singer Pauline Viardot organized a private performance in Paris of Act II at which she sang Dalila and the composer played the orchestral part on the piano, but the audience, including the director of the Opéra, remained unconvinced: the biblical subject would not do. Rameau and Voltaire had had similar difficulties 150 years earlier with a projected *Samson*. There was a public concert performance of the first act at the Châtelet theatre in 1875, but the opera was not performed on the French stage until 3 March 1890, at the Théâtre des Arts at Rouen. That production was brought to Paris, not to the Opéra but to the nearby Théâtre Eden, in October the same year. The Opéra was at last emboldened to accept *Samson*, and it was first seen there on 23 November 1892 with Deschamps-Jehin, Vergnet and Lassalle, conductor Colonne. (Viardot, for whom the role of Dalila was designed, and to whom the opera is dedicated, was now over 70.) Success with the general public in Paris was great and prolonged but was overshadowed for progressives by the vogue for Wagner. Audiences outside Paris, however, were enthralled: *Samson* became one of the most widely popular of operas.

SYNOPSIS

Act I: A public place at Gaza, before the temple of Dagon. The Hebrews lament their subjugation by the Philistines. They fear their God has forsaken them. Samson, claiming that God speaks through his mouth ('Arrêtez, ô mes frères!'), attempts to raise their spirits. The satrap Abimélech rebukes the Hebrews for praying to the wrong deity – Dagon would help them. His words incite Samson and the Hebrews to a fervent outburst ('Israël! Romps ta chaîne!'). Abimélech attacks Samson, who slays him. The Hebrews melt away as the temple gates open, revealing the high priest of Dagon, heavily guarded. As he scolds his followers for showing fear, a messenger brings news of an uprising among the Hebrews. The high priest curses Israel. Ready to celebrate the turn of events, Dalila and a group of priestesses advance, ostensibly to crown the victor Samson. Vowing that he reigns in her heart, she beseeches him to visit her again in her lonely dwelling. An old Hebrew warns Samson against the wiles of Dalila. As she dances among her priestesses the troubled Samson is compelled against his will to follow her voluptuous movements. She sings provocatively ('Printemps qui commence') of her nocturnal vigil, waiting for the hero.

Act II: Outside Dalila's house in the valley of Sorek. Night is falling and a storm is brewing. Dalila, sensing Samson's perplexity, calls on Love to help her ('Amour! Viens aider ma faiblesse!'). Her first visitor is the high priest, to inform her that since the Israelites have recaptured the city, the downfall of Samson is essential. He reminds Dalila that her previous encounter with the hero had not brought his total submission. She admits that her attempts to prise from him the secret of his strength were unsuccessful. She is their only hope, the high priest assures her; through her Samson must be enslaved and die. When the coast is clear, Samson steals in, the more shamefully because God has smiled on the Hebrews. This must be the lovers' farewell. Dalila dismisses thoughts of Israel's fate and invokes a more powerful god – Love. Samson dares the lightning to strike him down as he confesses his love. Dalila demands total surrender ('Mon coeur s'ouvre à ta voix'), adding that he must entrust her with his secret. Assuming that the thunder is the voice of God, Samson refuses, but finally follows her indoors. Philistine soldiers approach silently. Dalila signals to them to enter the house.

Act III, Tableau 1: The prison in Gaza. Blinded, his hair shorn, Samson turns the treadmill ('Vois ma misère, hélas'), while Hebrew voices are heard bemoaning his apparent betrayal of them and their God for a woman's charms. Tableau 2: Interior of the temple of Dagon with two marble columns in the centre. A celebration is in progress. The high priest, Dalila and their followers watch a bacchanal. Samson is led in by a small boy. The high priest mocks the hero's weakness. Dalila reminds him of her successful extraction of his secret (the nature of this secret is never revealed in words). At the sacrificial table they invoke their god ('Gloire à Dagon vainqueur!'). A flame appears, signifying the god's presence. The high priest commands Samson to kneel and worship. Samson asks the boy to lead him to the two columns, prays to God to give him back his old strength and, pushing them outwards, brings the temple roof crashing down.

Lemaire's libretto is an intelligent compression of the established five-act formula of Meyerbeerian grand opera. The customary spectacle and ballets form a logical part of the action. The clash between the austere Hebrews and the pleasure-loving Philistines is kept well in the foreground. In Act I the entry of Dalila and her maidens brings refreshment after the Hebrews' lament and Samson's killing of the satrap. In Act III the pathetic scene of Samson at the treadmill is followed by the appropriately superficial tinklings of Philistine rejoicing. Saint-Saëns made use of his knowledge of the classics: Bach (experienced perhaps through Mendelssohn) goes mainly to the Hebrews, Handel (his light, pagan side) to the Philistines, for instance in the canonic duet for the high priest and Dalila. In Act II the conflict is left to the protagonists. In the interview between Dalila and her master, Saint-Saëns works short, jagged instrumental phrases in a manner that makes one understand how theatre people in the 1870s were put off by the 'symphonic' nature of the writing in addition to the, to them, unacceptable subject matter. The symphonic aspect blinded them to the attraction of the set numbers. The eventual popularity of these numbers, ground out by café orchestras and pulled out of context, diverted serious musicians from the score's finer qualities. The orchestration is masterly throughout, especially in the second act where the dramatic tension is heightened by the sultry atmosphere – a summer storm circling round and breaking at the climax, the cooing of doves transformed into rushing storm scales.

The character of Dalila is carefully drawn. Each of her three arias adds something. The first is the most purely feminine. The second is an appeal for help and reassurance. In the third, Dalila, who has Samson in her power but still has not discovered his secret, gives him the full works. One may doubt her professions of love. Any tender feelings she may harbour disappear once he is helpless. Her gloating over him at this point and her earlier refusal of the high priest's offer of money imply that patriotism is a motive but, although as an expert she may appreciate Samson's physique, deeper feelings than endangered amour propre seem unlikely.

RECORDINGS 1. Bouvier, Luccioni, Cabanel, Paris Op Ch & O, Fourestier, Naxos, 1946; 2. Gorr, Vickers, Blanc, R. Duclos Ch, Paris Op O, Prêtre, EMI, 1962; 3. Borodina, Cura, Lafont, LSO & Ch, C. Davis, Erato, 1998
OTHER OPERAS *La princesse jaune*, 1872; *Le timbre d'argent*, 1877; *Etienne Marcel*, 1879; *Henry VIII*, 1883; *Proserpine*, 1887; *Ascanio*, 1890; *Phryné*, 1893; *Frédégonde* (completion, with Dukas, of opera by Guiraud), 1895; *Les barbares*, 1901; *Hélène*, 1904; *L'ancêtre*, 1906; *Déjanire*, 1911

R.H.C.

Arnold Schoenberg

Arnold Franz Walter Schoenberg [Schönberg]; *b* 13 September 1874, Vienna; *d* 13 July 1951, Los Angeles, US

The son of a Hungarian-born father and a Czech-born mother (both Jews), Schoenberg was brought up in straitened circumstances and had little academic musical training. He learned the violin and taught himself the cello, and for a time in the mid-1890s he had composition lessons from Zemlinsky, but he was otherwise self-taught. He played in a string quartet, and his earliest surviving works are mainly for string groups, including the sextet *Verklärte Nacht* (Op. 4, 1899). Their style is late Romantic and complicatedly tonal, like contemporary works by Richard Strauss, Max Reger or Zemlinsky. But they also have an extreme melodic and motivic density, and it was in developing this idea to its limits that Schoenberg found himself, within ten years, consciously abandoning tonality. In the D minor String Quartet (1905) and Chamber Symphony No. 1 (1906) the relentless working of melodic motifs tends to pull the harmony out of focus. So it was logical of Schoenberg, if characteristically intransigent, to ditch tonal harmony altogether and instead, in works such as the song-cycle *Das Buch der hängenden Gärten* and the *Three Piano Pieces*, Op. 11, to allow the chords as well as the melodies to emerge from the motivic process.

In 1906 Schoenberg sketched a first opera, based on Gerhard Hauptmann's play *Und Pippa tanzt*, but abandoned it when Hauptmann held out for a stiff percentage (Alban Berg had a similar experience with this play in 1928). Two unconventional one-act works date from the early atonal period: the so-called 'monodrama' *Erwartung* (1909) and the 'drama with music' *Die glückliche Hand* (1910–13). These are characteristic products of Expressionism, inhabiting a world of neurotic hypersensibility. They belong to a group of vocal works, including *Pierrot lunaire* (1912) and the *Four Orchestral Songs*, Op. 22 (1913–16), in which Schoenberg attempted to resolve certain problems of form, syntax and harmony arising from his rejection of tonality. In the course of writing his next work, the oratorio *Jacob's Ladder* (never completed), he began to evolve the more systematic processes that led, in a series of instrumental works of the early and mid-1920s to the 12-note, or serial, method that was to have such profound consequences for subsequent 20th-century music.

By this time, Schoenberg was already an established enfant terrible, surrounded by a small but fervent group of admiring disciples (including Berg and

Anton Webern, who had become his pupils in 1904, and remained attached to him as apostles and assistants until 1933). In Vienna before the First World War performances of his music were greeted with incomprehension and sometimes disruption, and he was the victim of open anti-Semitism. In Berlin, where he settled in 1911, he fared better, and *Pierrot lunaire* had a successful run there in the autumn of 1912. But the outbreak of war curtailed such activities, and in 1915 Schoenberg returned to Vienna and volunteered for military service (within ten months he was invalided out). There in 1919 he founded his Society for Private Musical Performance, which for three seasons gave concerts of new works to member audiences, with the notoriously factious Viennese press specifically excluded. Schoenberg, Berg and Webern themselves did much of the organizing and took part in performances. But the worsening inflation put paid to the venture after 1921. In 1926 Schoenberg returned to Berlin as professor of composition at the Prussian Academy of Arts, and he remained there until driven out by the Nazis in 1933. Among several substantial works composed during these Berlin years were two further operas: the one-act *Von Heute auf Morgen* (1928–9) and his single attempt at a full-length opera, *Moses und Aron* (1930–32, but incomplete). In October 1933 he and his family took ship for the USA, where he taught briefly at the Malkin Conservatory in Boston before preferring the more benign climate of the West Coast. He spent the last 17 years of his life in Hollywood and Los Angeles.

While there may still be debate about Schoenberg's artistic stature, there is none about his influence, which has been vast. This is partly because of the innate strength of his best music, but it is also because he took procedural decisions that later composers saw as axiomatic, and because he managed to invest these decisions with a sense of moral and historical necessity that has gone on impressing lesser composers faced with similar decisions in their own work. Schoenberg saw the rejection of tonality and the reliance on dense motivic workings as a logical and inevitable consequence of the music of Wagner and Brahms. His serial method was worked out directly from his existing atonal music: the idea of giving equal status to the 12 semitones; the idea of avoiding letting any one note take precedence (as a 'keynote'); the idea of deriving melody and harmony from the same material; the idea of free dissonance; even the idea of a fixed note order, which follows from the concept of an all-pervading motif – all this was already implicit, if unsystematic, in the works he wrote between 1908 and 1915.

This earnest and doctrinaire thinking might not encourage confidence in Schoenberg's potential as a theatre composer. But in fact his theatre music is some of his most brilliant and innovative. This is especially true of *Erwartung*, with its mercurial psychic scenario and spectacular orchestration, and *Pierrot lunaire*, with its witty adaptation of the idea of a cabaret sequence to a cycle of gruesome Symbolist poems accompanied by a small mixed band. During these years, Schoenberg also painted. He exhibited with the Blaue Reiter group and corresponded energetically with its co-founder, Vassily Kandinsky. Though apparently worked out quite independently, Schoenberg's *Die glückliche Hand* is close in concept to Kandinsky's so-called 'stage composition' *Der gelbe Klang*. There is valuable information on both works in their published correspondence, one of the most fascinating exchanges on any aspect of modern music. The later operas perhaps suffer from the streak of academicism in Schoenberg's serial writing, with its tendency towards stereotyping. Even so, *Moses und Aron* has remained his most staged opera, thanks to its vivid crowd scenes, which admirably (and relevantly) offset the somewhat abstract discussions of the issues of language and artistic integrity that form its basic subject matter.

Erwartung

Expectation

Monodrama in one act (30m)
Libretto by Marie Pappenheim
Composed 1909
PREMIERES 6 June 1924, Prague; UK: 9 January 1931, BBC broadcast conducted by the composer; 25 April 1960, Sadler's Wells, London (stage); US: 28 December 1960, Lisner Auditorium, George Washington University, Washington DC
CAST A Woman *s*

Schoenberg met Marie Pappenheim, a young medical student and poet, in the summer of 1909 and asked her to write an opera text for him. It seems that the choice of subject, and also possibly the idea of limiting the drama to a single character, were hers, though at that time Schoenberg had already sketched *Die glückliche Hand*, which, in its final form, also has only one solo singer. He had recently been setting Expressionist poems by Stefan George (the last two movements of the String Quartet No. 2 and the cycle *Das Buch der hängenden Gärten*). Perhaps Fräulein Pappenheim also knew that the previous year Schoenberg's wife Mathilde (the sister of Zemlinsky) had run off with his and her painting teacher, Richard Gerstl. Mathilde had been persuaded to return, and Gerstl had committed suicide.

Such events may find oblique echoes in the nightmarish dramaturgy of *Erwartung*, with its unfaithful lover slain (possibly) by the 'expectant' protagonist. But the literary apparatus and symbolic imagery (forest, moon, blood) are in fact conventional for the time, as is the Freudian dramatization of guilt. The most striking thing about *Erwartung*, apart from its sheer musical brilliance, is the sense of helpless striving for clarity: for self-knowledge followed by self-communication, in the face of an overwhelmingly alien yet terrifyingly familiar environment. The idea that profound experience is a dream inaccessible to logical explanation or description crops up regularly in the work of the Symbolists and Expressionists of the 1910s (in opera it is the theme of Debussy's *Pelléas*, a subject Schoenberg had used for an early symphonic poem, as well as Paul Dukas's *Ariadne* and Bartók's *Bluebeard*). It would be hard to imagine a better musical analogy than Schoenberg's free-association atonality – all haunted atmosphere and elusive substance.

According to the draft short score, Schoenberg composed this complex work between 27 August and 12 September (the orchestral score took a further three weeks). But it had to wait 15 years for its first performance, at the 1924 ISCM Festival in Prague, conducted by Zemlinsky (with Marie Gutheil-Schoder). Since then stage productions have been rare.

SYNOPSIS

Scene 1: In moonlight, the woman approaches the edge of a dark forest. She is looking for her lover, and knows this means entering the forest, but fears to do so. She plucks up courage and enters.

Scene 2: Groping in the darkness, she feels something crawling, and hears someone weeping. She thinks longingly of the peaceful garden where she had vainly awaited her lover. She hears a rustling and the screech of a night-bird and starts to run, but trips over what she at first thinks is a body but then recognizes as a tree trunk.

Scene 3: She approaches a moonlit clearing. She is startled by her own shadow and imagines it crawling towards her with goggling yellow eyes on stalks. She cries out for help.

Scene 4: On the edge of a forest, by a broad, moonlit road. The woman is exhausted and dishevelled; there is blood on her face and hands. She has not found him, and cannot return home for fear of 'the stranger woman'. Then she touches something; it is her lover's bloodstained corpse. She tries to convince herself that it is a figment of the moonlight. Then she tries to rouse him, remembering that they were to have spent the night together. She imagines it is day, and that the moonlight is sunlight. She lies down beside him and kisses him. But in his staring eyes she finds a memory of his suspected infidelity. She tries to banish the memory. Why was he killed? Where is the other woman? She becomes hysterically angry and kicks the body; then again self-pitying, grieving for her love. What is she to do now, since her existence was defined by him? And as she awaits the 'eternal day of waiting', she feels again the darkness, his presence and his kiss.

Erwartung is rare among Schoenberg's early atonal works in being one long continuous movement. There is little doubt that he saw the text as a crucial element in the musical syntax, and that Pappenheim's long-drawn interior monologue was exactly what he needed. Much of the setting is slow, but with rapid instrumental figuration within the texture. But the music moves swiftly from idea to idea, often with little obvious pattern. Linking motifs are hard to detect, though certain harmonies recur. The woman's consciousness – flickering between dream and reality – is reflected in the endlessly varied melodic and rhythmic figures, while her lurking derangement finds a potent metaphor in the tonal instability, incessant tempo changes and general lack of repose of the musical language.

All the same, much of the musical vocabulary is that of late-Romantic German music. The interval of a third is fundamental, just as it is to classical and Romantic harmony, though some chords are based on the fourth, in a way remote from textbooks such as Schoenberg's own *Harmonielehre*, published, curiously enough, a mere two years after he wrote *Erwartung*. Locally, continuity is sometimes achieved by repeated melodic/rhythmic patterns (ostinati). But the main thread is always the voice, with the orchestra providing sympathetic commentary. The vocal writing itself is strenuous, but Schoenberg generally avoids the huge leaps of some of his other Expressionist works for soprano, and there is no sprechgesang. The orchestra is huge, but much of the scoring is of chamber dimensions, with a kaleidoscopic variety of colouring and sudden explosions of full orchestra.

RECORDINGS 1. Martin, BBC SO, Boulez, Sony, 1977; 2. Silja, VPO, Dohnányi, Decca, 1980

Moses und Aron

Moses and Aaron

Opera in three acts (Acts I and II: 1h 45m)
Libretto by the composer
Composed 1930–32
PREMIERES 12 March 1954, Hamburg (concert); 6 June 1957, Zurich (stage); UK: 28 June 1965, Covent Garden, London; US: 2 November 1966, Black Bay Theater, Boston
CAST Moses *spoken role*, Aaron *t*, Young Girl *s*, Invalid Woman *c*, Young Man *t*, Naked Youth *t*, Another Man *bar*, Ephraimite *bar*, Priest *b*, 4 Naked Virgins 2 *s*, 2 *c*; *satb* chorus of Voice(s) from the Burning Bush, beggars, elderly persons, elders, tribal leaders, bricklayers, priests, tribeswomen, butchers, guardsmen, herdsmen

The first drafts of the libretto were made in October 1928, just as Schoenberg was also starting work on *Von Heute auf Morgen*. He then composed the *Accompaniment to a Film Scene* and the *Six Pieces* for male chorus, before starting serious composition on *Moses und Aron* (so spelt because he was superstitious about a title with 13 letters) in the summer of 1930. We have his own account, in a letter to Berg of 8 August 1931, of progress on the work. With chorus parts to write out and the libretto to revise as he went along, he was finding composition more laborious than usual. Nevertheless Acts I and II were complete by March 1932. Work on Act III did not proceed beyond a few sketches; Schoenberg was suffering from severe asthma, and instead of returning to Berlin he spent the winter of 1931–2 in Barcelona. By the spring of 1933, with the Prussian Academy being purged of Jewish elements, Schoenberg's position in Berlin had become untenable. He left Germany and in October sailed for the USA, where he again (in 1934) revised the text of Act III but could not find time to compose the music. In 1944 he applied to the Guggenheim Foundation for a grant to enable him to complete the work, but his application was turned down.

There may also, however, have been internal, creative reasons why the music for Act III eluded him. In a letter to Walter Eidlitz (15 March 1933) he complained of contradictions in the biblical account of Moses's smiting of the rock, and mentioned that he was engaged on his (at least) fourth revision of the text for Act III. Because this final act consists almost entirely of an extended diatribe by Moses against Aaron's love of graven images, details of the argument were obviously crucial. And yet in sung drama such things cut little ice. If the only meaning of Act III was one the audience would be unlikely to grasp in performance, then it is not surprising that Schoenberg found it hard to compose. Nor would it have escaped him that his difficulty was precisely Moses': how to put a lofty, abstract vision into words and images without distorting and ultimately destroying it.

SYNOPSIS

Act I, Scene 1: Moses hears the Voice in the burning bush, instructing him to free the Israelites and lead them to the Promised Land. Moses objects that he lacks eloquence, but God tells him that three miracles will serve as a sign, aided by Aaron's eloquence. (Moses 'speaks' throughout in sprechgesang, which stands for his lack of articulacy: the voice of God is given to six singers, backed here by a sprechgesang group, standing for the two aspects of God: the word, and the hidden meaning.) Scene 2: Moses and Aaron meet in the wilderness. Aware of his role, Aaron (a fluid, lyric tenor) consistently interprets Moses' words in a superficial, concrete sense, while Moses insists on God's unknowability. Scene 3: The Israelites discuss the meeting of Moses and Aaron, expressing various attitudes to the new god: the Young Girl sees him as the embodiment of love, the Young Man of spiritual aspiration, and an older man of political hope. A priest reminds them that Moses is a murderer. Two chorus groups sum up the different reactions, for and against. Moses and Aaron are seen approaching, and the chorus describes their contrasting ways of moving. Scene 4: Aaron interprets Moses' idea of the only, infinite, invisible God, but the people are hostile to an invisible god, even one who, Aaron says, is visible to the righteous. Moses expresses his helplessness in the face of Aaron's simplifications and the people's ridicule. But Aaron wins them over by changing Moses' staff ('the Law') into a writhing snake. Can the power of Moses and the new god force Pharaoh's hand? Aaron now turns Moses' hand leprous, then cures it, as a sign that the sickly, spiritless Israelites must make themselves whole in order to challenge Pharaoh. The people are now on the point of breaking their bonds. But what will they live on in the desert? Pure contemplation, says Moses. But Aaron promises that God will provide for his children by turning 'sand into fruit, fruit into gold, gold into ecstasy, and ecstasy into spirit'; he shows how God has changed the water in his pitcher to blood. God will lead them to a land flowing with milk and honey. The chorus takes up the ideas of the Chosen People and the Promised Land.

Interlude: In the darkness, the people ask after Moses (who has been absent on the Mount of Revelation for 40 days).

Act II, Scene 1: The people are restive, and the rule of law is beginning to break down. The Elders tell Aaron that they will not wait for Moses' return from the mountain with the new Law. Scene 2:

The people demand their old gods back. Aaron tries to calm them but lets slip that God might have killed Moses. As the people threaten to slaughter their priests, Aaron gives way and promises to build them a visible image of gold. Scene 3: Aaron calls on the people to worship the Golden Calf. First, animals are brought in for slaughter, and the people devour hunks of raw meat. Then a crippled woman is healed; beggars dedicate their last scraps of food to the calf; old men sacrifice their last moments of life; the Ephraimite and Tribal Chieftains ride in and bow down to the image. The spiritual young man of Act I, Scene 3 remonstrates with them and is slaughtered. Next comes an orgy of drunkenness, characterized by mutual generosity. Finally four naked virgins are embraced by priests and stabbed at the moment of ecstasy. This leads to an orgy of self-destruction and sexual excess. At the end, lassitude takes over. Scene 4: Moses is seen descending the mountain. He dismisses the calf with a gesture. The people flee. Scene 5: Aaron defends himself against Moses' reproof. Even Moses, he claims, needs images, like the tablets of the Commandments which he holds in his hands. In response, Moses smashes the tablets. Aaron reproaches him for his frailty. The Vision, he says, is not so easily falsified. In the background the Israelites are seen following the fiery and cloudy pillars. Aaron follows them, leaving Moses in an agony of frustration at his inarticulacy.

[Act III (uncomposed; late in his life, Schoenberg suggested it might be spoken): Aaron is brought in in chains. Once more, Moses reproves him for preferring the image to the idea. The guards ask if they should kill Aaron, but Moses orders his release, whereupon Aaron instantly falls dead.]

The obvious predecessor of *Moses und Aron* in Schoenberg's work is the unfinished oratorio *Jakobsleiter*, and *Moses* itself has attributes of oratorio. The chorus is consistently treated like the *turba* in Bach's Passion settings. Individual characters emerge from it, but in essence it is a symbolic group, reacting collectively to the central dilemma. Much of the choral writing is fugal, as in Bach or Handel. But even in the freer sections, the serial method constantly throws up melodic similarities that suggest the imitative vocal styles of earlier times. This 'strictness' of technique is offset by the perhaps surprising vitality of the choral dramaturgy (considering that Schoenberg had never written for a stage chorus before). The final scene of Act I, in particular, is a brilliantly co-ordinated piece of extended ensemble writing. The notorious *Dance round the Golden Calf* is also skilfully paced, though it contains relatively little vocal writing, while as an orchestral piece it has the vividness of detail and colour, but not the melodic or rhythmic thrust, of the greatest stage dance tableaux, such as the *Danse sacrale* in Stravinsky's *Rite of Spring*. Like all Schoenberg's other serial works, *Moses* is entirely based on a single 12-note row.

Since the 1950s *Moses* has had several stage productions, without ever quite establishing itself as a repertoire piece. Its dramatic complexities make it difficult to put on, but it also lacks the ingredients for even highbrow popularity. This would not have worried Schoenberg (he expected it), but it is worrying to his admirers. They look, without much hope, for any previous example of great music drama that has not, in the long run, achieved a wide audience. The irony of this is that Schoenberg always saw history as his main justification and support as an artist, yet in his determined unapproachability it gives him no support at all.

RECORDINGS 1. Palmer, Reich, Cassilly, BBC Singers, Orpheus Boys Ch, BBC SO, Boulez, Sony, 1974; 2. Fontana, Pittman-Jennings, Merritt, Ch of Netherlands Op, Concertgebouw O, Boulez, DG, 1995

OTHER OPERATIC WORKS *Die*

glückliche Hand, 1924; *Von Heute auf Morgen*, 1930

S.W.

Franz Schubert

Franz Peter Schubert; *b* 31 January 1797, Vienna; *d* 19 November 1828, Vienna

Though Schubert's songs and instrumental music place him among the greatest composers, none of his operas has joined the standard repertoire. Musically they contain fine moments, but are generally regarded as dramatically weak. Both an innate inability to construct large-scale dramatic works and a lack of stage experience have been suggested as reasons for this. Schubert evidently felt constrained by theatrical demands and conventions, which hampered the boundless creativity that found a natural and sublime expression in his songs. But there are elements in his last operas which suggest that, had he lived longer, he might have arrived at a highly original conception of opera.

Schubert's exceptional musical talents were already apparent when he became a pupil at the K. K. Stadtkonvikt in 1808, and his composition studies under Salieri were continued after he left the school in 1813. Salieri impressed on him that a composer should prove himself primarily through his dramatic works: it was certainly expected that composers should write operas. At the Stadtkonvikt Schubert had already made an abortive attempt at a singspiel, *Der Spiegelritter*, but his first substantial operatic work, *Des Teufels Lustschloss*, was composed during the 12 months immediately after he left. In 1815, when he was working as an assistant master in his father's school, he wrote no fewer than four stage works, which, following the current popular trend, were all singspiels. The influences of Mozart and of Beethoven's *Fidelio* on these are clear; Schubert was also evidently familiar with the work of contemporary French composers such as Le Sueur, Dalayrac and Méhul as well as the popular Viennese singspiels of the day by such composers as Wenzel Müller, Weigl and Hummel.

From 1816, when he gave up teaching, to 1818 Schubert made only abortive operatic efforts, but in 1819, as a result of the influence of his friend the singer Johann Michael Vogl, he was commissioned to write *Die Zwillingsbrüder*. The 1820 productions of this and the melodrama *Die Zauberharfe*, with its spectacular magic effects, though by no means resounding successes, brought his stage works to public notice.

Schubert wrote four further complete stage works between 1821 and 1823. Only the incidental music to Helmina von Chezy's *Rosamunde* was performed during his lifetime. His last opera, *Fierrabras*, and sketches for an unfinished work, *Der Graf von Gleichen*, show how far Schubert had progressed since his apprentice days. An individual theatrical style was beginning to emerge that in more than one respect (for example stage settings, instrumental accompaniments) anticipates later developments in German Romantic opera.

Fierrabras

Opera in three acts (2h 30m)
Libretto by Josef Kupelwieser, after the play *La Puente de Mantible* by Pedro Calderón de la Barca (1640) and an old German legend, *Eginhard und Emma*
Composed [May–October] 1823
PREMIERES 7 May 1835, Josefstadt Theatre, Vienna (three numbers; concert); 9 February 1897, Hoftheater, Karlsruhe (shortened version); US: 9 May 1980, Walnut Street Theater, Philadelphia; UK: 6 November 1938, London (excerpts; concert); 10 April 1971, BBC Radio (studio recording); 19 February 1986, Playhouse, Oxford (stage)
CAST King Karl *b*, Emma *s*, Eginhard *t*, Roland *bar*, Ogier *t*, Boland *b*, Fierrabras

t, Florinda *s*, Maragond *ms*, Brutamonte *b*; *satb* chorus of ladies, knights, soldiers

Late in 1821 Domenico Barbaja, director of the Kärntnertortheater, asked Schubert for a German opera for the 1822–3 season. The composer offered both *Alfonso und Estrella* and *Die Verschworenen* (neither of which had yet been performed), but they were rejected, and Schubert, anxious to see his stage works performed, set to work on a new full-length opera. Although it was completed in time, *Fierrabras* too was rejected and its 26-year-old composer did not live to see his last – and most individual – opera performed. *Fierrabras* disappeared until its publication in 1886. It has enjoyed a few revivals since the 1970s (including a significant production at the 1988 Vienna Festival).

SYNOPSIS

Act I: Emma, daughter of King Karl, and Eginhard, a young knight, are secretly in love. After a victory against the Moors, Karl sends a mission of peace led by his general, Roland, and including Eginhard. He declares an amnesty for the Moorish prisoners. Among these is Fierrabras, son of the Moorish leader Boland, whose valour has won Roland's admiration. It transpires that Fierrabras has loved Emma since seeing her during a visit to Rome and that Roland had simultaneously fallen in love with Fierrabras's sister Florinda. That night Fierrabras observes a secret meeting between Eginhard and Emma. Despite his jealousy he does not give them away, even when he is wrongly blamed for trying to abduct Emma and is imprisoned.

Act II: Eginhard and the rest of the peace mission are incarcerated by Boland. Florinda, recognizing Roland, determines to save them. She unlocks their prison and provides weapons, but only Eginhard escapes, while the rest of the knights remain barricaded in the tower.

Act III: Karl, having discovered the truth about Emma and Eginhard, orders Fierrabras's release. Eginhard, arriving with news of the knights' plight, begs to lead a rescue party. Fierrabras accompanies him. The rescue party arrives just in time to prevent the executions of the knights and Florinda. The opera ends with the couples united and Fierrabras accepted into the chivalric brotherhood of the Frankish knights.

While Schubert employed many of the stock-in-trade devices of contemporary German opera (for example the women's spinning chorus, the men's unaccompanied patriotic hymn), *Fierrabras*, undeniably Schubert's strongest stage work, rises above the commonplace and presents a tantalizing example of the composer's fully formed theatrical style. Elements familiar from other composers are here not so much borrowed or copied as assimilated into Schubert's own musical language. Much of the most effective writing is for Florinda (the best-drawn female character in Schubert's theatrical music), whose numbers include an aria accompanied by male-voice chorus ('Des Jammers herbe Qualen') and a highly dramatic melodrama, as she watches her beloved Roland in battle. Particularly haunting too is the serenade between Eginhard and Emma, 'Der Abend sinkt aus stiller Flor', which begins the Act I finale.

RECORDING Mattila, Studer, Protschka, Gambill, Hampson, Holl, Polgár, Arnold Schoenberg Ch, COE, C. Abbado, DG, 1988 (live, omits dialogue)
OTHER OPERATIC WORKS *Der Spiegelritter*, (inc.) (1812), 1949; *Des Teufels Lustschloss*, (1814), 1879; *Der vierjährige Posten*, (1815), 1896; *Fernando*, (1815), 1907; *Claudine von Villa Bella*, (inc.) (1815), 1913; *Die Freunde von Salamanka*, (1815), 1928; *Die Bürgschaft*, (inc.) (1816), 1908; *Adrast*, (inc.) (1820), 1985; *Die Zauberharfe*, 1820 (inc.); *Die Zwillingsbrüder*, 1820; *Sakuntala*, (inc.) (1820), 1971; *Alfonso und Estrella*, (1822), 1854; *Die Verschworenen*, (1823) 1861; *Rüdiger*, (inc.) (1823), 1868; *Der Graf von Gleichen*, (inc.) (1827)

C.A.B.

Robert Schumann

Robert Alexander Schumann; *b* 8 June 1810, Zwickau, Saxony; *d* 29 July 1856, Enderich, Saxony

One of the greatest of all 19th-century composers, Schumann's reputation today is founded upon his piano works (alongside Chopin's the most important of the Romantic era), songs and, to a lesser extent, his orchestral music. But until the late 20th century his choral works, especially *Das Paradies und die Peri* (1842) and *Scenes from Goethe's 'Faust'* (1853), were neglected, dismissed as lacking in dramatic energy and evenness of musical invention, and the same criticisms have been consistently levelled against his only opera, *Genoveva*.

Schuman had nurtured the ambition to write an opera since 1830, when he considered making a libretto from *Hamlet*, but having abandoned the idea, he devoted the next decade exclusively to the piano. It was only after his long-delayed marriage to Clara Wieck in 1840, which he celebrated in a great outpouring of song, including the cycles *Dichterliebe* and *Frauenliebe und -leben*, that the idea of a stage work surfaced again. He considered the possibilities of *Doge und Dogaresse* by E. T. A. Hoffmann, whose fantastical writings underpin his greatest piano work *Kreisleriana* (1838), but that too was soon abandoned, and over the next seven years he made ultimately fruitless attempts on a whole range of possible subjects. In 1844 he got as far as composing the first chorus of a work based upon Byron's *The Corsair*, while he also passingly considered *Faust*, the *Nibelungenlied* and the stories of Tristan and Isolde, Till Eulenspiegl, Abelard and Héloïse, Mazeppa and even the Blacksmith of Gretna Green; in 1845 he was piqued to discover that Wagner had published a libretto for *Lohengrin*, claiming that he had been considering a similar work on Arthurian myths for some time. Two years later, however, he read Tieck's *Das Leben und Tod der heiligen Genoveva* and immediately settled upon that, perhaps identifying Geneviève of Brabant, its virtuous heroine, with his own idolized wife Clara.

Genoveva

Genevieve

Opera in four acts (2h 15m)
Libretto by Robert Reinick and the composer, after the plays *Das Leben und Tod der heiligen Genoveva* by Ludwig Tieck (1799) and *Genoveva* by Friedrich Hebbel (1843)
Composed 1847–9
PREMIERES 25 June 1850, Stadt Theater, Leipzig; UK: 6 December 1893, Drury Lane, London
CAST Genoveva *s*, Siegfried *bar*, Golo *t*, Drago *b*, Margaretha *s*, Hidulfus *bar*, Balthasar *b*, Caspar *bar*, Angelo *silent*, Conrad *silent*; *satb* chorus of knights, squires, priests, servants, people, spirits

Schumann had already commissioned Reinick to prepare a libretto based upon Tieck's text when he discovered Hebbel's *Genoveva*, which offered a much less sentimental perspective on the French legend. He asked Reinick to combine both sources, but after two drafts were rejected by Schumann, their collaboration ceased. After failing to interest Hebbel in writing the libretto, Schumann decided to compile it himself, conflating Reinick's two versions and attempting to reconcile the sober intensity and coherence of Hebbel with the more protean, episodic quality of Tieck.

SYNOPSIS

Act I: Bishop Hidulphus commissions Siegfried, Count of Palatine, to join the war against the invading Moors. Siegfried entrusts his young bride Genoveva to the care of his servant Golo, who is secretly infatuated with her. Genoveva faints as Siegfried leaves, and Golo leads her inside; his former nurse, Margaretha, now a sorceress, agrees to help him win Genoveva's affections.

Act II: In her bedroom, Genoveva hears from Golo that Siegfried has been victorious and will soon return. She asks Golo to sing to her, and in the course of their duet, he confesses his passion; she is appalled and rebuffs his advances. Golo decides to take his revenge and, hearing gossip that Genoveva is unfaithful, he asks Drago, Siegfried's steward, to hide in her room to keep watch. The servants then discover Drago there and kill him; Genoveva is imprisoned as an adulteress.

Act III: Siegfried has been wounded in the victory, but is recovering at an inn in Strasbourg, nursed by Margaretha in disguise. All her efforts to poison him have failed, and she cannot sway his belief in Genoveva's fidelity, even when she offers to let him see the past in her magic mirror. Golo brings news of Genoveva's adultery. Siegfried vows never to return to his castle, and gives Golo his ring and sword, with the order that his wife should be executed. Golo now realizes the consequences of his treachery, but Siegfried now asks to look into the magic mirror, which shows increasing intimacy between Genoveva and Drago. Siegfried smashes the mirror and rushes off with Golo; Drago's ghost appears to Margaretha and warns her that unless she reveals the truth she will be burned alive.

Act IV: The servants Balthazar and Caspar take Genoveva to a rocky wilderness to kill her. She prays for deliverance, calling out for Siegfried, and has a vision of the Virgin Mary, while angelic voices promise she will find peace. Golo offers to save her, but she rejects his advances again; he leaves her to her fate. Margaretha brings Siegfried to the site of the execution just as the fatal blow is about to fall. He begs Genoveva for forgiveness, but she says he is blameless; everything was fate. In the castle courtyard Siegfried's retinue greets the returning couple; Hidulphus blesses Siegfried and Genoveva, committing them to God's grace.

Schumann wrote *Genoveva* at a transitional point in German opera; Wagner was still to prove himself, while lesser composers were still in thrall to Weber's *Die Freischütz*, and were repeatedly trying to replicate its spectacular effects. Yet Schumann did not attempt the kind of German grand opera that audiences had been craving since *Freischütz*: 'German composers', he wrote, 'usually fail through trying to please the public.' His instincts as a great lieder composer led him inevitably to explore the inner life of his operatic characters in his music, rather than to illustrate their actions in vividly pictorial music, and that, for the public and the critics at the time of the premiere (which Schumann himself conducted), was a fatal flaw.

Yet the plot of *Genoveva* is no more flimsy than that of many more celebrated operas, while from a 21st-century perspective, Schumann's dramaturgy and treatment of character seem to have much more in common with the Wagnerian approach to music drama than anyone, certainly Wagner himself, would have conceded at that time. In rejecting the use of spoken dialogue and recitative in his score Schumann placed all the responsibility for projecting character and motive on to the orchestra, and bound his almost symphonic construction together with a network of motifs, all of them derived from the chorale with which the opera opens. These are not leitmotifs in the strict Wagnerian sense of the term, for they do not have a specific signalling function; they operate instead by suggestion, so that, for instance, the music associated with Golo is permeated with a sense of malevolence, while Genoveva's exudes pristine virtue. Together with Schumann's acute sensitivity to words and their colouring, this web of connections creates wonderfully nuanced psychological portraits of the protagonists and their motivations. There is something very modern about *Genoveva*, and audiences today are in a better position to appreciate it for what the composer intended.

RECORDINGS 1. E. Moser, Schröter, Schreier, Fischer-Dieskau, Lorenz, Vogel, Berlin RCh, Leipzig Gewandhaus O, Masur, Berlin Classics, 1976; 2. Ziesak, Lipovsek, Van der Walt, Gilfry, O. Widmer, Quasthoff, Arnold Schoenberg Ch, COE, Harnoncourt, Teldec, 1996 (live)

A.C.

Dmitry Shostakovich

Dmitry Dmitriyevich Shostakovich; *b* 25 September 1906, St Petersburg; *d* 9 August 1975, Moscow

Shostakovich's mother was a professional pianist, and he entered the Petrograd (St Petersburg) Conservatory as a pianist at the age of 13. But he also developed rapidly as a composer, under Maximilian Steinberg, the Rimsky-Korsakov pupil. He was still only 19 when his First Symphony was premiered in the again renamed Leningrad in May 1926 (he had already destroyed a student opera based on Pushkin's *The Gypsies*); within two years this brilliant, if derivative, symphony had made him world famous. A Second and Third Symphony followed – both quite experimental in style – and several theatre works, including the sparkling Gogol opera *The Nose*, two or three ballets and incidental music to Mayakovsky's play *The Bedbug*. By the early 1930s Shostakovich was already moderating his style (as many west European progressives of the 1920s were also doing), and his second opera, *Lady Macbeth of the Mtsensk District*, mixes modernism and biting satire with revived Romantic-cum-Expressionist elements.

Shostakovich was not yet 30 when this work was violently attacked in *Pravda* in January 1936 and its composer left shattered and fearful – at a time when even artists were beginning to pay with their lives for deviating from the new ideal of Socialist Realism. Thereafter, he seldom risked serious theatre work. An operetta, *The Silly Little Mouse*, composed early in 1939, is lost, as is the film material of a miniature Pushkin comic opera, *The Tale of a Priest and His Servant Balda*, composed in 1941 but destroyed in the Leningrad bombing that year (a concert suite survives). His setting of Gogol's *The Gamblers* was left unfinished, he tells us in *Testimony*, because he suddenly realized it was morally unacceptable in wartime Russia (and it would certainly have been so in post-war Russia, when in 1948 Shostakovich was carpeted, along with most of his gifted compatriots, for 'formalism and anti-democratic tendencies'). He seems to have made little progress with an opera based on Tolstoy's *Resurrection* (1940). Later he composed only the operetta *Moscow, Cheryomushki*, though at the time of his death he was planning an opera on Chekhov's *The Black Monk*. The core of his work post-1936 is symphonic, with a parallel stream of chamber works dominated by 15 string quartets. But even while seeking safety in 'abstract' forms, or in film music or cantatas on officially acceptable topics, Shostakovich found it hard to deny his theatrical talent. Both his symphonies and his chamber works are full of essentially graphic writing and barely concealed psychological drama. Though he never wrote an unmistakable operatic masterpiece, it seems quite possible that he would have been one of the great modern opera composers – a worthy successor to Musorgsky and Tchaikovsky – if circumstances had allowed.

The Nose

Nos

Opera in three acts and an epilogue (1h 45m)
Libretto by the composer, after the short story by Nikolai Gogol (1835)

Composed 1927–8

PREMIERES 16 June 1929, Leningrad (concert); 18 January 1930, Leningrad (stage); UK: 21 October 1972 (broadcast); 4 April 1973, Sadler's Wells, London (stage); US: 11 August 1965, Opera Theater, Santa Fe

CAST Kovalyov *bar*, Yakovlevich *b-bar*, Police Inspector *very high t*, Ivan *t*, Nose *t*, Madame Podtochina *ms*, her daughter *s*, old countess *c*, Praskovya Ossipovna *s*, advertising employee *b-bar*, *s*, 7 *t*, 9 *b*; *satb* chorus of worshippers, poor matrons, travellers, passers-by, onlookers, eunuchs, policemen (also spoken roles) – numbers depend on various possibilities of role-doubling

Shostakovich wrote his first opera at the height of the 'anything-goes' period of early Soviet art. For a few years after the end of the Civil War the Soviet Union was in a ferment of artistic experiment, as seemed to befit an emerging revolutionary state. In music, the influence of western avant-gardists, such as Schoenberg, Hindemith and Stravinsky, was strong. Berg's *Wozzeck* was staged in Leningrad while Shostakovich was writing *The Nose*, and its influence is apparent, as is that of Prokofiev's *Love of Three Oranges* (Leningrad, 1926). At the same time the work's absurdism and unremitting grotesquerie suggest a knowledge of Cocteau and Les Six, though its satire against civil servants is purely Russian. In tone and outline it follows Gogol's short story closely, while incorporating material from other books by Gogol, as well as a song from Dostoevsky's *Brothers Karamazov*.

The Nose enjoyed some success in Leningrad, but was not taken up elsewhere. The political climate was already turning against such things, and in any case the piece is forbiddingly hard to stage, with its spiky and difficult orchestral writing and its cast of 70 characters. It returned to favour in the Soviet Union in the 1970s but has had only occasional productions abroad.

SYNOPSIS

Act I: After a brief prologue (Kovalyov being shaved by the barber Yakovlevich), we see Yakovlevich at breakfast. To his (moderate) surprise he finds a nose in his roll, but manages – not without difficulty – to dispose of it in the river Neva. Meanwhile, Kovalyov discovers his loss. He tracks the Nose down to Kazan Cathedral, where it appears dressed as a state councillor.

Act II: Kovalyov tries to report the loss to the police and to place a newspaper advertisement.

Act III: Eventually the Nose is apprehended trying to board the Riga coach, and the Police Inspector returns it to Kovalyov. But the Doctor is unable to reattach it. Kovalyov writes to Madame Podtochina, accusing her of masterminding the theft to blackmail him into marrying her daughter. Everyone discusses the rumours about Kovalyov's nose walking the streets.

Epilogue: The Nose suddenly reappears in its rightful place. The delighted Kovalyov is again able to hold his head up in St Petersburg.

Shostakovich maintained that his music for *The Nose* was not comical. But this may have been to pre-empt the criticism of unseriousness. The work is in fact rich in satire and grotesquerie, and the music is generally graphic rather than symphonic. Its structure is a montage of short scenes with orchestral interludes (compare *Wozzeck*, whose Captain may also have inspired Shostakovich's Police Inspector, with his ludicrously high-tenor squeak), and there is little sustained dramatic growth or psychological development.

Although he never again wrote music so dependent on parody, many typical Shostakovichisms appear in *The Nose* for the first time. The spiky scherzo ostinati were to become standard in his symphonies, and the jogging minimalism of episodes, such as Ivan's balalaika-playing scene (with flexatone) or the final scene on the Nevsky Prospect, was to serve Shostakovich much later in serious or ironic contexts. In general the ability to absorb naive musical styles into a sophisticated idiom was to prove one of his most individual traits and greatest strengths. *The Nose* may not be a masterpiece, but it is remarkably rich in musical possibilities.

RECORDING Sasulova, Belykh, Lomonosov, Akimov, Moscow C Th Ch & O, Rozhdestvensky, Melodiya, 1975

Lady Macbeth of the Mtsensk District

Ledi Makbet Mtsenskovo uyezda

Opera in four acts, nine scenes (2h 30m)
Libretto by Alexander Preis and the composer, after the short story by Nikolay Leskov (1865)
Composed 1930–32; rev. 1935, and (as *Katerina Ismailova*) 1956–63
PREMIERES *Lady Macbeth*: 22 January 1934, Maly Opera House, Leningrad; UK: 18 March 1936, Queen's Hall, London (concert); 22 May 1987, Coliseum, London (stage); US: 31 January 1935, Cleveland, Ohio (semi-staged); *Katerina Ismailova*: 26 December 1962, Stanislavsky-Nemirovich-Danchenko Music Theatre, Moscow; UK: 2 December 1963, Covent Garden, London; US: 23 October 1964, War Memorial Opera House, San Francisco
CAST Katerina Ismailova *s*, Boris Ismailov *high b*, Zinovy Ismailov *t*, Sergei *t*, Mill-hand *bar*, Coachman *t*, Aksinya *s*, Shabby Peasant *t*, Porter *b*, Steward *b*, 3 Foremen 3 *t*, Priest *b*, Chief of Police *bar*, Policeman *b*, Teacher *t*, Drunken Guest *t*, Old Convict *b*, Sentry *b*, Sonyetka *c*, Woman Convict *s*, Sergeant *b*; *satb* chorus of workers, policemen, guests, convicts

Shostakovich first encountered Leskov's brutal tale (published a few years after the emancipation of the serfs) through his artist friend Boris Kustodiev, who illustrated an edition of 1930. But from the start he reacted very differently from Leskov to the tragic heroine. The original Katerina is irredeemably cruel and self-seeking, and is treated by Leskov ironically, whereas Shostakovich saw her as a sympathetic figure driven to crime by intolerable boredom and despair. The social and psychological implications of her predicament struck him as important; it clearly never occurred to him that his graphic treatment of her actions would be taken as signifying approval.

'As a Soviet composer,' he wrote in 1934, 'I determined to preserve the strength of Leskov's novel, and yet, approaching it critically, to interpret its events from our modern point of view.' 'So little was socialist realism understood at first,' Gerald Abraham wrote in *Eight Soviet Composers*, 'that *Lady Macbeth of Mtsensk* was accepted as an embodiment of it.' In 1934–5 the work was a considerable popular success and was widely performed in and out of the Soviet Union, attracting generally appreciative notices. But on 28 January 1936 there appeared in *Pravda* a lengthy editorial denouncing the opera as 'Muddle instead of Music', attacking its 'deliberately discordant, confused stream of sounds . . . [its] din, grinding and screaming' and its sexual naturalism, in which '"love" is smeared all over the opera in the most vulgar manner'. 'Is its success abroad not explained,' *Pravda* demanded smugly, 'by the fact that it tickles the perverted bourgeois taste with its fidgety, screaming, neurotic music?'

The editorial apparently reflected the opinion of Stalin himself, who had attended a performance in December 1935. In any case, the denunciation was official, and the opera was instantly withdrawn, followed in December by the composer's Fourth Symphony, which had just gone into rehearsal. His Fifth Symphony, which followed in 1937, was subtitled 'the practical reply of a Soviet artist to justified criticism' and is certainly more direct and transparent than either of the withdrawn works, though less of a reaction against their style than is often said. *Lady Macbeth* vanished from the Soviet scene (there was a post-war production in Düsseldorf) until, in the more tolerant early 1960s, Shostakovich produced a major revision under the title *Katerina Ismailova*. This revision is a compromise. It purges textual and scenic details that would still have offended Soviet primness in 1962, but it also makes purely musical changes, especially to vocal lines, as well as somewhat lightening the orchestral texture. However, some of these changes already appear in the published edition of 1935. In particular, the orchestral depiction of Katerina's love-making with Sergei in Act I, Scene 3 is toned down (it completely disappears in 1962). Moreover the passacaglia interlude after the murder of Boris is reduced for solo organ, and the stage band is cut (both these changes were cancelled in 1962). Since the composer's death, the original (1932) version has returned to favour, both on record and on the stage, and today there seems little reason to prefer the expurgated score.

SYNOPSIS (ORIGINAL VERSION)

Act I, Scene 1: Katerina is lying on her bed, bored and frustrated. Boris, her father-in-law, nags her for not giving his son Zinovy a child. Zinovy meanwhile leaves to attend to a burst mill-dam, but before going he presents a new labourer, Sergei, to his father. Boris forces Katerina to swear fidelity in her husband's absence. Aksinya, a cook, tells Katerina that Sergei lost his previous job for carrying on with his master's wife. Boris berates her for not weeping at Zinovy's departure. Scene 2: Sergei and the men are brutally molesting Aksinya when Katerina appears and threatens Sergei with a thrashing. He in turn challenges her to a wrestling match, whose thinly veiled sexual intention takes them both to the ground as Boris comes in. He promises to report her behaviour to Zinovy. Scene 3: Boris orders Katerina to bed and goes out. She undresses, but as she lies down Sergei knocks on the door and asks to borrow a book. He complains of boredom, and she too admits she is bored and would like a child. He makes a pass at her and they make love. Boris is heard calling Katerina, but Sergei refuses to leave.

Act II, Scene 4: A week later Boris is walking about outside, musing on his sexual prowess when young. Seeing a light in Katerina's window, he decides to pay her a visit, and catches Sergei leaving her room. He at once calls in the workers, and personally whips Sergei, watched by Katerina, who slides down the drainpipe and tries to stop him. Sergei is taken away to the storeroom, while Boris orders Katerina to prepare him some mushrooms and sends the porter for Zinovy. Katerina slips rat poison into the mushrooms, and as Boris collapses, she takes the storeroom keys from his pocket. A gang of workers arrives, and one of their foremen brings a priest. Boris manages to get out a garbled accusation against Katerina before dying. The priest pronounces a (somewhat light-hearted) requiem. Scene 5: Katerina and Sergei are in bed, but Sergei warns her that when Zinovy returns their love will end. She promises that all will be well. But as he sleeps, Boris's ghost appears to her and curses her. Suddenly Katerina senses Zinovy's return. Sergei hides, and she admits Zinovy, who remonstrates with her for her philandering. Seeing Sergei's belt, he whips her with it, but Katerina and Sergei batter him to death with a candlestick and shove his body into the cellar.

Act III, Scene 6: Katerina and Sergei are about to get married, though Zinovy's body is still in the cellar. The Shabby Peasant sings a drunken song and breaks into the cellar in search of wine. Finding Zinovy's putrid corpse, he rushes off to the police station. Scene 7: At the station, the police sing a jolly hymn to bribery and corruption. They are incensed at not being invited to Katerina's wedding. A 'socialist' teacher is brought in and questioned. When the Shabby Peasant arrives with news of the corpse, the police see it as 'a gift from God'. Scene 8: At the wedding, the guests are drunk and the Priest makes lascivious advances to Katerina. Suddenly Katerina notices that the storeroom lock is broken, but as she suggests to Sergei that they steal the money and run away, the police arrive and the two give themselves up.

Act IV, Scene 9: In the convict line by a river on the road to Siberia, Katerina bribes the sentry to let her through to Sergei. But Sergei rejects her, and goes instead to Sonyetka, a convict who demands that he bring her Katerina's stockings. He tricks Katerina and takes the stockings to Sonyetka, while the other women convicts, and then Sonyetka herself, taunt Katerina. As the convicts begin to move off, Katerina pushes Sonyetka into the river and jumps in after her. The remaining convicts trudge off.

Technically *Lady Macbeth* is a major advance on *The Nose*. Shostakovich himself drew attention to its symphonic character. The crucial orchestral interludes link the scenes into an unbroken musico-dramatic thread, as well as adding psychological depth and tragic foreboding to the superficially crude narrative. The same expansiveness is apparent in the Fourth Symphony, but it might well be argued that the opera is the more successful work. Its few satirical episodes – the two appearances of the Priest, and the scene in the police station – only mildly disrupt the melodramatic texture; indeed, they lighten it usefully. Overall, the pacing is astonishingly assured for a first serious opera.

At the same time, the musical invention is consistently brilliant. Among several superb interludes, the passacaglia (Scenes 4/5) is equal to anything in the symphonies; but so is much else, particularly the bedroom scenes, where Shostakovich shows a rare and astonishing ability to use sustained orchestral counterpoint dramatically. This skill he combines with a strong sense of harmonic architecture and a mastery of ostinato (in *The Nose* an amusing mannerism) as a device for generating tension. Even more unexpectedly, the vocal writing is grateful and effective, notwithstanding a few passages where screaming takes over. Like Britten, Shostakovich devised a vocal style that adheres to traditional principles without limiting the musical idiom. One of the work's most memorable vocal melodies served him again (in the String Quartet No. 8: Katerina's 'Seryozha, khoroshi moy' in the last scene of the opera). But there are others as good. It is easy to understand why *Lady Macbeth* was popular until Stalin took against it.

Shostakovich had planned a tetralogy of operas about women. That the other three were never written must be accounted one of the major losses of 20th-century opera, even if his choice of heroines (the fourth was to be a Stakhanovite worker at the Dnieper Hydroelectric Works) might seem less than ideally promising. After completing *Lady Macbeth*, late in 1932, he worked instead on a comic opera, *The Big Lightning*, but soon laid it aside (the fragments were glued together by Gennadi Rozhdestvensky and performed in Leningrad in 1981).

RECORDINGS *Lady Macbeth* (1932): 1. Vishnevskaya, Valjakka, Gedda, Krenn, Petkov, Ambrosian Op Ch, LSO, Rostropovich, EMI, 1978; 2. Ewing, Kristine Ciesinski, Larin, Langridge, Haugland, Paris Opéra-Bastille Ch & O, Chung, DG, 1992; *Katerina Ismailova*: Andreyeva, Yefimov, Bulavin, Moscow Musical Th Ch & O, Provatorov, EMI/ Melodiya, 1964

OTHER OPERATIC WORKS *The Gamblers* (*Igroki*), (1942), 1978; *Moscow, Cheryomushki* (*Moskva, Cheryomushki*), 1958

S.W.

Bedřich Smetana

b 2 March 1824, Litomyšl, Bohemia (now Czech Republic); *d* 12 May 1884, Prague

Smetana is the outstanding figure in Czech opera of the 19th century. Before him there were only spasmodic and inconsistent attempts to write operas in Czech and together they form no continuous tradition. Smetana bequeathed to the Czech nation a work taken to be the very embodiment of 'Czechness' in opera (*The Bartered Bride*) and explored a variety of contrasting operatic genres as a basis for the future course of Czech opera. These range from large-scale historical and legendary operas to village operas, though his most personal contribution may well be the bitter-sweet questing dramas of his last years. Smetana's legacy was zealously defended after his death and turned into a cult that was used to stifle the works of his contemporaries and successors, Dvořák and Janáček in particular.

Smetana's musical education, at the Proksch Institute in Prague (1844–7), allied him to the Liszt–Wagner school, and his earliest mature orchestral works were a series of Lisztian tone poems, striking in their harmonic freedom and their use of thematic transformation. After working abroad in Sweden (1856–61), Smetana returned to Prague at a crucial stage in the city's operatic history: the opening of the Provisional Theatre in 1862, the first theatre built exclusively for Czech use. In 1866, after his first opera, *The Brandenburgers in Bohemia*, was given at the Provisional Theatre and won first prize in the Harrach Competition for new Czech operas, he was quickly taken on at the theatre as chief conductor, ousting Jan Nepomuk Maýr, who had built up the company from scratch. Smetana remained at the Provisional Theatre for eight years (1866–74) in an increasingly embittered tenure, during which his musicianship was unchallenged, but conservative factions, unhappy with his Wagnerian orientation, questioned his ability as a conductor and as music director of an opera company. This period saw more Smetana premieres, though only his second opera, *The Bartered Bride*, in its final reduction of 1870, achieved real popularity.

What Smetana's critics sought to achieve, however, came about through the sudden onslaught of deafness in 1874. He resigned his post as conductor and courageously set about a career exclusively as a composer. During this period he composed his First String Quartet (which depicts the tragic interruption of his working life by the high-pitched tinnitus, which was now all he heard), completed his cycle of six tone poems, *Má vlast*, and wrote three new operas. The first of these, *The Kiss*, became his most popular opera after *The Bartered Bride*. But his later years were increasingly unhappy as his illness took its toll, slowing down the rate of composition until he was able to compose only for short stretches at a time. At his death he left incomplete an earlier opera, *Viola* (after *Twelfth Night*), to which he had returned in his final years.

For all Smetana's Wagnerian affiliation and inclination, his operas derive from the French and Italian tradition of opera cultivated in the Provisional Theatre. (The German repertoire was the mainstay of the rival German Opera in Prague.) There is evidence of cabaletta technique and concertato in his first opera, and such elements can be found even in his later operas. He never abandoned resources such as the chorus or ensemble singing. With its ability for genre painting, the chorus was the core of Czech national opera and far too popular to sacrifice; even a serious historical opera such as *Dalibor* has a popular drinking chorus for the soldiers. The use of solo ensemble is a feature of Smetana's later operas and derives in part from the fervent belief of his last librettist, Eliška Krásnohorská, in simultaneous singing. Such ensembles are not found in *Dalibor*, which has a more austere libretto, though there are important duets even in this work.

Smetana's operas are Italianate also in their use of voice types. He employed tessituras more in keeping with Verdian voices, relying on lighter, brighter voices, rather than the lower, heldentenor dramatic voice types of Wagner. In this, he was guided by the voices available in the small pool of solo singers at the Prague Provisional Theatre. No dramatic soprano or heldentenor was a regular or long-lived member of the ensemble. Similarly the absence of low bass parts is related to the early departure of the finest (and lowest) Czech bass, Josef Paleček. Smetana's passive baritone roles, in contrast to Verdi's villainous baritones or German demonic baritones, are connected with the long-term presence in the company of Josef Lev, a poor actor, but the possessor of a baritone voice of great beauty, heard at its best in slow lyrical music.

The character of Smetana's operas varies noticeably with the different strengths and concerns of his four librettists. The historical operas *Dalibor* and *Libuše*, with much emphasis on patriotic sentiments, had librettos from a conservative patriot Josef Wenzig. Eliška Krásnohorská, the librettist of *The Kiss*, *The Secret* and *The Devil's Wall*, preferred small-scale exploration of character psychology and the evocation of typical Czech milieus. Smetana seemed happy to take over the subjects offered him. He never suggested a libretto topic himself and seldom went against the conventions implicit in each libretto.

Smetana was emphatically against the direct use of folksong in his operas as a means of conveying 'Czechness', and there are only a handful of documented borrowings in his operas. He had less hesitation in writing imitation folksongs, from Ludiše's 'Byl to krásný sen' in *The Brandenburgers in Bohemia* to Blaženka's 'Což ta voda' in *The Secret*. Mostly, however, the national character that most Czechs find in his works derives from Czech dance patterns, such as the polka (not just in actual dances, but as the basis for other numbers), and from an identification of 'national style' with that of Smetana himself.

The Bartered Bride

Prodaná nevěsta

Comic opera in three acts (2h 15m)
Libretto by Karel Sabina
Composed July 1863–spring 1865; orch. by 15 March 1866; rev. 1869–70
PREMIERES two-act version with spoken dialogue: 30 May 1866, Provisional Theatre, Prague; definitive three-act version, sung throughout: 25 September 1870, Provisional Theatre, Prague; US: 20 August 1893, Haymarket, Chicago; UK: 26 June 1895, Drury Lane, London
CAST Krušina *bar*, Ludmila *s*, Mařenka *s*, Mícha *b*, Háta *ms*, Vašek *t*, Jeník *t*, Kecal *b*, Circus-master *t*, Esmeralda *s*, Red Indian *b*, 2 circus artistes *silent*; *satb* chorus of villagers

The Bartered Bride was not especially popular when it was first given, seeming not to achieve the success of its predecessor, *The Brandenburgers in Bohemia*. But while the latter opera dropped out of the repertoire after 1870, *The Bartered Bride* maintained its place with a steadily increasing number of performances each year. From the 1870s it was recognized as the quintessential Czech national opera, setting a standard by which other operas, including those by Smetana himself, were judged. By 1927 it had been performed 1000 times in Prague.

Especially in its original version, with spoken dialogue and without the dances, it made only modest demands. Unlike the ambitious *Brandenburgers in Bohemia* (with three tenor parts) or the later *Dalibor* (which called for a dramatic soprano and a heldentenor), voice parts were written around the fledgling Czech company, which then included an operetta component. The first Esmeralda was a well-known soubrette; the first circus-master was a Czech actor, Jindřich Mošna, who got through his undemanding part in a sort of parlando, playing it altogether 446 times over 30 years.

Smetana tinkered with the opera from the third performance onwards. The first change was the omission of an ironic couplet for the circus-master and Esmeralda (thought to be too risky to be played before Emperor Franz Josef) and its replacement by the ballet from Act I of *The Brandenburgers in Bohemia*, an unnecessary precaution since the emperor left after the first act. A more drastic revision followed on 29 January 1869, when the first act was divided into two scenes, the first ending with the duet for Mařenka and Vašek, and the second beginning with the newly written drinking chorus. Act II began with a newly composed polka, and Mařenka acquired a new aria ('Ten lásky sen'). The Esmeralda–circus-master couplet was omitted for good.

After four performances, Smetana produced another version (1 June 1869) in which the opera was split into the present three acts, Act I ending with a newly written furiant. The circus scene in Act III was expanded with a march and a *skočná*, a fast dance in duple time of a light or comic nature. It was not until the final version of 25 September 1870, however, that the spoken dialogue was replaced by sung recitatives (written for a performance in St Petersburg) and the furiant received its final position in Act II, after the drinking chorus.

SYNOPSIS

Act I: The action takes place at a village fair in Bohemia. During a lull in the opening chorus ('Proč bychom se netěšili'), Mařenka confesses her fears to her lover Jeník. She cannot love anyone but Jeník, but her father is obliged to Mícha, and so she may be forced to marry Mícha's son. Jeník seems strangely unconcerned. Mařenka is also puzzled by Jeník's mysterious past. Why did he leave his home, she asks in the following aria ('Kdybych se co takového')? Jeník explains that after the death of his mother, his father married again and his stepmother soon sent him packing: he went off into the world and worked among foreigners. In a duet they swear eternal love ('Věrné milování'). The next scene introduces Mařenka's parents, Krušina and Ludmila, and the ebullient marriage-broker Kecal ('Jak vám pravím, pane kmotře'), who gives them a glowing picture of Vašek, the bridegroom proposed for their daughter. Mařenka, who now returns, is less enthusiastic, and to the strains of 'Věrné milování' in the orchestra she declares she loves another. Kecal resolves to seek out Jeník, whom he regards as the chief obstacle. The act ends in a polka with a choral conclusion.

Act II: After the opening drinking chorus and furiant, Mařenka's would-be suitor makes his appearance on an empty stage. Vašek is dressed up for the occasion but is nervous and stammers: his mother has told him that if he does not marry, the whole village will laugh at him ('Má ma-ma-matička'). Mařenka accosts him and, having established that he is her proposed bridegroom (he has no idea who she is), informs him that everyone is sorry for him. Mařenka, she tells him, loves another and will make sure that Vašek meets an early death. She coquettishly woos him in a duet ('Známt' já jednu dívčinu'), in which she makes the infatuated Vašek swear that he will not marry 'Mařenka'. Meanwhile Kecal has found Jeník, and in an extended duet attempts to bribe him into renouncing Mařenka. Jeník agrees to a final figure of 300 gulden on condition that Mařenka marry no one but Mícha's son and that Krušina's debt to Mícha will be cleared. Afterwards Jeník wonders how Kecal could believe that he would have sold his Mařenka ('Jak možná věřit'). Kecal, however, brings back Krušina and the chorus to witness his negotiating triumph. The chorus is angry about the 'sale' of Jeník's bride.

Act III: Vašek's confusion ('To to mi v hlavě leží') is brushed away by the arrival of the circus people, who give a preview of their skill in a lively *skočná*. Disaster has struck, however. The man appearing as the star attraction ('the big American bear') is too drunk to perform. Esmeralda the dancer and the circus-master persuade Vašek to take his place ('Milostné zvířátko'). Vašek's parents are astonished to hear that he does not want to marry Mařenka, but as soon as Vašek discovers that the girl who charmed him earlier is actually the feared Mařenka, he gladly agrees to marry her. Mařenka, now downcast at Jeník's supposed perfidy, agrees to think things over. The pathos of her predicament is underlined in a slow sextet ('Rozmysli si, Mařenko') and in the moving aria she sings after it ('Ten lásky sen'). When Jeník joins her to explain, she will not listen ('Tak tvrdošijná, divko, jsi'). Kecal calls the company to announce his final success. But Vašek's parents, Háta and Mícha, are amazed to see Jeník, now insisting on his rights as 'Mícha's son' to marry Mařenka. Mařenka realizes how Jeník has outwitted the others and gladly forgives him. Kecal is humiliated, but it is only when Vašek makes his appearance as the 'bear', that Mícha finally concedes that Vašek is too young and foolish to marry and gives his blessing to the union of Jeník and Mařenka.

The Bartered Bride is so full of spontaneous charm that it is hard to credit how long it took to reach its final form. The fact that the dances were a late addition is particularly surprising since dance rhythms underline much of the basic substance of the opera. Many of the numbers are based on polka-type rhythms (fast two-in-a-bar) or *sousedská* rhythms (slow three-in-a-bar). Very few have complex forms, introductions or changes of tempo and metre: isolated by the spoken dialogue, they must have seemed especially dancelike in the original version. Surprisingly in a 'folk opera', the chorus is given comparatively little to do (the male drinking chorus was another late addition), and instead the heart of the opera is the dazzling succession of duets: a loving duet for hero and heroine at the beginning and an angry one at the end; an immensely skilful one for Mařenka and the stuttering Vašek and, in another contrast of opposites, the brilliant duet for the high-spirited Jeník and the ponderous Kecal. Smetana's character drawing was especially sharp in this opera, and the self-important Kecal, established in just a few notes of limited range in his opening solo, spawned a whole generation of Czech comic successors. The overture, in Smetana's most brilliant fugal scherzando style, is a frequently performed concert piece in its own right. The opera's successful production by the Prague National Theatre at the Vienna Music and Theatre Exhibition in June 1892 initiated its popularity abroad, the only Czech opera to achieve this before the advent of Janáček.

RECORDING Beňačková, Dvorský, Novák, Kopp, Czech PO, Košler, Supraphon, 1980/81

OTHER OPERAS *The Brandenburgers in Bohemia* (*Braniboři v Čechhách*), 1866; *Dalibor*, 1868; *Libuše*, (1872), 1881; *The Two Widows* (*Dvě vdovy*), 1874; *Viola*, (inc.) (1884), 1900; *The Kiss* (*Hubička*), 1876; *The Secret* (*Tajemství*), 1878; *The Devil's Wall* (*Čertova stěna*), 1882

J.T.

Gaspare Spontini

Gaspare Luigi Pacifico Spontini; *b* 14 November 1774, Maiolati; *d* 24 January 1851, Maiolati

Spontini played a vital part in the formation of early Romantic opera. He enjoyed his greatest success under Napoleon. Like many Italians he found France a propitious place to work, for although he had composed a dozen operas in Italy, mostly comedies, he made little impression as a composer until he won the patronage of the Empress Josephine in Paris. His career there began with three opéras comiques and then blossomed overnight with the appearance of *La vestale* in 1807. This was his masterpiece, and it caught the imagination of the times. Its simple plot and its strongly expressive musical language give it an important place in the development of French opera leading from the tradition of Gluck and Piccinni towards the styles of Berlioz and Meyerbeer.

Two years later he produced *Fernand Cortez*, in which a tendency towards spectacular staging is evident, perhaps reflecting the grandeur of Napoleonic ambition; and the same emphasis on scenic effect is found in the last of his Parisian operas, *Olimpie* of 1819. His centre of activity then moved to Berlin, as Generalmusikdirektor to the King of Prussia, where his work never equalled the standard of his Parisian operas and he found himself embroiled in controversy. Politically conservative and inclined to touchiness, he was a difficult colleague. Yet Berlioz, to whom he was always generous in his support, declared that he loved Spontini; he was a widely respected figure, especially in France. Berlioz's early music owes much to Spontini, and Wagner too drew ideas freely from Spontini's scores.

He was advanced as an orchestrator, often trying new groupings, new effects, especially with mutes, and managing offstage bands with considerable care to create the illusion of distance. He was one of the first to use the metronome. He had an Italian's gift of melody but a Frenchman's care for the expressive projection of words. His operas contributed much to the increasing power required of leading singers, since they not only had to compete with a louder, larger orchestra but were also expected to maintain a high level of intensity. His heroic tenors already belong to the modern type. Spontini exercised a powerful influence over the following generation, but his work did not survive beyond the end of the 19th century; revivals and recordings in modern times have been rare.

La vestale

The Vestal Virgin

Tragédie lyrique in three acts (3h)
Libretto by Etienne de Jouy
Composed 1805
PREMIERES 15 December 1807, Opéra, Paris; US: 17 February 1828, Théâtre d'Orléans, New Orleans; UK: 9 June 1842, Covent Garden, London
CAST Licinius *t*, Cinna *t*, Julia *s*, High Priestess *ms*, Supreme Pontiff *b*, Chief Soothsayer *b*, *satb* chorus of vestal virgins, priests, matrons, young women, senators, consuls, lictors, warriors, gladiators, children, prisoners

La vestale was Spontini's first work for the Paris Opéra and his greatest success. It was accepted only through the intervention of the Empress Josephine. He had composed no opera in Italy or France that gave any foretaste of this modern brand of Gluckian serious opera, and it set a standard that was to be incorporated into French grand opera after the Napoleonic period. It remained in the repertoire during the first half of the 19th century and profoundly influenced both Berlioz and Wagner. The drama presents the classic conflict of love and duty in the person of Julia, the vestal virgin whose vows forbid her to yield to Licinius' passion.

SYNOPSIS

Act I: Licinius, the victorious Roman general, confides to his friend Cinna that he cannot enjoy acclamation and honour since Julia, whose hand he has long sought to win, has been forced by her father to become a priestess of Vesta, sworn to chastity. Julia still loves Licinius, despite her vows, and it falls to her to place the crown of victory on Licinius' head. During the ceremony Licinius learns that Julia has to guard the sacred flame at night.

Act II: Licinius visits the temple where Julia is on watch. In the excitement of passion they allow the flame to go out. With Cinna's help Licinius escapes, but Julia is stripped of her insignia and condemned to death, refusing to name the man who was with her.

Act III: Licinius attempts to persuade the Supreme Pontiff to exercise his mercy, even admitting his part in Julia's guilt, but is rebuffed. Julia prepares to be entombed alive, when suddenly a storm breaks and a thunderbolt strikes the altar, relighting the sacred flame and proving Vesta's forgiveness. The lovers are reunited.

The tragédie has a happy ending, but the emotional intensity of the opera, especially in Act II, is on a high dramatic level, worthy of a genuine tragedy. The scenes of solemnity and celebration are inherited from a long tradition in French opera, including Gluck, but the expressive intensity of Julia's music belongs truly to the new century. Its orchestration was considered noisy in its time, but it simply reflects the grandiose tastes of the Empire. In *La vestale* Spontini first revealed his striking gift for dramatic recitative, absorbing elements found in Gluck and Cherubini. The role of Julia, first sung by Madame Branchu, is particularly taxing in its high tessitura.

RECORDINGS 1. Callas, Stignani, Corelli, La Scala Ch & O, Votto, DiVa, 1954; 2. Hufstodt, Graves, Michaels-Moore, Raftery, La Scala Ch & O, Muti, Sony, 1993 (live)
OTHER OPERATIC WORKS *I puntigli delle donne*, 1796; *Adelina Senese, o sia L'amore secreto*, 1797; *L'eroismo ridicolo*, 1798; *Il Teseo riconosciuto*, 1798; *La finta filosofa*, 1799; *La fuga in maschera*, 1800; *Gli Elisi delusi*, 1800; *La petite maison*, 1804; *Milton*, 1804; *Julie, ou Le pot de fleurs*, 1805; *Fernand Cortez, ou La conquête du Méxique*, 1809; *Pélage, ou Le roi et la paix*, 1814; *Les dieux rivaux, ou Les fêtes de Cythère*, 1816; *Olimpie*, 1819; *Nurmahal, oder Das Rosenfest von Caschmir*, 1822; *Alcidor*, 1825; *Agnes von Hohenstaufen*, 1829; 4 lost operas

H.M.

Johann Strauss II

Johann Baptist Strauss; *b* 25 October 1825, Vienna; *d* 3 June 1899, Vienna

Johann Strauss II, the celebrated waltz king, was also the composer of the greatest of all Viennese operettas, *Die Fledermaus*, and a few others that still hold the stage. Although he chose his libretti foolishly and often set them mindlessly, the charge that Strauss had no theatrical instinct remains patently false. His music remains for millions the chief embodiment of the last glittering years of the Austro-Hungarian Empire.

Johann Strauss (the first waltz king) discouraged his son from becoming a professional musician. However, after his father left the family in 1842, the younger Strauss took a thorough musical training and his persistence soon paid off among the Viennese music publishers and dance halls, where he conducted his own orchestra. Soon Strauss II was as famous a composer, violinist and conductor as his father, and by the mid-1860s, when the huge success of Offenbach's operettas in Vienna aroused his interest, had also built up an international reputation through concert tours.

Strauss's first wife, Jetty Treffz, had taken some musical sketches to the director of the Theater an der Wien, Maximilian Steiner, who was able to convince the composer that his music was stageworthy. In 1869 Strauss composed *Die lustigen Weiber von Wien*, which was never produced, but his next operetta, *Indigo und die vierzig Räuber* (1871), was staged at the Theater an der Wien, conducted by the composer. Wags discussing the uncredited, unoriginal libretto referred to the '40 librettists'. But the public went crazy. There were productions abroad. The Paris version included the 'Blue Danube' waltz, whose phenomenal popularity is paralleled in the influence Strauss exerted not only on two generations of Viennese operetta, but on 'serious' composers. Brahms wrote of it: 'Not, unfortunately, by Johannes Brahms.' Wagner was an admirer, and among those who felt the influence of Strauss *fils* were Richard Strauss (no relation) and Maurice Ravel.

Der Karneval in Rom, the first of Strauss's operettas with an Italian setting, was an even bigger critical and commercial success in 1873. Both works were revised and remounted early in the 20th century but have rarely been seen again. Not so the next work, *Die Fledermaus*. Though not an immediate triumph, it would become the most celebrated operetta of all time, performed not only in the popular theatre but also in the temples of high art, rubbing shoulders with the works of Mozart, Verdi and Wagner.

Thereafter *Cagliostro in Wien* (1875) wedded Italian and Austrian elements, but was distinguished – like its successors – mainly for its principal waltz. For *Prinz Methusalem* (1877) Strauss did not even wait for the German translation of the original French libretto he was setting. This did not prevent the work from doing quite well in Austria and in the USA. The next work was even more popular with American audiences: *Das Spitzentuch der Königin* (1880), which had as its principal characters Cervantes and the Queen of Portugal. For every operetta Strauss composed, he also wrote various dance arrangements of their tunes, the sales of which were hugely lucrative for him and his publishers, and which served as publicity for the stage productions. Out of motifs from *Das Spitzentuch* came one of Strauss's greatest waltzes, 'Rosen aus dem Süden'. In the mid-1880s Strauss scored two of his greatest triumphs with *Eine Nacht in Venedig* and *Der Zigeunerbaron*; the latter is, after *Die Fledermaus*, the composer's most successful stage work.

None of Strauss's later operettas enjoyed the same acclaim, however, and despite sporadic attempts to revive them these works have for the most part passed into theatrical oblivion. In 1892 there were nine performances at the Hofoper of *Ritter Pázmán*, a through-composed work, set once again in Hungary. The *Waldmeister* overture is still occasionally aired, but little if anything is heard today from *Simplicius*, *Fürstin Ninetta*, *Jabuka* or *Die Göttin der Vernunft*. In recent years an authoritative edition of Strauss's autograph scores has shed new light on the major operettas, and it is hoped that the minor works will be re-examined on stage as well as in print.

Textual deviations must be tolerated; certainly, all manner of pasticcios using Strauss's tunes appeared after the composer's death. The most famous was *Wiener Blut* (1899), which has been accepted as a genuine Strauss operetta because Strauss authorized its composition and vetted the music chosen before he died. It remains popular as a kitsch paean to early 19th-century Vienna, despite a tiresome book, insipid characters and lyrics that are often ill-fitted to the music. *Walzer aus Wien* was a barely biographical study of the Strausses, father and son. A worldwide hit from 1931, it has usually been produced with great splendour. In New York it was *The Great Waltz*; in Paris, *Valses de Vienne*; in London, *Waltzes from Vienna*, where it was unimaginatively filmed by Alfred Hitchcock. A Hollywood spin-off entitled *The Great Waltz* (1938) was more popular.

Die Fledermaus

The Bat

Comic operetta in three acts (2h 15m)
Libretto by Carl Haffner and Richard Genée, based on the vaudeville *Le réveillon* by Henri Meilhac and Ludovic Halévy (1872)
Composed 1873–4
PREMIERES 5 April 1874, Theater an der Wien; US: 21 November 1874, Stadt Theater, New York; UK: 18 December 1876, Alhambra Theatre, London
CAST Gabriel von Eisenstein *t*, Alfred *t*, Dr Falke *bar*, Frank *bar*, Dr Blind *t*, Frosch *spoken role*, Rosalinde von Eisenstein *s*, Adele *s*, Prince Orlofsky *ms*; *satb* chorus of party guests, servants

Strauss's most brilliant stage work is universally regarded as the Austrian operetta *in excelsis*. Originally planned for the Carltheater in Vienna as a strict translation of the play *Le réveillon*, it was then proposed by a publisher–agent as an operetta with music by Strauss for the rival Theater an der Wien. The play's more risqué elements – consorting with a prostitute, for one – were eliminated and most of the original names changed. The initial reception was quite favourable, but by 1880 the work had been seen in over 170 German-language theatres and after the Vienna Opera admitted it into its repertoire in the 1890s it was performed all over the world. Curiously, *Die Fledermaus* was not at first as popular in the USA as some other Strauss operettas.

SYNOPSIS

Act I: In a spa near a large city (Vienna), Eisenstein has been sentenced to prison for a minor offence. Rosalinde, his wife, is serenaded by a singing teacher, Alfred ('Täubchen, das entflattert ist'), who promises to return after Eisenstein has begun his sentence. Adele, Rosalinde's maid, discloses to the audience that she wants to attend a party that evening given by the young Russian prince, Orlofsky. She tells her mistress she wants the night off to visit her sick aunt, but Rosalinde refuses. Eisenstein enters, furious with his inept lawyer, Dr Blind, for extending his gaol sentence ('Nein, mit solchen Advokaten'), but his friend Dr Falke cheers him up by recalling the time Eisenstein left him to walk home from a party in broad daylight in a bat costume. He then mentions the ball to be held at Prince Orlofsky's. If Eisenstein turns up at the prison at six the following morning, after the ball, the governor won't mind. Eisenstein agrees and dresses for the evening, but tells his wife that he is about to begin his sentence. They bid one another an ironically tearful farewell. Rosalinde, who has dismissed her maid for the night after all, looks forward to her tryst with Alfred. The singing teacher arrives, and they settle down to a cosy supper ('Trinke, Liebchen, trinke schnell') but are interrupted by the arrival of the prison governor, Frank, who, assuming Rosalinde's companion to be her husband, takes Alfred off to prison. Rosalinde, not wishing to be compromised, encourages this misunderstanding ('Mein Herr, was dachten Sie von mir?'): who else but her husband would be in his dressing-gown?

Act II: At Orlofsky's, the prince exhorts his guests to enjoy themselves ('Ich lade gern mir Gäste ein'); Dr Falke explains to the bored prince that he has created the 'bat's revenge', a scheme to embarrass Eisenstein, who has just arrived in the guise of the Marquis Renard. Eisenstein recognizes Adele, who laughingly denies to the guests that she resembles his chambermaid ('Mein Herr Marquis'). Eisenstein is introduced first to a 'compatriot', 'Chevalier Chagrin' (Frank), and then to a mysterious, masked Hungarian countess; he flirts with her using his repeater watch, little realizing she is his own wife ('Dieser Anstand, so manierlich'). The 'countess' sings of her Magyar homeland to the party guests ('Klänge der Heimat'), and Eisenstein boasts of his practical joke years before which had had Dr Falke walking home from a ball in a bat costume, to the derision of the townsfolk. Orlofsky proposes a toast to King Champagne the First ('Im Feuerstrom der Reben'), and as the guests become more and more mellow, Dr Falke praises the spirit of brotherly (and sisterly) love that has come over them ('Brüderlein und Schwesterlein'). A ballet display (in many productions, a small gala performance with guest stars and interpolated numbers) is followed by a general waltz. As the clock strikes six, Eisenstein – and Frank – hurriedly depart.

Act III: At the gaol, Alfred sings in his cell. The gaoler, Frosch, tries to keep him quiet. In a melodrama Frank, thoroughly drunk, sits at his desk and falls asleep. Adele and her sister enter in search of the 'Chevalier Chagrin'; Adele is sure he can help her become an actress ('Spiel' ich die Unschuld vom Lande'). Eisenstein arrives to serve his sentence. He is surprised to see his party friend as the prison warden, and more surprised to hear that this man personally arrested Eisenstein the previous evening and that the prisoner has already begun serving his sentence. Determined to find out who the culprit cavorting with his wife is, Eisenstein disguises himself as Blind, and questions both Alfred and Rosalinde – who has come to the gaol – about their evening together. In a fury, he reveals himself, but is confronted with his own wife's fake Hungarian accent and the watch she cleverly snatched from him. The other party-goers enter the gaol, and Falke admits the whole set-up. Rather than pursue the evening's indiscretions, the principals decide to blame everything on the champagne ('O Fledermaus, o Fledermaus').

In *Die Fledermaus* Strauss couples the Parisian tendency to parody with a Viennese charm that never lapses into sentimentality. The libretto inspired a succession of happy ideas: Adele's high-spirited laughter becomes one of the great soubrette arias, 'Mein Herr Marquis', while the subterfuges of the various characters result, as in Mozart's *Le nozze di Figaro*, in some brilliant ensembles, notably the ironic farewells in Act I ('So muss allein ich bleiben . . . o je, o je, wie rührt mich dies!') and the finales to Acts I and II. Rosalinde's Hungarian disguise provides the excuse for the spirited csárdás 'Klänge der Heimat', while the original ballet sequence comprised a sequence of national dances (now usually replaced by a popular Strauss polka). Alfred's transformation from the orchestra leader of the French original to singing teacher made possible the curtain-raising serenade. Productions that preserve the role of Eisenstein as a tenor further lift the flavour of the piece. Only in Act III do the exuberant pacing and invention seem momentarily to falter; here the antics of the drunken Frosch can form an embarrassing weak link, though a skilled performance can equally provide the icing on the cake, as interpreters such as Franz Muxeneder and Frankie Howerd have proved.

Quite how Strauss himself saw the work within the tradition of great opera is uncertain, though the stuttering Dr Blind is a clear descendant of Mozart's Don Curzio, as also is Eisenstein of Count Almaviva; and the Act III melodrama in the gaol recalls comically (and surely unconsciously) *Fidelio*. But ever since Max Reinhardt's Berlin production of 1928, *Die Fledermaus* has been a fully fledged member of the operatic repertoire, with memorable interpretations from such distinguished names as Krauss, Karajan and Carlos Kleiber.

RECORDINGS 1. Gueden, Lipp, Wagner, Patzak, Dermota, Poell, Vienna State Op Ch, VPO, Krauss, Decca, 1950 (omits dialogue); 2. Schwarzkopf, Streich, Christ, Gedda, Krebs, Philharmonia Ch & O, Karajan, EMI, 1955 (with dialogue); 3. Varady, Popp, Rebroff, Prey, Kollo, Weikl, Bavarian State Op Ch & O, C. Kleiber, DG, 1976 (with dialogue)

OTHER OPERATIC WORKS *Die lustigen Weiber von Wien* (1869); *Indigo und die vierzig Räuber*, 1871; *Der Carneval* *in Rom*, 1873; *Cagliostro in Wien*, 1875; *Prinz Methusalem*, 1875; *Blindekuh*, 1878; *Das Spitzentuch der Königin*, 1880; *Der lustige Krieg*, 1881; *Eine Nacht in Venedig*, 1883; *Der Zigeunerbaron*, 1885; *Simplicius*, 1887; *Ritter Pázmán*, 1892; *Fürstin Ninetta*, 1893; *Jabuka*, 1894; *Waldmeister*, 1895; *Die Göttin der Vernunft*, 1897; *Wiener Blut*, 1899

R.T.

Richard Strauss

Richard Georg Strauss; *b* 11 June 1864, Munich, Bavaria; *d* 8 September 1949, Garmisch-Partenkirchen

Strauss achieved mastery in three musical genres: opera, of which he composed 15, orchestral tone poems and lieder. He was also one of the great conductors of his day, not only of his own works but also of those by Mozart, Wagner, Beethoven and many others. His father was the principal horn-player in the Bavarian Court Opera orchestra for nearly half a century and his mother was a member of the wealthy brewing family of Pschorr. His childhood, therefore, was comfortable and he grew up in a household devoted to music. He composed copiously from the age of five; by the time he was 16 he had heard his first symphony played by his father's orchestra conducted by Hermann Levi. His music attracted the attention of Hans von Bülow who, in 1885, offered Strauss a post as his assistant at Meiningen. There he met Alexander Ritter, a passionate Wagnerian, who persuaded the younger man, brought up on a rigid classical diet, to become a follower of the 'music of the future'. In 1886 Strauss was appointed third conductor at the Munich opera house and moved to the Weimar Court Opera in 1889, where his adventurous choice of repertoire brought him much publicity. Meanwhile the success of his tone poems *Don Juan* and *Tod und Verklärung* had led Bülow to dub him 'Richard the Third' (since, he said, after Wagner there could be no 'Richard the Second').

While at Weimar, he conducted the world premieres of Humperdinck's *Hänsel und Gretel* (1893) and of his own first opera *Guntram* (1894). In the latter the principal soprano role was sung by Pauline de Ahna who had been Strauss's pupil for several years; they were married in September 1894. He portrayed her capricious, tempestuous nature in several of his works, notably *Intermezzo* (Christine) and *Die Frau ohne Schatten* (the Dyer's Wife). She was a fine interpreter of his lieder, and Strauss's special sympathy for the female voice undoubtedly owes much to her influence and example. Strauss returned to the Munich Opera in 1894, becoming chief conductor there in 1896, and in 1898 was appointed chief conductor of the Royal Opera in Berlin, where he remained until 1908, a tenure almost exactly parallel with his friend Mahler's directorship of the Vienna Court Opera. Strauss was chief guest conductor at Berlin until 1919, when he agreed to be co-director at Vienna with Franz Schalk. He also played a leading part in 1920 in establishing the Salzburg Festival. Like many before and after him, Strauss fell foul of Viennese opera politics and resigned in 1924. But in his five years there, with some legendary singers, he conducted important new productions of his own and others' operas. Those who heard him conduct *Così fan tutte*, *Fidelio* and *Tristan und Isolde* counted those performances among the great musical experiences of a lifetime.

Mention should also be made of the two arrangements Strauss made of other composers' operas. For Gluck's *Iphigénie en Tauride*, which he arranged at Weimar in September 1890, he provided a new German translation, made some cuts, rewrote many of the recitatives and enlarged the ending. He reorchestrated some passages but added no extra instruments. Strauss is said to have conducted his version in Berlin shortly after he went there in 1898 (mentioned in letters to his father), but the only documented performance is at Weimar on 9 June 1900, conducted by Rudolf Krzyzanowski. It has been revived several times and recorded.

He was more drastic with Mozart's *Idomeneo*, which he rearranged in 1930 to mark the 150th anniversary the following year of the premiere in 1781. Lothar Wallerstein translated the libretto; Strauss made many cuts, eliminated Elettra (replacing her with a priestess, Ismene), deleted a lot of recitative and composed two new numbers, an orchestral interlude and a Straussian quartet in the final scene. He conducted the premiere in Vienna on 16 April 1931 and was accused of sacrilege, but he replied that he loved the work (which at that date was practically unknown) and said he would 'answer for my impiety to the divine Mozart if I ever get to heaven'.

Strauss's first opera, *Guntram*, composed during the first rapture of Wagner-worship, was not a success and seven years passed before Strauss embarked on another opera. It is significant that *Feuersnot*, *Salome* and *Elektra* were one-act operas, stage equivalents of the tone poems with which, between 1888 and 1898, Strauss had established himself among the leaders of contemporary orchestral music. With *Salome* and *Elektra*, emotional blockbusters, he triumphed equally in the opera house, the former encountering resistance in some cities on moral grounds but winning public favour whenever it was performed. *Elektra* is a setting of the version of Sophocles' play by the Austrian poet and playwright Hugo von Hofmannsthal. Thus began the long and fruitful collaboration between composer and librettist, which posterity can vicariously share through their absorbingly frank and detailed correspondence – 'We were born for one another,' Strauss wrote.

In *Elektra* Strauss went, in a few passages, as near to the frontier of atonality as he was ever to go in the name of Expressionism. But to interpret the subsequent operas as a retreat from modernism is seriously to misjudge and misunderstand Strauss's achievement. He and Hofmannsthal followed *Elektra* with their biggest popular success, *Der Rosenkavalier*, a Viennese comedy of 18th-century manners. But for all its waltzes and luscious melodies, it also has harmonic progressions as advanced as any in *Elektra*. Strauss's principal operatic ambition, evolved through his experience as a conductor, was for a perfect and democratic fusion of words and music. With this in mind he strove to develop an endless melodic recitative that flowed as naturally as conversation. The beginnings of this style can be detected in *Feuersnot* and throughout much of Act I of *Der Rosenkavalier*.

Indeed, Strauss and Hofmannsthal wanted to break fresh ground in the opera house. 'New ideas must search for new forms,' Strauss wrote, and in *Ariadne auf Naxos* they attempted a bold marriage between straight theatre and chamber opera. But on practical and economic grounds alone this was doomed to failure, and in a revised version they substituted a short operatic prologue for the play. In this form the opera has become firmly established. They followed it with their most ambitious venture, the fairy tale-cum-allegory *Die Frau ohne Schatten*, in which Hofmannsthal's verbose flights of fancy were matched by music of outstanding intensity and opulence.

Strauss wrote his own libretto for *Intermezzo*, his dramatization of an episode in his married life, in which the melodic recitative style, developed in the prologue to *Ariadne*, fits the narrative like a glove. The fluidity of this style also ensured the success of *Arabella*, a return to romantic period comedy and the last collaboration with Hofmannsthal (who died before it was complete). Strauss could scarcely envisage the continuation of his operatic career without Hofmannsthal, but by a stroke of luck he met the novelist Stefan Zweig. Their opera buffa *Die schweigsame Frau*, based on Ben Jonson, is one of Strauss's happiest scores, a celebration of his delight in finding a new and congenial partner. But the advent of the Nazis meant the end of Strauss's collaboration with a Jew. On his next three operas he worked, grudgingly, with the Viennese theatre historian Joseph Gregor. In *Friedenstag* and *Daphne* he reverted to the one-act form. For the former, an anti-war opera banned in Germany after 1939, he forged a new and tougher style, while in the pastoral lyricism of *Daphne* can be heard the beginning of his last phase, the so-called Indian Summer, in which his music combined richness and simplicity. The autumnal splendour continued in *Die Liebe der Danae*, based on a discarded Hofmannsthal sketch, but achieved its operatic apogee in *Capriccio*. Here, in collaboration with the conductor Clemens Krauss, Strauss used the conflict between words and music as the theme of the opera itself. With its aristocratic 18th-century setting, its adorable heroine, its touches of broad comedy and its undercurrent of valediction, *Capriccio* was the perfect vehicle for all the best of Strauss to come together in the last chapter of his important contribution to the development of opera as a vital and progressive form.

Salome

Drama in one act (1h 45m)
Libretto by the composer from Hedwig Lachmann's German translation of the tragedy by Oscar Wilde (1893)
Composed November 1904–June 1905
PREMIERES 9 December 1905, Semper Opernhaus, Dresden; US: 22 January 1907, Metropolitan, New York; UK: 8 December 1910, Covent Garden, London
CAST Herod *t*, Herodias *ms*, Salome *s*, Jokanaan *bar*, Narraboth *t*, page to Herodias *a*, 5 Jews 4 *t*, *b*, First Nazarene *t*, Second Nazarene *b*, 2 soldiers 2 *b*, a Cappadocian *b*

Strauss saw Max Reinhardt's production of Wilde's French play *Salomé* (in a German translation) in Berlin in November 1902, with Gertrud Eysoldt in the title role. He was already sketching themes for an operatic setting, having been sent the play by the Austrian poet Anton Lindner, who offered to fashion a verse libretto for him. But Strauss was not impressed by the first few scenes and decided that he himself would adapt Hedwig Lachmann's translation, which he shortened by about a third.

Strauss offered the first performance to Ernst von Schuch at Dresden. Some of the singers at first read-through wanted to return their parts as too difficult, but the Czech tenor Karel Burian (uncle of the composer Emil Burian), who created Herod, already knew his by heart. The Salome, Marie Wittich, regarded the opera as improper and refused to perform the Dance of the Seven Veils – 'I won't do it, I'm a respectable woman.' A dancer stood in for her in this scene (a solution sometimes adopted since). In spite of moralistic objections, *Salome* was a sensational success at Dresden (except with the critics) and was performed at 50 other opera houses within two years.

But the Church's and others' objections to the work were still strong. At the Berlin Court Opera, where Strauss was employed as chief conductor, the Kaiser would allow it to be performed only if the Star of Bethlehem was shown in the sky (even though Christ's birth took place 30 years before the action of the opera). After its Metropolitan premiere in New York, there was such an outcry, led by the daughter of the financier J. Pierpont Morgan, that further performances were cancelled. Mahler, who regarded it as 'one of the greatest masterpieces of our time', was only dissuaded by Strauss from resigning his directorship of the Vienna Court Opera after the censor refused to allow him to stage it (and it was not performed in Vienna until October 1918). The Kaiser said: 'I like this fellow Strauss, but *Salome* will do him a lot of damage.' Strauss's retort was: 'The damage enabled me to build my house in Garmisch.'

After completing the full score of *Salome*, Strauss also worked on a version with Wilde's original French text. In order to adapt his music to this text, he consulted his friend the novelist and poet Romain Rolland. This version (1930) is rarely performed but was revived at Lyons in 1990 and subsequently recorded.

SYNOPSIS

On the terrace of the palace of the tetrarch Herod Antipas, the Syrian captain of the guard, Narraboth, is looking into the banqueting hall, captivated by the beauty of the 16-year-old Salome, daughter of Herod's second wife Herodias by her first marriage ('Wie schön ist die Prinzessin Salome heute Nacht!'). Herodias's page warns him that something terrible may happen if he looks at Salome too much. The page has been alarmed by how strange the moon seems, 'like a woman rising from a tomb'. Two soldiers are guarding the cistern beneath the terrace where Jokanaan (John the Baptist) is imprisoned for denunciation of Herodias's marriage to her husband's brother. They hear his voice uttering prophecies. Salome leaves the banquet to evade her stepfather's lascivious glances and to escape from the religious arguments among the Jews and from the Roman soldiers whom she hates. She hears Jokanaan and wheedles Narraboth into defying Herod's orders and bringing the prophet to meet her.

Jokanaan launches into a tirade against Herod and his wife. When Salome tells him she is the daughter of Herodias, he rails at her ('Zurück, Tochter Babylons!'), but she is fascinated by his voice and longs to touch his body and his hair and to kiss his mouth. At this point, Narraboth, horrified by her conduct, kills himself, but she hardly notices. Jokanaan tells her to seek salvation from the Son of Man and retreats into the cistern, cursing her as he goes.

Herod, Herodias and their attendants come on to the terrace. Herod, too, is disturbed by the strangeness of the moon. He slips in Narraboth's blood and orders the body to be removed. He feels a cold wind blowing and 'the beating of vast wings', but Herodias tells him he is ill. Herod offers Salome wine and fruit, but she refuses. Jokanaan's voice is heard again. Herodias urges that he be handed over to the Jews, but Herod says, 'He is a holy man who has seen God.' This prompts a heated argument among the five Jews over the question of whether anyone has seen God. After Jokanaan's reference to the 'Saviour of the world' the two Nazarenes tell Herod of the Messiah's miracles, including raising a woman from the dead. This alarms Herod ('I will not allow him to raise the dead'), but when Herodias complains that Jokanaan is reviling her, Herod replies, 'He did not speak your name'.

Herod commands Salome to dance for him. She refuses, despite promises of lavish gifts, but agrees when he says she can have whatever she desires. After the dance she claims her reward – Jokanaan's head on a silver charger. Herodias is delighted, but Salome says she wants it for her own pleasure not to please her mother. Herod tries everything to dissuade her, but she obsessively repeats her demand ('Gib mir den Kopf des Jokanaan!'). Eventually Herod gives in, saying, 'Truly she is her mother's child'. The executioner descends into the cistern and returns with the prophet's head on a silver shield. Salome seizes it and sings a long aria to it, taunting it for being unable to reply to her. 'If you had seen me, you would have loved me. I am hungry for your body.' Herod refuses to stay, and as he climbs the staircase looks back to see Salome lost in ecstasy as she kisses Jokanaan's mouth. Horrified, he orders the soldiers to kill her ('Man töte dieses Weib!'). They crush her beneath their shields.

Salome is a study in obsessions, wrought by a composer whose powers of description in his orchestral tone poems had equipped him to depict in the theatre the strangeness of the happenings on this oriental night, with the moon lighting the scene and inducing an atmosphere of impending violence and madness. There is no overture. A rising arpeggio on the clarinet launches Narraboth into his rapturous vision of Salome and, from then to the end, there is no let-up in the intensity and tension of the score. The 105-strong orchestra is used with an imaginative power that was new to opera in 1905, the exotic tone colours reflecting the action on the stage both graphically and psychologically. The passage of nearly a century has not diminished the startling novelty of the sound as Salome awaits Jokanaan's execution, an effect created by four double-basses 'pinching' the string with thumb and forefinger and striking it with the bow. There are many other equally dramatic moments, with dissonances no less far-reaching in their tendency towards atonality than those that were to follow in *Elektra*.

The role of Salome is a tremendous challenge for a soprano, who ideally should combine a Wagnerian weight of tone with a girlish quality. In 1930 Strauss reduced the orchestration so that a light soprano could sing the part. The 20-minute final aria moves from animal frenzy to a demented erotic yearning. Yet it is not only Salome's obsession that Strauss presents with such calculated vividness. The religious zeal of Jokanaan is equally obsessive and is conveyed in music of lofty and noble quality. The music for Herod also brilliantly delineates the tetrarch's personality: neurotic, superstitious, lascivious – a gift of a part for a character tenor. Whatever the mood in this opera, whether it be sultry, savage, sadistic or sensuous, Strauss finds the orchestral colours to convey it to the listener with overwhelming intensity.

RECORDINGS 1. Nilsson, Hoffman, Stolze, Waechter, VPO, Solti, Decca, 1961; 2. Studer, Rysanek, Hiestermann, Terfel, Berlin Deutsch Op O, Sinopoli, DG, 1990; 3. I. Nielsen, Silja, Goldberg, Hale, Danish Nat RSO, Schønwandt, Chandos, 1998

Elektra

Electra

Tragedy in one act (1h 45m)
Libretto by Hugo von Hofmannsthal, based on his own play (1903) after the tragedy by Sophocles (411 or 410 BC)
Composed June 1906–September 1908
PREMIERES 25 January 1909, Semper Opernhaus, Dresden; US: 1 February 1910, Manhattan Opera, New York; UK: 19 February 1910, Covent Garden, London
CAST Elektra *s*, Klytemnästra *ms*, Chrysothemis *s*, Aegisth *t*, Orest *bar*, Tutor to Orest *b*, Confidante *s*, Trainbearer *s*, Young Servant *t*, Old Servant *b*, Overseer *s*, First Maid *c*, Second and Third Maids 2 *ms*, Fourth and Fifth Maids 2 *s*; *satb* chorus of servants

Hugo von Hofmannsthal wrote his play *Elektra*, an adaptation of Sophocles, in three weeks in August 1903, when he was 28. It was produced in Berlin the following October by Max Reinhardt and was a major success. Strauss probably saw it there or a few years later and recognized its potential as an operatic subject. He and Hofmannsthal met in November 1905, and the poet gave him a free hand to cut the play to make a libretto. Hofmannsthal wrote new lines for two episodes, the recognition scene and the duet between Elektra and Chrysothemis after the murders.

Strauss was at first wary of setting *Elektra* immediately after *Salome*, feeling (not unjustifiably) that the emotional contents were similar. But Hofmannsthal pressed him, and the opera was performed at Dresden early in 1909. There and elsewhere it enjoyed a *succès d'estime* rather than a popular success, but its title role was soon to attract a series of superb dramatic sopranos, while the role of Klytemnästra was also to become a favourite. *Elektra* is often spoken of in Freudian terms, but it is by no means certain that Hofmannsthal had read Freud at the time he wrote his play. His main source was Sophocles, and the strength of the work is in its modern adaptation of Greek tragedy to which Strauss's music added a fearful strength.

SYNOPSIS

The courtyard of the royal palace at Mycenae, where Clytemnestra lives with Aegisthus. Serving women, drawing water from a well, are discussing Electra, daughter of King Agamemnon and Clytemnestra, who lives like a wild, unkempt animal. They all mock her, except one who is whipped for her loyalty. Electra, left alone, laments her loneliness ('Allein! Weh, ganz allein') and recalls the murder of her father Agamemnon by Aegisthus and Clytemnestra. Calling on her father's spirit to help her, Electra dreams of vengeance after which she will dance for joy. Her reverie is interrupted by her younger sister, Chrysothemis, with news that Clytemnestra and Aegisthus plan to imprison Electra in a tower. She sings of her own longing for a husband and children ('Ich hab's wie Feuer in der Brust').

A procession approaches; Clytemnestra and her entertainers are on their way to the ritual altar. The queen, bedecked with jewels and amulets, decides to consult Electra about how she can stop the horrible nightmares that disrupt her sleep. Electra brings the subject round to her brother Orestes. She does not believe reports that he has gone mad. Electra tells her mother that a sacrificial victim will stop her dreams – Clytemnestra herself. The queen's terror gives way to maniacal laughter when her confidante whispers to her that Orestes is dead.

The same news is given to Electra by Chrysothemis, who refuses to join Electra in killing Aegisthus and their mother. Electra resolves she must act alone ('Nun denn, allein!') and digs frantically for the axe with which Agamemnon was killed and which she has buried in the courtyard. As she digs, a man enters the courtyard. He says he awaits a summons to bring news of Orestes' death. Electra berates him for being alive while a better man is dead. When he discovers who she is, he whispers, 'Orestes lives'. She does not recognize her questioner until servants kiss his garments: 'The dogs in the courtyard know me, but my sister does not.' After the powerful recognition scene that follows, she impresses on him what must be done. He enters the palace, and Electra realizes that she has not given him the axe. But screams from the palace indicate Clytemnestra's death. These bring Aegisthus into the courtyard. Electra, chillingly amiable to him, lights him to the palace door. He shouts for help, to which Electra replies, 'Agamemnon hears you!' Electra begins her dance of joy, dropping dead at its climax. Chrysothemis beats vainly on the doors of the palace for admission, crying, 'Orest.' But Orestes is already being pursued by the Furies.

From the opening onomatopoeic fanfare, 'Agamemnon', it becomes plain that the dead king is the opera's principal leitmotif. *Elektra* is a huge crescendo from start to finish, less lyrical and tonal than *Salome*. The work sounds better organized than its predecessor, probably because the libretto is tauter and less rhapsodic than Wilde's play. It is feasible to regard *Elektra* as a symphonic structure, and it is firmly based on a tonal plan presenting each of the characters and their emotional states in a particular key. Both Electra and Clytemnestra, the most obsessive characters in the opera, are projected bitonally. Clytemnestra relates her dream in near-atonal harmonies as a kind of psychodrama, but it is inaccurate to describe *Elektra* in terms of the Schoenbergian Expressionism of *Erwartung* (1924). *Elektra* is near to being a number-opera, with formal introductions to the arias. Although the level of dissonance is higher in *Elektra* than in *Feuersnot* or *Der Rosenkavalier*, it has many points of contact with these works, not least in its use of the waltz in various guises. The music to which Electra leads Aegisthus to his doom might have been written for Baron Ochs in *Der Rosenkavalier*.

If Strauss wrote nothing again like *Elektra*, it was not because he had consciously retreated from avant-garde procedures. He instinctively knew that, with this work and *Salome*, he had gone as far as he could in depicting obsessed heroines of this kind. To have continued would have been to invite the charge of repeating himself, which had at first deterred him from setting *Elektra*.

Another important point to note about *Elektra* is that Strauss uses the orchestra to provide the opera with a wordless climax. Not until *Daphne*, nearly 30 years later, was he again to give the orchestra its head so completely. Music here triumphs over words, echoing Electra's opening of her final dance (a waltz) with the words 'Ob ich die Musik nicht höre? Sie kommt doch aus mir' ('You ask if I hear the music? It comes from me').

RECORDINGS 1. Varnay, Rysanek, Fischer, Hotter, WDR Ch & O, Kraus, Gala, 1953; 2. Borkh, Schech, Madeira, Fischer-Dieskau, Dresden Staatskapelle Op Ch & O, Böhm, 1960; 3. Nilsson, Collier, Resnik, Krause, Vienna State Op Ch, VPO, Solti, Decca, 1966/7

Der Rosenkavalier

The Knight of the Rose

Comedy for music in three acts (3h 15m)
Libretto by Hugo von Hofmannsthal
Composed April 1909–September 1910
PREMIERES 26 January 1911, Hofoper, Dresden; UK: 29 January 1913, Covent Garden, London; US: 9 December 1913, Metropolitan, New York
CAST Feldmarschallin, Princess Werdenberg *s*, Octavian, Count Rofrano *s*, Baron Ochs auf Lerchenau *b*, Herr von Faninal *bar*, Sophie *s*, Marianne Leitmetzerin, Sophie's duenna *s*, Valzacchi *t*, Annina *c*, Police Commissioner *b*, Marschallin's Major-domo (Struhan) *t*, Faninal's Major-domo *t*, Notary *b*, Innkeeper *t*, Italian Singer *t*, 3 Noble Orphans *s*, *ms*, *c*, Dressmaker *s*, Pet-seller *t*, 4 Marschallin's footmen 2 *t*, 2 *b*, 4 waiters *t*, 3 *b*, Mahomet *mime*; *silent*: Leopold, scholar flautist, hairdresser, hairdresser's assistant, widow of noble family; *satb* chorus of footmen, couriers, heyducks, cookboys, guests, musicians, 2 watchmen, 4 little children, various personages of suspicious appearance

The plot of *Der Rosenkavalier* was concocted within a few days in February 1909 by Hofmannsthal and his friend Count Harry Kessler. They borrowed ideas from many literary sources, including Molière, based some of the characters on operatic prototypes (Mozart's Countess and Cherubino in *Le nozze di Figaro*, and Verdi's *Falstaff*) and also drew inspiration from the graphic arts (Hogarth's *Mariage à la mode*). Strauss was delighted by the resulting libretto for Act I and set it page by page as he received it. He was highly critical of parts of the plot in Acts II and III, and these were adjusted to accommodate his ideas. Hofmannsthal created a mid-18th-century Vienna in considerable detail, but many of the customs (including the crucial idea of the presentation of a silver rose to the bride-to-be) were his own invention. The sense of class distinction and the subtlety of the language are prime features of the work's 'realism'.

The opera ran into censor trouble in Dresden and Berlin, but the principal threat to the Dresden premiere came from the inadequacy of the producer there. Strauss sent Max Reinhardt to supervise the carrying out of his own ideas, which he did without any credit in the programme. The opera was a huge success, with special trains being run to Dresden from various parts of Germany. The stage designs and production book prepared by Alfred Roller, who had been Mahler's scenic artist in Vienna, played a large part in the success and were used for several decades. London, Vienna, New York, Milan and many other operatic centres were quick to take up a work that remains in the repertoire of every major opera house and shows no sign of losing its popular appeal.

SYNOPSIS

Act I: Vienna, during the reign of the Empress Maria Theresa. The bedroom of the Princess Werdenberg, wife of the Field Marshal (hence 'Marschallin'). She has spent the night with her 17-year-old lover Count Octavian. Their breakfast is interrupted by her cousin, Baron Ochs auf Lerchenau, described by Strauss as a 'rural Don Juan'. Octavian disguises himself as a chambermaid ('Mariandel'), with whom Ochs flirts. The baron has come to ask the Marschallin to recommend a young nobleman as bearer of the traditional silver rose – a *Rosenkavalier* – to his fiancée, Sophie von Faninal, daughter of a recently ennobled arms dealer. It is then time for the Marschallin's *levée*. The stage is filled with tradesmen, various petitioners, a widow and her three daughters, a hairdresser, two intriguers (Valzacchi and Annina) and an Italian tenor who sings an aria ('Di rigori armato il seno'), which is a pastiche of Mozart's Italian song settings. The song is cut short by an argument over a dowry between Ochs and a lawyer. Valzacchi and Annina offer Ochs their services and Leopold, Ochs's bastard son (a non-speaking part), hands the silver rose to the Marschallin. Left alone, the Marschallin reflects on Ochs's conceit ('Da geht er hin') and compares herself when young with Sophie. At 32 she is acutely conscious of growing old, and when Octavian returns he finds her in a melancholy mood, aware that he will soon leave her for a younger woman. She tells him that time ('Die Zeit, die ist ein sonderbar Ding') slips by so quickly that she often gets up in the night and stops the clocks. When Octavian leaves her, the Marschallin realizes they have not even kissed goodbye. She sends her little black page Mahomet to him with the casket containing the silver rose.

Act II: In Herr von Faninal's palatial home Sophie, Faninal and her duenna are awaiting the rose-bearer's arrival by coach. Octavian ceremoniously presents her with the rose, and they are mutually attracted at first sight. Ochs is ushered in by Faninal and fondles Sophie lecherously. Meanwhile, his disreputable bodyguard causes chaos in the household. Sophie is appalled, and Octavian vows to prevent the marriage. Their love duet ('Mit Ihren Augen voll Tränen') is abruptly ended when they are apprehended by Valzacchi and Annina, who send for Ochs. Octavian challenges Ochs to a duel and wounds him slightly. Ochs acts as if he has been severely injured, and Sophie tells Faninal she refuses to marry this oaf. Octavian has meanwhile won over Valzacchi and Annina. While Ochs, bandaged, is left alone, Annina brings him a message from the Marschallin's chambermaid 'Mariandel' agreeing to a meeting. Ochs, delighted, sings his favourite waltz ('Ohne mich').

Act III: In a private room at an inn Valzacchi, Annina and others, under Octavian's supervision, rehearse the opening of trapdoors and other devices with which they plan to scare Ochs. Octavian dons his disguise as 'Mariandel' and goes to meet the baron. They sit down to supper, served by Leopold. To the music of an offstage band's waltzes, Ochs tries vainly to seduce the 'girl', who refuses wine and his advances ('Nein, nein! Ich trink kein Wein'). Every time he approaches her, apparitions appear at windows or through trapdoors. Annina, dressed in black as a widow, enters to claim Ochs as her husband and father of her children, who burst in noisily shouting 'Papa!' Ochs calls the police and tells the suspicious commissioner that he is dining with his fiancée Sophie. Octavian has ordered Valzacchi to send for Faninal and Sophie, who refute Ochs's story. Octavian tells the commissioner the truth and sheds his female attire. Meanwhile the Marschallin (summoned by Leopold) enters, recognizes the police commissioner as her husband's ex-orderly and assures him that the affair was 'just a masquerade'. She advises Ochs to leave, which he does, pursued by creditors, children and tavern staff. In the sublime trio for the three soprano voices ('Hab mir's gelobt'), the young lovers sing of their delight and the Marschallin accepts the situation with a good grace. She leaves them together ('Ist ein Traum') while she invites Faninal to ride home with her. The stage is empty, but Mahomet runs in to search for a handkerchief Sophie has dropped. Waving it above his head, he rejoins them and the curtain falls.

Although Hofmannsthal imagined *Der Rosenkavalier* as a neo-Mozartian opera in the *Figaro* mould, Strauss's music is post-Wagnerian in its subtle symphonic development of leitmotifs and its use of the orchestra in a richly allusive fashion. The score is both heavy and light, and the vocal writing carries a stage further Strauss's development of a lyrical conversational style that is neither aria nor recitative. The exquisite illustrative detail – whether it be the high polytonal chords for flutes, harps, celesta and three violins, which depict the silver rose, the fast movement of the hairdresser's hands as he adjusts the Marschallin's coiffure or the graphic love-making of the prelude to Act I – shows Strauss the tone poet at the height of his creative powers.

All three leading female roles reveal Strauss's extraordinary musical affinity with the soprano voice – the Act III trio is one of the finest ensemble pieces in all opera – while the bass and baritone roles of Ochs and Faninal are also richly rewarding. The role of the Marschallin is one of the greatest of all operatic creations and has attracted a line of distinguished interpreters. Strauss bound the whole work together with a string of memorable waltz tunes (which he later arranged in two sequences for concert performance), and although both he and Hofmannsthal admitted in later years that there were longueurs in *Der Rosenkavalier*, they never quite recaptured its lyrical élan. With its perennial themes of melancholy at growing old, love at first sight and nostalgia for a vanishing age threatened by social upheaval, *Der Rosenkavalier* had every ingredient for a lasting popular success. But what has ensured that success is the matchless blend between a marvellous libretto and the music it called into being.

RECORDINGS 1. Reining, Jurinac, Gueden, Weber, Vienna State Op Ch, VPO, E. Kleiber, Decca, 1954; 2. Stich-Randall, Schwarzkopf, Ludwig, Edelmann, Philharmonia Ch & O, Karajan, EMI, 1956; 3. Donath, Crespin, Minton, Jungwirth, Vienna State Op Ch, VPO, Solti, Decca, 1968

Ariadne auf Naxos

Ariadne on Naxos

Second version
Opera in one act, with prologue (2h)
Libretto by Hugo von Hofmannsthal
Prologue composed 1911–July 1912; second version, May–June 1916
PREMIERES first version: 25 October 1912, Hoftheater, Stuttgart; UK: 27 May 1913, His Majesty's Theatre, Haymarket, London; second version: 4 October 1916, Hofoper, Vienna; UK: 27 May 1924, Covent Garden, London; US: 1 November 1928, Civic Opera, Philadelphia
CAST Composer *s*, Music Master *bar*, Dancing Master *t*, Wig-maker *b*, Lackey *b*, Prima Donna/Ariadne *s*, Tenor/Bacchus *t*, Zerbinetta *s*, Harlequin *bar*, Scaramuccio *t*, Truffaldino *b*, Brighella *t*, Officer *t*, Naiad *s*, Dryad *c*, Echo *s*, Major-domo *spoken role*

Both Hofmannsthal and Strauss were indebted to the producer Max Reinhardt who, without official credit, had transformed the Dresden production of *Der Rosenkavalier*. As a thank-offering, Hofmannsthal devised a novel combination of play and 30-minute opera, the former to be his adaptation of Molière's *Le bour-*

geois gentilhomme, with incidental music for the dances, the latter *Ariadne auf Naxos*, with Strauss's music, which would interweave elements of opera seria with those of the commedia dell'arte. The opera was conceived as a divertissement after the dinner that concludes the play and was to be performed in the presence of Monsieur Jourdain, the 'bourgeois gentilhomme'. Between the play and opera came a short scene in prose in which those responsible for arranging the entertainments for Jourdain – the Composer and the Dancing Master – were told by Jourdain's footman that the two pieces must be performed simultaneously. This first version was performed in Stuttgart on 25 October 1912, but the evening lasted over six hours (the '30-minute opera' had become a 90-minute opera), and it was obvious to composer and librettist that in this form the work was impracticable, requiring both a drama company and an opera company to perform it.

In 1913 Hofmannsthal hit on a new version, with the opera preceded by a short sung prologue based on the linking scene. He eliminated Monsieur Jourdain and transferred the action of the prologue from 17th-century Paris to the 19th-century house of 'the richest man in Vienna'. Strauss at first was not interested, but in 1916 he composed the prologue. At the Vienna premiere the *travesti* role of the young Composer was sung by Lotte Lehmann, her first outstanding success. Although the original version is occasionally revived, it is the second version that has become part of the international repertoire.

SYNOPSIS

Prologue: In the house of the richest man in Vienna, where a sumptuous banquet is to be held in the evening, two theatrical groups are busy preparing their entertainments. The Music Master protests to the Major-domo about the decision to follow his pupil's opera seria, *Ariadne auf Naxos*, with 'vulgar buffoonery'. The Major-domo makes it plain that he who pays the piper calls the tune and that the fireworks display will begin at nine o'clock. The Composer wants a last-minute rehearsal with the violinists, but they are playing during dinner. The soprano who is to sing Ariadne is not available to go through her aria; the tenor cast as Bacchus objects to his wig. There is typical backstage chaos. Seeing the attractive Zerbinetta and inquiring who she is, the Composer is told by the Music Master that she is leader of the commedia dell'arte group that is to perform after the opera. Outraged, the Composer's wrath is turned aside when a new melody occurs to him ('Du, Venus' Sohn'). The Major-domo returns to announce that his master now requires both entertainments to be performed simultaneously and still to end at nine o'clock sharp. More uproar, during which the Dancing Master suggests that the Composer should cut his opera to accommodate the harlequinade's dances.

The plot of *Ariadne* is explained to Zerbinetta, who mocks the idea of 'languishing in passionate longing and praying for death'. To her, another lover is the answer. Zerbinetta and the Composer find they have something in common when Zerbinetta tells him 'A moment is nothing – a glance is much' ('Ein Augenblick ist wenig – ein Blick ist viel'). 'Who can say that my heart is in the part I play?' Heartened, the Composer sings of music's power ('Musik ist eine heilige Kunst'). But when he sees the comedians scampering about, he cries, 'I should not have allowed it.'

Opera: On the island of Naxos, where Ariadne has been abandoned by Theseus, who took her with him from Crete after she had helped him to kill the Minotaur. Ariadne is asleep, watched over by three nymphs, Naiad, Dryad and Echo. They describe her perpetual, inconsolable weeping. Ariadne wakes. She can think of nothing except her betrayal by Theseus and she wants death to end her suffering. Zerbinetta and the comedians cannot believe in her desperation and Harlequin vainly tries to cheer her with a song about the joys of life. She sings of the purity of the kingdom of death ('Es gibt ein Reich') and longs for Hermes to lead her there. The comedians again try to cheer her up with singing and dancing, but to no avail. Zerbinetta sends them away and tries on her own, with her long coloratura aria ('Grossmächtige Prinzessin'), the gist of which is that there are plenty of other men besides Theseus. In the middle of the aria Ariadne goes into her cave. Zerbinetta and her troupe then enact their entertainment in which the four comedians court her.

The three nymphs excitedly announce the arrival of the young god Bacchus, who has just escaped from the sorceress Circe. At first he mistakes Ariadne for another Circe, while she mistakes him for Theseus and then Hermes. But in the duet that follows, reality takes over and Ariadne's longing for death becomes a longing for love as Bacchus becomes aware of his divinity. As passion enfolds them, Zerbinetta comments that she was right all along: 'Off with the old, on with the new.'

The second version necessitated considerable revision of the score. Comments on the action by M. Jourdain and others, characters now eliminated, had to be deleted. Zerbinetta's aria was eased by dropping its pitch a whole tone for most of its duration: two major cuts amounting to about 80 bars of music were made, although Strauss replaced the second cut (in the closing section of the aria) by a new coda less than half as long, which contains a duet for voice and flute. A scene just before Bacchus' arrival, in which Zerbinetta interrupts Ariadne's address to her as yet invisible liberator, was deleted.

But the biggest alteration was the ending. In the first version, after the Ariadne–Bacchus love duet, the comedians return and Jourdain's guests depart. Part of Zerbinetta's aria is recapitulated as she points out that what has just occurred supports her view of life and love. The comedians' waltz returns as the four clowns and Zerbinetta sing and dance. Jourdain, who has been asleep, is wakened by a servant who asks if the firework display should begin. Jourdain ignores him and repeats his admiration for the true nobility. His trumpet tune ends the opera.

In *Ariadne auf Naxos* the two contrasting elements in Strauss's musical personality – the rococo and the heroic – are interwoven much as the opera seria and the harlequinade are intermingled or, more accurately, juxtaposed, in the plot of the opera itself. It represents a major step forward in Strauss's defence of the musical territory he had mapped out for himself, the antithesis of the Schoenbergian revolution. Yet it is no backward step. The neo-baroque music of the harlequinade belongs as inescapably to the 20th century as does Stravinsky's *Pulcinella*.

A virtuoso feature of the work is Strauss's use of a small orchestra (37 players). So skilful is his scoring that in the passionate final duet for Ariadne and Bacchus it is rich enough to give the impression of a large orchestra. Part of the unique flavour of the second version of *Ariadne auf Naxos* derives from Strauss's brilliant juxtaposition of low comedy and high tragedy. In the prologue, where he made a spectacular advance in his development of a melodic conversational recitative, he is at home depicting the quarrels and chaos of backstage theatrical life. In the opera, he slips easily from the heroic style in which Ariadne's part is composed to the buffooning of the commedia dell'arte characters.

RECORDINGS 1. Streich, Schwarzkopf, Seefried, Schock, Philharmonia O, Karajan, EMI, 1954; 2. Janowitz, Geszty, Zylis-Gara, King, Dresden Staatskapelle, Kempe, EMI, 1968; 3. Norman, Gruberova, Varady, Frey, Fischer-Dieskau, Leipzig Gewandhaus O, Masur, Philips, 1988

Die Frau ohne Schatten
The Woman without a Shadow

Opera in three acts (3h 30m)
Libretto by Hugo von Hofmannsthal
Composed July 1914–June 1917
PREMIERES 10 October 1919, Staatsoper, Vienna; US: 18 September 1959, War Memorial Opera House, San Francisco; UK: 2 May 1966, Sadler's Wells, London
CAST Emperor *t*, Empress *s*, Nurse *ms*, Spirit Messenger *bar*, Guardian of the Threshold of the Temple *s* or *ct*, Apparition of a Youth *t*, Voice of the Falcon *s*, Voice from Above *c*, Barak the Dyer *bar*, Dyer's Wife *s*, Barak's brothers: One-Eyed *b*, One-Armed *b*, Hunchback *t*, children's voices 3 *s*, 3 *c*, voices of the nightwatchmen 3 *b*; *satb* chorus of imperial servants, children, attendant spirits, spirit voices

Hofmannsthal first outlined his idea for a 'magic fairy tale' in March 1911. He told Strauss that in it two men would confront two women and 'for one of the women your wife might well, in all discretion, be taken as a model'. Progress on the libretto was slow and was interrupted by the composition of the first version of *Ariadne auf Naxos*. Composer and librettist discussed the project in detail during a trip to Italy in the spring of 1913. Hofmannsthal explained that *Die Frau ohne Schatten* would veer between the world of spirits and the world of humans with an intermediate plane inhabited by the Emperor and Empress. He described it as standing 'in general terms, to *Zauberflöte* as *Rosenkavalier* does to *Figaro*'. Although the principal subject of the opera is infertility – the 'shadow' is the symbol of parenthood – its main dramatic interest is in the Empress's development from a fairy-tale creature into a human being through her realization that other people matter. She is prepared to sacrifice her own and her husband's life rather than allow the humble Barak and his shrewish wife to be forced apart. The libretto is heavy with symbolism and has often been dismissed as pretentious and incomprehensible, but Strauss himself had no difficulty with it and regarded it as Hofmannsthal's masterpiece. The outbreak of the First World War caused further delays, with Hofmannsthal unable to complete the third act until the spring of 1915.

In March 1919 Strauss became joint director of the post-war Vienna State Opera with Franz Schalk. He gave the first performance of the new opera to Vienna but later admitted that it was a mistake, in spite of a cast headed by Maria Jeritza, Lotte Lehmann and Richard Mayr. With the poverty and hunger attendant upon the end of hostilities, this was no time for such a difficult and complicated work to be performed. In addition, Alfred Roller, the director and set designer, surprisingly failed to realize some of the magical effects that were required. Few German theatres were equipped to stage it satisfactorily (the Dresden premiere was a disaster). Consequently the opera made its way slowly and was not staged in New York and London, for example, until 1966. Even in Munich it is still cut in performance, but it has gradually come to be regarded by many Strauss enthusiasts as his greatest opera.

SYNOPSIS
Before the action of the opera begins, the Emperor of the South Eastern Islands was hunting with his falcon and pursued a gazelle. Just as he was about to kill it, it resumed its real form as the daughter of Keikobad, master of the spirit world. The Emperor married her, but she has remained neither spirit nor human and has borne no children.

Act I: The Nurse is guarding the room where the royal couple are sleeping. Keikobad's messenger appears to tell her that if the Empress does not cast a shadow – that is, become pregnant – within three days, the Emperor will be turned to stone and the Empress reclaimed by her father. The Emperor goes hunting for three days to try to find his falcon. In his absence, the falcon comes to the Empress and tells her what Keikobad has threatened. She knows she can obtain a shadow only from a human woman and forces the Nurse to help her find one. They fly down to the earth and go to the impoverished home of the Dyer Barak, whose Wife is quarrelling with her husband's deformed brothers. She is discontented and knows that Barak wants children. The Nurse plans to turn the Wife's unhappiness to her advantage. She tries to buy her shadow, promising a life of luxury in return. The Wife agrees to refuse her husband's advances for three days, during which time the Empress and Nurse will be her servants. Barak returns from market to find he has been provided with a single bed.

Act II: While Barak is at work, the Nurse continues her temptation of his Wife, conjuring up the young man of her dreams. But the Dyer's Wife pushes the youth away when he tries to touch her. Barak returns with a huge bowl of food for his brothers and the beggar children who have followed him home. His Wife refuses to eat. In his falcon-house, the Emperor awaits the Empress, having been told she will be there. He sees her and the Nurse slip secretly into the house, senses they have been in the world of humans and decides to kill the Empress. But he cannot bring himself to do it and flees. Before Barak leaves for work, the Nurse gives him a sleeping draught. She again causes the young man to appear. But the Wife takes fright and wakens Barak, rebuking him for sleeping in the daytime and leaving her a prey to robbers. The Empress, asleep in the falcon-house, is overcome with remorse for Barak. She hears the falcon's cry: 'The woman casts no shadow! The Emperor must turn to stone!' She laments: 'Whatever I touch I kill!' Barak's Wife taunts him by telling him she was unfaithful while he slept and has sold her shadow. Barak wants to kill her, and the Nurse provides a sword. The Wife realizes that she loves him, and the Empress repudiates the shadow bargain. Barak lifts the sword but it is snatched from him. The earth swallows him and his Wife while the Nurse leads the Empress to safety.

Act III: Imprisoned in separate cells, Barak and his Wife realize that they belong together. They are freed by servants of the spirit world to seek one another. The Empress and the Nurse go by boat to Keikobad's temple. The Empress recognizes its door from a dream. The Nurse tries to dissuade her from entering, warning her that she will be punished, but the Empress dismisses the Nurse – 'I part from you for ever' – and enters the temple. The voices of Barak and his Wife are heard as they search for each other. The Nurse says she hates all mankind and deliberately misleads the couple, sending them in opposite directions. She then tries to enter the temple, but Keikobad's messenger bars her way and throws her into the boat, condemning her to wander henceforth among those she hates. In the temple the Empress wants to face Keikobad. The Keeper of the Threshold tempts her with a drink from the water of life, after which the Dyer's Wife's shadow will be hers. She can hear the voices of Barak and his Wife. She refuses to drink and is shown the Emperor turned to stone, only his terrified eyes remaining alive. She offers to die with him and still refuses to drink. The stage goes dark and when the light returns the Empress is seen to cast a shadow and the Emperor is restored to life. Because the Empress has learned human feeling, Keikobad has forgiven her. Emperor and Empress, Barak and Wife are reunited while the voices of their unborn children sing their praises.

Die Frau ohne Schatten is Strauss's largest and most ambitious opera and the one in which the genius he lavished on description and characterization in his tone poems is most literally applied to the stage. The composer of the opening horn-call of *Till Eulenspiegel* is very obviously the same composer who invented the haunting and unforgettable cry of the falcon in this opera; and there are other striking instrumental effects, such as the use of a glass harmonica to depict the Empress's acquisition of a shadow. While some passages are on an opulent, Wagnerian scale, much of the score has the delicacy of chamber music. In this respect it closely resembles the Mahler of the Eighth Symphony and *Das Lied von der Erde* (of all his scores it comes closest to a homage to his colleague and friend). The exotic, oriental flavour is a further link with *Das Lied von der Erde*.

The score is another refutation of the widespread allegation that Strauss 'went soft' after *Elektra*. While there are such exquisite diatonic episodes as the orchestral interlude in the first scene between Barak and his Wife – a simple melodizing around the chord of D♭ to illustrate the Dyer's compassionate and loving nature – there are also any number of examples of rootless harmony and near atonality. The Empress's dream, for instance, ends with an orchestral epilogue in which nightmarish harmonies sum up the anguish she has expressed.

Like *Der Rosenkavalier* the opera contains three great roles for women – the Empress, Barak's Wife and the Nurse – and a typically fine Strauss baritone part for Barak. We may wonder if Strauss's supposed hostility to the tenor voice was anything more than a joke on his part when we hear the magnificent music he wrote for the Emperor, notably his Act II aria in the hunting-lodge. Although Strauss told Hofmannsthal that he found it difficult to fill the Emperor, Empress and Nurse with musical red corpuscles as he had the characters in *Der Rosenkavalier*, he nevertheless gave all three characters some of the most powerful and elevated music he ever composed.

RECORDINGS 1. Rysanek, Goltz, Höngen, Hopf, Schöffler, Vienna State Op Ch, VPO, Böhm, Decca, 1955; 2. Rysanek, Ludwig, Hoffmann, Thomas, Berry, Vienna State Op Ch, VPO, Karajan, DG, 1964 (live, cut); 3. Varady, Behrens, Runkel, Domingo, Van Dam, Vienna State Op Ch, VPO, Solti, Decca, 1989/91

Arabella

Lyric comedy in three acts (2h 30m)
Libretto by Hugo von Hofmannsthal
Composed 1930–October 1932
PREMIERES 1 July 1933, Staatsoper, Dresden: UK: 17 May 1934, Covent Garden, London; US: 10 February 1955, Metropolitan, New York
CAST Count Waldner *b*, Adelaide, his wife *ms*, Arabella *s*, Zdenka *s*, Mandryka *bar*, Matteo *t*, Count Elemer *t*, Count Dominik *bar*, Count Lamoral *b*, Fiakermilli *s*, Fortune-teller *s*, 3 players 3 *b*; *spoken roles*: Welko, Djura, Jankel, hotel porter; *silent*: Arabella's companion, a doctor, groom; *satb* chorus of cabmen, ball guests, hotel guests, waiters

Hofmannsthal based his last libretto for Strauss on his novel *Lucidor* (1910), with some elements added from a proposed comedy, *Fiaker als Graf* ('Cabbie as Count'). Strauss had been pressing him for some time for 'a second *Rosenkavalier* without its mistakes and longueurs'. In what became *Arabella*, Hofmannsthal believed he had found the formula his collaborator required: a Viennese setting with a background of waltzes and a plot based on his favourite theme of love at first sight. He sent the libretto of Act I to Strauss in May 1928. Adjustments were made, and the complete libretto was ready by Christmas 1928. Further revisions were delayed by Hofmannsthal's illness. Strauss wanted a substantial monologue for Arabella with which to end Act I, and 'Mein Elemer!' was supplied on 10 July 1929. Strauss telegraphed his thanks and congratulations from Garmisch to Rodaun. But the telegram was not opened. It arrived on 15 July, the day of the funeral of Hofmannsthal's son Franz, who had committed suicide.

An hour or so before the service, Hofmannsthal had a stroke and died.

Strauss began to compose *Arabella* in 1930. He dedicated it to Alfred Reucker and Fritz Busch, intendant and conductor of the Dresden State Opera where it was to be premiered. But in March 1933 the Nazis dismissed both men. Strauss withdrew the score, but Dresden held him to his contract and Clemens Krauss conducted the first performance with Viorica Ursuleac (who later became his wife) as Arabella. In Vienna Lotte Lehmann sang the title role. The critical response was cool, the general attitude being that it was an attempt to imitate *Rosenkavalier*, and was not as good. This attitude has gradually given way to admiration for the opera on its own terms, and it has become one of the best loved of Strauss's stage works. It is generally performed in the original three-act version, but Munich favours the producer Rudolf Hartmann's 1939 device of linking Acts II and III by omitting the final waltz and chorus of Act II.

SYNOPSIS

Act I: Count Waldner, a retired cavalry officer, and his wife live in a slightly seedy Vienna hotel. They are hard up. Waldner gambles at the card table but rarely wins. They have two daughters, Arabella and Zdenka, but the latter is passed off as a boy because they cannot afford to bring out both girls in Vienna society. It is Carnival Day (Shrove Tuesday) 1860, and Countess Waldner (Adelaide) is consulting a fortune-teller who says that Arabella's successful suitor will be a foreigner, summoned by letter. Left alone, Zdenka admits an army officer, Matteo. He believes Arabella loves him because of the letters he receives from her, but these are written by Zdenka, who adores him. He leaves, threatening suicide or exile. When Arabella enters, Zdenka quarrels with her about her coldness to Matteo. Arabella says she will know the right man when she meets him. In fact she saw a stranger looking at her in the street that morning and wishes he would send her flowers. Count Elemer, one of three suitors, arrives to escort Arabella for a drive. She tells him she must choose a husband before the night is out while she is queen of the Cabbies' Ball. Before they leave, Arabella sees her stranger in the street outside. Waldner tells Adelaide he's been hoping for a letter from a former army comrade, Mandryka, a Croatian. He has sent the rich old man a portrait of Arabella. Sure enough, a waiter says a Mandryka is waiting to see him. But this is a tall, handsome young man, nephew of Waldner's friend, who is now dead. He has inherited his uncle's lands and wealth and, having seen her portrait, has come to woo Arabella. He shows his bulging wallet to Waldner and tells him to help himself to its contents. After he has left, Arabella sings of the impossibility of marriage with Elemer ('Mein Elemer!').

Act II: At the Cabbies' Ball, Arabella is presented to Mandryka, whom she recognizes as her stranger in the street. They declare their love, and Mandryka tells her of the custom in his village whereby betrothed girls present a cup of clear Danube water to their fiancé as a token of chastity and allegiance. Arabella says she will dance farewell to her girlhood. The cabbies' mascot, the Fiakermilli, hails Arabella as the queen of the ball. Arabella has a final dance with each of her three suitors, Elemer, Dominik and Lamoral. Matteo has been hovering nearby and is assured by Zdenka of Arabella's love. She gives him a letter, supposedly from Arabella. This exchange is overheard by Mandryka. In the letter, Zdenka says, is the key to Arabella's bedroom (in reality, her own). Mandryka cannot believe this deception, but when he is given a letter from Arabella excusing herself from the remainder of the evening, he gets drunk, flirts with the Fiakermilli and insults the Waldners.

Act III: From the main hall of the Waldners' hotel we see Matteo on the landing at the top of the staircase, emerging from what he believes to be Arabella's room. He cannot believe his eyes when he sees Arabella, in her ball gown, in the lobby. He tells her he cannot understand how she can be so distant after what has just passed between them. Arabella is mystified and annoyed. She denies she was upstairs 15 minutes ago. The Waldners and Mandryka arrive. Seeing Matteo, Mandryka is convinced of Arabella's fickleness and orders his servants to pack for departure. Arabella denies that Matteo is her lover. The silence is broken by a cry as Zdenka, in a nightdress, runs downstairs to say farewell to her family before she jumps into the river. She tells Arabella what has happened and reveals to Matteo that she is a girl and that it was her to whom he has just made love. Mandryka, ashamed, asks Waldner to accept Matteo as a son-in-law. Everyone disperses, leaving Arabella with Mandryka. She asks that his servant should bring her a glass of water to her room to quench her thirst. Mandryka soliloquizes on his stupidity. Then he sees Arabella descending the stairs bringing him the glass of water as in his village custom. 'Take me as I am!' she declares.

Arabella is Strauss's most romantic opera. For their last collaboration, Hofmannsthal eschewed his tendency to overload his libretti with symbols, mysticism and psychological insights. Instead he was content with a tale of love at first sight involving a strange and eccentric but very human group of characters. Just as *Die ägyptische Helena* seemed to reflect the cinema's preoccupation in the 1920s with sheikhs and desert songs, so in *Arabella* there is suggestion of a cinematic plot – waiting for Mr Right. But Strauss's music is of such charm and warmth that the improbabilities of the plot as they involve Matteo and Zdenka in Act III are of no account – one accepts it all. The scoring has a transparency and sweetness rare in 20th-century opera.

In setting the libretto, Strauss continued the parlando style he had been developing so successfully since the *Ariadne* prelude (though it can be found in *Feuersnot* in an embryonic state). *Arabella* created a new kind of music theatre, combining the finest qualities of opera, operetta and musical.

Too much is made of the fact that Hofmannsthal died before he could revise Acts II and III. Although there are dramatic weaknesses in Act II, they are not fatal – and the Munich habit of running the last two acts together is no improvement in any respect. The comparison with *Der Rosenkavalier* is also overworked. Vienna and waltzes are about the only genuine similarities, both treated in very different ways in *Arabella*.

A feature of the score is Strauss's use of Slavonic folk music to give special flavour to the music for Mandryka. Lyricism is all in *Arabella*, both in the libretto and the music. If it is not Strauss's most profound opera, it is in many ways the most uncomplicatedly enjoyable, which is not to say that it lacks complexities. The heroine herself is a fascinating figure, as Strauss realized when he demanded a big aria for her to end Act I. In 'Mein Elemer!', he and Hofmannsthal provide a character study of Arabella that is the key to the whole opera.

RECORDINGS 1. Gueden, della Casa, Dermota, London, Edelmann, Vienna State Op Ch, VPO, Solti, Decca, 1957; 2. Donath, Varady, Dallapozza, Fischer-Dieskau, Berry, Bavarian State Op Ch & O, Sawallisch, Orfeo, 1981; 3. Grundheber, Te Kanawa, Seiffert, Grundheber, Covent Garden Ch & O, Tate, Decca, 1986

Capriccio

Conversation piece for music in one act (2h 15m)
Libretto by Clemens Krauss and the composer
Composed July 1940–August 1941
PREMIERES 28 October 1942, Nationaltheater, Munich; UK: 22 September 1953, Covent Garden, London; US: 2 April 1954, Juilliard School of Music, New York

CAST Countess *s*, Count *bar*, Flamand *t*, Olivier *bar*, La Roche *b*, Clairon *c*, M. Taupe *t*, Italian Singer *s*, Italian tenor *t*, Major-domo *b*, 8 servants 4 *t*, 4 *b*, ballet dancer

Strauss's last opera was on the subject that had exercised him for most of his life: the relationship between words and music in opera. In 1935 Zweig had suggested reshaping Casti's comedy *Prima la musica, poi le parole*, which had been set by Salieri (1786). Zweig passed on his idea to Gregor and together they devised a scenario. Over the next four years Strauss rejected two libretti by Gregor and consulted Clemens Krauss, who wrote a scenario but suggested that Strauss should write the text himself. Gregor was dismissed, and together Strauss and Krauss completed *Capriccio*. Although Krauss is credited with the libretto in the printed score, much of it is by Strauss. The first performance was given in Munich with Ursuleac as the Countess, Hotter as Olivier and Georg Hann as La Roche. In spite of the nightly air raids, each performance was fully attended and enthusiastically received. Krauss made several attempts to interest Strauss in writing another opera, but he replied, 'One can only leave one testament'. At Hamburg in 1957 Rudolf Hartmann, the producer of the Munich premiere, divided the opera into two acts, making a break at the point where the Countess orders chocolate in the drawing room. This version has been widely adopted elsewhere, including at Glyndebourne.

SYNOPSIS

In a château near Paris *c.*1775, the young widowed Countess Madeleine, with her brother the Count, is listening to a string sextet written in honour of her forthcoming birthday by the composer Flamand. Other members of the house party are the poet Olivier, who has written a play for the occasion, and the theatrical director La Roche, who is to produce it. The Count is to act in the play mainly because he is infatuated with the Parisian actress Clairon, who has recently broken off her affair with Olivier and is expected at any moment. On arrival, she inquires pointedly if Olivier has yet written the love scene. He has that morning written a sonnet as its climax, and this is declaimed from manuscript by the Count and Clairon. While a rehearsal of his play begins, from which La Roche excludes him, Olivier reads the sonnet to the Countess, for whom it is intended ('Kein Andres, das mir so im Herzen loht'). Flamand, to Olivier's annoyance, promptly sets it to music and sings it to Madeleine and Olivier. Poet and composer quarrel over whose work it now is – the Countess says it is hers, a present from them both. Olivier is summoned by La Roche, and Flamand declares his love to the Countess. He demands an answer from her. She says she will meet him next morning at eleven, in the library. Chocolate is now served and La Roche introduces a young ballerina to entertain the company. After the dances (imitations of Couperin), fugal discussion of the relative merits of words and music begins. La Roche then introduces an Italian soprano and tenor, who sing a duet, after which La Roche describes the lavish entertainment he plans for the Countess's birthday. This is received with ribald comments, which lead to two octets, the first a laughing ensemble, the second a quarrel (during which the Italian soprano eats too many cakes and drinks too much wine). La Roche replies with a long monologue in which he defines the work of a director and asks where the great artists of today are (the text was written by Strauss and its sentiments are obviously his). The Countess suggests Flamand and Olivier should collaborate on an opera for La Roche to direct. Various subjects (*Ariadne* and *Daphne* among them) are rejected. The Count suggests that it should be 'about all of us and the events of today'. This is agreed and the company disperses to return to Paris. The servants tidy the salon and discuss what has been happening. The Major-domo gives them the evening off after they have prepared the Countess's supper. A voice is heard – it is the prompter, M. Taupe, who had fallen asleep and has been left behind. As he is led off to be given a meal, the Countess enters, dressed for supper, and stands on the terrace in the moonlight. The Major-domo gives her a message from Olivier – he will be in the library at eleven next morning to learn how the opera should end. 'How should it end?' she ponders. Is she more moved by words or music, does she love Olivier or Flamand? Can there be an ending that is not trivial? She curtsies to her reflection in a mirror and goes into supper – humming the melody of the sonnet.

In what he expected to be a dry, academic subject for opera, written for his own amusement – a theatrical fugue, as he described it to Krauss – and unlikely to appeal to a wide audience, Strauss paradoxically found in *Capriccio* a libretto to suit all that he did best. It drew from him a fresh fount of inspiration and has become one of his most popular works. His technical virtuosity is demonstrated in three vocal octets, the laughing and quarrelling ensembles and the servants' scherzo-like commentary on the day's proceedings. In the music for the Italian singers and the ballerina his gift for parody is at its keenest and most affectionate. In the strange, half-lit scene for the prompter and the Major-domo, with its shifting harmonies and air of mystery, he recaptured something of the poetic fantasy of his *Don Quixote* variations (1897). The instrumental sextet that opens the opera and the scoring throughout the rest of the work are examples of Strauss at his most lyrical and sensitive, but suffused with autumnal melancholy, and in the role of the Countess he created one of his most adorable heroines and wrote for her music of intense melodic beauty in which the finest qualities of his lieder and arias are combined to provide the ideal final 20 minutes for a last opera by Strauss.

The Strauss who was able to cut his musical cloth as the dramatic situation dictated is perfectly accommodated in *Capriccio*. Like *Der Rosenkavalier*, the work is gorgeously anachronistic. Although it is set in the late 18th century and a mock-rococo style is sometimes affected, the music belongs inescapably to Strauss's own era, which is one reason why productions updated to the 1920s and 1930s are successful, give or take the resulting ludicrousness of the libretto's references to Goldoni and Gluck as contemporary figures. As in the prologue to *Ariadne auf Naxos* and in *Intermezzo* and *Arabella*, the continuously melodic conversational recitative is here raised to a fine art. All the greatest features of his operas from *Der Rosenkavalier* onwards were filtered through the experience and wisdom gained over 30 years to find their apogee in *Capriccio*. Its resonances and delights increase at each hearing.

RECORDINGS 1. Schwarzkopf, Gedda, Waechter, Fischer-Dieskau, Hotter, Philharmonia O, Sawallisch, EMI, 1957/8; 2. Janowitz, Schreier, Fischer-Dieskau, Prey, Ridderbusch, Bavarian RSO, Böhm, DG, 1971; 3. Lott, Kunde, Allen, Genz, Kannen, South West German Vocal Ens, RSO, Prêtre, Forlane, 1999

OTHER OPERATIC WORKS *Guntram*, 1894; *Feuersnot*, 1901; *Intermezzo*, 1924; *Die ägyptische Helena*, 1928; *Die schweigsame Frau*, 1935; *Friedenstag*, 1938; *Daphne*, 1938; *Die Liebe der Danae*, (1940), 1944

M.K.

Igor Stravinsky

Igor Fyodorovich Stravinsky; *b* 17 June 1882, Oranienbaum (now Lomonosov), Russia; *d* 6 April 1971, New York

Stravinsky owed his meteoric early success to his association with Diaghilev and the Paris-based Ballets Russes. His upbringing might well have directed him more readily towards opera. His father was leading bass at the Mariinsky

Theatre in St Petersburg, and his teacher was Rimsky-Korsakov, at the time when the master was writing his last operas. But Diaghilev wanted a ballet score (for *The Firebird*, 1910), and the result was so brilliant in its vitality of movement and fantastic orchestral colouring that Stravinsky was diverted into a genre that Diaghilev was busy pushing to the forefront of the modern aesthetic movement. Between then and his death in 1929, Diaghilev put on nine further stage works by Stravinsky, six of them ballets. For much of this period Stravinsky was a leading light of the Paris artistic scene (after spending the war years in Switzerland, he settled in France in 1920); and, while often on bad terms with Diaghilev, he numbered many of the prominent artists and thinkers of the day among his friends, including Debussy (until his death in 1918), Picasso, Cocteau, Valéry and Maritain. *Perséphone* was the climax of this French stage of Stravinsky's life, completed in the year he became a French citizen (1934). His subsequent theatre works were nearly all written for the US, where he settled in 1940.

Of Stravinsky's 20 or so works for the theatre, perhaps four are definitely operas: *The Nightingale*, *Mavra*, *Oedipus Rex* and *The Rake's Progress*. But many of his best works are hard to categorize, since it was an essential part of his genius to invent genres to suit his subject matter. In 1913 he told a reporter: 'I dislike opera. Music can be married to gesture or to words – not to both without bigamy.' Yet between 'pure' ballet, like *Petrushka*, and 'pure' opera, like *The Rake's Progress*, are several works that combine dance with speech and/or singing, with or without narrative in the conventional sense. In such matters Stravinsky was evidently influenced by his compatriot Meyerhold, the theatre director, who rejected the 19th-century notion of stage realism in favour of an open-ended theatre where any resource is legitimate if it serves the central idea of the action. The use of masks (in *Pulcinella*, *Renard* and *Oedipus Rex*), ritualized action (*The Rite of Spring*, *Les Noces*, *Oedipus Rex*), deliberate breaks in style (*Petrushka*, *The Soldier's Tale*, *Perséphone*), objectivization in the form of spoken or sung commentaries (*Renard*, *The Soldier's Tale*, *Oedipus Rex*) and other such devices, all originate in the Symbolist techniques of Meyerhold.

In trying to form a picture of Stravinsky's contribution to opera, it is obvious that one cannot wholly isolate his works in that form from his ballets and mixed-media pieces. His whole approach to opera was nourished by the spirit of magic and the intimate artifice he found in the ballets of Tchaikovsky, and *The Nightingale* is much closer in spirit to *The Nutcracker* than to *The Queen of Spades* or even the late magical operas of Rimsky-Korsakov (to which, however, it owes something musically). *Renard* is a vocal piece only in the sense that *The Wedding*, on which Stravinsky was stuck at the time, is a vocal piece; and *The Wedding* is vocal because the idea for it came from a reading of Kireyevsky's collection of folk verse and is inextricably bound up with the verbal exchanges, the risqué jokes and ritual sayings of the traditional peasant wedding.

Later, however, after the end of the war and the Russian Revolution, which cut him off from his home and roots, he turned against this ethnic strain. The songs in *Pulcinella* (1919), a Stravinskyization of music by, or at that time attributed to, Pergolesi, are in a courtly musical and linguistic Italian. *Mavra* (1921–2), though it has a Russian story, studiously avoids peasant types and instead takes as its subject a comic bourgeois tale by Pushkin, and for its musical models Glinka and Tchaikovsky. This is the real start of Stravinsky's neoclassical phase. Now his music is tonal, formal and vocally ornate. *Mavra* is a number opera, like Mozart's or Weber's. The instrumental works of the time allude to Bach, Haydn and Beethoven. In *Oedipus Rex* (1926–7) Handelian choruses and Verdian or Bellinian arias serve to dramatize a bookish and statuesque presentation of Sophocles, with a Latin text (explained somewhat patronizingly by a narrator in evening dress), immobile characters in masks and a two-dimensional set. For some reason this unpromising mixture produces one of the most powerful and moving operas in the history of the genre.

After emigrating to America, Stravinsky fell temporarily into a rut in which his neoclassicism became somewhat routine and predictable. *The Rake's Progress* (1947–51), for all its wit and polished craftsmanship, is conventional in a way no previous Stravinsky theatre piece had been; and, according to his new associate Robert Craft, it was partly out of depression at the lack of newness in his work that Stravinsky let himself be persuaded to study the music of the serial composers Schoenberg and Webern. The vitality of Stravinsky's own serial period (roughly from 1952) is one of the most startling aspects of a career marked by almost continuous renewal. The main thrust of these late works is religious, and it is symptomatic that the one sung drama of the period, *The Flood* – a typically geometric, diamantine piece of writing – should be on a biblical subject.

Oedipus Rex

King Oedipus

Opera-oratorio in two acts (50m)
Libretto (in French) by Jean Cocteau (Latin sections translated by Jean Daniélou), after the play *Oedipus Tyrannus* by Sophocles (*c.* 430 BC)
Composed 1926–7, rev. 1948
PREMIERES 30 May 1927, Théâtre Sarah-Bernhardt, Paris (concert); 23 February 1928, Staatsoper, Vienna (stage); US: 24 February 1928, Boston (concert); 21 April 1931, Metropolitan, New York (stage); UK: 12 May 1928 (radio broadcast); 12 February 1936, Queen's Hall, London (concert); 21 August 1956, King's Theatre, Edinburgh (stage)
CAST Oedipus *t*, Jocasta *ms*, Creon *b-bar*, Tiresias *b*, the Shepherd *t*, the Messenger *b-bar*, Speaker *spoken role*; *tb* chorus

The idea for 'an opera in Latin on the subject of a tragedy of the ancient world, with which everyone would be familiar' was Stravinsky's own, as a letter to Cocteau of 11 October 1925 proves. He himself dated the inspiration for *Oedipus Rex* to the chance discovery of Joergenson's *Life of St Francis* on a Genoa bookstall in September of that year. On the other hand, the device of a spoken narration in the language of the audience (for which Stravinsky later 'blamed' Cocteau) was probably worked out between them, as was the intended visual handling, with the main characters immobile, like statues, able to gesture only with head and hands, within a monumental, tableau-like, two-dimensional setting (a style that goes back to Cocteau's 1922 version of Sophocles' *Antigone*). The conception of a heroic tragedy immured within an antique convention is obviously fundamental, as is the idea of enriching such a conception from various heroic traditions: not only Greek, but Handelian and even Verdian–Bellinian. In one sense, this is no more than the translation into the theatre of the synthetic techniques of early neoclassicism; in another sense it updates the idea of symbolic re-enactment already present in *Renard* and *The Wedding*. The argument over whether *Oedipus* is opera or oratorio is thus specious. The subtitle merely refers to the various elements in the work as a whole, while it was first performed in concert because money could not be found in time for a stage version to be prepared.

SYNOPSIS

The speaker introduces each scene, describing the events we are about to witness. He 'is in a black suit . . . [and] expresses himself like a lecturer, presenting the story with a detached voice'.

Act I: The Thebans implore their King Oedipus, who vanquished the Sphinx, to rescue them from the plague ('Liberi, vos liberabo'); Oedipus boastfully promises to do so. He reports that Creon, his brother-in-law, has been sent to consult the Delphic Oracle ('Respondit deus'); Creon arrives and announces that the murderer of King Laius is hiding in Thebes and must be hunted out before the plague will go. Oedipus undertakes to find the murderer ('Non reperias vetus scelas'). The people implore the blind seer, Tiresias, to tell what he knows ('Delie, exspectamus'). Tiresias refuses ('Dicere non possum'), but when Oedipus accuses him directly of the murder, he retorts that Laius' murderer is another king, now hiding in Thebes. Oedipus angrily accuses both Tiresias and Creon of plotting to seize the throne. At this moment the people hail the arrival of Oedipus' wife, Queen Jocasta.

Act II: The final 'Gloria' chorus of Act I is repeated; the score indicates this before the speaker's introduction, but Stravinsky stated in *Dialogues* that he preferred the reprise to follow the introduction and lead straight into Jocasta's aria. Jocasta rebukes the princes for quarrelling ('Non erubescite, reges'). The oracle, she says, is a liar. It prophesied that Laius would be killed by her son, but in fact he was killed at a crossroads by thieves. Suddenly afraid, Oedipus tells Jocasta that once he killed an old man at a crossroads ('Pavesco subito'). He determines to find out the truth. The chorus greets the arrival of the shepherd and the messenger from Corinth ('Adest ominiscius pastor'). The messenger announces the death of King Polybus of Corinth. Oedipus, he reports, was not Polybus' son, but a foundling, discovered on a mountainside and brought up by a shepherd. Jocasta understands and tries to draw Oedipus away. Oedipus accuses her of shame at the discovery that he is not the son of a king ('Nonne monstrum rescituri'), but the shepherd and messenger spell out the truth: that Oedipus was the son of Laius and Jocasta, abandoned to die. Oedipus acknowledges the truth, that he has killed his father and married his mother ('Natus sum quo nefastum est'). The messenger, helped by the chorus, relates the death of Jocasta and Oedipus' self-blinding with her golden brooch ('Divum Jocastae caput mortuum'). Oedipus appears, a figure of revulsion. He is firmly but gently expelled from Thebes by the people.

Cocteau's treatment of the story assumes a knowledge of Sophocles and cannot be properly understood without it. Here is the essential outline. The oracle warned King Laius that, as a punishment for stealing Pelops' son, Chrysippus, he would be killed by his own son; so, when Oedipus was born, Laius and Jocasta exposed him on a mountainside, piercing his feet with leather thongs. There he was found and brought up by a shepherd of the Corinthian King Polybus. Polybus, being childless, adopted (and named) Oedipus; later, Oedipus was taunted about his parentage and, when he consulted the oracle, was told that he would kill his father and marry his mother. To avoid these crimes and, naturally supposing them to refer to Polybus and his wife, he left Corinth for Thebes. On the way he killed an old man he met at a crossroads, not recognizing him, of course, as King Laius. At Thebes he solved the riddle of the Sphinx, winning the hand of the now-widowed Queen Jocasta. It is crucial that, even when he begins to suspect that he is the murderer of King Laius and thus the cause of the plague in Thebes, Oedipus still does not realize that he is Laius' son. He simply believes his crime to be usurping the marital bed of a man he has killed. One other obscurity is his accusation of Tiresias' complicity with Creon, which is explained by the fact that, in Sophocles, it is Creon who first suggests consulting Tiresias.

Oedipus Rex is one of Stravinsky's greatest works and a climax both of his early synthetic (neoclassical) style and of his lifelong experimentation with theatrical technique. Like *Mavra*, it is a number opera in the classical tradition, though the numbers often evolve into substantial scenes, separated by the narration. The monumental character of each scene goes with the statuesque, sculptural design idea and with the impersonal grandeur of the Latin text. But many details of style break into this monumentality. The most obvious is the spoken narration, which is at first strictly separate from the music but later intrudes into it to some limited extent. Stravinsky makes rich use of the ironic possibilities of this device. For instance, when (in the narration) Tiresias reveals that 'the murderer of the king is a king', the last four words are set rhythmically to the motif of the chorus's anxious anticipation of the seer's arrival, in which they do not, of course, yet know what he will reveal.

Another obvious 'break' is the mixture of musical styles. Handel seems to have been a conscious influence, but that of Italian opera is more striking, because more surprising. There are clear reminiscences of Verdi, Bellini and even Puccini, and Stravinsky uses the idea of operatic vocalism itself to a dramatic end. Oedipus' coloratura diminishes with his self-confidence, and his last utterances, when the truth has struck him, are unadorned. These and other associative devices seem to act as a bridge between modern perception and the musically disembodied world of Greek tragedy: through what they sing and what accompanies them, the characters take on an extra dimension of humanity, like statues whose heads turn at the sound of music that is, so to speak, ours rather than theirs.

Both tonally and rhythmically, *Oedipus Rex* contains some of the plainest music Stravinsky ever wrote. The squarely cut choral ostinati (with their persistent minor-third motif) are worlds away from the subtleties of his previous opera, *Mavra*. Much of the score uses fixed tonal centres, contrasted by terracing rather than classical modulation. Moreover the work marks Stravinsky's use of a 'standard' symphony orchestra for the first time since *The Rite of Spring* and *The Nightingale*.

Stravinsky and Cocteau planned to stage *Oedipus Rex* in 1927 in honour of Diaghilev's 20th season, but the financial arrangements became immersed in Parisian social politics, and in the end the premiere was given in concert form. The first stagings were in February the following year in Vienna and Berlin (Kroll Opera, under Klemperer). In the 1950s Stravinsky came to favour omitting the speaker altogether. But one of the most famous post-war (concert) performances, by Stravinsky in London's Festival Hall in 1959, had Cocteau as the speaker.

RECORDINGS 1. Mödl, Pears, Rehfuss, Cocteau, Cologne RCh & O, Stravinsky, CBS, 1951; 2. von Otter, Cole, Gedda, Estes, Swedish RCh & RSO, Salonen, Sony, 1991

The Rake's Progress

Opera in three acts (2h 15m)
Libretto by W. H. Auden and Chester Kallman, after the cycle *A Rake's Progress* by William Hogarth (1735)
Composed 1947–51
PREMIERES 11 September 1951, La Fenice, Venice; UK: 2: January 1953 (radio); 25 August 1953, Edinburgh Festival; US: 14 February 1953, Metropolitan, New York
CAST Trulove *b*, Anne Trulove *s*, Tom Rakewell *t*, Nick Shadow *bar*, Mother Goose *ms*, Baba the Turk *ms*, Sellem *t*, Keeper of the Madhouse *b*; *satb* chorus of whores, roaring boys, servants, citizens, madmen

After settling in the USA in 1940, Stravinsky went through an uneasy time, in which the pressure to fulfil commissions of a 'typically' American, commercial sort went hand in hand with changes in style that were to lead to a complete new direction in his work of the 1950s. One important catalyst of change was his growing interest in pre-classical music.

This is the period of the Mass (1944–8), and of the ballet *Orpheus* (1947), with its mixture of neoclassical mannerisms and contrapuntal austerities. *The Rake's Progress*, which looks like a summation, is therefore also partly a work of transition.

Stravinsky saw the Hogarth prints at an exhibition in Chicago in May 1947. Later that year he contacted W. H. Auden and proposed a collaboration (Auden soon brought in Chester Kallman as co-author). Auden was to prove a brilliant collaborator. His gift for investing verse in simple metres with rich meanings perfectly suited Stravinsky's need for variable patterns and a clear ethical thrust, and Auden's virtuosity made him uniquely quick at responding to specific requirements. Beyond question the libretto is one of the best ever written.

Although the work seems at first sight like a straight 18th-century pastiche, complete with secco recitative accompanied by harpsichord, it is one of Stravinsky's most complex and many-tiered scores. The influence of Mozart is obvious and well documented, but the actual subject is quite un-Mozartian; it rather suggests the urban world of *The Beggar's Opera*, as do the plain, lilting cut of its melodies and its preference for strophic or verse-and-refrain forms. But while the dramatic setting of *The Beggar's Opera* clearly has a lot in common with Hogarth, the verse-and-refrain idea also recalls Stravinsky's lifelong interest in ritual forms, where repetition and recurrence are more in evidence than organic development in the classical sense. That this was hardly a limitation is shown by the fact that the longest and most serious of the three acts, the third, proceeds almost entirely by interlocking verse forms. Here *The Rake* anticipates the proto-serial works of the 1950s, where the refrain form is ubiquitous.

Auden's view of the subject fitted this aspect of Stravinsky like a glove. Starting with the idea that Tom's downfall comes from his denial of Nature (Anne and ordered country life), he constructed a moving allegory in which the gruesome materialism of the city increasingly usurps the natural virtues – love, marriage, procreation, the ordinary rhythm of life. The opera begins and ends in spring; against Hogarth's London, Auden set up a pastoral idyll in the tradition of Theocritus. Tom is Adonis, who comes to a bad end for disobeying the command of his goddess lover, Venus. Cut off from his moral roots, he falls prey to philosophies of despair – existentialism, moral nihilism – and is about to succumb when the still small voice of love brings him back to his senses, or at least to life (since he does in fact lose his senses). Thus a mixture of antique conventions provides a frame for a strictly modern fable, just as in the music.

SYNOPSIS

'The action takes place in 18th-century England.'

Act I, Scene 1 (the garden of Trulove's home in the country): A short prelude leads into a duet for Anne and Tom about the joys of spring ('The woods are green'). Later it becomes a trio, with Trulove voicing his fears about the marriage. Trulove suggests that Tom take a job, but Tom has other plans ('Here I stand' and 'Since it is not by merit'). At his words 'I wish I had money', a messenger (Nick Shadow) appears with news that he has inherited a fortune (quartet: 'I wished but once'). Tom agrees to go to London to settle his affairs, with Shadow as his servant. In a trio, Tom, Anne and Trulove voice their respective attitudes to easy money ('Laughter and light'). Scene 2 (Mother Goose's brothel, London): Roaring boys and whores sing of the joys of debauchery ('With air commanding'). Shadow and Mother Goose rehearse Tom in the catechism of vice. Only when love is mentioned does he falter and beg to be released. Shadow now introduces Tom as a would-be initiate, though Tom's cavatina ('Love, too frequently betrayed' with obbligato clarinet) sustains his regret at betraying true love, to the delight of the sentimental whores. As Mother Goose takes Tom off to her bed, the chorus sings the Lanterloo Chorus. Scene 3 (as Scene 1): Anne laments Tom's infidelity but makes up her mind to rescue him ('I go to him').

Act II, Scene 1 (Rakewell's house in London): Tom, at breakfast, is already bored with fashionable life ('Vary the song'). Shadow enters with a newspaper report about the bearded lady, Baba the Turk, whom he proposes Tom should marry in order to demonstrate his freedom from 'those twin tyrants of appetite and conscience' ('In youth the panting slave pursues'). They sing of appetite and coming notoriety ('My tale shall be told'). Scene 2 (street in front of Rakewell's house): Anne has found Tom's house, but falters in front of the door. Tom enters in a sedan chair, preceded by servants. He presses Anne to leave him to his fate. From the sedan chair Baba demands to be handed down, and when Tom introduces her as his wife, Anne turns away (trio: 'Could it then have been known'). To the strains of a sarabande, Baba descends from the chair, and briefly gratifies the assembled crowd with a sight of her flowing black beard. Scene 3 (as Act II, Scene 1, but the room now cluttered with Baba's possessions): Baba chatters away about her life ('As I was saying'), ending with a lyrical appeal to Tom's finer feelings. Rebuffed, she breaks into a classic rage aria ('Scorned! Abused!'), smashing the china as she sings, until Tom silences her by putting his wig over her face, then himself falls asleep. Enter Shadow with a 'bread-making machine', which he demonstrates to the audience. Tom wakes up, having dreamed of just such a machine, which he imagines will abolish misery in the world (duet: 'Thanks to this excellent device').

Act III, Scene 1 (the same, but covered with cobwebs and dust; Baba still where she was left): The populace has gathered for the sale of Tom's property. Anne also arrives, looking for Tom. Sellem, the auctioneer, begins ('Who hears me, knows me') with the sale of various curios, culminating in Baba herself, who, as the wig is removed, continues her rage aria where it left off. Offstage, Tom and Shadow are heard in a ballad song ('Old wives for sale!'). The sale grinds to a halt, as Baba advises Anne to go to Tom. Scene 2 (a churchyard; night): A short prelude for string quartet (the first music to be composed) leads to the final confrontation between Tom and Shadow. Shadow claims Tom's soul as wages. He proposes suicide on the stroke of twelve, but relents on the ninth stroke and instead suggests a game of cards to decide Tom's fate. Unexpectedly Tom wins, by trusting the voice of love (that is, Anne, heard offstage). Shadow departs in a fury but condemns Tom to insanity. Scene 3 (Bedlam): Tom, now insane, imagines himself as Adonis soon to be visited by Venus ('Prepare yourselves, heroic shades'), but the other inmates refuse to participate ('Leave all love and hope behind'). But Anne does come, sings him to sleep ('Gently, little boat'), and then departs with her father ('Every wearied body must'). Waking to find her gone, Tom seems to die of grief ('Mourn for Adonis'). Like Mozart's *Don Giovanni*, the opera ends with a moralistic epilogue ensemble ('Good people, just a moment').

The Rake's Progress is generally considered the culminating work of Stravinsky's neoclassicism. Its use of a standard 18th-century orchestra and of various operatic formal conventions, of clear tonal schemes and rhythmic periods perpetuates the tradition of the Symphony in C and the Concerto in D. The formal schemes and some of its instrumental textures anticipate the *Cantata*, but there is no trace of serialism or any other conscious modernism. *The Rake* was Stravinsky's first setting of an English text (apart from the short cantata *Babel*). Its eccentric prosody has been criticized, but Auden himself pointedly defended it. The fact is that

Stravinsky saw words as an element of rhythm and was always ready to distort natural accentual patterns to enrich the musical movement. His *Rake* technique is essentially no different from his earlier handling of Russian, French or Latin.

Stravinsky worked on the opera for three years, to the exclusion of all else (except negotiations as to where it should be premiered and for how much money). The Venice premiere was fixed up by him over everyone's head and with disastrous consequences in Italian musical politics. (La Scala, Milan, had to be placated by a shared role in the production.) It was a *succès d'estime*, but artistically uneven. Stravinsky conducted effectively, but the cast was variable and Carl Ebert's production pleased neither the composer nor the librettists.

RECORDINGS 1. Raskin, Sarfaty, Young, Reardon, Sadler's Wells Op Ch, RPO, Stravinsky, Sony, 1964; 2. Upshaw, Bumbry, Hadley, Ramey, Op Nat de Lyon Ch & O, Nagano, Erato, 1995
OTHER OPERATIC WORKS *The Nightingale* (*Solovyei*), 1914; *Renard* (*Baika*), (1916), 1922; *Mavra*, 1922; *Perséphone*, 1934; *The Flood*, 1962

S.W.

Arthur Sullivan

(Sir) Arthur Seymour Sullivan; *b* 13 May 1842, London; *d* 22 November 1900, London

Until the advent of Lloyd Webber, Sullivan was by far the most performed and internationally the best-known British composer for the theatre. In his early professional life he was an all-rounder, winning fame before he was 20 with his incidental music to *The Tempest* (1861) and proceeding to, among other works, a symphony and a cello concerto. But the financial rewards to be reaped from operetta, as well as his own proven mastery of it, led him later to concentrate almost entirely on the theatre and on large-scale choral works. Operetta is the internationally recognized term for the type of work on which William Schwenck Gilbert and Sullivan collaborated under Richard D'Oyly Carte's management (1875–96), but they themselves used the term 'comic opera'.

Carte built the Savoy Theatre in 1882 to house Gilbert's and Sullivan's chain of successes, though he himself did not confine the term 'Savoy Opera' to their works. In early days, and later during and after a period of personal estrangement from Gilbert, Sullivan worked with other librettists, notably Francis Cowley Burnand and Basil Hood, later the librettist of Edward German's *Merrie England* (1902). He used the term 'light opera' for *Haddon Hall* (libretto by Sydney Grundy). But his sole venture into what was then called grand opera was *Ivanhoe*, for which Carte built the Royal English Opera House (now the Palace Theatre) in 1891. For Carte, who failed to profit from his investment and had to sell the theatre, *Ivanhoe* spelt failure, despite an initial run of 160 consecutive performances unrivalled for a 'serious' work. The music and libretto received weighty adverse criticism, and it has not been successfully revived.

Curiously, the operettas, though so often tied to satire on British social life of their own day (the 'aesthetic' craze in *Patience*, parliamentary anomalies in *Iolanthe*), have maintained a perennial life quite unparalleled by any other body of work from the Victorian theatre. They were original works, not adaptations from others. If Gilbert's extraordinary dexterity of language did much for these works, and added not a few proverbial phrases in doing so, Sullivan's scores likewise caught popular taste – and exhibited musical subtleties as well. In every one of the operettas there are numbers that, in contrapuntal wit or harmonic subtlety or musical allusiveness, have continued to make their appeal to sophisticated taste. The contrapuntal yoking of two apparently unrelated tunes became a Sullivan trademark, while his patter songs, extended in *Ruddigore* to a patter trio, are no less effective than their predecessors in Rossini and Donizetti.

Recurrence of a musical motif as a dramatic indicator to the audience is rare; where found, it corresponds more to Bizet's and Gounod's usage than to Wagner's. A deeper level of musical linking has been demonstrated for *The Mikado* and is perhaps waiting to be discovered in others of the operetta scores. The fact that, in the non-English-speaking world, *The Mikado* has been the most widely performed of the operettas (with many translations) is puzzling. The butt of its satire is Britain, not Japan, yet its musical and costumed orientalisms seem to have exerted their own attraction and gained it a place in that special sequence of operatic exotica that ranges from Meyerbeer's *L'Africaine* to Puccini's *Madama Butterfly*.

Trial by Jury

Comic opera (originally dramatic cantata) in one act (45m)
Libretto by W. S. Gilbert
Composed 1875
PREMIERES 25 March 1875, Royalty Theatre, London; US: 15 November 1875, Eagle Theater, New York
CAST Plaintiff *s*, Defendant *t*, Learned Judge *bar*, Usher *b*, Counsel for the Plaintiff *bar*, Foreman of the Jury *bar*; *satb* chorus of jurymen and bridesmaids

The first time Gilbert and Sullivan collaborated under Richard D'Oyly Carte's management (though Carte had not yet set up his own company) produced an all-sung work, oddly designated in the score as a dramatic cantata. In no subsequent collaboration with Gilbert did Sullivan retain the all-sung form. It is based on the comical extravagance of setting a court action to verse and to music, the action being that of breach of promise of marriage, a type of legal case that was already liable to ridicule. In addition to the impassioned statements of the point at issue, even routine matters such as the swearing in of the (all-male) jury are subjected to full musical treatment. The character of the Learned Judge (originally taken with much success by Sullivan's brother Fred, who was to die young) is the first of a famous line of comic parts with self-descriptive songs that often reveal moral ambiguities.

SYNOPSIS

The jury is waiting to try the case of 'Edwin, sued by Angelina'. The jurymen are addressed by the Usher: he and the jurors are already prejudiced against the Defendant, who enters and states his case to guitar accompaniment. The Learned Judge enters, is greeted, and gives an account of himself ('When I, good friends, was called to the Bar'). The Plaintiff enters in bridal dress and attended by bridesmaids. Her Counsel tells how she was courted, then jilted for another. The Defendant offers, 'I'll marry this lady today, and marry the other tomorrow'. The Judge is disposed to agree until reminded that such a step would constitute 'burglaree' ('A nice dilemma we have here'). No solution emerging to satisfy both sides, the Judge (who has taken a fancy to the Plaintiff from her first entrance) dismisses the court: 'Put your briefs upon the shelf: I will marry her myself!'

In the choral greeting to the Judge before his self-revelatory song, Sullivan parodies Handel's grandest oratorio manner, complete with word-repetition. A more specific parody, not merely of a composer but of an actual operatic number, is the climactic ensemble, 'A nice dilemma': in its imitative vocal entries, in general style and even key, it is directly modelled on 'D'un pensiero', the Act I finale to Bellini's *La sonnambula*.

RECORDING Evans, Banks, Savidge, Suart, WNO Ch & O, Mackerras, Telarc, 1995

HMS Pinafore, or The Lass that Loved a Sailor

Comic opera in two acts (1h 45m)
Libretto by W. S. Gilbert
Composed 1878
PREMIERES 25 May 1878, Opéra-Comique, London; US: 25 November 1878, The Boston Museum, Boston
CAST Sir Joseph Porter *bar*, Captain Corcoran *b-bar*, Ralph Rackstraw *t*, Josephine *s*, Dick Deadeye *b*, Mrs Cripps (Little Buttercup) *c, ms, bar, b, silent*; *satb* chorus of Sir Joseph's relatives, sailors, marines, etc.

Although Gilbert's and Sullivan's previous two collaborations, *Trial by Jury* and *The Sorcerer*, had been given present-day settings, only with *HMS Pinafore* was a pronounced note of political and social satire introduced. Class relations within the navy (and outside it) and the dubious machinations of political appointments are set forth. The character of Sir Joseph Porter was inevitably taken, despite Gilbert's (perhaps ironic) denials, as being aimed at W. H. Smith, the actual First Lord of the Admiralty. All this was set within a highly traditional theatrical frame featuring the upright sailor lad, his faithful sweetheart, and the blackhearted villain (Dick Deadeye: 'It's a beast of a name, ain't it?').

After an initially cautious reception at the box office, *HMS Pinafore* grew into Gilbert's and Sullivan's first major success and has remained one of their most popular and frequently revived works, the mock-patriotism of 'For he is an Englishman' becoming proverbial. This work, too, was the start of Gilbert's and Sullivan's North American (and wider) reputation: pirated performances of *HMS Pinafore* were so successful in Boston, New York and elsewhere that Carte decided to take the composer and librettist and their company across the Atlantic to present the work in authentic form (at the same time launching *The Pirates of Penzance*).

SYNOPSIS

Act I: A happy regime is maintained aboard HMS *Pinafore*, now anchored at Portsmouth. The bum-boat woman Mrs Cripps with her stock of useful and tasty wares is welcomed on board ('I'm called Little Buttercup'). To his sympathetic messmates, Ralph as a humble sailor discloses his audacity in his love for his captain's daughter, Josephine. Captain Corcoran, the ship's commander, declares in a self-introductory song that he never uses bad language to his crew ('What, never?'/'Hardly ever!'). But he is worried that Josephine is disinclined to accept a proposal of marriage from an exalted quarter, the First Lord of the Admiralty, Sir Joseph Porter. Sir Joseph arrives, escorted by sisters, cousins and aunts. An autobiographical song recounts his rise to Cabinet minister ('When I was a lad I served a term/As office boy to an attorney's firm'). He has composed a three-part glee, which is performed. Josephine, at first acting her rank, spurns Ralph's love, but after he threatens suicide she joyfully admits she loves him. All his mates, except the malevolent Deadeye, will help the pair get ashore that night to be married.

Act II: In the evening Captain Corcoran sings to the moon of his worry about Josephine. Mrs Cripps tries to warn him of some mystery, but he does not comprehend. Josephine herself is doubtful of the hardships that confront her. But Sir Joseph, thinking to promote his own case in condescending to marry a captain's daughter, tells her that 'Love levels all ranks'. She takes that as arguing Ralph's case and is ready to proceed with the elopement. Warned by Dick Deadeye, her father steps in to prevent it. Ralph speaks up for his rights: 'I am an Englishman' (echoed by the chorus, 'For he himself has said it,/And it's greatly to his credit,/That he is an Englishman'). In reprimanding Ralph, Captain Corcoran says, 'Damme, it's too bad!', a profanity for which Sir Joseph confines him to his cabin while the presumptuous Ralph is taken off to the ship's dungeon. Mrs Cripps makes a dramatic declaration in song: a former baby-farmer, she had both Ralph and Corcoran in her care as infants and mixed them up. They now re-emerge: Ralph as a captain, Corcoran as an able seaman. All is now serene for the lovers, Corcoran at the same time pairing off with Mrs Cripps and Sir Joseph with Hebe, one of his cousins.

Gilbert's strong characterization is so well fulfilled in Sullivan's music as to override the occasional weakness. The Act I finale, though it gathers a splendid momentum (with a remarkable artifice of rhythmical structure), does not get two opposing sides into dramatic and musical conflict as most of its successors do. The 'Buttercup' waltz is tediously plugged as an entr'acte and a mere medley of previous tunes serves to end Act II. But Ralph, Captain Corcoran, Sir Joseph and Josephine all live in their interactive music (particularly 'Never mind the why and wherefore'), and almost as much musical resource is lavished on two characters parodied from opera or melodrama, Little Buttercup with 'gypsy blood in her veins' and the heavy-treading Dick Deadeye.

RECORDING Evans, F. Palmer, Schade, Allen, Suart, WNO Ch & O, Mackerras, Telarc, 1994 (omits dialogue)

The Pirates of Penzance, or The Slave of Duty

Comic opera in two acts (1h 45m)
Libretto by W. S. Gilbert
Composed 1879
PREMIERES in skeleton form: 30 December 1879, Royal Bijou Theatre, Paignton; 3 April 1880, Opéra-Comique, London; US: 31 December 1879, New Fifth Avenue Theater, New York
CAST Major-General Stanley *bar*, Pirate King *b*, Frederic *t*, Mabel *s*, Ruth *c*, Sergeant of Police *b-bar*, *s*, *ms*, *b*; *satb* chorus of pirates, police and General Stanley's daughters

Very much in the pattern of its highly successful predecessor, *The Pirates of Penzance* satirized not naval but military anomalies (in the person of the Major-General) and the police as well. Mock-patriotism is also invoked once again. The mainspring of the plot, however, arises from a recurrent target of Gilbert's satire, the idiocy and sometimes the hypocrisy of a literal-minded devotion to duty: here the knife is artfully twisted, with Frederic rigorously functioning as the 'slave of duty' of the opera's subtitle.

The piece received its formal premiere at the hands of the British company brought by Carte to New York, a mere token staging having been previously given at Paignton, Devon, to establish British copyright. After the American performances Gilbert and Sullivan made several alterations, which bore fruit in the London production.

SYNOPSIS

Act I: Frederic, apprenticed to the pirate band as a boy, has reached the age of 21 and is congratulated: his apprenticeship over, he can be considered a full member of the band. But, though loyal while he had to be, he has decided to leave and oppose the Pirate King and his followers. Ruth, his former nurserymaid, who had led him to the apprenticeship through mishearing 'pilot' as 'pirate' and had herself become a maid-of-all-work to the pirates, hopes to persuade Frederic to marry her. (He has seen no other females to make comparison.) But to his enraptured view a group of young women appears, the daughters of the Major-General, on an outing to the beach. To prevent their unknowingly exposing as much as a leg, Frederic announces his presence. He begs any one of them to accept him in marriage – and Mabel, considering it her duty, accepts ('Poor wand'ring one'). Suddenly the pirates appear and are about to abduct the young women when the Major-General himself arrives. He persuades them not to rob him, an orphan, of his daughters. Their better nature is touched. Only in an aside does the Major-General confess his fib – he is no orphan.

Act II: That night, the Major-General is not abed as usual; his conscience is tormented by his fib. Under Frederic's command the police are now to take the vengeance of the law on the pirates. The Sergeant of Police and his men are disquieted by Mabel's fervent exhortation ('Go, ye heroes, go and die!'). Frederic is confronted by the Pirate King and Ruth who explain 'a most ingenious paradox': having been born on 29 February in leap year, and apprenticed not for 21 years but until his 21st birthday (which will not arrive till 1940) he is still bound to them. Frederic switches his 'duty' and bids a tearful farewell to Mabel. The police re-enter, the Sergeant proclaiming that 'A policeman's lot is not a happy one'. The pirates, now informed by Frederic of the Major-General's deception, are intent on revenge. The Major-General, still conscience-ridden, sings a song ('Softly sighing to the river') accompanied by the police and pirates, of whose presence he is ignorant. The pirates overpower the police but yield when challenged 'in Queen Victoria's name'. The pirates themselves are revealed to be all 'noblemen who have gone wrong'; their crimes are forgiven, since 'peers will be peers', and they can marry the Major-General's daughters while Frederic and Mabel can get married too.

Musically *The Pirates* is, as Sullivan himself recognized, stronger than *Pinafore*. Nowhere in the whole Gilbert and Sullivan canon is anything more deft than the dovetailing of the love duet in waltz time into the chattering 2/4 women's chorus, 'How beautifully blue the sky' in Act I, the whole modulating from B to G and back again. The Major-General's song in Act II, with its Schubertian water-rippling accompaniment, is placed as an absolutely straight number within a hilarious comic context – the Major-General's unawareness of the male choruses surely parodying a similar situation in *Il trovatore*. The process by which, some time after 1900, the melody of 'Come, friends, who plough the sea' was metamorphosed into the American song 'Hail, hail, the gang's all here' has still not been clarified.

RECORDINGS 1. Masterson, Potter, Adams, Reed, D'Oyly Carte Op Ch, RPO, Godfrey, Decca, 1968 (with dialogue); 2. Evans, Ainsley, Adams, Suart, WNO Ch & O, Mackerras, Telarc, 1992 (omits dialogue)

Iolanthe, or The Peer and the Peri

Comic opera in two acts (2h)
Libretto by W. S. Gilbert
Composed 1882
PREMIERES 25 November 1882, Savoy Theatre, London; US: 25 November 1882, Standard Theater, New York
CAST Lord Chancellor *bar*, Earl of Mountararat *b*, Earl Tolloller *t*, Private Willis *b*, Strephon *bar*, Queen of the Fairies *c*, Iolanthe *ms*, Phyllis *s*, 2 *s*, *ms*; *satb* chorus of dukes, marquises, earls, viscounts, barons and fairies

Iolanthe was the first of the operettas written expressly for the Savoy Theatre (though Carte had moved his company there in the middle of the run of *Patience*), and it is hard to resist the idea that Sullivan found a new musical stimulus in the prospect. Gilbert's dramaturgical scheme is exceptionally strong, especially the counter-marching and conflict of peers and fairies at the end of Act I; an unusual richness of characterization invests the Lord Chancellor (in other respects the successor of mere patter-song professionals such as Sir Joseph Porter and the Major-General) with real pathos at the climax of the plot. The initial staging of the work displayed a helmeted, spear-carrying Queen of the Fairies as a kind of parodied Brünnhilde, but allegations of Wagnerism in Sullivan's music for the scene of Iolanthe's pardon should be met with scepticism.

SYNOPSIS

Act I: For the chorus of fairies there is little gaiety in life because one of their number, Iolanthe, was banished 25 years ago for marrying a mortal, a crime normally punished by death. The Queen of the Fairies is persuaded to pardon her, on condition that she does not communicate with her husband. Iolanthe appears, followed by her 24-year-old son, Strephon, who is a fairy only 'down to the waist'. He earns the approval of the Queen. His beloved Phyllis, a shepherdess and a ward in Chancery, enters with a solo, followed by a duet with Strephon ('None shall part us from each other'). They leave. Preceded with military pomp by a chorus of peers ('Loudly let the trumpet bray'), the Lord Chancellor introduces himself ('The law is the true embodiment'). All the peers are smitten with love for Phyllis, and Lords Tolloller and Mountararat in particular lay suit to her. Her declaration that she loves Strephon causes anger: his application to marry a ward in Chancery has already been dismissed. Distraught, Strephon consults his young-looking fairy mother; Phyllis takes Iolanthe for a rival and, thinking Strephon unfaithful, declares her willingness to wed a peer. The Queen of the Fairies, summoned by Strephon and insulted by the Lord Chancellor, announces vengeance: Strephon shall go into Parliament and upset its cherished institutions. Fairies and peers exchange defiance.

Act II opens to display the Palace of Westminster: On sentry duty, Private Willis ponders the strange fact of 'ev'ry boy and ev'ry gal' becoming 'either a little Liberal or else a little Conservative' ('When all night long a chap remains'). The fairies are delighted at the legislative havoc being caused now that 'Strephon's a Member of Parliament', but Mountararat points out the dangers of the House of Lords becoming a house of intellectuals ('When Britain really rul'd the waves'). The fairies having begun to love the peers, their Queen endeavours to steady them by pointing out ('Oh, foolish fay') how she resists the 'simply godlike' charms of Private Willis. The Lord Chancellor discloses in a nightmare song ('When you're lying awake with a dismal headache') how his love for Phyllis – a ward of his own court – is upsetting him. Tolloller and Mountararat embolden him, so although Phyllis and Strephon have removed their mutual misunderstanding, the Lord Chancellor now decides to claim Phyllis for himself. The only one who can stop him is his former wife Iolanthe (whom he believes dead). She declares herself, thus inviting her own death sentence from the Queen. The Lord Chancellor persuades the Queen to alter fairy law so that every fairy shall die 'who don't marry a mortal': she engages herself to Private Willis and all depart for fairyland.

Instead of being a mere medley of tunes (often assembled by one of Sullivan's musical assistants) the overture here is an accomplished sonata-type movement in which the tune of 'Oh, foolish fay' is combined by Sullivan with another tune of Mendelssohnian grace which does not occur in the operetta itself. And so the richness of this score continues, with a romantic pathos for Iolanthe's pardon and her later danger, and with a tiny, changing motif for the Lord Chancellor. The military strains, though they belong to peers rather than soldiers, are even more imposing than those in *Patience*. The sweetest and subtlest of all Sullivan's love duets (a soprano heroine paired with a baritone rather than a tenor hero) is 'None shall part us', its on-running melody underpinned by delicate harmonic progression.

RECORDING Suart, Creasy, Rath, Richard, Pert, D'Oyly Carte Ch & O, Pryce-Jones, TER, 1991 (omits dialogue)

The Mikado, or The Town of Titipu

Comic opera in two acts (2h 15m)
Libretto by W. S. Gilbert
Composed 1884–5
PREMIERES 14 March 1885, Savoy Theatre, London; US: 6 July 1885, Chicago (unauthorized); 19 August 1885, Fifth Avenue Theater, New York (D'Oyly Carte)
CAST The Mikado *b*, Nanki-Poo *t*, Ko-Ko *bar*, Pooh-Bah *b-bar*, Pish-Tush *bar*, Yum-Yum *s*, Pitti-Sing *ms*, Peep-Bo *ms*, Katisha *c*, (Go-To *b* sometimes added); *satb* chorus of schoolgirls, nobles, guards and coolies

The Mikado was the collaborators' longest-running work (672 performances) and, on its revival in 1896, became the first to achieve 1000 performances at the Savoy. Praised by the Viennese critic Hanslick, translated into many languages, including Russian (for a performance under Stanislavsky's auspices), it is often considered Sullivan's masterpiece. Perhaps Gilbert's too: characters such as Pooh-Bah, phrases such as 'modified rapture!' and 'let the punishment fit the crime' became proverbial.

It was the first Gilbert and Sullivan piece set in a recognized and strongly identified foreign location, but the 'Japanese' names are all English, obviously in cases such as Ko-Ko, less obviously with Pitti-Sing (baby talk for 'pretty thing'). Through the Japanese mask Gilbert satirized English abuses or absurdities, the more effectively because Sullivan's music is (typically of him) straight and not grotesque. Seemingly perfect in balance, the score has come down to us in a form not exactly that of the original. Shortly after the opening night the author and composer made two important structural changes, advancing Ko-Ko's 'little list' song within Act I and moving Yum-Yum's 'The sun, whose rays' from Act I to Act II.

SYNOPSIS

Act I: Nanki-Poo, a wandering minstrel arriving in the town of Titipu ('A wand'ring minstrel I'), learns from Pish-Tush that Yum-Yum, whom he hoped to marry, is engaged to her guardian, Ko-Ko, a tailor who has become Lord High Executioner. Ko-Ko expounds his 'little list' of 'society offenders' who could usefully be decapitated. Yum-Yum and her friends Pitti-Sing and Peep-Bo ('Three little maids from school') are cheeky towards the colossal dignity of Pooh-Bah, 'Lord High Everything Else'. Nanki-Poo reveals to Yum-Yum that he is really the son of the Mikado, fleeing the amorous attentions of the elderly Katisha. After an edict from the Mikado, Ko-Ko nerves himself to begin decapitations. Since Nanki-Poo is about to commit a love-sick suicide, a bargain is drawn: he will be permitted to marry Yum-Yum on condition of consenting to be beheaded in a month's time. Rejoicing is in order, and even the terrifying appearance of Katisha is defied ('For he's going to marry Yum-Yum'). She threatens the Mikado's vengeance.

Act II: Yum-Yum, decked for her wedding, sings naively of her own beauty ('The sun, whose rays are all ablaze'). Joined in a madrigal by Pitti-Sing and Pish-Tush the lovers rejoice ('Brightly dawns our wedding day'). But expectations are dampened when Ko-Ko discovers a law by which, when a man is executed, his bride is buried alive. The Mikado's arrival is announced: he identifies himself ('A more humane Mikado never did in Japan exist') and catalogues his own system of justice: 'to let the punishment fit the crime.' Ko-Ko, Pooh-Bah and Pitti-Sing regale him with an account of a supposed recent execution. But the Mikado learns that the 'victim' was Nanki-Poo, his own son: the penalty for encompassing the death of the heir apparent is 'something lingering, with boiling oil in it'. Nanki-Poo refuses to come back to life to exonerate his 'executioners' unless Katisha's amorous attentions can be diverted by Ko-Ko's marrying her, a prospect Ko-Ko views with the utmost distaste (duet: 'The flowers that bloom in the spring, tra-la'). Katisha enters ('Alone, and yet alive!'). By a cunning fable ('Tit-willow') Ko-Ko persuades her to accept him, on the supposition that Nanki-Poo has indeed been executed. When Nanki-Poo appears, now married to Yum-Yum, rejoicing is resumed and even the Mikado is pacified.

The interplay between the supposed Japanese scene and the real England satirized by Gilbert is kept up not merely in words ('The Japanese equivalent for "Hear, hear, hear!"') but in music. The score finds place for a madrigal in Sullivan's 'old English' style, and also for a glee ('See how the Fates their gifts allot'), as well as an authentic Japanese tune for the entrance of the Mikado. Its immediately captivating aspects, from patter to love duet, are underpinned by musical subtleties. In a trio for Pooh-Bah ('I am so proud'), Ko-Ko and Pish-Tush three dissimilar tunes are deftly counterpointed (the suggestion for such treatment came from Gilbert), and later a Bach fugue is cross-rhythmically quoted with the Mikado's reference to 'masses and fugues and ops,/By Bach, interwoven/ With Spohr and Beethoven'.

RECORDINGS 1. Garrett, Palmer, Bullock, Bottone, Idle, Angas, Van Allen, Richardson, ENO Ch & O, Robinson, TER, 1987 (cut, omits dialogue); 2. McLaughlin, Palmer, Rolfe Johnson, Suart, Adams, Van Allan, WNO Ch & O, Mackerras, Telarc, 1992 (omits dialogue)

The Yeomen of the Guard, or The Merryman and his Maid

Comic opera in two acts (2h 15m)
Libretto by W. S. Gilbert
Composed 1888
PREMIERES 3 October 1888, Savoy Theatre, London; US: 17 October 1888, Casino Theater, New York
CAST Colonel Fairfax *t*, Sergeant Meryll *bar*, Jack Point *bar*, Wilfred Shadbolt *bar*, Elsie Maynard *s*, Phoebe Meryll *ms*, Dame Carruthers *c*, *s*, 3 *t*, 3 *bar*, 2 spoken roles; *satb* chorus of Yeomen of the Guard, gentlemen, citizens, etc.

With *The Yeomen of the Guard* Sullivan came as near as he could to a serious opera within what had been established as the Savoy convention. At the end the jester Jack Point, disappointed in love, falls 'insensible' amid the merry-making of the rest. Gilbert's plot, though originally criticized as uncomfortably close to that of William Vincent Wallace's opera *Maritana* (1845), achieves force as a serious drama in which comic elements are kept subordinate and not allowed to break from the Tudor period to introduce modern satire. None the less the comic juxtaposition of the quick-witted jester and the slow, would-be-funny Shadbolt ('Head Gaoler and Assistant Tormentor' at the Tower of London) gives brilliant contrast to the pathos of the rest. The opening is, for once, not an assertive chorus but a gentle soliloquy in song.

SYNOPSIS

Act I: Phoebe, daughter of Sergeant Meryll of the Yeomen of the Guard at the Tower of London, sings at her spinning-wheel ('When maiden loves'). Secretly in love with the unjustly imprisoned Colonel Fairfax, she repulses the clumsy advances of the gaoler Shadbolt. Dame Carruthers, housekeeper of the Tower, sings of its valiant history ('When our gallant Norman foes'). Anxious to rescue Fairfax (who once saved his life) from execution, Meryll plans with Phoebe to release him from his cell and pass him off as Phoebe's brother Leonard, himself due to join the Yeomen. Fairfax appears, reconciled to his fate ('Is life a boon?'), but asks the Lieutenant of the Tower to procure him a blindfold bride so that his possessions do not fall into the hands of his persecuting relatives.

The arrival of two strolling players, Jack Point and Elsie ('I have a song to sing, O'), is auspicious; Elsie consents to be the blindfold bride. Phoebe wheedles the keys of the cells from Shadbolt ('Were I thy bride'); Fairfax is released and introduced as Leonard. When the time for the execution arrives there is uproar; Fairfax has vanished. Point, loving Elsie, now cannot court her since her husband Fairfax has not been executed.

Act II: Point persuades Shadbolt to say he saw Fairfax in the river and shot him, in return for which Point will teach Shadbolt the jester's art. A quartet 'Strange adventure!' for Fairfax, Sergeant Meryll, Dame Carruthers and her niece Kate, discloses that Elsie (who has been heard talking in her sleep) was the mysterious blindfold bride. Elsie herself, still not realizing whom she has married, has fallen in love with the supposed 'Leonard' but may not permit his advances because she must keep her wifely duty to Fairfax. A shot rings out, and Shadbolt and Point tell their cooked-up story. Fairfax now being assumed dead, Point courts Elsie – clumsily; Fairfax offers to show him how – but makes the proposal on his own account as 'Leonard' and is accepted. Phoebe, still in love with Fairfax, shows her annoyance, and Shadbolt, realizing that this can be no brother of Phoebe's, sees the extent of the deception. Phoebe is obliged to promise to marry Shadbolt as the price of his silence; similarly Sergeant Meryll buys Dame Hannah's silence by ending his long resistance to marrying her. A reprieve for Fairfax arrives: he claims his bride, and only after an anguished moment does Elsie realize that her beloved 'Leonard' and her hitherto unseen husband Fairfax are the same. The jester Point, broken-hearted, falls insensible.

A formally unified sonata-type overture (as in the case of *Iolanthe* but not of most of the Savoy pieces) opens with a rising, fanfare-like figure which intermittently serves as a kind of representational theme for the stern Tower of London itself. The strolling players' ballad, 'I have a song to sing, O' is a cumulative structure (like that of the folksong 'Green grow the rushes, O'), a pattern that seems exceptionally to have been suggested by Gilbert himself, though the 'archaic' drone effect of the harmony is a brilliant touch of Sullivan's own. There is not a weak number in *The Yeomen*, and the Act II duet for Dame Carruthers and Sergeant Meryll (omitted in some performances and recordings) is a perfect comic foil to the prevailing seriousness: note the introduction of the lugubrious bassoon when her 'Rapture, rapture!' is replaced by his 'Doleful, doleful!'

RECORDING Mellor, Archer, Suart, Adams, Savidge, WNO Ch & O, Mackerras, Telarc, 1995

The Gondoliers, or The King of Barataria

Comic opera in two acts (2h 15m)
Libretto by W. S. Gilbert
Composed 1889
PREMIERES 7 December 1889, Savoy Theatre, London; US: 7 January 1890, New Park Theater, New York
CAST Duke of Plaza-Toro *bar*, Luiz *t*, Don Alhambra del Bolero *b-bar*, Marco Palmieri *t*, Giuseppe Palmieri *bar*, Duchess of Plaza-Toro *c*, Casilda *s*, Tessa *ms*, Gianetta *s*, 2 *ms*, *c*, *t*, *bar*, *b*, *spoken role*; *satb* chorus of gondoliers and contadine, men-at-arms, heralds and pages

The Gondoliers marks a reversion, after *The Yeomen of the Guard*, to the fully comic work with topical references introduced into the supposedly 18th-century setting in Venice and the island of Barataria (a location mentioned in *Don Quixote*). The plot treads some old ground, notably in the baby-swapping and the revelation of a secret at the end, but the satire on ultra-democratic sentiments (with the implication of hypocrisy thrown in) marked a subtly fresh turn of the Gilbertian knife. Sullivan rose to the opportunity to impart first an Italian, then a Spanish, flavour. By the design of Gilbert himself, responding to what he knew Sullivan craved in musical autonomy, the piece begins with about 18 minutes of music uninterrupted by speech.

SYNOPSIS

Act I: The gondoliers Marco and Giuseppe choose their brides by a game of blind man's buff; by judicious cheating Giuseppe catches Tessa and Marco, Gianetta. The impoverished Duke of Plaza-Toro, 'that celebrated, cultivated, underrated nobleman', arrives accompanied by his overweening Duchess, his loyal drummer Luiz, and his daughter Casilda, who was married in infancy to the heir of the throne of Barataria. Where is that husband now? Don Alhambra the Grand Inquisitor knows him well ('no possible doubt whatever') – he is one of two gondoliers. Luiz's mother, who was their nurse, will declare which. This brings consternation to Luiz and Casilda, secretly in love. Marco and Giuseppe return with their new wives: learning that one of them is King of Barataria, they find it easy to drop their republican principles. Reigning jointly as an interim arrangement, they will set sail for Barataria forthwith, leaving their wives behind.

Act II: In Barataria the court is said to display 'a despotism strict, combined with absolute equality': in fact the new monarchs are slaves to their courtiers. They pine for their wives (Marco: 'Take a pair of sparkling eyes'), who unexpectedly arrive from Venice. Celebrations are interrupted by the arrival of the Grand Inquisitor, who criticizes their egalitarian regime ('When everyone is somebodee, then no one's anybody!'). Only now do Marco and Giuseppe learn to their dismay that one of them had contracted a marriage in infancy (quartet with Tessa and Gianetta: 'In a contemplative fashion'). The Duke of Plaza-Toro arrives with his usual entourage; the Duchess gives her recipe for duke-taming ('On the day when I was wedded to your admirable sire'). The embarrassment of the three young women (Casilda, Tessa, Gianetta) vis-à-vis the two young gondoliers is evident. At last Luiz's mother is shown in and recounts the deft interchange of babies by which her own son now emerges as the true king. Luiz re-enters, crowned. All is now disentangled and Venetian music recurs to end the opera.

If 'Take a pair of sparkling eyes' has by sheer lyrical grace become the most famous number of the opera, Sullivan's cleverest contribution was the Act II quartet, where individual voices break out furiously from the artificial calm. Gilbert himself in a letter had modestly suggested some elements of the musical treatment. The Italian and Spanish touches in songs and dances are enhanced by particularly brilliant orchestration, the quick repeated notes on the cornet (at that time used in the theatre in place of trumpets) giving extra excitement to 'Dance a cachucha' (the celebration of the wives' arrival in Barataria).

RECORDING Reed, Skitch, Sandford, Round, Styler, Knight, Toye, Sansom, Wright, D'Oyly Carte Ch, New SO, Godfrey, Decca, 1961 (with dialogue)
OTHER OPERAS *The Sapphire Necklace* (inc.) (later *The False Heiress*), (1864), overture, 1866, one further number published 1898 (lost); *Cox and Box, or The Long-lost Brothers*, 1866; *The Contrabandista, or The Law of the Ladrones*, 1867; *Thespis, or The Gods Grown Old*, 1871; *The Zoo*, 1875; *The Sorcerer*, 1877; *Patience, or Bunthorne's Bride*, 1881; *Princess Ida, or Castle Adamant*, 1884; *Ruddigore, or The Witch's Curse*, 1887; *Ivanhoe*, 1891; *Haddon Hall*, 1892; *Utopia Limited, or The Flowers of Progress*, 1893; *The Chieftain*, 1894; *The Grand Duke, or The Statutory Duel*, 1896;

The Beauty Stone, 1898; *The Rose of Persia, or The Story-teller and the Slave*, 1899; *The Emerald Isle, or the Caves of Carrig-Cleena*, 1901

A.J.

Karol Szymanowski

Karol Maciej Szymanowski; *b* 6 October 1882, Tymoszówka, Ukraine; *d* 29 March 1937, Lausanne, Switzerland

Szymanowski was the most important Polish composer to follow Chopin and Stanisław Moniuszko. He was taught music by his father, then later by Gustav Neuhaus and finally by Zygmunt Noskowski in Warsaw. From 1911 to 1914 he lived mainly in Vienna where he made contact with Universal, who became his main publishers.

Szymanowski was an energetic traveller. Before the First World War he visited Sicily and North Africa, and these journeys stimulated the interest in ancient and oriental cultures that was to colour works such as the opera *King Roger*, the Third Symphony, *Myths* and *Songs of an Infatuated Muezzin*. Szymanowski also wrote poems and left sketches and fragments of six novels. The libretto for *King Roger*, written in collaboration with Jarosław Iwaszkiewicz, is derived from his novel *Ephebos*. From 1930 his home was at Zakopane in the Tatra Mountains, and the local folk music influenced his late compositions. At this time, he was also rector of the Warsaw Conservatory (1927–9, 1930–32), and from 1933 to 1936 he worked as a touring musician, playing his own piano music all over Europe. Apart from these episodes, Szymanowski devoted himself wholly to composition and writing.

He wrote music in many genres: four symphonies, two violin concertos, two string quartets, music for violin and for piano, operas, incidental music, a ballet-pantomime, vocal and choral music and many songs. They display a variety of influences and tendencies easily divisible into three periods. Up to 1914, Chopin and Skryabin are strong influences, but most obviously Richard Strauss, and later Reger. With the late-Romantic strain there is also a classical tendency, which is manifested in his fascination with counterpoint and the use of dances, such as the gavotte and minuet (in the Second Symphony) or the sarabande and minuet (in the Second Piano Sonata). The one-act *Hagith* derives from the spirit of German Expressionism as manifested in Strauss's *Salome*, though Szymanowski's harmony and texture are denser than Strauss's, and his emotional tension even more unrelenting.

In his middle period (1914–20) colour assumed greater importance, and Szymanowski's music became more impressionistic, reflecting his interest in oriental and ancient cultures. His most important opera, *King Roger*, belongs to this period. While working on it, Szymanowski was also composing works, such as the song-cycle *Słopiewnie*, that anticipate his so-called 'national' last period, when his music became simpler in structure and texture, with harmony that uses folk modes and is less chromatic. The major works of this final period are the Fourth Symphony, the Second Violin Concerto and the ballet *Harnasie*, whose Paris performance in 1936 was the composer's last great international success.

Through all his apparent changes of style, Szymanowski's attitude remained Romantic. Emotion is central to his music. As a composer he was prolific, but he was also an influential writer on music, touching on crucial contemporary musical issues and expressing strong views on, for example, the social role of music and on Chopin as a living musical tradition for the 20th century.

King Roger
Król Roger

Opera in three acts, Op. 46 (1h 45m)
Libretto by Jarosław Iwaszkiewicz and the composer, after the novel *Ephebos* by the composer, in its turn after the play *The Bacchae* by Euripides (*c*.404 BC)
Composed 1918–24
PREMIERES 19 June 1926, Wielki Theatre, Warsaw; UK: 14 May 1975, Sadler's Wells, London
CAST King Roger II *bar*, Roxana *s*, Shepherd *t*, *c*, *t*, *b*; children's choir of acolytes; *satb* chorus of priests, monks, nuns, king's guard, Norman knights

In *King Roger* Szymanowski planned an integrated musical spectacle in which music, words and design would form part of a single concept in the manner of the Wagnerian ideal. The composer not only collaborated on the libretto but also gave detailed instructions for the sets. The drama is symbolic: the characters represent ideals, and the dramatic conflict is between the Pagan (personified by the Shepherd) and the Christian (personified by Roger).

SYNOPSIS
Act I: Twelfth-century Sicily. In the cathedral at Palermo, the priests ask King Roger to imprison an unknown Shepherd, who has proclaimed a philosophy of beauty and pleasure which they see as threatening Christianity. The king is willing to comply, but his beloved wife Roxana begs him to hear the Shepherd before deciding. Roger agrees, and invites the Shepherd to his castle.

Act II: The Shepherd, who comes from India, enters the castle with a group of disciples. They begin to dance. Roxana and the courtiers are won over by the Shepherd's charismatic personality and teaching, and when he leaves they follow.

Act III: In the ruins of an ancient theatre Roger searches for Roxana and the Shepherd. Soon they appear, and he follows them like a pilgrim. Suddenly the Shepherd becomes Dionysus, and his disciples bacchantes and maenads. They dance ecstatically and then depart with Roxana. Roger remains alone, singing a hymn to the rising sun. He has resisted a powerful temptation, and has thereby achieved wholeness.

King Roger combines elements of opera and oratorio. Its statuesque action and important choral part suggest Stravinsky's *Oedipus Rex* or Schoenberg's *Moses und Aron*, but the music itself has little in common with those works. Each act presents a different world – the first Byzantine, the second Arabic–Indian, the third Ancient Greek – and these characteristics determine the musical stylizations, which are not historically or geographically exact but amount rather to suggestions of old church or oriental music (such as antiphonal psalmody or organum) in Act I; asymmetry of phrase, irregular metre, a narrow melodic range but with much ornamentation and free use of percussion in Act II. There are no quotations and no authentic scales. In Act III the stylization is achieved mainly through the scenery. There is some flavour of Tatra folksong, a symptom of Szymanowski's growing interest in folklore.

The music is extremely varied in texture. Though much of the choral music is archaic in character, the orchestra is sometimes treated as one vast instrument in the late-Romantic manner, offering dense textures and complex modern harmony. It is sometimes divided into smaller chamber ensembles, or there are instrumental solos, in the style of French Impressionism. The dense chromatic harmony is contrasted with the sound of parallel fifths and plain common chords, sometimes in order to differentiate character (King Roger, chromatic; Roxana, modal). This combination of styles produced a work with a unique atmosphere, which has no real parallel in either earlier or contemporary music. The best-known number in the opera is Roxana's Act II aria, which is often performed as a violin solo in a transcription by Pawel Kochański.

RECORDING Szmytka, Langridge, Hampson, Gierlach, City of Birmingham Youth Ch, Ch & SO, Rattle, EMI, 1988

OTHER OPERATIC WORKS *Lottery for a Husband* (*Loteria na mężów*) (operetta), (1909); *Hagith*, (1913), 1922; 2 lost operas

Z.C.

T

Pyotr Tchaikovsky

Pyotr Ilyich Tchaikovsky; *b* 7 May 1840, Kamsko-Votkinsk (Vyatka Province); *d* 6 November 1893, St Petersburg

Though only two of his operas, *Eugene Onegin* and *The Queen of Spades*, are regularly performed outside Russia, Tchaikovsky occupied himself more with opera than with any other musical genre. He wrote operas at every stage of his career, and they were invariably given productions within a reasonably short time. Much more than ballet, opera charts his development as a composer, even where it does not represent his very best work.

The son of a mining engineer in Votkinsk, some 600 miles east of Moscow, Tchaikovsky moved with his family to St Petersburg when he was eight. As a child, he was almost excessively attached to his mother, and when she died in 1854 he suffered an emotional trauma from which he never completely recovered. Relations with women were a problem for the rest of his life. In 1868 it seems he came close to marrying the Belgian opera singer, Désirée Artôt, and in 1877 he allowed himself to be drawn into a disastrous marriage by the desperation of the woman and by his own feelings of guilt. These and his curious epistolary friendship with his patroness Nadezhda von Meck, whom he never met in person, were his only attempts at close relationships with the female sex outside his own family, and his letters, including some only recently made available, show that, as a homosexual, he felt much guilt and self-reproach. The mountain of contradictory evidence makes it impossible to say with certainty how he died, but raises a strong possibility of suicide.

There is little sign that Tchaikovsky's student years under Anton Rubinstein at the St Petersburg Conservatory (1862–5) prepared him for operatic composition, and the Russian repertoire in the 1860s offered few models by native composers. Not surprisingly, Tchaikovsky's first experiment with the form, *The Voyevoda* (1867–8), was unsuccessful, while *Undine* (1869) was rejected outright by the Imperial Theatres, and the composer subsequently destroyed it. But he had a good dramatic instinct that could rise to greatness when his personal sympathies were fully engaged, and by the time he tackled his third subject, *The Oprichnik*, he had greatly developed his craft in instrumental music, and had magnificently revealed a highly personal style in his fantasy overture, *Romeo and Juliet* (1869, revised 1870 and 1880). In fact, *The Oprichnik* (1870–72) was not only a great audience success, but a notable achievement (though Tchaikovsky's own hostility to it came to exceed even what he felt for its two predecessors). Its individuality was reinforced by its very pronounced Russianness, and in the old Boyarina he created the first of those 'suffering women' who were to prove the most memorable characters in his operas.

But already he was being drawn towards his nationalist contemporaries, led by Balakirev, and the Second ('Little Russian') Symphony (1872) especially revealed a radical shift in manner, which was confirmed in his fourth opera, *Vakula the Smith* (1874), in which the score's four identified folksongs are supplemented with passages of folksong pastiche. With *Vakula*, however, Tchaikovsky's nationalist phase came to an abrupt end. While the First Piano Concerto (1874–5) signalled a return towards his earlier manner, the heightened turbulence and pathos of the symphonic fantasy *Francesca da Rimini* (1876) seemed almost to foretell the disastrous events of the following year.

Eugene Onegin (1877–8) is inextricably entangled with that traumatic episode: its story had uncanny parallels with Tchaikovsky's own life. It is undoubtedly his greatest opera and also his most characteristic, both in its content and its musico-dramatic technique. Composed under the impression of Bizet's *Carmen*, which Tchaikovsky saw in Paris in 1876 and adored, his handling of Pushkin's ironic verse tale also projects Bizet's concept of happy domesticity and social virtue undermined by inexorable personal tragedy. Especially crucial is the design of its scenario. Three of Tchaikovsky's last six operas are based on Pushkin, and it is in these that the episodic structure to which Russian libretti incline becomes most explicit. It was perhaps because *Eugene Onegin*, *Mazeppa* and *The Queen of Spades* were literary classics, known to all educated Russians, that their scenarios could be more selective, relying on the listener's knowledge to fill any gaps in the plots. Be that as it may, all three (like Musorgsky's *Boris Godunov*, also drawn from Pushkin) use a 'strip cartoon' structure, each scene dwelling on a crucial incident in the story, thus giving the composer time to explore in depth the psychological states of his characters. In *Onegin* Tchaikovsky rose to such opportunities magnificently – above all in Tatyana's letter monologue, the finest scene in all his operas. Some consider *Onegin* his masterpiece.

No such claim could be made for *The Maid of Orleans* (1878–9; rev. 1882). *The Maid* suffered from Tchaikovsky's clear determination to compose a grandiose, Meyerbeerish work that would appeal to the taste of Western operatic audiences. But it was not only that 'commercial' considerations seem to have shaped *The Maid*; the traumatic events of 1877 had stunned his creative individuality. He shrank from society as far as possible to live mostly abroad or with his sister in the Ukraine, and few of the compositions of the next seven years are among his most powerful or characteristic. He attempted no symphony, turning instead to the freer form of the suite and serenade, and only two works are truly outstanding: the Piano Trio (1881–2) and the opera *Mazeppa* (1881–3).

In the *Manfred Symphony* of 1885 Tchaikovsky rediscovered his full, most individual powers, and it might have been hoped that his next opera, *The Enchantress* (1885–7), would be a masterpiece matching *Onegin*. But for all its undeniable fluency and stretches of excellent music, it was crippled by its implausibly melodramatic subject. The Fifth Symphony (1888) and especially the great ballet *The Sleeping Beauty* (1888–9) are on a very different plane, and completely at one stylistically. Yet the most striking feature of *The Queen of Spades* (1890), Tchaikovsky's third Pushkin opera, is the savage stylistic dichotomy between the sombre, sometimes menacing music prompted by the remorseless obsession of the main character, and the bright, cheerful music of the elegant society within which events are set. In several earlier works, most notably the *Rococo Variations* for cello and orchestra (1876), Tchaikovsky had allowed 'Mozartean' style to mate with his own; now he himself confessed that some music in this opera was no more than 18th-century pastiche. Elsewhere, in the darker scenes and passages, the tragic pessimism of the Sixth Symphony (1893) is anticipated.

For the three years after *The Queen of Spades* it seems that Tchaikovsky's creative resources were husbanding themselves for the stupendous achievement of this final symphony. Certainly all the intervening compositions are relatively relaxed, and his last opera, *Iolanta* (1891), is little more than a charming, though at times very affecting, piece.

Eugene Onegin

Yevgenii Onegin

Lyrical scenes in three acts (seven scenes) (2h 30m)
Libretto by the composer, after the verse novel by Aleksandr Pushkin (1828); Triquet's couplets by Konstantin Shilovsky
Composed May 1877–February 1878; *écossaise* added 1885
PREMIERES 29 March 1879, Maly Theatre, Moscow Conservatory; UK: 17 October 1892, Olympic Theatre, London; US: 24 March 1920, Metropolitan, New York
CAST Larina *ms*, Tatyana *s*, Olga *c*, Filippevna *ms*, Eugene Onegin *bar*, Lensky *t*, Prince Gremin *b*, Captain *b*, Zaretsky *b*, Triquet *t*, Guillot *silent*; *satb* chorus of peasants, fruit-pickers (female) and ball guests

In May 1877 Tchaikovsky had received a letter from a former Moscow Conservatory student, Antonina Milyukova, who was quite unknown to him, claiming she had been secretly in love with him for some years. Then on 25 May the singer Elizaveta Lavrovskaya suggested to him Pushkin's novel in verse, *Eugene Onegin*, as the subject for an opera. After initial hesitation Tchaikovsky's enthusiasm was aroused and, working from his own scenario and libretto (using Pushkin's lines as far as possible), he set to work on the scene that he had always found the most compelling: that in which the inexperienced Tatyana writes to Onegin confessing her love (which he rejects). While engaged on this he received a second letter from Antonina. Determined not to play Onegin to her Tatyana, he agreed to meet her, proposed marriage and on 10 June left for a friend's country estate. When he returned five weeks later for the wedding, he had already composed two-thirds of the opera.

His appalling marital situation drove him to attempt suicide, and in early October he fled from Antonina and was taken abroad by his brother, Anatoly, to recover. At first he was capable only of scoring what he had composed, and in November he proposed to his friend and the head of the Moscow Conservatory, Nikolay Rubinstein, that students should perform the first four scenes. A year later, in December 1878, these scenes were presented at a dress rehearsal, and three months later the entire opera was premiered.

It was Tchaikovsky's express wish that conservatory students should give the first performance, for he feared that the work's special qualities would be smothered by the habits and routine of the professional opera houses. Though a minority immediately perceived the work's rare qualities (Tchaikovsky insisted it should be published as 'lyrical scenes'), and though it received a number of modest productions in Russia during the early 1880s, it was not until the Imperial Opera produced it in St Petersburg in 1884 that it suddenly began to enjoy the success that has made it the most popular of all Russian operas. (In 1885, during this production's run, Tchaikovsky added the écossaise in the ballroom scene.) The opera reached Prague in 1888, and in 1892 Tchaikovsky himself was much impressed by a performance in Hamburg conducted by the young Gustav Mahler.

SYNOPSIS

Act I, Scene 1: In the garden of her country house Mrs Larina gossips with the old nurse, Filippevna, as she listens to her daughters, Tatyana and Olga, singing a sentimental duet inside the house. A group of peasants approaches, bringing in the last of the harvest. They perform a choral dance for Mrs Larina, who orders them be given wine. Meanwhile Tatyana and Olga have entered. Olga draws attention to Tatyana's pallor; she herself, she observes, is always carefree. But Tatyana attributes her own condition to the romantic novel she is reading. Suddenly their neighbour, Lensky, and his friend, Onegin, are seen approaching. Mrs Larina receives them, then withdraws. The young people join in a quartet, Onegin comparing Olga unfavourably with Tatyana, Tatyana seeing in Onegin the man fate has chosen for her. Onegin comments patronizingly to Tatyana on the limitations of the world she inhabits; then they retire, leaving Lensky to voice his happiness with Olga. Mrs Larina and the nurse return to invite everybody indoors, and notice that Onegin and Tatyana are missing. As the couple re-enter, the nurse sees that Tatyana is under Onegin's spell. Scene 2: That night, as Filippevna helps her prepare for bed, Tatyana asks about the nurse's past, then suddenly confesses she is in love. Requesting writing materials and dismissing the nurse, she writes to Onegin declaring her love. By the time she has finished it is morning, and she begs the nurse to send her grandson to deliver the letter. Scene 3: A few days later Onegin returns to give his reply; Tatyana flees into the garden, where he rejects her confession with appalling, if unintended, condescension, telling her, in effect, to grow up. Tatyana is humiliated.

Act II, Scene 1: Mrs Larina is holding a name-day party for Tatyana. A number of military men are present, as well as Lensky and Onegin. The latter is bored with the occasion, annoyed with Lensky for having brought him, and to get his revenge flirts with Olga by dancing with her. Olga abets him. Triquet, a Frenchman, sings some couplets he has written in Tatyana's honour, to her great embarrassment. During the following mazurka Onegin continues his flirtation with Olga; subsequently the two men exchange words, Lensky becoming increasingly heated until he loses his self-control and denounces Onegin. The guests have to separate them. Lensky rushes out, bidding farewell for ever to Olga, who faints. Scene 2: Next morning on a riverbank Lensky and his second, Zaretsky, are awaiting Onegin. Lensky sings of his love for Olga. Onegin arrives late, bringing his valet, Guillot, as his second. Lensky and Onegin reflect separately on the situation in which they are caught. Preparations for the duel are completed; Onegin fires and Lensky falls dead. Onegin is horrified at what he has done.

Act III, Scene 1: In a splendid St Petersburg mansion Onegin is watching other guests dance a polonaise. After the duel he had left the area and some years have passed, but he remains troubled by what he has done and bored with the society he finds himself in. An écossaise is danced; the arrival of Princess Gremina is announced. When she enters on her elderly husband's arm Onegin recognizes Tatyana. Prince Gremin tells Onegin of his love for Tatyana, then introduces his wife to him. Tatyana cuts short the meeting by pleading fatigue, and she and Gremin leave. Onegin confesses his love for Tatyana and leaves as the écossaise is resumed. Scene 2: The last encounter between Onegin and Tatyana takes place at her home. She enters distraught, holding the most recent of his letters. Onegin rushes in and falls on his knees. She reminds him how he had rejected her and asks bitterly whether it is her new status that has induced Onegin to lay siege to her now. She reflects how close happiness had once been for both of them, but says firmly she will remain faithful to her husband. Telling him to go, she confesses she still loves him. He embraces her, but she orders him out. In despair he leaves.

Pushkin's verse novel had concerned itself with the clash between the decadent mores of an opulent St Petersburg society and the simple, wholesome ways of a rural family. However, though the dance scenes (the rural 'hop' of Tatyana's name-day party with its boisterous, unsophisticated dances, and the ballroom scene with its grand polonaise) define this social divide, Tchaikovsky's attention was focused implacably on the pain and suffering endured by individuals whose relationships are twisted or destroyed by the differences of these worlds. The opera's greatest riches lie not in these two tableaux nor in the slightly rambling first scene, which establishes both the base for later events and, in the peasant choruses, the thoroughly Russian milieu, but in the intimate encounters of the remaining four scenes, where Tchaikovsky realizes with supreme sensitivity the inner worlds of his characters.

Though Lensky is simply a country squire who has been to university, and his music has at first no more than youthful freshness, when he is about to face Onegin's pistol a depth of pain is revealed that is deeply affecting. Much of Onegin himself remains concealed behind a mask of aloof sophistication until the belated awakening of his love for Tatyana suddenly exposes his helplessness when he becomes the victim of an irrepressible and truthful emotion. Tatyana's transformation, from the ingenuous but deeply serious adolescent of her great letter scene into the mature yet desperately unhappy woman who finally dismisses the man she loves, is disclosed with supreme mastery. The creation of Tatyana is the greatest single achievement of all Tchaikovsky's operas.

Nor should his deft handling of lesser roles be overlooked: the old nurse, Filippevna, the adoring husband, Gremin, and the 'very insipid' (Tchaikovsky's own words) Olga are all very clearly projected.

RECORDINGS 1. Vishnevskaya, Lemeshev, Belov, Bolshoi Th Ch & O, Khaikin, Melodiya, 1955; 2. Focile, Shicoff, Hvorostovsky, St Petersburg CCh, Paris O, Bychkov, Philips, 1990

Mazeppa

Mazepa

Opera in three acts (six scenes) (2h 45m)
Libretto by the composer and Viktor Burenin, after the epic poem *Poltava* by Aleksandr Pushkin (1829)
Composed summer 1881–April 1883

PREMIERES 15 February 1884, Bolshoi Theatre, Moscow; UK: 6 August 1888, Liverpool; US: 14 December 1922, Opera House, Boston

CAST Mazepa *bar*, Kochubei *b*, Lyubov Kochubei *ms*, Mariya *s*, Andrei *t*, Orlik *b*, Iskra *t*, Drunken Cossack *t*; *satb* chorus of young girls, Cossacks, guests, Kochubei's servants, Mazepa's bodyguards, monks, executioners

In 1709 the bid of the Cossack hetman, Mazepa, to gain Ukrainian independence from Russia ended in the defeat of himself and Charles XII of Sweden by Peter the Great at Poltava. This was one theme of Pushkin's *Poltava*; the other was the romantic relationship, also based on fact, of the elderly Mazepa with his own goddaughter, Mariya (Mazepa's apocryphal ride bound to a wild horse is ignored by Pushkin, though it conditioned part of Tchaikovsky's orchestral introduction). Viktor Burenin's libretto, drawn from Pushkin's epic poem, had been prepared for Karl Davidov, but he had made little progress, and in 1881 Tchaikovsky asked Davidov to assign it to him. Over the next year he composed a few numbers, but systematic composition did not begin until an enforced seven-week stay on a friend's country estate in the summer of 1882. The sketches were completed in late September, but because of the extra attention Tchaikovsky had been giving to the special problems of scoring for the opera house, this operation was protracted, and it was April the following year before the opera was ready. By now Tchaikovsky's reputation in his native Russia was such that the Imperial Theatres in both Russia's leading cities competed for the piece, and it opened in St Petersburg only three days after its Moscow premiere. In both productions the staging was excellent, the performance at least adequate, and the opera enjoyed some success. But though it was also produced in Tiflis in 1885, *Mazeppa* failed to secure a place in the repertoire.

SYNOPSIS

Act I, Scene 1: Mariya, Kochubei's daughter, is in love with Mazepa and gently rejects the advances of Andrei. Meanwhile Kochubei is entertaining Mazepa, who asks for Mariya's hand. Kochubei is horrified because of their difference in age, but Mazepa protests his love – and he knows Mariya shares his feelings. A quarrel grows. Mariya agonizes over the choice she will have to make between her parents and her beloved. But when finally Mazepa demands she choose, in terrible agitation she leaves with him. Scene 2: Lyubov, Mariya's mother, exhorts her husband to move directly against Mazepa, but Kochubei has a better plan. Mazepa has confided to him his scheme to join the Swedish king against Peter the Great in the cause of Ukrainian independence; now Kochubei will inform the tsar. Andrei begs to be sent as messenger, despite all the risks. All join in a chorus of hate against Mazepa.

Act II, Scene 1: In a dungeon beneath Mazepa's castle Kochubei is chained to the wall. The tsar has not believed his accusations against Mazepa, and has delivered him and his associate, Iskra, into Mazepa's hands. He is to be executed the next day. Mazepa's henchman, Orlik, enters to interrogate him further, for he has not disclosed where his secret treasure is. Bitterly Kochubei tells Orlik to ask Mariya; she will show him everything. Orlik summons the torturer. Scene 2: In the castle Mazepa is comparing the calm of the night with the turmoil within his own soul. Kochubei must die – but how will Mariya react when she discovers all that has happened? Orlik enters to tell him Kochubei will not give way, and Mazepa confirms the execution. Mariya appears and reproaches him for being so preoccupied. Pressed by her, he reveals his plans for a free Ukraine; soon, he says, he could occupy a throne. Mariya is excited at the prospect and vows she will die with him if necessary. He then asks how she would act if required to choose between her husband and father. Totally ignorant of her father's plight, she affirms her choice would be for Mazepa. Mazepa leaves, deeply troubled. Lyubov quietly slips in. When she realizes her daughter knows nothing of what has happened, she discloses the situation. As the appalling truth dawns upon Mariya a march is heard offstage; the execution is already beginning. The two women rush out to try to prevent it. Scene 3: At the place of execution a crowd has gathered; a drunken Cossack is reproved for untimely merriment. The execution procession enters. Kochubei and Iskra kneel to pray, then mount the scaffold. The people crowd round, and the axes fall as Mariya and Lyubov rush in.

Act III: The Battle of Poltava (depicted in a symphonic tableau using the well-known 'Slava' folktune) has been fought. Andrei enters the ruined garden of Kochubei's house. He had been searching for Mazepa; now, painfully, he recognizes where he is. Mazepa and Orlik enter as fugitives, and Andrei confronts Mazepa, but is fatally wounded. Mariya, now demented, emerges into the moonlight. There follows a mad scene. Finally Orlik persuades Mazepa to leave without her. Mariya perceives the dying Andrei, thinking he is a child, and cradling his head in her lap, sings him to sleep, staring blankly in front of her.

Though uneven and unashamedly melodramatic, *Mazeppa* is one of Tchaikovsky's best operas. As in the Pushkin-based *Eugene Onegin*, its finest passages are those which focus on the predicaments and feelings of one or two characters; like Tatyana and Onegin in the earlier opera, Mariya and Mazepa are seen as victims of fate. Especially impressive is the dungeon scene at the opening of Act II, virtually a grim monologue for Kochubei, which drew from Tchaikovsky some of the darkest music he ever wrote. In complete contrast Mazepa's musings on the night and his love aria in the next scene are remarkably beautiful, while the ensuing love duet is tender, yet reveals much of the other emotions that affect the spirited Mariya and tormented Mazepa. The following encounter between Mariya and her mother is also admirably handled. Though the first scene sprawls, the full choral sections in this and the following scene being no more than efficiently conventional, the execution scene is splendidly taut and as fine as any of Tchaikovsky's crowd scenes (its first part, using two folksongs and labelled 'folk scene', is self-consciously national in flavour). The characters of Kochubei and Lyubov are well projected, but as in *Onegin*, it is the young tragic heroine who most engaged Tchaikovsky's creative sympathies, while Mazepa fades in interest. The final mad scene for Mariya is deeply affecting. The opera had originally concluded with Mariya's suicide and a crowded stage, but for the 1885 revival Tchaikovsky cut this, extending Mariya's lullaby instead. It is an ending whose pathos is absolutely right.

RECORDINGS 1. Gorchakova, Dyadkova, Larin, Leiferkus, Kotscherga, Stockholm Royal Op Ch, Gothenburg SO, Järvi, DG, 1993; 2. Losutova, Diadkova, Lutsiuk, Putilin, Alexashkin, Kirov Op Ch & O, Gergiev, Philips, 1996

The Queen of Spades

Pikovaya dama

Opera in three acts (seven scenes), Op. 68 (2h 45m)
Libretto by Modest Tchaikovsky and the composer, after the novel by Aleksandr Pushkin (1834); with incorporations from Pyotr Karabanov (the pastoral interlude in Scene 3), Vasily Zhukovsky and Konstantin Batyushkov
Composed January–June 1890
PREMIERES 19 December 1890, Mariinsky Theatre, St Petersburg; US: 5 March 1910, Metropolitan, New York; UK: 29 May 1915, London Opera House, London
CAST Herman *t*, Count Tomsky (also Zlatogor) *bar*, Prince Eletsky *bar*, Chekalinsky *t*, Surin *b*, Chaplitsky *t*, Narumov *b*, Master of Ceremonies *t*, the Countess *ms*, Liza *s*, Polina (also Milovzor) *c*, Governess *ms*, Masha *s*, Prilepa *s*, Child-commander *spoken role*; *satb* chorus of nurses and governesses, boys, promenaders, girls, guests and gamblers; offstage: church choir

Pushkin's ironic yet chilling short novel *The Queen of Spades* is a masterpiece of clarity and conciseness and an almost ideal basis for a libretto. In fact, Tchaikovsky had disclaimed any interest in the subject when in 1887 his brother, Modest, had started drawing from it a libretto for Nikolay Klenovsky. But Modest had turned the piece into a romantic melodrama, and in the autumn of 1889, after Klenovsky had made little or no progress, Tchaikovsky himself was attracted to it. Because it was hoped to produce the opera during the following season, in January 1890 he settled in Florence where he could work undisturbed; the only problem was delays occasioned by Modest, who was completing the libretto back in Russia. The sketches were finished on 15 March, and the scoring was begun in Rome on 9 April. So close was Tchaikovsky's identification with his central character, Herman, that he confessed he had wept while composing his death scene, and he was pleased with his friends' enthusiasm when he played the opera through to some of them on his return to Russia. Even more was he delighted with the response of Nikolay Figner, then the darling of the St Petersburg operatic public, who was to create the role of Herman. The premiere was splendidly mounted and performed and was highly successful, though critical reaction was less approving, and the pregnancy of Medea Figner, Nikolay's wife, who created the part of Liza, meant the opera was suspended from the repertoire two months later.

The Queen of Spades was first produced in Kiev only 12 days after the St Petersburg premiere, and in Moscow on 16 November 1891. By this time critical reaction was becoming more favourable; in 1892 it was mounted in Odessa and Saratov and also in Prague.

SYNOPSIS

Act I: The opera is set in St Petersburg in the late 18th century. Scene 1: In the Summer Garden, while others stroll and children play at soldiers, Chekalinsky, a gambler, and Surin, an officer, discuss Herman; this officer of German extraction obsessively watches others gamble but will not join in. To a third officer, Tomsky, Herman confesses he is in love, though he does not know the lady's name. Eletsky is congratulated by Chekalinsky and Surin on his engagement. Asked who his fiancée is, the prince points to Liza, who has just entered with her grandmother, the old Countess. Herman is in despair, for Liza is his secret beloved. Tomsky tells how in her youth in Paris the old Countess had lost heavily at cards. To restore her fortune St Germain, at the price of a 'rendezvous', had given her the secret of three cards that would always win. She had confided the secret to her husband and one of her lovers, but then a ghost had appeared to her, telling her she would die at the hand of a third man who would come as a lover to wring it from her. Herman rejects the temptation this offers. He vows Eletsky shall never have Liza. Scene 2: In her room Liza and her friend Polina are entertaining some other girls. Liza, however, is very preoccupied. The others try to raise her spirits, but the governess bustles in to reprove them for unbecoming merriment. Left alone Liza reflects on her secret obsession. And suddenly that obsession is standing before her: Herman has entered through the balcony's open door. Liza is confused, but Herman begins to plead with her. He is interrupted when the Countess is heard outside, and he hides. The old woman wants to know why Liza is still dressed; she orders her to bed, then leaves. Herman emerges muttering the ghost's words, then resumes his declaration of love. Liza finally yields.

Act II, Scene 1: In a great hall a masked ball is in progress. After the others have withdrawn while the room is prepared for the interlude, the prince asks Liza why she is out of spirits and reaffirms his love. Herman enters carrying a letter from Liza: he is to meet her after the interlude. The guests are invited to witness the story of Prilepa and her rival lovers, the poor Milovzor and the wealthy Zlatogor. When this pastoral interlude is over Liza slips Herman a key; next day he is to come to her room where everything will be settled. But Herman insists he will come that night. The master of ceremonies suddenly announces that the empress herself is approaching. All line up to receive her. Scene 2: Herman surveys the Countess's empty bedroom. Midnight strikes. On hearing footsteps he hides. The Countess's maids lead their mistress through into her dressing room and Liza passes on to her own room. Prepared for bed, the old woman chooses to sit in a chair, muses to herself, then dismisses her maids. Herman emerges and tries to persuade her to reveal her secret, then draws a pistol and threatens her. She dies of fright. Liza returns from her room and realizes how Herman has been using her. Desperately hurt and enraged, she dismisses him.

Act III, Scene 1: In his room, to the distant sounds of trumpet calls and a church choir, Herman recalls with horror how he had gone to gaze on the Countess's body in her open coffin – and how the corpse had winked at him. Suddenly there is a noise outside, and the Countess's ghost enters. She has come to give him the secret of the three cards: 'Three . . . seven . . . ace!' Scene 2: Liza, still in love with Herman, has begged him to meet her beside the Winter Canal at midnight. Finally he appears, and they sing of their mutual love. But when she asks him to leave with her, he wants only to go to the gambling table. She realizes that he no longer recognizes her and throws herself into the canal. Scene 3: In a gambling house, Eletsky has joined the others. Tomsky entertains the company with a song, and as play resumes Herman appears, announçing he wants to play for a very high stake. Choosing three, he wins, then stakes his winnings. Playing on seven, he wins again. When he insists on playing a third time, Eletsky demands to play against him. Herman stakes on ace, but when he picks up his card it is the queen of spades – and the Countess's ghost passes across the stage, smiling. Herman stabs himself, and begs Eletsky's forgiveness. The male chorus prays for the peace of his soul.

Tchaikovsky himself invented the sixth (Winter Canal) scene of *The Queen of Spades*, arguing that the audience would need to know what had happened to Liza. In fact, his decision was also a measure of how completely Modest's libretto had transformed Pushkin's objectively observed characters into hot-blooded mortals. Pushkin had been able to let Liza slip away almost casually, but the opera's audience was bound to identify closely with her and demand to know her destiny. There can be no doubt that it was this 'humanizing' of Pushkin's tale that made it attractive to Tchaikovsky.

The opera uniquely reverses Tchaikovsky's normal preference, for this time it is Herman, a male character, who grips him. Nor among the female characters is his chief fascination with the young doomed woman, but rather with the aged and totally unsympathetic Countess, whose presence, because she is not only a victim but also the agent of fate (for by her own death she achieves fate's purpose), looms over them all. The work is also unique for its extreme stylistic dichotomy, for it incorporates a very large element of rococo pastiche – there are even two substantial quotations from other composers (the aria the Countess sings to herself in Act II from André Grétry's *Richard Coeur-de-lion* (1784) and a polonaise by Józef Kozlowski (1791) to end the ballroom scene) – which contrasts savagely with the dark, mysterious, sometimes sinister music to which the tragic destinies of the three main characters run their course. Even more, perhaps, than in *Eugene Onegin* it is the more intimate scenes that make this opera memorable, especially the scene in the Countess's bedroom; only the dungeon scene in *Mazeppa* can match this for its harrowing intensity. But that had had a single dramatic concern – the suffering of Kochubei; this one manifests a complete mastery in projecting a changing dramatic and psychological situation. If Tatyana's letter scene in *Eugene Onegin* is the most moving scene in all Tchaikovsky's operas, this one is the most totally gripping.

RECORDINGS 1. Freni, Forrester, Atlantov, Hvorostovsky, Leiferkus, Tanglewood Festival Ch, Boston SO, Ozawa, RCA, 1991; 2. Guleghina, Arkhipova, Grigorian, Chernov, Putilin, Kirov Op Ch & O, Gergiev, Philips, 1992

OTHER OPERAS *The Voyevoda* (*Voyevoda*), 1869; *Undine* (*Undina*), (1869); *The Oprichnik* (*Oprichnik*), 1874; *Vakula the Smith*, rev. as *The Slippers* (*Kuznets Vakula*, rev. as *Cherevichki*), 1876; *The Maid of Orleans* (*Orleanskaya Dyeva*), 1881; *The Enchantress* (*Charodeika*), 1887; *Iolanthe* (*Iolanta*), 1892

D.B.

Ambroise Thomas

Charles Louis Ambroise Thomas;
b 5 August 1811, Metz, France;
d 12 February 1896, Paris

The career of Ambroise Thomas mingled success and failure to a remarkable degree over a long period of time. His fame as an opera composer and his status as an Establishment figure, apparently unassailable, were not proof against reaction, neglect and indifference lasting long after his death. A Conservatoire pupil of Jean-François Le Sueur, Thomas won the Prix de Rome in 1832. A series of mainly comic operas, including notably *Le Caïd*, *Le songe d'une nuit d'été* (not after Shakespeare but about him) and *Psyché*, was followed by a pause before the resounding achievements of *Mignon* and *Hamlet*. Those triumphs were not repeated. After becoming director of the Conservatoire in 1871 Thomas wrote only one major opera, *Françoise de Rimini*. Years later, in honour of the 1000th performance of *Mignon* in 1894, Thomas became the first composer to receive the Grand Cross of the Légion d'honneur. By then, while the public stayed faithful to *Mignon* and *Hamlet*, his reputation, whether with Wagnerites and Debussyists or the merely fashionable, was extinguished. Chabrier's remark about 'three kinds of music – good, bad and Ambroise Thomas' contains a gleam of truth. He was more follower than originator. There is in Thomas a deeper vein of lyrical sentiment than can be found in the comic operas of the first half of the century, but he did little to expand the genre. Gounod, Saint-Saëns and Bizet had more personal styles, yet Thomas possessed an amount of skill in writing opera from which they and others after them profited. His melodic gift went with a kind of inspired ordinariness to the heart of the public. For that he was not quickly forgiven.

Hamlet

Opera in five acts (seven tableaux) (2h 45m)
Libretto by Michel Carré and Jules Barbier, after the play by William Shakespeare (1601)
PREMIERES 9 March 1868, Opéra, Paris; UK: 19 June 1869, Covent Garden, London; US: 22 March 1872, Academy of Music, New York
CAST Hamlet *bar*, Claudius *b*, Gertrude *ms*, Ophélie *s*, Laërte *t*, Le spectre *b*, 2 *t*, 3 *b*; *satb* chorus of courtiers, soldiers, players, peasants

Expectations of the poetic and philosophical richness and dramatic scope of Shakespeare must be disappointed by Carré's and Barbier's drastic but ingenious reduction, from which familiar characters and incidents are omitted. Thomas's *Hamlet* obeys the laws not of Elizabethan tragedy but of French 19th-century opera. In many ways it is a model of its kind, combining powerful drama (the scene on the battlements and the confrontation between Hamlet and his mother) with more conventionally conceived episodes. Ophélie's mad scene may be 'floridly inconsequential' (Philip Robinson) by later standards, but it is an effective and affecting example of the genre. The first interpreters of Hamlet and Ophélie, Jean-Baptiste Faure and Christine Nilsson, had many distinguished successors. *Hamlet*, the composer's single great success at the Opéra, remained in the repertoire until 1938.

SYNOPSIS

Act I: Elsinore (Denmark). Prince Hamlet is shocked by the unseemly haste of the marriage, just celebrated, of his mother Gertrude, widow of the late king, to his brother and successor, Claudius. Hamlet affirms his love for Ophélie, whom her brother Laërte, about to leave for Norway, entrusts to Hamlet's care. Hamlet learns that his father's ghost has been seen on the battlements. The ghost appears to Hamlet and reveals that he was murdered by Claudius. Hamlet swears vengeance.

Act II: Hamlet's strange behaviour alarms Ophélie. The queen tries to comfort her. Hamlet has invited strolling players to entertain the court. He instructs them to perform a play about the murder of a king. Hamlet and the players carouse together. During the performance the king rises in confusion. In a frenzy Hamlet snatches the crown.

Act III: Hamlet broods over his inability to take action. He overhears the prayers of the guilt-stricken king. The queen implores Hamlet to marry Ophélie, but he cruelly rejects her. She returns his ring. Hamlet forces his mother to consider the portraits of her two husbands and reveals that he knows the truth. The ghost materializes, urging Hamlet to slay the king but spare his mother.

Act IV: Peasants dancing by a lake are joined by Ophélie, her reason gone, distributing flowers from a garland. After singing a melancholy ballad she subsides gently into the water.

Act V: Hamlet muses in the cemetery on Ophélie's madness. He is still unaware of her death: the gravediggers do not know whose grave they are preparing. Laërte, returned from his journey, reproaches Hamlet. As they prepare to fight a procession appears, headed by the king and queen, with Ophélie's bier. Hamlet is commanded by the ghost to kill Claudius forthwith and assume the crown. Hamlet does his bidding and is acclaimed king.

For English audiences the original ending, which follows a French version of Shakespeare by Dumas *père* and Paul Maurice, was revised for Covent Garden. The ghost does not return: Hamlet kills the king and then kills himself. Richard Bonynge devised a compromise for Sydney (1982, later recorded) in which Hamlet, mortally wounded by Laërte, is reminded by the ghost of his vow, kills the king and dies on Ophélie's body.

RECORDING Anderson, Kunde, Hampson, Ramey, Ambrosian Op Ch, LPO, de Almeida, EMI, 1993

OTHER OPERAS *La double échelle*, 1837; *Le perruquier de la Régence*, 1838; *Le panier fleuri*, 1839; *Carline*, 1840; *Le Comte de Carmagnola*, 1841; *Le Guerrillero*, 1842; *Angélique et Médor*, 1843; *Mina*, 1843; *Le Caïd*, 1849; *Le songe d'une nuit d'été*, 1850; *Raymond*, 1851; *La Tonelli*, 1853; *La cour de Célimène*, 1855; *Psyché*, 1857; *Le carnaval de Venise*, 1857; *Le roman d'Elvire*, 1860; *Gille et Gillotin*, (1859), 1874; *Mignon*, 1866; *Françoise de Rimini*, 1882

R.H.C.

Michael Tippett

(Sir) Michael Kemp Tippett; *b* 2 January 1905, London; *d* 8 January 1998, London

Tippett was brought up in the Suffolk countryside and educated at first privately and then, from the age of nine, at various boarding schools. His father was a lawyer who became the proprietor of a hotel in the south of France, his mother a nurse who became a novelist and a suffragette. After the First World War his parents lived abroad, and from the age of 14 he had no real home, spending the holidays in those parts of southern Europe where his parents had temporarily settled. From this unusual and stimulating background, coloured not least by his parents' agnosticism, he gained a marked independence of outlook, which was to stand him in good stead. He was expected to become a lawyer, but even at preparatory school he had decided to become a composer. Apart from piano lessons he had no formal training until he went to the Royal College of Music in London in 1923. From then on he developed not only a passionate interest in music of all kinds but also the patience to accept that his compositional apprenticeship would take a long time. He was 30 when he completed his first characteristic work, his String Quartet No. 1 (1934–5), before which he had returned to the RCM for a second period of study, this time with R. O. Morris.

During the 1930s Tippett experimented with opera composition in four unpublished stage works. While these reveal little evidence of his mature style, they none the less show how he had been testing his ability to apply operatic techniques. His concert music from 1935 until 1946, when he started composing his first opera, *The Midsummer Marriage*, likewise shows him experimenting within the other principal musical genres. He wrote a Second String Quartet, a First Sonata for Piano, his well-known Concerto for Double String Orchestra, his oratorio *A Child of Our Time* and his First Symphony. *The Midsummer Marriage*, completed in 1952, can be seen therefore as the culmination of an extended compositional programme.

This very deliberate approach to composition shows how important the acquisition of technical skill was to him at a time when, in his opinion, English music was suffering from a lack of it. His early works also reveal his attitude towards the force of tradition. In this respect he was greatly influenced by the theoretical writings of T. S. Eliot. In 1937 Tippett met Eliot, who for a while became his 'spiritual and artistic mentor'. It was Eliot who advised him to write his own text for what became *A Child of Our Time*: having seen Tippett's draft he thought it was already a text in embryo and that any 'poetry' he wrote would be obtrusive and impede the music. Eliot was thus largely responsible for Tippett's subsequent decision to write his own libretti. This has aroused criticism, though Tippett's operatic subject matter, as well as his writing style, is so individual that collaboration could only have resulted in damaging compromises.

Tippett's five operas offer a very distinctive interpretation of the nature of opera, in general proposing that the genre should explore deeper layers of human understanding than can be revealed through the interactions of a conventional plot. His characters may be sharply defined, but they tend towards the representational rather than the individual; while two of his operas, *King Priam* and *The Ice Break*, do have strong 'story lines', these are ultimately no less symbolic than the others. Tippett's prime justification for this approach is that if dramatic music is poorly equipped to conduct narrative, it is peculiarly well equipped to give perceptible shape to the emotional feelings, forces and intuitions that prompt human behaviour. It follows that opera might also have a socially therapeutic role to play, in enabling its listeners to discover more about their own psychology.

Tippett's commitment to this idea took root in 1938, when, as a result of the break-up of a tumultuous love affair and of problems with his homosexuality, as well as his disillusionment at the menacing political situation in Europe, he undertook a course of Jungian self-analysis. The result of this was not only that he felt better balanced as a person but also that he drew back from his involvement in the left-wing politics of the 1930s (when he had been a Trotskyist sympathizer) and devoted himself to his fundamental vocation as composer. The work in which his new-found attitude is most explicit is *A Child of Our Time*, when he first showed his readiness to address in music large and seemingly intractable problems, here man's inhumanity to man. What gave him the confidence to do so – and also to become a pacifist and a conscientious objector during the Second World War (he was imprisoned in 1943 for refusing to comply with the conditions imposed by a tribunal) – was his Jungian understanding of the 'shadow' and 'light', reflected in the text of the penultimate section of the oratorio: 'I would know my shadow and my light,/so shall I at last be whole./Then courage, brother, dare the grave passage.' These lines enabled him to reach a characteristically affirmative, if in this case restrained, conclusion to the oratorio, even though it was written in wartime (1939–41). They provide the key to much of his subsequent output. *The Midsummer Marriage* is, in effect, a dramatization of them.

From 1940 until 1951 Tippett achieved prominence as director of music at Morley College, where his concert programmes proved to be the most adventurous heard in London during the war and for some years after. He then devoted himself almost entirely to composition.

Not until the 1960s did his music achieve proper recognition, having been frequently dismissed as the product of an impractical, if occasionally inspired, dilettante. This may be ascribed to the originality and complexity of his thought in general (as can also be seen in his published essays and his libretti), as well as to the fact that his musical language seemed to have been overtaken by post-war styles. But from the successful premiere of his second opera, *King Priam*, in 1962, and a BBC broadcast in 1963 of *The Midsummer Marriage*, a reassessment began, and it became apparent that here was a composer of international stature. This judgement was reinforced by the inexhaustible invention of those major works that were to flow from his creativity for the next thirty years: symphonies, concertos, sonatas, quartets, not to mention operas, which remain at the core of his output.

The Midsummer Marriage

Opera in three acts (2h 30m)
Libretto by the composer
Composed 1946–52
PREMIERES 27 January 1955, Covent Garden, London; US: 15 October 1983, War Memorial Opera House, San Francisco
CAST Mark *t*, Jenifer *s*, King Fisher *bar*, Bella *s*, Jack *t*, Sosostris *c*, The Ancients *b*, *ms*, Strephon *dancer*; *satb* chorus of Mark's and Jenifer's friends; dancers

The first performance of *The Midsummer Marriage* has acquired legendary status. Conducted by John Pritchard, produced by Christopher West, with scenery and costumes by Barbara Hepworth and choreography by John Cranko, it also had a strong cast, including Joan Sutherland, Richard Lewis and Otakar Kraus. Yet most press notices were violently hostile, at least to the libretto. This was dismissed variously as meaningless, amateurish or absurdly self-indulgent: Tippett, cripplingly inexperienced as an opera composer, paying the price for an ill-considered pursuit of the vogue for British opera that had followed the success of Britten's *Peter Grimes* in 1945. *The Midsummer Marriage*'s music, however, had not failed to win its admirers, and after a second Covent Garden production in 1968 conducted by Colin Davis, the opera rapidly gained ground and entered the international repertoire.

The opera is closely related to Mozart's *Die Zauberflöte*, having two pairs of lovers, one more elevated than the other but both in quest of enlightenment. Further correspondences are less clear, for, in essence, Tippett's libretto comprises a journey into the world of Jungian archetypes, a dreamlike, imaginative realm where a mythological ritual of sacrifice and rebirth can be enacted, and the hero and heroine undergo the experiences that enable them to understand their full selves and embark on a true marriage. As such, it sets out an abiding theme in Tippett's output, which is the power of music to overcome ignorance and illusion about the human psyche and so effect a better understanding of human relationships. In tone the opera is exuberant, lyrical and emphatically affirmative throughout, even though written during the austere post-war years. In this respect it can be seen as Tippett's compensating message of vitality and rejuvenation – against the general character of the period and much of its music.

SYNOPSIS

Act I: Dawn on Midsummer's Day, the scene a clearing on a wooded hilltop. The chorus is arriving for the runaway marriage of Mark and Jenifer. They notice a strange temple, at the centre of which sounds strange music. They hide, as dancers, led by Strephon (Mark's alter ego) and followed by the Ancients, emerge. Mark interrupts their dance, demanding a new one for his wedding day. The Ancients order a repeat of the old dance, during which the He-Ancient trips Strephon, demonstrating that change can be destructive and painful. The dancers and Ancients return to the temple. Mark puts the whole episode aside, settling down to wait for Jenifer. When she arrives, she announces there will be no wedding: 'It isn't love I want, but truth.' Their quarrel is cut short when she notices a spiral staircase by the temple and makes her decision: 'For me, the light! for you, the shadow!' She climbs the staircase and disappears from sight. Distraught, Mark plunges into a hillside cave. As its gates close, King Fisher, the businessman, with Bella his secretary, arrives in pursuit of his absconding daughter, Jenifer. He agrees to Bella's suggestion that Jack, her boyfriend who is a mechanic, should be asked to help open the gates. King Fisher bribes the men of the chorus to search for Mark. The women are not to be bought off. Jack's first attempt to open the gates fails, and with King Fisher and then with Bella he prepares for a second attempt. As he raises his hammer a warning voice (Sosostris) tells King Fisher not to interfere. At the height of his frustration, Jenifer is revealed at the top of the staircase, then Mark at the mouth of the cave. The Ancients appear, with the dancers, to announce a contest: the two will sing of their experiences. Jenifer sings of the spiritual purity of hers, Mark of the bodily abandon of his. Jenifer, convinced of her moral superiority, holds up a mirror to Mark so he can see the beast he has become. But his gaze shatters her mirror and she now enters the cave to seek what has given him such power. In turn Mark decides to share Jenifer's experience, and while King Fisher is left nonplussed, the chorus happily leaves spiritual journeys to Mark and Jenifer.

Act II: Afternoon. Strephon is at the temple, listening. He is frightened by distant voices and hides. Among the voices are Jack and Bella. It being Midsummer's Day, Bella proposes to Jack, and the two sing about their future life together. Three ritual dances follow, in which Strephon in various transformations is pursued by a female dancer similarly transformed. In the first (*The Earth in Autumn*) Strephon is a hare, hunted by a hound; he escapes. In the second (*The Waters in Winter*) he is a fish, is nearly caught by an otter and is injured. In the third (*The Air in Spring*) he is a bird with a broken wing and cannot escape the swooping hawk. At this point Bella cries out in terror, not knowing whether what she has seen is real or her own dreams. The dancers vanish. Jack comforts her, and, her composure regained, she leaves with him, while the chorus is again heard singing behind the hill.

Act III: Evening and night. The chorus is enjoying a party. King Fisher sends them away to collect Sosostris, his private clairvoyante, who will outwit the Ancients and restore Jenifer to him. The chorus reappears, not however with Sosostris but with a figure dressed as a jester and carrying a crystal bowl. The impostor turns out to be Jack. In the ensuing confusion the veiled figure of the real Sosostris appears. Jack places the bowl before her. She summons up her oracular powers and describes a vision of Mark and Jenifer making love. King Fisher is incensed, smashes the bowl and commands Jack to unveil Sosostris. Jack defies him, choosing instead to go off with Bella. King Fisher is left to unveil Sosostris himself. What emerges is not Sosostris but a lotus flower, whose petals unfold to reveal the transfigured Mark and Jenifer in mutual embrace. King Fisher aims a pistol at Mark. Mark and Jenifer turn their gaze towards him and he falls, dead. King Fisher's body is carried into the temple. Strephon and his dancers perform the fourth ritual dance (*Fire in Summer*) before the transfigured couple. Strephon sinks at their feet and is absorbed into the flower, which closes and bursts into flame. The scene becomes dark and cold. Dawn breaks. Mark and Jenifer enter. She accepts the wedding ring and, as they disappear into the distance, the sun rises.

The Midsummer Marriage presents Tippett's 'early', tonal style at its most developed – irrepressibly vital and inventive, lyrical, richly textured and with light-footed rhythmic momentum. The opera's relatively traditional design, separate numbers linked in a continuous flow, disguises a very original dramaturgy, in which the action proceeds to the point of Jenifer's arrival and then shifts into a dream realm, not broken until the lovers reappear a few minutes from the end. So the bulk of the opera takes place in a period 'out of time'. This is a context in which Tippett can plausibly delve into the purely imaginative, the mythological and psychological, and in which another individual feature of the work, the integral use of dance, can find its place. The opera is not however entirely set in a fantasy world, for the chorus, as well as some other characters, notably Jack and Bella but including King Fisher, continually relate the action to the everyday.

Among the musical high points are the Act I arias of Jenifer and Mark, in which they sing respectively of their experiences of the Jungian animus and anima, the enchanting Act II duets of Bella and Jack and the extended Act III aria of Sosostris, a rare instance of an operatic aria for alto and remarkable evidence of the workings of the creative process. The *Ritual Dances* (the first three linked to the fourth) have become one of Tippett's most frequently performed works as a concert suite, and if in this guise their operatic function as further projections of the animus and anima is lost, their brilliant narrative imagery and their culminating expression, in the fourth dance, of ecstatic sexual and psychological fulfilment is amply realized, even when the last dance is performed without the voices and chorus.

RECORDING Carlyle, Harwood, Watts, Remedios, Burrows, Herincx, Covent Garden Ch & O, C. Davis, Philips, 1970

King Priam

Opera in three acts (2h)
Libretto by the composer
Composed 1958–61
PREMIERES 29 May 1962, Coventry Theatre, Coventry; US: 1 July 1994, Theatre Artaud, San Francisco
CAST Priam *b-bar*, Hecuba *s*, Hector *bar*, Andromache *s*, Paris (as boy) *treble*, Paris (as man) *t*, Helen *ms*, Achilles *t*, Patroclus *bar*, Nurse *ms*, Old Man *b*, Young Guard *t*, Hermes *t*; *satb* chorus of hunters, wedding guests, serving women, etc.

King Priam is exceptional in Tippett's output, not so much because it marked a more radical break with his previous music than at any subsequent stage in his career, or even because its story is traditional, but because it is a tragedy. As such it can be seen as a critique of, or a reaction to *The Midsummer Marriage*. Now it is shown that no matter how honourable, human and deeply self-aware someone's actions might be, they may still lead to catastrophe. This is the essential message of an opera that on the surface seems a straightforward, if selective retelling of Homer's story of how Priam, King of Troy, reversed his decision to have his son Paris killed and thereby set in motion the Trojan War. The death of Priam may be cathartic, in the Aristotelian sense described by Hermes in the opera's last interlude, but it is final: it releases no possibility of life recharged or reborn, as with the endings of his other operas. It remains a profoundly inspiriting work however, because Tippett lights up the opera's mounting sequence of violence with moments of human insight and passion. Its accent on violence and brutality can be seen therefore not only as a means by which human values can be dramatized and upheld at times when the gods are at their most capricious, but also as a challenge to the mood of reconciliation that characterized the 1960s. Tippett's attitude in this latter respect was set in sharp relief at the opera's first performance, which took place just one day before that of Britten's *War Requiem*.

SYNOPSIS

Act I, Scene 1: Priam's palace. The birth of Paris. The baby is restless, as is Hecuba, his mother and queen of Troy. The Old Man interprets Hecuba's dream: Paris will cause his father's death. Hecuba's reaction is immediate. The young Priam hesitates, troubled by his conflicting responsibilities as father and king, before commanding that the child be killed. Interlude: The Nurse, Old Man and Young Guard comment on Priam's decision and introduce the course of the opera. Scene 2: Paris was not killed but given to a shepherd. As a young boy he meets his father and brother Hector while they are on a bull hunt. At the moment of recognition, Priam hesitates again, and then reverses his decision. He takes Paris to Troy. Interlude: Further comment. Wedding guests announce Hector's marriage with Andromache and report friction between the brothers and Paris' departure for Greece, where he falls in love with Helen, wife of Menelaus of Sparta. Scene 3: Paris and Helen. The answer to Paris' dilemma – whether to provoke war by abducting Helen – is given in a vision (*The Judgement of Paris*). The god Hermes tells him to give the apple to the most beautiful of three goddesses. Two, Athene and Hera, remind him of his mother and sister-in-law: he gives it to Aphrodite. Despite the curses of Athene and Hera, he takes Helen to Troy.

Act II, Scene 1: Hector taunts his brother for not fighting the Greeks. Priam encourages both his sons and, separately, they rush off to battle. Interlude: Through the agency of Hermes, the Old Man is taken to the Greek camp to gloat over the inertia of Achilles. Scene 2: Achilles, refusing to fight because of a quarrel with Agamemnon, his chief, sings nostalgically of his homeland. His friend Patroclus persuades him of the desperate situation on the battlefield, and Achilles allows Patroclus to fight Hector wearing Achilles' armour. Interlude: The Old Man asks Hermes to tell Priam of the danger. Scene 3: Hector has killed Patroclus and, with his father and brother, sings a hymn of thanksgiving, interrupted by the war cries of Achilles, who has been roused to action.

Act III, Scene 1: The war causes antagonism between the three women, but they are powerless and pray to their tutelary goddesses. Andromache senses the death of Hector. Interlude: Serving women comment on the impending collapse of Troy, and on the condition of Priam, who has been shielded from news of the war. Scene 2: Paris tells Priam of Hector's death. In torment, Priam relives his decision of the first scene. He begins to accept his own death. Interlude: instrumental. Scene 3: Priam visits the Greek camp to beg the body of Hector from Achilles, who feels pity for the old man and grants him his wish. They drink to their own deaths at the hands of their respective sons. Interlude: Hermes announces the imminent death of Priam and sings of the power of music to express cathartic experience. Scene 4: Paris tells Priam he has killed Achilles. Priam is unmoved. He dismisses everyone and speaks only to the mysterious Helen. Before he is killed by Neoptolemus, he has a momentary vision.

King Priam rejects the burgeoning tonal paragraphs of *The Midsummer Marriage* and is constructed in a series of short scenes and sung interludes (a method owing something to Brecht); in these the orchestra is split up into small ensembles, each character (and many of the concepts) has its own immediately recognizable sound quality and the musical language is more taut and dissonant. Only once, in the penultimate interlude, does Tippett treat his full orchestra as a unit. So there is little of the carefully modulated textures of *The Midsummer Marriage*, rather a rapid shifting of sound spectrum, between, for example, the horns and piano of Priam and the violins of Hecuba, or between the trumpets and percussion representing war, and the guitar of Achilles. Some of the characters – Hecuba and Andromache (cellos) for instance – are always represented by the same instruments. But Tippett does not stick rigidly to his methods and others, notably Priam and the semi-divine Helen and Achilles, also have a rich variety of associated instrumentation.

While there is no lack of lyrical music, Tippett's writing for voices in *King Priam* is typically declamatory in style, especially in the questing monologues which are a feature of the work and which emphasize the characters' individual predicaments and their isolation from one another. The moments of human compassion, between Achilles and Patroclus, or between Priam and Achilles, are correspondingly more poignant, their dramatic impact nicely counterpointed against the stark momentum of the rest of the opera and against its more obviously theatrical (and masterly) moments – such as the ends of Act I and Act II. Tippett's methods in *King Priam* became the source of much, if not all, of his subsequent output, both for the theatre and the concert hall.

RECORDING Harper, Palmer, Minton, Murray, Langridge, Tear, Bowen, Allen, Roberts, Wilson-Johnson, Bailey, London Sinfonietta Ch & O, Atherton, Argo, 1980

The Knot Garden

Opera in three acts (1h 30m)
Libretto by the composer
Composed 1966–9
PREMIERES 2 December 1970, Covent Garden, London; US: 22 February 1974, Northwestern University Opera Theater, Cahn Auditorium, Evanston, Illinois
CAST Faber *bar*, Thea *ms*, Flora *s*, Denise *s*, Mel *b-bar*, Dov *t*, Mangus *t-bar*

Between *King Priam* and *The Knot Garden* Tippett wrote three important concert works, of which the first two, his Piano Sonata No. 2 (1962) and Concerto for Orchestra (1963), explore the style, structural methods and even some of the material of *King Priam*. The third, *The Vision of Saint Augustine* (1965), ventures into realms of mystical experience and the perception of time. With *The Knot Garden* Tippett abruptly returned to earth. It is set in 'the present' and deals with directly contemporary problems – those stemming from a lifeless marriage and touching also on race relations, homosexuality and the torture of political prisoners, while in general exploring the inner as opposed to the public lives of its seven characters. If this bold subject matter was perhaps not unexpected of Tippett, and the brilliantly faceted musical language, its rapid sequence of short scenes and its gritty style a natural development from *King Priam*, the opera's intimate yet intensely concentrated dramaturgy shows him at his most original. Its speed of movement is a product of his adaptation of television techniques (notably the little 'dissolve' sections which break up one scene in preparation for the next) and of contemporary stage-lighting techniques; its essential substance is a product of contemporary psychotherapeutic techniques and of Shakespeare's *The Tempest*, this latter a conspicuous instance of his instinct to draw on cultural tradition while shaping it to his own purposes. Of all Tippett's operas, *The Knot Garden* is the most radical in its rejection of conventional narrative explanation. The whys and wherefores of the 'plot' have therefore to be deduced from what hints the libretto does provide. For all these reasons the opera was immediately recognized as strikingly original in conception and execution.

SYNOPSIS

Thea, a gardener, and Faber, a civil engineer, are a married couple in their mid-thirties. They have a ward, Flora. Thea has asked Mangus, a psychoanalyst, to stay with them so that he can help with Flora's adolescent problems. Mangus realizes, however, that it is the marriage that needs attention, and he plans a therapy in which his charges will be persuaded to project their feelings on to characters from *The Tempest* and act them out in a series of 'charades' he has derived from the play. Faber will be Ferdinand and Flora Miranda. He has asked Thea to invite two friends to be Ariel and Caliban. These are a homosexual couple, Dov, a composer, and Mel, a black writer. Mangus himself will be Prospero, who with his 'magic art' will solve the problems. Thea, tactfully, will not be included. The scene is a high-walled house garden shutting out an industrial city. The garden changes shape metaphorically according to the situations – from a boxed-in knot garden to a tangled labyrinth or to a rose garden.

Act I: The characters are introduced, Mangus testing his ability to summon up a tempest and a magic island, Thea and Faber locked in bitter confrontation, Flora neurotic, Dov and Mel ready to play-act though unsure of themselves. Thea's attempt to attract Mel begins to break open the entrenched positions but what really does so is the unexpected arrival of Denise, Thea's sister and a 'dedicated freedom fighter'. Disfigured from torture, she denounces them all.

Act II: Mangus is understood to be manipulating a nightmarish tempest, in which the characters, in a series of duets, give vent to their suppressed desires and antagonisms. Eventually the two most hurt, Flora and Dov, are left to console each other.

Act III: Before an audience of Thea and Denise, Mangus now masterminds four charades. The characters, including Thea and Denise, are able to some extent to come to terms with themselves – except Dov, who is isolated, and Mangus himself, who suddenly discovers that his behaviour has been grossly presumptuous. He stops the proceedings, all the cast comes forward and tentatively sings of the human qualities that, after all, can bind them, and the audience, together. In an epilogue Thea and Faber are about to embrace.

The emotional drama of *The Knot Garden* is dynamic and fast moving, but within its pattern of little arias and ensembles Tippett also leaves room for large set pieces. Act I is geared to lead up to the first of them, a harrowing aria for Denise ('O you may stare in horror'), answered by the second, a septet for the whole cast, which since it is set in motion by Mel, is a blues, with a boogie-woogie middle section. Although some of Tippett's early music, notably his Concerto for Double String Orchestra, absorbs jazz into his style, this was the first time his interest in popular culture had been shown so directly in one of his operas. Naturally it also affected *The Knot Garden*'s instrumentation, which includes jazz kit and electric guitar. The guitar features prominently in the song Dov sings to Flora at the end of Act II, one of the most conspicuous moments of lyric warmth Tippett places in an otherwise sharp-edged and even astringent score. Flora's song to Dov, immediately before, is another such moment, an exquisitely orchestrated version of Schubert's 'Die liebe Farbe'. Of all the solos in the opera Thea's Act III aria ('Now I am no longer afraid') is the most beautiful, and of all the ensembles the concluding quintet the most typical of the opera's intrinsic irony: a humanistic statement ('If for a timid moment we submit to love') punctuated by mocking quotations from some songs for Ariel Tippett had himself written for an earlier Old Vic production of *The Tempest.*

RECORDING Gomez, Barstow, Minton, Tear, Carey, Herincx, Hemsley, Covent Garden Ch & O, C. Davis, Philips, 1973
OTHER OPERAS *The Ice Break*, 1977; *New Year*, 1989
UNPUBLISHED WORKS *The Village Opera*, 1928 (arr. of ballad opera by C. Johnson, 1729); *Robin Hood*, 1934 (folksong opera); *Robert of Sicily*, 1938 (play for children); *Seven at One Stroke*, 1939 (play for children)

I.K.

Mark-Anthony Turnage

b 10 June 1960, Corringham, Essex

Turnage studied composition with Knussen from the age of 14, and later worked with John Lambert at the RCM; a scholarship to the Tanglewood summer school in 1983 also brought him into contact with Gunther Schuller and Henze. With his first orchestral work, *Night Dances*, which won the Guinness Prize in 1981, he had revealed his very personal stylistic synthesis, in which a language derived from Stravinsky and Britten was combined with elements of rock and jazz, but it was the premiere of *Greek*, commissioned by Henze for the 1988 Munich Biennale, that established Turnage at the forefront of European composers of his generation and gave him the label, however inaccurate, of the 'angry young man' of British music.

The years after the composition of *Greek* were dominated by orchestral music. After the premiere of *Three Screaming Popes* in Birmingham in 1989 Turnage was invited to become composer-in-association with the City of Birmingham Symphony Orchestra; he held the post for four years, writing a series of works for the orchestra and its conductor Simon Rattle, which culminated in the large-scale *Drowned Out* (1993). The same year he completed a saxophone concerto, *Your Rockaby*, and began the evening-long suite, *Blood on the Floor*, for three jazz soloists and ensemble (1996), before he returned to music theatre. The one-act *The Country of the Blind* (1997, withdrawn) was conceived as part of a double-bill with the scena for mezzo-soprano, *Twice through the Heart* (1996), to poems by Jackie Kay, and that was immediately followed by the composition of *The Silver Tassie*, commissioned by English National Opera, his first work to use the full resources of an opera house.

Greek

Opera in two acts (1h 30m)
Libretto by the composer and Jonathan Moore, after the play by Steven Berkoff (1980)
Composed 1987–88
PREMIERES 17 June 1988, Carl-Orff Saal, Munich; UK: 25 August 1988, Leith Theatre, Edinburgh; US: 25 July 1998, Wheeler Opera House, Aspen, Colorado
CAST Eddy *bar*, Dad/Café Manager/ Chief of Police *bar*, Wife/Doreen/ Waitress 1/Sphinx 2 *ms*, Mum/Waitress 2/Sphinx 1 *ms*; spoken chorus

Berkoff's reworking of the Oedipus myth translates the story to London's East End sometime in the late 20th century, but in their libretto Turnage and Moore defined it more precisely, turning some of the references into an explicit attack on the social injustices in Britain under the Thatcher government.

SYNOPSIS
Act I: Eddy is bored by family life in the East End. When his Dad remembers that a fortune-teller once told him that Eddy would murder his father and marry his mother, Eddy decides it's time to leave home. He wanders around the city, gets

involved in a riot and is beaten up by the police. Taking refuge in a café, he complains about the service, gets into a fight with the Manager and kicks him to death. As he falls in love with the Manager's wife, she remarks that he reminds her of a child she lost years ago off Southend Pier.

Act II: Ten years later. Eddy and his Wife have prospered in the café. Mum and Dad arrive and remind him that plague continues to ravage the land; a Sphinx outside the city is thought to be the cause. Eddy decides to confront the Sphinx, which turns out to be two women; he successfully answers their riddles and kills them both. Returning home in triumph, he discovers that he is not his parents' natural son; they found him floating off Southend Pier. Though Mum, Dad and Wife tell him it does not matter, Eddy is horror-struck and contemplates blinding himself. After a mock funeral procession, though, he changes his mind, and decides to subvert the Oedipal myth; love, he proclaims, is what counts.

The action juxtaposes moments of black, scabrous comedy with savage violence, just as Berkoff's prose veers between high-flown, almost Shakespearean imagery and raw, demotic directness. The pungent score, in which wind instruments predominate, is constructed out of a series of short, tightly focused scenes and employs a wide range of vocal modes, from speech through sprechgesang to fully winged arioso. The biggest set pieces – the percussion-dominated riot in Act I, Eddy's confrontation with the Sphinxes in Act II – are also the dramatic pivots of the work. While much of the text is declaimed rather than sung and the textures are often abrasive, the lyrical moments, such as the love duet between Eddy and Wife and his final aria, are unmistakably operatic and look forward a decade to the set pieces of Turnage's later opera.

RECORDING Charnock, Kimm, Hayes, Suart, Greek Ens, Bernas, Argo, 1992
OTHER OPERA *The Silver Tassie*, 2000

A.J.C.

U

Viktor Ullmann

b 1 January 1898, Prague; *d* 18 October 1944, ?Auschwitz

Ullmann studied with Schoenberg in Vienna and later in Prague with Alois Hába in the quarter-tone department of the Prague Musikhochschule. He also worked under Zemlinsky on the music staff of the Deutsches Theater, Prague, and was a member of Schoenberg's Society for Private Musical Performances (two of his song-cycles were performed by the Society in 1924). Like Hába, he was greatly interested in the teachings of Rudolf Steiner. In 1942 he was arrested by the Nazis and interned in Theresienstadt; on 16 October 1944 he was transferred to Auschwitz.

Der Kaiser von Atlantis, oder Die Tod-Verweigerung

The Emperor of Atlantis, or The Refusal to Die

Legend in four scenes, Op. 49 (1h)
Libretto by Peter Kien
Composed *c.*1943
PREMIERES 16 December 1975, Bellevue Centre, Amsterdam; US: 21 April 1977, San Francisco; UK: 7 May 1985, Imperial War Museum, London

The precise circumstances under which *Der Kaiser von Atlantis* was composed are uncertain. In Theresienstadt a fellow prisoner was the poet and painter Peter Kien. He and Ullmann set out to write an opera, drawing on the limited resources available (some distinguished singers and an orchestra of 13 players, including banjo, harpsichord and harmonium). Evidently the work was rehearsed, but the text was interpreted by the authorities as being anti-Hitler and its performance prohibited. Ullmann and Kien were both subsequently transferred to Auschwitz and met their deaths in the gas chamber. In 1972 an exhibition was devoted to Ullmann in Prague. Documents came to light that suggested that autograph material had by some miracle survived the Holocaust. Two years later, while working on Theresienstadt documentation, H. G. Adler discovered the performing materials, the manuscript score as well as a handwritten and a typed copy of the libretto in London. Kerry Woodward collated the diverse sources, completing sketchy or illegible passages to produce a performing edition of the score, which he himself conducted at the world premiere.

The Kaiser of Atlantis has proclaimed a 'holy war'. Death abdicates his duties in protest, and the Kaiser's authority is further undermined by a rebellion. A girl and a soldier from opposing sides fall in love. Finally Death agrees to return to work, but only on condition that the Kaiser should be his first victim. During the course of the action the Kaiser loses touch with reality and becomes an almost sympathetic figure. The supposed analogy to contemporary events is shown to be superficial: anyway, it is Death who dominates the entire action.

The dramatic circumstances under which *Der Kaiser von Atlantis* was composed were an obvious bonus for the work's posthumous promoters. However, the powerful libretto needs no special pleading and, despite stylistic allegiances to Hanns Eisler and Weill, moments of Straussian harmony and jazz influence, Ullmann's score has sufficient individuality to stand on its own. Since its rediscovery it has been widely performed, recorded and televised.

RECORDING Oelze, Lippert, Kraus, Berry, Mazura, Leipzig Gewandhaus O, Zagrosek, Decca, 1993
OTHER OPERATIC WORKS *Peer Gynt*, (1928) (music lost); *Der Sturz des Antichrist*, (1936), 1995; *Der zerbrochene Krug*, (1942), 1996

A.B.

V

Giuseppe Verdi

Giuseppe Fortunino Francesco Verdi; *b* 9/10 October 1813, Roncole, nr Busseto, Italy; *d* 27 January 1901, Milan

Verdi is one of a tiny group of composers who set the supreme standards by which the art of opera is judged; of his 28 operas – several of which exist in more than one version – about a dozen form the backbone of the standard operatic repertoire. He was the dominant figure in Italian opera for 50 years and was largely responsible for a radical transformation of its character. But in many ways his revolution was a deeply conservative one, and he carried popular audiences with him almost to the end.

Born in a village in the rural depths of what is now the province of Parma, Verdi received his earliest musical education from church organists in Roncole and Busseto. His gifts made a deep impression on local music-lovers, and in 1832 one of them, a merchant named Antonio Barezzi, undertook to finance a year of study for him at the Milan Conservatory. Though Verdi did sit an entrance examination, he was in fact too old to be admitted and had to study privately instead, working under Vincenzo Lavigna. Lavigna was, Verdi recounted many years later, 'very good at counterpoint, a little pedantic, and didn't care for any music but Paisiello'.

Having completed his studies Verdi returned to Busseto to take up a position as director of music in the commune and marry Barezzi's daughter Margherita. Three years later he was back in Milan with his family, for he had been able to arrange for his first opera, *Oberto*, to be staged at La Scala. The premiere, in November 1839, was successful enough for the publisher Giovanni Ricordi to want to purchase it and for Bartolomeo Merelli, impresario of La Scala, to offer Verdi a contract for three further operas. Between August 1838 and June 1840, however, both his two children and his wife died; in September 1840, his second opera, *Un giorno di regno*, was an inglorious fiasco, and Verdi's life, personal and professional, lay in ruins. Merelli's confidence in him did not falter, and his faith was rewarded when *Nabucco* triumphed in March 1842. This third opera established Verdi as a national figure; it also marked the beginning of what he was to call his *anni di galera* (years in the galleys), for impresarios from all over Italy were now eager to engage the rising star, and he was inescapably drawn into a life of grinding routine, composing, rehearsing and staging operas all over Italy and sometimes further afield. In the 17 years from *Nabucco* to *Un ballo in maschera* he composed 20 operas.

With its central theme of a chosen nation dreaming of deliverance from foreign bondage, *Nabucco* had a certain topicality in Risorgimento Italy; and the eloquence with which Verdi's music expressed moods of religious and national fervour played no small part in its success. Such Risorgimento overtones recur again and again during the *anni di galera*. Fastidious music-lovers of an older generation were sometimes repelled by the violence and noisiness of the young Verdi, but the majority of his operas enjoyed huge popular success and made an important contribution to Italian national self-awareness. It was a providential coincidence that the name Verdi formed an acronym for Vittorio Emanuele, Re D'Italia; and during the 1850s, as the Savoy monarchy became the focus for Italian national aspirations, the commonplace acclamation 'Viva Verdi' acquired a thrilling patriotic resonance.

This nationalist dimension contributed little, however, to the deepening of his art that took place between *Nabucco* and the so-called 'popular trilogy' – *Rigoletto*, *Il trovatore* and *La traviata* – of the early 1850s. *Nabucco* had given Verdi entrée to the best social and artistic circles: among the friends he made were Andrea Maffei, whose wife Clara was hostess of Milan's most cultivated salon, and Giulio Carcano, Italian translators of, respectively, Schiller and Shakespeare. During the 1840s Verdi developed into something of a literary connoisseur, an avid reader of dramatic literature from all over Europe. Inspired by this reading, his dramatic vision deepened; he acquired a sense of the potentialities of poetic drama, and hence of musical drama, that extended far beyond the conventions of Romantic opera. In his Hugo operas – *Ernani* (1844) and *Rigoletto* (1851) – his Schiller operas – particularly *Luisa Miller* (1850) – and his Shakespeare opera – *Macbeth* (1847) – we find Verdi stretching and bending the conventions inherited from his predecessors to give his operas an expressive range and a uniqueness of characterization and atmosphere that matched that of the greatest dramatists. Another Shakespearean project, *Re Lear* (*King Lear*), had first attracted Verdi as early as 1843. A libretto was written (by Somma, based on preliminary work by Cammarano); but though Verdi returned to the subject frequently and sketched much music for it, the scheme remained unrealized.

The repertoire of opera on which Verdi had been brought up as a student in the 1830s had been almost exclusively Italian. It was, however, infiltrated by French elements, mediated primarily through the operas written by Rossini in the late 1820s. It was Verdi's emulation of such models that gave both *Nabucco* and *I lombardi* something of the cut of French grand operas. As his reputation spread and invitations took him to London and Paris, he had the opportunity to experience grand opera at first hand, and made his first attempt at composing it himself – significantly *Jérusalem* (1847) is a revised version of *I lombardi*. His attitude to Parisian grand opera proved to be ambivalent; but the genre, and its greatest exponent, Giacomo Meyerbeer, certainly exerted a profound influence on his music in the 1850s and 1860s. After *Jérusalem* he composed two more French grand operas, *Les vêpres siciliennes* (1855) and *Don Carlos* (1867), and two of his Italian operas are based either on grand opera libretti (*Un ballo in maschera*, 1859) or on French scenarios in the grand opera manner (*Aida*, 1871). It was while he was in Paris in 1847 that he met up again with Giuseppina Strepponi, who had sung in the first performances of *Nabucco* and who in due course (1859) was to become his second wife.

With *Un ballo in maschera* the *anni di galera* came to an end. Verdi was world famous and very wealthy, and had begun to enjoy the life of a country gentleman. In 1848 he had bought, in an 'unimproved' state, a property (Sant' Agata) near Busseto; he moved there in 1851 and worked for decades developing and beautifying it. Since he had by now earned an outstandingly honourable place in the life of his resurgent nation, Cavour – prime minister of the united Italy that finally materialized in 1860 – persuaded him to become a deputy in the Turin parliament: he represented his local district, Borgo San Donnino (now Fidenza), from 1861 to 1865. Verdi was now less productive as a composer, accepting new commissions only when they really interested him. Between 1860 and 1870 he wrote three operas; their performance venues – St Petersburg, Paris, Cairo – vividly express the reach of his reputation. Each opera is on a huge scale, and the last of them, *Aida*, achieves to perfection that fusion of the Italian and French traditions of opera that Verdi had long pursued. He was by now nearly 60, and many assumed that *Aida* marked the end of his operatic career. In 1874 he produced the *Messa da Requiem* in memory of Alessandro Manzoni.

Unlike Wagner, Verdi left no theoretical writings, but from his vast correspondence, particularly from his letters to his librettists and his publishers, it is not difficult to extract a Verdian 'aesthetics of opera' that rivals Wagner's in comprehensiveness and perhaps surpasses it in clarity. He never wavered in his loyalty to values inherited in his youth: a good opera was an opera that was acclaimed all over Italy by enthusiastic audiences in packed theatres; its object was the exploration of human passions and human behaviour in situations of extreme dramatic tension; and its principal means of expression was the fusion of poetry and music in dramatic song. He sought out subjects bolder than anything an earlier generation would have dared, and characters became more idiosyncratic, but his sense of values was in the classical Italian tradition. In rehearsal he was a rigorous disciplinarian, demanding absolute compliance with his demands; and these extended beyond the music to virtually every element of the staging. From *Les vêpres siciliennes* onward, his publisher Ricordi issued production books – *disposizioni sceniche* – which record how his operas were staged.

The 1870s were, for the most part, years of disillusion. The reality of the new Italian state did not match up to the dreams of those who had come to maturity in the heroic decades of the Risorgimento; its chronic financial difficulties had plunged opera houses into crisis, and many were closing. Worst of all for Verdi was his feeling that a younger generation was abandoning the traditions of Italian civilization to pursue fashions or ideals emanating from France and Germany. Wagner had become a major force among the avant-garde, and though there was much in Wagner that Verdi admired, he did not see him as a good model for Italian composers. The primacy of song, the clarity of form and luminosity of sound to which Italian art had always aspired, a firm basis in humanist ethics – all seemed under threat.

His friendship with two remarkable men a generation younger than himself – the publisher Giulio Ricordi and the poet and composer Arrigo Boito – did much to draw Verdi out of this unhappy phase and make possible the glorious Indian summer of the 1880s and 1890s. He composed three operas in collaboration with Boito, to each of which Ricordi served as a kind of midwife – a second version of *Simon Boccanegra* (1881), and the two operas that stand as the most eloquent testimony to his lifelong veneration of Shakespeare, *Otello* (1887) and *Falstaff* (1893). None was to rival *Rigoletto, Il trovatore* or *La traviata* in popularity, but the very sophistication (especially in matters of harmony and instrumentation) that popular audiences sometimes found a little taxing appealed deeply to those educated in the German musical tradition, and many musicians came to love and admire *Ernani* and *Nabucco* via an enthusiasm for the late Verdi.

By the 1890s Verdi had, in the words of Giuseppe Depanis, a Turin journalist, come to be seen as 'the patriarch, the guardian deity of the fatherland'. His rare public appearances were occasions of astonishing demonstrations of affection and veneration; at his funeral close on 30,000 people are reported to have lined the streets of Milan and to have joined spontaneously in singing 'Va pensiero' from *Nabucco*.

Nabucco

Nebuchadnezzar

Dramma lirico in four parts (2h 15m)
Libretto by Temistocle Solera, after the play *Nabucodonosor* (1836) by Anicet-Bourgeois and Francis Cornue, and the scenario of the ballet *Nabucodonosor* by Antonio Cortesi (1838)
Composed 1841; rev. August and December 1842
PREMIERES 9 March 1842, La Scala, Milan; UK: 3 March 1846, Her Majesty's Theatre, Haymarket London (as *Nino*); US: 4 April 1848, Astor Opera House, New York
CAST Nabucco, King of Babylon *bar*, Ismaele *t*, Zaccaria *b*, Abigaille *s*, Fenena *s*, High Priest of Baal *b*, Abdallo *t*, Anna *s*; *satb* chorus of Babylonian and Hebrew soldiers, Levites, Hebrew virgins, Babylonian women, magi, grandees of the Kingdom of Babylon, populace, etc.

Nabucco occupies in Verdi's career very much the position that *Der fliegende Holländer* occupies in Wagner's: 'With this opera,' he remarked, in the *Autobiographical Sketch* dictated to Giulio Ricordi in 1879, 'it is fair to say my career began.' After the humiliation of *Un giorno di regno* (1840), whose premiere was hissed from the stage, Verdi seriously considered giving up all ambitions for a career in opera. But Merelli, the impresario of La Scala, did not lose faith in his talent. Early in 1841 he brought off a psychological masterstroke by suddenly thrusting a new libretto into the unsuspecting composer's hand and bundling him out of his office. Verdi later insisted that he read Solera's libretto very reluctantly; but its biblical grandeur and pathos moved him deeply, haunted and finally obsessed him. By the autumn the opera was finished.

After the premiere, Milan's leading newspaper acclaimed a 'clamorous and total success'; *Nabucco* revealed Verdi as a major new force in the Italian theatre and gave the rather gauche young provincial entrée into the best social and artistic circles in the city. By the end of the year it had enjoyed 65 performances at La Scala, and within two years had been sung all over north and central Italy and as far afield as Vienna, Cagliari, Barcelona and Lisbon. More than any other Verdi opera, *Nabucco* – by virtue of its great central theme of national humiliation and renewal – was to prove a major spiritual experience for Italians during the Risorgimento era; in later decades it became an indispensable element of Risorgimento mythology.

SYNOPSIS

The scene is set in Jerusalem (Part I) and Babylon (Parts II, III and IV) in 587 BC.

Part I: Jerusalem, inside Solomon's Temple. As Nabucco's Assyrian hordes press upon Jerusalem, the Hebrews take refuge in the temple. Zaccaria, the high priest, has taken hostage Nabucco's daughter, Fenena; he urges the Hebrews to trust God and fight bravely ('D'Egitto là sui lidi' – 'Come notte a sol fulgente'). Fenena is left in the care of Ismaele; they have been lovers since he once led an embassage to Babylon, and she has become sympathetic to the Hebrew god. A group of soldiers bursts into the temple, led by the warlike Abigaille, Nabucco's elder daughter. She too loves Ismaele and tries to woo him away from Fenena, promising to spare the otherwise doomed Jewish people. These now stream back into the temple, and Nabucco rides triumphantly in on horseback. Zaccaria threatens to kill Fenena ('Tremin gl'insani'), but Ismaele saves her from the high priest's sword, and she flees to the arms of her father. Nabucco and Abigaille shout for plunder and slaughter, while Zaccaria and the Hebrews anathematize Ismaele ('Mio furor, non più costretto' – 'Dalle genti sii reietto').

Part II The Wicked Man, Scene 1: Apartments in the palace. It has emerged that Abigaille is the offspring of slaves, and in the king's absence it is Fenena who is invested with his authority. But Abigaille has stolen the document that betrays her secret; moreover she has an ally in the High Priest of Baal, who circulates a rumour that Nabucco has died in battle and leads demands for Abigaille to become queen ('Anch'io dischiuso un giorno' – 'Salgo già del trono aurato'). Scene 2: Another room in the palace. Zaccaria reads holy scripture and prays for the gift of prophecy ('Tu sul labbro dei reggenti'). He reveals that Fenena has embraced the faith and is now a fellow Jew. Rumour of Nabucco's death reaches them, but when Abigaille and her priests arrive and dispute Fenena's authority, they are confounded by the return of the king himself ('S'appressan gl'istanti'). Nabucco orders Babylonians and Jews alike to worship him as god and is struck mad by a thunderbolt. He querulously calls for help ('Chi mi toglie il regio scettro?'), but Abigaille snatches up his fallen crown and reaffirms the glory of Baal.

Part III The Prophecy, Scene 1: The Hanging Gardens. Babylonians acclaim Abigaille. The High Priest demands that all Jews be killed, beginning with the traitorous Fenena. Nabucco appears, unkempt and still out of his wits, and attempts to reimpose his authority, but alone with Abigaille ('Donna, chi sei?'), he is tricked into putting his seal to the death warrant. When he realizes what he has done and then sees Abigaille destroy the proof of her lowly birth, he pathetically, but fruitlessly, appeals for compassion ('O di qual'onta aggravasi' – 'Deh perdona, deh perdona'). Scene 2: The banks of the Euphrates. The Hebrews dream nostalgically of their distant homeland ('Va, pensiero, sull'ali dorate'). Zaccaria prophesies the downfall of Babylon.

Part IV The Broken Idol, Scene 1: An apartment in the palace. Nabucco awakes from his deranged slumbers (portrayed in an extended orchestral prelude) to hear the sounds of the procession conducting Fenena to her death. In a flash of inspiration he recognizes that Jehovah is the one omnipotent god and kneels in prayer ('Dio di Giuda!'); then, his reason restored, he summons his warriors ('O prodi miei, seguitemi'). Scene 2: The Hanging Gardens. Fenena and the condemned Hebrews seek strength in prayer ('Oh, dischiuso è il firmamento!'). When Nabucco arrives the statue of Baal crumbles to dust. All join in worship of Jehovah ('Immenso Jehova'). Meanwhile, Abigaille has taken poison; she begs forgiveness from Fenena, and dies in the fear of the Lord ('Su me . . . morente . . . esanime'). (After the first two performances the closing scene was regularly cut, presumably with Verdi's authorization, to finish with 'Immenso Jehova'.)

Nabucco is a thrilling opera, but it has little of the urgent theatrical élan that was soon to become a hallmark of Verdi's style; its musical structure is altogether more massive than that of most of the operas he wrote in the 1840s, owing something to French grand opera, especially Rossini's *Moïse*. Each act contains at least one substantial tableau, and it is in these that the typical Risorgimento intermingling of religion and nationhood is clearest. Part I, for example, begins with a huge choral movement in which the Jews bewail the desecration of their land by Nabucco and are exhorted by their high priest to remain true to the faith. The preoccupation with nationhood in Solera's text is matched in Verdi's music by the emphasis laid on the chorus which, whether in lament, denunciation or worship, represents the whole national and religious community. Early Milanese audiences were so enthusiastic about the choral music in *Nabucco* and its successor *I lombardi* that they styled Verdi *il padre del coro*. Much of it, including the greater part of 'Va pensiero', is in unison and, in view of its dramatic and expressive function, might appropriately be described as community singing.

Contemporaries were also struck – sometimes disconcerted – by the brassiness of Verdi's orchestral palette. A stage band appears for no fewer than four formal marches, and choral melodies and even solo arias are often doubled on trumpet and/or trombone; like those of Moses in Rossini's opera, many of Zaccaria's recitatives are accompanied by brass. At the same time *Nabucco* is the first of Verdi's operas in which certain scenes – Abigaille's death scene, for example – are given a more intimate intensity by being accompanied by a small ensemble of instruments. Verdi's genius for musical characterization comes to a first climax in the turbulent rhythms and the vaulting and plunging melodies of Abigaille's music and in its radical contrast with the bland cantabiles of Fenena.

RECORDINGS 1. Suliotis, Prevedi, Gobbi, Cava, Vienna State Op Ch & O, Gardelli, Decca, 1965; 2. Dimitrova, Domingo, Cappuccilli, Nesterenko, Berlin Deutsche Op Ch & O, Sinopoli, 1983

Ernani

Dramma lirico in four acts (parts) (2h 15m)
Libretto by Francesco Maria Piave, after the tragedy *Hernani* by Victor Hugo (1830)
Composed November 1843–February 1844, rev. September and December 1844
PREMIERES 9 March 1844, La Fenice, Venice; UK: 8 March 1845, Her Majesty's Theatre, Haymarket, London; US: 13 April 1847, Park Theater, New York
CAST Ernani *t*, Don Carlo, King of Spain *bar*, Don Ruy Gomez de Silva *b*, Elvira *s*, Giovanna *s*, Don Riccardo *t*, Jago *b*; *satb* chorus of rebel highlanders and bandits, knights and members of Silva's household, maids in attendance on Elvira, knights in attendance on Don Carlo, Spanish and German noblemen and their ladies; extras: highlanders and bandits, electors and grandees of the imperial court, pages of the imperial court, German soldiers, ladies, male and female followers

By now theatres all over Italy were keen to engage Verdi. Having seen his first four operas staged at La Scala, he decided the time had come to accept an invitation from La Fenice, Venice, next to La Scala the leading opera house in northern Italy. And since much of the correspondence that now began to flow between Milan and Venice survives, *Ernani* provides us with a vivid picture of how the young Verdi went about his work. It is not surprising to find that he expects to be well paid; he insists on selecting his own singers and on having time to rehearse thoroughly; he explains – and this was rare in Italy at the time – that he began to compose only when the libretto was completed to his satisfaction, because 'when I have a general conception of the whole poem the music always comes of its own accord.'

After the grandiosities of *Nabucco* and *I lombardi* (1843), Verdi was looking for a different kind of drama, faster moving and more fiery in its passions. And he embarked on what was to become a typical procedure, reading widely in Byron and Dumas and other heroes of Romanticism, until he came across something – in this case one of the landmarks of French Romantic theatre – in which, in a flash of intuition, he sensed an opera was latent. The librettist for *Ernani*, the Venetian poetaster Francesco Maria Piave, whom Verdi did not yet know personally, was soon to become his most trusted collaborator; not because he had more talent than Solera or Cammarano, but because he was so compliant. Already Verdi had very precise ideas about what he wanted from his librettist; and in his letters about *Ernani* we find him emphasizing two issues that were to remain obsessions for the rest of his life: the poet must be as concise as possible, and he must remain as faithful as possible to the situations and the words of the original play. Despite *Hernani*'s notoriety, it was possible, thanks to the comparatively liberal censorship in Venice, to get the libretto approved without too much aggravation. The censors were exercised by a few passages, notably the conspiracy scene. They insisted that this should be as brief as possible, that the conspirators should not draw their swords and that the king's words of pardon should be 'liberal and impressive'; and they drew something of the republican sting from Piave's text 'Si ridesti il Leon di Castiglia', which, however, was still able to inspire one of the most spine-tingling of the hymns to liberty that stud Verdi's early operas.

Verdi arrived in Venice at the start of December, allowing himself three months to compose, orchestrate and rehearse the opera, as well as supervising a revival of *I lombardi*. It was a trying winter: there were acute difficulties over assembling a suitable cast; *I lombardi* flopped, and Verdi became increasingly apprehensive as the Venetians hissed two more operas off the stage; last-minute hitches meant that neither sets nor costumes were quite ready for the premiere.

Nevertheless, *Ernani* was an immediate and lasting triumph. The first Verdi opera to be performed in Britain, it did more than any other to spread his reputation internationally during the 1840s, and it remained a repertoire work for half a century. In the post-war Verdi renaissance it has proved to be, with *Nabucco*, the most resilient of his pre-*Macbeth* scores.

SYNOPSIS

The action takes place in 1519.

Act I (Part I: The Bandit), Scene 1: The mountains of Aragon; Don Ruy Gomez de Silva's Moorish castle is visible in the distance. Ernani joins his roistering company of outlaws. He loves Elvira, and has just heard that her guardian, Silva, is to marry her himself on the morrow; the outlaws plan to abduct her ('Come rugiada al cespite' – 'O tu, che l'alma adora'). Scene 2: Elvira's richly appointed room in Silva's castle. Night. Elvira fears and detests Silva; his gifts serve only to sharpen her longing for Ernani ('Ernani! . . . Ernani, involami' – 'Tutto sprezzo che d'Ernani'). Don Carlo also loves Elvira, and in Silva's absence makes one last attempt to persuade her to elope with him ('Da quel dì che t'ho veduta'/'Fiero sangue d'Aragona'). They are interrupted by Ernani, the king's deadly enemy in politics as in love. As Elvira struggles to keep them from one another's throats ('Tu se' Ernani!'), Silva returns. Finding his bride-to-be in the company of two strange men, he bewails his shame and prepares to avenge himself ('Infelice! e tu credevi'; the cabaletta 'Infin che un brando vindice' is a later addition). When the king's identity is revealed, however, Silva changes his tone ('Oh cielo! è desso il re!!!'). Quixotically moved to help Ernani escape, Carlo describes him as one of his own servants; then in an ensemble, as Ernani and Elvira plan their elopement, and Ernani vows to avenge his father's death (for which Carlo was responsible), the king and Silva discuss political affairs.

Act II (Part II: The Guest): A magnificent hall in Don Ruy Gomez de Silva's castle. Rumours of Ernani's death are rife; Elvira has despaired of delaying her marriage any longer, and Silva's household is celebrating the wedding day. Ernani has, however, escaped; disguised as a pilgrim, he gains admission to the castle, where he hears that Silva and Elvira are about to be married. Once alone with him, Elvira persuades him of her undying love, and Silva returns to find them embracing passionately; the arrival of the king delays the execution of his vengeance ('Ah morir potessi adesso' – 'No . . . vendetta più tremenda'). Carlo has come in pursuit of Ernani, but Silva, ever punctilious in the laws of hospitality, refuses to surrender him. The king orders his men to search the castle; as they find nothing, he takes Elvira hostage ('Lo vedremo, o veglio audace' – 'Vieni meco, sol di rose'). Silva releases Ernani from his hiding place, presents him with a sword and demands the instant satisfaction of honour. Ernani refuses to fight an old man, and points out what Silva had not previously realized: that the king is their rival for

Elvira's love. Silva agrees to let Ernani help him rescue Elvira, but only on the grimmest condition: Ernani gives him a hunting horn, and pledges that if he wishes him dead, he need only sound it; they ride off in pursuit ('Ecco il pegno: nel momento' – 'In arcione, in arcion, cavalieri').

Act III (Part III: Clemency): Subterranean vaults enclosing the tomb of Charlemagne at Aquisgrana (Aachen). The new Holy Roman Emperor is about to be named. Carlo, knowing that a group of conspirators is to meet in the vaults by Charlemagne's tomb, hides himself. Ambitious now for eternal glory, he bids farewell to the follies of youth ('Oh de' verd'anni miei'). The conspirators assemble – Ernani and Silva among them; Ernani is chosen to kill Carlo, and refuses, even when offered his own life in exchange, to yield the privilege to Silva; all conspirators join in a hymn to freedom ('Si ridesti il Leon di Castiglia'). Then, as three cannon shots announce Carlo's election, he steps from Charlemagne's tomb and denounces the conspirators. Electors, nobles and soldiers stream into the vaults; Carlo condemns the rebels to condign punishment, but Elvira persuades him to emulate the clemency of Charlemagne ('Oh sommo Carlo').

Act IV (Part IV: The Mask): The terrace of Don Giovanni d'Aragona's (Ernani's) palace in Saragossa. A crowd of guests, momentarily troubled by a masked figure in black, celebrates the wedding of Ernani and Elvira. Hardly are the lovers left alone before a horn is heard in the distance; the mask approaches and reveals himself as Silva, come to demand the honouring of the pledge; unable to soften his obduracy, Ernani stabs himself and Elvira swoons ('Cessaro i suoni, disparì ogni face' – 'Solingo, errante e misero' – 'Ferma . . . crudele, estinguere').

With *Ernani* Verdi moved from the high-minded communal concerns of *Nabucco* and *I lombardi* to a world of passionate individualism. His attention focuses on the possibilities of musical characterization, and in particular – given a dramatic situation in which three men pay court to one woman – the expressive qualities of the three types of male voice. *Ernani* provides the archetypal pattern for a whole tradition of opera: the tenor, a youthful, suffering lover; the bass, an elderly ruthless egotist; and, most distinctively, the baritone, a psychologically more complex type, torn between tenderness and violence, self-indulgence and idealism.

Ernani is not a sophisticated work, but in scene after scene it shows the young Verdi at his most effective. The magnificent breadth of conception of the conspiracy scene (despite the censors) and its evocative orchestral colouring; the lyrical fervour of the arias ('Ernani! . . . Ernani involami', 'Vieni meco, sol di rose', etc.) and the enthralling expressive details of the recitatives (especially in Act IV) set standards that he was not to surpass for some years. And if the prelude that henceforth generally takes the place of the overture is intended to act as a microcosm of the drama, no later example does it more effectively than *Ernani*'s, with its juxtaposition of tender lyricism and tragic solemnity (the motif associated with Ernani's oath).

RECORDINGS 1. L. Price, Bergonzi, Sereni, Flagello, RCA Italiana Ch & O, Schippers, RCA, 1967; 2. Freni, Domingo, Bruson, Ghiaurov, La Scala Ch & O, Muti, EMI, 1982 (live)

Macbeth

Opera (melodramma) in four acts (2h 30m)

Original version: libretto by Francesco Maria Piave (with additions by Andrea Maffei), after the tragedy by William Shakespeare (1606)

Revised version: French text translated from Piave (who revised the 1847 text himself) and Maffei by Charles Nuittier Alexandre Beaumont

Composed September 1846–February 1847, rev. November 1864–February 1865
PREMIERES original version: 14 March 1847, Teatro della Pergola, Florence; US: 24 April 1850, Niblo's Garden, New York; Ireland: 30 March 1859, Theatre Royal, Dublin; UK: 2 October 1860, Theatre Royal, Manchester; revised version: 21 April 1865, Théâtre-Lyrique, Paris; UK: 21 May 1938, Glyndebourne, Sussex; US: 24 October 1941, 44th Street Theater, New York
CAST Duncan, King of Scotland *silent*, Macbeth *bar*, Banco *b*, Lady Macbeth *s*, Lady Macbeth's lady-in-waiting *ms*, Macduff *t*, Malcolm *t*, Fleanzio *silent*, Doctor *b*, Macbeth's servant *b*, assassin *b*, 3 apparitions 2 *s*, *b*, (rev. version: herald *b*, Hecate, goddess of the night *silent*); *satb* chorus of witches, king's messengers, Scottish noblemen and exiles, assassins, English soldiers, bards, aerial spirits; (rev. version: ballet)

The breakdown of Verdi's health at the time of *Attila* (1846) was a blessing in disguise: during the six-month convalescence that followed he was able to recover an artistic idealism he had been in danger of losing in the relentless routine of the previous two years. *Macbeth*, conceived at this time, was the boldest, the most consistently inventive and the most idealistic opera he had yet written. Verdi was already an ardent Shakespearean and was determined to do all he could to make his opera worthy of its model. Sending Piave a first synopsis, he described Macbeth as 'one of mankind's grandest creations' and demanded from the librettist 'extravagance and originality . . . brevity and sublimity'.

Macbeth is the first of Verdi's operas in which we find him taking as minute an interest in the staging as in the text and music. He would not commit himself to writing it until he knew he could have Felice Varesi – a supremely intelligent singer and actor – for the title role; he warned the Florence impresario, Alessandro Lanari, that no production expenses could be spared, since chorus and stage machinery were so important; and he paid scrupulous attention to such details as lighting, the historical accuracy of the settings, the gestures and movements of the singers. In her memoirs Marianna Barbieri-Nini, the first Lady Macbeth, described the unprecedented demands Verdi made on his performers: working on the sleepwalking scene, she found herself 'for three months, morning and evening, attempting to impersonate someone who speaks in her sleep, who (as the maestro put it) utters words . . . almost without moving her lips, the rest of the face motionless, the eyes shut'.

At the Florence premiere *Macbeth* was very warmly received. There was some critical unease that an Italian artist should have invested such enthusiasm in a subject in the *genere fantastico* – a transalpine aberration of taste, to the minds of many Italians – but the extraordinary quality of Verdi's dramatic vision was recognized and admired on all sides. The special place the opera held in his own affections is shown, first, in his dedication of it to Antonio Barezzi, the father-in-law to whom he owed so much, and, second, in the fact that it was the first opera for which he refused to provide *puntature* (adaptations of the arias for singers with different types of voice).

In 1863 Léon Carvalho, director of the Théâtre-Lyrique in Paris, asked Verdi to compose a ballet and a new choral finale for *Macbeth*. Returning to the score, Verdi found himself being drawn into a more radical revision than either he or Carvalho had anticipated. Despite the fine quality of this new music, the Paris *Macbeth* was relatively unsuccessful and has established itself as a repertoire work only during the last half-century.

SYNOPSIS

The scene is Scotland, principally Macbeth's castle.

Act I, Scene 1: A wood. As Macbeth and Banquo, two generals in Duncan's army, make their way home from battle, they come across a coven of witches. The witches foretell, among other prophecies, that Macbeth will be king of Scotland and Banquo the father of future kings – prophecies that chime strangely with Macbeth's own secret ambitions ('Due vaticini compiuti or sono' – 'Oh, come s'empie costui d'orgoglio'). The witches disperse ('S'allontanarono!'). Scene 2: A hall in Macbeth's castle. Lady Macbeth reads a letter telling of her husband's military successes and of the witches' prophecy. She doubts if, without her prompting, he is ruthless enough to attain his ambitions. When a messenger announces that Duncan is accompanying Macbeth to the castle that night, she realizes that the time has come to act ('Vieni! t'affretta!' – 'Or tutti sorgete, ministri infernali'), and on Macbeth's return, he is soon persuaded that Duncan must be killed. After nightfall the vision of a bloody dagger leads him on to the murder ('Mi si affaccia un pugnal?!'). He returns, already racked by conscience. His wife chides him for his faint-heartedness and goes to Duncan's chamber to incriminate the guards ('Fatal mia donna! un murmure'). Macduff, a Scottish nobleman, and Banquo come to attend on the king; the murder is discovered ('Schiudi, inferno, la bocca ed inghiotti').

Act II, Scene 1: A room in the castle. Macbeth is now king of Scotland, and Duncan's son Malcolm has taken refuge in England. Since the witches have prophesied that Banquo's sons will succeed to the throne, Macbeth and his wife resolve that they too must be killed (1847: 'Trionfai! securi alfine'; 1865: 'La luce langue, il faro spegnesi'). Scene 2: A park. Banquo and his son, Fleance, make their way towards Macbeth's castle ('Come dal ciel precipita'); they are attacked by assassins, but Fleance escapes. Scene 3: A magnificent hall. Macbeth and his queen welcome their guests, and the wine is soon flowing ('Si colmi il calice'). An assassin enters to tell Macbeth what happened in the park. As the king rejoins the banquet he is appalled to see the figure of Banquo sitting in his appointed place. Lady Macbeth tries to dispel the gathering shadows, but the ghost of Banquo returns. By now Macbeth's behaviour is filling his guests with suspicion; Macduff decides to join the exiles ('Sangue a me quell'ombra chiede').

Act III: A gloomy cavern. The witches are brewing potions and casting spells. (In the 1865 version there follows a ballet of spirits, devils and witches, in honour of Hecate.) Macbeth enters, and in response to his questioning the witches conjure up a series of visions. These warn him to beware Macduff but assure him that he need fear no man born of woman and that he will be invincible until Birnam Wood (*sic*) moves against him. But then, terrified by the apparition of eight kings, followed by Banquo carrying a mirror ('Fuggi, regal fantasima'), Macbeth swoons, and the witches dance around him. When he recovers, he determines to exterminate Macduff and his family (1847: 'Vada in fiamme, e in polve cada'; 1865: 'Ora di morte e di vendetta').

Act IV, Scene 1: A deserted place on the borders of Scotland and England; in the distance Birnam Wood. Scottish refugees bewail the plight of their country under Macbeth's rule ('Patria oppressa! il dolce nome'). Macduff, heartbroken to hear of the deaths of his wife and children, is urged by Malcolm to seek comfort in revenge ('Ah, la paterna mano' – 'La patria tradita'). Plucking branches from the trees, they advance towards Macbeth's castle. Scene 2: A room in Macbeth's castle. A doctor and lady-in-waiting watch in horror as the sleepwalking Lady Macbeth muses over the murders she and her husband have committed ('Una macchia è qui tuttora'). Scene 3: A room in the castle. Macbeth is already so overwhelmed with melancholy ('Pietà, rispetto, amore') that the news of his wife's death leaves him unaffected. When his men report the moving of Birnam Wood, however, and when later, on the battlefield, Macduff tells how he was 'from his mother's womb untimely ripp'd', Macbeth realizes that he is doomed. 1847: he dies at Macduff's hands, cursing the ambition that he had delivered his soul to the powers of Hell ('Mal per me che m'affidai'); 1865: Macbeth and Macduff exeunt fighting; a few minutes later Malcolm's victorious troops enter, rejoicing in the liberation of their country ('Macbeth, Macbeth ov'è?').

Verdi's insistence that as much as possible of the quality of Shakespeare's tragedy should be preserved in the libretto had a transfiguring effect on his music, most clearly in what he called 'the two most important pieces in the opera'. In the great duet that follows the murder of Duncan in Act I a densely packed sequence of poetic images taken from the play inspires a matching sequence of musical images, creating an exceptionally flexible operatic design, whose dramatic intensity never flags. And in the sleepwalking scene, where Shakespeare writes a highly charged prose, periodically lit up with phrases of shocking expressive power, Verdi contrives to match him by composing an orchestral backcloth packed with mysterious patterings and sighs, against which Lady Macbeth sings broken declamatory phrases, periodically opening up into great arches of cantabile melody. Both scenes are landmarks in Verdi's development as a master of dramatic orchestration, the broad daubs of his early style giving way to a more scrupulous selection and blending of colours.

A criticism sometimes directed at the 1865 revision is that the greater sophistication of the new music makes it impossible for the climactic scenes of the original to stand out as the dramatic peaks they were obviously intended to be. The greatest gains from a musical point of view are, first, Lady Macbeth's 'La luce langue', an aria of gloomy magnificence replacing an icily virtuosic cabaletta; and, second, the rewritten scene of the apparitions (Act III) where, with subtler phrasing, harmony and instrumentation, the strangeness of atmosphere is sustained with fewer lapses into the commonplace. The magnificent choral music in the last act is also largely a result of the Paris revision.

RECORDINGS 1. Cossotto, Carreras, Milnes, Raimondi, Ambrosian Op Ch, Philharmonia O, Muti, EMI, 1976; 2. Verrett, Domingo, Cappuccilli, Ghiaurov, La Scala Ch & O, C. Abbado, DG, 1976; 3. 1847 version: Hunter, Glossop, Tomlinson, Collins, BBC Singers, BBC Concert O, Mathjeson, Opera Rara, 1978 (live)

Luisa Miller

Melodramma tragico in three acts (2h 15m)
Libretto by Salvatore Cammarano, after the 'bourgeois tragedy' *Kabale und Liebe* by Johann Christoph Friedrich von Schiller (1784)
Composed August–October 1849
PREMIERES 8 December 1849, Teatro San Carlo, Naples; US: 27 October 1852, Academy of Music, Philadelphia; UK: 3 June 1858, Her Majesty's Theatre, Haymarket, London
CAST Count Walter *b*, Rodolfo *t*, Federica, Duchess of Ostheim *c*, Wurm *b*, Miller *bar*, Luisa *s*, Laura *ms*, peasant *t*; *satb* chorus of maids-in-waiting to Federica, pages, members of the household, bowmen (bodyguards), villagers

The idea of composing an opera based on *Kabale und Liebe* originated in the summer of 1846, when Verdi was convalescing at Recoaro and much in the company of Andrea Maffei, Schiller's Italian translator. As usual when he found a subject that excited him, he at first imagined an opera that would follow closely in the steps of its literary model. But the opera was intended for Naples, the most old-fashioned of the major operatic centres of Italy, and Cammarano recognized at once that they would never get it past the censors without eliminating some episodes and raising some of the characters 'to a nobler plane'. There is no doubt that the composer would have been more completely happy about *Luisa Miller* had it proved possible to keep closer to Schiller. He particularly regretted the sacrifice of Lady Milford, the prince's mistress (replaced by Federica, a 'respectable' widow), but Cammarano explained that, quite apart from the problem of censorship, no leading singer in Naples would be prepared to undertake such a role.

The opera was warmly received at its premiere, and has always been admired without ever quite gaining for itself the central place in the repertoire that most Verdians feel it deserves.

SYNOPSIS

The action takes place in the Tyrol, in the first half of the 17th century.

Act I: Love. Scene 1: A pleasant village. Luisa Miller, daughter of a retired and widowed soldier, is touched by the birthday greetings of the villagers but no longer feels truly happy when separated from her beloved 'Carlo'. She assures Miller that there never was a more honourable young man ('Lo vidi, e'l primo palpito'), and when 'Carlo' joins the celebrations her happiness is complete ('T'amo d'amor ch'esprimere'). In conversation with Wurm, castellan to Count Walter, and another admirer of Luisa, Miller insists that his daughter must choose for herself whom she will marry, but he is dismayed to learn that 'Carlo' is in fact Rodolfo, Walter's son ('Sacra la scelta è d'un consorte' – 'Ah! fu giusto il mio sospetto!'). Scene 2: A room in Count Walter's castle. Walter, musing over his tormented relationship with Rodolfo ('Il mio sangue, la vita darei'), hears of his love for Luisa and insists that the wedding planned for him with Federica, a young widow, must go ahead without delay. Left alone with Federica, a friend since childhood, Rodolfo decides to confess the truth, but she loves him too much to react with anything but indignation ('Dall'aule raggianti di vano splendor' – 'Deh! la parola amara' – 'Arma, se vuoi, la mano'). Scene 3: Inside Miller's house. As Miller is telling Luisa what he has learned from Wurm, Rodolfo enters and swears that he will keep faith with her. Walter himself now appears. His insults prompt Miller to draw his sword on him, and Walter's bodyguard takes both Miller and Luisa prisoner. Rodolfo tries every means to persuade his father to release them. Finally, vowing that he will make known to all the world how Walter came to his title, he hurries away. The count orders the Millers to be freed.

Act II: Intrigue. Scene 1: Inside Miller's house. Wurm tells Luisa that her father, a prisoner in Walter's castle, will die unless she does exactly what she is told. At his dictation she writes a letter, professing that she has always known who Rodolfo was and that ambition prompted her association with him. Initially she recoils from the task ('Tu puniscimi, o Signore'), but when Wurm reminds her of the consequences, she completes and signs the letter ('A brani, a brani, o perfido'). She is then made to swear that, when necessary, she will publicly proclaim her love for Wurm. Scene 2: The castle, Walter's apartment. Walter promises Wurm that he has nothing to fear, even though Rodolfo has found out about the murder they plotted together to seize the title ('L'alto retaggio non ho bramato'). Federica enters, and Luisa is brought in to confirm that there are no longer any ties between herself and Rodolfo. Finally, she professes to love Wurm ('Come celar le smanie'). Scene 3: Hanging gardens in the castle. Luisa's letter has destroyed all Rodolfo's hopes of happiness ('Quando le sere al placido'). Wurm is challenged to a duel, but by discharging his pistol into the air he brings Walter and attendants rushing to the scene. Rodolfo is persuaded that the fittest way to be revenged is to marry Federica ('L'ara o l'avello apprestami').

Act III: Poison. Inside Miller's house.

Resolved to take her life, Luisa is writing a last letter to Rodolfo when her father enters, released from prison. She confesses what she intends to do, but such is the old man's despair that she relents and agrees to join him in a life of exile from their old home ('La tomba è un letto' – 'Andrem, raminghi e poveri'). Music sounds from the church where Rodolfo and Federica are about to be married, but a moment later Rodolfo appears, brandishing Luisa's letter. As he questions her, he contrives for both of them to drink poison. Via accusations, tears and solemn warnings the ghastly truth emerges ('Piangi, piangi il tuo dolore' – 'Maledetto, maledetto il dì ch'io nacqui'). Miller returns to the scene only to receive the embraces of his dying daughter and Rodolfo's prayers for forgiveness ('Padre ricevi l'estremo addio'). By now all have assembled. Rodolfo, with one last effort, runs Wurm through with his sword, then falls dead beside Luisa.

After the stylistic adventures of *Macbeth* and the French-inspired operas of the late 1840s, Verdi returns to the mainstream of Italian melodrama but at a higher level of sophistication and expressiveness. The music is more consistently inventive, such purely conventional elements as formal introductions and cadences are pared away or given expressive meaning, and the structures of aria and ensemble become more various and flexible. The wonderful duets in Act III best illustrate Verdi's habit of fashioning the musical forms to match the dramatic purpose: in the final section of 'Andrem, raminghi e poveri' Luisa does not, in the customary fashion, sing on equal terms with Miller; instead, in an ethereal, 'barely perceptible' descant, she hovers over him, guardian-angel-like; in 'Piangi, piangi il tuo dolore' no musical reconciliation is brought about between the pure-heartedness of Luisa and the blasphemous despair of Rodolfo: to the bitter end, the music of each remains distinct in melodic style, colour and texture.

The opera owes much of its distinctive ethos to the simple eloquence of its choruses, notably those that open each of the three acts. In using the chorus so charmingly to evoke a vision of an idyllic and harmonious community Verdi was surely remembering Bellini's *La sonnambula*.

The full-length overture, one of Verdi's finest, is a monothematic sonata movement, based on a theme that recurs in various guises throughout the opera – but especially in Act III – as a symbol of the malign fate that destroys the lovers' happiness.

RECORDINGS 1. Caballé, Pavarotti, Milnes, Giaiotti, London Op Ch, Nat PO, Maag, Decca, 1975; 2. Ricciarelli, Domingo, Bruson, Howell, Covent Garden Ch & O, Maazel, DG, 1979; 3. Millo, Domingo, Chernov, Plishka, Ch & O of Metropolitan, New York, Levine, RCA, 1991

Stiffelio

Stiffelius

Dramma lirico in three acts (1h 45m)
Libretto by Francesco Maria Piave, after the play *Le pasteur, ou L'évangile et le foyer* (1849) by Emile Souvestre and Eugène Bourgeois
Composed July–November 1850
PREMIERES 16 November 1850, Teatro Grande, Trieste; 26 December 1968, Teatro Regio, Parma (uncensored); UK: 14 February 1973, Collegiate Theatre, London; US: 17 February 1978, Opera House, Boston
CAST Stiffelio *t*, Lina *s*, Stankar *bar*, Raffaele *t*, Jorg *b profondo*, *ms*, *t*, *spoken role*; *satb* chorus of members of Stankar's household, friends and followers of Stiffelio

Of all Verdi's many bold choices of subject, that of Stiffelio, a tale of treachery and adultery, revenge and forgiveness among the members of an extreme Protestant sect, is surely the most unusual.

The opera's viability was utterly destroyed when, at the last moment, the ecclesiastical censor in Trieste inflicted a series of bowdlerizations – notably in the final church scene – that made it dramatically pointless and in large measure unintelligible. Not surprisingly, it was coolly received, and it fared little better with a rewritten libretto (which incurred the composer's grave displeasure) in which the problematic central character became a German politician, Guglielmo Wellingrode. Fond of *Stiffelio* as Verdi was, it soon became clear that it had no future in the censor-ridden Italy of the 1850s, and by 1854 he had decided that the only way to salvage its remarkable music was by adapting it to a new libretto, *Aroldo* (1857). As a consequence of this rewriting, *Stiffelio* disappeared from view entirely; a full score was discovered only in the 1960s, and the opera received its belated uncensored Italian premiere in 1968.

SYNOPSIS
The scene is set in and near to Count Stankar's castle in Germany on the banks of the river Salzbach (*sic*) at the beginning of the 19th century.

Act I: While Stiffelio is away on a preaching mission, his wife Lina is lured into an adulterous liaison with Raffaele. On Stiffelio's return, Lina's father, Stankar, prevents her from confessing her wrongdoing; he does, however, challenge Raffaele to a duel.

Act II: The duel is interrupted by Stiffelio; but when he hears what is at issue, he insists on fighting Raffaele himself. Psalm-singing from the nearby church and the solemn words of Jorg, an elderly minister, recall him to his duty as a man of God.

Act III: Stiffelio offers Lina the chance of a divorce; she persuades him that she has always loved him, but had been treacherously seduced. When he goes to administer condign punishment on Raffaele, Stiffelio finds that Stankar has already killed him. Joining his flock in church he tries to recover his serenity of mind by reading from the Bible. It falls open at the story of the woman taken in adultery.

Verdi's music, in keeping with the dramatic theme, is as boldly unconventional as anything he had yet composed. Typical of this opera are movements in which the overall musical effect seems less important than a profusion of expressive detail designed to heighten the tensions of the moment. Stiffelio's Act I aria 'Vidi dovunque gemere' is so sensitive to the changing moods of the troubled Lina, to whom it is addressed, that it has the effect of a whole series of sharply contrasting ariosi. The finale, the Bible-reading scene so mauled by the censor, marks the most radical break with the stylistic conventions of the day: its single lyrical phrase, the climactic 'Perdonata! Iddio lo pronunziò', stands out electrifyingly from an austere context of recitative intonation and quietly reiterated instrumental ostinati. Such textural bleakness marks only one extreme of a wide spectrum of colours, some of which – the elaborately subdivided string patterns in Lina's Act II aria 'Ah, dagli scanni eternei', for example – are exceptionally rich.

RECORDING Sass, Carreras, Manuguerra, Ganzarolli, Austrian R Ch, Gardelli, Philips, 1979

Rigoletto

Melodramma in three acts (2h)
Libretto by Francesco Maria Piave, after the tragedy *Le roi s'amuse* by Victor Hugo (1832)
Composed November 1850–March 1851
PREMIERES 11 March 1851, La Fenice, Venice; UK: 14 May 1853, Covent Garden, London; US: 19 February 1855, Academy of Music, New York
CAST Duke of Mantua *t*, Rigoletto *bar*, Gilda *s*, Sparafucile *b*, Maddalena *a*, Giovanna *ms*, Count Monterone *bar*, Marullo *bar*, Matteo Borsa *t*, Count Ceprano *b*, Countess Ceprano *ms*, court

usher *t*, Duchess's page *ms*; *tb* chorus of gentlemen of the court; extras: ladies, pages, halberdiers

If the ruination of *Stiffelio* was the most crushing blow Verdi ever received at the hands of the censors, the triumph of *Rigoletto* marked his most famous victory over them. In this instance problems were anticipated from the start – even in liberal Paris *Le roi s'amuse* had been banned after a single performance – and Verdi's determination to produce a worthy operatic version of Hugo's notorious play was resourcefully abetted by the Venetian theatre management. *Le roi s'amuse* thrilled him as no other subject since *Macbeth* had done. He found it 'the greatest subject and perhaps the greatest drama of modern times' and deemed Triboulet (who became Rigoletto) 'a creation worthy of Shakespeare'. Recognizing that the motif of the curse was both the seed and the moral of the drama, Verdi proposed to call the opera *La maledizione*, and probably during November 1850 it was fully sketched under that title, using the setting and the names of Hugo's play. Despite earlier assurances that the subject was acceptable, when the censors read Piave's libretto they were appalled, expressed their regrets that he and the 'celebrated maestro' had squandered their talents on a subject of 'such repellent immorality and obscene triviality' and forbade absolutely the performance of such an opera in Venice. Only after two rewritings was Piave able to produce a libretto that satisfied both Verdi and the censors. The first, *Il duca di Vendome*, though acceptable to the censors, was dismissed out of hand by the composer because it eliminated everything that was original and powerful. The second, however – *Rigoletto* – satisfied both parties. By such ruses as shifting the action from the French court of François I to the court of an anonymous duke and by eliminating some of the more flagrantly libertine passages, Piave soothed the political and moral sensibilities of the censors; but in all essentials Hugo's grotesque and macabre drama emerged unscathed. After his experience with *Stiffelio* Verdi would have accepted nothing less.

The premiere was a brilliant popular success, and within ten years *Rigoletto* had been staged in some 250 opera houses all over the world. But its early history was more problematic than that might suggest. Not all censors were as accommodating as those in Venice, and for a decade and more a number of alternative versions of the opera – *Viscardello*, *Lionello*, *Clara di Perth* – were all that could be seen in many theatres. Sometimes the ending had to be altered, and Gilda emerged from her sack in good health to join Rigoletto in giving thanks for the 'clemenza del cielo'. Nor was censorship always the problem. In Bergamo in September 1851 it was withdrawn from the repertoire after only one and a half performances because of audience protests. Nevertheless, *Rigoletto* is the earliest of Verdi's operas whose popularity has survived essentially unimpaired from its first performance to the present.

SYNOPSIS

The scene is set in and near Mantua during the 16th century.

Act I, Scene 1: A magnificent hall in the ducal palace. A party is in progress. The libertine Duke proclaims his philosophy of taking his pleasure where he finds it ('Questa o quella per me pari sono'). He flirts with the Countess Ceprano, a sardonic commentary being provided by his jester, the hunchback Rigoletto. Enraged by Rigoletto's insults, Ceprano arranges for a group of courtiers to meet at his palace that night. The revelry is interrupted by Monterone, a political opponent whose daughter has been ravished by the Duke. Mocked by Rigoletto, Monterone lays a solemn curse on the Duke and his jester. Scene 2: The end of a blind alley. Rigoletto, haunted by Monterone's curse ('Quel vecchio maledivami!'), is accosted by

Sparafucile, a professional assassin. He converses long with him, then compares his own way of life with that of his new acquaintance ('Pari siamo! io la lingua, egli ha il pugnale'). Unknown to the world at large, Rigoletto is a widower, who, all too familiar with the vices of the court, keeps his daughter Gilda in the strictest seclusion. He tells her of her mother and solemnly enjoins the duenna Giovanna to guard her vigilantly ('Deh, non parlare al misero' – 'Veglia, o donna, questo fiore'). As they are speaking, the Duke (in disguise – he later introduces himself as a poor student, Gualtier Maldè) creeps into the courtyard and is astonished to learn that his new flame is Rigoletto's daughter. When Rigoletto has gone indoors, he steps forward with a passionate avowal of love ('È il sol dell' anima'). Sounds of footsteps in the street disturb them, and the Duke bids a hasty farewell, leaving Gilda in ecstatic reverie ('Caro nome'). The footsteps were those of the courtiers gathering at Ceprano's house. They trick Rigoletto into allowing himself to be blindfolded; then he unwittingly helps them ransack his own house ('Zitti, zitti, moviamo a vendetta'), carrying off Gilda. Rigoletto hears her cries in the distance, tears off his blindfold and recognizes in what has happened the force of Monterone's curse.

Act II: A reception room in the ducal palace. The Duke fears he has lost Gilda. Returning to her house shortly after their parting he had found it deserted ('Ella mi fu rapita!' – 'Parmi veder le lagrime'). But when the courtiers tell him of their night's exploits, he realizes that she is in his power and hastens away to take his pleasure ('Possente amor mi chiama'). Rigoletto enters, searching anxiously for Gilda. Overhearing the courtiers' evasive replies when a page asks for the Duke, he realizes that she must be with him. He turns on them, denouncing them as contemptible hirelings ('Cortigiani, vil razza dannata'). Gilda appears, burning with shame. Rigoletto drives out the courtiers and weeps as he hears her story ('Tutte le feste al tempio'). Monterone is escorted through the room on his way to prison. To Gilda's horror, Rigoletto assures the departing figure that he will soon be avenged ('Sì, vendetta, tremenda vendetta').

Act III: The right bank of the Mincio. Having engaged the services of Sparafucile, Rigoletto brings Gilda to a half-ruined tavern where they observe the Duke settling down for an evening's drinking and whoring ('La donna è mobile'). He has been lured there by Maddalena, Sparafucile's sister, and now begins to make love to her, Gilda despairs, while Rigoletto meditates revenge ('Bella figlia dell' amore'). Rigoletto sends his daughter home, then arranges with Sparafucile to return at midnight for the Duke's body. A storm rises. Gilda returns in disguise and hears Sparafucile and Maddalena arguing. Maddalena has fallen for the young man, now asleep upstairs, and wants to spare him. Sparafucile agrees that if someone else calls at the inn before Rigoletto's return, he can be murdered instead. With a short prayer, Gilda resolves to sacrifice herself. As the storm reaches its height she enters the tavern ('Se pria ch'abbia il mezzo la notte toccato'). Rigoletto returns for the body, which is handed over in a sack. The sound of the Duke's singing in the distance arouses him from his meditations. He tears open the sack and discovers Gilda, still just alive. As she dies, she tries to comfort her distraught father ('V'ho ingannato! colpevole fui'). Monterone's curse is fulfilled.

Rigoletto marks Verdi's most radical break yet with the conventions of ottocento opera: there are no formal entrance arias (*sortite*) for the principal characters and no ensemble finales; for long stretches there is no conventional recitative; and – part of its unique colouring – female voices are excluded from the chorus. Perhaps the most Verdian touch of all is that this revolutionary opera is, on the surface, simpler, more tuneful and more popular than anything he had written before.

The key to *Rigoletto* is to be found in the characterization in Hugo's play and Verdi's attempt to re-create it in musical terms. The split personality of the central character – 'grossly deformed and absurd but inwardly passionate and full of love', as Verdi put it – is the source of those veerings of tone, from darkness to light, from comedy to tragedy, which give *Rigoletto* an almost Shakespearean expressive range and a breadth of sympathy typical of all Verdi's greatest operas from this time forward. The hedonistic Duke makes his entry, not with the customary formal aria, but with a *ballata* (dance song) that falls naturally into place as part of the festivities of the opening scene, and follows this with a duet, accompanied by an instrumental minuet, whose echoes of *Don Giovanni* are unlikely to be accidental. Gilda, a girl wholly lacking in prima donna-ish egotism, finds her proper medium of expression in a series of duets with the two men she loves. Her only aria, 'Caro nome', is a single movement in a unique form: a series of delicately musing variations on a theme, first played by the flutes, that serves as an emblem of her lover's (pretended) name. The Act III quartet, 'Bella figlia dell'amore', is one of Verdi's greatest and most characteristic achievements, resolving a situation of excruciating emotional complexity into a torrent of passionate but exquisitely shaped song.

The impression of some early critics that the vocal writing in *Rigoletto* was 'less splendid' than the orchestration seems largely unintelligible today. But it does highlight the remarkable originality of Verdi's score and the freedom with which he avails himself of colouristic and harmonic resources rarely accorded high priority in the Italian tradition. The Rigoletto–Sparafucile dialogue in Act I, probably inspired by the duettino 'Qui che fai?' from Donizetti's *Lucrezia Borgia*, demonstrates his art of conjuring atmospheric colours from the orchestra and underlining certain phrases ('Sparafucil mi nomino') with harmonic progressions of rare audacity.

RECORDINGS 1. Callas, di Stefano, Gobbi, Zaccaria, La Scala Ch & O, Serafin, EMI, 1955; 2. Cotrubas, Domingo, Cappuccilli, Ghiaurov, Vienna State Op Ch & O, Giulini, DG, 1981

Il trovatore

The Troubadour

Dramma in four parts (2h 15m)
Libretto by Salvatore Cammarano and Leone Emanuele Bardare, after the play *El trovador* by Antonio García Gutiérrez (1836)
Composed ?September 1851–January 1853; rev. for Paris 1856
PREMIERES 19 January 1853, Teatro Apollo, Rome; US: 2 May 1855, Academy of Music, New York; UK: 10 May 1855, Covent Garden, London
CAST Il Conte di Luna *bar*, Leonora *s*, Azucena *ms*, Manrico *t*, Ferrando *b profondo*, Ines *s*, Ruiz *t*, old gypsy *b*, messenger *t*; *satb* chorus of companions of Leonora, nuns, members of the count's household, men-at-arms, gypsies

When Verdi first read García Gutiérrez's play it was, as usual, the strong situations and the characters, especially the gypsy Azucena, that fired his imagination. He saw in the bizarre plot and the insane passions of the protagonists a pretext for more operatic boldness along the lines of *Rigoletto*. He wrote to a friend: 'The more Cammarano provides me with originality and freedom of form, the better I shall be able to do.' And he went on to speculate about an operatic ideal 'in which there were neither cavatinas, nor duets, nor trios, nor choruses . . . and the whole opera was (if I might express it this way) one single piece'. Cammarano had his usual sobering effect on Verdi's revolutionary impulses, but the collaboration on *Il trovatore* was singularly harmonious, and it was tragic that the librettist died in July 1852, when composition was still at an early stage. He had completed a first version of the libretto virtually on his deathbed, but all revisions and additions that Verdi later found necessary were made by a young friend of Cammarano, Leone Emanuele Bardare. They include several of the best-loved numbers, including 'Stride la vampa!', 'Il balen del suo sorriso' and 'D'amor sull'ali rosee'.

The success of the premiere surpassed even that of *Rigoletto*, and the speed with which *Il trovatore* swept the world, literally from Scotland to the South Pacific, was even more sensational. Street-theatre parodies were widely enjoyed (by Verdi as much as anyone) for decades. Despite, indeed in part because of, its demotic tone, *Il trovatore* has come to be seen as one of the composer's supreme achievements, and the Verdian critic – especially if he is Italian – is likely to extol its sublime vulgarity with an enthusiasm that soars to mystic heights: 'the definitive melodrama . . . the Via Crucis of Italian song . . . this is where Verdi's art, which is all in subversion, deformation, sublime caricature, sets the four corners of the world on fire' (B. Barilli). The opera's irrational magical power is encapsulated in a familiar anecdote told of the first Italian prime minister, the utterly unmusical Count Cavour, who, on receiving the Austrian ultimatum that was to bring France into alliance with Piedmont in the war of Italian Unity, could find no more effective way of expressing his excitement than throwing open the window and singing 'Di quella pira' at the top of his voice.

In 1856 Verdi was commissioned to adapt *Il trovatore* for the Paris Opéra by adding an extended ballet to the third act; this version, *Le trouvère*, which included a number of other revisions, was staged under the composer's direction in January 1857.

SYNOPSIS

The action takes place partly in Biscay, partly in Aragon, during the early 15th century.

Part I: The Duel. Scene 1: A hall in the palace of Aliaferia. Ferrando tells the story of Azucena, daughter of a woman who, 20 years before, had been burned for witchcraft because she cast the 'evil eye' on Luna's infant brother. To avenge her, Azucena allegedly threw the infant on the embers of the pyre ('Di due figli vivea padre beato'). Scene 2: The gardens of the palace. In the days before the civil war began, an unknown knight won Leonora's love by his bravery at a tournament. Since then he has sometimes returned in the guise of a troubadour to serenade her ('Tacea la notte placida' – 'Di tale amor che dirsi'). Through the garden her two admirers approach: Luna (quietly) and Manrico (in full-throated song – 'Deserta sulla terra'). Hastening to greet Manrico, Leonora blunders into the arms of Luna. The count is enraged to discover that his rival is Manrico, a rebel in the civil war. The men rush away to duel ('Di geloso amor sprezzato').

Part II: The Gypsy. Scene 1: A ruined hovel at the foot of a mountain in Biscay. Manrico has defeated Luna in the duel but spared his life. In turn wounded by Luna in the wars, he has been nursed back to health by Azucena, supposedly his mother. She sings a ballad about a woman – it proves to be her mother – who was burned at the stake ('Stride la vampa!') and goes on to tell the ghastly story of how, seeking to avenge her, she had thrown into the flames not the infant Luna but her own baby son ('Condotta ell'era in ceppi'). Then, confused, she tries to reassure Manrico: of course he is her son. A messenger brings news that Leonora, believing her beloved dead, is about to take the veil. Manrico hastens away ('Perigliarti ancor languente'). Scene 2: The porch of a place of retreat near Castellor. Luna has also heard of Leonora's intention and plans to abduct her ('Il balen del suo sorriso' – 'Per me, ora fatale'). As Leonora bids farewell to her companions, Luna steps from the shadows. But he is confounded by the appearance of Manrico ('E deggio

. . . e posso crederlo?'), who with his own followers hurries Leonora away.

Part III: The Gypsy's Son. Scene 1: An encampment. Luna's troops prepare to assault Manrico's stronghold ('Squilli, echeggi la tromba guerriera'). Some soldiers have arrested a gypsy on suspicion of spying, and Ferrando recognizes her as Azucena. In terror she calls out for Manrico, so revealing that he is her son ('Giorni poveri vivea'). Luna is exultant. By burning her before the walls of Manrico's fortress, he can torment his rival and at the same time avenge his brother's death ('Deh, rallentate, o barbari'). Scene 2: A room adjacent to the chapel at Castellor. In the beleaguered castle Manrico and Leonora are about to be married ('Ah! sì, ben mio'). Ruiz reports that a pyre has been erected outside the walls and that Azucena is being dragged towards it in chains. Manrico leads off his men to the rescue ('Di quella pira').

Part IV: The Execution. Scene 1: A wing of the palace of Aliaferia. Leonora comes, armed with a phial of poison, to rescue Manrico, who is now imprisoned with his mother. From the castle she hears monkish chants of death and Manrico's own singing (the so-called 'Miserere' scene: 'D'amor sull'ali rosee' – 'Miserere d'un alma già vicina' – 'Ah, che la morte ognora' – 'Tu vedrai che amore in terra'). She accosts Luna. At first deaf to her appeal, he assents when she offers herself as the price for Manrico's freedom. She takes the poison ('Mira, di acerbe lagrime' – 'Vivrà! . . . contende il giubilo'). Scene 2: A horrid dungeon. Manrico comforts the fearful Azucena and she sleeps ('Si, la stanchezza m'opprime, o figlio' – 'Ai nostri monti . . . ritorneremo'). Leonora comes to free Manrico. Refusing to leave without her, he begins to suspect the bargain she may have made with Luna and, since she makes no denial, denounces her ('Parlar non vuoi? . . . Balen tremenda!'). When she sinks dying at his feet, he is overcome with remorse. Luna enters ('Prima che d'altri vivere') and consigns Manrico to immediate execution, forcing Azucena to watch from her prison window. As Manrico dies, she reveals to Luna that he has killed his own brother. Her mother is avenged!

Despite Verdi's first thoughts on the subject, *Il trovatore* is an opera that rejoices unashamedly in the peculiar strengths of traditional Romantic melodrama and generally makes fewer demands of the singers' acting skills or intelligence than does *Rigoletto*. Caruso once famously, if discouragingly, remarked that all one needed for a good performance were the four greatest singers in the world. In most scenes the traditional forms are clearly audible, contributing much to the sense of concentrated emotional intensity so characteristic of the score. Many numbers owe much of their expressive force to a style of melody that the composer had been developing from his earliest years and that in *Il trovatore* reaches full maturity. Typically the arias start from quiet, sometimes even unremarkable openings, gradually unfolding in mounting waves of melody to culminate in grand engulfing phrases employing the full extension of the voice. The opera's extraordinary range of scenic, psychological and musical expression is best seen in the so-called 'Miserere' scene, where the customary ingredients of scena, cantabile and cabaletta are enriched by episodes of ecclesiastical chanting, by a declamatory soliloquy for Leonora accompanied by shuddering ostinato rhythms for the full orchestra, and by the heart-broken ecstasy of Manrico's offstage troubadour song. The masterly juxtaposition and combination of these elements make the 'Miserere' scene a supreme moment not only of Italian Romantic melodrama but of the whole art of opera.

For some years the rebel, the nonconformist and the outcast had been favourite figures in Verdi's operas. In *Il trovatore* a matching sense of alienation is vividly expressed in the music. The finely nuanced cantabiles of Leonora and Luna leave no doubt of their aristocratic breeding, but the music of Azucena and (more equivocally) Manrico is popular and balladesque in manner – particularly distinctive are the pervasive strumming rhythms in 3/8 metre.

RECORDINGS 1. Callas, Barbieri, di Stefano, Panerai, La Scala Ch & O, Karajan, EMI, 1956 (cut); 2. Stella, Cossotto, Bergonzi, Bastianini, La Scala Ch & O, Serafin, DG, 1962; 3. L. Price, Cossotto, Domingo, Milnes, Ambrosian Op Ch, NPO, Mehta, RCA, 1969

La traviata

The Fallen Woman

Melodramma in three acts (2h)
Libretto by Francesco Maria Piave, after the play *La dame aux camélias* by Alexandre Dumas *fils* (1852)
Composed January–February 1853, rev. March–April 1854
PREMIERES 6 March 1853, La Fenice, Venice; rev. version: 6 May 1854, Teatro Gallo di San Benedetto, Venice; UK: 24 May 1856, Her Majesty's Theatre, Haymarket, London; US: 3 December 1856, Academy of Music, New York
CAST Violetta Valéry *s*, Flora Bervoix *ms*, Annina *s*, Alfredo Germont *t*, Giorgio Germont *bar*, Gastone, Viscomte de Letorières *t*, Baron Douphol *bar*, Marquis d'Obigny *b*, Doctor Grenvil *b*, Giuseppe *t*, Flora's servant *b*, messenger *b*; *satb* chorus of ladies and gentlemen, friends of Violetta and Flora, matadors, picadors, gypsies, servants of Violetta and Flora, masquers; dancers

For extended periods between August 1847 and March 1852 Verdi lived in Paris, It was the time when the new artistic vogue of realism was emerging, and *La traviata* is the most eloquent witness to the movement's influence on him. He may well have seen Dumas's *La dame aux camélias* when it was first staged in February 1852, but it was not until October, when he eventually acquired a copy of the play, that he decided to make an opera of it.

Warm memories of the *Rigoletto* premiere made it easy for the management of La Fenice in Venice to engage Verdi for another opera. In addition to its high musical standards, Venice had the advantage of an unusually liberal censorship, without which *La traviata* would hardly have been possible at all. Nevertheless, despite the fact that this opera is one of his most intimate and personal creations, Verdi, having heard bad reports of the singers, approached its premiere with less eagerness than might have been expected.

There is no truth in the oft-repeated tale that the opera's initial failure was due to its contemporary setting. In fact, despite Verdi's wish to have it performed in modern dress, it was set '*c.*1700', and it was not until the 1880s – by which time, of course, the 1850s were a generation distant – that 'realistic' productions were attempted. Nor is there anything to support the claim that the plump Fanny Salvini-Donatelli made a laughably inept consumptive heroine: her performance in the role of Violetta was one of the few things at the premiere that met with general approval. The root of the problem, according to Felice Varesi, the distinguished baritone for whom Verdi had already composed the roles of Macbeth and Rigoletto and who now appeared as the first Giorgio Germont, was that Verdi had composed the opera with sublime disregard for the vocal capabilities of his principals and that 'this caused much strong feeling among the Venetian public'. After the premiere, Verdi withdrew the opera until the opportunity arose to stage it with an ideal cast and/or to revise it.

Antonio Gallo, impresario of the Teatro San Benedetto, had meanwhile been impressed with *La traviata* and bombarded the publisher, Ricordi, with requests to stage the work in his own theatre. Eventually Verdi consented, and took back five movements of his autograph score for revision (all from

Acts II and III: the Violetta–Germont duet, the cabaletta of Germont's aria, the largo of the Act II finale, the Violetta–Alfredo duet and the Act III finale). In this revised form *La traviata* was enthusiastically received, and it soon rivalled *Il trovatore* in popularity, even in Victorian England, where its premiere had been greeted by a denunciatory leading article in *The Times* and where early Covent Garden productions refrained from supplying translations, out of consideration – it was implied – for patrons' moral wellbeing.

SYNOPSIS

The scene is set in Paris and its vicinity in about 1850.

Act I: A salon in Violetta's house, August. At a party given by the notorious courtesan, Violetta Valéry, Alfredo is introduced as an admirer. After a *brindisi* ('Libiam ne' lieti calici'), the guests move to an adjoining room for dancing. Violetta, afflicted by a fit of consumptive coughing, remains behind and finds herself attended by a solicitous Alfredo. He urges her to abandon a way of life that can lead only to an early grave ('Un dì felice'). The party guests leave, and Violetta muses: could Alfredo really be the redeemer of whom she has dreamed ('È strano! . . . è strano!' – 'Ah, fors'è lui')? She shrugs off her foolish fancy ('Sempre libera degg'io').

Act II, Scene 1: A country house near Paris, January. For three months Alfredo and Violetta have lived together in the country. But Alfredo's happiness turns to shame when by chance he learns that Violetta has been selling her possessions to maintain them ('De' miei bollenti spiriti' – 'O mio rimorso! o infamia!'), and he hastens away to Paris to rearrange his affairs. Violetta is visited by an elderly gentleman, who proves to be Germont senior. He begs her to leave Alfredo for the sake of a younger daughter, whose prospects are threatened by her brother's liaison ('Pura siccome un angelo'), He dismisses all Violetta's hopes of happiness as delusions, transient as youth and beauty ('Non sapete quale affetto' – 'Un dì, quando le veneri'). Finally, he extracts from her a promise to renounce Alfredo for ever ('Dite alla giovine' – 'Morrò! . . . la mia memoria'). When Alfredo returns, Violetta bids him a passionate farewell, pretending that she is absenting herself only for a few hours. A little later he is brought a letter telling the truth: she is returning to a former protector, Baron Douphol. While Germont tries to comfort him ('Di Provenza il mar, il suol' – 'No, non udrai rimproveri'), Alfredo broods on vengeance. Scene 2: A gallery in Flora's palace. Flora's guests are entertained with masquerades of gypsies and bullfighters. Alfredo arrives, followed by Violetta and Douphol, and wins large sums of money at cards. The guests are summoned to dinner, but a moment later Violetta and Alfredo return alone. Fearing for his life, she urges him to leave the party. Instead, he summons the revellers and, announcing that he is paying off Violetta for services rendered, hurls the money he has just won at her feet. At that moment his father arrives. In the finale the multitude of different passions provoked by Alfredo's insult are expressed.

Act III: Violetta's bedroom, February. Despite Dr Grenvil's encouraging words, Violetta knows that she has only a few hours to live. She reads over a letter from Germont. Alfredo, who fled abroad after wounding Douphol in a duel, has been told of her sacrifice and is hurrying back to Paris for her forgiveness. But alone and dying, Violetta has, realistically, only God's mercy to depend upon ('Addio, del passato'). The sound of Shrove Tuesday revels in the street contrasts ironically with the desolation within. Alfredo does return, however, and the lovers dream of escape from Paris, of health and happiness. But as Violetta tries to dress she collapses, and both realize she is on the point of death ('Parigi, o cara, noi lasceremo' – 'Gran Dio! morir sì giovane'). Grenvil returns, and Germont too arrives, anxious to make amends for the suffering he has caused. Giving Alfredo a medallion to remember her by and praying that he will find a wife more worthy of him, Violetta dies ('Prendi; quest'è l'immagine').

La traviata shares with *Rigoletto* and *Il trovatore* a magnificent directness of utterance. The three operas embody the principles of ottocento opera with sovereign mastery and freedom and an unerring sense of dramatic purpose, and popular opinion is not deceived in seeing in them the ripest harvest of Italian Romantic melodrama. *La traviata* is the most elegant and refined of the three. Typically its profusion of 3/8 rhythms – as common here as in *Il trovatore* – are evocative less of the primitive strummings of popular music than of the sensual swaying of the waltz. Its scoring is also the most delicate, its translucence serving in part (in the prelude and in much of Act III) as a musical symbol of the consumptive Violetta.

The clarity of the plot and the overwhelming presence of a single moral idea – that of an ideal of love that survives all man's attempts to exploit and corrupt it – prompt Verdi to make fuller use than in any earlier opera of a single recurring theme. In the cantabile of the Act I duet Alfredo and Violetta are characteristically contrasted, the hesitant phrases of the shy idealist being juxtaposed and later counterpointed with the fickle brilliance of the 'woman of pleasure'. Alfredo's solo rises to a magnificent climactic hymn to love ('Di quell'amor'), and in Violetta's great solo scena at the close of Act I, she takes up the same theme at the climax to the cantabile ('Ah, fors'è lui'), where she dreams of the true love that might one day redeem her. Between the two statements of her cabaletta ('Sempre libera'), it returns again, sung by Alfredo from the street below her window; and this is a masterstroke of dramatic psychology as well as a coup de théâtre, for to remind Violetta of Alfredo's love as she is in the midst of reasserting her philosophy of pleasure is to turn what might have been merely a brilliant cabaletta into a conflict of hedonism and idealism. In Act III the same theme recurs twice more, now in purely orchestral form, for all illusory hope has vanished, and Violetta cherishes only the memory of what might have been.

Germont is as vividly characterized as the two lovers, his music made up in part of nostalgic Bellinian memories ('Pura siccome un angelo', 'Di Provenza il mar, il suol'), in part of songs in which his didactic manner is suggested by downbeats heavy with flurries of short notes ('Un dì, quando le veneri', 'No, non udrai rimproveri'). His Act II duet with Violetta is as magnificent a musico-dramatic achievement as anything Verdi ever wrote. The inexorable tragic thrust of the argument is embodied with rare finesse in a seemingly kaleidoscopic, but in fact masterfully controlled, sequence of short movements.

RECORDINGS 1. Callas, Kraus, Sereni, Lisbon San Carlos Th Ch & O, Ghione, EMI, 1958 (cut, live); 2. Cotrubas, Domingo, Milnes, Bavarian State Op Ch & O, C. Kleiber, DG, 1977 (cut); 3. Gheorghiu, Lopardo, Nucci, Covent Garden Ch & O, Solti, Decca, 1994 (live)

Un ballo in maschera

A Masked Ball

Melodramma in three acts (2h 15m)
Libretto by Antonio Somma, after the libretto *Gustave III* by Augustin Eugène Scribe (1833)
Composed autumn 1857–early 1858
PREMIERES 17 February 1859, Teatro Apollo, Rome; US: 11 February 1861, Academy of Music, New York; UK: 15 June 1861, Lyceum (English Opera House), London
CAST 'American' version: Riccardo, Count of Warwick *t*, Renato *bar*, Amelia *s*, Ulrica *c*, Oscar *s*, Silvano *b*, Samuel *b*, Tom *b*, judge *t*, Amelia's servant *t*; 'Swedish' version: Gustavus III *t*, Count Anckarstroem *bar*, Amelia *s*,

Mademoiselle Arvidson *c*, Oscar *s*, Christian *b*, Count Ribbing *b*, Count Horn *b*, judge *t*, Amelia's servant *t*; *satb* chorus of deputies, officers, sailors, guards, men, women and children of the populace, gentlemen, followers of Samuel/Ribbing and Tom/Horn, servants, masquers and dancing couples

While in Venice in 1853 for the production of *La traviata*, Verdi became friendly with the lawyer and playwright Antonio Somma; and he was delighted when Somma, a poet of some distinction in his day, volunteered to write a libretto for him. But the subject proposed did not, Verdi explained, have 'the variety my crazy brain would like'. And therefore, though the poet knew next to nothing about the technicalities of libretto-writing and needed a great deal of detailed advice, Verdi put him to work on *King Lear*, the libretto of which he managed to complete to the composer's satisfaction. Having signed a contract with the San Carlo at Naples early in 1857, Verdi spent several months negotiating with the theatre with a view to producing an opera on this theme. The plan eventually foundered, ostensibly because of his lack of confidence in the cast. With time running out, he now resorted to desperate measures, abandoning the search for a new subject and taking up an old libretto by Scribe, *Gustave III, ou Le bal masqué*, first set by Auber in 1833.

First approaches to the Neapolitan censors resulted in a crop of irritating demands: the king must become a duke, resident anywhere in the north 'except Norway or Sweden'; the action must be set in an age that believed in witchcraft; the hero must be tormented by remorse, etc. So when Verdi arrived in Naples early in 1858 to start rehearsals, the libretto, now called *Una vendetta in domino*, was set in 17th-century Pomerania; but the prospects of even this version being permitted vanished on 13 January, when an assassination attempt was made on the life of Napoleon III. The censors now demanded more fundamental alterations and engaged a Neapolitan poet to rewrite the libretto (*Adelia degli Adimari*, set in 14th-century Florence). When the composer refused to have anything to do with a text that was quite alien to the spirit of his music, he was sued for breach of contract. The case was eventually settled out of court, but meanwhile Verdi had been in touch with the impresario Jacovacci about the possibility of staging the opera in Rome. Here, after some preliminary skirmishing, the censors agreed to let the subject stand, provided only that the hero be downgraded to a count and the action be removed from Europe altogether. It was Somma who, from the alternatives offered, chose colonial Boston; but he remained piqued with the indignities to which his libretto had been subjected and refused to let his name appear on it.

Despite some shortcomings in the casting, *Un ballo in maschera* was an immediate triumph. Though it was too sophisticated a score to find ready acceptance in smaller or provincial theatres, it is the only Verdi opera between *La traviata* and *Aida* to have been regularly performed and consistently admired through all changes of taste and fashion. Among the more 'interesting' revivals may be mentioned the opera's Boston premiere, when patrons were invited to join in the masked ball, extended for the occasion by a specially composed galop by the conductor, Verdi's pupil and friend, Emanuele Muzio. Verdi was quite happy with the Americanization of his opera and never expressed any desire to transfer it back to Sweden, but, since a Danish production in Copenhagen in 1935, there has been an increasing tendency to restore the opera to its original setting.

SYNOPSIS ('AMERICAN' VERSION)

The action takes place in Boston and its vicinity at the end of the 17th century.

Act I, Scene 1: A hall in the governor's residence. Officials attend on Riccardo, the easy-going governor of Boston. Most are devoted to him, but there are among them some conspirators, led by Samuel and Tom. Riccardo's chief concern is the guest list for a forthcoming ball; the name of Amelia plunges him into romantic reverie ('La rivedrà nell'estasi'), and he is embarrassed to be interrupted by her husband Renato, his friend and secretary. Renato brings news of a conspiracy and reminds him that his people's destiny depends upon him ('Alla vita che t'arride'). A judge demands an order of banishment on the enchantress Ulrica, but Riccardo heeds rather the pleas for clemency voiced by the pageboy Oscar ('Volta la terrea'). He proposes that he and his officials disguise themselves and visit Ulrica to discover what she really does ('Ogni cura si doni al diletto'). Scene 2: The enchantress's dwelling. Disguised as a fisherman, Riccardo enters Ulrica's hovel and finds her at her conjuring watched by a throng of women and children ('Re dell'abisso, affrettati'). She prophesies wealth for Silvano, a sailor, and Riccardo drops a commission into his pocket. One of Amelia's servants requests a private audience for his mistress: she seeks a cure for a guilty love that torments her. Ulrica's remedy involves picking herbs at midnight at the foot of the gallows. Amelia is determined to do what duty demands ('Segreta, acerba cura' – 'Della città all'occaso' – 'Consentimi, o Signore'), and the eavesdropping Riccardo resolves to join her. Amelia departs. Court officials now crowd into the cave, and Riccardo asks to be told his fortune ('Dì tu se fedele'). When Ulrica warns of imminent death at the hands of the man who first shakes his hand, Riccardo laughs it off ('È scherzo od è follia'). Renato joins them and is greeted by a handshake. Riccardo's identity is revealed, and Silvano leads an anthem in his praise ('O figlio d'Inghilterra').

Act II: A solitary field on the outskirts of Boston. Amelia is terrified by spectral imaginings and tormented by the conflict of love and duty ('Ecco l'orrido campo' – 'Ma dall'arido stelo divulsa'). When Riccardo appears, she repulses him. Let him spare her good name and keep faith with his friend, but he presses her to confess her love ('Non sai tu che se l'anima mia' – 'Oh, qual soave brivido'). Renato arrives to warn Riccardo that conspirators are closing an ambush round him. Seconded by Amelia, who has veiled herself at her husband's approach, he persuades Riccardo to take an indirect route to the city; meanwhile, he will escort the veiled lady back without speaking to her ('Odi tu come fremono cupi'). But they are waylaid by the conspirators, and in the ensuing argument Amelia lets fall her veil. Renato's humiliation is a source of ribald mirth ('Ve', se di notte qui colla sposa'). Determined to avenge himself, he invites Samuel and Tom to his house on the morrow; then he leads his wife home.

Act III, Scene 1: A study in Renato's house. Finding Renato determined to kill her, Amelia begs to be allowed to bid their son farewell ('Morrò, ma prima in grazia'). Left alone, Renato reflects that death is too severe a fate for her, but not for Riccardo, who has poisoned every source of his friend's happiness ('Eri tu'). When Samuel and Tom arrive, he demands to join in their conspiracy ('Dunque l'onta di tutti sol una'). An argument about who should kill Riccardo is resolved in Renato's favour by the drawing of lots. Oscar brings an invitation to a masked ball at the governor's residence, and Amelia is filled with foreboding ('Di che fulgor, che musiche'). The conspirators agree on costumes and a password. Scene 2: A sumptuous small apartment in Riccardo's residence. Riccardo is resolved to send Amelia and Renato back to England ('Ma se m'è forza perderti'). Oscar brings a letter warning him that an assassination attempt will be made during the evening, but, as this will be his last farewell to Amelia, he hastens recklessly to the ball. Scene 3: A huge and richly decorated ballroom, splendidly illuminated and adorned for the ball. The conspirators despair of finding Riccardo, but Renato detects Oscar who, after some teasing ('Saper vorreste'), unwittingly betrays his disguise. Amelia urges Riccardo to escape. He tells her his plans and is bidding farewell when Renato stabs him. In the finale, the dying Riccardo swears that Amelia is chaste, Renato is overcome with remorse, and all mourn the death of their beloved governor.

The central moment in any Italian Romantic opera was the ensemble – the *pezzo concertato* – at the heart of its Act I or Act II finale: some revelation or confrontation freezes the action, and the tension is discharged in ecstatic song. What is extraordinary in *Un ballo in maschera* is that in both *pezzi concertati* – that in Act I prompted by Ulrica's prophecy that Riccardo is soon to die, and that in Act II occurring when the veiled lady escorted by Renato proves to be his own wife – the tension is resolved not merely in song, but in laughter too, nervous in Act I, mocking in Act II. This is Verdi's most successful essay in the blending of tragedy and comedy in Shakespeare's manner. The sombre tale of guilty passion and murderous jealousy is lit up by flashes of 'brilliance and chivalry', and by an all-pervasive 'aura of gaiety' (Verdi).

This distinctive chiaroscuro is already unmistakable in the prelude and introduction. In both movements a darkly muttering theme, associated throughout the opera with the conspirators, casts its shadow over the otherwise serene harmonies and impulsive lyricism. The opera's ambivalent tone owes much to the blending of Verdi's native style with traits borrowed from French opera, such as the rhythmic élan of the galop-like Act I ensemble 'Ogni cura si doni al diletto'. French influence is particularly clear in the music of the pageboy, Oscar – a projection of the insouciant gaiety of Riccardo's own character – whose arias are in the French couplet form (strophes with refrain). Both numbers, like several others in the opera, seem to borrow hints from Auber's setting of the text.

If the opera has nevertheless sometimes been described as Verdi's *Tristan* it is because no other of his mature operas places the love duet so centrally or makes of it the dramatic fulcrum of the score or invests it with such flaming incandescence. The transfiguring of the link between cantabile and cabaletta ('La mia vita . . . l'universo' etc.) into an ecstatic lyrical climax, and the subtly transformed recurrence of this before the duet verse of the cabaletta help ensure that the emotional exaltation achieved in the early part of the scene is sustained to the close, without interruption or anticlimax.

RECORDINGS 1. Callas, Ratti, di Stefano, Gobbi, La Scala Ch & O, Votto, EMI, 1956 (live); 2. L. Price, Verrett, Bergonzi, Merrill, RCA Italiana Ch & O, Leinsdorf, RCA, 1967; 3. M. Price, Ludwig, Pavarotti, Bruson, London Op Ch, Nat PO, Solti, Decca, 1982/3

La forza del destino

The Force of Destiny

Opera in four acts (3h 15m)
Libretto by Francesco Maria Piave, based on the drama *Don Alvaro, o La fuerza del sino* (1835) by Angel de Saavedra, Duke of Rivas, and incorporating material adapted from *Wallensteins Lager* (1799) by Johann Christoph Friedrich von Schiller, translated by Andrea Maffei (1869 revisions by Antonio Ghislanzoni)
Composed, but not fully orchestrated, August–November 1861; rev. autumn 1868–early 1869
PREMIERES 22 November 1862, Imperial (Bolshoi) Theatre, St Petersburg; US: 24 February 1865, Academy of Music, New York; UK: 22 June 1867, Her Majesty's Theatre, Haymarket, London; rev. version: 27 February 1869, La Scala, Milan
CAST Il Marchese di Calatrava *b*, Leonora *s*, Don Carlo di Vargas *bar*, Don Alvaro *t*, Preziosilla *ms*, Father Superior (Padre Guardiano) *b*, Fra

Melitone *bar*, Curra *s*, Alcalde *b*, Mastro Trabuco *t*, Spanish military surgeon *t*; *satb* chorus of muleteers, Spanish and Italian peasants, Spanish and Italian soldiers of various ranks and their orderlies, Italian recruits, Franciscan friars, peasant girls, *vivandières*; ballet: Spanish and Italian peasant women and *vivandières*, Spanish and Italian soldiers; extras: host, hostess, inn servants, muleteers, Italian and Spanish soldiers of all ranks, drummers, buglers, peasants, peasant women and girls of both nations, tumbler, various pedlars

The 16 'years in the galleys' had ended with *Un ballo in maschera*. By the close of the 1850s Verdi was leading the life of a country gentleman, prosperous, world famous, with no obligation to compose operas except on his own terms, when a commission really interested him. *La forza del destino* resulted from the first such commission: an invitation from the Imperial Theatre of St Petersburg for the 1861–2 season. Verdi was in theory given a free hand over the choice of subject, though in fact his first proposal, Victor Hugo's *Ruy Blas*, was unceremoniously rejected by the censor. His choice eventually alighted on *Don Alvaro* by one of Hugo's Spanish imitators, the Duke of Rivas, an already rambling play, which Verdi elaborated further by incorporating into the encampment scene episodes from Schiller's *Wallensteins Lager*. The premiere was delayed by almost a year; for when Verdi arrived in Russia late in 1861, he found the prima donna unsatisfactory and refused to proceed if she could not be replaced.

The opera stands alone in the Verdi canon in having an abstract idea for its title. By now, Verdi was more insistent than ever that the age of 'operas of cavatinas, duets, etc.' was past and that the future belonged to 'operas of ideas'. *La forza del destino*, inspired by what he called a 'powerful, singular and truly vast' play, is one of the clearest demonstrations of this conviction. And because the 'idea' concerns chance – the sheer random fortuitousness with which fate chooses its victims – the normal cut of a Verdian opera, which is concentrated, concise and thrusting, is replaced by a vast, shambling panorama of loosely related episodes during which the principals disappear from the scene for whole acts at a time.

Staged at a period when Russian musical life was in ferment, *La forza del destino* met with a confused reception. It earned the composer the Order of St Stanislas, but most critics found it wearisomely long, and it did not escape a hostile demonstration – apparently from a nationalist faction – at the third performance. Nevertheless, it is tempting to see in its chronicle-like panorama of life in time of war one of the prototypes of *Boris Godunov* and thus of a whole tradition of Russian opera. Early performances in Italy were also only equivocally successful, largely because of dissatisfaction with the carnage at the opera's blasphemous and nihilistic close. After much thought, Verdi and the librettist Ghislanzoni (Piave had been incapacitated by a stroke in 1867) arrived at a visually more discreet and spiritually more resigned denouement, in which the influence of Alessandro Manzoni, the revered grand old man of Italian literature, has plausibly been detected. At the same time the events in Act III were reordered; many scenes were revised in detail, and the familiar full-length overture was composed to replace the original prelude. Even in revised form, the opera established itself slowly, probably because it needed a first-rate conductor to co-ordinate it successfully. A famous production at Dresden in 1926 under Fritz Busch was a milestone in the 20th-century Verdi renaissance. By the early 1990s some interest was being shown in reintroducing the original St Petersburg version.

SYNOPSIS

The scene is set in Spain and Italy towards the middle of the 18th century.

Act I: Seville. Leonora, daughter of the

Marchese di Calatrava, has agreed to elope with Alvaro, a South American half-caste prince. The thought of abandoning her home fills her with remorse ('Me pellegrina ed orfana'), but when Alvaro arrives, she soon declares herself ready to follow him to the ends of the earth ('Seguirti fino agli ultimi' – 'Sospiro, luce ed anima'). They are interrupted by her father. Alvaro throws his pistol at the Marchese's feet as a gesture of surrender. The gun goes off, fatally wounding the old man, who dies cursing his daughter.

Act II: The village of Hornachuelos and vicinity. Scene 1: Large kitchen in the inn. The muleteer Trabuco arrives with an unknown youth (Leonora in disguise). Among the crowd is her brother Carlo, who is pursuing Leonora and Alvaro, intent on avenging his father's death; he too is disguised, as a student. The gypsy girl Preziosilla tells of the wars in Italy, singing the praises of military life ('Al suon del tamburo'). Pilgrims pass by, and those in the inn join in their prayer ('Su noi prostrati e supplici'). The Alcalde now suggests that the student tell them who he is. Posing as one Pereda, Carlo claims to have left university to help a friend hunt down his sister and her seducer, but the villain has escaped across the seas ('Son Pereda, son ricco d'onore'). Scene 2: The monastery of Our Lady of the Angels, outside Hornachuelos. Having overheard her brother's story Leonora feels betrayed by Alvaro's flight. She prays for forgiveness and a quiet mind ('Madre, pietosa Vergine'). The Father Superior, Padre Guardiano, has been forewarned of her visit and after questioning her ('Più tranquilla l'alma sento') agrees to help her live as an anchorite in a nearby cave ('Sull'alba il piede all'eremo' – 'Tua grazia, o Dio'). The friars vow to respect the young penitent's solitude. The Father Superior leads them in prayer ('La Vergine degli Angeli'), and Leonora hastens to her hiding place.

Act III: In Italy, near to Velletri. Scene 1: A wood at night. Alvaro, now in the Spanish army, muses on the harshness of destiny and, believing Leonora to be dead, prays to her ('O tu che in seno agl'angeli'). Cries for help send him hurrying to the rescue. He returns with Carlo. They introduce themselves (using false names), and vow eternal comradeship. A surgeon and some orderlies watch the battle: the Italian–Spanish forces carry the day, but they are dismayed to see 'Don Federico Herreros' (Alvaro) fall injured. He is borne in, attended by Carlo, who is astonished by his violent reaction to the name Calatrava. Before Alvaro receives medical attention, he entrusts to Carlo some papers, to be destroyed in the event of his death ('Solenne in quest'ora'). The suspicion dawns on Carlo that his new friend is the long-pursued Alvaro. He resists the temptation to read the papers ('Urna fatale del mio destino'), but looking through Alvaro's other belongings finds a portrait of his sister, Leonora. When the surgeon pronounces Alvaro safe, Carlo exults: now for revenge! ('Egli è salvo! oh gioia immenso'). Scene 2: A military encampment near Velletri. Carlo challenges Alvaro to a duel. Reminding Carlo of their oath of friendship, Alvaro protests his innocence; he learns that Leonora is alive, and joyfully imagines that all may yet be well. But Carlo is adamant: both Alvaro and Leonora must die to satisfy family honour. The two men are soon fighting furiously ('No, d'un imene il vincolo' – 'Stolto! fra noi dischiudesi'). They are separated by a patrol, and Alvaro decides to retreat to a monastery. As reveille sounds, the camp comes to life. Preziosilla is telling fortunes ('Venite all'indovina'), Trabuco is bargaining with some soldiers, peasants are begging for food, and new recruits are consoled by the *vivandières* (Tarantella). The merry-making is interrupted by Melitone's 'sermon' ('Toh, toh! . . . Poffare il mondo!'), which incenses the soldiers. Preziosilla beats the drum to turn their thoughts to serious business ('Rataplan, rataplan, della gloria'). [1862: the scene between Alvaro and Carlo follows the encampment scene and ends differently. They fight their duel to the bitter end, Alvaro, as he imagines, killing his adversary. In despair he returns to the battlefield to seek death ('S'affronti la morte').]

Act IV: In the vicinity of Hornachuelos. Scene 1: A courtyard inside the monastery of Our Lady of the Angels. Five years have elapsed. Melitone is serving soup to the poor. As he and the Father Superior talk of one 'Padre Rafaello', we realize that this mysterious friar must be Alvaro ('Del mondo i disinganni'). The bell rings, and Carlo enters. He demands to see 'Rafaello', and brusquely announces his intention of killing him. Alvaro's saintly behaviour provokes only insult. Finally, he snatches the sword Carlo offers, and they hasten away to duel. Scene 2: A gorge between precipitous rocks. Leonora has found no peace of mind ('Pace, pace, mio Dio!'). She hears the sound of fighting, and Alvaro rushes in, entreating the hermit to give absolution to a dying man. As Leonora rings the bell to summon the Father Superior, she and Alvaro recognize one another. He speeds her away to comfort her brother. A moment later a scream is heard: Carlo, even as he died, could not forgive Leonora and stabbed her as she bent over him. Alvaro's blasphemous despair is softened by her prayers and the grave words of the Father Superior ('Non imprecare; umiliati'), and as Leonora dies Alvaro too glimpses some hope of redemption. [1862: the duel and the stabbing of Leonora take place on stage. The opera ends with Alvaro throwing himself into a ravine as the Father Superior and monks approach.]

The nature of the subject means that in *La forza del destino* episodic genre scenes and 'character songs' play a more conspicuous part than in any other Verdi opera. At the same time the overriding dramatic idea of a malevolent destiny is embodied in a theme – often described as the leitmotif of Destiny – that pervades much of the opera: it launches the overture, is heard at the tragic climax of Act I when Calatrava disturbs the eloping lovers and is accidentally killed, and recurs in several later scenes, particularly those in which Leonora is haunted by a pursuing nemesis. No other theme is used as extensively, but the long clarinet concertino that prefaces Act III and punctuates its opening scene – it was composed for St Petersburg's star clarinettist, Ernesto Cavallini, an old acquaintance from Verdi's student days – is a remarkable example of a thematic reminiscence (from the Act I duet, where Alvaro dreams of a happy future with Leonora) developed into an independent movement (in a context of heart-broken memories).

For all the novelty of the overall design, the familiar Verdi is present in every scene, and his musical language is developing in the most idiosyncratic ways. Act I, one of the fastest-moving and most densely packed acts in all Verdi, is full of such individual touches. Its opening scene, pitching the spectator into the middle of the dramatic action, is a casual dialogue set against a quietly sustained orchestral backcloth and marks the composer's final rejection of the formal, decorative introductions of operatic tradition. Even when he does use traditional forms, his fast-developing musical language transfigures them. This is especially the case with the cabalettas – where once they derived their energy from pounding rhythmic repetitions, most of them now acquire their urgency from the fleetly moving basses and rapidly changing harmonies. Leonora's Act I aria 'Me pellegrina ed orfana' is one of the few pieces that has tangible links with the long-pondered *King Lear*. The text is taken directly from Somma's *Lear* libretto, though obviously that does not prove that the music was intended for *Lear*. In the improvisatory freedom of form, the chromatic nuances of the harmony and the flexibility of the instrumentation, it encapsulates much of Verdi's mature lyrical style.

RECORDINGS (1862 version) Gorchakova, Borodina, Grigorian, Putilin, Kit, Kirov Op Ch & O, Gergiev, Philips, 1995; (1869 version) 1. L. Price, Cossotto, Domingo, Milnes, Giaiotti, John Alldis Ch, LSO, Levine, RCA, 1986; 2. Freni, Zajic, Domingo, Zancanaro, Plishka, La Scala Ch & O, Muti, EMI, 1986 (live)

Don Carlos/Don Carlo

Grand opera in five acts (3h 30m)/
Opera in four acts (3h)
French libretto by Joseph Méry and Camille du Locle, based on the dramatic poem *Don Carlos, Infant von Spanien* by Johann Christoph Friedrich von Schiller (1787) and on the play *Philippe II, roi d'Espagne* by Eugène Cormon (1846); libretto of four-act version rev. du Locle; Italian translation by Angelo Zanardini, based on Achille de Lauzières's translation of the original five-act opera
Composed early 1866–February 1867, rev. November–December 1872; rev. (four-act) version June 1882–March 1883
PREMIERES 11 March 1867, Opéra, Paris; UK: 4 June 1867, Covent Garden, London; US: 12 April 1877, Academy of Music, New York; four-act version: 10 January 1884, La Scala, Milan; hybrid five-act version: 29 December 1886, Modena
CAST Philip II *b*, Don Carlos *t*, Rodrigo, Marquis of Posa *bar*, Grand Inquisitor *b*, monk *b*, Elisabeth de Valois *s*, Princess Eboli *ms*, Thibault *s*, voice from Heaven *s*, Countess d'Aremberg *silent*, woman in mourning *silent*, Count de Lerma *t*, royal herald *t*, 6 Flemish Deputies 6 *b*, 6 Inquisitors 6 *b*; *satb* chorus of lords and ladies of the French and Spanish courts, woodcutters, populace, pages, guards of Henri II and Philip II, monks, officers of the Inquisition, soldiers

Together with Shakespeare and Hugo, Schiller was one of the playwrights Verdi most revered, but the size and ideological complexity of his plays made operatic adaptation difficult and, *I masnadieri* and *Luisa Miller* notwithstanding, it is not until *Don Carlos* that we find Verdi getting to grips with the great German dramatist in all his rambling magnificence. The death of Meyerbeer in 1864 prompted the management of the Opéra to approach Verdi with a libretto found among Meyerbeer's papers in the hope of persuading him to make a return to Paris. He dismissed the libretto out of hand, but when they returned to the charge the following year and offered him a scenario for *Don Carlos*, it 'really thrilled him'. He went to Paris in November 1865, signed a contract and spent some four months there, hammering out a libretto with Méry and du Locle, before returning to Busseto in the spring to complete the composition. The Fontainebleau scene and the *auto da fé* were the most substantial of several incidents borrowed from a contemporary play on Philip II by Eugène Cormon.

In its stirring depiction of the conflict between libertarianism and dogmatism Schiller's play appealed to some of Verdi's deepest convictions. Every scene of the opera breathes a passionate high-mindedness that makes it, for many listeners, the most inspiring of all his works. Sadly, as in the past, the Paris Opéra disappointed the composer's hopes, and the endless tedium of the rehearsals, the lack of spontaneity and enthusiasm in the performance and the multitude of opinionated busybodies who hung about the place were to provide him with material for satirical reflection for many a year.

No other Verdi opera has so complicated a stage history and none survives in so many different forms. The *edizione integrale* distinguishes eight 'authentic' versions of the score. For all practical purposes these may be reduced to three, all of which now have a place in the repertoire: the five-act French grand opera (1867), the four-act Italian *Don Carlo* (1884) and the hybrid Modena version (1886), which, broadly speaking, reinstates the original Act I while leaving the remaining acts in their revised 1884 form. What exactly constitutes the 1867 score is a complicated question. The immense length of the opera led to cuts being made during rehearsals, and when at the first dress rehearsal it was found to be still well over three and a half hours long (excluding intervals) it was cut more drastically (it had to finish before midnight, as the last trains to the Paris suburbs left at 12.35 a.m.). The most ruthless excisions involved the opening chorus of Act I, and the duet in Act IV in which Philip and Carlos mourn the dead Posa. (Some of the deleted material from this served as the seed for the *Lacrymosa* in the Requiem, and all the abandoned material was recovered and reconstructed by Verdi scholars in the 1960s and 1970s.) Cuts continued to be made, especially when the opera began to appear in Italy, and for a Naples production in 1872–3 Verdi himself revised and abbreviated several scenes. But *Don Carlos* stubbornly resisted popular success, and in 1882 the composer embarked on a more drastic rewriting. Only Carlos's romance 'Je l'ai vu' (revised) survives from the original Act I, and much else – notably the Philip–Posa duet in Act II and the closing scene of the opera – was radically revised. In the process the opera draws closer to its Schiller model. This 1884 version is certainly 'more concise and vigorous' (Verdi), but the desire to reinstate the Fontainebleau act, which led to the hybrid Modena version of 1886, is understandable. It restores much superb music (some of it drawn on in episodes of reminiscence later in the opera), and it makes plot and motivation much clearer.

Perhaps not surprisingly, despite the passionate admiration of some connoisseurs, *Don Carlos* was for long regarded as a 'problem opera'. In Paris it disappeared completely from the repertoire after 1869; even during the Verdi renaissance between the wars – indeed as late as the 1950s and 1960s – many opera houses felt it necessary to stage adaptations that 'improved' it in some way or another. It was not until well into the second half of the 20th century that *Don Carlos* came to be recognized, not only as Verdi's most ambitious opera but as one of his supreme achievements.

SYNOPSIS

Act I takes place in France, Acts II–V in Spain; the period is *c.*1560.

Act I: The forest of Fontainebleau. France and Spain have long been at war. Carlos has come to France, impatient to be with Elisabeth, to whom he is betrothed ('Je l'ai vu et dans son sourire'). Elisabeth has lost her way in the forest during a hunt, and Carlos, introducing himself as a member of the Spanish diplomatic mission – for Elisabeth does not yet know him – undertakes to protect her while Thibault goes for help. He produces a portrait that shows that he is the man she is to marry. When the sound of cannon from the palace confirms that a peace has been concluded, their joy is complete ('De quels transports poignants et doux'). Thibault returns, followed by courtiers and people. As a pledge of the peace Elisabeth is to marry Carlos's widowed father, the great King Philip himself, and recognizing that the well-being of her people depends upon her, Elisabeth assents ('L'heure fatale est sonnée' – 'O chants de fête').

Act II, Scene 1: The cloisters at the monastery of Saint-Just. Monks meditate by the tomb of the Emperor Charles V ('Charles-Quint, l'auguste Empereur'), Carlos is startled by the resemblance of one of the monks to his late grandfather. He is joined by his dearest friend, Rodrigo, Marquis of Posa. Just returned from the Netherlands, Posa paints a grim picture of the oppression it suffers, and when he hears of Carlos's hopeless passion for Elisabeth, he urges him to go to Flanders and learn there to be a king. They renew their vows of fellowship in the service of liberty ('Mon compagnon, mon ami' – 'Dieu, tu serras dans nos âmes'). Scene 2: A pleasant spot by the gates of the monastery of Saint-Just. Thibault, Eboli and the ladies of the court shelter from the heat ('Sous ces bois au feuillage immense') and pass the time with song ('Au palais des fées', the so-called 'Song of the Veil'). The queen joins them, then Posa, who delivers two letters, one from her father, the other, which she reads while he engages Eboli in gallantries, from Carlos. Posa requests an audience for Carlos ('L'infant Carlos, notre espérance'), for Philip is unsympathetic to his troubles; Eboli imagines Carlos may be in love with her. Carlos appears and, dismissing her attendants, Elisabeth struggles to remain calm. She agrees to help persuade Philip to send him to Flanders, but, to her distress, he swoons and raves ('O bien perdu . . . Trésor sans prix') then hurries away. Philip is angry to find his queen unattended and orders the guilty lady-in-waiting, Countess D'Aremberg, back to France. Elisabeth bids her farewell ('O ma chère compagne'). Posa is detained by the king and seizes the opportunity to protest about the plight of Flanders ('O Roi! j'arrive de Flandre'). He urges him to give his people freedom. Impressed by Posa's integrity, Philip warns him to beware the Grand Inquisitor and confides his worries about Carlos and Elisabeth and asks him to keep a watch on them. (The Philip–Posa scene is always performed in the 1884 form.)

Act III, Scene 1: The Queen's Gardens, an enclosed grove. Festivities have been arranged for the eve of Philip's coronation, but Elisabeth wishes to spend the night in prayer and, entrusting Eboli with her mantilla, necklace and mask, asks her to stand in for her. Eboli, seeing the chance to make sure of Carlos's love ('Pour une nuit me voilà reine'), writes him a hasty note. A sumptuous ballet ('La Peregrina') is staged. (This opening scene is commonly omitted in favour of the Act II preludio of the 1884 version.) Mistaking Eboli for Elisabeth, Carlos declares his love ('C'est vous, c'est vous! ma bien-aimée'). When she unmasks, his confusion perplexes her. She warns him that Posa is now a confidant of the king and that only she can protect him ('Hélas! votre jeunesse ignore'). Suddenly it dawns on her that Carlos and Elisabeth are lovers. At the same moment Posa appears. Despite his threats, she is determined to exact revenge by exposing the queen's liaison with her stepson ('Malheur sur toi, fils adultère'). Scene 2: A large piazza in front of the cathedral at Valladolid. A throng of people, gathered for an auto da fé, sings the king's praises ('Ce jour heureux'). Philip's coronation oath requires him to act as God's avenger with sword and fire. Carlos presents a group of deputies from Flanders and Brabant. They beg Philip to show clemency, a prayer in which the queen, Posa and most of the crowd join, but Philip's persecuting obduracy is encouraged by the monks ('Sire, la dernière heure'). Carlos now demands that his father entrust to him the regency of Flanders. When Philip dismisses the request, he draws his sword and vows to be the saviour of that unhappy land. All are scandalized by this breach of etiquette. Posa disarms Carlos, and is elevated to a dukedom by Philip. The auto da fé continues: an angelic voice is heard comforting the dying.

Act IV, Scene 1: The king's cabinet at Valladolid. Philip muses wretchedly over his failure to win Elisabeth's love ('Elle ne m'aime pas!' – 'Je dormirais dans mon manteau royal'). The Grand Inquisitor is led in. He assures Philip that, if it is for the good of the faith, there can be no objection to having Carlos killed. But Posa represents a greater danger, and if Philip persists in protecting a heretic, he will have to answer for it to the Holy Office ('Dans ce beau pays'). Elisabeth is indignant to find her jewel box stolen. Philip has it on his table, and when she refuses to open it, forces it himself: a portrait of Carlos is found among her treasures. When he denounces her as an adulteress, she faints. At the king's summons, Eboli and Posa enter. He realizes that immediate action must be taken to save Carlos ('Maudit soit le soupçon infame'). Left alone with the queen, Eboli begs forgiveness. She stole the casket, and, what is worse, she is herself guilty of the sin of which Elisabeth stands suspected. The queen banishes her from the court: she must choose exile or the cloister. Eboli curses her own beauty, but before taking leave of the world she resolves to save Carlos ('O don fatal et détesté'). (The original French version makes no mention of the fact that Eboli is the king's mistress.) Scene 2: Carlos's prison. Posa comes to bid Carlos farewell and encourage him in his great libertarian mission. Two men appear at the cell door and Posa is shot. As he dies, he tells Carlos that Elisabeth will be at Saint-Just the next day ('Ah! je meurs, l'âme joyeuse'). The king enters and returns Carlos's sword, but his son repulses him. (Omitted before the Paris premiere: Philip and Carlos mourn Posa, 'Qui me rendra ce mort'.) The clanging of the tocsin signals a popular uprising. For a moment Philip seems in danger, but the appearance of the Grand Inquisitor reduces the mob to submission. Meanwhile Eboli enables Carlos to make his escape. (The whole scene following the death of Posa is normally performed in the shorter 1884 form.)

Act V: The monastery of Saint-Just. Elisabeth recognizes that her earthly task will soon be done ('Toi qui sus le néant'). Carlos comes to bid farewell, Elisabeth blesses his Flanders mission, and they look forward to meeting again in a better world ('Oui, voilà l'héroïsme' – 'Au revoir dans un monde'). The king appears, attended by the Grand Inquisitor, and his officers. Carlos is anathematized. As he tries to evade the inquisitors he retreats towards Charles V's tomb, which suddenly opens. The monk from Act II reappears and is recognized as Charles V himself. Carlos is hurried away into the monastery. (The whole scene from Carlos's arrival is normally performed in the revised 1884 version, which does not include the anathematizing of Carlos by the inquisitors.)

'Severe and terrible like the savage monarch who built it,' wrote Verdi of the Escurial on a visit to Spain in 1863. As a dramatic character Philip enthralled Verdi, and it was at his insistence that *Don Carlos* included two of the king's great scenes of confrontation – with Posa in Act II and with the Grand Inquisitor in Act IV – which offered negligible scope for the conventionally operatic. The confidence that he could hold an audience spellbound with a scene of ideological debate was amply justified in the latter case: the fearsome clash of private sorrow and ruthless dogmatism, the whole expressed in vocal and orchestral colours of a chilling blackness, is one of the things in opera that, once heard, is never likely to be forgotten. The Philip–Posa scene, on the other hand, cost Verdi endless trouble (its alternative forms occupy almost 90 pages of vocal score in the *edizione integrale*); but every revision had the effect of eliminating relics of traditional lyricism and bringing the scene closer to Schiller's thrilling dialectic.

Not only in the Grand Inquisitor scene but throughout *Don Carlos* Verdi's genius for the dramatic exploitation of colour, which had appeared fitfully as early as *Macbeth* or even *Ernani*, is revealed in full splendour: colours of garish magnificence in the auto da fé, otherworldly colours like the mysterious chords (high woodwind and deep horn pedal note) set against male voices in the prayer at the start of Act II, colours of desolating melancholy in Philip's incomparable 'Elle ne m'aime pas'. Nothing, however, contributes more to the dramatic colouring than the fact that the opera is, or should be, sung in French (even the 1884 version was conceived with a French text, then translated into Italian). Of course it is not Verdi's first French opera, but never before has it seemed so to matter that French imposes certain constraints on the manner of singing, which in turn make possible an inwardness and a type of sensibility new to Italian opera. The consequences are particularly remarkable in Carlos's music – far less extrovert, far more delicate in nuance than that of any earlier Verdi tenor.

All of which is not to imply any lack of lyrical abundance. On the contrary, what has been called Verdi's '*Aida* manner' (Julian Budden) might with equal justice be called his '*Don Carlos* manner'. The nervous sensibility of the principal characters is expressed in a lyrical style of exceptional richness, for in arias and ensembles alike every nuance of every experience calls forth its own melody.

RECORDINGS five-act Italian version: Caballé, Verrett, Domingo, Milnes, Raimondi, Foiani, Ambrosian Op Ch, Covent Garden O, Giulini, EMI, 1970; original French version: 1. Ricciarelli, Valentini-Terrani, Domingo, Nucci, Raimondi, Ghiaurov, La Scala Ch & O, Abbado, DG, 1985 (incl. appendices); 2. Mattila, Meier, Alagna, Hampson, Van Dam, Halfvarson, Th du Châtelet Ch, Paris O, Pappano, EMI, 1996 (live)

Aida

Opera (melodramma) in four acts (2h 15m)
Libretto by Antonio Ghislanzoni, after a scenario by Auguste Mariette and a French prose version by Camille du Locle
Composed July 1870–after November 1870 (rev. continued until December 1871)
PREMIERES 24 December 1871, Opera House, Cairo; Italy: 8 February 1872, La Scala, Milan; US: 26 November 1873, Academy of Music, New York; UK: 22 June 1876, Covent Garden, London
CAST The King *b*, Amneris *ms*, Aida *s*, Radamès *t*, Ramfis *b*, Amonasro *bar*, High Priestess *s*, messenger *t*; *satb* chorus of priests, priestesses, ministers, captains, soldiers, functionaries, slaves and Ethiopian prisoners, Egyptian people

In November 1869, during celebrations to mark the completion of the Suez Canal, a new opera house was opened in Cairo with a performance of *Rigoletto*. But the khedive of Egypt, abetted by the distinguished French Egyptologist Auguste Mariette, was also determined to commission a specially composed opera for his theatre; since Mariette was a friend of Camille du Locle, one of the *Don Carlos* librettists, it was through him that Verdi was approached. In April 1870 Mariette sent du Locle a scenario he had written. Though conventional in plot, it was rich in local colour and scenic detail, and Verdi liked it. In fact he was to show an almost Puccinian curiosity about the ambience of this drama, seeking advice on Egyptian religion, music, history and geography and experimenting with flutes and trumpets specially constructed in a spurious ancient Egyptian style for the scenes of ritual and celebration. Du Locle, working under Verdi's supervision, elaborated Mariette's synopsis into a French prose libretto, which in turn was rendered into Italian verse by Ghislanzoni. Dozens of letters between composer and librettist show Verdi taking as full a part as ever in planning the text: conceiving certain scenes himself (Amneris and her attendants and slaves in Act II, Scene 1); urging Ghislanzoni boldly to cast away convention when it did not serve the dramatic purpose (Aida–Amonasro duet in Act III); dictating the metrical details in arias and ensembles (Act IV finale: 'You can't imagine what a beautiful melody can be written in so strange a form').

Originally scheduled for January 1871, the premiere had to be delayed until the following season, for Mariette – who had gone to Paris in July 1870 to advise du Locle and the designers, so that the opera would be 'composed and executed in a strictly Egyptian style' – found himself immured in the city when the Franco-Prussian War broke out a few days later. The Prussian victory at Sedan (Verdi contributed part of his fee for *Aida* for the benefit of the French wounded) formed a suggestive background for the composition of the 'Triumph' scene (Act II, Scene 2). With some distaste, Verdi referred Ghislanzoni to King Wilhelm's victory telegram as a suitable model for the priests' chorus!

Both in Cairo, where it was conducted by the double-bass virtuoso Giovanni Bottesini, and Milan, where it was in the trusty hands of Franco Faccio, *Aida* was enthusiastically received. It has remained one of Verdi's most popular operas and in particular a natural first choice for open-air festival performances, such as those that began at Verona in the early 20th century. For the Paris Opéra premiere (in French) in 1880 the Act II ballet was extended by some 90 bars; this expanded version of the scene at once became the standard form. On the other hand, the full-length overture written at Ricordi's suggestion for the Milan premiere was discarded before the performance even took place and was first heard under Toscanini in 1940. Another abandoned movement was a chorus 'alla Palestrina', placed at the start of Act III; the definitive Act III *introduzione* was composed only in August 1871.

SYNOPSIS

The action takes place in Memphis, in the time of the pharaohs.

Act I, Scene 1: A hall in the royal palace at Memphis. In the wars with Ethiopia, Aida has been captured and brought to Memphis as a slave for Amneris, daughter of the Egyptian king. Her father, the Ethiopian king Amonasro, has launched an invasion to rescue her. The young captain Radamès dreams of being chosen to lead the Egyptian forces. Ironically, his longing for glory is inspired by Aida, whom he loves ('Celeste Aida'). Radamès in turn is loved by Amneris, who suspects that Aida may be her rival. The Egyptian king receives a report on the invasion. He announces that Isis has declared Radamès commander of the army and leads the assembly in patriotic song ('Su! del Nilo al sacro lido'). Aida is torn between love of Radamès and love of her homeland ('Ritorna vincitor!'). Scene 2: The interior of the Temple of Vulcan at Memphis. The divinity is invoked with mystic song and dance, and the high priest Ramfis consecrates Radamès for his mission.

Act II, Scene 1: A room in Amneris' apartments. Amneris is arrayed for the triumphal return of the Egyptian army ('Chi mai fra gl'inni e i plausi'). In a long dialogue ('Fu la sorte dell'armi a' tuoi funesta') she poses as Aida's friend, tricks her into admitting her love for Radamès and finally exults arrogantly over her. Scene 2: One of the gateways into the city of Thebes. The victorious host passes before the king ('Gloria all'Egitto, ad Iside'). Radamès is crowned with the victor's wreath and offered any gift he chooses. The Ethiopian prisoners are led in, and though Amonasro is disguised as a common soldier Aida at once recognizes him. He tells the Egyptian king a false tale about his own death and begs him to show magnanimity and release the prisoners ('Ma tu, Re, tu signore possente'). Despite the warnings of the priests, the crowd takes up his plea, and the issue is settled when Radamès adds his voice. The king bestows Amneris' hand on the young warrior, and the scene ends with a resumption of the triumphal anthems with which it commenced.

Act III: The banks of the Nile. Ramfis escorts Amneris to the temple where she is to spend the night before her marriage in prayer. Aida comes down to the river to meet Radamès. She fears she will never see her homeland again ('O patria mia'). To her astonishment, Amonasro suddenly appears. Once more he has invaded Egypt. This time, with Aida's help, the Ethiopians can win, and with a relentless barrage of moral blackmail, he forces her to agree to get Radamès to reveal the Egyptians' military plans ('Rivedrai le foreste imbalsamate'). Amonasro hides, and Aida sets about persuading her lover to elope with her. Reluctantly, he accepts her argument ('Pur ti riveggo, mia dolce Aida' – 'Fuggiam gli arbori inospiti' – 'Sì, fuggiam da queste mura'). If they make their getaway tonight, they will be able to pass the Napata gorges before the army moves into them. When he realizes that Amonasro has overheard him, Radamès is overcome with shame. Amneris and Ramfis re-emerge from the temple. Radamès saves Amneris from a murderous attack by Amonasro, then surrenders himself as Aida and her father escape.

Act IV, Scene 1: A hall in the royal palace. The Ethiopians have been routed again, and Amonasro has been killed. Aida has disappeared. Amneris halts the procession escorting Radamès to his trial: if only he will make some effort to explain himself, she will plead for mercy. But Radamès has lost all he values in life and is resolved to die ('Già i sacerdoti adunansi' – 'Chi ti salva, sciagurato'). Amneris listens in mounting anguish to the progress of the trial. Radamès is sentenced to be buried alive under the altar of the god he has offended. Scene 2: The Temple of Vulcan. Anticipating Radamès' fate, Aida has hidden herself in the vault, and as he is entombed there, she emerges from the shadows. She consoles him with her vision of a paradise where love will be unalloyed ('Morir! sì pura e bella' – 'Vedi? di morte l'angelo'), and as Amneris prays for Radamès, Aida dies in his arms ('O terra addio, addio o valle di pianti').

Aida is a summation of all that Verdi had hitherto achieved, brilliantly combining the strengths of Italian Romantic melodrama with those of French grand opera. No work epitomizes more splendidly the qualities the world admires in grand opera. But its dramatic pace belongs to his native tradition, as does its sense of priorities, for in Acts III and IV the external splendours recede, and we have to concern ourselves solely with the tormented humanity of the protagonists. Contemporaries saw signs of Wagner's influence too, probably in the comparatively superficial fact that recurring themes play a large part in the score. Both Aida and Amneris have their identifying themes – each in its own way sensuous and alluring – and another theme, severe and contrapuntal in character, is associated with Ramfis and the priests. A more distinctive feature of the opera is its uniquely powerful sense of time and place: the prominence of flutes, trumpets and harps helps evoke a world of bardic antiquity, while modal inflexions (most evident in the scene of Radamès' consecration) often colour the harmony.

The interaction of tradition and innovation that perplexed some early critics is best seen in the magnificent series of duets that runs through the opera, in all of which the starting point was a text in basically conventional form. It is fascinating to see how Verdi elaborated and varied this, sometimes playing up to, sometimes frustrating the audience's expectations. In the Aida–Amneris duet, for example (Act II, Scene 1), the 'cabaletta' is in large part a kind of descant set against an offstage reprise of the chorus 'Su! del Nilo', while in the duet finale of Act IV the (slow) cabaletta is provided with a supremely ironic commentary from Amneris. This closing scene occasioned Verdi some anxiety. He questioned Bottesini closely about the effect of what he described as an experiment in the 'ethereal genre'. Thomas Mann, using Hans Castorp in *The Magic Mountain* as his mouthpiece, saw it as a supreme instance of music's idealizing tendency, its power to transfigure and beautify even the harshest realities.

RECORDINGS 1. Milanov, Barbieri, Björling, Warren, Christoff, Rome Op Ch & O, Perlea, RCA, 1955; 2. L. Price, Gorr, Vickers, Merrill, Tozzi, Rome Op Ch & O, Solti, Becca, 1961; 3. Caballé, Cossotto, Domingo, Cappuccilli, Ghiaurov, Covent Garden Ch, NPO, Muti, EMI, 1974

Simon Boccanegra (II)

Melodramma in a prologue and three acts (2h 15m)
Libretto by Francesco Maria Piave and Arrigo Boito (a rewriting by Boito of Piave's 1857 libretto of the same name)
Composed December 1880–February 1881
PREMIERES 24 March 1881, La Scala, Milan; US: 28 January 1932, Metropolitan, New York; UK: 27 October 1948, Sadler's Wells, London
CAST Simon Boccanegra *bar*, Jacopo Fiesco *b*, Paolo Albiani *b*, Pietro *bar*, Maria Boccanegra (under the name of Amelia Grimaldi) *s*, Gabriele Adorno *t*, captain of the crossbowmen *t*, Amelia's maidservant *ms*; *satb* chorus of soldiers, sailors, people, Fiesco's servants, senators, the doge's court

In November 1880 Verdi's publisher Giulio Ricordi raised the question of reviving *Simon Boccanegra*. Verdi was interested, but the opera would need revision – it was 'too sad, too desolate' as it stood – and he went on to mention, as a means of lightening the gloom, 'two stupendous letters' by the 14th-century poet Petrarch. Addressing himself to the doges of Genoa and Venice, Petrarch had rebuked them for embarking on a fratricidal war, when they were 'both born of the same mother, Italy . . . how wonderful' – remarked Verdi – 'this feeling for an Italian fatherland at that time!' Boito, already well advanced on a libretto for *Otello*, was at first reluctant to undertake the revision, but Verdi had not yet committed himself to *Otello*, and almost certainly the shrewd Ricordi encouraged the *Simon Boccanegra* collaboration so that the two men could have the experience of working together on something slightly less momentous than a new opera. Verdi was not prepared to contemplate rewriting on the scale Boito suggested, so apart from a number of comparatively minor revisions, the librettist had to limit himself to creating a new second scene for Act I, the great council chamber scene. But the admiration Verdi felt for the way he did that – the general conception, the distinction of the verses, the ingenuity in solving niggling little problems of detail – was a major factor in persuading the composer that Boito was an ideal colleague. The poet himself 'attributed no artistic or literary merit to the patchwork I have made from poor Piave's libretto' and refused to allow his name to be publicly linked with the revised *Simon Boccanegra*.

Except for Act II, the least revised and therefore the most old-fashioned in style, the new *Simon Boccanegra* was warmly received. But for all Boito's ingenuity and for all the magnificence of the 'late Verdi' style that here emerges for the first time, it remains a perplexing and sombre drama – an opera for connoisseurs rather than a popular favourite. Brahms, who saw it in Vienna in 1882, spoke for many. He found 'something talented and gripping everywhere, but after a while . . . ceased all investigations into the meaning of the libretto'.

SYNOPSIS
The action takes place in Genoa and its vicinity, about the middle of the 14th century. Twenty-five years elapse between the prologue and the drama.

Prologue: A piazza in Genoa. A new doge is about to be elected; the goldsmith Paolo persuades Pietro, leader of the plebeian party, to vote for Simon Boccanegra, a corsair in the service of the republic. The sight of the darkened Fiesco palace prompts speculation on the fate of the unhappy Maria ('L'atra magion vedete?'), incarcerated there because her father disapproves of her love for Simon. Fiesco emerges from the palace. Maria has died ('Il lacerato spirito'), but his pride is unbroken, and he scorns Simon's offer of reconciliation. Only if he entrusts to Fiesco the daughter Maria has borne to Simon will he be forgiven, but the young Maria has disappeared without trace ('Del mar sul lido'). Simon enters the palace determined to see Maria once more. He discovers her corpse just as a throng of plebeians proclaims him doge.

Act I, Scene 1: The garden of the Grimaldi palace outside Genoa. Amelia impatiently awaits her beloved, Gabriele Adorno ('Come in quest'ora bruna' – 'Cielo di stelle orbato'). She is worried at the dangers he and her guardian Andrea – in fact Fiesco – are running by conspiring against Boccanegra. Learning that the doge (Simon), whose visit is now announced, is likely to seek her hand for Paolo, Gabriele agrees to ask Andrea to bless them as man and wife ('Vieni a mirar la cerula' – 'Sì, sì, dell'ara il giubilo'). His love is unshaken when the supposed Amelia Grimaldi proves to be an orphan girl, and Andrea blesses him ('Vieni a me, ti benedico'). Greeting the doge, Amelia tells him her heart is already engaged. As Simon questions her, he recognizes her as his long-lost daughter Maria ('Orfanella il tetto umile' – 'Figlia! a tal nome io palpito'). The spurned Paolo plots to abduct Amelia. Scene 2: The council chamber in the Palazzo degli Abati. A council meeting is interrupted by the sound of a brawl; a mob of plebeians drags in Gabriele and Fiesco. Gabriele tells the doge that Amelia has been abducted. He has killed the man who did it, but believes the abductor was acting on Simon's instructions. He now tries to kill Simon but is prevented by the appearance of Amelia. Simmering hostility between patricians and plebeians threatens to break out into open fighting. Appealing to ideals of brotherhood and patriotism, Simon re-establishes his authority ('Plebe! Patrizi! Popolo'); then he compels Paolo to anathematize the traitor in their midst.

Act II: The doge's room in the ducal palace in Genoa. Paolo puts poison in Simon's water jug. He fails to enlist Fiesco in his plan to murder Simon, but enrages Gabriele by claiming that Amelia is the plaything of the doge's lust. Meeting Amelia, Gabriele denounces her bitterly, but she cannot yet explain her feelings for Simon ('Parla, in tuo cor virgineo'). As Simon approaches, Gabriele hides. Despite new evidence of Gabriele's plots, Amelia persuades her father to forgive him. He insists on being left alone, drinks from the poisoned water and falls asleep. Amelia, fearful of what might happen, has only pretended to leave, and when her lover emerges bent on murder, she intervenes. Their argument wakens the doge. His relationship to Amelia can be concealed no longer, and Gabriele is appalled by what he has tried to do ('Perdon, perdon, Amelia'). Again insurrection is heard in the streets, and Simon is determined to seek reconciliation. If Gabriele can negotiate a peace, Amelia shall be his reward.

Act III: Within the doge's palace. The Guelphs have been routed, and Paolo captured. As he is led to execution he meets Fiesco, who expresses his loathing of the poisoner and abductor. The sounds of the wedding of Amelia and Gabriele are heard from a distant part of the palace. Simon enters, the effects of the poison already far advanced. As he gazes out to sea, Fiesco emerges from the shadows. When Simon recognizes the old man, he surprises him by claiming the reconciliation that had been offered 25 years before. Now he can fulfil the conditions: Amelia Grimaldi is Fiesco's long-lost granddaughter, and he gladly restores her to him. Fiesco's pride is broken at last, and, weeping, he embraces the dying Simon ('Piango, perchè mi parla'). The doge blesses the newly married couple and nominates Gabriele his successor ('Gran Dio, ti benedici').

Once Verdi had Boito's revised text, he composed/revised 'everything in sequence, just as if it were a matter of a new opera'. The more mechanical conventions of the 1850s now seemed intolerable to him, and there were few scenes – even where the libretto remained unaltered – that he did not scrutinize rigorously and, where necessary, rewrite. In the broadest terms the musical continuity is more skilfully sustained (thanks particularly to a more sophisticated use of the orchestra). The new material is of course in a riper and richer style, and the dramatic characterization is more interesting. Fiesco, through his Act I duet with Gabriele, acquires a warmer humanity, and Paolo becomes one of Boito's mephistophelean villains. Good examples of Verdi's musical transformation of an unaltered text are to be found in the first scene of the prologue, where the dialogue, instead of being punctuated by the customary figurations of accompanied recitative, is set against a gravely flowing orchestral theme (made much of in Liszt's *Réminiscences de Boccanegra*, 1882), and in the duet 'Orfanella il tetto umile', where the conventional cadenza is replaced by an exquisitely tender and poetic coda. Nevertheless, discrepancies between Verdi's 1857 manner and his 1880 manner are an inescapable feature of the opera and have a singular effect, for Verdi, we must suppose, was moved to revise most radically those scenes he felt most deeply. At such critical moments, the characters might be said to rise to the occasion and express themselves with a subtlety and power unknown in the 1857 score.

The most substantial new number is the Act I finale, the council chamber scene. Inspired by those Petrarch letters, Verdi, who as a young composer had had a positive genius for music in the most demotic manner, finds a voice worthy of his by now patriarchal status in Italian society. The magnificent declamatory fervour of Simon's solo, the radiance of Amelia's lyricism, the searching harmonies, the consummate craftsmanship of the whole ensemble combine to make the scene one of the noblest visions of social idealism in music.

RECORDINGS 1. de los Angeles, Campora, Gobbi, Christoff, Rome Op Ch & O, Santini, EMI, 1957; 2. Freni, Carreras, Cappuccilli, Ghiaurov, La Scala Ch & O, Abbado, DG, 1977

Otello

Othello

Dramma lirico in four acts (2h 15m)
Libretto by Arrigo Boito, after the tragedy *Othello* by William Shakespeare (1604–5)
Composed December 1884–November 1886; rev. April 1887
PREMIERES 5 February 1887, La Scala, Milan; US: 16 April 1888, Academy of Music, New York; UK: 5 July 1889, Lyceum, London
CAST Otello *t*, Iago *bar*, Cassio *t*, Roderigo *t*, Lodovico *b*, Montano *b*, herald *b*, Desdemona *s*, Emilia *ms*; *satb* chorus of soldiers and sailors of the Venetian Republic, Venetian ladies and gentlemen, Cypriot people, Greek men-at-arms, Dalmatians, Albanians, children of the island trebles; an innkeeper, 4 inn servants, ship's crew

During the last 20 years of Verdi's life, Arrigo Boito was to become one of his closest friends, and their working relationship was one of the most remarkable in the history of opera. It was a position he did not win easily: almost 30 years Verdi's junior, Boito had deeply offended him with a foolish poem published in the 1860s, and it took all his generosity of spirit and all Ricordi's diplomacy to bring about a reconciliation. Their two Shakespearean operas, *Otello* and *Falstaff*, are widely regarded as the twin peaks of the whole Italian tradition of opera. A few critics, however, judge the collaboration more captiously and deplore what they see as the artificiality and self-conscious intellectualism of Verdi's last operas.

In adapting *Othello*, Boito omitted the first, Venetian act – save for a number of hints that are ingeniously recapitulated later, notably in the love duet in Act I; otherwise he follows the play closely. But his understanding of Shakespeare's characters had its roots in Continental sources – in the writings of August Wilhelm von Schlegel and François-Victor Hugo (whose French translation was his primary source), and in the style of Shakespeare performance growing up in Italy around the actors Ernesto Rossi and Tommaso Salvini. With Othello, Boito's emphasis lies on the 'Ethiopian' core of savage passion only fragilely contained beneath a veneer of Mediterranean civility; Desdemona, on the other hand, is a saintly idealization, 'a type of goodness, of resignation, of self-sacrifice' (Verdi). For Iago too, Boito and Verdi draw on this interpretative tradition; but, equally, his diabolical cynicism makes him one with a whole family of mephistophelean villains conceived by Boito for his opera libretti. The peculiar fascination Iago exerted over both men is seen from one of Boito's additions to Shakespeare's play, the 'Credo' in Act II – which Verdi found 'most beautiful and wholly Shakespearean' – and from the fact that for years they were disposed to call the opera *Jago*. They finally resolved to challenge comparison with Shakespeare by using his title only in January 1886, not much more than a year before the premiere.

No other opera, if one excepts *King Lear*, occupied Verdi so long. The possibility of composing *Otello* had first been put to him in earnest during a visit to Milan in June 1879, and a first draft of Boito's libretto was written during the summer and autumn. But it was not until November 1886 that Verdi was ready to declare the opera finished, and he continued to tinker with details even during the rehearsals. Faccio rehearsed his cast with exemplary zeal, and no detail of casting, *mise-en-scène* or general organization was too tiny for Ricordi's attention. Even so, to the last moment Verdi reserved the right to withdraw the opera if anything failed to satisfy him. In the event he was not pleased with the premiere, but it was recognized internationally as an artistic occasion of the first importance and prompted scenes of wild enthusiasm: *The Times* critic reported that at one o'clock in the morning the streets outside Verdi's hotel were still full of 'an eager multitude . . . shouting and yelling'.

For the first performance at the Paris Opéra in October 1894, Verdi composed a short ballet; it forms part of the ceremony of welcome for the Venetian ambassadors in the Act III finale.

SYNOPSIS

The scene is set in a maritime city on the island of Cyprus at the end of the 15th century.

Act I: Outside the castle. A crowd watches as the ship bearing Otello, the new governor, battles into harbour through a hurricane. The Venetians have routed the Turks, and a celebratory bonfire is prepared. Otello's ensign, Iago, who hates both Otello and the young officer Cassio, promises to help Roderigo enjoy the love of Otello's wife, Desdemona, and, as the bonfire dies down ('Fuoco di gioia!'), sets his plan in motion. Wine flows freely in honour of the nuptials of Otello and Desdemona ('Inaffia l'ugola!'), and Cassio is soon drunk. When Montano, the retiring governor, orders him to the ramparts, Roderigo and Iago easily provoke a brawl. Roderigo goes to raise havoc through the city, alarm bells clang, and Otello reappears, roused from his bed. Furious to find Montano wounded and believing what 'honest Iago' tells him, he dismisses Cassio, appoints Iago in his stead and sends him to re-establish order in the streets. Desdemona has also been roused by the pandemonium. The lovers are left alone, to recall the strange chances of fortune that brought them together ('Già nella notte densa').

Act II: A hall on the ground floor of the castle. Having advised Cassio to ask Desdemona to intercede for him with Otello, Iago confesses his nihilistic creed ('Credo in un Dio crudel'). He urges Otello to watch Desdemona's behaviour with Cassio: it may be less innocent than he supposes. Otello is disturbed, but when he sees the islanders paying homage to his wife in the garden ('Dove guardi splendono'), his suspicions are disarmed. When Desdemona pleads with him for Cassio, he is reminded of

Iago's warning, becomes irritable and throws down the handkerchief she offers him. Emilia picks it up. In the quartet ('Dammi la dolce e lieta parola del perdono') Desdemona beseeches Otello to forgive her for any offence given; he muses gloomily; Iago snatches Desdemona's handkerchief from Emilia. Otello's dreams of love and glory are fast evaporating ('Nell'ore arcane della sua lussuria' – 'Ora è per sempre addio'), and he demands proof of his wife's guilt. Iago recounts how he had recently slept with Cassio, who, in his dreams, had unmistakably been making love to Desdemona ('Era la notte'). What is more, only the day before, he was carrying the handkerchief Otello had once given her. Otello swears to exact bloody vengeance ('Sì, pel ciel marmoreo giuro!').

Act III: The great hall of the castle. Iago outlines a plan to make Cassio chatter about Desdemona while Otello eavesdrops. Otello greets Desdemona with elaborate courtesy ('Dio ti giocondi, o sposo'), but as soon as she mentions Cassio, he becomes agitated, and after an argument about her handkerchief, drives her away. The grief occasioned by her falseness is unendurable ('Dio! mi potevi scagliar'). Iago re-enters, followed by Cassio, who is soon talking about his mistress Bianca ('Essa t'avvince coi vaghi rai'). Otello, unable to catch Bianca's name, imagines the ribald laughter to be about Desdemona, and when Cassio produces the handkerchief, no further proof is required. While a distant chorus is heard greeting ambassadors from Venice, Otello and Iago plan how to kill the guilty pair. The ambassadors have come to recall Otello; Cassio is appointed his successor. But affairs of state are overshadowed by Otello's behaviour ('A terra! . . . sì . . .'); soon he is delirious. He drives everyone but Iago from the scene, curses Desdemona, and swoons. Cries of 'Viva Otello!' resound in the distance, while Iago spurns the prostrate figure with his heel.

Act IV: Desdemona's bedroom. While she prepares for bed, Desdemona sings the willow song ('Piangea cantando nell'erma landa') she once learned from her mother's maid. She bids Emilia goodnight and having said her prayers ('Ave Maria') lies down to sleep. Otello enters, extinguishes the lamp and kisses Desdemona. She realizes that he has come to kill her. Her entreaties are in vain, and he smothers her just as Emilia comes hammering at the door to announce that Cassio has killed Roderigo. Aghast to find Desdemona dying, she raises the alarm: Cassio, Iago, Lodovico and later Montano enter. As the truth emerges, Iago makes his escape and Otello is disarmed. But he has a dagger hidden in his robes, and having bidden a solemn farewell to his comrades and a heart-broken one to the dead Desdemona, he stabs himself and falls dying beside her.

As so often in Verdi the musical characterization is the key to the opera's individuality. Otello, he remarked, 'now the warrior, now the passionate lover, now crushed to the point of baseness, now ferocious like a savage, must sing and shout'; Desdemona 'must always, always sing'; but Iago 'has only to declaim and mock'. Again and again in Otello, Desdemona's pure-hearted and passionate lyricism, an expression of all that love and idealism the art of opera had been invented to express, is juxtaposed with, counterpointed against and undermined by Iago's nonchalant parlando, which is graced only with a few slithering and trilling touches of arioso and which could, Verdi noted, 'with the exception of a few outbursts, be sung mezza voce throughout' – an unforgettable musical image of the mephistophelean 'spirit of denial'.

In 1882, when work on the opera was still at an early stage, Verdi predicted that *Otello* would be 'Italian in scale and Italian in who knows how many other ways . . . Perhaps a few melodies . . . (if I can find any) . . . and melody is always Italian . . .'. A few critics were deluded by the opera's seamless continuity, the sumptuousness of the orchestral writing and the sophistication of the harmony into imagining that he was at last coming round to a Wagnerian ideal of music drama. But the essence of his art remained the wedding of poetry and song in balanced lyrical forms. What is different in the later Verdi is that these forms are not confined to arias and ensembles, but blossom wherever poetry and the spirit of the drama suggest. In the opening scene, for example, two distinct musical shapes – one a prayer ('Dio, fulgor della bufera'), one an exclamation of joy ('Vittoria! vittoria!') – materialize out of the orchestral turmoil of the hurricane. Conversely, it is out of the songs and celebrations marking Otello's safe arrival that the dramatic action re-emerges: Iago's *brindisi* is the source of the musical figures that propel the brawl, just as the wine he sings of is the source of the drunkenness that causes it.

Many sections of the score draw inspiration directly from Shakespeare's poetry – for example, Otello's two great solos, in Act II 'Nell'ore arcane' ('What sense had I of her stol'n hours of lust?') and in Act III 'Dio! mi potevi scagliar' ('Had it pleas'd heaven to try me with affliction'). No Shakespeare-inspired detail is more telling than the threefold recurrence – at the close of the Act I love duet, when Otello enters Desdemona's bedchamber to kill her, and at the end of the opera – of the so-called 'kiss' motif: 'I kiss'd thee ere I kill'd thee; no way but this, killing myself to die upon a kiss.'

RECORDINGS 1. Nelli, Vinay, Valdengo, NBC Ch & SO, Toscanini, RCA, 1947; 2. Rysanek, Vickers, Gobbi, Rome Op Ch & O, Serafin, RCA, 1960; 3. Scotto, Domingo, Milnes, Ambrosian Opera Ch, Nat PO, Levine, RCA, 1978

Falstaff

Commedia lirica in three acts (2h)
Libretto by Arrigo Boito, after the comedy *The Merry Wives of Windsor* by William Shakespeare (1597) and incorporating material from the histories *Henry IV*, Parts I and II (1597/1598)
Composed ?August 1889; March 1890–December 1892; major revs March 1893 and January 1894
PREMIERES 9 February 1893, La Scala, Milan; UK: 19 May 1894, Covent Garden, London; US: 4 February 1895, Metropolitan, New York
CAST Sir John Falstaff *bar*, Ford *bar*, Fenton *t*, Dr Caius *t*, Bardolph *t*, Pistol *b*, Mrs Alice Ford *s*, Nannetta *s*, Mrs Quickly *ms*, Mrs Meg Page *ms*, Host of the Garter Inn *silent*; Robin, Falstaff's page *silent*; *satb* chorus of burghers and commoners, Ford's servants, masquerade of elves, fairies, witches, etc.

Falstaff was Verdi's first comic opera since *Un giorno di regno* (1840). There were those who felt, as Rossini did, that he was 'too melancholy and serious' to compose a successful one; but since *Luisa Miller* he had used elements of comedy to set off the prevailing tragic mood in his operas, and at various times since the 1860s he had considered making another attempt at comedy, if a suitable subject could be found. He was not interested in buffoonery. For all its Latin spirit, *Falstaff* was not an opera buffa, Verdi insisted, but a depiction of character.

As a result of their collaboration on *Otello*, Verdi now had complete trust in Boito, and embarked on this new enterprise – at first a secret between the two of them – with much zest. Shortly after receiving a first draft of the plot (summer 1889) he was experimenting with 'comic fugues' (it is likely that the opera's finale was conceived at this time), and when he received the complete libretto (March 1890) he drafted the whole of Act I in little more than a week. Such bursts of intense activity were to recur throughout the three and a half years he worked on *Falstaff*; but there were distractions and sorrows too (particularly the deaths of several of his closest friends) that drove music out of his head for months on end. It is obvious from the manuscripts and early printed sources that Verdi worked over every scene again and again, refining the craftsmanship, enriching the musical fabric, sharpening the wit. The process of revision continued while the score was being printed, throughout the period of rehearsals and even during the first run of performances. Further rewriting, sometimes quite substantial, took place before the Rome performances in April 1893 and before the French premiere the following year.

Falstaff had long been one of Verdi's favourite characters – a supreme embodiment of Shakespeare's genius for 'inventing truth' – and Boito's libretto is the most brilliant of all operatic adaptations of Shakespeare. He adroitly condenses and clarifies the plot of *The Merry Wives*, while drawing freely on the two parts of *Henry IV* to give us a Falstaff in all his prodigious abundance of personality; at the same time Shakespeare's quintessential Englishness is translated to 'the gardens of the *Decameron*', the verse given an antique tang and raciness with vocabulary drawn from Boccaccio and the satirists of the Italian Renaissance. The libretto is beautifully formed: each act subdivided into one scene of character depiction for a small group of soloists and one of teeming action and elaborate ensembles.

No production book for *Falstaff* survives, but there is plenty of evidence that Verdi, who supervised a huge number of rehearsals in January and February 1893, insisted on a more naturalistic style of performance than in his tragic operas (a newspaper account survives of him demonstrating to Fenton how to kiss Nannetta with suitable ardour), and the designer Adolph Hohenstein was sent off to London and Windsor to ensure that sets and costumes were as authentic as possible. The premiere was a brilliant occasion and aroused worldwide excitement. But a high proportion of opera-lovers, especially perhaps in Italy, were frankly bewildered, and the admiration of connoisseurs was not matched by the kind of popular enthusiasm that had attended the greater part of Verdi's career. It was in large part due to Toscanini, who made his superlatively drilled performances cornerstones of the repertoire in every opera house he directed, that *Falstaff* came to be regarded as a national classic rather than an object of bewildered admiration.

SYNOPSIS

The scene is set in Windsor, in the reign of Henry IV of England.

Act I, Part 1: Inside the Garter Inn. Falstaff's carousing is interrupted by Dr Caius, who threatens to report him to the Star Chamber. Unable to ruffle Falstaff's bibulous calm, Caius turns on Bardolph and Pistol who, the previous night, had made him drunk and emptied his purse. The charges are denied, and Caius storms out. Finding they have no money to pay the bill, Falstaff blames his companions. Bardolph's glowing nose means they can economize on lanterns, but the savings are more than consumed in wine bills. He outlines a new enterprise: two wealthy citizens, Ford and Page, have beautiful wives; he will lay siege to their virtue as a means of getting at their husbands' money ('V'è noto un tal'). Bardolph and Pistol refuse to assist so dishonourable an enterprise. Falstaff harangues them on the subject of Honour ('L'Onore! Ladri!' – 'Puo l'onore riempirvi la pancia?'), before kicking them out. Part 2: The garden by Ford's house. Alice and Meg have received identical love letters from Falstaff ('Fulgida Alice! amor t'offro') and decide he must be taught a lesson. Ford enters with Fenton and Caius (rivals for Nannetta's hand), and Bardolph and Pistol, from whom he learns that Falstaff is bent on seducing his wife and emptying his money bags. While the women engage Mistress Quickly to lure Falstaff to an assignation, Ford plans to visit the Garter Inn in disguise to investigate these tales. Twice Nannetta and Fenton break away from their companions to kiss in the shadow of the trees ('Labbra di foco!').

Act II, Part 1: Inside the Garter Inn. Mistress Quickly arrives with the answer to Falstaff's letters ('Reverenza!'): both wives love him, but only Alice is able to receive him – any day between two and three, when her husband is always out. Bardolph announces 'Mastro Fontana' ('Master Brook'). 'Fontana' introduces himself as a wealthy man accustomed to want for nothing, but he has fallen in love with Ford's wife and all his wooing has been in vain ('C'è a Windsor una dama'). The gold he has brought with him is Falstaff's if he can seduce her, for once she has fallen to a man of the world like Sir John, she is more likely to listen to his own suit. Falstaff accepts the challenge – indeed, it is almost won already, for he has an assignation with the lady in half an hour. He excuses himself a moment, and Ford is left alone, a prey to jealousy ('E sogno? o realtà?' – 'L'ora è fissata'). Falstaff returns, dressed to kill, and they go out together. Part 2: A room in Ford's house. Mistress Quickly reports on the success of her mission ('Giunta all'Albergo della *Giarrettiera*'). A screen is set up, a lute laid ready, and servants carry in a laundry basket. They all look forward to the adventure ('Gaie comari di Windsor'). Falstaff arrives, woos Alice ardently and recalls the days of his slender youth ('Quand'ero paggio'). But Ford is heard approaching. Falstaff hides behind the screen, while Ford, assisted by Caius, Bardolph and Pistol, seeks high and low for the intruder. He soon rushes off to another part of the house, Falstaff is bundled into the laundry basket, and Fenton and Nannetta retreat behind the screen. While Ford closes in on – as he supposes – his wife and Falstaff, Nannetta and Fenton continue their romantic tête-à-tête. The screen is snatched away, to reveal only the young lovers, and a new hunt for Falstaff begins on a false scent laid by Bardolph. The laundry basket is hauled to the window, and as soon as Ford returns Falstaff is tipped into the river.

Act III, Part 1: A courtyard outside the Garter Inn. Falstaff broods over his humiliation ('Mondo ladro'); but the consolations of steaming wine are infallible. Mistress Quickly brings a letter inviting him to a midnight assignation in Windsor Park, but he must come disguised as the 'Black Huntsman' who haunts the forest. The conversation is overheard by the other wives and by Ford, Caius and Fenton, and while Falstaff accompanies Mistress Quickly into the inn they plan the details of the midnight masquerade. Mistress Quickly reappears to hear Ford plotting Nannetta's marriage with Caius. Part 2: Windsor Great Park. Fenton's musings ('Dal labbro il canto estasiato vola') are interrupted by the wives: to outwit Ford and Caius last-minute changes of mask and costume are necessary. As midnight strikes, Falstaff enters; but his wooing of Alice is interrupted by the approach of a horde of spirits. With Falstaff prostrate on the ground in terror, Nannetta, disguised as the queen of the fairies, and her attendants weave a spell in solemn song and dance ('Sul fil d'un soffio etesio'). Then, while she and Fenton are hurried away, fantastically garbed figures torment Falstaff and conduct him through a litany of repentance. In the excitement Bardolph loses his hood; further unmaskings follow, and Falstaff realizes he has been made an ass of. Ford proposes that the betrothal of the queen of the fairies be celebrated. Caius's bride proves, when unveiled, to be Bardolph, while another masked couple brought forward for blessing are revealed as Nannetta and Fenton. Ford accepts the situation philosophically, and Falstaff leads the company in a fugal chorus celebrating the absurdity of the human condition ('Tutto nel mondo è burla').

It is not difficult to see why early audiences were sometimes bemused. By far the greater part of *Falstaff* moves at such a giddy pace that only the most fleeting glimpses of musical forms are perceived. The choicest melodies are come and gone with teasing rapidity, giving an effect that is at once virtuosic and tender, and beautifully suggestive of the spirit of Shakespearean comedy. Only in the final scene, as order returns and reconciliation is achieved, does the musical pace broaden out into a sequence of almost ceremonial movements: serenade, dance, litany, fugue. In many passages musical continuity is achieved by the orchestral development of short melodic and rhythmic figures, a procedure more 'symphonic' than anything heard in Verdi's operas hitherto. Some of these symphonic passages are based on trenchant vocal phrases – 'dalle due alle tre' and 'te lo cornifico' in Act II, Part 1 for example – in which Verdi shows that his vaunted *parola scenica* – the 'theatrical word' that 'carves out a situation or a character' – can be as brilliantly apt in the comic vein as in the heroic or tragic.

With the passage for muted double-basses in the final scene of *Otello*, Verdi had become the first Italian since Spontini to earn a place in Berlioz's *Treatise on Orchestration*, as revised by Richard Strauss. Many an episode in *Falstaff* – Falstaff's self-portraits in the opening scene, his ruminations on his ducking in the river culminating in the celebrated trill cum tremolo for virtually every instrument in the orchestra, and the fairy music in the last act – demonstrates that for sheer virtuosity in tone-painting the elderly Verdi rivalled Strauss himself. But it is orchestration of exquisite translucency: instruments are virtually never used simply to reinforce the voices. To sing unsupported by the orchestra was only one of the unfamiliar demands Verdi made on his performers; he knew that Italian singers in particular would be severely tested, for there was, he declared, no room in *Falstaff* for 'artists who want to sing too much . . . and fall asleep on the notes'; above all they would need to 'loosen up their tongues and clarify their pronunciation'.

RECORDINGS 1. Nelli, Stich-Randall, Elmo, Madasi, Valdengo, Guarrera, Robert Shaw Ch, NBC SO, Toscanini, RCA, 1950 (radio); 2. Schwarzkopf, Moffo, Barbieri, Alva, Gobbi, Panerai, Philharmonia Ch & O, Karajan, EMI, 1956; 3. Ligabue, Freni, Simionato, Kraus, Evans, Merrill, RCA Italiana Op Ch & O, Solti, Decca, 1963

OTHER OPERAS *Oberto, conte di San Bonifacio*, 1839; *Un giorno di regno/Il finto Stanislao*, 1840; *I lombardi alla prima crociata*, 1843; *I due Foscari*, 1844; *Giovanna d'Arco*, 1845; *Alzira*, 1845; *Attila*, 1846; *I masnadieri*, 1847; *Jérusalem*, 1847; *Il corsaro*, 1848; *La battaglia di Legnano*, 1849; *Les vêpres siciliennes*, 1855; *Simon Boccanegra (I)*, 1857; *Aroldo*, 1857

D.K.

W

Richard Wagner

Wilhelm Richard Wagner; *b* 22 May 1813, Leipzig; *d* 13 February 1883, Venice

Wagner is a major figure in the history of opera and one of the most controversial (and written about) figures of the 19th century. Late photographs of him show an expensively dressed man wearing a velvet beret whose calm and stately expression is that of a prince among artists. The carefully nurtured image of the distinguished 'reformer', however, disguises his mercurial nature and nervous disposition (though they were noticed by Renoir in a startling portrait sketched as late as 1882) and above all is given the lie by a turbulent career, marked almost from the start by radical ideas and actions.

No detail of Wagner's life was too sordid to be aired in public in the 19th century (his liking for silk underwear and supposedly homosexual relations with his patron Ludwig II of Bavaria were two favourites). Yet this lurid fascination would have been unthinkable without the two things that will always be most important about him: the power of his music and the ambitious artistic claim he made for opera. In a sense he marks a return to the noble spirit of court opera in the 17th century – opera, that is, as a festive, unique and spectacular event. Seen in this light, his sheer good luck in finding in Ludwig II a modern royal patron prepared to sponsor him on a reasonably lavish scale seems only logical given the nature of the Wagnerian enterprise. Through the agency of history and myth and the universal humanity he saw in them, the 'extraordinary' operatic occasion, as opposed to the day-to-day opera routinely organized in the public sphere according to market demands, was to be a celebration not so much of royal dynasties as of a notion of art as redemption and catharsis addressed to the entire human race. Drama on the highest level and music aspiring to the condition of the symphony combined with a passion for allegory in a bid to reconcile the modern age of science with some highly ambivalent feelings about it. In other words, a performance of a Wagner 'drama' (posterity is still oblivious to the fact that he rejected the term 'music drama') was not just a special occasion transcending the everyday commercial success of 'modern' opera by, for example, Rossini or Meyerbeer. It was also intended as a drastic form of cultural therapy.

Wagner's worldly polemics (which he set down in 16 substantial volumes of prose works) look clumsy now next to the unshakeable distinction of his art. His defence of the Gesamtkunstwerk – a utopian idea adapted from Herder and the early Romantics proposing the inherent unity of all the arts – and his crusade against opera-as-a-business and the decline of German culture pale before the intoxicating effects of his music and his daring modernity. That he discovered the world of dreams and the unconscious long before Freud, or that he is 'indisputably the father of the structural analysis of myth' (Lévi-Strauss) are claims that have long since been inscribed in tablets of stone in some areas of modernist lore. The German philosopher Adorno even spoke of 'the birth of film out of the spirit of [Wagner's] music', though the remark was intended more as a polemical paradox than as a compliment. (Adorno meant that the seamless musical continuity of Wagner's works, each seductively flaunting its unique identity and the artistic individuality of its creator, had actually anticipated a technological art and subtle means of persuasion that is essentially anonymous and mass produced.)

Wagner's influence both on the development of opera and on purely instrumental music is immense. He began writing operas in the early 1830s. The bloated dimensions of his early efforts (which are often explained away as youthful inexperience) are already a sign of an attempt to push opera to its limits. The decisive breakthrough came with the huge local success of *Rienzi* in Dresden in 1842 (in a heavily cut version), though it was Wagner's fourth opera, *Der fliegende Holländer*, first performed to less enthusiastic audiences a few months later in the same city, that marked his break with provincialism and the real beginning of his distinctive style.

Wagner's greatest musical hero was unquestionably Beethoven, and especially the Beethoven of the symphonies. Wagner emulated him in parts of his operas up to *Lohengrin* (and in many early instrumental works now mercifully forgotten) but developed a large-scale, quasi-symphonic style of his own only by the time he began work on the music of the *Ring*. The symphonic element in Wagner's operas is said to have ensured their international success because it was 'the essence of what had been expected of German music since the time of Haydn and Beethoven' (Carl Dahlhaus). But arguably the much vaunted symphonic 'unity' of Wagner's famous system of leitmotifs was less crucial than the way his leitmotifs imprinted themselves on the memory (Adorno likened them to advertising jingles). Indeed, his uncanny sense of musical metaphor, which he refined through an intense study of early Romantic lieder and then applied on a much larger and hence more public scale in his stage works, probably did more than anything else to establish his enormous fame by attracting ears previously deaf to opera and the classical style.

One of Wagner's principal aims was to make music come of age, so to speak, by proceeding from the notion of the sublime (as opposed to the beautiful) and by fusing music in an unprecedented way with literary and philosophical ideas. For Wagner this meant nothing less than the end of opera with its schematic sequence of set pieces (during the first stages of writing the *Ring* he declared publicly that he was going to write 'no more operas') and a widening of tonality and thematic continuity. To put it another way, Wagner found a cogent justification for taking music beyond its perceived limits of expression by cutting opera loose from its traditional moorings. Whatever the validity of his rationale now, the historical impact of the music that resulted from it is undeniable. He was able to organize vast tracts of continuously flowing music in which swift changes in stylistic level and syntax were possible – a bold adventure in harmony and large-scale structure that left an indelible mark on the late 19th-century symphony. On a subjective level, his musical innovations led to new extremes of sensibility and for many a dangerous feeling of disorientation, which Nietzsche likened to the sense of losing one's depth in a large ocean. Others have simply compared his music to a drug.

In almost every respect Wagner's most radical work is *Tristan und Isolde*. Based on a medieval source noted for its vivid depiction of existential love and 'eternal death' and overlaid with a provocative interpretation of Schopenhauer's 'Metaphysics of Sexual Love', it was a cause célèbre by the end of the 19th century mainly on account of the explicit eroticism of its music. It is still Wagner's most incandescent work, standing on the threshold of musical modernity with its daring harmonies and open-ended musical syntax. At the same time its stubborn individuality and hot-house aestheticism – the sensual yearning for death and nothingness that has prompted its critics to accuse Wagner of cultural exhaustion and a pernicious nihilism – are at odds with Wagner's ideal of opera as a unique and revitalizing communal experience. Not surprisingly Wagner retreated from the extreme position of *Tristan*. Schopenhauer's negation of the will and denial of life (or rather Wagner's version of them) are transformed in subsequent works into a more conciliatory and beguiling form of world-sorrow by the inclusion of more obviously humanistic themes – such as the popularity of art and the principle of nation (*Die Meistersinger*) and the conquering of sensuality by a divine moral code (*Parsifal*). Wagner's music became more accessible after *Tristan* too, but paradoxically also much richer and more refined than before.

Wagner was an outstanding performer and producer of his own works as well as those of others, including Gluck, Mozart and Beethoven. He influenced a whole generation in the art of conducting. But perhaps the most significant thing he did, apart from composing several masterpieces, was to organize the building of the Bayreuth Festival Theatre. It was constructed according to his specifications, with an auditorium in the form of an amphitheatre (the opposite of the hierarchical seating arrangement in the court theatres with their tiers of boxes), a sunken and invisible orchestra, and a double proscenium, which creates an illusion of perspective concentrating attention on to the stage image. It was an experiment in what Wagner called 'public art' that attempted to evade the then prevailing social and commercial conditions of opera in order to turn each performance of his works into something 'special' and available to all. From the first it could never be entirely independent of the conditions it sought to escape, as Wagner himself came to realize. But it still stands as a monument to that ideal.

Wagner's description of vocal parts is sometimes confusing and frequently inconsistent. Wotan in *Die Walküre* is a 'high bass', for instance, although now he would be called a 'bass baritone' or even a 'heroic baritone'. Alberich, Fasolt and Gunther in the *Ring* are also each described as a 'high bass'. This does not mean of course that they are to be cast with the same kind of voice. Wagner's descriptions usually refer to the vocal range, as opposed to the character, of a role. In *Siegfried* the Wanderer (Wotan) is thus a straightforward bass, as the tessitura of the part is lower than the Wotan in *Die Walküre*. In the following entries the voice specifications used by Wagner in his manuscript scores and first printed editions have been retained without further comment.

Der fliegende Holländer
The Flying Dutchman

Romantic opera in three acts (2h 15m)
Libretto by the composer
Composed: libretto 1840, 1841; music 1840, 1841, rev. 1842, 1846, 1852, 1860
PREMIERES 2 January 1843, Royal Saxon Court Theatre, Dresden; UK: 23 July 1870, Drury Lane, London (in Italian); US: 8 November 1876, Academy of Music, Philadelphia (in Italian)
CAST Daland *b*, Senta *s*, Erik *t*, Mary *c*, Daland's Steersman *t*, the Dutchman *high b*; *tb* choruses of sailors from the Norwegian ship, the Flying Dutchman's crew, *sa* chorus of young women

It is not certain when Wagner decided to turn the subject of the Flying Dutchman into an opera. However, there is no doubt that his chief model was Heinrich Heine's *Memoirs of Herr von Schnabelewopski*, though he could have been acquainted with other sources such as Wilhelm Hauff's fairy tale *Geschichte vom Gespensterschiff* (1825). The first surviving document is a prose scenario in French written during May 1840. Wagner's intention was to offer it to Meyerbeer's librettist Eugène Scribe, who would turn it into a libretto for a one-act curtain-raiser to a larger ballet (a practice then in vogue in Paris), which he, Wagner, would then be commissioned by the Opéra to compose. The plan was not new. Indeed, with a similar goal in mind Wagner had already sent Scribe a detailed scenario for a projected opera, *Die hohe Braut*, from Königsberg as early as 1836. But like practically all Wagner's Paris plans, this one fell on stony ground. Wagner received promises from the Opéra for an audition of three numbers (Senta's ballad, and the two sailors' songs in what is now Act III), which he composed between May and July 1840. The audition, however, never took place.

In 1841 Wagner sold the original scenario to the Paris Opéra for 500 francs. The Opéra then commissioned two librettists and the composer Pierre-Louis-Philippe Dietsch, later the conductor of the ill-fated Paris *Tannhäuser* performances in 1861, to turn Wagner's draft into *Le vaisseau fantôme*, which after only 11 performances sank, like the ship of its title, into eternal oblivion. According to Wagner's biography, he was forced to sell the scenario in order to rent the piano he needed to compose the opera himself. Much has been made of Wagner's 'humiliation' at having to do this, but the French prose scenario and the opera he eventually made out of it are actually very different. Wagner not only expanded the scale of the work but also altered its 'tone' in order to introduce, or to elaborate on, several literary motifs in a way that went far beyond the scope of the first version, not to say notions of opera current at the time. The Dutchman's nihilism and yearning for death; the quasi-Christian idea of redemption; Senta's preoccupation with dreams and folly or illusion (*Wahn*); the transformation of Senta's suitor into a hunter whose humble profession and clumsy demeanour serve as a foil to her utopian release (in effect a *Liebestod à la Tristan*) from the narrow world he represents: all these elements meant that by the time Wagner had finished the libretto of *Holländer* in May 1841 he had included, at least in embryo, many of the major themes that were to dominate his later works.

The new version was so much more ambitious than the first that Wagner had no hesitation in offering it to the Court Opera in Berlin as a fully fledged opera that could fill an entire evening. With Meyerbeer's help, it was accepted in March 1842. But delays, and a counter-offer from Dresden following the huge success of *Rienzi* there in October 1842, prompted Wagner to withdraw it. The opera was eventually given four performances in Dresden under Wagner's direction with Johann Michael Wächter as the Dutchman and Wilhelmine Schröder-Devrient in the role of Senta. It was only a moderate success. A few performances followed in 1843 in Riga and Kassel (where it was conducted by Spohr) and then in Berlin in 1844. The opera quickly disappeared from the repertoire before Wagner himself revived it in Zurich in April and May 1852.

SYNOPSIS

Act I: The Norwegian coast, a steep cliff. Forced by fierce weather to cast anchor, Daland has gone ashore to reconnoitre. He recognizes Sandwike, a bay just seven miles from his home. He curses the wind – 'blowing out of the devil's crevice' – that prevents him from seeing Senta, his daughter. He returns on board and retires to his cabin, assuring his crew that all is well. The steersman is left on watch. He too sings of a loved one tantalizingly close. As he falls asleep, the storm revives and the Flying Dutchman's ship appears. The Dutchman, dressed in black Spanish costume, comes ashore. He is condemned to travel the seas for ever, returning to land every seven years in a hopeless search for salvation ('Die Frist ist um'). Only the Day of Judgement can save him, when the world will shatter and eternal oblivion will be his. Daland returns on deck and shakes his steersman awake. He catches sight of the Dutchman, who asks him for hospitality and the hand of his daughter in return for unimaginable riches. Daland readily agrees. The steersman announces a favourable wind from the south, and the rest of the Norwegian crew join in a jubilant final verse of his song.

Act II: A large room in Daland's house. A picture of a pale, bearded man wearing a black Spanish costume hangs on the wall. Senta is transfixed by it. Her governess Mary and the other women sit round a fire, spinning. The women sing of their spinning wheels creating enough wind to bring their lovers home. They mock Senta for falling in love with the old picture. She retorts by singing the ballad of the legendary Dutchman ('Traft ihr das Schiff im Meere an'). Salvation awaits him only if he can find a woman faithful unto death. 'I am that woman,' Senta declares, to the consternation of all. Only Erik's announcement of Daland's return brings her to her senses. Erik and Senta are alone. Erik is convinced that his hunter's livelihood will not qualify him in Daland's eyes as Senta's suitor and begs her to persuade her father otherwise. She feels more for the picture than for him, he complains. When she leads him close to the portrait to convey her feelings, he is certain that the devil has taken possession of her. He tells her of his dream ('Auf hohem Felsen lag ich träumend'). Senta listens enraptured: a strange ship; two men, one Senta's father, the other pale, wearing a black cloak; she kisses the stranger wildly; they both flee out to sea. Senta knows the dream is true. Daland and the stranger arrive. As Senta now gazes on the real Dutchman, Daland formally introduces them ('Mögst du, mein Kind'), but they ignore his banal speech about marriage and wealth. After Daland has discreetly withdrawn in amazement, the Dutchman expresses his mixed feelings about Senta ('Wie aus der Ferne'). Is she a long-lost dream come true? Or one of Satan's tricks? Senta asks if this is folly, an illusion ('ist's ein Wahn?'). She is deeply moved by the Dutchman's suffering. In turn, the Dutchman is touched by her compassion. She is an angel. He warns her of the terrible sacrifices she must make if she promises eternal faithfulness ('Ach! könntest das Geschick du ahnen'). But Senta is overcome by a powerful magic and does not flinch from her resolve to save him. Daland returns with a curious crowd. They are delighted at what they think is going to be a successful marriage.

Act III: A bay on a rocky shore. In the foreground to one side is Daland's house. The Norwegian ship, light and festive, is in the background with the Dutchman's vessel, shrouded in darkness, anchored nearby. The sailors celebrate ('Steuermann, lass' die Wacht!') and joke that the crew of the other ship are either all dead or like dragons guarding their hoard. Despite the Norwegian sailors' taunts, the strange vessel stays silent. Suddenly a fierce storm flares up around the Dutchman's ship, and its crew sing that Satan has charmed it so that it will sail until eternity. The Norwegians flee in terror. Erik is horrified that Senta has agreed to marry the Dutchman. Does she not remember embracing him, as if to confess her love? ('Willst jenes Tag's du nicht dich mehr entsinnen'). The Dutchman overhears the conversation and misinterprets it. As he suspected, Senta is unfaithful: he will never find salvation. Senta frantically tries to convince him that he is wrong. Erik calls for help. The Dutchman reveals his true identity and in ecstasy Senta cries out to him as he departs ('Preis deinen Engel'). She leaps into the ocean and immediately the Dutchman's ship sinks. Against the rising sun, Senta and the Dutchman appear transfigured, soaring upwards hand in hand above the wreck of the vessel.

Wagner always insisted that *Der fliegende Holländer* was the opera that marked the real beginning of his career. From a critical point of view he was undoubtedly right. Historians have protested that *Rienzi* (in which the sublime and the unspeakably banal are disconcertingly entwined) has been seriously misjudged largely because of Wagner's over-negative and highly influential critique of it. Yet despite the magnificent moments in *Rienzi* and the fact that it is close to *Holländer* chronologically (at one point Wagner was working on both operas simultaneously) there is no denying that *Holländer* is in almost every respect a superior work.

Exactly how Wagner turned virtually overnight into a composer of genius is not an easy question to answer. The change from the historical subject matter of *Rienzi* to the more suggestive, and for Wagner always more sympathetic, world of myth and legend in *Holländer* clearly made a difference. So, too, did the dire circumstances of his life. An exile in Paris suffering endless setbacks in the fight for recognition, Wagner was arguably more deeply touched by the image of 'the Wandering Jew of the ocean' (Heine) than he ever had been by Rienzi's grandiose idealism. To see experiences in life as sources of artistic inspiration may no longer be fashionable, but it would be a cold critic who ignored a possible connection between Wagner's serious existential doubts in his early Paris years and the bleak intensity of some of the best music in *Holländer*. The words 'in need and care' (*in Noth und Sorgen*) written at the end of the composition draft on 22 August 1841 meant exactly what they said.

Wagner was preoccupied at regular intervals with the Dutchman throughout a major period of his life. For the first performances he transposed Senta's ballad from A minor into G minor and relinquished his original idea of playing the three acts as one without an interval. (The current fashion for producing the opera in its original, supposedly 'authentic' one-act version should be weighed against the fact that Wagner never conducted, or encouraged, a performance of the opera in this form.) He undertook major revisions of the orchestration in 1846, and again in 1852 when he retouched the instrumentation of the ending of the overture. For a performance in Weimar in 1853, he expressly asked Liszt, who was to conduct the opera, to change the orchestration of a single chord: the accompaniment of Senta's cry at the start of the Act II finale. For his Paris concerts in 1860 he made two major additions to the ending of the overture and added a trumpet and two harps to its orchestration. He even began a completely new version of Senta's ballad (a sketch of which has survived) for a model performance of *Holländer* in Munich commissioned in 1864 by King Ludwig. Cosima von Bülow (later Wagner) reported to Ludwig in 1866 that Wagner was intending to revise *Holländer* so that it would be 'worthy to stand alongside *Tannhäuser* and *Lohengrin*'. During Wagner's last years, she noted in her diary (9 April 1880) that he 'wants to postpone the dictation of the autobiography until after the performance of *Parsifal* when he also wants to revise *Der fliegende Holländer*'. Not long afterwards, Cosima recorded one of his most famous remarks: 'He says that he still owes the world *Tannhäuser*' (23 January 1883). Wagner might have added that he still owed the world *Der fliegende Holländer* as well.

RECORDINGS 1. Varnay, Lustig, Uhde, Weber, Bayreuth Festival Ch & O, Keilberth, Teldec, 1955 (live); 2. Rysanek, Liebl, London, Tozzi, Covent Garden Ch & O, Dorati, Decca, 1960; 3. Silja, Kozub, Unger, Adam, Talvela, BBC Ch, NPO, Klemperer, EMI, 1968

Tannhäuser und der Sängerkrieg auf Wartburg

Tannhäuser and the Song Contest on the Wartburg

Grand romantic opera in three acts; from 1859/60 onwards: Handlung in three acts (*c*.3h; so-called Paris version: 3h 15m)
Libretto by the composer
The genesis and revisions of the work (libretto and music) have been divided into four stages as follows: Stage 1 (June 1842–premiere (19 October 1845)): libretto June 1842–April 1843; music July 1843–October 1845. Stage 2 (the preparations for the second performance (27 October 1845) – the first engraved f.s. (June 1860)): libretto spring 1847; music October 1845–May 1847, September 1851. Stage 3 (the preparations for staging the work in Paris (from autumn 1859) – the Paris performances (13, 18, 24 March 1861)): Wagner translates libretto into French September 1859–March 1861; music August/September 1860–March 1861. Stage 4 (August 1861 – the Vienna premiere (22 November 1875)): Wagner reworks libretto into German August/September 1861–spring 1865; music from summer/autumn 1861 (the so-called Paris version played today is actually this version)
PREMIERES 19 October 1845, Royal Saxon Court Theatre, Dresden; US: 4 April 1859, Stadt Theater, New York; UK: 6 May 1876, Covent Garden, London (in Italian)
CAST Herrmann *deep b*, Tannhäuser *t*, Wolfram von Eschinbach *high b*, Walther von der Vogelweide *t*, Biterolf *b*, Heinrich der Schreiber *t*, Reinmar von Zweter *b*, Elisabeth *s*, Venus *s*, a Young Shepherd *s*, 4 Pages 2 *s*, 2 *a*; *satb* chorus of Thuringian knights, counts and nobles, noblewomen, older and younger pilgrims, sirens, naiads, nymphs, maenads; in stages 3 and 4 also: the three Graces, young men, cupids, satyrs, fauns

According to Wagner's autobiography, he was already making plans for *Tannhäuser* in 1841–2 during his first sojourn in Paris. The earliest surviving document is a prose scenario begun on 28 June 1842 after he had returned to Dresden. Here, and in the first libretto (completed in April 1843), the opera is called *Der Venusberg*. Wagner appears to have changed the title soon after finishing the libretto. In a letter to Schumann of 13 June 1843 he referred to the project as *Tannhäuser und der Wartburgkrieg* and in a letter written to his brother the next day simply as *Tannhäuser*.

The word 'and' (as opposed to the conventional 'or') in the opera's final title reflects its derivation from two separate legends: the theme of Tannhäuser and Venus on the one hand and Heinrich von Ofterdingen's defeat in the Wartburg song contest on the other. Wagner was less interested in the epic accounts of the two stories he found in his sources (of which there are more for *Tannhäuser* than any of his previous works) than in bringing them into dramatic conflict with one another. Two key texts were Heine's *Tannhäuser: A Legend* in the *Salon* (1837) – the same collection in which Wagner found the tale of *Der fliegende Holländer* – and Tieck's story *Der getreue Eckart und der Tannenhäuser* from the *Phantasus* collection (1812–17). Wagner never acknowledged his debt to Heine, though he does mention Tieck and E. T. A. Hoffmann's *Der Kampf der Sänger* from *Die Serapionsbrüder* of 1819. But he is disparaging about them and silent, too, about another source he must have known: Ludwig Bechstein's *Sagenschatz des Thüringerlandes* (a 'treasury of tales from Thuringia') of 1835 in which the song contest on the Wartburg and its hero Heinrich von Ofterdingen and the legend of Tannhäuser and the Venusberg are loosely connected. In his Paris years Wagner came across an obscure monograph, *Der Krieg von Wartburg* by C. T. L. Lucas (1838), which boldly claimed that Ofterdingen and Tannhäuser were one and the same person. The bizarre notion was immediately pilloried by the academic establishment, but for Wagner (as he more or less admitted in his autobiography) it was the key to a brilliant idea: the antithesis of two worlds dividing the hero against himself in a tragic conflict between sensuality and asceticism.

Tannhäuser has been described as Wagner's 'most medieval work' (Volker Mertens). This may be true in the sense that Wagner returned via German Romanticism to the spirit of the medieval tale of penance with (for instance) the idea of redemption through love in an afterlife that is deemed to be real, and with the image of the burgeoning staff as a symbol of God's grace for all mankind (including the worst of sinners). Yet Wagner's synthesis of his materials is so strikingly original and modern (the fear that it would be perceived otherwise may have been one reason why he was so coy in acknowledging some of his sources) that to see the opera as medieval at all is to miss its point. The pre-modern world of miracles and burning Christian faith becomes in Wagner's hands an allegory of a modern society impoverished by precisely those Christian values it claims to represent. The dialectical strategy (which Wagner later perfected in *Parsifal*) embraced other modernist issues, including the alienated artist who yearns for the world of the imagination, yet is fatally attracted to the real world as well. For the first time, the opera also betrays Wagner's uninhibited (and masochistic) attitude to sex, especially in his portrayal of Venus, whom he made even more explicit by contrasting her with Elisabeth, her exact opposite. Elisabeth is remotely related to a real historical character, the wife of Landgrave Ludwig IV (1200–27). But as a virgin and quasi-Christian antithesis to Venus, the pagan goddess of love, she is entirely Wagner's invention.

SYNOPSIS

The action takes place in Thuringia and the Wartburg at the beginning of the 13th century.

Act I: A subterranean grotto inside the Venusberg (Hörselberg, near Eisenach). Sirens, naiads, nymphs and bacchantes dance ecstatically. The song of the sirens ('Naht euch dem Strande') interrupts the wild movement at its orgiastic climax, and exhaustion and calm ensue. (In the Paris–Vienna versions, stages 3 and 4, Wagner added satyrs, fauns, young men and an allegory in which the three Graces, with the help of cupids, quell the orgy. An image of the 'rape of Europe', riding on a white bull drawn through a blue sea by tritons and nereids, emerges through the mist at the end.) Tannhäuser, half-kneeling before Venus, his harp at his side, yearns for release from the endlessly pleasurable, artificial world of the Venusberg. Human society and death, measured by real time and marked by pain and freedom, are drawing him away. Full of burning admiration for Venus and her charms ('Dir töne Lob!'), he begs her to let him leave. In despair, she curses him and the cold humans tempting him to abscond. Death will rebuff him, she warns; but he may return when it does. Invoking the Virgin Mary, Tannhäuser breaks away from the magic of the Venusberg. He finds himself at the foot of the Wartburg. A shepherd is singing and playing a pipe in praise of spring. A chorale sung by passing pilgrims moves Tannhäuser to kneel in prayer, as if to atone for his sins. Hunting horns are heard, and the Landgrave appears with a large retinue. Astonished, the knights recognize Tannhäuser, who long ago parted from their company. He refuses their invitation to rejoin them. Only when Wolfram mentions the name of Elisabeth and tells of how much she misses him does he change his mind.

Act II: Elisabeth greets the hall in the Wartburg where at last she is to see Tannhäuser again ('Dich, teure Halle, grüss' ich wieder'). Tannhäuser is led by Wolfram to Elisabeth. They rejoice at their reunion while Wolfram remains in the background, convinced that he has lost Elisabeth's love. The Landgrave sees that Elisabeth is perturbed. He tells her to keep her feelings to herself, at the same time announcing the forthcoming song contest, in which Tannhäuser will once again participate. The power of song, he suggests, may offer a solution. The local nobles with their wives arrive at the Wartburg for the contest. The Landgrave gives the competing singers the task of defining the essence of love in song. Elisabeth will give the winner as his prize whatever he is bold enough to demand. The contest begins. Wolfram, Walther and Biterolf conceive love as something abstract and moral, while Tannhäuser, with increasing vehemence, opposes them with an image of love as a joyous, sensual experience. A fight nearly ensues, prevented only by a pious and conciliatory song from Wolfram ('O Himmel, lass dich jetzt erflehen'). But this merely goads Tannhäuser into singing a fourth verse of the song he sang to Venus at the beginning of the opera, this time with words praising the lusts of the flesh and culminating in the demand that all should hasten to the Venusberg to learn the real meaning of love. The assembled company is scandalized. In the ensuing tumult, Elisabeth shields Tannhäuser from the knights rushing forward to kill him ('Zurück von ihm! Nicht ihr seid seine Richter'). She implores the Landgrave to pardon the sinner, for whose salvation she is prepared to offer her life. Tannhäuser is expelled and ordered to go to Rome to seek forgiveness. As the hymn of the young pilgrims on their way to Rome sounds in the distance, Tannhäuser kisses the hem of Elisabeth's robe and rushes out to join them.

Act III: The Wartburg valley. It is autumn; evening is approaching. Elisabeth looks in vain for Tannhäuser among the pilgrims returning from Rome. She prays to the Virgin to take her from this earth ('Allmächt'ge Jungfrau, hör mein Flehen'), insisting to Wolfram that she must go her way alone. Wolfram is distraught at Elisabeth's decision to sacrifice her life. To calm himself, he begs the evening star to greet Elisabeth as she ascends to heaven ('O du, mein holder Abendstern'). Night has fallen. Tannhäuser, his pilgrim's garb torn, enters with faltering steps. He tells Wolfram of his journey to Rome ('Inbrunst im Herzen') and in particular of the Pope's harsh words to him: 'Just as this staff in my hand can never blossom, so can you never be redeemed from the flames of hell.' Tannhäuser is convinced he is damned and seeks to return to the Venusberg. In the first Dresden version (stage 1) his 'Rome narration' gradually turns into a delirious vision of the Venusberg. In desperation, Wolfram invokes the name of Elisabeth, at which point a chorus behind the scenes announces her blessed martyrdom. Tannhäuser has found salvation through her death and expires in Wolfram's arms. In the revised Dresden version and all later versions (stages 2, 3 and 4) Venus appears in person and calls Tannhäuser to her. At Wolfram's naming of Elisabeth, a funeral procession with chorus appears from the direction of the Wartburg carrying her body on an open bier. Tannhäuser is transfixed at the sound of her name, whereupon Venus vanishes, lamenting that she has lost him. No longer spurned by death and redeemed at last, Tannhäuser sinks down dying over Elisabeth's body. The younger pilgrims enter with a staff that has put forth leaves, celebrating God's miracle with hallelujahs as the rising sun bathes the scene in the morning light.

Wagner did not break entirely with operatic convention in *Tannhäuser*; but by building the opera out of complex scenic units (which often resemble jumbled baroque allegories) he did move several steps beyond it. The richly suggestive dramaturgy, however, was not easy to translate into music. Already in 1843 Wagner hinted to friends that he was having difficulties with the composition of the opera. Considering the musical demands placed on him by the dialectical structure of the action this was hardly surprising. (Tannhäuser's song to Venus, for instance, not only had to sound noble and earnest as he longs for the real world in Act I, but also deliriously sensual when he yearns again for Venus in Act II.) The full score was completed in April 1845 and the first performance took place in Dresden in the following October under Wagner's baton with Joseph Tichatschek in the title role and Wilhelmine Schröder-Devrient as Venus. Audience reaction to the premiere was lukewarm, and Wagner immediately began to revise the score with cuts in the finales of Acts I and II and a new orchestral introduction to Act III. Other alterations followed with the revival in Dresden on 1 August 1847, including a radical recomposition of the ending. Following Liszt's lead in Weimar in 1849, the opera was taken up in the 1850s by nearly every theatre in Germany, which prompted an unceasing flow of instructions and interpretations from Wagner's pen and still more changes to the score. Wagner reserved his most drastic revisions for the three notorious Paris performances of 1861 in French (which were all different from each other) and still persisted in tinkering with the opera for the productions he supervised in Munich (1 August 1867) and Vienna (22 November 1875). The Paris revisions included the expansion and recomposition of the opening bacchanal and the second scene, as well as extensive modifications to the song contest. Except for the Vienna production, the overture was played in full by popular demand in the Paris and Munich performances, even though Wagner had insisted on cutting it and merging it without a break into the bacchanal (ironically a practice now familiar from the so-called Paris version). The version known today as the Paris version is in fact the Vienna version of 1875.

To the end of Wagner's life the preoccupation with the music of *Tannhäuser* never left him, as numerous remarks in Cosima's diaries prove. With the possible exception of *Der fliegende Holländer*, it is his only major score, in a sense, that he never finished composing.

RECORDINGS 1. Dresden version: Grümmer, Schech, Hopf, Fischer-Dieskau, Frick, Berlin State Op Ch, Berlin Staatskapelle, Konwitschny, EMI, 1961; 2. conflation of Dresden & Paris versions: Silja, Bumbry, Windgassen, Waechter, Greindl, Bayreuth Festival Ch & O, Sawallisch, Philips, 1962 (live); 3. Paris version: Dernesch, Ludwig, Kollo, Braun, Sotin, Vienna St Op Ch, VPO, Solti, Decca, 1970

Lohengrin

Romantic opera in three acts (3h 30m)
Libretto by the composer
Composed: libretto 1845; music 1846–8
PREMIERES 28 August 1850, Grand Ducal Court Theatre, Weimar; US: 3 April 1871, Stadt Theater, New York; UK: 8 May 1875, Covent Garden, London (in Italian)
CAST Heinrich der Vogler, deutscher König *b*, Lohengrin *t*, Elsa von Brabant *s*, Duke Gottfried *silent*, Friedrich von Telramund *bar*, Ortrud *s*, King's Herald *b*, 4 Brabantine Nobles 2 *t*, 2 *b*, 4 Pages 2 *s*, 2 *a*; *satb* chorus of Saxon and Thuringian counts and nobles, Brabantine counts and nobles, noblewomen, pages, vassals, women, servants

Written between summer 1845 and April 1848, *Lohengrin* was intended originally for Dresden. To prepare the way for the premiere, Wagner conducted a concert performance of the finale of Act I at the Royal Saxon Court Theatre on 22 September 1848. The scenery was duly commissioned and a full-scale production announced to the press in January 1849. Wagner's involvement in the events leading to the ill-fated Dresden revolution of May 1849 prevented the project from going ahead. The eventual first performance in Weimar was conducted by Liszt, the opera's dedicatee, on the 101st anniversary of Goethe's birth. The place and date were symbolic. After the failed revolutions of 1848–9, increasing nostalgia for Weimar's former cultural glory and Wagner's burgeoning reputation as the radically new hope of German art focused critical attention on the event. The authorities inadvertently played their part by refusing to grant Wagner clemency. He was in political exile in Switzerland, and in the eyes of Germany's cultural vanguard his conspicuous absence only made the premiere yet more significant. (According to Wagner's autobiography, he spent the evening in Lucerne in a tavern called the Swan 'watching the clock and closely following the hour of the opera's beginning and its presumed end'.) Though Wagner conducted excerpts in concerts in Zurich (1853), London (1855), Paris (1860) and Brussels (1860), nearly 11 years elapsed before a partial amnesty enabled him to hear the whole opera for the first time in a dress rehearsal in Vienna in May 1861.

In contrast to the idealism symbolized by the place and date of the premiere of *Lohengrin*, Wagner found its subsequent popularity irksome, especially the fame of its most celebrated item, the Bridal Chorus. Wagner introduced it to English audiences in his London concerts in 1855. Three years later at the marriage of Queen Victoria's daughter, Princess Victoria, to Frederick Wilhelm of Prussia it earned a permanent place in the history of popular culture when it was coupled for the first time with the Wedding March from Mendelssohn's *A Midsummer Night's Dream*. In its original context the Bridal Chorus is a masterpiece of sweet foreboding and a prelude to marital disaster. The irony of its transformation into a much-loved public symbol of faith in the institution of marriage was not lost on Wagner, who sensed almost from the start that undue focus of attention on the best-known 'numbers' in *Lohengrin* left it open to serious misinterpretation. In 1853, when the opera was taken up by several German houses (and not long after by several foreign companies as well), he persuaded Breitkopf und Härtel to publish a brochure with production details and illustrations of scenery and costumes, which he described as 'according to my wishes'. Perhaps rightly resisting this somewhat peremptory authorial vigilance, hardly a single producer responded. Wagner continued to complain of inadequate performances and publicly expressed his dissatisfaction in an open letter of 7 November 1871 to Boito. Though Wagner conducted the opera several times, he personally supervised only two productions of it. The first (conducted by Hans von Bülow) was given on 16 June 1867 in Munich; the second (conducted by Hans Richter) took place in Vienna on 15 December 1875. The Munich production, Wagner told Boito, was the first time the work had been rehearsed according to its 'rhythmic-architectonic structure'.

SYNOPSIS

Act I: The first half of the 10th century. A meadow on the bank of the river Scheldt near Antwerp. After a nine-year truce, the Hungarians are again threatening to attack Germany. King Heinrich I of Saxony (Heinrich der Vogler) has come to Brabant to recruit men to help fend off an attack from the east. He finds the country in disarray and demands to know what is wrong. Friedrich von Telramund explains that he was granted the right to care for Elsa and her younger brother Gottfried, the children of the deceased Duke of Brabant. Gottfried has disappeared, and Friedrich now formally accuses Elsa of murdering him at the instigation of a secret lover. Friedrich is so convinced that Elsa has lost her heart to another man that he has renounced his right to her and married Ortrud, the daughter of Radbod, Prince of Friesland. Elsa is guilty of fratricide, Friedrich argues, and as he is himself next of kin to the dead duke, he has a legitimate claim to be ruler of Brabant in her stead. Elsa is summoned and declares with a powerful radiance that she has dreamed of a knight who will come to protect her. Friedrich, certain that the knight is Elsa's secret lover, agrees to a trial by combat. In the distance a swan is seen drawing a boat carrying a knight in shining armour. The swan appears, accompanied by the growing excitement of the onlookers. Lohengrin steps on shore, and Elsa, at first spellbound by his presence, throws herself enraptured at his feet. He asks her whether she will marry him if he wins on her behalf and lays down his conditions: never is she to ask about, or brood upon, his origin, his lineage or his name. Heinrich leads a prayer ('Mein Herr und Gott'): may God weaken the strength of the liar and give power to the true hero. Lohengrin wins the fight and magnanimously spares Friedrich's life. All rejoice, while Ortrud broods ominously on the mysterious knight who is thwarting her plans.

Act II: The citadel of Antwerp. Night. Friedrich and Ortrud, both shabbily dressed, are sitting on the steps of the minster in the foreground. The windows of the knights' dwelling at the back are brightly lit as the celebrations continue. Friedrich accuses Ortrud of lying to him about Elsa's supposed murder of Gottfried. Ortrud retaliates by calling Friedrich a coward. To regain his honour he must sow doubts in Elsa's mind by accusing Lohengrin of sorcery. If that fails, force must be used: those made strong by magic lose their strength merely by losing the smallest limb. Elsa appears on a balcony and tells the breezes of her happiness ('Euch, Lüften, die mein Klagen'). Her pity is cunningly aroused by Ortrud. As Elsa retires for a moment to let Ortrud inside, Ortrud's false pathos rapidly disappears in an abrupt and violent passage during which she invokes the pagan gods to help her regain power ('Entweihte Götter'). Elsa returns and Ortrud begins to insinuate doubt into her mind with the almost casual warning that her nameless protector could one day leave her just as mysteriously as he came. As day breaks the herald makes four announcements: Friedrich is banished; Brabant is given to Lohengrin who has relinquished the title of duke for that of 'protector'; the wedding between Lohengrin and Elsa is to take place that day; on the next, Lohengrin will lead the men of Brabant into battle. A small group of four nobles dissents. As Elsa approaches the minster where she is to marry her protector, Ortrud interrupts the procession to demand the revelation of Lohengrin's identity. No sooner has Lohengrin tried to comfort Elsa when Friedrich steps forward as well to accuse him of sorcery. Elsa manages to suppress her darkening dismay but not before she receives unwelcome attention from Friedrich. He whispers to her that he can enter the bridal chamber that night to remove a fingertip from Lohengrin, which would break his magic strength. Lohengrin intervenes: he leads his bride solemnly into the minster and, as they reach the highest step, Elsa turns to him in deep emotion, only to catch a glimpse of Ortrud, her arm raised, as if certain of victory.

Act III: The bridal chamber. An exuberant orchestral introduction leads into the gentle Bridal Chorus ('Treulich geführt'). It reflects the transition from highly public events to an intimate space where, after the wedding trains have left, the sense of claustrophobia increases as Elsa's doubts gain control. Nuptial bliss gradually turns insidiously into marital trauma. Elsa finally asks Lohengrin his name and origin, at which point Friedrich and the four disaffected nobles burst in to attack him. Lohengrin kills Friedrich and orders the four nobles to carry the body before Heinrich where, in front of the people of Brabant, Elsa's questions will be answered. Day breaks as the scene changes to the meadow as in Act I. Lohengrin announces that he cannot now lead the Brabantines into battle. He justifies the slaying of Friedrich and announces that Elsa, poisoned by treachery, has broken her vow. He reveals that in a wondrous castle in a far-away place is the holy cup carried to earth by an angel host ('In fernem Land'). Once a year a dove is sent to renew its strength: it is the Grail and it imparts supernatural power to the knights it selects. The Grail sends the knights to distant lands on errands of chivalry, but only on condition that they depart once their identity is known. Lohengrin announces that he is the son of Parsifal, King of the Grail, and utters his own name. The swan is seen returning. Lohengrin tells Elsa that had he been able to stay for only one year at her side the power of the Grail would have returned her brother to her. Lohengrin gives Elsa three objects to pass on to her brother if he ever returns: a horn to assist him in danger, a sword to make him victorious in battle and a ring to remind him of his sister's protector. Ortrud gloats on her apparent triumph ('Fahr' heim, du stolzer Helde!'), bragging that it was she who made Gottfried disappear by using a magic chain to turn him into a swan. Lohengrin answers her with a prayer. The white dove of the Grail hovers over the boat, and the swan is miraculously transformed into Gottfried, a beautiful youth in gleaming silver apparel. As Lohengrin proclaims him leader of Brabant, Ortrud sinks powerless to the ground. Gottfried bows to Heinrich and rushes into the arms of his sister, while Lohengrin, standing with head bowed in the boat now being drawn by the dove, recedes into the distance. Elsa's soul leaves her body as she gradually collapses in her brother's arms.

The music of *Lohengrin* is hard to describe as forward-looking, yet equally difficult to dismiss as reactionary. In the first editions of the libretto and full score Wagner called *Lohengrin* a romantic opera, though he later withdrew the designation. The aura of chivalrous romance in *Lohengrin* notwithstanding, the opera also has an oddly 'classical' air about it. The polyphonic orchestral writing much admired by Richard Strauss, the close motivic relationships and, above all, the neat, often uncomfortably schematic dramatic and musical symmetries – the recapitulation of the Grail music in Act III, for instance – are all evidence of Wagner's ambition to inject into the medium of opera something of the spirit of the great classical symphonists.

The musical details of *Lohengrin*, however, are rarely judged properly, mainly because Wagner's progressive tendencies, usually traced by historians with depressing regularity exclusively to *Tristan* and *Parsifal*, are said to consist of near-atonal chromaticism and irregular phrase structure. In fact, the anti-chromatic moments of *Lohengrin* are often the most striking (the opening of the prelude, for instance) and even the regular phrases of the Bridal Chorus can seem daring and ambivalent in context. In a sense, *Lohengrin* is a contradiction in terms: it mixes genres that do not mix (fairy-tale opera and grand historical drama) and its music can still sound original precisely where, according to the conventional view of musical progress, it is least avant-garde.

With the exception of the Prelude, which was written last, *Lohengrin* is the first work Wagner composed systematically from beginning to end with almost polemical disregard for clear demarcations between operatic set pieces. (Ernest Newman's statement that the last act was composed first and the second act last is contradicted by the sketches.) The new method added irony to the initial success of the opera as a series of popular concert pieces, though it must be pointed out that Wagner's indulgence in allowing its large-scale formal rhythm (more akin to a symphony than an opera) to co-exist with more short-winded 'numbers' that could satisfy the most conservative of operatic tastes was part and parcel of his aesthetic strategy from the start. Wagner always rightly insisted, however, that *Lohengrin* is closer to the grand designs and seamless continuity of his later music dramas than it is usually thought to be. This may account for the fact that, in contrast to his other early operas, he was never tempted to revise it. The only substantial change he made was a cut in Lohengrin's Grail narration in Act III, which he communicated to Liszt shortly before the first performance.

RECORDINGS 1. Steber, Varnay, Windgassen, Uhde, Greindl, Bayreuth Festival Ch & O, Keilberth, Teldec, 1953; 2. Grümmer, Ludwig, Thomas, Fischer-Dieskau, Frick, Vienna State Op Ch, VPO, Kempe, EMI, 1962/3; 3. Studer, Meier, Jerusalem, Welker, Moll, Vienna State Op Concert Ch, VPO, C. Abbado, DG, 1991/2

Der Ring des Nibelungen

Ein Buhnenfestspiel fur drei Tage und einen Vorabend

The Ring of the Nibelung
A stage festival play for three days and a preliminary evening

Libretto by the composer
PREMIERES as a cycle: 13–17 August 1876, Festspielhaus, Bayreuth; UK: 5–9 May 1882, Her Majesty's Theatre, Haymarket, London; US: 4–11 March 1889, Metropolitan, New York

Der Ring des Nibelungen is the biggest work in the history of Western music. It took 28 years to write, rewrite, rehearse and finally to perform in its entirety at the first Bayreuth Festival in 1876. Wagner conceived it initially as an allegory of the social unrest in Europe that began with the Paris uprisings in February 1848. (The first documented reference to the project is 1 April of that year.) It soon turned into a parable of riddles and emotional conflict that dissolved politics into philosophical poetry, as it were, and reached far beyond the political upheavals that first inspired it. Even before the revolutions of 1848–9 Wagner's political views had been part of a utopian quest for a new kind of theatre that could reflect different truths about society that were less acute and yet – clouded by paradox and contradiction as they often were – more suggestive than politics or philosophy ever could be. Wagner saw the *Ring* as his *summum opus*, which represented this ideal in its most radical form.

The *Ring* began relatively simply as the libretto of a single work, *Siegfrieds Tod* (later revised and retitled *Götterdämmerung*), which was first sketched in October 1848. Wagner's main source was the Middle High German *Nibelungenlied*, though he was by no means the first to consider its operatic possibilities. The philosopher F. T. Vischer had already published an essay in 1844 suggesting that the epic poem – regarded since its discovery in the mid-1700s as a kind of German *Iliad* – could be used as the subject of a new kind of musical drama, which he called 'a grand heroic opera'. Probably following Vischer's example, Wagner designated *Siegfrieds Tod* in the same way and based the opera mainly on the first half of the *Nibelungenlied*, amplifying it with details from the second and from other versions of the legend.

In 1851 Wagner made the momentous decision to expand *Siegfrieds Tod* into a cycle of four dramas, which he called collectively *Der Ring des Nibelungen*. By this time he had undertaken a much more thorough study of the older oral tradition of the Nibelung myth. Among the works he examined and re-examined were the Old Norse Eddic poems, the so-called *Poetic Edda*, Snorri Sturluson's 13th-century explanatory account of Scandinavian myth known as the *Prose Edda*, and the ancient narrative accounts in the *Völsunga Saga* and *Thidreks Saga*. From the *Poetic Edda* Wagner adapted the technique of *Stabreim* (the linking of words and lines by alliteration instead of end rhyme) as a new way of writing the texts for the additional dramas *Das Rheingold*, *Die Walküre* and *Der junge Siegfried* (as *Siegfried* was then called). The wealth of mythical situations that Wagner found in the older sources – the trials, contracts, riddles and prophecies, to name only a few – were also bound to tempt him to try something more than just another series of operas in the German Romantic tradition. His utopian journey from 'grand heroic opera' to a complex world myth or 'drama of the future', as he liked to refer to the new project, was inseparable from his discovery of the Nibelung myth in what he believed to be its most archaic form.

Another reason for Wagner's decision to write a four-part cycle (or more precisely a trilogy with a preliminary evening) was his conception of the project as a festival event. Here his model was the ancient Greek festival of Dionysus at Athens. His intention was not to imitate the awesome Athenian spectacles, but rather to revive their sense of communal celebration (as opposed to art as mere entertainment), which in his view the modern theatre totally lacked. Certain dramatic techniques, however, and even the idea of a thematically related cycle of festival dramas itself, were borrowed directly from Aeschylus. The blending of politics and myth; the interplay of gods and humans; the curse that drives the action forward with the oppressive memories of past events; the rule of law and the resolution of guilt; the cosmic mythical presentation of nature: the shaping of the *Ring* drama clearly owed a good deal to the *Oresteia* and to *Prometheus Bound*.

Almost from the start, the idea of the Ring project as a festival occasion went hand in hand with the notion of a theatre built specially for its performance. Two years after writing the libretto of *Siegfrieds Tod*, Wagner was already seriously thinking of designing and building a temporary theatre for it outside Zurich to which he would 'invite the most suitable singers and organize everything necessary for a special event' (letter to E. B. Kietz, 14 September 1850). The idea was not carried out; nor did a later, far more ambitious, project fare much better when Ludwig II placed Wagner under contract in the mid-1860s to complete the *Ring* and ordered plans to proceed for a festival theatre to be built on the Gasteig in Munich, only to see the scheme aborted through political intrigue. The realization of this, for its creator extremely important, aspect of the *Ring* had to wait until the building of the Bayreuth Festival Theatre in the 1870s, which Wagner managed to bring about largely through private initiative and the co-operation of the Bayreuth authorities. Ludwig II, irritated that Wagner had relinquished Munich as a festival site, was eventually persuaded to support the project.

In many other respects, however, the *Ring* is not at all like Greek drama. Nor in the course of its history has it ever really been dependent on Wagner's original festival concept. In a sense it is a return to the detailed scenic images of nature and mythological symbolism characteristic of 17th-century opera and also to what Walter Benjamin has called the 'allegorical drapery' of the baroque *Trauerspiele* (literally 'sorrow-plays') to which the *Ring* text, richly embroidered as it is with powerfully suggestive icons, is by no means unrelated. (Wagner was a great admirer, for instance, of the allegorical plays of the Spanish dramatist Calderón.) The *Ring* is also a strange amalgam of poetic and musical imagery borrowed from the early Romantic lied, techniques indebted to Beethoven's monumental symphonic style, modernist ideas about politics and myth inherited mainly from Hegel's critics (the so-called Young Hegelians), the world of fairy tale and, last but not least, a wonderfully inventive harmonic language indebted in part to the works of Franz Liszt.

Wagner published the *Ring* libretto in a private edition early in 1853, several months before he began composing the music for it. He read the entire text several times to groups of friends and acquaintances (many of whom later reported on the riveting power of his delivery) and published it again in revised form in 1863, this time with a preface containing an appeal to a 'princely patron' who might be found to help finance the project. It was this first public edition of the *Ring* text that drew the attention of the young Ludwig II and led to the famous association between the two men that changed the course of Wagner's life. Repercussions from the earlier private edition, however, had not been so positive. Without music, the words of the *Ring* on their own either seemed gratuitously artificial and inept (even to some of Wagner's friends) or gave the impression of an arcane, neo-gothic disinterment of medieval legend that was of merely academic interest. Indeed, a not insignificant detail in the history of the *Ring* is the fact that the first book about it to appear (by Franz Müller) was not so much about the cycle and its wider implications but rather an introduction to its medieval sources and, moreover, one published as early as 1862 before a note of the music had been performed in public. It is true that not long afterwards Wagner conducted excerpts from the music he had composed so far in two concerts in Vienna. But misunderstanding – and ridicule – of the *Ring* libretto persisted and was certainly a factor in Wagner's negative reaction to the premieres of *Das Rheingold* and *Die Walküre* ordered to take place by Ludwig II and conducted by Franz Wüllner in Munich in 1869 and 1870. Wagner did not attend the performances (though a large portion of Europe's musical intelligentsia did), partly on the reasonable grounds that an incomplete production of the cycle, which he had not even finished composing, could only lead to further misapprehension. He refused access to the full score of the third act of *Siegfried*, without which the premiere of the third drama in the cycle planned by Ludwig for 1871 could not take place. And in blatant breach of his 1864 contract with the king, he undermined all attempts by Munich to procure *Götterdämmerung*, the full score of which was finally finished on 21 November 1874.

Eventually, after superhuman efforts on Wagner's part, the first performance of all four dramas as a cycle took place under his direction in the newly built Festival Theatre in Bayreuth in August 1876 with a cast that included Amalie Materna as Brünnhilde, Franz Betz as Wotan and Albert Niemann as Siegmund. Wagner entrusted the conducting to his protégé Hans Richter, among other reasons because of his immense knowledge of instruments, which proved invaluable in helping the orchestral musicians to solve some formidable technical problems in a score that at the time counted as one of the most modern and sophisticated in existence. Financially, the event was so disastrous that Wagner had to close the Festival Theatre for the next six years. The performances themselves were a different matter. Uneven as they were, they convinced many critics and observers that, far from simply resurrecting an archaic legend that for years had been the preserve of university professors, Wagner had successfully created, largely through the power of his music, a completely new myth that could provide a key to an interpretation and deeper understanding of the contemporary world for a wider audience.

Das Rheingold (Preliminary Evening)

The Rhinegold

In one act (2h 30m)
Composed: libretto 1851–2; music 1853–4
PREMIERES 26 December 1862, Theater an der Wien, Vienna (excerpts from Scenes 1, 2 and 4; concert); 22 September 1869, Royal Court and National Theatre, Munich (stage); 13 August 1876, Festspielhaus, Bayreuth (as part of the *Ring* cycle); UK: 5 May 1882, Her Majesty's Theatre, Haymarket, London; US: 4 January 1889, Metropolitan, New York
CAST Gods: Wotan *high b*, Donner *high b*, Froh *t*, Loge *t*; Goddesses: Fricka *low s*, Freia *high s*, Erda *low s*; Nibelungs: Alberich *high b*, Mime *t*;

Giants: Fasolt *high b*, Fafner *low b*; Rhinedaughters: Woglinde *high s*, Wellgunde *high s*, Flosshilde *low s*; *tb* chorus of Nibelungs

SYNOPSIS

Scene 1: At the bottom of the Rhine. In greenish twilight steep rocks are visible. Water swirls around them at the top while the waves dissolve into a damp mist lower down. The Rhinedaughters circle round the central reef, which points upward to the brighter light above. Alberich comes out of a cleft in the rocks and makes advances to the Rhinedaughters, who cruelly lead him on. Alberich eventually realizes that he is being ridiculed. Silenced by anger, he catches sight of the gleaming Rhinegold high on the central reef. Wellgunde imprudently reveals that whoever can fashion an all-powerful ring from the gold will inherit the world ('Der Welt Erbe gewänne zu eigen'). To the accompaniment of the famous Wagner tubas (sounding here for the first time), Woglinde adds that the required magic can be attained only by renouncing love ('Nur wer der Minne Macht entsagt'). Alberich curses love with hideous passion and snatches the gold before vanishing into the depths.

Scene 2: An open space high in the mountains. The light of dawn reflects off the battlements of a magnificent castle. Wotan dreams of eternal power and a fortress for the gods. His wife Fricka rudely awakens him. While Wotan gazes enraptured at the magnificent edifice he has just been dreaming about, Fricka bluntly reminds him of its price. Built by the giant brothers Fasolt and Fafner, the fortress is to be paid for by giving them Freia, keeper of the golden apples of eternal youth. Freia rushes in, complaining that she has been threatened by Fasolt. The giants enter, and Fasolt proceeds to lecture Wotan on the significance of contracts. The more pragmatic Fafner, however, knowing that Freia is indispensable to the gods, proposes to abduct her by force. Donner and Froh, Freia's brothers, hurry in to protect their sister, but the giants invoke their contract. The long-awaited god of fire, Loge, on whom Wotan is relying to find a way out of the dilemma, joins the gods at last and tells of many things ('So weit Leben und Weben'), including Alberich's theft of the gold and the mighty ring he has fashioned from it. The giants agree to take Freia away as a provisional hostage until evening and then to hand her over in exchange for the gold. A pallid mist fills the stage. The gods begin to age, fearfully looking to Wotan for a way out of their plight. Wotan decides to travel with Loge to Nibelheim to take possession of the gold.

Scene 3: A subterranean cavern. Tormented in the first scene, Alberich is now the tormenter. With great skill, his brother Mime has created the Tarnhelm, a magic helmet that enables its wearer to assume any form at will. Alberich takes it from him by force and vanishes in a column of mist. Mime writhes in agony from Alberich's invisible whiplashes. Alberich takes off the Tarnhelm and drives a pack of Nibelung dwarfs laden with treasure before him. Eventually he notices Wotan and Loge. Unable to resist a demonstration of his power, he kisses the ring on his finger, causing the screaming Nibelungs to scatter, and dons the Tarnhelm again to turn himself into a monstrous dragon. Loge cunningly suggests to Alberich that a small creature would better escape danger but that the transformation would probably be too hard to accomplish. Alberich rises to the challenge and turns himself into a toad. Loge and Wotan easily capture him and drag him away.

Scene 4: An open space high in the mountains. Alberich is forced to give up the hoard, which is dragged up through a cleft by the Nibelungs. Already humiliated in front of his own slaves, Alberich is completely ruined when Wotan violently takes the ring from him. Driven to confront Wotan, among other things with the telling argument that his own theft of the gold was a peccadillo compared with Wotan's present betrayal of the laws he supposedly upholds, Alberich curses the ring just as he cursed love in order to create it ('Wie durch Fluch er mir geriet, verflucht sei dieser Ring'). Henceforth no one who possesses the ring will escape death. The giants enter with Freia and plant two stakes in the ground on either side of her. They demand that the hoard be piled up until her shape is concealed. Now it is Wotan's turn to be humiliated: to fill the final crack the giants demand the ring. Wotan refuses until Erda, the goddess of earth, intervenes to deliver a sphinx-like warning about the end of the gods ('Ein düstrer Tag dämmert den Göttern'), advising him to discard the prize. With sudden resolve he throws the ring on to the pile. Freia is free and the gods return to their immortal state, at least for the moment, but to their horror they witness the first effects of the curse as Fafner kills Fasolt in the ensuing struggle for the ring. Donner conjures up a storm to clear the sultry air. Valhalla lies gleaming in the evening sun at the end of a rainbow bridge, which the gods begin to cross in triumph. Diffidently joining the procession, Loge remarks that the gods are really hastening to their end ('Ihrem Ende eilen sie zu'). Their refurbished glory is also dimmed momentarily by the Rhinedaughters, who lament from the depths that their demand that the gold be returned to its original purity has gone unheeded.

Die Walküre (First Day)

The Valkyrie

In three acts (3h 45m)
Composed: libretto 1851–2; music 1854–6
PREMIERES 26 December 1862, Theater an der Wien, Vienna (excerpts from Acts I and III; concert); 26 June 1870, Royal Court and National Theatre, Munich (stage); 14 August 1876, Festspielhaus, Bayreuth (as part of the *Ring* cycle); US: 2 April 1877, Academy of Music, New York, UK: 6 May 1882, Her Majesty's Theatre, Haymarket, London
CAST Siegmund *t*, Hunding *b*, Wotan *high b*, Sieglinde *s*, Brünnhilde *s*, Fricka *s*, Valkyries: Gerhilde, Ortlinde, Waltraute, Schwertleite, Helmwige, Siegrune, Grimgerde, Rossweisse, *s* and *c*

SYNOPSIS

Act I: The interior of a house at the centre of which stands the trunk of a huge ash tree. A man is being pursued. He enters the house and staggers towards the hearth. The wife of Hunding, the absent master of the house, gives him water. The stranger explains that a storm has driven him there and prepares to leave. But the woman begs him to stay. A secret bond begins to grow between them. Hunding returns from combat. He is instinctively distrustful of the stranger but reluctantly grants him hospitality for the night. Hunding insists on knowing his guest's name. The stranger says he calls himself 'Woeful' (*Wehwalt*) and explains by telling the story of his childhood. He and his father Wolf returned one day from the hunt to find his mother murdered and his twin sister abducted. He eventually lost track of his father and has been cursed with bad luck ever since, hence his name. A woman forced to marry someone she did not love had asked him for help, whereupon he killed her brothers whose kinsmen are now hunting him. Hunding, realizing that 'Woeful' is the killer, reveals that he is one of the hunters and challenges the stranger to combat the next day. Only the laws of hospitality protect him for the moment. Hunding's wife has tried to intervene, but Hunding orders her to leave to prepare his nightly drink. Alone, the stranger recalls his father's promise to provide him with a sword when in direst need ('Ein Schwert verhiess mir der Vater'). The woman returns. She has put a sleeping draught in Hunding's drink and proceeds to show the stranger a sword thrust into the tree. It was put there by a one-eyed man during her wedding to Hunding. None of the guests, nor anyone since, has had the strength to draw it out. She believes that the hero who can will more than make up for the shame she has had to endure since robbers forced her to marry Hunding. She embraces the stranger passionately as the great door opens to let in a beautiful spring night. The stranger sings in praise of spring, which, like a brother, has freed love, its sister, from the storms of winter ('Winterstürme wichen dem Wonnemond'). The metaphor soon turns into a reality. The woman knew from the single eye of the old man who planted the sword that she was his daughter. Seeing the same look in the stranger's eyes, she suspects that she is related to him too. The stranger asks her to give him a name she loves. When he tells her that his father's name was not Wolf, but Wälse, she knows for certain that he is the Wälsung for whom the sword is intended. She calls him Siegmund. Revelling in his name ('Siegmund heiss ich und Siegmund bin ich'), Siegmund pulls the sword from the tree with a mighty wrench. Rapt with wonder and delight, the woman tells him that she is his twin sister Sieglinde. They embrace in ecstasy as Siegmund calls for the blossoming of the Wälsung race.

Act II: A wild and rocky mountainside. Wotan knows that Siegmund and Sieglinde are fleeing from Hunding and that Hunding will eventually overtake them. He charges his favourite daughter Brünnhilde (borne to him by the earth goddess Erda) with the task of ensuring Siegmund's victory in his forthcoming duel with Hunding. Brünnhilde warns Wotan of the 'violent storm' in store for him from his wife Fricka, the guardian of marriage, who is approaching in a chariot drawn by a pair of rams. Fricka insists that Hunding has a right to vengeance. She upholds the law in the face of Wotan's advocacy of nature. The power of spring may have brought the twins together, but their incestuous union is a monstrous affront to reason. As for Wotan's grand idea of a free hero who would allow the gods to escape their guilty complicity in the theft of the Rhinegold, this is just false: Siegmund is not free, but merely a pawn in a game invented by Wotan, who is himself severely compromised by his promiscuity. Humbled by the sheer force of Fricka's reasoning, Wotan agrees to forbid Brünnhilde to let Siegmund win the battle against Hunding. The hero must be sacrificed to preserve the divine law. Alone with Brünnhilde, Wotan confesses that all along he has been deceiving himself. Master of the laws of the universe, he is also their victim. Only the end of everything he has built will cleanse the guilt of the gods ('Auf geb' ich mein Werk: nur eines will ich noch: das Ende!'). And for that end Alberich is working. He has created a son whom Wotan now blesses: may the hate of Alberich's child feed on the empty glory of the gods' divinity. Brünnhilde cannot accept Wotan's bleak nihilism and argues to protect Siegmund. Wotan threatens her with the direst consequences if she rebels. Siegmund and Sieglinde enter. Sieglinde is haunted by nightmarish visions of Hunding and his dogs in pursuit of them. She faints in Siegmund's arms. Brünnhilde appears to Siegmund and announces his impending death ('Siegmund! Sieh auf mich!'). But he refuses to go to Valhalla if Sieglinde cannot join him. Rather than put her and their unborn child at the mercy of a hostile world, he threatens to kill them. Brünnhilde is overcome by this display of human emotion and promises to defy her father's command. Hunding's horn is heard summoning Siegmund to battle. Sieglinde's nightmare is now a reality. Brünnhilde protects Siegmund with her shield. But Wotan intervenes and forces Siegmund's sword to shatter on his spear. Hunding drives his spear into the breast of the unarmed Siegmund. Wotan looks in anguish at Siegmund's body and with a dismissive wave of the hand causes Hunding to fall down dead. Meanwhile Brünnhilde has fled with Sieglinde on horseback after gathering up the pieces of the broken sword. In a thunderous rage Wotan storms off in pursuit of them.

Act III: On the summit of a rocky mountain. The Valkyries gather together with warlike exuberance, each with a slain hero destined for Valhalla on the saddle of her horse. To their astonishment Brünnhilde arrives with a woman. The Valkyrie sisters, fearful of Wotan's wrath, refuse to protect them. Brünnhilde tells Sieglinde to flee to a forest in the east where she will be safe. There she will give birth to the noblest hero of the world ('den hehrsten Helden der Welt'). Brünnhilde gives her the shattered pieces of the sword and names the hero Siegfried, one joyous in victory, predicting that he will one day forge the fragments anew. Sieglinde sings a striking motif in reply ('O hehrstes Wunder! Herrlichste Maid!'), which Wagner called the 'Glorification of Brünnhilde'. Brünnhilde faces Wotan without the protection of her sisters. To their horror, he condemns her to lie defenceless in a magic sleep, vulnerable to the first man who finds her. The Valkyries gallop away wildly. Left alone with Wotan, Brünnhilde justifies her actions. Although she is not wise, she knew in her heart that Wotan loved Siegmund ('Nicht weise bin ich, doch wusst'ich das eine, dass den Wälsung du liebst'), which is why she disobeyed his order. Wotan is moved against his better judgement by her courage. Reluctantly he grants her only request. She is to be surrounded by a magic fire that only the freest hero who knows no fear can penetrate. With great emotion, Wotan bids farewell to his daughter and summons Loge to encircle her with fire: only one freer than himself will be able to win her.

Siegfried (*Second Day*)

In three acts (4h 15m)
Composed: libretto 1851–2; music 1856–7 (to end of Act II in second draft), 1864–5 (orchestration of Act II), 1869–71 (Act III)
PREMIERES 1 January 1863, Theater an der Wien, Vienna (excerpts from Act I; concert); 16 August 1876, Festspielhaus, Bayreuth (as part of the *Ring* cycle); UK: 8 May 1882, Her Majesty's Theatre, Haymarket, London; US: 9 November 1887, Metropolitan, New York
CAST Siegfried *t*, Mime *t*, the Wanderer (Wotan) *b*, Fafner *b*, Erda *c*, Brünnhilde *s*, Woodbird *boy s*

SYNOPSIS
Act I: The opening of a cave in the forest. Mime is frustrated that he can neither forge a sword strong enough for Siegfried nor piece together the shattered fragments of Notung ('Zwangvolle Plage'). Notung is the only weapon adequate for the task Mime has in mind for his powerful charge: the killing of the dragon Fafner in order to win back the ring. Siegfried enters boisterously from the forest. He has no respect for the puny dwarf who pretends to be his father. Siegfried forces him to confess the truth. A dying woman emerged from the forest to give birth in the cave. She entrusted the child to Mime, insisting that he should be called Siegfried, and gave him the fragments of Notung, which had been shattered when the child's father was slain. Siegfried is thrilled by the story and, before racing back into the forest from which he senses freedom at last ('Aus dem Wald fort in die Welt ziehn'), orders Mime to mend the sword. The Wanderer, dressed in a dark blue-grey cloak, appears uninvited at Mime's hearth. Mime can be rid of him only by agreeing to a game of riddles. The Wanderer stakes his head on three questions from his unwilling host, who, overconfident in his own cunning, agrees to ask them ('Drei der Fragen stell' ich mir frei'). The unwanted guest answers correctly and insists that Mime stake his own head on three questions in turn. But Mime, panic-stricken, cannot solve the third riddle: who will weld Notung together again? The Wanderer solves it for him: 'only one who has never felt fear' and the one to whom, he adds casually, Mime's head is now forfeit. Mime promises to take Siegfried to Fafner's lair to teach him fear. Disconcertingly

for Mime, Siegfried is only too willing to co-operate. Siegfried starts to forge Notung himself, deliberately ignoring Mime's expertise. Dimly aware of Siegfried's destiny, Mime brews a poison to kill him once he has slain the dragon. Siegfried sings lustily of Notung as he forges ('Notung! Notung! Neidliches Schwert'), and Mime skips around the cave in delight at the secret plan he has concocted to save his head. With the finished sword, Siegfried cuts the anvil in two and exultantly lifts Notung high in the air as Mime falls to the ground in fright.

Act II: Deep in the forest at night. Alberich is on watch outside Fafner's cave. The Wanderer enters and stops to face Alberich, who, as a shaft of moonlight illuminates the scene, quickly recognizes his adversary. Alberich, suspicious of the Wanderer's nonchalance, confronts him with his main weakness: his inability to steal the hoard yet again – an act that would shatter the rule of law once and for all. As if to prove his indifference, the Wanderer generously tells Alberich of Mime's plans to get the hoard for himself and suggests warning Fafner, who, to avoid being murdered, might relinquish the ring to Alberich before Mime arrives. The Wanderer even offers to waken the dragon himself. He knows full well, however, that everything is set on a course that no one, not even Alberich, can alter ('Alles ist nach seiner Art, an ihr wirst du nichts ändern'). Predictably the dragon refuses to listen and goes back to sleep. Siegfried and Mime arrive as day breaks. Mime conjures up threatening images of Fafner. But Siegfried is more intent on ridding himself of his guardian, whom he finds increasingly repulsive. Mime leaves Siegfried beneath a linden tree to muse on his origins. Siegfried cuts a reed pipe and tries to play it in order to converse with the birds. He loses patience and instead uses his silver horn. As the sounds of the horn grow faster and louder, Fafner begins to stir. Spewing venom out of its nostrils, the dragon heaves itself up to crush the interloper, only to expose its heart into which Siegfried swiftly plunges his sword. Realizing that his killer is only a naïve boy being used by someone more sinister, the dying Fafner warns Siegfried of Mime's true plans. Some of the dragon's blood spills on to Siegfried's hand. After involuntarily licking it, Siegfried can at last understand the song of one of the birds, who tells him that the hoard is now his ('Hei! Siegfried gehört nun der Niblungen Hort!'). After Siegfried has gone into the cave to look for the treasure, Mime and Alberich scuttle into sight, quarrelling about their right to the hoard. Siegfried emerges from the cave looking thoughtfully at the ring and the Tarnhelm he is carrying. Alberich withdraws as Mime persuades Siegfried to take the poisonous drink. But the dragon's blood also enables Siegfried to hear the murderous intent beneath Mime's ingratiating phrases. In a moment of disgust Siegfried kills Mime with a single stroke of his sword. Alberich's mocking laughter echoes in the background, but Siegfried, oblivious, simply asks the Woodbird for a new and preferably more congenial companion. The Woodbird obliges by telling him of Brünnhilde, who, asleep on a high rock and imprisoned by a magic fire, awaits a fearless hero to set her free. The Woodbird flies off to show Siegfried the way.

Act III: A wild region at the foot of a rocky mountain. The Wanderer arouses Erda from a deep sleep. Bleakly observing that nothing can change the destiny of the world, he still wants her advice on 'how to slow down a rolling wheel' ('wie zu hemmen ein rollendes Rad?'). She replies that her mind is growing 'misty with the deeds of men' ('Männertaten umdämmern mir den Mut'). She was raped by Wotan and bore him Brünnhilde. She is confused and not even clear who her rude awakener is. Irritated but not surprised, the Wanderer announces the coming end of her wisdom, and the triumph of his will: the fall of the gods. The Wanderer awaits

Siegfried, who enters in high spirits. Their banter is good-humoured until the old man asks the young hero who it was who created Notung. The Wanderer laughs at Siegfried's ignorance, and Siegfried, hurt by the condescension, in turn pours scorn on the Wanderer. With a single blow Siegfried cuts the Wanderer's spear in two. The Wanderer picks up the pieces and disappears in total darkness. Siegfried puts his horn to his lips and plunges into the billowing fire spreading down from the mountain. On the tip of Brünnhilde's rock, Siegfried has reached the sleeping Brünnhilde, whom he mistakes at first for a male warrior. He cuts away the armour to discover a feminine form that fills him with a strange emotion that he knows is fear. He sinks down, as if he were about to die ('wie ersterbend') and with closed eyes places a kiss on Brünnhilde's lips. She awakens slowly from the darkness of sleep, sitting up gradually to praise the sun and the earth. Siegfried and Brünnhilde are lost in delight, until she realizes that his love for her (not to mention his destruction of her armour) will impede the fierce independence she knew as a Valkyrie. Miraculously regaining his fearlessness, Siegfried overcomes Brünnhilde's qualms. Together they become ecstatically blind to the world, welcoming its destruction and the death of the gods with the delirium of 'radiant love, laughing death' ('leuchtende Liebe, lachender Tod').

Götterdämmerung (*Third Day*)

Twilight of the Gods

Prologue and three acts (4h 15m)
Composed: libretto 1848–52; music (sketches for *Siegfrieds Tod* 1850) 1869–74
PREMIERES 1 March and 6 May 1876, Musikvereinssaal, Vienna (excerpts from Prologue and Acts I and III; concerts); 17 August 1876, Festspielhaus, Bayreuth (stage, as part of the *Ring* cycle); UK: 9 May 1882, Her Majesty's Theatre, Haymarket, London; US: 25 January 1888, Metropolitan, New York
CAST Siegfried *t*, Gunther *high b*, Alberich *high b*, Hagen *low b*, Brünnhilde *s*, Gutrune *s*, Waltraute *low s*, First Norn *c*, Second Norn *s*, Third Norn *s*; Rhinedaughters: Woglinde *s*, Wellgunde *s*, Flosshilde *c*; *tb* chorus of vassals, *s* chorus of women

SYNOPSIS

Prologue: On the Valkyries' rock. The three Norns, daughters of Erda, spin the golden rope of world knowledge that binds past, present and future. The rope was once tied to the World Ash Tree until Wotan desecrated the Tree to create his spear and establish his rule of order over the universe. The Norns try to keep the rope taut. But the threads tangle and it snaps. The continuum between past and future is broken: the Norns' primeval wisdom is at an end. Outside a cave, Brünnhilde and Siegfried emerge with the rising of the sun, he in full armour, she leading her horse Grane. Brünnhilde sings that her love for Siegfried would not be true if she refused to let him go forth into the world to perform new deeds ('Zu neuen Taten'). Siegfried leaves Brünnhilde the ring as a token, and she in turn gives him Grane. Carrying his sword, he begins his descent from the rock and vanishes with the horse. His horn is heard from below as Brünnhilde bids him farewell.

Act I: The hall of Gunther's court on the Rhine. Hagen, the illegitimate son of Alberich and Grimhild, is plotting to regain the ring for his father. His legitimate half-siblings, Gunther and Gutrune, who have inherited their kingdom from their dead parents Gibich and Grimhild, sit on a throne to one side. Hagen gives them some (seemingly) sensible advice. If they are to retain the respect of their subjects, they must marry without delay. Hagen suggests Siegfried for Gutrune and Brünnhilde for Gunther. The lacklustre Gibichungs are overwhelmed with the thought but sceptical until Hagen suggests a way of attracting their powerful partners-to-be. Gutrune is to give Siegfried a potion that will erase his memory of all other women. Once Gutrune has captured his heart, it will be easy for her brother to persuade him to woo Brünnhilde. Siegfried's horn sounds from his boat on the Rhine. Hagen calls out to him to come ashore. Siegfried steps on to land with his sword and Grane. He tells Gunther of the Tarnhelm and the ring. As planned, Gutrune offers him the potion of forgetfulness, which he unwittingly accepts, dedicating his first drink to Brünnhilde and faithful love. Its effect is immediate: spellbound by Gutrune, he hears Gunther talk of the woman Gunther desires, but cannot win because she lives on a high mountain surrounded by a fire. Siegfried shows no sign of recognition. Knowing that he can penetrate the fire, he offers to woo the woman, using the Tarnhelm to disguise himself as his host. After sealing his promise with an oath of blood brotherhood, he sets off with Gunther for Brünnhilde's rock, leaving Hagen to guard the hall. Hagen savours the plot he has set in motion ('Hier sitz' ich zur Wacht'). On the Valkyries' rock, Brünnhilde sits in front of the cave gazing rapturously at the ring. Dark storm clouds appear as Waltraute, one of the Valkyries, arrives to tell her of Wotan seated morosely in Valhalla, waiting passively for the end of the gods ('Höre mit Sinn, was ich dir sage'). Despite Waltraute's pleading, Brünnhilde refuses Wotan's only remaining wish: to free the gods from the curse by returning the ring to the Rhinedaughters. Brünnhilde vows never to renounce the ring or the love it supposedly symbolizes ('Die Liebe liesse ich nie'). Waltraute hastens away, distraught. The brightening flames and the sound of a horn herald the arrival of Siegfried. But to Brünnhilde's horror a different figure steps out of the fire. In Gunther's shape, Siegfried wrestles with her and wrenches the ring from her finger. He forces her into the cave and lays his sword between them as witness that his wooing of Gunther's bride is chaste.

Act II: In front of the hall of Gunther's court, Hagen is asleep. As the moon suddenly appears, Alberich can be seen in front of him, resting his arms on his son's knees. He exhorts Hagen to keep faith with their plan to ruin Siegfried and win back the ring ('Sei treu, Hagen, mein Sohn! Trauter Helde!'). With the help of the Tarnhelm, Siegfried arrives at the Gibichungs' court ahead of Gunther and Brünnhilde. In a detailed dialogue with Hagen and Gutrune, he describes his successful wooing of Brünnhilde for Gunther and announces their imminent arrival. As if calling the Gibichung vassals to battle, Hagen summons them to greet Gunther and his bride. The vassals do not understand Hagen's warlike tone or the need for the sharp weapons and bellowing horns. Hagen explains by proposing a barbaric feast, including the slaughter of animals for the gods, and uninhibited drunkenness. Solemnly, the vassals greet Gunther and Brünnhilde as they disembark. Brünnhilde appears crushed and humiliated until she sees the ring on Siegfried's finger. Roused to furious anger, she declares that Siegfried is her husband and flings desperate charges at him. To clear his name Siegfried swears an oath on Hagen's spear that its point may pierce his body if he is lying about who he is. Brünnhilde dedicates the sharp blade to Siegfried's downfall. After Siegfried has left to prepare for his marriage, Brünnhilde tells Hagen that she did not protect Siegfried's back with her magic as he would never have turned it towards an enemy. Now his enemy, she reveals that his back is the only place where he can be mortally wounded. Gunther, the deceived deceiver, is convinced of Siegfried's treachery by Hagen but worried about the effect Siegfried's death will have on Gutrune. Hagen decides to make it look like a hunting accident. All are now dedicated to Siegfried's death. Calling on Wotan, guardian of vows, Brünnhilde and Gunther swear an oath of vengeance. Hagen in turn invokes the spirit of his father, Alberich, lord of the ring ('des Ringes Herrn'). Siegfried returns with Gutrune and the bridal procession, while Hagen forces Brünnhilde to join Gunther to prepare for a double wedding they know will never take place.

Act III: A forest area on the banks of the Rhine. An elf has lured Siegfried away from his hunting companions to the riverbank where the Rhinedaughters are playing. They tell him he will die later that day if he keeps the ring. Laughing, he ignores them. They lament his blindness and swim away to 'a proud woman' ('ein stolzes Weib'), who will soon inherit his treasure and give them a better hearing. Siegfried has rejoined his hunting companions who sit down to rest and drink. At Hagen's prompting he regales them with stories of Mime and Notung, of Fafner and the Woodbird. But Hagen has a servant slip an antidote into Siegfried's drink that enables him to tell the true story of Brünnhilde as well. Siegfried gives a rapturous account of how he learned about her from the Woodbird and how passionately she embraced him after his bold kiss. Wotan's two ravens fly up out of a bush. Hagen asks Siegfried if he can understand them too. Siegfried turns, and immediately Hagen thrusts his spear into Siegfried's back. Perjury is avenged, Hagen gloats to the horrified onlookers. The vassals take up Siegfried's body to form a solemn cortège as the magnificent funeral march recollects and reflects on the hero's life. In the hall of Gunther's court, Gutrune has been plagued by disturbing dreams and the sight of Brünnhilde walking to the banks of the Rhine. When she discovers Siegfried's body, brought back by the hunters, she nearly faints with shock. Hagen freely admits the murder and kills Gunther in a fight over the ring. But when Hagen reaches for the ring, the dead Siegfried's hand rises menacingly to prevent him from taking it. Brünnhilde comes forward to silence Gutrune's lament and to contemplate the dead Siegfried. She orders his body to be placed on a funeral pyre ('Starke Scheite schichtet mir dort am Rande des Rheines zuhauf'). Now, after talking to the Rhinedaughters, she understands Wotan's will to end the gods, to rid them of the curse that also ensnared her innocent lover. She takes the ring, puts it on her finger and casts a torch on the pyre. To cleanse the ring from the curse with fire before it is returned to the Rhinedaughters, she leaps with her horse into the burning pyre, united with Siegfried in death. The Rhine overflows its banks and pours over the flames. As the Rhinedaughters appear on the waves, Hagen rushes headlong into the flood to demand the return of the ring. Woglinde and Wellgunde draw him into the depths, while Flosshilde holds up the ring in triumph. The hall has collapsed, and in its ruins the men and women watch apprehensively as an increasingly bright glow appears in the sky. Gradually the hall of Valhalla becomes visible, filled with gods and heroes just as Waltraute described it in Act I. As the orchestra recalls Erda's prophecy in *Das Rheingold* of the end of the gods ('Ein düstrer Tag dämmert den Göttern'), the hall appears to be completely consumed by bright flames.

Wagner's *Ring* has been interpreted in so many wildly contradictory ways that it probably counts as the most ingratiating work ever written for the operatic stage. Yet the fact that it has far transcended its original destiny as a 'stage festival play' and German national epic is testimony not only to the potency of Wagner's self-made myth, but also to the consistently superior quality of his music. The search for archetypal images and mythical heroes in the forging of the *Ring* libretto would have been unthinkable without the assistance of pioneering works such as Jacob Grimm's *German Mythology* (1835) and Karl Simrock's *Lay of the Amelungs* (1843–9), which provided the building blocks of, and methods of linking, the various stories and legends Wagner needed to create his own myth. But for the composition of the music there was no such help. Wagner's five-and-a-half-year musical silence between the completion of *Lohengrin* in April 1848 and the start of work on the *Ring* in November 1853 suggests that the difficulties were formidable: at no other point in his life was Wagner musically silent for so long.

Once a start had been made on the music, however, the composition proceeded so rapidly that it is hard to believe that Wagner had no premeditated strategy in mind. Astonishingly, he finished the first drafts of *Das Rheingold* and *Die Walküre* in (respectively) only two and a half and six months. Wagner himself, and most of his biographers since, have explained this rush of invention with certain events in his (usually turbulent) private life. Seventeen coded messages to Mathilde Wesendonck, for instance, the wife of a rich friend and benefactor, with whom he fell in love in 1854, were inserted into the first draft of Act I of *Die Walküre*. But Wagner surely must have used some of his long musical silence to think out, at least in broad terms, strategies that were determined to a large extent by the interaction of the different levels of his myth. The network of leitmotifs, the highly original use of keys and form that usurps all sense of traditional operatic set numbers, not to mention the mirroring of the drama through extremely differentiated orchestration, are worked out too carefully and consistently (at least in the first half of the cycle) for anything else to seem possible.

The sheer quantity of motifs alone (there are over a hundred) Wagner needed to fill out about 15 hours of music suggests an important difference between the leitmotif system he invented specifically for the *Ring* and the well-tried operatic device of the so-called reminiscence motif he had used, albeit with great originality, in his earlier operas. (In *Lohengrin*, for instance, there are only six main motifs in the entire opera, fewer than in the first scene of *Das Rheingold* alone.) In short, the necessity of another kind of motivic network arose because of Wagner's decision in the *Ring* finally to abolish the contrast between unstructured recitative and musically highly organized 'set pieces' typical of conventional opera. Usually for reasons of dramatic irony, Wagner reinvented the contrast at certain places in the *Ring* – the start of Loge's laconic narration to the gods in the second scene of *Das Rheingold*, for instance – but basically set out to create a continuous musical–dramatic dialogue that relies for its coherence not on predictable stylistic changes but on a steady interchange of related motifs that can be joined, combined and varied in countless ways without loss of identity. The technique is fundamentally an extension of Berlioz's *idée fixe* (a resilient theme symbolizing a central figure in a story that returns in different shapes and sizes during the course of the narrative). This is not to deny the originality of Wagner's daring concept of motifs in series that not only represent significant aspects of the unfolding drama but also relate to each other to provide the narrative with a semblance of logic and a scaffold for its monumental structure on a musical level.

Contrary to a widely held belief, Wagner named a few of the leitmotifs in the *Ring* in his sketches and occasionally to friends. The practice, usually thought to be the invention of Hans von Wolzogen, the compiler of the first leitmotif guides, has often been misused and misunderstood. Wagner called the motif sung by Alberich when he renounces love to steal the gold in the opening scene of *Das Rheingold* the 'curse on love' (*Liebesfluch*). But he did not intend to suggest (and arguably neither did Wolzogen) that the meaning of the motif stays literally the same later in the cycle. Avid leitmotif watchers have all noticed Wagner's 'inconsistency' and apparently lamentable lack of rigour in Act I of *Die Walküre* when he allows Siegmund to sing the motif in its original key of C minor as he pulls the sword out of the ash tree – a moment leading to a triumphant announcement of the so-called 'sword' motif in C major, when Siegmund, far from having cursed love, seems to have discovered it for the first time. Few have considered the reverse parallel (of which there are many in the *Ring*) with the opening scene of *Das Rheingold* when, after the dazzling presentation of the gold in C major by the Rhinedaughters, the music shifts gradually to C minor and Alberich's snatching of the treasure. By moving emphatically in the opposite direction, Siegmund's music in *Die Walküre* promises to negate the consequences of Alberich's primal crime – a possible reading that suggests that Siegmund's singing of the motif is not a 'mistake' but an attempt to exorcize its original meaning. That Siegmund turns out to be the wrong hero for the task and the promise a false one only adds irony to the moment in retrospect. Indeed, after Siegmund is killed, the memory of the past weighs so oppressively on the motif that Wagner can use it again to great ironic effect in Act I of *Götterdämmerung* when Brünnhilde tells Waltraute in all sincerity that she will never renounce her love for Siegfried, only to do just that at the end of Act II. Nearly all the motifs in the *Ring* resonate similarly with memories of past events that, though the actual notes of the motifs may stay exactly the same, never cease to accumulate and hence to be gradually transformed as the tragedy unfolds.

Wagner deliberately used one motif so sparingly that there could be no mistake about it. Bernard Shaw was puzzled by it (as many later commentators have been), calling it 'the most trumpery phrase in the entire tetralogy', the sole valuable quality of which was its 'gushing effect'. He was referring to the motif that, 'since it undoubtedly does gush very emphatically', dominates the concluding moments of the cycle. In effect the ending of the *Ring* is a vast musical recapitulation. Salient motifs, cadences, keys, fragments of form and even details of orchestration return from earlier parts of the tetralogy to sum up a great parable of human existence. The feeling of circular movement, of going back over the whole cycle to the beginning, could be seen as a metaphor for Wotan's pessimism – a static, spatial image that is filled with what Walter Benjamin called 'the disconsolate chronicle of world history'. At the same time the motif Wagner chose to end the *Ring* has been heard only once before, when Sieglinde sings it to Brünnhilde in Act III of *Die Walküre* after Brünnhilde has alluded to Siegfried's future destiny. The last-minute development of it in the final moments of the *Ring* is so unexpected that it appears to cut across the feeling of endless return, as if to break the circle of history, by celebrating instead Siegfried's victory in reconciling, through his death, the conflict between nature and society at the root of the myth. The motif is certainly triumphant, as Wagner stressed when, in contrast to the leitmotif guides, he called it not the 'redemption through love' but the 'glorification of Brünnhilde' – a perfectly logical description since it is Brünnhilde who successfully brings the story to an end by announcing that its true hero has completed his task.

RECORDINGS 1. Mödl, Konetzni, Cavelti, Klose, Malaniuk, Windgassen, Suthaus, Patzak, Frantz, Neidlinger, Frick, Greindl, Rome Radio Ch & O, Furtwängler, EMI, 1953; 2. Nilsson, Crespin, Flagstad/Ludwig, Windgassen, King, Svanholm, Stolze, London/Hotter, Frick, Böhme, Vienna State Op Ch, VPO, Solti, Decca, 1957–66; 3. Evans, Secunde, Finnie, Jerusalem, Elming, Clarke, Pampuch, Tomlinson, Höller, Kang, Bayreuth Festival Ch & O, Barenboim, Teldec, 1991/2

Tristan und Isolde

Handlung in three acts (3h 45m)
Libretto by the composer
Composed: libretto 1857; music 1856–9

PREMIERES 12 March 1859, Prague (Prelude with concert ending by Hans von Bülow; concert); 25 January 1860, Theatre Italien, Paris (Prelude with concert ending by Wagner; concert); 10 March 1863, St Petersburg (Prelude and Transfiguration; concert); 10 June 1865, Royal Court and National Theatre, Munich (stage); UK: 20 June 1882, Drury Lane, London; US: 1 December 1886, Metropolitan, New York
CAST Tristan *t*, King Marke *b*, Isolde *s*, Kurwenal *bar*, Melot *t*, Brangäne *s*, Shepherd *t*, Steersman *bar*, voice of Young Sailor *t*; *tb* chorus of ship's crew, knights and pages

Inspired by his reading of the philosopher Arthur Schopenhauer, Wagner first conceived *Tristan und Isolde* in the autumn of 1854. Another immediate stimulus was a dramatization of the story by his friend Karl Ritter of which he was extremely critical, calling it too elaborate and packed with 'adventurous incidents'. One of two operatic foretastes of Wagner's masterpiece is the famous light-hearted account of Tristan and Isolde in Donizetti's opera *L'elisir d'amore*, the title of which is itself an allusion to the tale. (Wagner probably knew the opera, as it was in the repertoire of the Dresden Court Opera when he was conductor there in the 1840s.) The other is a scenario of an opera *Tristan und Isolde* in five acts written in 1846 by the poet Robert Reinick for Schumann, who eventually decided not to compose it. (In all likelihood Wagner knew this too since he conversed regularly with Schumann in 1845 and 1846 at the Engelklub in Dresden about their respective artistic plans.) As an operatic venture and in terms of its sheer rigour and boldness, however, Wagner's *Tristan* is without precedent, even when compared with his previous works.

Wagner's main source was Gottfried von Strassburg's medieval epic *Tristan* (*c.*1215), in the 19th century a work admired for its style and pilloried for its suspect morality in about equal measure. There were several reasons for Wagner's sudden decision to adapt it, including its (for medieval texts) unusual subject of fated and enchanted, as opposed to courtly, love that leads to physical destruction and 'eternal death' (*êweclîchez sterben*). The idea was in tune not only with Wagner's newly awakened interest in Schopenhauer, who believed that the preconscious Will was an expression of the sexual drive and its negation the road to salvation, but also with his increasing love for Mathilde Wesendonck, the wife of his long-suffering patron Otto Wesendonck – a love that Wagner knew, because of his dependence on the latter, would be unlikely to become a reality. This interpretation is at least not hard to read into a famous letter about *Tristan* he wrote to Liszt in December 1854: 'Since I have never enjoyed the real happiness of love in my life, I want to erect another monument to this most beautiful of dreams in which love will be properly sated from beginning to end.'

Wagner called *Tristan* 'the most full-blooded musical conception'. In the end the musical challenge was perhaps his most important reason for writing it. (His wife Cosima later wrote in her diaries on 11 December 1878 – carefully omitting to mention the role of Mathilde Wesendonck – that 'he had felt the urge to express himself symphonically for once, and that led to *Tristan*'.) In 1857 Wagner interrupted work on the *Ring* at the end of *Siegfried* Act II and finished *Tristan* two years later, often working at breakneck speed to deliver each act to the printer on time before moving on to the next. Indeed, half the score was already in print before he finished composing it – an odd situation that had to do with the comical fact that he was desperate for cash from the publisher who would pay him only an act at a time. After its publication in 1860 the work was widely regarded as unperformable. The first performance was planned for the Vienna Court Opera in 1861, but abandoned after 77 rehearsals. The premiere eventually took place in Munich in 1865, conducted by Hans von Bülow with Ludwig Schnorr von Carolsfeld and his wife Malwina in the leading roles. Nine years elapsed before a second production was attempted in Weimar.

SYNOPSIS

Act I: An awning on board Tristan's ship during a crossing from Ireland to Cornwall. Isolde is being taken to Cornwall against her will to marry King Marke. Resolved to die, she tells her confidante Brangäne to call Tristan to speak to her. Tristan is politely evasive and, when Brangäne insists, his trusted companion Kurwenal leaps up to sing a mocking song about Morald, a knight of Ireland who came to Cornwall to collect its tribute, only to be killed by Tristan. Now Morald's head hangs in Ireland as payment. The knights and the ship's crew join lustily in the refrain. A furious Isolde confides to Brangäne her version of the story ('Wie lachend sie mir Lieder singen'). Morald was her fiancé who in his fatal battle with Tristan seriously wounded him. Sick and dying, Tristan returned to Ireland in a small boat, where he was found by Isolde and nursed back to health. Disguised as 'Tantris', he went unrecognized by her until she noticed a notch in his sword that perfectly matched a splinter extracted from Morald's body. She raised a sword to kill him, but as he looked longingly into her eyes she let it fall. Now he has repaid her kindness by returning to claim her as a bride in a loveless marriage. Brangäne tries to calm her by reminding her of her mother's elixir of love. But Isolde will hear of only one of her mother's magic potions: the elixir of death. Kurwenal enters to announce their imminent landing and the approach of Tristan. Isolde demands vengeance for the death of Morald and offers Tristan a drink of atonement. Recognizing the elixir of death, Tristan drinks to Isolde. She wrenches the cup from his hand and drains it herself. Grimly expecting to die, they are overcome by passionate love instead, oblivious to the cries of the knights and the sailors as the ship prepares to land. Brangäne confesses in despair that she has substituted the elixir of love. Isolde, dismayed that she is now condemned to live, falls unconscious on to Tristan's breast.

Act II: A garden with tall trees in front of Isolde's apartment in King Marke's royal fortress in Cornwall. It is a summer night and the king's hunting party can be heard setting out. Isolde is impatiently waiting for Brangäne to extinguish the torch burning by the door as a signal to Tristan that he can come to her safely. But Brangäne is hesitant, believing that Tristan's best friend Melot, who has arranged the hunt so that the lovers can meet, has actually set a trap. Isolde is scornful, impatiently putting out the torch herself and ordering Brangäne to stand watch in the tower. Tristan enters and the lovers fall passionately into each other's arms. Both deliver a curse on 'the spiteful day' ('dem tückischen Tage') that has bedazzled them, and a hymn to the night, a symbol of death that will ensure the eternal existence of their love ('O sink hernieder, Nacht der Liebe'). They ignore Brangäne's warnings about the imminent break of day and enter into an ecstatic duet, which is brutally interrupted at its climax by the sudden entrance of Kurwenal who warns of King Marke's approach. Marke enters with Melot and the hunting party. In an extended monologue, the bewildered king asks in vain how his faithful nephew could betray him ('Dies, Tristan, mir?'). Tristan yearns for the night. As he bends down to kiss Isolde, Melot draws his sword. Instead of defending himself, Tristan lets his guard fall and sinks wounded into the arms of Kurwenal.

Act III: Tristan's fortress in Brittany. The sound of a melancholy tune played by an old shepherd awakes Tristan from a deep coma. Overjoyed, Kurwenal tells how he brought Tristan back to his homeland to recover. Kurwenal is hourly awaiting Isolde's ship, and the shepherd will play a joyful melody when it is sighted. In demented excitement Tristan curses the terrible elixir of love ('verflucht sei, furchtbarer Trank!') and imagines he sees the ship approaching with Isolde on it transfigured and full of grace. Suddenly the shepherd sounds his joyful melody. Tristan rips the bandages off his wound and leaps from the sickbed to struggle forward to meet Isolde as she enters, only to die in her arms with her name on his lips. A second ship arrives, and King Marke, Melot and their retinue pour into the castle. In a rage Kurwenal kills Melot, but collapses seriously wounded, dying at the feet of the dead Tristan. Brangäne tells Isolde that she has explained everything about the fatal elixir of love to the king who has come to Brittany to forgive Tristan. But Isolde is deaf to her words. She sees Tristan awakened to new life in eternal death ('Mild und leise, wie er lächelt') and falls, as if transfigured, into Brangäne's arms.

Bernard Shaw once admitted that Wagner had retraced 'poetic love' to its 'alleged origin in sexual passion, the emotional phenomena of which he has expressed in music with a frankness and forcible naturalism which would possibly have scandalized Shelley'. Shaw was thinking especially of *Tristan und Isolde*, which from the first, with its graphic 'translation into music of the emotions which accompany the union of a pair of lovers', posed a moral as well as a musical challenge to 19th-century audiences. That Duchess Sophie of Bavaria was not allowed to attend the first performance of *Tristan* in 1865 out of moral considerations, despite the fact that she was a mature 20-year-old woman married to Duke Carl Theodor of Bavaria, is only one historical detail illustrating the point. Wagner's need to present unquenchable yearning and sexual passion in a convincing way, however, led him to widen the scope of his musical resources so drastically that *Tristan* almost inevitably soon became one of the most important musical works of the 19th century. In 1878 he explained to Cosima his need at the time of *Tristan* 'to push himself to the limit musically'. And indeed the unprecedented expansion of harmonic possibilities audible in the very first chord of the work (the so-called 'Tristan chord' is by far the most widely analysed collection of four notes in Western music) and the sheer freedom and invention in the handling of individual chromatic lines mean that it is quite justifiable to speak of the music of *Tristan* as a harbinger of the new music of the 20th century. (The music of *Tristan* is never actually atonal, though it energizes the tonal system from within to near breaking-point.) Composers have frequently acknowledged and parodied the modernist ambition of *Tristan* by using its opening phrase in their own works, including Wagner himself who, in Act III of *Die Meistersinger*, was the first to cite it. Perhaps the subtlest use of it is in the final movement of Alban Berg's *Lyric Suite*, where it recalls not only the avant-garde aspect of *Tristan*, but also its erotic raison d'être. Berg blended Wagner's music into a 12-note movement in such a way that it can be explained, as Berg himself pointed out, in terms of the working of the 12-note row. At the same time it was intended as part of a secret programme referring to his affair with Hanna Fuchs-Robettin, the sister of Franz Werfel and wife of a rich industrialist. The parallel with Wagner's infatuation with Mathilde Wesendonck, one of the inspirations behind *Tristan* and also the wife of a wealthy businessman, was obviously not a coincidence.

RECORDINGS 1. Flagstad, Thebom, Suthaus, Fischer-Dieskau, Greindl, Covent Garden Ch, Philharmonia O, Furtwängler, HMV, 1952; 2. Nilsson, Ludwig, Windgassen, Waechter, Talvela, Bayreuth Festival Ch & O, Böhm, Philips, 1966 (live); 3. Meier, Lipovšek, Jerusalem, Struckmann, Salminen, Berlin State Op Ch, BPO, Barenboim, Teldec, 1994

Die Meistersinger von Nürnberg

The Mastersingers of Nuremberg

In three acts (4h 15m)
Libretto by the composer
Composed: libretto 1845, 1861–2, 1866–7; music 1862–4, 1866–7

PREMIERES 1 November 1862, Gewandhaus, Leipzig (Prelude; concert); 26 December 1862, Theater an der Wien, Vienna (excerpts from Act I, Scene 3 Assembly of the Mastersinger Guild for orchestra alone and Pogner's address; concert); 5 November 1863, Prague (Sachs's Shoemaker Song from Act II; concert); 12 July 1865, Residenztheater, Munich (excerpts from Act I, Scene 3, including Walther's Trial Song; concert); 4 April 1868, Liedertafel Frohsinn, Linz (Sachs's closing address and final chorus from Act III; concert, conducted Anton Bruckner); 21 June 1868, Royal Court and National Theatre, Munich; UK: 30 May 1882, Drury Lane, London; US: 4 January 1886, Metropolitan, New York

CAST Mastersingers: Hans Sachs (shoemaker) *b*, Veit Pogner (goldsmith) *b*, Kunz Vogelgesang (furrier) *t*, Konrad Nachtigall (tinsmith) *b*, Sixtus Beckmesser (town clerk) *b*, Fritz Kothner (baker) *b*, Balthasar Zorn (pewterer) *t*, Ulrich Eisslinger (grocer) *t*, Augustin Moser (tailor) *t*, Hermann Ortel (soap-boiler) *b*, Hans Schwarz (stocking weaver) *b*, Hans Foltz (coppersmith) *b*; Walther von Stolzing *t*, David *t*, Eva *s*, Magdalene *s*, Night Watchman *b*; *satb* chorus of men and women from every guild, journeymen, apprentices, young women, populace

Die Meistersinger is an exception among Wagner's works in that it is not substantially based on any narrative source, though no end of literary and historical detail was lavished on it. Characterizations of its main figure, Hans Sachs, and other background material were provided by Goethe's poem 'An Account of an Old Woodcut Showing Hans Sachs's Poetic Calling' and Gervinus's influential *History of German Literature*, as well as Lortzing's 1840 opera *Hans Sachs* (an adaptation of a play written in 1827 by the Viennese court dramatist J. L. F. Deinhardstein). Ironically, Wagner had no hesitation in resorting to the well-known methods of his arch-rival Meyerbeer with some painstaking research into local colour, including details of medieval Nuremberg, various folk traditions, and the doctrine and practices of the historical mastersingers, which he gleaned mostly from J. C. Wagenseil's *Book of the Master-Singers' Gracious Art* (1687). But apart from some ideas taken from E. T. A. Hoffmann's *Master Martin the Cooper and His Apprentices* (1819) and a few other sources, the story of the opera is largely Wagner's own invention.

Wagner first sketched out a scenario for *Die Meistersinger* in 1845. He wrote later that he conceived it then as a work that stood in relation to the song contest on the Wartburg in *Tannhäuser* 'like a richly textured satyr play', just as in ancient Athens 'a comic satyr play would follow a tragedy'. Not long after the fiasco of the revised Paris *Tannhäuser* in 1861 the idea reasserted itself, but with the key difference that it took its bearings this time from *Tristan* and the philosophy of Schopenhauer. The passion of the young nobleman for the woman he wins in the singing competition in the first version became a blind urge driven by fate in the second (at one point Eva explains to Sachs that she did not choose to love Walther, rather her love 'chose' her and became an 'unheard-of torment'), and Sachs was transformed into a far more substantial figure who beneath his jovial appearance is himself distracted by irrational feelings for the same woman. But Wagner also deliberately turned the tables on *Tristan* and Schopenhauer's pessimism by (among other things) fleshing out the conclusion of *Die Meistersinger* until it glowed with robust health and life. Sachs announces warmly that Walther's prize song has 'strength to live', resigning himself cheerfully to his loss of Eva with noble thoughts on the 'folly' (*Wahn*) of the world at the mercy of the blind Will. Despite their compulsive attraction to one another, Walther and Eva are prevented from renouncing society – that is (in the language of *Tristan*) from experiencing an inevitable love-death – and live happily ever after. The 'richly textured satyr play' to *Tannhäuser*, in other words, became a richly ironic counterpart to *Tristan* instead.

The premiere in Munich of *Die Meistersinger* was conducted by Hans von Bülow with a cast including Franz Betz (Sachs), Gustav Hölzel (Beckmesser), Franz Nachbaur (Walther) and Mathilde Mallinger (Eva). It was a resounding triumph comparable only to the first performance of *Rienzi* in Dresden in 1842. Over the years the mellow irony of the 'internal' drama of *Die Meistersinger* has proved to be its most enduring quality. But its immediate success was due more to its extrovert nationalism, which had enormous resonance in the years leading up to the 1870 Franco-Prussian War. There is a world of difference between this and Hitler's misappropriation of *Die Meistersinger* as the official opera of the Nuremberg party congresses during the Nazi period. Even though the sheer genius of the work transcends that part of it that has its origins in the growing nationalist fervour in Germany in the 1860s, its concluding propaganda on behalf of the hegemony of German art is for some still hard to accept, despite efforts to see it in historical perspective.

SYNOPSIS

Act I: Nuremberg; mid-16th century. St Catherine's Church. Walther von Stolzing, a young Franconian knight who has sold his estate with the help of the goldsmith Veit Pogner, has made his home in Nuremberg and fallen in love with Pogner's daughter Eva. After the afternoon service on the eve of Midsummer's Day, Eva and her nurse Magdalene tell Walther that Pogner has promised the hand of his daughter to the mastersinger who wins the singing competition due to take place on the morrow. Walther has no alternative but to join the mastersingers' guild. An examination for membership is about to take place, and Magdalene persuades her sweetheart David to initiate Walther into the mastersingers' rules and regulations without delay. Pogner is flattered that a nobleman wishes to join the guild and lends Walther his support. Walther tells the assembled masters that his singing teacher was an ancient book by Walther von der Vogelweide and his school the depths of the forest ('Am stillen Herd in Winterszeit'). But the reaction is sceptical: only Hans Sachs senses something out of the ordinary. Walther is allowed to proceed to a formal trial song, and the town clerk Sixtus Beckmesser, a mastersinger who is just as determined to win Eva's hand, acts as marker to note each fault. Out of Beckmesser's formal invitation to begin ('Fanget an') Walther improvises a dithyramb in praise of nature and love. But Beckmesser soon chalks up enough mistakes to exceed the statutory limit. Sachs's admiration for the boldness and originality of the candidate falls on deaf ears. Walther is declared by the majority to have failed the test.

Act II: A street with the houses of Pogner and Sachs. Eva hears the bad news about Walther from Magdalene. Snatches of Walther's trial song continue to haunt Sachs, who cannot grasp how the song could sound old, yet at the same time so new ('Es klang so alt, und war doch so neu'). Walther and Eva decide to flee, only to find their escape thwarted by Sachs. Beckmesser appears with his lute, ready to try out his prize song on Eva who, already forewarned, has asked Magdalene to take her place at her window. Sachs constantly interrupts Beckmesser with a deliberately coarse shoemaker's song (a delicious parody of Siegfried's forging songs in the *Ring*) and finally agrees to listen only if Beckmesser lets him act as marker. Sachs strikes the soles of the shoes he is making every time Beckmesser makes a mistake. Beckmesser tries to drown the blows by singing louder, only to wake the neighbours, including David who, at the sight of Beckmesser apparently serenading Magdalene, becomes furiously jealous. David attacks Beckmesser and their fight quickly escalates into a violent free-for-all during which Walther and Eva again try to escape. Sachs intervenes to separate them, giving the half-swooning Eva into the protection of her father, while he quickly leads Walther into his workshop. At the sound of the approaching night-watchman's horn, the tumult ends almost as suddenly as it began.

Act III: Sachs's workshop the next morning. David comes to offer his apologies for the night before. Left alone, Sachs continues reading a large folio, musing on the folly he sees everywhere beneath the self-torment of the human race ('Wahn, Wahn! Überall Wahn!'). Walther enters and sings Sachs a song that has just come to him in a dream. Sachs helps him to shape the first two verses, sensing something new at last that can be reconciled with the mastersingers' rules. After they have left Beckmesser limps into the workshop and discovers a sheet of paper on which Sachs has written the song. He immediately takes it to be a prize song by Sachs, who suddenly looks like yet another dangerous rival. On his return Sachs calms Beckmesser's fears and generously gives him the manuscript, though cannily forgetting to mention its real author. Eva enters and Walther, transfixed by the sight of her, improvises the third verse of his song. Sachs knows he will never realize his love for Eva but prefers to be nobly cheerful about it. The woes of King Marke in the sad story of Tristan and Isolde, he tells Eva, are not for him (at which point Wagner cites his own *Tristan*). After a moving quintet in celebration of the 'baptism' of Walther's prize song by Sachs ('Selig, wie die Sonne'), the scene changes to the festival meadow outside Nuremberg where the singing competition is to take place. The first candidate is Beckmesser, who proceeds to bowdlerize the words of the song given to him by Sachs ('Morgen ich leuchte in rosigem Schein'). He is ridiculed by the townspeople and in a rage declares that Sachs is the author of the poem. But this only gives Sachs an ideal opportunity to call on the true author. Walther delivers an impassioned rendering of his song ('Morgenlich leuchtend im rosigen Schein'), which wins unanimous approval from populace and mastersingers alike. The prize and Eva's hand are Walther's, though he instinctively recoils from accepting the guild's chain of honour. After Sachs voices his opinion about the importance of the masters and their art for Germany ('Verachtet mir die Meister nicht'), Walther changes his mind and joins in the celebration of Sachs as the embodiment of 'holy German art'.

Wagner's original intention in 1861 after the *Tannhäuser* debacle in Paris was to complete the *Ring*, which he had abandoned four years before to write *Tristan*. Suddenly in October he wrote to his publisher that he had decided instead to cheer himself up with 'something lighter' that would be finished much faster, in a year. That year turned into six – the last note of the score of *Die Meistersinger* was written on 24 October 1867 at eight o'clock in the evening – and probably no other single fact about the opera is more eloquent than this about the difficulties Wagner had in composing it. Finding a musical style for *Die Meistersinger* that stood in the same relation to *Tristan* as its libretto – a style, that is, which would turn the earlier work on its head without letting the ironic reversal descend into emptiness or banality – proved to be a trickier task than Wagner had anticipated.

Simplicity was hard for Wagner. The overture and Act I of *Die Meistersinger* took four and a half years to complete which, even accounting for interruptions, was for him a surprisingly long time. If he found it difficult at first to write music that concealed its highly advanced technique so well that the most distinctive thing about it would be its apparent lack of sophistication, once he had discovered the right stylistic balance for the work, or – in the language of the mastersingers – its correct 'tone', it took him only another year and a half to finish it. One of the results of this hard thinking is that large sections of *Die Meistersinger* are written in inverted commas, so to speak, yet retain a powerful semblance of immediacy in spite of – or perhaps even because of – the fact that they are historical stylizations. The music of *Tristan* is placed inside the robust diatonicism of Lutheran chorales and quasi-baroque counterpoint, which become richly tinged with chromatic harmony as a result. The new is passed through the filter of the old, just as Walther's prize song in the last act is subjected by Sachs to the rules of the mastersingers' guild. Though he took longer than usual to do it, Wagner had once more discovered an ingenious musical metaphor that mirrored a central concern of the drama: the widening divide between high art and popular culture and the fracturing of tradition by the radically new.

RECORDINGS 1. Grümmer, Höffgen, Hopf, Unger, Frantz, Kusche, Frick, St Hedwig's Cathedral Ch, Deutsche Op O, Kempe, EMI, 1956; 2. Donath, Hesse, Kollo, Schreier, Adam, G. Evans, Dresden Stat Op Ch, Leipzig RCh, Dresden Staatskapelle, Karajan, EMI, 1970; 3. Mattila, Heppner, Opie, Van Dam, Pape, Chicago SO & Ch, Solti, Decca, 1995 (live)

Parsifal

Buhnenweihfestspiel ('stage dedication play') in three acts (4h–4h 30m)
Libretto by the composer
Composed: libretto 1865, 1877; music 1877–82

PREMIERES 25 December 1878, Haus Wahnfried, Bayreuth (Prelude; concert); 12 November 1880, Royal Court and National Theatre, Munich (Prelude; concert); 26 July 1882, Festspielhaus, Bayreuth (stage) ; UK: 10 November 1884, London (concert); 2 February 1914, Covent Garden, London (stage); US: 3 March 1886, New York (concert); 24 December 1903, Metropolitan New York (stage)
CAST Amfortas *bar*, Titurel *b*, Gurnemanz *b*, Parsifal *t*, Klingsor *b*, Kundry *s*, First and Second Knights of the Grail *t*, *b*, First and Second Squires 2 *s*, Third and Fourth Squires 2 *t*, an alto voice *c*, Klingsor's flower maidens: 6 *s*, 2 *sa* choruses; *tb* brotherhood of the knights of the Grail, *at* young men, *sa* boys

Parsifal has never been a work to attract moderate comment. Variously described as sublime, vicious or merely decadent, it has always fascinated critics, who have seen it as a 'superior magic opera' that 'revels in the wondrous' (Eduard Hanslick) or as a 'profoundly inhuman spectacle, glorifying a barren masculine world whose ideals are a combination of militarism and monasticism' (Peter Wapnewski). Given the suggestive allegory Wagner designed for what he called his 'last card' and 'farewell to the world', the controversy is hardly surprising. However, whether *Parsifal* is a sinister millenarianist fantasy about the redemption of an Aryan Jesus from Judaism (as Germany's most vociferous post-war anti-Wagnerite Hartmut Zelinsky seems to think) or just a feeble Armageddon cocktail with large twists of Schopenhauer, critics of its supposed inhumanity will always find it hard to account for the fascinating beauty of its score and the inconvenient fact that militancy and aggression could not be further removed from its central idea.

Parsifal is based on the notion of compassion (*Mitleid*) borrowed from the philosophy of Schopenhauer and subjected to some characteristically Wagnerian variations. Schopenhauer and Wagner saw compassion as a specific moral response to the violent chaos of the world – a beatific annihilation of the Will, so to speak, achieved through a denial of Eros and (in Wagner's personal version of the doctrine) a deep sympathy with the suffering in others caused by the torment of sexual desire. *Parsifal* has been called anti-*Tristan* (where salvation depends on the opposite notion of consummated sexual longing), though it is probably best understood as a dialectical counterpart offering a different solution to the same, and for Wagner always extremely important, problem of blind carnality and the pain it inflicts. In fact, Wagner's first idea in 1856 had been to introduce Parsifal into Act III of *Tristan* where, during his wanderings in search of the Grail, he visits Tristan on his sickbed. But Parsifal's compassionate response to Tristan's suffering had so many implications of its own (at one point in the early *Tristan* sketches he asks whether the whole world is not just 'unquenchable longing' and how it can ever be 'stilled') that Wagner decided to drop the plan and to make Parsifal the subject of a separate work.

The idea of compassion also influenced Wagner's radical treatment of his main literary source, Wolfram von Eschenbach's early 13th-century romance *Parzival*. Wagner discussed Wolfram and sexual asceticism at length in his letters to Mathilde Wesendonck in the late 1850s (in view of his rapidly cooling feelings towards her after finishing *Tristan* this was perhaps to be expected) and came to the conclusion that he would have to compress the enormous 24,810-line poem into just 'three climactic situations'. In the final work these have been turned in effect into three successive stages of compassion (a concept foreign to Wolfram's poem, incidentally, at least as Schopenhauer and Wagner understood it) that begins as a vague and unformed feeling in Parsifal's response to the Grail ceremony in Act I, that progresses to a burning insight into Amfortas's suffering at the moment of Kundry's kiss in Act II and that, with the baptism of Kundry and the healing of Amfortas's wound in Act III, is finally and miraculously transformed into an act of redemption. *Parsifal* is fundamentally a cathartic ritual that unfolds in three cycles, each more intense than the last. The melancholy history of the Grail community, however, which has taken place before the action begins, slowly asserts itself too as the work progresses. *Parsifal* is by no means just a comforting vision of a possible future state of grace. The gradual fulfilment of the prophecy announced at the start – the coming of the redeemer made wise through compassion – is also precariously balanced against irrevocably painful memories of the past. It is therefore important first to explain the past events weighing on the action of the drama.

The action takes place in Spain in two contrasting worlds on the same mountain range. To the north on the Christian side lies Monsalvat, the castle of the knights of the Grail. It was built by Titurel as a shrine for the chalice (the Grail) used at the Last Supper in which Joseph of Arimathea caught the blood of Christ on the cross, and for the spear that pierced Christ's side. Only those who are chaste through spiritual self-examination may take part in the life-giving ritual of the unveiling of the Grail by Titurel's son Amfortas, the present king. On the southern slope facing Moorish (that is, heathen) Spain is Klingsor's castle. Klingsor, once a pious hermit unable to suppress sinful desire through reflection, castrated himself and was spurned by the Grail community. Determined to possess the chalice and the spear for himself, he turned to paganism and magic in order to lure the Grail knights into his magic garden where his seductive flower maidens trap them with the very power they have learned to repress.

Linking the two worlds is Kundry, who once laughed at Christ on the cross and is condemned to live for eternity, both as a decoy and prostitute in Klingsor's castle, and as a repentant slave in the kingdom of the Grail. Klingsor has absolute power over her, as only he knows of her history and her tormented double existence, from which she seeks in vain to be delivered through death. On his orders she once seduced Amfortas, who had set out with the holy spear to put an end to Klingsor's threat. Klingsor stole the spear with which he seriously wounded Amfortas in the side. Amfortas was led home by his trusty knight Gurnemanz to administer the unveiling of the Grail. But his wound refuses to heal, with the consequence that the ritual has become a torture and his kingdom increasingly desolate.

SYNOPSIS

Act I: A shady forest in the region of the Grail castle. After recounting the oppressive past weighing on the Grail community to some of its younger members, Gurnemanz tells of a prophetic saying that came to Amfortas in a vision: a blameless fool made wise through compassion ('durch Mitleid wissend, der reine Tor') will one day redeem him and become king of the Grail. The young knights are disturbed by the arrival of a youth who has killed a swan. Gurnemanz questions him, but the intruder is aware of nothing, not even his name: only Kundry knows he is an orphan. Gurnemanz thinks he may have found the innocent fool who will redeem Amfortas. During a long transformation scene he leads him into the castle of the Grail. They witness Amfortas's torment as, under pressure from his father Titurel, he unwillingly unveils the Grail. The stranger is moved by the event, but cannot grasp its deeper meaning.

Act II: Klingsor's magic castle. Klingsor wakes Kundry and commands her to trap the simple youth approaching his domain, against whom he will again wield the holy spear. After easily resisting the flower maidens, the youth is transfixed when Kundry calls out 'Parsifal' – the name his mother once gave him in a dream. Kundry inveigles him with her charm, cleverly exploiting his deep feelings of guilt about his mother's death. She gives him a long kiss on the mouth. He jumps up in shock: now he senses the terrible consequences of sinful longing, the torment of Amfortas's wound that burns in his own heart ('Amfortas! – Die Wunde!'). Furious that he continues to reject her sensual allure, Kundry summons Klingsor. But Parsifal regains the spear and Klingsor's castle crumbles to dust.

Act III: In the region of the Grail castle. Years have passed. Amfortas has refused to unveil the Grail, and the knights, debilitated and distressed, await their deliverer. Gurnemanz is an old man living as a hermit on the edge of the forest. He discovers Kundry again, almost dead. Parsifal enters in black armour with the holy spear at his side. Gurnemanz knows that the moment of salvation has come. He anoints Parsifal as the new king of the Grail while Kundry washes the feet of the new king and receives from him the baptism of absolution. It is the magic of Good Friday: nature has regained its lost innocence. Kundry's tears of repentance are tears of benediction, Parsifal tells her gently, and the meadow smiles ('du weinest – sieh! es lacht die Aue'). The scene changes gradually into the castle of the Grail, as in Act I. The knights urge Amfortas to unveil the Grail, but he refuses and demands that they kill him. This time Parsifal understands. He takes the spear and places its tip on Amfortas's side. The wound heals, and the power of the holy spear is restored (the spear was deconsecrated the moment it pierced Amfortas, who had sullied the purity of Christ through his transgression in Kundry's arms). Now the taint of sin has been removed from the spear, the symbol of Christ's sacrifice. Parsifal orders the unveiling of the Grail. Kundry dies, and the chorus quietly intones a new saying: 'Redemption to the Redeemer' ('Erlösung dem Erlöser').

Although the first performance of *Parsifal*, conducted by Hermann Levi, made a profound impression, Wagner insisted, as he had already agreed with Ludwig II in 1880, that the work be performed only in Bayreuth. Ironically, the first to ignore the stipulation was Ludwig himself, who ordered three performances of the Bayreuth production to take place in the Munich Court Opera in 1884 and 1885. The whole work was occasionally given in concert in countries that were not signatories to the Berne Convention (London, 1884; New York, 1886; Boston, 1891; Amsterdam, 1896), and there were unauthorized productions at the New York Metropolitan on 24 December 1903 and in Amsterdam on 20 June 1905 respectively. (The New York production was also taken on tour throughout the United States, when it was performed no fewer than 130 times.) As the full score of *Parsifal* had been widely available since 1883, however, it is actually more surprising that the 'rape of the Grail' (as the New York production became known to the Bayreuth faithful) had not happened much sooner. Cosima Wagner petitioned the Reichstag twice to extend the copyright beyond the statutory 30 years after the composer's death, first in 1901 and again in 1912, this time armed with 18,000 signatures, but her efforts were unsuccessful. When the copyright lapsed in 1914 nearly every major opera house rushed to mount its own production. *Parsifal* was deconsecrated and its secular existence began.

Before 1914 modern composers who wanted to hear *Parsifal* (and most of them did) had to make the pilgrimage to the Bayreuth shrine to witness its yearly unveiling. Debussy went in 1888, Berg in 1909, and Stravinsky was easily tempted by Diaghilev to go with him in 1912, even though it meant interrupting work on *Le sacré du printemps*. Berg complained of the 'empty-headed folly' (*leerer Wahn*) of Bayreuth, and Stravinsky noted in dismay that the inside of the theatre was like a crematorium (and a very old one at that). Indeed, the fading iconic world of the German empire the Festival Theatre represented seems to have been repellent to many of Europe's visiting intelligentsia. For Berg, however, the sophisticated refinement and sheer loveliness of the music of *Parsifal* was worth the trip. Stravinsky, who is wrongly supposed to have rejected *Parsifal* out of hand during his visit, deliberately stayed silent about the music, preferring to lambast the audience and the cult-like atmosphere of the performance. Debussy saw the gulf between Wagner's musical genius and the rest of his Bayreuth legacy in the work itself. The score is 'one of the most beautiful monuments ever raised to music', he wrote a few years after his visit, while the 'moral and religious ideas' represented by the allegory 'are completely false'. The startling volte-face is a suspect critical strategy, though it has been used by other prominent critics, including Nietzsche and Adorno, and tends to reflect modern opinion. The baroque-like rhetorical figures and highly intricate musical textures in *Parsifal*, however, are metaphorical reflections on its supposedly creaky allegory that are arguably still only imperfectly understood.

RECORDINGS 1. Dalis, Thomas, London, Neidlinger, Hotter, Bayreuth Festival Ch & O, Knappertsbusch, Philips, 1962 (live); 2. Vejzovic, Hofmann, Van Dam, Nimsgern, Moll, Berlin Deutsche Op Ch, BPO, Karajan, DG, 1979/80; 3. Meier, Jerusalem, Van Dam, von Kannen, Hölle, Berlin State Op Ch, BPO, Barenboim, Teldec, 1990
OTHER OPERAS *Die Feen*, 1835; *Das Liebesverbot, oder Die Novize von Palermo*, 1835; *Rienzi, der Letzte der Tribunen*, 1842

J.D.

Carl Maria Von Weber

Carl Maria Friedrich Ernst [von] Weber; *b* ?18 November 1786, Eutin; *d* 5 June 1826, London

Weber played a key role in the development of German Romantic opera. His most enduringly successful work, *Der Freischütz*, combines national characteristics in both plot and music with dramatic vitality, vivid musical imagery and appealing directness of style. These qualities ensured not only that it enjoyed extraordinary popularity in its own day but also that, alone of early Romantic German operas, it still retains a firm place in the standard operatic repertoire. Weber's later operas, *Euryanthe* and *Oberon*, though they contain some of his finest music, are, for very different reasons, flawed masterpieces.

Weber's childhood was spent in a theatrical environment, accompanying his father's touring theatre company as it travelled around Bavaria performing fashionable plays and singspiels. His education was haphazard; he received some instruction in music from his half-brother Fridolin and sporadic lessons from teachers in the various towns where the troupe performed. In Hildburghausen J. P. Heuschkel laid the foundations of his later pianistic virtuosity, in Salzburg he took lessons from Michael Haydn, and in Munich he took singing and composition lessons. With the help of the Munich court organist, Johann Nepomuk Kalcher, the 13-year-old Weber composed his first opera, a singspiel, *Die Macht der Liebe und des Weins*, in 1798. The score was destroyed in a fire at Kalcher's house shortly after its composition. His second opera, *Das Waldmädchen*, was composed shortly afterwards in Freiberg, to a libretto by Carl von Steinsberg, by whose travelling company it was performed.

By 1801 Weber was continuing his studies with Michael Haydn back in Salzburg, where he wrote his third opera, *Peter Schmoll und seine Nachbarn*. Early in 1803 it was staged in Augsburg, where his half-brother Edmund was conducting at the theatre. Later that year Weber moved to Vienna, intending to study with Joseph Haydn, but he came instead under the influence of the Abbé Vogler, whose impact on Weber's musical development was profound and lasting.

At Vogler's recommendation, the 17-year-old Weber was offered the post of kapellmeister at the Breslau theatre in 1804. During his two years in Breslau he attempted to reform the repertoire but encountered considerable opposition. He began another opera, on a libretto based on Musäus's 'Rübezahl' story, but only three numbers, which show no perceptible advance in his creative power, survive. Weber's departure from Breslau was precipitated when he accidentally drank engraving acid. Returning to work after a two-month convalescence, he found that most of his reforms had been undone, and he resigned.

After a sojourn in Carlsruhe, where he composed his two symphonies, Weber moved in 1807 to Stuttgart as secretary to Duke Ludwig of Württemberg. Encouraged by the hofkapellmeister there, Franz Danzi, Weber continued to compose for the theatre, writing incidental music for Schiller's *Turandot* (1809) and working on the opera *Silvana*, which he completed after he had moved to Stuttgart in 1810. The first ideas for *Der Freischütz* came later that year in Darmstadt when, on a visit to Stift Neuberg, he and Alexander von Dusch got as far as sketching a scenario. But Dusch, an amateur cellist, had insufficient time to prepare a libretto, and the project was postponed. Apart from the singspiel *Abu Hassan*, Weber composed no stage works during this period, turning his attention instead to instrumental works and to his own tours as a concert pianist. Early in 1813, however, he was persuaded to accept the post of kapellmeister at the Prague opera. Here, as earlier in Breslau, he immersed himself in his work of reforming the running of the opera house and its repertoire (basing it on the works of Mozart and on French opera), a task that left him little time to pursue his own compositions and that took its toll on his health. Disagreements with the opera's directors were constant, and in October 1816 he handed in his resignation and left for Berlin.

Within a few months he had secured himself a position as Royal Saxon kapellmeister in Dresden. While this gave him authority over the city's German opera, local taste favoured Italian opera, so the challenge set Weber in fostering an indigenous opera was substantial. He set about the task with his customary diligence and enthusiasm, once again leaving himself little time for composition. But, meeting Friedrich Kind, the idea of an opera on the *Freischütz* story was rekindled. Work proceeded fitfully – interruptions included a royal commission for an opera *Alcidor* (later cancelled) – but by May 1820 *Der Freischütz*, Weber's first opera for nine years, was complete (except for one aria, added the following year). The premiere was a triumph, and it was rapidly taken up throughout Europe, making Weber an international celebrity.

The success of *Der Freischütz* led to a commission for a new opera for the 1822–3 season at the Kärntnertortheater in Vienna. Weber embraced the project with enthusiasm and, laying aside his work on *Die drei Pintos* (a comic work he had begun in the summer of 1820), began seeking a suitable subject. Unfortunately, both his choice of Helmina von Chezy as librettist and *Euryanthe* as subject proved disastrous. Despite a respectfully received Vienna premiere, the opera's weaknesses soon became apparent, and it was withdrawn after 20 performances.

For more than a year after the premiere of *Euryanthe*, Weber composed almost nothing. But, in August 1824, he was invited by Charles Kemble to write a new opera for London, and, persuaded that by this means he would be able to provide for his family's financial security after his death, he accepted the commission. Against his doctor's advice, he travelled to London in February 1826 for the production of *Oberon*; he died on the day before he had planned to travel home.

Der Freischütz

The Free-Shooter

Romantic opera in three acts (2h 30m)
Libretto by Johann Friedrich Kind, after *Gespensterbuch* by Johann August Apel and Friedrich Laun (1811)
Composed 1817–21
PREMIERES 18 June 1821, Schauspielhaus, Berlin; UK: 22 July 1824, Lyceum, London; US: 2 March 1825, New York
CAST Max *t*, Kilian *bar*, Cuno *b*, Caspar *b*, Ännchen *s*, Agathe *s*, Samiel *spoken role*, 4 bridesmaids 4 *s*, Ottokar *bar*; *satb* chorus of hunters, peasants, spirits, bridesmaids, followers of the Prince

Weber considered writing an opera on the *Freischütz* story in 1811, after reading the tale in Apel's and Laun's newly published *Gespensterbuch*. When he became kapellmeister in Dresden in 1817 he revived the idea and discussed it with Friedrich Kind, who rapidly produced the draft of a libretto. At this stage it was entitled *Der Probeschuss* ('The Test Shot'). The story had already been used as the basis of a number of other theatrical pieces: by Franz Xaver von Caspar with music by Carl Neuner (1812); by Ferdinand Rosenau (1816); by Aloys Gleich with music by Franz Roser (1816). In 1818 Spohr, with the collaboration of Georg Döring, also began to compose an opera based on Apel's tale but, on hearing that Weber was working on the same subject, abandoned it in favour of *Zemire und Azor*.

Weber's poor health, his efforts on behalf of the German opera in Dresden and the pressure of other commissions slowed down the composition of *Der Freischütz*. In 1819 he began to work more intensively on the score – by then known as *Die Jägersbraut* ('The Hunter's Bride') – after he had reached an agreement that it should open the newly rebuilt Schauspielhaus in Berlin. (In fact, the Schauspielhaus was opened with a Goethe play, but *Der Freischütz* was the first musical piece to be performed there.) The premiere was a triumph, and the opera was soon being performed throughout Europe.

Der Freischütz was by far the most popular German opera of the first half of the 19th century. But its tremendous popularity is only partly explained by its musical and dramatic characteristics. It came at an opportune moment in German history, when the upsurge of patriotic feeling, following the defeat of Napoleon, was at its height. With its powerfully German character, in both drama and music, *Der Freischütz* seized the German imagination and remained a significant symbol of national identity throughout the difficult times that followed.

By 1830 *Der Freischütz* had been translated into Danish, Swedish, Czech, Russian, English, French, Hungarian, Polish and Dutch. It was also produced in many severely mutilated versions and its success led to a number of parodies. In 1824 a piece was published under the title *Samiel, oder Die Wunderpille*, and in England 'Septimus Globus' issued '*Der Freischütz*, a new muse-sick-all and see-nick performance from the new German uproar. By the celebrated Funnybear'. In the same year Castil-Blaze also produced his French version as *Robin des Bois*, which infuriated the young Berlioz. But Berlioz was later persuaded, albeit reluctantly, to supply recitatives and a ballet for a Paris production of *Der Freischütz* in 1841.

SYNOPSIS

Act I: In front of an inn in the Bohemian forest, peasants are congratulating Kilian on his victory over Max, a forester, in a shooting competition ('Victoria, victoria'). They taunt Max and only the arrival of Cuno, the head forester, prevents a fight. Caspar, another forester (who has made a compact with Samiel, the Black Huntsman), mockingly suggests that Max should call on the dark powers for assistance. Cuno rebukes Caspar, but warns Max that if he fails in the shooting test, he will not be allowed to marry his daughter Agathe. The peasants exit to a waltz. Alone, Max ponders his lack of success ('Durch die Wälder') while Samiel observes him. Caspar joins Max and insists on drinking several toasts with him; his coarse drinking song ('Hier im ird'schen Jammerthal') enrages Max. Caspar offers to help Max pass the test and proves the point by giving him his gun, with which he miraculously shoots an almost invisible eagle. Caspar explains that it was loaded with a magic bullet, and that seven more can be cast if he will come to the Wolf's Glen at midnight. Caspar plans to offer Max as a victim to Samiel in place of himself and exults in Max's impending damnation ('Schweig, schweig').

Act II: In Cuno's house Ännchen is rehanging a portrait that had fallen down, hitting Agathe. She cheers her cousin in a lively arietta ('Kommt ein schlanker Bursch gegangen'), and Agathe relates how, that morning, the Hermit, warning her of impending danger, gave her holy roses for her protection. Agathe's uneasiness gives way to joy when she hears Max approaching ('Leise, leise'). Her uneasiness returns, however, when Max explains that he must collect a stag that he has shot near the Wolf's Glen ('Wie? Was? Entsetzen!'). In the Wolf's Glen, as midnight strikes, Caspar summons Samiel, who accepts the substitute victim. Max arrives and, together, they cast seven bullets. Between each of the castings there are increasingly horrific supernatural manifestations; finally Samiel himself appears. Caspar and Max fall unconscious and calm returns.

Act III: The following day Max, out hunting, has made three magnificent shots and has only one magic bullet left;

Caspar has used all his three. Agathe is praying ('Und ob die Wolke'). She dreamed that she was a white dove; when Max fired his gun she fell, but the dove vanished and she was Agathe again, while a black bird lay bleeding at her feet. Ännchen tries to dispel Agathe's anxiety with a merry tale ('Einst träumte'). The bridesmaids arrive and sing a folksong ('Wir winden dir den Jungfernkranz'). Ännchen arrives with a box containing flowers, but a funeral wreath has been sent instead of a wedding wreath. They decide to make a new wreath from the Hermit's roses. The shooting test is about to begin. Prince Ottokar chooses a white dove as target. As Max takes aim Agathe enters and cries to him to hold fire since she is the dove. The Hermit causes the dove to fly off to another tree behind which Caspar is hiding. Max shoots, and both Agathe and Caspar fall. Everyone thinks Max has shot Agathe ('Schaut, o schaut'), but the bullet has hit Caspar; he dies cursing. Max makes a full confession, and, after the intervention of the Hermit, the prince pardons him.

The overture sets the scene for the opera; its two principal tonalities – C minor and C major – represent the opposing forces of good and evil. The appearance of the diminished seventh chord, associated with Samiel (F♯, A, C, E♭), foreshadows the dark side of the drama. The molto vivace section is based on passages to come later in the opera: Max's 'Doch mich umgarnen finstre Mächte' (from 'Durch die Wälder'), full of foreboding, and Agathe's exultant 'Süss entzückt entgegen ihm' (from 'Leise, leise').

Throughout the opera, keys play an important part in underlining the conflict between good and evil. The major keys, particularly the sharp keys, are associated with simplicity and goodness, while the minor keys, especially C minor, characterize the dark powers. Samiel's diminished seventh chord appears periodically and acts as a leitmotif, warning of the approaching evil. The whole of the Wolf's Glen scene is built round tonalities based on the individual notes of this chord: the music begins in F♯ minor; at Samiel's appearance it moves to C minor; as Max arrives it modulates to E♭; it returns to C minor and they begin casting the bullets, then, as the bullets are cast, the music alternates between C minor and A minor with copious use of diminished sevenths; at the end, when Caspar and Max fall unconscious, the tonality returns to F♯ minor.

Weber's brilliant orchestration creates dramatic atmospheric effects. In the opening section of the overture horns conjure up a vision of forests and hunting, while low clarinets and timpani create a sense of foreboding. The shrill piccolo is used to give a devilish quality to the end of Caspar's aria and masterly orchestration plays a significant part in creating the powerful atmosphere of the Wolf's Glen scene, which was regarded as a *locus classicus* of German Romantic imagery and imagination during the 19th century. Perhaps the most important musical contribution to the enduring success of the opera, however, is the vigour of Weber's melodic invention. His handling of both the folksong-like choruses and solos and the weightier arias and ensembles is equally successful.

RECORDINGS 1. Grümmer, Otto, Schock, Kohn, Frick, Berlin Deutsche Op Ch, BPO, Keilberth, EMI, 1958 (with dialogue); 2. Janowitz, Mathis, Schreier, Adam, Crass, Leipzig RCh, Dresden Staatskapelle, C. Kleiber, DG, 1973 (with dialogue); 3. Orgonášová, Schafer, Wottrich, Salminen, Moll, Berlin RCh, BPO, Harnoncourt, Teldec, 1995

OTHER OPERAS *Die Macht der Liebe des Weins* (1778), (singspiel); *Das Waldmädchen* (fragments of 2 arias survive), 1800; *Peter Schmoll und seine Nachbarn*, 1803; *Rübezahl, oder Der Beherrscher der Geister* (3 numbers survive), (1805); *Silvana*, 1810; *Abu*

Hassan, 1811; *Euryanthe*, 1823; *Die drei Pintos*, (inc.) (1824), 1888 (completed by Mahler); *Oberon, or The Elf King's Oath*, 1826; 1 lost opera

C.A.B.

Kurt Weill

Kurt Julian Weill; *b* 2 March 1900, Dessau, Saxony; *d* 3 April 1950, New York

Weill was the third child of the chief cantor at the Dessau synagogue. He received his musical education first from the conductor Albert Bing (a pupil of Pfitzner) in Dessau and in 1918 from Humperdinck at the Berlin Hochschule für Musik. After a year's practical work at the opera house in his home town (where Hans Knappertsbusch was the music director) and as staff conductor at the Lüdenscheid opera in Westphalia, he returned to Berlin in 1920 to join Busoni's composition masterclass.

By the time he started to collaborate with Bertolt Brecht in 1927, Weill was established as one of the leading composers in Weimar Germany, with four successful stage works under his belt; it was indeed Weill who gave the unknown writer his first chance of fame with the sensational premiere of the *Mahagonny Songspiel* at Baden-Baden. Brecht continued to ride on Weill's coattails with *Die Dreigroschenoper* (1928), *Aufstieg und Fall der Stadt Mahagonny* (1930), *Happy End* (1929) and *Der Jasager* (1930), after which they drifted apart; as Lotte Lenya, whom the composer had married in 1926, was to put it later, her husband was not interested in setting the Communist manifesto to music, and Weill resumed collaboration with the Expressionist playwright Georg Kaiser in *Der Silbersee* (February 1933). This was simultaneously premiered in three cities (which gives some idea of the composer's status), but was to be the last Weill premiere in Germany. Nazi thugs disrupted early performances, and nine days after the first night the Reichstag fire gave them the opportunity to assume power. Weill fled precipitately from Berlin to Paris in March, with few belongings and none of his music.

The Nazis seem to have feared him more than any other composer, and for years went to inordinate lengths through diplomatic channels worldwide to have his scores, orchestral parts and records destroyed. Weill himself believed that all his German works save for *Dreigroschenoper* were irretrievably lost, and reused some of the music in later pieces.

Weill spent 18 months in Paris, which saw a brief reunion with Brecht for *Die sieben Todsünden* and the incidental music for Jacques Deval's play *Marie Galante* (which included one of his greatest songs, 'J'attends un navire', later used as a signal by the French resistance), and went to the US in 1935 to complete the score for the Franz Werfel–Max Reinhardt pageant of Jewish history, *Der Weg der Verheissung*, eventually staged as *The Eternal Road* (New York, 1937). He remained in the States for the rest of his life, composing for Broadway and Hollywood, and died from a heart condition in 1950 while embarking on a musical version of *Huckleberry Finn*.

Weill is beyond any doubt one of the most important composers for the theatre – a more accurate designation than 'opera composer' – of the 20th century. His precise place in the history of Western music in general and opera in particular is still impossible to assess. The cultural upheaval caused by the short-lived but still reverberating Nazi tyranny in the very heartland of European music; a generally left-wing political and critical stance, allied to knee-jerk anti-American sentiment in post-war Europe that bolstered accusations of a progressive composer 'selling out' to Broadway commercialism (his US works are loathed in Germany); and Weill's tragically premature death aged only 50: all contribute to clouding a highly complex issue.

At the time, the end of the First World War seemed like a watershed, though today we may see it as only the first act of a European drama that is still being played out. But it afforded an opportunity for composers to grapple with the post-Wagnerian legacy. Wagner had pushed tonality as far as it could go: what next? Strauss largely wrote neo-Wagnerian operas; Schoenberg devised a new musical language, dodecaphony; Stravinsky and Busoni advanced – or retreated – into neoclassicism; Schreker, Zemlinsky and others nudged Wagnerianism over the edge into no-holds-barred Expressionism. Most composers embraced without question an aesthetic of linear progress: music could only get more complicated, more demanding, more remote from everyday audiences, more dependent on a state-subsidized system of presentation. The artificial separation of high art and popular art is still a very real problem, and it seems to be only in music that this linear progress has been accepted virtually without question. Few would regard the path in painting from, say, Giotto to Raphael, as one of smooth, uninterrupted progress.

Weill's early works are conventionally Expressionist; there is a vitally important neoclassical element in *Dreigroschenoper* and *Mahagonny*. The latter was rejected by Otto Klemperer – later a leading exponent of the 'sell-out' school of Weill criticism – at the Krolloper, and Weill took it instead to Berlin's equivalent of Broadway, the Kurfürstendamm, for a commercial run. *Dreigroschenoper* and *Happy End* were commercial ventures, and although there were still projects for subsidized theatres (*Die Bürgschaft* and *Der Silbersee*) he had taken the basic decision to write for a mass audience long before he went to America. In Germany he transformed into high art familiar song and dance idioms of the time and place, and the mass popularity of *Dreigroschenoper* cannot be overstressed. In America he naturally turned to the popular and folk idioms of his new homeland – to have done otherwise would have been senseless – and it is this that has stuck in sensitive European throats. But as Weill wrote in 1949, 'The American popular song, growing out of American folk music, is the basis of the American musical theatre, just as the Italian song was the basis of Italian opera.'

The notion that a radical, left-wing composer 'sold out' to naked commerce does not bear serious examination. The people Weill collaborated with in the US were, for the main part, committed radicals of the kind who got into serious trouble in the McCarthy era, and *Johnny Johnson*, *Knickerbocker Holiday*, *Street Scene*, *Love Life* and *Lost in the Stars* are works brimming over with political and social concern. The collaboration with Brecht cannot be taken as evidence that Weill was in any sense a conventional left-winger: the break coincided with the playwright's conversion to orthodox communism. Weill, on the evidence in particular of his US output as well as his later German works, could best be described as a militant humanist, a man set on using popular theatre to combat intolerance, prejudice, deprivation and injustice wherever they were to be found.

His compositional aesthetic is neatly summed up in an interview he gave to the *New York Sun* in 1940. 'I have never acknowledged the difference between "serious" music and "light" music. There is only good music and bad music,' he said, and continued with a direct challenge to critical orthodoxy: 'Schoenberg has said he is writing for a time 50 years after his death. But the great classical composers wrote for their contemporary audiences. They wanted those who heard their music to understand it, and they did. For myself, I write for today. I don't give a damn about writing for posterity.'

Weill was above all a great writer of tunes: the Ballad of Mack the Knife has become an authentic 20th-century folksong, and he composed many others worthy of that status. He was a tirelessly inventive orchestrator, varying the accompaniments to each verse of his songs and, almost uniquely on Broadway, doing virtually all his own scoring and devising his own dance sequences. Yet his melodic genius should not be taken to imply the smallest degree of facileness: David Drew's analysis of *Dreigroschenoper* in the Cambridge Opera Handbook suggests a personal, highly complex serialist technique.

An of necessity interim report must credit Weill with at least four masterpieces: *Dreigroschenoper*, *Mahagonny* and *Die sieben Todsünden* have never lost their hold on the repertoire, and after regular revival *Street Scene* has now been accepted as one of the great American operas, a work to set beside *Porgy and Bess* and one he considered to be his first complete technical success. A pleasing new critical stance holds that it was with *Street Scene* that he reached full maturity as a composer for the theatre.

When the rest of his output is investigated now that prejudice against his later works is fading, other masterpieces may emerge. As it is, his importance in having shown that popular theatre can – or rather must – be serious is now generally accepted, and his influence on later Broadway composers, from Bernstein to Sondheim, is incalculable.

Die Dreigroschenoper

The Threepenny Opera

Play with music in three acts (music: 1h 15m; full-length play)
Libretto and play text by Bertolt Brecht, based on the translation by Elisabeth Hauptmann of *The Beggar's Opera* by John Gay (1728), with interpolated ballads by François Villon and Rudyard Kipling
PREMIERES 31 August 1928, Theater am Schiffbauerdamm, Berlin; US: 13 April 1933, Empire Theater, New York; UK: 9 February 1956, Royal Court Theatre, London
CAST Jonathan Jeremiah Peachum *bar*, Mrs Peachum *ms*, Polly Peachum *s*, Macheath *t*, Tiger Brown/Streetsinger *bar*, Lucy *s*, Jenny Diver *s*, Macheath's gang; *satb* chorus of whores, beggars and police

Weill composed the score of *Die Dreigroschenoper* in the spring and summer of 1928 for the impresario J. E. Aufricht, who had unexpectedly come into money and taken a lease of the Theater am Schiffbauerdamm. Final rehearsals were chaotic – the piece did not find its final form until well after the premiere – and the theatre was not full on the first night. Those involved were half expecting a flop. But despite mixed notices word of mouth ensured a hit of near-unprecedented proportions (the triumph of *The Merry Widow* a quarter of a century earlier provides a nicely ironic parallel), and the piece was soon staged throughout Europe (save for Britain) and in the US. Only the advent of the Nazis in 1933 interrupted its near continuous run in Berlin and countless productions all over Germany.

SYNOPSIS

Act I: In a prologue set in London's Soho, the Streetsinger sings the Ballad of Mack the Knife, admiringly cataloguing the petty criminal's crimes. Mr and Mrs Peachum briefly interrupt the business-like organization of the band of beggars and thieves they control to note the absence of their daughter Polly. It emerges that she has eloped with Mack, a highly unsuitable son-in-law. In the second scene Polly and Mack celebrate their wedding in a stable surrounded by stolen goods and the gang. Polly entertains the company with a song she recently heard a bedraggled hotel chambermaid singing (Pirate Jenny). Among the guests is the police chief Tiger Brown, Mack's old schoolfriend. They reminisce over happy days in the Indian Army (Cannon Song). Left alone, the newly-weds sing a love duet of sickly sentimentality. Back with her parents, Polly seeks to explain her new liaison via the Barbara Song, but they are determined to force Brown to arrest Mack. In the First Threepenny Finale, the three comment on the intractability of human existence.

Act II: In the stable, Mack and Polly sing a duet of farewell: he has 'business' to attend to. Meanwhile, Mrs Peachum bribes the whore Jenny to betray Mack to the police (Song of Sexual Dependency), which Jenny duly does in a brothel in Turnbridge, having first joined with him in the Tango Ballad, in which they remember affectionately the good old days when he was her pimp. In the Old Bailey, Mack sings the Ballad of the Good Life (based on Villon). Brown's daughter Lucy, feigning pregnancy, reproaches Mack and sings a furious Jealousy Duet with Polly, but nevertheless helps her seducer to escape. The Second Threepenny Finale, sung by the entire company, returns to the problems of human existence: man survives only by suppressing his humanity and exploiting his fellow man.

Act III: Peachum blackmails Brown: if Mack is not rearrested, his army of beggars will disrupt the forthcoming coronation. Mack is found with another whore and returned to the Old Bailey. Polly and his gang are unable, or unwilling, to come up with the necessary bribe to prevent his hanging. He takes bitter farewell of the world. But Peachum announces that the company has thought up a different ending (Third Threepenny Finale): the King's Messenger (Brown) brings news that in honour of the coronation the queen grants Mack a reprieve, a peerage, a grace-and-favour castle and a pension. The company sings a mock-Bach chorale of ironic relief: 'Don't prosecute crime: it will die out of its own accord.'

The action was never intended to be in any way naturalistic: décor and acting style were non-representational, and the plot came to a halt for the musical numbers, which were differently lit. This was 'epic theatre' after the manner of the day and, in Weill's words, 'the most consistent reaction to Wagner . . . the complete destruction of the concept of music drama'. *The Beggar's Opera* satirized the 18th-century ruling classes by putting them in a low-life setting (Hogarth's painting shows the original cast still very grandly dressed); *The Threepenny Opera*'s target is the solid bourgeoisie of post-war Europe. It has become customary to play both works as low-life extravaganzas, which weakens their impact: the characters should be instantly, inescapably recognizable as, and to, the audience.

Weill wrote the music not for opera singers, but for artists from the fields of cabaret, musical comedy and (in the case of Macheath) operetta. The dart of his satire is poisoned by the beauty and catchiness of the tunes. As you hum or listen to them, the cheerful, subversive obscenity of the words inevitably sinks in, nowhere more devastatingly than in the Tango Ballad, the Song of Sexual Dependency (which the first Mrs Peachum refused to sing), or – more pointfully – the finales. The songs nevertheless need to be sung properly, not snarled or shouted as has become the custom in low-life productions: early recordings (hoarded and secretly played by liberal Germans under Nazi rule) reveal a sweetness and innocence of approach that makes their appeal all the more insinuating.

Brecht revised both the libretto and the lyrics after the premiere, bringing them into line with his own growing Marxist convictions and by 1931 establishing the text as usually played today. The original is shorter, funnier, more anarchic and less didactic, but is unlikely to be revived before Brecht's copyright runs out.

The New York revival of 1954, which ran for 2,611 performances in Marc Blitzstein's translation, marked a significant stage in the revival of interest in Weill's work – revivals and recordings of his other European scores followed – and confirmed *Dreigroschenoper* as one of the most important (and in the right circumstances enjoyable) pieces of music theatre composed in the 20th century.

RECORDINGS 1. Koczian, Lenya, Wolffberg, Hesterburg, Schellow, Grunert, Trenk-Trebitsch, Neuss, Sender Freies Berlin O, Brückner-Rüggeberg, CBS, 1958; 2. Lemper, Milva, Tremper, Dernesch, Kollo, Reichmann, Adorf, Boysen, RIAS Berlin Sinfonietta, Mauceri, Decca, 1990

Aufstieg und Fall der Stadt Mahagonny

The Rise and Fall of the City of Mahagonny

Opera in three acts (2h 15m)
Libretto by Bertolt Brecht
Composed 1927–9
PREMIERES 9 March 1930, Neues Theater, Leipzig; US: 23 February 1952, Town Hall, New York; UK: 16 January 1963, Sadler's Wells, London
CAST Leocadia Begbick *ms*, Fatty the Bookkeeper *t*, Trinity Moses *bar*, Jenny Smith *s*, Jim Mahoney *t*, Jakob Schmidt *t*, Bankroll Bill *bar*, Alaska Wolf Joe *b*, Tobby Higgins *t*; *satb* chorus of people of Mahagonny

The full-length *Mahagonny* opera, conceived early in 1927, received a preview in the form of the so-called *Mahagonny Songspiel*, a music-theatre setting of a group of loosely linked poems from Brecht's *Hauspostille* about an imaginary US city. God consigns its licentious citizens to hell, but they truculently reply that they are there already. The *Songspiel* fulfilled a commission to Weill from the Baden-Baden Deutsche Kammermusik festival, and the premiere there on 17 July 1927 was an enormous *succès de scandale* – an audience expecting respectable avant-garde experiment was regaled with raucous music-hall songs set in a boxing ring.

SYNOPSIS

Act I: A desert in America. A battered truck drives on to the stage and breaks down. Its passengers are Begbick, Fatty and Trinity Moses, fugitives from justice on charges of white-slaving and fraud. Noting that it is easier to extract gold from men than from the dried-up riverbed they are stranded on, Begbick decides to found Mahagonny, a 'city of nets' given over to pleasure since life is so miserable everywhere else. Jenny and her friends – the first 'sharks' – enter: 'Oh show us the way to the next whisky bar' (Alabama Song). Fatty and Moses recruit emigrants from the industrial cities of the world, and Jimmy Mahoney and his friends Jake, Bill and Joe, four 'simple lumberjacks from Alaska', arrive to a sprightly parody of the Bridesmaids' Chorus from *Der Freischütz*. They are offered their choice of girls, and Jimmy buys Jenny Smith for 30 dollars. She asks him whether or not he would like her to wear knickers. He answers in the negative. Mahagonny suffers a recession, and Jimmy is only just dissuaded from leaving by his friends. In the saloon he rails (to a parody of 'The Maiden's Prayer') against too much peace and quiet. An approaching typhoon is the answer to his prayer. As they await its arrival, Jimmy protests that the city is hemmed in by too many regulations: society should be founded on total permissiveness, on laissez-faire and each man for himself – 'as you make your bed, so you lie on it' ('Wie man sich bettet so liegt man').

Act II: Mahagonny is miraculously spared and its citizens follow Jimmy's precepts in four tableaux: gluttony, in which Jake eats himself to death; lechery, in which Begbick presides over a brothel; fighting, in which Jimmy puts all his money on Joe in a boxing match with Trinity Moses (Joe is killed); and drinking, in which Jimmy buys rounds of drinks for which he cannot pay. When Begbick demands payment, Jenny refuses his appeal for a loan and throws 'Wie man sich bettet' back at him. Imprisoned, he dreads the dawn of a new day.

Act III: In the courts, Tobby Higgins is cleared of murder after handing money over to the bench. Jimmy asks Bill for a loan so that his case may similarly be heard fairly; Bill replies that he is fond of him, but money is something else. So Jimmy has no defence against accusations of subversion, the violation of Jenny, the death of Joe for financial gain and – the most serious crime of all in Mahagonny – inability to pay, for which he is sentenced to death. The remaining principals dream of another city, Benares, only to hear that it has been destroyed by an earthquake. Jimmy bids farewell to Jenny and exhorts the citizens to continue living life to the full: there is no afterlife, and he has no regrets. As he is strapped into the electric chair, they enact God's visit to Mahagonny. Following his execution, there are mass demonstrations and counter-demonstrations against the rising cost of living while the city burns. Jimmy's relics are paraded, but there is no way of helping a dead man.

Following the Leipzig premiere and stagings in other German cities, *Mahagonny* was turned down by Klemperer at the Berlin Krolloper; Weill responded by organizing a commercial run on the Kurfürstendamm in December 1931 conducted by Zemlinsky. Revisions were made, and rehearsals saw the not-quite-final break with Brecht, who resented the dominance of the music and accused the composer of writing 'phoney Richard Strauss'. After the war Brecht supervised a drastically cut, ideologically more acceptable version for performance in East Germany. Weill himself allowed substantial cuts for a Vienna production in 1932, and had performances not been interrupted by the Nazi regime would surely have worked to tighten the action more systematically and resolve the conflict between the need for operatically trained voices and decidedly unoperatic material.

Nevertheless, *Mahagonny* as it stands remains one of the great 20th-century operas, a beguiling mixture of lively neoclassical formulae and music-hall songs, melodically prodigiously rich. The expressionistically grotesque trial scene builds up unstoppable dramatic momentum, and the finale with its marches and counter-marches, in which all the hit tunes are brought back, has a pole-axing effect. This is in a way a 20th-century equivalent to *Die Zauberflöte*, a journey not from darkness to light, but from darkness to even greater darkness, one in which the eternal truths proposed are distinctly less comfortable than Mozart's and Schikaneder's. No easy answers are given (Brecht had not yet quite embraced Marxist fundamentalism), which makes the work all the more disturbing. At the final curtain the cast is, as it were, addressing the audience with the title of Weill's lost musical of 1927, *Na und?* ('And so?'). The fact that that question remains unanswered 60 years later suggests that *Mahagonny* has by no means had its day.

RECORDING Lenya, Litz, Sauerbaum, Günter, Markwort, Mund, NW German RCh & O, Brückner-Rüggeberg, CBS, 1956

Die sieben Todsünden

The Seven Deadly Sins

Ballet chanté in one act (35m)
Scenario by Edward James and Boris Kochno; choreography by George Balanchine; libretto by Bertolt Brecht
PREMIERES 7 June 1933, Théâtre des Champs-Elysées, Paris; UK: 28 June 1933, Savoy Theatre, London (as *Anna-Anna*); US: 4 December 1958, City Center, New York
CAST Anna I *s*, Anna II *dancer*, the Family 2 *t*, *bar*, *b*

Within a month of arriving in Paris in 1933 Weill had been commissioned to compose a ballet by the English philanthropist Edward James. He was funding the first season of Balanchine's and Kochno's dance company Les Ballets 1933, which had just broken away from Diaghilev's Ballets Russes. James insisted on a role for his estranged wife, the dancer Tilly Losch, in the hope that it would lead to a reconciliation (it didn't – they divorced spectacularly the following year), and when the basic idea of dividing a split personality between a dancer and a singer, between flesh and spirit, was established, James in turn suggested Lotte Lenya for the singing role, although Weill and Lenya were at the time in the middle of their own divorce proceedings (they remarried in the USA in 1937). Lenya's lover at the time, Otto von Pasetti, was given one of the tenor roles in the family.

When Cocteau declined to write the libretto, James urged Brecht on a none-too-willing Weill: they had fallen out over the Kurfürstendamm *Mahagonny* 18 months earlier. Brecht was at first unenthusiastic about the scenario, but managed to feed enough social criticism into it to salve his conscience. When the libretto was included in his collected works after the war, he expanded the title to *Die sieben Todsünden der Kleinbürger* ('of the Petty-Bourgeois'), lest anyone miss the point.

SYNOPSIS

In the prologue the two Annas, sisters from Louisiana, introduce themselves. Anna I, the singer, is the practical, down-to-earth one; her dancing sister Anna II, she warns us, is a bit dizzy (*etwas verrückt*). 'But we're really one person, not two, with one past and one future, one heart and one savings bank account.' Their mission is to travel to seven cities in America to earn enough money for their family to build a little house back in Louisiana, and the voices of the family quartet (the mother sung by the bass) are throughout heard singing biblical bromides warning them not to fall into sin. The basic joke is that the instinctive dancer Anna is tempted to give in to sin at each turn, but is prevented by the singer Anna: sin compromises their earning power. Thus, Anna II is too proud to take her clothes off in a strip-tease cabaret ('Pride is only for rich people,' warns Anna I); too wrathful over cruelty to an animal when working as a movie extra, and risking dismissal; too prone to gluttony when agents want only slim dancers; too much given to lust (a toy-boy), which upsets her sugar-daddy (named 'Edward', an obvious in-joke); and so on. Bourgeois morality is wittily turned on its head. In the epilogue the sisters return to the little house in Louisiana, the practical Anna I triumphant, Anna II's human spirit utterly crushed.

Weill here achieved a perfect synthesis of popular form and weightiness of content. The tunes beguile, the dance rhythms sparkle, yet the score is rigorously organized along traditional symphonic lines. The sardonic musical wit balances that in the text, but the composer triumphs decisively over the detached librettist in the compassion he shows for human, instinctive, near-wordless Anna II. The final bars are heart-rending.

The premiere, attended by the Parisian *beau monde*, was an artistic triumph, but the season as a whole was a financial disaster. Among those who attended the first run was Lincoln Kirstein, who recognized Balanchine's genius and was to lure the choreographer to the US and found the New York City Ballet for him. The company gave the US premiere (and first post-war performance) of Weill's ballet in 1958, with Lenya. It has been given numerous productions since. When Lenya was engaged for the premiere, Weill sanctioned downward transpositions of parts of the score to accommodate her limited resources. It has been recorded mostly in that form.

RECORDINGS 1. Lenya, NW German Radio O, Brückner-Rüggeberg, Philips/CBS, 1960: with transpositions; 2. Ross, CBSO, Rattle, EMI, 1983: original pitch

Street Scene

'An American Opera' in two acts
(2h 30m)
Book by Elmer Rice, based on his own play (1929); lyrics by Langston Hughes

Composed 1946
PREMIERES 9 January 1947, Adelphi Theater, New York; UK: 6 June 1983, Royal Academy of Music, London (semi-staged and much cut); 26 April 1987, Palace Theatre, London
CAST Anna Maurrant *s*, Rose Maurrant *s*, Mrs Jones *ms*, Mrs Fiorentino *s*, Mrs Olsen *c*, Sam Kaplan *t*, Frank Maurrant *b*, Harry Easter *bar*, Willy Maurrant *boy s*, Henry Davis *bar*, Mr Buchanan *t*, Mr Fiorentino *t*, Jennie Hildebrand *ms*, Mrs Hildebrand *ms*, Mr Jones *bar*, Mr Kaplan *t*, 2 Nursemaids *s, ms, spoken roles; satb* chorus of neighbours

Weill had known the playwright Elmer Rice since his earliest days in America – they met during rehearsals of *Johnny Johnson* in 1936, and he wrote incidental music for Rice's play *Two on an Island* in 1939 – and the possibility of turning Rice's social-realist study of life in a slum tenement block into an opera had been at the back of his mind since seeing a performance of *Street Scene* in Europe before being driven into exile. 'It seemed like a great challenge to me,' he wrote later, 'to find the inherent poetry in these people and to blend my music with the stark realism of the play.'

Other composers had seen operatic possibilities in *Street Scene*, but Rice was fiercely protective of his material. He turned down Deems Taylor's projected setting for the Met because it strayed too far from the original. Weill secured the playwright's agreement in 1945, and the result is remarkably faithful; the composer from the land of *Fidelio* and *Freischütz* saw no problem with long passages of spoken dialogue in serious music drama, and his use of Hollywood rather than Benda-inspired mélodrame helped bind music and speech into an indissoluble whole. 'Not until *Street Scene* did I achieve a real blending of drama and music,' wrote Weill at the time of the premiere.

The black poet Langston Hughes was engaged to supply the lyrics, and the collaboration was close if not always easy. Hughes took Weill to Harlem to gather material for the Janitor's Song, and together they roamed New York listening to vendors' cries and children's street games. After a less than successful try-out in Philadelphia, *Street Scene* ran in New York for 148 performances (a modest first run compared to *Lady in the Dark*, but not bad for an opera – Gershwin's *Porgy and Bess* managed only 126). The leading roles were taken by trained opera singers: Polyna Stoska of the City Opera as Anna, Norman Cordon of the Met as Frank, Anne Jeffreys as Rose and Brian Sullivan, a future Lohengrin, as Sam.

SYNOPSIS

Act I: The sidewalk outside a tenement block in New York City; early evening in June (the action is contained within 24 hours). The inhabitants of the block, half stifled by the humidity ('Ain't it awful, the heat'), are introduced: the black Janitor ('I got a marble and a star'); the tenement bitch, Mrs Jones, who leads the gossip about Anna Maurrant's affair with the milk collector, Mr Sankey; Sam Kaplan, a shy, bookish boy in calf love with the Maurrant daughter, Rose; Sam's father Abraham, an elderly socialist firebrand, and his sister Shirley, a teacher; Mr Buchanan, whose wife is about to give birth for the first time; finally the Maurrants, Frank, an inarticulate, reactionary theatre electrician, and his wife Anna, who expresses her disillusion in the extended aria 'Somehow I never could believe' – she contrasts her romantic girlhood dreams with the bitter reality of life. The solace of her affair with Mr Sankey is known to all except her husband, who nevertheless starts to suspect something during the course of Act I. Mr Fiorentino – the block is authentically multiracial – leads the Ice Cream Sextet, likening a cone to the torch held by the Statue of Liberty glimpsed by all European immigrants as they sail into New York. Jennie Hildebrand returns from her graduation ceremony to general rejoicing ('Wrapped in a ribbon'). The cheerful optimism of the concerted number is tempered by the knowledge that the Hildebrand family, deserted by the father, is to be evicted for non-payment of rent the following day. Maurrant leaves for an evening's drinking; gossip resumes. Sam attacks the gossipers before singing of his misery in 'Lonely house'. Rose Maurrant enters with Harry Easter, a married man from her office with plans to set her up as his mistress. He tempts her with the sleazy 'Wouldn't you like to be on Broadway'; she counters with 'What use would the moon be'; like her mother before her, she nurtures romantic ideals. Easter prudently withdraws when Maurrant returns drunk from the bar. Buchanan's wife goes into labour; Anna Maurrant runs to help her. Mrs Jones's daughter Mae enters with an admirer, Dick; their love is anything but romantic ('Moon-faced, starry eyed', an energetic jitterbug). In a long duet ('Pain! Nothing but pain') Rose and Sam sing of the possibility of escape to a better life, taking as a symbol Walt Whitman's Lilac Bush ('In the dooryard fronting an old farmhouse') before bidding each other a tender goodnight.

Act II: Early the next morning. Raucous children's street games carry a whiff of the class war. Buchanan thanks Anna, who has been up all night with his wife. Frank leaves for work, after gruffly rejecting Rose's plea to him to be kinder to her mother (trio: 'You've got no right'). Anna sends her son Willy off to school. Rose tells Sam about Harry Easter's importunings, and they sing of running away together. Easter arrives to accompany Rose to an office funeral. Anna Maurrant invites Mr Sankey up to her apartment. City marshalls start to put the Hildebrands' belongings out on the sidewalk. The suspicious Maurrant returns unexpectedly, and Sam's shouted warning to Anna is too late: shots ring out. Maurrant escapes, but Rose returns with an excited crowd to see her dying mother being carried out to the ambulance (ensemble: 'The woman who lived up there'). Sankey is dead. The eviction of the Hildebrands proceeds. Some hours later, Scene 2 is launched by two nursemaids from uptown gawking at the scene of the double murder with their charges ('Sleep, baby dear') – the other side of the class war. Maurrant is caught, and before being led away by the police tells Rose he killed her mother out of jealousy and panic at the thought of losing her. The crowd disperses, leaving Rose and Sam alone. She plans to go away to start a new life and kindly but firmly refuses to let the lovelorn Sam go with her. The experience of her parents' tragedy makes her unwilling to enter any such commitment. She leaves. Two prospective tenants come to view the Hildebrands' empty apartment. The neighbours drift back to the sidewalk ('Ain't it awful, the heat'). Life goes on.

The technical brilliance of *Street Scene* cannot be overstressed, nor the way Weill sets Rice's intentionally flat prose to music of charm, colour and dramatic power. Some commentators have found Hughes's lyrics banal, but underprivileged, barely literate people tend to express themselves in cliché – they know no other way. To that extent, Hughes's verses are as social-realist as Rice's prose. The action is set among – to borrow a phrase from *Dreigroschenoper* – 'the poorest of the poor', which is rare enough in opera (Charpentier's *Louise* is one of the very few other operatic studies of working-class life). The tenement represents a trap, and the action examines various ways of coming to terms with, or escaping from, it. Mae and Dick resort to dope and sex; Anna to adultery; Sam to study and self-improvement; many of the others – including Frank Maurrant – to drink. For a moment Rose seriously considers Harry Easter's offer: anything to escape the grinding, cheerless spiritual and material poverty of the tenement. Otherwise Rose dreams with Sam of Whitman's Lilac Bush, which remains a dream, since *Street Scene*'s creators heroically declined to settle for the Broadway Happy End. The fact that it ends with two young lives irretrievably ruined – this is not a cheerful evening in the theatre – may account for its slow acceptance into the general operatic repertoire; Weill couldn't quite, like Janáček, turn physical disaster into spiritual triumph. On the other hand, Weill's musical treatment of all the inhabitants of the tenement trap (save perhaps for the monstrous Mrs Jones, a villain of Begbick or Frau von Luber proportions) is notable for its compassion, its anger and its total lack of condescension.

In *Mahagonny* Brecht's doggerel line 'Is here no telephone' has been proposed as the catch-phrase of 20th-century alienation; the last words of 'Ain't it awful, the heat', which opens and closes Street Scene, are 'Don't know what I'm gonna do' – just as powerful an image of the hopelessness of the 20th-century human condition. Nowhere else is the voice of Weill the militant humanist heard so clearly.

RECORDINGS 1. Barstow, Réaux, Mackillop, Dickinson, Hadley, Mee, Ramey, Scottish Op O, Mauceri, Decca, 1990; 2. Kristine Ciesinski, Kelly, Bullock, Dickinson, Bottone, Bronder, Van Allan, ENO O, Carl Davis, That's Entertainment, 1991
OTHER OPERATIC WORKS *Der Protagonist*, 1926; *Royal Palace*, 1927; *Na und?* (lost), (1927); *Der Zar läßt sich photographieren*, 1928; *Happy End*, 1929; *Der Jasager*, 1930; *Die Bürgschaft*, 1932; *Der Silbersee*, 1933; *Der Kuhhandel*, (1934), 2000; *Johnny Johnson*, 1936; *The Eternal Road*, 1937; *Knickerbocker Holiday*, 1938; *Davy Crockett* (inc.), (1938); *Ulysses Africanus* (inc.), (1939); *Lady in the Dark*, 1941; *One Touch of Venus*, 1943; *The Firebrand of Florence*, 1945; *Down in the Valley*, 1948; *Love Life*, 1948; *Lost in the Stars*, 1949; *Huckleberry Finn* (unfinished at the composer's death), (1950)

R.M.

Judith Weir

b 11 May 1954, Cambridge

Weir first studied with John Tavener, then with Robin Holloway at Cambridge and Gunther Schuller at Tanglewood. *A Night at the Chinese Opera* (1987), her first full-length opera, put her firmly on the map as a composer with a distinct theatrical aptitude and an accessible yet individual musical language. These qualities had been discernible in a string of earlier concert works that perhaps could be termed 'concert-theatre' or opera-in-embryo; works that involve narrative and dramatic techniques of an operatic kind but, for reasons of scale, inhabit a concert hall rather than a theatre. The most reductionist of these is *King Harald's Saga* (1979), a ten-minute 'Grand Opera in three acts' for unaccompanied soprano singing eight solo roles and one representing the Norwegian Army. In all her works, Weir uses her own texts derived from a variety of sources. In *Harald* she uses an Icelandic saga, and something fundamental to all her texts is in the tone of this original source: a deadpan narrative style that enables fantastic or epic events to be recounted with economy and speed. In *The Consolations of Scholarship* (1985), described as a 'music drama' for mezzo-soprano and nine instruments, the Yüan dynasty tale unfolds (the same story as *A Night at the Chinese Opera*) through plain narration and relevant philosophical discourse. This work has been convincingly staged, further confounding any attempt to classify what counts as opera within her oeuvre.

Weir's musical language is aphoristic and understated, developing in early works from a quasi-minimalist style to encompass more straightforwardly melodic ideas, which can assimilate all sorts of ethnic flavouring, whether Scottish (as Weir is herself), Chinese or Spanish, without resorting to parody and pastiche. Weir has cited Stravinsky's *Oedipus Rex* as a major influence on her work. Similar to Stravinsky in his neoclassical phase is an emotional distancing from her material that goes hand in hand with her idiosyncratic narrative style. This has led her work to be dubbed witty and ironic, and while these qualities are present, dark and sinister elements are pervasive, particularly in *The Black Spider* (1984), a children's opera, and *HEAVEN ABLAZE in his Breast* (1989), a retelling of E. T. A. Hoffmann's *The Sandman* for eight dancers, six singers and two pianos – an experimental mixture of dance, opera, extended vocal techniques and spoken theatre. Since *Blond Eckbert* (1994) she has not returned to opera, but her preoccupation with differing forms of narrative continues, notably in song-cycles: *Natural History* (1998), settings of fables by Chuang-Tze, and *woman.life.song* (2000), a commission from Jessye Norman, portraying stages in the lives of women. A new departure is a collaboration with Indian performing storyteller Vayu Naidu, *Future Perfect* (2000), where the music is incidental, but which includes written-in options to accommodate all outcomes of the improvised story.

A Night at the Chinese Opera

Opera in three acts (1h 30m)
Libretto by the composer, based on the 13th-century Yüan dynasty drama *The Chao Family Orphan* by Chi Chun-Hsiang
PREMIERES 8 July 1987, Everyman Theatre, Cheltenham; US: 29 July 1989, Opera Theater, Santa Fe

The setting is late 13th-century China, under the military rule of Mongolia, the era of Kublai Khan and of Marco Polo. It concerns Chao Lin, a Chinese collaborator with the Mongolian regime, who attends a performance of *The Chao Family Orphan*. He finds that the first half of the play mirrors his own life and strives to take steps to avoid his surmised fate. Acts I and III tell his story and origin, and Act II is an interrupted performance of the play, accompanied by a reduced orchestra (predominately flutes, violas, basses and percussion) imitating traditional Chinese music. This act adheres closely to the traditional style of Yüan drama in its mixture of speech and sung rhythmic declamation and in its fast and furious pace. The two narratives, that of Chao Lin and that of the play, essentially the same story, entwine in the final act with a double conclusion, one tragic and one more optimistic.

The music is economical, pictorial, spacious and brilliantly coloured. One instantly identifiable stylistic trait – a naturalistic speech rhythm duplicated simultaneously by the orchestra – aptly both supports and undermines the text, a fitting musical metaphor for a work where so much is double edged.

RECORDING Grummet, Lynch, McCafferty, Chance, Thompson, Robinson, Thomas, Daymond, George, Scottish CO, Parrott, NMC, 1999 (live)
OTHER OPERATIC WORKS *King Harald's Saga*, 1979; *The Black Spider*, 1984 (children's opera); *The Consolations of Scholarship*, 1985; *HEAVEN ABLAZE in his Breast*, 1989; *The Vanishing Bridegroom*, 1990; *Scipio's Dream*, 1991 (TV Mozart adaptation); *Blond Eckbert*, 1994

J.G.

Z

Alexander Zemlinsky

Alexander [von] Zemlinsky;
b 14 October 1871, Vienna; *d* 15 March 1942, Larchmont, New York

Zemlinsky grew up in a Vienna dominated by Brahms and Wagner and matured at a time when *Jugendstil* was the all-pervading influence. His knowledge of modern literature was wide-ranging, and his choice of song texts and opera libretti often eclectic. During the First World War and its aftermath of cultural and political turmoil, he reached his artistic zenith. Later he sympathized with the younger generation in their reaction against Expressionism, and he championed the music of Hindemith and Weill, Krenek and Malipiero. While continuing to support the achievements of Schoenberg (who was his brother-in-law), he himself never entirely abandoned the tonal system, which he considered an essential, indeed God-given, attribute of his art.

Having worked as principal conductor at the Carltheater from 1900 to 1903 and at the Theater an der Wien during the following season, in 1904 Zemlinsky was appointed musical director of the newly opened Kaiser-Jubiläumstheater (Vienna Volksoper). That same year he and Schoenberg founded a society to promote new Austro-German music. For part of the 1907–8 season he assisted Mahler at the Vienna Court Opera, but when Weingartner, Mahler's successor, cancelled the world premiere production of Zemlinsky's *Der Traumgörge*, he resigned. Returning to the Volksoper, he followed Mahler's example of innovative repertory planning, with the Viennese premieres of Paul Dukas's *Ariane et Barbe-Bleue*, Richard Strauss's *Salome* and his own *Kleider machen Leute*. From 1911 to 1927 he was opera director at the New German Theatre in Prague. Here, while continuing to champion contemporary music (including the world premiere of Schoenberg's *Erwartung*), he wrote his own most substantial and significant works, including two operas based on texts by Oscar Wilde, *Eine florentinische Tragödie* and *Der Zwerg*. In 1927 Zemlinsky moved to the Krolloper in Berlin as deputy to Klemperer. Despite the offer of musical directorship at the Leningrad State Opera, he remained there until the company was disbanded in 1931.

Liberation from full-time theatre commitments offered Zemlinsky greater scope as a guest conductor and, above all, more time to compose. He taught at the Akademie der Künste until 1933, when, like many of his colleagues, he had to leave Germany. Returning to Vienna, he worked on his last opera, *Der König Kandaules*. Soon after the Anschluss he fled via Prague to New York where, within a few months of arrival, ill health put an end to his career. He remained a neglected figure until the 1970s, when his music experienced a remarkable renaissance.

Der Zwerg

The Dwarf

Tragic folk tale for music in one act (1h 30m)
Libretto by Georg C. Klaren, after the story *The Birthday of the Infanta* by Oscar Wilde (1888)
Composed 1920–24 January 1921
PREMIERES 28 May 1922, Theater am Habsburger Ring, Cologne; US: 29 May 1993, Gaillard Municipal Auditorium, Charleston; UK: 22 August 1983, King's Theatre, Edinburgh
CAST Infanta *s*, The Dwarf *t*, Ghita *s*, Don Estoban *b*, 3 ladies-in-waiting *s*, *s*, *c*; *sa* chorus of the Infanta's entourage (playmates, maids and ladies); beggars; servants *silent*

Der Zwerg is the tragedy of an ugly man, a theme that depicts Zemlinsky's personal predicament. Alma Schindler taunted him on account of his diminutive stature and chinless physiognomy and by rejecting him in 1901 to marry Mahler dealt a severe blow to his self-respect. The opera recounts these traumatic experiences in parable form.

SYNOPSIS
The most extravagant of gifts for the Infanta on her eighteenth birthday is a hideous dwarf. The creature is self-possessed and entirely unaware of his grotesque appearance, indeed the servants are instructed to cover up the mirrors to prevent him seeing himself. Presenting himself to the court, he explains that he knows neither parents nor homeland – as a child he was sold to the Sultan – but claims to be of noble birth and a fine singer. As proof of his skill, he sings a ditty about a blood-orange. Dismissing her retinue, the Infanta declares her love and gives him a white rose from her hair. On the dance-floor, the Dwarf smothers the rose in kisses. Capriciously, the Infanta orders her maid Ghita to show him a mirror. The kind-hearted girl cannot bring herself to do so, but when the Dwarf himself accidentally uncovers a mirror and sees his reflection, he is shattered. Repeatedly he begs the Infanta to tell him he is handsome, but she saunters back to the dance-floor, leaving him alone with his misery. As he dies, broken-hearted, he begs Ghita for the white rose.

Cast in a form that encompasses elements of number-opera and dance-suite, the score is a feast of orchestral colour. The Infanta's music is often synthetic in character, while that of the Dwarf vacillates between growling parody, to portray his outward appearance, and fervid lyricism, to depict his innermost hopes and fears. The love theme itself is based on a piano piece written in 1891, which Zemlinsky had dedicated (unofficially) to Alma. The Dwarf's final confrontation with the Infanta quotes and distorts the Princess's 'miracle-world' theme from Act I of *Der Traumgörge*. For the production that relaunched the work, by the Hamburg State Opera in 1981, the score was abridged and the text brought in line with Wilde's original story, making the Dwarf a simple peasant-boy. Many subsequent performances have reverted successfully to the original libretto.

RECORDINGS as *Der Geburtstag der Infantin* (abridged): Nielsen, Riegel, Berlin RSO, Albrecht, Koch, Schwann, 1984; as *Der Zwerg*: Isokoski, Kuebler, Frankfurter Kantorei, Gürzenich O of Cologne Phil, Conlon (EMI, 1996): complete, orig. version
OTHER OPERAS *Sarema*, 1897; *Es war einmal*, 1900; *Der Traumgörge*, (1907), 1980; *Kleider machen Leute*, 1910; *Eine florentinische Tragödie*, 1917; *Der Kreidekreis*, 1933; *Der König Kandaules*, (1936), 1996
INCOMPLETE OPERAS (all MSS in the Library of Congress, Washington DC): *Fridl* (1901, singspiel); *Malwa*, (1912); *Raphael*, (1918); *Der heilige Vitalis*, (1926); *Circe*, (1939); numerous shorter fragments

A.B.

Bernd Alois Zimmermann

b 20 March 1918, Bliesheim, Cologne;
d 10 August 1970, Königsdorf, Cologne

Brought up under the Nazis, Zimmermann is the classic instance in music of the psychological instabilities of post-war Germany. A pupil of Philipp Jarnach during the war, and of Wolfgang Fortner and René Leibowitz after it, he emerged as a composer at a time when a slightly younger generation of new composers was adopting extreme solutions to the problems of recent European history. Zimmermann was trained in serial method. He attended the Darmstadt Ferienkurse in 1948–50, and much of his early music shares the angular lines and intellectual schemes cultivated there. But there is always a feeling in these instrumental works that a tortured spirit is fighting to escape from mental prison. In his only opera, *Die Soldaten*, the spirit finally breaks out, and on its many levels this work is one of the most characteristic products of early 1960s Germany, with its desperate need to reject its own intellectual and military history while rummaging in that history for causes, explanations and scapegoats.

Die Soldaten established a pluralist, associative style which was to become Zimmermann's trademark, and was to serve him in several striking works during the last decade of his life. These works show increasing intellectual as well as stylistic anxiety. It could well be that the generous use of quotation in the *Requiem für einen jungen Dichter* shows too much faith in the artistic power of good credentials. It certainly looks, in any case, as if Zimmermann was personally overtaken by the menace of history. In August 1970 he took his own life, apparently in blank despair at the state of the world.

Die Soldaten

The Soldiers

Opera in four acts (1h 45m)
Libretto by the composer, after the play by Jakob Michael Reinhold Lenz (1776)
Composed 1958–60, rev. 1963–4
PREMIERES 15 February 1965, Opernhaus, Cologne; UK: 21 August 1972, King's Theatre, Edinburgh; US: 22 January 1982, Opera House, Boston
CAST Wesener *b*, Marie *very dramatic coloratura s*, Charlotte *ms*, Wesener's Old Mother *low c*, Stolzius *youthful high bar*, Stolzius's Mother *very dramatic c*, Obrist *b*, Desportes *very high t*, Pirzel *high t*, Eisenhardt *heroic bar*, Haudy *heroic bar*, Mary *bar*, Countess de la Roche *ms*, Her Son *very high lyrical t*, 3 *very high t* (or *dramatic s*), 4 *actors, dancers*, 18 officers and cadets *spoken roles*, and stage percussion

Lenz's play was based on an incident he himself had witnessed in Strasbourg. A friend – an aristocratic soldier in the French garrison – had failed to honour a marriage contract with the daughter of a Strasbourg jeweller. The play is a bitter attack on the tendency of an idle and peripatetic soldiery to ruin local girls in this way, but attributes the problem partly to the fact that the soldiers were on oath to remain unmarried. Zimmermann characteristically generalizes this plot into a rambling attack on soldiers everywhere, with the setting transferred to French Flanders.

SYNOPSIS

Act I, Scene 1 (Strofe): After a long opening prelude, the curtain rises on the house of the fancy-goods dealer, Wesener, in Lille. His daughter Marie is writing to the mother of her fiancé, the draper Stolzius, in Armentières. Scene 2 (Ciacona I): The letter is received and Stolzius is teased by his mother. Scene 3 (Ricercari I): Back in Lille, Marie is courted by Desportes, a French officer. But Wesener refuses him permission to take Marie to the theatre. Later he lectures her on the dubious morals of soldiers. Scene 4 (Toccata I): On the old town moat in Armentières, French officers discuss their leisure activities. Captain Haudy defends the theatre and its attendant debauchery against the disapproval of the chaplain Eisenhardt. Scene 5 (Nocturno I): Back in Lille Wesener advises Marie to discourage neither the aristocratic Desportes nor Stolzius.

Act II, Scene 1 (Toccata II): In the crowded Armentières coffee house, Eisenhardt deplores Haudy's plot to lure Marie away from Stolzius. The officers tease Stolzius about Desportes's designs on his fiancée. Scene 2 (Capriccio, Corale and Ciacona II) has three simultaneous settings. In Lille Desportes seduces Marie, who has received a scolding letter from Stolzius; in the same place, but on a darkened stage, Marie's grandmother sings of her coming ruin; in Armentières Stolzius and his mother receive Marie's reply, written with Desportes's help.

Act III, Scene 1 (Rondino): Eisenhardt remarks with concern to Captain Pirzel that Captain Mary has also taken lodgings in Lille. Scene 2 (Rappresentazione): Meanwhile, in Lille, Stolzius takes a post as Mary's batman. Scene 3 (Ricercari II): Mary arrives with Stolzius to take Marie for a drive. She only half-recognizes Stolzius. Scene 4 (Nocturno II) introduces the Countess de la Roche, a philanthropic aristocrat. Her son, too, is involved with Marie, and the Countess determines to save her. In Scene 5 (Tropi) she visits Marie and engages her as companion.

Act IV, Scene 1 (Toccata III): Marie has run away and threatens to rejoin Desportes (who is now in prison); wanting to be rid of her, he offers Marie to his gamekeeper, who rapes her. This is shown on film, while a complex stage action, in the Armentières coffee house, suggests various levels of interpretation, culminating in the question, 'Must those who suffer evil be afraid?' Scene 2 (Ciacona III): Mary and Desportes are at dinner, waited on by Stolzius. They discuss Marie contemptuously, but Stolzius has poisoned Desportes. As he dies, Stolzius walks on to Mary's sword. Scene 3 (Nocturno III): Wesener is accosted by a beggarwoman by the river Lys. He fails to recognize his own daughter. As he hands her a coin she sinks to the ground.

In its montage of short scenes and savage anti-military satire, the play looks forward half a century to *Woyzeck* (whose author, Georg Büchner, wrote a novel about Lenz). Zimmermann took the hint, and the Berg of *Wozzeck* (as well as of *Lulu*) is an obvious father figure of *Die Soldaten*. Zimmermann not only uses film but also various musical layering techniques. Berg's associative methods (dance music in *Wozzeck*, film in *Lulu*) are greatly extended, while his touches of quasi-cinematic montage become a standard device. Zimmermann uses actual film, both to extend the scope of Lenz's action and to bring in newsreel associations. More interestingly, he has multi-level scenes depicting simultaneous or non-sequential actions. Finally, he adopts Berg's device of associating each scene with a musical genre (chaconne, toccata, ricercar, etc.); moreover, by giving different scenes the same generic name, he suggests connections between them, a procedure not found in Berg. Bach chorales pop up in more or less straightforward arrangements to suggest an apocalyptic view of the action. Pop music and jazz accompany a ballet sequence in Act II, Scene 1. The dense overlaying of styles and texts comes to a climax in the final act, where Eisenhardt's voice intones the Lord's Prayer in Latin to the accompaniment of tapes of military commands, the sound of 'unrestrained weeping', 'hopeless moaning' and so forth. Pop music emanates (along with a crowd of drunken soldiers) from a dance hall, while film of military equipment, tanks, etc., reminds us that all evil is ultimately one: a valid if not startling observation.

Is *Die Soldaten* more than the sum of its parts? It hardly seems so now that its early vogue (especially in Germany) has subsided. Dramatically it is one-paced, and Zimmermann's own angular vocal style and undifferentiated orchestral textures convey little interest in the human significance of the actual plot. In a review of the British premiere, Winton Dean compared the work with Meyerbeer, quoting Wagner's dictum, 'effects without causes'. As a document of its time it certainly has importance, but that is unlikely to guarantee it a permanent place in the repertoire.

RECORDING Vargas, Shade, Ebbecke, Cochran, Munkittrick, Wolansky, Stuttgart State Op Ch & O, Kontarsky, Teldec, 1989

S.W.

List of Contributors

A.B.
Antony Beaumont (b. 1949, London), conductor, broadcaster, lecturer and writer, read music at Cambridge. Since 1972 he has lived in Germany, where for nearly twenty years he worked as opera conductor in Zurich, Saarbrücken, Bremen (Deutsche Kammerphilharmonie) and Cologne. His most substantial publications are his studies of Busoni, Zemlinsky and Alma Mahler. He has reconstructed two of the great unfinished torsos of the 20th-century operatic repertoire, Busoni's *Doktor Faust* and Zemlinsky's *Der König Kandaules*, and recorded in Munich (Bavarian Radio), Hamburg (NDR) and Prague (Czech Philharmonic).

A.C.
Andrew Clements (b. 1950, Gloucester) studied natural sciences at Cambridge University. He has been chief music critic of the *Guardian* since 1993, was music critic of the *New Statesman* (1977–88), editor of *The Musical Times* (1987–88), and wrote for the *Financial Times* (1979–93). He is a trustee of the Holst Foundation.

A.H.
Amanda Holden studied music at Oxford and at the Guildhall School in London, where she subsequently taught for several years. In 1987 she began work on the first edition of this book (published as the *Viking Opera Guide*) and wrote her first opera translation, of Verdi's *Falstaff*. Since then she has written many librettos, translations and texts for the opera stage, theatre and concert hall. Her librettos include *The Silver Tassie* for which – with the composer Mark-Anthony Turnage – she received the 2001 Olivier award for Outstanding Achievement in Opera.

A.J.
Arthur Jacobs (1922–96) worked at the RAM, London (1965–79), was head of the Department of Music at Huddersfield Polytechnic (1979–84) and lectured extensively at US, Canadian and Australian universities. He joined the editorial board of *Opera* in 1962 and translated many operas for performance. His books include *Arthur Sullivan: A Victorian Musician* and *Henry J. Wood: Maker of the Proms*.

B.D.
Basil Deane was born and educated in Northern Ireland. He was Professor of Music in the universities of Sheffield, Manchester and Birmingham, and held the posts of Music Director at the Arts Council of Great Britain and Foundation Director of the Hong Kong Academy for Performing Arts. His principal research interests are in French music and music of the classical period; his publications include books on Roussel, Cherubini and Hoddinott.

C.A.B.
Clive Brown studied at Cambridge (MA) and Oxford (D.Phil.) and is Professor of Applied Musicology at Bretton Hall, the

University of Leeds. Publications include *Louis Spohr, A Critical Biography* (CUP), *Selected Works of Louis Spohr* (10 vols., Garland) and *Classical and Romantic Performing Practice 1750–1900* (OUP). Forthcoming are a book on Mendelssohn and the critical edition of Mendelssohn's *Die Hochzeit des Camacho* for the *Leipziger Mendelssohn Ausgabe*. He is active as a violinist and as a conductor, particularly of rare operas.

C.B.
Clive Bennett was for ten years in charge of opera broadcasts on BBC Radio 3. He is now Executive Producer with the Decca Music Group responsible for planning the company's opera recordings.

C.I.P.
Charlotte Purkis is principal lecturer in drama and performing arts at University College Winchester, where she has been teaching since 1995. She was previously a lecturer in music and cultural history at the Open University and at Southampton University. She has written on Krenek and Brand for the *New Grove Dictionaries* and also published on Rutland Boughton and Rudolf Laban. Her current publications focus on late 19th- and early 20th-century women's writing on music, part of a broader project about modern and postmodern performance criticism.

C.P.
Curtis Price is a specialist on baroque and classical music and opera. He is the author of *Henry Purcell and the London Stage*, the Norton Critical Score of *Dido and Aeneas*, and co-author of *Italian Opera in London in the Late 18th Century*. In 1985 he received the Dent Medal of the Royal Musical Association. Since 1995 he has been Principal of the Royal Academy of Music, London. He is also past President of the Royal Musical Association and Chairman of the British Violin Making Association.

D.B.
David Brown was, after five years' schoolmastering, music librarian of London University for three years before joining the music staff of Southampton University in 1962. He retired as Professor of Musicology there in 1989. He has published books on Thomas Weelkes, John Wilbye, Glinka and Musorgsky; his four-volume study of Tchaikovsky was completed in 1990. He has also edited numerous editions of English Renaissance music, contributed many articles to periodicals, and has broadcast frequently.

D.C.
David Cairns (b. 1926) read history at Oxford. In 1950 he co-founded Chelsea Opera Group and sang in early performances. Since 1958 he has worked as music critic on, among other publications, the *Spectator*, *Financial Times* and *Sunday Times*. He was Classical Programme Coordinator, Philips Records (1967–72) and Distinguished Visiting Professor, University of California, Davis (1985). In 1983 he founded the Thorington Players, of which he is still conductor. He became Officier de l'Ordre des Arts et des Lettres in 1991. Publications include: *Berlioz's Memoirs* (translation, 1969, revised 2002); *Responses: Musical Essays and Reviews* (1973); *Berlioz: the Making of an Artist* (1989) and *Berlioz: Servitude and Greatness* (1999).

D.J.B.
Donald Burrows is Professor of Music at the Open University and an internationally known Handel scholar, being a vice-president of the Handel-Gesellschaft and a founding council member of the Handel Institute. He is author of 'The Master Musicians' biography of Handel, co-author of *A Catalogue of Handel's Musical Autographs* (OUP) and editor of *The Cambridge Companion to Handel*. He has written on many aspects of Handel's music, as well as editing *Messiah*, *Alexander's Feast* and

Handel's violin sonatas for publication. In 2000 he was awarded the Handel Prize from the city of Halle, Handel's birthplace.

D.K.

David Kimbell, by birth a Man of Kent, has spent the whole of his professional life in Scotland; he has recently retired as Professor of Music and Dean of the Faculty of Music at the University of Edinburgh. Author of *Verdi in the Age of Italian Romanticism* and *Italian Opera* (both CUP), he also contributed to *The New Oxford History of Music* and the Halle edition of the *Collected Works of Handel*.

D.L-J.

David Lloyd-Jones has conducted over 100 different operas in Britain and abroad in his career as freelance conductor, Assistant Music Director of English National Opera (1972–8) and Artistic Director of Opera North (1978–90). He has made critical editions of *Boris Godunov* (OUP and Muzyka), *The Gondoliers* (Eulenberg) and *La Jolie Fille de Perth* (UMP). He is an acknowledged authority on Russian music and has made widely used singing translations of operas by Musorgsky, Borodin, Tchaikovsky and Prokofiev.

D.M.

David Murray (b. Halifax, Nova Scotia) studied music and philosophy in Canada (and played the piano professionally), then more philosophy at Oxford, meanwhile writing scores for radio plays and theatre. For 27 years he lectured in philosophy at the University of London, while also reviewing music for the *Financial Times*, the BBC and various journals; he continues to do the last. He has contributed to several books on music.

D.O-S.

David Osmond-Smith (b. 1946) completed his education at the universities of Cambridge and York. In 1970 he went to Milan to study with Umberto Eco but also worked with Cathy Berberian and with Luciano Berio, of whose music he has made a special study. Since 1973 he has taught at the University of Sussex, where he is now Professor of Music. He has published two books on Berio, plus numerous other essays and translations. He broadcasts regularly and lectures in Italy and France, and at Glyndebourne.

E.F.

Elizabeth Forbes, an autodidact, is a musical journalist who specializes in opera. She has contributed to many encyclopedias, including the *New Grove Dictionary of Music* (1980) and the *New Grove Dictionary of Opera* (1992), and has published the following books: *Opera from A to Z* (1977), *The Observer's Book of Opera* and *Mario and Grisi: a Biography* (1985). She has translated opera librettos from French, German and Swedish.

E.G.

Edward Garden is Professor Emeritus of Music at Sheffield University. He has written extensively on Russian music; books include the definitive one in English on Balakirev (Faber, 1967) and 'The Master Musicians' biography of Tchaikovsky (Dent, 2nd edn. 1993), which has been translated into German and Spanish. He is also co-editor of *To My Best Friend: the Correspondence between Tchaikovsky and Nadezhda von Meck, 1876–8* (OUP, 1993).

E.H.

Elizabeth Hudson is Associate Professor of Music at the University of Virginia. She is the editor of *Il Corsaro* in the 'Verdi Critical Edition' and is preparing a book on the performance history of *La traviata*.

E.S.

Erik Smith (MA Cantab, 1954) is the son of German conductor Hans Schmidt-Isserstedt but grew up in England. He has worked for Universal Edition (Vienna,

1957), as record producer for Decca (1968), Head of A & R (until 1989) and record producer for Philips: his many recordings include 80 operas. He was musical organizer of the 1991 Philips Complete Mozart Edition, for which he also orchestrated several sketches. His publications include many record-sleeve notes and articles (mainly on Mozart), BBC Music Guide on Mozart Serenades and Dances and the music section of the Cambridge University Press Guide to *Die Zauberflöte*.

F.A.
Felix Aprahamian (1914–2005) began his career as a musical journalist in 1931. He was deputy music critic of the *Sunday Times* (1948–89) and for many years a leading reviewer for the *Gramophone* – he appeared in Schlesinger's film *Darling* (1965) in the role of a critic. An authority on French music, he was also adviser to the Delius Trust and vice president of the Delius Society. He edited the essays of Ernest Newman and was co-editor of the 20th-century volume of *The Heritage of Music* (1989).

G.H.
George Hall is the UK correspondent of *Opera News* and also contributes regularly to *Opera*, *Opera Now*, *BBC Music Magazine*, *Gramophone* and other publications. Following a degree at the Royal College of Music, he worked as an editor for the Decca record company for seven years, then in a similar capacity at the BBC for twelve. As well as a number of opera translations and many programme notes and articles, he has also published *The Proms in Pictures* (with Matías Tarnopolsky) and a new English edition of the autobiography of Darius Milhaud (with the late Christopher Palmer).

G.S.
Graham Sadler was educated at the universities of Nottingham and London. Reader in Music at the University of Hull, he is co-author of *The New Grove French Baroque Masters* (Macmillan, 1986) and *French Baroque Opera: A Reader* (Ashgate, 2000), and has written numerous articles and broadcasts on Rameau and his period. Editions include music by M-A. Charpentier, Campra, Leclair, Lully and Rameau, many of which have been recorded and/or broadcast.

H.M.
Hugh Macdonald is Avis Blewett Professor of Music at Washington University, St Louis. He has taught at Cambridge, Oxford and Glasgow, where he was Professor of Music, 1980–87. He has been general editor of the *New Berlioz Edition* since its inception in 1967 and has published books on Berlioz and Skryabin. He has edited Berlioz's three operas and has made a number of opera translations, including Debussy's *Pelléas et Mélisande*.

I.K.
Ian Kemp is retired as Professor of Music at the University of Manchester, having previously held appointments at the universities of Aberdeen, Cambridge and Leeds. In 1965 he edited the first book to be published on Tippett and is the author of a major study: *Tippett: The Composer and his Music*. He has also written on Berlioz, Hindemith and Weill.

J.A.C.
Jon Alan Conrad teaches music theory and literature at the University of Delaware. He has been a contributing editor of *Opus* magazine, and has written articles and reviews for *The Kurt Weill Newsletter*, *Opera Quarterly*, the *New York Times* and *Opera News*. He is a contributor to *The New Grove Dictionary of Opera*, the *Metropolitan Opera Guide to Recorded Opera* and the *Metropolitan Opera Guide to Opera on Video*.

J.A.S.
Jan Smaczny studied at Oxford University and the Charles University in Prague. A specialist in Czech music, in particular the life and music of Dvořák, he has written and broadcast extensively. In 1996 he became Hamilton Harty Professor of Music at the Queen's University, Belfast. His books include studies of the Prague Provisional Theatre and Dvořák's Cello Concerto.

J.C.G.W.
John C. G. Waterhouse (1939–98) studied at Oxford University, where his D.Phil. thesis was 'The Emergence of Modern Italian Music' (up to 1940). He was a lecturer in music in the extramural departments of the universities of Belfast (1966–72) and Birmingham (1973–98), and spent much time in Italy. His many publications on 20th-century Italian music include *Gian Francesco Malipiero (1882–1973), The Life, Times and Music of a Wayward Genius.*

J.D.
John Deathridge, formerly Reader in Music at Cambridge University and Fellow of King's College, is King Edward Professor of Music at King's College London. His books include *Wagner's Rienzi* (1977) and the source catalogue of Wagner's works – the *Wagner-Werk-Verzeichnis* (WWV) – co-edited with Martin Geck and Egon Voss (1986). He has written extensively about German music, including a collection of essays about German opera, and edited Wagner's *Lohengrin* with Klaus Döge (1996–2000).

J.G.
Julian Grant lives in London and Shelter Island, NY. He is a composer, writer and broadcaster and is currently Director of Music at St Paul's Girls' School.

J.R.
Julian Rushton took his Mus.B. at Cambridge and D.Phil. at Oxford, his thesis being 'Music and Drama at the Académie royale de musique, Paris, 1774–1789' (1969). He taught at the Universities of East Anglia and Cambridge until 1982, when he became Professor of Music at the University of Leeds. He has taught and lectured in Canada, Germany, the United States and Israel. Publications include Cambridge Opera Handbooks on *Don Giovanni* (1981) and *Idomeneo* (1993); *The Music of Berlioz* (2001); four volumes of *The New Berlioz Edition* (including *La Damnation de Faust*) and two prefaces for the *Pendragon French Opera* edition. He was President of the Royal Musical Association, 1994–9, and is Chairman of the Editorial Committee of *Musica Britannica.*

J.S.
Jeremy Sams is a freelance composer, translator and director.

J.T.
John Tyrrell (b. Harare, Zimbabwe) studied at Cape Town, Oxford and Brno Universities. He worked at the *New Grove Dictionary of Music and Musicians* and *The Musical Times*, and taught at the University of Nottingham (1976–96). After serving as Executive Editor for the second edition of the *New Grove* (1996–2000), he was appointed Professor at Cardiff University. His books include *Leoš Janáček: Kát'a Kabanová* (1982), *Czech Opera* (1988, published in Czech, 1992) and *Janáček's Operas: a Documentary Account* (1992). He is also translater/editor of Janáček's letters to Kamila Stösslová (*Intimate Letters*, 1994) and of Zdenka Janácková's *My Life with Janácek* (1998). He is co-author of the catalogue *Janáček's Works* (1998) and, with Sir Charles Mackerras, co-editor of authentic editions of *Jenůfa* (1996) and *From the House of the Dead.*

J.W.B.
Jennifer Williams Brown (Ph.D. Cornell, 1992) specializes in 17th-century Venetian opera. Her dissertation exam-

ines the problems of aria borrowing, revivals and revisions in the late 17th century. She has also presented papers on 17-century source studies, opera production and harmonic organization. She taught part time at the Eastman School of Music (1987–90), where she prepared an edition of Cavalli's *La Calisto* for productions at Eastman and in New York. She is assistant professor of musicology at Louisiana State University.

K.P.
Keith Potter is Head of Department and Senior Lecturer in Music at Goldsmiths College, University of London and a music critic for the *Independent*. A writer on many aspects of contemporary music, he has particular interests in American and British composition since 1945. His book, *Four Musical Minimalists: La Monte Young, Terry Riley, Steve Reich and Philip Glass*, was published by CUP in 2000 (and in paperback in 2002). He was Founding and Chief Editor of *Contact: a journal of contemporary music* (1971–88).

L.A.W.
Lesley A. Wright is Professor of Music at the University of Hawaii. After her doctoral dissertation on Bizet's compositional process (Princeton University), she published various studies of Bizet and his contemporaries. More recently she has also turned her attention to the institutions that supported musicians in 19th-century Paris, French music criticism, Berlioz's posthumous fame and the Paris Exposition of 1900. She has prepared editions of Bizet's works and his letters and has published articles in dictionaries and scholarly journals in Europe, North America, Australia and Asia.

M.E.P.
Marvin E. Paymer received his Ph.D. from the City University of New York, where he has taught at York and Hunter Colleges. His interests have centred on the authenticity of the hundreds of works attributed to Giovanni Battista Pergolesi, and to this end he has received fellowships from the Andrew W. Mellon Foundation and the National Endowment for the Humanities. Paymer is co-founder of the Pergolesi Research Center and of the new Pergolesi Complete Works.

M.J.K.
Martin Kettle is an assistant editor of the *Guardian*. He previously worked for *New Society* and the *Sunday Times* and is a regular freelance writer and broadcasts on politics and the arts. He was US bureau chief of the *Guardian* (1997–2001).

M.K.
Michael Kennedy (b. 1926, Manchester) has been a music critic for the *Daily Telegraph* and, latterly, the *Sunday Telegraph* since 1948. He has written biographical studies of Elgar, Vaughan Williams, Britten, Walton, Mahler and Strauss, histories of the Hallé Orchestra and the Royal Manchester College of Music, biographies of Sir John Barbirolli and Sir Adrian Boult, and the *Oxford Dictionary of Music*. He is a regular broadcaster and contributor to *Opera* and other periodicals. He is the author of the Strauss entry in the *New Grove Dictionary of Music and Musicians* and of a BBC music guide to the Strauss tone-poems. He was appointed OBE in 1981 and CBE in 1997 for services to music.

N.G.
Noel Goodwin, now retired from newspaper reviewing, was a regular critic for *The Times* (1978–98) and music critic for the *Daily Express* (1956–78). He was a member of the editorial board of *Opera* (1990–99), following a stint as the magazine's Overseas News Editor, London correspondent for *Opera News* (New York, 1975–90) and a Council Member and Deputy Chairman of the Music Advisory Panel, Arts Council of Great Britain (1979–81). He collaborated with

Sir Geraint Evans on *A Knight at the Opera* (1984), was Editor of the Royal Opera Yearbooks (1978–80) and has written for several works of reference.

P.A.G.
Paul Griffiths (b. 1947) was educated in Birmingham and at Oxford. He started as a critic in the early 1970s and was chief music critic of *The Times*, 1982–92. Among his publications are several books on music, including *The Penguin Companion to Classical Music* (2004), and librettos for operas by Mozart (*The Jewel Box*), Tan Dun and Elliott Carter.

P.B.B.
Patricia B. Brauner (Ph.D., Yale University, 1970) is a member of the editorial committee of the *Edizione critica della opere di Gioachino Rossini* (Fondazione Rossini and G. Ricordi) and Coordinator of the Center for Italian Opera Studies at the University of Chicago. She was a contributor to the *New Grove Dictionary of Music* and editor of Rossini's *Ermione* (with Philip Gossett), *Armida* (with Charles S. Brauner) and *La riconoscenza/Il vero omaggio* for the critical edition.

P.D.
Peter Dickinson, composer, writer and pianist, is Head of Music at the Institute of United States Studies, University of London. He is an Emeritus Professor of the universities of Keele, where he started the Music Department with its Centre for American Music in 1974, and London, where he was Professor at Goldsmiths' College (1991–7). His recorded compositions include the concertos for organ and for piano; a series of song-cycles; and rags, blues and parodies. His books include *The Music of Lennox Berkeley* (1989) and *Marigold: the Music of Billy Mayerl* (1999).

P.G.
Philip Gossett (Ph.D., Princeton University, 1970) is Robert W. Reneker Distinguished Service Professor in the Department of Music at the University of Chicago, where he was for ten years dean of the Division of Humanities, and Professor of the History of Music at the University of Rome 'La Sapienza'. He is general editor of *The Works of Giuseppe Verdi* (University of Chicago Press and G. Ricordi) and *direttore dell'edizione* of the *Edizione critica delle opere di Gioachino Rossini* (Fondazione Rossini and G. Ricordi). His writings include *'Anna Bolena' and the Maturity of Gaetano Donizetti* (OUP, 1985), *Performing Italian Opera* (University of Chicago Press, 2005) and the critical editions of Rossini's *Tancredi*, *Ermione* (with Patricia Brauner) and *Semiramide*. For his service to Italian culture, he was named a Cavaliere di Gran Croce of the Italian Republic in 1999.

P.J.
Peter Jonas is general director of the Bavarian State Opera and Chairman of the German Association of Opera Houses. Previously, he was general director, English National Opera (1985–93); Director of Artistic Administration, Chicago Symphony Orchestra and Orchestral Association of Chicago (1974–85). He has been a Fellow of the Royal College of Music since 1990 and was a Member of the Council there (1988–93); he is also a Fellow of the Royal Northern College of Music and of the Royal Society of Arts. He was educated at the University of Sussex (who awarded him a D.Mus. in 1994), the Royal Northern College of Music and the Royal College of Music. He is also on the board of trustees for the three Berlin opera companies and a member of the board of governors of Bavarian Radio and TV. He was awarded a CBE in 1992 and knighted in 2000.

R.G.H.
Robin Holloway (b. 1943) was a chorister at St Paul's Cathedral, then a schoolboy at King's Wimbledon. At Cambridge he read English then Music. He has held a fellowship at Caius College since 1969, a

university lectureship since 1975 and a readership since 1999. His numerous compositions include two operas – *Clarissa* (1976, ENO 1990) and its buffa complement, inspired by the life and work of Cynthia Payne (1991). He writes a monthly music review in the *Spectator*. A selection of these, with many longer pieces (many of them on opera) is in *On Music: Essays and Diversions* (Claridge/ Continuum, 2003).

R.H.C.
Ronald Crichton (b. 1913, Scarborough) worked in London on Anglo-French cultural relations (1938–40). After war service (1940–46) and work for the British Council in Greece, Belgium, West Germany and London (1946–67) he joined the *Financial Times* as music critic in 1967 and continued to contribute after reaching retiring age. He was co-editor of the *Dictionary of Modern Ballet* (1959) and has written for many publications. His work includes *Manuel de Falla – A Descriptive Catalogue of his Works* (1976), *Falla* (BBC Music Guides, 1982) and the abridged edition of *The Memoirs of Ethel Smyth* (1987).

R.L.H.
Robert Henderson was for many years music critic of the *Daily Telegraph*. He studied at the universities of Durham and Oxford (with Egon Wellesz, the medievalist Frank Harrison and the art historian Edgar Wind), and after graduating worked as a freelance writer and broadcaster, specializing in medieval and 20th-century music. He has written extensively on the music of Henze, for *Opera* magazine and wrote on Monteverdi and Offenbach in Alan Blyth's *Opera on Record*. He retired in 1997.

R.L.
Richard Luckett is Pepys Librarian and Precentor of Magdalene College, Cambridge, and a University Lecturer in English. He has published *Handel's Messiah: a Celebration* (1992) and has edited, with Christopher Hogwood, *English Music in the Eighteenth Century*, a collection of essays. His contributions to *The Companion to the Latham and Matthews Edition of Pepys's Diary* include the article on music and the biographies of musicians.

R.M.
Rodney Milnes read history at Oxford and after a short career in publishing moved into musical journalism. He has been associated with *Opera* magazine since 1971, and was Editor 1986–99. He was opera critic of the *Spectator* (1970–90), and after two years with the London *Evening Standard* served as chief opera critic of *The Times* from 1992 to 2002. He has translated many operas, including *Rusalka* (Dvořák), *Osud* (Janáček) and *Tannhäuser* (Wagner). He was appointed Knight of the Order of the White Rose of Finland in 1987 and in 2001 both OBE and HonRAM.

R.P.
Roger Parker is Professor of Music at Cambridge University, having formerly taught at Cornell and Oxford. He has written numerous articles on 19th-century Italian opera and is co-author (with Arthur Groos) of *Giacomo Puccini: La Bohème* (CUP, 1986). He is the editor of *Nabucco* in the 'Verdi Critical Edition', and was for ten years founding co-editor of the *Cambridge Opera Journal*. His latest books are *Leonora's Last Act: Essays in Verdian Discourse* (Princeton, 1997) and *Arpa d'or: the Verdian Patriotic Chorus* (Parma, 1997).

R.S.
Robert Samuels is a Lecturer in the Music Department of the Open University. He studied English and Music at Cambridge, graduating with a BA (1985) and a Ph.D. (1994) supervised by Derrick Puffett. He is translator of *The Boulez–Cage Correspondence* (CUP, 1993) and author of *Mahler's Sixth Symphony: A Study in Musical Semiotics* (CUP, 1995). His pub-

lished work centres on analysis of music from the 19th and 20th centuries and the relationship between music and literature.

R.T.
Richard Traubner is the author of *Operetta: A Theatrical History* (Gollancz) and a frequent contributor to the *New York Times*, *Opera News*, the *Economist*, *Stagebill*, *American Record Guide* and other publications. He has lectured and broadcast on operetta and film throughout the US and the UK. His four Offenbach translations have been produced around the US, and he has directed and designed several operettas. He restored material for the New York Shakespeare Festival *Pirates of Penzance* and wrote new lyrics for the 1991 Houston Grand Opera production of *Babes in Toyland*.

S.H.
Steven Huebner holds a Ph.D. degree from Princeton University and is Professor of Music at McGill University in Montreal, Canada. He is the author of *The Operas of Charles Gounod* (1990) and *French Opera at the Fin de Siècle: Wagnerism, Nationalism, and Style* (1999).

S.W.
Stephen Walsh (b. 1942) was educated at St Paul's School, London and Gonville and Caius College, Cambridge. From 1963 to 1976 he worked as a music critic and broadcaster in London, writing regularly for *The Times*, the *Daily Telegraph* and the *Financial Times*. He was deputy music critic of the *Observer* (1966–85). Since 1976 he has taught at Cardiff University, where he is now a professor of music. He is the author of several books on music, including *The Music of Stravinsky* (Routledge/OUP, 1988/1993) and the first volume of a biography of the composer, *Stravinsky: A Creative Spring* (Knopf/Cape, 1999/2000).

T.C.
Tim Carter (b. Sydney, Australia) studied in the UK at Durham and Birmingham Universities. He is well known as an author, lecturer and broadcaster: his books include the Cambridge Opera Handbook on *Le nozze di Figaro* (1987), *Jacopo Peri (1561–1633): His Life and Works* (1989), *Music in Late Renaissance and Early Baroque Italy* (1992) and *Monteverdi's Musical Theatre* (2002). He taught at the Universities of Leicester and Lancaster and was Professor of Music at Royal Holloway and Bedford New College, University of London before becoming, in 2001, David G. Frey Distinguished Professor of Music, University of North Carolina at Chapel Hill.

W.A.
William Ashbrook (b. 1922, Philadelphia) was educated at the Universities of Pennsylvania and Harvard. After a 40-year career teaching Humanities, mostly at Indiana State University, he is Distinguished Professor Emeritus of Humanities. He continues to teach part time, to lecture, and to write copiously on the subject of Italian opera of the ottocento. His studies of Donizetti and Puccini are well known. Though retired as editor of *The Opera Quarterly*, he is engaged on a critical biography of Arrigo Boito.

Z.C.
Zofia Chechlinska is a professor of musicology and the author of books on Polish 19th-century music, including Chopin. Since 1969 she has worked in the Music Department of the Institute of Art of the Polish Academy in Warsaw, and since 1989 also at the Institute of Musicology of the Jagiellonian University, Krakow. She is the editor of a series devoted to 19th-century musical culture and an editor of the Chopin Studies, published by the Chopin Society in Warsaw. She contributed to the *New Grove Dictionaries*.

Index